# DOMAINS AND LAMBDA-CALCULI

**Cambridge Tracts in Theoretical Computer Science**

Editorial Board

S. Abramsky, *Department of Computing Science, University of Edinburgh*
P. H. Aczel, *Department of Computer Science, University of Manchester*
J. W. de Bakker, *Centrum voor Wiskunde en Informatica, Amsterdam*
Y. Gurevich, *Department of Electrical Engineering and Computer Science, University of Michigan*
J. V. Tucker, *Department of Mathematics and Computer Science, University College of Swansea*

**Titles in the series**

# DOMAINS AND LAMBDA-CALCULI

Roberto M. Amadio
*Université de Provence, Marseille*

Pierre-Louis Curien
*Ecole Normale Supérieure, Paris*

CAMBRIDGE
UNIVERSITY PRESS

PUBLISHED BY THE PRESS SYNDICATE OF THE UNIVERSITY OF CAMBRIDGE
The Pitt Building, Trumpington Street, Cambridge CB2 1RP, United Kingdom

CAMBRIDGE UNIVERSITY PRESS
The Edinburgh Building, Cambridge CB2 2RU, UK http://www.cup.cam.ac.uk
40 West 20th Street, New York, NY 10011–4211, USA http://www.cup.org
10 Stamford Road, Oakleigh, Melbourne 3166, Australia

First published 1998

A catalogue record for this book is available from the British Library

ISBN 0 521 62277 8 hardback


Transferred to digital printing 2003

# Contents

# Preface

Denotational semantics is concerned with the mathematical meaning of programming languages. Programs are to be interpreted in categories with structure by which we mean initially sets and functions, and later, suitable topological spaces and continuous functions. The main goals of this branch of computer science are, in our belief:

- To provide rigorous definitions that abstract away from implementation details, and that can serve as an implementation independent reference.

- To provide mathematical tools for proving properties of programs: as in logic, semantic models are guides in designing sound proof rules, that can then be used in automated proof-checkers like LCF.

Historically the first goal came first. In the sixties Strachey was writing semantic equations involving recursively defined data types without knowing if they had mathematical solutions. Scott provided the mathematical framework, and advocated its use in a formal proof system called LCF. Thus denotational semantics has from the beginning been applied to the two goals.

In this book we aim to present in an elementary and unified way the theory of certain topological spaces, best presented as order theoretical structures, that have proved to be useful in the modelling of various families of typed λ-calculi considered as core programming languages and as meta-languages for denotational semantics. This theory is now known as Domain Theory, and has been founded as a subject by Scott and Plotkin.

The notion of continuity used in domain theory finds its origin in recursion theory. Here the works of Platek and Ershov come to mind: in Stanford and Novosibirsk, independently, they both exploited the continuity properties of recursive functionals to build a theory of higher order recursive functions. Recursion theory is implicit in the basics of domain theory, but becomes again explicit when *effective* domains are considered.

The topic is indebted to lattice theory and topology for ideas and techniques, however the aims are different. We look for theories that can be usefully applied to programming languages (and logic). Therefore a certain number of complications arise that are not usually considered. Just to name a few:

- The topologies we are interested in satisfy only a weak separation axiom ($T_0$). This stands in sharp contrast with classical topology based on $T_2$, or Hausdorff spaces, but it relates to the subject of pointless topology [Joh82].

- In applications it is difficult to justify the existence of a greatest element, hence the theory is developed without assuming the existence of arbitrary lub's, that is, we will not work with complete lattices.

- There are several models of computation, certainly an important distinction is the possibility of computing in parallel or in series, hence the development of various notions of *continuous*, *stable*, and *sequential* morphisms.

- There is a distinction between an explicitly typed program and its untyped run time representation, hence the connection with *realizability interpretations*.

One of our main concerns will be to establish links between mathematical structures and more syntactic approaches to semantics, often referred to as operational semantics. The distinction of operational vs. denotational is reminiscent of the distinction between 'function as extension, or as a graph' (say, of a partial recursive function) and 'function as a rule, or as an algorithm' (say, the specification of a Turing machine). The qualities of a denotational semantics can be measured in the way it matches an independently defined operational semantics. Conversely, an operational semantics, like any formal system, can be 'blessed' by soundness or even completeness results with respect to some denotational semantics.

We shall therefore describe operational semantics as well as denotational semantics. In our experience it is essential to insist on these two complementary views in order to motivate computer scientists to do some mathematics and in order to interest mathematicians in structures that are somehow unfamiliar and far away from the traditional core of mathematics.

A description of the contents of each chapter follows. Unless stated otherwise we do not claim any novelty for the material presented here. We highlight this by mentioning some of the papers which were most influential in the writing of each chapter.

Chapter 1 introduces the first concepts in domain theory and denotational semantics: *directed complete partial orders*, *algebraicity*, and *Scott topology*. A basic link between Scott continuity and computability (the Myhill-Shepherdson theorem) is established. As an application, the denotational semantics of two simple imperative languages are presented, and are shown to be equivalent to their formal operational semantics [Sco72, Plo83].

Chapter 2 introduces the *untyped $\lambda$-calculus*. We establish several of the fundamental theorems of $\lambda$-calculus using a labelling technique due to Lévy. In this way we prove the Church-Rosser property, the standardization theorem, and the finite developments theorem. The same technique also yields the strong normalization property for the simply typed $\lambda$-calculus. Finally, we show the syntactic continuity theorem (a further evidence of the role of continuity in the semantics of programming languages) and the sequentiality theorem, which motivates the semantic study of sequentiality [Lev78, Ber79].

Chapter 3 is a case study of the fundamental domain equation $D = D \to D$, which provides models of the untyped $\lambda$-calculus. We detail the construction of the $D_\infty$ models, obtained as suitable limits. The chapter is also a case study of Stone duality: the $D_\infty$ models can also be constructed out of certain theories of 'types', or functional characters [Bar84, CDHL82].

Chapter 4 is an introduction to the interpretation of simply typed and untyped $\lambda$-calculi in categories. In particular we develop the *categorical models* of simply typed and type free $\lambda$-calculus and illustrate the techniques needed to prove the soundness and completeness of the related interpretations [LS86, Sco80].

Chapter 5 gives a complete presentation of the problem of classifying the largest cartesian closed categories of algebraic directed complete partial orders and continuous morphisms, which was solved by Jung, following earlier work by Smyth. Two important classes of algebraic cpo's come out of this study: bifinite domains, and L-domains [Jun88, Smy83a].

Chapter 6 presents the language PCF of Scott-Plotkin-Milner. This is a simply typed $\lambda$-calculus extended with fixpoints and arithmetic operators. For this calculus we discuss the *full abstraction* problem, or the problem of the correspondence between denotational and operational semantics [Sco93, Plo77].

Chapter 7 presents the basic apparatus for the solution of *domain equations*. It also includes material on the construction of *universal domains*, and on the representation of domains by *projections* [Sco72, SP82, DR93, Sco76, ABL86].

Chapter 8 studies $\lambda$-calculi endowed with a reduction strategy that stops at $\lambda$-abstractions. We analyse in particular a *call-by-value* $\lambda$-calculus and a $\lambda$-calculus with *control operators*. We introduce the semantic aspects of these calculi via a unifying framework proposed by Moggi and based on the idea of computation-as-monad [Plo75, Plo85, Mog89, Bou94].

Chapter 9 concentrates on the construction of *powerdomains* (loosely speaking a powerset construction in domain theory) and their applications to the semantics of non-deterministic and concurrent computations. On the denotational side we develop the theory of Plotkin's convex powerdomain. On the syntactic side we introduce a process calculus (Milner's CCS) and its operational semantics based on the notion of *bisimulation*. We interpret CCS using a domain equation which involves the convex powerdomain and relate the denotational semantics to the operational one [Plo76, Mil89, Abr91a].

Chapter 10 presents *Stone duality* (originally the correspondence between Boolean algebras and certain topological spaces), applied to domains. Algebraic domains can be reconstructed from their compact elements, or from the opens of their Scott topology, which can be viewed as observable properties. Elements are then certain kinds of filters of properties. This idea can be exploited to the point of presenting domain theory in logical form, as advocated by Martin-Löf (a program which was carried out systematically by Abramsky) [Joh82, ML83, Abr91b].

Chapter 11 introduces the problem of the categorical interpretation of a typed $\lambda$-calculus with *dependent* and *second order* types along the lines established in chapter 4. We first develop some guidelines in a categorical framework, and then we apply them to the specific cases of categories of complete partial orders and Scott domains. Two popular fragments of this typed $\lambda$-calculus are considered in greater detail: the system LF of dependent types, and the system F of polymorphic types [Gir86, CGW88, AL87, Gir72, Rey74, HHP93].

Chapter 12 presents another theory of domains based on the notion of *stable morphism*. Stability was introduced by Berry, as an approximation of the sequential behaviour of λ-calculus. The definition of a stable function formalizes the property that there is always a *minimum* part of a given input needed to reach a given finite output. We develop the theory along the lines of chapters 1 and 5: we study stability on meet cpo's, dI-domains and event structures (and coherence spaces), stable bifinite domains (with an application to the construction of a retraction of all retractions), and continuous L-domains [Ber79, Ama91a, Ama95].

Chapter 13 is devoted to *linear logic*. The simplest framework for stability, coherence spaces, led Girard to the discovery of a new resource-sensitive logic. In linear logic, hypotheses, or data are consumed exactly once, and multiple uses (including no use) are re-introduced by explicit connectives. Linear logic has a rich model theory. We present only a few models: the stable model, Ehrhard's hypercoherence model (which is closer to capturing sequential behaviour), and Winskel's bistructures model (which combines the continuous and the stable models). Also continuity can be recast in the light of linear logic, as shown by Lamarche [Gir87, Ehr93, Win80].

Chapter 14 addresses the semantic notion of *sequentiality*, which is aimed at capturing sequential computation, as opposed to inherently parallel computation. We start with Kahn-Plotkin sequential functions, which do not lead to a cartesian closed category. But sequential algorithms, which are pairs (function, computation strategy) yield a model of PCF. They actually model, and are fully abstract for an extension of PCF with a control operator *catch*. Sequential algorithms lend themselves to a game interpretation. On the other hand, a term model of PCF, from which a fully abstract model of PCF is obtained by a quotient, can also be described in a syntax-independent way using games. Games semantics therefore appear as a powerful unifying framework, which is largely undeveloped at the time this book is written [Cur86, AJ92].

Chapter 15 is an elementary introduction to the ideas of *synthetic domain theory* via the category of partial equivalence relations (per's). The category of per's is a useful tool in semantics; we exhibit an interpretation of system F, of a type assignment system, and of a subtyping system. Towards the interpretation of recursion we introduce various reflective subcategories of per's. In this context we prove a generalized Myhill-Shepherdson theorem [Hyl88, Ros86, FMRS92, Ama91b].

Chapter 16 discusses some connections between the functional and concurrent computational paradigms. As a main tool for this comparison we introduce the basics of π-calculus theory, a rather economical extension of Milner's CCS. We show that this calculus is sufficiently expressive to adequately encode a call-by-value λ-calculus enriched with parallel composition and synchronization operators [MPW92, ALT95].

Two appendices provide the basic material on recursion theory and category theory (see [Rog67, Soa87] for the former and [ML71, BW85, AL91, Poi92] for the latter). We refer to [Smy92] for an introduction to topological structures in computer science, and to [Bar84, GLT89] for more advanced results on the syntactic aspects of $\lambda$-calculus.

Most people never manage to read a scientific book from the beginning to the end. We guess this book will be no exception. In first approximation a precedence relation $\succ$ among the chapters can be defined as follows.

$$1, 2 \succ 3 \succ 4 \succ 6 \succ 8 \succ 9 \succ 16$$
$$4 \succ 5 \succ 9, 10$$
$$6 \succ 12 \succ 13 \succ 14$$
$$5 \succ 7 \succ 11 \succ 15$$

Clearly there are plenty of possible shortcuts. When using the book in an introductory graduate course or seminar it is perhaps a good idea to modulate the amount of domain theoretical constructions which are presented. The sections marked with a * contain more advanced or less fundamental material. By avoiding all sections marked with a * and by doing some selection it is possible to cover the contents of the book in about 40 one-hour lectures.

This book arises out of a joint effort to develop and integrate lecture notes for graduate courses taught by the authors in the years 1991-1996 in a number of research institutions. A preliminary report of our work had appeared in [AC94]. We are grateful to the following colleagues for providing comments, corrections, and encouragement: Antonio Bucciarelli, Gérard Boudol, Franck van Breugel, Solange Coupet, Manfred Droste, Thomas Ehrhard, Pierre Lescanne, Giuseppe Longo, Eugenio Moggi, Fritz Müller, Davide Sangiorgi, and Guoqiang Zhang.

Special thanks go to David Tranah of Cambridge University Press for the excellent management of the publishing process.

Constructive criticisms and corrections are welcome and can be addressed to `amadio@gyptis.univ-mrs.fr` and `curien@dmi.ens.fr`. We plan to maintain a page with corrections at the following address `http://protis.univ-mrs.fr/~amadio/`.

# Notation

**Starred sections and exercises.** Sections and exercises marked with a * contain more advanced or less fundamental material.

## Set theoretical

| | |
|---|---|
| $\emptyset$ | empty set |
| $\omega$ | natural numbers |
| $\mathbf{B}$ | two elements set |
| $\cup, \cap$ | union, intersection of two sets |
| $\bigcup, \bigcap$ | union, intersection of a family of sets |
| $X^c$ | complement of $X$ |
| $\mathcal{P}(X)$ | subsets of $X$ |
| $\mathcal{P}_{fin}(X)$ | finite subsets of $X$ |
| $X \subseteq_{fin} Y$ | $X$ is a finite subset of $Y$ |
| $X \subseteq^\star_{fin} Y$ | $X$ is a finite and non-empty subset of $Y$ |
| $\sharp X$ | cardinality of $X$ |
| $R^*$ | reflexive and transitive closure of $R$ |
| $\{d_i\}_{i \in I}$ | indexed set |
| $\{x_n\}_{n<\omega}, \{x_n\}_{n\in\omega}, \{x_n\}_{n\geq 0}$ | equivalent notations for an enumerated set |
| $x \mapsto f(x), \lambda x.f(x)$ | equivalent functional notations |

## Recursion theoretical

| | |
|---|---|
| $\{n\}, \phi_n$ | function computed by the $n^{th}$ Turing machine |
| $\downarrow, \uparrow$ | convergence, divergence predicate |
| $\cong$ | Kleene's equality on partially defined terms, where $s \cong t$ iff $(s \downarrow$ and $t \downarrow$ and $s = t)$ or $(s \uparrow$ and $t \uparrow)$ |
| $f(x) \downarrow y$ | is equivalent to $f(x) \downarrow$ and $f(x) = y$ ($f$ function) |

## Category theoretical

| | |
|---|---|
| $\mathbf{C}, \mathbf{D}$ | categories |
| $\mathbf{C}[a, b]$ | morphisms from $a$ to $b$ |
| $f \circ g$ | composition of morphisms |
| $\langle f, g \rangle$ | pairing of morphisms |
| $L \dashv R$ | $L$ left adjoint to $R$ |

## Order theoretical

| | |
|---|---|
| $(P, \leq)$ | preorder (reflexive and transitive) |
| poset | or partial order: a preorder such that $x \leq y$, $y \leq x \Rightarrow x = y$ |
| $f : (P, \leq) \to (P', \leq')$ | $f$ is monotonic if it preserves the preorder |
| $UB(X)$ | upper bounds of $X$ |
| $MUB(X)$ | minimal upper bounds (mub's) of $X$ |
| $\bigvee X$ | least upper bound (lub) |
| $\bigwedge X$ | greatest lower bound (glb) |
| $x \uparrow y$ | elements with an upper bound (compatible elements) |
| $x \prec y$ | immediate predecessor |
| $\uparrow X,$ | smallest upper (or upward closed) set containing $X$ |
| $\downarrow X$ | smallest lower (or downward closed) set containing $X$ |
| $\mathbf{O}$ | poset $\{\bot, \top\}$ with $\bot < \top$ |

## Syntax

| | |
|---|---|
| BNF | Backus-Naur form for grammars |
| $V[U/x]$ | substitution of $U$ for $x$ in $V$ |
| $FV(M)$ | free variables of $M$ |
| $\vec{M}$ | vector of terms |

## Semantics

$$f[e/d] \quad \text{environment update, } f[e/d](x) = \begin{cases} e & \text{if } x = d \\ f(x) & \text{otherwise} \end{cases}$$

# 1

# Continuity and computability

As the computation of a program proceeds, some (partial) information is read from the input, and portions of the output are gradually produced. This is true of mathematical reasoning too. Consider the following abstraction of a typical highschool problem for simple equation solving. The student is presented with three numerical figures – the data of the problem (which might themselves be obtained as the results of previous problems). Call them $u, v$, and $w$. The problem has two parts. In part 1, the student is required to compute a quantity $x$, and in the second part, using part 1 as a stepping stone, he (or she) is required to compute a quantity $y$. After some reasoning, the student will have found that, say, $x = 3u + 4$, and that $y = x - v$. Abstracting away from the actual values of $u, v, w, x$, and $y$, we can describe the problem in terms of information processing. We consider that the problem consists in computing $x$ and $y$ as a function of $u, v, w$, i.e., $(x, y) = f(u, v, w)$. A first remark is that $w$ is not used. In particular, if computing $w$ was itself the result of a long, or even diverging, computation, the student would still be able to solve his problem. A second remark is that $x$ depends on $u$ only. Hence, again, if finding $v$ is very painful, the student may still achieve at least part 1 of his problem. Finally, $y$ depends on both $u$ and $v$.

We use the symbol $\perp$ to mark the absence of information. What we have described with English words can be formalized as follows (we assume $u, v \neq \perp$):

$$
\begin{aligned}
f(\perp, \perp, \perp) &= (\perp, \perp) \\
f(u, \perp, \perp) &= (3u + 4, \perp) \\
f(u, v, \perp) &= (3u + 4, (3u + 4) - v) \, .
\end{aligned}
$$

Input and output data may be ordered according to their information contents. Therefore we write:

$$
\begin{aligned}
(\perp, \perp, \perp) &\leq (u, \perp, \perp) \leq (u, v, \perp) \\
(\perp, \perp) &\leq (3u + 4, \perp) \leq (3u + 4, (3u + 4) - v) \, .
\end{aligned}
$$

The function $f$ is monotonic with respect to this order, i.e., if $(x, y, z) \leq (x', y', z')$, then $f(x, y, z) \leq f(x', y', z')$. Notice that we are not concerned here with the order relation between numbers: we do not focus on the actual operations performed, but only on the underlying flow of information.

Another example involving an open-ended view of computation is offered by some popular programs running in the background at many academic institutions, which compute larger and larger prime numbers. In this case, larger and larger lists of prime numbers are obtained from scanning larger and larger portions of the (infinite) list of natural numbers, and making the appropriate primality checks. The currently produced list of prime numbers is an approximation of the infinite sorted list of all prime numbers, which is the ideal total output information. Continuity arises as the formalization of the slogan: 'any finite part of the output can be reached through a finite computation'. The primality of an arbitrarily large number can be (in principle) checked in finite time and by scanning a finite portion of the sorted list of natural numbers.

Thus our basic **objects** of study are certain partial orders called complete partial orders and continuous functions over them (section 1.1). The following two sections sketch links with topology and recursion theory. In section 1.2, we show that complete partial orders can be viewed as (quite special) topological spaces. In section 1.3, we indicate where all this came from: a theorem of recursion theory, due to Myhill and Shepherdson, shows that, in a suitable sense, computability implies continuity. In section 1.4, we come back to the order theoretical treatment, and present basic domain constructions (product, function space, smash product, lifting, and different kinds of sums). In section 1.5, we apply the material of the previous sections to give a denotational semantics to a toy imperative language. In section 1.6, we consider a small extension of this language, and we introduce continuation semantics (continuations will be considered again in chapter 8).

## 1.1    Directed completeness and algebraicity

After giving the basic definitions concerning directed complete partial orders and continuous functions, we immediately arrive at a simple, but fundamental fixpoint theorem, which will be used to give meaning to loops (section 1.5) and to recursive definitions (section 6.1).

**Definition 1.1.1 (dcpo)** *Given a partial order* $(D, \leq)$, *a non-empty subset* $\Delta \subseteq D$ *is called* directed *if*

$$\forall x, y \in \Delta \; \exists z \in \Delta \; x \leq z \text{ and } y \leq z .$$

*In the sequel,* $\Delta \subseteq_{dir} D$ *stands for: '$\Delta$ is a directed subset of $D$' (when clear from the context, the subscript is omitted). A partial order $(D, \leq)$ is called a* directed complete partial order *(dcpo) if every* $\Delta \subseteq_{dir} D$ *has a least upper bound (lub), denoted* $\bigvee \Delta$. *If moreover* $(D, \leq)$ *has a least element (written* $\bot$), *then it is called a* complete partial order *(cpo).*

*If* $(D, \leq)$ *is a dcpo, a subset* $E \subseteq D$, *ordered by the restriction of* $\leq$ *(also called the induced ordering), is called a* subdcpo *if it is closed under directed lub's, i.e., for each* $\Delta \subseteq_{dir} E$, *E contains the lub of* $\Delta$ *in* $D$. *Clearly, a subdcpo is a dcpo. If, furthermore, $D$ is a cpo and if* $\bot \in E$, *then* $E$ *is called a* subcpo.

**Definition 1.1.2 (monotonic, continuous)** *Let* $(D, \leq)$ *and* $(D', \leq)$ *be partial orders. A function* $f : D \to D'$ *is called* monotonic *if*

$$\forall x, y \in D \; x \leq y \Rightarrow f(x) \leq f(y) .$$

*If $D$ and $D'$ are dcpo's, a function $f : D \to D'$ is called continuous if it is monotonic and preserves directed lub's:*

$$\forall \Delta \subseteq_{dir} D \ f(\bigvee \Delta) = \bigvee f(\Delta) .$$

*(Notice that a monotonic function maps directed sets to directed sets.)* A fixpoint *of $f : D \to D$ is an element $x$ such that $f(x) = x$. A prefixpoint of $f : D \to D$ is an element $x$ such that $f(x) \leq x$. If $f$ has a least fixpoint, we denote it by* fix$(f)$.

The most noteworthy example of a directed set is an infinite ascending sequence $x_0 \leq x_1 \leq \cdots \leq x_n \cdots$ . Actually they are the ones that matter. Most of domain theory can be formulated with partial orders that are complete only with respect to denumerable ascending chains.

**Definition 1.1.3 ($\omega$-dcpo)** *A partial order $(D, \leq)$ is called an $\omega$-dcpo if every (denumerable) ascending sequence $\{x_n\}_{n<\omega}$ has a lub. If $D$ and $D'$ are $\omega$-dcpo's, a monotonic function $f : D \to D'$ is called $\omega$-continuous if it preserves the lub's of ascending sequences.*

Clearly, dcpo's are $\omega$-dcpo's. We will stick to directed sets, which have a more abstract flavour.

**Exercise 1.1.4** *Show that the identity functions are continuous, and that the composition of two continuous functions is continuous.*

**Definition 1.1.5** *The category **Dcpo** is the category of directed complete partial orders and continuous functions. The category **Cpo** is the full subcategory of **Dcpo** whose objects are the cpo's.*

**Example 1.1.6** (1) *Given any set $X$, define $X_\perp = X \cup \{\perp\}$ (where $\perp \notin X$), and $x \leq y \Leftrightarrow (x = \perp$ or $x = y)$. Cpo's defined in this way are called flat. The flat domain $\{\perp, \top\}$ is written **O**. The boolean flat domain $\{\perp, tt, ff\}$ is written $\mathbf{B}_\perp$.*

(2) *All partial orders without infinite ascending chains are dcpo's (this includes all finite partial orders).*

(3) *$X \rightharpoonup Y$ (the set of partial functions between two sets $X, Y$), endowed with the following order, is a cpo:*

$$f \leq g \Leftrightarrow (f(x) \downarrow \Rightarrow (g(x) \downarrow \ and \ f(x) = g(x)))$$

*(where $\downarrow$ means 'defined'). Equivalently, $f \leq g \Leftrightarrow$ graph$(f) \subseteq$ graph$(g)$ (where graph$(f) = \{(x,y) \mid f(x) \downarrow \ and \ f(x) = y\}$). The least element is the everywhere undefined function, and lub's are set theoretical unions (of graphs).*

The following proposition is the key to the interpretation of recursively defined programs or commands.

**Proposition 1.1.7 (Kleene's fixpoint)** *If $D$ is a cpo and $f : D \to D$ is continuous, then $\bigvee_{n\in\omega} f^n(\perp)$ is a fixpoint of $f$, and is the least prefixpoint of $f$ (hence it is the least fixpoint of $f$).[1]*

---

[1]Why this fact is named after Kleene is explained in remark 1.3.3.

PROOF. From $\perp \leq f(\perp)$, we get by monotonicity that $\perp, f(\perp), \ldots, f^n(\perp), \ldots$ is an ascending chain, thus is directed. By continuity of $f$, we have:

$$f(\bigvee_{n\in\omega} f^n(\perp)) = \bigvee_{n\in\omega} f^{n+1}(\perp) = \bigvee_{n\in\omega} f^n(\perp) \, .$$

Suppose $f(x) \leq x$. We show $f^n(\perp) \leq x$ by induction on $n$. The base case is clear by minimality of $\perp$. Suppose $f^n(\perp) \leq x$: by monotonicity, $f^{n+1}(\perp) \leq f(x)$, and we conclude by transitivity. $\square$

It is actually possible to prove the existence of least fixpoints for all monotonic functions. We propose two different proofs, based on different assumptions, in the following two exercises.

**Exercise 1.1.8 (Tarski's fixpoint)** *Let $D$ be a complete lattice (i.e., $D$ is a partial order in which every subset has a lub). Show that any monotonic function $f : D \to D$ has a least fixpoint, which is $\bigwedge \{x \mid f(x) \leq x\}$ (see exercise 5.5.2 for a converse), and that the set of fixpoints of $f$ is a complete lattice.*

**Exercise 1.1.9** *Let $D$ be a cpo, and $f : D \to D$ be a monotonic function. Set $f^0 = \perp$, $f^{\kappa+1} = f(f^\kappa)$, and $f^\lambda = \bigvee_{\kappa<\lambda} f^\kappa$, where $\kappa$ is an ordinal, and $\lambda$ is a limit ordinal. Show that there is an ordinal $\mu$ such that $f^\mu$ is the least prefixpoint of $f$. Describe a dual construction (with dual assumptions) for the greatest fixpoint. Hint: The above transfinite induction cannot go beyond the cardinal of $D$.*

Next we introduce compact elements, which are used to model the notion of finite information.

**Definition 1.1.10 (compact)** *Let $D$ be a dcpo. An element $d \in D$ is called compact (some authors say isolated) if the following implication holds, for each directed $\Delta$:*

$$d \leq \bigvee \Delta \Rightarrow \exists x \in \Delta \ d \leq x \, .$$

*We write $\mathcal{K}(D)$ for the collection of compact elements of $D$, and we let $d, e$ range over compact elements.*

**Exercise 1.1.11** *Show that the lub of two compact elements, if any, is compact.*

**Definition 1.1.12 (algebraic)** *A dcpo $D$ is called algebraic if for all $x \in D$ the set $\{d \in \mathcal{K}(D) \mid d \leq x\}$, is directed and has lub $x$. It is called an $\omega$-algebraic dcpo if it is algebraic and $\mathcal{K}(D)$ is denumerable. The elements of $\{d \in \mathcal{K}(D) \mid d \leq x\}$ are called the approximants of $x$, and $\mathcal{K}(D)$ is called the basis of $D$. We denote by* **Adcpo** *and* $\omega$**Adcpo** *the full subcategories of* **Dcpo** *consisting of algebraic and $\omega$-algebraic dcpo's, respectively. We also write:*

$$\mathbf{Acpo} = \mathbf{Cpo} \cap \mathbf{Adcpo} \, , \quad \omega\mathbf{Acpo} = \mathbf{Cpo} \cap \omega\mathbf{Adcpo} \, .$$

Thinking of a directed set $\Delta$ as describing the output of a possibly infinite computation and of the elements of $\Delta$ as describing the larger and larger portions of the output produced as time passes, then the property of $d$ being compact means that only a finite computing time is required to produce at least $d$. The algebraicity requirement says that we want to bother only about those abstract elements which can be described as the 'limits' of their finite approximations.

**Example 1.1.13** (1)   *We have seen that $X \to Y$ is a cpo. It is actually an algebraic cpo: the compact elements are the functions that have a finite domain of definition.*

(2)   *The powerset of natural numbers, $\mathcal{P}(\omega)$, ordered by inclusion, is an $\omega$-algebraic cpo.*

(3)   *Consider a signature $\Sigma$ consisting of symbols $f$ with an associated arity $arity(f)$. Define possibly infinite terms as partial functions $S$ from $\omega^\star$ to $\Sigma$ satisfying the following property:*

$$S(un) \downarrow \Rightarrow \exists f \; S(u) \;\; = \;\; f \; with \; n < arity(f) \,.$$

*The order is the restriction of the graph inclusion order on $\omega^\star \to \Sigma$.*

(4)   *The following is a minimal example of a non-algebraic cpo:*

$$D = \omega_\perp \cup \{a, b\} \; with \; x \leq y \;\; iff \quad \begin{cases} x = \perp \; or \\ y = b \; or \\ x = y = a \; or \\ x = m, y = n, m, n \in \omega, \; and \; m \leq n \,. \end{cases}$$

**Exercise 1.1.14** *Let $D$ be a dcpo, and $\mathcal{K} \subseteq \mathcal{K}(D)$ be such that for any $x \in D$ the set $\{d \in \mathcal{K} \mid d \leq x\}$ is directed and has lub $x$. Show that $D$ is algebraic, and that $\mathcal{K} = \mathcal{K}(D)$.*

**Exercise 1.1.15** *Define a notion of $(\omega-)$algebraic $\omega$-dcpo (cf. definition 1.1.3), and show that $\omega$-algebraic $\omega$-dcpo's and $\omega$-algebraic dcpo's are the same.*

The following proposition formalizes the idea that continuous means 'finite input only is needed to produce finite output'.

**Proposition 1.1.16** ($\varepsilon\delta$-continuity)   *Let $D$ and $E$ be algebraic dcpo's.*

(1)   *A function $f : D \to E$ is continuous iff it is monotonic, and for each $e \in \mathcal{K}(E)$ and $x \in D$ such that $e \leq f(x)$, there exists $d \leq x$ such that $d \in \mathcal{K}(D)$ and $e \leq f(d)$.*

(2)   *$\{(d, e) \in \mathcal{K}(D) \times \mathcal{K}(E) \mid e \leq f(d)\}$, denoted by $graph(f)$ and called the* graph *of $f$, determines $f$ entirely.*[2]

PROOF. (1) We first prove ($\Leftarrow$). Let $\Delta$ be directed. We have $\bigvee f(\Delta) \leq f(\bigvee \Delta)$ by monotonicity. To show $f(\bigvee \Delta) \leq \bigvee f(\Delta)$, it is enough to prove that for any compact $e \leq f(\bigvee \Delta)$ there exists $\delta \in \Delta$ such that $e \leq f(\delta)$. By assumption there exists $d \leq \bigvee \Delta$ such that $d \in \mathcal{K}(D)$ and $e \leq f(d)$, and the conclusion follows by compactness of $d$. Conversely, if $f$ is continuous and $e \leq f(x)$, take a directed $\Delta \subseteq \mathcal{K}(D)$ such that $x = \bigvee \Delta$. Then by continuity we can rephrase $e \leq f(x)$ as $e \leq \bigvee f(\Delta)$, and we conclude by compactness of $e$. For the second part of the statement, notice:

$$\begin{aligned} f(x) \;\; &= \;\; \bigvee \{e \in \mathcal{K}(E) \mid e \leq f(x)\} \\ &= \;\; \bigvee \{e \in \mathcal{K}(E) \mid \exists d \in \mathcal{K}(D) \; d \leq x \; and \; e \leq f(d)\} \,. \end{aligned}$$   □

---

[2]This definition of *graph* is a variant of the set theoretical definition used in example 1.1.6(3), which is well suited for continuous functions over algebraic cpo's.

**Definition 1.1.17 (effective continuity)** *If $D$ and $E$ are $\omega$-algebraic dcpo's, and if two surjective enumerations $\{d_n\}_{n<\omega}$ and $\{e_n\}_{n<\omega}$ of the compact elements of $D$ and $E$ are given, an element $x$ of, say, $D$, is called computable if $\{n \mid d_n \leq x\}$ is recursively enumerable. A function $f : D \to E$ such that $\{(m,n) \mid e_n \leq f(d_m)\}$ is recursively enumerable, is called computable, or effectively continuous.*

Since a continuous function is determined in terms of compact elements, it is natural to ask for a characterization of those sets of pairs that arise as graph of a continuous function.

**Definition 1.1.18 (approximable relation)** *If $D$ and $E$ are algebraic dcpo's, a relation $R \subseteq \mathcal{K}(D) \times \mathcal{K}(E)$ is called an approximable relation if it satisfies:*

$(AR_1)$ $(d, e_1), (d, e_2) \in R$ $\qquad \Rightarrow \exists e \ (e_1, e_2 \leq e \text{ and } (d, e) \in R)$
$(AR_2)$ $(d, e) \in R, d \leq d_1, e_1 \leq e \Rightarrow (d_1, e_1) \in R$.

**Proposition 1.1.19** *The approximable relations are exactly the graphs of continuous functions.*

PROOF. Clearly, the graph of a continuous function satisfies $(AR_1)$ and $(AR_2)$. Conversely, let $R$ be an approximable relation. We define $f$ by:

$$f(x) = \bigvee \{e \mid \exists d \leq x \ (d, e) \in R\} .$$

We show that $f$ is well-defined. We have to check that $\{e \mid \exists d \leq x \ (d, e) \in R\}$ is directed. Let $(d_1, e_1), (d_2, e_2) \in R$, with $d_1, d_2 \leq x$. By algebraicity there exists a compact $d$ such that $d_1, d_2 \leq d \leq x$. We have:

- $(d, e_1), (d, e_2) \in R$ by $(AR_2)$,

- $(d, e) \in R$ for some $e$ such that $e_1, e_2 \leq e$ by $(AR_1)$.

Hence $e$ fits. The proofs that $f$ is continuous and $graph(f) = R$ are easy.  $\square$

Next we show how algebraic dcpo's correspond to a completion process, similar to that for obtaining real numbers from rationals.

**Definition 1.1.20 (ideal)** *Given a preorder $(P, \leq)$, an ideal $I$ is a directed, lower subset of $P$ (i.e., if $x \leq y \in P$, then $x \in P$). Write $Ide(P)$ for the collection of ideals over $P$, ordered by set theoretical inclusion. An ideal $I$ is called principal if $(\exists x \in P \ I = \downarrow x)$.*

**Proposition 1.1.21 (ideal completion)** (1) *If $P$ is a preorder, then $Ide(P)$ is an algebraic dcpo whose compact elements are exactly the principal ideals.*

(2) *If $D$ is an algebraic dcpo, then $D$ and $Ide(\mathcal{K}(D))$ are isomorphic in **Dcpo**.*

PROOF. (1) Let $\Delta$ be a directed set of ideals. Define $\bigvee \Delta$ as the set theoretical union of the ideals in $\Delta$. It is easily checked that this is an ideal, thus it is the lub of $\Delta$ in $Ide(P)$. The rest of (1) follows from the following obvious facts:

$I = \bigcup\{\downarrow x \mid \downarrow x \subseteq I\}$, and principal ideals are compact. (The directedness of $\{\downarrow x \mid \downarrow x \subseteq I\}$ follows from the directedness of $I$.)

(2) The two inverse functions are $x \mapsto \{d \in \mathcal{K}(D) \mid d \leq x\}$ and $I \mapsto \bigvee I$.     □

Ideal completion is a universal construction, characterized by an adjunction (cf. definition A2.4.4).

**Proposition 1.1.22 (ideal completion free)** *Ideal completion is left adjoint to the forgetful functor* Forget : **Dcpo** → **P**, *where* **P** *is the category of partial orders and monotonic functions, and where* Forget *takes a dcpo to the underlying partial order and a continuous function to the underlying monotonic function. Less abstractly, given a partial order $X$ and a dcpo $D$, every monotonic function $f : X \to D$ extends uniquely to a continuous function $\hat{f} : Ide(X) \to D$.*

PROOF. We define the counity of the adjunction by $\eta(x) = \downarrow x$. Take a monotonic $f : X \to D$. The unique continuous extension $\hat{f}$ of $f$ to $Ide(X)$ is defined by $\hat{f}(I) = \bigvee_{x \in I} f(x)$.     □

In a different perspective, ideal completion determines an equivalence of categories.

**Proposition 1.1.23** *The ideal completion and the transformation $D \mapsto \mathcal{K}(D)$ determine an equivalence between* **Adcpo** *and the category of partial orders and approximable relations.*

PROOF. First we make sure that partial orders and approximable relations form a category. Composition is defined as graph composition:

$$R' \circ R = \{(d, d'') \mid \exists d' \ (d, d') \in R \text{ and } (d', d'') \in R'\}.$$

We only check that $R' \circ R$ satisfies $(AR_1)$. Let $(d, d_1') \in R$, $(d_1', d_1'') \in R'$, $(d, d_2') \in R$, and $(d_2', d_2'') \in R'$. Then:

$$
\begin{array}{ll}
(d, d') \in R \text{ for some } d' \geq d_1', d_2' & \text{(by } (AR_1)) \\
(d', d_1'') \in R', (d', d_2'') \in R' & \text{(by } (AR_2)) \\
(d', d'') \in R' \text{ for some } d'' \geq d_1'', d_2'' & \text{(by } (AR_1)).
\end{array}
$$

The rest of the proposition follows easily from propositions 1.1.21 and 1.1.19. □

**Exercise 1.1.24** *Consider the finite partial terms over a signature $\Sigma \cup \{\Omega\}$ (disjoint union) including a special symbol $\Omega$ of arity 0, ordered as follows: $s \leq t$ iff $\vdash s \leq t$ can be established by the following rules:*

$$\frac{}{\vdash \Omega \leq t} \qquad \frac{\vdash s_1 \leq t_1 \ \cdots \ \vdash s_n \leq t_n}{f(s_1, \ldots, s_n) \leq f(t_1, \ldots, t_n)}.$$

*Show that the ideal completion of this partial order is isomorphic to the set of finite and infinite terms as defined in example 1.1.13.*

## 1.2   Dcpo's as topological spaces

Any partial order $(X, \leq)$ may be endowed with a topology, called the *Alexandrov topology*, whose open sets are the upper subsets of $X$ (i.e., the subsets $U$ such that $(x \in U$ and $x \leq y) \Rightarrow y \in U)$. It has as a basis the sets $\uparrow x$, where $x$ ranges over $X$. Conversely, with every topological space $(X, \Omega X)$, one may associate a preorder, called the *specialization preorder*, defined by:

$$x \leq y \quad \text{iff} \quad \forall U \in \Omega X \ \ x \in U \Rightarrow y \in U \ .$$

A $T_0$ topology is by definition a topology whose associated preorder is a partial order, i.e., if $x \neq y$, then either there exists an open set $U$ such that $x \in U$ and $y \notin U$, or there exists an open set $U$ such that $y \in U$ and $x \notin U$. Classical topology assumes a much stronger separation axiom, known as $T_2$ or Hausdorff: if $x \neq y$, then there exist disjoint open sets $U$ and $V$ such that $x \in U$ and $y \in V$. The topological spaces arising from dcpo's are not Hausdorff. They are not even $T_1$, where $T_1$ is the following intermediate property: if $x \neq y$, then there exists an open set $U$ such that $x \in U$ and $y \notin U$. (Clearly, if $T_1$ holds, and if $\leq$ is the specialization order, then $x \leq y \Rightarrow x = y$.) We seek a $T_0$ topology associated with a dcpo in such a way that:

- the specialization order is the dcpo order,

- order theoretical continuity coincides with topological continuity.

Recall that the open sets of a topological space $X$ are in one-to-one correspondence with the continuous functions $X \to \{\bot, \top\}$, where $\{\bot, \top\}$ is endowed with the topology $\{\emptyset, \{\top\}, \{\bot, \top\}\}$. Precisely, the correspondence associates with an open set its characteristic function, and maps any $f$ to $f^{-1}(\top)$. The specialization order on $\{\bot, \top\}$ yields the flat cpo $\mathbf{O}$ (cf. example 1.1.6). So the open sets of a dcpo $D$ must be the sets of the form $f^{-1}(\top)$, for $f$ continuous from $D$ to $\mathbf{O}$, in the order theoretical sense. This motivates the following definition.

**Definition 1.2.1 (Scott topology)** *A subset $A \subseteq D$ of a dcpo $D$ is called Scott open if:*

(1) $x \in A$ *and* $x \leq y \Rightarrow y \in A$.

(2) $\Delta$ *directed and* $\bigvee \Delta \in A \Rightarrow \exists x \in \Delta \ \ x \in A$.

*The collection $\Omega_S(D)$ of Scott open sets (which is clearly a topology) is called the Scott topology over $D$.*

**Exercise 1.2.2** *Show that $U_x = \{y \in D \mid y \not\leq x\}$ is Scott open.*

**Lemma 1.2.3** *The specialization order on $(D, \Omega_S)$ is $(D, \leq)$. In particular, $\Omega_S$ is $T_0$.*

PROOF. Call the specialization order $\leq'$. It is obvious from the definition of Scott topology that $\leq \subseteq \leq'$. Conversely, let $x \leq' y$ and suppose $x \not\leq y$, i.e., $x \in U_y$ (cf. exercise 1.2.2). Then $y \in U_y$ by definition of $\leq'$, contradicting reflexivity.   $\square$

**Proposition 1.2.4** *Let $D$, $E$ be dcpo's. The continuous functions (in the topological sense) from $(D, \Omega_S)$ to $(E, \Omega_E)$ are exactly the morphisms in* **Dcpo**.

PROOF. Let $f$ be continuous with respect to the Scott topologies. By lemma 1.2.3, $f$ is monotonic (a continuous function is always monotonic with respect to the specialization order). Suppose $f(\bigvee \Delta) \not\leq \bigvee f(\Delta)$, i.e., $\bigvee \Delta \in f^{-1}(U_{\bigvee f(\Delta)})$. Thus $f(\delta) \in U_{\bigvee f(\Delta)}$ for some $\delta \in \Delta$, since $f^{-1}(U_{\bigvee f(\Delta)})$ is Scott open. But this contradicts $f(\delta) \leq \bigvee f(\Delta)$. The converse is easy and left to the reader. $\square$

**Proposition 1.2.5 (Scott basis)** *If $D$ is algebraic, then the sets $\uparrow d$, for $d$ compact, form a basis of $\Omega_S$.*

PROOF. The sets $\uparrow d$ are Scott open, by definition of compactness. We have to show that if $\uparrow d \cap \uparrow d' \neq \emptyset$, then $\uparrow d'' \subseteq \uparrow d \cap \uparrow d'$, for some $d''$, that is, $d, d' \leq d''$. Let $x \in \uparrow d \cap \uparrow d'$, that is, $d, d' \in \{e \in \mathcal{K}(D) \mid e \leq x\}$. We find $d''$ by directedness. We also have to show that if $U$ is open and $x \in U$, then $x \in \uparrow d \subseteq U$ for some $d$: this trivially follows from the definition of open sets and by algebraicity. $\square$

Exercise 1.2.6 gives a topological justification of ideal completion. Recall that the open sets of a topological space can be viewed as the morphisms from that space into **O**. Suppose that we are interested in the dual exercise. We have an abstract topology, consisting of a partial order of 'open sets' with arbitrary lub's and finite greatest lower bounds (glb's) distributing over them. Such a structure is called a frame. (The set of open sets of a topological space, ordered by inclusion, is a frame.) Dually to the way of obtaining open sets out of points, a way to recover points from (abstract) open sets is to take the frame morphisms from $A$ to **O** (i.e., those that preserve the frame structure), where **O** is considered as a frame. The construction that takes a topological space to its frame of open sets, then to the set of points of this frame, is called soberification. All these notions of abstract topology will be developed in section 10.1.

**Exercise 1.2.6** *Let $(X, \leq)$ be a partial order. Show that ideals of $X$ are in one-to-one correspondence with the points of the Alexandrov topology over $X$, i.e., the frame homomorphisms from $\Omega X$ to* **O**. *In other words, ideal completion is an instance of soberification.*

The following exercise, based on [EH96], hints at recent developments connecting classical topology with domain theory, with applications to effective integration and effective computations over real numbers [Eda95b, Eda95a, Esc95]. The basic idea, due to Scott, is to look at, say, real numbers as the maximal points of a partial order of suitable neighborhoods, for example, the interval $[1/2, 3/2]$ is an approximation of the real number 1 represented as the interval $[1, 1]$ (see also exercise 5.1.4).

**Exercise\* 1.2.7 (Edalat-Heckmann)** *(This exercise requires some elementary knowledge of metric spaces.) Let $X$ be a metric space. A formal ball on $X$ is a pair $(x, r)$, with $x \in X$ and $r \geq 0$ a positive real number. Formal balls are ordered by $(x, r) \leq (y, s) \Leftrightarrow d(x, y) \leq r - s$. The set of formal balls is denoted by* **B**$X$. *(1) Show* that $\mathbf{B}X$ is a poset. (2) Show that an ascending chain $\{(x_n, r_n)\}_{n\in\omega}$ in $\mathbf{B}X$ has $(y, s)$ as lub iff $y$ and $s$ are the limits of $\{(x_n)\}_{n\in\omega}$ and $\{(r_n)\}_{n\in\omega}$, respectively. Show that $\mathbf{B}X$ is an $\omega$-dcpo iff $X$ is complete (i.e., if every Cauchy sequence converges in $X$). (4) Show that $X \times \{0\}$ is the subset of maximal elements of $\mathbf{B}X$, and that the induced subspace (with respect to the Scott topology on $\mathbf{B}X$) is homeomorphic to $X$. (5) Exploit this embedding of $X$ into $\mathbf{B}X$ to prove Banach's fixpoint theorem as a consequence of Kleene's fixpoint theorem (cf. 1.1.7). We recall that a function $f : X \to X$ such that $d(f(x), f(y)) \leq c\, d(x, y)$ for some $c < 1$ and for all $x, y \in X$ is called contractive, and that Banach's fixpoint theorem asserts that in a complete metric space every contractive function has a (unique) fixpoint. Hint: Associate with $f, c$ the function $\mathbf{B}(f, c)$ defined by $\mathbf{B}(f, c)(x, r) = (f(x), cr)$. (See also exercise 5.1.3.)

## 1.3   Computability and continuity

We give a recursion theoretical characterization of the set $(\omega \rightharpoonup \omega) \to_{\mathit{eff}} (\omega \rightharpoonup \omega)$ of effectively continuous functions from $\omega \rightharpoonup \omega$ to $\omega \rightharpoonup \omega$. Let $\{\phi_n\}_{n<\omega}$ be an enumeration of the set $PR$ of partial recursive functions. We have:

$$\mathcal{K}(\omega \rightharpoonup \omega) \subseteq PR \subseteq \omega \rightharpoonup \omega\,.$$

We recall theorem A1.3.1: if $A$ is a subset of $PR$ such that $\{x \mid \phi_x \in A\}$ is recursively enumerable, then for any partial recursive $f$:

$f \in A$ iff there exists a finite function $\theta \leq f$ such that $\theta \in A$.

This statement says that we can view $A$ as a Scott open. In particular, $A$ is an upper subset.

**Theorem 1.3.1 (Myhill-Shepherdson)** (1) *Let $f$ be a total recursive function that is extensional, i.e., $\phi_{f(m)} = \phi_{f(n)}$ whenever $\phi_m = \phi_n$. Then there is a unique continuous function $F : (\omega \rightharpoonup \omega) \to (\omega \rightharpoonup \omega)$ 'extending' $f$, i.e., such that $F(\phi_n) = \phi_{f(n)}$ for all $n$. Moreover, $F$ is effectively continuous.*

(2) *Conversely, any effectively continuous function $F : (\omega \rightharpoonup \omega) \to (\omega \rightharpoonup \omega)$ maps partial recursive functions to partial recursive functions, and there is a total (extensional) recursive function $f$ such that $F(\phi_n) = \phi_{f(n)}$ for all $n$.*

PROOF. (1) Define $F_0 : PR \to PR$ by $F_0(\phi_n) = \phi_{f(n)}$. The key property of $F_0$ is:

$$F_0(g)(m) \downarrow n \quad \text{iff} \quad F_0(\theta)(m) \downarrow n \text{ for some finite } \theta \leq g \quad (g \in PR)\,. \tag{1.1}$$

We get this by theorem A1.3.1, taking:

$$A = \{g \in PR \mid F_0(g)(m) \downarrow n\} \quad (m, n \text{ fixed})\,.$$

A procedure in $p$ that terminates when $\phi_p \in A$ is given by:

- computing $f(p)$,
- computing $\phi_{f(p)}(m)$ and checking $\phi_{f(p)}(m) = n$.

By continuity, there is no choice for the definition of $F$:

$$F(g)(m) \downarrow n \quad \text{iff} \quad F_0(\theta)(m) \downarrow n \text{ for some finite } \theta \le g \quad (g \in \omega \to \omega) \, .$$

(Hereafter $\theta$ always ranges over finite functions.) We show that $F$ is well-defined. Suppose that $F_0(\theta)(m) \downarrow n$ and $F_0(\theta')(m) \downarrow n'$ for some finite $\theta, \theta' \le g$. Let $\theta''$ be a finite upper bound of $\theta$ and $\theta'$. By 1.1, we have $F_0(\theta'')(m) \downarrow n$ and $F_0(\theta'')(m) \downarrow n'$, which forces $n = n'$. The function $F$ extends $F_0$ and is continuous by definition. We show finally that $F$ is effectively continuous. A procedure in (encodings of) $\theta$, $\theta'$, which terminates when $\theta' \le F(\theta) = F_0(\theta)$, is obtained as a sequence of procedures in $\theta$, which terminate when $F_0(\theta)(m) \downarrow n$, for all $m$, $n$ such that $\theta'(m) = n$. Such procedures can be obtained by prefixing the procedure considered above with a (total) procedure taking $\theta$ to an index $p$ such that $\theta = \phi_p$.

(2) Conversely, let $F$ be effectively continuous. We build $f$ as in the statement by a simple application of the s-m-n theorem (see A1.1.5): it is enough to show that $(p, m) \mapsto F(\phi_p)(m)$ is partial recursive. This in turn is equivalent to proving that $F(\phi_p)(m) \downarrow n$ is recursively enumerable in $p$, $m$, $n$. We know from the effectivity of the continuity of $F$ that the predicate $F(\theta)(m) \downarrow n$ is recursively enumerable in $\theta$, $m$, $n$. Whence the following procedure for $p$, $m$, $n$: try in parallel the successive $\theta$'s, checking whether $\theta \le \phi_p$ and $F(\theta)(m) \downarrow n$, and stop when one such $\theta$ has been found. Continuity guarantees that the procedure will succeed if $F(\phi_p)(m) \downarrow n$. $\square$

**Exercise 1.3.2** *Let $F$ be as in the statement of Myhill-Shepherdson's theorem 1.3.1. Show that the least fixpoint of $F$ is partial recursive.*

**Remark 1.3.3** *Forgetting about minimality, exercise 1.3.2 can be reformulated as follows: for any total and extensional recursive function $f : \omega \to \omega$, there exists $n_0$ such that $\phi_{f(n_0)} = \phi_{n_0}$. This is known as Kleene's recursion theorem. The proof followed here uses the (computable $\Rightarrow$ continuous) direction of theorem 1.3.1 and proposition 1.1.7.*

# 1.4 Constructions on dcpo's

In this section, we show how to construct new dcpo's out of dcpo's. First we consider the product and function space constructions. Then we consider other basic domain constructions: lifting, smash product, and sum.

Let $D$, $E$ be two dcpo's. The product $D \times E$ of $D$ and $E$ in the category of sets becomes a product in the category of dcpo's (for the categorical notion of product, see appendix 2), when endowed with the following componentwise order:

$$(x, y) \le (x', y') \quad \text{iff} \quad x \le x' \text{ and } y \le y' \, .$$

**Proposition 1.4.1 (dcpo of pairs)** *If $D$, $E$ are dcpo's, then $D \times E$ ordered as above is a dcpo. The statement also holds, replacing 'dcpo' by 'cpo'.*

PROOF. If $\Delta$ is directed in $D \times E$, define $\Delta_D = \{x \mid \exists y \ (x, y) \in \Delta\}$, and symmetrically $\Delta_E$. Then $(\bigvee \Delta_D, \bigvee \Delta_E)$ is the lub of $\Delta$. If $D$, $E$ are cpo's, then

$(\bot, \bot)$ is the minimum of $D \times E$.         $\square$

If the dcpo's are algebraic, the product in **Dcpo** coincides with the product in **Top**, the category of topological spaces.

**Exercise 1.4.2** *Let $D$, $E$ be dcpo's, let $\Omega_S$ be the Scott topology on $D \times E$, and let $\tau$ be the product of the Scott topologies on $D$ and $E$ (a basis of $\tau$ is $\{U \times V \mid U, V \text{ Scott open}\}$). Show $\tau \subseteq \Omega_S$. Show that if $D$, $E$ are algebraic, then $\tau = \Omega_S$. (See exercise 1.3.12 in [Bar84] for a situation where $\tau \neq \Omega_S$.)*

In general topology, it is not true that a continuous function of several arguments is continuous as soon as it is continuous in each argument, but this is true for dcpo's.

**Proposition 1.4.3 (argumentwise continuity)** *Let $D$, $D'$, and $E$ be dcpo's. A function $f : D \times D' \to E$ is continuous iff for all $x \in D$ the functions $f_x : D' \to E$, and for all $y \in D'$ the functions $f_y : D \to E$, defined by $f_x(y) = f(x, y)$ and $f_y(x) = f(x, y)$, respectively, are continuous.*

PROOF. Let $f : D \times D' \to E$ be continuous, and $\Delta$ be a directed subset of $D'$. Then $(x, \Delta) = \{(x, \delta) \mid \delta \in \Delta\}$ is a directed subset of $D \times D'$. Thus:

$$f_x\left(\bigvee \Delta\right) = f\left(\bigvee(x, \Delta)\right) = \bigvee f(x, \Delta) = \bigvee f_x(\Delta).$$

Suppose conversely that $f$ is continuous in each argument separately. Let $\Delta$ be directed in $D \times D'$. Let $\Delta_D$ and $\Delta_{D'}$ be as in the proof of proposition 1.4.1. Then:

$$
\begin{aligned}
f\left(\bigvee \Delta\right) &= f\left(\bigvee \Delta_D, \bigvee \Delta_{D'}\right) = \bigvee f(\Delta_D, \bigvee \Delta_{D'}) \\
&= \bigvee\{\bigvee f(\delta, \Delta_{D'}) \mid \delta \in \Delta_D\} = \bigvee f(\Delta_D, \Delta_{D'}).
\end{aligned}
$$

It remains to show $\bigvee f(\Delta_D, \Delta_{D'}) = \bigvee f(\Delta)$. One side is obvious since $\Delta \subseteq \Delta_D \times \Delta_{D'}$. Conversely, one uses directedness of $\Delta$ to check that each element of $\Delta_D \times \Delta_{D'}$ has an upper bound in $\Delta$.     $\square$

Next we consider the construction of function spaces.

**Proposition 1.4.4 (dcpo of functions)** *The set $D \to_{cont} E$ of continuous functions from a dcpo $D$ to a dcpo $E$ is a dcpo, when endowed with the* pointwise ordering *defined by*

$$f \leq_{ext} f' \quad \text{iff} \quad \forall x \; f(x) \leq f'(x)$$

*is a dcpo. Moreover, if $E$ is a cpo, then $D \to_{cont} E$ is a cpo. (We shall omit the subscripts $_{cont}$ and $_{ext}$ until chapter 12.)*

PROOF. Let $\Delta$ be a directed set of functions. Define $f(x) = \bigvee \Delta(x)$. Let $\Delta'$ be a directed subset of $D$. Then:

$$
\begin{aligned}
f\left(\bigvee \Delta'\right) &= \bigvee \Delta\left(\bigvee \Delta'\right) = \bigvee\{\bigvee g(\Delta') \mid g \in \Delta\} = \bigvee \Delta(\Delta') \\
&= \bigvee\{\bigvee \Delta(\delta') \mid \delta' \in \Delta'\} = \bigvee f(\Delta').
\end{aligned}
$$

For the last part of the statement, notice that the constant function $\lambda x. \bot$ is the minimum of $D \to E$.     $\square$

**Exercise 1.4.5 (fix continuous)** *Show that the fixpoint functional* fix : $(D \to D) \to D$ *of proposition 1.1.7 is continuous.*

The material needed to show that $D \times E$ and $D \to E$ are categorical product and function spaces is collected in exercises 1.4.6 and 1.4.7. We refer to section 4.2, and in particular to exercises 4.2.11 and 4.2.12, for the full treatment.

**Exercise 1.4.6** *Show the following properties: (1) The projections $\pi_1$ and $\pi_2$, defined by $\pi_1(x, y) = x$ and $\pi_2(x, y) = y$, are continuous. (2) Given continuous functions $f : D \to E$ and $g : D \to E'$, the pairing $\langle f, g \rangle$ defined by $\langle f, g \rangle(x) = (f(x), g(x))$ is continuous.*

**Exercise 1.4.7** *Show the following properties: (1) The evaluation defined by $ev(x, y) = x(y)$ is continuous. (2) Given $f : D \times D' \to E$, show that $\Lambda(f) : D \to (D' \to E)$ defined by $\Lambda(f)(x)(y) = f(x, y)$ is well-defined and continuous.*

What is the situation for algebraic dcpo's? Unfortunately, if $D$, $E$ are algebraic, $D \to E$ may fail to be algebraic. The story seems to begin well, though, at least for cpo's (notice the use of $\bot$ in definition 1.4.8). The following lemma shows how compact functions can be naturally constructed out of compact input and output elements.

**Lemma 1.4.8 (step functions)** (1) *Let $D$, $E$ be cpo's, $d \in \mathcal{K}(D)$ and $e \in \mathcal{K}(E)$. Then the step function $d \to e$, defined as follows, is compact:*

$$(d \to e)(x) = \begin{cases} e & \text{if } x \geq d \\ \bot & \text{otherwise}. \end{cases}$$

(2) *If $D$ and $E$ are algebraic, then $f = \bigvee\{d \to e \mid (d \to e) \leq f\}$, for any $f$.*

PROOF. First we observe that the compactness of $d$ implies that $d \to e$ is continuous and that $d \to e \leq f$ iff $e \leq f(d)$, for any $f : D \to E$.

(1) If $d \to e \leq \bigvee \Delta$, then $e = (d \to e)(d) \leq \bigvee\{f(d) \mid f \in \Delta\}$. Since $e$ is compact, we get $e \leq f(d)$ for some $f \in \Delta$, i.e., $d \to e \leq f$.

(2) Notice that $\{d \to e \mid (d \to e) \leq f\} \leq g$ iff $(e \leq f(d) \Rightarrow e \leq g(d))$ for all $d, e$ iff $f \leq g$. $\qquad \square$

The trouble is that the sets $\{g \mid g \leq f \text{ and } g \text{ compact}\}$ are not directed in general (see exercise 1.4.15). They become directed under a further assumption on the domains. The next definition is motivated by the following observation: if $d \to e \leq f$, $d' \to e' \leq f$, and $d \uparrow d'$, then also $e \uparrow e'$.

**Definition 1.4.9 (Scott domain)** *A dcpo satisfying the following axiom is called* bounded complete *(some authors say* consistently complete*):*

$$x \uparrow y \Rightarrow x \vee y \text{ exists, for any } x \text{ and } y.$$

*Bounded complete and algebraic cpo's are called* Scott domains. *The full subcategory of* **Cpo** *whose objects are Scott domains is called* **S**.

**Exercise 1.4.10** *(1) Show that a dcpo $D$ is bounded complete iff any non-empty upper bounded subset of $D$ has a lub iff any non-empty subset of $D$ has a glb. (2) Show that if $D, E$ are bounded complete, and if $f : D \to E$ is continuous, then $f$ preserves all existing lub's. Hint: Given a bounded subset $M$, consider $M' = \{\bigvee X \mid X \subseteq_{fin} M\}$.*

**Exercise 1.4.11** *Show that an algebraic dcpo $D$ is bounded complete iff $d \uparrow d' \Rightarrow d \vee d'$ exists, for any compact $d$ and $d'$ of $D$.*

Suppose that $E$ is bounded complete; then define, for $d \to e$ and $d' \to e'$ such that if $d \uparrow d'$, then also $e \uparrow e'$:

$$h(x) = \begin{cases} e \vee e' & \text{if } x \geq d \text{ and } x \geq d' \\ e & \text{if } x \geq d \text{ and } x \not\geq d' \\ e' & \text{if } x \not\geq d \text{ and } x \geq d' \\ \bot & \text{otherwise} . \end{cases}$$

It is easily checked that $h$ is the lub of $d \to e$ and $d' \to e'$.

**Theorem 1.4.12** *If $D$ is algebraic and $E$ is a Scott domain, then $D \to E$ is a Scott domain. The compact elements of $D \to E$ are exactly the functions of the form $(d_1 \to e_1) \vee \cdots \vee (d_n \to e_n)$ such that whenever $I \subseteq \{1, \ldots, n\}$ is such that $\{d_i \mid i \in I\}$ is bounded, then so is $\{e_i \mid i \in I\}$.*

PROOF. Let $\Delta$ be the set of lub's of such finite non-empty sets of step functions (which always exist by a straightforward extension of the above construction of $h$). Then $f = \bigvee\{d \to e \mid (d \to e) \leq f\}$ implies $f = \bigvee\{g \in \Delta \mid g \leq f\}$, which shows that $D \to E$ is algebraic, since $\{g \in \Delta \mid g \leq f\}$ is directed by definition, and since $\Delta$ is a set of compact elements (cf. exercise 1.1.14). Bounded completeness for compact elements obviously follows from the definition of $\Delta$. $\qquad\square$

**Remark 1.4.13** *The lub's of finite sets of step functions, when they exist, are described by the following formula:*

$$((d_1 \to e_1) \vee \cdots \vee (d_n \to e_n))(x) = \bigvee\{e_i \mid d_i \leq x\} .$$

**Exercise 1.4.14** *Show that an algebraic cpo is a lattice (i.e., it has all finite lub's and glb's) iff it has all finite lub's (cf. exercise 1.4.10). Show that if $D, E$ are algebraic lattices, then so is $D \to E$.*

There are larger full subcategories of algebraic dcpo's and algebraic cpo's that are closed under the function space construction. This will be the subject matter of chapter 5.

**Exercise 1.4.15** *Consider example (A) in figure 5.1. Show that $D$ is $\omega$-algebraic and that $D \to D$ is not algebraic. Hints: (1) Show:*

$$a \to a, b \to b \leq f \leq id \;\Rightarrow\; f(\overline{\omega}) \subseteq \overline{\omega}, f(a) = a \text{ and } f(b) = b$$
$$\Rightarrow\; \bigvee_{n \in \omega} f_n = f ,$$

*where $f_n(x) = \begin{cases} f(x) & \text{if } x \notin \omega \text{ or } (x = \overline{m} \text{ and } m \leq n) \\ f(\overline{m+1}) & \text{if } x = \overline{m} \text{ and } m > n . \end{cases}$*

*(2) Notice that $f = f_p$ entails that $f$ is constant on $\{\overline{q} \mid q > p\}$, contradicting $f \leq id$. (3) Conclude that the set of approximants of the identity is not directed.*

The following constructions play an essential role in the semantics of call-by-value, which is addressed in chapter 8. Most of the proofs are easy and omitted.

**Definition 1.4.16 (lifting)** *Let $D$ be a partial order. Its lifting $D_\perp$ is the partial order obtained by adjoining a new element $\perp$ (implicitly renaming the $\perp$ element of $D$, if any) below all the elements of $D$:*

$$x \leq y \text{ in } D_\perp \quad \Leftrightarrow \quad x = \perp \text{ or } (x, y \in D \text{ and } x \leq y \text{ in } D).$$

In particular, the flat domains, introduced in example 1.1.6, are liftings of discrete orders.

**Definition 1.4.17 (partial continuous, strict)** *Let $D$, $E$ be dcpo's.*

(1) *A partial function $f : D \rightharpoonup E$ is called continuous if $dom(f)$ (the domain of definition of $f$) is Scott open, and if $f$ restricted to $dom(f)$ is continuous, i.e., if $f(\bigvee \Delta) \downarrow$ implies $f(\bigvee \Delta) = \bigvee\{f(\delta) \mid \delta \in \Delta \text{ and } f(\delta) \downarrow\}$ (notice that since $dom(f)$ is open, the right hand set is non-empty).*

(2) *If $D$ and $E$ are cpo's, a continuous function $f : D \to E$ is called strict if $f(\perp) = \perp$.*

(3) *If $D$, $D'$, and $E$ are cpo's, a continuous function $f : D \times D' \to E$ is called:*

$$\begin{array}{lll} \text{left strict} & \text{if} & \forall x' \subset D' \ f(\perp, x') = \perp, \\ \text{right strict} & \text{if} & \forall x \in D \ f(x, \perp) = \perp. \end{array}$$

**Exercise 1.4.18** *Show that a partial function $f : D \rightharpoonup E$ between two dcpo's is continuous if and only if $f : dom(f) \to E$ is continuous in the topological sense, where $dom(f)$ is endowed with the subspace topology, i.e., open sets are of the form $dom(f) \cap U$, where $U$ is Scott open in $D$ (cf. proposition 1.2.4).*

Given two dcpo's $D, E$, the following sets are in bijective correspondence (in fact, they are order-isomorphic):

(1) The set of partial continuous functions from $D$ to $E$.

(2) The set of continuous functions from $D$ to $E_\perp$.

(3) The set of strict continuous functions from $D_\perp$ to $E_\perp$.

The transformations (all denoted as $f \mapsto \hat{f}$) are:

(1) to (2) $\hat{f}(x) = \begin{cases} f(x) & \text{if } f(x) \downarrow \\ \perp & \text{otherwise}. \end{cases}$

(2) to (1) $\hat{f}$ is the restriction of $f$ to $\{x \mid f(x) \neq \perp\}$ (notice that this set is open, cf. exercise 1.2.2).

(2) to (3) $\hat{f}(x) = \begin{cases} f(x) & \text{if } x \neq \perp \\ \perp & \text{if } x = \perp. \end{cases}$

(3) to (2) $\hat{f}$ is the restriction of $f$ to $D$.

**Exercise 1.4.19** *(1) Show that if $D, E$ are dcpo's, then the (pointwise ordered) set $D \to E$ of partial continuous functions from $D$ to $E$ is a cpo. (2) Show that if $D, E$ are cpo's, then $D \to_{\perp} E$, the set of strict continuous functions from $D$ to $E$, is a subcpo of $D \to E$ (cf. definition 1.1.1).*

The following proposition characterizes this relationship in a more abstract manner. We define the image of a functor $F : \mathbf{C} \to \mathbf{C}'$ as the subcategory of $\mathbf{C}'$ whose objects are (the objects isomorphic to) $Fa$ for some $a \in Ob_{\mathbf{C}}$, and whose arrows are the morphisms $Ff$ for some morphism $f$ of $\mathbf{C}$.

**Proposition 1.4.20 (lifting as adjunction)** *(1) The lifting of a dcpo is a cpo. Lifting is right adjoint to the inclusion functor from **Dcpo** to the category **pDcpo** of dcpo's and partial continuous functions.*

*(2) The lifting functor is faithful, and its image is the category **Scpo** of cpo's and strict continuous functions.*

*(3) Lifting is left adjoint to the inclusion functor from **Scpo** to **Cpo**.*

PROOF. We only show how (3) follows from (1) and (2) by categorical 'abstract nonsense'. Suppose that we have an adjunction $F \dashv G$, with $F : \mathbf{C} \to \mathbf{C}'$ and $G : \mathbf{C}' \to \mathbf{C}$, Then call $\mathbf{C_1}$ the image of $G$, and $\mathbf{C_2}$ the full subcategory of $\mathbf{C}$ whose objects are those of $\mathbf{C_1}$. There are inclusion functors $Inc_1 : \mathbf{C_1} \to \mathbf{C_2}$ and $Inc_2 : \mathbf{C_2} \to \mathbf{C}$. It is easy to see that $F \circ Inc_2 \dashv Inc_1 \circ G$, where $G$ is now considered from $\mathbf{C}'$ to $\mathbf{C_1}$. If moreover $G$ is faithful, and faithful on objects (i.e., if $Ga' = Gb'$ implies $a' = b'$), then $G : \mathbf{C}' \to \mathbf{C_1}$ is actually an isomorphism of categories, so that, composing with $G$, $G^{-1}$, respectively, the adjunction becomes:

$$G \circ F \circ Inc_2 \dashv Inc_1 \circ G \circ G^{-1} = Inc_1 \,.$$

If we take $\mathbf{C} = \mathbf{Dcpo}$, $\mathbf{C}' = \mathbf{pDcpo}$, and the inclusion and lifting functors as $F$ and $G$, respectively, we obtain (3). $\qquad\qquad\qquad\qquad\qquad\qquad\qquad\square$

The first adjunction is at the root of a more abstract definition of lifting, which will be given in section 8.1.

**Definition 1.4.21 (smash product)** *Let $D$ and $E$ be two cpo's. Their smash product is the subset $D \otimes E$ of $D \times E$ defined by:*

$$D \otimes E = \{(x, y) \mid (x \neq \perp \text{ and } y \neq \perp) \text{ or } (x = \perp \text{ and } y = \perp)\} \,,$$

*and ordered by the induced pointwise ordering.*

Smash products enjoy a universal property.

**Exercise 1.4.22** *(1) Show that the smash product of two cpo's $D, D'$ is a cpo, and that the function $\otimes : D \times D' \to D \otimes D'$ defined as follows is continuous:*

$$\otimes(x, x') = \begin{cases} (x, x') & \text{if } (x, x') \in D \otimes D' \\ (\perp, \perp) & \text{otherwise} \,. \end{cases}$$

*(2) Show that the function $\otimes$ is universal in the following sense: for any $E$ and any continuous function $f : D \times D' \to E$ that is both left strict and right strict, there exists a unique strict continuous function $\hat{f} : D \otimes D' \to E$ such that $\hat{f} \circ \otimes = f$.*

Several notions of sums have been used in the literature to give meaning to sum types.

**Definition 1.4.23 (coalesced, separated sum)** *Let $D, E$ be two cpo's. Their coalesced sum $D + E$ is defined by:*

$$D + E = \{(1, x) \mid x \in D\backslash\{\bot\}\} \cup \{(2, y) \mid y \in E\backslash\{\bot\}\} \cup \{\bot\},$$

*and is ordered as follows: $z_1 \leq z_2$ iff*

$$
\begin{aligned}
z_1 = \bot \quad &or \quad (z_1 = (1, x_1), z_2 = (1, x_2) \text{ and } x_1 \leq x_2) \\
&or \quad (z_1 = (2, y_1), z_2 = (2, y_2) \text{ and } y_1 \leq y_2).
\end{aligned}
$$

*The separated sum of $D$ and $E$ is defined as $D_\bot + E_\bot$.*

Thus, in a coalesced sum, the two $\bot$'s are identified, while in the separated sum, a new $\bot$ element is created and acts as a switch, because any two elements above $\bot$ are either incompatible or come from the same component $D$ or $E$.

**Exercise 1.4.24** *(1) Let $D$ and $E$ be two dcpo's. Show that their disjoint union, ordered in the obvious way, is a categorical coproduct in* **Dcpo**. *(2) Let $D$ and $E$ be two cpo's. Show that their coalesced sum, ordered in the obvious way, is a categorical coproduct in* **Scpo**. *(3) Show that neither the coalesced nor the separated sum yield a categorical coproduct in* **Cpo**.

Exercise 1.4.24 suggests that sums do not fit as categorical coproducts in a cartesian closed category of cpo's. We refer to exercise 6.1.10 for precise negative results.

## 1.5   Toy denotational semantics

We illustrate the use of domains by giving a denotational semantics for a simple imperative language IMP, whose set of commands is given by the following grammar:

$$c ::= a \mid skip \mid c; c \mid if \ b \ then \ c \ else \ c \mid while \ b \ do \ c,$$

where $b$ and $a$ range over two unspecified sets *Bexp* and *Act* of boolean expressions and of actions, respectively. The set of commands is written *Com*. We define the meaning of the commands of this language, first by means of rules, second by means of mathematical objects: sets and functions with structure. Thus we specify their operational and denotational semantics, respectively, as discussed in the preface. In IMP, these two semantics agree. We shall see later that it is difficult to achieve this goal in general (see section 6.4).

With the unspecified syntactic domains *Bexp* and *Act* we associate unspecified denotation functions $[\![ \_ ]\!] : Bexp \rightarrow (\Sigma \rightarrow \mathbf{B})$ and $[\![ \_ ]\!] : Act \rightarrow (\Sigma \rightarrow \Sigma)$, where $\Sigma$ is an unspecified set of states (for example an environment assigning values to identifiers), and $\mathbf{B} = \{tt, ff\}$ is the set of truth values.

The operational semantics of IMP is given by the formal system described in figure 1.1. In this figure, there are so-called judgments of the form $\langle c, \sigma \rangle \rightarrow \sigma'$,

$$\frac{[\![a]\!]\sigma = \sigma'}{\langle a, \sigma \rangle \to \sigma'}$$

$$\frac{}{\langle skip, \sigma \rangle \to \sigma} \qquad\qquad \frac{\langle c_0, \sigma \rangle \to \sigma' \quad \langle c_1, \sigma' \rangle \to \sigma''}{\langle c_0; c_1, \sigma \rangle \to \sigma''}$$

$$\frac{[\![b]\!]\sigma = tt \quad \langle c_0, \sigma \rangle \to \sigma'}{\langle if\ b\ then\ c_0\ else\ c_1, \sigma \rangle \to \sigma'} \qquad \frac{[\![b]\!]\sigma = f\!f \quad \langle c_1, \sigma \rangle \to \sigma'}{\langle if\ b\ then\ c_0\ else\ c_1, \sigma \rangle \to \sigma'}$$

$$\frac{[\![b]\!]\sigma = f\!f}{\langle while\ b\ do\ c, \sigma \rangle \to \sigma} \qquad \frac{[\![b]\!]\sigma = tt \quad \langle c, \sigma \rangle \to \sigma' \quad \langle while\ b\ do\ c, \sigma' \rangle \to \sigma''}{\langle while\ b\ do\ c, \sigma \rangle \to \sigma''}$$

Figure 1.1: The operational semantics of IMP

which should be read as: 'starting with state $\sigma$, the command $c$ terminates and its effect is to transform the state $\sigma$ into the state $\sigma'$'. A proof, or derivation, of such a judgment is a tree, all of whose nodes are instances of the inference rules. The rules show that IMP has no side effects: the evaluation of expressions does not change the state.

**Lemma 1.5.1** *Set $w = while\ b\ do\ c$. Then:*

$$w \ \approx \ if\ b\ then\ (c; w)\ else\ skip\ ,$$

*where $\approx$ is defined by: $c_0 \approx c_1$ iff $\forall \sigma, \sigma' \ \langle c_0, \sigma \rangle \to \sigma' \Leftrightarrow \langle c_1, \sigma \rangle \to \sigma'$.*

PROOF. By a simple case analysis on the last rule employed to show $\langle c, \sigma \rangle \to \sigma'$, where $c$ stands for $w$ and for $if\ b\ then\ c; w\ else\ skip$, respectively. □

**Exercise 1.5.2** *The following is a specified version of Bexp and Act (the actions are assignment commands, therefore we introduce a syntactic category Aexp of arithmetical expressions):*

$$\begin{aligned} Bexp \quad &b ::= tt \mid f\!f \mid e = e \mid e \le e \mid \neg b \mid b \wedge b \mid b \vee b \\ Aexp \quad &e ::= i \mid X \mid e + e \mid e - e \mid e \times e \\ Act \quad &a ::= (X := e)\ , \end{aligned}$$

*where $i$ ranges over the set $\omega$ of natural numbers, and $X$ ranges over a set Loc of locations. The set $\Sigma$ is defined by $\Sigma = Loc \to \omega$. (1) Complete the description of the operational semantics, by rules like:*

$$\frac{\langle b, \sigma \rangle \to tt}{\langle \neg b, \sigma \rangle \to f\!f} \qquad \frac{}{\langle X, \sigma \rangle \to \sigma(X)}\ .$$

*(2) Prove $\langle e, \sigma \rangle \to m$ and $\langle e, \sigma \rangle \to n \Rightarrow m = n$ (similarly for Bexp) (determinism of expression evaluation). Hint: Use structural induction, that is, induction on the size of expressions. (3) Prove $\langle c, \sigma \rangle \to \sigma'$ and $\langle c, \sigma \rangle \to \sigma'' \Rightarrow \sigma' = \sigma''$ (determinism of command evaluation). Hint: Use induction on the size of derivations. (4) Prove $\nexists \sigma' \ \langle while\ tt\ do\ c, \sigma \rangle \to \sigma'$. Hint: Reason by contradiction, with a minimal derivation.*

$$
\begin{array}{lcl}
[\![skip]\!] & = & id \\
[\![c_0; c_1]\!] & = & [\![c_1]\!] \circ [\![c_0]\!] \\
[\![if\ b\ then\ c_0\ else\ c_1]\!] & = & cond \circ \langle [\![b]\!], \langle [\![c_0]\!], [\![c_1]\!] \rangle \rangle \\
[\![while\ b\ do\ c]\!] & = & fix(\lambda\phi.cond \circ \langle [\![b]\!], \langle \phi \circ [\![c]\!], id \rangle \rangle)
\end{array}
$$

- $\langle \_, \_ \rangle$ is the set theoretical pairing of $f$ and $g$ (cf. exercise 1.4.6).

- $cond : \mathbf{B} \times (\Sigma \times \Sigma) \to \Sigma$ is the conditional function: $cond(tt, (\sigma, \sigma')) = \sigma$, and $cond(ff, (\sigma, \sigma')) = \sigma'$.

- $fix : ((\Sigma \rightharpoonup \Sigma) \to (\Sigma \rightharpoonup \Sigma)) \to (\Sigma \rightharpoonup \Sigma)$ is the least fixpoint function (cf. proposition 1.1.7).

Figure 1.2: The denotational semantics of IMP

The denotational semantics of IMP is given by a function:

$$
[\![\_]\!] : Com \to (\Sigma \rightharpoonup \Sigma),
$$

i.e., a function that associates with every command $c$ a partially defined function $[\![c]\!]$ from states to states. This function extends $[\![\_]\!] : Act \to (\Sigma \to \Sigma)$. The semantics employs the type $\Sigma \rightharpoonup \Sigma$ of *partial* functions, because loops may cause non-termination, as in *while tt do skip*. The meaning of *skip* and command sequencing are given by the identity and by function composition, respectively. The meaning of conditionals is defined by cases. In other words, the meanings of these three constructs are an obvious rephrasing of the operational semantics:

$$
\begin{array}{lcl}
[\![skip]\!]\sigma & = & \sigma \\
[\![c_0; c_1]\!]\sigma & = & [\![c_1]\!]([\![c_0]\!]\sigma) \\
[\![if\ b\ then\ c_0\ else\ c_1]\!]\sigma & = & \left\{ \begin{array}{ll} [\![c_0]\!]\sigma & \text{if } [\![b]\!]\sigma = tt \\ [\![c_1]\!]\sigma & \text{if } [\![b]\!]\sigma = ff \end{array} \right. .
\end{array}
$$

The denotational meaning of *while* is a fixpoint construction suggested by lemma 1.5.1. The full definition of $[\![\_]\!]$ by structural induction is given in figure 1.2.

**Theorem 1.5.3** *The following equivalence holds, for any $c$, $\sigma$, $\sigma'$: $\langle c, \sigma \rangle \to \sigma' \Leftrightarrow [\![c]\!]\sigma = \sigma'$.*

PROOF HINT. ($\Rightarrow$) This is easily shown by induction on derivations.

($\Leftarrow$) This is proved by structural induction (cf. exercise 1.5.2), and in the *while* case by mathematical induction. Let $[\![while\ b\ do\ c]\!]\sigma = \sigma'$, i.e., $fix(\Phi)(\sigma) = \sigma'$, where:

$$
\Phi = \lambda\phi.cond \circ \langle [\![b]\!], \langle \phi \circ [\![c]\!], id \rangle \rangle .
$$

Then since $graph(fix(\Phi)) = \bigcup_{n \geq 0} graph(\Phi^n(\bot))$, we have $(\sigma, \sigma') \in graph(\Phi^n(\bot))$ for some $n$. Hence it is enough to prove:

$$
\forall n\ (\Phi^n(\bot)(\sigma) \downarrow \Rightarrow \langle while\ b\ do\ c, \sigma \rangle \to \Phi^n(\bot)(\sigma)),
$$

by induction on $n$. The base case is obvious, because $\Phi^0(\bot) = \bot$ has an empty graph. For the induction step, there are two cases:

(1) $[\![b]\!]\sigma = tt$. then $\Phi^{n+1}(\bot)(\sigma) = \Phi^n(\bot)(\sigma')$, where $[\![c]\!]\sigma = \sigma'$; by induction $\langle b, \sigma \rangle \to tt$, $\langle c, \sigma \rangle \to \sigma'$, and $\langle while\ b\ do\ c, \sigma' \rangle \to \Phi^n(\bot)(\sigma')$. Hence, by the definition of the operational semantics:

$$\langle while\ b\ do\ c, \sigma \rangle \to \Phi^n(\bot)(\sigma') = \Phi^{n+1}(\bot)(\sigma) .$$

(2) $[\![b]\!]\sigma = ff$. then $\Phi^{n+1}(\bot)(\sigma) = \sigma$, and by induction $\langle b, \sigma \rangle \to ff$. Hence, by definition of the operational semantics, $\langle while\ b\ do\ c, \sigma \rangle \to \sigma = \Phi^{n+1}(\bot)(\sigma)$. □

## 1.6   Continuation semantics *

Control operators are programming constructs that allow us to break the textual line-to-line order of execution of a program. In this section, we modify the language IMP replacing loops by *goto* commands. A *goto* command is an example of control operator. In chapter 8, we shall discuss control operators in the setting of functional programming. The commands of IMP$'$ are written using the following grammar:

$$c ::= a \mid skip \mid c; c \mid if\ b\ then\ c\ else\ c \mid goto\ l \mid l : c\,,$$

where *Bexp* is as in IMP, and where $l$ ranges over a set *Lab* of labels. We impose a further condition: in a command, any occurrence of *goto l* must always be in the scope of the declaration of $l$: e.g., $(l : c); goto\ l$ is ruled out, and $l : (\cdots (goto\ l) \cdots)$ is acceptable. Formally, we define the following simple deductive system, whose judgments have the form $L \vdash c$, where $L$ is a (finite) subset of labels:

$$\frac{}{L \vdash a} \qquad\qquad \frac{}{L \vdash skip}$$

$$\frac{L \vdash c_0 \quad L \vdash c_1}{L \vdash c_0; c_1} \qquad\qquad \frac{L \vdash c_0 \quad L \vdash c_1}{L \vdash if\ b\ then\ c_0\ else\ c_1}$$

$$\frac{l \in L}{L \vdash goto\ l} \qquad\qquad \frac{L \cup \{l\} \vdash c}{L \vdash l : c} .$$

The set *Com$'$* of the commands of the language IMP$'$ is defined as $\{c \mid \exists L\ (L \vdash c)\}$.

The semantics of IMP$'$ is more difficult than that of IMP. The inclusion of *goto* complicates the task of determining 'what to do next'. In our first language, a command acted as a state transformer, and handed its resulting state to the next command. The presence of *goto* creates a new situation. In a command $c_0; c_1$, $c_0$ may jump to a completely different area of the program, so that $c_1$ is possibly not the 'next command'. Consequently, we can no longer consider an interpretation where $c_0$ produces a state that $c_1$ can start with. An appropriate way of approaching the semantics of *goto* is by means of *continuations*. The main idea is that, since possible jumps make future – or continuation – of the program unpredictable, then future must become a parameter of the semantics. This guides us to the definition of the following sets:

$$Cont = \Sigma \to \Sigma$$
$$Env = Lab \to Cont .$$

$$
\begin{aligned}
[\![a]\!]'\rho\theta &= \theta \circ [\![a]\!] \\
[\![skip]\!]' &= id \\
[\![c_0; c_1]\!]'\rho &= [\![c_0]\!]'\rho \circ [\![c_1]\!]'\rho \\
[\![if\ b\ then\ c_0\ else\ c_1]\!]'\rho\theta\sigma &= cond([\![b]\!]\sigma, [\![c_0]\!]'\rho\theta\sigma, [\![c_1]\!]'\rho\theta\sigma) \\
[\![goto\ l]\!]'\rho\theta &= \rho(l) \\
[\![l : c]\!]'\rho\theta &= fix(\lambda\theta'.[\![c]\!]'\rho[\theta'/l]\theta)
\end{aligned}
$$

Figure 1.3: The denotational semantics of IMP$'$

*Cont* is called the set of command continuations, and *Env* is called the set of environments. We let $\theta$, $\rho$ range over *Cont*, *Env*, respectively. The semantic function $[\![\_]\!]'$ for IMP$'$ has the following type:

$$[\![\_]\!]' : Com' \to (Env \to (Cont \to Cont)) .$$

Moreover, when we write $[\![c]\!]'\rho$, it is intended that $L \vdash c$ for some $L$ such that $\rho(l)$ is defined for all $l \in L$. First, we define $[\![\_]\!]'$ on the subset *Act* of *Com'*, for which the function $[\![\_]\!] : Act \to (\Sigma \to \Sigma)$ is available. Then the definition of $[\![\ ]\!]'$ is extended to *Com'*. The full definition is given in figure 1.3. The boolean expressions are interpreted with the predefined function $[\![\_]\!] : Bexp \to (\Sigma \to \mathbf{B})$ of section 1.5.

**Exercise 1.6.1** *Show that if $L \vdash c$, then $[\![c]\!]'\rho_1 = [\![c]\!]'\rho_2$ if $\rho_1(l) = \rho_2(l)$ for all $l \in L$.*

**Exercise 1.6.2** *A while command can be encoded in IMP$'$. Specifically, the effect of (while b do c) can be achieved by ($l$ : if b then ($c$; goto $l$) else skip). Use this encoding to define a translation $(\_)^*$ from IMP to IMP$'$, and show $[\![c]\!] = [\![c^*]\!]'\bot id$, for every $c \in Com$.*

**Exercise\* 1.6.3** *Design an operational semantics for IMP$'$ and prove an equivalence result similar to theorem 1.5.3. Hints: Replace the judgments $\langle c, \sigma \rangle \to \sigma'$ by judgments $\langle (c, \rho, S), \sigma \rangle \to \sigma'$, where $\rho$ and $S$ are syntactic versions of environments and continuations, respectively. Take as syntactic environments functions from labels to triples $(c, \rho, S)$, and as syntactic continuations lists of pairs $(c, \rho)$. The equivalence result to prove is of the form $\langle (c, \rho), S, \sigma \rangle \to \sigma' \Leftrightarrow [\![c]\!]\,[\![\rho]\!]\,[\![S]\!]\,\sigma = \sigma'$ .*

# 2

# Syntactic theory of the λ-calculus

This chapter introduces the untyped λ-calculus. We establish some of its fundamental theorems, among which we count the syntactic continuity theorem, which offers another indication of the relevance of Scott continuity (cf. section 1.1 and theorem 1.3.1).

The λ-calculus was introduced around 1930 by Church as part of an investigation in the formal foundations of mathematics and logic [Chu41]. The related formalism of combinatory logic had been introduced some years earlier by Schönfinkel and Curry. While the foundational program was later relativized by such results as Gödel's incompleteness theorem, λ-calculus nevertheless provided one of the concurrent formalizations of partial recursive functions. Logical interest in λ-calculus was resumed by Girard's discovery of the second order λ-calculus in the early seventies (see chapter 11).

In computer science, the interest in λ-calculus goes back to Landin [Lan66] and Reynolds [Rey70]. The λ-notation is also important in LISP, designed around 1960 by MacCarthy [Mac60]. These pioneering works have eventually led to the development of functional programming languages like Scheme or ML. In parallel, Scott and Strachey used λ-calculus as a meta-language for the description of the denotational semantics of programming languages. The most comprehensive reference on λ-calculus is [Bar84]. A more introductory textbook is [HS86]. We refer to these books for more historical pointers.

In section 2.1, we present the untyped λ-calculus. The motivation to prove a strong normalization theorem leads us to the simply typed λ-calculus. Typed λ-calculi, and extensions of them, will be considered later in the book, particularly in chapters 4, 11, and 16. In section 2.2, we present Lévy's labelled λ-calculus, a powerful tool for proving many fundamental theorems of the λ-calculus. One of them is the syntactic continuity theorem, whose proof is rather technical and is the subject of section 2.3. Finally, section 2.4 motivates the study of sequentiality, which will be undertaken in section 6.5 and in chapter 14. Another fundamental theorem of the λ-calculus is Böhm's theorem. It will stated (but not proved in detail) as theorem 3.2.10 in the next chapter.

## 2.1 Untyped λ-calculus

We present the λ-calculus and its basic computation rule – the β-reduction. A proof of the confluence property is sketched, and the notion of standardization is defined.

**Definition 2.1.1 (λ-calculus)** *The syntax of the untyped λ-calculus (λ-calculus for short) is given by the following grammar:*

$$M ::= x \mid MM \mid \lambda x.M,$$

*where $x$ is called a variable, $M_1 M_2$ is called an application, and $\lambda x.M$ is called an abstraction. The set of all λ-terms is denoted by $\Lambda$.*

The following are frequently used abbreviations and terms:

$$\lambda x_1 \cdots x_n.M = \lambda x_1.(\cdots \lambda x_n.M \cdots)$$
$$MN_1 \cdots N_n = (\cdots (MN_1) \cdots N_n)$$

$$I = \lambda x.x \quad K = \lambda xy.x$$
$$\Delta = \lambda x.xx \quad S = \lambda xyz.(xz)(yz).$$

**Definition 2.1.2 (head normal form)** *A term $\lambda x_1 \cdots x_n.x M_1 \cdots M_p$, where $x$ may or may not be equal to one of the $x_i$'s, is called a head normal form (hnf for short).*

**Remark 2.1.3** *Any λ-term has exactly one of the following two forms: either it is a hnf, or it is of the form $\lambda x_1 \cdots x_n.(\lambda x.M)M_1 \cdots M_p$ ($n \geq 0$, $p \geq 1$).*

Occurrences and contexts, which we introduce next, provide a notation allowing us to manipulate subterms.

**Definition 2.1.4 (occurrence)** *Let $M$ be a term, and $u$ be a word over the alphabet $\{0, 1, 2\}$. The subterm of $M$ at occurrence $u$, written $M/u$, is defined as follows:*

$$\frac{}{M/\epsilon = M} \qquad \frac{M/u = N}{\lambda x.M/0u = N}$$

$$\frac{M_1/u = N}{M_1 M_2/1u = N} \qquad \frac{M_2/u = N}{M_1 M_2/2u = N} \quad ,$$

*where $\epsilon$ is the empty word. The term $M/u$ may well not be defined. If it is defined, we say that $u$ is an occurrence of $M$. The result of replacing the subterm $M/u$ by another term $N$ is denoted $M[N/u]$. We often write $M[N/u]$ just to say that $M/u = N$. We write:*

- $u \leq v$ *($u$ is a prefix of $v$) if $\exists w$ $(v = uw)$;*

- $u \nleq v$ *($u$ and $v$ are disjoint) if neither $u \leq v$ nor $v \leq u$, or equivalently if $\nexists w_1, w_2$ $(uw_1 = vw_2)$.*

$$\begin{aligned}
[\,]_i[N_1 \cdots N_n] &= N_i \\
x[\vec{N}] &= x \\
(C_1 C_2)[\vec{N}] &= C_1[\vec{N}]C_2[\vec{N}] \\
(\lambda x.C)[\vec{N}] &= \lambda x.(C[\vec{N}])
\end{aligned}$$

Figure 2.1: Filling the holes of a context

**Example 2.1.5**   $(\lambda x.xy)/02 = y$   $(\lambda x.xy)[x/02] = \lambda x.xx$ .

**Definition 2.1.6 (context)** *The contexts with numbered holes are defined by the following grammar (where $i \in \omega$):*

$$C ::= [\,]_i \mid x \mid CC \mid \lambda x.C \ .$$

*If all the occurrences of holes bear the same subscript in a term, we denote them $[\,]$ for short.*

In figure 2.1, we define the operation of filling the holes of a context by a (sufficiently long) vector of terms. Occurrences and contexts are related as follows.

**Proposition 2.1.7 (occurrences/contexts)** *For every term $M$ and every occurrence $u$ of $M$, there exists a unique context $C$ with a unique hole occurring exactly once, such that $M = C[M/u]$. Such contexts are called* occurrence contexts.

Free occurrences of variables are defined in figure 2.2 through a predicate $Free(u, M)$. We define $Bound(u, v, M)$ ($u$ is bound by $v$ in $M$) by:

$$\frac{M/v = \lambda x.P \quad u = v0w \quad M/u = x \quad Free(w, P)}{Bound(u, v, M)} \ .$$

If we are not interested in the actual occurrences at which variables appear bound or free, we can define the sets $FV(M)$ and $BV(M)$ of free and bound variables of $M$ by:

$$\begin{aligned}
FV(M) &= \{x \mid \exists u \ M/u = x \text{ and } Free(u, M)\} \\
BV(M) &= \{x \mid \exists u, v \ M/u = x \text{ and } Bound(u, v, M)\} \ .
\end{aligned}$$

If $BV(M)$ is empty, we say that $M$ is closed, or ground. If $M$ is a term and $x \notin FV(M)$, we often say that $x$ is fresh (relative to $M$).

The definition of substitution of a term for a (free) variable raises a difficulty (there is a similar difficulty for the quantifiers in predicate calculus). We expect $\lambda y.x$ and $\lambda z.x$ to be two different notations for the same thing: the constant function with value $x$. But careless substitution leads to:

$$(\lambda y.x)[y/x] = \lambda y.y \qquad (\lambda z.x)[y/x] = \lambda z.y \ ,$$

$$\frac{}{\mathit{Free}(\epsilon, x)} \qquad \frac{\mathit{Free}(u, M) \qquad M/u \neq x}{\mathit{Free}(0u, \lambda x.M)}$$

$$\frac{\mathit{Free}(u, M)}{\mathit{Free}(1u, MN)} \qquad \frac{\mathit{Free}(u, N)}{\mathit{Free}(2u, MN)}$$

Figure 2.2: Free occurrences

$$
\begin{aligned}
x[N/x] &= N \\
y[N/x] &= y && (y \neq x) \\
(M_1 M_2)[N/x] &= (M_1[N/x])(M_2[N/x]) \\
(\lambda y.M)[N/x] &= \lambda z.(M[z/y][N/x]) && (z \notin FV(M) \cup FV(N))
\end{aligned}
$$

Figure 2.3: Substitution in the λ-calculus

only the second of which is intended. What has gone wrong is that, in the first equality, the free variable $y$ of the substituted term has been captured. This leads to the capture-avoiding definition of substitution given in figure 2.3. The choice of $z$ satisfying the side condition in the last clause of figure 2.3 is irrelevant: we manipulate terms up to the following equivalence $\equiv$, called α-conversion:

$$(\alpha) \quad C[\lambda x.M] \equiv C[\lambda y.(M[y/x])] \quad (y \notin FV(M)) ,$$

for any occurrence context $C$ and any term $M$.

We now introduce the basic computation rule of the λ-calculus.

**Definition 2.1.8 (β-rule)** *The β-rule is the following relation between λ-terms:*

$$(\beta) \quad C[(\lambda x.M)N] \to C[M[N/x]] ,$$

*where $C$ is an occurrence context and $M, N$ are arbitrary terms. A term of the form $(\lambda x.M)N$ is called a redex. The arrow $\to$ may be given optional subscripts: $u$ (to witness the occurrence of the redex being reduced), or $\beta$ (to clarify that the reduction is a β-reduction).*

In figure 2.4, we give an alternative presentation of β-reduction, by means of an axiom and inference rules.

**Exercise 2.1.9** *Show that the substitution algorithm as specified in figure 2.3 is correctly defined, i.e., terminates.*

$$\frac{}{(\lambda x.M)N \to M[N/x]} \qquad (\xi) \quad \frac{M \to M'}{\lambda x.M \to \lambda x.M'}$$

$$(\nu) \quad \frac{M \to M'}{MN \to M'N} \qquad\qquad (\mu) \quad \frac{N \to N'}{MN \to MN'}$$

Figure 2.4: $\beta$-reduction

**Definition 2.1.10 (derivation)** *We denote by $\to_\beta^*$ (or simply $\to^*$) the reflexive and transitive closure of $\to_\beta$, and use $\to^+$ to express that at least one step is performed. The reflexive, symmetric, and transitive closure of $\to_\beta$ is denoted simply with $=_\beta$. A derivation is a sequence $M \to_{u_1} M_1 \to_{u_2} \cdots \to_{u_n} M_n$, written $D : M \to^* M_n$, with $D = u_1 \cdots u_n$.*

**Example 2.1.11** (1) $II \to I$.

(2) $SKK \to^* I$.

(3) $\Delta\Delta \to \Delta\Delta$.

(4) $(\lambda x.f(xx))(\lambda x.f(xx)) \to f((\lambda x.f(xx))(\lambda x.f(xx)))$.

*The last two examples show that there are infinite reduction sequences. Moreover, the last example indicates how fixpoints can be encoded in the λ-calculus. If we set:*

$$Y = \lambda f.(\lambda x.f(xx))(\lambda x.f(xx)),$$

*then we have $Yf =_\beta f(Yf)$. The term $Y$ is known as Curry's fixpoint combinator.*

Another rule, in addition to $\beta$, is often considered:

$$(\eta) \quad C[\lambda x.Mx] \to C[M] \quad (x \notin FV(M)).$$

This is an extensionality rule, asserting that 'every term is a function' (if it is read backwards). The $\eta$-rule is not studied further in this chapter, but will be considered in chapter 4.

**Remark 2.1.12** *Any reduction sequence starting from a hnf*

$$\lambda x_1 \cdots x_n.xM_1 \cdots M_p$$

*consists of an interleaving of independent reductions of $M_1, \ldots, M_p$. By this we mean:*

$$(\lambda x_1 \cdots x_n.xM_1 \cdots M_p \to^* P) \Rightarrow \exists N_1, \ldots N_p \left\{ \begin{array}{l} P = \lambda x_1 \cdots x_n.xN_1 \cdots N_p \text{ and} \\ \forall i \le p \ M_i \to^* N_i \,. \end{array} \right.$$

We omit most details of the proofs of the next results (see e.g., [HS86]).

$$\frac{}{M \Rightarrow M} \qquad \frac{M \Rightarrow M' \quad N \Rightarrow N'}{(\lambda x.M)N \Rightarrow M'[N'/x]}$$

$$\frac{M \Rightarrow M' \quad N \Rightarrow N'}{MN \Rightarrow M'N'} \qquad \frac{M \Rightarrow M'}{\lambda x.M \Rightarrow \lambda x.M'}$$

Figure 2.5: Parallel $\beta$-reduction

**Lemma 2.1.13** (1) *If $M \to M'$, then $M[N/x] \to M'[N/x]$.*
(2) *If $N \to N'$, then $M[N/x] \to^* M[N'/x]$.*

Lemma 2.1.13 is the key to the proof of the following property, called the local confluence.

**Proposition 2.1.14 (local confluence)** *The $\beta$-reduction is locally confluent: if $M \to N$ and $M \to P$, then $N \to^* Q$ and $P \to^* Q$ for some $Q$.*

The following is one of the fundamental theorems of the $\lambda$-calculus.

**Theorem 2.1.15 (Church-Rosser)** *The $\beta$-reduction is confluent: If $M \to^* N$ and $M \to^* P$, then $N \to^* Q$ and $P \to^* Q$ for some $Q$.*

PROOF HINT. In section 2.2, the theorem will be proved completely as a consequence of a powerful labelling method. Here we sketch an elegant direct proof due to Tait and Martin-Löf. A strongly confluent relation is a relation $\Rightarrow$ that satisfies:

$$M \Rightarrow N, M \Rightarrow P \quad \text{implies} \quad \exists Q \ N \Rightarrow Q \text{ and } P \Rightarrow Q \, .$$

By a straightforward paving argument, the strong confluence of a relation $\Rightarrow$ implies the confluence of $\Rightarrow^*$. Unfortunately, $\beta$-reduction is not strongly confluent:

$$
\begin{array}{llll}
(\lambda x. \cdots x \cdots x \cdots)N & \to & (\lambda x. \cdots x \cdots x \cdots)N' & \to & \cdots N' \cdots N' \cdots \\
(\lambda x. \cdots x \cdots x \cdots)N & \to & \cdots N \cdots N \cdots & \to^{\geq 2} & \cdots N' \cdots N' \cdots
\end{array}
$$

(by $\to^{\geq 2}$, we mean that the reduction from $\cdots N \cdots N \cdots$ to $\cdots N' \cdots N' \cdots$ takes at least two steps). But parallel reduction, defined in figure 2.5, is strongly confluent. In a parallel reduction, several redexes can be simultaneously reduced in one step. For example, we have $\cdots N \cdots N \cdots \Rightarrow \cdots N' \cdots N' \cdots$. Finally, the confluence of $\to$ easily follows from the following inclusions, which hold by definition of parallel reduction: $\to \, \subseteq \, \Rightarrow \, \subseteq \, \to^*$. □

The following exercise (based on [CH94]) states a negative result due to Klop [Klo85].

**Exercise\* 2.1.16** *Suppose that three constants $D, F, S$ are added to the λ-calculus, together with the following new rewriting axiom:*

$$(SP) \quad D(Fx)(Sx) \to x .$$

*Show that confluence fails for $\beta + (SP)$. Hints: Consider the following so-called Turing fixpoint combinator:*
$$Y_T = (\lambda xy.y(xxy))(\lambda xy.y(xxy)) .$$

*The advantage of this term over $Y$ (cf. example 2.1.11) is that $Y_T f$ is not only convertible to, but reduces to, $f(Y_T f)$. Set $C = Y_T(\lambda xy.D(F(Ey))(S(E(xy))))$ and $B = Y_T C$, where $E$ is a free variable. Notice that $B \to^* A$ and $B \to^* CA$, where $A = E(CB)$. Show that $A$ and $CA$ have no common reduct, by contradiction, taking a common reduct with a minimum number of $E$'s in head position.*

Another fundamental theorem of the λ-calculus is the standardization theorem. It will fall out from the general technique of section 2.2, but we shall need part of it to develop this technique. As a first approximation, a reduction from $M$ to $N$ is standard when it does not reduce a redex when there is no need to reduce it in order to reach $N$. The standardization theorem asserts that any derivation $M \to^* N$ can be transformed to a standard derivation from $M$ to $N$. To define precisely the notion of standard reduction, we need the notion of residual, which formalizes what a redex in a term $M$ becomes after the reduction of another redex of $M$.

**Definition 2.1.17 (residual)** *If $u$, $v$ are redex occurrences in a term $M$, and if $M \to_u N$, then $v/u$, the set of residuals of $v$ after the reduction of $u$, is defined by:*

$$v/u = \begin{cases} \{v\} & (u \not{/} v \text{ or } v < u) \\ \emptyset & (v = u) \\ \{uw'w \mid Bound(u10w', u1, M)\} & (v = u2w) \\ \{uw\} & (v = u10w) . \end{cases}$$

*The notation is extended to $V/D$, where $V$ stands for a set of redex occurrences, and $D$ for a derivation, as follows:*

$$\begin{aligned} V/u &= \bigcup \{v/u \mid v \in V\} \\ V/(uD) &= (V/u)/D . \end{aligned}$$

Here is an informal description of $v/u$ (let $M/u = (\lambda x.P)Q$ and $M/v = (\lambda y.R)S$):

• The second case is obvious: a redex is entirely 'consumed' when it is reduced.

• The first case and the last case of the definition correspond to the situation where the redex at $v$ 'remains in place'.

− If $u \not{/} v$, then $N/v = M/v$.

− If $v < u$, then $M/u$ is a subterm of $R$ or $S$, say of $R$, and $N/v$ has the form $(\lambda y.R')S$ for some $R'$.

—  If $v = u10w$, the occurrence of the redex at $v$ has to be readjusted, and moreover the redex gets instantiated:

$$P/w = ((\lambda x.P)Q)/10w = M/v = (\lambda y.R)S$$
$$N/uw = (P[Q/x])/w = (P/w)[Q/x] = (\lambda y.R[Q/x])(S[Q/x]) \ .$$

• In the third case, the subterm at occurrence $v$ is a subterm of $Q$, and gets copied by the substitution which replaces $x$ by $Q$. In particular the redex $(\lambda y.R)S$ may be duplicated if there is more than one free occurrence of $x$ in $P$. If on the contrary $x \notin FV(P)$, then $v$ has no residual.

**Example 2.1.18** *For $M = I((\lambda x.(Ix)x)(\lambda x.Ix))$, we have:*

$$220/2101 = \{220\} \quad \epsilon/2 = \{\epsilon\} \quad 2/2 = \emptyset \quad 2101/2 = \{21\} \quad 220/2 = \{212, 22\} \ .$$

**Definition 2.1.19 (left)** *If $u$, $v$ are redex occurrences of $M$, we say that $u$ is to the left of $v$ if*

$$u < v \quad or \quad \exists w, u', v' \ (u = w1u' \ and \ v = w2v'),$$

*or equivalently, if the first symbol of the redex at $u$ is textually to the left of the first symbol of the redex at $v$.*

**Definition 2.1.20 (standard)** *A derivation $D : M_0 \to_{u_1} M_1 \to_{u_2} \cdots \to_{u_n} M_n$ is called standard if*

$$\forall i, j \ 1 \leq i < j \leq n \ \Rightarrow \ \not\exists u \text{ to the left of } u_i \text{ such that } u_j \in u/D_{ij} \ ,$$

*where $D_{ij} : M_{i-1} \to_{u_i} M_i \to_{u_{i+1}} \cdots \to_{u_{j-1}} M_{j-1}$. We then write $M_0 \overset{stnd}{\longrightarrow} {}^*M_n$. A special case of standard derivation is the normal derivation, which always derives the leftmost outermost redex (leftmost redex for short), defined as follows: the leftmost redex of $\lambda x_1 \cdots x_n.(\lambda x.M)M_1 \cdots M_p$ is $(\lambda x.M)M_1$, and the leftmost redex of $\lambda x_1 \cdots x_n.xM_1 \cdots M_p$, if any, is the leftmost redex of the first $i$ such that $M_j$ is in normal form for $j < i$ and $M_i$ is not in normal form. We write $M \overset{norm}{\longrightarrow} {}^*N$ if $N$ is reached from $M$ by the normal derivation. We denote with $Val(M)$ the first abstraction (if any) met along the normal derivation from $M$, i.e.:*

$$M = M_0 \overset{norm}{\longrightarrow} M_1 \overset{norm}{\longrightarrow} \cdots \overset{norm}{\longrightarrow} M_n = Val(M),$$

*where $M_n$ is an abstraction and $M_1, \ldots, M_{n-1}$ are not abstractions.*

**Example 2.1.21** *The derivation $(\lambda x.y)(\Delta\Delta) \to_2 (\lambda x.y)(\Delta\Delta) \to_\epsilon y$ is not standard. Set $u_1 = 2$ and $u_2 = \epsilon$. Then $\epsilon = \epsilon/2$, and $\epsilon$ is to the left of $2$ in $(\lambda x.y)(\Delta\Delta)$. Informally, the derivation is not standard because the final term $y$ could have been reached without reducing the redex at occurrence $2$ in $(\lambda x.y)(\Delta\Delta)$, since we have, directly:*

$$(\lambda x.y)(\Delta\Delta) \to_\epsilon y \ .$$

**Lemma 2.1.22** *If $D : M \overset{stnd}{\longrightarrow} {}^*\lambda x.N$, then $D$ decomposes into:*

$$M \overset{norm}{\longrightarrow} {}^* Val(M) \overset{stnd}{\longrightarrow} {}^*\lambda x.N \ .$$

PROOF. By induction on the length of $D$. If $M$ is already an abstraction, then the statement holds vacuously. If $M = xM_1 \cdots M_p$, then all its reducts have the form $xN_1 \cdots N_p$, hence the statement again holds vacuously. If $M = (\lambda x.M)M_1 \cdots M_p$, and if the first step in $D$ does not reduce the leftmost redex, then the definition of standard implies that the terms in $D$ all have the form $M = (\lambda x.P)P_1 \cdots P_p$. Hence the first step of $D$ must be the first step of the normal derivation. The conclusion then follows by induction (a subderivation of a standard derivation is standard). □

## 2.2   The labelled λ-calculus

In this section, we introduce simple types, and show that simply typed terms are strongly normalizable. Next we introduce Lévy's labelled λ-calculus, and prove a more general strong normalization theorem. The following fundamental theorems of the λ-calculus appear as simple consequences of this general theorem:

- the confluence of $\beta$-reduction,
- the standardization theorem,
- the finite developments theorem,
- the syntactic continuity theorem.

In this section and in the following one, we rely on [Lev78] and [Ber79].

**Definition 2.2.1 (strongly normalizable)** *A λ-term M is called strongly normalizable if there is no infinite β-derivation starting from M. We denote by SN the set of strongly normalizable terms. A term which cannot be further reduced is called a* normal form.

**Definition 2.2.2 (size, reduction depth)** *The size of a term M is defined as follows:*

$$size(x) = 1 \,, \ size(MN) = size(M) + size(N) + 1 \,, \ size(\lambda x.M) = size(M) + 1 \,.$$

*If M $\in$ SN, the maximal length of a derivation starting from M is called the* reduction depth *of M, and is denoted depth(M).*

Confluence and normalization are the cornerstones of (typed) λ-calculus and rewriting theory. They ensure that any term has a unique normal form, which is a good candidate for being considered as the final result of the computation. The two properties[1] imply the decidability of the equality, defined as the reflexive, transitive, and symmetric closure of $\rightarrow$: to decide whether two terms $M$, $N$ are $\beta$-equal, reduce $M$, $N$ to their normal form, and check whether these normal forms coincide (up to $\alpha$-conversion). As a stepping stone for our next results, we show the standardization theorem for strongly normalizable terms.

---

[1] Actually, only the existence of an effective way to reduce a term to a normal form is sufficient for this purpose.

**Lemma 2.2.3** *If $M \in SN$ and $M \to^* N$, then $M \xrightarrow{stnd} {}^*N$.*

PROOF. By induction on $(depth(M), size(M))$. The only non-trivial case is $M = M_1 M_2$.

- If $N = N_1 N_2$ and $M_1 \to^* N_1$, $M_2 \to^* N_2$, then $M_1 \xrightarrow{stnd} {}^*N_1$, $M_2 \xrightarrow{stnd} {}^*N_2$ by induction, and we have $M_1 M_2 \xrightarrow{stnd} {}^*N_1 M_2 \xrightarrow{stnd} {}^*N_1 N_2$.

- Otherwise, $M_1 M_2 \to^* (\lambda x.N_1) N_2 \to N_1[N_2/x] \to^* N$, with $M_1 \to^* \lambda x.N_1$ and $M_2 \to^* N_2$. By induction and lemma 2.1.22:

$$M_1 \xrightarrow{norm} {}^*\lambda x.P \xrightarrow{stnd} {}^*\lambda x.N_1 .$$

Hence $M_1 M_2 \xrightarrow{norm^+} P[M_2/x]$. Also, by lemma 2.1.13, $P[M_2/x] \to^* N$ follows from $P \to^* N_1$, $M_2 \to^* N_2$, and $N_1[N_2/x] \to^* N$. Since $depth(P[M_2/x]) < depth(M)$, we get $P[M_2/x] \xrightarrow{stnd} {}^*N$ by induction. We conclude by observing that prefixing a standard derivation with a normal derivation yields a standard derivation. $\square$

**Lemma 2.2.4** *The following implication holds:*

$$M[N/x] \xrightarrow{stnd} {}^*\lambda y.P \Rightarrow \begin{cases} (M \to^* \lambda y.Q \text{ and } Q[N/x] \to^* P) \text{ or} \\ M \to^* M' = xP_1 \cdots P_n \text{ and } M'[N/x] \to^* \lambda y.P . \end{cases}$$

PROOF HINT. The statement follows quite easily from lemma 2.1.22. $\sqcap$

We now engage in an attempt to show that any term $M$ is strongly normalizable. We know by the example $\Delta\Delta \to \Delta\Delta$ that this property does *not* hold for arbitrary terms. But it holds for *typed* terms (and more generally for labelled terms whose labels are bounded, as we shall see in section 2.2). Types will be introduced right after we discover a failure in our proof attempt.

We proceed by induction on $size(M)$. We examine all the reduction paths originating from $M$. The only non-trivial case is $M = M_1 M_2$. If $M_1$ and $M_2$ never interact, then we conclude by induction. Otherwise, we have $M_1 \to^* \lambda x.N_1$, $M_2 \to^* N_2$, and $M \to^* N_1[N_2/x]$. By induction, $N_1$, $N_2$ are strongly normalizable. Hence, strong normalization can be proved from the following property:

$$(\sigma SN) \quad M, N \in SN \Rightarrow M[N/x] \in SN .$$

Let us see how an attempt to prove $(\sigma SN)$ by induction on $(depth(M), size(M))$ fails. The only interesting case is (as above):

$$M = M_1 M_2, \ M_1[N/x] \to^* \lambda y.P \text{ and } M_2[N/x] \to^* N_2.$$

We want to prove $P[N_2/y] \in SN$. By induction and lemma 2.2.3, we have $M_1[N/x] \xrightarrow{stnd} {}^*\lambda y.P$. Following lemma 2.2.4, we thus consider two cases:

(A) $M_1 \to^* \lambda y.Q$ and $Q[N/x] \to^* P$. Consider $M' = Q[M_2/y]$. We have $M \to^+ M'$, hence $depth(M') < depth(M)$, and $M'[N/x] \in SN$ by induction. On the other hand:

$$\left. \begin{array}{l} M'[N/x] = Q[N/x][M_2[N/x]/y] \\ Q[N/x] \to^* P \text{ and } M_2[N/x] \to^* N_2 \end{array} \right\} \Rightarrow M'[N/x] \to^* P[N_2/y] .$$

Hence $P[N_2/y] \in SN$.

(B) $M_1 \to^* M' = xP_1 \cdots P_n$ and $M'[N/x] \to^* \lambda y.P$. This is where we get stuck. Think of $\Delta\Delta$.

To get around the difficulty, it would be enough to have a new measure $\phi$ for which we could show, in case (B):

$$\phi(N_2) < \phi(N) . \tag{2.1}$$

Then we could carry the whole argument, by induction on:

$$(\phi(N), depth(M), size(M)) .$$

Let us briefly revisit the proof attempt. Case (A) is unchanged, since the induction is applied to $M'[N/x]$, for which the first component of the ordinal is the same as for $M$ and $N$. Case (B) is now settled because the first component of the ordinal decreases. The simply typed λ-calculus offers such a measure $\phi$.

**Definition 2.2.5 (simple types)** *The simple types are defined by the following grammar:*

$$\sigma ::= \kappa \mid \sigma \to \sigma,$$

*where $\kappa$ ranges over a collection $K$ of basic (or ground) types. The size of a type $\sigma$ is defined by:*

$$size(\kappa) = 1 \quad size(\sigma \to \tau) = size(\sigma) + size(\tau) + 1 .$$

In other words, types are built from a collection of basic types (like natural numbers, or booleans) by a unique constructor, the function space constructor. Next we introduce a syntax of raw typed terms.

**Definition 2.2.6 (raw typed)** *The raw simply typed λ-terms are λ-terms all of whose occurrences are labelled by a type. Formally, they are the terms $P$ declared by the following mutually recursive clauses:*

$$M ::= x \mid PP \mid \lambda x.P$$
$$P ::= M^\sigma .$$

*To a raw typed term $P$ we associate an untyped term by stripping all type superscripts. We denote the resulting term by $er(P)$.*

**Definition 2.2.7 (typed)** *The typed λ-terms, or $\lambda^\to$-terms, are the raw typed terms $P$ satisfying the following constraints:*

(1) *All the occurrences of $x$ that are free in $er(P)$ have the same superscript.*

(2) *If $P = (M^{\sigma_1} M^{\sigma_2})^{\sigma_3}$, then $\sigma_1 = \sigma_2 \to \sigma_3$.*

(3) *If $P = (\lambda x.M^{\sigma_1})^{\sigma_2}$, then $\sigma_2 = \sigma_3 \to \sigma_1$ for some $\sigma_3$, and all free occurrences of $x$ in $M$ have superscript $\sigma_3$.*

*The typed β-reduction is defined by:*

$$(\beta^\to) \quad C[((\lambda x.M^\tau)^{\sigma\to\tau} N^\sigma)^\tau /u] \to_u C[M^\tau[N^\sigma/x^\sigma]/u] .$$

In this chapter, we consider typed $\lambda$-calculus only in passing, on our way to Lévy's labelled $\lambda$-calculus. The significance of the simply typed $\lambda$-calculus will appear more clearly in section 4.1, where it will be described as a language of proofs in a natural deduction system.

**Lemma 2.2.8 (subject reduction)** *If $er(M^\sigma) \to N$, then $M^\sigma \to N'^\sigma$ for some $N'^\sigma$ such that $er(N'^\sigma) = N$.*

**Theorem 2.2.9 (strong normalization – simple types)** *All simply typed $\lambda$-terms are $\beta^\to$-strongly normalizable.*

PROOF. The argument attempted above now goes through. We prove:

$$(\sigma SN^\to) \quad M^\tau, N^\sigma \in SN \Rightarrow M^\tau[N^\sigma/x^\sigma] \in SN \;,$$

by induction on $(size(\sigma), depth(M), size(M))$. The typed version of the crucial case (B) is:

$$M^\tau = M_1^{\sigma' \to \tau} M_2^{\sigma'}$$
$$M_1^{\sigma' \to \tau} \to^* M'^{\sigma' \to \tau} = (\cdots (x^{\sigma_1 \to \cdots \to \sigma_n \to \sigma' \to \tau} P_1^{\sigma_1})^{\sigma_2 \to \cdots \to \sigma_n \to \sigma' \to \tau} \cdots P_n^{\sigma_n})^{\sigma' \to \tau}$$
$$M'^{\sigma' \to \tau}[N^\sigma/x^\sigma] \to^* \lambda y.P^\tau$$
$$M_2^{\sigma'}[N^\sigma/x^\sigma] \to^* N_2^{\sigma'} \;,$$

with $\sigma = \sigma_1 \to \cdots \to \sigma_n \to \sigma' \to \tau$. Then $size(\sigma') < size(\sigma)$. Hence, defining $\phi(N^\sigma)$ as the size of the type of $N$, condition 2.1, i.e., $\phi(N_2^{\sigma'}) < \phi(N^\sigma)$, holds. □

We now turn to a more general system of labels.

**Definition 2.2.10 (labels)** *We define a calculus of labels by the following grammar:*

$$\alpha ::= e \mid \underline{\alpha} \mid \overline{\alpha} \mid \alpha\alpha \;,$$

*where $e$ ranges over an infinite alphabet $E$ of atomic labels ($E$ stands for 'étiquette'). We let $\alpha, \beta$ range over labels. The height of a label $l$ is defined as follows:*

$$height(e) = 0 \quad (e \in E)$$
$$height(\underline{\alpha}) = height(\overline{\alpha}) = height(\alpha) + 1$$
$$height(\alpha\beta) = \max\{height(\alpha), height(\beta)\} \;.$$

Hence labels are defined from atomic labels $e \in E$ by underlining, overlining and concatenation. Underlining and overlining will be put to use in induction arguments (see theorem 2.2.13 and exercise 2.2.21, respectively). Labelled terms are defined in the same way as (raw) typed terms.

**Definition 2.2.11 (labelled terms)** *Labelled terms $P$ are defined by the following mutually recursive grammar:*

$$M ::= x \mid PP \mid \lambda x.P$$
$$P ::= M^\alpha \;.$$

*We write $\alpha \cdot M^\beta = M^{\alpha\beta}$, and $height(M^\alpha) = height(\alpha)$.*

$$\begin{array}{rcll}
x^\alpha[P/x] & = & \alpha \cdot P & (P \text{ is a labelled term}) \\
x^\alpha[z/x] & = & z^\alpha & \\
y^\alpha[Q/x] & = & y^\alpha & (y \neq x) \\
(P_1 P_2)^\alpha[Q/x] & = & (P_1[Q/x]P_2[Q/x])^\alpha & \\
(\lambda y.P)^\alpha[Q/x] & = & (\lambda z.P[z/y][Q/x])^\alpha & (z \notin FV(M) \cup FV(N))
\end{array}$$

Figure 2.6: Substitution in the labelled $\lambda$-calculus

Substitution for labelled terms is defined in figure 2.6. In this figure, $P$ ranges over labelled terms and $Q$ ranges over labelled terms or unlabelled variables (the latter arise from $\alpha$-conversion). As for the typed terms, the erasure of a labelled term is obtained by stripping off the labels.

The labelled version $\beta^l_{\mathcal{P}}$ of $\beta$-reduction is defined relatively to a predicate $\mathcal{P}$ on labels:

$$(\beta^l_{\mathcal{P}}) \quad C[((\lambda x.P)^\alpha Q)^\beta/u] \to_u C[\beta \cdot \overline{\alpha} \cdot P[(\underline{\alpha} \cdot Q)/x]/u] \quad \text{if } \mathcal{P}(\alpha) \text{ holds.}$$

The label $\alpha$ is called the degree of the redex. Unrestricted labelled restriction is defined as the labelled reduction with respect to the full predicate consisting of all labels.

**Definition 2.2.12 (q-bounded)** *Let $q \in \omega$. A q-bounded predicate is a predicate $\mathcal{P}$ such that $(\forall \alpha \ (\mathcal{P}(\alpha) \Rightarrow height(\alpha) \leq q))$.*

**Theorem 2.2.13 (strong normalization − labels)** *If $\mathcal{P}$ is q-bounded for some $q$, then all labelled terms are strongly $\beta^l_{\mathcal{P}}$-normalizable.*

PROOF HINT. We prove (cf. theorem 2.2.9):

$$(\sigma SN^l_{\mathcal{P}}) \quad M^\delta, N^\alpha \in SN \Rightarrow M^\delta[N^\alpha/x] \in SN \ ,$$

by induction on $(q\text{-}height(\alpha), depth(M^\delta), size(er(M^\delta)))$. The labelled version of the crucial case (B) is:

$$\begin{array}{l}
M^\delta = (M_1^\epsilon M_2^\eta)^\delta \\
M_1^\epsilon \to^* P' = (\cdots (x^\gamma P_1)^{\alpha_1} \cdots P_n)^{\alpha_n} \\
P'[N^\alpha/x] \to^* (\lambda y.P)^\beta \\
M_2^\eta[N^\alpha/x] \to^* Q_2 \ .
\end{array}$$

Since $M^\delta[N^\alpha/x] \to^* ((\lambda y.P)^\beta Q_2)^\delta \to \delta \cdot \overline{\beta} \cdot P[\underline{\beta} \cdot Q_2/y]$, condition 2.1 is rephrased here as $height(\alpha) < height(\underline{\beta} \cdot Q_2)$. *A fortiori* it is enough to prove $height(\alpha) \leq height(\underline{\beta})$ (notice the use of the underlining in $\underline{\beta}$), which is a consequence of the following claim:

**Claim.** $(\cdots (M^\zeta P_1)^{\beta_1} \cdots P_n)^{\beta_n} \to^* (\lambda y.P)^\beta \Rightarrow height(\zeta) \leq height(\beta).$

We prove the claim by induction on the length of the derivation. Suppose that $M = \lambda x.Q$ and that the first step reduces $(M^\varsigma P_1)^{\beta_1}$ (this is the only interesting case). If $n = 0$, then $\varsigma = \beta$. If $n > 0$, then:

$$(\cdots (M^\varsigma P_1)^{\beta_1} \cdots P_n)^{\beta_n} \to (\cdots (\beta_1 \cdot \overline{\varsigma} \cdot Q[\underline{\varsigma} \cdot P_1/x]) \cdots P_n)^{\beta_n},$$

and we conclude by induction, since $height(\varsigma) \leq height(\beta_1 \cdot \overline{\varsigma} \cdot Q[\underline{\varsigma} \cdot P_1/x])$. Applying the claim to $M^\varsigma = \gamma \cdot N^\alpha$, we get $height(\alpha) \leq height(\varsigma) \leq height(\beta)$. □

Now we indicate how confluence, standardization and finite developments follow from theorem 2.2.13. For full details, we refer to [AG].

**Lemma 2.2.14** *If $D : P \to^* Q$ and $v \in u/D$, then $P/u$ and $Q/v$ have the same degree.*

**Proposition 2.2.15** *If $\mathcal{P}$ is q-bounded, then $\beta_{\mathcal{P}}^l$-reduction is confluent.*

PROOF. We get local confluence by proving a labelled version of lemma 2.1.13, using lemma 2.2.14. Then we use Newman's lemma (see exercise 2.2.16): $\beta_{\mathcal{P}}^l$ is confluent, since it is locally confluent and strongly normalizing. □

**Exercise 2.2.16 (Newman)** *Prove that any locally confluent and strongly normalizing system is confluent. Hint: Use induction on the reduction depth of the term from which the two derivations originate.*

Next we transfer labelled confluence to the unlabelled calculus. We start with a term $M$, which we label arbitrarily. That is, we construct $P$ such that $er(P) = M$. If $M \to^* M_1$ and $M \to^* M_2$, then, with unrestricted labelled reduction, we get:

$$P \to^* P_1, \; P \to^* P_2 \text{ with } er(P_1) = M_1, \; er(P_2) = M_2 \;.$$

Next we construct a predicate $\mathcal{P}$ that fits the situation: $\mathcal{P}(\alpha)$ iff $\alpha$ is the degree of a redex reduced in $P \to^* P_1$ or $P \to^* P_2$. This predicate is finite, hence bounded. Thus we can complete $P_1 \to^* P_3$, $P_2 \to^* P_3$ by $\beta_{\mathcal{P}}^l$-reduction, by proposition 2.2.15, and we get $M_1 \to^* er(P_3)$ and $M_2 \to^* er(P_3)$. This gives an alternative proof of theorem 2.1.15.

**Theorem 2.2.17 (standardization)** *If $M \to^* N$, then $M \xrightarrow{stnd} {}^* N$.*

PROOF. By theorem 2.2.13 and (a labelled version of) lemma 2.2.3, using $\mathcal{P}$ defined as follows: $\mathcal{P}(\alpha)$ iff $\alpha$ is the degree of a redex reduced in $M \to^* N$. □

**Corollary 2.2.18 (normal)** *If $M$ has a normal form $N$, then $M \xrightarrow{norm} {}^* N$.*

PROOF. By theorem 2.2.17, we have $M \xrightarrow{stnd} {}^* N$. If at some step a redex different from the leftmost one is reduced, then the leftmost redex at this step has a residual in $N$, by definition of a standard reduction. This is a contradiction, since $N$ is a normal form. □

Next we define the notion of development, and we prove the finite developments theorem.

**Definition 2.2.19 (development)** *A derivation* $M \to_{u_1} M_1 \to_{u_2} \cdots \to_{u_n} M_n$
*is relative to a set $F$ of redex occurrences in $M$ if $u_1 \in F$, and if $u_i$ is a residual of
an occurrence in $F$, for all $i > 1$. If moreover $M_n$ does not contain any residual
of $F$, then $M \to_{u_1} M_1 \to_{u_2} \cdots \to_{u_n} M_n$ is called a complete development (or
development for short) of $M$ relative to $F$.*

**Theorem 2.2.20 (finite developments – 1)** *Let $M$, $F$ be as above. All reductions relative to $F$ terminate, and they terminate on the same term.*

PROOF. Take $P$ such that $er(P) = M$, and define $\mathcal{P}$ by: $\mathcal{P}(\alpha)$ iff $\alpha$ is the degree
of a redex of $F$. The conclusion then follows by lemma 2.2.14.                    □

In the following exercises, we propose a stronger version of the finite developments theorem, and we indicate how simple types can be related to labels.

**Exercise\* 2.2.21 (finite developments – 2)** *If $M \to_u N$ and if $v$ is a redex occurrence of $N$ that is not a residual of a redex occurrence in $M$, we say that $v$ is
created by $u$. (1) Let $\alpha$, $\beta$ be the degrees of the redexes $u$ in $M$ and $v$ in $N$. Show
$height(\beta) > height(\alpha)$. (2) Extend the definition of $v/u$ (cf. definition 2.1.17) to a definition of $G/D$, for two derivations originating from the same term. Hint: Define first
$G/V$ for a set $V$ of redex occurrences. (3) Show that if $D : M \to^* N$ and $D' : M \to^* N$
are two developments of $M$ relative to $F$, then $G/D = G/D'$ for any derivation $G$
originating from $M$. Hints: There are three cases of redex creation:*

$$(\lambda xy.M)N_1 N_2 \qquad (u = 1, v = \epsilon)$$
$$I(\lambda x.M)N \qquad (u = 1, v = \epsilon)$$
$$(\lambda x.C[xN])(\lambda x.M) \qquad (u = \epsilon, v = \text{any occurrence of } [\,]) \,.$$

*Overlining is crucial in the proof of (1). Choose the initial labelling of $M$ such that the
degrees of the redexes in $F$ are distinct letters of $E$.*

**Exercise\* 2.2.22** *Derive theorem 2.2.9 as a corollary of theorem 2.2.13. Hints: Take
as $E$ the finite collection of the types of the subterms of $M$ (the term we start from).
Define $\Xi$ from labels to types by:*

$$\Xi(\sigma) = \sigma \qquad \frac{\Xi(\alpha) = (\sigma \to \tau)}{\Xi(\overline{\alpha}) = \tau} \qquad \frac{\Xi(\alpha) = (\sigma \to \tau)}{\Xi(\underline{\alpha}) = \sigma} \qquad \frac{\Xi(\alpha) = \Xi(\beta)}{\Xi(\alpha\beta) = \Xi(\alpha)} \; .$$

*Define $\mathcal{P}(\alpha)$ as $\Xi(\alpha) \downarrow$. For $P$ whose labels all satisfy $\mathcal{P}$, define $\Xi(P)$ as the term
obtained by applying $\Xi$ to all labels. Say that $P$ is well-typed if all its labels satisfy
$\mathcal{P}$ and if $\Xi(P)$ is well-typed. Show that any $\beta_{\mathcal{P}}^l$-reduct $Q$ of a well-typed term $P$ is
well-typed, and that $\Xi(P)$ $\beta^{\to}$-reduces to $\Xi(Q)$.*

There exist many other proofs of finite developments, of confluence, and of
standardization. In exercise 2.2.23, we propose a particularly simple recent proof
of finite developments due to Van Raamsdonk [vR96]. In exercises 2.2.24 and
2.2.25, we propose proofs of confluence and of standardization based on finite
developments.

**Exercise 2.2.23** *Consider the set of underlined λ-terms, defined by the following grammar:*

$$M ::= x \mid MM \mid \lambda x.M \mid (\underline{\lambda} x.M)M .$$

*Consider the least set $\mathcal{FD}$ of underlined λ-terms containing the variables, closed under (ordinary) abstraction and application, and such that, for all underlined $M, N$:*

$$(M[N/x] \in \mathcal{FD} \text{ and } N \in \mathcal{FD}) \Rightarrow (\underline{\lambda} x.M)N \in \mathcal{FD} .$$

*Show that $\mathcal{FD}$ is the set of all underlined terms, and exploit this to show the finite developments theorem. Hint: Finite developments amount to the strong normalization of underlined β-reduction $(\underline{\lambda} x.M)N \rightarrow M[N/x]$. Prove strong normalization by an induction following the definition of $\mathcal{FD}$.*

**Exercise 2.2.24** *Show confluence as a consequence of finite developments. Hint: Consider any development as a new notion of one step reduction.*

**Exercise 2.2.25** *Show the standardization theorem as a consequence of the finite developments theorem, by the following technique, which goes back to Curry. Let $D : M_0 \rightarrow_{u_0} M_1 \rightarrow_{u_1} M_2 \rightarrow^* M_n$ be the reduction sequence to standardize. Take a leftmost (cf. definition 2.1.19) occurrence $u$ in the set of redex occurrences of $M$ that have a residual reduced in $D$. Let $M \rightarrow_u M_{01}$, and build the reduction sequence $M_{01} \rightarrow^* M_{j1} = M_{j+1}$ where each step is a finite development of $u/u_i$ (cf. exercise 2.2.24), where (because $u$ is leftmost) $M_i \rightarrow_u M_{1i}$, and where $u = u_j$. Continue the construction, applying it to the sequence $D_1 : M_{01} \rightarrow^* M_{j1} \rightarrow M_{j+2} \rightarrow^* M_n$, which is shorter than $D$.*

We end the section by sketching an interpretation of labels as computation paths. Labels allow us to keep track of the history of a reduction, and are a powerful tool for analysing the properties of derivations. As Asperti and Laneve showed [AL93], labels appearing in any reduct $Q$ of a λ-term $M$ all of whose subterms are labelled by distinct atomic labels can be read as paths in a graph representation of $M$, where arrows have been added from the bound occurrences to their binder. In this interpretation, concatenation means concatenation of paths, underlining means reversing of paths, while overlining is ignored. We sketch this interpretation for the labelled term $((\lambda x.(x^d x^e)^c)^b (\lambda y.(y^h y^k)^g)^f)^a$ whose erasure is $\Delta\Delta$. We read, say, $b$ indifferently as a name for the node $\lambda x$ or as a name for the edge leading to it, i.e. the edge from node $a$ to node $b$. After one step of labelled β-reduction, we obtain:

$$((\lambda y.(y^h y^k)^g)^{d\underline{b}f} (\lambda y.(y^h y^k)^g)^{e\underline{b}f})^{\overline{abc}} .$$

The label $d\underline{b}f$ reads as the following path. From the edge leading to the occurrence of $x$ labelled with $d$, follow the binding arrow to the abstraction node $b$, follow the edge $b$ *backwards*, and go down the edge $f$. This path connects an application node of $M$ to an abstraction node of $M$, and encodes a redex that does not exist in $M$, but is created by the substitution of $\lambda y.yy$ for $x$ in $xx$. We can give a direct computational explanation of the path $d\underline{b}f$. Consider the following question: will the application node $c$ ever become a redex? To answer this question is the same as determining whether the left son $d$ of $c$ will ever become an abstraction, through substitution. We therefore go up to the binder of $x$, reaching the abstraction node

$b$, and we try to answer a second question: will the node $b$ ever be the abstraction part of a redex? For investigating this, we go up and reach the node $a$: the path so far is $d\underline{b}$. Since node $a$ is an application node, we have a positive answer to the second question. Then we know that $x$ is bound to the term whose root is $f$, the right son of $a$. The path is now $d\underline{b}f$, and the initial question has been answered since the node $f$ is an abstraction.

We leave it to the reader to analyse the path corresponding to the degree $hd\underline{b}fe\underline{b}f$ of the next redex in the (labelled version) of the derivation from $\Delta\Delta$.

Hence all the future reductions can be 'read', or recorded, by following paths in the initial term of a derivation. Girard has developed this general idea in the framework of linear logic under the name of Geometry of Interaction.

We should also mention that labelled reductions were not designed for the purpose of proving a powerful strong normalization theorem only. They served in a more ambitious program of defining a sensible notion of optimal reduction for the λ-calculus. An optimal computation is one which reaches its goal in a minimum number of steps. Neither the call-by-name reductions nor the call-by-value computations are optimal. In call-by-name, one reduces a redex $(\lambda x.M)N$ before computing the argument $N$. This may result in duplications of computations, if $x$ occurs more than once free in $M$. In call-by-value, $N$ should be evaluated first. But if $x$ does not occur free in $M$, this computation is not needed. In his thesis, Lévy found a theoretical solution to the problem of optimality by decreeing that all redexes of the same degree should be considered as being reduced simultaneously. He left open the question of finding an actual graph structure allowing to physically share these reductions. Such a structure and a corresponding algorithm were proposed by Lamping [Lam80].

Neither the Geometry of Interaction nor the theory and practice of optimal reductions are in the scope of this book. We refer to [AG] for an up-to-date account of both subjects, with an eye on their applications to implementation issues.

## 2.3　Syntactic continuity *

Recall that a head normal form is a term of the form $\lambda x_1 \cdots x_n.x M_1 \cdots M_p$. We define an algebraic (or symbolic) semantics for the λ-calculus. We interpret the (finite) λ-terms as (potentially) infinite terms. For this purpose, we need to introduce partial terms (cf. exercise 1.1.24) to allow for a description of finite approximations.

**Definition 2.3.1 (Böhm trees)** *The set $\mathcal{N}$ is defined by:*

$$\frac{}{\Omega \in \mathcal{N}} \qquad \frac{A_1 \in \mathcal{N} \ \cdots \ A_p \in \mathcal{N}}{\lambda x_1 \cdots x_n.x A_1 \cdots A_p \in \mathcal{N}} \ .$$

*This is a subset of the set of partial λ-terms, also called the $\Omega$-terms, which are defined by:*

$$M ::= \Omega \mid x \mid MM \mid \lambda x.M \ .$$

*It inherits the order on $\Omega$-terms, defined by:*

$$\frac{}{\Omega \leq M} \qquad \frac{M_1 \leq M_1' \quad M_2 \leq M_2'}{M_1 M_2 \leq M_1' M_2'} \qquad \frac{M \leq M'}{\lambda x.M \leq \lambda x.M'} \ .$$

*The elements of the ideal completion (cf. proposition 1.1.21) $\mathcal{N}^\infty$ of $\mathcal{N}$ are called the Böhm trees. For any $\lambda$-term $M$, we define $\omega(M) \in \mathcal{N}$, called the immediate approximation of $M$, as follows:*

$$\omega(M) = \begin{cases} \Omega & \text{if } M = \lambda x_1 \cdots x_n.(\lambda x.M)M_1 \cdots M_p \\ \lambda x_1 \cdots x_n.x\omega(M_1) \cdots \omega(M_p) & \text{if } M = \lambda x_1 \cdots x_n.xM_1 \cdots M_p, \end{cases}$$

*where $p \geq 1$ is assumed in the first case. The function $\omega$ is extended to $\Omega$-terms by setting $\omega(\lambda x_1 \cdots x_n.\Omega M_1 \cdots M_p) = \Omega$.*

**Lemma 2.3.2** *If $M \to N$, then $\omega(M) \leq \omega(N)$.*

PROOF. By induction on the size of $M$. If $M = \lambda x_1 \cdots x_n.xM_1 \cdots M_p$, then the reduction occurs in one of the $M_i$'s, and induction can be applied. $\square$

**Definition 2.3.3** *For any $\lambda$-term $M$ we define:*

$$BT(M) = \bigvee \{\omega(N) \mid M \to^* N\}.$$

*$BT(M)$ is called the Böhm tree of $M$.*

By lemma 2.3.2 and by confluence, $\{\omega(N) \mid M \to^* N\}$ is directed, for fixed $M$, hence Böhm trees are well-defined. The immediate approximation $\omega(M)$ can be understood as the current approximation of $BT(M)$, obtained (roughly) by replacing the redexes with $\Omega$'s. If computation proceeds, with $M \to^* N$, then $\omega(N)$ may be a better approximation of $BT(M)$.

**Example 2.3.4** (1) *If $M \in SN$, then $BT(M)$ is the normal form of $M$.*

(2) $BT(\Delta\Delta) = \Omega$.

(3) $BT((\lambda x.f(xx))((\lambda x.f(xx)))) = \bigvee_{n \geq 0} f^n(\Omega)$.

The last example shows that Böhm trees can be infinite.

**Proposition 2.3.5** *If $M \to N$, then $BT(M) = BT(N)$.*

PROOF HINT. Use the confluence property. $\square$

**Lemma 2.3.6** *If $M$ and $N$ differ only by the replacement of some (disjoint) occurrences of subterms of the form $\lambda x_1 \cdots x_n.\Omega M_1 \cdots M_p$ by $\Omega$ or vice-versa, then $BT(M) = BT(N)$.*

PROOF HINT. If $M$, $N$ are as in the statement, then $\omega(M) = \omega(N)$; moreover, if $M \to M'$, then either $\omega(M') = \omega(N)$ or $(\exists N' \; N \to N'$ and $\omega(M') = \omega(N'))$. $\square$

Let $M$ be a $\lambda$-term and $F$ be a set of redex occurrences in $M$. Then $F$ determines a context $C_{M,F}$ such that $M = C_{M,F}[\vec{R}]$, where $\vec{R}$ enumerates

$$\{M/u \mid u \in F \text{ and } (v < u \Rightarrow v \notin F)\}.$$

**Lemma 2.3.7** *Let $M$, $F$ be as above. Then $\omega(C_{M,F}[\vec{\Omega}]) = \omega(M)$.*

PROOF. By the definition of $\omega$ and by simple induction on the size of $M$.  □

We say that a derivation $M \to_{u_1} M_1 \to_{u_2} \cdots \to_{u_n} M_n$ does not touch a set $F$ of redex occurrences in $M$ if none of the $u_i$'s is a residual of an occurrence in $F$. We write $M \xrightarrow{\neg F} {}^* M_n$.

**Lemma 2.3.8** *If* $D : M \xrightarrow{\neg F} {}^* N$, *then* $C_{M,F}[\vec{\Omega}] \to^* C_{N,F/D}[\vec{\Omega}]$.

PROOF. The one step case implies the multistep case straightforwardly. Thus let $D = u$. There are two cases:

(a) $\exists u_1 \in F \ u_1 < u$. Then $u_1/u = \{u_1\}$, hence $C_{N,F/u}[\vec{\Omega}] = C_{M,F}[\vec{\Omega}]$.

(b) $\forall u_1 \in F \ (u < u_1$ or $u \not< u_1)$. Then $C_{M,F}[\vec{\Omega}] \to_u C_{N,F/u}[\vec{\Omega}]$.  □

When $F$ is the set of all redexes in $\vec{M}$, we write $C[\vec{M}] \xrightarrow{\neg \vec{M}} {}^* N$ for $C[\vec{M}] \xrightarrow{\neg F} {}^* N$.

**Lemma 2.3.9 (inside-out)** *If* $C[\vec{M}] \to^* P$, *then there exist* $\vec{N}$, $Q$ *such that:*

$$\vec{M} \to^* \vec{N}, \ C[\vec{N}] \xrightarrow{\neg \vec{N}} {}^* Q, \ \text{and} \ P \to^* Q,$$

*where* $\vec{M} \to^* \vec{N}$ *has the obvious componentwise meaning.*

PROOF. Once more, we use labelled reduction. Assume that $C[\vec{M}]$ is labelled. Let $\mathcal{P}$ consist of the degrees of the redexes reduced in $C[\vec{M}] \to^* P$. Let $\vec{N}$ be the $\beta_{\mathcal{P}}^l$-normal forms of $\vec{M}$. By $\beta_{\mathcal{P}}^l$-confluence, we have $P \to^* Q$ and $C[\vec{N}] \to^* Q$, for some $Q$. Let $u$ be an occurrence of a $\beta$-redex in $\vec{N}$. Since the components of $\vec{N}$ are $\beta_{\mathcal{P}}^l$-normal, the degree of $u$, which by lemma 2.2.14 is the degree of all its residuals, does not satisfy $\mathcal{P}$, hence no residual of $u$ is reduced in the derivation $C[\vec{N}] \to^* Q$.  □

Informally, the lemma says that reductions can be first carried out 'inside' (in the terms $\vec{M}$), and then 'outside' only. In this outside phase, the actual nature of the redexes in $\vec{N}$ is irrelevant, as formalized by the next lemma.

**Lemma 2.3.10** *If* $D : C[\vec{N}] \xrightarrow{\neg \vec{N}} {}^* Q$, *then* $\omega(Q) \leq BT(C[\omega(\vec{N})])$.

PROOF. Let $F$ be the family of all the redex occurrences in $\vec{N}$. By lemma 2.3.8 we have $C_{C[\vec{N}],F}[\vec{\Omega}] \to^* C_{Q,F/D}[\vec{\Omega}]$. Hence $\omega(Q) = \omega(C_{Q,F/D}[\vec{\Omega}]) \leq BT(C_{C[\vec{N}],F}[\vec{\Omega}])$, by lemma 2.3.7 and by definition of Böhm trees. We are left to prove:

$$BT(C_{C[\vec{N}],F}[\vec{\Omega}]) = BT(C[\omega(\vec{N})]),$$

which follows from lemma 2.3.6.  □

Finally, we can prove the main result of the section: the context operation is continuous. This result is due to Hyland and Wadsworth, independently [Wad76, Hyl76]. We follow the proof of Lévy [Lev78].

**Theorem 2.3.11 (syntactic continuity)** *For all contexts* $C$, *for any* $\vec{M}$ *and any* $B \in \mathcal{N}$, *the following implication holds:*

$$B \leq BT(C[\vec{M}]) \Rightarrow (\exists \vec{A} \in \vec{\mathcal{N}} \ (\vec{A} \leq BT(\vec{M}) \ \text{and} \ B \leq BT(C[\vec{A}]))) .$$

PROOF. If $B \leq BT(C[\vec{M}])$, then $C[\vec{M}] \rightarrow^* P$ for some $P$ such that $B \leq \omega(P)$. By lemma 2.3.9, there exist $\vec{N}$, $Q$ such that $\vec{M} \rightarrow^* \vec{N}$, $C[\vec{N}] \xrightarrow{\neg \vec{N}} {}^* Q$, and $P \rightarrow^* Q$. We have:

$$\omega(P) \leq \omega(Q) \qquad \text{(by lemma 2.3.2)}$$
$$\omega(Q) \leq BT(C[\omega(\vec{N})]) \quad \text{(by lemma 2.3.10)} \,.$$

Take $\vec{A} = \omega(\vec{N})$. Then $B \leq \omega(P) \leq \omega(Q) \leq BT(C[\vec{A}])$, and $\vec{A} \leq BT(\vec{M})$ (by definition of Böhm trees). $\square$

Thus, informally, the proof proceeds by organizing the reduction in an inside-out order, allowing us to gather sufficient information about the Böhm trees of $\vec{M}$ during the inside phase.

**Exercise 2.3.12 (_C_-cont)** *Let $M$, $N$ be $\Omega$-terms such that $M \leq N$. Show that $BT(M) \leq BT(N)$. This allows us to define $\underline{C} : \mathcal{N}^\infty \rightarrow \mathcal{N}^\infty$, for any context $C$, by:*

$$\underline{C}(A) = \bigvee \{BT(C[B]) \mid B \leq A \text{ and } B \text{ is finite}\} \,.$$

*Show that $\underline{C}(BT(M)) = BT(C[M])$, for any $M$.*

# 2.4   The syntactic sequentiality theorem *

The context operation is not only continuous, but also sequential. The syntactic sequentiality theorem, due to Berry [Ber79], which we present in this section, motivates a semantic investigation of sequentiality, which is covered in section 6.5 and chapter 14. Two technical lemmas are needed before we can state the theorem.

**Lemma 2.4.1** *If $M$ is an $\Omega$-term and $M \rightarrow^* M'$, then there exists a mapping [†] from the set $\{v_1, \ldots v_n\}$ of occurrences of $\Omega$ in $M'$ to the set of occurrences of $\Omega$ in $M$ such that $N \rightarrow^* M'[(N/v_1^{\dagger})/v_1, \ldots, (N/v_n^{\dagger})/v_n]$, for any $N > M$.*

In particular, if $M \rightarrow^* M'$ and $N > M$, then there exists $N' > M'$ such that $N \rightarrow^* N'$.

**Lemma 2.4.2** *If the normal derivation sequence from $M$ contains only terms of the form $M' = \lambda x_1 \cdots x_n.(\lambda x.P')M_1' \cdots M_k'$, then $BT(M) = \Omega$.*

PROOF. We reason as in the proof of corollary 2.2.18. Suppose $BT(M) \neq \Omega$. Then there exists a derivation:

$$M \rightarrow^* M'' = \lambda x_1 \cdots x_n.y M_1'' \cdots M_k'',$$

and we can suppose that this derivation is standard, by theorem 2.2.17. But the shape of $M''$ forces this derivation to be actually normal. $\square$

The following theorem asserts that the function $BT$ is sequential. A general definition of sequential functions will be given in section 14.1.

**Theorem 2.4.3 (syntactic sequentiality)** *The Böhm tree function is such that for any $\Omega$-term $M$ and any $u$ such that $BT(M)/u = \Omega$ and $BT(P)/u \neq \Omega$ for some $P > M$, there exists $v$, depending on $M$, $u$ only, such that whenever $N > M$ and $BT(N)/u \neq \Omega$, then $N/v \neq \Omega$.*

PROOF. By induction on the size of $u$. Suppose $BT(M)/u = \Omega$, $M < N$, and $BT(N)/u \neq \Omega$. We distinguish two cases:

(1) $BT(M) \neq \Omega$. Then:

$$M \to^* M' = \lambda x_1 \cdots x_n.y M_1' \cdots M_k' \text{ and}$$
$$BT(M) = BT(M') = \lambda x_1 \cdots x_n.y BT(M_1') \cdots BT(M_k') \,.$$

We observe that any $N' > M'$ has the form $N' = \lambda x_1 \cdots x_n.y N_1' \cdots N_k'$, and also that $BT(N') = \lambda x_1 \cdots x_n.y BT(N_1') \cdots BT(N_k')$. We have $BT(M')/u = BT(M_i')/u'$ $(= \Omega)$, for an appropriate $i$ and a proper suffix $u'$ of $u$. On the other hand, let $N > M$ with $BT(N)/u \neq \Omega$, and let $N' > M'$ be such that $N \to^* N'$. Then $N_i' > M_i'$ and $BT(N_i')/u' = BT(N')/u = BT(N)/u \neq \Omega$. We can thus apply induction to $M_i'$, $u'$, and obtain an index $v$ at $M'$, $u$. It remains to bring this index back to $M$. We show that the index at $M$, $u$ is $v^\dagger$, in the terminology of lemma 2.4.1. Indeed, if $N > M$ and $N/v^\dagger = \Omega$, then, setting $N' = M'[(N/v_1^\dagger)/v_1, \ldots, (N/v_n^\dagger)/v_n]$:

$$N \to^* N' \qquad \text{(hence } BT(N) = BT(N'))$$
$$N' > N \text{ and } N'/v = \Omega \quad \text{(hence } BT(N')/u = \Omega) \,.$$

Putting this together, we have $BT(N)/u = \Omega$, which shows that $v^\dagger$ is a sequentiality index.

(2) $BT(M) = \Omega$. Suppose that the leftmost reduction sequence from $M$ contains only terms of the form $M' = \lambda x_1 \cdots x_n.(\lambda x.P') M_1' \cdots M_k'$. Then the normal sequence from $N$ is the sequence described by lemma 2.4.1, whose terms are of the same shape, which entails $BT(N) = \Omega$ by lemma 2.4.2. Hence the leftmost reduction sequence from $M$ contains a term $M' = \lambda x_1 \cdots x_n.\Omega M_1' \cdots M_k'$. The only chance of getting $BT(N') \neq \Omega$ for an $N' > M'$ is to increase $M'$ by replacement of its head $\Omega$, which is therefore a sequentiality index at $M'$, $u$. As above, we use lemma 2.4.1 to bring this index back to $M$. □

Exercise 2.4.4 ($\underline{C}$-seq) *Show, as a corollary of theorem 2.4.3, that the function $\underline{C}$ defined in exercise 2.3.12 is sequential. (The reader can refer to definition 14.1.9, or guess a definition.)*

# 3

# $D_\infty$ models and intersection types

In this chapter we address the fundamental domain equation $D = D \to D$ which serves to define models of the untyped $\lambda$-calculus. By 'equation', we actually mean that we seek a $D$ together with an order-isomorphism $D \cong D \to D$. Taking $D = \{\bot\}$ certainly yields a solution, since there is exactly one function $f : \{\bot\} \to \{\bot\}$. But we are interested in a non-trivial solution, that is a $D$ of cardinality at least 2, so that not all $\lambda$-terms will be identified! Domain equations will be treated in a general setting in chapter 7.

In section 3.1, we construct Scott's $D_\infty$ models as order theoretical limit constructions. In section 3.2, we first define a general notion of $\lambda$-model, and then discuss some specific properties of the $D_\infty$ models: Curry's fixpoint combinator is interpreted as the least fixpoint operator, and the theory induced by a $D_\infty$ model can be characterized syntactically, using Böhm trees. In section 3.3, we present a class of $\lambda$-models based on the idea that the meaning of a term should be the collection of properties it satisfies in a suitable 'logic'. This point of view will be developed in more generality in chapter 10. In section 3.4, we relate the constructions of sections 3.1 and 3.3, following [CDHL82]. Finally, in section 3.5, we use intersection types as a tool for the syntactic theory of the $\lambda$-calculus [Kri91, RdR93].

## 3.1 $D_\infty$ models

In chapter 1, we have considered products and function spaces as constructions on cpo's. They actually extend to functors (cf. exercises 1.4.6 and 1.4.7). Here is the action of $\to$ on pairs of morphisms of **Cpo**.

**Definition 3.1.1** ($\to$ **functor**) *Let $D, D', E, E'$ be dcpo's and $f : D' \to D$ and $g : E \to E'$ be continuous. Then $f \to g : (D \to E) \to (D' \to E')$ is defined by:*

$$(f \to g)(h) = g \circ h \circ f.$$

Notice the 'reversal' of the direction: $f$ goes from $D'$ to $D$, not from $D$ to $D'$: we have defined a functor which is contravariant in its first argument and covariant in its second argument (cf. appendix 2). This entails that the association $D \mapsto (D \to D)$ is not functorial in **Cpo**. But it becomes functorial in the category of cpo's and injection-projection pairs.

**Definition 3.1.2 (injection-projection pair)** *An injection-projection pair between two cpo's $D$ and $D'$ is a pair $(i : D \to D', j : D' \to D)$, written $(i,j) :$ $D \to_{ip} D'$ (or simply $(i,j) : D \to D'$), such that:*

$$j \circ i = id \quad and \quad i \circ j \leq id,$$

*where $\leq$ is the pointwise ordering, cf. proposition 1.4.4. We call $i$ the injection and $j$ the projection of the pair $(i,j)$. If only $j \circ i = id$ holds, we say that $(i,j)$ is a retraction pair and that $D'$ is a retract of $D$. Injection-projection pairs are composed componentwise:*

$$(i_1, j_1) \circ (i_2, j_2) = (i_1 \circ i_2, j_2 \circ j_1),$$

*and the identity injection-projection pair is $(id, id)$.*

Examples of injection-projection pairs will be given in definition 3.1.10 and remark 3.1.11. The following exercise proposes another one, which will be used in section 15.7.

**Exercise 3.1.3** *Show that if $D, E$ are cpo's, the injection $i$ from $D$ to $D + E$ (the coalesced sum of $D, E$, cf. definition 1.4.23), defined by $i(\bot) = \bot$ and $i(x) = (1,x)$ if $x \neq \bot$, is the first component of an injection-projection pair.*

**Remark 3.1.4** *Definition 3.1.2 makes sense in the larger category of posets and monotonic functions, as well as in a more general categorical context (see section 7.1).*

**Proposition 3.1.5** (1) *If $(i,j) : D \to_{ip} D'$ is an injection-projection pair, then $i$ determines $j$.*

(2) *Moreover, $j$ is defined as follows: $j(x) = \bigvee \{y \mid i(y) \leq x\}$.*

PROOF. (1) Suppose that $(i, j')$ is another pair. Then observe:

$$j' = id \circ j' = j \circ i \circ j' \leq j \circ id = j,$$

and symmetrically $j \leq j'$.

(2) An injection-projection pair is *a fortiori* an adjunction (cf. section A2.4), i.e., $i(y) \leq x$ iff $y \leq j(x)$. Hence $\bigvee \{y \mid i(y) \leq x\} = \bigvee \{y \mid y \leq j(x)\} = j(x)$. □

**Proposition 3.1.6** (1) *For any injection-projection pair $(i,j) : D \to_{ip} D'$, the injection $i$ maps compact elements of $D$ to compact elements of $D'$.*

(2) *If $D, D'$ are algebraic dcpo's, a function $i : D \to D'$ is the injection part of an injection-projection pair $(i,j)$ iff $i$ restricted to $\mathcal{K}(D)$ is a monotonic injection into $\mathcal{K}(D')$ such that for any finite $M \subseteq \mathcal{K}(D)$, if $i(M)$ is bounded by $d'$ in $\mathcal{K}(D')$, then $M$ is bounded in $\mathcal{K}(D)$ by some $d$ such that $i(d) \leq d'$.*

PROOF. (1) If $i(d) \leq \bigvee \Delta'$, then $d = j(i(d)) \leq j(\bigvee \Delta') \doteq \bigvee j(\Delta')$ implies $d \leq j(\delta')$ for some $\delta' \in \Delta'$. Then $i(d) \leq i(j(\delta')) \leq \delta'$.

(2) Let $(i, j)$ be an injection-projection pair. By (1), $i$ restricted to $\mathcal{K}(D)$ is a monotonic injection into $\mathcal{K}(D')$. Suppose $i(M) \leq d'$. Then $M = j(i(M)) \leq j(d')$. Hence $M$ is bounded in $D$, from which we deduce $M \leq d$ for some compact $d \leq j(d')$, by algebraicity and by finiteness of $M$. Then $d$ fits since $i(d) \leq i(j(d')) \leq d'$. Conversely, let $i : \mathcal{K}(D) \rightarrow \mathcal{K}(D')$ be as in the statement. It extends to a continuous function $i : D \rightarrow D'$: $i(x) = \bigvee \{i(d) \mid d \leq x\}$. Let $j : D' \rightarrow D$ be defined by:

$$j(x) = \bigvee \{d \mid i(d) \leq x\}.$$

We prove that $j$ is well-defined. We have to check that $\{d \mid i(d) \leq x\}$ is directed. If $i(d_1), i(d_2) \leq x$, then by algebraicity $i(d_1), i(d_2) \leq d'$ for some compact $d' \leq x$, and by the assumption $\{d_1, d_2\} \leq d$ for some compact $d$ such that $i(d) \leq d'$. This $d$ fits since *a fortiori* $i(d) \leq x$. It is easy to check $j \circ i = id$ and $i \circ j \leq id$. $\square$

**Exercise 3.1.7** *Show that if $D$ and $D'$ are bounded complete (cf. definition 1.4.9 and exercise 1.4.11), then, in proposition 3.1.6(2), 'if $i(M)$ is bounded by $d'$ in $\mathcal{K}(D')$, then $M$ is bounded in $\mathcal{K}(D)$ by some $d$ in $\mathcal{K}(D)$ such that $i(d) \leq d'$ ' can be replaced by: 'if $i(M)$ is bounded in $\mathcal{K}(D')$, then $M$ is bounded in $\mathcal{K}(D)$ and $i(\bigvee M) = \bigvee i(M)$ '.*

**Definition 3.1.8** *Let $(i, j) : D \rightarrow_{ip} D'$ be an injection-projection pair. We define $(i', j') = (i, j) \rightarrow (i, j) : (D \rightarrow D) \rightarrow_{ip} (D' \rightarrow D')$ by:*

$$i'(f) = i \circ f \circ j \quad j'(f') = j \circ f' \circ i.$$

**Exercise 3.1.9** *Show that definition 3.1.8 turns $D \mapsto (D \rightarrow D)$ into a functor in the category of injection-projection pairs.*

**Definition 3.1.10** ($D_\infty$) *Given a cpo $D$, we define the standard injection-projection pair $(i_0, j_0) : D \rightarrow_{ip} (D \rightarrow D)$ by:*

$$i_0(x)(y) = x \quad j_0(f) = f(\bot).$$

*The cpo $D_\infty$ is defined as follows:*

$$D_\infty - \{(x_0, \ldots, x_n, \ldots) \mid \bigvee n \ x_n \in D_n \ and \ x_n = j_n(x_{n+1})\},$$

*where $(x_0, \ldots, x_n, \ldots)$ is an infinite tuple, standing for a map from $\omega$ to $\bigcup_{n \in \omega} D_n$, and where:*

$$D_0 = D \quad D_{n+1} = D_n \rightarrow D_n \quad (i_{n+1}, j_{n+1}) = (i_n, j_n) \rightarrow (i_n, j_n),$$

*so that $(i_n, j_n) : D_n \rightarrow_{ip} D_{n+1}$ for all $n$. We write $x_n$ for the $n^{th}$ component of $x \in D_\infty$. In the description of an element of $D_\infty$ we can omit the first components, for example $(x_1, \ldots, x_n, \ldots)$ determines $(j_0(x_1), x_1, \ldots, x_n, \ldots)$.*

**Remark 3.1.11** *There may be other choices for the initial pair $(i_0, j_0)$. For example the pair $(i_0, j_0)$ of definition 3.1.10 is just the instance $(i_\bot, j_\bot)$ of the family $(i_d, j_d)$ $(d \in \mathcal{K}(D))$ defined by:*

$$\begin{aligned} i_d(e) &= d \rightarrow e \quad (step \ function) \\ j_d(f) &= f(d). \end{aligned}$$

*Hence the construction of $D_\infty$ is parameterized by $D$ and $(i_0, j_0)$.*

The lub's in $D_\infty$ are defined pointwise: $(\bigvee \Delta)_n = \bigvee \{x_n \mid x \in \Delta\}$ (the continuity of the $j_n$'s guarantees that $\bigvee \Delta$ indeed belongs to $D_\infty$). The minimum element of $D_\infty$ is $(\bot, \ldots, \bot, \ldots)$.

**Lemma 3.1.12** *The following define injection-projection pairs from $D_n$ to $D_\infty$:*

$$i_{n\infty}(x) = (k_{n0}(x), \ldots, k_{nn}(x), \ldots, k_{nm}(x), \ldots)$$
$$j_{n\infty}(x) = x_n,$$

*where $k_{nm} : D_n \to D_m$ is defined by:*

$$k_{nm} = \begin{cases} k_{(n-1)m} \circ j_{n-1} & (n > m) \\ id & (n = m) \\ k_{(n+1)m} \circ i_n & (n < m). \end{cases}$$

*We shall freely write $x$ for $i_{n\infty}(x)$. Under this abuse of notation, we have:*

$$\begin{array}{llll}
x \in D_n & \Rightarrow \ x_n = x & m \le n & \Rightarrow \ x_m \le x_n \\
x \in D_n & \Rightarrow \ i_n(x) = x & (x_n)_m & = \ x_{\min(n,m)} \\
x \in D_{n+1} & \Rightarrow \ j_n(x) \le x & x & = \ \bigvee_{n \ge 0} x_n \, .
\end{array}$$

PROOF. We check only the second implication and the last equality.

- $x \in D_n \Rightarrow i_n(x) = x$. $i_n(x)$ stands for $i_{(n+1)\infty}(i_n(x))$, that is,

$$(k_{(n+1)0}(i_n(x)), \ldots, k_{(n+1)n}(i_n(x)), i_n(x), \ldots, k_{(n+1)m}(i_n(x)), \ldots),$$

which is $(k_{n0}(x), \ldots, x, i_n(x), \ldots, k_{nm}(x), \ldots)$, that is, $x$.

- $x = \bigvee_{n \ge 0} x_n$. By the continuity of $j_{n\infty}$, we have:

$$(\bigvee_{n \ge 0} x_n)_p = (\bigvee_{n \ge p} x_n)_p = \bigvee_{n \ge p} (x_n)_p = \bigvee_{n \ge p} x_p = x_p. \qquad \square$$

**Lemma 3.1.13** *The following properties hold:*

(1) $\forall n \le p, x \in D_{n+1}, y \in D_p \quad x(y_n) = x_{p+1}(y)$.

(2) $\forall n \le p, x \in D_{p+1}, y \in D_n \quad x_{n+1}(y) = x(y_p)_n$.

PROOF. We check only the case $p = n + 1$.

(1) By definition of $i_{n+1}$, we have $i_{n+1}(x) = i_n \circ x \circ j_n$. Hence, as claimed, we have $i_{n+1}(x)(y) = i_n(x(j_n(y))) = i_n(x(y_n)) = x(y_n)$.

(2) $(x(i_n(y))_n = j_n(x(i_n(y))) = j_{n+1}(x)(y) = x_{n+1}(y)$. $\qquad \square$

The following lemma will be needed in the proof of lemma 3.4.7(3).

**Lemma 3.1.14** *For any $f \in D_{n+1}$, we have $G(i_{n\infty} \circ f \circ j_{n\infty}) = f$.*

PROOF. We have $G(i_{n\infty} \circ f \circ j_{n\infty}) = \bigvee_{p \geq n} G_p(i_{n\infty} \circ f \circ j_{n\infty})$. Let $y \in D_p$. From:

$$G_p(i_{n\infty} \circ f \circ j_{n\infty})(y) = i_{n\infty}(f(j_{n\infty}(y)))_p \, ,$$

we get $G_p(i_{n\infty} \circ f \circ j_{n\infty})(y) = f(y_n)$ (with our abuse of notation), hence, by lemma 3.1.13, $G_p(i_{n\infty} \circ f \circ j_{n\infty}) = k_{(n+1)(p+1)}(f)$, and the conclusion follows. □

**Definition 3.1.15** *We define* $\bullet : D_\infty \times D_\infty \to D_\infty$ *and* $G : (D_\infty \to D_\infty) \to D_\infty$ *by:*

$$x \bullet y = \bigvee_{n \geq 0} x_{n+1}(y_n) \qquad G(f) = \bigvee_{n \geq 0} G_n(f) \, ,$$

*where* $G_n(f) \in D_{n+1}$ *is defined by* $G_n(f)(y) = f(y)_n$.

It is straightforward to check that these mappings are continuous.

**Lemma 3.1.16** *The following properties hold:*

(1) *If* $x \in D_{n+1}$, *then* $x \bullet y = x(y_n)$ *(and hence* $x \bullet y = (x \bullet y)_n$).

(2) *If* $y \in D_n$, *then* $(x \bullet y)_n = x_{n+1}(y)$.

PROOF. (1) Using lemma 3.1.13, we have:

$$x \bullet y = \bigvee_{p \geq n} x_{p+1}(y_p) = \bigvee_{p \geq n} x((y_p)_n) = x(y_n).$$

(2) By continuity of $j_{n\infty}$ and by lemma 3.1.13, we have:

$$(x \bullet y)_n = \bigvee_{p \geq n} (x_{p+1}(y_p))_n = \bigvee_{p \geq n} x_{n+1}(y) = x_{n+1}(y).$$ □

**Theorem 3.1.17** *Let* $F(x)(y) = x \bullet y$. *The maps* $F$ *and* $G$ *are inverse isomorphisms between* $D_\infty$ *and* $D_\infty \to D_\infty$.

PROOF. • $G \circ F = id$. Thanks to lemma 3.1.16, we have $G_n(F(x)) = x_{n+1}$. Hence $G(F(x)) = \bigvee_{n \geq 0} x_{n+1} = x$.

• $F \circ G = id$. We have to prove $G(f) \bullet x = f(x)$ for any $f : D_\infty \to D_\infty$ and $x \in D_\infty$. By continuity, we have $G(f) \bullet x = \bigvee_{n \geq 0} G_n(f) \bullet x$. Since $G_n(f) \bullet x = G_n(f)(x_n)$ by lemma 3.1.16, we have $G(f) \bullet x = \bigvee_{n \geq 0} f(x_n)_n$. On the other hand we have $f(x) = \bigvee_{n \geq 0} f(x_n)$ by continuity, hence $f(x) = \bigvee_{n \geq 0, p \geq n} f(x_n)_p$. Finally, observing that $f(x_n)_p \leq f(x_p)_p$, we have:

$$G(f) \bullet x = \bigvee_{n \geq 0} f(x_n)_n = \bigvee_{n \geq 0, p \geq n} f(x_n)_p = f(x).$$ □

We have thus obtained a solution to the equation $D = D \to D$. The heuristics has been to imitate Kleene's fixpoint construction, and to build an infinite sequence $D_0 = D, \ldots, H^n(D_0), \ldots$, with $H(D) = D \to D$. In fact it can be formally shown (in a suitable sense) that:

• $D_\infty$ is the least upper bound of the $D_n$'s, and, as a consequence,

• $D_\infty$ is the least $D'$ 'above' $D$ for which '$H(D') \leq D'$' holds, and that moreover '$H(D') = D'$' holds.

This is fairly general, and will be addressed in chapter 7 (see also exercises 3.1.18, 3.1.19 for an anticipation).

**Exercise 3.1.18** *(1) Show that, for any $D'$ with a collection of $(\phi_{n\infty}, \psi_{n\infty}) : D_n \to_{ip} D'$ such that $(\forall n \ (\phi_{n\infty}, \psi_{n\infty}) = (\phi_{(n+1)\infty}, \psi_{(n+1)\infty}) \circ (i_n, j_n))$, there exists a unique pair $(\phi, \psi) : D_\infty \to_{ip} D'$ such that:*

$$\forall n \ (\phi, \psi) \circ (i_{n\infty}, j_{n\infty}) = (\phi_{n\infty}, \psi_{n\infty}).$$

*Hint: Define $\phi(x) = \bigvee \phi_{n\infty}(x_n)$, $\psi(y)_n = \psi_{n\infty}(y)$. (2) Show that the definition of $(F, G) : D_\infty \to_{ip} (D_\infty \to D_\infty)$ is recovered by taking:*

$$D' = D_\infty \to D_\infty \qquad (\phi_{(n+1)\infty}, \psi_{(n+1)\infty}) = (i_{n\infty}, j_{n\infty}) \to (i_{n\infty}, j_{n\infty}) .$$

**Exercise 3.1.19** *We define an $(i_0, j_0)$-$H$-algebra (where $HD = D \to D$) as a pair of two injection-projection pairs $(\alpha, \beta) : D_0 \to_{ip} D'$ and $(\gamma, \delta) : HD' \to_{ip} D'$ such that:*

$$(\gamma, \delta) \circ H(\alpha, \beta) \circ (i_0, j_0) = (\alpha, \beta) .$$

*A morphism from $((\alpha, \beta), (\gamma, \delta))$ to $((\alpha_1, \beta_1) : D_0 \to_{ip} D'_1, (\gamma_1, \delta_1) : HD'_1 \to_{ip} D'_1)$ is a pair $(\mu, \nu) : D' \to_{ip} D'_1$ such that:*

$$(\mu, \nu) \circ (\alpha, \beta) = (\alpha_1, \beta_1) \ and \ (\mu, \nu) \circ (\gamma, \delta) = (\gamma_1, \delta_1) \circ H(\mu, \nu).$$

*Show that $((i_{0\infty}, j_{0\infty}), (G, F))$ is an initial $(i_0, j_0)$-$H$-algebra, i.e., that it has a unique morphism into each $(i_0, j_0)$-$H$-algebra.*

## 3.2    Properties of $D_\infty$ models

We have not yet explained precisely why a solution to $D = D \to D$ gives a model of the $\lambda$-calculus. We shall first give a few definitions: applicative structure, pre-reflexive domain, functional $\lambda$-model, and reflexive domain. The $D_\infty$ models are reflexive domains. A fully general (and more abstract) definition of model will be given in chapter 4. In the rest of the section, we discuss some specific properties of $D_\infty$ models.

**Definition 3.2.1 (pre-reflexive)** *An applicative structure $(X, \bullet)$ is a set $X$ equipped with a binary operation $\bullet$. The set of representable functions $X \to_{rep} X$ is the set of functions from $X$ to $X$ defined by:*

$$X \to_{rep} X = \{f \in X \to X \mid \exists y \in X \ \forall x \in X \ f(x) = y \bullet x\} .$$

*A pre-reflexive domain $(D, F, G)$ is given by a set $D$, a set $[D \to D]$ of functions from $D$ to $D$, and two functions $F : D \to [D \to D]$ and $G : [D \to D] \to D$ such that $F \circ G = id$. Denoting $\bullet$ the uncurried form of $F$, a pre-reflexive domain is an applicative structure, with $D \to_{rep} D = F(D) = [D \to D]$. If moreover (i) $D$ is a partial order, (ii) $[D \to D]$ contains only monotonic functions, (iii) $F, G$ are monotonic, and (iv) $(G, F)$ forms an injection-projection pair (cf. remark 3.1.4), then $(D, F, G)$ is called* coadditive.

Notice that the conjunction of $F \circ G \geq id$ and $G \circ F \leq id$ is a poset adjunction situation (cf. section A2.4). In coadditive pre-reflexive domains, we thus have:

$$G(f) \leq x \Leftrightarrow f \leq F(x),$$

$$\begin{array}{rcl}
[\![x]\!]\rho & = & \rho(x) \\
[\![MN]\!]\rho & = & F([\![M]\!]\rho)([\![N]\!]\rho) \\
[\![\lambda x.M]\!]\rho & = & G(\lambda d.[\![M]\!]\rho[d/x])
\end{array}$$

Figure 3.1: The semantic equations in a functional $\lambda$-model

which entails that:

- $G$ preserves lub's (cf. proposition A2.5.1).

- $G$ maps compact elements to compact elements (cf. proposition 3.1.6).

The functions $F$ and $G$ can serve to interpret untyped $\lambda$-terms. As in universal algebra and in logic, the meaning of a term is given relative to a so-called environment $\rho$ mapping variables to elements of the model. Thus the meaning of a term is to be written as an element $[\![M]\!]\rho$ of $D$, read as: 'the meaning of $M$ at $\rho$'. This motivates the following definition (see also remark 4.6.11).

**Definition 3.2.2 ($\lambda$-model)** *A functional $\lambda$-model ($\lambda$-model for short) is a pre-reflexive domain $(D, F, G)$ such that the interpretation of $\lambda$-terms given by the equations of figure 3.1 is correctly defined. In these equations, the point is to make sure that $\lambda d.[\![M]\!]\rho[d/x] \in [D \to D]$.*

**Proposition 3.2.3 (soundness)** *In a $\lambda$-model, the following holds:*

$$\text{if } M \to_\beta N, \text{ then } [\![M]\!]\rho = [\![N]\!]\rho \text{ for any } \rho.$$

PROOF HINT. Since $F \circ G = id$, we have:

$$\begin{array}{rcl}
[\![(\lambda x.M)N]\!]\rho & = & F(G(\lambda d.[\![M]\!]\rho[d/x]))([\![N]\!]\rho) \\
& = & [\![M]\!]\rho[[\![N]\!]\rho/x] .
\end{array}$$

Then the conclusion follows from the following substitution property, which can be proved by induction on the size of $M$: $[\![M[N/x]]\!]\rho = [\![M]\!]\rho[[\![N]\!]\rho/x]$. $\square$

We refer to chapter 4 for a more detailed treatment of the validation of $\beta$ (and $\eta$), in a categorical setting.

**Definition 3.2.4 (reflexive)** *A pre-reflexive domain $(D, F, G)$ is called reflexive if $D$ is a cpo, if $[D \to D] = D \to_{cont} D$, and if $F, G$ are continuous.*

In other words, a reflexive domain is a pre-reflexive domain whose representable functions are exactly the continuous functions.

**Proposition 3.2.5** *A reflexive domain is a functional $\lambda$-model.*

PROOF. One checks easily by induction on $M$ that $\lambda \vec{d}.[\![M]\!]\rho[\vec{d}/\vec{x}]$ is continuous. It follows by currying that $\lambda d.[\![M]\!]\rho[d/x] \in [D \to D]$.                    □

The $D_\infty$ models are reflexive. The additional property $G \circ F = id$ which they satisfy amounts to the validation of the $\eta$-rule (see chapter 4).

**Remark 3.2.6** *It should come as no surprise that the $D_\infty$ models satisfy $\eta$ as well as $\beta$, since for $\beta$ we expect a retraction from $D_\infty \to D_\infty$ to $D_\infty$, while the construction exploits retractions from $D_n$ to $D_n \to D_n$ which are the other way around.*

We now come back to $D_\infty$ and prove a result originally due to Park: Curry's fixpoint combinator (cf. example 2.1.11) is interpreted by the least fixpoint operator in $D_\infty$. The proof given here is inspired by recent work of Freyd (and Pitts) which will be briefly discussed in section 7.2.

**Proposition 3.2.7** *Let $\delta_J : (D_\infty \to D_\infty) \to (D_\infty \to D_\infty)$ be the function defined by:*

$$\delta_J(e) = G \circ (e \to id) \circ F,$$

*where $\to$ is used in the sense of definition 3.1.1. The function $\delta_J$ has the identity as unique fixpoint.*[1]

PROOF. Let $\epsilon$ be a fixpoint of $\delta_J$. Considering $\epsilon, id$ as elements of $D_\infty$, we shall prove that, for any $n$, $\epsilon_n = id_n$, i.e., for $n \geq 1$, $\epsilon_n = id : D_{n-1} \to D_{n-1}$. The general case ($n \geq 2$) is handled as follows, using lemma 3.1.16:

$$\epsilon_{n+2}(x)(y) = (\epsilon \to id)_{n+2}(x)(y) = ((\epsilon \to id)(x))_{n+1}(y)$$
$$= (x \circ \epsilon)_{n+1}(y) = ((x \circ \epsilon)(y))_n .$$

On the other hand, also by lemma 3.1.16:

$$(x \circ \epsilon_{n+1})(y) = x(\epsilon_{n+1}(y)) = x(\epsilon(y)_n) = (x \circ \epsilon)(y) = ((x \circ \epsilon)(y))_n .$$

Then we can use induction:

$$\epsilon_{n+2}(x)(y) = ((x \circ \epsilon)(y))_n = (x \circ \epsilon_{n+1})(y) = (x \circ id)(y) = x(y).$$

Hence $\epsilon_{n+2}(x) = x$, and $\epsilon_{n+2} = id$. We leave the base cases $n = 0, 1$ to the reader, with the following hint: establish first that $\bot \cdot y = \bot$, and $x_0 \cdot y = x_0 = x \cdot \bot_0$.                    □

**Remark 3.2.8** (1) *Proposition 3.2.7 does not depend on the initial choice of $D_0$, but the proof uses the fact that the initial pair $(i_0, j_0)$ is the standard one (this is hidden in the hint).*

(2) *The functional $\delta_J$ may seem a bit ad hoc. A more natural functional would be $\delta$ defined by: $\delta(e) = G \circ (e \to e) \circ F$. More generally, for a domain equation of the form $D = H(D)$, with a solution given by inverse isomorphisms $F : D \to H(D)$*

---

[1] The subscript $J$ in $\delta_J$ comes from the term $J = Y(\lambda fxy.x(fy))$ (see the discussion on the relations between $D_\infty$ and Böhm trees, later in this section).

*and $G : H(D) \to D$, we can set $\delta(e) = G \circ H(e) \circ F$. But replacing $\delta_J$ by $\delta$ in the proof of proposition 3.2.7 fails to work in the base cases $n = 0, 1$. On the other hand, we shall see (proposition 7.1.24) that the functional $\delta$ works well with the* initial *solution of $D = H(D)$. (In the case of $H(D) = D \to D$, the initial solution, which is $\{\perp\}$, is of little interest.)*

A fortiori, the identity is the least fixpoint of $\delta_J$. This fact can be used as a tool to prove properties of $D_\infty$. We illustrate this with a simple proof (adapted from [Pit96]) of Park's result.

**Proposition 3.2.9 (Park)** *Let $Y = \lambda y.(\lambda x.y(xx))(\lambda x.y(xx))$. In $D_\infty$, $[\![Y]\!]$ is the least fixpoint operator (cf. proposition 1.1.7 and exercise 1.4.5).*

PROOF. Let $f : D_\infty \to D_\infty$. Let $\Delta_f = [\![\lambda x.y(xx)]\!]\rho[f/y] = G(\lambda x.f(x{\bullet}x))$. We have to prove $\Delta_f{\bullet}\Delta_f \leq \mathit{fix}(f)$ (the other direction follows from soundness, since $YM =_\beta M(YM)$). Consider:

$$E = \{e : D_\infty \to D_\infty \mid e \leq id \text{ and } e(\Delta_f){\bullet}\Delta_f \leq \mathit{fix}(f)\}.$$

By continuity, $E$ is closed under directed lub's. We have to show that $id \in E$. By proposition 3.2.7, it is enough to show that $\delta_J^n(e) \in E$, for all $n \geq 0$. We proceed by induction on $n$. The property is obvious for $n = 0$. Set $e = \delta_J^n(e)$, and suppose $e \in E$. We have:

$$
\begin{aligned}
\delta_J(e)(\Delta_f){\bullet}\Delta_f &= G((e \to id)(\lambda x.f(x{\bullet}x))){\bullet}\Delta_f \\
&= (e \to id)(\lambda x.f(x{\bullet}x))(\Delta_f) \\
&= f(e(\Delta_f){\bullet}e(\Delta_f)) \\
&\leq f(e(\Delta_f){\bullet}\Delta_f) \qquad && \text{since } e \leq id \\
&\leq f(\mathit{fix}(f)) \qquad && \text{since } e \in E \\
&= \mathit{fix}(f) . && \qquad\qquad \square
\end{aligned}
$$

**$D_\infty$ models and Böhm trees.** The rest of the section is an overview of early fundamental (and independent) work of Wadsworth and Hyland that relates $D_\infty$ models and Böhm trees (cf. definition 2.3.1) [Wad76, Hyl76]. They proved that the following are equivalent for any two $\lambda$-terms $M$ and $N$:

(1)  For all contexts:

$$(C[M] \text{ has a head normal form } \Rightarrow C[N] \text{ has a head normal form})$$

(cf. definitions 2.1.2 and 2.1.6).

(2)  $BT(M) \leq^\eta BT(N)$ (the meaning of $\leq^\eta$ is sketched below).

(3)  $[\![M]\!] \leq [\![N]\!]$ in $D_\infty$ (for any choice of $D_0$, but with the standard initial $(i_0, j_0)$).

If $M, N$ satisfy the property (1), we write $M \leq_{obs} N$, and $\leq_{obs}$ is called the observational, or operational preorder. The equivalence (1)$\Leftrightarrow$(3) is called a full-abstraction property (cf. section 6.4). We briefly indicate the techniques used to prove these equivalences.

(1) $\Rightarrow$ (2) This is the hard core of the theorem. It is proved by contradiction, using the so-called Böhm-out technique. Consider an occurrence $u$ where the two Böhm trees of $M$ and $N$ differ. We sketch how the technique works if $BT(M)/u \neq \Omega$ and $BT(N)/u = \Omega$. Then there exist $M', N'$ such that $M \to^* M'$, $N \to^* N'$, $M'/u$ and $N'/u$ are defined, $BT(M'/u) \neq \Omega$ and $BT(N'/u) = \Omega$ (i.e., $M'/u$ has a head normal form and $N'/u$ has no head normal form). The Böhm-out technique consists in associating with $u$ a context $C$ such that $C[P] =_{\beta\eta} P/u$ for all $P$ such that $P/u$ is defined. Then the context associated with $u$ witnesses $M \not\leq_{obs} N$, since we have $C[M] \to^* C[M'] =_{\beta\eta} M'/u$ and $C[N] \to^* C[N'] =_{\beta\eta} N'/u$. (If $BT(M)/u \neq \Omega$ and $BT(N) \neq \Omega$, then the proof is similar to the proof of theorem 3.2.10.)

The following example should suggest the contents of $\leq^\eta$. Consider (cf. proposition 3.2.7):

$$I = \lambda x.x \text{ and } J = Y(\lambda fxy.x(fy)).$$

It can be proved (by the technique used in the proof of proposition 3.2.9) that $[\![I]\!] = [\![J]\!]$ in $D_\infty$. But the Böhm tree of $I$ is just $I$, while the Böhm tree of $J$ is infinite:

$$\lambda x z_0.x(\lambda z_1.z_0(\lambda z_2.z_1 \dots .$$

These two Böhm trees get equalized through infinite $\eta$-expansion of $I$:

$$I = \lambda x z_0.x z_0 = \lambda x z_0 x(\lambda z_1.z_0 z_1) = \dots .$$

The relation $\leq^\eta$ formalizes '$\leq$ modulo (infinite) $\eta$-conversions'.

(2) $\Rightarrow$ (3) This follows from the following so-called approximation theorem (see exercise 3.5.22):

$$[\![M]\!] = \bigvee \{[\![A]\!] \mid A \leq BT(M)\}.$$

(3) $\Rightarrow$ (1) A corollary of the approximation theorem is the following property, called adequacy:

$$[\![M]\!] = \bot \Leftrightarrow M \text{ has no head normal form} \Leftrightarrow BT(M) = \Omega.$$

Let $M, N$ be such that $[\![M]\!] \leq [\![N]\!]$. By adequacy, $M \leq_{obs} N$ can be rephrased as:

$$\forall C \ ([\![C[N]]\!] = \bot) \Rightarrow ([\![C[M]]\!] = \bot).$$

The implication holds, because we have $[\![C[M]]\!] \leq [\![C[N]]\!]$, by the compositionality of the interpretation in $D_\infty$.

The Böhm-out technique was first used in the proof of Böhm's theorem, which we now state.

**Theorem 3.2.10 (Böhm)** *Let $M, N$ be $\lambda$-terms which have both a $\beta\eta$-normal form, and whose $\beta\eta$-normal forms are distinct. Then any equation $P = Q$ is derivable from the system obtained by adding the axiom $M = N$ to $\beta\eta$.*

PROOF HINT. Let $M, N$ be two distinct $\beta\eta$-normal forms. The proof consists in associating with any pair of terms $P, Q$ a context $C_{P,Q}$ ($C$ for short) such that $C[M] =_{\beta\eta} P$ and $C[N] =_{\beta\eta} Q$. The induction is based on the size of $M, N$. We only describe a few typical situations. We can assume without loss of generality that $M$ and $N$ have no head $\lambda$'s, since they can be brought to that form by contexts of the form $[\ ]x_1 \ldots x_n$. Here $\eta$-interconvertibility is crucial: to prove $Mx_1 \ldots x_n \neq_{\beta\eta} Nx_1 \ldots x_n$, we use $M =_\eta \lambda\vec{x}.M\vec{x}$. There are three cases:

(1) Base case: $M = x\vec{M}$ and $N = y\vec{N}$ ($y \neq x$). Then we take:

$$C = (\lambda xy.[\ ])(\lambda\vec{u}.P)(\lambda\vec{v}.Q).$$

(2) $M = xM_1$ and $N = xN_1N_2$. We turn this difference in the number of arguments into a base case difference, in two steps. First, a context $[\ ]y_1y_2$, with $y_1, y_2$ distinct, yields $xM_1y_1y_2$ and $xN_1N_2y_1y_2$. Second, we substitute the term $\alpha_2 = \lambda z_1z_2z.zz_1z_2$, called an *applicator*, for $x$. Altogether, we set $D = (\lambda x.[\ ]y_1y_2)\alpha_2$, and we have:

$$D[M] =_{\beta\eta} y_2M_1y_2 \quad \text{and} \quad D[N] =_{\beta\eta} y_1N_1N_2y_2 \,,$$

which is a base case situation.

(3) $M = xM_1M_2$, $N = xN_1N_2$: Then $M \neq_{\beta\eta} N$ implies, say, $M_2 \neq_{\beta\eta} N_2$. It is enough to find $D$ such that $D[M] =_{\beta\eta} M_2$ and $D[N] =_{\beta\eta} N_2$, because then one may conclude by an induction argument. In first approximation, we are inclined to substitute the projection term $\pi_2 = \lambda z_1z_2.z_2$ for $x$, yielding $M_2[\pi_2/x]$ and $N_2[\pi_2/x]$. But we do not want the substitution of $\pi_2$ for $x$ in $M_2$ and $N_2$. To avoid this, we proceed in two steps: First we apply the two terms to a fresh variable $z$ and substitute $\alpha_2$ for $x$, then we substitute $\pi_2$ for $z$. Formally, we take $D = D_2[D_1]$, where $D_1 = (\lambda x.[\ ]z)\alpha_2$, and $D_2 = (\lambda z.[\ ])\pi_2$. Then:

$$D[M] =_{\beta\eta} M_2[\alpha_2/x] \quad \text{and} \quad D[N] =_{\beta\eta} N_2[\alpha_2/x].$$

The substitution of $\alpha_2$ turns out to be harmless. Such substitutions can be turned into a parameter of the induction, together with $P, Q$. For full details on the proof, we refer to [Kri91]. $\square$

In other words, adding $M = N$ leads to inconsistency. As a last remark, we observe that Böhm's theorem gives us already a limited form of 'full abstraction'.

**Corollary 3.2.11** *Let $M, N$ be $\lambda$-terms which have a $\beta\eta$-normal form. Then $[\![M]\!] = [\![N]\!]$ in $D_\infty$ iff $M =_{\beta\eta} N$.*

PROOF. ($\Leftarrow$) By soundness.

($\Rightarrow$) If $M, N$ have distinct normal forms and if $[\![M]\!] = [\![N]\!]$, then by Böhm's theorem and by soundness we have $[\![P]\!] = [\![Q]\!]$, for all $P, Q$; in particular $[\![x]\!] = [\![y]\!]$, which is contradicted by interpreting these terms with a $\rho$ such that $\rho(x) \neq \rho(y)$ ($D_\infty$ contains at least two elements). $\square$

## 3.3   Filter models

In this section, we introduce the syntax of intersection types, which leads to the definition of a class of reflexive domains. Coppo and Dezani's characters, or types, are the simple types (built with $\to$ only, cf. definition 2.2.5), supplemented by two new constructions: binary intersection and a special type $\omega$, with the following informal typing rules (see exercise 3.3.14):

- any term has type $\omega$,
- a term has type $\sigma \wedge \tau$ iff it has both types $\sigma$ and $\tau$.

This extension of the simple types allows us to type all terms of the $\lambda$-calculus. As an illustration, to type a self application of a variable $x$ to itself, we can give to $x$ the type $(\sigma \to \tau) \wedge \sigma$, and we get that $xx$ has type $\tau$ (but see exercise 3.5.2). In section 3.5, we shall further discuss the use of intersection types in the investigation of normalization properties.

Turning to semantics, functional characters can be used to give meaning to terms. Characters are then seen as properties satisfied by terms, in particular, the property $\sigma \to \tau$ is the property which holds for a term $M$ if and only if, whenever $N$ satisfies $\sigma$, $MN$ satisfies $\tau$. The meaning of a term is then the collection of properties that it satisfies.

Another way to understand the language of intersection types is as a formal language for presenting the compact elements of the domain $D$ which they serve to define. Recall that the topological presentation of domains (section 1.2) provides us with a collection of properties: the open sets of the Scott topology, or more specifically the open sets in the basis of Scott topology, that is, the sets of the form $\uparrow d$, where $d$ is a compact element of $D$. Hence, in this approach:

- Types $\sigma, \tau$ represent compact elements $d, e$ of $D$, the association being bijective, but *antimonotonic* (observe that $d \leq e$ iff $(\uparrow e) \subseteq (\uparrow d)$).

- $\sigma \to \tau$ represents the step function (cf. lemma 1.4.8) $d \to e : D \to D$, which is a (compact) element of $D$, since it is intended that $D = D \to D$.

- $\sigma \wedge \tau$ represents $d \vee e$, and $\omega$ represents $\bot$ (intersection types give a lattice: all finite lub's exist).

These remarks should motivate the following definition.

**Definition 3.3.1 (eats)** *An extended abstract type structure (eats for short) $S$ is given by a preorder $(S, \leq)$, called the carrier, whose elements are often called types, which:*

(1) *has all finite glb's, including the empty one, denoted by $\omega$, and*

(2) *is equipped with a binary operation $\to$ satisfying:*

$$(\to_1) \quad (\sigma \to \tau_1) \wedge (\sigma \to \tau_2) \leq \sigma \to (\tau_1 \wedge \tau_2)$$

$$(\to_2) \quad \frac{\sigma' \leq \sigma, \tau \leq \tau'}{(\sigma \to \tau) \leq (\sigma' \to \tau')}$$

$$(\omega) \quad \omega \leq \omega \to \omega \,.$$

**Remark 3.3.2** (1) *The structure of a preorder having all finite glb's can be axiomatized as follows:*

$$\sigma \le \sigma \qquad\qquad \frac{\sigma_1 \le \sigma_2, \sigma_2 \le \sigma_3}{\sigma_1 \le \sigma_3}$$

$$\sigma \le \omega$$

$$\sigma \wedge \tau \le \sigma \quad \sigma \wedge \tau \le \tau \qquad \frac{\sigma \le \sigma' \quad \tau \le \tau'}{(\sigma \wedge \tau) \le (\sigma' \wedge \tau')}$$

$$\sigma \le \sigma \wedge \sigma$$

(2) *Inequation* $(\to_2)$ *expresses contravariance in the first argument and covariance in the second argument (cf. definition 3.1.1).*

(3) *Thanks to inequation* $(\to_2)$, *the two members of* $(\to_1)$ *are actually equivalent.*

**Lemma 3.3.3** *In any eats, the following inequality holds:*

$$(\sigma_1 \to \tau_1) \wedge (\sigma_2 \to \tau_2) \le (\sigma_1 \wedge \sigma_2) \to (\tau_1 \wedge \tau_2).$$

PROOF. The statement is equivalent to:

$$(\sigma_1 \to \tau_1) \wedge (\sigma_2 \to \tau_2) \le ((\sigma_1 \wedge \sigma_2) \to \tau_1) \wedge ((\sigma_1 \wedge \sigma_2) \to \tau_2),$$

which holds since $\sigma_1 \to \tau_1 \le (\sigma_1 \wedge \sigma_2) \to \tau_1$ and $\sigma_2 \to \tau_2 \le (\sigma_1 \wedge \sigma_2) \to \tau_2$, by $(\to_2)$. $\qquad\square$

A way to obtain an eats is via a theory.

**Definition 3.3.4** *Let $T$ be the set of types constructed from a non-empty set At of atoms and from a signature $\{\omega^0, \wedge^2, \to^2\}$ (with the arities in superscript). Consider formulas of the form $\sigma \le \tau$, for $\sigma, \tau \in T$. A theory consists of a set Th of formulas closed under the rules defining an eats, making $T$ an eats (the preorder is described by Th, $\to$ is the term constructor). We denote this eats also by Th. For any set $\Sigma$ of formulas, $Th(\Sigma)$ denotes the smallest theory containing $\Sigma$. We denote with $Th_0$ the free theory $Th(\emptyset)$.*

**Remark 3.3.5** *The assumption At $\ne \emptyset$ is important: otherwise everything collapses, since $\omega = \omega \wedge \omega = \omega \to \omega$, reading $=$ as the equivalence associated with the preorder $\le$.*

Another way to obtain an eats is by means of an applicative structure.

**Definition 3.3.6 (ets)** *Let $(D, \cdot)$ be an applicative structure. Consider the following operation on subsets of $D$:*

$$A \to B = \{d \in D \mid \forall e \in A \ d \cdot e \in B\}.$$

*A subset of $\mathcal{P}(D)$ is called an extended type structure (ets for short) if it is closed under finite set theoretical intersections and under the operation $\to$ just defined.*

**Lemma 3.3.7** *An ets, ordered by inclusion, is an eats.*

We have already observed that the order between types is reversed with respect to the order in the abstract cpo semantics. Accordingly, the role of ideals is played here by filters.

**Definition 3.3.8 (filter)** *A filter of an inf-semi-lattice $S$ is a nonempty subset $x$ of $S$ such that:*

(1) $\sigma, \tau \in x \Rightarrow \sigma \wedge \tau \in x$,

(2) $\sigma \in x$ *and* $\sigma \leq \tau \Rightarrow \tau \in x$.

*The filter domain of an eats $S$ is the set $\mathcal{F}(S)$ of filters of $S$, ordered by inclusion.*

**Remark 3.3.9** *Equivalently, in definition 3.3.8, the condition of non-emptyness can be replaced by $\omega \in x$.*

The following properties are easy to check:

- For each $\sigma \in S$, $\uparrow \sigma$ is a filter.

- Given $A \subseteq S$, the filter $\overline{A}$ generated by $A$ (i.e., the least filter containing $A$) is the intersection of all filters containing $A$. It is easily seen that:

$$\overline{A} = \bigcup \{\uparrow (\tau_1 \wedge \cdots \wedge \tau_n) \mid \tau_1, \ldots, \tau_n \in A\}.$$

- In particular for a finite $A = \{\tau_1, \ldots, \tau_n\}$, we have $\overline{A} = \uparrow (\tau_1 \wedge \cdots \wedge \tau_n)$.

**Proposition 3.3.10** *If $S$ is an eats, then $\mathcal{F}(S)$ is a complete algebraic lattice.*

PROOF. The minimum and maximum elements are $\uparrow \omega$ and $S$, respectively. The nonempty glb's are just set theoretical intersections. The lub's are obtained by $\bigvee A = \overline{\bigcup A}$. Two instances of lub's can be given explicitly:

- If $A$ is directed, then $\bigcup A$ is a filter, hence $\bigvee A = \bigcup A$. To see this, let $\sigma, \tau \in \bigcup A$. Then $\sigma \in x$, $\tau \in y$ for some $x, y \in A$. By directedness $\sigma, \tau \in z$ for some $z \in A$; since $z$ is a filter, we have $\sigma \wedge \tau \in z$, hence $\sigma \wedge \tau \in \bigcup A$.

- $(\uparrow \sigma) \vee (\uparrow \tau) = \overline{\{\sigma, \tau\}} = \uparrow (\sigma \wedge \tau)$.

It follows that $\{\uparrow \sigma \mid \sigma \in x\}$ is directed, for any filter $x$, and since it is clear that $x = \bigcup \{\uparrow \sigma \mid \sigma \in x\}$, we obtain that $\mathcal{F}(S)$ is algebraic and that the compact elements are the principal filters $\uparrow \sigma$. □

**Definition 3.3.11** *Let $S$ be an eats, let $x, y \in \mathcal{F}(S)$, and $f$ be a function from $\mathcal{F}(S)$ to $\mathcal{F}(S)$. We define:*

$$x \cdot y = \{\tau \mid \exists \sigma \in y \ \sigma \to \tau \in x\} \qquad G(f) = \overline{\{\sigma \to \tau \mid \tau \in f(\uparrow \sigma)\}}.$$

*We write $F$ for the curried form of $\cdot$.*

**Lemma 3.3.12** *For any $x, y \in \mathcal{F}(S)$, $x \cdot y$ is a filter, and the operation $\cdot$ is continuous. The function $G$ (restricted to $\mathcal{F}(S) \to_{cont} \mathcal{F}(S)$) is continuous.*

$$\frac{x : \sigma \in \Gamma}{\Gamma \vdash x : \sigma} \qquad \frac{\Gamma \vdash M : \sigma \to \tau \quad \Gamma \vdash N : \sigma}{\Gamma \vdash MN : \tau} \qquad \frac{\Gamma, x : \sigma \vdash M : \tau}{\Gamma \vdash \lambda x.M : \sigma \to \tau}$$

$$\frac{}{\Gamma \vdash M : \omega} \qquad \frac{\Gamma \vdash M : \sigma \quad \Gamma \vdash M : \tau}{\Gamma \vdash M : \sigma \wedge \tau} \qquad \frac{\Gamma \vdash M : \sigma \quad \sigma \leq \tau}{\Gamma \vdash M : \tau}$$

Figure 3.2: Intersection type assignment

PROOF. We check only that $x \cdot y$ is a filter:

- $\omega \in x \cdot y$. Take $\sigma = \omega$. Then $\omega \in x \cdot y$ since $\omega \leq \omega \to \omega$ implies $\omega \to \omega \in x$.

- Closure under intersections. Let $\tau_1, \tau_2 \in x \cdot y$, and let $\sigma_1, \sigma_2 \in y$ such that $\sigma_1 \to \tau_1, \sigma_2 \to \tau_2 \in x$. Then $\sigma_1 \wedge \sigma_2 \to \tau_1 \wedge \tau_2 \in x$, by lemma 3.3.3, hence $\tau_1 \wedge \tau_2 \in x \cdot y$.

- Upward closedness. by covariance. □

**Remark 3.3.13** *Notice the role of the axiom $\omega < \omega \to \omega$, which guarantees the non-emptyness of $x \cdot y$.*

**Exercise 3.3.14** *Consider the following interpretation of $\lambda$-terms:*

$$[\![x]\!]\rho = \rho(x) \quad [\![MN]\!]\rho = ([\![M]\!]\rho) \cdot ([\![N]\!]\rho) \quad [\![\lambda x.M]\!]\rho = G(\lambda d.[\![M]\!]\rho[d/x]) ,$$

*where $F$ and $G$ are as in definition 3.3.11 and where $\rho$ maps variables to filters. (Unlike in definition 3.2.2, we do not suppose $F \circ G = id$.) On the other hand, consider the formal typing system of figure 3.2, involving judgments of the form $\Gamma \vdash M : \sigma$, where $M$ is an untyped $\lambda$-term, $\sigma \in S$, and $\Gamma$ is a partial function from (a finite set of) variables to $S$, represented as a list of pairs of the form $x : \sigma$. (A slightly different typing system will be considered in section 3.5.) Show:*

$$[\![M]\!]\rho = \{\sigma \mid \Gamma \vdash M : \sigma\},$$

*where $\rho(x) = \uparrow \sigma$ whenever $x : \sigma$ is in $\Gamma$.*

We next examine how $F$ and $G$ compose.

**Lemma 3.3.15** *In an eats, the following holds for any $\sigma, \tau \in S, x \in \mathcal{F}(S)$:*

$$\sigma \to \tau \in x \Leftrightarrow \tau \in x \cdot (\uparrow \sigma) .$$

PROOF. ($\Rightarrow$) This follows obviously from $\sigma \in \uparrow \sigma$. Conversely, $\tau \in x \cdot (\uparrow \sigma)$ implies $\sigma' \to \tau \in x$ for some $\sigma' \geq \sigma$, hence $\sigma \to \tau \in x$ by contravariance. □

**Lemma 3.3.16** *Let $F, G$ be as in definition 3.3.11. Then $G \circ F \leq id$.*

PROOF. Let $f = F(y)$. If $\sigma \in G(f)$, then $\sigma \geq (\sigma_1 \to \tau_1) \wedge \cdots \wedge (\sigma_n \to \tau_n)$, where $\tau_i \in y \cdot (\uparrow \sigma_i)$ $(1 \leq i \leq n)$, or, equivalently, $\sigma_i \to \tau_i \in y$, from which $\sigma \in y$ follows, by definition of a filter. $\qquad\square$

**Proposition 3.3.17** *Let $F, G$ be as in definition 3.3.11. We have:*

$$F \circ G \geq id \quad on \; \mathcal{F}(S) \to_{cont} \mathcal{F}(S)$$
$$F \circ G = id \quad on \; \mathcal{F}(S) \to_{rep} \mathcal{F}(S) \,.$$

PROOF. • $F \circ G \geq id$. We have to prove $f(x) \subseteq G(f) \cdot x$, for all $f, x$. If $\tau \in f(x)$, then by continuity $\tau \in f(\uparrow \sigma)$ for some $\sigma \in x$. Hence $\sigma \to \tau \in G(f)$ by definition of $G$, and $\tau \in G(f) \cdot x$ by definition of •.

• $F \circ G \leq id$. Since $\mathcal{F}(S) \to_{rep} \mathcal{F}(S) = F(\mathcal{F}(S))$, we can reformulate the statement as $F \circ G \circ F \leq F$; it then follows from lemma 3.3.16. $\qquad\square$

The situation so far is as follows. An eats gives rise to a coadditive pre-reflexive domain based on the representable functions. This domain does not necessarily give rise to a $\lambda$-model, because there may not exist enough representable functions to guarantee that $\lambda d.[\![M]\!]\rho[d/x]$ is always representable. The following proposition characterizes the eats's which give rise to reflexive domains, with the above choice of $F, G$.

**Proposition 3.3.18** *For any eats $S$, $\mathcal{F}(S) \to_{rep} \mathcal{F}(S) = \mathcal{F}(S) \to_{cont} \mathcal{F}(S)$ (and hence $(\mathcal{F}(S), F, G)$ is reflexive) if and only if (for any types):*

$$(\mathcal{F}refl) \quad (\sigma_1 \to \tau_1) \wedge \cdots \wedge (\sigma_n \to \tau_n) \leq \sigma \to \tau \Rightarrow \bigwedge\{\tau_i \mid \sigma \leq \sigma_i\} \leq \tau.$$

PROOF. We begin with two observations:

(1) By proposition 3.3.17, any representable function $f$ is represented by $G(f)$.

(2) The compact continuous functions in $\mathcal{F}(S) \to_{cont} \mathcal{F}(S)$ are the functions of the form $f = (\uparrow \sigma_1 \to \uparrow \tau_1) \vee \cdots \vee (\uparrow \sigma_n \to \uparrow \tau_n)$, i.e., such that:

$$f(x) \;=\; \bigvee\{\uparrow \tau_i \mid \sigma_i \in x\} \;=\; \uparrow \bigwedge\{\tau_i \mid \sigma_i \in x\}$$

(cf. remark 1.4.13). In particular, $\tau_i \in f(\uparrow \sigma_i)$, hence $\sigma_i \to \tau_i \in G(f)$ (for all $i$).

Suppose first that all continuous functions are representable. Then the above $f$ is represented by $G(f)$. Let $\sigma, \tau$ be as in the assumption of $(\mathcal{F}refl)$. Then $\sigma \to \tau \in G(f)$, since $\sigma_i \to \tau_i \in G(f)$ for all $i$. Moreover, since $F \circ G = id$, we have:

$$\tau \;\in\; G(f) \cdot (\uparrow \sigma) \;=\; f(\uparrow \sigma) \;=\; \uparrow \bigwedge\{\tau_i \mid \sigma \leq \sigma_i\}.$$

Hence $\bigwedge\{\tau_i \mid \sigma \leq \sigma_i\} \leq \tau$.

Conversely, suppose that $(\mathcal{F}refl)$ holds. We show that the compact functions $f$ (cf. observation (2)) are representable. We first show:

$$G(f) \;=\; \uparrow ((\sigma_1 \to \tau_1) \wedge \cdots \wedge (\sigma_n \to \tau_n)).$$

- $\uparrow ((\sigma_1 \to \tau_1) \wedge \cdots \wedge (\sigma_n \to \tau_n)) \subseteq G(f)$. This follows from $\sigma_i \to \tau_i \in G(f)$, shown above.

- $G(f) \subseteq \uparrow ((\sigma_1 \to \tau_1) \wedge \cdots \wedge (\sigma_n \to \tau_n))$. It is enough to show that $\tau \in f(\uparrow \sigma)$, implies $(\sigma_1 \to \tau_1) \wedge \cdots \wedge (\sigma_n \to \tau_n) \leq \sigma \to \tau$ (the converse of $(\mathcal{F}refl)$). This is proved using lemma 3.3.3:

$$
\begin{aligned}
(\sigma_1 \to \tau_1) \wedge \cdots \wedge (\sigma_n \to \tau_n) &\leq \bigwedge_{\{i | \sigma \leq \sigma_i\}} (\sigma_i \to \tau_i) \\
&\leq \bigwedge_{\{i | \sigma \leq \sigma_i\}} \sigma_i \to \bigwedge_{\{i | \sigma \leq \sigma_i\}} \tau_i \\
&\leq \sigma \to \tau .
\end{aligned}
$$

Now we can prove that $G(f)$ represents $f$, that is, for all $\sigma$:

$$
G(f) \cdot (\uparrow \sigma) = \uparrow \bigwedge \{\tau_i \mid \sigma \leq \sigma_i\}.
$$

- $G(f) \cdot (\uparrow \sigma) \subseteq f(\uparrow \sigma)$. Let $\tau \in G(f) \cdot (\uparrow \sigma)$, that is, let $\sigma' \geq \sigma$ be such that $\sigma' \to \tau \in G(f)$. Then $(\sigma_1 \to \tau_1) \wedge \cdots \wedge (\sigma_n \to \tau_n) \leq \sigma' \to \tau$. By $(\mathcal{F}refl)$, we have $\bigwedge \{\tau_i \mid \sigma' \leq \sigma_i\} \leq \tau$. A fortiori $\bigwedge \{\tau_i \mid \sigma \leq \sigma_i\} \leq \tau$, that is, $\tau \in f(\uparrow \sigma)$.

- $f(\uparrow \sigma) \subseteq G(f) \cdot (\uparrow \sigma)$. This always holds, by proposition 3.3.17.

Finally, consider an arbitrary continuous function $f$, and let $\Delta$ be the set of its approximants. Then, using lemma 3.3.12:

$$
G(\bigvee \Delta) \cdot x = (\bigvee G(\Delta)) \cdot x = \bigvee_{\delta \in \Delta} G(\delta) \cdot x = \bigvee_{\delta \in \Delta} \delta(x) = (\bigvee \Delta)(x). \qquad \square
$$

Many eats's satisfy $(\mathcal{F}refl)$, including $Th_0$ (next exercise), and the theories $Th_V$ defined in section 3.4.

**Exercise 3.3.19** *Show that $Th_0$ satisfies $(\mathcal{F}refl)$. Hint: Reformulate the goal for an arbitrary formula $\sigma \leq \tau$, exploiting the fact that an arbitrary formula can be written as an intersection of formulas which are each either $\omega$, or an atom, or of the form $\sigma_1 \to \sigma_2$.*

## 3.4   Some $D_\infty$ models as filter models *

We are now interested in recasting some $D_\infty$ models in terms of 'logic', that is in terms of filter models built on a theory. We restrict our attention to an initial $D_0$ which is an algebraic lattice.

**Exercise 3.4.1** *Show that if $D_0$ is an algebraic cpo or an algebraic lattice, then so is $D_\infty$, for an arbitrary choice of $(i_0, j_0)$, and that $\mathcal{K}(D_\infty) = \bigcup_{n \in \omega} \mathcal{K}(D_n)$.*

**Definition 3.4.2** *Let $(D, F, G)$ be a pre-reflexive domain. Let $v : D \to D'$ and $w : D' \to D$ be inverse order-isomorphisms. Let $F', G'$ be defined by:*

$$
F'(x') = v \circ F(w(x')) \circ w \qquad G'(f') = v(G(w \circ f' \circ v)) .
$$

*Then we say that $(D', F', G')$ is isomorphic to $(D, F, G)$.*

If $(D, F, G)$ and $(D', F', G')$ are isomorphic, then they satisfy the same properties, e.g., one of them is reflexive if and only if the other is, or one of them satisfies ($\mathcal{F}$ refl) if and only if the other does.

In the following definition we 'officialize' the inversion of order involved in the logical treatment.

**Definition 3.4.3** *Let $D$ be an algebraic lattice. We set:*

$$K(D) = \{\uparrow d \mid d \in \mathcal{K}(D)\},$$

*and order it by inclusion. (Hence, up to isomorphism, $K(D)$ is $(\mathcal{K}(D), \geq)$.)*

**Theorem 3.4.4** *If $D$ is an algebraic lattice and if $(D, F', G')$ is a reflexive coadditive domain, then $K(D)$ can be equipped with an eats structure in such a way that the associated $(\mathcal{F}(K(D)), F, G)$ is isomorphic to $(D, F', G')$.*

PROOF. By lemma 3.3.7 applied to the applicative structure $D$, it is enough to prove that $K(D)$ is closed under finite intersections and under the $\rightarrow$ operation. We have:

$$(\uparrow d) \wedge (\uparrow e) = \uparrow (d \vee e) \qquad \uparrow \bot = D.$$

We show:

$$\uparrow d \rightarrow \uparrow e \;=\; \uparrow G'(d \rightarrow e),$$

where the left $\rightarrow$ denotes the operation introduced in definition 3.3.6, and where $d \rightarrow e$ is a step function. Indeed, we have:

$$z \in (\uparrow d \rightarrow \uparrow e) \Leftrightarrow z{\bullet}d \geq e \Leftrightarrow F'(z) \geq d \rightarrow e \Leftrightarrow z \geq G'(d \rightarrow e),$$

where the last equivalence holds by coadditivity. Hence $K(D)$ forms an ets (notice that $G'(d \rightarrow e)$ is compact by coadditivity). The filters over $K(D)$ are in order-isomorphic correspondence with the ideals over $\mathcal{K}(D)$. We finally check that the operations $F, G$ are the operations $F', G'$, up to isomorphism. For $x, y \in D$, we have:

$$\{\uparrow f \mid f \leq x\}{\bullet}\{\uparrow d \mid d \leq y\} = \{\uparrow e \mid \exists d \leq y \; (G'(d \rightarrow e) \leq x)\}.$$

So what we have to show is:

$$e \leq x{\bullet}y \Leftrightarrow \exists d \leq y \; (G'(d \rightarrow e) \leq x),$$

which by coadditivity is equivalent to:

$$e \leq F'(x)(y) \Leftrightarrow \exists d \leq y \; (d \rightarrow e \leq F'(x)),$$

which follows by continuity of $F'(x)$. Matching $G$ against $G'$ amounts to showing:

$$\{\uparrow f \mid f \leq G'(g)\} = \overline{\{\uparrow d \rightarrow \uparrow e \mid e \leq g(d)\}},$$

which can be rephrased as:

$$\{\uparrow f \mid f \leq G'(g)\} = \overline{A} \quad \text{where } A = \{\uparrow G'(d \rightarrow e) \mid d \rightarrow e \leq g\}.$$

- $\{\uparrow f \mid f \leq G'(g)\} \subseteq \overline{A}$. By the continuity of $G'$, if $f \leq G'(g)$, then:

$$f \leq G'(d_1 \rightarrow e_1 \vee \cdots \vee d_n \rightarrow e_n)$$

for some $d_1, e_1, \ldots, d_n, e_n$ such that $d_1 \rightarrow e_1 \le g, \ldots, d_n \rightarrow e_n \le g$. Hence:

$$\uparrow G'(d_1 \rightarrow e_1), \ldots, \uparrow G'(d_n \rightarrow e_n) \in A.$$

Then, since $G'$ preserves lub's:

$$
\begin{aligned}
\uparrow G'(d_1 \rightarrow e_1 \vee \cdots \vee d_n \rightarrow e_n) &= \uparrow (G'(d_1 \rightarrow e_1) \vee \cdots \vee G'(d_n \rightarrow e_n)) \\
&= \uparrow G'(d_1 \rightarrow e_1) \cap \cdots \cap \uparrow G'(d_n \rightarrow e_n) \in \overline{A},
\end{aligned}
$$

from which we get $\uparrow f \in \overline{A}$.

- $\overline{A} \subseteq \{\uparrow f \mid f \le G'(g)\}$. It is obvious that $A \subseteq \{\uparrow f \mid f \le G'(g)\}$.    □

Now we investigate under which conditions a filter domain can be presented by a theory (recall definition 3.3.4).

**Definition 3.4.5** *Suppose that $S$ is an eats, and that an interpretation $V : At \rightarrow S$ (which obviously extends to $V : T \rightarrow S$) is given. Then $S, V$ induce a theory $Th_V = \{\sigma \le \tau \mid V(\sigma) \le V(\tau)\}$.*

**Lemma 3.4.6** *If $S$ is an eats and $V : At \rightarrow S$ is such that its extension $V : T \rightarrow S$ is surjective, then the pre-reflexive domains of filters associated with $Th_V$ and $S$ are isomorphic.*

PROOF. The inverse maps between the sets of filters are $x \mapsto V(x)$ and $y \mapsto V^{-1}(y)$. The surjectivity of $V$ guarantees that $V(V^{-1}(y)) = y$. In the other direction, $x \subseteq V^{-1}(V(x))$ holds obviously. If $\sigma \in V^{-1}(V(x))$, then $V(\sigma) = V(\tau)$ for some $\tau \in x$, hence $\tau \le \sigma \in Th_V$, from which $\sigma \in x$ follows since $x$ is a filter.    □

Summarizing, to get a presentation of a domain $D$ by a theory, we should make sure that $D$ is an algebraic lattice, is reflexive and coadditive, and we should find a surjection from types to the compact elements of the domain. We apply this discussion to the $D_\infty$ models $(D_\infty, F, G)$ constructed from a lattice $D_0$.

**Lemma 3.4.7** *If $V : At \rightarrow K(D_\infty)$ is such that for each $d \in K(D_0)$ there exists $\sigma \in T$ such that $V(\sigma) = \uparrow d$, then $V : T \rightarrow K(D_\infty)$ is surjective.*

PROOF. A compact element of $D_\infty$ is a compact element of $D_n$ for some $n$ (cf. exercise 3.4.1). We use induction over $n$. The case $n = 0$ is the assumption. Take a compact element $c = (a_1 \rightarrow b_1) \vee \cdots \vee (a_n \rightarrow b_n)$ of $D_{n+1}$. By induction there exist $\sigma_1, \ldots, \sigma_n, \tau_1, \ldots, \tau_n$ such that:

$$\uparrow a_1 = V(\sigma_1), \ldots, \uparrow a_n = V(\sigma_n) \quad \text{and} \quad \uparrow b_1 = V(\tau_1), \ldots, \uparrow b_n = V(\tau_n).$$

Hence:

$$
\begin{aligned}
V(\sigma_i \rightarrow \tau_i) &= \uparrow a_i \rightarrow \uparrow b_i \\
&= \uparrow G'(a_i \rightarrow b_i) && \text{(cf. the proof of theorem 3.4.4)} \\
&= \uparrow G'(i_{n\infty} \circ (a_i \rightarrow b_i) \circ j_{n\infty}) && \text{(since } a_i \le x \Leftrightarrow a_i \le x_n) \\
&= \uparrow (a_i \rightarrow b_i) && \text{(by lemma 3.1.14) .}
\end{aligned}
$$

We conclude that $\uparrow c = V((\sigma_1 \rightarrow \tau_1) \wedge \cdots \wedge (\sigma_n \rightarrow \tau_n))$.    □

We now define a theory for the $D_\infty$ model based on $D_0 = \{\perp, \top\}$ and the standard pair $(i_0, j_0)$ (cf. definition 3.1.10). We take $At = \{\kappa\}$, and define $V(\kappa) = \uparrow \top$. Then obviously $V$ satisfies the assumption of lemma 3.4.7. So all we need now is a syntactic characterization of $Th_V$ as $Th(\Sigma)$ for some finite set $\Sigma$ of axioms.

**Theorem 3.4.8** *Let $D_\infty, V$ be as above. Set $\Sigma = \{\kappa \leq \omega \rightarrow \kappa, \omega \rightarrow \kappa \leq \kappa\}$. Then $Th_V = Th(\Sigma)$ and $D_\infty$ is isomorphic to $\mathcal{F}(Th(\Sigma))$.*

PROOF. We have the following isomorphisms:

$$
\begin{array}{lll}
D_\infty & \text{is isomorphic to} & \mathcal{F}(K(D_\infty)) \quad \text{(by theorem 3.4.4)} \\
\mathcal{F}(K(D_\infty)) & \text{is isomorphic to} & \mathcal{F}(Th_V) \quad \text{(by lemma 3.4.6)} .
\end{array}
$$

We deduce from these isomorphisms that $Th_V$ satisfies ($\mathcal{F}refl$), by proposition 3.3.18 (since $D_\infty$ is reflexive), and that the second part of the statement follows from the first part.

- $Th(\Sigma) \subseteq Th_V$. It suffices to check $V(\kappa) = V(\omega \rightarrow \kappa)$:

$$
x \in V(\omega \rightarrow \kappa) \; (= (\uparrow \bot) \rightarrow (\uparrow \top)) \; \Leftrightarrow \; \forall y \; x \bullet y = \top \; \Leftrightarrow \; x = \top.
$$

The latter equivalence follows from the fact that $D_\infty$'s $\top$ element $(\top, \ldots, \top, \ldots)$ is $D_0$'s $\top$, since $i_0(\top) = \lambda x.\top$ is $D_1$'s $\top$ element, and since it is easily seen that $i(\top) = \top$ implies $i'(\top) = \top$ where $(i', j') = (i, j) \rightarrow (i, j)$.

- $Th_V \subseteq Th(\Sigma)$. We pick $(\sigma \leq \tau) \in Th_V$ and proceed by induction on $size(\sigma) + size(\tau)$, where the size of a type is the number of nodes in its tree representation (cf. definition 2.2.5). Clearly, it is enough to prove $\sigma' \leq \tau' \in Th(\Sigma)$ for some $\sigma', \tau'$ such that $(\sigma = \sigma'), (\tau = \tau') \in Th(\Sigma)$ (where = is the equivalence associated with $\leq$, i.e., the conjunction of $\leq$ and $\geq$). Clearly, from any $\sigma$ we can extract a type $\sigma' =_0 \sigma$ (where $=_0$ is the equivalence associated with the preorder $\leq_0$ of $Th_0$) such that $size(\sigma') \leq size(\sigma)$ and $\sigma'$ has one of the following forms:

$$
\begin{array}{l}
\omega \\
(\sigma_1^1 \rightarrow \sigma_2^1) \wedge \cdots \wedge (\sigma_1^n \rightarrow \sigma_2^n) \; (n \geq 1) \\
(\sigma_1^1 \rightarrow \sigma_2^1) \wedge \cdots \wedge (\sigma_1^n \rightarrow \sigma_2^n) \wedge \kappa \; (n \geq 0) .
\end{array}
$$

Similarly for $\tau$. Exploiting this fact, the problem of verifying $(\sigma \leq \tau) \in Th(\Sigma)$ can be limited without loss of generality to $\tau \equiv \kappa$ and $\tau \equiv \tau_1 \rightarrow \tau_2$ (where $\equiv$ means 'identical'):

- $\tau \equiv \kappa$. We consider the three possible forms of $\sigma$:

  - $\sigma \equiv \omega$. This case is impossible, since $\omega \leq \kappa \notin Th_V$.

  - $\sigma \equiv (\sigma_1^1 \rightarrow \sigma_2^1) \wedge \cdots \wedge (\sigma_1^n \rightarrow \sigma_2^n)$. Then $\sigma \leq (\omega \rightarrow \kappa) \in Th_V$, since $(\sigma \leq \kappa) \in Th_V$. Let $I = \{i \mid \omega \leq \sigma_1^i \in Th_V\}$. By ($\mathcal{F}refl$), we have: $\bigwedge_{i \in I} \sigma_2^i \leq \kappa \in Th_V$. We can apply induction to both $\omega, \bigwedge_{i \in I} \sigma_1^i$ and $\bigwedge_{i \in I} \sigma_2^i, \kappa$, from which $\sigma \leq \tau' \in Th(\Sigma)$ follows by lemma 3.3.3, where $\tau' \equiv \omega \rightarrow \kappa = \kappa \equiv \tau$.

  - $\sigma \equiv (\sigma_1^1 \rightarrow \sigma_2^1) \wedge \cdots \wedge (\sigma_1^n \rightarrow \sigma_2^n) \wedge \kappa$. Then obviously $\sigma \leq_0 \tau$.

- $\tau \equiv \tau_1 \rightarrow \tau_2$. We consider the three possible forms of $\sigma$:

  - $\sigma \equiv \omega$. Replacing $\omega$ by $\omega \rightarrow \omega$, we get $\omega \leq \tau_2$ by ($\mathcal{F}refl$), and $\omega \leq \tau_2 \in Th(\Sigma)$ by induction applied to $\omega, \tau_2$. Hence $\sigma' \leq \tau \in Th(\Sigma)$, with $\sigma' \equiv \omega \rightarrow \omega = \sigma$.

  - $\sigma \equiv (\sigma_1^1 \rightarrow \sigma_2^1) \wedge \cdots \wedge (\sigma_1^n \rightarrow \sigma_2^n)$. The reasoning is the same as for the corresponding case for $\tau \equiv \kappa$. We define now $I = \{i \mid \tau_1 \leq \sigma_1^i \in Th_V\}$, and we apply induction to $\tau_1, \bigwedge_{i \in I} \sigma_1^i$ and $\bigwedge_{i \in I} \sigma_2^i, \tau_2$.

$- \ \sigma \equiv (\sigma_1^1 \to \sigma_2^1) \wedge \cdots \wedge (\sigma_1^n \to \sigma_2^n) \wedge \kappa$. The reasoning is a variation of the previous case. We replace $\kappa$ by $\omega \to \kappa$, we keep the same $I$, and we apply induction to $\tau_1, \bigwedge_{i \in I} \sigma_1^i$ and $\bigwedge_{i \in I} \sigma_2^i \wedge \kappa, \tau_2$. □

There are more liberal conditions allowing us to get $Th = Th(\Sigma)$ for some finite $\Sigma$.

**Exercise\* 3.4.9** *Let $Th$ be a theory satisfying $(\mathcal{F}refl)$, and in which every atom $\kappa$ is equivalent to a finite conjunction $\sigma_\kappa$ of types of the form $\omega \to \kappa$ or $\kappa_1 \to \kappa_2$. Show that $Th = Th(\Sigma)$, where:*

$$\Sigma = (Th \cap \{\kappa_1 \wedge \cdots \wedge \kappa_m \le \kappa \mid \kappa_1, \ldots, \kappa_m, \kappa \in At\}) \cup \{\kappa = \sigma_\kappa \mid \kappa \in At\}.$$

*Hints: Reason by induction on the number of occurrences of $\to$. The inequations $\kappa_1 \wedge \cdots \wedge \kappa_m \le \kappa$ might lead to loops when replacing $\kappa_1, \ldots, \kappa_m, \kappa$ by $\sigma_{\kappa_1}, \ldots, \sigma_{\kappa_n}, \sigma_\kappa$, hence they are added explicitly.*

**Exercise\* 3.4.10 (Park's $D_\infty$)** *Apply exercise 3.4.9 to show that the $D_\infty$ model based on $D_0 = \{\bot, \top\}$ and $(i_\top, j_\top)$ (cf. remark 3.1.11) is isomorphic to $\mathcal{F}(Th(\Sigma^{Park}))$, with $\Sigma^{Park} = \{\kappa = \kappa \to \kappa\}$. Hint: Use the same function $V$, but notice that (unlike in the standard $D_\infty$ model) it is not the case here that $D_0$'s $\top$ is $D_\infty$'s $\top$, since $i_\top(\bot) = \lambda x.x$ is not $D_1$'s $\top$ element.*

We refer to exercise 4.6.6 for a related characterization of some $D^\infty$ models as initial segment models. We end our investigation of $D_\infty$ models with an important remark.

**Remark 3.4.11** *Remarks 3.1.11, 3.2.8, and 3.3.5 indicate the rather ad hoc nature of $D_\infty$ models. It would be nicer to be in a situation where just one initial, or canonical, model would exist, which could be captured logically in a 'pure' theory such that $At = \emptyset$. Such a model has been first proposed by Abramsky for the lazy $\lambda$-calculus [Abr90] (see exercise 7.1.23). Another such model is presented in section 8.4.*

# 3.5   More on intersection types  *

In this section, following original work of Coppo and Dezani [CD78, CDC80], we study intersection types from a syntactic point of view. Intersection types are used to give characterizations of the following predicates over $\lambda$-terms: 'has a head normal form', 'has a normal form', and 'is strongly normalizable'. The first two characterizations can be derived as corollaries of a logical formulation of the approximation theorem (cf. section 3.2). Our presentation follows [Kri91].

**Systems $\mathcal{D}\Omega$ and $\mathcal{D}$.**   Recall the set $T$ of intersection types from definition 3.3.4. The typing system $\mathcal{D}\Omega$ is defined in figure 3.3. A judgment $\Gamma \vdash M : \sigma$ reads as: $M$ has type $\sigma$ in context $\Gamma$. A context is a list of pairs of the form $x : \sigma$ of type declarations (at most one for a given variable $x$). If $x : \sigma$ appears in $\Gamma$, we write $x : \sigma \in \Gamma$ and we say that $x$ is declared in $\Gamma$. The only difference with the system presented in figure 3.2 is the replacement of the last rule by the more restricted rules $(\wedge E1)$ and $(\wedge E2)$. We do not need here an explicit preordering on types, as we did in order to construct a model. Also, we let now $M$ range over $\Omega$-terms (cf. definition 2.3.1). The rule $(\omega)$ allows us to type $\Omega$.

The restriction of $\mathcal{D}\Omega$ obtained by removing $\omega$ in the BNF grammar of $T$, as well as the rule $(\omega)$, is called $\mathcal{D}$. In $\mathcal{D}$, only $\lambda$-terms, i.e., terms without occurrences of $\Omega$, can be typed.

(Asmp)   $\dfrac{x : \sigma \in \Gamma}{\Gamma \vdash x : \sigma}$

$(\to_E)$   $\dfrac{\Gamma \vdash M : \sigma \to \tau \quad \Gamma \vdash N : \sigma}{\Gamma \vdash MN : \tau}$          $(\to_I)$   $\dfrac{\Gamma, x : \sigma \vdash M : \tau}{\Gamma \vdash \lambda x.M : \sigma \to \tau}$

$(\omega)$   $\dfrac{}{\Gamma \vdash M : \omega}$          $(\wedge I)$   $\dfrac{\Gamma \vdash M : \sigma \quad \Gamma \vdash M : \tau}{\Gamma \vdash M : \sigma \wedge \tau}$

$(\wedge E1)$   $\dfrac{\Gamma \vdash M : \sigma \wedge \tau}{\Gamma \vdash M : \sigma}$          $(\wedge E2)$   $\dfrac{\Gamma \vdash M : \sigma \wedge \tau}{\Gamma \vdash M : \sigma}$

Figure 3.3: System $\mathcal{D}\Omega$

---

**Remark 3.5.1** *Because of axiom* $(\omega)$*, in a provable judgment* $\Gamma \vdash M : \sigma$ *of* $\mathcal{D}\Omega$*, some or even all free variables of M may not be declared in* $\Gamma$*. This property holds however in* $\mathcal{D}$*.*

**Exercise 3.5.2** *Show that* $\Delta\Delta = (\lambda x.xx)(\lambda x.xx)$ *can only be typed by* $\omega$*.*

We state a number of syntactic lemmas that hold in $\mathcal{D}\Omega$.

**Lemma 3.5.3 (weakening)** *If* $\Gamma \vdash M : \sigma$ *and* $\Gamma \subseteq \Gamma'$ *(that is, if* $x : \sigma \in \Gamma$*, then* $x : \sigma \in \Gamma'$*), then* $\Gamma' \vdash M : \sigma$*.*

**Lemma 3.5.4** *If* $\Gamma, x_1 : \sigma_1, \ldots, x_k : \sigma_k \vdash M : \sigma$ *and if* $\Gamma \vdash N_i : \sigma_i$ *for all i's such that* $x_i \in FV(M)$*, then* $\Gamma \vdash M[N_1/x_1, \ldots, N_k/x_k] : \sigma$*.*

PROOF. By induction on the length of the proof of $\Gamma, x_1 : \sigma_1, \ldots, x_k : \sigma_k \vdash M : \sigma$.   □

**Remark 3.5.5** *Lemma 3.5.4 encompasses both substitution and* strengthening*. Substitution corresponds to the situation where* $\Gamma \vdash N_i : \sigma_i$ *for all* $i \leq k$*. Strengthening corresponds to the situation where* $x_1, \ldots, x_k \notin FV(M)$*: then* $\Gamma, x_1 : \sigma_1, \ldots, x_k : \sigma_k \vdash M : \sigma$ *implies* $\Gamma \vdash M : \sigma$*.*

**Lemma 3.5.6** *If* $\Gamma, x : \sigma \vdash M : \tau$*, then* $\Gamma, x : \sigma \wedge \sigma' \vdash M : \tau$ *for any* $\sigma'$*.*

PROOF. By induction on the length of the proof of $\Gamma, x : \sigma \vdash M : \tau$. We only look at the base cases:

$\Gamma, x : \sigma \vdash x : \sigma$: Then $\Gamma, x : \sigma \wedge \sigma' \vdash x : \sigma \wedge \sigma'$, and $\Gamma, x : \sigma \wedge \sigma' \vdash x : \sigma$ follows by $(\wedge E)$.

$\Gamma, x : \sigma \vdash y : \tau$ $(y \neq x)$: Then also $\Gamma, x : \sigma \wedge \sigma' \vdash y : \tau$.   □

**Lemma 3.5.7** *If* $\Gamma \vdash M : \sigma$ *and* $\Gamma' \vdash M : \sigma$*, then* $\Gamma \uplus \Gamma' \vdash M : \sigma$*, where the variables declared in* $\Gamma \uplus \Gamma'$ *are those declared in* $\Gamma$ *or* $\Gamma'$*, and where (viewing the environments as functions):*

$$\Gamma \uplus \Gamma'(x) = \begin{cases} \tau \wedge \tau' & \text{if } \Gamma(x) = \tau \text{ and } \Gamma'(x) = \tau' \\ \tau & \text{if } \Gamma(x) = \tau \text{ and } \Gamma'(x) \text{ is undefined} \\ \tau' & \text{if } \Gamma'(x) = \tau' \text{ and } \Gamma(x) \text{ is undefined} . \end{cases}$$

PROOF. The statement follows from lemma 3.5.3 and from a repeated application of lemma 3.5.6.      □

**Definition 3.5.8 (prime type)** *An intersection type is called prime if it is either an atomic type $\kappa$ or an arrow type $\sigma \to \tau$. Every type is thus a conjunction of prime types (called its prime factors) and of some $\omega$'s, and, by $(\wedge E)$, if $\Gamma \vdash M : \sigma$ and if $\sigma'$ is a prime factor of $\sigma$, then $\Gamma \vdash M : \sigma'$.*

**Lemma 3.5.9** *Let $\Gamma \vdash M : \sigma$, with $\sigma$ prime. Then:*

(1) *If $M = x$, then $x : \sigma' \in \Gamma$, where $\sigma$ is a prime factor of $\sigma'$,*

(2) *If $M = \lambda x.N$ , then $\sigma = \sigma_1 \to \sigma_2$ and $\Gamma, x : \sigma_1 \vdash N : \sigma_2$,*

(3) *If $M = M_1 M_2$, then $\Gamma \vdash M_2 : \tau$ and $\Gamma \vdash M_1 : \tau \to \sigma'$, for some $\tau, \sigma'$, such that $\sigma$ is a prime factor of $\sigma'$.*

PROOF. First we claim that a proof of $\Gamma \vdash M : \sigma$ contains a proof $\Gamma \vdash M : \sigma'$ which does not end with a $(\wedge I)$ or $(\wedge E)$ rule and is such that $\sigma$ is a prime factor of $\sigma'$. To prove the claim, we generalize the assumption 'a proof of $\Gamma \vdash M : \sigma$' to: 'a proof of $\Gamma \vdash M : \sigma''$ where $\sigma$ is a prime factor of $\sigma''$'. We proceed by induction on the length of the proof of $\Gamma \vdash M : \sigma''$ and consider the last rule used:

$(\wedge I)$ Then $\sigma'' = \sigma_1 \wedge \sigma_2$, and $\sigma$, being a prime factor of $\sigma''$, is a prime factor of $\sigma_1$ or $\sigma_2$, thus we can apply induction to the left or right premise of the $(\wedge I)$ rule.

$(\wedge E)$ Then the premise of the rule is of the form $\Gamma \vdash M : \sigma'' \wedge \tau$ or $\Gamma \vdash M : \tau \wedge \sigma''$, and $\sigma$, being a prime factor of $\sigma''$, is also prime factor of $\sigma'' \wedge \tau$ or $\tau \wedge \sigma''$.

The claim is proved. Let $\Gamma \vdash M : \sigma'$ be as in the claim; it is a conclusion of one of the three rules of the simply typed $\lambda$-calculus (without intersection types):

$\quad M = x$. Then $x : \sigma' \in \Gamma$.
$\quad M = \lambda x.N$. Then $\sigma' = \sigma_1 \to \sigma_2$, hence $\sigma'$ is prime, which entails $\sigma = \sigma'$.
$\quad M = M_1 M_2$. Obvious.      □

**Proposition 3.5.10 (subject reduction)** *The following implication holds in $\mathcal{D}\Omega$, for all $\Gamma, M, M', \sigma$: if $\Gamma \vdash M : \sigma$ and $M \to_\beta M'$, then $\Gamma \vdash M' : \sigma$.*

PROOF HINT. In the crucial case ($M = (\lambda x.P)Q$ and $M' = P[Q/x]$), we use lemmas 3.5.9(2) and 3.5.4.      □

**Lemma 3.5.11 (expansion)** (1) *In $\mathcal{D}\Omega$, if $\Gamma \vdash M[N/x] : \tau$, then $\Gamma \vdash (\lambda x.M)N : \tau$.*

(2) *In $\mathcal{D}$, if $\Gamma \vdash M[N/x] : \tau$ and if $\Gamma \vdash N : \sigma$ for some $\sigma$, then $\Gamma \vdash (\lambda x.M)N : \tau$.*

PROOF. We prove (1), indicating where the additional assumption comes in for (2). We may assume that $x$ is not declared in $\Gamma$. The statement follows obviously from the following claim:

$$\exists \sigma \ (\Gamma \vdash N : \sigma \text{ and } \Gamma, x : \sigma \vdash M : \tau).$$

The claim is proved by induction on $(size(M), size(\tau))$:

- $\tau = \omega$. Obvious, taking $\sigma = \omega$.

- $\tau = \tau_1 \wedge \tau_2$. By $(\wedge E)$ and by induction, we have:

$$\Gamma \vdash N : \sigma_1 \quad \Gamma, x : \sigma_1 \vdash M : \tau_1$$
$$\Gamma \vdash N : \sigma_2 \quad \Gamma, x : \sigma_2 \vdash M : \tau_2 \,.$$

We set $\sigma = \sigma_1 \wedge \sigma_2$, and we conclude by $(\wedge I)$ and lemma 3.5.6.

- $\tau$ prime.

  - $M = x$. Then the assumption is $\Gamma \vdash N : \tau$. Take $\sigma = \tau$.
  - $M = y \neq x$. Then the assumption is $\Gamma \vdash y : \tau$. Take $\sigma = \omega$ (in $\mathcal{D}$, take the assumed type of $N$).
  - $M = \lambda y.P$ (with $y \notin FV(N)$). By lemma 3.5.9(2) we have $\tau = \tau_1 \to \tau_2$ and:

    $$\Gamma, y : \tau_1 \vdash P[N/x] : \tau_2.$$

    By induction we have:

    $$\Gamma, y : \tau_1 \vdash N : \sigma \quad \text{and} \quad \Gamma, x : \sigma, y : \tau_1 \vdash P : \tau_2.$$

    The conclusion follows from lemma 3.5.4.

  - $M = M_1 M_2$. We can apply induction since $size(M_1), size(M_2) \leq size(M)$. Using lemma 3.5.9(3), we have:

    $$\Gamma \vdash N : \sigma_1 \quad \Gamma, x : \sigma_1 \vdash M_1 : \tau'' \to \tau'$$
    $$\Gamma \vdash N : \sigma_2 \quad \Gamma, x : \sigma_2 \vdash M_2 : \tau'' \,,$$

    with $\tau$ a prime factor of $\tau'$. As above, we set $\sigma = \sigma_1 \wedge \sigma_2$.  $\square$

**Remark 3.5.12** *Unlike subject reduction, which holds widely in type systems, lemma 3.5.11 is peculiar to intersection types.*

**Theorem 3.5.13 (subject equality)** *In $\mathcal{D}\Omega$, if $\Gamma \vdash M : \sigma$ and $M =_\beta M'$, then $\Gamma \vdash M' : \sigma$.*

PROOF. One direction is proposition 3.5.10 and the other is easily proved by induction using lemmas 3.5.11 and 3.5.9.  $\square$

We now introduce an important and quite general technique called the computability method. Here, the technique serves to prove a strong normalization and a logical approximation theorem (theorem 3.5.18 and exercise 3.5.19, respectively). The computability method will be used again in sections 6.3 and 11.5, and is related to the notion of logical relation introduced in section 4.5.

**Definition 3.5.14 ($\mathcal{N}$-saturated)** *Let $\mathcal{N} \subseteq \Lambda$. (Recall that $\Lambda$ is the set of all $\lambda$-terms.) A subset $\mathcal{X} \subseteq \Lambda$ is called $\mathcal{N}$-saturated if*

$$\forall N \in \mathcal{N} \; \forall M, N_1, \ldots, N_n \in \Lambda \quad (M[N/x]N_1 \ldots N_n \in \mathcal{X} \Rightarrow (\lambda x.M)NN_1 \ldots N_n \in \mathcal{X})$$

*(in this implication $n$ is arbitrary, in particular it can be 0).*

We consider $\Lambda$ as an applicative structure, with $M \cdot N = MN$.

**Proposition 3.5.15** *The $\mathcal{N}$-saturated sets form an ets (cf. definition 3.3.6).*

PROOF HINT. The statement is obvious for intersections. As for function types, the $N_i$'s in the definition of saturated set serve precisely that purpose.                    □

**Lemma 3.5.16** *For any interpretation $V$ (cf. definition 3.4.5) by $\mathcal{N}$-saturated sets such that $V(\sigma) \subseteq \mathcal{N}$ for all $\sigma$, for any provable $x_1 : \sigma_1, \ldots, x_k : \sigma_k \vdash M : \sigma$, and for any $N_1 \in V(\sigma_1), \ldots, N_k \in V(\sigma_k)$, we have $M[N_1/x_1, \ldots, N_k/x_k] \in V(\sigma)$.*

PROOF. We proceed by induction on the length of the proof of $x_1 : \sigma_1, \ldots, x_k : \sigma_k \vdash M : \sigma$.

(Asmp) The conclusion is one of the assumptions.

($\to_E$) By induction we have:

$$M[N_1/x_1, \ldots, N_k/x_k] \in V(\sigma \to \tau) \quad \text{and} \quad N[N_1/x_1, \ldots, N_k/x_k] \in V(\sigma) \, ,$$

hence $(MN)[N_1/x_1, \ldots, N_k/x_k] \in V(\tau)$ by definition of $V(\sigma \to \tau)$.

($\to_I$) We have to prove $(\lambda x.M[N_1/x_1, \ldots, N_k/x_k])N \in V(\tau)$, for any $N \in V(\sigma)$. By induction we have $M[N_1/x_1, \ldots, N_k/x_k][N/x] \in V(\tau)$, and the conclusion follows by the definition of $\mathcal{N}$-saturated set, using the assumption $V(\sigma) \subseteq \mathcal{N}$.

($\omega$) Obvious, since $V(\omega) = \Lambda$.

($\wedge I$) Obvious by induction, since $V(\sigma \wedge \tau) = V(\sigma) \wedge V(\tau)$.

($\wedge E1$) (or ($\wedge E2$)) Here we use the implicit order: $V(\sigma \wedge \tau) \subseteq V(\sigma)$.                    □

**Remark 3.5.17** *Notice that we have used induction on types to construct $V(\sigma)$ at all types, and that we have used induction on (typing proofs of) terms to prove the statement. The core of the computability method indeed resides in this elegant separation of inductions, to be contrasted with their combinatorial combination in the proof of theorem 2.2.9.*

The following characterization of strongly normalizable terms, provides in particular an alternative proof of strong normalization for the simply typed $\lambda$-calculus (theorem 2.2.9).

**Theorem 3.5.18 (strong normalization – intersection types)** *For a $\lambda$-term $M$, the following properties are equivalent:*

(1) *$M$ is strongly normalizable,*

(2) *$\Gamma \vdash M : \sigma$ is provable in $\mathcal{D}$ for some $\Gamma, \sigma$.*

PROOF. ($\Leftarrow$) We take $\mathcal{N} = SN$, the set of strongly normalizable terms, and we interpret the atomic types $\kappa$ by setting $V(\kappa) = \mathcal{N}$. Our proof plan goes as follows. We show, for all $\sigma$:

(1) $V(\sigma)$ is $\mathcal{N}$-saturated,

(2) $x \in V(\sigma)$ for all variables $x$,

(3) $V(\sigma) \subseteq \mathcal{N}$.

By these conditions lemma 3.5.16 can be applied, with $N_1 = x_1, \ldots, N_k = x_k$ (where $x_1, \ldots, x_k$ are the variables declared in $\Gamma$), yielding $M \in \mathcal{N}$. Therefore all we have to do is to prove the three conditions.

(1) By lemma 3.5.15, the condition boils down to the verification that $\mathcal{N}$ is $\mathcal{N}$-saturated. We proceed by induction on $depth(N) + depth(M[N/x]N_1 \ldots N_n)$ (cf. definition 2.2.1). It is enough to prove that all the one step reducts $P$ of $(\lambda x.M)NN_1 \ldots N_n$ are in $\mathcal{N}$:

- $P = M[N/x]N_1 \ldots N_n$. By assumption.
- $P = (\lambda x.M')NN_1 \ldots N_n$. By induction, since

$$depth(M'[N/x]N_1 \ldots N_n) < depth(M[N/x]N_1 \ldots N_n).$$

- If the reduction takes place in one of the $N_i$'s, the reasoning is similar.
- $P = (\lambda x.M)N'N_1 \ldots N_n$. By induction, since $depth(N') < depth(N)$ (notice that if $x \notin FV(M)$, then the depth of $M[N/x]N_1 \ldots N_n$ does not change; whence the notion of $\mathcal{N}$-saturated).

(2) and (3)  We actually strengthen (2) into:

(2') $\mathcal{N}_0 \subseteq V(\sigma)$,

where $\mathcal{N}_0 = \{xM_1 \ldots M_p \mid p \geq 0 \text{ and } \forall i \leq p \ M_i \in \mathcal{N}\}$. We shall prove (2') and (3) together, as a consequence of the following properties, which we shall establish first:

$$\text{(A) } \mathcal{N}_0 \subseteq \mathcal{N} \qquad \text{(B) } \mathcal{N}_0 \subseteq (\mathcal{N} \to \mathcal{N}_0) \qquad \text{(C) } (\mathcal{N}_0 \to \mathcal{N}) \subseteq \mathcal{N} \,.$$

(A)  Any reduct of $xM_1 \ldots M_p$ is of the form $xN_1 \ldots N_p$ where the $N_i$'s are reducts of the $M_i$'s. Therefore all elements of $\mathcal{N}_0$ are strongly normalizable.

(B)  The terms $M_1, \ldots, M_p$ in the definition of $\mathcal{N}_0$ serve precisely that purpose.

(C)  Let $M \in \mathcal{N}_0 \to \mathcal{N}$. Then $Mx \in \mathcal{N}$, and *a fortiori* $M \in \mathcal{N}$.

Now we can prove (2') and (3). The two properties hold at basic types because we have chosen $V(\kappa) = \mathcal{N}$, and by (A). The intersection case is obvious. Let thus $\sigma = \sigma_1 \to \sigma_2$. By induction we have $V(\sigma_1) \subseteq \mathcal{N}$ and $\mathcal{N}_0 \subseteq V(\sigma_2)$, hence $\mathcal{N} \to \mathcal{N}_0 \subseteq V(\sigma)$, and (2') at $\sigma$ then follows by (B). Similarly, we use induction and (C) to prove (3) at $\sigma$.

($\Rightarrow$)  By induction on $(depth(M), size(M))$, and by cases:

- $M = \lambda x_1 \ldots x_m.xN_1 \ldots N_n$, with $x \neq x_1, \ldots, x_m$. By induction and by lemmas 3.5.7 and 3.5.3, we have $\Delta \vdash N_1 : \sigma_1, \ldots, \Delta \vdash N_n : \sigma_n$ for some $\Delta = \Gamma, x_1 : \tau_1, \ldots, x_m : \tau_m, x : \tau$. Then we have, using lemma 3.5.6:

$$\Gamma, x : \tau \wedge (\sigma_1 \to \cdots \to \sigma_n \to \kappa) \vdash M : \tau_1 \to \cdots \to \tau_m \to \kappa \,.$$

- $M = \lambda x_1 \ldots x_m.x_iN_1 \ldots N_n$. Similar to the previous case.
- $M = \lambda x_1 \ldots x_m.(\lambda x.N)PN_1 \ldots N_n$. Then, by induction:

$$\Delta \vdash P : \sigma \text{ and } \Delta \vdash N[P/x]N_1 \ldots N_n : \tau,$$

for some $\Delta = \Gamma, x_1 : \tau_1, \ldots, x_m : \tau_m$. We claim that $\Delta \vdash (\lambda x.N)PN_1 \ldots N_n : \tau$, from which $\Gamma \vdash M : \tau_1 \to \cdots \to \tau_m \to \tau$ follows. This is proved by induction on $n$, the base case being lemma 3.5.11(2). □

In the following three exercises, we present the logical approximation theorem, and derive as corollaries characterizations of the terms having a head normal form and of the terms having a normal form. We follow [RdR93].

**Exercise\* 3.5.19 (logical approximation)** *We define the following relation $\overset{norm}{\Longrightarrow}$:*

$$\frac{}{(\lambda x.P)QM_1\dots M_n \overset{norm}{\Longrightarrow} P[Q/x]M_1\dots M_n} \qquad \frac{M \overset{norm}{\Longrightarrow} N}{\lambda x.M \overset{norm}{\Longrightarrow} \lambda x.N}$$

$$\frac{P \overset{norm}{\Longrightarrow} Q}{xM_1\dots M_{i-1}PM_{i+1}\dots M_n \overset{norm}{\Longrightarrow} xM_1\dots M_{i-1}QM_{i+1}\dots M_n}.$$

*Show that the following implication holds, for any $\Gamma, M, \sigma$:*

$$\Gamma \vdash M : \sigma \quad\Rightarrow\quad \exists N \ M \overset{norm}{\Longrightarrow} {}^*N \text{ and } \Gamma \vdash \omega(N) : \sigma.$$

*Hints (referring to the proof of theorem 3.5.18): The following easy property is useful: in $\mathcal{D}\Omega$, if $\Gamma \vdash M : \sigma$ and $M \leq N$, then $\Gamma \vdash N : \sigma$. One should now deal with typed versions of the predicates $\mathcal{N}$ and $\mathcal{N}_0$. Specifically, set:*

$$\begin{aligned}
\mathcal{N}(\Gamma, \sigma) &= \{M \in \Lambda \mid \exists N \ (M \overset{norm}{\Longrightarrow} {}^*N \text{ and } \Gamma \vdash \omega(N) : \sigma)\} \\
\mathcal{N}_0(\Gamma, \sigma) &= \{M \in \mathcal{N}(\Gamma, \sigma) \mid M \text{ has the form } xM_1\dots M_p\}.
\end{aligned}$$

*Formulate and prove typed versions of properties (A) (B), and (C) (plus a property saying that the predicates at $\sigma \wedge \tau$ are the intersections of the predicates at $\sigma$ and $\tau$), as well as of properties (1), (2′), and (3) (in the latter, the type should be restricted to a non-trivial one, see exercise 3.5.20). In the proof of (C), observe that if*

$$Mx \overset{norm}{\Longrightarrow} {}^*(\lambda y.M)x \overset{norm}{\Longrightarrow} M[x/y] \overset{norm}{\Longrightarrow} {}^*P\,,$$

*then*

$$M \overset{norm}{\Longrightarrow} {}^*\lambda y.M \overset{norm}{\Longrightarrow} {}^*\lambda y.P[y/x].$$

*Formulate interpretations of the form $V(\Gamma, \sigma)$ (making use of the operation $\uplus$ defined in proposition 3.5.7 for the arrow case), and prove a version of lemma 3.5.16.*

**Exercise\* 3.5.20** *Show that the following are equivalent for a $\lambda$-term $M$:*

(1) *$M =_\beta N$ for some head normal form $N$,*

(2) *$M \overset{norm}{\longrightarrow} {}^*N$ for some head normal form $N$ (cf. definition 2.1.20),*

(3) *$M$ is typable with a non-trivial type in $\mathcal{D}\Omega$,*

*where the non-trivial types are defined as follows: atomic types are non-trivial, $\sigma \wedge \tau$ is non-trivial provided one of $\sigma$ or $\tau$ is non-trivial, and $\sigma \to \tau$ is non-trivial provided $\tau$ is non-trivial. Hints: The term $\Omega$ can only have a trivial type. Any term $xM_1\dots M_n$ is typable in any environment $x : \omega \to \cdots \to \omega \to \sigma$.*

**Exercise\* 3.5.21** *Show that the following are equivalent for a $\lambda$-term $M$:*

(1) *$M$ is normalizable,*

(2) *the leftmost reduction from $M$ terminates (cf. proposition 2.2.18),*

(3) *$\Gamma \vdash M : \sigma$ in $\mathcal{D}\Omega$ for some $\Gamma, \sigma$ where $\omega$ does not occur.*

*On the way, show the following properties:*

• *If $\Gamma \vdash M : \sigma$, where $M$ is a $\beta$-normal form and where $\omega$ does not occur in $\Gamma, \sigma$, then $\Omega$ does not occur in $M$.*

• *Every $\beta$ normal form $M$ is typable in $\mathcal{D}$.*

**Exercise 3.5.22** *(1) Show that the logical approximation theorem still holds, replacing the type system $\mathcal{D}\Omega$ by the type system of figure 3.2. (Warning: this involves revisiting a number of syntactic lemmas, typically lemma 3.5.9.) (2) Show the approximation theorem for the $D_\infty$ model based on $D_0 = \{\bot, \top\}$ and the standard pair $(i_0, j_0)$, i.e., $[\![M]\!] = \bigvee\{[\![A]\!] \mid A \leq BT(M)\}$ (cf. exercise 3.3.14 and theorem 3.4.8).*

# 4

# Interpretation of λ-calculi in CCC's

In first approximation, typed λ-calculi are *natural deduction* presentations of certain fragments of minimal logic (a subsystem of intuitionistic logic). These calculi have a natural computational interpretation as core of typed functional languages where computation, intended as $\beta\eta$-reduction, corresponds to proof normalization. In this perspective, we reconsider in section 4.1 the simply typed λ-calculus studied in chapter 2. We exhibit a precise correspondence between the simply typed λ-calculus and a natural deduction formalization of the implicative fragment of propositional implicative logic.

Next, we address the problem of *modelling* the notions of $\beta\eta$-reduction and equivalence. It turns out that simple models can be found by interpreting types as sets and terms as functions between these sets. But, in general, which are the structural properties that characterize such models? The main problem considered in this chapter is that of understanding what is the *model theory* of simply typed and untyped λ-calculi. In order to answer this question, we introduce in section 4.2 the notion of cartesian closed category (CCC). We present CCC's as a natural categorical generalization of certain adjunctions found in Heyting algebras. As a main example, we show that the category of directed complete partial orders and continuous functions is a CCC.

The description of the models of a calculus by means of category theoretical notions will be a central and recurring topic of this book. We will not always fully develop the theory but in this chapter we can take advantage of the simplicity of the calculus to go into a complete analysis. In section 4.3, we describe the interpretation of the simply typed λ-calculus into an arbitrary CCC, and we present some basic properties such as the substitution theorem. The interpretation into a categorical language can be seen as a way of implementing α-renaming and substitution. This eventually leads to the definition of a *categorical abstract machine*.

In section 4.4, we address the problem of understanding which equivalence is induced on terms by the interpretation in a CCC. To this end, we introduce the notion of λ-theory. Roughly speaking, a λ-theory is a congruence over λ-terms (i.e., an equivalence relation closed under λ-abstraction and application) which includes $\beta\eta$-equivalence. It turns out that every CCC induces a λ-theory. Vice versa, one may ask: does any λ-theory come from the interpretation in a CCC? We answer this question positively by showing how to build a suitable CCC from any λ-theory. This concludes our development of a *model theory* for the simply typed λ-calculus. Related results will be presented in chapter 6 for PCF, a simply typed λ-calculus extended with arithmetical operators and fixpoint combinators.

In section 4.5 we introduce *logical relations* which are a useful tool to establish links between syntax and semantics. In particular, we apply them to the problem of characterizing equality in the set theoretical model of the simply typed λ-calculus, and to the problem of understanding which elements of a model are definable by a λ-term.

In section 4.6 we regard the untyped λ-calculus as a typed λ-calculus with a *reflexive type*. We show that every CCC with a reflexive object gives rise to an untyped λ-theory. We present a general method to build a category of retractions out of a reflexive object in a CCC. We give two applications of this construction. First, we hint at the fact that every untyped λ-theory is induced by a reflexive object in a CCC (this is similar to the result presented in section 4.4 for the simply typed λ-calculus). Second, following Engeler, we adopt the category of retractions as a frame for embedding algebraic structures in λ-models.

This chapter is mainly based on [LS86, Sco80, Cur86] to which the reader seeking more advanced results is directed.

## 4.1   Simply typed λ-calculus

In chapter 2, we have presented a simply typed λ-calculus in which every subterm is labelled by a type. This was well-suited to our purposes but it is probably not the most illuminating treatment. So far, we have (mainly) discussed the λ-calculus as a core formalism to represent functions-as-algorithms. The simply typed λ-calculus receives an additional interpretation: it is a language of proofs for minimal logic. Let us revisit simple types first, by considering basic types as atomic propositions and the function space symbol as implication:

$$At \quad ::= \kappa \mid \kappa' \mid \cdots$$
$$\sigma \quad ::= At \mid (\sigma \to \sigma) \,.$$

Forgetting the terms for a while, we briefly describe the provability of formulas for this rudimentary logic. We use a deduction style called *natural deduction* [Pra65]. A formula $\sigma$ is proved relative to a list $\sigma_1, \ldots, \sigma_n$ of assumptions. The formal system described in figure 4.1 allows us to derive judgments of the form $\sigma_1, \ldots, \sigma_n \vdash \sigma$, which are called sequents.

An important remark with a wide range of possible applications [How80] is that proofs in natural deduction can be encoded precisely as λ-terms. To this aim hypotheses are named by variables. Raw terms are defined by the following syntax (in the following, we feel free to be sparing with parentheses):

$$v \quad ::= x \mid y \mid \ldots$$
$$M \quad ::= v \mid \lambda v : \sigma.M \mid MM \,.$$

A *context* $\Gamma$ is a list of pairs, $x : \sigma$, where $x$ is a variable and $\sigma$ is a type, and where all variables are distinct. We write $x : \sigma \in \Gamma$ to express that the pair $x : \sigma$

$$\frac{1 \leq i \leq n}{\sigma_1, \ldots, \sigma_n \vdash \sigma_i} \qquad \frac{\sigma_1, \ldots, \sigma_n, \sigma \vdash \tau}{\sigma_1, \ldots, \sigma_n \vdash \sigma \to \tau} \qquad \frac{\sigma_1, \ldots, \sigma_n \vdash \sigma \to \tau \quad \sigma_1, \ldots, \sigma_n \vdash \sigma}{\sigma_1, \ldots, \sigma_n \vdash \tau}$$

Figure 4.1: Natural deduction for minimal implicative logic

$$(\text{Asmp}) \quad \frac{x : \sigma \in \Gamma}{\Gamma \vdash x : \sigma}$$

$$(\to_I) \quad \frac{\Gamma, x : \sigma \vdash M : \tau}{\Gamma \vdash \lambda x : \sigma.M : \sigma \to \tau} \qquad (\to_E) \quad \frac{\Gamma \vdash M : \sigma \to \tau \quad \Gamma \vdash N : \sigma}{\Gamma \vdash MN : \tau}$$

Figure 4.2: Typing rules for the simply typed λ-calculus

occurs in $\Gamma$. A judgment has the shape $\Gamma \vdash M : \sigma$. Whenever we write $\Gamma \vdash M : \sigma$ it is intended that the judgment is provable. We also write $M : \sigma$ to say that there exists a context $\Gamma$ such that $\Gamma \vdash M : \sigma$. A term $M$ with this property is called well-typed. Provable judgments are inductively defined in figure 4.2. We may omit the labels on the λ-abstractions when the types are obvious from the context. It is easily seen that any derivable judgment admits a unique derivation, thus yielding a one-to-one correspondence between proofs and terms.

Yet another presentation of the typing rules omits all type information in the λ-terms. The corresponding typing system is obtained from the one in figure 4.2 by removing the type $\sigma$ in $\lambda x : \sigma.M$. In this case a term in a given context can be given several types. For instance the term $\lambda x.x$ can be assigned in the empty context any type $\sigma \to \sigma$, for any $\sigma$. To summarize, we have considered three styles of typing:

(1) A totally explicit typing where every subterm is labelled by a type (see section 2.2).

(2) A more economic typing, where only the variables bound in abstractions are labelled by a type. This style is known as 'typing à la Church'.

(3) A type assignment system, where an untyped term receives a type. This is known as 'typing à la Curry'.

In the first system, the term itself carries all the typing information. We note that once we have labelled free variables and λ-abstractions, the label of each subterm can be reconstructed in a unique way. In the two other systems, à la Church and à la Curry, a separate context carries type information for the free variables. In the system à la Church, the context together with the types of bound variables carry all the necessary information to reconstruct uniquely the type of the term. In the system à la Curry, a term, even in a given context, may have many types. In general, the problem of deciding if an untyped λ-term has a type in a given context is a non-trivial one. This is referred to as the *type inference* or *type reconstruction* problem.

Type reconstruction algorithms are quite relevant in practice as they relieve the programmer from the burden of explicitly writing all type information and allow for some form of polymorphism. For the simply typed discipline presented here, it can be shown that the problem is decidable and that it is possible to represent by a type schema (a type with type variables) all derivable solutions to a given type reconstruction problem [Hin69]. On the other hand, the type inference problem turns out to be undecidable in certain relevant type disciplines (e.g., second order [Wel94]).

In this chapter, we concentrate on the interpretation of λ-terms with *explicit* type information. We regard these calculi à la Church as central, by virtue of their strong ties with category theory and proof theory. The interpretation of type assignment systems has already been mentioned in chapter 3, and it will be further developed in section 15.3.

**Exercise 4.1.1** *Let $M^\sigma$ be a totally explicitly typed term. Let $x_1^{\sigma_1}, \ldots, x_n^{\sigma_n}$ be its free variables. Let erase be the function that erases all type information in a λ-term. Show that $x_1 : \sigma_1, \ldots, x_n : \sigma_n \vdash erase(M) : \sigma$ is à la Curry derivable. Define a function semi-erase such that $x_1 : \sigma_1, \ldots, x_n : \sigma_n \vdash semi\text{-}erase(M) : \sigma$ is à la Church derivable. Conversely, from a derivation à la Curry of $x_1 : \sigma_1, \ldots, x_n : \sigma_n \vdash M : \sigma$, construct a totally explicitly typed term $N^\sigma$, whose free variables are $x_1^{\sigma_1}, \ldots, x_n^{\sigma_n}$, and such that $erase(N^\sigma) = M$. Design a similar transformation from a derivation à la Church. Investigate how these transformations compose.*

**Exercise 4.1.2** *Show that the structural rules of exchange, weakening, and contraction are derived in the system above, in the sense that, if the premises are provable, then the conclusion is provable.*

$$(exch) \quad \Gamma, x : \sigma, y : \tau, \Gamma' \vdash M : \rho \;\; \Rightarrow \;\; \Gamma, y : \tau, x : \sigma, \Gamma' \vdash M : \rho$$
$$(weak) \quad \Gamma \vdash M : \tau \text{ and } x : \sigma \notin \Gamma \;\; \Rightarrow \;\; \Gamma, x : \sigma \vdash M : \tau$$
$$(contr) \quad \Gamma, x : \sigma, y : \sigma \vdash M : \tau \;\; \Rightarrow \;\; \Gamma, z : \sigma \vdash M[z/x, z/y] : \tau \;\; (z \text{ fresh}) \,.$$

We consider two basic axioms for the reduction of terms (cf. section 2.1):

$$(\beta) \quad (\lambda x : \sigma.M)N \to M[N/x]$$
$$(\eta) \quad \lambda x : \sigma.(Mx) \to M \quad \text{if } x \notin FV(M) \,.$$

We denote with $\to_{\beta\eta}$ their compatible (or contextual) closure (cf. figure 2.4), and with $\to_{\beta\eta}^*$ the reflexive and transitive closure of $\to_{\beta\eta}$.

**Exercise 4.1.3 (subject reduction)** *Show that well-typed terms are closed under reduction, formally:*

$$(\Gamma \vdash M : \sigma \text{ and } M \to_{\beta\eta} N) \;\; \Rightarrow \;\; \Gamma \vdash N : \sigma \,.$$

*and that if $M^\sigma$ and $N^\sigma$ are the totally explicitly typed terms associated to $M$ and $N$ (cf. exercise 4.1.1) then $M^\sigma$ reduces to $N^\sigma$ (cf. definition 2.2.7).*

**Theorem 4.1.4 (confluence and normalization)** (1) *The reduction relation* $\rightarrow^*_{\beta\eta}$ *is confluent (both on typed and untyped $\lambda$-terms).*

(2) *The reduction system $\rightarrow_{\beta\eta}$ is strongly normalizing on well-typed terms, that is, if $M : \sigma$ then all reduction sequences starting from $M$ lead to a $\beta\eta$-normal form.*

We have already proved these properties in chapter 2 for $\beta$-reduction and the totally explicit typed variant. The results are easily adapted to the present à la Church setting (cf. exercise 4.1.3). The following exercise provides enough guidelines to extend the results to $\beta\eta$-reduction.

**Exercise 4.1.5** *In the following $\rightarrow^{\leq 1}$ means reduction in 0 or 1 step. Show the following properties.*

(1) *If $M \rightarrow_\eta M_1$ and $M \rightarrow_\eta M_2$, then there exists an $N$ such that $M_1 \rightarrow^{\leq 1}_\eta N$ and $M_2 \rightarrow^{\leq 1}_\eta N$.*

(2) *If $M \rightarrow_\eta M_1$ and $M \rightarrow_\beta M_2$, then there exists an $N$ such that $M_1 \rightarrow^{\leq 1}_\beta N$ and $M_2 \rightarrow^*_\eta N$.*

(3) *If $M \rightarrow_\eta \cdot \rightarrow_\beta N$, then $M \rightarrow_\beta \cdot \rightarrow_\beta N$ or $M \rightarrow_\beta \cdot \rightarrow^*_\eta N$, where $M \rightarrow_{R_1} \cdot \rightarrow_{R_2} N$ stands for $\exists P \ (M \rightarrow_{R_1} P$ and $P \rightarrow_{R_2} N)$.*

# 4.2 Cartesian closed categories

The reader will find in appendix 2 some basic notions of category theory. Next, we motivate the introduction of CCC's as the combination of two more elementary concepts.

**Example 4.2.1 (conjunction and binary products)** *Let us consider a simple calculus in which we can pair two values or project a pair to one of its components.*

$$
\begin{array}{rll}
\textit{Types} & At & ::= \kappa \mid \kappa' \mid \cdots \\
& \sigma & ::= At \mid (\sigma \times \sigma) \\
\textit{Terms} & v & ::= x \mid y \mid \cdots \\
& M & ::= v \mid \langle M, M \rangle \mid \pi_1 M \mid \pi_2 M \ .
\end{array}
$$

*This calculus corresponds to the conjunctive fragment of minimal logic. Its typing rules are shown in figure 4.3.*

It is intuitive that a cartesian category (i.e., a category with a terminal object and binary products) has something to do with this calculus. Let us make this intuition more precise:

(1) We interpret a type $\sigma$ as an object $[\![\sigma]\!]$ of a cartesian category $\mathbf{C}$. The interpretation of the type $\sigma \times \tau$ is the cartesian product $[\![\sigma]\!] \times [\![\tau]\!]$.

(2) If types are objects, it seems natural to associate terms to morphisms. If $M$ is a closed term of type $\sigma$, we may expect that its interpretation is a morphism $f : 1 \rightarrow [\![\sigma]\!]$, where 1 is the terminal object. But what about a term $M$ such that

$$(\text{Asmp}) \quad \frac{x : \sigma \in \Gamma}{\Gamma \vdash x : \sigma} \qquad (\times_I) \quad \frac{\Gamma \vdash M : \sigma \quad \Gamma \vdash N : \tau}{\Gamma \vdash \langle M, N \rangle : \sigma \times \tau}$$

$$(\times_{E1}) \quad \frac{\Gamma \vdash M : \sigma \times \tau}{\Gamma \vdash \pi_1 M : \sigma} \qquad (\times_{E2}) \quad \frac{\Gamma \vdash M : \sigma \times \tau}{\Gamma \vdash \pi_2 M : \tau}$$

Figure 4.3: Typing rules for a calculus of conjunction

---

$x_1 : \sigma_1, \ldots, x_n : \sigma_n \vdash M : \sigma$? The idea is to interpret this term as a morphism $f : (\cdots (1 \times \llbracket \sigma_1 \rrbracket) \times \cdots \times \llbracket \sigma_n \rrbracket) \to \llbracket \sigma \rrbracket$.

This example suggests that types can be seen as objects and terms as morphisms. We do not wish to be more precise at the moment (but see section 3) and leave the following as an exercise.

**Exercise 4.2.2** *Define an interpretation of the typed terms of the calculus of conjunction into a cartesian category.*

There is a well-known correspondence between classical propositional logic and boolean algebras: a formula is provable iff it is valid in every boolean algebra interpretation. *Heyting algebras* play a similar role for intuitionistic (or minimal) logic.

**Definition 4.2.3 (Heyting algebra)** *A Heyting algebra $H$ is a lattice with lub operation $\vee$, glb operation $\wedge$, greatest element $1$, least element $0$, and with a binary operation $\to$ that satisfies the condition*

$$(x \wedge y) \leq z \quad \text{iff} \quad x \leq (y \to z) .$$

**Exercise 4.2.4** *Heyting algebras abound in nature. Show that the collection $\Omega$ of open sets of a topological space $(X, \Omega)$ ordered by inclusion can be seen as a Heyting algebra by taking:*

$$U \to V = \bigcup \{ W \in \Omega \mid W \subseteq (X \backslash U) \cup V \} .$$

For our purposes the important point in the definition of Heyting algebra is that the implication is characterized by an adjoint situation (in a poset case, see section A2.4), as for any $y \in H$ the function $\_ \wedge y$ is left adjoint to the function $y \to \_$:

$$\forall y \in H \quad (\_ \wedge y) \dashv (y \to \_) .$$

In poset categories the interpretation of proofs is trivial. For this reason Heyting algebras cannot be directly applied to the problem of interpreting the simply typed λ-calculus. However, combined with our previous example they suggest a natural generalization: consider a cartesian category in which each functor $\_ \times A$ has a right adjoint $(\_)^A$. In this way we arrive at the notion of CCC. The adjunction condition can be reformulated in a more explicit way, as shown in the following definition.

**Definition 4.2.5 (CCC)** *A category* **C** *is called* cartesian clôsed *if it has:*

(1) *A terminal object* 1.

(2) *For each* $A, B \in \mathbf{C}$ *a product given by an object* $A \times B$ *with projections* $\pi_A : A \times B \to A$ *and* $\pi_B : A \times B \to B$ *such that:*

$$\forall C \in \mathbf{C} \, \forall f : C \to A \, \forall g : C \to B \, \exists! h : C \to A \times B \, (\pi_A \circ h = f \text{ and } \pi_B \circ h = g) \, .$$

*The morphism* $h$ *is often denoted by* $\langle f, g \rangle$*, where* $\langle \_, \_ \rangle$ *is called the pairing operator. Other (most frequently used) notations for* $\pi_A$ *and* $\pi_B$ *are* $\pi_1$ *and* $\pi_2$.

(3) *For each* $A, B \in \mathbf{C}$ *an* exponent *given by an object* $B^A$ *with* $ev : B^A \times A \to B$ *such that:*

$$\forall C \in \mathbf{C} \, \forall f : C \times A \to B \, \exists! h : C \to B^A \, (ev \circ (h \times id) = f) \, .$$

*The morphism* $h$ *is often denoted by* $\Lambda(f)$*,* $\Lambda$ *is called the currying operator, and* $ev$ *the evaluation morphism.*

In the following $B^A$ and $A \Rightarrow B$ are interchangeable notations for the exponent object in a category.

**Exercise 4.2.6** *Given a CCC* **C***, extend the functions* $Prod(A, B) = A \times B$ *and* $Exp(A, B) = B^A$ *to functors* $Prod : \mathbf{C} \times \mathbf{C} \to \mathbf{C}$ *and* $Exp : \mathbf{C}^{op} \times \mathbf{C} \to \mathbf{C}$.

**Exercise 4.2.7** *Show that a CCC can be characterized as a category* **C** *such that the following functors have a right adjoint: (i) the unique functor* $! : \mathbf{C} \to \mathbf{1}$*, (ii) the diagonal functor* $\Delta : \mathbf{C} \to \mathbf{C} \times \mathbf{C}$ *defined by* $\Delta(c) = (c, c)$ *and* $\Delta(f) = (f, f)$*, (iii) the functors* $\_ \times A : \mathbf{C} \to \mathbf{C}$*, for any object* $A$.

It is possible to *skolemize* the definition of CCC, that is, to eliminate the existential quantifications, using the type operators 1, $(\_ \times \_)$, $(\_)^{(\_)}$ and the term operators $*$, $\langle \_, \_ \rangle$, $\Lambda(\_)$. In this way, the theory of CCC's can be expressed as a typed equational theory.

**Exercise 4.2.8** *Show that a CCC can be characterized as a category* **C** *such that the following equations hold.*

- *There are* $1 \in \mathbf{C}$ *and* $*_A : A \to 1$*, such that for all* $f : A \to 1$,

$$(!) \quad f = *_A \, .$$

- *There are* $\pi_1 : A \times B \to A$ *and* $\pi_2 : A \times B \to B$*, for any* $A, B \in \mathbf{C}$*, and* $\langle f, g \rangle : C \to A \times B$ *for any* $f : C \to A$*,* $g : C \to B$*, such that for all* $f : C \to A$*,* $g : C \to B$*,* $h : C \to A \times B$,

$$\begin{array}{llll} (Fst) & \pi_1 \circ \langle f, g \rangle & = & f \\ (Snd) & \pi_2 \circ \langle f, g \rangle & = & g \\ (SP) & \langle \pi_1 \circ h, \pi_2 \circ h \rangle & = & h \, . \end{array}$$

- *There are* $ev : B^A \times A \to B$ *for any* $A, B \in \mathbf{C}$*, and* $\Lambda(f)$ *for any* $f : C \times A \to B$*, such that for all* $f : C \times A \to B$*,* $h : C \to B^A$,

$$\begin{array}{llll} (\beta_{cat}) & ev \circ (\Lambda(f) \times id) & = & f \\ (\eta_{cat}) & \Lambda(ev \circ (h \times id)) & = & h \, , \end{array}$$

*where* $f \times g = \langle f \circ \pi_1, g \circ \pi_2 \rangle$.

**Exercise 4.2.9** *Referring to exercise 4.2.8 prove that (SP) is equivalent to:*

$$(DPair) \quad \langle f, g \rangle \circ h \;=\; \langle f \circ h, g \circ h \rangle$$
$$(FSI) \quad \langle \pi_1, \pi_2 \rangle \;=\; id\,,$$

*and that ($\beta_{cat}$) and ($\eta_{cat}$) are equivalent to:*

$$(Beta) \quad ev \circ \langle \Lambda(f), g \rangle \;=\; f \circ \langle id, g \rangle$$
$$(D\Lambda) \quad \Lambda(f) \circ h \;=\; \Lambda(f \circ (h \times id))$$
$$(AI) \quad \Lambda(ev) \;=\; id\,.$$

**Exercise 4.2.10** *Show that the following categories are cartesian closed: (1) (finite) sets, (2) (finite) posets and monotonic functions. On the other hand prove that the category* **pSet** *of sets and partial functions is not cartesian closed. Hint: Consider the existence of an isomorphism between* **pSet**$[2 \times 2, 1]$ *and* **pSet**$[2, 4]$.

One can now formally prove that the category of directed complete partial orders (dcpo's) and functions preserving lub's of directed sets is cartesian closed using propositions 1.4.1 and 1.4.4. Exercise 1.4.6 does not say directly that the product construction in **Dcpo** yields a categorical product. This follows from the following general (meta-)property.

**Exercise 4.2.11** *Let* **C**, **C'** *be categories, and* $F : \mathbf{C} \to \mathbf{C'}$ *be a faithful functor. Suppose that* **C'** *has products, and that for any pair of objects A and B of* **C** *there exists an object C and two morphisms* $\alpha : C \to A$ *and* $\beta : C \to B$ *in* **C** *such that:*

$$F(C) = F(A) \times F(B), \quad F(\alpha) = \pi_1, \quad F(\beta) = \pi_2\,,$$

*and for any object D and morphisms* $f : D \to A$, $g : D \to B$, *there exists a morphism* $h : D \to C$ *such that* $F(h) = \langle F(f), F(g) \rangle$. *Show that* **C** *has products. Explain why this general technique applies to* **Dcpo**.

In a similar way one can verify that the function space construction in **Dcpo** yields a categorical exponent. The check is slightly more complicated than for the product, due to the fact that the underlying set of the function space in **Dcpo** is a proper subset of the function space in **Set**.

**Exercise 4.2.12** *Let* **C**, **C'** *be categories, and* $F : \mathbf{C} \to \mathbf{C'}$ *be a faithful functor. Suppose that the assumptions of exercise 4.2.11 hold, and use* $\times$ *to denote the cartesian product in* **C**. *Suppose that* **C'** *has exponents, and that for any pair of objects A and B of* **C** *there exists an object C of* **C**, *a mono* $m : FC \to FB^{FA}$ *and a morphism* $\gamma : C \times A \to B$ *such that: (1)* $F(\gamma) = ev \circ (m \times id)$, *and (2) for any object D and arrow* $f : D \times A \to B$, *there exists a morphism* $k : D \to C$ *such that* $m \circ F(k) = \Lambda(F(f))$. *Show that* **C** *has exponents. Apply this to* **Dcpo**.

**Theorem 4.2.13 (Dcpo CCC)** **Dcpo** *is a cartesian closed category. The order for products is componentwise, and the order for exponents is pointwise.* **Cpo** *is cartesian closed too.*

PROOF. We can apply the exercises 1.4.6 and 4.2.12. A direct proof of cartesian closure is also possible and easy. □

$$
\begin{array}{lll}
\text{(Asmp)} & [\![ x_1 : \sigma_1, \ldots, x_n : \sigma_n \vdash x_i : \sigma_i ]\!] & = & \pi_{n,i} \\
(\to_I) & [\![ \Gamma \vdash \lambda x : \sigma.M : \sigma \to \tau ]\!] & = & \Lambda([\![ \Gamma, x : \sigma \vdash M : \tau ]\!]) \\
(\to_E) & [\![ \Gamma \vdash MN : \tau ]\!] & = & ev \circ \langle [\![ \Gamma \vdash M : \sigma \to \tau ]\!], [\![ \Gamma \vdash N : \sigma ]\!] \rangle
\end{array}
$$

Figure 4.4: Interpretation of the simply typed λ-calculus in a CCC

## 4.3   Interpretation of λ-calculi

We explain how to interpret the simply typed λ-calculus in an arbitrary CCC. Suppose that **C** is a CCC. Let us choose a terminal object 1, a product functor $\times : \mathbf{C} \times \mathbf{C} \to \mathbf{C}$ and an exponentiation functor $\Rightarrow : \mathbf{C}^{op} \times \mathbf{C} \to \mathbf{C}$. Then there is an obvious interpretation for types as objects of the category, which is determined by the interpretation of the atomic types. The arrow is interpreted as exponentiation in **C**. Hence given an interpretation $[\![ \kappa ]\!]$ for the atomic types, we have:

$$
[\![ \sigma \to \tau ]\!] = [\![ \sigma ]\!] \Rightarrow [\![ \tau ]\!] .
$$

Consider a provable judgment of the shape $x_1 : \sigma_1, \ldots, x_n : \sigma_n \vdash M : \sigma$. Its interpretation will be defined *by induction on the length of the proof* as a morphism from $[\![ \Gamma ]\!]$ to $[\![ \sigma ]\!]$, where we set $\Gamma = x_1 : \sigma_1, \ldots, x_n : \sigma_n$ and $[\![ \Gamma ]\!] = 1 \times [\![ \sigma_1 ]\!] \times \ldots \times [\![ \sigma_n ]\!]$. We will take the convention that $\times$ associates to the left. We denote with $\pi_{n,i} : [\![ \Gamma ]\!] \to [\![ \sigma_i ]\!]$ $(i = 1, \ldots, n)$ the morphism: $\pi_2 \circ \pi_1 \circ \cdots \circ \pi_1$, where $\pi_1$ is iterated $(n - i)$ times.

The interpretation is defined in figure 4.4. The last two rules need some explanation. Suppose $C = [\![ \Gamma ]\!]$, $A = [\![ \sigma ]\!]$, and $B = [\![ \tau ]\!]$.

$(\to_I)$ If there is a morphism $f : C \times A \to B$ then there is a uniquely determined morphism $\Lambda(f) : C \to B^A$.

$(\to_E)$ If there are two morphisms $f : C \to B^A$ and $g : C \to A$, then one can build the morphism $\langle f, g \rangle : C \to B^A \times A$ and composing with $ev$ one gets $ev \circ \langle f, g \rangle : C \to A$.

Sometimes, we write $[\![ M ]\!]$ as an abbreviation for $[\![ \Gamma \vdash M : \sigma ]\!]$. We shall mostly use this abbreviation when $M$ is closed. When composing the interpretation of the judgment $\Gamma \vdash M : \tau$ with an environment, that is, a morphism in $\mathbf{C}[1, [\![ \Gamma ]\!]]$, we will freely use the notation $[\![ M ]\!] \circ \langle d_1, \ldots, d_n \rangle$ which relies on an n-ary product.

In section 4.5 we will work with a simply typed λ-calculus enriched with a set of constants $C$. We suppose that each constant is labelled with its type, say $c^\sigma$. The typing system is then enriched with the rule:

$$
\frac{}{\Gamma \vdash c^\sigma : \sigma} . \tag{4.1}
$$

We denote with $\Lambda(C)$ the collection of well-typed terms. The interpretation is fixed by providing for each constant $c^\sigma$ a morphism $f_c : 1 \to [\![ \sigma ]\!]$. The judgment

$\Gamma \vdash c^\sigma : \sigma$ is then interpreted by composing with the terminal morphism:

$$[\![\Gamma \vdash c^\sigma : \sigma]\!] = f_c \circ \, ! \, . \qquad (4.2)$$

The interpretation in figure 4.4 is defined by induction on the structure of a proof of a judgment $\Gamma \vdash M : \sigma$. In the simple system we presented here, a judgment has a *unique* proof. However, in general, there can be several ways of deriving the same judgment, therefore a problem of *coherence* of the interpretation arises, namely one has to show that different proofs of the same judgment receive the same interpretation. Note that in the simply typed calculus the coherence problem is avoided by getting rid of the structural rules. This trick does not suffice in more sophisticated type theories like *LF* (see chapter 11) where the derivation is not completely determined by the structure of the judgment. In this case term judgments and type judgments are inter-dependent.

**Exercise 4.3.1** *Show that* $[\![\Gamma, x : \sigma \vdash M : \tau]\!] = [\![\Gamma \vdash M : \tau]\!] \circ \pi_1$ *if* $\Gamma \vdash M : \tau$ *and* $x : \sigma \notin \Gamma$ *(cf. exercise 4.1.2).*

**Exercise 4.3.2** *Given two contexts* $\Gamma, x : \sigma, y : \tau, \Gamma'$ *and* $\Gamma, y : \tau, x : \sigma, \Gamma'$ *define an isomorphism* $\phi$ *between the corresponding objects. Hint: If* $\Gamma \equiv z : \rho$ *and* $\Gamma'$ *is empty then* $\phi \equiv \langle \langle \pi_1 \circ \pi_1, \pi_2 \rangle, \pi_2 \circ \pi_1 \rangle : (C \times A) \times B \to (C \times B) \times A$. *Show that (cf. exercise 4.1.2):*

$$[\![\Gamma, x : \sigma, y : \tau, \Gamma' \vdash M : \rho]\!] = [\![\Gamma, y : \tau, x : \sigma, \Gamma' \vdash M : \rho]\!] \circ \phi \, .$$

The next step is to analyse the interpretation of substitution in a category.

**Theorem 4.3.3 (substitution)** *Let* $\Gamma, x : \sigma \vdash M : \tau$, *and* $\Gamma \vdash N : \sigma$. *The following properties hold.*

(1) $\Gamma \vdash M[N/x] : \tau$.

(2) $[\![\Gamma \vdash M[N/x] : \tau]\!] = [\![\Gamma, x : \sigma \vdash M : \tau]\!] \circ \langle id, [\![\Gamma \vdash N : \sigma]\!]\rangle$.

PROOF. (1) By induction on the length of the proof of $\Gamma, x : \sigma \vdash M : \tau$. The interesting case arises when the last deduction is by $(\to_I)$:

$$\frac{\Gamma, x : \sigma, y : \tau \vdash M : \tau'}{\Gamma, x : \sigma \vdash \lambda y : \tau.M : \tau \to \tau'} \, .$$

We observe $(\lambda y : \tau.M)[N/x] \equiv \lambda y : \tau.M[N/x]$. We can apply the inductive hypothesis on $\Gamma, y : \tau, x : \sigma \vdash M : \tau'$ (note the exchange on the assumptions) to get $\Gamma, y : \tau \vdash M[N/x] : \tau'$ from which $\Gamma \vdash (\lambda y : \tau.M)[N/x] : \tau \to \tau'$ follows by $(\to_I)$.

(2) We will use the exercises 4.3.1 and 4.3.2 on the interpretation of weakening and exchange. Again we proceed by induction on the length of the proof of $\Gamma, x : \sigma \vdash M : \tau$ and we just consider the case $(\to_I)$. We set $B = [\![\tau]\!]$, $B' = [\![\tau']\!]$, $C = [\![\Gamma]\!]$, and:

$$
\begin{aligned}
f_1 &= [\![\Gamma \vdash \lambda y : \tau.M[N/x] : \tau \to \tau']\!] &&: C \to B'^B \\
g_1 &= [\![\Gamma, y : \tau \vdash M[N/x] : \tau']\!] &&: C \times B \to B' \\
f_2 &= [\![\Gamma, x : \sigma \vdash \lambda y : \tau.M : \tau \to \tau']\!] &&: C \times A \to B'^B \\
g_2 &= [\![\Gamma, y : \tau, x : \sigma \vdash M : \tau']\!] &&: (C \times B) \times A \to B' \\
f_3 &= [\![\Gamma \vdash N : \sigma]\!] &&: C \to A \\
g_3 &= [\![\Gamma, y : \tau \vdash N : \sigma]\!] &&: C \times B \to A \\
g_2' &= [\![\Gamma, x : \sigma, y : \tau \vdash M : \tau']\!] &&: (C \times A) \times B \to B' \, .
\end{aligned}
$$

We have to show $f_1 = f_2 \circ \langle id, f_3 \rangle$, knowing by induction hypothesis that $g_1 = g_2 \circ \langle id, g_3 \rangle$. We observe that $f_1 = \Lambda(g_1)$, $f_2 = \Lambda(g_2')$, and $g_2' = g_2 \circ \phi$, where $\phi$ is the iso given by exercise 4.3.2. Moreover $g_3 = f_3 \circ \pi_1$ (cf. exercise 4.3.1). We then compute (cf. exercise 4.2.8):

$$
\begin{aligned}
f_2 \circ \langle id, f_3 \rangle &= \Lambda(g_2') \circ \langle id, f_3 \rangle \\
&= \Lambda(g_2' \circ (\langle id, f_3 \rangle \times id)) \ .
\end{aligned}
$$

So it is enough to show $g_1 = g_2' \circ (\langle id, f_3 \rangle \times id)$. We compute on the right hand side:

$$
\begin{aligned}
g_2' \circ (\langle id, f_3 \rangle \times id) &= g_2 \circ \phi \circ \langle\langle \pi_1, f_3 \circ \pi_1 \rangle, \pi_2 \rangle \\
&= g_2 \circ \phi \circ \langle\langle \pi_1, g_3 \rangle, \pi_2 \rangle \\
&= g_2 \circ \langle\langle \pi_1, \pi_2 \rangle, g_3 \rangle \\
&= g_2 \circ \langle id, g_3 \rangle \ .
\end{aligned}
$$

$\square$

The categorical interpretation can be seen as a way of compiling a language with variables into a language without variables. The slogan is that *variables are replaced by projections*, for instance $[\![ \emptyset \vdash \lambda x : \sigma.x : \sigma \to \sigma ]\!] = \Lambda(\pi_2)$. In other words, rather than giving a symbolic reference in the form of a variable, one provides a path for accessing a certain information in the context.[1] As a matter of fact the *compilation* of the λ-calculus into the categorical language has been taken as a starting point for the definition of an abstract machine (the *Categorical Abstract Machine* (CAM), see [CCM87]) in the style of Landin's classical *SECD* machine [Lan64] (see [Cur86] for a comparison). The purpose of these machines is to provide a high-level description of data structures and algorithms used to efficiently reduce λ-terms. In the CAM approach, a fundamental problem is that of orienting the equations that characterize CCC's as defined in exercise 4.2.8. In the following we drop all type information and we restrict our attention to the simulation of β-reduction (the treatment of the extensional rules raises additional problems). Hardin [Har89] has studied the term rewriting system $\mathcal{E} + Beta$ described in figure 4.5. The most important results are:

- $\mathcal{E}$ is confluent and strongly normalizing.

- $\mathcal{E} + Beta$ is confluent (on a subset of categorical terms which is large enough to contain all the compilations of λ-terms).

The proof of strong normalization of $\mathcal{E}$ is surprisingly difficult [CHR96]. The proof of confluence for $\mathcal{E} + Beta$ uses the strong normalization property of $\mathcal{E}$ and the confluence of β in the λ-calculus. The key connection is given by the following fact: if $M \to_\beta N$, if $f$ and $g$ are the compilations of $M$ and $N$, then there is an $h$ such that $f \to_{Beta} h$ and $g$ is the $\mathcal{E}$ normal form of $h$. The system $\mathcal{E}$ takes care of explicitly carrying the substitution involved in the β-reduction.

Simpler results have been obtained with a related calculus called λσ-calculus [ACCL92, CHL96]. More results on abstract machines which are related to the CAM are described in section 8.3.

---

[1]de Bruijn conventions for the representation of variables as distances from the respective binders (see, e.g., [ACCL92]), as well as standard implementations of environments in abstract machines (see section 8.3) follow related ideas.

$$(Beta) \quad ev \circ \langle \Lambda(f), g \rangle \rightarrow f \circ \langle id, g \rangle$$

$$(\mathcal{E}) \quad \begin{cases} (f \circ g) \circ h & \rightarrow & f \circ (g \circ h) \\ id \circ f & \rightarrow & f \\ \pi_1 \circ id & \rightarrow & \pi_1 \\ \pi_2 \circ id & \rightarrow & \pi_2 \\ \pi_1 \circ \langle f, g \rangle & \rightarrow & f \\ \pi_2 \circ \langle f, g \rangle & \rightarrow & g \\ \langle f, g \rangle \circ h & \rightarrow & \langle f \circ h, g \circ h \rangle \\ \Lambda(f) \circ h & \rightarrow & \Lambda(f \circ \langle h \circ \pi_1, \pi_2 \rangle) \end{cases}$$

Figure 4.5: A rewriting system for the $\beta$-categorical equations

**Exercise 4.3.4** *Show that two λ-terms are compiled into the same categorical term if and only if they are α-convertible (cf. section 2.1).*

## 4.4 From CCC's to λ-theories and back

We study the equivalence induced by the interpretation of the simply typed λ-calculus in a CCC. It turns out that the equivalence is closed under $\beta\eta$-conversion and forms a congruence.

**Definition 4.4.1 (λ-theory)** *Let $T$ be a collection of judgments of the shape $\Gamma \vdash M = N : \sigma$ such that $\Gamma \vdash M : \sigma$ and $\Gamma \vdash N : \sigma$. $T$ is called a λ-theory if it is closed under the rules in figure 4.6.*

We note that the congruence generated by the axioms $\beta$ and $\eta$ is the smallest λ-theory, we call it the pure $\lambda\beta\eta$ theory. To every CCC we can associate a λ-theory.

**Theorem 4.4.2** *Let $\mathbf{C}$ be a CCC and let $[\![\ ]\!]$ be an interpretation in the sense of figure 4.4 of the simply typed λ-calculus defined over $\mathbf{C}$. Then the following collection is a λ-theory.*

$$Th(\mathbf{C}) = \{ \Gamma \vdash M = N : \sigma \mid \Gamma \vdash M : \sigma, \Gamma \vdash N : \sigma \text{ and } [\![ \Gamma \vdash M : \sigma ]\!] = [\![ \Gamma \vdash N : \sigma ]\!] \} \, .$$

PROOF. We have to check that $Th(\mathbf{C})$ is closed under the rules presented in figure 4.6. For ($\alpha$) we observe that $[\![\ ]\!]$ is invariant with respect to the names of bound variables (cf. exercise 4.3.4).

($\beta$) Let $[\![ \Gamma \vdash (\lambda x : \sigma.M)N : \tau ]\!] = ev \circ \langle \Lambda(f), g \rangle$, where $f = [\![ \Gamma, x : \sigma \vdash M : \tau ]\!]$ and $g = [\![ \Gamma \vdash N : \sigma ]\!]$. By the substitution theorem, $[\![ \Gamma \vdash M[N/x] : \tau ]\!] = f \circ \langle id, g \rangle$, and (cf. exercise 4.2.9) $f \circ \langle id, g \rangle = ev \circ \langle \Lambda(f), g \rangle$.

$$(\alpha) \quad \frac{\Gamma \vdash \lambda x : \sigma.N : \sigma \to \tau \quad y \notin FV(N)}{\Gamma \vdash \lambda y : \sigma.N[y/x] = \lambda x : \sigma.N : \sigma \to \tau}$$

$$(\beta) \quad \frac{\Gamma \vdash (\lambda x : \sigma.M)N : \tau}{\Gamma \vdash (\lambda x : \sigma.M)N = M[N/x] : \tau}$$

$$(\eta) \quad \frac{\Gamma \vdash \lambda x : \sigma.(Mx) : \sigma \to \tau \quad x \notin FV(M)}{\Gamma \vdash \lambda x : \sigma.(Mx) = M : \sigma \to \tau}$$

$$(\xi) \quad \frac{\Gamma, x : \sigma \vdash M = N : \tau}{\Gamma \vdash \lambda x : \sigma.M = \lambda x : \sigma.N : \sigma \to \tau}$$

$$(appl) \quad \frac{\Gamma \vdash M = N : \sigma \to \tau \quad \Gamma \vdash M' = N' : \sigma}{\Gamma \vdash MM' = NN' : \tau}$$

$$(Asmp) \quad \frac{\Gamma \vdash M = N : \sigma \in T}{\Gamma \vdash M = N : \sigma} \qquad\qquad (weak) \quad \frac{\Gamma \vdash M = N : \sigma \quad x : \tau \notin \Gamma}{\Gamma, x : \tau \vdash M = N : \sigma}$$

$$(refl) \quad \frac{\Gamma \vdash M : \sigma}{\Gamma \vdash M = M : \sigma} \qquad\qquad (sym) \quad \frac{\Gamma \vdash M = N : \sigma}{\Gamma \vdash N = M : \sigma}$$

$$(trans) \quad \frac{\Gamma \vdash M = N : \sigma \quad \Gamma \vdash N = P : \sigma}{\Gamma \vdash M = P : \sigma}$$

Figure 4.6: Closure rules for a typed λ-theory

($\eta$)  We have:

$$\begin{aligned}
\llbracket \Gamma \vdash \lambda x : \sigma.Mx : \sigma \to \tau \rrbracket &= \Lambda(ev \circ \langle \llbracket \Gamma, x : \sigma \vdash M : \sigma \to \tau \rrbracket, \llbracket \Gamma, x : \sigma \vdash x : \sigma \rrbracket \rangle) \\
&= \Lambda(ev \circ \langle \llbracket \Gamma \vdash M : \sigma \to \tau \rrbracket \circ \pi_1, \pi_2 \rangle) \\
&= \Lambda(ev \circ (\llbracket \Gamma \vdash M : \sigma \to \tau \rrbracket \times id)) \\
&= \llbracket \Gamma \vdash M : \sigma \to \tau \rrbracket .
\end{aligned}$$

For (*weak*) we use the exercise 4.3.1. The rules (*refl*), (*sym*), (*trans*) hold since $Th(\mathbf{C})$ is an equivalence. Finally, (ξ), (*apl*) follow by the definition of the interpretation of abstraction and application. □

**Exercise 4.4.3** *Show that there are infinitely many λ-theories. Hints: Interpret the atomic types as finite sets and consider the resulting λ-theory. Then analyse the βη-normal forms of type $(\kappa \to \kappa) \to (\kappa \to \kappa)$.*

Next, we show how to generate a CCC starting from a λ-theory. The construction consists essentially in taking types as objects of the category and (open) terms quotiented by the λ-theory as morphisms (cf. Henkin's term model [Hen50]). It is convenient to work in an extended setting combining λ-calculus with product types. We take the following steps:

(1) We extend the language with constructors for terminal object and product, as well as the relative equations:

$$\text{Types} \quad At \ ::= \ \kappa \mid \kappa' \mid \ldots$$
$$\sigma \quad ::= \ At \mid 1 \mid \sigma \times \sigma \mid \sigma \to \sigma$$
$$\text{Terms} \quad v \quad ::= \ x \mid y \mid \ldots$$
$$M \quad ::= \ v \mid * \mid \langle M, M \rangle \mid \pi_1 M \mid \pi_2 M \mid \lambda v : \sigma.M \mid MM \ .$$

1. Typing rules. The rules of the simply typed calculus (figure 4.2), plus the rules for conjunction (figure 4.3), plus:

$$(*) \quad \frac{}{\Gamma \vdash * : 1} \ .$$

2. Equations. A theory is now a set of equality judgments closed under the rules of the pure λβη-theory (figure 4.6) plus:

$$(*) \quad \frac{\Gamma \vdash M : 1}{\Gamma \vdash M = *} \qquad\qquad (SP) \quad \frac{\Gamma \vdash M : \sigma \times \tau}{\Gamma \vdash \langle \pi_1 M, \pi_2 M \rangle = M : \sigma \times \tau}$$

$$(\pi_1) \quad \frac{\Gamma \vdash \langle M, N \rangle : \sigma \times \tau}{\Gamma \vdash \pi_1 \langle M, N \rangle = M : \sigma} \qquad (\pi_2) \quad \frac{\Gamma \vdash \langle M, N \rangle : \sigma \times \tau}{\Gamma \vdash \pi_2 \langle M, N \rangle = N : \tau} \ .$$

(2) We associate to a theory $T$ a CCC $\mathbf{C}(T)$ as follows.

1. The objects are the types of the extended language.

2. The morphisms are equivalences classes of *open* terms according to the equivalence induced by $T$. More precisely:

$$\mathbf{C}(T)[\sigma, \tau] \ = \ \{[M] \mid \exists \Gamma \ \Gamma \vdash M : \tau\}$$
$$[M] \quad\quad = \ \{N \mid \exists \Gamma, \tau \ \Gamma \vdash M = N : \tau \in T\} \ .$$

3. The structure associated to every CCC is defined as follows (we omit the type labels):

$$(id) \quad [\lambda x.x]$$
$$(comp) \quad [M] \circ [N] = [\lambda x.M(Nx)] \quad (x \text{ fresh})$$
$$(term) \quad !_\sigma = [\lambda x.*]$$
$$(proj) \quad \pi_1 = [\lambda x.\pi_1 x] \quad \pi_2 = [\lambda x.\pi_2 x]$$
$$(pair) \quad \langle [M], [N] \rangle = [\lambda x.\langle Mx, Nx \rangle] \quad (x \text{ fresh})$$
$$(eval) \quad ev = [\lambda x.(\pi_1 x)(\pi_2 x)]$$
$$(curry) \quad \Lambda([M]) = [\lambda y.\lambda z.M\langle y, z \rangle] \quad (y, z \text{ fresh}) \ .$$

4. We leave to the reader the verification of the equations associated to a CCC.

(3) Finally we have to verify that the $\lambda$-theory associated to $\mathbf{C}(T)$ is exactly $T$. To this end one checks that:

$$[\![x_1 : \sigma_1, \ldots, x_n : \sigma_n \vdash M : \sigma]\!] = [\lambda x : \tau.M[\pi_{n,1}x/x_1, \ldots \pi_{n,n}x/x_n]\,],$$

where $\tau \equiv (\cdots(1 \times \sigma_1) \times \cdots \times \sigma_n)$.

We can summarize our constructions as follows.

**Theorem 4.4.4 (from $\lambda$-theories to CCC's)** *Given any $\lambda$-theory $T$ over the simply typed calculus with products and terminal object we can build a CCC $\mathbf{C}(T)$ such that the $\lambda$-theory associated to $\mathbf{C}(T)$ coincides with $T$.*

**Remark 4.4.5** (1) *It is possible to see the constructions described here as representing an equivalence between a category of CCC's and a category of $\lambda$-theories [LS86].*

(2) *It is possible to strengthen the previous theorem by considering a theory $T$ over the simply typed $\lambda$-calculus (without products and terminal object). Then one needs to show that it is possible to add conservatively to $T$ the equations $(*)$, $(\pi_1)$, $(\pi_2)$, and $(SP)$, i.e., that adding these new equations does not allow us to prove new equalities between two simply typed $\lambda$-terms. We refer to [Cur86, chapter 1] for a description of suitable proof techniques.*

# 4.5 Logical relations

Logical relations are a quite ubiquitous tool in semantics and in logic. They are useful to establish links between syntax and semantics. In this section, logical relations are defined and applied to the proof of three results of this sort: Friedman's completeness theorem [Fri73], which characterizes $\beta\eta$-equality, and Jung-Tiuryn's and Sieber's theorems [JT93, Sie92] on the characterization of $\lambda$-definability.

Logical relations are predicates relating models of a given $\lambda$-calculus with constants $\Lambda(C)$, defined by induction over types. To simplify matters, throughout the rest of this section, we make the assumption that there is only one basic type $\kappa$. We define next (binary) logical relations, to this end we fix some terminology. Recall that an interpretation of simply typed $\lambda$-calculus in a CCC $\mathbf{C}$ is given as soon as the basic type $\kappa$ is interpreted by an object $D^\kappa$ of $\mathbf{C}$. We shall summarize this by calling the pair $\mathcal{M} = (\mathbf{C}, D^\kappa)$ a model. We write $[\![\sigma]\!] = D^\sigma$, hence $D^{\sigma \to \tau} = D^\sigma \Rightarrow D^\tau$.

If there are constants, then the constants must also be interpreted, but we leave this implicit to keep notation compact. We shall make repeated use of the hom-sets of the form $\mathbf{C}[1, D]$. It is thus convenient to use a shorter notation. We shall write, for any object $D$ of $\mathbf{C}$:

$$\mathbf{C}[1, D] = \underline{D}\,.$$

As a last preliminary to our definition, we point out the following instrumental isomorphisms which hold in any CCC, for any objects $A$ and $B$:

$$\mathbf{C}[A, B] \cong \mathbf{C}[1, B^A] \ .$$

Here is the right-to-left direction (the other is left to the reader):

$$\hat{f} = \Lambda(f \circ \pi_2) \ .$$

**Definition 4.5.1 (logical relation)** *Let $\mathcal{M} = (\mathbf{C}, D^\kappa)$ and $\mathcal{M}' = (\mathbf{C}', D'^\kappa)$ be two models. A logical relation is given by relations $\mathcal{R}^\kappa \subseteq \underline{D^\kappa} \times \underline{D'^\kappa}$ at each basic type $\kappa$. These relations are extended to all types (including product types) by the following definitional equivalences:*

$$\mathcal{R}^1 \ = \ \{(id, id)\}$$
$$\langle d, e \rangle \, \mathcal{R}^{\sigma \times \tau} \, \langle d', e' \rangle \ \Leftrightarrow \ (d \, \mathcal{R}^\sigma \, d' \ and \ e \, \mathcal{R}^\tau \, e')$$
$$\mathcal{R}^{\sigma \to \tau} \ = \ \mathcal{R}^\sigma \to \mathcal{R}^\tau \ ,$$

*where $f \, (R \to S) \, f' \Leftrightarrow \forall d, d' \ (d \, R \, d' \Rightarrow (ev \circ \langle f, d \rangle) \, S \, (ev \circ \langle f', d' \rangle))$ (cf. definition 3.3.6). Thus: $\forall \sigma \ \ \mathcal{R}^\sigma \subseteq \underline{D^\sigma} \times \underline{D'^\sigma}$. We shall write, for any $f, f' : D^\sigma \to D^\tau$:*

$$f \, \mathcal{R}^{\sigma, \tau} \, f' \quad whenever \quad \hat{f} \, \mathcal{R}^{\sigma \to \tau} \, \hat{f'} \ .$$

*A logical relation is called C-logical if $[\![c]\!]_\mathcal{M} \, \mathcal{R}^\sigma \, [\![c]\!]_{\mathcal{M}'}$, for all constants (where $\sigma$ is the type of $c$). Notice that if $C$ is empty, i.e., if our language is the simply typed λ-calculus without constants, then C-logical is the same as logical.*

**Remark 4.5.2** *The above definition is much in the spirit of the computability predicates used in section 3.5. The only difference is that computability predicates are defined on terms, while logical relations are defined on elements of models. There are also relations mixing terms and syntax (see theorems 6.3.6 and 8.2.6).*

The following is known as the fundamental lemma of logical relations (cf. lemmas 3.5.16 and 11.5.18).

**Lemma 4.5.3 (fundamental lemma)** *Let $\mathcal{R}$ be a C-logical relation. Then, for any closed term $M$ of type $\sigma$:*

$$[\![M]\!]_\mathcal{M} \, \mathcal{R}^\sigma \, [\![M]\!]_{\mathcal{M}'} \ .$$

PROOF HINT. We extend the statement to open terms as follows. For any $x_1 : \sigma_1, \ldots, x_n : \sigma_n \vdash M : \tau$, and for any $d_1 \, \mathcal{R}^{\sigma_1} \, d'_1, \ldots, d_n \, \mathcal{R}^{\sigma_n} \, d'_n$:

$$[\![M]\!] \circ \langle d_1, \ldots, d_n \rangle \quad \mathcal{R}^\tau \quad [\![M]\!] \circ \langle d'_1, \ldots, d'_n \rangle \ .$$

The proof of this extended statement is by induction on the size of $M$. For the abstraction case, one uses the following equation, which is consequence of the equations characterizing CCC's (cf. exercise 4.2.8): $ev \circ \langle \Lambda(f) \circ d, e \rangle = f \circ \langle d, e \rangle$. $\square$

A more concrete description of models, and of logical relations, can be given when the models are extensional, i.e., when the morphisms of the model can be viewed as functions.

**Definition 4.5.4 (enough points)** *A category* **C** *with terminal object 1 is said to have enough points if the following holds, for any* $a, b$ *and any* $f, g \in \mathbf{C}[a, b]$:

$$\forall h : 1 \to a \ (f \circ h = g \circ h) \ \Rightarrow \ f = g .$$

*If the underlying category of a model* $\mathcal{M}$ *has enough points, we say that* $\mathcal{M}$ *is extensional.*

Extensional models and logical relations over them can be described without using the vocabulary of category theory. The price to pay is that the definition is syntax-dependent. We leave it to the reader to convince himself that the following constructions indeed define (all) extensional models and logical relations.

A simply-typed extensional applicative structure (cf. section 3.1) $\mathcal{M}$ consists of a collection of sets $D^\sigma$, such that, for all $\sigma, \tau$, $D^{\sigma \to \tau}$ is (in bijection with) a set of functions from $D^\sigma$ to $D^\tau$. We write $\mathcal{M} = \{D^\sigma\}$.

With any sequence $\sigma_1, \ldots, \sigma_n$ of types we associate a set $D^{\sigma_1, \ldots, \sigma_n}$ (abbreviated as $D^{\vec{\sigma}}$) as follows. With the empty sequence we associate a singleton set $\{*\}$, and we define $D^{\vec{\sigma}, \tau} = D^{\vec{\sigma}} \times D^\tau$ (for $n \geq 1$, we shall freely consider $D^{\sigma_1, \ldots, \sigma_n}$ as $D^{\sigma_1} \times \cdots \times D^{\sigma_n}$).

An interpretation function is a function $[\![ \_ ]\!]$ mapping any typing judgment $x_1 : \sigma_1, \ldots, x_n : \sigma_n \vdash M : \tau$ to a function from $D^{\vec{\sigma}}$ to $D^\tau$ (for closed terms $\vdash M : \tau$, we consider freely $[\![ \vdash M : \tau ]\!]$ as an element of $D^\tau$), which has to satisfy the following (universally quantified) properties:

$$
\begin{aligned}
[\![ \vdash c : \sigma ]\!] &\in D^\sigma \\
[\![ x_1 : \sigma_1, \ldots, x_n : \sigma_n \vdash x_i : \sigma_i ]\!](\vec{d}) &= d_i \\
[\![ \Gamma \vdash MN : \tau ]\!](\vec{d}) &= ([\![ \Gamma \vdash M : \sigma \to \tau ]\!](\vec{d}))([\![ \Gamma \vdash N : \sigma ]\!](\vec{d})) \\
([\![ \Gamma \vdash \lambda x : \sigma. M : \sigma \to \tau ]\!](\vec{d}))(e) &= [\![ \Gamma, x : \sigma \vdash M : \tau ]\!](\vec{d}, e) .
\end{aligned}
$$

There is an additional condition dealing with weakening, which we omit here, and which serves in the proof of theorem 4.5.13. These clauses characterize the interpretation function.

An extensional model $\mathcal{M}$ consists of an extensional applicative structure together with an interpretation function $[\![ \_ ]\!]_{\mathcal{M}}$ (the subscript is omitted when clear from the context).

In this concrete framework, a logical relation is now a relation $\mathcal{R}^\kappa \subseteq D^\kappa \times D'^\kappa$, extended to all types (using function types only) by the following definitional equivalence:

$$f \, \mathcal{R}^{\sigma \to \tau} \, f' \ \Leftrightarrow \ (\forall d, d' \ (d \, \mathcal{R}^\sigma \, d') \Rightarrow (f(d) \, \mathcal{R}^\tau \, f(d'))) .$$

We shall freely use this concrete presentation in the sequel, when dealing with extensional models.

**Exercise 4.5.5** *Establish formal links between extensional models as defined above and categories with enough points. Hint: Given a model described concretely, consider the category whose objects are sequences* $(\sigma_1, \ldots, \sigma_m)$ *of types and whose morphisms are vectors* $(d_1, \ldots, d_n) : (\sigma_1, \ldots, \sigma_m) \to (\tau_1, \ldots, \tau_n)$ *where* $d_i \in D^{\sigma_1 \to \cdots \to \sigma_m \to \tau_i}$ *for all* $i$.

**Exercise 4.5.6 (extensional collapse)** *Let $\mathcal{M} = (C, D^\kappa)$ be a model, and consider the logical relation $\mathcal{R}$ defined by $\mathcal{R}^\kappa = \{(d,d) \mid d \in \underline{D^\kappa}\}$. (1) Show that, for all $\sigma$, $\mathcal{R}^\sigma$ is a partial equivalence relation, i.e., is symmetric and transitive (cf. definition 15.1.3. (2) Consider the category [C] whose objects are the types built freely from $\kappa$ using finite products and function types, and whose arrows from $\sigma$ to $\tau$ are equivalence classes with respect to $\mathcal{R}^{\sigma,\tau}$. Show that [C] is a CCC with enough points, called the extensional collapse of C.*

Next we give two applications of logical relations. The first application is in fact itself a family of applications. Logical relations may be useful to prove inclusions of theories, thanks to the following lemma.

**Lemma 4.5.7** *Let $\mathcal{R}$ be a logical relation between two models $\mathcal{M}$ and $\mathcal{M}'$. Suppose that $\mathcal{R}^\sigma$ is functional for all $\sigma$, i.e., for all $d, d', d''$:*

$$(d\, \mathcal{R}^\sigma\, d'\ and\ d\, \mathcal{R}^\sigma\, d'') \ \Rightarrow\ d' = d'' .$$

*Then, for any closed terms $M, N$ of the same type:*

$$[\![M]\!]_\mathcal{M} = [\![N]\!]_\mathcal{M} \ \Rightarrow\ [\![M]\!]_{\mathcal{M}'} = [\![N]\!]_{\mathcal{M}'} .$$

PROOF. Let $\sigma$ be the common type of $M, N$ and let $d$ be the common value of $[\![M]\!]_\mathcal{M}$ and $[\![N]\!]_\mathcal{M}$. By two applications of lemma 4.5.3 we have $d\, \mathcal{R}^\sigma\, [\![M]\!]_{\mathcal{M}'}$ and $d\, \mathcal{R}^\sigma\, [\![N]\!]_{\mathcal{M}'}$, and we conclude by the assumption that $\mathcal{R}$ is functional. $\square$

**Characterization of $\beta\eta$-equality.** First, we consider the following issue: we seek conditions on $\mathcal{R}^\kappa$ to prove that $\mathcal{R}$ is functional. Clearly, one should require $\mathcal{R}^\kappa$ to be functional to start with. In practice $\mathcal{R}^\kappa$ may be more than functional. Often we want to compare (extensional) models which interpret basic types the same way and which differ in the choice of the functions (or morphisms) in the interpretation of function types. In other words, $\mathcal{R}^\kappa$ is often the identity (an example is provided by exercise 4.5.6). It turns out that surjectivity (a property *a fortiori* enjoyed by the identity) is a useful property to carry along an induction. Indeed, let us attempt to prove that if $\mathcal{R}^\kappa$ is functional and surjective, then $\mathcal{R}^\sigma$ is functional and surjective for all $\sigma$.

Once we know that $\mathcal{R}^\sigma$ is functional, we freely say that $\mathcal{R}^\sigma(d)$ is defined and equal to $d'$ if $d\, \mathcal{R}^\sigma\, d'$. Also, we assume that we have proved surjectivity at type $\sigma$ by building a function $i^\sigma : D'^\sigma \to D^\sigma$ such that $i^\sigma(d')\mathcal{R}^\sigma d'$ for all $d'$. Equivalently, we assume that at type $\sigma$, there exists a partial function $\mathcal{R}^\sigma : D^\sigma \to D'^\sigma$ and a total function $i^\sigma : D'^\sigma \to D^\sigma$ such that $\mathcal{R}^\sigma \circ i^\sigma = id$. Similarly, we suppose that these data exist at type $\tau$. We want to show that $\mathcal{R}^{\sigma\to\tau}$ is functional, and to construct $i^{\sigma\to\tau}$ such that $\mathcal{R}^{\sigma\to\tau} \circ i^{\sigma\to\tau} = id$.

• **Functional.** Using the formulation of $\mathcal{R}^\sigma$ and $\mathcal{R}^\tau$ as partial functions, the definition of $f\, \mathcal{R}^{\sigma\to\tau}\, f'$ reads:

$$\forall d \in D^\sigma \quad \mathcal{R}^\sigma(d) \downarrow\ \Rightarrow f'(\,\mathcal{R}^\sigma(d)) = \mathcal{R}^\tau(f(d)) .$$

Suppose that $f\ \mathcal{R}^{\sigma\to\tau}\ f'$. Then, for any $d' \in D'^\sigma$:

$$
\begin{aligned}
f'(d') &= f'(\mathcal{R}^\sigma(i^\sigma(d'))) && \text{(by surjectivity at } \sigma) \\
&= \mathcal{R}^\tau(f(i^\sigma(d'))) && \text{(by the definition of } \mathcal{R}^{\sigma\to\tau}) .
\end{aligned}
$$

Hence $f'$ is unique. More precisely:

$$
\mathcal{R}^{\sigma\to\tau}(f) \downarrow \;\Rightarrow\; \mathcal{R}^{\sigma\to\tau}(f) = \mathcal{R}^\tau \circ f \circ i^\sigma .
$$

- Surjective. We claim that all we need to know about $i^{\sigma\to\tau}$ is the following, for any $f' \in D'^{\sigma\to\tau}$:

$$
\forall d \in D^\sigma\ \mathcal{R}^\sigma(d) \downarrow \Rightarrow i^{\sigma\to\tau}(f')(d) = i^\tau(f'(\mathcal{R}^\sigma(d))) . \tag{4.3}
$$

Let us prove that if $i^{\sigma\to\tau}$ satisfies 4.3, then, for any $f' : D'^{\sigma\to\tau}$, $i^{\sigma\to\tau}(f')\ \mathcal{R}^{\sigma\to\tau}\ f'$, that is, by the definition of $\mathcal{R}^{\sigma\to\tau}$:

$$
\forall d \in D^\sigma\ \mathcal{R}^\sigma(d) \downarrow \Rightarrow f'(\mathcal{R}^\sigma(d)) = \mathcal{R}^\tau(i^{\sigma\to\tau}(f')(d)) .
$$

Indeed, we have, under the assumption that $\mathcal{R}^\sigma(d) \downarrow$:

$$
\begin{aligned}
\mathcal{R}^\tau(i^{\sigma\to\tau}(f')(d)) &= \mathcal{R}^\tau(i^\tau(f'(\mathcal{R}^\sigma(d)))) && \text{(by 4.3)} \\
&= f'(\mathcal{R}^\sigma(d)) && \text{(by surjectivity at } \tau) .
\end{aligned}
$$

The above proof schema, which uses the extensionality of both $\mathcal{M}$ and $\mathcal{N}$, is instantiated in the proof of the following theorem.

**Theorem 4.5.8 (Friedman)** *Let* $\mathcal{F} = \{\mathcal{D}^\sigma\}$ *be the full type hierarchy over an infinite set* $D^\kappa$, *i.e.,* $\mathcal{F} = \{\mathcal{D}^\sigma\}$ *is the extensional model for which* $D^{\sigma\to\tau}$ *is the set of all functions from* $D^\sigma$ *to* $D^\tau$. *Then, for any* $\lambda$-*terms:*

$$
[\![M]\!]_\mathcal{F} = [\![N]\!]_\mathcal{F} \;\Leftrightarrow\; M =_{\beta\eta} N .
$$

Proof. ($\Leftarrow$) Since $\mathcal{F}$ is extensional, it validates $\beta\eta$.

($\Rightarrow$) We turn syntax into an extensional model $\mathcal{M}'$, defining $D'^\sigma$ as the set of all $\beta\eta$ equivalence classes of (open) terms of type $\sigma$ (cf. construction developed for the proof of theorem 4.4.4). That this makes an extensional model is proved as follows. We define an application function $\bullet$ by $[M]\bullet[N] = [MN]$. Suppose that for all $[P]$, $[M]\bullet[P] = [N]\bullet[P]$. Then in particular, for a fresh $x$, $[Mx] = [Nx]$, i.e., $Mx =_{\beta\eta} Nx$. Then:

$$
M =_{\beta\eta} \lambda x.Mx =_{\beta\eta} \lambda x.Nx =_{\beta\eta} N .
$$

Therefore we have an extensional model. Now we are ready to use the proof schema, with the term model as $\mathcal{M}'$, and $\mathcal{F}$ as $\mathcal{M}$. We need a surjection from $D^\kappa$ to $D'^\kappa$. It is clearly enough to live with a denumerable set of variable names. Therefore we can consider the set of terms as denumerable. The sets $D'^\sigma$ are then at most denumerable. They are not finite, since we can have infinitely many different $\beta\eta$-normal forms $x, xx_1, xx_1 \cdots x_n, \ldots$ at any given type $\sigma$. In particular, $D'^\kappa$ is infinite and denumerable. Then, given any infinite $D^\kappa$, we can pick a (total) surjection $\mathcal{R}^\kappa : D^\kappa \to D'^\kappa$. More precisely, we can pick a function $i^\kappa : D'^\kappa \to D^\kappa$ such $\mathcal{R}^\kappa \circ i^\kappa = id$. We are left to exhibit a definition of $i^{\sigma \to \tau}$ satisfying 4.3. But property 4.3 actually gives a definition of the restriction of $i^{\sigma \to \tau}(f')$ to the domain of $\mathcal{R}^\sigma$. Since we are in the full type hierarchy, we can choose any value for $i^{\sigma \to \tau}(f')(d)$ when $\mathcal{R}^\sigma(d) \uparrow$. Hence $\mathcal{R}$ is functional, and we conclude by lemma 4.5.7. □

The above proof, which is essentially the original proof of [Fri73], uses the fullness of the model $\mathcal{F}$ quite crudely. There exists another proof of Friedman's theorem, as a corollary of a powerful theorem known as Statman's 1-section theorem, whose range of applications to various completeness theorems seems wider than what can be achieved by the above proof schema.

Statman's theorem states that in order to prove a completeness theorem, it suffices to prove it for terms of type $\alpha = (\kappa \to \kappa \to \kappa) \to \kappa \to \kappa$. What is special about this type? If there are no constants, the closed normal forms of type $\alpha$ are exactly the terms of the form $\lambda g c.t$, where $t$ is the (curried form) of a first order term constructed over the signature $\{g, c\}$ consisting of a symbol $g$ of arity 2 and a symbol $c$ of arity 0.

**Theorem 4.5.9 (1-section)** *Let $C$ be a class of models of the simply-typed $\lambda$-calculus. The following properties are equivalent:*

(1) *For any type $\sigma$, and any closed terms $M, N$ of type $\sigma$:*

$$\forall \mathcal{M} \in C \;\; [\![M]\!]_\mathcal{M} = [\![N]\!]_\mathcal{M} \;\; \Leftrightarrow \;\; M =_{\beta\eta} N .$$

(2) *For any closed terms $M, N$ of type $\alpha = (\kappa \to \kappa \to \kappa) \to \kappa \to \kappa$:*

$$\forall \mathcal{M} \in C \;\; [\![M]\!]_\mathcal{M} = [\![N]\!]_\mathcal{M} \;\; \Leftrightarrow \;\; M =_{\beta\eta} N .$$

PROOF. Statement (1) obviously implies (2). The other direction is an immediate consequence of the following lemma 4.5.11. □

**Definition 4.5.10 (rank)** *The rank of a simple type $\tau$ is defined as follows:*

$$rank(\kappa) = 0 \quad (\kappa \text{ base type})$$
$$rank(\tau_1 \to \cdots \to \tau_k \to \kappa) = 1 + (\max\{rank(\tau_i) \mid i = 1 \ldots k\}) .$$

*We say that a type $\tau$ is of rank at most $n$ if $rank(\tau) \leq n$. If there is only one base type $\kappa$, the types of rank at most 1 are thus the types $\kappa^n$, where:*

$$\kappa^0 = \kappa \quad \kappa^{n+1} = \kappa \to \kappa^n .$$

*Types of rank at most 1 are often called first order types, according to the use of 'first order' in, say, 'first order terms' or 'first order signature'. We shall use both terminologies.*[2]

---

[2]Note that 'first order' may sometimes also refer to all simply-typed $\lambda$-terms, as opposed to 'second order' that designates quantification over types; second order types in this sense are introduced in chapter 11.

**Lemma 4.5.11** *If $M, N$ are closed simply-typed $\lambda$-terms of type $\sigma$, and if $M \neq_{\beta\eta} N$, then there exists a closed simply-typed $\lambda$-term $P$ of type $\sigma \to \alpha$ (where $\alpha$ is as in the statement of theorem 4.5.9) such that $PM \neq_{\beta\eta} PN$.*

PROOF HINT. The proof makes use of the notion of extended $\beta\eta$-normal form. An extended $\beta\eta$-normal form of type $\sigma_1 \to \cdots \to \sigma_n \to \kappa$ is a term of the form $\lambda x_1 \cdots x_n.u(M_1 x_1 \cdots x_n) \cdots (M_k x_1 \cdots x_n)$, where each $M_j$ is itself an extended $\beta\eta$-normal form. Note that extended $\beta\eta$-normal forms are not normal forms in general, whence the qualification 'extended'. Using strong $\beta\eta$ normalization, it is easily shown that for any $M$ there exists a unique extended $\beta\eta$-normal form $N$ such that $M =_{\beta\eta} N$. The proof of the statement is decomposed into two claims.

(1) Let $M, N$ be two different closed extended $\beta\eta$-normal forms of a type $\sigma$ of rank at most 2. Then there exists a closed term $L^\sigma$ ($L$ for short) of type $\sigma \to \alpha$ depending only on $\sigma$, such that $LM \neq_{\beta\eta} LN$.

(2) Let $M, N$ be two different closed extended $\beta\eta$-normal forms of type $\sigma_1 \to \cdots \to \sigma_n \to \kappa$. Then there exist terms $V_1, \ldots, V_n$, whose free variables have types of rank at most 1, such that $MV_1 \cdots V_n \neq_{\beta\eta} NV_1 \cdots V_n$.

The statement follows from these claims, taking:

$$P = \lambda x.L^\sigma(\lambda \vec{y}.xV_1 \cdots V_n)$$

where $V_1, \ldots, V_n$ are obtained by claim (2) applied to $M, N$, where $\vec{y}$ is a list of the free variables in $V_1, \ldots, V_n$, where $\sigma$ is the common type of $\lambda \vec{y}.MV_1, \ldots V_n$ and $\lambda \vec{y}.NV_1, \ldots V_n$, and where $L^\sigma$ is obtained by (1).

Both claims are proved by induction on the size of $M, N$. For claim 1 let us fix $\sigma = \sigma_1 \to \cdots \to \sigma_n \to \kappa$. We pick free variables $x : \kappa$ and $g : \kappa \to \kappa \to \kappa$ and define the following terms:

$$\mathbf{0} = x \qquad (\mathbf{i+1}) = (gx\mathbf{i}) \ .$$

Suppose, say, that $\sigma_i = \kappa \to \kappa \to \kappa$. Then we set:

$$P_i = \lambda y_1 y_2.g\mathbf{i}(gy_1 y_2) \ .$$

Finally, we take:

$$L = \lambda wgx.wP_1 \cdots P_n \ ,$$

which depends on $\sigma$ only. Suppose, say, that $M = \lambda \vec{x}.\, x_i(M_1 \vec{x})(M_2 \vec{x})$. Then:

$$LM =_{\beta\eta} \lambda gx.g\mathbf{i}(g(M_1 \vec{P})(M_2 \vec{P})) \ .$$

If $N$ has a different head variable, say $x_j$, then similarly $LN$ is $\beta\eta$-equal to a term that starts with $\lambda gx.g\mathbf{j}$, which cannot be $\beta\eta$ equal to a term starting with $\lambda gx.g\mathbf{i}$ (these prefixes are preserved until the normal form is reached). Suppose thus that $N$ has the same head variable, i.e., $N = \lambda \vec{x}.\, x_i(N_1 \vec{x})(N_2 \vec{x})$. Since the type of $x_i$ has rank 1, $M_1 \vec{x}$ has type $\kappa$, i.e., $M_1$ has type $\sigma$. Similarly, $M_2, N_1$, and $N_2$ have type $\sigma$. On the other hand $M \neq_{\beta\eta} N$ implies, say, $M_1 \neq_{\beta\eta} N_1$. We can thus apply induction to $M_1$ and $N_1$:

$$M_1 \vec{P} =_{\beta\eta} LM_1 gx \neq_{\beta\eta} LN_1 gx =_{\beta\eta} N_1 \vec{P} \ .$$

On the other hand, since

$$LN =_{\beta\eta} \lambda gx.gi(g(N_1\vec{P})(N_2\vec{P})),$$

$LM =_{\beta\eta} LN$ would imply $M_1\vec{P} =_{\beta\eta} N_1\vec{P}$ and $M_2\vec{P} =_{\beta\eta} N_2\vec{P}$. Contradiction.

We turn to the second claim. The interesting case is again when $M$ and $N$ have the same head variable. We suppose as above that:

$$M = \lambda\vec{x}.\ x_i(M_1\vec{x})(M_2\vec{x})\quad N = \lambda\vec{x}.\ x_i(N_1\vec{x})(N_2\vec{x})\ ,$$

and $M_1 \neq_{\beta\eta} N_1$. But now $\sigma_i = \tau_1 \to \tau_2 \to \kappa$, where $\tau_1, \tau_2$ are arbitrary types, hence, say, $M_1\vec{x}$ is not necessarily of basic type. By induction applied to $M_1$ and $N_1$, there exists a vector $\vec{U}$ of terms $U_1, \ldots, U_m$ such that $M_1\vec{U} \neq_{\beta\eta} N_1\vec{U}$ at type $\kappa$. In particular $m \geq n$, where $n$ is the length of $\vec{x}$. We set (with $h, y_1, y_2$ fresh and of rank at most 1):

$$V_i = \lambda y_1 y_2.h(y_1 U_{n+1} \cdots U_m)(U_i y_1 y_2)\ ,$$

and $V_p = U_p$ if $p \neq i$ and $p \leq n$. The trick about $V_i$ is the following property:

$$(\star)\quad V_i[\lambda uv.v/h] =_{\beta\eta} U_i\ ,$$

from which $(M_1\vec{V}U_{n+1} \cdots U_m)[\lambda uv.v/h] = M_1\vec{U}$ follows, and similarly for $N_1$. Therefore:

$$M_1\vec{V}U_{n+1} \cdots U_m \neq_{\beta\eta} N_1\vec{V}U_{n+1} \cdots U_m\ ,$$

which entails the claim, since $M\vec{V}$ reduces to a term which starts with

$$h(M_1\vec{V}U_{n+1} \cdots U_m)\ ,$$

and similarly for $N_1$. □

We now show how theorem 4.5.9 yields Friedman's theorem as a corollary. All we have to check is that if two terms $s$ and $t$ built only using application from variables $g : \kappa \to \kappa \to \kappa$ and $c : \kappa$ are different, then $[\![\lambda gc.s]\!]_{\mathcal{F}} \neq [\![\lambda gc.t]\!]_{\mathcal{F}}$. We assume more precisely that $D^\kappa$ is $\omega$, and we pick a pairing function *pair* which is injective and such that:

$$\forall m, n\ (m < pair(m,n)\ \text{and}\ n < pair(m,n))\ .$$

Then we interpret $g$ by (the curried version of) *pair*, and $c$ by any number, say 0. It is easy to prove by induction that if $s, t$ are two distinct terms, then $[\![s]\!]_{\mathcal{F}}(pair, 0) \neq [\![t]\!]_{\mathcal{F}}(pair, 0)$, using these two properties of *pair*. This shows the hard implication in the equivalence stated in theorem 4.5.9, and thus completes our second proof of Friedman's theorem.

**Definability.** As a second application of logical relations, we consider the so-called definability problem. Given an extensional model $\mathcal{M}$, is it possible to characterize the elements $d$ such that $d = [\![M]\!]$ for some closed $M$? A positive answer was given by Jung and Tiuryn [JT93]. It is an elegant construction, based on Kripke logical relations, which we define next (in the particular setting we need).

**Definition 4.5.12** *A Kripke logical relation over an extensional model $\mathcal{M}$ is given by a family of sets $\mathcal{R}_{\vec{\sigma}}^{\kappa} \subseteq (D^{\vec{\sigma}} \to D^{\kappa})$ satisfying the following so-called Kripke monotonicity condition:*

$$f \in \mathcal{R}_{\vec{\sigma}}^{\kappa} \;\Rightarrow\; (\forall \vec{\sigma}' \; f \circ \pi \in \mathcal{R}_{\vec{\sigma},\vec{\sigma}'}^{\kappa}) \,,$$

*where $\pi(\vec{d},\vec{d}') = \vec{d}$. A Kripke logical relation is extended to all types as follows:*

$$f \in \mathcal{R}_{\vec{\sigma}}^{\tau_1 \to \tau_2} \subseteq (D^{\vec{\sigma}} \to D^{\tau_1 \to \tau_2}) \;\Leftrightarrow\; \forall \vec{\sigma}', \, g \in \mathcal{R}_{\vec{\sigma},\vec{\sigma}'}^{\tau_1} \; \lambda \vec{d}\vec{d}'. \, f(\vec{d})(g(\vec{d},\vec{d}')) \in \mathcal{R}_{\vec{\sigma},\vec{\sigma}'}^{\tau_2} \,.$$

*We write $\mathcal{R}^{\tau}$ for $\mathcal{R}_{\vec{\sigma}}^{\tau}$ when $\vec{\sigma}$ is of length 0. An element $d \in D^{\sigma}$ is called invariant under $\mathcal{R}$ if $d \in \mathcal{R}^{\sigma}$. A Kripke C-logical relation is a Kripke logical relation such that $[\![c]\!]$ is invariant for all $c \in C$.*

Each set $\mathcal{R}_{\vec{\sigma}}^{\tau}$ can be viewed as a relation over $D^{\tau}$ whose arity is the cardinality of $D^{\vec{\sigma}}$. In this sense, Kripke logical relations are of variable arities. It is easy to check that Kripke monotonicity extends to all types:

$$f \in \mathcal{R}_{\vec{\sigma}}^{\tau} \;\Rightarrow\; (\forall \vec{\sigma}' \; f \circ \pi \in \mathcal{R}_{\vec{\sigma},\vec{\sigma}'}^{\tau}) \,.$$

**Theorem 4.5.13** *Let $\mathcal{M}$ be an extensional model. Then $d$ is definable, i.e., $d = [\![M]\!]$ for some closed term $M \in \Lambda(C)$, if and only if $d$ is invariant under all Kripke C-logical relations.*

PROOF. ($\Rightarrow$) This is a variant of the fundamental lemma of logical relations. The statement needs to be extended to subscripts $\vec{\sigma}$ and to open terms. The following extended statement is proved straightforwardly by induction on $M$.
For any $x_1 : \tau_1, \ldots, x_n : \tau_n \vdash M : \tau$, for any $\vec{\sigma}$, for any $f_1 \in \mathcal{R}_{\vec{\sigma}}^{\tau_1}, \ldots, f_n \in \mathcal{R}_{\vec{\sigma}}^{\tau_n}$:

$$[\![M]\!](f_1, \ldots, f_n) \in \mathcal{R}_{\vec{\sigma}}^{\tau} \,.$$

($\Leftarrow$) We actually prove a stronger result. We exhibit a single Kripke logical relation that characterizes definability. This relation $\mathcal{S}$ is defined as follows:

$$\mathcal{S}_{\vec{\sigma}}^{\kappa} = \{[\![M]\!] \mid \vec{x} : \vec{\sigma} \vdash M : \kappa\} \,.$$

The proof that $\mathcal{S}$ satisfies Kripke monotonicity requires an additional assumption on the interpretation function in the concrete description of extensional model, which we detail now. If $\vec{x} : \vec{\sigma} \vdash M : \tau$ is a provable judgment, then $\vec{x} : \vec{\sigma}, \vec{x}' : \vec{\sigma}' \vdash M : \tau$ is also provable, for any $\vec{\sigma}'$. We require:

$$[\![\vec{x} : \vec{\sigma}, \vec{x}' : \vec{\sigma}' \vdash M : \tau]\!] = [\![\vec{x} : \vec{\sigma} \vdash M : \tau]\!] \circ \pi \,.$$

Kripke monotonicity follows straightforwardly. We next claim:

$$\forall \tau, \vec{\sigma} \quad S_{\vec{\sigma}}^{\tau} = \{ [\![M]\!] \mid \vec{x} : \vec{\sigma} \vdash M : \tau \} \ .$$

Then the statement follows, taking the empty $\vec{\sigma}$. We prove the two inclusions of the claim by mutual induction on the size of the type $\tau$, for $\tau = \tau_1 \to \tau_2$:

($\subseteq$) By induction applied at $\tau_1$ ($\supseteq$), we have:

$$[\![\vec{x} : \vec{\sigma}, y : \tau_1 \vdash y : \tau_1]\!] \in S_{\vec{\sigma}, \tau_1}^{\tau_1} \ .$$

Let $f \in S_{\vec{\sigma}}^{\tau_1 \to \tau_2}$ . By definition of $S$ at $\tau_1 \to \tau_2$, we have:

$$\lambda \vec{d} d_1. \, f(\vec{d})(d_1) \in S_{\vec{\sigma}, \tau_1}^{\tau_2} \ .$$

By induction applied at $\tau_2$ ($\subseteq$), there exists $\vec{x} : \vec{\sigma}, y : \tau_1 \vdash M : \tau_2$ such that, for all $\vec{d}, d_1$:

$$[\![\vec{x} : \vec{\sigma}, y : \tau_1 \vdash M : \tau_2]\!](\vec{d}, d_1) = f(\vec{d})(d_1) \ .$$

It follows that $[\![\lambda y. M]\!] = f$.

($\supseteq$) Let $\vec{x} : \vec{\sigma} \vdash M : \tau_1 \to \tau_2$. Let $g \in S_{\vec{\sigma}, \vec{\sigma'}}^{\tau_1}$ . By induction applied at $\tau_1$ ($\subseteq$), there exists $\vec{x} : \vec{\sigma}, \vec{x'} : \vec{\sigma'} \vdash N : \tau_1$ such that $g = [\![N]\!]$. We have to prove:

$$[\![\vec{x} : \vec{\sigma}, \vec{x'} : \vec{\sigma'} \vdash MN : \tau_2]\!] \in S_{\vec{\sigma}, \vec{\sigma'}}^{\tau_2} \ ,$$

which holds by induction applied at $\tau_2$ ($\supseteq$).　　　　　　　　　　□

If we restrict our attention to terms whose type has at most rank 2, and if we require that the constants in $C$ also have a type of rank at most 1, then we can get around variable arities. The following theorem is due to Sieber. It was actually obtained before (and provided inspiration for) theorem 4.5.13. Given an extensional model $\mathcal{M} = \{ D^{\sigma} \}$, and a function $f \in D^{\sigma_1 \to \cdots \to \sigma_n \to \kappa}$, given a matrix $\{ d_{ij} \}_{i \leq p, j \leq n}$, we wonder whether there exists a closed term $M$ such that, for each line of the matrix, i.e., for all $i \leq p$:

$$[\![M]\!](d_{i1}) \cdots (d_{in}) = f(d_{i1}) \cdots (d_{in}) \ ,$$

and we consider to this aim $C$-logical relations of arity $p$, containing the columns of the matrix. If we can exhibit such a logical relation which moreover does not contain the vector $(f(d_{11}) \cdots (d_{1n}), \ldots, f(d_{p1}) \cdots (d_{pn}))$, then the answer to our question is negative, by the fundamental lemma. Sieber's theorem asserts that this method is complete.

**Theorem 4.5.14** *Consider a set $C$ of constants whose types have at most rank 1. Let $\mathcal{M}$ be an extensional model for $\Lambda(C)$, and let $\sigma = \sigma_1 \to \cdots \to \sigma_n \to \kappa$ be a type with rank at most 2. Let $\{ d_{ij} \}_{i \leq p, j \leq n}$ be a matrix where $d_{ij} \in D^{\sigma_j}$, for any $i, j$, let $f \in D^{\sigma}$, and let, for all $i \leq p$:*

$$e_i = f(d_{i1}) \cdots (d_{in}) \ .$$

*The following properties are equivalent:*

(1) *There exists* $\vdash M : \sigma$ *such that, for all* $i \le p$:

$$[\![M]\!](d_{i1}) \cdots (d_{in}) = e_i \ .$$

(2) *For every p-ary C-logical relation* $\mathcal{R}$, *the following implication holds:*

$$(\forall j \le n \ (d_{1j}, \ldots, d_{pj}) \in \mathcal{R}^{\sigma_j}) \ \Rightarrow \ (e_1, \ldots, e_p) \in \mathcal{R}^\kappa \ . \tag{4.4}$$

(3) *The logical relation* $\mathcal{S}$ *defined at* $\kappa$ *by*

$$\mathcal{S}^\kappa = \{(a_1, \ldots, a_p) \mid \exists \vdash N : \sigma \ \forall i \le p \ [\![N]\!](d_{i1}) \cdots (d_{in}) = a_i\}$$

*contains* $(e_1, \ldots, e_p)$.

PROOF. (1) $\Rightarrow$ (2) This implication holds by the fundamental lemma.

(2) $\Rightarrow$ (3) Suppose that we have shown that $\mathcal{S}$ is $C$-logical. Then, by (2), $\mathcal{S}$ satisfies 4.4. The conclusion will follow if we prove that $\mathcal{S}$ in fact satisfies the hypothesis of 4.4. If $N$ and $(a_1, \ldots, a_p)$ are as in the definition of $\mathcal{S}^\kappa$, it is convenient to call $N$ a witness of $(a_1, \ldots, a_p)$. If $(d_{1j}, \ldots, d_{pj})$ is at a base type, then we take $\lambda \vec{x}.x_j$ as witness. If $(d_{1j}, \ldots, d_{pj})$ have types of rank at most 1, say $\kappa^2$, we have to check, for any $(a_1, \ldots, a_p), (b_1, \ldots, b_p) \in \mathcal{S}^\kappa$ :

$$(d_{1j}(a_1)(b_1), \ldots, d_{pj}(a_p)(b_p)) \in \mathcal{S}^\kappa \ .$$

Since $\vec{a}$ and $\vec{b}$ are at a base type (this is where we use the restriction on types of rank 2 in the statement), by definition of $\mathcal{S}^\kappa$ there are witnesses $N$ and $P$ for them. Then $\lambda \vec{x}.x_j(N\vec{x})(P\vec{x})$ is a witness for $(d_{1j}(a_1)(b_1), \ldots, d_{pj}(a_p)(b_p))$.

The argument to show that $\mathcal{S}$ is $C$-logical is similar to the argument just used (left to the reader).

(3) $\Rightarrow$ (1) Obvious by definition of $\mathcal{S}$. □

If the base domain $D^\kappa$ is finite, then all the $D^\sigma$'s are finite, and the complete behaviour of $f$ can be described by a matrix. By the characterization (2) of theorem 4.5.14, the definability problem is then decidable at rank at most 2: try successively all $C$-logical relations $\mathcal{R}$ (there are finitely many of them).

The following proposition, due to Stoughton [Sto94], paves the way towards a more realistic decision procedure. We call intersection of two logical relations $\mathcal{S}_1$ and $\mathcal{S}_2$ the relation $\mathcal{S}$ defined at $\kappa$ by:

$$\mathcal{S}^\kappa = \mathcal{S}_1^\kappa \cap \mathcal{S}_2^\kappa \ .$$

We write $\mathcal{S} = \mathcal{S}_1 \cap \mathcal{S}_2$. (Notice that $\mathcal{S}^\sigma$ has no reason to be the intersection of $\mathcal{S}_1^\sigma$ and $\mathcal{S}_2^\sigma$ at types of rank $> 0$.) We can similarly define an arbitrary intersection of logical relations. When $C$ consists of constants whose types have at most rank 1, then any intersection of $C$-logical relations is $C$-logical.

**Proposition 4.5.15** *Let $S'$ be the intersection of all the $C$-logical relations satisfying $(\forall j \leq n \ (d_{1j}, \ldots, d_{pj}) \in \mathcal{R}^{\sigma^j})$. Then $S' = S$, where $S$ is the relation defined in theorem 4.5.14(3).*

PROOF. Let $S'$ be the intersection mentioned in the statement. We have $S'^{\kappa} \subseteq S^{\kappa}$, since $S$ satisfies $(\forall j \leq n \ (d_{1j}, \ldots, d_{pj}) \in \mathcal{R}^{\sigma^j})$ (cf. proof of theorem 4.5.14). Conversely, if $(a_1, \ldots, a_p) \in S^{\kappa}$, then, by definition of $S$, there exists an $N$ such that $\forall i \leq p \ [\vdash N](d_{i1}) \cdots (d_{in}) = a_i$, which implies $(a_1, \ldots, a_p) \in S'^{\kappa}$ by the fundamental lemma, and by the definition of $S'$. □

By this proposition, it is enough to progressively construct $S'$, starting from the assumptions that $S'$ contains the vectors $(d_{1j}, \ldots, d_{pj})$ $(j \leq n)$. If the construction terminates without having met $\vec{e}$, then there is no $M$ for $f$ and $\{d_{ij}\}_{i \leq p, j \leq n}$. We illustrate this with an example which will be important in the sequel.

**Very finitary PCF.** We set $C = \{\bot, \top, if \_ then \_\}$. We set $D^{\kappa} = \mathbf{O}$, the flat domain $\{\bot, \top\}$, and we build the model in the category of partial orders and monotonic functions. The meanings of $\vdash \bot : \kappa$ and $\vdash \top : \kappa$ are $\bot \in D^{\kappa}$ and $\top \in D^{\kappa}$. The last constant is a unary test function:

$$if \bot then \ d = \bot \qquad if \top then \ d = d \quad (d \in D).$$

This language is known as Very Finitary PCF (Finitary PCF is coming next, and PCF is the subject of chapter 6). We claim that there is no closed term $M$ in this language such that:

$$[M](\bot)(\top) = \top$$
$$[M](\top)(\bot) = \top$$
$$[M](\bot)(\bot) = \bot.$$

We begin the construction of $S'$. It should contain the two columns $(\bot, \top, \bot)$ and $(\top, \bot, \bot)$. Since it has to be a $C$-logical relation, it also has to contain $(\bot, \bot, \bot)$ and $(\top, \top, \top)$. It is easy to see that this set of pairs makes *if _ then _* invariant. We have completed the definition of $S'$, since we have obtained a $C$-logical relation containing $(\bot, \top, \bot)$ and $(\top, \bot, \bot)$. Since $S'$ does not contain $(\top, \top, \bot)$, there is no $M$ meeting the above specification.

On the other hand, if the decision procedure yields a positive answer, it would be nice to produce the defining term as well. Here is an indication of how this may be done. We refer to [Sto94] for details. We now consider a function $F : (\kappa \to \kappa \to \kappa) \to \kappa$ such that:

$$F(g_1) = \top \quad F(g_2) = \top \quad F(\bot) = \bot,$$

where $g_1$ is a function such that $g_1(\top)(\bot) = \top$, $g_2$ is a function such that $g_2(\bot)(\top) = \top$, and $\bot$ is the constant $\bot$ function. We exhibit a closed term $M$ such that:

$$[M](g_1) = \top \quad [M](g_2) = \top \quad [M](\bot) = \bot.$$

We begin the construction of $S'$ as we did in the previous example, but now we build pairs $(\vec{d}, P)$, where $\vec{d}$ is a member of $S'$, and where $P$ is a term. We start with $((\bot,\bot,\bot),\bot)$, $((\top,\top,\top),\top)$, and $((g_1,g_2,\bot),g)$, where $g$ is a variable of type $\kappa \to \kappa \to \kappa$. By definition of a logical relation, $\mathcal{S}'$ has to contain

$$(g_1(\top)(\bot),g_2(\top)(\bot),\bot(\top)(\bot)) = (\top,\bot,\bot) .$$

We form the pair $((\top,\bot,\bot),g(\top)(\bot))$ to keep track of how we obtained this new vector. Similarly, we obtain $((\bot,\top,\bot),g(\bot)(\top))$. Finally, taking these two new vectors as arguments for $g$, we build the vector which we are seeking:

$$((\top,\top,\bot),g(g(\top)(\bot))(g(\bot)(\top))) .$$

The term $M = \lambda g.g(g(\top)(\bot))(g(\bot)(\top))$ satisfies the requirements, by construction.

**Finitary PCF.** The same counter-example and example also live in the following language, called Finitary PCF. We now set $C = \{\bot, tt, ff, if \_ then \_ else \_\}$. We set $D^\kappa = \mathbf{B}_\bot$, the flat domain $\{\bot, tt, ff\}$. Again, we build the model in the category of partial orders and monotonic functions. The meanings of $\vdash \bot : \kappa$, $\vdash tt : \kappa$, and $\vdash ff : \kappa$ are $\bot \in D^\kappa$, $tt \in D^\kappa$, and $ff \in D^\kappa$. The last constant is the usual conditional:

$$if \perp then \ d \ else \ e = \perp \quad if \ tt \ then \ d \ else \ e = d \quad if \ ff \ then \ d \ else \ e = e .$$

We next give an elegant characterization of the $C$-logical relations for Finitary PCF (also due to Sieber).

**Definition 4.5.16 ((Sieber-)sequential)** *The $C$-logical relations for Finitary PCF and its monotonic function model are called sequential relations. Consider the following $n$-ary relations $\mathcal{S}^n_{A,B}$ over $\mathbf{B}_\bot$, where $A \subseteq B \subseteq \{1,\dots,n\}$:*

$$(d_1,\dots,d_n) \in \mathcal{S}^n_{A,B} \quad \Leftrightarrow \quad (\exists\, i \in A \ \ d_i = \bot) \ or \ (\forall\, i,j \in B \ \ d_i = d_j) .$$

*A Sieber-sequential relation is an $n$-ary logical relation $\mathcal{S}$ such that $\mathcal{S}^\kappa$ is an intersection of relations of the form $\mathcal{S}^n_{A,B}$.*

The word 'sequential' will be justified in section 6.5.

**Theorem 4.5.17** *A logical relation over Finitary PCF is sequential if and only if it is Sieber-sequential.*

PROOF. $(\Leftarrow)$ All base type constants are invariant, since constant vectors trivially satisfy the second disjunct in the definition of $\mathcal{S}^n_{A,B}$. We check only that the conditional is invariant. If its first argument $d = (d_1,\dots,d_n)$ satisfies the first disjunct, or the second disjunct with the common value equal to $\bot$, then the result vector $e = (e_1,\dots,e_n)$ satisfies the same property by strictness of the conditional function. Otherwise, if, say, $d_i = 0$ for all $i \in B$, then the coordinates $e_i$ for $i \in B$ are those of the second argument. Since $A \subseteq B$, this entails $e \in \mathcal{S}^n_{A,B}$.

($\Rightarrow$) Let $\mathcal{R}$ be $n$-ary and sequential, and let $\mathcal{S}$ be the intersection of all $\mathcal{S}_{A,B}^n$'s containing $\mathcal{R}^\kappa$. We prove $\mathcal{S} \subseteq \mathcal{R}^\kappa$. We pick $d = (d_1, \ldots, d_n) \in \mathcal{S}$, and we show, by induction on the size of $C \subseteq \{1, 2, \ldots, n\}$:

$$\exists e = (e_1, \ldots, e_n) \in \mathcal{R}^\kappa \quad (\forall i \in C \; e_i = d_i) \,.$$

If $C = \{i\}$ is a singleton, then we choose $e = (d_i, \ldots, d_i)$. We suppose now that $\sharp C \geq 2$, and we distinguish cases.

1. $d_i = \perp$ for some $i \in C$.

    (a) $\mathcal{R}^\kappa \subseteq \mathcal{S}_{C\setminus\{i\},C}^n$. Then $d \in \mathcal{S}_{C\setminus\{i\},C}^n$, by definition of $\mathcal{S}$, and either $d_k = \perp$ for some $k \in C\setminus\{i\}$, or all $d_j$'s are equal, for $j \in C$. Since $d_i = \perp$, the latter case is rephrased as: all $d_j$'s are $\perp$. Recalling that $\sharp C \geq 2$, we have thus, in either case:

$$\exists k \in C\setminus\{i\} \; d_k = \perp \,.$$

We apply induction to both $C\setminus\{i\}$ and $C\setminus\{k\}$, obtaining $v \in \mathcal{R}^\kappa$ and $w \in \mathcal{R}^\kappa$, respectively. There are again two cases:

      i. If $v_i = d_i (= \perp)$, then $v$ works for $C$.

      ii. If $v_i \neq \perp$, say, $v_i = tt$, consider the term:

$$M = \lambda xy. \; if \; x \; then \; y \; else \; x,$$

and set $f = [\![M]\!]$ and $e = (f(v_1)(w_1), \ldots, f(v_n)(w_n))$. First, $e \in \mathcal{R}^\kappa$ since $\mathcal{R}$ is $C$-logical. Second, we show that $e$ coincides with $d$ over $C$. By definition of $M$, for any $x, y$, we have $f(x)(y) = x$ or $f(x)(y) = y$. This implies that $e$ does the job over $C\setminus\{i, k\}$, over which $v$ and $w$ coincide. Since $v$ coincides with $d$ over $C\setminus\{i\}$, we have $v_k = d_k = \perp$, hence $f(v_k)(w_k) = \perp = d_k$, since $f$ is strict in its first argument. Finally, since $v_i = tt$, we have $f(v_i)(w_i) = w_i = d_i$.

    (b) $\mathcal{R}^\kappa \nsubseteq \mathcal{S}_{C\setminus\{i\},C}^n$: Let $u \in \mathcal{R}^\kappa \setminus \mathcal{S}_{C\setminus\{i\},C}^n$. By definition of $\mathcal{S}_{C\setminus\{i\},C}^n$, there exists $k \in C$ such that:

$$u_k \neq u_i \quad \text{(negation of } \forall j, k \in C \; u_j = u_k)$$
$$u_k \neq \perp \quad \text{(negation of } \exists j \in C\setminus\{i\} \; u_j = \perp) \,.$$

We suppose, say, that $u_k = tt$. Let, as in the previous case, $v$ and $w$ be relative to $C\setminus\{i\}$ and $C\setminus\{k\}$, respectively. We now consider the term $N = \lambda xyz. \; if \; x \; then \; y \; else \; z$, and we set:

$$g = [\![N]\!] \quad \text{and} \quad e = (g(u_1)(v_1)(w_1), \ldots, g(u_n)(v_n)(w_n)) \,.$$

We check that $e$ works for $C$. Let $j \in C\setminus\{i\}$, since $u \notin \mathcal{S}_{C\setminus\{i\},C}^n$, we have $u_j \neq \perp$. Hence $g(u_j)(v_j)(w_j)$ passes the test, and is either $v_j$ or $w_j$. For $j \in C\setminus\{i, k\}$, both are equal to $d_j$. Suppose now that $j = k$. We have $g(u_k)(v_k)(w_k) = v_k = d_k$. Finally, let $j = i$. We know from above that $u_i \neq u_k$. If $u_i = \perp$, then $g(u_i)(v_i)(w_i) = \perp = d_i$ since $g$ is strict in its first argument. If $u_i \neq \perp$, then $u_i = ff$, hence $g(u_i)(v_i)(w_i) = w_i = d_i$.

2. $\forall i \in C \ d_i \neq \bot$. We treat this case more briefly. There are two cases:

(a) $\mathcal{R}^\kappa \subseteq \mathcal{S}^n_{C,C}$. Then $d \in \mathcal{S}^n_{C,C}$ by the definition of $\mathcal{S}$, which forces $d$ to be a constant vector by the assumption ($\forall i \in C \ d_i \neq \bot$). Hence we can take $e = d$.

(b) $\mathcal{R}^\kappa \nsubseteq \mathcal{S}^n_{C,C}$. We take $u \in \mathcal{R}^\kappa$ such that $u_i \neq \bot$ for all $i \in C$ and such that $u_i \neq u_j$ for some $i, j$ in $C$, say, $u_i = tt$ and $u_j = ff$. Let:

$$C_1 = \{k \in C \mid u_k = u_i\} \quad C_2 = \{k \in C \mid u_k = u_j\} \ .$$

We can apply induction to $C_1$ and $C_2$, obtaining $v$ and $w$. Then the proof is completed with the help of $N = \lambda xyz. \ if \ x \ then \ y \ else \ z$. □

In the next exercise we propose an application of Sieber's technique to a proof of non-definability of a functional known as Curien's 'third counter-example' [Cur86, section 4.4] (see the discussion at the end of section 14.3).

**Exercise 4.5.18** *Show that there is no term of Finitary PCF of type* $(\kappa \to \kappa \to \kappa) \to \kappa$ *such that:*

$$F(g_1) = tt \quad F(g_2) = tt \quad F(g_3) = tt \quad F(\bot) = \bot \ ,$$

*where* $g_1, g_2, g_3$ *are such that:*

$$g_1(\bot)(ff) = tt \quad g_1(ff)(tt) = tt$$
$$g_2(tt)(\bot) = tt$$
$$g_3(\bot)(tt) = tt \ .$$

*Hints: (1) Notice that* $(0, 0, 0, \bot) \notin \mathcal{S}^4_{\{1,2,3\},\{1,2,3,4\}}$. *(2) The relations* $\mathcal{S}^4_{\{1,2\},\{1,2\}}$ *and* $\mathcal{S}^4_{\{1,3\},\{1,3\}}$ *arise when trying to prove that* $(g_1, g_2, g_3, \bot) \in \mathcal{S}^4_{\{1,2,3\},\{1,2,3,4\}}$.

**Exercise 4.5.19** *Let* $g_1, g_2$ *be the functions whose minimal points are described by:*

$$g_1(ff)(\bot)(\bot) = ff \quad g_1(tt)(tt)(tt) = tt$$
$$g_2(\bot)(ff)(\bot) = ff \quad g_2(tt)(tt)(ff) = tt \ .$$

*Show that there is no closed term* $M$ *of Finitary PCF of type* $(\kappa \to \kappa \to \kappa \to \kappa) \to \kappa$ *such that* $g_1$ *and* $g_2$ *are the only minimal points of* $[\![M]\!]$. *Generalize this to (uncurried) first order functions* $g_1$ *et* $g_2$ *(of the same type) whose minimal points are described by:*

$$g_1(A_0) = a_0 \quad g_1(B_0) = b_0$$
$$g_2(A_1) = a_0 \quad g_2(B_1) = b_1 \ ,$$

*where* $a_0 \neq b_0$, $a_0 \neq b_1$, $A_0 \uparrow A_1$ *(i.e.,* $\exists A \ A \geq A_0, A_1$*),* $B_0 \nmid B_1$, $B_0 \nmid A_1$ *and* $A_0 \nmid B_1$. *Hint: Find* $g_3$ *such that* $(g_1, g_2, g_3) \in \mathcal{S}^3_{\{1,2\},\{1,2,3\}}$.

On the negative side, it has been shown by Loader that the definability problem (at arbitrary ranks) is undecidable for Finitary PCF [Loa97] (see exercise 6.4.8).[3]

---

[3]In earlier work, Loader had shown that definability is undecidable for 'finitary $\lambda$-calculus', that is, $\lambda$-calculus without constants, and whose basic types are interpreted by finite sets [Loa94].

# 4.6    Interpretation of the untyped λ-calculus

We recall the grammar and the basic computation rule of the untyped λ-calculus (cf. chapter 2).

$$Terms: \qquad v ::= x \mid y \mid \dots$$
$$M ::= v \mid \lambda v.M \mid MM$$

$$\beta\text{-reduction}: \quad (\lambda x.M)N \to M[N/x] \ .$$

In order to use the work done in the typed case, it is useful to represent the untyped calculus as a typed calculus with a special type $\delta$, and the following typing rules:

$$\frac{x : \delta \in \Gamma}{\Gamma \vdash x : \delta} \qquad \frac{\Gamma, x : \delta \vdash M : \delta}{\Gamma \vdash \lambda x : \delta.M : \delta} \qquad \frac{\Gamma \vdash M : \delta \quad \Gamma \vdash N : \delta}{\Gamma \vdash MN : \delta} \ .$$

Observe that if a type $\delta \to \delta$ could contract into a type $\delta$ in the introduction rule, and vice versa, if the type $\delta$ could expand into a type $\delta \to \delta$ in the elimination rule, then we would have the same rules as in the simply typed λ-calculus. In other words, we can apply the standard apparatus provided we have a type whose elements can be seen both as arguments and as functions. The following definition makes this intuition formal.

**Definition 4.6.1** *An object $D$ in a CCC* **C** *is called* reflexive *if there is a pair $(i, j)$, called a* retraction pair *(or simply a* retraction*), such that:*

$$i : D^D \to D, \quad j : D \to D^D, \quad j \circ i = id \ .$$

*We write $D^D \lhd D$ to indicate the existence of a retraction pair.*

The above definition generalizes definition 3.2.4: a reflexive object in **Cpo** is exactly what we have called there a reflexive domain. In section 3.1 we have seen how to use domain theoretical methods to build reflexive objects in that category. Next, we describe a different construction with a set theoretical flavour that serves the same purpose. The resulting models are usually called *graph models*.∎

**Example 4.6.2 (graph model)** *Let $A$ be a non-empty set equipped with an injective coding $\langle \_, \_ \rangle : \mathcal{P}_{fin}(A) \times A \to A$. In the following we denote with $a, b, \dots$ elements of $A$; with $\alpha, \beta, \dots$ elements of $\mathcal{P}_{fin}(A)$; and with $X, Y, \dots$ elements of the powerset $\mathcal{P}(A)$. We define for $f \in \mathbf{Dcpo}[\mathcal{P}(A), \mathcal{P}(A)]$:*

$$Graph(f) = \{\langle \alpha, a \rangle \mid a \in f(\alpha)\} \in \mathcal{P}(A) \ .$$

*Vice versa for $X \in \mathcal{P}(A)$, we define $Fun(X) : \mathcal{P}(A) \to \mathcal{P}(A)$ as follows:*

$$Fun(X)(Y) = \{a \mid \exists \alpha \ (\langle \alpha, a \rangle \in X \text{ and } \alpha \subseteq Y)\} \ .$$

**Proposition 4.6.3** *Given any non-empty set $A$ with an injective coding $\langle \_, \_ \rangle : \mathcal{P}_{fin}(A) \times A \to A$, the complete lattice $\mathcal{P}(A)$, ordered by inclusion, is a reflexive object in* **Dcpo***, via the morphisms Graph and Fun.*

PROOF. We take the following elementary steps:

- *Graph* is monotonic. $f \leq g \Rightarrow Graph(f) \subseteq Graph(g)$.

- *Graph* preserves directed lub's, namely $\{f_i\}_{i \in I}$ directed implies $Graph(\bigvee_{i \in I}\{f_i\})$ $\subseteq \bigcup_{i \in I} Graph(f_i)$. We observe $\langle \alpha, a \rangle \in Graph(\bigvee_{i \in I}\{f_i\})$ iff $a \in (\bigvee_{i \in I}\{f_i\})(\alpha) = \bigcup_{i \in I} f_i(\alpha)$ iff $a \in f_i(\alpha)$, for some $i \in I$.

- *Fun* is monotonic in both arguments. If $X \subseteq X'$, $Y \subseteq Y'$ then $Fun(X)(Y) \subseteq Fun(X')(Y')$.

- *Fun* is continuous in both arguments. If $\{X_i\}_{i \in I}$, $\{Y_j\}_{j \in J}$ are directed then $Fun(\bigcup_{i \in I} X_i)(\bigcup_{j \in J} Y_j) \subseteq \bigcup_{i \in I, j \in J} Fun(X_i)(Y_j)$.

- $(Graph, Fun)$ is a retraction. $Fun(Graph(f))(X) = f(X)$. This is the only condition that depends on the assumption that the coding is injective. □

The construction of the graph model is parametric with respect to the choice of the set $A$ and of the coding $\langle \_, \_ \rangle$. If we define a coding $\langle \_, \_ \rangle : \mathcal{P}_{fin}(\omega) \times \omega \to \omega$ where $\omega$ is the collection of natural numbers, then we obtain a family of reflexive objects also known as $\mathcal{P}(\omega)$ graph models.

**Exercise 4.6.4** *Build an example of injective coding* $\langle \_, \_ \rangle : \mathcal{P}_{fin}(\omega) \times \omega \to \omega$.

The so-called $D_A$ graph models are obtained by a 'free construction' of the coding function. Let $At$ be a non empty set of atoms. We define $A$ as the set of 'terms' generated as follows:

> if $a \in At$, then $a$ is a term,
> if $a$ is a term and if $\alpha$ is a finite set of terms, then $(\alpha, a)$ is a term.

**Exercise 4.6.5** *Verify that* $\langle \_, \_ \rangle : \mathcal{P}_{fin}(A) \times A \to A$ *defined as* $\langle \alpha, a \rangle = (\alpha, a)$ *is the desired coding.*

The graph models, and particularly the free construction just given, are related to the filter model constructions of chapter 3, as the following exercise based on [Kri91] shows. The basic idea is to read $\langle \{a_1, \ldots, a_n\}, a \rangle$ as $a_1 \wedge \cdots \wedge a_n \to a$.

**Exercise\* 4.6.6** *Consider the following variant of the construction of graph models. We now suppose that $A$ is a preorder $(A, \leq)$, we preorder $\mathcal{P}_{fin}(A)$ by the relation $\alpha \leq_l \beta$ iff $(\forall a \in \alpha \ \exists b \in \beta \ a \leq b)$ (this is called the lower preorder, see theorem 9.1.8), and we replace $\mathcal{P}(A)$ by the set $Dcl(A)$ of lower subsets of $A$ (this is called the lower set completion of $A$, see lemma 10.2.4). (1) Adapt proposition 4.6.3 to the present setting. Hint: The following compatibility condition has to be imposed: if $\langle \alpha, a \rangle \leq \langle \beta, b \rangle$, then $a \leq b$ and $\beta \leq_l \alpha$ (cf. the condition (Frefl) in proposition 3.3.18). (2) The full benefit of this preorder enrichment comes here. Show that the retraction is actually an isomorphism (and hence that we have a model of $\beta\eta$, see theorem 4.6.8), provided the condition stated in the hint for (1) is actually an iff condition, and that $\langle \_, \_ \rangle$ is surjective up to the equivalence induced by the preorder. After Krivine, such models are called initial segment models ('initial segment' being synonymous for 'lower set'). (3) Provide suitable free constructions of initial segment models isomorphic to the $D^\infty$ models considered in section 3.4. Hint: In constructing 'terms' as above, one has to identify $\langle \emptyset, a \rangle$ and $a$, for any atom $a$.*

| (Asmp) | $[\![x_1 : \delta, \ldots, x_n : \delta \vdash x_i : \delta]\!]$ | $=$ | $\pi_{n,i}$ |
|---|---|---|---|
| $(\to_I)$ | $[\![\Gamma \vdash \lambda x : \delta.M : \delta]\!]$ | $=$ | $i \circ \Lambda([\![\Gamma, x : \delta \vdash M : \delta]\!])$ |
| $(\to_E)$ | $[\![\Gamma \vdash MN : \delta]\!]$ | $=$ | $ev \circ \langle j \circ [\![\Gamma \vdash M : \delta]\!], [\![\Gamma \vdash N : \delta]\!] \rangle$ |

Figure 4.7: Interpretation of the untyped λ-calculus in a CCC

---

Having verified the existence of various techniques to build reflexive objects in CCC's, we introduce in figure 4.7 the interpretation of the untyped $\lambda\beta$-calculus in those structures. This is the same as the interpretation of the simply typed λ-calculus up to insertion of the maps $i, j$ which collapse the hierarchy of types to $D$. The notion of λ-theory (cf. definition 4.4.1) is readily adapted to the untyped case.

**Definition 4.6.7** *A collection of judgments of the shape $\Gamma \vdash M = N : \delta$ such that $\Gamma \vdash M : \delta$ and $\Gamma \vdash N : \delta$ is called an untyped λ-theory if it is closed under the rules obtained from figure 4.6 by replacing all types with the type $\delta$. The rule $(\eta)$ is not included unless explicitly stated.*

Every interpretation induces an untyped λ-theory.

**Theorem 4.6.8** *Let **C** be a CCC with a reflexive object $D$ and $[\![\ ]\!]$ be an interpretation of the untyped λ-calculus defined over **C** in the sense of figure 4.7. Then the following collection is an untyped λ-theory:*

$$Th(\mathbf{C}) = \{\Gamma \vdash M = N : \delta \mid \Gamma \vdash M : \delta, \Gamma \vdash N : \delta, [\![\Gamma \vdash M : \delta]\!] = [\![\Gamma \vdash N : \delta]\!]\} \ .$$

*If the retraction making $D$ a reflexive object is in fact an isomorphism, then the rule $(\eta)$ is also valid.*

PROOF HINT. The proof of this result follows the same schema as in the typed case. We just show how $i$ and $j$ cancel each other. We have, setting $f = [\![\Gamma, x : \delta \vdash M : \delta]\!]$ and $g = [\![\Gamma \vdash N : \delta]\!]$:

$$[\![\Gamma \vdash (\lambda x : \delta.M)N : \delta]\!] = ev \circ \langle j \circ (i \circ \Lambda(f)), g \rangle = ev \circ \langle \Lambda(f), g \rangle \ .$$

$\square$

Next we describe a general construction, called *Karoubi envelope*, that given a reflexive object $D$ in a CCC produces a new CCC of *retractions over $D$*.

**Definition 4.6.9 (Karoubi envelope)** *Let **C** be a CCC and $D$ be a reflexive object in **C**. The Karoubi envelope is the category **Ret**$(D)$ of retractions over $D$ defined as follows:*

$$\mathbf{Ret}(D) \quad = \quad \{r : D \to D \mid r \circ r = r\}$$
$$\mathbf{Ret}(D)[r, s] \quad = \quad \{f : D \to D \mid s \circ f \circ r = f\} \ .$$

**Theorem 4.6.10** *If* **C** *is a CCC and* $(D, i, j)$ *is a reflexive object in* **C**, *then* **Ret**$(D)$ *is a CCC.*

PROOF. First, it is easy to check that **Ret**$(D)$ is a category, thanks to the following easy observation:

$$f : r \to s \Leftrightarrow (f \circ r = f \text{ and } s \circ f = f) .$$

The rest of the proof is a matter of translating λ-calculus encodings into the categorical language and checking that everything goes through. Here we just remind the reader of the encoding. When we write λ-terms for building morphisms it is intended that one has to take the *interpretations* of such λ-terms.

In the untyped λβ-calculus we can define a fixpoint combinator $Y$ (cf. example 2.1.11), as well as terms for pairing and projections:

$$\langle \_, \_ \rangle = \lambda x.\lambda y.\lambda p.pxy, \quad p_1 = \lambda p.p(\lambda x.\lambda y.x), \quad p_2 = \lambda p.p(\lambda x.\lambda y.y) ,$$

so that $p_1\langle x, y \rangle = x$, $p_2\langle x, y \rangle = y$. These terms describe morphisms in **C**, e.g., we can consider $\langle \_, \_ \rangle$ as a description of the morphism $[\![ x : \delta, y : \delta \vdash \lambda p.pxy : \delta ]\!]$ : $D \times D \to D$.

- Terminal object. In a CCC we have a unique morphism $* : D \to 1$. Moreover if we take $Y(\lambda x.x)$ we get a morphism from 1 to $D$. From this follows $1 \lhd D$. Then we take the retraction determined by 1 as the terminal object in **Ret**$(D)$.

- Product. The pairing and projections defined above show that $D \times D \lhd D$ via the retraction $(\langle \_, \_ \rangle, \lambda x.(\pi_1(x), \pi_2(x)))$. If $r$ and $s$ are retractions then we define their product as:

$$r \times s = \lambda x.\langle r(\pi_1(x)), s(\pi_2(x)) \rangle .$$

- Exponent. If $r$ and $s$ are retractions then we define their exponent as:

$$r \to s = \lambda x.i(s \circ j(x) \circ r) .$$

$\square$

**Remark 4.6.11** *The Karoubi envelope construction can also serve to reverse the previous theorem 4.6.8, namely to show that every untyped λ-theory is the theory induced by a reflexive object in a CCC; a result very much in the spirit of theorem 4.4.4. The construction is similar to that described above in the proof of theorem 4.6.10. The difference is that, rather than starting with a reflexive object in a CCC, one starts from a λ-theory and the related monoid of terms and composition (see [Sco80] for details).*

*In a similar vein, one can apply the Karoubi envelope construction to relate λ-models (cf. definition 3.2.2) to reflexive objects. More precisely, given a λ-model, one may build its Karoubi envelope, which turns out to be a CCC with enough points (cf. definition 4.5.4) and with a reflexive object. Conversely, given a reflexive object $D$ in a CCC* **C**, **C**$[1, D]$ *can be turned into a λ-model. Moreover, composing the two transformations yields a λ-model which is isomorphic to the original λ-model. We refer to [Bar84, chapter 5] for details on these correspondences.*

As an application, we use $\mathbf{Ret}(D)$ as a frame for an abstract formulation of Engeler's theorem [Eng81, Eng95] on the embedding of algebras in λ-models. In the following, $\mathbf{C}$ is a CCC with enough points (cf. definition 4.5.4) and $D$ is a reflexive object in $\mathbf{C}$. Let $\Sigma \equiv \{\sigma_i^{n_i}\}_{i \in I}$ be a finite signature, where $n_i$ is the arity of $\sigma_i$. We are interested in a notion of $\Sigma$-algebra in which the carriers are objects in $\mathbf{Ret}(D)$ and the operators are maps in $\mathbf{Ret}(D)$ of the appropriate type.

**Definition 4.6.12 ($\Sigma_D$-algebra)** *A $\Sigma_D$-algebra is a pair $(r, \{f_i\}_{i \in I})$ where $r \in \mathbf{Ret}(D)$, $f_i : D^{n_i} \to D$ and $r \circ f_i \circ (r \times \cdots \times r) = f_i$, for all $i \in I$. A morphism of $\Sigma_D$-algebras $h : (r, \{f_i\}_{i \in I}) \to (r', \{g_i\}_{i \in I})$ is a morphism $h : r \to r'$ in $\mathbf{Ret}(D)$ such that $h \circ f_i = g_i \circ (h \times \cdots \times h)$, for all $i \in I$.*

**Theorem 4.6.13 (embedding)** *There exists a $\Sigma_D$-algebra $(id, \{F_i\}_{i \in I})$ such that any other $\Sigma_D$-algebra $(r, \{f_i\}_{i \in I})$ can be embedded into it by a monomorphism.*

PROOF. For the sake of simplicity we just consider the case $\Sigma = \{\sigma^2\}$. Assume that $\langle \_, \_ \rangle$, and $\pi_1, \pi_2$ are, respectively, the pairing and the projections definable in the λ-calculus as in the proof of theorem 4.6.10. We take $F = \lambda(x_1, x_2).(\pi_2 x_1)x_2$. We note that recursive definitions are available in the untyped λ-calculus thanks to the fixpoint combinator. Given the $\Sigma_D$-algebra $(r, \{f\})$ we recursively define a morphism $\rho : D \to D$ as follows:

$$\rho(a) = \langle a, \lambda x.\rho(f(a, \pi_1 x)) \rangle \ .$$

The basic idea of the embedding is to put into the data the information on the behaviour of the operations defined on them. In the first place, let us observe that $\rho$ is a mono as (using the enough points hypothesis):

$$\rho(a) = \rho(b) \ \Rightarrow \ a = \pi_1(\rho(a)) = \pi_2(\rho(b)) = b \ .$$

Clearly $\rho \circ r : r \to id$ in $\mathbf{Ret}(D)$ as $\rho \circ r = id \circ \rho \circ r \circ r$. Also since $r(f(x,y)) = f(x,y) = f(rx, ry)$ we have:

$$
\begin{aligned}
F(\rho(ra), \rho(rb)) &= (\lambda x.\rho(f(ra, \pi_1 x)))\rho(rb) &=& \ \rho(f(ra, \pi_1\rho(rb))) \\
&= \rho(f(ra, rb)) &=& \ (\rho \circ r)(f(a,b)).
\end{aligned}
$$

Therefore $\rho \circ r : (r, \{f\}) \to (id, \{F\})$ is a morphism of $\Sigma_D$-algebras. □

**Exercise 4.6.14** *Extend the proof just given to an arbitrary finite signature. Hint: Given $\Sigma = \{f_1, f_2, f_3, \ldots\}$, define $\rho(a) = \langle a, \langle \underline{f_1}, \langle \underline{f_2}, \langle \underline{f_3}, \ldots$ where:*

$$
\underline{f_i} = \begin{cases} \lambda x_1 \ldots \lambda x_j.\rho(f_i a)(\pi_1 x_1) \cdots (\pi_1 x_j) & \text{if } f_i \text{ has arity } j+1 \\ a & \text{if } f_i \text{ has arity } 0 \ . \end{cases}
$$

# 5

# CCC's of algebraic dcpo's

In this chapter, we provide a finer analysis of algebraicity. The central result –
which was conjectured by Plotkin and was first proved in [Smy83a] – is that there
exists a maximum cartesian closed full subcategory (full sub-CCC) of $\omega$**Acpo** (the
category of $\omega$-algebraic cpo's). Jung has extended this result: he has characterized
the maximal cartesian closed full subcategories of **Acpo** and **Adcpo** (and of
$\omega$**Adcpo** as well).

In section 5.1, we define continuous dcpo's, which are dcpo's where approximations exist without being necessarily compact. Continuous lattices have been
investigated in depth from a mathematical perspective [GHK+80]. Our interest
in continuous dcpo's arises from the fact that retracts of algebraic dcpo's are not
algebraic in general, but are continuous. Much of the technical work involved in
our quest of maximal full cartesian closed subcategories of (d)cpo's involves retracts. In section 5.2, we introduce two cartesian closed categories: the category of
profinite dcpo's and the category of L-domains, both with continuous functions as
morphisms. In section 5.3, we show that the algebraic L-domains and the bifinite
domains form the two maximal cartesian closed full subcategories of **Acpo**, and
derive Smyth's result for $\omega$**Acpo** with little extra work. In section 5.4, we treat
more sketchily the situation for **Adcpo**. The material of sections 5.3 and 5.4 is
based on [Jun88]. In section 5.5, we show a technical result needed in section 5.3:
a partial order is a dcpo if and only if all its well-founded subsets have a lub.

## 5.1   Continuous dcpo's

In order to define algebraic dcpo's, we first introduced the notion of compact
element, and then we defined algebraicity. The definition of continuous dcpo's is
more direct, and more general.

**Definition 5.1.1 (continuous dcpo)** *Let $D$ be a dcpo. For elements $x, y \in D$,
we say that $x$ is way-below $y$, and write $x \ll y$, if*

$$\Delta \text{ directed, } y \leq \bigvee \Delta \Rightarrow \exists \delta \in \Delta \ x \leq \delta .$$

*$D$ is called continuous if, for any $x$ in $D$, $\Downarrow x = \{y \mid y \ll x\}$ is directed and has
$x$ as lub.*

Notice that by definition $x$ is compact iff $x \ll x$. We leave the proof of the following easy properties as an exercise:

$$x \ll y \qquad \Rightarrow \quad x \leq y$$
$$x' \leq x \ll y \leq y' \Rightarrow \quad x' \ll y' \; .$$

Clearly, algebraic dcpo's are continuous, but the converse does not hold.

**Exercise 5.1.2** *Show that the interval* $[0,1]$ *of real numbers is continuous but not algebraic. Hint: Prove that* $x \ll y$ *iff* $x = 0$ *or* $x < y$.

**Exercise 5.1.3** *Let* $\mathbf{B}X$ *be the partial order defined in exercise 1.2.7. Show that* $(x,r) \ll (y,s)$ *iff* $d(x,y) < r - s$. *Show that* $\mathbf{B}X$ *is continuous.*

**Exercise 5.1.4** *Endow the set of closed intervals* $[a,b]$ *of the real line with a suitable order turning it into a continuous dcpo whose subset of maximal elements endowed with the induced Scott topology is homeomorphic to the real line (cf. exercises 1.2.7 and 5.1.3).*

**Lemma 5.1.5** *In a continuous dcpo,* $x \ll y$ *holds iff the following implication holds:*

$$\Delta \text{ directed}, \; y = \bigvee \Delta \Rightarrow \exists \delta \in \Delta \; x \leq \delta \; .$$

PROOF. Suppose $(y = \bigvee \Delta \Rightarrow \exists \delta \in \Delta \; x \leq \delta)$, for all $\Delta, y$. Since $y = \bigvee(\Downarrow y)$, we have $x \leq y'$ for some $y' \ll y$. Hence $x \ll y$ since $x \leq y' \ll y$. $\qquad \square$

**Lemma 5.1.6** *Let* $D$ *be a dcpo and* $x \in D$. *If* $\Delta \subseteq \Downarrow x$ *is directed and* $x = \bigvee \Delta$, *then* $\Downarrow x$ *is directed and* $x = \bigvee(\Downarrow x)$.

PROOF. If $y \ll x$, $y' \ll x$, then by definition $y \leq a$, $y' \leq a'$ for some $a, a' \in \Delta$. By directedness we have $a, a' \leq y''$ for some $y'' \in \Delta$. Hence $y, y' \leq y'' \in \Downarrow x$. The inequality $x \leq \bigvee(\Downarrow x)$ follows from the obvious inequality $\bigvee \Delta \leq \bigvee(\Downarrow x)$. $\qquad \square$

The density property of the real line is generalized as follows.

**Lemma 5.1.7 (interpolation)** *In a continuous dcpo* $D$, *if* $x \ll y$ , *then there exists* $z \in D$ *such that* $x \ll z \ll y$.

PROOF. Consider $\Delta = \{a \in D \mid \exists a' \in D \; a \ll a' \ll y\}$. If we show that $\Delta$ is directed and $\bigvee \Delta = y$, then we can conclude, since by definition $x \ll y$ implies $x \leq a$ for some $a \in \Delta$, hence $x \in \Delta$. We show that $\Delta$ is non-empty. Since $\Downarrow y$ is directed, it is not empty, so we can find at least an $a' \ll y$, and in turn, by directedness of $\Downarrow a'$, we can find at least an $a \ll a'$. Suppose that $a \ll a' \ll y$ and $b \ll b' \ll y$. By directedness, there exists $c' \in D$ such that $a', b' \leq c' \ll y$. Hence $a, b \ll c'$, and by directedness again $a, b \leq c \ll c'$ for some $c$, which is in $\Delta$ since $c \ll c' \ll y$. Hence $\Delta$ is directed. Since $a \ll a' \ll y$ implies $a \ll y$, we have $\bigvee \Delta \leq \bigvee \Downarrow y$. Conversely, if $y' \ll y$, then $\Downarrow y' \subseteq \Delta$, hence $\bigvee \Downarrow y = \bigvee_{y' \in \Downarrow y} \bigvee \Downarrow y' \leq \bigvee \Delta$. $\qquad \square$

**Lemma 5.1.8** *In a continuous dcpo* $D$, *minimal upper bounds (mub's) of finite sets of compact elements are compact.*

PROOF. Let $A \subseteq \mathcal{K}(D)$ be finite, and $x \in MUB(A)$. Let $a \in A$. Since $a \ll a \leq x$, we have $a \ll x$. By directedness of $\Downarrow x$, there exists $x' \in (\Downarrow x) \cap UB(A)$. Then $x' \leq x$ and $x \in MUB(A)$ imply $x' = x$. Finally, $x = x' \ll x$ means exactly that $x$ is compact. □

We move on to retractions and projections. Recall that a retraction is an idempotent function $r : D \to D$, i.e., $r$ is such that $r \circ r$ (cf. theorem 4.6.10). The image of $r$, endowed with the induced ordering, is called a retract of $D$.

**Definition 5.1.9 (projection)** *Let $D$ be a dcpo. If a retraction $r : D \to D$ is such that $r \leq id$, we say that $r$ is a projection.*

Linking up with definition 3.1.2, any injection-projection pair $(i,j) : D \to_{ip} D'$ induces a projection $i \circ j$ on $D'$. Projections are determined by their images.

**Proposition 5.1.10** *For two projections $p$, $p'$ over the same dcpo $D$, one has $p \leq p'$ iff $p(D) \subseteq p'(D)$.*

PROOF. Suppose $p \leq p'$. If $y \in p(D)$, then $y = p(y) \leq p'(y) \leq y$ since $p \leq p' \leq id$, hence $y = p'(y) \in p'(D)$. Conversely, notice that for any projection $p$ and any $x \in D$ one has $p(x) = \max\{y \in p(D) \mid y \leq x\}$. Then $p \leq p'$ follows obviously. □

**Lemma 5.1.11** *Let $D$ be a dcpo.*

(1) *Let $x \in D$. Then $\downarrow x = r_x(D)$ is a retract of $D$, where:*

$$r_x(y) = \begin{cases} y & \text{if } y \leq x \\ x & \text{otherwise}. \end{cases}$$

(2) *Let $d \in \mathcal{K}(D)$. Then $\uparrow d = s_d(D)$ is a retract of $D$, where:*

$$s_d(x) = \begin{cases} x & \text{if } x \geq d \\ d & \text{otherwise}. \end{cases}$$

PROOF. (1) We check that $r_x$ is continuous. If $\bigvee \Delta \leq x$, then $\forall \delta \in \Delta \ \delta \leq x$, hence $r_x(\bigvee \Delta) = \bigvee \Delta = \bigvee r_x(\Delta)$. If $\bigvee \Delta \not\leq x$, then $\exists \delta \in \Delta \ \delta \not\leq x$. Then we have $r_x(\delta) = x$, which implies $\bigvee r_x(\Delta) = x = r_x(\bigvee \Delta)$.

(2) If $\bigvee \Delta \geq d$, then $\exists \delta \in \Delta \ d \leq \delta$, by compactness. We set $\Delta' = \Delta \cap (\uparrow \delta)$; since obviously $s_d(\bigvee \Delta') = \bigvee s_d(\Delta')$, we deduce $s_d(\bigvee \Delta) = \bigvee s_d(\Delta)$. If $\bigvee \Delta \not\geq d$, then $\forall \delta \in \Delta \ \delta \not\geq d$, so that $s_d(\bigvee \Delta) = d$ and $s_d(\Delta) = \{d\}$, hence $s_d(\bigvee \Delta) = \bigvee s_d(\Delta)$. □

Retractions are at the heart of our interest in continuous dcpo's. Indeed, retracts of algebraic dcpo's are not algebraic in general, but only continuous (see exercise 5.1.13).

**Proposition 5.1.12 (continuous retracts)** *A retract $r(D)$ of a dcpo $D$ is a subdcpo, i.e., $r(D)$ is a cpo whose directed lub's are those in $D$. If $D$ is continuous, then $r(D)$ is continuous.*

PROOF. Let $\Delta \subseteq r(D)$ be directed. Then $r(\bigvee \Delta) = \bigvee r(\Delta) = \bigvee \Delta$, since $\forall \delta \in \Delta \; r(\delta) = \delta$. Suppose that $x \ll y \in r(D)$. If $y \leq \bigvee \Delta$, with $\Delta \subseteq r(D)$, then $x \ll y$ implies $x \leq \delta$ for some $\delta \in \Delta$; hence $r(x) \leq r(\delta) = \delta$. Thus $r(x)$ is way-below $y$ in $r(D)$. Since $y = r(y) = r(\bigvee \Downarrow y) = \bigvee\{r(x) \mid x \ll y\}$, we conclude by lemma 5.1.6. $\qquad\square$

**Exercise 5.1.13** *Show that any continuous dcpo $D$ is isomorphic to a projection of $Ide(D)$.*

We end the section with a topological exercise. Continuous lattices were met (and named so) by Scott in his quest of spaces whose topology could be entirely understood from an underlying partial order [Sco72, GHK+80].

**Exercise 5.1.14** *Let $D$ be a continuous dcpo. Show the following properties:*

(1) *$\Uparrow x$ is Scott open, and these open sets form a basis of Scott topology.*

(2) *If $D$ is a complete lattice, then $\forall x \in D \; x = \bigvee\{\bigwedge U \mid x \in U\}$.*

(3) *$x \ll y \Leftrightarrow y \in (\uparrow x)^\circ$ (the interior of $\uparrow x$).*

**Exercise\* 5.1.15 (injective spaces)** *A topological space $D$ is called injective if whenever $X, Y \subseteq X$, and $f : Y \to D$ are given, with $X$ a topological space and $f$ continuous for the induced subspace topology, there exists a continuous extension $\overline{f} : X \to D$ of $f$. Show that the following properties are equivalent for a $T_0$ space:*

(1) *$D$ is injective.*

(2) *$D$ is a retract of a product of copies of $\mathbf{O}$.*

(3) *$D$ is a continuous lattice endowed with its Scott topology.*

*Hints: Every space $X$ is homeomorphic to a subspace of a product $\Pi_{U \in \Omega X} \mathbf{O}$ of copies of $\mathbf{O}$. An injective subspace $Y$ of a space $X$ is a retract of $X$: take $\overline{id_Y} : X \to Y$. $\mathbf{O}$ is continuous, and continuous lattices are stable under products and retractions (cf. proposition 5.1.12). If $D$ is a continuous lattice, $Y \subseteq X$, and $f : Y \to D$, then define $\overline{f}$ by: $\overline{f}(x) = \bigvee\{\bigwedge\{f(y) \mid y \in Y \cap U\} \mid x \in U\}$.*

## 5.2  Bifinite domains and L-domains

Recall that, if $D$ and $E$ are algebraic, then the step functions $d \to e$ are compact (lemma 1.4.8), but $D \to E$ need not be algebraic (exercise 1.4.15). One way to ensure algebraicity is to impose bounded completeness (cf. theorem 1.4.12). But it is not the only way, nor a 'minimal' one, to reach this goal.

**Definition 5.2.1** *Let $(P, \leq)$ be a preorder, and let $A \subseteq P$. The set $MUB(A)$ of minimal upper bounds (mub's) of $A$ is called complete if*

$$\forall y \in UB(A) \; \exists x \in MUB(A) \; x \leq y \,.$$

Consider a continuous function $f$, and step functions $d \to e \leq f$, $d' \to e' \leq f$. We want to construct a compact upper bound $h$ of $d \to e$ and $d' \to e'$ such that $h \leq f$. It turns out that there are essentially two ways to achieve this. We may assume $d \uparrow d'$ as otherwise $(d \to e) \vee (d' \to e')$ exists trivially.

(1) In section 1.4, we focused on $E$ and required bounded completeness of the codomain. In fact a local form of bounded completeness is enough. Namely, all we need is that a pair like $(e, e')$, which is bounded by $f(x)$ (where $x$ is an upper bound of $d, d'$), has a unique minimal upper bound under $f(x)$. If we denote it by $e \vee_{f(x)} e'$, then we obtain the desired upper bound as the following variant of the function considered in section 1.4:

$$h(x) = \begin{cases} e \vee_{f(x)} e' & \text{if } x \geq d \text{ and } x \geq d' \\ e & \text{if } x \geq d \text{ and } x \not\geq d' \\ e' & \text{if } x \not\geq d \text{ and } x \geq d' \\ \bot & \text{otherwise} . \end{cases}$$

(2) One may instead focus on $D$. Suppose that $MUB(d, d')$ is complete. Then we may choose $e''$ such that $e \leq e''$, $e' \leq e''$ and $e'' \leq f(d'')$ for each $d'' \in MUB(d, d')$, and set $h_1(d'') = e''$. In general, one has to consider in turn the compatible pairs $d_1'', d_2'' \in MUB(d, d')$, leading to the construction of a new function $h_2$, and so on. At each step we have by construction $h_n \leq f$. We need further assumptions to allow us to stop this chain, and to ensure that each $h_n$ is monotonic (hence is continuous by construction) and compact. We impose finiteness conditions on minimal upper bounds: if $MUB(d, d')$ is finite, and if the process of taking minimal upper bounds of minimal upper bounds, and so on, terminates, then the above construction stops at some $h_n$. Moreover, the finiteness of the description of $h_n$ entails that it is compact.

The two kinds of assumptions correspond to L-domains and profinite dcpo's, respectively. The rest of the section is devoted to their study. We first introduce the profinite dcpo's (a terminology due to Gunter) and show that they form a cartesian closed full subcategory of **Adcpo**. We recall that **Dcpo** is a cartesian closed category and that lub's of functions are defined pointwise.

**Definition 5.2.2 (profinite)** *Let $D$ be a dcpo. A projection is called finite if its image is finite. We say that $D$ is profinite if the finite projections $p : D \to D$ form a directed set whose lub is the identity. (In particular, any finite dcpo is profinite.) We denote with* **Prof** *the category of profinite dcpo's and continuous functions. A profinite dcpo which is moreover a cpo is called* bifinite. *We denote with* **Bif** *the full subcategory of bifinite cpo's.*

*If $id : D \to D$ is actually the lub of an ascending sequence $\{p_n\}_{n \in \omega}$ of finite projections, then we say that $D$ is $\omega$-profinite (or $\omega$-bifinite if $D$ is a cpo). We denote with $\omega$***Prof** *and $\omega$***Bif** *the full subcategories of $\omega$-profinite dcpo's and of $\omega$-bifinite cpo's, respectively. In the sequel, $(\omega-)$bifinite cpo's will be most often called $(\omega-)$bifinite domains.*

The terminology 'bifinite', due to Taylor, comes from a more categorical characterization of profinite dcpo's and bifinite cpo's to be found in chapter 7: they are limits and colimits at the same time (whence 'bi') of families of finite (d)cpo's. The bifinite domains have been first explored in [Plo76], under the name SFP (Sequence of Finite Projections). The following proposition justifies the name of finite projections.

**Proposition 5.2.3** *Let $D$ be a cpo and $p : D \to D$ be a projection such that $im(p)$ is finite. Then every element in $im(p)$ is compact in $D$ and $p$ is compact in $D \to D$. Moreover, if $D$ is profinite, then all compact projections over $D$ have a finite image.*

PROOF. We suppose $x = p(x)$ and $x \leq \bigvee \Delta$, with $\Delta$ directed in $D$. Then:

$$x \leq \bigvee \Delta \;\Rightarrow\; x = p(x) \leq p(\bigvee \Delta) = \bigvee p(\Delta) \;.$$

Since $im(p)$ is finite, there is $\delta \in \Delta$ such that $\bigvee p(\Delta) = p(\delta)$, hence $x \leq p(\delta) \leq \delta$. Next, we suppose $p \leq \bigvee A$, with $A \subseteq_{dir} (D \to D)$. We have just proven that:

$$\forall x \in im(p) \; \exists f_x \in A \; (x = p(x) \leq f_x(x)) \;.$$

Since $im(p)$ is finite, there exists $f \in A$ such that $(\forall x \in im(p) \; (x \leq f(x)))$. Hence $p(y) \leq f(p(y)) \leq f(y)$, for all $y \in D$. Conversely, first observe that for any projection $q$ we have:

$$q = (\bigvee\{p \mid p \text{ finite projection}\}) \circ q = \bigvee\{p \circ q \mid p \text{ finite projection}\}.$$

Hence if $q$ is compact, then $q = p \circ q$ for some finite projection $p$. Hence $im(q) \subseteq im(p)$ is finite.                    □

**Proposition 5.2.4 (profinite – CCC)** (1) *Every profinite dcpo $D$ is algebraic, and $\mathcal{K}(D) = \{p(x) \mid x \in D \text{ and } p \text{ is a finite projection}\}$.*

(2) *Profinite dcpo's (bifinite cpo's, respectively) and continuous maps form a cartesian closed category. The full subcategories $\omega\mathbf{Prof}$ and $\omega\mathbf{Bif}$ are also cartesian closed.*

PROOF. (1) If $D$ is profinite, then $x = \bigvee\{p(x) \mid p \text{ finite projection}\}$, for any $x$, and we know by proposition 5.2.3 that $p(x)$ is compact, for any finite projection $p$, whence the conclusion follows.

(2) It is enough to check that if $D, E$ are profinite, then so are $D \times E, D \to E$. For $D \times E$, take the set of projections $p \times q = \langle p \circ \pi_1, q \circ \pi_2 \rangle$, where $p, q$ are finite projections. For $D \to E$, define, for any pair of finite projections $p, q$ on $D, E$:

$$r(f) = \lambda x.q(f(p(x))))$$

(cf. theorem 4.6.10). Clearly, these $r$'s are all projections, and $id$ is their lub. The finiteness of $im(r)$ follows from the following observations:

(i) There are finitely many functions from $p(D)$ to $q(E)$.

(ii) every $f$ such that $r(f) = f$ restricts to a function $f : p(D) \to q(E)$, and is determined by this restriction, because $f(x) = f(p(x))$ for any $x$.

The last part of the statement follows obviously from the fact that if $p, q$ range over a denumerable set, then so do $p \times q$ and $r$.                    □

**Exercise 5.2.5** *Show that an $\omega$-profinite dcpo is $\omega$-algebraic.*

We next give an alternative characterization of profinite dcpo's that corresponds to the heuristic constructions given at the beginning of the section.

**Definition 5.2.6 (properties $m$, $M$)** *We say that a partial order $(Y, \leq)$*

- *satisfies property $m$ (notation $Y \models m$) if for all $X \subseteq_{fin} Y$ the set $MUB(X)$ of mub's of $X$ is complete, i.e., $\forall y \in UB(X) \; \exists x \in MUB(X) \; x \leq y$.*

- *satisfies property $M$ (notation $Y \models M$) if it satisfies property $m$, with the additional condition that $MUB(X)$ is finite for any $X \subseteq_{fin} Y$.*

**Theorem 5.2.7** *An algebraic cpo $D$ is profinite iff the following properties hold:*

(1) $\mathcal{K}(D) \models m$.

(2) $\mathcal{K}(D)$ *satisfies the property $M^{\infty}$, where property $M^{\infty}$ is defined as follows:* $U^{\infty}(X) = \bigcup_{n \in \omega} U^n(X)$ *is finite for any $X \subseteq_{fin} \mathcal{K}(D)$, where $U$ is an operator on subsets defined by:*

$$U(X) = \bigcup \{MUB(Y) \mid Y \subseteq_{fin} X\} .$$

PROOF. Notice that in particular, $X \subseteq U(X)$ for any $X$, and $MUB(X) \subseteq U(X)$ if $X$ is finite. Therefore properties (1) and (2) imply that $\mathcal{K}(D) \models M$.[1]

($\Rightarrow$) Let $D$ be profinite. We recall that $\mathcal{K}(D) = \bigcup \{p(D) \mid p \text{ finite projection}\}$. If $X \subseteq_{fin} \mathcal{K}(D)$, then $X \subseteq p(D)$ for some $p$, by directedness and proposition 5.1.10. Call $Z$ the set of mub's of $X$ in $p(D)$, which exists, is finite, and is complete in $p(D)$, since $p(D)$ is finite. We first show: $Z \subseteq MUB(X)$. Indeed suppose $z \in Z$, $z' \in UB(X)$, and $z' < z$. Then:

$$\begin{aligned} p(z') &\in UB(X) \quad \text{(since } p(X) = X) \\ p(z') &< z \quad \text{(since } p(z') \leq z') . \end{aligned}$$

This contradicts the definition of $Z$. Thus $Z \subseteq MUB(X)$. We next show that $Z$ is a complete set of mub's of $X$ in $D$. Take $y \in UB(X)$; then, as argued above, $p(y) \in UB(X)$, and by completeness of $Z$ one may find $z \in Z$ such that $z \leq p(y)$, and a fortiori $z \leq y$. The completeness of $Z$ forces $Z = MUB(X)$. Therefore $MUB(X)$ is finite and complete, and $MUB(X) \subseteq p(D)$. Similarly, $MUB(Y) \subseteq p(D)$ for any $Y \subseteq_{fin} X$. From there we deduce easily that $U^n(X) \subseteq p(D)$ for any $n$.

($\Leftarrow$) Let $A$ be a finite set of compact elements. Then we claim:

$$\forall y \in D \quad U^{\infty}(A) \cap \downarrow y \text{ is directed}$$

(i.e., $U^{\infty}(A)$ is normal, according to a terminology that will be introduced in definition 7.4.6).

The claim is shown as follows: if $x, x' \in U^{\infty}(A) \cap \downarrow y$, then $MUB(x, x') \subseteq U^{\infty}(A)$, and by completeness $MUB(x, x') \cap \downarrow y \neq \emptyset$. By the claim we can set:

$$p_A(y) = \bigvee (U^{\infty}(A) \cap \downarrow y) .$$

---

[1] Algebraic dcpo's $D$ such that $\mathcal{K}(D)$ satisfies property $M$ are sometimes called 2/3 SFP.

It is left to the reader to check that this gives a directed set of finite projections having *id* as lub. □

Notice that, in the proof of ($\Leftarrow$), we have used only mub's of pairs. The following result, which will be used in the proof of proposition 5.3.6, goes in the same direction.

**Lemma 5.2.8** *Let* $(D, \leq)$ *be a partial order. If* $MUB(X)$ *is complete and finite for every subset* $X$ *such that* $\sharp X \leq 2$, *then* $MUB(X)$ *is complete and finite for every finite subset* $X$.

PROOF. Let $X = \{a_1, \ldots, a_n\}$. We construct:

$$M_2 = MUB(a_1, a_2), \ldots, M_n = \bigcup_{x \in M_{n-1}} MUB(x, a_n).$$

If $x$ is an upper bound of $X$, then by completeness $x$ dominates an element of $M_2$. Continuing in the same way, we find an element $y$ of $M_n$ below $x$. Suppose moreover $x \in MUB(X)$: then $x = y$, since by construction $M_n \subseteq UB(X)$. We have proved $MUB(X) \subseteq M_n$. Since $M_n$ is finite, $MUB(X)$ is *a fortiori* finite. □

**Exercise 5.2.9** *Let* $X$ *be finite. Show that if there exists* $Y \subseteq_{fin} \uparrow X$ *such that* $\forall x \in \uparrow X$ $\exists y \in Y$ $y \leq x$, *then* $MUB(X)$ *is finite and complete.*

**Exercise 5.2.10** *Show that* $D$ *is profinite iff the conditions stated in theorem 5.2.7 hold, replacing the operator* $U$ *by the operator* $U'(X) = \bigcup \{MUB(Y) \mid Y \subseteq X \text{ and } \sharp Y \leq 2\}$. *Show that if* $D$ *is profinite, then* $U^\infty(X) = U'^\infty(X)$.

Figure 5.1 illustrates how an algebraic dcpo may fail to be profinite. The function spaces of examples (A) and (C) are not algebraic (cf. exercise 1.4.15 and proposition 5.3.7). The function space of example (B) is algebraic, but not $\omega$-algebraic. It is an example of an L-domain, which we introduce next.

**Definition 5.2.11 (L-domain)** *An L-domain*[2] *is a cpo* $D$ *such that:*

$$\forall A \subseteq_{fin} D \ \forall x \in UB(A) \ \exists! y \leq x \ y \in MUB(A).$$

Notice that in the definition of L-domain we have traded the finiteness condition of property $M$ against a uniqueness assumption.

**Example 5.2.12** *The following is an example of a finite cpo which is not an L-domain:* $D = \{\bot, a, b, c, d, e\}$ *with* $(a, b \leq c), (a, b \leq d)$ *and* $(c, d \leq e)$.

**Exercise 5.2.13** *(1) Show that one can restrict definition 5.2.11 to the A's which have cardinal 2 without loss of generality. Hint: The uniqueness is essential. (2) Show that, if* $D$ *is algebraic, we may restrict ourselves to compact elements, i.e.,* $A \subseteq_{fin} \mathcal{K}(D)$.

Hence L-domains are 'locally' bounded complete: any bounded subset is bounded complete.

---

[2]See also definition 12.5.4 and exercise 12.5.6.

(A)  $D = \overline{\omega} \cup \{a, b\}$ (where $\overline{\omega} = \{\overline{n} \mid n \in \omega\}$ is a copy of $\omega$), ordered as follows:

$$x \leq y \text{ iff } \begin{cases} x = a \text{ and } y \in \overline{\omega} \text{ or} \\ x = b \text{ and } y \in \overline{\omega} \text{ or} \\ x = \overline{n}, y = \overline{m}, \text{ and } m \leq n \,. \end{cases}$$

In this example, property $m$ fails.

(B)  $D = \{a, b\} \cup \omega$, ordered as follows:

$$\forall n \; a, b < n.$$

In this example, property $M$ fails.

(C)  $D = \omega_L \cup \omega_R$ (where $\omega_L = \{n_L \mid n \in \omega\}$ and $\omega_R = \{n_R \mid n \in \omega\}$), ordered as follows:

$$m \leq n \Rightarrow m_L \leq n_L \text{ and } m_R \leq n_R$$
$$m < n \Rightarrow m_L < n_R \text{ and } m_R < n_L \,.$$

In this example, $U^\infty(\{0_L, 0_R\})$ fails to be finite.

Figure 5.1: Dcpo's that fail to be profinite

---

**Proposition 5.2.14** *A cpo $D$ is an L-domain iff*

$$D \models m \text{ and } U^\infty(A) = U(A) \text{ for all finite subsets } A \text{ of } D.$$

PROOF. ($\Rightarrow$) Property $m$ holds *a fortiori*. To show $U^\infty(A) = U(A)$, it is enough to prove $U^2(A) \subseteq U(A)$. Let $x \in MUB(B)$, for a finite $B \subseteq U(A)$, and let $A_b$ be a finite subset of $A$ of which $b$ is a mub, for any $b \in B$. We show $x \in MUB(\bigcup_{b \in B} A_b)$. By construction $x \in UB(\bigcup_{b \in B} A_b)$. Suppose $x \geq y \in UB(\bigcup_{b \in B} A_b)$. By property $m$, $y \geq b'$ for some mub $b'$ of $A_b$. By uniqueness of the mub of $A_b$ below $x$, we get $b' = b$. Hence $y \geq B$, and $y = x$ follows from $x \in MUB(B)$.

($\Leftarrow$) Let $x \geq A \subseteq_{fin} D$. By property $m$ there exists $a \in MUB(A)$ such that $a \leq x$. Let $a' \leq x$ be such that $a' \in MUB(A)$. By applying $m$ again, there exists $b \in MUB(a, a')$ such that $b \leq x$. Since $U^\infty(A) = U(A)$, we have $b \in U(A)$, i.e., $b \in MUB(A')$ for some $A' \subseteq A$. Since $a, a' \in UB(A)$, we get $a = b = a'$. This proves the uniqueness of $a$. $\square$

So far, we have made use of the dcpo structure only. The following proposition involves step functions, which are defined with the help of $\bot$.

**Proposition 5.2.15 (L − CCC)** *The category of L-domains and continuous functions is cartesian closed. The full subcategory **L** of algebraic L-domains is cartesian closed.*

(A)  The following is both an L-domain and a bifinite domain and is not a Scott domain:

$$D_A = \{\perp, a, b, c, d\} \quad \text{where } a, b \leq c \text{ and } a, b \leq d \;.$$

(B)  The cpo $D_B$ obtained by adding a top element $\top$ to $D_A$ is an example of a bifinite domain that is not an L-domain.

Example (B) of figure 5.1 (with a $\perp$ added) is an example of an L-domain that is not bifinite.

Figure 5.2: Scott domains versus L-domains and bifinite domains

---

PROOF. The proof is similar to the proof of theorem 1.4.12. Suppose that $f, g \leq h$ are in $D \to E$. Then $f(x), g(x) \leq h(x)$, for all $x$. Define $k(x)$ as the least upper bound of $f(x), g(x)$ under $h(x)$. This function $k$ is the least upper bound of $f, g$ under $h$ (to check the continuity of $k$, given $\Delta$, one works in $\downarrow h(\bigvee \Delta)$). If $D$ and $E$ are algebraic, then we already know that any $h$ is the lub of the set of compact functions below it. We have to check that this set is directed. This follows from the bounded completeness of $\downarrow h$ that we just proved.          □

So far, we have seen three cartesian closed categories of algebraic cpo's: **S** (cf. definition 1.4.9), **Bif**, and **L**. In exercise 5.2.16 and in figure 5.2, we investigate how these categories compare with respect to inclusion.

**Exercise 5.2.16** *Show that* **S** *is a full subcategory of* **Bif** *and of* **L**. *Hint: To show* **S** $\subseteq$ **Bif**, *use proposition 5.2.14.*

As a last result in this section we show that the terminal object, products, and exponents in a full subcategory of **Dcpo**, if any, must be those of **Dcpo**.

**Proposition 5.2.17** *Let* **C** *be a full subcategory of* **Dcpo**. *We denote by* $\times$, $\to$ *the product and the exponent in* **Dcpo**. *Then the following properties hold (where* $\cong$ *means 'isomorphic in* **Dcpo**'):

(1)  *If* **C** *has a terminal object* $\hat{1}$, *then* $\hat{1}$ *is a one point cpo.*

(2)  *If* **C** *has a terminal object* $\hat{1}$ *and products* $D \hat{\times} E$, *then* $D \hat{\times} E \cong D \times E$.

(3)   *If* **C** *has terminal object* $\hat{1}$, *binary products, and exponents* $D \hat{\to} E$, *then* $D \hat{\to} E \cong D \to E$.

PROOF. (1)  If $\hat{1}$ is terminal and has distinct elements $x, y$, then the constant functions $z \mapsto x, z \mapsto y : \hat{1} \to \hat{1}$ are continuous and distinct: contradiction. In the sequel we freely confuse $x \in D$ and $x : \hat{1} \to D$.

(2)  Let $D, E \in$ **C**. Consider the products:

$$(D \hat{\times} E, \hat{\pi}_1, \hat{\pi}_2) \text{ in } \mathbf{C} \qquad \text{with pairing denoted by } \widehat{\langle , \rangle}$$
$$(D \times E, \pi_1, \pi_2) \text{ in } \mathbf{Cpo} \quad \text{with pairing } \langle , \rangle \;.$$

We show that $\langle \widehat{\pi_1}, \widehat{\pi_2} \rangle : D \hat{\times} E \to D \times E$ is an isomorphism in **Cpo**:

- $\langle \widehat{\pi_1}, \widehat{\pi_2} \rangle$ is injective. We have, for any $x, x' \in \hat{1} \to D \hat{\times} E$:

$$\langle \widehat{\pi_1}, \widehat{\pi_2} \rangle \circ x = \langle \widehat{\pi_1}, \widehat{\pi_2} \rangle \circ x' \iff \widehat{\pi_1} \circ x = \widehat{\pi_1} \circ x' \text{ and } \widehat{\pi_2} \circ x = \widehat{\pi_2} \circ x'$$
$$\iff x = \widehat{\langle \widehat{\pi_1}, \widehat{\pi_2} \rangle} \circ x = \widehat{\langle \widehat{\pi_1}, \widehat{\pi_2} \rangle} \circ x' = x' .$$

- $\langle \widehat{\pi_1}, \widehat{\pi_2} \rangle$ is surjective. Let $(y, z) \in D \times E$. We have: $(y, z) = \langle \widehat{\pi_1}, \widehat{\pi_2} \rangle (\widehat{\langle y, z \rangle})$, since $\widehat{\pi_1}(\widehat{\langle y, z \rangle}) = y$ and $\widehat{\pi_2}(\widehat{\langle y, z \rangle}) = z$.

- $\langle \widehat{\pi_1}, \widehat{\pi_2} \rangle$ is order-reflecting, i.e., if $(y, z) \leq (y', z')$, then $\widehat{\langle y, z \rangle} \leq \widehat{\langle y', z' \rangle}$. We can assume the existence of an object $C \in \mathbf{C}$ containing at least two elements $c, c'$, such that $c < c'$: indeed, if $\mathbf{C}$ only admits objects of cardinality 1 then the proposition is trivially true, and if $\mathbf{C}$ contains only discretely ordered sets, then in particular $D, E$ are discretely ordered, and so are $D \hat{\times} E$ (as an object of $\mathbf{C}$) and $D \times E$ (by the definition of product in **Dcpo**). With this fixed $C$, for any $D$ and $x, x' \in D$ such that $x \leq x'$, we can build a continuous map $f_{x,x'} : C \to D$ as follows:

$$f_{x,x'}(y) = \begin{cases} x & \text{if } y \leq c \\ x' & \text{otherwise} . \end{cases}$$

With the help of these functions, we have:

$$\widehat{\langle y, z \rangle} = \widehat{\langle f_{y,y'}, f_{z,z'} \rangle} \circ c \quad \widehat{\langle y', z' \rangle} = \widehat{\langle f_{y,y'}, f_{z,z'} \rangle} \circ c' .$$

Thus, by monotonicity of $\widehat{\langle f_{y,y'}, f_{z,z'} \rangle}$, we get $\widehat{\langle y, z \rangle} \leq \widehat{\langle y', z' \rangle}$.

(3) Given (1) and (2), we may work directly with the standard product $\times$. Consider the exponents:

$$(D \hat{\to} E, \hat{ev}) \quad \text{in } \mathbf{C}, \text{ with currying denoted by } \hat{\Lambda}$$
$$(D \to E, ev) \quad \text{in } \mathbf{Cpo}, \text{ with currying denoted by } \Lambda .$$

We show that $\Lambda(\hat{ev}) : (D \hat{\to} E) \to (D \to E)$ is an iso.

- $\Lambda(\hat{ev})$ is injective. If $\Lambda(\hat{ev})(h) = \Lambda(\hat{ev})(h')$, then $\hat{ev} \circ (h \times id) = \hat{ev} \circ (h' \times id)$ by the bijectivity of $\Lambda$. This entails:

$$h = \hat{\Lambda}(\hat{ev} \circ (h \times id)) = \hat{\Lambda}(\hat{ev} \circ (h' \times id)) = h' .$$

- $\Lambda(\hat{ev})$ is surjective. Let $f : D \to E$. We have $f = \Lambda(\hat{ev})(\hat{\Lambda}(ev)(f))$ since

$$\Lambda(\hat{ev}) \circ \hat{\Lambda}(ev) = \Lambda(\hat{ev} \circ (\hat{\Lambda}(ev) \times id)) = \Lambda(ev) = id .$$

- $g \leq g' \Rightarrow \hat{\Lambda}(ev)(g) \leq \hat{\Lambda}(ev)(g')$. Consider $f_{g,g'} : C \to (D \to E)$. We have:

$$\begin{aligned} \hat{\Lambda}(ev)(g) &= \hat{\Lambda}(ev \circ (g \times id)) \\ &= \hat{\Lambda}(ev \circ ((f_{g,g'} \circ c) \times id)) \\ &= \hat{\Lambda}(ev \circ (f_{g,g'} \times id) \circ (c \times id)) \\ &= \hat{\Lambda}(ev \circ (f_{g,g'} \times id))(c) . \end{aligned}$$

Let $k = \hat{\Lambda}(ev \circ (f_{g,g'} \times id))$. Then $\hat{\Lambda}(ev)(g) = k(c)$ and $\hat{\Lambda}(ev)(g') = k(c')$. The conclusion follows. $\square$

# 5.3   Full sub-CCC's of Acpo *

This section is devoted to Jung's classification theorem for algebraic dcpo's. Both L-domains and bifinite domains satisfy property $m$. We shall first prove that this property is necessary. Actually we prove that bicompleteness is necessary (which is stronger).

**Definition 5.3.1 (bicomplete)** *A partial order* $(D, \leq)$ *is called bicomplete if both $D$ and $D^{op} = (D, \leq)$ are directed complete.*

**Proposition 5.3.2** *If $(D, \leq)$ is bicomplete, then it satisfies property $m$.*

PROOF. By Zorn's lemma. Consider $A \subseteq_{fin} D$ and $x \in UB(A)$. Let $B = \downarrow x \cap UB(A)$. In $B$, every totally ordered subset is *a fortiori* codirected in $D$, and its glb is clearly in $B$. Hence $B$ has a minimal element, which is a minimal upper bound of $A$.          □

Jung's theorem relies on three propositions: 5.3.3, 5.3.6, and 5.3.7. We shall also need a result whose proof is given in section 5.5: a partial order is a dcpo if and only if any non-empty well-ordered subset of $D$ has a lub.

**Proposition 5.3.3** *A continuous dcpo $D$ with continuous function space $D \to D$ is bicomplete.*

PROOF. The proof is by contradiction. By proposition 5.5.1, we may assume that there exists a non-empty op-well-ordered subset $B$ of $D$ which has no glb. Let $A$ be the (possibly empty) set of lower bounds of $B$. Notice that by the assumption on $B$ we have $A \cap B = \emptyset$. We define the following function $r$ on $D$ by:

$$r(x) = \begin{cases} x & \text{if } x \in A \\ \bigwedge\{b \in B \mid b \geq x\} & \text{if } x \notin A \end{cases} \quad \text{(where the glb is meant in } B \text{)} .$$

- $r$ is well-defined. We first prove that the set $C$ of lower bounds in $B$ of $\{b \in B \mid b \geq x\}$ is not empty. Since $x \notin A$, we have $x \not\leq b'$ for some $b' \in B$. *a fortiori*, if $b \geq x$, then $b \not\leq b'$. But $B$ is a total order, hence $b' < b$, which proves $b' \in C$. Thus, since we assumed that $B$ is op-well-ordered, the maximum of $C$ exists and is $\bigwedge\{b \in B \mid b \geq x\}$. In particular we have $x \notin A \Rightarrow r(x) \in B$.

- $r \circ r = r$: $r(D) \in A \cup B$, and $r$ is the identity on $A \cup B$.

- $r$ is continuous. If $\bigvee \Delta \in A$, then $\Delta \subseteq A$, hence $r(\bigvee \Delta) = \bigvee \Delta = \bigvee r(\Delta)$. If $\bigvee \Delta \notin A$, then $\delta \not\leq b$ for some $b \in B$, $\delta \in \Delta$ (i.e., $\delta \notin A$). Hence $\Delta' \cap A = \emptyset$, where $\Delta' = \Delta \cap \uparrow \delta$, and $r(\Delta') \subseteq B$. Clearly $\bigvee \Delta' = \bigvee \Delta$ and $\bigvee r(\Delta') = \bigvee r(\Delta)$. Hence it is enough to prove $\bigvee r(\Delta') \geq r(\bigvee \Delta')$. We proceed by contradiction. Let $b' = r(\bigvee \Delta')$. If $\bigvee r(\Delta') \not\geq b'$, then *a fortiori* $r(\delta) \not\geq b'$ for all $\delta \in \Delta'$. But we have:

$$r(\delta) \not\geq b' \quad \Leftrightarrow \quad b' \not\leq \{b \in B \mid b \geq \delta\} \quad \Leftrightarrow \quad (\exists b_\delta \in B \; b' > b_\delta \geq \delta) .$$

(For the last equivalence, notice that $\bigvee \Delta \notin A$ implies $b' \in B$, and recall that $B$ is totally ordered.) Since $B$ is op-well-ordered, the non-empty set $\{b_\delta \mid \delta \in \Delta\}$ has a maximum $b_{\delta''}$ for some $\delta'' \in \Delta$. But then we have:

- $b' > b_{\delta''} \geq \bigvee \Delta$ by construction,

- $b' = r(\bigvee \Delta') \leq \{b \in B \mid b \geq \bigvee \Delta'\}$ implies $b' \leq b_{\delta''}$ .

Contradiction. Hence $r$ is continuous. We know from exercise 4.6.10 that $D' \to D'$ is a retract of $D \to D$, where $D' = r(D) = A \cup B$. It is continuous, by proposition 5.1.12. The rest of the proof consists in obtaining a contradiction to the continuity of $D' \to D'$. It goes via successive claims:

**Claim 1.** If $A \neq \emptyset$, then there exist $x' \ll x \in A$ and $y' \ll y \in A$ such that $x'$ and $y'$ have no upper bound in $A$.

We first show that $A' = \Downarrow A$ is not directed. By continuity of $D$, the lub of $A'$ would be larger than any element of $A$, and still belong to $A$; but since $A$ is not empty, we know that it has no maximum by the assumption on $B$: contradiction. Hence there exist $x'' \ll x \in A$ and $y'' \ll y \in A$ such that $x''$ and $y''$ have no upper bound in $A'$. Let $x'$ and $y'$ be obtained by interpolation: $x'' \ll x' \ll x$ and $y'' \ll y' \ll y$. Suppose that $x'$ and $y'$ have an upper bound $z$ in $A$: then, by directedness of $\Downarrow z$, $x''$ and $y''$ would have an upper bound in $A'$. This completes the proof of claim 1.

**Claim 2.** $\exists f \in D' \to D'$  $f \ll id$ and $f(B) \subseteq B$.

Claim 2 is obvious if $A$ is empty, since then $B = D'$. If $A \neq \emptyset$, let $x', y'$ be as in claim 1. Since $x' \ll x = \bigvee\{f(x) \mid f \ll id\}$, we have $x' \leq g(x)$ for some $g \ll id$. Similarly $y' \leq h(y)$ for some $h \ll id$. Let $f$ be an upper bound of $g, h$ in $\Downarrow id$. Then $x' \leq f(x)$ and $y' \leq f(y)$. Let $b$ be an element of $B$. Then $b$ is an upper bound of $x$ and $y$, since $x, y \in A$. Hence $f(b) \geq f(x) \geq x'$. Similarly $f(b) \geq y'$. Thus, by claim 1, $f(b) \in D' \setminus A = B$. This completes the proof of claim 2.

Since $B$ is op-well-ordered, we can define a predecessor function: $pred(b)$ is the maximum $b'$ such that $b' < b$ (there is at least one such $b'$, otherwise $b$ would be a minimum of $B$, contradicting our assumption on $B$). Define, for each $b \in B$, a function $g_b : D' \to D'$ by:

$$g_b(x) = \begin{cases} pred(f(x)) & \text{if } x \in B \text{ and } x \leq b \\ x & \text{otherwise}, \end{cases}$$

where $f$ is given by claim 2.

**Claim 3.** (1)  $g_b$ is continuous, for all $b \in B$.

(2)  $\{g_b \mid b \in B\}$ is directed and has $id$ as lub.

(3)  There is no $g_b$ such that $f \leq g_b$.

Claim 3 contradicts $f \ll id$. Thus we are left with the proof of claim 3.

(3) If $f \leq g_b$, then $f(b) \leq g_b(b) = pred(f(b))$, a contradiction to the definition of $pred$.

(2) We prove that $\{g_b \mid b \in B\}$ is actually a chain, i.e., is totally ordered, by proving $b' \leq b \Rightarrow g_b \leq g_{b'}$. The only interesting case is when $x \in B$ and $b' < x \leq b$. Then $g_b(x) = pred(f(x)) \leq f(x) \leq x = g_{b'}(x)$. The equality $id = \bigvee\{g_b \mid b \in B\}$ follows from the remark that $g_{pred(b)}(b) = b$ for all $b \in B$.

(1) It is easily checked that $g_b$ is monotonic. Let $\Delta$ be directed in $D'$. The interesting case is $\bigvee \Delta \in B$. Then $\delta \in B$ for some $\delta \in \Delta$, as otherwise we would have $\Delta \subseteq A$ (and hence $\bigvee \Delta \in A$). We can choose $\delta$ to be the maximum of $B \cap \Delta$, since $B$ is well-ordered. Then $\bigvee \Delta = \delta \in \Delta$, and the continuity of $g_b$ follows by monotonicity.  $\square$

**Remark 5.3.4** *This proof generalizes the situation presented in exercise 1.4.15.*

The hypotheses of the previous proposition are actually redundant.

**Exercise 5.3.5** *Show that a dcpo with continuous function space is continuous. Hint: Use the claim in the proof of proposition 5.3.7.*

**Proposition 5.3.6 (L/M)** *Let $D$ and $E$ be algebraic cpo's satisfying property $m$. If $D \to E$ is continuous, then $E$ is an L-domain or $\mathcal{K}(D) \models M$.*

PROOF. By contradiction. Suppose that $E$ is not an L-domain and that $\mathcal{K}(D) \not\models M$. Then (cf. exercise 5.2.13) there exists $c$ in $E$, two compact $a_1, a_2 \leq c$, and two distinct mub's $b_1, b_2$ of $\{a_1, a_2\}$ below $c$. Since $D \models m$, also $\mathcal{K}(D) \models m$ by lemma 5.1.8. Since $\mathcal{K}(D) \not\models M$, by lemma 5.2.8 there exist $d_1$ and $d_2$ in $\mathcal{K}(D)$ such that $MUB(d_1, d_2)$ is infinite. Assume moreover that $D \to E$ is continuous. Then we define $g : D \to E$ by:

$$
g(x) = \begin{cases} \bot & \text{if } x \not\geq d_1 \text{ and } x \not\geq d_2 \\ a_1 & \text{if } x \geq d_1 \text{ and } x \not\geq d_2 \\ a_2 & \text{if } x \not\geq d_1 \text{ and } x \geq d_2 \\ b_1 & \text{if } x \geq d_1 \text{ and } x \geq d_2 \,. \end{cases}
$$

We leave the reader check that $g$ is continuous and is a mub of the step functions $d_1 \to a_1$ and $d_2 \to a_2$. In particular $g$ is compact. We shall contradict the compactness of $g$. We define $f$ by replacing $b_1$ by $c$ in the last line of the definition of $g$. Clearly $g \leq f$. We shall exhibit a directed set of functions which has $f$ as lub, but none of which dominates $g$. For each finite subset $A$ of $MUB(d_1, d_2)$, define a function $f_A : D \to E$ by:

$$
f_A(x) = \begin{cases} \bot & \text{if } x \not\geq d_1 \text{ and } x \not\geq d_2 \\ a_1 & \text{if } x \geq d_1 \text{ and } x \not\geq d_2 \\ a_2 & \text{if } x \not\geq d_1 \text{ and } x \geq d_2 \\ b_2 & \text{if } x \in MUB(d_1, d_2) \backslash A \\ c & \text{otherwise} \,. \end{cases}
$$

We have to check that the $f_A$'s are continuous, and form a directed set with lub $f$. We leave this to the reader, with the following hint: to prove the continuity, observe that:

$$
d_1, d_2 \text{ compact}, \bigvee \Delta \in MUB(d_1, d_2) \Rightarrow \Delta \text{ has a maximum}.
$$

Suppose $g \leq f_A$ for some $A$, and pick $d \in MUB(d_1, d_2) \backslash A$. We should have $b_1 = g(d) \leq f_A(d) = b_2$. Since we assumed $b_1 \neq b_2$, this contradicts the minimality of $b_2$.  $\square$

**Proposition 5.3.7** *Let $D$ be a dcpo with algebraic function space and such that $\mathcal{K}(D) \models M$. Then $D$ is profinite.*

PROOF. Suppose that $U^\infty(A)$ is infinite, for some $A \subseteq_{fin} \mathcal{K}(D)$. We set $B^0 = A, B^{n+1} = U^{n+1}(A) \backslash U^n(A)$. By our assumption, for each $n$, $B^{n+1} \neq \emptyset$. We construct a tree in the following way. The nodes are finites sequences $b_n \cdots b_0$ where $b_i \in B^i$ for all $i$, and where, for each $i < n$, $b_i$ belongs to a subset of $U^i(A)$ of which $b_{i+1}$ is a mub. The root is the empty sequence, the predecessor of $b_n \cdots b_0$ is $b_{n-1} \cdots b_0$. By construction, and by property $M$, this is a finitely branching tree. We show that for any $b \in U^\infty(A)$ there exists a node $b_n \cdots b_0$ such that $b = b_n$, which entails that the tree is infinite. Let $n$ be minimum such that $b \in U^n(A)$; we have *a fortiori* $b \in B^n$. By definition of $U^n(A)$ we can find a subset $B$ of $U^{n-1}(A)$ of which $b$ is a mub. If $B$ were also a subset of $U^{n-2}(A)$, then we would not have $b \in B^n$. Hence we can build $b_{n-1} \in B^{n-1}, \ldots, b_0 \in B^0$ as desired. Since the tree is infinite and finitely branching, by König's lemma it has an infinite branch $\cdots b_n \cdots b_0$, which in particular forms an infinite strictly increasing sequence in $U^\infty(A)$. Now we use the algebraicity of $D \to D$. We have:

$$id = \bigvee \{f \mid f \text{ is compact and } f \le id\} .$$

In particular $a = \bigvee \{f(a) \mid f \text{ is compact and } f \le id\}$, for $a$ compact, implies $a = f(a)$ for some $f$. By directedness we can find a compact $f \le id$ for which $\forall a \in A$ $(a = f(a))$. We prove that in fact:

$$\forall a \in U^\infty(A) \ (a = f(a)) .$$

Suppose that we know $\forall a \in U^n(A)$ $(a = f(a))$. Let $a'$ be a mub of $A' \subseteq U^n(A)$. Then $a' \ge f(a') \ge f(A') = A'$ implies $f(a') = a'$.

Hence we have in particular $f(b_n) = b_n$ for all $n$, and $f(c) = c$ follows by continuity for $c = \bigvee b_n$. We shall get a contradiction by proving the following claim:

**Claim.** If $D$ is a dcpo which has a continuous function space, and if $f \ll id$, then $f(x) \ll x$ for all $x \in D$.

If the claim is true, then $c = f(c) \ll c$, hence $c$ is compact. But a lub of a strictly increasing sequence is not compact: contradiction.

We prove the claim by appealing again to a 'retract' trick. Let $\Delta$ be such that $x \le \bigvee \Delta$. Set $z = \bigvee \Delta$. Since $\downarrow z = D'$ is a retract of $D$ (cf. lemma 5.1.11), $D' \to D'$ is continuous, as a retract of $D \to D$. We show that $f \ll id$ also holds in $D' \to D'$ (notice that since $f \le id$, $f$ maps $D'$ into $D'$). For this, it is enough by lemma 5.1.5 to consider a directed $\Delta' \subseteq D' \to D'$ such that $id = \bigvee \Delta'$ in $D' \to D'$. Each $g$ in $\Delta'$ can be extended to $D$ by setting:

$$g(x) = x \text{ whenever } x \not\le z .$$

Hence $\Delta'$ can be viewed as a directed subset in $D \to D$, and has clearly $id$ as lub there too. It follows that $f \le g$ for some $g \in \Delta'$, and the inequality holds *a fortiori* in $D' \to D'$. We have proved $f \ll id$ in $D' \to D'$. Consider the family of constant functions $x \mapsto \delta$ for each $\delta \in \Delta$. It forms a directed set with lub the constant $x \mapsto z$. We have $(x \mapsto z) \ge id$ (in $D' \to D'$). Hence $f \le (x \mapsto \delta)$ for some $\delta \in \Delta$. In particular $f(x) \le \delta$, hence $f(x) \ll x$. This ends the proof of the claim and of the proposition. $\square$

**Theorem 5.3.8 (Jung)** *Any cartesian closed full subcategory of* **Acpo** *is either a subcategory of* **Bif** *or a subcategory of* **L**.

PROOF. We have already proved that **Bif** and **L** are cartesian closed. By proposition 5.2.17, if **C** is a cartesian closed full subcategory of **Acpo**, we know that the exponents of **C** are the exponents of **Cpo**. Let $D \in$ **C**. Since both $D$ and $D \to D$ are algebraic, $D$ is bicomplete by proposition 5.3.3, hence, by proposition 5.3.2, $D \models m$. Thus we can apply proposition 5.3.6 to any $D, E \in$ **C**. Combining with proposition 5.3.7 applied to $D$, we get, for any $D, E \in$ **C**:

$$D \text{ is bifinite or} E \text{ is an algebraic L-domain.}$$

Suppose now that **C** is neither a subcategory of **L** nor a subcategory of **Bif**. Then there is an object $D$ of **C** which is not bifinite and an object $E$ of **C** which is not an L-domain: contradiction. $\square$

The analysis is simplified in the case of $\omega$-algebraic cpo's, thanks to the following proposition.

**Proposition 5.3.9** *If $D$ is an (algebraic) cpo and $D \to D$ is $\omega$-algebraic, then $\mathcal{K}(D) \models$*
$M$.

PROOF. We already know from proposition 5.3.3 that $D$ is bicomplete, hence that
$\mathcal{K}(D) \models m$. Assume that $MUB(a_1, a_2)$ is infinite for some compacts $a_1, a_2$. We build
uncountably many mub's of $a_1 \to a_1$ and $a_2 \to a_2$. Since they are all compact, this
contradicts the $\omega$-algebraicity of $D$. We pick two distinct mub's $b_1, b_2$ of $a_1, a_2$. For any
$S \subseteq MUB(a_1, a_2)$, we define $f_S : D \to D$ by:

$$f_S(d) = \begin{cases} \perp & \text{if } d \not\geq a_1 \text{ and } d \not\geq a_2 \\ a_1 & \text{if } d \geq a_1 \text{ and } d \not\geq a_2 \\ a_2 & \text{if } d \not\geq a_1 \text{ and } d \geq a_2 \\ b_1 & \text{if } \exists\, s \in S \;\; d \geq s \\ b_2 & \text{if } \exists\, s \in MUB(a_1, a_2) \backslash S \;\; d \geq s \,. \end{cases}$$

To see that $f_S$ is well-defined, we use the fact that $D$ is an L-domain by proposition
5.3.6: if $d \in UB(a_1, a_2)$, there is exactly one mub of $a_1, a_2$ below $d$. We omit the rest of
the proof.                                                                                          $\square$

**Exercise 5.3.10 (Smyth)** *Show that the category $\omega$**Bif** of $\omega$-bifinite domains and continuous functions is the largest cartesian closed full subcategory of $\omega$**Acpo***. Hint: Use
proposition 5.3.9 instead of proposition 5.3.6.*

# 5.4   Full sub-CCC's of Adcpo *

In this section, we present a brief account of Jung's results in the case of algebraic dcpo's,
that is, when relaxing the assumption that the domains have a $\perp$. Then $MUB(\emptyset)$ is not
a singleton, and lends itself to the same sort of dichotomy of finiteness versus uniqueness
that have led us to the two maximal cartesian closed categories of section 5.3. There
are four maximal cartesian closed full subcategories of **Adcpo**. The duplication with
respect to the previous section comes from the following discrimination, which is both
similar and 'orthogonal' to the discrimination in proposition 5.3.6.

**Proposition 5.4.1 (F/U)** *Let $D$ and $E$ be continuous dcpo's satisfying property $m$.
If $D \to E$ is continuous, then $D$ has finitely many minimal elements or $E$ is a disjoint
union of cpo's.*

PROOF. Let us assume by contradiction that $D$ has infinitely many minimal elements
and that $E$ is not a disjoint union of cpo's. First notice that the collection of minimal
elements of $E$ can be alternatively described as $MUB(\emptyset)$. Hence, by property $m$, $E$ can
be described as $E = \bigcup \{\uparrow e \mid e$ is a minimal element of $E\}$. Our assumption implies
that there exists an upper bounded pair $\{e_1, e_2\}$ of distinct minimal elements of $E$. By
property $m$ one can find a mub $e$ of $e_1, e_2$. The constant function $x \mapsto e_1$ is minimal,
hence compact in $D \to E$ (minimal implies compact in a continuous dcpo). For any
finite set $A$ of minimal elements of $D$, we define a function $f_A$ by:

$$f_A(x) = \begin{cases} e & \text{if } x \in \uparrow A \\ e_2 & \text{otherwise} \,. \end{cases}$$

This defines a directed family of continuous functions which has $x \mapsto e$ as lub (the
monotonicity of $f_A$ follows from $e_2 \leq e$). Hence one must have $(x \mapsto e_1) \leq f_A$ for some

$A$, which entails $e_1 \leq e_2$. But $e_2$ is minimal and $e_1 \neq e_2$: contradiction. □

The property of finiteness of the set of minimal elements is not strong enough to be closed under function spaces. But a strengthening will do.

**Definition 5.4.2 (root)** *Given a dcpo $D$, the set $U^\infty(\emptyset)$ is called the root of $D$.*

**Proposition 5.4.3** *If $D$ is a dcpo and if $D \to D$ is such that $MUB(\emptyset)$ is complete and finite, then $D$ has a finite root.*

PROOF. With each element $d$ of the root we associate the retraction $r_d$ onto $\downarrow d$ defined in lemma 5.1.11. We show that if $d \neq d'$, then $r_d$ and $r_{d'}$ have no common lower bound. We can assume, say, $d \not\leq d'$. Then if $f \leq r_d, r_{d'}$, we have:

$$f \leq r_d \;\Rightarrow\; f(d) \leq d$$
$$f \leq r_{d'} \;\Rightarrow\; f(d) \leq r_{d'}(d) = d' \;.$$

In fact, because $d$ is in the root of $D$, $f(d) \leq d$ implies $f(d) = d$ (cf. the proof of proposition 5.3.7). Hence $d = f(d) \leq d'$, contradicting the assumption. Since $D \to D \models m$, there exists a minimal function $m_d$ below each $r_d$. The $m_d$'s are all distinct, since $m_d = m_{d'}$ would entail that $\{r_d, r_{d'}\}$ has a lower bound. Hence if the root of $D$ is infinite, then $D \to D$ has infinitely many minimal elements: contradiction. □

We now show how the results of the previous section can be exploited.

**Corollary 5.4.4 ($\forall$L/$\forall$B)** *If $D$ and $E$ are algebraic dcpo's satisfying property $m$ and if $D \to E$ is an algebraic dcpo, then either all basic Scott open sets $\uparrow d$ ($d \in \mathcal{K}(D)$) are bifinite or all $\uparrow e$'s ($e \in \mathcal{K}(E)$) are L-domains.*

PROOF. We first prove the following claim.

**Claim.** Under the assumptions of the statement, either all basic Scott open sets $\uparrow d$ are such that $\mathcal{K}(\uparrow d) \models M$ or all $\uparrow e$'s ($e \in \mathcal{K}(E)$) are L-domains.

Suppose that there exist Scott open sets $\uparrow d$ and $\uparrow e$ such that $\mathcal{K}(\uparrow d) \not\models M$ and $\uparrow e$ is not an L-domain. Then, by proposition 5.3.6, $(\uparrow d) \to (\uparrow e)$ is not continuous. This contradicts our assumption, since $(\uparrow d) \to (\uparrow e)$ is a retract of $D \to E$.

The statement follows from the claim and from proposition 5.3.7. □

**Theorem 5.4.5** *Any cartesian closed full subcategory of **Adcpo** is a subcategory of one of the following four cartesian closed full subcategories of **Adcpo**, described by their respective classes of objects:*

**(UL)** *the disjoint unions of algebraic L-domains,*

**(UB)** *the disjoint unions of bifinite domains,*

**(FL)** *the dcpo's with a finite root whose basic Scott open sets are algebraic L-domains,*

**(FB)** *the profinite dcpo's.*

PROOF. We omit the verification that these four categories are cartesian closed. We also leave it to the reader to verify that the profinite dcpo's are the dcpo's with a finite root such that all $\uparrow d$'s are bifinite. The proof proceeds like the proof of theorem 5.3.8, exploiting not only the discrimination L/M (in its variant $\forall$L/$\forall$B), but also the discrimination F/U. In the rest of the proof, **B** and **L**, **F**, **U** will stand for the following classes of objects:

(**B**)  the dcpo's whose basic Scott open sets are bifinite,

(**L**)  the dcpo's whose basic Scott open sets are algebraic L-domains,

(**F**)  the dcpo's with a finite root,

(**U**)  the disjoint union of cpo's.

Let **C** be a cartesian closed full subcategory of **Adcpo**. By corollary 5.4.4, and by combining proposition 5.4.1 (applied to $D \to D$ and $E$) and 5.4.3, we get, as in the proof of theorem 5.3.8:

$$(\mathbf{C} \subseteq \mathbf{B} \text{ or } \mathbf{C} \subseteq \mathbf{L}) \text{ and } (\mathbf{C} \subseteq \mathbf{F} \text{ or } \mathbf{C} \subseteq \mathbf{U}) \,.$$

Assume now that **C** is not included in any of **UL**, **UB** and **FL**. Let $D_1, D_2, D_3 \in \mathbf{C}$ witness these non inclusions, and let $D$ be an arbitrary object of **C**. Then we proceed by cases:

- $D_1 \notin \mathbf{U}$. Then $D, D_3 \in \mathbf{F}$ since $\mathbf{C} \subseteq \mathbf{F}$ or $\mathbf{C} \subseteq \mathbf{U}$. By non inclusion, we have $D_3 \notin \mathbf{L}$, which implies $D \in \mathbf{B}$ since $\mathbf{C} \subseteq \mathbf{B}$ or $\mathbf{C} \subseteq \mathbf{L}$.

- $D_1 \notin \mathbf{L}$. Similarly we deduce that $D \in \mathbf{B}$ and $D \in \mathbf{F}$, using witness $D_2$.  □

**Exercise 5.4.6** *Show that the category* $\omega$**Prof** *of* $\omega$*-profinite dcpo's and continuous functions is the largest cartesian closed full subcategory of* $\omega$**Adcpo**.

# 5.5   Completeness of well-ordered lub's *

We prove the result used in the proof of proposition 5.3.3 . The proof (adapted from [Mar76]) assumes some familiarity with ordinals and cardinals. We simply recall that every set can be well-ordered, that ordinals are canonical representatives of isomorphisms classes of well-orderings, and that cardinals are the least ordinals of a given cardinality. We write $\sharp\Delta$ for the cardinal of $\Delta$

**Proposition 5.5.1** *A partial order* $D$ *is a dcpo iff any non-empty well-ordered subset of* $D$ *has a lub.*

PROOF. ($\Rightarrow$) This is obvious, since well-ordered subsets are *a fortiori* totally ordered, hence directed.

($\Leftarrow$) We first prove the following claim.

**Claim.** Let $\Delta$ be an infinite directed set. There is a family $\{\Delta_\alpha\}_{\alpha<\gamma}$ of directed subsets of $\Delta$ indexed over the cardinal $\gamma$ of $\Delta$, such that:

(A)  $\alpha < \beta \Rightarrow \Delta_\alpha \subset \Delta_\beta$,

(B)  $\Delta_\alpha$ is finite if $\alpha$ is finite, $\sharp\Delta_\alpha = \sharp\alpha$ if $\alpha$ is infinite,

(C)  $\Delta = \bigcup_{\alpha<\gamma} \Delta_\alpha$.

In order to prove the claim, we first fix a choice $u_F$ of an upper bound of $F$ for any $F \subseteq_{fin} \Delta$, with the property that $u_F \leq u_{F'}$ if $F \subseteq F'$ (proceeding by induction on $\sharp F$). Let $\{x_\alpha\}_{\alpha<\gamma}$ be a bijective indexing of $\Delta$. We construct $\Delta_\alpha$ and we prove properties (A), (B), and (C) together by transfinite induction:

- $\alpha = 0$. $\Delta_0 = \{x_0\}$.

- $\alpha = \beta + 1$. We set:

$$\Delta'_\alpha = \Delta_\beta \cup \{x_\delta\} \text{ where } \delta \text{ is the least index such that } x_\delta \in \Delta \backslash \Delta_\beta$$
$$\Delta_\alpha = \Delta'_\alpha \cup \{u_F \mid F \subseteq_{fin} \Delta'_\alpha\} \,.$$

(It will be part of the proof to show that $\Delta \backslash \Delta_\beta$ is indeed non-empty.)

- $\alpha$ is a limit ordinal. We set $\Delta_\alpha = \bigcup_{\beta < \alpha} \Delta_\beta$.

By construction, the sets $\Delta_\alpha$ are directed and property (A) holds. Property (C) can be rephrased as $\Delta = \Delta_\gamma$, and thus follows from property (B) by minimality of $\gamma$. Property (B) clearly holds for $\alpha = 0$. For a finite ordinal $\alpha = \beta + 1$, the finiteness of $\Delta_\alpha$ follows from the finiteness of $\{F \mid F \subseteq_{fin} \Delta'_\alpha\}$. For infinite ordinals, the limit case is obvious (notice that $\Delta_\omega$ is infinite because the inclusions $\Delta_i \subseteq \Delta_{i+1}$ are strict). If $\alpha = \beta + 1$, then $\sharp \Delta_\alpha = \sharp \Delta_\beta$ follows from the fact that $\sharp \mathcal{P}_{fin}(X) = \sharp X$, for any infinite set $X$.

This completes the proof of (B). We next prove that property (B) at $\beta$ ensures the well-definedness of $\Delta_{\beta+1}$. This is clear for finite $\beta$. Suppose that $\beta$ is infinite, that $\beta + 1 = \alpha \le \gamma$, and that $\Delta = \Delta_\beta$. Then $\gamma = \sharp \Delta = \sharp \Delta_\beta = \sharp \beta$, which contradicts the minimality of $\gamma$ since $\beta < \gamma$.

We reason by contradiction. Let $\gamma$ be the least ordinal for which there exists a directed $\Delta$ of cardinal $\gamma$ such that $\bigvee \Delta$ does not exist, and let $\{\Delta_\alpha\}$ be as in the claim. Then $\bigvee \Delta_\alpha$ exists for each $\alpha < \gamma$, by the minimality of $\gamma$. The collection $\{\bigvee \Delta_\alpha \mid \alpha < \gamma\}$ is well-ordered by (A), and its lub is the lub of $\Delta$ by (C). Contradiction. □

**Exercise 5.5.2** *Show that a poset $D$ such that any monotonic function $f : D \to D$ has a least fixpoint is a cpo. Hints: Use proposition 5.5.1. Given a well-ordered subset $A$, define $f_A$ as follows: $f_A(x) = x$ if $x \ge A$, otherwise $f_A(x) = y$, where $y$ is the least element of $A$ such that $y \not\le x$. Consider $id : D \to D$.*

# 6

# The Language PCF

In chapter 4, we have provided semantics for both typed and untyped $\lambda$-calculus. In this chapter we extend the approach to typed $\lambda$-calculus with fixpoints ($\lambda Y$-calculus), we suggest formal ways of reasoning with fixpoints, and we introduce a core functional language called PCF [Sco93, Plo77]. PCF has served as a basis for a large body of theoretical work in denotational semantics. We prove the adequacy of the interpretation with respect to the operational semantics, and we discuss the full abstraction problem, which has triggered a lot of research, both in syntax and semantics.

In section 6.1, we introduce the notion of *cpo-enriched* CCC's, which serves to interpret the $\lambda Y$-calculus. In section 6.2, we introduce fixpoint induction and show an application of this reasoning principle. In section 6.3, we introduce the language PCF, define its standard denotational semantics and its operational semantics, and we show a computational adequacy property: the meaning of a closed term of basic type is different from $\bot$ if and only if its evaluation terminates. In section 6.4, we address a tighter correspondence between denotational and operational semantics, known as the full abstraction property. In section 6.5, we introduce Vuillemin's sequential functions, which capture first order PCF definability. In section 6.6, we show how a fully abstract model of PCF can be obtained by means of a suitable quotient of an (infinite) term model of PCF.

## 6.1 The $\lambda Y$-calculus

The $\lambda Y$-calculus is the typed $\lambda$-calculus extended with a family of constants $Y^\sigma$ of type $(\sigma \to \sigma) \to \sigma$ for each type $\sigma$ ($Y$ for short), with the following reduction rule:

$$(Y) \quad YM \to M(YM) \,.$$

It is also convenient to introduce a special constant $\Omega^\sigma$ at each type (to be interpreted by $\bot$).

**Definition 6.1.1 (cpo-enriched-CCC)** *A cartesian closed category* **C** *is called a cpo-enriched cartesian closed category if all its homsets are cpo's, if composition is continuous, if pairing and currying are monotonic, and if the following strictness conditions hold (for all $f$ of the appropriate type):*

$$\bot \circ f = \bot \qquad ev \circ \langle \bot, f \rangle = \bot \,.$$

**Remark 6.1.2** (1) *Notice that our definition of a cpo-enriched CCC involves the cartesian closed structure of the category: thus in our terminology a cpo-enriched CCC is not just a cpo-enriched category (see definition 7.1.5) that happens to be cartesian closed.*

(2) *The strictness conditions of definition 6.1.1 will be used in the proof of theorem 6.3.6.*

**Lemma 6.1.3** *In a cpo-enriched CCC pairing and currying are continuous.*

PROOF. We consider the case of currying only (the argument is similar for pairing, which has to be established first). In order to prove $\Lambda(\bigvee \Delta) = \bigvee \{\Lambda(f) \mid f \in \Delta\}$, it is enough to check that $\bigvee \{\Lambda(f) \mid f \in \Delta\}$ satisfies the characterizing equation:

$$ev \circ (\bigvee \{\Lambda(f) \mid f \in \Delta\} \times id) = \bigvee \Delta .$$

The monotonicity of $\Lambda$ guarantees that $\{\Lambda(f) \mid f \in \Delta\}$ is directed. Hence by continuity of composition and pairing we have:

$$ev \circ (\bigvee \{\Lambda(f) \mid f \in \Delta\} \times id) = \bigvee \{ev \circ (\Lambda(f) \times id) \mid f \in \Delta\} = \bigvee \Delta .$$
□

The following definition was first given by Berry [Ber79].

**Definition 6.1.4 (least fixpoint model)** *A least fixpoint model is a cpo-enriched cartesian closed category where $\Omega$ and $Y$ are interpreted as follows:*

$$[\Omega] = \bot \qquad [Y] = \bigvee_{n < \omega} [\lambda f . f^n \Omega] ,$$

*where $M^n \Omega = M(\cdots (M\Omega) \cdots)$, $n$ times.*

The fact that the sequence of the $[\lambda f . f^n \Omega]$'s is increasing follows from the assumptions of monotonicity in the definition of cpo-enriched CCC.

**Proposition 6.1.5** *In a least fixpoint model, the $(Y)$-rule is valid.*

PROOF. Exploiting the continuity of the composition and pairing, we have:

$$[YM] = ev \circ \langle \bigvee_{n<\omega}[\lambda f.f^n\Omega], [M]\rangle = \bigvee_{n<\omega}[M^n\Omega]$$
$$[M(YM)] = ev \circ \langle [M], \bigvee_{n<\omega}[M^n\Omega]\rangle = \bigvee_{n<\omega}[M^{n+1}\Omega] .$$
□

**Proposition 6.1.6 Cpo** *is a cpo-enriched CCC. In particular, for any cpo $D$, $Fix : (D \to D) \to D$, defined by $Fix(f) = \bigvee_{n \in \omega} f^n(\bot)$, is continuous.*

PROOF. Notice that in a category with enough points, the interpretation of $Y$ given in definition 6.1.4 is precisely $Fix$. □

In chapter 2 we have seen so-called fixpoint combinators (cf. example 2.1.11 and exercise 2.1.16). Thus, the $\lambda Y$-calculus can be simulated in the untyped $\lambda$-calculus. But the semantics of $\lambda Y$-calculus is easier, since it involves only fixpoints of functions, not domain equations (cf. chapter 3).

**Exercise 6.1.7** *Consider the extension of the simply typed $\lambda$-calculus with a collection of constants $Y_n$ $(n \geq 0)$ and rules:*

$$(Y_n) \quad Y_{n+1}M \to M(Y_nM) .$$

*Prove that the system obtained by adding these rules to the $\beta$-rule is strongly normalizing. Hint: Adapt the proof of theorem 2.2.9.*

**Exercise 6.1.8** *Let $\mathbf{C}$ be a cpo-enriched cartesian-closed category such that currying is strict, i.e., $\Lambda(\bot) = \bot$. Adapt the definition of Böhm tree given in chapter 2 to the $\lambda Y$-calculus by setting $\omega(\lambda \vec{x}.Y M_1 \ldots M_p) = \Omega$ $(p \geq 1)$. Show that the following holds:*

$$\llbracket M \rrbracket = \bigvee \{ \llbracket \omega(N) \rrbracket \mid M \to^* N \} .$$

*Hints: Extend the meaning function by setting: $\llbracket Y_n \rrbracket = \llbracket \lambda f.f^n \Omega \rrbracket$. Show that $\llbracket M \rrbracket = \bigvee_{n < \omega} \llbracket M_n \rrbracket$, where $M_n$ is obtained from $M$ by replacing all its occurrences of $Y$ by $Y_n$. Consider the normal form $N_0$ of $M_n$. Show that it is the result of replacing all the occurrences of $Y$ by $Y_0$ in a reduct $N$ of $M$, and use the strictness assumptions to show $\llbracket N_0 \rrbracket = \llbracket \omega(N) \rrbracket$.*

**Exercise 6.1.9** *A class of continuous functionals $F_D : (D \to D) \to D$, ranging over all cpo's $D$, is called a fixpoint operator if $F_D(f)$ is a fixpoint of $f$, for any $D$ and $f : D \to D$. Moreover, it is called uniform if the following holds:*

$$\forall f : D \to D, g : E \to E, h : D \to E \quad (h \circ f = g \circ h \Rightarrow h(F_D(f)) = F_D(g)) ,$$

*where $h$ is supposed strict. Show that Fix is the unique uniform fixpoint operator.*

The following exercise, based on [HP90], shows that fixpoints cannot coexist with coproducts in a cartesian closed category.

**Exercise 6.1.10** *We say that a category $\mathbf{C}$ with a terminal object $1$*

- *has fixpoints if for every $A$ and $f : A \to A$ there exists a morphism $Y(f) : 1 \to A$ such that $f \circ Y(f) = Y(f)$;*

- *is inconsistent if all objects in $\mathbf{C}$ are isomorphic to $1$.*

*(1) Show that any cartesian closed category that has an initial object $0$ and fixpoints is inconsistent. Hints: Consider $Y(id_0)$, and use exercise A2.7.4. (2) Show that any cartesian closed category that has binary coproducts and fixpoints is inconsistent. Hints: Show that the two injections, call them tt and ff, from $1$ to $2 = 1 + 1$ are equal, by 'implementing' in the categorical language the following reasoning (where $\neg = [ff, tt] : 2 \to 2$):*

$$
\begin{aligned}
tt &= (Y(\neg) \text{ or } \neg(Y(\neg))) &&= (Y(\neg) \text{ or } Y(\neg)) &&= Y(\neg) \\
&= (Y(\neg) \text{ and } Y(\neg)) &&= (Y(\neg) \text{ and } \neg(Y(\neg))) &&= ff .
\end{aligned}
$$

*(In [HP90], incompatibility with equalizers and with a natural number object is also proved.)*

# 6.2   Fixpoint induction

A key motivation for denotational semantics lies in its applications to the proof of properties of programs. An important tool is fixpoint induction. If we want to show that a property $\mathcal{P}$ holds of a term $YM$, then, knowing that the meaning of $YM$ is the lub of the sequence $\bot, F(\bot), F(F(\bot)), \ldots$, where $F$ is the meaning of $M$, it is enough to check the following properties.

- The (meaning of) property $\mathcal{P}$, is an $\omega$-subdcpo of the domain $D$ associated to the type of $YM$, i.e., $\mathcal{P}$ is closed under lub's of non-decreasing chains; such predicates are called *inclusive*.

- Both properties $\bot \in \mathcal{P}$ and $\forall x(x \in \mathcal{P} \Rightarrow F(x) \in \mathcal{P})$ hold.

This is summarized by the following inference rule, known as the fixpoint induction principle

$$\frac{\mathcal{P} \text{ inclusive} \quad \bot \in \mathcal{P} \quad \forall x \ (x \in \mathcal{P} \Rightarrow F(x) \in \mathcal{P})}{Fix(F) \in \mathcal{P}},$$

where $\mathcal{P} \subseteq D$, for a given cpo $D$, and $F : D \to D$ is continuous. Such an inference rule is a step towards mechanizing proofs of programs. What is needed next is a formal theory for proving that some predicates are inclusive (see exercise 6.2.2).

**Remark 6.2.1** *The sufficiency of the above conditions, hence the validity of fixpoint induction, follows immediately from the Peano induction principle on natural numbers. Thus, mathematically speaking, it is not strictly necessary to formulate the above principle explicitly. One can prove $\bot \in \mathcal{P}$, $F(\bot) \in \mathcal{P}$, $F(F(\bot)) \in \mathcal{P}, \ldots$ and use Peano induction to conclude (if $\mathcal{P}$ is inclusive). The interest of stating an explicit induction principle is to enable one: (1) to write lighter proofs, as $F(x)$ is easier to write than $F(F(\ldots(\bot)\ldots))$; and (2) to insert it in a mechanical proof-checker like LCF [Pau87].*

**Exercise 6.2.2** *(1) Let $D$ be a cpo. Show that $\emptyset$ and $D$ are inclusive predicates in $D$. Show that $x = x$ and $x \le y$ are inclusive in $D \times D$. (2) Let $D$ and $E$ be cpo's and $f : D \to E$ be continuous. Let $\mathcal{R}$ be inclusive in $E$. Show that $f^{-1}(\mathcal{R})$ is inclusive. (3) Let $D$ be a cpo and $\mathcal{P}, \mathcal{Q}$ be inclusive in $D$. Then show that $\mathcal{P} \cap \mathcal{Q}$ and $\mathcal{P} \cup \mathcal{Q}$ are inclusive. (4) Let $D$ and $E$ be cpo's and $\mathcal{R}$ be inclusive on $D \times E$ in its first argument. Show that the predicate $\forall y \ (x\mathcal{R}y)$ is inclusive on $D$. (5) Let $D$ and $E$ be dcpo's and $\mathcal{P}, \mathcal{Q}$ be inclusive in $D, E$ respectively. Show that $\mathcal{P} \times \mathcal{Q}$ is inclusive in $D \times E$, and that $\mathcal{P} \to \mathcal{Q}$ is inclusive in $D \to E$, where $\mathcal{P} \to \mathcal{Q} = \{f : D \to E \mid \forall d \in \mathcal{P} \ f(d) \in \mathcal{Q}\}$.*

As an illustration, we carry out in some detail the proof of the following proposition, due to Bekič, which shows that $n$-ary fixpoints can be computed using unary fixpoints.

**Proposition 6.2.3** *Let $D, E$ be cpo's and $f : D \times E \to D$, $g : D \times E \to E$ be continuous. Let $(x_0, y_0)$ be the least fixpoint of $\langle f, g \rangle$. Let $x_1$ be the least fixpoint of $f \circ \langle id, h \rangle$, where $h = Fix \circ \Lambda(g) : D \to E$ (hence $h(x_1)$ is such that $g(x_1, h(x_1)) = h(x_1)$). Then $x_0 = x_1$ and $y_0 = h(x_1)$.*

PROOF. $(x_0, y_0) \leq (x_1, h(x_1))$. Define the predicate $\mathcal{Q}(u, v)$ as $(u, v) \leq (x_1, h(x_1))$. This is an inclusive predicate (see exercise 6.2.2). Thus we may start the fixpoint induction engine. The base case is obvious. Suppose that $(u, v) \leq (x_1, h(x_1))$. We want to show that $f(u, v) \leq x_1$ and $g(u, v) \leq h(x_1)$. By monotonicity we have $f(u, v) \leq f(x_1, h(x_1))$ and $g(u, v) \leq g(x_1, h(x_1))$. But $f(x_1, h(x_1)) = x_1$ since $x_1$ is a fixpoint of $f \circ \langle id, h \rangle$. This settles the inequality $f(u, v) \leq x_1$. By definition of $h$, we have $h(x_1) = g(x_1, h(x_1))$, which settles the other inequality.

$(x_1, h(x_1)) \leq (x_0, y_0)$. We define a second predicate $\mathcal{R}(u)$ as $(u, h(u)) \leq (x_0, y_0)$. We leave the base case aside for the moment, and suppose that $\mathcal{R}(u)$ holds. We have to prove $\mathcal{R}(f(u, h(u)))$. We have $f(u, h(u))) \leq f(x_0, y_0) = x_0$ by monotonicity, and by definition of $(x_0, y_0)$. We need a little more work to obtain $h(f(u, h(u))) \leq y_0$. It is enough to check $h(x_0) \leq y_0$. We define a third inclusive predicate $\mathcal{S}(u)$ as $u \leq y_0$, remembering that $h(x_0)$ is the least fixpoint of $\Lambda(g)(x_0)$. The base case is obvious. Suppose that $u \leq y_0$. Then $g(x_0, u) \leq g(x_0, y_0) = y_0$. Hence fixpoint induction with respect to $\mathcal{S}$ allows us to conclude $h(x_0) \leq y_0$. We are left with the base case with respect to $\mathcal{R}$: $(\bot, h(\bot)) \leq (x_0, y_0)$ follows *a fortiori* from $h(x_0) \leq y_0$. □

In this proof: we have focused in turn on each of the least fixpoint operators involved in the statement, exploiting just the fact that the other least fixpoints are fixpoints.

# 6.3  The programming language PCF

Scott [Sco93], and then Plotkin [Plo77], introduced a simply typed $\lambda Y$-calculus, PCF, which has become a quite popular language in studies of semantics. It has two basic types: the type $\iota$ of natural numbers, and the type $o$ of booleans. Its set of constants is given in figure 6.1. The language PCF is interpreted in **Cpo** as specified in figure 6.2 (for the interpretation of $\Omega$ and $Y$, cf. definition 6.1.4). We use the same notation for the constants and for their interpretation. This interpretation is called the *continuous model* of PCF. More generally, we define the following notion of standard model.

**Definition 6.3.1 (standard model)** *Let* **C** *be a least fixpoint model. If we interpret $\iota$ and $o$ by objects $D^\iota$ and $D^o$ such that* **C**$[1, D^\iota]$ *and* **C**$[1, D^o]$ *are (order-isomorphic) to $\omega_\bot$ and $\mathbf{B}_\bot$, if the basic constants are interpreted as in figure 6.2, and if the first order constants behave functionally as specified in figure 6.2 (replacing, say, $succ(x)$ by $ev \circ \langle succ, x \rangle$), then we say that we have a standard model of PCF.*

Recall that if **C** has enough points (cf. definition 4.5.4), then the model is called extensional.

**Definition 6.3.2 (order-extensional)** *Let* **C**, *$D^\iota$, and $D^o$ be as in definition 6.3.1. Moreover, suppose that* **C** *has enough points and that the order between the morphisms is the pointwise ordering, as in* **Cpo**. *Then the model is called order-extensional.*

$$n \qquad\qquad : \iota \qquad\qquad\qquad (n \in \omega)$$
$$tt, f\!f \qquad\quad : o$$
$$succ, pred \quad : \iota \to \iota$$
$$zero? \qquad\; : \iota \to o$$
$$if \;\; then \;\; else \;\; : o \to \iota \to \iota \to \iota$$
$$if \;\; then \;\; else \;\; : o \to o \to o \to o$$

$$\Omega \qquad\qquad : \sigma \qquad\qquad\qquad \text{for all } \sigma$$
$$Y \qquad\qquad : (\sigma \to \sigma) \to \sigma \quad \text{for all } \sigma$$

Figure 6.1: The constants of PCF

$$D^o = \mathbf{B}_\perp \qquad\qquad \text{where } \mathbf{B}_\perp = \{\perp, tt, f\!f\}$$
$$D^\iota = \omega_\perp \qquad\qquad \text{flat domain on natural numbers}$$
$$D^{\sigma \to \tau} = D^\sigma \to_{cont} D^\tau \quad \text{exponent in } \mathbf{Cpo}$$

$$succ(x) = \begin{cases} \perp & if \; x = \perp \\ x+1 & if \; x \neq \perp \end{cases} \qquad pred(x) = \begin{cases} \perp & if \; x = \perp \text{ or } x = 0 \\ x-1 & \text{otherwise} \end{cases}$$

$$zero?(x) = \begin{cases} \perp & \text{if } x = \perp \\ tt & \text{if } x = 0 \\ f\!f & \text{otherwise} \end{cases} \qquad if \; x \; then \; y \; else \; z = \begin{cases} \perp & \text{if } x = \perp \\ y & \text{if } x = tt \\ z & \text{if } x = f\!f \end{cases}$$

Figure 6.2: Interpretation of PCF in **Cpo**

**Operational semantics of PCF.** We equip PCF with an operational semantics which is adequately modelled by any standard model. It is described in figure 6.3 by means of a deterministic evaluation relation $\to_{op}$.

**Exercise 6.3.3** Let $add_\iota = Y(\lambda f xy.if \; zero?(x) \; then \; y \; else \; succ(f(pred(x))y))$. Compute $add_\iota\, 4\, 3$ using the rules in figure 6.3.

**Exercise 6.3.4** Imitate the techniques of chapter 2 to establish that the rewriting system $\to$ specified by the eight axioms of figure 6.2 (applied in any context) is confluent, and that if $M \to^* N$ and $N$ is a normal form, then $M \to_{op}^* N$. Hint: Prove suitable versions of the standardization and Church-Rosser theorems presented in chapter 2.

Next we investigate the relationships between the denotational and the operational semantics of PCF.

$$(\lambda x.M)N \to_{op} M[N/x] \qquad YM \to_{op} M(YM)$$
$$zero?(0) \to_{op} tt \qquad zero?(n+1) \to_{op} f\!\!f$$
$$succ(n) \to_{op} n+1 \qquad pred(n+1) \to_{op} n$$
$$if\ tt\ then\ N\ else\ P \to_{op} N \qquad if\ f\!\!f\ then\ N\ else\ P \to_{op} P$$

$$\frac{M \to_{op} M'}{MN \to_{op} M'N} \qquad \frac{M \to_{op} M'}{if\ M\ then\ N\ else\ P \to_{op} if\ M'\ then\ N\ else\ P}$$

$$\frac{M \to_{op} M'}{f(M) \to_{op} f(M')} \qquad (for\ f \in \{succ, pred, zero?\})$$

Figure 6.3: Operational semantics for PCF

**Definition 6.3.5 (PCF program)** *We call programs the terms of PCF which are closed and of basic type.*

For example, $(\lambda x.x)3$ and $add_\iota\,4\,3$ (cf. exercise 6.3.3) are programs.

**Theorem 6.3.6 (adequacy)** *Any standard model* **C** *of PCF is adequate, i.e., for all programs of type $\iota$ (and similarly for type $o$):*

$$(\exists n\ P \to_{op}^* n) \Leftrightarrow [\![P]\!] = n\,.$$

PROOF. ($\Rightarrow$) This follows by soundness of the continuous model.

($\Leftarrow$) We use the notation of section 4.5, and write $\underline{D^\sigma} = \mathbf{C}[1, D^\sigma]$. The induction on types comes into play by a definition of a family of so-called *adequacy relations* $\mathcal{R}^\sigma \subseteq \underline{D^\sigma} \times PCF_\sigma^o$, for each type $\sigma$, where $PCF_\sigma^o$ is the set of closed terms of type $\sigma$. Here is the definition of these (logical-like) relations ($\mathcal{R}^o$ is analogous to $\mathcal{R}^\iota$):

$$\mathcal{R}^\iota = \{(x,M) \mid x = \bot\ or\ (x = n\ and\ M \to_{op}^* n)\}$$
$$\mathcal{R}^{\sigma \to \tau} = \{(f,M) \mid \forall e, N\ (e\,\mathcal{R}^\sigma\,N \Rightarrow ev \circ \langle f, e\rangle\,\mathcal{R}^\tau\,MN)\}\,.$$

The statement is a part of the following claim.

**Claim.** For each provable judgment $x_1 : \sigma_1, \ldots, x_n : \sigma_n \vdash M : \sigma$, for each n-tuple $(d_1, N_1), \ldots, (d_n, N_n)$ such that $d_i\,\mathcal{R}^{\sigma_i}\,N_i$ for $i = 1, \ldots, n$, we have:

$$[\![\vec{x} : \vec{\sigma} \vdash M]\!] \circ \langle d_1, \ldots, d_n\rangle\,\mathcal{R}^\sigma\,M[N_1/x_1, \ldots, N_n/x_n]\,.$$

We set $M' = M[N_1/x_1, \ldots, N_n/x_n]$, etc. We proceed with the simplest cases first.

- $M = x_i$. Then $[\![M]\!] \circ \langle d_1, \ldots, d_n\rangle = d_i$, and $M[N_1/x_1, \ldots, N_n/x_n] = N_i$, hence the sought result is $d_i\,\mathcal{R}^{\sigma_i}\,N_i$, which is among the assumptions.

- $M = NQ$. By induction $[\![N]\!] \circ \langle d_1, \ldots, d_n \rangle \, \mathcal{R}^{\sigma \to \tau} \, N'$ and $[\![Q]\!] \circ \langle d_1, \ldots, d_n \rangle \, \mathcal{R}^\sigma \, Q'$. By definition of $\mathcal{R}^{\sigma \to \tau}$, $ev \circ \langle [\![N]\!] \circ \langle d_1, \ldots, d_n \rangle, [\![Q]\!] \circ \langle d_1, \ldots, d_n \rangle \rangle \, \mathcal{R}^\tau \, N'Q'$, i.e., $[\![M]\!] \circ \langle d_1, \ldots, d_n \rangle \, \mathcal{R}^\tau \, M'$.

- $M = \lambda x.Q$. We have to show, for each $d \, \mathcal{R}^\sigma \, N$:

$$ev \circ \langle [\![M]\!] \circ \langle d_1, \ldots, d_n \rangle, d \rangle \, \mathcal{R}^\tau \, M'N \quad i.e. \quad [\![Q]\!] \circ \langle d_1, \ldots, d_n, d \rangle \, \mathcal{R}^\tau \, (\lambda x.Q')N.$$

By induction we have:

$$[\![Q]\!] \circ \langle d_1, \ldots, d_n, d \rangle \, \mathcal{R}^\tau \, Q[N_1/x_1, \ldots, N_n/x_n, N/x] \ .$$

Since $(\lambda x.Q')N \to_{op} Q[N_1/x_1, \ldots, N_n/x_n, N/x]$, we can conclude provided the following property holds, for all $\sigma$:

$$(Q_1) \quad f \, \mathcal{R}^\sigma \, M \text{ and } M' \to_{op} M \quad \Rightarrow \quad f \, \mathcal{R}^\sigma \, M' \ .$$

- $M = n$. In this case, $n \, \mathcal{R}^\iota \, M$ holds trivially. Similarly for $tt$ and $ff$.

- $M = succ$. Let $d \, \mathcal{R}^\iota \, P$. We have to show $ev \circ \langle succ, d \rangle \, \mathcal{R}^\iota \, succ(P)$. There are two cases:

$d = \bot$. Then $ev \circ \langle succ, d \rangle = ev \circ \langle succ, \bot \rangle = \bot$

$d = n$. Then $ev \circ \langle succ, d \rangle = n + 1 \ .$

In both cases $ev \circ \langle succ, d \rangle \, \mathcal{R}^\iota \, succ(P)$. The reasoning is similar for *pred*, *zero?*, and *if then else*.

- $M = Y$. We have to show $[\![Y]\!] \, \mathcal{R}^{(\sigma \to \sigma) \to \sigma} \, Y$, that is, $ev \circ \langle [\![Y]\!], g \rangle \, \mathcal{R}^\sigma \, YM$, for all $g \, \mathcal{R}^{\sigma \to \sigma} \, M$. We assume the following properties (cf. inclusive predicates), for all (fixed) $\sigma, M$:

$(Q_2) \quad \bot \, \mathcal{R}^\sigma \, M$

$(Q_3) \quad \{f_n\}_{n < \omega}$ non decreasing implies $(\forall n \ f_n \, \mathcal{R}^\sigma \, M) \Rightarrow (\bigvee_{n < \omega} f_n) \, \mathcal{R}^\sigma \, M$.

By $(Q_3)$, the conclusion follows if we show:

$$ev \circ \langle [\![\lambda f.f^n \Omega]\!], g \rangle \, \mathcal{R}^\sigma \, YM \quad \text{(for all } n) \ .$$

We set $d_n = ev \circ \langle [\![\lambda f.f^n \Omega]\!], g \rangle$. Since $d_n = [\![f^n \Omega]\!] \circ g$, we have $d_{n+1} = ev \circ \langle g, d_n \rangle$ for all $n$. Therefore, we only have to show:

(1) $d_0 \, \mathcal{R}^\sigma \, YM$. Since $d_0 = [\![\Omega]\!] \circ g$, this follows from $(Q_2)$ and from the left strictness of composition.

(2) $(d \, \mathcal{R}^\sigma \, YM) \Rightarrow (ev \circ \langle g, d \rangle \, \mathcal{R}^\sigma \, YM)$. Since $g \, \mathcal{R}^{\sigma \to \sigma} \, M$ by assumption, we have $ev \circ \langle g, d \rangle \, \mathcal{R}^\sigma \, M(YM)$, and the conclusion then follows by $(Q_1)$.

Properties $(Q_1)$ and $(Q_2)$ are obvious at basic types. For a type $\sigma \to \tau$, $(Q_1)$ follows by induction from the inference: $(M' \to_{op} M) \Rightarrow (M'N \to_{op} MN)$ and $(Q_2)$ follows from the strictness equation $ev \circ \langle \bot, d \rangle = \bot$. Property $(Q_3)$ follows at basic types from the fact that non-increasing sequences are stationary in a flat domain, and at functional types from the preservation of limits by continuity. This completes the proof of the claim. $\qquad\square$

**Remark 6.3.7** *The adequacy relations used in the proof of theorem 6.3.6 combine ideas from the computability technique (cf. theorem 3.5.18, remark 3.5.17, and remark 4.5.2) and from the inclusive predicates technique (cf. section 6.2).*

# 6.4     The full abstraction problem for PCF

In general, given a programming language, the specification of the operational semantics is given in two steps:

(1) Evaluation: a collection of *programs* is defined, usually a collection of closed terms, on which a partial relation of evaluation is defined. The evaluation is intended to describe the dynamic evolution of a program while running on an abstract machine.

(2) Observation: a collection of admissible observations is given. These observations represent the only means to record the behavior of the evaluation of a program.

In this fashion, an observational equivalence can be defined on arbitrary terms $M$ and $N$ as follows: $M$ is observationally equivalent to $N$ if and only if whenever $M$ and $N$ can be plugged into a piece of code $P$, so to form correct programs $P[M]$ and $P[N]$, then $M$ and $N$ are not separable (or distinguishable) by any legal observation. On the other hand any interpretation of a programming language provides a theory of program equivalence. How does this theory compare to observational equivalence? We will say that an interpretation (or a model) is adequate whenever it provides us with a theory of equivalence which is contained in the observational equivalence. Moreover, we call an adequate model (equationally) fully abstract if the equivalence induced by the model coincides with the observational equivalence.

In section 3.2, we discussed a full abstraction result for $D_\infty$ models. There, all terms were considered programs, and the observation was the existence of a head normal form. In this section, we discuss the situation for PCF. We have defined the programs as the closed terms of basic type. We have defined an evaluation relation $\to_{op}$. What can be observed of a program is its convergence to a natural number or to a boolean value. The principal reason for focusing on programs is that they lead to observable results. This stands in contrast with expressions like $\lambda x.x$, which are just code, and are not evaluated by $\to_{op}$ unless they are applied to an argument, or more generally unless they are plugged into a program context. A program context for a PCF term is a context $C$ (cf. definition 2.1.6) such that $C[M]$ is a program.

**Definition 6.4.1 (observational preorder)** *We define a preorder $\leq_{obs}$, called the observational preorder, between PCF terms $M, N$ of the same type, as follows:*

$$M \leq_{obs} N \quad \Leftrightarrow \quad \forall C \ (C[M] \to_{op}^* c \ \Rightarrow \ C[N] \to_{op}^* c) \ ,$$

*where $C$ ranges over all the contexts which are program contexts for both $M$ and $N$, and where $c ::= n \mid tt \mid ff$.*

**Remark 6.4.2** *By exercise 6.3.4 and by theorem 6.3.6, equivalent definitions for $\leq_{obs}$ are:*

$$M \leq_{obs} N \quad \Leftrightarrow \quad \forall C \ (C[M] \to^* c \ \Rightarrow \ C[N] \to^* c)$$
$$M \leq_{obs} N \quad \Leftrightarrow \quad \forall C \ (\llbracket C[M] \rrbracket \leq \llbracket C[N] \rrbracket) \ .$$

**Definition 6.4.3 (fully abstract)** *A cpo-enriched CCC is said to yield an inequationally fully abstract (fully abstract for short) model of PCF if the following equivalence holds for any PCF terms of the same type:*

$$M \leq_{obs} N \Leftrightarrow [\![M]\!] \leq [\![N]\!] \ .$$

It is a consequence of the adequacy theorem that the direction ($\Leftarrow$) holds for the continuous model (and in fact for any standard model). But the converse direction does not hold for the continuous model. There are several proofs of this negative result, all based on a particular continuous function $por : \mathbf{B}_\perp \times \mathbf{B}_\perp \to \mathbf{B}_\perp$ defined by:

$$por(x, y) = \begin{cases} tt & \text{if } x = tt \text{ or } y = tt \\ f\!f & \text{if } x = f\!f \text{ and } y = f\!f \\ \perp & \text{otherwise} \ . \end{cases}$$

(1) Plotkin first proved that the continuous model is not fully abstract. He gave the following terms, both of type $(o \to o \to o) \to o$:

$$M_1 = \lambda g.\text{if } P_1 \text{ then if } P_2 \text{ then if } P_3 \text{ then } \Omega \text{ else } tt \text{ else } \Omega \text{ else } \Omega$$
$$M_2 = \lambda g.\text{if } P_1 \text{ then if } P_2 \text{ then if } P_3 \text{ then } \Omega \text{ else } f\!f \text{ else } \Omega \text{ else } \Omega \ ,$$

where $P_1 = g\, tt\, \Omega$, $P_2 = g\, \Omega\, tt$, and $P_3 = g\, f\!f\, f\!f$. These terms are designed in such a way that:

$$tt = [\![M_1]\!](por) \neq [\![M_2]\!](por) = f\!f \ .$$

On the other hand $M_1 =_{obs} M_2$. This is proved thanks to two key syntactic results:

(a) Milner's context lemma [Mil77]. This lemma, proposed as exercise 6.4.4, states that in the definition of $\leq_{obs}$ it is enough to let $C$ range over so-called applicative contexts, of the form $[\ ]N_1 \dots N_p$. Applying this lemma to $M_1, M_2$, we only have to consider contexts $[\ ]N$. By the definition of $\to_{op}$, we have for $i = 1, 2$:

$$[M_i]N \to^*_{op} c \Rightarrow \begin{cases} N\, tt\, \Omega \to^*_{op} tt \\ N\, \Omega\, tt \to^*_{op} tt \\ N\, f\!f\, f\!f \to^*_{op} f\!f \ . \end{cases}$$

(b) There is no $N$ such that $N\, tt\, \Omega \to^*_{op} tt$, $N\, \Omega\, tt \to^*_{op} tt$ and $N\, f\!f\, f\!f \to^*_{op} f\!f$. This result is a consequence of the following more general result. PCF is a *sequential* language, in the following sense: If $C$ is a program context with several holes, if

$$[\![\vdash C[\Omega, \dots, \Omega]]\!] = \perp \quad \text{and} \quad \exists\, M_1, \dots, M_n \ [\![\vdash C[M_1, \dots, M_n]]\!] \neq \perp,$$

then there exists an $i$ called a sequentiality index, such that

$$\forall N_1, \dots, N_{i-1}, N_{i+1}, \dots, N_n \ [\![\vdash C[N_1, \dots, N_{i-1}, \Omega, N_{i+1}, \dots, N_n]]\!] = \perp \ .$$

This result is an easy consequence of (the PCF version of) Berry's syntactic sequentiality theorem 2.4.3 (see exercise 6.4.5) and of the adequacy theorem 6.3.6. Here, it is applied to $C = N[\ ][\ ]$, observing that we can use $N\, f\!f\, f\!f \to^*_{op} f\!f$ to deduce that there is no $c$ such that $N\Omega\Omega \to^*_{op} c$.

Another way to prove the non-existence of $N$ is by means of logical relations. We have treated essentially the same example when we discussed Very Finitary PCF (cf. section 4.5).

(2) Milner has shown that in an extensional standard fully abstract model of PCF, the interpretations of all types are algebraic, and their compact elements must be definable, i.e., the meaning of some closed term. This is called the definability theorem (for a proof, we refer to [Cur86]). One can use this result to cut down the path followed in (1) and go directly to step (b). In reality, there is no cut down at all, since the proof of the definability theorem uses the context lemma, and exploits terms in the style of $M_1, M_2$.

**Exercise\* 6.4.4 (context lemma)** *Let $M$ and $M'$ be two closed PCF terms of the same type such that, for all closed terms $N_1, \ldots, N_n$ such that $MN_1 \cdots N_n$ is of basic type, the following holds:*

$$MN_1 \cdots N_n \to_{op}^* c \quad \Rightarrow \quad M'N_1 \cdots N_n \to_{op}^* c \,.$$

*Show that $M \leq_{obs} M'$, by induction on (length of the reduction $C[M] \to_{op}^* c$, size of $C[M]$).*

**Exercise 6.4.5 (syntactic sequentiality for PCF)** *Prove the PCF version of theorem 2.4.3, and show the corresponding corollary along the lines of exercise 2.4.4.*

The converse of the definability theorem also holds, and is easy to prove.

**Proposition 6.4.6** *If $\mathbf{C}$ is an order-extensional standard model of PCF in which all $\mathbf{C}[1, D^\sigma]$'s are algebraic and are such that all their compact elements are definable, then $\mathbf{C}$ is fully abstract.*

PROOF. Suppose that $M \leq_{obs} M'$. It is enough to check $[\![M]\!](\vec{d}) \leq [\![M']\!](\vec{d})$ for all compact $\vec{d} = d_1 \cdots d_n$. Then the conclusion follows using contexts of the form $[\ ]N_1 \cdots N_n$.                                                    □

**Exercise 6.4.7 (uniqueness)** *Show, as a consequence of proposition 6.4.6 and of the definability theorem, that all order-extensional standard models of PCF are isomorphic (in a suitable sense).*

In fact, this (unique) fully abstract model exists, and was first constructed by Milner (essentially) as a quotient of the term model of PCF. (see section 6.6, and in particular remark 6.6.11). Since then, lots of efforts have been made in order to provide 'more semantic' constructions of this model (this is known as the full abstraction problem for PCF [BCL85]). In particular, the non-definability of *por* prompted the study of sequentiality, which is the subject of section 6.5 and of chapter 14. A weaker notion, stability, appeared on the way, and is the subject of chapter 12. By 'more semantic' constructions, the contributors in this area certainly meant at least the following two informal requirements:

(1) The model should consist explicitly of cpo's of a certain sort and of functions or function-like morphisms of a certain sort.

(2) The model should throw some light on the operational preorder of PCF. In particular, it was hoped to show that the operational preorder for PCF could be shown to be effectively presented.

As regards the last point, we now know that there is no hope: Loader has proved that the observational preorder on Finitary PCF is undecidable [Loa97]. But not all efforts have been lost: the sequential model of chapter 14 is fully abstract for an extension of PCF with a family of control operators (see section 14.4). The stable and sequential models are also interesting for other reasons. For example, stability is at the root of linear logic (see chapter 13).

**Exercise 6.4.8** *Show that the undecidability of the observational equivalence for Finitary PCF implies the undecidability of the definability problem for Finitary PCF (cf. section 4.5).*

**Remark 6.4.9** *Gunter has proposed a simple semantic proof of $M_1 =_{obs} M_2$. In the stable model of PCF, to be defined in chapter 12, one retains only functions which satisfy the following property (specified here for a type like $o \times o \to o$):*

$$\forall x \ f(x) \neq \perp \ \Rightarrow \ \exists y \ minimum \ s.t. \ (y \leq x \ and \ f(y) \neq \perp) \ .$$

*In particular, por is rejected (take $x = (tt, tt)$, then $(\perp, tt)$ and $(tt, \perp)$ are both minimal, but there is no minimum), and as a consequence we have $[\![M_1]\!] = [\![M_2]\!]$. Now, because the direction ($\Leftarrow$) holds for the stable model, which is standard, we have $M_1 =_{obs} M_2$.*

# 6.5 Towards sequentiality

We have already pointed out that the $\lambda$-calculus is sequential (theorem 2.4.3). In sections 4.5 and 6.4, we have exhibited examples of inherently parallel functions that are not definable in a (finitary version of) PCF. In this section, we give further evidence of the sequential nature of PCF. We define sequential functions in a restricted setting, which will be extended in chapter 14. We show that the compact definable first order functions of the continuous model of PCF are exactly the (compact) first order sequential functions.

But before we engage in the semantic investigation of sequentiality, we should mention that another approach to full abstraction is to stick to the continuous model and seek a suitable extension of PCF for which the continuous model is fully abstract. Such a simple extension exists, as was first shown by Plotkin, who added a parallel conditional to PCF [Plo77]. Later it was shown in [Cur86] that the more natural extension of PCF with a constant *por* (with the rules *por x tt* $\to_{op}$ *tt*, *por tt x* $\to_{op}$ *tt* and *por ff ff* $\to_{op}$ *ff*) has the continuous model as fully abstract model. The proof goes via definability (cf. proposition 6.4.6). Plotkin has also given a strengthened form of definability: if the language is further extended with a *parallel existential* operator, then the language is universal for the continuous model, i.e., every computable element of the model (cf. definition 1.1.17) is definable (see [Plo77] for details, and see remark 14.4.18 for a similar, more satisfactory result in a sequential framework).

**Definition 6.5.1 (sequential function (Vuillemin))** *Let $D, D_1, \ldots, D_n$ be flat cpo's, and let $f : D_1 \times \cdots \times D_n \to D$ be monotonic (hence continuous). Let $x = (x_1, \ldots, x_n) \in D_1 \times \cdots \times D_n$, and suppose that $f(x) = \bot$. We say that $f$ is sequential at $x$ if either $f(z) = \bot$ for all $z \geq x$, or there exists $i$ such that $x_i = \bot$, and:*

$$\forall y = (y_1, \ldots, y_n)\ (y > x \text{ and } f(y) \neq \bot) \Rightarrow y_i \neq \bot.$$

*We say then that $i$ is a sequentiality index for $f$ at $x$.*

The above definition goes back to [Vui74]. The following easy proposition offers an alternative definition of sequential functions over flat cpo's.

**Proposition 6.5.2** *Let $D = X_\bot$ be a flat cpo. The sets of sequential functions from products of flat domains to $D$ are alternatively defined as follows, by induction on their arity $n$:*

*Arity $1$ : Any monotonic function $f : D \to D$ is sequential.*

*Arity $n \geq 2$ : Given $D_1, \ldots, D_n$, $i \leq n$, $X \subseteq D_i \backslash \{\bot\}$, and a set*

$$\{f_x : D_1 \times \cdots \times D_{i-1} \times D_{i+1} \times \cdots \times D_n \to D \mid x \in X\}$$

*of sequential functions, the following function $f$ is sequential:*

$$
\begin{aligned}
f(x_1, \ldots, x_{i-1}, x, x_{i+1}, \ldots, x_n) &= \bot && \text{if } x \notin X \\
f(x_1, \ldots, x_{i-1}, x, x_{i+1}, \ldots, x_n) &= f_x(x_1, \ldots, x_{i-1}, x_{i+1}, \ldots, x_n) && \text{if } x \in X .
\end{aligned}
$$

*Moreover, the compact sequential functions are exactly the functions obtained as above, with $X$ finite at each induction step, and with a finite graph in the base case.*

PROOF. In both directions, the proof goes by induction on the arity. The two parts of the statement are proved together. If $f$ is sequential, then we pick a sequentiality index $i$ at $\bot$, and we define the $f_x$'s by the second equation in the statement. They are clearly sequential, hence induction applies to them. If $f$ is compact, $X$ cannot be infinite, as otherwise $f$ would be the lub of an infinite sequence of functions obtained by cutting down $X$ to finite subsets. Conversely, let $f$ be constructed as in the statement and $x$ such that $f(x) = \bot$ and $f(z) \neq \bot$ for some $z > x$. There are two cases:

(1) $x_i = \bot$. Then $i$ is a sequentiality index at $x$.

(2) $x_i = j \neq \bot$. Then $j \in X$ and by induction $f_j$ has a sequentiality index at $(x_1, \ldots, x_{i-1}, x_{i+1}, \ldots, x_n)$, which is a sequentiality index of $f$ at $x$.

If the $X$'s are all finite, then the description of $f$ is finite, from which compactness follows easily. $\square$

**Exercise 6.5.3** *Show that the $C$-logical relations, where $C$ is the set of all the constants of PCF (including $Y$), are exactly the Sieber-sequential relations of definition 4.5.16. Hint: Show that at each type $\sigma$, the set of invariant elements of a Sieber-sequential relation forms an inclusive predicate.*

Hence (compact) sequential functions on flat domains can be described by sequential 'programs', which can actually be written as PCF terms, as the following theorem shows.

**Theorem 6.5.4** *For a compact first order function $f$ of a standard extensional model of PCF, the following properties are equivalent:*

(1) *$f$ is sequential.*

(2) *$f$ is definable in the following restriction $\Lambda(C')$ of PCF (with $\Omega$ of basic type):*

$$C' = \{\Omega, n, tt, ff, pred, zero?, if \quad then \quad else \}\ .$$

(3) *$f$ is definable in PCF.*

(4) *$f$ is invariant under all $k+1$-ary relations $S_{k+1}$ $(k \geq 1)$ defined at basic type by:*

$$(x_1, \ldots, x_{k+1}) \in S_{k+1} \quad \Leftrightarrow \quad (\exists j \leq k \ x_j = \bot) \ or \ (x_1 = \ldots = x_{k+1} \neq \bot))\ .$$

*These relations are special cases of Sieber-sequential relations, cf. definition 4.5.16. More precisely: $S_{k+1} = \mathcal{S}^{k+1}_{\{1,\ldots,k\},\{1,\ldots,k+1\}}$.*

PROOF. (1) $\Rightarrow$ (2) The restricted syntax allows us to encode all compact sequential functions, as characterized in proposition 6.5.2 (cf. the proof of theorem 6.6.6). Hence the interpretation function is a surjection from the restricted syntax to the set of compact first order sequential functions.

(2) $\Rightarrow$ (3) Obvious by inclusion.

(3) $\Rightarrow$ (4) This follows from lemma 4.5.3 and from exercise 6.5.3.

(4) $\Rightarrow$ (1) Suppose that $f$ is not sequential. Then there exists $x = (x_1, \ldots, x_n)$ such that:

$$f(x) = \bot$$
$$J = \{j \leq n \mid x_j = \bot\} \neq \emptyset$$
$$\forall j \in J \ \exists y_j = (y_{1j}, \ldots, y_{nj}) \ ((\forall i \notin J \ y_{ij} = x_i) \text{ and } y_{jj} = \bot \text{ and } f(y_j) \neq \bot)\ .$$

Without loss of generality, we can assume that $J - \{1, \ldots, k\}$ for some $k \geq 1$ (and $\leq n$). We claim that $(y_{i1}, \ldots, y_{ik}, x_i) \in S_{k+1}$ for all $i \leq n$. This follows from the following easy case analysis.

$i \notin J$. Then $y_{i1} = \ldots = y_{ik} = x_i$.

$i \in J$. Then $y_{ii} = \bot$.

Hence, by invariance: $(f(y_1), \ldots, f(y_k), f(x)) \in S_{k+1}$, which contradicts the definition of $S_{k+1}$, since we have assumed $f(y_j) \neq \bot$ for all $j \leq k$ and $f(x) = \bot$. $\square$

The semantic treatment of sequentiality at higher orders will be the subject of chapter 14 (see also section 13.3).

**Exercise 6.5.5** *Show that every PCF definable first order function in a standard model of PCF is sequential. Hint: Given a closed term $M$, call $M_n$ the term obtained by replacing $Y$ by $\lambda f.f^n\Omega$ (cf. exercise 6.1.8), and let $P_n$ be the normal form of $M_n$. Show that the $P_n$'s form a directed set, and exploit this to show that they all contribute to a single sequential function defined as in proposition 6.5.2.*

# 6.6   PCF Böhm trees *

In this section, we sketch a construction of the fully abstract model of PCF, based on a notion of Böhm tree for PCF due independently to Hyland and Ong, and to Abramsky, Jagadeesan and Malacaria [HO94, AJM95]. Often, our definitions are given for types built over $\iota$ only. The extension of the constructions to the full PCF type hierarchy is straightforward.

**Definition 6.6.1 (PCF Böhm tree)**  *We define the set $T^{raw}$ of raw PCF Böhm trees, and the auxiliary set $B^{raw}$ as follows (T ranges over $T^{raw}$, and B ranges over $B^{raw}$ ):*

$$T ::= \lambda \vec{x} : \vec{\sigma}.B$$
$$B ::= \Omega \mid n \mid case\ x\vec{T}\ [F] \quad (n \in \omega)$$
$$F : \omega \rightarrow B^{raw} \qquad\qquad (dom(F)\ finite)\ .$$

*We endow $T^{raw}$ with a subtree ordering, which is the least congruence satisfying:*

$$\Omega \leq T \ (for\ any\ T) \qquad \frac{F(n) \downarrow \Rightarrow F(n) \leq F'(n)\ for\ any\ n \in \omega}{F \leq F'}\ .$$

*The set $T^{raw}$ can be viewed as a subset of the set of (raw) terms in $\Lambda(C)$, with:*

$$C = \{\Omega, n, case_X \mid n \in \omega, X \subseteq_{fin} \omega\},$$

*taking $case_{dom(F)}$ to encode $case\ x\vec{T}\ [F]$. The constants are typed as follows:*

$$\vdash \Omega : \iota \quad \vdash n : \iota \quad \vdash case_X : \iota^{\sharp X + 1} \rightarrow \iota\ .$$

*Notice that we include the constants $\vdash \Omega : \sigma$ at basic types only. A correctly typed raw PCF Böhm tree is called a finite Böhm tree. The sets of correctly typed terms of $T^{raw}$ and $B^{raw}$ are denoted $T$ and $B$. We denote with $T^{\infty}$ the ideal completion of $(T, \leq)$ (cf. proposition 1.1.21). The elements of $T^{\infty}$ are called the PCF Böhm trees. We use $P, Q$ to range over $T^{\infty}$, while $S, T, B$ always denote finite trees. The completion is done at every type, and we write $\Gamma \vdash P : \tau$ whenever $\Gamma \vdash S : \tau$ for any finite approximation of $P$.*

Next we define a category whose morphisms are PCF Böhm trees.

**Definition 6.6.2**  *The category $\mathbf{BT}_{PCF}$ has the following objects and morphisms:*

- *The objects of $\mathbf{BT}_{PCF}$ are the sequences $\vec{\sigma}$ of PCF types.*

- *$\mathbf{BT}_{PCF}[\vec{\sigma}, \vec{\tau}]$, with $\vec{\tau} = \tau_1, \ldots, \tau_n$, consists of a vector of trees $\vec{x} : \vec{\sigma} \vdash P_i : \tau_i$ in $T^{\infty}$, for $i = 1, \ldots, n$.*

*Given $\vec{\sigma}$ and $\sigma$ in the list $\vec{\sigma}$, we define a projection morphism $\vec{x} : \vec{\sigma} \vdash \pi_{\vec{\sigma}, \sigma} : \sigma$ by induction on $\sigma = \tau_1 \rightarrow \cdots \rightarrow \tau_p \rightarrow \iota$, as follows:*

$$\pi_{\vec{\sigma}, \sigma} = \lambda \vec{y}.\ case\ x(\pi_{\vec{\tau}, \tau_1}) \cdots (\pi_{\vec{\tau}, \tau_p})\ [id]\ ,$$

*where id is the identity function mapping $n \in \omega$ to $\vdash n : \iota$. If $\vec{\sigma} = \sigma_1, \ldots, \sigma_n$, then the identity morphism $id : \vec{\sigma} \rightarrow \vec{\sigma}$ is defined by: $id = \pi_{\vec{\sigma}, \sigma_1}, \ldots, \pi_{\vec{\sigma}, \sigma_n}$.*

**Remark 6.6.3**  *The projection and identity morphisms are infinite trees, due to the presence of the identity function $\lambda n.n$ in their definition, which introduces infinite horizontal branching.*

In order to define composition, we proceed in two stages. First, we define the composition of finite morphisms, i.e., finite trees. Given $T \in \mathbf{BT}_{PCF}[\vec{\sigma}, \vec{\sigma'}]$ and $S \in \mathbf{BT}_{PCF}[\vec{\sigma'}, \sigma'']$, we form $(\lambda \vec{x}.S)\vec{T}$, and reduce it to its normal form $R$, applying $\beta$, as well as the following rules:

$$
\begin{aligned}
(\delta) \quad & case\, n\ [F] \rightarrow \begin{cases} F(n) & \text{if } F(n) \downarrow \\ \Omega & \text{otherwise} \end{cases} \\
(\Omega) \quad & case\, \Omega\ [F] \rightarrow \Omega \\
(\gamma) \quad & case\,(case\, M\ [F])\ [G] \rightarrow case\, M\ [H]\ ,
\end{aligned}
$$

where $H$ has the same domain as $F$ and $H(n) = case\, F(n)\ [G]$. We set:

$$
S \circ (\vec{T}) = R\ .
$$

Finally, composition is extended to infinite trees by continuity:

$$
P \circ (\vec{Q}) = \bigvee \{ S \circ (\vec{T}) \mid S \leq P, \vec{T} \leq \vec{Q} \}\ .
$$

We now have to justify all this carefully. We have to show that:

(1)  $R$ always exists.

(2)  $R \in \mathcal{T}$.

(3)  The lub in the definition of $P \circ (\vec{Q})$ exists.

(4)  Composition satisfies the monoid laws.

As for (1), we rely on the following theorem due to Breazu-Tannen and Gallier [BTG91].

**Theorem 6.6.4** *Let $\Lambda(C)$ be a simply-typed[1] $\lambda$-calculus with constants whose type has rank at most 1. Let $\mathcal{R}$ be a set of strongly normalizing rewriting rules for first order terms written with the (uncurried) signature $C$. Then the rewriting system $\beta + \mathcal{R}$ (with the curried version of $\mathcal{R}$) over $\Lambda(C)$ is strongly normalizing.*

We instantiate $\mathcal{R}$ as $(\delta) + (\Omega) + (\gamma)$.

**Proposition 6.6.5** *The system $(\delta) + (\Omega) + (\gamma)$, considered as a first order rewriting system, is strongly normalizing.*

PROOF. We use a technique inspired from exercise 2.2.23. We call $\Phi$ the set of first order terms built over the uncurried signature $C = \{\Omega, n, case_X \mid n \in \omega, X \subseteq_{fin} \omega\}$. Let $\Psi$ be the least subset of $\Phi$ closed under the following rules, where $F \in \Psi$ stands for $\forall n\ (F(n) \downarrow \Rightarrow F(n) \in \Psi)$:

(1)  $s \in \Psi$ if $s = \Omega, n$, or $x$.

(2)  $case\, s\ [F] \in \Psi$ if $s = \Omega, n$, or $x$ and if $F \in \Psi$.

(3)  $case\,(case\, s\ [F])\ [G] \in \Psi$ if $G \in \Psi$ and if $case\, s\ [H] \in \Psi$, where $H$ is as in rule $(\gamma)$.

We claim that for all $s$ and $F$, if $s \in \Phi$ and $G \in \Psi$, then $case\, s\ [G] \in \Psi$. We prove this by induction on the size of $s$ only:

• If $s = \Omega, n$, or $x$, then $case\, s\ [G] \in \Psi$ by (2).

---

[1]This theorem is actually proved in [BTG91] for the polymorphic $\lambda$-calculus.

- If $s = case\ t\ [F]$, then we have to prove $case\ t\ [H] \in \Psi$, which holds by induction, provided we prove first $H \in \Psi$. But this holds by induction too, since $H(n) = case\ F(n)\ [G]$.

The claim *a fortiori* implies that $\Psi$ is closed under $case\ _-[\ ]$, hence $\Psi = \Phi$. The interest of the presentation of $\Phi$ as $\Psi$ is that we can prove strong normalization of $s$ by induction on the proof of $s \in \Psi$, as follows:

(1) Then $s$ is in normal form.

(2) Then we know by induction that $F(n)$ is strongly normalizing whenever $F(n)$ is defined, and we conclude by noticing that a reduct of $s$ is either $case\ s\ [F']$ (where $F$ pointwise reduces to $F'$), or $\Omega$, or $t$, where $t$ is a reduct of $F(n)$ for some $n$.

(3) We know by induction that $G$ is pointwise strongly normalizing, and that $case\ s\ [H]$ is strongly normalizing. In particular, $s$ is strongly normalizing, and, by the definition of $H$, $F$ is pointwise strongly normalizing. Therefore an infinite reduction from $case\ (case\ s\ [F])\ [G]$ can only be of the form:

$$case\ (case\ s\ [F])\ [G] \to^* case\ (case\ s'\ [F'])\ [G'] \to case\ s'\ [H'],$$

where $H'$ is defined from $F'$ and $G'$ as $H$ is defined from $F$ and $G$. It follows that $case\ s'\ [H']$ is a reduct of $case\ s\ [H]$, and is therefore strongly normalizing. $\quad\square$

To establish that $R \in \mathcal{T}$, we define a subset $\Xi$ of $\Lambda(C)$ (with $C$ as above), within which all the reductions which interest us take place. The raw terms of $\Xi$ are defined by the following grammar:

$$
\begin{array}{ll}
T ::= \lambda\vec{x}.B \mid (\lambda\vec{x}.T)\vec{S} & (length(\vec{S}) = length(\vec{x})) \\
B ::= \Omega \mid n \mid case\ A\ [F] & (n \in \omega) \\
A ::= xT_1 \cdots T_n \mid B \mid (\lambda\vec{x}.B)\vec{S} & (length(\vec{S}) = length(\vec{x})) \\
F : \omega \to \mathcal{B} & (dom(F)\ \text{finite}) .
\end{array}
$$

We define the following multiple version $\vec{\beta}$ of $\beta$-reduction:

$$(\vec{\beta}) \quad (\lambda\vec{x}.T)\vec{S} \to T[\vec{S}/\vec{x}] .$$

The following properties are easily checked:

- The set $\Xi$ is stable under the reductions $\vec{\beta}$, $(\delta)$, $(\Omega)$ and $(\gamma)$.

- The $\vec{\beta}\delta\Omega\gamma$ normal form of a term of $\Xi$ is a $\beta\delta\Omega\gamma$-normal form, and belongs to $T$.

Hence $R \in \mathcal{T}$. The fact that $P \circ (\vec{Q})$ is well-defined is a consequence of the following property, which is easy to check: if $S \to S'$ and if $S \leq T$, then there exists $T'$ such that $S' \leq T'$ and $T \to T'$, where $\to$ is $\vec{\beta}\delta\Omega\gamma$ reduction. It follows that $\{S \circ (\vec{T}) \mid S \leq P, \vec{T} \leq \vec{Q}\}$ is directed.

We now show that the monoid laws hold. We examine associativity first. By definition, $(S \circ (T_1 \cdots T_n)) \circ (\vec{T'})$ is the normal form of

$$(\lambda\vec{x'}.(\lambda\vec{x}.S)T_1 \cdots T_n)\vec{T'},$$

while $S \circ (T_1 \circ (\vec{T'}) \cdots T_n \circ (\vec{T'}))$ is the normal form of

$$(\lambda\vec{x}.S)(((\lambda\vec{x'}.T_1)\vec{T'}) \cdots ((\lambda\vec{x'}.T_n)\vec{T'})),$$

and these two terms are $\vec{\beta}$ equal to $(\lambda\vec{x}.S)(T_1[\vec{T'}/\vec{x'}]\cdots T_n[\vec{T'}/\vec{x'}])$. Hence associativity holds for finite trees, which implies associativity for infinite trees by continuity.

As for the identity laws, consider, say, $S \circ id$. We construct by induction on $S$ a finite subtree $id_S \leq id$ such that $S \circ id_S = S$. We only examine the essential case $S = case\ x_i\vec{T}\ [F]$. We choose $id_S$ to be (the minimum) such that $id_T \leq id_S$ for each $T \in \vec{T}$ and such that the $i^{th}$ component of $id_S$ has the form $case\ \_\ [G]$ with $dom(F) \subseteq dom(G)$ (and of course $G(n) = n$ whenever $G(n) \downarrow$). One reasons similarly for the other identity law.

The product structure is trivial by construction, since the morphisms of the category are vectors: products of objects and pairing of arrows are their concatenations, while projection morphisms are defined with the help of the morphisms $\pi_{\vec{\sigma},\sigma}$. Finally, the exponent structure is also obvious. We set:

$$\vec{\sigma} \to (\tau_1, \cdots, \tau_n) = (\vec{\sigma} \to \tau_1, \cdots, \vec{\sigma} \to \tau_n),$$

and use multiple abstraction to define currying.

**Theorem 6.6.6** *The category* $\mathbf{BT}_{PCF}$ *is a standard model of PCF, in which all compact elements of the interpretations of all types are definable (by terms without Y).*

PROOF HINT. We have already sketched the proof that $\mathbf{BT}_{PCF}$ is a CCC. The homsets are cpo's by construction, and it is easy to check that $\mathbf{BT}_{PCF}$ is a cpo-enriched CCC. The only closed trees of basic type are the trees $n$ and $\Omega$. The PCF constants are given their obvious interpretation, e.g. $[\![succ]\!] = \lambda x.case\ x\ [succ]$, where the second occurrence of $succ$ is the usual successor function on $\omega$. The fact that all compact elements are definable follows from tedious and easy encodings. For example, the tree $T = case\ x\ [F]$ where $F(1) = 4$ and $F(3) = 1$ is defined by:

$$if\ zero?(pred\ x)\ then\ 4\ else\ (if\ zero?(pred(pred(pred\ x)))\ then\ 1\ else\ \Omega)\ .$$

In order to show that the interpretation of this term is actually $T$, one has to cut the interpretation of the constants like $zero?$ or $pred$ and the projections interpreting the variables to finite approximations (this is similar to what we did to justify the identity laws). □

We have thus obtained a standard model whose compact elements are all definable. What we lack is extensionality. By extensional collapse (cf. exercise 4.5.6), we can obtain a category $[\mathbf{BT}_{PCF}]$ with enough points. It remains to see whether this category is cpo-enriched. It turns out that it has enough limits to make it possible to interpret $Y$ and the $(Y)$-rule, and thus to obtain a fully abstract model of PCF because the category $[\mathbf{BT}_{PCF}]$ inherits from $\mathbf{BT}_{PCF}$ the property that all its 'compact' elements are definable (see exercises 6.6.7 and 6.6.8). However $[\mathbf{BT}_{PCF}]$ is (a priori) not a cpo-enriched CCC, and therefore is not the unique cpo-enriched order-extensional model of PCF (cf. exercise 6.4.7). To obtain the latter, we go through a slightly more involved construction. We build a logical-like collapse relation over finite PCF Böhm trees, and we then perform an ideal completion of the quotient. This guarantees by construction that the resulting category $[\mathbf{BT}_{PCF}]^\infty$ is cpo-enriched. However there is still a subtle point in showing that extensionality is preserved by the completion. For this, we have to resort to finite projections (cf. section 5.2). We give more details in exercises 6.6.9 and 6.6.10.

**Exercise 6.6.7** *Let* **C** *be a cpo-enriched CCC, and let* [**C**] *be its extensional collapse (cf. exercise 4.5.6), whose homsets are ordered pointwise. (1) Show that* [**C**] *is rational (in the terminology of [AJM95]), i.e. satisfies the following properties: all homsets have a $\bot$; for any $A, B$ and any $f : A \times B \to B$, the sequence $\{f^n\}_{n<\omega}$ defined by $f^0 = \bot$ and $f^{k+1} = f \circ \langle id, f^k \rangle$ has a lub; those lub's are preserved by left and right composition. (2) Show that if* **C** *is a standard model of PCF, then* [**C**] *is an order-extensional model of PCF.*

**Exercise 6.6.8** *Show that* [**BT**$_{PCF}$] *is a fully abstract model of PCF. Hints: Use exercise 6.6.7, and adapt the proof of proposition 6.4.6 to the rational case.*

**Exercise 6.6.9** *Let* **C** *be a cpo-enriched CCC whose homsets are all algebraic, and which satisfies:*

(1) *Compact morphisms are closed under composition, currying, and uncurrying.*

(2) *For any compact $f$ there exists a compact morphism $id_f \leq f$ such that $f \circ id_f = id_f \circ f = f$.*

(3) *For any type $\sigma$, interpreted by $D^\sigma$, there exists a sequence of compact morphisms $\psi_n^{D^\sigma} : \mathbf{C}[D^\sigma, D^\sigma]$ such that $\bigvee_{n<\omega} \psi_n^{D^\sigma} = id$ and (for all $\sigma, \tau$) $\psi_n^{D^{\sigma \to \tau}} = [\![\lambda f x. g(f(h(x)))]\!] \circ \langle \psi_n^{D^\sigma}, \psi_n^{D^\tau} \rangle$.*

(4) *Moreover, at basic types, $\{\psi_n^{D^\kappa} \circ h \mid h : 1 \to D^\kappa\}$ is finite, for all $n$.*

*Define a logical-like relation $\mathcal{R}$ on compact morphisms (hence such that $\mathcal{R}^\sigma \subseteq \mathcal{K}(\underline{D^\sigma}) \times \mathcal{K}(\underline{D^\sigma})$, where $D^\sigma$ is the interpretation of $\sigma$ and where $\underline{A} = \mathbf{C}[1, A]$), by setting:*

$$\mathcal{R}^\kappa = \{(d, d) \mid d \in \mathcal{K}(\underline{D^\kappa})\},$$

*and by extending $\mathcal{R}$ to all types as in definition 4.5.1. Define a category $[\mathbf{C}]^\infty$ whose objects are the types and whose homsets are the ideal completions of the sets of $\mathcal{R}^{\sigma,\tau}$ equivalence classes (in the terminology of definition 4.5.1), ordered pointwise. Show that $[\mathbf{C}]^\infty$ is an order-extensional cpo-enriched CCC, and that there is a functor from* **C** *to $[\mathbf{C}]^\infty$ which preserves the cartesian closed structure. Show that the functor maps compact morphisms surjectively onto compact morphisms. Hint: Show that $[\psi_n]$ has a finite image (cf. proof of proposition 5.2.4), and exploit the fact that for any compact $f$ there exists $n$ such that $\psi_n \circ f = f$, by (2) and (3).*

**Exercise 6.6.10** *Show that* **BT**$_{PCF}$ *satisfies the conditions stated in exercise 6.6.9, and that* [**BT**$_{PCF}$]$^\infty$ *is the unique fully abstract model of exercise 6.4.7.*

**Remark 6.6.11** *What we have done to construct the fully abstract model can be summarized as: 'approximate, then quotient, and finally complete'. Originally, Milner did not go through the first of these steps. Instead of working on finite approximations, he worked directly on PCF terms. Focusing on finite Böhm trees has the following advantages:*

(1) *It is reasonable (and simpler than Milner's original construction) to 'complete first, and then quotient' (cf. exercise 6.6.8).*

(2) *It is mathematically cleaner to first construct a least fixpoint model (the PCF Böhm tree model), and then to apply a general construction allowing us to obtain an extensional least fixpoint model out of a least fixpoint model (cf. exercise 6.6.9).*

**Exercise 6.6.12** *Show that for any simply typed $\lambda$-terms $M, N$, considered as PCF terms, $M =_{obs} N$ iff $M =_{\beta\eta} N$. Hint: Proceed as in the proof of Friedman's theorem via the 1-section theorem 4.5.9.*

**Game semantics.** The category $\mathbf{BT}_{PCF}$ is a full subcategory of two categories of games constructed recently by Hyland and Ong [HO94], and by Abramsky, Jagadeesan, and Malacaria (AJM for short) [AJM95]. In this brief discussion, we shall call these categories of games $\mathbf{G}$ (collectively). The striking point about the categories $\mathbf{G}$ is that their construction does not refer to the syntax. The identification of PCF Böhm trees was even a side effect of the game theoretical work. The basic idea behind this interpretation is to understand computations as exchanges of questions and answers, or as alternations of opponent's moves and player's moves. A typical player's move is a head variable, while an opponent's move is the bunch of abstractions that precedes it. More precisely, the root of a finite PCF tree $T = \lambda \vec{x} : \vec{\sigma}.B$ corresponds to an opponent's move, while the root of $B$ corresponds to a player's move. If $B$ has the form $case\ x\vec{T}\ [F]$, then we can think of $x$ as the answer to the question: 'what is the head variable of $T$?'. The sequential model of chapter 14 also gives rise to such a game theoretical interpretation (see in particular remark 14.3.52).

The categories $\mathbf{G}$ do not meet the informal criteria (1) and (2) that we stated at the end of section 6.4 to qualify 'more semantic' constructions of the fully abstract model.

(1) Because their morphisms are in bijective correspondence with terms, they are very far from being 'functions of some sort'.

(2) Because the extensional collapse is the result of a construction which is the exact counterpart of the syntactic observational equivalence, no particularly new insight is gained in the understanding of observational equivalence.

On the other hand, the categories $\mathbf{G}$ offer lots of promising prospects towards a 'more dynamic' understanding of computation. For example, Hyland-Ong's games link up nicely with environment abstract machines (like the one described in figure 8.9), while AJM games have close links with Girard's Geometry of Interaction (which we briefly mentioned in section 2.2) [DHR96].

Finally, we mention that game semantics arose earlier in logic as a particular model of provability according to which a formula is considered valid if the player can defend it against 'attacks' of an opponent who doubts it or any of the lemmas that lead to it. We refer to [Hyl97] for a survey of game semantics and to [Coq97] for a classical logic perspective.

# 7

# Domain equations

This chapter presents general techniques for the solution of domain equations and the representation of domains and functors over a universal domain. Given a category of domains $\mathbf{C}$ we build the related category $\mathbf{C}^{ip}$ (cf. chapter 3) that has the same objects as $\mathbf{C}$ and *injection-projection pairs* as morphisms (section 7.1). It turns out that this is a suitable framework for the solution of domain equations. The technique is applied in section 7.2 in order to solve a *predicate equation*. In turn, the solution of the predicate equation is used in proving an adequacy theorem for a simple declarative language with dynamic binding.

The category of injection-projection pairs is also a suitable framework for the construction of a *universal homogeneous object* (section 7.3). The latter is a domain in which every other domain (not exceeding a certain size) can be embedded. Once a universal object $U$ is built, it is possible to *represent* the collection of domains as the domain $FP(U)$ of *finitary projections* over $U$, and functors as continuous functions over $FP(U)$. In this way, one obtains a rather handy poset theoretical framework for the solution of domain equations (section 7.4). If, moreover, $FP(U)$ is itself (the image of a) projection, then projections can be used to give a model of second order typed $\lambda$-calculus (see exercise 7.4.8 and section 11.3).

A third approach to the solution of domain equations consists in working with concrete representations of domains like information systems, event structures, or concrete data structures (introduced in definitions 10.2.11, 12.3.3 and 14.1.1, respectively). At this level, domain approximation can be modelled by means of inclusions relating the representing structures, and domain equations can be then solved as ordinary fixpoint equations. As in the finitary projections approach the solutions obtained are exact solutions ($F(D) = D$, and not merely $F(D) \cong D$). This was first remarked by Berry in the framework of concrete data structures. We do not detail this approach here (a good reference is [Win93, Chapter12]). See, however, exercises 10.2.14, 13.1.20 and 14.1.15.

## 7.1   Domain equations

One of the earliest problems in denotational semantics was that of building a model of the untyped $\lambda\beta\eta$-calculus. This boils down to the problem of finding a non-trivial domain $D$ isomorphic to its functional space $D \rightarrow D$ (cf. chapter

3). Following work by Wand, Smyth and Plotkin [Wan79, SP82], we present
a generalization of the technique proposed by Scott [Sco72] for the solution of
domain equations.

An $\omega$-chain is a sequence $\{B_n, f_n\}_{n \in \omega}$ such that $f_n : B_n \to B_{n+1}$ for all $n$.
The general categorical definition of colimit specializes to $\omega$-colimits as follows.
A *cocone* $\{B, g_n\}_{n \in \omega}$ of the $\omega$-chain $\{B_n, f_n\}_{n \in \omega}$ is given by an object $B$, and a
sequence $\{g_n : B_n \to B\}_{n \in \omega}$ satisfying $g_{n+1} \circ f_n = g_n$ for all $n$. A cocone $\{B, g_n\}_{n \in \omega}$
is a *colimit* if it is an initial object in the category of cocones, that is, if for any
other cocone $\{C, h_n\}_{n \in \omega}$ there exists a unique morphism $k : B \to C$ such that
$k \circ g_n = h_n$ for all $n$. We shall also use the dual notions of $\omega^{op}$-chain and $\omega^{op}$-limit:
an $\omega^{op}$-chain is a sequence $\{B_n, g_n\}_{n \in \omega}$ such that $g_n : B_{n+1} \to B_n$ for all $n$, and
an $\omega^{op}$-limit is a limit cone of an $\omega^{op}$-chain (cf. section A2.2).

Let $T : \mathbf{K} \to \mathbf{K}$ be a functor. We outline some rather general results that
guarantee the existence of an *initial* solution for the equation $TX \cong X$. It will be
shown next that these results can be usefully applied to the solution of domain
equations.

**Definition 7.1.1 ($T$-algebra)** *Let* $T : \mathbf{K} \to \mathbf{K}$ *be a functor. A $T$-algebra is
a morphism* $\alpha : TA \to A$. *The $T$-algebras form a category. If* $\alpha : TA \to A$
*and* $\beta : TB \to B$ *are $T$-algebras then a morphism from* $\alpha$ *to* $\beta$ *is a morphism*
$f : A \to B$ *such that* $f \circ \alpha = \beta \circ Tf$.[1]

**Lemma 7.1.2** *Every initial $T$-algebra is an isomorphism.*

PROOF. Let $\alpha : TA \to A$ be initial. Then $T\alpha : TTA \to TA$ is also a $T$-algebra
and by initiality there is an $i : A \to TA$ such that:

$$i \circ \alpha = T\alpha \circ Ti = T(\alpha \circ i) . \tag{7.1}$$

We observe that $\alpha$ is a morphism (of $T$-algebras) from $T\alpha$ to $\alpha$. By composition
and initiality we get $\alpha \circ i = id$. By the equation 7.1 above we derive:

$$T(\alpha \circ i) = T(id) = id = i \circ \alpha .$$

So $i$ is the inverse of $\alpha$. □

The following proposition will appear natural if one thinks of categories as cpo's
and of functors as continuous functions.

**Proposition 7.1.3** *Let* $\mathbf{C}$ *be a category with initial object and $\omega$-colimits and*
$T : \mathbf{C} \to \mathbf{C}$ *be an $\omega$-cocontinuous functor, i.e., a functor that preserves $\omega$-colimits.
Then there is an initial $T$-algebra.*

PROOF. Let 0 be the initial object. Consider the uniquely determined morphism $z : 0 \to T0$. By iterating $T$ on this diagram we get an $\omega$-diagram

---
[1] A stronger notion of $T$-algebra is given in definition A2.8.3 in the case $T$ is the functor
component of a monad.

$D = \{T^i 0, T^i z\}_{i<\omega}$. By assumption there is an $\omega$-colimit of $D$, say $C = \{A, f_i\}_{i<\omega}$, satisfying $f_i = f_{i+1} \circ T^i z$, for all $i$.

Now consider $TC = \{TA, Tf_i\}_{i<\omega}$. By assumption $TC$ is an $\omega$-colimit of $TD = \{TT^i 0, TT^i z\}_{i<\omega}$. Since we can restrict $C$ to a cocone of $TD$, there exists a unique morphism $h : TC \to C$.

Moreover, we want to prove that the $T$-algebra $h : TA \to A$ is initial. The proof exploits a close relationship between $T$-algebras and cocones over $D$.

(1)  We show that any $T$-algebra, $\beta : TB \to B$, gives rise to a cocone $\{B, g_i^B\}_{i<\omega}$ where:

$$g_i^B = \beta \circ T\beta \circ TT\beta \circ \cdots \circ T^{i-1}\beta \circ T^i z_B \quad i < \omega, \; z_B : 0 \to B \; .$$

It is enough to check that $g_{i+1}^B \circ T^i z = g_i^B$, which follows from $\beta \circ Tz_B \circ z = z_B$.

Moreover, $\beta$ is a morphism from $\{TB, Tg_i^B\}_{i<\omega}$ to $\{B, g_i^B\}_{i\geq 1}$ of cocones over $TD$ as $g_{i+1}^B = \beta \circ Tg_i^B$. Also, specializing this equality to $B = A$ and $\beta = h$, we get by induction on $i$ that $g_i = f_i$, and hence that the cocone associated to $h : TA \to A$ is the cone $C$.

(2)  Any morphism $u : \alpha \to \beta$ of $T$-algebras, where $\alpha : TA' \to A'$ and $\beta : TB \to B$, induces a morphism between the related cocones over $D$, as defined in (1). Suppose $\beta \circ Tu = u \circ \alpha$. Then:

$$
\begin{aligned}
u \circ g_i^{A'} &= u \circ \alpha \circ T\alpha \circ \cdots \circ T^{i-1}\alpha \circ T^i z_{A'} \\
&= \beta \circ Tu \circ T\alpha \circ \cdots \circ T^{i-1}\alpha \circ T^i z_{A'} \\
&= \cdots \\
&= \beta \circ T\beta \circ \cdots \circ T^{i-1}\beta \circ T^i u \circ T^i z_{A'} \\
&= \beta \circ T\beta \circ \cdots \circ T^{i-1}\beta \circ T^i z_B \\
&= g_i^B \; .
\end{aligned}
$$

By (1) and (2), there is at most one $T$-algebra morphism $u : h \to \beta$.

(3)  To prove existence, we go the other way around. By initiality there exists a (unique) cocone morphism $l : A \to B$ from $C$ to $\{B, g_i^B\}_{i<\omega}$. We show that $l$ is a $T$-algebra morphism. We observe that $Tl$ is a morphism from $\{TA, Tf_i\}_{i<\omega}$ to $\{TB, Tg_i^B\}_{i<\omega}$ of cocones over $TD$. We have seen (cf. (1)) that $\beta$ is a morphism from $\{TB, Tg_i^B\}_{i<\omega}$ to $\{B, g_i^B\}_{i\geq 1}$. By initiality of $TC$ on $TD$, it follows that $l \circ h = \beta \circ Tl$. $\qquad\square$

When solving domain equations, we may wish to start the construction of the $\omega$-diagram with some morphism $z : X \to TX$, where $X$ is not necessarily an initial object. For example, if we apply the construction of definition 3.1.10, we get a non-trivial $D_\infty$ model only if $D_0 \neq \{\bot\}$. In the poset case this corresponds to looking for the least fixpoint of a function $f : D \to D$, above a given point $d$ such that $d \leq f(d)$. If $D$ is an $(\omega\text{-})$dcpo, and $f$ is $(\omega\text{-})$continuous then we can compute the solution as $\bigvee_{n<\omega} f^n(d)$. This is the least element of the set $\{e \in D \mid f(e) \leq e \text{ and } d \leq e\}$.

We provide a categorical generalization of this fact. Suppose that the category $\mathbf{C}$ and the functor $F$ satisfy the conditions in proposition 7.1.3. Given a morphism $z : X \to TX$ we can build an $\omega$-diagram $D = \{T^i X, T^i z\}_{i < \omega}$. Using the hypotheses we can build its colimit $\{A, f_i\}_{i < \omega}$ and a morphism $h : TA \to A$. The problem is now to determine in which framework $h$ is initial. In first approximation it is natural to consider $T$-algebras $\beta : TB \to B$ together with a morphism $z_B : X \to B$ (as $B$ has to be 'bigger' than $X$). If we mimic step (1) in the proof of proposition 7.1.3, that builds a cocone out of a $T$-algebra, we see that we need the following property:

$$z_B = \beta \circ T z_B \circ z . \tag{7.2}$$

Generalizing step (2) presents a new difficulty. It appears that a $T$-algebra morphism $l : \beta \to \gamma$, where $\beta : TB \to B$, and $\gamma : TC \to C$, should also satisfy:

$$l \circ z_B = z_C . \tag{7.3}$$

The following exercise shows that this is just an instance of the problem we have already solved, but with respect to a related category $\mathbf{C} \uparrow X$, and a related functor $T_z$.

**Exercise 7.1.4** *Given a category $\mathbf{C}$ and an object $X \in \mathbf{C}$, we define the* slice *category $\mathbf{C} \uparrow X$ as follows (there is a related slice category $\mathbf{C} \downarrow X$ which is introduced in example A2.1.5):*

$$\mathbf{C} \uparrow X = \{f : X \to B \mid B \in \mathbf{C}\} \qquad (\mathbf{C} \uparrow X)[f, g] = \{h \mid h \circ f = g\} .$$

*Also, given a functor $T : \mathbf{C} \to \mathbf{C}$, and a morphism $z : X \to TX$, we define a new functor $T_z : \mathbf{C} \uparrow X \to \mathbf{C} \uparrow X$ as follows:*

$$T_z(f) = Tf \circ z \qquad T_z(h) = Th .$$

*Show that if $\mathbf{C}$ has an initial object and $\omega$-colimits and if $T : \mathbf{C} \to \mathbf{C}$ preserves $\omega$-colimits, then the category $\mathbf{C} \uparrow X$ has an initial object and $\omega$-colimits, and that for every morphism $z : X \to TX$ the functor $T_z$ preserves $\omega$-colimits. Hint: The commutation conditions displayed in equations 7.2 and 7.3 arise as a consequence of the abstract definitions. The above morphism $h : TA \to A$ yields the initial $T_z$-algebra.*

Consider the functor $\Rightarrow: \mathbf{C}^{op} \times \mathbf{C} \to \mathbf{C}$, defined in every CCC, that given objects $A$, $B$ returns the exponent $A \Rightarrow B$ (with the standard extension to morphisms). We would like to find solutions to equations such as $X = X \Rightarrow D$, or $X = X \Rightarrow X$. We recall from chapter 3 that there is no way we can look at $\lambda X.X \Rightarrow D$, or $\lambda X.X \Rightarrow X$ as (covariant) functors. We will introduce new structures that allow us to see the problem as an instance of the one solved by proposition 7.1.3. In the first place we present the notion of injection-projection pair in an *O-category* [Wan79].

**Definition 7.1.5 (O-category)** *A category $\mathbf{C}$ is called an O-category if it is $\omega$-cpo enriched, i.e., if every homset is an $\omega$-cpo and if composition of morphisms is a continuous operation with respect to the orders of the homsets (cf. definition 6.1.1).*

Next we formulate some familiar notions (cf. section 3.1, and in particular definition 3.1.2) in the framework of O-categories.

**Definition 7.1.6 (retraction, injection, projection)** *Let* C *be an O-category, and let* $A, B \in$ C.

(1) *A retraction from* $A$ *to* $B$ *is a pair* $(i, j)$ *such that* $i : A \to B$, $j : B \to A$, $j \circ i = id_A$. *We then write* $A \lhd B$ *(cf. definition 4.6.1).*

(2) *An injection-projection from* $A$ *to* $B$ *is a pair* $(i, j)$ *which is a retraction as above and such that* $i \circ j \leq id_B$ *We write then* $A \unlhd B$ *and* $(i, j) : A \to_{ip} B$ *(or* $(i, j) : A \to B$ *for short). We shall also use the notation* $f = (f^+, f^-)$ *for an injection-projection pair.*

(3) *A projection on* $A$ *is a morphism* $p : A \to A$ *such that* $p \circ p = p$ *and* $p \leq id_A$.

**Example 7.1.7 Cpo** *is an O-category, ordering the morphisms pointwise. Stable functions, strongly stable functions, sequential algorithms, introduced in later chapters, provide other examples of O-categories.*

We point out two basic properties of any injection-projection pair $(i, j)$:

- $i$ determines $j$ and $j$ determines $i$ (cf. proposition 3.1.5);

- $i$ and $j$ are strict functions (cf. definition 1.4.17): indeed, $i(\perp) \leq i(j(\perp)) \leq \perp$ and $\perp = j(i(\perp)) = j(\perp)$.

**Definition 7.1.8** *Let* C *be an O-category. The category* $\mathbf{C}^{ip}$ *has the same objects as* C *and injection-projection pairs as morphisms:*

$$\mathbf{C}^{ip}[A, B] = \{(i, j) \mid (i, j) : A \to_{ip} B\} .$$

*Composition is given by* $(i, j) \circ (i', j') = (i \circ i', j' \circ j)$, *identities by* $(id, id)$.

**Proposition 7.1.9** *Let* C *be an O-category. Then:*

(1) $\mathbf{C}^{ip}$ *is a category in which all morphisms are monos.*

(2) *If* C *has a terminal object, if each homset* $\mathbf{C}[A, B]$ *has a least element* $\perp_{A,B}$, *and if composition is left strict (i.e.,* $f : A \to A'$ *implies* $\perp_{A',A''} \circ f = \perp_{A,A''}$), *then* $\mathbf{C}^{ip}$ *has an initial object.*

PROOF. (1) Suppose: $(i, j) \circ (i', j') = (i, j) \circ (i'', j'')$. That is $(i \circ i', j' \circ j) = (i \circ i'', j'' \circ j)$. Since $i$ is a mono, $i \circ i' = i \circ i''$ implies $i' = i''$ (and hence $j' = j''$ since $i', i''$ determine $j', j''$).

(2) Let 1 be the terminal object in C. We show that 1 is initial in $\mathbf{C}^{ip}$. Given $A \in$ C, we first show $(\perp_{1,A}, \perp_{A,1}) \in \mathbf{C}^{ip}[1, A]$. On one hand, $\perp_{A,1} \circ \perp_{1,A} = id_1$ since 1 is terminal, on the other hand $\perp_{1,A} \circ \perp_{A,1} = \perp_{A,A} \leq id_A$ since composition is left strict. There are no other morphisms in $\mathbf{C}^{ip}[1, A]$ since $\perp_{A,1}$ is the unique element of $\mathbf{C}[A, 1]$. □

We are now in a position to suggest what the category of injection-projection pairs is good for. Given a functor $F : \mathbf{C}^{op} \times \mathbf{C} \to \mathbf{C}$, we build a functor $F^{ip} : \mathbf{C}^{ip} \times \mathbf{C}^{ip} \to \mathbf{C}^{ip}$ which coincides with $F$ on objects. In particular the exponent functor is transformed into a functor which is covariant in both arguments. We then observe that $F^{ip}(D, D) \cong D$ in $\mathbf{C}^{ip}$ implies $F(D, D) \cong D$ in $\mathbf{C}$.

In other words, we build a related structure, $\mathbf{C}^{ip}$, and we consider a related problem, $F^{ip}(D, D) \cong D$, whose solutions can be used for the original problem. The advantage of the related problem is that we only have to deal with covariant functors and therefore we are in a favorable position to apply proposition 7.1.3. Towards this goal, it is natural to look for conditions on $\mathbf{C}$ that guarantee that $\mathbf{C}^{ip}$ has $\omega$-colimits (we already know that under certain conditions it has an initial object) as well as for conditions on $F$ that guarantee that $F^{ip}$ is $\omega$-cocontinuous.

The following result points out that the $\omega$-colimit of $\{D_n, (i_n, j_n)\}_{n \in \omega}$ in $\mathbf{C}^{ip}$ can be derived from the $\omega^{op}$-limit of $\{D_n, j_n\}_{n \in \omega}$ in $\mathbf{C}$. One often refers to this situation as limit-colimit coincidence (see exercise 7.1.12).

**Theorem 7.1.10 (limit-colimit coincidence)** *Let $\mathbf{C}$ be an O-category. If $\mathbf{C}$ has $\omega^{op}$-limits then $\mathbf{C}^{ip}$ has $\omega$-colimits.*

PROOF. Consider an $\omega$-chain $\{D_n, f_n\}_{n \in \omega}$ in $\mathbf{C}^{ip}$ where we denote with $f_n^+ : D_n \to D_{n+1}$ the injection and with $f_n^- : D_{n+1} \to D_n$ the projection.

Let $\{C, g_n^-\}_{n \in \omega} = lim_{\mathbf{C}}\{D_n, f_n^-\}_{n \in \omega}$. We show that $D_m$ can be made into a cone for $\{D_n, f_n^-\}_{n \in \omega}$, for all $m$. There is a natural way to go from $D_m$ to $D_n$ via the morphism $h_{m,n} : D_m \to D_n$ which is defined as follows:

$$h_{m,n} = \begin{cases} id & \text{if } m = n \\ f_n^- \circ \cdots \circ f_{m-1}^- & \text{if } m > n \\ f_{n-1}^+ \circ \cdots \circ f_m^+ & \text{if } m < n \ . \end{cases}$$

It is enough to check that $f_n^- \circ h_{m,n+1} = h_{m,n}$. Hence there exists a unique cone morphism $g_m^+ : D_m \to C$. We note that $g_m^- \circ g_m^+ = id$, since $h_{m,m} = id$. We now prove that $\{g_m^+ \circ g_m^-\}_{m \in \omega}$ is an ascending chain. We claim that $g_m^+ = g_{m+1}^+ \circ f_m^+$ and $g_m^- = f_m^- \circ g_{m+1}^-$. The second equality is immediate since $\{C, g_n^-\}_{n \in \omega}$ is a cone. To prove the first equality, it is enough to show $g_{m+1}^+ \circ f_m^+$ is a cone morphism from $\{D_m, h_{m,n}^-\}_{n \in \omega}$ to $\{C, g_n^-\}_{n \in \omega}$, since there is a unique such morphism. This is proved by induction as follows:

$$g_n^- \circ g_{m+1}^+ \circ f_m^+ = h_{m+1,n} \circ f_m^+ = h_{m,n} \ .$$

By the claim, we have:

$$g_m^+ \circ g_m^- = g_{m+1}^+ \circ f_m^+ \circ f_m^- \circ g_{m+1}^- \leq g_{m+1}^+ \circ g_{m+1}^- \ .$$

Hence $\{g_m^+ \circ g_m^-\}_{m \in \omega}$ is a chain and we write $k = \bigvee_{m \in \omega} g_m^+ \circ g_m^-$. We next prove that (1) $k = id$, and (2) if $\{C', g_n'\}_{n \in \omega}$ is a cocone of $\{D, f_n\}_{n \in \omega}$ in $\mathbf{C}^{ip}$ such that $\bigvee_{m \in \omega} g_m'^+ \circ g_m'^- = id$ then the cocone is a colimit.

(1) It is enough to remark that $k$ is a cone morphism over $\{C, g_m^-\}_{m \in \omega}$ as:

$$\begin{aligned} g_m^- \circ k &= g_m^- \circ (\bigvee_{i \in \omega} g_i^+ \circ g_i^-) = g_m^- \circ (\bigvee_{i \geq m} g_i^+ \circ g_i^-) \\ &= \bigvee_{i \geq m} g_m^- \circ g_i^+ \circ g_i^- = \bigvee_{i \geq m} h_{i,m} \circ g_i^- = g_m^- \ . \end{aligned}$$

(2) Let $\{B, l_m\}_{m \in \omega}$ be a cocone. We define:

$$p^+ = \bigvee_{m \in \omega} l_m^+ \circ g_m'^- : C' \to B \quad p^- = \bigvee_{m \in \omega} g_m'^+ \circ l_m^- : B \to C' .$$

It is easy to check that $p : C' \to B$ in $\mathbf{C}^{ip}$. Moreover $p$ is a morphism of cocones between $\{C', g_m'\}_{m \in \omega}$ and $\{B, l_m\}_{m \in \omega}$. Finally suppose $q$ is another morphism beween these two cocones. Then:

$$\begin{aligned}
(q^+, q^-) &= (q^+ \circ (\bigvee_{m \in \omega} g_m'^+ \circ g_m'^-), (\bigvee_{m \in \omega} g_m'^+ \circ g_m'^-) \circ q^-) \\
&= (\bigvee_{m \in \omega} q^+ \circ g_m'^+ \circ g_m'^-, \bigvee_{m \in \omega} g_m'^+ \circ g_m'^- \circ q^-) \\
&= (\bigvee_{m \in \omega} l_m^+ \circ g_m'^-, \bigvee_{m \in \omega} g_m'^+ \circ l_m^-) \\
&= (p^+, p^-) .
\end{aligned}$$

Hence, by (1) and (2) $\{C, g_n\}_{n \in \omega}$ is a colimit of $\{D_n, f_n\}_{n \in \omega}$.  □

We can extract from the previous proof the following useful information.

**Proposition 7.1.11** *Let* $\mathbf{C}$ *be an O-category, and let* $\{D_n, f_n\}_{n \in \omega}$ *be an* $\omega$*-chain in* $\mathbf{C}^{ip}$*. A cocone* $\{C, g_n\}_{n \in \omega}$ *is a colimit of* $\{D_n, f_n\}_{n \in \omega}$ *iff* $\bigvee_{n \in \omega} g_n^+ \circ g_n^- = id$.

The following exercise shows that there is also an initial algebra—final algebra coincidence. This observation has been the starting point of a more axiomatic treatment of domain equations [Fre91a, Fre91b], which is itself part of a wider program called *axiomatic domain theory* that aims at establishing some of the basic principles underlying the various categories of domains or realizability universes (considered in chapter 15) [Fio96].

**Exercise 7.1.12** *(1) Referring to theorem 7.1.10, show that the* $\omega$*-colimit in* $\mathbf{C}^{ip}$ *gives also an* $\omega$*-colimit in* $\mathbf{C}$*. (2) Show that when proposition 7.1.3 is applied to a category* $\mathbf{C}^{ip}$ *obtained from an O-category* $\mathbf{C}$*, then the initial T-algebra in* $\mathbf{C}^{ip}$ *gives both an initial algebra and a final coalgebra in* $\mathbf{C}$ *(where a coalgebra is a morphism* $\beta : B \to TB$*).*

We now show how to build $\omega^{op}$-limits in the category $\mathbf{Cpo}$.

**Proposition 7.1.13** *The category* $\mathbf{Cpo}$ *has* $\omega^{op}$*-limits.*

PROOF. Consider an $\omega^{op}$-chain $\{D_n, f_n\}_{n \in \omega}$ in $\mathbf{Cpo}$ (with $f_n : D_{n+1} \to D_n$). We define:

$$D = \{\alpha : \omega \to \bigcup_{n \in \omega} D_n \mid \alpha(n) \in D_n \text{ and } f_n(\alpha(n+1)) = \alpha(n)\} ,$$

with the pointwise ordering $\alpha \leq_D \beta$ iff $\forall n \in \omega \; (\alpha(n) \leq_{D_n} \beta(n))$. It is easy to verify that this makes $D$ into a cpo. Now $\{D, g_n\}_{n \in \omega}$ is a cone with $g_n(\alpha) = \alpha(n)$. Suppose $\{E, h_n\}_{n \in \omega}$ is another cone. Then a morphism $k : \{E, h_n\}_{n \in \omega} \to \{D, g_n\}_{n \in \omega}$ is completely determined by the equations $k(e)(n) = (g_n \circ k)(e) = h_n(e)$. It is easily checked that this function $k$ is continuous.  □

Therefore, as an instance of theorem 7.1.10, we obtain:

$$colim_{\mathbf{Cpo}^{ip}}\{D_n, f_n\}_{n \in \omega} = lim_{\mathbf{Cpo}}\{D_n, f_n^-\}_{n \in \omega} .$$

This result is applied to bifinite domains in the following.

**Proposition 7.1.14** *The categories* $\mathbf{Bif}^{ip}$ *and* $\omega\mathbf{Bif}^{ip}$ *(cf. definition 5.2.2) have* $\omega$*-colimits.*

PROOF. Given an $\omega$-chain in $\mathbf{Bif}^{ip}$ $\{D_n, f_n\}_{n\in\omega}$ let $\{D, g_n\}_{n\in\omega}$ be its $\omega$-colimit in $\mathbf{Cpo}^{ip}$ which exists by proposition 7.1.13 and theorem 7.1.10. It remains to verify that $D$ is bifinite. Since $D_n$ is bifinite for any $n \in \omega$, we have $\bigvee_{i\in I_n} p_{n,i} = id$ where $\{p_{n,i}\}_{i\in I_n}$ is a directed set of finite projections over $D_n$. We compute:

$$
\begin{aligned}
id \;=\; \bigvee_{n\in\omega}(g_n^+ \circ g_n^-) \;&=\; \bigvee_{n\in\omega}(g_n^+ \circ (\bigvee_{i\in I_n} p_{n,i}) \circ g_n^-) \\
&=\; \bigvee_{n\in\omega}\bigvee_{i\in I_n}(g_n^+ \circ p_{n,i} \circ g_n^-) \\
&=\; \bigvee_{n\in\omega, i\in I_n}(g_n^+ \circ p_{n,i} \circ g_n^-) \,.
\end{aligned}
$$

We note that $\{g_n^+ \circ p_{n,i} \circ g_n^-\}_{n\in\omega, i\in I_n}$ is directed (and is denumerable if the $I_n$'s are denumerable) and that $g_n^+ \circ p_{n,i} \circ g_n^-$ is a finite projection, and hence is compact by proposition 5.2.3. $\qquad\square$

We now turn to functors.

**Definition 7.1.15 (locally continuous)** *Let* $\mathbf{C}$ *be an O-category and* $F : \mathbf{C}^{op} \times \mathbf{C} \to \mathbf{C}$ *be a functor (the generalization to several arguments is immediate). We say that* $F$ *is locally monotonic (continuous) if it is monotonic (continuous) w.r.t the orders on the homsets.*

**Example 7.1.16** *The following are locally continuous functors over* $\mathbf{C}$*, where* $\mathbf{C}$ *is* $\mathbf{Cpo}$ *or a full subcategory of* $\mathbf{Cpo}$ *like the category* $\mathbf{S}$ *of Scott domains or the category* $\mathbf{Bif}$ *of bifinite domains or the category* $\omega\mathbf{Bif}$ *of* $\omega$*-bifinite domains: the product, the tensor product, the function space, the lifting, the partial function space, the strict function space (cf. exercise 1.4.19), the coalesced sum, the separated sum.*

There is a standard technique to transform a contravariant-covariant monotonic functor on $\mathbf{C}$ into a covariant functor on $\mathbf{C}^{ip}$.

**Definition 7.1.17** *Given* $F : \mathbf{C}^{op} \times \mathbf{C} \to \mathbf{C}$ *define* $F^{ip} : \mathbf{C}^{ip} \times \mathbf{C}^{ip} \to \mathbf{C}^{ip}$ *as follows:*

$$
\begin{aligned}
F^{ip}(c, c') \;&=\; F(c, c') \\
F^{ip}((i, j), (i', j')) \;&=\; (F(j, i'), F(i, j')) \,.
\end{aligned}
$$

**Exercise 7.1.18** *Verify that* $F^{ip}$ *as defined above is a functor. Show that the same definition works for contravariant-covariant functors and retractions instead of contravariant-covariant monotonic functors and injection-projection pairs.*

The following result relates local continuity and preservation of $\omega$-colimits.

**Proposition 7.1.19** *Let* $\mathbf{C}$ *be an O-category with* $\omega^{op}$*-limits. If* $F : \mathbf{C}^{ip} \times \mathbf{C} \to \mathbf{C}$ *is a locally continuous functor then* $F^{ip} : \mathbf{C}^{ip} \times \mathbf{C}^{ip} \to \mathbf{C}^{ip}$ *preserves* $\omega$*-colimits.*

PROOF. We have already observed that if $F$ is locally monotonic then $F^{ip}$ is a functor. Let $\{(D_n, E_n), (f_n, g_n)\}_{n \in \omega}$ be an $\omega$-diagram in $\mathbf{C}^{ip} \times \mathbf{C}^{ip}$ with colimit $\{(D, E), (h_n, k_n)\}_{n \in \omega}$ built as in the previous theorem 7.1.10. To show that the cocone $\{F^{ip}(D, E), F^{ip}(h_n, k_n)\}_{n \in \omega}$ is a colimit for $\{F^{ip}(D_n, E_n), F^{ip}(f_n, g_n)\}_{n \in \omega}$ it is enough to verify that (cf. proposition 7.1.11 and definition 7.1.17):

$$\bigvee_{n \in \omega} F(h_n^-, k_n^+) \circ F(h_n^+, k_n^-) = id_{F(D, E)} .$$

This is proven as follows:

$$
\begin{aligned}
\bigvee_{n \in \omega} F(h_n^-, k_n^+) \circ F(h_n^+, k_n^-) &= \bigvee_{n \in \omega} F(h_n^+ \circ h_n^-, k_n^+ \circ k_n^-) \\
&= F(\bigvee_{n \in \omega} h_n^+ \circ h_n^-, \bigvee_{n \in \omega} k_n^+ \circ k_n^-) \\
&= F(id_D, id_E) = id_{F(D, E)} . \qquad \square
\end{aligned}
$$

To summarize the method, we suppose given:

- an O-category $\mathbf{C}$ that has a terminal object and (certain) $\omega^{op}$-limits, and is such that the homsets have a least element and such that composition is left strict,

- a locally continuous functor $F : \mathbf{C}^{op} \times \mathbf{C} \to \mathbf{C}$.

We can apply the previous constructions and build:

- the category $\mathbf{C}^{ip}$ which has an initial object and $\omega$-colimits,

- the functor $F^{ip} : \mathbf{C}^{ip} \times \mathbf{C}^{ip} \to \mathbf{C}^{ip}$ which preserves $\omega$-colimits.

Therefore we find an initial solution for $F^{ip}(X, X) \cong X$ in $\mathbf{C}^{ip}$. The initial solution also gives a solution for the equation $F(X, X) \cong X$ in $\mathbf{C}$.

**Exercise 7.1.20** *Show the existence of a non-trivial domain $D$ such that $D \cong D \times D \cong D \Rightarrow D$. Hint: Consider the system $D \cong D \Rightarrow E$ and $E \cong E \times E$.*

**Exercise 7.1.21** *Explain how to build two non-isomorphic, non-trivial solutions of the equation $D \cong D \Rightarrow D$. Hint: One can start the construction with a cpo which is not a lattice.*

**Exercise 7.1.22** *The cpo of lazy natural numbers is the set*

$$\omega_L = \{s^n(\bot) \mid n \in \omega\} \cup \{s^n(0) \mid n \in \omega\} \cup \{s^\omega(\bot)\}$$

*(with $s^0(\bot) = \bot$, $s^0(0) = 0$), ordered by:*

$$x \le y \Leftrightarrow (x = \bot \text{ or } x = y \text{ or } (x = s^m(\bot) \text{ and } \exists z \ y = s^m(z)))$$

*(the last case includes $y = s^\omega(\bot)$, setting $s^\omega(\bot) = s^m(s^\omega(\bot))$). (1) Show that $\omega_L$ is $\omega$-algebraic, and determine which are the compact and the maximal elements, respectively. (2) Show that $\omega_L$ is isomorphic to the initial solution of the domain equation $D = \{0\} + D$ (where $+$ is the separated sum, cf. definition 1.4.23).*

**Exercise\* 7.1.23** *Let $(\_)_\perp$ be the lifting functor (cf. definitions 1.4.16 and 8.1.6). (1) Show that the equations $D \cong (D \Rightarrow D)_\perp$ and $D \cong D \Rightarrow (D)_\perp$ have a non-trivial initial solution in $\mathbf{Cpo}^{ip}$. (2) Adapt the proofs of section 3.4 to show that the initial solution of $D \cong (D \Rightarrow D)_\perp$ is isomorphic to the filter domain*

$$\mathcal{F}(Th(\{(\sigma \to \omega) \leq (\omega \to \omega) \mid \sigma \in T\}))$$

*(cf. definition 3.3.4 and remark 3.4.11). (A similar intersection type interpretation of the second equation is undertaken in section 8.4.)*

The following proposition gives a powerful tool for reasoning in recursively defined domains [Pit96] (cf. proposition 3.2.7 and remark 3.2.8).

**Proposition 7.1.24** *Let $\mathbf{C}$ be an $O$-category with a terminal object and $\omega^{op}$-limits, and such that each homset has a least element, and composition is left strict. Let $F : \mathbf{C}^{op} \to \mathbf{C}$ be locally continuous. Let $i : F(C) \to C$ be an isomorphism constructed as indicated in the proof of proposition 7.1.3 (applied to $F^{ip}$). We define $\delta : \mathbf{C}[C, C] \to \mathbf{C}[C, C]$ as follows:*

$$\delta(f) = i \circ F(f) \circ i^{-1} .$$

*The function $\delta$ is continuous and has id as least fixpoint.*

PROOF. The statement follows from proposition 7.1.11 and from the following claim:

$$\forall n \geq 0 \quad \delta^n(\perp) = g_n^+ \circ g_n^- ,$$

where $\{C, g_n\}_{n\in\omega}$ is constructed as in the proof of theorem 7.1.10. The base case follows from left strictness of composition. The induction case follows from the fact that $(i, i^{-1})$ is an iso from $\{F(C), h_n\}_{n\in\omega}$ to $\{C, g_{n+1}\}_{n\in\omega}$, with $h_{n+1}^+ = F(g_n^-)$ and $h_{n+1}^- = F(g_n^+)$:

$$\delta^{n+1}(\perp) = i \circ F(\delta^n(\perp)) \circ i^{-1} = i \circ F(g_n^-) \circ F(g_n^+) \circ i^{-1} = g_{n+1}^+ \circ g_{n+1}^- .\qquad \square$$

Proposition 7.1.24 will serve in a proof of an adequacy result in section 7.2. One can actually strengthen proposition 7.1.24 if one restricts attention to strict functions, as the following exercise (based on [Pit96]) shows.

**Exercise 7.1.25** *We use the notation of proposition 7.1.24. (1) Consider two strict functions $f : A \to F(B)$ and $g : F(A) \to B$ (think of the functor $H : \mathbf{C}^{op} \times \mathbf{C} \to \mathbf{C}^{op} \times \mathbf{C}$ defined by $H(A, B) = (F(B), F(A))$). Show that there exists a unique pair of strict functions $h : A \to C$ and $k : C \to B$ such that:*

$$F(k) \circ f = i^{-1} \circ h \quad and \quad g \circ G(h) = k \circ i .$$

*Hint: For existence, take as $(h, k)$ the least fixpoint of a suitable function. For uniqueness, use proposition 7.1.24 and exercise 6.1.9 (this is where strictness comes in). (2) Show that id is in fact the unique fixpoint of the restriction to strict functions of $\delta$. Hint: Take $f = i^{-1}, g = i$. (3) Prove a version of (1) and (2) and of proposition 7.1.24 for a functor $F : \mathbf{C}^{op} \times \mathbf{C} \to \mathbf{C}$. (Consider again, as a heuristic, an associated functor $H' : \mathbf{C}^{op} \times \mathbf{C} \to \mathbf{C}^{op} \times \mathbf{C}$.)*

**Remark 7.1.26** (1) *The unique fixpoint property of proposition 7.1.24 (in the strengthened form given by exercise 7.1.25), which has been called the minimal invariant property by Freyd [Fre91a], is quite similar to the initial $T$-algebra property of proposition 7.1.3 (think of a fixpoint of $\delta$ as a 'morphism' from $i$ to $i$). There is an essential difference, though. While the category of concern in the application of proposition 7.1.24 is $\mathbf{C}^{ip}$, one deals here directly with the original category $\mathbf{C}$ (cf. exercise 7.1.12).*

(2) *The uniqueness property of minimal invariants allows for proofs by coinduction as well as by induction (see [Pit96] which presents a powerful mixed induction-coinduction principle for reasoning in recursively defined domains).*

We conclude this section with a version of Cantor's theorem on spaces of monotonic functions. Cantor's theorem states that there is no surjection from $D$ to $\mathcal{P}(D)$ in the category of sets. It follows that the problem $(D \Rightarrow D) \lhd D$ has no nontrivial solution in this category (otherwise $\mathcal{P}(D) = (D \Rightarrow 2) \lhd (D \Rightarrow D) \lhd D$). This result can be generalized to the category of partially ordered sets and monotonic morphisms (cf. [GD62]). (*A posteriori*, this provides a justification for jumping directly from set theoretical to continuous functions.) In the following $\mathbf{O} = \{\bot, \top\}$ is the two point poset with $\bot < \top$, and $[D \to E]$ denotes the poset of monotonic morphisms from $D$ to $E$, ordered pointwise.

**Proposition 7.1.27** *Let $P$ be a poset. There is no monotonic surjection $e : P \to [[P \to \mathbf{O}] \to \mathbf{O}]$.*

PROOF. First we build a monotonic surjection $e_1 : [[P \to \mathbf{O}] \to \mathbf{O}] \to [P^{op} \to \mathbf{O}]$. To this end we define:

$$f : P^{op} \to [P \to \mathbf{O}] \qquad fxy = \begin{cases} \top & \text{if } x \leq y \\ \bot & \text{otherwise .} \end{cases}$$

We observe that $f$ is monotonic and injective as:

$$fx \leq fz \text{ iff } \forall y \ (x \leq y \Rightarrow z \leq y) \text{ iff } z \leq x .$$

Next we define $e_1(F) = F \circ f$. We verify the surjectivity. Suppose $d : P^{op} \to \mathbf{O}$, let:

$$H_d : [P \to \mathbf{O}] \to \mathbf{O} \qquad H_d(h) = \bigvee\{dx \mid fx \leq h\} .$$

$H_d$ is clearly monotonic. Surjectivity follows from the computation:

$$e_1(H_d)(z) = H_d(fz) = \bigvee\{dx \mid fx \leq fz\} = \bigvee\{dx \mid z \leq x\} = dz .$$

Suppose that there exists a monotonic surjection $e : P \to [[P \to \mathbf{O}] \to \mathbf{O}]$. By composition with $e_1$ we derive the existence of a surjection $s : P \to [P^{op} \to \mathbf{O}]$. We apply a diagonalization trick defining:

$$c, c' : P^{op} \to \mathbf{O} \qquad c(x) = \overline{s(x)(x)} \quad c'(x) = \bigvee\{c(y) \mid x \leq y\} ,$$

where $\overline{\bot} = \top$ and $\overline{\top} = \bot$. Note that $c'$ is monotonic. Let $w$ be such that $c' = s(w)$. We claim that $c(y) = \top$ for some $y \geq w$. If $c(w) = \top$ take $w$.

Otherwise, if $c(w) = \bot$ then $s(w)(w) = \top$, that is $c'(w) = \top$. Hence $c(y) = \top$ for some $y \geq w$. We then derive a contradiction as follows:

- $s(y)(y) = \bot$ by definition of $c$.
- $s(y)(y) = \top$ because:

$$
\begin{aligned}
c(y) = \top &\Rightarrow& c'(y) = \top \quad &\text{(by definition of } c') \\
&\Rightarrow& s(w)(y) = \top \quad &\text{(since } c' = s(w)) \\
&\Rightarrow& s(y)(y) = \top \quad &\text{(by monotonicity of } s \text{ and since } y \geq w) . \qquad \square
\end{aligned}
$$

**Corollary 7.1.28** *If $[P \to P] \lhd P$ in the category of posets and monotonic morphisms then $\sharp P = 1$.*

PROOF. Since the empty poset is not a solution suppose $\sharp P \geq 2$. If all elements in $P$ are incomparable then Cantor's theorem applies. Otherwise, let $x_1 < x_2 \in P$. Then the pair $(i, \mathbf{O} \to P, j : P \to \mathbf{O})$ defined by:

$$
i(y) = \begin{cases} x_2 & y = \top \\ x_1 & y = \bot \end{cases} \qquad\qquad j(x) = \begin{cases} \top & x_2 \leq x \\ \bot & \text{otherwise} \end{cases}
$$

shows $\mathbf{O} \lhd P$. We observe that $D \lhd D'$ and $E \lhd E'$ implies $[D \to E] \lhd [D' \to E']$ (cf. exercise 7.1.18). Then:

$$
[P \to \mathbf{O}] \lhd [P \to P] \lhd P \quad \Rightarrow \quad [[P \to \mathbf{O}] \to \mathbf{O}] \lhd [P \to \mathbf{O}] \lhd P ,
$$

contradicting the previous proposition 7.1.27. $\qquad\qquad\square$

# 7.2   Predicate equations *

In proving properties of programs, one is often faced with predicates or relations (cf. chapter 6, and in particular theorem 6.3.6). If the semantics of a language involves recursively defined domains, then proving properties of programs may involve recursively defined predicates, and the existence of the solutions to these predicate equations may be troublesome, just as we had troubles with contravariance in solving domain equations. We treat an example of Mulmuley [Mul89], borrowing our techniques from Pitts [Pit96], to which we refer for a general treatment. Our example consists of proving an adequacy theorem for a simple declarative language DYN, based on dynamic binding, whose syntax is given by:

$$
M \quad ::= n \mid Ide \mid \text{let } Ide \text{ bedyn } M \text{ in } M ,
$$

where $n$ ranges over natural numbers and $x, y \dots$ range over a set $Ide$ of identifiers. The intended value of

$$
\text{let } x \text{ bedyn } 3 \text{ in let } y \text{ bedyn } x \text{ in let } x \text{ bedyn } 5 \text{ in } y
$$

is 5, because in computing the value of $y$ it is the last value of $x$, namely 5, which is used. In contrast, the $\lambda$-term $(\lambda x.(\lambda y.(\lambda x.y)5)x)3$ evaluates to 3. We say that $\lambda$-calculus is static. In the static discipline, the declaration of $x$ which is used when evaluating $y$ is the one which is immediately above $y$ in the program text.

$$
\begin{array}{rcl}
n[\sigma] & \to & n \\
x[\sigma] & \to & \sigma(x)[\sigma] \\
(\text{let } x \text{ bedyn } M \text{ in } N)[\sigma] & \to & N[\sigma[M/x]]
\end{array}
$$

Figure 7.1: Operational semantics of DYN

$$
\begin{array}{rcl}
[\![n]\!](\rho) & = & n \\
[\![x]\!](\rho) & = & \rho(x)(\rho) \qquad (\text{if } \rho(x)(\rho) \downarrow) \\
[\![\text{let } x \text{ bedyn } M \text{ in } N]\!](\rho) & = & [\![N]\!](\rho[[\![M]\!]/x])
\end{array}
$$

Figure 7.2: Denotational semantics of DYN

The operational semantics of DYN is described via rewriting rules on pairs $(M, \sigma)$, written $M[\sigma]$, until eventually a constant $n$ is reached. In the pairs $M[\sigma]$, $M$ ranges over the set *Exp* of terms and $\sigma$ ranges over the set of syntactic environments which are functions from *Ide* to *Exp*. The rules are given in figure 7.1. These rules should be contrasted with the rules for the environment machines described in section 8.3. In both cases a natural implementation relies on a stack to pile up unevaluated expressions. However, in dynamic binding we just save the code, whereas in static binding we memorize the code with its environment (a closure).

A denotational semantics of this language can be given with the help of a semantic domain $D$ satisfying the equation $D = Ide \to (D \to \omega)$. The meaning $[\![M]\!]$ of a term $M$ is a partial function from $D$ (ranged over by $\rho$) to $\omega$, defined in figure 7.2 (without an explicit mention of the isomorphism $i : D = Ide \to (D \to \omega)$).

These semantic equations look 'the same' as the rules defining the operational semantics. It requires however a non-trivial proof to show the following adequacy property of the denotational semantics with respect to the operational semantics:

If $M$ is a closed term of DYN, then $M[] \to^* n$ iff $[\![M]\!](\bot) = n$,

where $[]$ is the identity syntactic environment and $\bot$ is the constant $\bot$ function.

We first need to formulate adequacy for any term. We define a semantic mapping from syntactic environments to semantic environments in the following way:

$$
[\![\sigma]\!](x) = [\![\sigma(x)]\!] .
$$

The general adequacy result that we want to prove is:

$$
\forall M, \sigma \ (M[\sigma] \to^* n \ \Leftrightarrow \ [\![M]\!]([\![\sigma]\!]) = n) . \tag{7.4}
$$

($\Rightarrow$) We proceed by induction on the length of the derivation of $M[\sigma]$ to $n$:

- $n$. We have $[\![n]\!]([\![\sigma]\!]) = n$ by the first semantic equation.
- $x$.

$$\begin{aligned}
[\![x]\!]([\![\sigma]\!]) &= [\![\sigma]\!](x)([\![\sigma]\!]) \\
&= [\![\sigma(x)]\!]([\![\sigma]\!]) \\
&= n \qquad \text{(by induction) .}
\end{aligned}$$

- let $x$ bedyn $M$ in $N$.

$$[\![\text{let } x \text{ bedyn } M \text{ in } N]\!]([\![\sigma]\!]) = [\![N]\!]([\![\sigma]\!][[\![M]\!]/x]) = [\![N]\!]([\![\sigma[M/x]]\!]) = n .$$

($\Leftarrow$) The proof involves a predicate $\Theta$ satisfying the following mutually recursive specification:

$$\begin{aligned}
\Theta &= \{(f, M) \in (D \to \omega) \times Exp \mid \forall (\rho, \sigma) \in \Pi \ (f(\rho) \uparrow \text{ or } M[\sigma] \to^* f(\rho))\} \\
\Pi &= \{(\rho, \sigma) \in D \times (Ide \to Exp) \mid \forall x \in Ide \ (\rho(x), \sigma(x)) \in \Theta\} .
\end{aligned}$$

The whole point of this section is to prove that $\Theta$ exists. Meanwhile, assuming its existence, we end the proof of adequacy. We prove by induction on the size of $M$ that $([\![M]\!], M) \in \Theta$.

- $n$. This case holds vacuously since we always have $[\![n]\!](\rho) = n$ and $n[\sigma] \to n$, regardless of what $\rho$ and $\sigma$ are.
- $x$. Let $(\rho, \sigma) \in \Pi$. In particular, $(\rho(x), \sigma(x)) \in \Theta$. By the specification of $\Theta$, we have thus:

$$\rho(x)(\rho) \uparrow \text{ or } \sigma(x)[\sigma] \to^* \rho(x)(\rho) ,$$

which by the definition of the two semantics can be rephrased as:

$$[\![x]\!](\rho) \uparrow \text{ or } x[\sigma] \to^* [\![x]\!](\rho) .$$

Hence $([\![x]\!], x) \in \Theta$.

- let $x$ bedyn $M$ in $N$. Let $(\rho, \sigma) \in \Pi$. First, exploiting induction on $M$, we get $(\rho[[\![M]\!]/x], \sigma[M/x]) \in \Pi$. The conclusion follows by applying induction to $N$.

From $(\forall M \ ([\![M]\!], M) \in \Theta)$ we deduce immediately $(\forall \sigma \ ([\![\sigma]\!], \sigma) \in \Pi)$, by definition of $\Pi$ and of $[\![\sigma]\!]$. Then 7.4 follows from $([\![M]\!], M) \in \Theta$, taking $\rho = [\![\sigma]\!]$.

We are now left with the proof of the existence of $\Theta$. We set:

$$H(E) = Ide \to (E \to \omega) \qquad G(E) = (E \to \omega) \times Exp .$$

We have $H : \mathbf{Cpo}^{op} \to \mathbf{Cpo}$. The ordering on $H(E)$ is obtained as follows: $E \to \omega$ is isomorphic to $E \to \omega_\perp$ (cf. definitions 1.4.16 and 1.4.17), and given a domain $D'$, $Ide \to D'$ is the product of copies of $D'$ indexed over $Ide$, ordered pointwise. Remark that $\{\perp\} \to \omega$ (and hence $H(\{\perp\})$) has infinitely many elements, which makes the initial solution of $H(D) = D$ non-trivial.

We 'extend' $H$ to predicates as follows. For $R \subseteq G(E)$, we define $H(R) \subseteq G(H(E))$ as the set of pairs $(f, M)$ such that:

$$\forall \rho \in H(E), \sigma \in Ide \to Exp \ (\forall x \ (\rho(x), \sigma(x)) \in R) \Rightarrow (f(\rho) \uparrow \text{ or } M[\sigma] \to^* f(\rho)) .$$

The predicate $\Theta$ is a fixpoint for the following function $K : \mathcal{P}(G(D)) \to \mathcal{P}(G(D))$:

$$K(R) = \{(f, M) \mid (f \circ i, M) \in H(R)\},$$

where $i : H(D) \to D$ is the isomorphism associated with the functor $H$ (cf. proposition 7.1.24).

The trouble is that, because $H$ is contravariant in $E$, the function $K$ is antimonotonic. The sequence $\{K^n(\emptyset)\}_{n<\omega}$ is a zigzag $\emptyset \subseteq K(\emptyset) \supseteq K^2(\emptyset) \cdots$, and therefore we cannot build a fixpoint for $K$ right away. However, $K$ gives rise to a continuous function:

$$L : ((\mathcal{P}(G(D)), \supseteq) \times (\mathcal{P}(G(D)), \subseteq)) \to ((\mathcal{P}(G(D)), \supseteq) \times (\mathcal{P}(G(D)), \subseteq)) ,$$

defined by $L(S_1, S_2) = (K(S_2), K(S_1))$, which has a fixpoint $(R_1, R_2)$ (cf. exercise 7.1.25). For reasons linked with the particular $K$ we have at hand, we in fact have $R_1 = R_2$ (and hence we can take $\Theta = R_1 = R_2$). It is enough to establish $R_1 \subseteq R_2$, by the symmetric specification of $R_1$ and $R_2$.

We introduce more ingredients. Since $H$ acts on relations as well as on objects and morphisms, we are led to examine the relationships between morphisms and relations more closely. Given $f : E \to E'$, $R \subseteq G(E)$ and $R' \subseteq G(E')$, we write:

$$f : R \to R' \Leftrightarrow \forall (g, M) \in R' ((g \circ f, M) \in R) .$$

The following are easily established facts:

(1) If $f : R \to R'$ and $f' : R' \to R''$, then $f' \circ f : R \to R''$.

(2) $id : R \to R'$ if and only if $R' \subseteq R$.

(3) If $f : R \to R'$, then $H(f) : H(R') \to H(R)$.

Moreover, we restrict our attention to predicates $R$ satisfying the following properties.

(I1) Closure under directed lub's: $(\forall \delta \in \Delta \ (\delta, M) \in R) \Rightarrow (\bigvee \Delta, M) \in R$.

(I2) $\forall M \ (\bot, M) \in R$.

(I3) $\forall n \in \omega \ ((\lambda u.n, M) \in R \Leftrightarrow M[] \to^* n)$.

We denote with $I(E)$ ($I$ for 'inclusive', cf. section 6.2) the collection of predicates over $G(E)$ satisfying properties (I1) through (I3). Clearly, $I(E)$ has a bottom element, which is:

$$\{(\lambda\rho.n, M) \mid M[] \to^* n\} \cup \{(\bot, M) \mid M \in Exp\} .$$

Moreover, we have:

(4) $H$ maps $I(E)$ to $I(H(E))$.

We only check that $H(R)$ satisfies (I3). If $(\lambda\rho.n, M) \in H(R)$, then since $(\bot, x) \in R$ for all $x$, we have $M[] \to^* (\lambda\rho.n)(\lambda x.\bot) = n$. The converse direction follows from the fact that $M[] \to^* n$ implies $M[\sigma] \to^* n$ for any $\sigma$.

From now on, we shall assume that all predicates satisfy (I1) through (I3). The following further facts will be needed.

(5) For any directed $\Delta \subseteq (E \to E')$, $(\forall \delta \in \Delta \ \delta : R \to R') \Rightarrow \bigvee \Delta : R \to R'$.

(6) $\bot : R \to R'$, for any $R, R'$.

Fact (5) is a consequence of (I1), by the continuity of the composition operation. Properties (I2) and (I3) serve to establish (6), as we show now. Let $(d, M) \in R'$. There are two cases. If $d$ is strict, then $d \circ \bot = \bot$, and $(d \circ \bot, M) \in R$ follows by (I2). Otherwise, since $\omega_\bot$ is flat, $d = \lambda\rho.n$ for some $n$, the conclusion follows by (I3). We now have all the needed material.

By property (4), the function $K$ restricts to a function from $I(D)$ to $I(D)$. Hence we can take the solution $(R_1, R_2)$ in $(I(D), \supseteq) \times (I(D), \subseteq)$. By (2), by proposition 7.1.24, and by (5), our goal can be reformulated as:

$$\forall n \geq 0 \ \delta^n(\bot) : R_2 \to R_1 \ .$$

The base case holds by (6). By fixpoint induction (cf. section 6.2), we are left to show:

$$f : R_2 \to R_1 \Rightarrow \delta(f) = i \circ H(f) \circ i^{-1} : R_2 \to R_1 \ ,$$

which by (1) is proved as follows:

$$
\begin{array}{ll}
i^{-1} : R_2 \to H(R_1) & \text{(since } K(R_1) = R_2) \\
H(f) : H(R_1) \to H(R_2) & \text{(by (3))} \\
i : H(R_2) \to R_1 & \text{(since } K(R_2) = R_1) \ .
\end{array}
$$

**Remark 7.2.1** *Our proof uses only the fact that $(R_1, R_2)$ is a fixpoint (in $I(D)$), not that this is the least one. So, in the end, we get not only that $\Theta$ exists, but also that it is the 'unique' solution of $K(R) = R$ (cf. exercise 7.1.25).*

# 7.3 Universal domains *

We discuss a technique for the construction of a *universal* domain and we apply it to the category of $\omega$-bifinite domains and continuous functions. In the first place, we introduce the notion of *algebroidal* category [BH76] which generalizes to categories the notion of algebraicity already considered for domains.

**Definition 7.3.1** *A category $\mathbf{K}$ is called a* category of monos *if every morphism of $\mathbf{K}$ is mono.*

**Example 7.3.2** *Sets with injections form a category of monos.*

**Definition 7.3.3** *Let $\mathbf{K}$ be a category of monos. An object $A \in \mathbf{K}$ is called* compact *if, for each $\omega$-chain $\{B_n, f_n\}_{n \in \omega}$ with colimit $\{B, g_n\}_{n \in \omega}$ and any $h : A \to B$, there exists $n$ and $k_n : A \to B_n$ such that $h = g_n \circ k_n$. We denote with $\mathcal{K}(\mathbf{K})$ the collection of compact objects.*

**Remark 7.3.4** *We note that for any $n$ there is at most one $k_n$, as $\mathbf{K}$ is a category of monos and therefore $g_n \circ k_n = g_n \circ k_n' = h$ implies $k_n = k_n'$. Moreover, if $g_n \circ k_n = h$ then we can set $k_{n+1} = f_n \circ k_n$ as $g_{n+1} \circ f_n \circ k_n = g_n \circ k_n = h$.*

**Definition 7.3.5** *A category of monos $\mathbf{K}$ is called* algebroidal *if:*

(1) $\mathbf{K}$ *has an initial object.*

(2) *Every $\omega$-chain of compact objects has a colimit.*

(3) *Every object is the colimit of an $\omega$-chain of compact objects.*

*An algebroidal category is called $\omega$-algebroidal if the collection of compact objects, $\mathcal{K}(\mathbf{K})$, is countable up to isomorphism and so is the homset between any two compact objects.*

Next we define the notion of universal object. In particular we will be interested in universal, *homogeneous* objects, as they are determined up to isomorphism. In this section, we follow quite closely [DR93] (see also [GJ90]). More generally, the terminology and the techniques used in this section are clearly indebted to model theory.

**Definition 7.3.6** *Let $U$ be an object in a category $\mathbf{K}$ of monos, and let $\mathbf{K}^*$ be a full subcategory of $\mathbf{K}$. Then we say that:*

(1) *$U$ is $\mathbf{K}^*$-universal if $\forall A \in \mathbf{K}^*$ $\exists f : A \to U$.*

(2) *$U$ is $\mathbf{K}^*$-homogeneous if*

$$\forall A \in \mathbf{K}^* \ \forall f : A \to U \ \forall g : A \to U \ \exists h : U \to U \ (h \circ g = f) .$$

(3) *$U$ is $\mathbf{K}^*$-saturated if*

$$\forall A, B \in \mathbf{K}^* \ \forall f : A \to U \ \forall g : A \to B \ \exists k : B \to U \ (k \circ g = f) .$$

(4) *$\mathbf{K}^*$ has the* amalgamation property *if*

$$\forall A, B, B' \in \mathbf{K}^* \ \forall f : A \to B \ \forall f' : A \to B'$$
$$\exists C \in \mathbf{K}^* \ \exists g : B \to C \ \exists g' : B' \to C \ (g \circ f = g' \circ f') .$$

*When $\mathbf{K}^* = \mathbf{K}$, we simply speak of a universal, homogeneous, or saturated object.*

**Remark 7.3.7** *Definition 7.3.6 requires the existence of certain morphisms but not their uniqueness.*

**Proposition 7.3.8** *The category $\omega\mathbf{Bif}^{ip}$ is $\omega$-algebroidal. Moreover, the collection of compact objects of $\omega\mathbf{Bif}^{ip}$ has the amalgamation property.*

PROOF. To check that $\omega\mathbf{Bif}^{ip}$ is a category of monos with an initial object it is enough to verify that $\omega\mathbf{Bif}$ has a terminal object, the homsets have a least element and composition is left strict (cf. proposition 7.1.9).

By proposition 7.1.14, each $\omega$-diagram of (compact) objects in $\omega\mathbf{Bif}^{ip}$ has a colimit. It is easily checked that finite cpo's are compact, using the fact that for any colimit $\{B, g_n\}_{n\in\omega}$ of any $\omega$-chain $\{B_n, f_n\}_{n\in\omega}$ we have $\mathcal{K}(B) = \bigcup_{n\in\omega}\{g_n^+(B_n)\}$ (cf. proposition 5.2.4). Moreover, by definition of bifinite domain, each object in $\omega\mathbf{Bif}^{ip}$ is an $\omega$-colimit of finite cpo's. If follows that the compact objects are the finite cpo's, since if $D \trianglelefteq E$ and $E$ is finite then $D$ is finite.

Next we verify that $\omega\mathbf{Bif}^{ip}$ has the amalgamation property. Let us consider three finite posets $(E, \leq)$, $(D_1, \leq_1)$, $(D_2, \leq_2)$ with morphisms $h_i = (h_i^+, h_i^-) : E \to_{ip} D_i$, $i = 1, 2$, in $\omega\mathbf{Bif}^{ip}$. Without loss of generality we assume $E = D_1 \cap D_2$, then:

$$\forall e, e' \in E \ (e \leq e' \text{ iff } e \leq_1 e' \text{ iff } e \leq_2 e') .$$

Now we define the amalgam as the set $F = E \cup (D_1\backslash E) \cup (D_2\backslash E)$ where $f \leq_F f'$ iff

$$\exists i \in \{1, 2\} \ (f, f' \in D_i \text{ and } f \leq_i f') \text{ or}$$
$$\exists e \in E \ (f \leq_i e \leq_j f') \ (\text{with } i \neq j, i, j \in \{1, 2\}) .$$

It is easy to verify that $\leq_F$ is a partial order. We are left with the definition of the morphisms $k_i = (k_i^+, k_i^-) : D_i \to_{ip} F$, $i = 1, 2$. We take the inclusions for $k_i^+$, and we define:

$$k_1^-(f) = \begin{cases} f & f \in D_1 \\ h_2^-(f) & \text{otherwise} . \end{cases}$$

$k_2^-$ is defined symmetrically. It can be easily checked that $k_i$ is a morphism in $\omega\mathbf{Bif}^{ip}$, and that $k_1 \circ h_1 = k_2 \circ h_2$. □

**Exercise 7.3.9** *Show that* **Bif**$^{ip}$ *is not an algebroidal category. Hint: Consider an uncountable flat domain. How would you modify the definition in order to include* **Bif**$^{ip}$ *(or* **S**$^{ip}$*) among the algebroidal categories? Hint: A directed diagram in a category* **C** *is a functor* $D : I \to \mathbf{C}$*, where* $I$ *is a directed set. Show that* **Bif**$^{ip}$ *has colimits of directed diagrams, and that each object is the colimit of a directed diagram of compact objects.*

**Theorem 7.3.10** *Let* **K** *be an* $\omega$*-algebroidal category of monos. The following properties are equivalent:*

(1)   *There is a* **K***-universal,* $\mathcal{K}(\mathbf{K})$*-homogeneous object (universal homogeneous for short).*

(2)   *There is a* $\mathcal{K}(\mathbf{K})$*-saturated object.*

(3)   $\mathcal{K}(\mathbf{K})$ *has the amalgamation property.*

*Moreover a* **K***-universal,* $\mathcal{K}(\mathbf{K})$*-homogeneous object is uniquely determined up to isomorphism.*

PROOF. The proof of this theorem is an immediate consequence of the following lemmas. The main difficulty lies in the proof of (3) $\Rightarrow$ (2) (see lemma 7.3.14). □

**Lemma 7.3.11** *Let* **K** *be an algebroidal category of monos and let* $U, V$ *be* $\mathcal{K}(\mathbf{K})$*-saturated. Then:*

$$\forall A \in \mathcal{K}(\mathbf{K}) \ \forall f : A \to U \ \forall g : A \to V \ \exists i : U \to V \ (i \circ f = g) \ .$$

PROOF. Let $\{(U_i, f_i)\}_{i \in \omega}$ and $\{(V_j, g_j)\}_{j \in \omega}$ be $\omega$-diagrams of compact objects whose colimits are $\{U, l_i\}_{i \in \omega}$ and $\{V, l'_i\}_{i \in \omega}$ respectively. Given $f : A \to U$ and $g : A \to V$, we have:

$$\exists f^*_{n_0} : A \to U_{n_0} \ (l_{n_0} \circ f^*_{n_0} = f) \quad \text{(by compactness)}$$
$$\exists p_{n_0} : U_{n_0} \to V \ (p_{n_0} \circ f^*_{n_0} = g) \quad \text{(by saturation)}$$
$$\exists h^*_0 : U_{n_0} \to V_{n_1} \ (l'_{n_1} \circ h^*_0 = p_{n_0}) \quad \text{(by compactness)} \ .$$

We show how to iterate this construction once more. By saturation and by compactness we can build $p_{n_1} : V_{n_1} \to U$ and $h^*_1 : V_{n_1} \to U_{n_2}$ such that $p_{n_1} \circ h^*_0 = l_{n_0}$ and $l_{n_2} \circ h^*_1 = p_{n_1}$, respectively. We proceed inductively, building $V_{n_3}, U_{n_4}, \dots$ . We may suppose $n_0 < n_1 < \dots$ . We observe $l_{n_2} \circ h^*_1 \circ h^*_0 = p_{n_1} \circ h^*_0 = l_{n_0}$. Since $l_{n_2}$ is a mono, this equality entails $h^*_1 \circ h^*_0 = f_{n_2-1} \circ \dots \circ f_{n_0}$. Since we also have $p_{n_2} \circ h^*_1 \circ h^*_0 = l'_{n_1} \circ h^*_0 = p_{n_0}$, it is then possible, using the $p_{n_{2i}}$'s, to see $V$ as (the object of) a cocone for $\{(U_i, f_i)\}_{i \in \omega}$, by which the existence of $i$ such that $i \circ f = g$ follows. □

**Remark 7.3.12** *In the notation of definition 7.3.6 (2) and lemma 7.3.11, the morphisms* $h$ *and* $i$ *are actually isos. This follows from the fact that* **K** *is a category of monos, and from the observation that* $f$ *and* $g$ *play symmetric roles.*

**Lemma 7.3.13** *Let* **K** *be an algebroidal category of monos. The following properties hold:*

(1)   *For any object* $U$ *the following are equivalent: (a)* $U$ *is* **K***-universal and* $\mathcal{K}(\mathbf{K})$*-homogeneous. (b)* $U$ *is* $\mathcal{K}(\mathbf{K})$*-universal and* $\mathcal{K}(\mathbf{K})$*-homogeneous. (c)* $U$ *is* $\mathcal{K}(\mathbf{K})$*-saturated.*

(2)   *A* **K***-universal,* $\mathcal{K}(\mathbf{K})$*-homogeneous object is determined up to isomorphism.*

(3)   *If there is a* **K***-universal and* $\mathcal{K}(\mathbf{K})$*-homogeneous object then* $\mathcal{K}(\mathbf{K})$ *has the amalgamation property.*

PROOF. (1)  We prove the equivalence as follows:

($a$) $\Rightarrow$ ($b$)  Immediate, by definition.

($b$) $\Rightarrow$ ($c$)  Let $A, B \in \mathcal{K}(\mathbf{K})$, $f : A \to U$, $g : A \to B$. By $\mathcal{K}(\mathbf{K})$-universality $\exists g' : B \to U$. By $\mathcal{K}(\mathbf{K})$-homogeneity $\exists h : U \to U$ ($h \circ g' \circ g = f$). So $h \circ g'$ gives saturation.

($c$) $\Rightarrow$ ($a$)  Since there is an initial object 0, $U$ is $\mathcal{K}(\mathbf{K})$-universal by saturation applied to the (unique) morphisms $f : 0 \to U$ and $g : 0 \to A$. The object $U$ is also $\mathcal{K}(\mathbf{K})$-homogeneous by lemma 7.3.11. It remains to show that $U$ is K-universal. Let $A \in \mathbf{K}$ and let $\{(A_i, f_i)\}_{i \in \omega}$ be an $\omega$-chain in $\mathcal{K}(\mathbf{K})$ whose colimit is $A$. Take advantage of $\mathcal{K}(\mathbf{K})$-saturation to build a cocone with object $U$ for this $\omega$-chain. Then there is a morphism from $A$ to $U$.

(2)  Apply lemma 7.3.11 and remark 7.3.12 with $A = 0$.

(3)  Let $A, B, B' \in \mathcal{K}(\mathbf{K})$, $f : A \to B$, $f' : A \to B'$. By $\mathcal{K}(\mathbf{K})$-universality $\exists h : B \to U$. By $\mathcal{K}(\mathbf{K})$-saturation $\exists h' : B' \to U$ ($h \circ f = h' \circ f'$). Now consider an $\omega$-chain in $\mathcal{K}(\mathbf{K})$ whose colimit is $U$ and use the compactness of $B$ and $B'$ to factorize $h$ and $h'$ along some element of the $\omega$-chain.  $\square$

In the next lemma we use (for the first time) the countability conditions that distinguish an $\omega$-algebroidal category from an algebroidal one.

**Lemma 7.3.14**  *Let* **K** *be an $\omega$-algebroidal category of monos. If $\mathcal{K}(\mathbf{K})$ has the amalgamation property then it is possible to build a $\mathcal{K}(\mathbf{K})$-saturated object.*

PROOF.  We use the hypothesis that **K** is $\omega$-algebroidal to build an enumeration $H_o = \{A_i\}_{i \in \omega}$ up to isomorphism of the compact objects of **K** and an enumeration of all quintuples $M_o = \{(B_i, C_i, g_i, h_i, j_i)\}_{i \in \omega}$, where $B_i, C_i \in H_o$, $g_i, h_i : B_i \to C_i$, and $j_i \in \omega$, such that each quintuple occurs infinitely often. We build an $\omega$-chain $\{(U_i, f_i)\}_{i \in \omega}$ such that $U_i \in H_o$ and such that the following properties hold, where we set $f_{j,i} = f_{i-1} \circ \cdots \circ f_j : U_j \to U_i$ ($j \leq i$):

(1)  $\forall i \in \omega$ $\exists k_i : A_i \to U_i$.

(2)  For all $j$, and for all $i \geq j$ such that $j = j_i$ and $U_j = C_i$, we have:

$$\exists k : U_i \to U_{i+1} \ (k \circ f_{j,i} \circ h_i = f_i \circ f_{j,i} \circ g_i) .$$

A consequence of (1) is that, for all $C \in H_o$ and $j$ sufficiently large, we can find $g : C \to U_j$. We also note that if $g, h : B \to C$ with $B, C \in H_o$, and $C = U_j$, then $(B, C, g, h, j)$ will appear infinitely often in the enumeration, so we can find an $i$ such that $(B, C, g, h, j) = (B_i, C_i, g_i, h_i, j_i)$ and $(j =) j_i \leq i$.

Then we define $U$ as the colimit $\{(U, f_{n\infty})\}_{n \in \omega}$ of the $\omega$-chain $\{(U_n, f_n)\}_{n \in \omega}$. First we observe that if we just want to build a $\mathcal{K}(\mathbf{K})$-universal object, then it is enough to check condition (1), as follows: one sets $U_0 = A_0$ and proceeds inductively using the amalgamation property on the (uniquely determined) morphisms $f : 0 \to U_i$ and $g : 0 \to A_{i+1}$. Condition (2) has to do with the fact that we want $U$ to be $\mathcal{K}(\mathbf{K})$-saturated. Let us see how this is used. Let $B, C \in H_o$ and $g : B \to U, h : B \to C$. By (1) and since $B \in \mathcal{K}(\mathbf{K})$ we have:

$$\exists j \ (h' : C \to U_j, g^* : B \to U_j, g = f_{j,\infty} \circ g^*) .$$

| in a cpo $D$ | in $\mathbf{Cpo}^{ip}$ | in $\mathbf{Cpo}$ |
|---|---|---|
| $\perp$ | initial object | terminal object |
| directed lub | $\omega$-colimits | $\omega^{op}$-limits |
| monotonic | functor $F^{ip}$ | functor $F$ (not always) |
| continuous | $\omega$-cocontinuous | locally continuous |
| algebraic | algebroidal | |

Figure 7.3: Domain theoretical versus category theoretical notions

Let $h^* = h' \circ h$. Choose $i$ large enough so that:

$$ j \leq i \text{ and } (B, U_j, g^*, h^*, j) = (B_i, C_i, g_i, h_i, j_i) \ . $$

By (2), $\exists k : U_i \rightarrow U_{i+1}$ $(k \circ f_{j,i} \circ h^* = f_i \circ f_{j,i} \circ g^*)$. From this, saturation follows. Indeed, setting $h'' = f_{(i+1)\infty} \circ k \circ f_{j,i} \circ h' : C \rightarrow U$, we have:

$$ h'' \circ h = f_{(i+1)\infty} \circ k \circ f_{j,i} \circ h^* = f_{(i+1)\infty} \circ f_i \circ f_{j,i} \circ g^* = f_{j\infty} \circ g^* = g \ . $$

Finally, we show how to build the $\omega$-chain $\{(U_i, f_i)\}_{i \in \omega}$. Set $U_0 = A_0$, the first element in the enumeration $H_o$. Next, suppose we have built $U_i$ and consider $A_{i+1}$. As observed above there are $f : 0 \rightarrow U_i$ and $g : 0 \rightarrow A_{i+1}$. By amalgamation we get, for some $U_i'$, two morphisms $f' : U_i \rightarrow U_i'$ and $g' : A_{i+1} \rightarrow U_i'$. Let $j = j_i$.

• If $j \leq i$ and $U_j = C_i$, then by applying amalgamation to $f' \circ f_{j,i} \circ h_i$ and $f' \circ f_{j,i} \circ g_i$ we obtain $k : U_i' \rightarrow U_{i+1}'$ and $k' : U_i' \rightarrow U_{i+1}'$. It just remains to select $U_{i+1}$ isomorphic to $U_{i+1}'$ and in $H_o$.

• Otherwise it is enough to choose an object $U_{i+1}$ in $H_o$ isomorphic to $U_i'$.

In both cases the morphism from $A_{i+1}$ to $U_{i+1}$ is then obtained by composition.     □

**Corollary 7.3.15** *The category $\omega\mathbf{Bif}^{ip}$ has a universal homogeneous object.*

PROOF. We have shown in proposition 7.3.8 that $\omega\mathbf{Bif}^{ip}$ is an $\omega$-algebroidal category with the amalgamation property. Hence theorem 7.3.10 can be applied.     □

Figure 7.3 draws a rough correspondence between domain theoretical and category theoretical notions.

We conclude by pointing out a drawback of the approach through the amalgamation property: we do not have a direct, concrete description of a universal domain. The first universal domains that were proposed in the literature are $\mathcal{P}(\omega)$ (cf. section 4.6) and $T^\omega$ [Sco76, Plo78]. Both $\mathcal{P}(\omega)$ and $T^\omega$ are rather concrete: their elements are sets of natural numbers and disjoint sets of natural numbers, respectively. On the other hand, these universal domains have no claim to be homogeneous. We refer to exercise 13.1.21 for a rather simple direct construction of a universal homogeneous object in the category of coherence spaces and stable injection-projection pairs.

# 7.4 Representation *

We are interested in the problem of representing *subdomains* of a domain $D$ as certain functions over $D$. In particular we concentrate on retractions and projections, the idea being that subdomains are represented by the image of such morphisms. When working with algebraic cpo's and continuous functions, not every retraction (or projection) corresponds to a domain (i.e., is algebraic). For this reason, one focuses on the collection of *finitary* retractions, which are by definition those retractions whose image forms a domain.

The theory is simpler when dealing with (finitary) projections. Then it is not difficult to show that the collection of finitary projections $FP(D)$ over an $\omega$-bifinite domain $D$ is again an $\omega$-bifinite domain. In other words the collection of subdomains of an $\omega$-bifinite domain can be again given a structure of $\omega$-bifinite domain. Having found a representation of domains, we address the problem of representing domain constructors, e.g., product, exponent, sum, and lifting. It turns out that the basic domain constructors we have considered so far can be represented in a suitable technical sense.

The collection $Ret(D)$ of retractions on a cpo $D$ is the collection of fixpoints of the functional $\lambda f.f \circ f$, and the image $r(D)$ of a retraction $r$ on $D$ coincides with the collection of its fixpoints. Hence general results on fixpoints can be immediately applied. We will see that under suitable hypotheses $Ret(D)$ and $r(D)$ enjoy certain algebraic properties.

**Proposition 7.4.1** *Let $D$ be a cpo. Then:*

(1) *If $f : D \to D$ is a continuous morphism then $Fix(f) = \{d \in D \mid f(d) = d\}$ is a cpo.*

(2) *$Ret(D) = Fix(\lambda f : D \to D.f \circ f)$ is a cpo.*

(3) *If $r \in Ret(D)$ then $r(D) = Fix(r)$ is a cpo.*

**Proposition 7.4.2** *Let $D$ be an algebraic cpo and $r \in Ret(D)$. Then $\mathcal{K}(r(D))$, the collection of compacts in $r(D)$, can be characterized as follows:*

$$\mathcal{K}(r(D)) = \{rd \mid d \in \mathcal{K}(D) \text{ and } d \leq rd\} \ .$$

*In particular, if $p$ is a projection then $\mathcal{K}(p(D)) = p(\mathcal{K}(D))$.*

PROOF. Let $ry \in \mathcal{K}(r(D))$. Since $D$ is algebraic, $ry = \bigvee \{x \in \mathcal{K}(D) \mid x \leq ry\}$. So:

$$ry = r(ry) = r(\bigvee\{x \in \mathcal{K}(D) \mid x \leq ry\}) = \bigvee\{rx \mid x \in \mathcal{K}(D) \text{ and } x \leq ry\} \ .$$

Since $ry \in \mathcal{K}(r(D))$, we have $\exists z$ $(ry = rz$ and $z \in \mathcal{K}(D)$ and $z \leq ry)$. This $z$ gives the desired representation of $ry$. Vice versa, suppose $d \in \mathcal{K}(D)$ and $d \leq rd$. Let $\Delta \subseteq r(D)$, $\Delta$ directed, be such that $rd \leq \bigvee \Delta$. Then:

$$d \leq \bigvee \Delta \ \Rightarrow \ \exists \delta \in \Delta \ (d \leq \delta) \ .$$

Hence $rd \leq r\delta = \delta$, which proves that $rd$ is compact in $r(D)$. The statement concerning projections follows from this characterization of the compact elements. $\quad\Box$

**Proposition 7.4.3** *If $D$ is a bounded complete cpo and $r \in Ret(D)$ then $r(D)$ is bounded complete.*

PROOF. Let $X \subseteq r(D)$ and suppose $y \in r(D)$ is an upper bound for $X$. Then $X$ is bounded in $D$ and therefore $\bigvee_D X$ exists. We show $\bigvee_{r(D)} X = r(\bigvee_D X)$.

- $\forall x \in X$ $(x \leq \bigvee_D X)$ implies $\forall x \in X$ $(x = rx \leq r(\bigvee_D X))$. So $r(\bigvee_D X)$ is an upper bound.

- If $y$ is an upper bound for $X$ in $r(D)$ then it is also an upper bound for $X$ in $D$, so $\bigvee_D X \leq y$. This implies $r(\bigvee_D X) \leq ry = y$. So $r(\bigvee_D X)$ is the lub in $r(D)$.    □

Let $D$ be an $(\omega\text{-})$algebraic cpo and $r \in Ret(D)$. Can we conclude that $r(D)$ is again an $(\omega\text{-})$algebraic cpo? The answer is *no*. In general it can only be shown that $r(D)$ is a continuous cpo (see chapter 5).

**Example 7.4.4** *Let $\mathcal{Q}$ and $\mathcal{R}$ be the rational and real numbers, respectively. Let $D = D_0 \cup D_1$ where $D_0 = \{[0, q] \mid q \in \mathcal{Q}\}$, and $D_1 = \{[0, r[ \mid r \in \mathcal{R} \cup \{\infty\}\}$, ordered by inclusion. Consider the projection $p$ defined by:*

$$p([0, q]) = [0, q[ \quad p([0, r[) = [0, r[ \, .$$

*The domain $D$ is an $\omega$-algebraic complete total order, and $D_0 = \mathcal{K}(D)$. On the other hand $im(p)$ fails to be algebraic.*

For the collection $Ret(D)$ things get even worse. For example it has been shown by Ershov (see exercise 18.4.10 in [Bar84]) that the collection of retractions over $\mathcal{P}(\omega)$ is not a continuous lattice, hence *a fortiori* not the image of a retraction. This also shows that the collection of fixpoints of a continuous function does not need to be a continuous cpo, as $Ret(D) = Fix(\lambda f. f \circ f)$.

We will consider retractions again in the context of stable domain theory (section 12.4). For the time being we will concentrate on the simpler case of *finitary projections*.

**Definition 7.4.5 (finitary)** *Let $D$ be an algebraic cpo and $r \in Ret(D)$. We say that $r$ is finitary if $r(D)$ with the induced order is an algebraic cpo.*

Finitary projections over an $\omega$-bifinite domain $D$ provide an adequate representation of the idea of subdomain, moreover the collection of finitary projections over $D$, $FP(D)$, is again an $\omega$-bifinite domain. This is a powerful result that has applications, for instance, to the interpretation of higher order calculi (see section 11.3). The following notion of normal subposet is useful in studying projections.

**Definition 7.4.6 (normal subposet)** *Let $(P, \leq)$ be a poset. A subset $N \subseteq P$ is called a normal subposet if $\forall x \in P$ $(\downarrow x) \cap N$ is directed. We denote with $\mathcal{N}(P)$ the collection of normal subposets of $P$ ordered by inclusion.*

**Theorem 7.4.7** *Let $D \in \textbf{Bif}$. Then:*

*(1) There is an isomorphism $\mathcal{N}(\mathcal{K}(D)) \cong FP(D)$ between the collection of normal subposets of $\mathcal{K}(D)$, ordered by inclusion, and the pointwise ordered set of finitary projections over $D$.*

*(2) $FP(D)$ is an $\omega$-algebraic complete lattice.*

PROOF. We prove only (1), leaving (2) as an exercise. We remark that if $p$ is a projection, $x \in D$ and $Z \subseteq p(D)$, then:

$$(\downarrow x) \cap Z = (\downarrow p(x)) \cap Z .$$

This applies in particular to $Z = p(\mathcal{K}(D)) = \mathcal{K}(p(D))$. Moreover, if $p$ is finitary, then $(\downarrow x) \cap \mathcal{K}(p(D)) = (\downarrow p(x)) \cap \mathcal{K}(p(D))$ is directed, and hence $\mathcal{K}(p(D))$ is normal. Vice versa, if $N \in \mathcal{N}(\mathcal{K}(D))$ we define (cf. proof of theorem 5.2.7):

$$p_N(d) = \bigvee ((\downarrow d) \cap N) .$$

This is well defined because $(\downarrow d) \cap N$ is directed. It is easy to check that the functions $\lambda p.\mathcal{K}(p(D))$ and $\lambda N.p_N$ are inverse isomorphisms between $FP(D)$ and $\mathcal{N}(\mathcal{K}(D))$ (cf. proposition 5.1.10). □

A natural question to ask is whether $FP(D)$ itself is the image of a projection. The answer is negative for bifinite domains in general, but is positive for Scott domains. This property of Scott domains will find an application in section 11.3.

**Exercise 7.4.8** *(1) Show that if $D$ is a Scott domain then $FP(D) \trianglelefteq (D \to D)$. Hint: Given $f : D \to D$ consider $X_f = \{x \in \mathcal{K}(D) \mid x \leq fx\}$ and define $N_f = U^\infty(X_f)$. The set $N_f$ corresponds to a finitary projection $p_{N_f}$. Set $\pi : (D \to D) \to (D \to D)$ as $\pi(f) = p_{N_f}$. (2) Show that the property may fail for bifinite domains (see also exercise 12.4.20). Hint: Consider the cpo given as example (A) of figure 5.2, consider the two projections whose images are $\{\bot, a\}$ and $\{\bot, b\}$, respectively, and use the function $f$ that exchanges $c$ and $d$ and is the identity elsewhere to witness the fact that $FP(D)$ is not normal.*

Let $U$ be a universal domain for some relevant category of domains, say $\omega\mathbf{Bif}$. Then every domain is isomorphic to the image of a finitary projection over $U$. Furthermore, it can be shown that certain basic operators over domains can be adequately represented as continuous functions over $FP(U)$. As a fall-out, one gets a technique to solve domain equations via the standard Kleene least fixpoint construction (cf. proposition 1.1.7).

Observe that there is an injective function $Im$ from the poset $FP(U)$ to the category $\omega\mathbf{Bif}^{ip}$ (this is immediately extended to a functor):

$$Im = \lambda p \in FP(U).p(U) .$$

Let $F : \omega\mathbf{Bif}^{ip} \times \omega\mathbf{Bif}^{ip} \to \omega\mathbf{Bif}^{ip}$ be a binary functor. The representation problem for $F$ consists of finding a continuous function $R_F : FP(U) \times FP(U) \to FP(U)$ such that the following holds, modulo order-isomorphism (for all $p, q \in FP(U)$):

$$F(p(U), q(U)) = R_F(p, q)(U) .$$

**Proposition 7.4.9** *Product and exponent are representable.*

PROOF. In showing that $\omega\mathbf{Bif}$ is a CCC (proposition 5.2.4), one uses the fact that if $p \in FP(D)$ and $q \in FP(D)$ then $\lambda(d, e).(p(d), q(e)) \in FP(D \times E)$ and $\lambda f.(q \circ f \circ p) \in FP(D \to E)$. If $U$ is a universal (homogeneous) domain for $\omega\mathbf{Bif}^{ip}$ then we may assume the existence of injection-projection pairs:

$$(\langle \_, \_ \rangle, \lambda u.(\pi_1(u), \pi_2(u))) : (U \times U) \to_{ip} U \quad (i, j) : (U \to U) \to_{ip} U .$$

It just remains to combine the two ideas to define the operators representing product and exponential (cf. the proof of theorem 4.6.10):

$$\lambda(p,q).\lambda u.\langle p(\pi_1(u)), q(\pi_2(u))\rangle \quad \lambda(p,q).\lambda u.i(q \circ j(u) \circ p) \ .$$

For instance, in the case of the exponential, we compose $\lambda(p,q).\lambda u.(q \circ u \circ p) : FP_U \times FP_U \to FP_{U \to U}$ with $\lambda r.i \circ r \circ j$. $\qquad\qquad\qquad\qquad\qquad\qquad\qquad\qquad\qquad\qquad\qquad$ $\Box$

**Remark 7.4.10** *It is good to keep in mind that Im is not an equivalence of categories between $FP(U)$ and $\omega\mathbf{Bif}^{ip}$, as $FP(U)$ is just a poset category. This point is important when one interprets second order types (see section 11.3).*

**Exercise 7.4.11** *(1) Verify in detail that we can apply proposition 1.1.7 to the domain $FP(U)$ in order to get initial solutions of domain equations in $\omega\mathbf{Bif}^{ip}$. (2) Consider the representation problem for all the type constructors listed in example 7.1.16. (3) Consider the representation problem in the case we replace (finitary) projections with (finitary) retractions.*

Finally, we point out that most of the constructions of this chapter can be carried over to categories of cpo's and stable functions (see proposition 12.4.21 and exercise 12.4.22).

# 8

# Values and computations

When considering the $\lambda$-calculus as the kernel of a programming language it is natural to concentrate on *weak* reduction strategies, that is, strategies where evaluation stops at $\lambda$-abstractions. In presenting the semantic counterpart of these calculi it is useful to emphasize the distinction between *value* and *computation*. A first example coming from recursion theory relies on the notions of total and partial morphism. In our jargon a total morphism when given a value always returns a value whereas a partial morphism when given a value returns a possibly infinite computation. This example suggests that the denotation of a partial recursive algorithm is a morphism from values to computations, and that values are particular kinds of computations.

In domain theory the divergent computation is represented by a bottom element, say $\bot$, that we add to the collection of values. This can be seen as the motivation for the shift from sets to flat domains. More precisely, we have considered three categories (cf. definition 1.4.17).

• The category **Dcpo** in which morphisms send values to values, say $D \to E$. This category is adapted to a framework where every computation terminates.

• The category **pDcpo** which is equivalent to the one of cpo's and strict functions, and in which morphisms send values to computations, say $D \to (E)_\bot$. This category naturally models *call-by-value* evaluation where functions' arguments are evaluated before application.

• The category **Cpo** in which morphisms send computations to computations, or $(D)_\bot \to (E)_\bot$. In the models of the untyped $\lambda$-calculus that we have presented the distinction value-computation can actually be hidden by regarding $\bot$ as an element with the same status of a value.

Another framework where the distinction between values and computations is useful is that of fixpoint extensions of typed $\lambda$-calculi. Consider for example a simply typed $\lambda$-calculus and its *Curry-Howard correspondence* with the minimal propositional logic of implication (cf. chapter 4). Suppose that we want to enrich the calculus with a fixpoint combinator on terms, say $Y$, allowing for fully recursive definitions. Which type should we assign to $Y$? One possibility considered in chapter 6 is to introduce a family of combinators $Y^\sigma$ of type $(\sigma \to \sigma) \to \sigma$. Then the correspondence with the logic is blurred as $Y^\sigma(\lambda x : \sigma.x)$ has type $\sigma$ for any type/proposition $\sigma$, i.e., every type is inhabited/provable. Another possibility is to regard $Y^\sigma(\lambda x : \sigma.x)$ as a *computation of a proof*, that is to assign to $Y^\sigma$ the type $(c(\sigma) \to c(\sigma)) \to c(\sigma)$, where $c(\sigma)$ is the type representing the computations over $\sigma$. Then, at the cost of a complication of the formal system, we may keep a correspondence between propositions and a subset of types.

In these examples, we have roughly considered computations as values enriched with an element denoting the divergent computations. There are, however, other possible notions of computations that arise in the study of programming languages. For instance, if we model non-determinism, then a computation may consist of a collection of values representing the possible outcomes of a program. On the other hand, if we model control operators (cf. section 1.6), then we may view a computation as a continuation.

Which are then the common properties of these notions of computation? The notion of monad that we describe in section 8.1 seems to provide a good general framework. We present a general technique to produce a monad out of a category of partial morphisms. In particular the familiar category of dcpo's is revisited in this perspective. In section 8.2 we introduce a call-by-value version of the language PCF studied in chapter 6 which reflects the properties of the function space in a category of partial morphisms. By a variant of the technique presented in theorem 6.3.6, we prove the *adequacy* of the semantic interpretation with respect to the operational semantics. In section 8.3 we describe a class of abstract machines, known as environment machines, for the mechanical evaluation of weak untyped $\lambda$-calculi. In section 8.4 we consider the full abstraction problem for the call-by-value $\lambda$-calculus. We show that a canonical filter model is fully abstract for the calculus enriched with a parallel join operator. In section 8.5 we revisit the continuation based semantics introduced in section 1.6 from a monadic viewpoint. We introduce a typed call-by-value $\lambda$-calculus enriched with *control operators* for the manipulation of the execution flow and study its *Continuation Passing Style* (CPS for short) translation into a standard $\lambda$-calculus. The typing of control operators allows us to push from intuitionistic to classical logic the Curry-Howard correspondence between typed $\lambda$-calculi and propositional calculi. In this respect CPS translations can be regarded as a way to extract an effective content from a classical proof. We also discuss simple variants of environment machines which can handle control operators.

# 8.1 Representing computations as monads

In this section, following [Mog89], we present the notion of computation-as-monad. The monads of *partial computations*, *continuations*, and *non-deterministic computations* will be our leading and motivating examples.

Monads (or triples) are an important category theoretical notion, we refer to section A2.8 for some basic constructions and to [BW85, ML71] for a deeper analysis. What is important here is to state which are the basic computational properties we wish to formalize. Suppose that $\mathbf{C}$ is our category of data types. An endofunctor $T : \mathbf{C} \to \mathbf{C}$ defines how to go from a collection of values to the collection of computations over such values. A natural transformation $\eta : id_\mathbf{C} \to T$ determines how a value can be seen as a computation. Another natural transformation $\mu : T^2 \to T$ explains how to flatten a computation of a computation to a computation. These requirements plus certain natural commutation properties are expressed by the following equations (cf. definition A2.8.1):

$$\mu_A \circ \eta_{TA} = \mu_A \circ T\eta_A = id_{TA} \qquad \mu_A \circ \mu_{TA} = \mu_A \circ T\mu_A .$$

We say that a monad satisfies the *mono requirement* if $\eta_A$ is a mono, for any object $A$.

**Example 8.1.1** *We give three basic examples of monads with a computational flavour in the category of sets. We leave to the reader the needed verifications and the check that these monads satisfy the mono requirement.*

- *Partial computations. Define* $(\_)_\perp : \mathbf{Set} \to \mathbf{Set}$ *as:*

$$
\begin{aligned}
(X)_\perp &= X \cup \{\perp_X\}, \ \text{where } \perp_X \notin X \\
(f)_\perp(z) &= \begin{cases} f(z) & \text{if } z \in X \\ \perp_Y & \text{otherwise} \end{cases} \quad (\text{where } f : X \to Y) \\
\eta_X(x) &= x \\
\mu_X(z) &= \begin{cases} z & \text{if } z \in X \\ \perp_X & \text{otherwise} . \end{cases}
\end{aligned}
$$

- *Non-deterministic computations. Define* $P : \mathbf{Set} \to \mathbf{Set}$ *as:*

$$
\begin{aligned}
P(X) &= \mathcal{P}_{fin}(X) & P(f)(a) &= f(a), \text{ where } f : X \to Y \\
\eta_X(x) &= \{x\} & \mu_X(z) &= \bigcup z .
\end{aligned}
$$

- *Continuations. We suppose given a set of results,* $R$*, containing at least two elements. In order to understand the basic trick behind the notion of computation, one should think of the double negation interpretation of classical logic into intuitionistic logic [TvD88]. Let* $\neg X \equiv (X \to R)$*, and define* $C : \mathbf{Set} \to \mathbf{Set}$ *as:*

$$
\begin{aligned}
C(X) &= \neg\neg X \\
C(f) &= \lambda g \in \neg\neg X.\lambda h \in \neg Y.g(h \circ f), \text{ where } f : X \to Y \\
\eta_X(x) &= \lambda h \in \neg X.h(x) \\
\mu_X(H) &= \lambda h \in \neg X.H(\lambda g \in \neg\neg X.g(h)) .
\end{aligned}
$$

First, let us concentrate on the monads of continuations and non-deterministic computations. We introduce two variants of the imperative language studied in chapter 1, and analyse their interpretations in suitable monads (for the sake of simplicity we leave out recursion and expressions).

$$
\begin{aligned}
L_C \quad c &::= a \mid skip \mid c; c \mid stop \\
L_N \quad c &::= a \mid skip \mid c; c \mid c + c .
\end{aligned}
$$

In $L_C$ we have introduced a statement *stop* whose intuitive effect is that of terminating immediately the execution of a program and return the current state. As already discussed in section 1.6, the 'direct' semantics used in section 1.5 is not adequate to interpret commands which alter in some global way the control flow. For instance we should have $[\![stop; c]\!] = [\![stop]\!]$, for any $c$, which is hopeless if we insist in stating $[\![stop; c]\!] = [\![c]\!] \circ [\![stop]\!]$. The notion of continuation was introduced in section 1.6 precisely to model operators that explicitly manipulate the control flow.

Let $\Sigma$ be the collection of states. It is natural to take $\Sigma$ as the collection of results. In particular, we have:

$$C(\Sigma) = (\Sigma \to \Sigma) \to \Sigma \ .$$

The semantics of a program is a morphism from $\Sigma$ to $C(\Sigma)$. The interpretation for $L_C$ is defined as follows:[1]

$$
\begin{aligned}
[\![skip]\!] &= \eta_\Sigma & [\![a]\!] &= \eta_\Sigma \circ \underline{a}, \text{ for } \underline{a} : \Sigma \to \Sigma \\
[\![c_1; c_2]\!] &= \mu_\Sigma \circ C([\![c_2]\!]) \circ [\![c_1]\!] & [\![stop]\!] &= \lambda\sigma.\lambda f.\sigma \ .
\end{aligned}
$$

**Exercise 8.1.2** *Verify that* $[\![a; b]\!] = \lambda\sigma.\lambda f.f(\underline{b}(\underline{a}\sigma))$, *and* $[\![stop; c]\!] = [\![stop]\!]$.

In $L_N$ we have introduced an operator $+$ for the non-deterministic composition of two statements. The intuition is that the statement $c_1 + c_2$ can choose to behave as either $c_1$ or $c_2$. It is then natural to consider the interpretation of a statement as a morphism from $\Sigma$ to $\mathcal{P}_{fin}(\Sigma)$, where $\Sigma$ is the collection of states. Hence, using the monad of non-deterministic computations we define:

$$
\begin{aligned}
[\![skip]\!] &= \eta_\Sigma & [\![a]\!] &= \eta_\Sigma \circ \underline{a}, \text{ for } \underline{a} : \Sigma \to \Sigma \\
[\![c_1, c_2]\!] &= \mu_\Sigma \circ \mathit{\Gamma}([\![c_2]\!]) \circ [\![c_1]\!] & [\![c_1 + c_2]\!] &= \lambda\sigma.[\![c_1]\!]\sigma \cup [\![c_2]\!]\sigma \ .
\end{aligned}
$$

An obvious remark is that the interpretations for $L_C$ and $L_N$ are formally identical but for the fourth clause. As a matter of fact we have been using a general pattern in these interpretations which goes under the name of *Kleisli category*. Given a monad $(T, \eta, \mu)$ over a category $\mathbf{C}$, the Kleisli category $\mathbf{K}_T$ is formed as follows (cf. section A2.8):

$$
\begin{aligned}
\mathbf{K}_T &= \mathbf{C} & \mathbf{K}_T[d, d'] &= \mathbf{C}[d, Td'] \\
id_d &= \eta_d : d \to Td & f \circ g &= \mu_{d''} \circ Tf \circ g \quad \text{for } g : d \to d', f : d' \to d'' \text{ in } \mathbf{K}_T \ .
\end{aligned}
$$

The reader will find in [Mog89] more information on this construction, and on its use in the interpretation of a meta-language where the notion of computation is treated abstractly, as a monad with certain desirable properties. The interpretation of the meta-language requires some additional structure to which we hint in the following exercise based on [Koc72, Mog89].

**Exercise 8.1.3** * *A monad* $(T, \eta, \mu)$ *over a category* $\mathbf{C}$ *with finite products and enough points is called* strong *if there is a family of morphisms* $t_{A,B} : A \times TB \to T(A \times B)$, *indexed over the objects* $A, B \in \mathbf{C}$ *such that, for all points* $a : 1 \to A$, $b : 1 \to TB$:

$$t_{A,B} \circ \langle a, b \rangle = T(\langle a \circ !_B, id_B \rangle) \circ b \ . \tag{8.1}$$

*Verify that by the enough points hypothesis, the family* $t_{A,B}$, *if it exists, is uniquely determined. Prove that the monads defined in example 8.1.1 are strong.*

---

[1]This definition differs slightly from the one presented in section 1.6. There, if we ignore environments and partiality, we have $[\![c]\!] : (\Sigma \to \Sigma) \to (\Sigma \to \Sigma)$, whereas here we take $[\![c]\!] : \Sigma \to C(\sigma)$. The two semantic domains are isomorphic as: $(\Sigma \to \Sigma) \to (\Sigma \to \Sigma) \cong (\Sigma \to \Sigma) \times \Sigma \to \Sigma$ $\cong \Sigma \times (\Sigma \to \Sigma) \to \Sigma \cong \Sigma \to C(\Sigma)$.

Going back to the monads of power-sets, we hint at an application to the modelling of parallel computation. We illustrate the idea on yet another variant of the imperative language considered above:

$$L_P \quad c ::= a \mid skip \mid c; c \mid c \parallel c \ .$$

An execution or run of the program $c_1 \parallel c_2$ is an interleaving of the state transformations performed by $c_1$ and by $c_2$. Since $c_1$ and $c_2$ share the same state, different orders of execution might generate different final results, as is clear, for instance, in the program $x := 0 \parallel x := 1$, which upon termination can associate to $x$ either 0 or 1.

In defining the semantics one has to establish what modifications of the state are *atomic*, i.e., are executed as non-interruptible operations. For instance, if we assume that assignment is an atomic operation, then the program $x := 0 \parallel x := 1$ will terminate with $x$ having value 0 or 1, and nothing else (simultaneous assignments are forbidden). The semantics of a program is a collection of sequences of state transformations. For instance we can take:

$$[\![c]\!] \in \mathcal{P}_{fin}((\Sigma \to \Sigma)^+),$$

where $(\Sigma \to \Sigma)^+$ are non-empty finite sequences of functions. In this case it is clear that we can distinguish the interpretations of, e.g., $x := 0; x := x + 1$ and $x := 1$ (due to the interleaving of the actions, the first program when put in parallel with the assignment $x := 1$ can associate 2 to $x$). The interpretation of a parallel composition is an operator that *shuffles* the sequences in all possible combinations.

**Exercise 8.1.4** *Define an interpretation of the language $L_P$ in $\mathcal{P}_{fin}((\Sigma \to \Sigma)^+)$.*

In the presence of divergent programs things are a bit more complicated. What is needed is an analogy of the power-set construction in a category of domains. Various solutions to this problem will be presented in chapter 9. Let us provisionally call $\mathcal{P}_D$ the *powerdomain* operator. The interpretation of a parallel imperative language with recursion is given in a domain of *resumptions* (see, e.g., [Plo83]) which is the least solution of the following equation:

$$R = \Sigma \to \mathcal{P}_D(\Sigma + (\Sigma \times R)) \ .$$

A resumption is a function that takes a state and returns a collection of elements that can be either a state or a pair (state, resumption). Intuitively, a program is interpreted as a possibly infinite sequence of state transformations (cf. exercise 8.1.4). Each state transformation in the sequence models an operation that the program can perform atomically on the memory.

**Partial morphisms.** In example 8.1.1 we have defined the monad of partial computations over **Set**. We show next that the monad of partial computations can be derived in a systematic way from a general notion of *partial morphism*. We then apply this connection between partial morphisms and monads of partial computations to the categories of domains introduced in the previous chapters.

It is standard to consider an equivalence class of monos on an object as a generalized notion of subset. A partial morphism from $a$ to $b$ can then be represented as a total morphism from a subset of $a$ to $b$. In most interesting examples the domain of convergence of a partial morphism is not arbitrary. For instance it is open (as in **Dcpo**), recursively enumerable, etc. It is then reasonable to look for a corresponding categorical notion of admissible mono as specified by the following definition.

**Definition 8.1.5** *An* admissible *family of monos* $\mathcal{M}$ *for a category* $\mathbf{C}$ *is a collection* $\{\mathcal{M}(a) \mid a \in \mathbf{C}\}$ *such that:*

(1) *If* $m \in \mathcal{M}(a)$ *then* $m$ *is a mono* $m : d \to a$.

(2) *The identity on* $a$ *is in* $\mathcal{M}(a)$: $id_a \in \mathcal{M}(a)$.

(3) $\mathcal{M}$ *is closed under composition i.e.:*

$$m_1 : a \to b \in \mathcal{M}(b), m_2 : b \to c \in \mathcal{M}(c) \quad \Rightarrow \quad m_2 \circ m_1 : a \to c \in \mathcal{M}(c) \ .$$

(4) $\mathcal{M}$ *is closed under pullbacks, i.e., if* $m : d \to b \in \mathcal{M}(b)$ *and* $f : a \to b$, *then the limit* $(m' : d' \to a, f' : d' \to d)$ *exists and* $m' \in \mathcal{M}(a)$.

An admissible family of monos $\mathcal{M}$ on $\mathbf{C}$ enjoys properties which are sufficient for the construction of a related category of partial morphisms $\mathbf{pC}$ (the pair $(\mathbf{C}, \mathcal{M})$ is called a partial category).[2] A *representative* for a partial morphism from $a$ to $b$ is a pair of morphisms in $\mathbf{C}$, $(m, f)$, where $m : d \to a \in \mathcal{M}(a)$ determines the domain and $f : d \to b$ the functional behavior. The category $\mathbf{pC}$ has the same objects as $\mathbf{C}$ and as morphisms equivalence classes of representatives of partial morphisms, namely:

$$\mathbf{pC}[a, b] = \{[m, f] \mid m : d \to a \in \mathcal{M}(a), f : d \to b\} \ ,$$

where $[m, f]$ denotes an equivalence class for the following relation: $(m : d \to a, f : d \to b)$ is *equivalent* to $(m' : d' \to a, f' : d' \to b)$ iff there is an iso $i : d \to d'$ in $\mathbf{C}$ such that $m' \circ i = m$ and $f' \circ i = f$.

To specify domain and codomain of a partial morphism, we write $[m, f] : a \rightharpoonup b$, and we write $(m, f) : a \rightharpoonup b$ for a representative. The identity is given by $[id, id] : a \rightharpoonup a$. To compose $[m' : d' \to b, f' : d' \to c] : b \rightharpoonup c$ with $[m : d \to a, f : d \to b] : a \rightharpoonup b$, we compute the pullback $(m'' : d'' \to a, f'' : d'' \to d')$ and obtain $[m \circ m'', f' \circ f''] : a \rightharpoonup c$.

Given $(\mathbf{C}, \mathcal{M})$ there is a canonical embedding functor, $Emb : \mathbf{C} \to \mathbf{pC}$, defined as:

$$Emb(a) = a, \quad Emb(f) = [id, f] \ .$$

**Definition 8.1.6 (lifting)** *Given a category enriched with a collection of admissible monos, say* $(\mathbf{C}, \mathcal{M})$ *and an object* $a$ *in* $\mathbf{C}$, *a lifting of* $a$ *is defined as a partial morphism, open* : $(a)_\perp \rightharpoonup a$, *such that (cf. definition 1.4.16):*

$$\forall b \in \mathbf{C} \ \forall f : b \rightharpoonup a \ \exists! f' : b \to (a)_\perp \ (f = open \circ f') \ . \tag{8.2}$$

---

[2]We refer to [CO88, Mog88, RR88] for extended information on the origins and the development of the theory. The definition of pCCC can already be found in [LM84].

The following theorem characterizes the lifting as the right adjoint of the embedding functor and shows that it induces a monad (cf. section 1.4).

**Theorem 8.1.7** (1) *The partial category* $(\mathbf{C}, \mathcal{M})$ *has liftings iff the embedding
functor has a right adjoint.*

(2) *The lifting functor induces a monad over* $\mathbf{C}$.

PROOF HINT. If $f : b \longrightarrow a$ then we define $f' : b \to (a)_\perp$ according to condition
8.2 (from the morphism *open* we can construct the co-unity of the adjunction).

(1) ($\Rightarrow$) We define a lifting functor, $Lift : \mathbf{pC} \to \mathbf{C}$, as:

$$Lift(a) = (a)_\perp, \quad Lift(f) = (f \circ open_a)', \text{ where } f : a \longrightarrow b .$$

Next we provide a natural iso: $\tau : \mathbf{pC}[\_, \_] \to \mathbf{C}[\_, Lift\_]$, $\tau_{a,b}(f) = f'$. ($\Leftarrow$) Given
the natural iso $\tau$, we define:

$$(a)_\perp = Lift(a), \quad open_a = \tau^{-1}(id_{(a)_\perp}) .$$

(2) This is a mechanical construction of a monad out of an adjunction (cf. section
A2.8). We define $\eta_a = (id_a)'$, and $\mu_a = \tau_{((a)_\perp)_\perp, a}(open_a \circ open_{(a)_\perp})$.  □

**Exercise 8.1.8** *Find a notion of admissible mono in* **Set** *that generates the monad of
partial computations defined in the example 8.1.1(1).*

The notion of partial cartesian closed category (pCCC) arises naturally when
requiring closure under the partial function space.

**Definition 8.1.9 (pCCC)** *Let* $\mathcal{M}$ *be an admissible collection of monos on the
category* $\mathbf{C}$. *The pair* $(\mathbf{C}, \mathcal{M})$ *is a pCCC (partial cartesian closed category) if* $\mathbf{C}$
*is cartesian and for any pair of objects in* $\mathbf{C}$, *say* $a, b$, *there is a pair*

$$(c, pev_{a,b} : c \times a \longrightarrow b)$$

*(pev for short) with the universal property that for any* $f : (d \times a) \longrightarrow b$ *there exists
a unique* $h : d \to c$ *(denoted* $p\Lambda_{a,b}(f)$, *or* $p\Lambda(f)$ *for short) such that* $pev \circ (h \times id_a) =
f$. *We write* $c = a \longrightarrow b$, *and call it the partial exponent of* $a, b$.

In other words, for any object $b$ there is a functor $b \longrightarrow \_ : \mathbf{pC} \to \mathbf{C}$ that is right
adjoint to the product functor $\_ \times b : \mathbf{C} \to \mathbf{pC}$:

$$\mathbf{pC}[\_ \times b, \_] \cong \mathbf{C}[\_, b \longrightarrow \_] .$$

By instantiating this natural isomorphism, we obtain the following version of
*currying*: $a \times b \longrightarrow c \cong a \to (b \longrightarrow c)$. By virtue of this isomorphism we can safely
confuse $b \longrightarrow c$ with $\mathbf{pC}[b, c]$.

**Remark 8.1.10** *In any pCCC the lifting can be defined as* $(a)_\perp = 1 \longrightarrow a$, *with
the morphism* $open = pev \circ \langle id, ! \rangle$.

Every pCCC has an object $\Sigma$, called the *dominance*, that classifies the admissible subobjects. This terminology comes from *topos theory* which is an intuitionistic generalization of set theory formalized in the language of category theory. In every topos there is an object of truth-values $\Omega$ which classifies arbitrary subobjects.

**Proposition 8.1.11** *In every pCCC the object* $\Sigma = (1)_\perp = 1 \rightharpoonup 1$, *called the dominance, classifies the admissible monos in the following sense, where* $\top = p\Lambda(!) : 1 \to \Sigma$:

$$\forall a \; \forall m \in \mathcal{M}(a) \; \exists! \chi : a \to \Sigma \quad \text{such that } (m, !) \text{ is a pullback for } (\chi, \top) \; . \quad (8.3)$$

PROOF HINT. The set $\mathcal{M}(a)$ of admissible monos on $a$ (modulo equivalence), is in bijective correspondence with $\mathbf{p}C[a, 1]$. □

**Exercise 8.1.12** *Given a partial category* $(\mathbf{C}, \mathcal{M})$, *define an admissible subobject functor* $\mathcal{M}(\_) : \mathbf{C}^{op} \to \mathbf{Set}$. *Show that the classifier condition 8.3 can be reformulated by saying that there is a natural isomorphism between the functor* $\mathcal{M}(\_)$, *and the hom-functor* $\mathbf{C}[\_, \Sigma]$.

**Exercise 8.1.13** *Show that in a pCCC the natural isomorphism* $a \to \Sigma \cong a \rightharpoonup 1$ *holds.*

In order to use these definitions, let us consider the familiar category of directed complete partial orders and continuous morphisms (Dcpo). In Dcpo we can choose as admissible monos (i.e., subobjects) the ones whose image is a Scott open. Then the dominance is represented by Sierpinski space $\mathbf{O}$, the two point cpo. The dominance $\mathbf{O}$ classifies the admissible monos because any Scott open $U$ over the dcpo $D$ determines a unique continuous morphism, $f : D \to \mathbf{O}$ such that $f^{-1}(\top) = U$ (this point was already discussed in section 1.2 and it will be fully developed in section 10.1).

**Definition 8.1.14** *Let* **Dcpo** *be the category of dcpo's and continuous morphisms. We consider the following class of monos in* **Dcpo**:

$$m : D \to E \in \mathcal{M}_S \quad \text{iff} \quad m \text{ is a mono and } im(m) \in \tau_S(E) \; .$$

We leave to the reader the simple proof of the following proposition (cf. section 1.4).

**Proposition 8.1.15** (1) *The class* $\mathcal{M}_S$ *is an admissible family of monos for the category* **Dcpo**.

(2) *The related category of partial morphisms is a pCCC with dominance isomorphic to Sierpinski domain* $\mathbf{O}$.

(3) *The following categories are equivalent: the partial category* $(\mathcal{M}_S, \mathbf{Dcpo})$, *the category of cpo's and strict continuous morphisms, and the category of dcpo's and partial continuous morphisms.*

## 8.2　Call-by-value and partial morphisms

We apply the idea of distinguishing between total and divergent computations which is implicit in the monad of *partial computations* to the design of a variant of the language PCF (see chapter 6). This gives us the opportunity to revisit the general problem of relating the interpretation of a programming language with the way the programming language is executed.

We may start from the following question (reversing the historical evolution of the topic): for which kind of simply typed $\lambda$-calculus does a pCCC provide an adequate interpretation? A crucial point is that we follow a call-by-value evaluation discipline, hence in an application the evaluator has to diverge if the argument diverges. To be more precise, we have to fix the rules of evaluation and observation. We stipulate the following:

(1)　The evaluator has to stop at $\lambda$-abstractions.

(2)　It is possible to observe the termination of a computation of a closed term at all types, equivalently one may say that programs have arbitrary, possibly functional, types.

Contrast these design choices with the definition of the evaluator $\to_{op}$ in section 6.3. There evaluation followed a call-by-name order and observation of termination was allowed only at basic types. As in chapter 6, we wish to relate operational and denotational semantics. The technical development of the adequacy proof goes through three main steps.

(1)　A language based on a fixpoint extension of the simply typed $\lambda$-calculus is introduced and a call-by-value evaluation of closed terms is defined.

(2)　A standard interpretation of the language in the pCCC **pDcpo** is specified.

(3)　A notion of *adequacy relation* is introduced (cf. the proof of theorem 6.3.6) which allows us to relate closed terms and denotations.

It is first proved that the evaluation of a closed term converges to a *canonical* term if and only if its denotation is a total morphism. As a corollary, a result of adequacy of the interpretation with respect to a natural observational preorder is obtained.

**Call-by-value $\lambda Y$-calculus.** We consider a variant of the $\lambda Y$-calculus defined in section 6.1 suited to the call-by-value viewpoint. Types and raw terms are defined by the following grammars. We distinguish a special type 1 which is inhabited by the constant $*$. This type corresponds to the terminal object and it is used to define a lifting operator, according to what can be done in every pCCC.

| | | |
|---|---|---|
| Type Variables | $tv$ | $::= t \mid s \mid \ldots$ |
| Types | $\sigma$ | $::= 1 \mid tv \mid (\sigma \to \sigma)$ |
| Term Variables | $v$ | $::= x \mid y \mid \ldots$ |
| Terms | $M$ | $::= * \mid v \mid \lambda v : \sigma.M \mid MM \mid Y^\sigma M$ . |

Contexts $\Gamma$ are defined as in chapter 4. Provable typing judgments are inductively defined in figure 8.1 (in the following we often omit the type label from the $Y$ combinator).

$$(*) \quad \frac{}{\Gamma \vdash * : 1} \qquad (Asmp) \quad \frac{x : \sigma \in \Gamma}{\Gamma \vdash x : \sigma}$$

$$(\to_I) \quad \frac{\Gamma, x : \sigma \vdash M : \tau}{\Gamma \vdash \lambda x : \sigma.M : \sigma \to \tau} \qquad (\to_E) \quad \frac{\Gamma \vdash M : \sigma \to \tau \quad \Gamma \vdash N : \sigma}{\Gamma \vdash MN : \tau}$$

$$(Y) \quad \frac{\Gamma \vdash M : (1 \to \sigma) \to \sigma}{\Gamma \vdash Y^\sigma M : \sigma}$$

Figure 8.1: Typing rules for the call-by-value typed $\lambda$-calculus

The types of the $Y$ clause may seem a bit puzzling at a first glance. One can give a semantic justification by recalling that in a pCCC we define the lifting as $(a)_\perp = (1 \to a)$, on the other hand the partial function space, say $\to$, relates to the total function space, say $\to$, as $a \to b = a \to (b)_\perp$. So $(1 \to \sigma) \to \sigma$ is the 'same' as $((\sigma)_\perp \to (\sigma)_\perp)$ and the implicit type we give to $Y$ is $((\sigma)_\perp \to (\sigma)_\perp) \to (\sigma)_\perp$, that is the usual type of a fixpoint combinator over $(\sigma)_\perp$. One good reason to restrict recursion to lifted objects is that these objects do have a least element! A continuous function over a directed complete partial order without a least element does not need to have a fixpoint.

**Evaluation.** In chapter 6 we defined the reduction relation as the reflexive, transitive closure of a one-step reduction relation $\to_{op}$. In the following we follow a different style of presentation in which evaluation is presented as a relation between programs, i.e., closed terms, and *canonical forms*. The definition of the relation $\mapsto$ directly gives a deterministic procedure to reduce, if possible, a closed term to a canonical form. By convention, canonical forms evaluate to themselves.

In the case considered here, the canonical forms are the closed, well-typed terms $C, C', \ldots$ that are generated by the following grammar (other examples of definition of evaluation relations can be found in section 8.3):

$$C ::= * \mid (\lambda v : \sigma.M) .$$

The evaluation relation $\mapsto$ relates closed terms and canonical forms of the same type. Its definition is displayed in figure 8.2. We write $M \downarrow$ if $\exists C \ (M \mapsto C)$.

**Interpretation.** In order to define an interpretation of our call-by-value $\lambda$-calculus we concentrate on the category of directed complete partial orders and partial continuous morphisms. Then, as usual, there is a least fixpoint operator over lifted objects that is calculated as the lub of an inductively defined chain.

We give a type interpretation that depends on an assignment $\eta : tv \to \mathbf{Dcpo}$

$$(*) \quad \frac{}{* \mapsto *}$$

$$(\rightarrow_I) \quad \frac{}{\lambda x : \sigma.M \mapsto \lambda x : \sigma.M}$$

$$(\rightarrow_E) \quad \frac{M \mapsto \lambda x : \sigma.M' \quad N \mapsto C' \quad M'[C'/x] \mapsto C}{MN \mapsto C}$$

$$(Y) \quad \frac{M(\lambda x : 1.YM) \mapsto C}{YM \mapsto C} \quad (x \text{ fresh})$$

Figure 8.2: Evaluation rules for the call-by-value $\lambda$-calculus

$$
\begin{array}{llll}
(*) & [\![\Gamma \vdash * : 1]\!] & = & !_{[\![\Gamma]\!]} \\
(Asmp) & [\![\Gamma \vdash x_i : \sigma_i]\!] & = & \pi_{n,i} \\
(\rightarrow_I) & [\![\Gamma \vdash \lambda x : \sigma.M : \sigma \rightharpoonup \tau]\!] & = & p\Lambda([\![\Gamma, x : \sigma \vdash M : \tau]\!]) \\
(\rightarrow_E) & [\![\Gamma \vdash MN : \tau]\!] & = & pev \circ \langle [\![\Gamma \vdash M : \sigma \rightharpoonup \tau]\!], [\![\Gamma \vdash N : \sigma]\!] \rangle \\
(Y) & [\![\Gamma \vdash YM : \sigma]\!] & = & \bigvee_{n < \omega} f_n
\end{array}
$$

where $g = [\![\Gamma \vdash M : (1 \rightharpoonup \sigma) \rightharpoonup \sigma]\!]$,
$f_0$ is the divergent morphism, and
$f_{n+1} = pev \circ \langle g, \underline{id} \circ f_n \rangle$.

Figure 8.3: Interpretation of the call-by-value $\lambda$-calculus in **pDcpo**

as follows:

$$
\begin{array}{lll}
[\![1]\!] & = 1 & \text{(the terminal object)} \\
[\![t]\!] & = \eta(t) & \\
[\![\sigma \rightharpoonup \tau]\!] & = [\![\sigma]\!] \rightharpoonup [\![\tau]\!] & \text{(the partial exponent)} .
\end{array}
$$

The interpretation of a judgment $\Gamma \vdash M : \sigma$, where $\Gamma \equiv (x_1 : \sigma_1), \ldots, (x_n : \sigma_n)$, is a partial morphism of type: $[\![1]\!] \times [\![\sigma_1]\!] \times \cdots \times [\![\sigma_n]\!] \rightharpoonup [\![\sigma]\!]$ ($\times$ associates to the left) as defined in figure 8.3 (we refer to figure 4.4 for the definition of the projection $\pi_{n,i}$).

- If $\vdash M : \sigma$, that is the term is closed, then the interpretation $f$ lives in $[\![1 \rightharpoonup \sigma]\!]$. Since 1 is a singleton, say $1 = \{*\}$, $f(*)$ is either undefined or a point in $[\![\sigma]\!]$. We write $f \uparrow$ in the first case and $f \downarrow$ in the second case. We denote with $\bot$ the diverging morphism.

- In $(*)$, $!_{[\![\Gamma]\!]}$ is the unique total morphism into 1.

- In $(\to_E)$, the operation $\langle \_, \_ \rangle$ is a *partial* pairing, that is, it is defined only if its arguments are both defined.

- In $(Y)$, the morphism $\underline{id} : a \to (1 \to a)$ is uniquely determined by the identity over $a$ and the morphism $open_a : (1 \to a) \to a$.

As in chapter 4 we can proceed by induction on the size of the typing proof to establish the following properties of substitution.

**Lemma 8.2.1 (substitution)** *If $\Gamma, x : \sigma \vdash M : \tau$, and $\Gamma \vdash C : \sigma$ then:*

(1) $\Gamma \vdash M[C/x] : \tau$.

(2) $[\![\Gamma \vdash M[C/x] : \tau]\!] = [\![\Gamma, x : \sigma \vdash M : \tau]\!] \circ \langle id, [\![\Gamma \vdash C : \sigma]\!] \rangle$.

**Adequacy.** We want to prove that given a well typed closed term $M$, $M \downarrow$ iff $[\![M]\!] \downarrow$. It is easy to show that if $M \downarrow$ then $[\![M]\!] \downarrow$ as the interpretation is invariant under evaluation and the interpretation of a canonical form is a total morphism. In the other direction the naive attempt of proving $([\![M]\!] \downarrow \Rightarrow M \downarrow)$ by induction on the typing of $M$ does not work. Therefore, we associate to every type $\sigma$ an *adequacy relation* $\mathcal{R}^\sigma$ relating denotations and closed terms of type $\sigma$ (cf. chapter 6). Adequacy relations enjoy the following property:

$$(f \, \mathcal{R}^\sigma \, M \text{ and } f \downarrow) \;\Rightarrow\; M \downarrow$$

Moreover they enjoy additional properties so that a proof by induction on the typing can go through. Let $\lambda Y_\sigma^o$ be the collection of closed terms of type $\sigma$.

**Definition 8.2.2** *A relation $S \subseteq [\![1 \to \sigma]\!] \times \lambda Y_\sigma^o$ is called an adequacy relation of type $\sigma$ if it satisfies the following conditions:*

$(C_1)$ $(fSM \text{ and } f \downarrow) \Rightarrow M \downarrow$

$(C_2)$ $(fSM \text{ and } M \mapsto C \text{ and } M' \mapsto C) \Rightarrow fSM'$

$(C_3)$ $\bot SM$, *for any $M \in \lambda Y_\sigma^o$*

$(C_4)$ $(\{f_n\}_{n<\omega} \text{ directed in } [\![1 \to \sigma]\!] \text{ and } \forall n \; f_n \, S \, M) \Rightarrow (\bigvee_{n<\omega} f_n)SM$ .

*We denote with $AR_\sigma$ the collection of adequacy relations of type $\sigma$. For any type $\sigma$, the relation $\{(\bot, M) \mid M \in \lambda Y_\sigma^o\}$ is an adequacy relation of type $\sigma$.[3]*

It is interesting to observe certain geometric properties of adequacy relations. To this end we make explicit a cpo structure on the collection of closed terms. Define an equivalence relation, say $\approx$, on terms by stating that:

$$M \approx N \text{ iff } (M \uparrow \text{ and } N \uparrow) \text{ or } \exists C \; (M \mapsto C \text{ and } N \mapsto C) \, .$$

Given a type $\sigma$ consider the quotient $\lambda Y_\sigma^o / \approx$, with a flat order obtained by assuming that the equivalence class of diverging terms is the least element, and all other equivalence classes are incomparable.

---

[3]The conditions $(C_2)$, $(C_3)$ and $(C_4)$ are the counterparts of the properties $(Q_1)$, $(Q_2)$ and $(Q_3)$ considered in the proof of theorem 6.3.6.

We can now consider $E = [\![1 \multimap \sigma]\!] \times (\lambda Y_\sigma^o / \approx)$ as the product cpo. By definition, a set $P \subseteq E$ is an *admissible predicate* (cf. inclusive predicates in section 6.3) if it is closed under directed sets. Note that any admissible predicate $P$ determines a relation $S_P$ over $[\![1 \multimap \sigma]\!] \times \lambda Y_\sigma^o$ as follows:

$$(f, M) \in S_P \text{ iff } (f, [M]_\approx) \in P .$$

Adequacy relations can be seen as a particular case of admissible predicates.

**Exercise 8.2.3** *Let $U = \{(f, [M]_\approx) \mid f \downarrow \Rightarrow M \downarrow\}$ and $L = \{(\bot, [M]_\approx) \mid M \text{ closed}\}$. Verify that $U$ and $L$ are admissible predicates. Next show that the admissible predicates $S$ such that $L \subseteq S \subseteq U$ are in bijective correspondence with the adequacy relations.*

**Definition 8.2.4** *Given an assignment $\theta : tv \to \bigcup_{t \in tv} AR_t$, such that $\theta(t) \in AR_t$ for any $t$, we associate to every type $\sigma$ a relation $\mathcal{R}^\sigma \subseteq [\![1 \multimap \sigma]\!] \times \lambda Y_\sigma^o$ as follows:*

$$\begin{aligned}
\mathcal{R}^1 &= \{(f, M) \mid f \uparrow \text{ or } (f \downarrow \text{ and } M \downarrow)\} \\
\mathcal{R}^t &= \theta(t) \\
\mathcal{R}^{\sigma \to \tau} &= \{(f, M) \mid (f \downarrow \Rightarrow M \downarrow) \text{ and } \forall d, N \ (d \mathcal{R}^\sigma N \Rightarrow (pev \circ \langle f, d \rangle) \mathcal{R}^\tau MN)\} .
\end{aligned}$$

**Proposition 8.2.5** *The relation $\mathcal{R}^\sigma$ is an adequacy relation of type $\sigma$, for any type $\sigma$.*

PROOF. We just consider the case $\sigma \to \tau$ and verify the four conditions:

$(C_1)$ By definition of $\mathcal{R}^{\sigma \to \tau}$.

$(C_2)$ Suppose $(f \mathcal{R}_{\sigma \to \tau} M$ and $M \mapsto C$ and $M' \mapsto C)$. First observe:

$$(M \mapsto C \text{ and } M' \mapsto C \text{ and } MN \mapsto C') \Rightarrow M'N \mapsto C' . \tag{8.4}$$

We have to show: $pev \circ \langle f, d \rangle \mathcal{R}^\tau MN$ implies $pev \circ \langle f, d \rangle \mathcal{R}^\tau M'N$; that follows by induction hypothesis on $\tau$ and property 8.4.

$(C_3)$ $\bot \mathcal{R}^{\sigma \to \tau} M$ because $pev \circ \langle \bot, d \rangle \cong \bot$, and $\bot \mathcal{R}^\tau MN$, by induction hypothesis on $\tau$.

$(C_4)$ $pev \circ \langle \bigvee_{n < \omega} f_n, d \rangle = \bigvee_{n < \omega} pev \circ \langle f_n, d \rangle$, but $\forall n \ (f_n \mathcal{R}^{\sigma \to \tau} M)$ and $d \mathcal{R}^\sigma N$ implies $\forall n \ (pev \circ \langle f_n, d \rangle \mathcal{R}^\tau MN)$. The thesis follows by $(C_4)$ over $\mathcal{R}^\tau$. $\square$

**Theorem 8.2.6** *If $\Gamma \vdash M : \sigma$, $\Gamma \equiv (x_1 : \sigma_1), \ldots, (x_n : \sigma_n)$, and $d_i \mathcal{R}^{\sigma_i} C_i$, $i = 1, \ldots, n$ then $([\![\Gamma \vdash M : \sigma]\!] \circ \langle d_1, \ldots, d_n \rangle) \mathcal{R}^\sigma M[C_1/x_1, \ldots, C_n/x_n]$.*

PROOF. By induction on the length of the typing judgment. We adopt the following abbreviations: $\langle d_1, \ldots, d_n \rangle \equiv \vec{d}$ and $[C_1/x_1, \ldots, C_n/x_n] \equiv [\vec{C}/\vec{x}]$. We just consider three cases (cf. proof of lemma 3.5.16).

$(*)$ $([\![\Gamma \vdash * : 1]\!] \circ \vec{d}) \mathcal{R}^1 *$, by definition of $\mathcal{R}^1$.

$(\to_I)$ We show $(p\Lambda([\![\Gamma, x : \sigma \vdash M : \tau]\!]) \circ \vec{d}) \mathcal{R}^{\sigma \to \tau} (\lambda x : \sigma.M[\vec{C}/\vec{x}])$. The first condition that defines $\mathcal{R}^{\sigma \to \tau}$ follows by the fact that $\lambda x : \sigma.M[\vec{C}/\vec{x}] \downarrow$. For the second, suppose $d \mathcal{R}^\sigma N$, $N \mapsto C$, and the application is defined, then by inductive hypothesis we have:

$$([\![\Gamma, x : \sigma \vdash M : \tau]\!] \circ \langle \vec{d}, d \rangle) \, \mathcal{R}^\tau \, M[\vec{C}/\vec{x}][C/x] \, .$$

We observe:

(1) $pev \circ \langle p\Lambda([\![\Gamma, x : \sigma \vdash M : \tau]\!]) \circ \vec{d}, d \rangle = ([\![\Gamma, x : \sigma \vdash M : \tau]\!]) \circ \langle \vec{d}, d \rangle$ .

(2) $M[\vec{C}/\vec{x}][C/x] \mapsto C'$ implies $(\lambda x : \sigma.M[\vec{C}/\vec{x}])N \mapsto C'$ .

(3) Hence by condition $(C_2)$:

$$(pev \circ \langle p\Lambda([\![\Gamma, x : \sigma \vdash M : \tau]\!]) \circ \vec{d}, d \rangle) \, \mathcal{R}^\tau \, (\lambda x : \sigma.M[\vec{C}/\vec{x}])N \, .$$

$(Y)$ We show $((\bigvee_{n<\omega} f_n) \circ \vec{d}) \, \mathcal{R}^\sigma \, YM[\vec{C}/\vec{x}]$. We prove by induction that, for each $n$, $(f_n \circ \vec{d}) \, \mathcal{R}^\sigma \, YM[\vec{C}/\vec{x}]$. The case $n = 0$ follows by $(C_3)$. For the induction step, let $g = [\![M]\!] \circ \vec{d}$. We observe:

$$(pev \circ \langle g, \underline{id} \circ f_n \rangle) \, \mathcal{R}^\sigma \, M(\lambda x : 1.YM[\vec{C}/\vec{x}]) \, ,$$

by induction hypothesis on $\Gamma \vdash M : (1 \to \sigma) \to \sigma$. Now we use $(C_2)$ to conclude $f_{n+1} = pev \circ \langle g, \underline{id} \circ f_n \rangle \, \mathcal{R}^\sigma \, YM[\vec{C}/\vec{x}]$. Hence by $(C_4)$ we have the thesis. $\quad\square$

**Corollary 8.2.7** (1) *If* $\vdash M : \sigma$ *then* $[\![M]\!] \downarrow$ *implies* $M \downarrow$.

(2) *If* $\Gamma \vdash M : \sigma$, $\Gamma \vdash N : \sigma$, *and* $[\![\Gamma \vdash M : \sigma]\!] \leq [\![\Gamma \vdash N : \sigma]\!]$, *then in any context* $C$ *such that* $\vdash C[M] : \tau$ *and* $\vdash C[N] : \tau$ *we have* $C[M] \downarrow$ *implies* $C[N] \downarrow$.

PROOF. (1) We apply the theorem 8.2.6 in the case the context is empty.

(2) We prove by induction on the structure of a context $C$ that for any $M, N$ such that $\vdash C[M] : \tau$ and $\vdash C[N] : \tau$,

$$[\![\Gamma \vdash M : \sigma]\!] \leq [\![\Gamma \vdash N : \sigma]\!] \quad \Rightarrow \quad [\![\vdash C[M] : \tau]\!] \leq [\![\vdash C[N] : \tau]\!] \, .$$

Next we apply the adequacy theorem to show $C[M] \downarrow \;\Rightarrow\; [\![C[M]]\!] \downarrow \;\Rightarrow\; [\![C[N]]\!] \downarrow \;\Rightarrow\; C[N] \downarrow$. $\quad\square$

# 8.3 Environment machines

The efficient reduction of $\lambda$-terms is an important research topic (see, e.g., [PJ87]). A central problem is the implementation of the substitution operation. In $\lambda$-calculus theory substitution is considered as a meta-operation whose definition involves renaming of bound variables and a complete visit of the term in which the substitution is carried on. In implementations, it is tempting to distribute the price of substitution along the computation. The idea is to record the substitution in a suitable data structure, the *environment*, which is kept on the side during the evaluation. The environment is accessed whenever the actual 'value' of a variable is needed.

$(\beta)$  $$\overline{(\lambda x.M)N \to M[N/x]}$$

$(\mu)$  $$\frac{M \to M'}{MN \to M'N}$$          $(\nu)$  $$\frac{N \to N'}{MN \to MN'}$$

Figure 8.4: Reduction rules for the weak $\lambda$-calculus

$$\overline{(\lambda x.M)V \to_v M[V/x]} \qquad \frac{M \to_v M'}{MN \to_v M'N} \qquad \frac{N \to_v N'}{VN \to_v VN'}$$

Figure 8.5: Call-by-value reduction strategy

**The weak $\lambda$-calculus.** Based on this idea we present a class of machines known as *environment machines* which are related to the Categorical Abstract Machine mentioned in section 4.3 (see [Cur91] for an exact connection). We concentrate on the implementation of the *weak* $\lambda$-calculus, a $\lambda$-calculus in which reduction cannot occur under $\lambda$'s. Terms are defined as usual, we omit types since they are not relevant to our discussion. The rules for weak reduction are shown in figure 8.4.

Note that the reduction relation $\to^*$ generated by these rules is *not* confluent. For instance consider $(\lambda y.\lambda x.y)(II)$, where $I$ is $\lambda z.z$. This term can be reduced to two distinct normal forms: $\lambda x.II$ and $\lambda x.I$. Call-by-name and call-by-value are two popular reduction strategies for the weak reduction.

• In the call-by-name strategy rule $(\nu)$ is omitted. We denote the resulting reduction relation with $\to_n$.

• By definition, a value $V$ is a term which begins with a $\lambda$-abstraction. The call-by-value reduction strategy is presented in figure 8.5.

**Exercise 8.3.1** *Formalize a call-by-name version of the typed $\lambda$-calculus defined in section 8.2. Define a translation of call-by-name into call-by-value according to the type translation $\sigma \to \tau = (1 \to \sigma) \to \tau$, where $\to$ is the exponentiation operator for the call-by-name calculus.*

In the study of abstract machines implementing a given strategy, one is often interested in the *evaluation relation* that we conventionally denote with $\mapsto$, in order to distinguish it from the reduction relation (an example of evaluation relation was given in figure 8.2). The evaluation relation relates terms to values (or canonical forms). The evaluation relations $\mapsto_n$ and $\mapsto_v$ for call-by-name and call-by-value, respectively, are shown in figure 8.6.

$$\frac{}{V \mapsto_n V} \qquad \frac{M \mapsto_n \lambda x.M' \quad M'[N/x] \mapsto_n V}{MN \mapsto_n V}$$

$$\frac{}{V \mapsto_v V} \qquad \frac{M \mapsto_v \lambda x.M' \quad N \mapsto_v V' \quad M'[V'/x] \mapsto_v V}{MN \mapsto_v V}$$

Figure 8.6: Evaluation relations for call-by-name and call-by-value

$$\frac{}{x[e] \to e(x)} \qquad \frac{M[e] \to^* (\lambda x.P)[e']}{(MN)[e] \to P[e'[N[e]/x]]} \qquad \frac{e(x) \to c}{M[e] \to M[e[c/x]]}$$

Figure 8.7: Weak reduction for the calculus of closures

**Exercise 8.3.2** *Let $s$ stand for $n$ or $v$. Show that: (i) $\mapsto_s \subset \to_s^*$, and (ii) the relations $\mapsto_s$ and $\to_s$ are incomparable with respect to the inclusion relation.*

**A weak calculus of closures.** Next we formalize the idea of environment. To this end we define a calculus of *closures* which are pairs of $\lambda$-terms and environments. Environments and closures are mutually defined as follows:

- An *environment* is a partial function $e : Var \rightharpoonup Closures$ where $Dom(e)$ is finite (in particular the always undefined function is an environment), and $Closures$ is the set of closures.

- A *closure* $c$ is a term $M[e]$ where $M$ is a term and $e$ is an environment.

We evaluate closures $M[e]$ such that $FV(M) \subseteq Dom(e)$. The evaluation rules for weak reduction are displayed in figure 8.7. In the second rule, $M[e]$ can be already of the form $(\lambda x.P)[e']$. Observe that the schematic formulation of this rule is needed in order to keep environments at top level.

It is shown in [Cur91] that the relation $\to^*$ is confluent on closures. Next we formalize the evaluation relations for the call-by-name and call-by-value strategies. By definition, a value $vc$ is a closure $(\lambda x.M)[e]$. The rules are shown in figure 8.8.

**Abstract machines.** The evaluation rules described in figure 8.8 are pretty close to the definition of an interpreter. What is still needed is a data structure which keeps track of the terms to be evaluated or waiting for their arguments to be evaluated. Not surprisingly, a *stack* suffices to this end. In the call-by-name strategy, we visit the term in a leftmost outermost order looking for a redex. During this visit the terms that appear as arguments in an application are piled

$$\frac{e(x) \mapsto_n vc}{x[e] \mapsto_n vc} \qquad \frac{M[e] \mapsto_n \lambda x.P[e'] \quad P[e'[N[e]/x]] \mapsto_n vc}{(MN)[e] \mapsto_n vc}$$

$$\frac{e(x) \mapsto_v vc}{x[e] \mapsto_v vc} \qquad \frac{M[e] \mapsto_v \lambda x.P[e'] \quad N[e] \mapsto_v vc' \quad P[e'[vc'/x]] \mapsto_n vc}{(MN)[e] \mapsto_n vc}$$

Figure 8.8: Evaluation rules for call-by-name and call-by-value

$$
\begin{aligned}
(x[e], s) &\quad\to\quad (e(x), s) \\
((MN)[e], s) &\quad\to\quad (M[e], N[e] : s) \\
((\lambda x.M)[e], c : s) &\quad\to\quad (M[e[c/x]], s)
\end{aligned}
$$

Figure 8.9: Environment machine for call-by-name

up with their environment in the stack. Therefore the stack $s$ can be regarded as a possibly empty list of closures that we denote with $c_1 : \ldots : c_n$. The related environment machine due to Krivine, is described in figure 8.9 as a rewriting system on pairs $(M[e], s)$ of closures and stacks. The machine operates on closed terms. At the beginning of the evaluation the stack is empty, and the environment can be conventionally taken as the everywhere undefined function.

In the call-by-value strategy, we need to know if what is on the top of the stack is a function or an argument. For this reason, we insert in the stack markers $l$ for left and $r$ for right that specify if the next closure on the stack is the left or right argument of the evaluation function. Therefore a stack is defined as a possibly empty list of markers $m \in \{l, r\}$ and closures: $m_1 : c_1 : \ldots m_n : c_n$. The related environment machine is described in figure 8.10.

$$
\begin{aligned}
(x[e], s) &\quad\to\quad (e(x), s) \\
((MN)[e], s) &\quad\to\quad (M[e], r : N[e] : s) \\
(vc, r : c : s) &\quad\to\quad (c, l : vc : s) \\
(vc, l : (\lambda x.M)[e] : s) &\quad\to\quad (M[e[vc/x]], s)
\end{aligned}
$$

Figure 8.10: Environment machine for call-by-value

**Exercise 8.3.3** *Formally relate the evaluation rules for call-by-name (call-by-value) in figure 8.8 to the reduction rules for the corresponding environment machine given in figure 8.9 (8.10).*

# 8.4 A FA model for a parallel λ-calculus

We build a filter model for an untyped, call-by-value λ-calculus adapting the techniques already introduced in chapter 3. Following [Bou94] we show that this model is fully abstract when the calculus is enriched with a join operator ($\sqcup$) allowing for the *parallel* evaluation of λ-terms. Evaluation converges as soon as *one* of the terms converges. The join operator fails to be sequential in the sense described in section 2.4 and so one can show that it cannot be defined in the pure λ-calculus. In the calculus extended with the join operator, every compact element of a canonical model based on Scott continuity is definable (i.e., it is the interpretation of a closed term of the $\lambda_\sqcup$-calculus, a similar result was stated in chapter 6 for PCF enriched with a parallel or). This result entails the full abstraction of the model.

**The $\lambda_\sqcup$-calculus.** We introduce a call-by-value, untyped λ-calculus enriched with a join operator $\sqcup$ and construct a model for it as the collection of filters over a specifically tailored *eats* (cf. definition 3.3.1). The language of terms is defined as follows:

$$v \quad ::= x \mid y \mid \ldots$$
$$M \quad ::= v \mid \lambda v.M \mid MM \mid M \sqcup M \ .$$

Canonical forms are the closed terms generated by the following grammar:

$$C ::= \lambda v.M \mid C \sqcup M \mid M \sqcup C \ .$$

Finally, the *evaluation relation* is defined inductively on closed terms as shown in figure 8.11. As usual we write $M \downarrow$ if $\exists C \ (M \mapsto C)$.

**Exercise 8.4.1** *Observe that a term may reduce to more than one canonical form. Consider the reduction relation naturally associated to the evaluation relation defined in figure 8.11. Observe that this relation is not confluent, e.g., $(\lambda x.\lambda y.x)(II \sqcup II) \mapsto \lambda y.(I \sqcup I)$ and $(\lambda x.\lambda y.x)(II \sqcup II) \mapsto \lambda y.(II \sqcup I)$. This is a typical problem of weak λ-calculi (cf. section 8.3). Define a suitable calculus of closures (where environments are evaluated) and show its confluence (a solution is described in [Bou94]).*

We have already proved in section 8.2 the adequacy of a model for a call-by-value λ-calculus in which the function space is composed of the *partial* continuous functions. In the following, we build a filter model over an eats for call-by-value, which is a solution of the equation $V = V \rightharpoonup V$. More precisely, we work with total functions and build the initial solution of the corresponding equation $D = D \rightarrow (D)_\perp$ in the category of algebraic complete lattices and injection-projection pairs (this solution exists by the techniques presented in chapter 3 and generalized in chapter 7).[4]

---

[4]Following Boudol [Bou94], an equivalent presentation of the domain $D$ is as $D_\perp = E$, where $E$ is the initial solution of the equation $E = (E \rightarrow_\perp E)_\perp$ (cf. exercise 1.4.19). Boudol also studies the situation for call-by-name, in this case one works with the equation $D = (D \rightarrow D)_\perp$.

$$\frac{M \mapsto \lambda x.M' \quad N \mapsto C' \quad M'[C'/x] \mapsto C}{MN \mapsto C}$$

$$\frac{M \mapsto M_1 \sqcup M_2 \quad M_1 N \sqcup M_2 N \mapsto C}{MN \mapsto C}$$

$$\overline{C \mapsto C} \qquad \frac{M \mapsto C \quad N \mapsto C'}{M \sqcup N \mapsto C \sqcup C'}$$

$$\frac{M \mapsto C}{M \sqcup N \mapsto C \sqcup N} \qquad \frac{N \mapsto C}{M \sqcup N \mapsto M \sqcup C}$$

Figure 8.11: Evaluation relation for the $\lambda_\sqcup$-calculus

In a lattice the $\sqcup$ operator can be simply interpreted as the lub. In the definition of eats for call-by-value we have to axiomatize the strict behaviour of the $\rightharpoonup$ operator.

**Definition 8.4.2 (v-eats)** *An eats for call-by-value (v-eats) is a preorder having all finite glb's and enriched with a binary operation $\rightharpoonup$ which satisfies the following properties (as usual $\omega$ denotes a top element):*

(1) $\dfrac{\sigma' \leq \sigma \quad \tau \leq \tau'}{\sigma \rightharpoonup \tau \leq \sigma' \rightharpoonup \tau'}$   (2) $\sigma \rightharpoonup (\tau \wedge \tau') \leq (\sigma \rightharpoonup \tau) \wedge (\sigma \rightharpoonup \tau')$

(3) $\sigma \rightharpoonup \omega \leq \omega \rightharpoonup \omega$   (4) $(\sigma \wedge (\omega \rightharpoonup \omega)) \rightharpoonup \tau \leq \sigma \rightharpoonup \tau$ .

Rule (1) and inequality (2) are inherited from the eats axiomatization. Inequality (3) says that $\omega \rightharpoonup \omega$ is the largest defined element. The inequality $\sigma \leq \omega \rightharpoonup \omega$ states that $\sigma$ is defined, this is used in the $\rightharpoonup$-elimination rule in figure 8.12. Inequality (4) states that functions are strict, in other terms the behaviour on undefined elements is irrelevant, for instance we can derive $\omega \rightharpoonup \tau = (\omega \rightharpoonup \omega) \rightharpoonup \tau$. Given a v-eats $S$, consider the collection of filters $\mathcal{F}(S)$ ordered by inclusion. We write $x \downarrow$ if $\omega \rightharpoonup \omega \in x$ and $x \uparrow$ otherwise. We define a strict application operation as follows.

**Definition 8.4.3 (strict application)** *Given a v-eats $S$ and $x, y \in \mathcal{F}(S)$ define*

$$x \bullet_v y = \begin{cases} \{\tau \mid \sigma \rightharpoonup \tau \in x, \sigma \in y\} & \text{if } x \downarrow \text{ and } y \downarrow \\ \uparrow \omega & \text{otherwise} . \end{cases}$$

**Definition 8.4.4 (representable function)** *Let $S$ be a v-eats. A strict function $f$ over $\mathcal{F}(S)$ is representable if $\exists x \; \forall y \; (f(y) = x \bullet_v y)$.*

**Proposition 8.4.5** *Let S be a v-eats. Then the following properties hold:*

(1) $\mathcal{F}(S)$ *is an algebraic complete lattice.*

(2) *The strict application operation is well-defined and continuous in both arguments. In particular every representable function is strict continuous.*

PROOF HINT. (1) Follow the corresponding proof in proposition 3.3.10. (2) Perform a simple verification. □

**Proposition 8.4.6** *Let T be the smallest theory including an element ω and satisfying the conditions in definition 8.4.2 (cf. definition 3.3.4). Then every strict continuous function over $\mathcal{F}(T)$ is representable.*

PROOF HINT. First show that in the initial v-eats $\wedge_{i\in I}(\sigma_i \rightharpoonup \tau_i) \leq \sigma \rightharpoonup \tau$ implies $\wedge_{\sigma \leq \sigma_i} \tau_i \leq \tau$, where $\sigma, \sigma_i \leq \omega \rightharpoonup \omega$. Then the proof follows the schema presented in proposition 3.3.18. □

**Exercise 8.4.7** *Show that if T is defined as in proposition 8.4.6 then $\mathcal{F}(T)$ is isomorphic to the initial solution of the equation $D = D \rightharpoonup (D)_\perp$ in the category of algebraic complete lattices and embedding projection pairs.*

**Definition 8.4.8 (interpretation)** *Let S be a v-eats. We define an interpretation function $[\![\_]\!] : \lambda_\sqcup\text{ term} \rightharpoonup (Env \rightharpoonup \mathcal{F}(S))$, where Var is the set of term variables, and $Env = Var \rightarrow \mathcal{F}(S)$ with generic element $\rho$. When interpreting a closed term we omit writing the environment as it is irrelevant. As usual if $x \subseteq S$ then $\overline{x}$ denotes the least filter containing $x$.*

$$[\![x]\!]\rho = \rho(x) \qquad\qquad [\![MN]\!]\rho = ([\![M]\!]\rho)\bullet_v([\![N]\!]\rho)$$

$$[\![\lambda x.M]\!]\rho = \overline{\{\sigma \rightharpoonup \tau \mid \tau \in [\![M]\!]\rho[(\uparrow \sigma)/x]\}} \quad [\![M \sqcup N]\!]\rho = \overline{[\![M]\!]\rho \cup [\![N]\!]\rho} \ .$$

Next we define a typing system that allows us to compute the interpretation, in the sense that the interpretation of a term is the collection of types that we can assign to it. Types $\sigma, \tau, \ldots$ are elements of a v-eats. Contexts $\Gamma$ are defined as usual. The typing system is displayed in figure 8.12. Note that to type the join of two terms we take the glb of the respective types.

An environment $\rho$ is *compatible* with a context $\Gamma$ if $x : \sigma \in \Gamma$ implies $\sigma \in \rho(x)$. In this case we write $\Gamma \uparrow \rho$.

**Proposition 8.4.9** *For any term of the $\lambda_\sqcup$-calculus the following holds:*

$$[\![M]\!]\rho = \{\sigma \mid \Gamma \vdash M : \sigma, \Gamma \uparrow \rho\} \ .$$

PROOF. ($\supseteq$) By induction on the length of the derivation we prove that:

$$\forall \rho \ \forall \Gamma \uparrow \rho \ (\Gamma \vdash M : \sigma \ \Rightarrow \ \sigma \in [\![M]\!]\rho) \ .$$

($\subseteq$) First we observe a weakening property of the typing system (cf. lemma 3.5.6):

$$\text{if } \Gamma, x : \sigma \vdash M : \tau \text{ then } \Gamma, x : \sigma \wedge \sigma' \vdash M : \tau \ . \tag{8.5}$$

$$\frac{x : \sigma \in \Gamma}{\Gamma \vdash x : \sigma} \qquad\qquad \Gamma \vdash M : \omega$$

$$\frac{\Gamma, x : \sigma \vdash M : \tau}{\Gamma \vdash \lambda x.M : \sigma \to \tau} \qquad\qquad \frac{\Gamma \vdash M : \sigma \to \tau \quad \Gamma \vdash N : \sigma \quad \sigma \le \omega \to \omega}{\Gamma \vdash MN : \tau}$$

$$\frac{\Gamma \vdash M : \sigma \quad \Gamma \vdash N : \tau}{\Gamma \vdash M \sqcup N : \sigma \wedge \tau}$$

$$\frac{\Gamma \vdash M : \sigma \quad \Gamma \vdash M : \tau}{\Gamma \vdash M : \sigma \wedge \tau} \qquad\qquad \frac{\Gamma \vdash M : \sigma \quad \sigma \le \tau}{\Gamma \vdash M : \tau}$$

Figure 8.12: Typing rules for the $\lambda_\sqcup$-calculus

We prove this by induction on the length of the proof. For instance, suppose we derive $\Gamma, x : \sigma \vdash M_1 \sqcup M_2 : \tau_1 \wedge \tau_2$, from $\Gamma, x : \sigma \vdash M_1 : \tau_1$ and $\Gamma, x : \sigma \vdash M_2 : \tau_2$. Then by induction hypothesis, $\Gamma, x : \sigma \wedge \sigma' \vdash M_1 : \tau_1$ and $\Gamma, x : \sigma \wedge \sigma' \vdash M_2 : \tau_2$, and we conclude $\Gamma, x : \sigma \wedge \sigma' \vdash M_1 \sqcup M_2 : \tau_1 \wedge \tau_2$ by the rule for $\sqcup$-introduction.

Second, we note that for any environment $\rho$, the following set is a filter:

$$\{\sigma \mid \exists \Gamma \ (\Gamma \uparrow \rho \text{ and } \Gamma \vdash M : \sigma)\} . \tag{8.6}$$

By induction on the structure of $M$ we show that for all $\rho$, $n \ge 0$:

$$\tau \in [\![M]\!]\rho[(\uparrow \sigma_1)/x_1, \ldots, (\uparrow \sigma_n)/x_n] \Rightarrow$$
$$\exists \Gamma \ (\Gamma \uparrow \rho \text{ and } \Gamma, x_1 : \sigma_1, \ldots, x_n : \sigma_n \vdash M : \tau) .$$

Let us consider the case $\lambda x.M$. Fix an environment $\rho$. By 8.6 it is enough to show that $\tau \in [\![M]\!]\rho[(\uparrow \sigma_1)/x_1, \ldots, (\uparrow \sigma_n)/x_n, (\uparrow \sigma)/x]$ implies $\Gamma, x_1 : \sigma_1, \ldots, x_n : \sigma_n \vdash \lambda x.M : \sigma \to \tau$, for some $\Gamma$. By induction hypothesis, $\Gamma, x_1 : \sigma_1, \ldots, x_n : \sigma_n, x : \sigma \vdash M : \tau$, and we conclude by $\to$-introduction. $\qquad\qquad\qquad \square$

**Full abstraction.** We outline the proofs of adequacy and full abstraction of the $\lambda_\sqcup$-calculus with respect to the filter model built on the initial v-eats. The adequacy proof follows the technique of adequacy relations (cf. sections 6.4 and 8.2). We start by specifying when a closed term *realizes* a type.

**Definition 8.4.10** *We define a family of predicates* $\mathcal{R}^\sigma$ *over closed terms as follows:*

$$\begin{aligned}
\mathcal{R}^\omega &= \Lambda_\sqcup^o \ \textit{(all closed terms)} \\
\mathcal{R}^{\sigma \wedge \tau} &= \mathcal{R}^\sigma \cap \mathcal{R}^\tau \\
\mathcal{R}^{\sigma \to \tau} &= \{M \mid M \downarrow \ \textit{and} \ \forall N \in \mathcal{R}^\sigma \ (N \downarrow \ \Rightarrow \ MN \in \mathcal{R}^\tau)\} .
\end{aligned}$$

$$
\begin{array}{llll}
M_\omega & = & \Omega & \\
M_{\sigma \wedge \tau} & = & M_\sigma \sqcup M_\tau & \\
M_{\sigma \to \tau} & = & \lambda x.(T_\sigma x) M_\tau & (\sigma \leq \omega \to \omega)
\end{array}
\qquad
\begin{array}{lll}
T_{\omega \to \omega} & = & \lambda f.I \\
T_{\sigma \wedge \tau} & = & \lambda f.(T_\sigma f)(T_\tau f) \quad (\sigma, \tau \leq \omega \to \omega) \\
T_{\sigma \to \tau} & = & \lambda f.T_\tau(f M_\sigma) \quad (\tau \leq \omega \to \omega)
\end{array}
$$

Figure 8.13: Defining compact elements

---

We write $\models M : \sigma$ if $M \in \mathcal{R}^\sigma$ and $x_1 : \sigma_1, \ldots, x_n : \sigma_n \models M : \sigma$ if for all $N_i$ such that $N_i \downarrow$ and $\models N_i : \sigma_i$ $(i = 1, \ldots, n)$ we have $\models M[N_1/x_1, \ldots, N_n/x_n] : \sigma$.

**Exercise 8.4.11** *Verify that $\sigma \leq \tau$ implies $\mathcal{R}^\sigma \subseteq \mathcal{R}^\tau$.*

**Proposition 8.4.12** *If $\Gamma \vdash M : \sigma$ then $\Gamma \models M : \sigma$.*

PROOF HINT. We prove the following properties by induction on $\sigma$:

(1) $(\lambda x.M)N\vec{Q} \in \mathcal{R}^\sigma$ iff $M[N/x]\vec{Q} \in \mathcal{R}^\sigma$ whenever $N, \vec{Q} \downarrow$.

(2) $(M \sqcup N)\vec{P} \in \mathcal{R}^\sigma$ iff $(M\vec{P} \sqcup N\vec{P}) \in \mathcal{R}^\sigma$.

We prove the statement by induction on the length of the typing proof, and relying on exercise 8.4.11. □

**Corollary 8.4.13** *For any closed $\lambda_\sqcup$-term $M$ the following properties are equivalent: (1) $M \downarrow$, (2) $[\![M]\!] \downarrow$, and (3) $\vdash M : \omega \to \omega$.*

PROOF. (1) $\Rightarrow$ (2) We prove that $M \mapsto C$ implies $[\![M]\!] = [\![C]\!]$ by induction on the length of the proof of the evaluation judgment.

(2) $\Rightarrow$ (3) If $(\omega \to \omega) \in [\![M]\!]$ then $\vdash M : \omega \to \omega$, by proposition 8.4.9.

(3) $\Rightarrow$ (1) We observe that for any canonical form $C$, $\vdash C : \omega \to \omega$, and that $\mathcal{R}^{\omega \to \omega}$ is the collection of convergent (closed) terms. □

This concludes the kernel of the adequacy proof. The full abstraction proof relies on the definability of the compact elements of the model (cf. proposition 6.4.6). To this end, we inductively define closed terms $M_\sigma$ of type $\sigma$, and auxiliary terms $T_\tau$, for $\tau \leq \omega \to \omega$, in figure 8.13.

**Exercise 8.4.14** *The definitions in figure 8.13 are modulo equality, where $\sigma = \tau$ if $\sigma \leq \tau$ and $\tau \leq \sigma$. Check that we associate a term to every type, and that equal types are mapped to the same term.*

**Theorem 8.4.15** *For all types $\sigma, \tau$ such that $\tau \leq \omega \to \omega$ the following holds:*

$$
[\![M_\sigma]\!] = \uparrow \sigma \qquad [\![T_\tau]\!] \bullet_v x = \begin{cases} [\![I]\!] & \text{if } \tau \in x \\ \uparrow \omega & \text{otherwise .} \end{cases}
$$

PROOF HINT. By induction on $\sigma$. We just consider two cases.

Case $M_{\sigma \to \tau}$. Then we have:

$$\begin{aligned}
[\![M_{\sigma \to \tau}]\!] &= \overline{\{\sigma' \to \tau' \mid \tau' \in [\![(T_\sigma x)M_\tau]\!][(\uparrow \sigma')/x]\}} \\
&= \overline{\{\sigma' \to \tau' \mid \tau' \in ([\![T_\sigma]\!]\bullet_v(\uparrow \sigma'))\bullet_v(\uparrow \tau)\}} \ .
\end{aligned}$$

If $\sigma' \not\leq \sigma$ then $([\![T_\sigma]\!]\bullet_v(\uparrow \sigma'))\bullet_v(\uparrow \tau) = \uparrow \omega$ and $\sigma \to \tau \leq \sigma' \to \omega$. If $\sigma' \leq \sigma$ then supposing $\tau' \in ([\![T_\sigma]\!]\bullet_v(\uparrow \sigma'))\bullet_v(\uparrow \tau) = \uparrow \tau$ we have $\sigma \to \tau \leq \sigma' \to \tau'$. We conclude that $[\![M_{\sigma \to \tau}]\!]\rho = \uparrow (\sigma \to \tau)$.

Case $M_{\sigma \wedge \tau}$. We use $\overline{\uparrow \sigma \cup \uparrow \tau} = \uparrow (\sigma \wedge \tau)$. $\qquad\square$

We have derived the adequacy of the interpretation from the soundness of the typing system with respect to the realizability interpretation (proposition 8.4.12). Symmetrically, the full abstraction result will be obtained from a completeness property of the typing system (which follows from the definability theorem 8.4.15).

**Definition 8.4.16** *Let $M, N$ be closed terms. A* logical preorder $M \leq_L N$ *is defined as:* $\forall \sigma \ (\models M : \sigma \ \Rightarrow \ \models N : \sigma)$.

**Corollary 8.4.17** *Let $M, N$ be closed terms. If $M \leq_L N$ then $[\![M]\!] \leq [\![N]\!]$.*

PROOF. It is enough to show by induction on $\sigma'$ that for all $M$, $\models M : \sigma'$ implies $\vdash M : \sigma'$. Let us consider the case for $\sigma' = \sigma \to \tau$. From $\vdash M_\sigma : \sigma$ we derive $\models M_\sigma : \sigma$, by proposition 8.4.12. We assume $\sigma \leq \omega \to \omega$, i.e., $\sigma$ is defined. Therefore $M_\sigma \downarrow$. It follows $\models M M_\sigma : \tau$. By induction hypothesis $\vdash M M_\sigma : \tau$. We conclude by the following chain of implications:

$$\begin{aligned}
\vdash M M_\sigma : \tau \ &\Rightarrow \ \tau \in [\![M]\!]\bullet_v(\uparrow \sigma) \qquad \Rightarrow \ \sigma' \to \tau \in [\![M]\!], \ \sigma \leq \sigma' \\
&\Rightarrow \ \vdash M : \sigma' \to \tau, \ \sigma \leq \sigma' \ \Rightarrow \ \vdash M : \sigma \to \tau \ .
\end{aligned}$$
$\qquad\square$

This result virtually concludes the full abstraction proof. It just remains to formally define an operational preorder and to verify that it coincides with the preorder induced by the model.

**Definition 8.4.18** *An* applicative simulation $S$ *is a binary relation on closed terms such that the following properties hold whenever $M S N$:*

(1) $M \downarrow$ *implies* $N \downarrow$,

(2) *for all $P$, $P \downarrow$ implies $(M P) S (N P)$.*

*Let $\leq_{sim}$ be the largest applicative simulation.*

**Proposition 8.4.19** *Let $M, N$ be closed terms. If $[\![M]\!] \leq [\![N]\!]$ then $M \leq_{sim} N$.*

PROOF. It follows from the observation that $\{(M, N) \mid [\![M]\!] \leq [\![N]\!]\}$ is a simulation. $\qquad\square$

**Proposition 8.4.20** *If $M \leq_{sim} N$ then $M \leq_L N$.*

PROOF. We suppose $M \leq_{sim} N$. We prove by induction on $\sigma$ that $\models M : \sigma$ implies $\models N : \sigma$. □

**Corollary 8.4.21** *Let $M, N$ be closed terms. Then $[\![M]\!] \leq [\![N]\!]$ iff $M \leq_{sim} N$ iff $M \leq_L N$.*

PROOF. By corollary 8.4.17 and propositions 8.4.19, 8.4.20. □

**Exercise 8.4.22** *(1) Let $M, N$ be closed $\lambda_\sqcup$-terms. Define:*

$$M \leq_{appl} N \quad \text{iff} \quad \forall n \in \omega \ \forall P_1, \ldots, P_n \ (MP_1 \ldots P_n \downarrow \ \Rightarrow \ NP_1 \ldots P_n \downarrow) \ .$$

*Show that $M \leq_{appl} N$ iff $M \leq_{sim} N$. (2) Let $M, N$ be arbitrary terms. Define:*

$$M \leq_{op} N \quad \text{iff} \quad \forall C \ \text{such that} \ C[M], C[N] \ \text{are closed} \ (C[M] \downarrow \ \Rightarrow \ C[N] \downarrow) \ .$$

*Show that for $M, N$ closed, $M \leq_{op} N$ iff $M \leq_{appl} N$ (this is a context lemma, cf. exercise 6.4.4).*

# 8.5 Control operators and CPS translation

Most programming languages whose kernel is based on typed $\lambda$-calculus, also include *control* operators such as *exceptions* or *call-with-current-continuation* (see for instance Scheme or ML). In the following we show how to type certain control operators and how to give them an adequate functional interpretation (another study of control operators in functional programming will be carried out in section 14.4). As already hinted in example 8.1.1, the monad of continuations is a useful technical device to approach these problems.

**A $\lambda$-calculus with control operators.** As in section 8.2, we consider a simply typed call-by-value $\lambda$-calculus. This language is enriched with a basic type *num*, numerals $0, 1, \ldots$ with generic element $n$, and two unary combinators: $\mathcal{C}$ for *control* and $\mathcal{A}$ for *abort*. Formally we have:

$$
\begin{array}{lll}
\text{Types} & \sigma & ::= \text{num} \mid (\sigma \rightharpoonup \sigma) \\
\text{Terms} & v & ::= x \mid y \mid \ldots \\
& M & ::= n \mid x \mid \lambda v : \sigma.M \mid MM \mid \mathcal{C}M \mid \mathcal{A}M \\
\text{Values} & V & ::= n \mid \lambda v : \sigma.M \ .
\end{array}
$$

We briefly refer to the related calculus as the $\lambda_{\mathcal{C}}$-calculus. We also use a subscript $\mathcal{C}$, e.g., $\vdash_{\mathcal{C}}$, $\rightarrow_{\mathcal{C}}$, to indicate that we refer to this calculus. In order to formalize the behaviour of the control operators $\mathcal{C}$ and $\mathcal{A}$ it is useful to introduce the notion of (call-by-value) *evaluation context* $E$ (cf. [FFKD87]):

$$E ::= [\,] \mid EM \mid (\lambda x : \sigma.M)E \ .$$

Note that an evaluation context is a context with exactly one hole which is not in the scope of a lambda abstraction. If we forget about type labels the *one step* reduction relation on terms is defined as follows:

$$
\begin{array}{lll}
(\beta_v) & E[(\lambda x.M)V] & \rightarrow \ E[M[V/x]] \\
(\mathcal{C}) & E[\mathcal{C}M] & \rightarrow \ M(\lambda x.\mathcal{A}E[x]) \quad x \notin FV(E) \\
(\mathcal{A}) & E[\mathcal{A}M] & \rightarrow \ M \ .
\end{array}
$$

We can now provide a syntactic intuition for what a continuation for a given term is, and for what is special about a control operator. A redex $\Delta$ is defined as follows:

$$\Delta ::= (\lambda v.M)V \mid CM \mid \mathcal{A}M .$$

Given a term $M \equiv E[\Delta]$, the *current continuation* is the abstraction of the evaluation context, that is $\lambda x.E[x]$. We will see later that there is at most one decomposition of a term into an evaluation context $E$ and a redex $\Delta$. A control operator is a combinator which can manipulate directly the current continuation. In particular the operator $\mathcal{A}$ disregards the current continuation and starts the execution of its argument, while the operator $C$ applies the argument to $\lambda x.\mathcal{A}E[x]$, when $\lambda x.E[x]$ is the current continuation.

We illustrate by an example the role of control operators in functional programming. We want to write a function $F : Tree(num) \rightharpoonup num$ where $Tree(num)$ is a given type of binary trees whose nodes are labelled by natural numbers. The function $F$ has to return the product of the labels of the tree nodes, but if it finds that a node has label 0, in this case it has to return zero in a constant number of steps of reduction. Intuitively the termination time has to be independent from the size of the current stack of recursive calls. There is a simple realization of this specification that just relies on the abort operator $\mathcal{A}$ (more involved examples can be found in exercise 16.2.4 and in [HF87]):

> let $\quad F(t) = F'(\lambda x.\mathcal{A}x)t$
> where $\quad F' = \lambda k.Y(\lambda f.\lambda t'. \quad$ if $empty(t')$ then 0
> $\qquad\qquad\qquad\qquad\qquad$ else if $val(t') = 0$ then $k0$
> $\qquad\qquad\qquad\qquad\qquad$ else $val(t') * f(left(t')) * f(right(t')))$

(*left*, *right*, and *empty* are the functions associated with the data type *Tree(num)*). At the beginning of the computation we have $F(t) \rightarrow F'[\lambda x.\mathcal{A}x/k]$. If at some point the exceptional branch 'if $val(t') = 0 \dots$' is selected, then the following computation is derived, in some evaluation context $E$:

$$E[(\lambda x.\mathcal{A}x)0] \rightarrow E[\mathcal{A}0] \rightarrow 0 .$$

By applying a CPS translation (to be defined next) it is possible to obtain a purely functional program with a similar behaviour. This is an interesting result which finds applications in compilers' design [App92]. On the other hand, one should not conclude that we can forget about control operators. CPS translations tend to be unreadable, and programming directly in CPS is a tricky business. In practice, control operators are directly available as primitives in functional languages such as ML and Scheme. We refer to [FFKD87] for a syntactic analysis of a $\lambda$-calculus with control operators.

**Typing control operators.** It is possible to type the operators $C$ and $\mathcal{A}$ coherently with the reduction rules as shown in figure 8.14 (this typing naturally arises in proving subject reduction, cf. proposition 8.5.2). A *program* is a closed term of type *num*. The reduction rules $(\beta_v)$, $(C)$, $(\mathcal{A})$ define a deterministic procedure to reduce programs.

$$(\mathcal{C}) \ \frac{\Gamma \vdash M : \neg\neg\sigma}{\Gamma \vdash \mathcal{C}M : \sigma} \qquad (\mathcal{A}) \ \frac{\Gamma \vdash M : num}{\Gamma \vdash \mathcal{A}M : num} \quad \text{where } \neg\sigma \equiv \sigma \rightharpoonup num .$$

$$
\begin{array}{lll}
(\beta_v) & E[(\lambda x : \sigma.M)V] & \rightarrow \quad E[M[V/x]] \\
(\mathcal{C}) & E[\mathcal{C}M] & \rightarrow \quad M(\lambda x : \sigma.\mathcal{A}E[x]) \quad \text{where } \mathcal{C}M : \sigma \\
(\mathcal{A}) & E[\mathcal{A}M] & \rightarrow \quad M
\end{array}
$$

Figure 8.14: Typing control operators and reduction rules

---

**Proposition 8.5.1 (unique decomposition)** *Suppose $\vdash_{\mathcal{C}} M : \sigma$ . Then either $M$ is a value or there is a unique evaluation context $E$ and redex $\Delta$ such that $M \equiv E[\Delta]$.*

PROOF. By induction on the structure of $M$. The only interesting case is when $M \equiv M'M''$. Then $M$ is not a value, $\vdash_{\mathcal{C}} M' : \tau \rightharpoonup \sigma$, and $\vdash_{\mathcal{C}} M'' : \tau$, for some $\tau$ (note that we cannot type $\mathcal{A}$, and $\mathcal{C}$ alone). There are two cases:

- $M'$ is a value. Then $M' \equiv \lambda x : \sigma.M_1$. If $M''$ is a value take $E \equiv [\ ]$ and $\Delta \equiv (\lambda x : \sigma.M_1)M''$. Otherwise, if $M''$ is not a value then, by inductive hypothesis, there are $E_1, \Delta_1$ such that $M'' \equiv E_1[\Delta_1]$. Then take $E \equiv M'E_1$ and $\Delta \equiv \Delta_1$.

- $M'$ is not a value. Then, by inductive hypothesis, there are $E_1, \Delta_1$ such that $M' \equiv E_1[\Delta_1]$. Note that if $M'$ is closed then $\Delta_1$ is closed. We take $E \equiv E_1M''$ and $\Delta \equiv \Delta_1$. □

**Proposition 8.5.2 (subject reduction)** *If $\vdash_{\mathcal{C}} M : num$ and $M \rightarrow_{\mathcal{C}} N$ then $\vdash_{\mathcal{C}} N : num$.*

PROOF. Suppose there are $E, \Delta$ such that $M \equiv E[\Delta]$. There are three cases to consider according to the shape of the redex.

- $\Delta \equiv (\lambda x : \sigma.M')V$. This requires a simple form of the substitution lemma. We observe that $x : \sigma \vdash_{\mathcal{C}} M' : \tau$ and $\vdash_{\mathcal{C}} V : \sigma$ implies $\vdash_{\mathcal{C}} M'[V/x] : \tau$.

- $\Delta \equiv \mathcal{C}M'$. Suppose $\vdash_{\mathcal{C}} \mathcal{C}M' : \sigma$. Then $\vdash_{\mathcal{C}} M' : \neg\neg\sigma$ and $x : \sigma \vdash_{\mathcal{C}} E[x] : num$. Hence $x : \sigma \vdash_{\mathcal{C}} \mathcal{A}E[x] : num$, which implies $\vdash_{\mathcal{C}} \lambda x : \sigma.\mathcal{A}E[x] : \neg\sigma$, and finally $\vdash_{\mathcal{C}} M'(\lambda x : \sigma.\mathcal{A}E[x]) : num$.

- $\Delta \equiv \mathcal{A}M'$. $\vdash_{\mathcal{C}} \mathcal{A}M : num$ forces $\vdash_{\mathcal{C}} M : num$. □

The previous propositions show that the rules $(\beta_V)$, $(\mathcal{C})$, $(\mathcal{A})$ when applied to a program define a deterministic evaluation strategy which preserves the well-typing.

**Remark 8.5.3** *One may consider other control operators. A popular one is the call-with-current-continuation operator (callcc). The typing and reduction rule for*

$$\underline{x} \;\; = \;\; \lambda k.kx \qquad \underline{MN} \;\; = \;\; \lambda k.\underline{M}(\lambda m.\underline{N}(\lambda n.mnk))$$
$$\underline{n} \;\; = \;\; \lambda k.kn \qquad \underline{CM} \;\; = \;\; \lambda k.\underline{M}(\lambda m.m(\lambda z.\lambda d.kz)(\lambda x.x))$$
$$\underline{\lambda x.M} \;\; = \;\; \lambda k.k(\lambda x.\underline{M}) \qquad \underline{AM} \;\; = \;\; \lambda k.\underline{M}(\lambda x.x)$$

Figure 8.15: CPS translation

*the callcc operators can be formalized as follows:*

$$\frac{\Gamma, k : \neg\sigma \vdash M : \sigma}{\Gamma \vdash callcc(\lambda k.M) : \sigma} \qquad E[callcc(\lambda k.M)] \to (\lambda k.kM)(\lambda x.\mathcal{A}E[x]) \; .$$

**Exercise 8.5.4** *(1) Find a simulation of the callcc operator using the $\mathcal{C}$ operator. (2) Show that call-by-name and call-by-value evaluations of the expression $\mathcal{C}(\lambda k.(\lambda x.n)(k\,m))$ give different results (this fact corresponds to the non-confluence of cut-elimination in classical logic).*

**CPS translation.** Next we describe an interpretation of the $\lambda_C$-calculus into the $\lambda$-calculus. We begin with a translation of types.

$$\underline{num} = num \qquad \underline{\sigma \to \tau} = \underline{\sigma} \to \neg\neg\underline{\tau} \; .$$

The interpretation of the arrow follows the monadic view where we take *num* as the *type of results*. From another point of view observe that replacing *num* with $\perp$ one obtains a fragment of the double-negation translation from classical logic to intuitionistic logic. The rule for typing the $\mathcal{C}$ operator can then be seen as stating the involutive behaviour of classical negation.

Note that the translation involves both types/formulas and terms/proofs. Indeed a variant of the translation considered here was used by Friedman to extract algorithmic content from a certain class of proofs in (classical) Peano arithmetic (see [Fri78, Gri90, Mur91] for elaborations over this point). We associate with a term $M$ a term $\underline{M}$ without control operators so that:

$$x_1 : \sigma_1, \ldots, x_n : \sigma_n \vdash_C M : \sigma \Rightarrow x_1 : \underline{\sigma_1}, \ldots, x_n : \underline{\sigma_n} \vdash \underline{M} : \neg\neg\underline{\sigma} \; .$$

The definition is presented in figure 8.15 (we omit types). This is known as the *Continuation Passing Style* translation.

Before giving the explicit typing of the translation we recall three basic combinators of the continuation monad.

$$M : \sigma \qquad \eta(M) = \lambda k : \neg\sigma .kM : \neg\neg\sigma$$
$$M : \sigma \to \tau \qquad \neg\neg M = \lambda k : \neg\neg\sigma .\lambda h : \neg\tau .k(\lambda x : num .h(Mx))$$
$$M : \neg\neg\neg\neg\sigma \qquad \mu(M) = \lambda k : \neg\sigma .M(\lambda h : \neg\neg\sigma .hk) : \neg\neg\sigma \; .$$

The explicitly typed CPS translation is given in figure 8.16.

It is now a matter of verification to prove the following, where conventionally $\underline{\Gamma, x : \sigma} \equiv \underline{\Gamma}, x : \underline{\sigma} \; .$

$$
\begin{array}{lll}
\underline{x} & = & \lambda k : \neg\sigma \ .kx : \neg\neg\underline{\sigma} \ \ \text{if } x : \sigma \\
\underline{n} & = & \lambda k : \neg num \ .kn : \neg\neg num \\
\underline{\lambda x : \sigma.M} & = & \lambda k : \neg\underline{\sigma \rightharpoonup \tau} \ .k(\lambda x : \underline{\sigma} \ .\underline{M}) : \neg\neg\underline{\sigma \rightharpoonup \tau} \\
\underline{MN} & = & \lambda k : \neg\underline{\tau} \ .\underline{M}(\lambda m : \underline{\sigma \rightharpoonup \tau} \ .\underline{N}(\lambda n : \underline{\sigma} \ .mnk)) : \neg\neg\underline{\tau} \\
\underline{CM} & = & \lambda k : \neg\underline{\sigma} \ .\underline{M}(\lambda m : \underline{\neg\neg\sigma} \ .m(\lambda z : \underline{\sigma} \ .\lambda d : \neg num \ .kz)(\lambda x : num \ .x)) : \neg\neg\underline{\sigma} \\
\underline{AM} & = & \lambda k : \neg num \ .\underline{M}(\lambda x : num \ .x) : \neg\neg num
\end{array}
$$

Figure 8.16: Typing the CPS translation

**Proposition 8.5.5 (typing CPS translation)** *With reference to the transla- tion in figure 8.15, if* $\Gamma \vdash_C M : \sigma$ *then* $\underline{\Gamma} \vdash_C \underline{M} : \neg\neg\underline{\sigma}$ .

**Exercise 8.5.6** *There are many possible CPS translations which from a logical view point correspond to different ways to map a proof in classical logic into a proof in constructive logic. In particular verify that, consistently with the proposed typing, one can give the following translation of application:*

$$
\underline{MN} = \lambda k : \neg\underline{\tau}.\underline{N}(\lambda n : \underline{\sigma}.\underline{M}(\lambda m : \underline{\sigma \rightharpoonup \tau}.mnk)) \ .
$$

The main problem is to show that the CPS translation adequately represents the intended behavior of the control operators. Suppose $\vdash_C M : num$, the desired result reads as follows:

$$
M \rightarrow^*_C n \ \text{iff} \ \underline{M}id \rightarrow^* n.
$$

The difficulty in proving this result consists in relating reductions of $M$ and $M\,id$.

**Example 8.5.7** *It is not the case that for a provable judgment* $\vdash M : num$, $M \rightarrow_C N$ *implies* $\underline{M}id \rightarrow^* \underline{N}id$. *Consider for instance* $M = (\lambda x.x)(An) \rightarrow_C n$. *Then* $\underline{M}id \rightarrow^* n$ *as* $\underline{(\lambda x.x)(An)} \rightarrow^* \lambda k.n$, *and* $\underline{n}id \rightarrow^* n$ *as* $\underline{n} = \lambda k.kn$. *However* $(\lambda k.n)id$ *does not reduce to* $\underline{n}id = (\lambda k.kn)id$.

**An optimized translation.** Given a term $M$, a new translation $\langle M \rangle \equiv \lambda k.M{:}k$ is defined with the following relevant properties:

(1) $\underline{M} \rightarrow^* \langle M \rangle$

(2) if $M : num$ and $M \rightarrow N$ then $M{:}id \rightarrow^* N{:}id$.

This optimized translation is instrumental to the proof of the adequacy of the CPS translation (cf. following theorem 8.5.14). We limit our attention to the fragment of the calculus without control operators (this is already enough to simulate call- by-value in call-by-name, cf. exercise 8.5.15). An extension of the results to the full calculus is possible but it would require a rather long detour (see [DF92]). The translation considered here, also known as colon translation (cf. [Plo75]) performs a more careful analysis of the term, the result is that a certain number of redexes can be statically reduced. By this, we can keep term and CPS translation in lockstep, hence avoiding the problem presented in example 8.5.7.

**Definition 8.5.8** *We define a translation $\psi$ from values to values, so that $\vdash \psi(V) : \underline{\sigma}$, if $\vdash V : \sigma$:*

$$\psi(n) = n \quad \psi(\lambda x : \sigma.M) = \lambda x : \underline{\sigma}.\underline{M} \ .$$

**Lemma 8.5.9** *For any $V$, $\underline{M}[\psi(V)/x] \equiv \underline{M[V/x]}$.*

PROOF. We just consider the representative case $M = x$, $V = \lambda y.N$. Then $\underline{M} = \lambda k.kx$, hence:

$$\underline{M}[\psi(V)/x] = \lambda k.k(\lambda y.\underline{N}) = \underline{V} = \underline{x[V/x]} \ .$$

$\square$

We note that every evaluation context $E$ can be written as either $[\,]$, or $E'[[\,]N]$, or $E'[V[\,]]$. Then, we associate to every evaluation context $E$ a well-typed closed term $\kappa(E)$ as follows:

$$\begin{aligned}
\kappa([\,]) &= \lambda x.x \\
\kappa(E[[\,]N]) &= \lambda m.\underline{N}(\lambda n.mn\kappa(E)) \\
\kappa(E[V[\,]]) &= \lambda n.\psi(V)n\kappa(E) \ .
\end{aligned}$$

Let $\mathcal{K}$ be the image of the function $\kappa$, with generic element $K$.

**Definition 8.5.10** *We define the* semi-colon *translation $M{:}K$, where $M$ is closed and $K \in \mathcal{K}$ as follows:*

$$\begin{aligned}
V{:}K &= K\psi(V) \\
V_1V_2{:}K &= \psi(V_1)\psi(V_2)K \\
V_1N{:}K &= N{:}\lambda n.\psi(V_1)nK \\
MN{:}K &= M{:}\lambda m.\underline{N}(\lambda n.mnK) \ .
\end{aligned}$$

*If $\vdash M : \sigma$ and $\vdash K : \neg\underline{\sigma}$ then $M{:}K : num$ (note the double use of ':').*

We observe that if $\Gamma \vdash M : \sigma$ then $\underline{\Gamma} \vdash \langle M \rangle : \neg\neg\underline{\sigma}$. Next we prove three technical lemmas that relate the standard and optimized CPS translations.

**Lemma 8.5.11** *If $\vdash M : \sigma$, $K \in \mathcal{K}$, and $\vdash K : \neg\underline{\sigma}$ then $\underline{M}K \rightarrow^+ M{:}K$.*

PROOF. By induction on $M$ and case analysis of the semi-colon translation. For instance let us consider:

$$\underline{MN}K = (\lambda k.\underline{M}(\lambda m.\underline{N}(\lambda n.mnk)))K \ .$$

By induction hypothesis on $M$, $\underline{MN}K \rightarrow^+ M{:}\lambda m.\underline{N}(\lambda n.mnK) = MN{:}K$. $\square$

**Lemma 8.5.12** *If $\vdash M : \sigma$ and $M$ is not a value, then:*

$$E[M]{:}\kappa(E') \equiv M{:}\kappa(E'[E]) \ .$$

*In particular, $E[M] : id \equiv M : \kappa E$.*

PROOF. By induction on $E$. For instance let us consider $E \equiv E_1[[\ ]N]$. By induction hypothesis on $E_1$:

$$
\begin{aligned}
E_1[MN]{:}\kappa(E') &\equiv MN{:}\kappa(E'[E_1]) \\
&\equiv M{:}\lambda m.\underline{N}(\lambda n.mn\kappa(E'[E_1])) \\
&\equiv M{:}\kappa(E'[E_1[[\ ]N]]) \, . \qquad \square
\end{aligned}
$$

**Lemma 8.5.13** *If* $\vdash V : \sigma$ *and* $\vdash \kappa(E) : \neg\underline{\sigma}$ *then* $V{:}\kappa(E) \to^* E[V]{:}id$.

PROOF. By induction on the structure of $E$.

- If $E[V]$ is a value then $E \equiv [\ ]$, and the statement holds since $\kappa([\ ]) = id$.

- Otherwise we distinguish three cases: (1) $E \equiv E_1[[\ ]N]$, $N$ not a value, (2) $E \equiv E_1[[\ ]V_1]$, and (3) $E \equiv E_1[V_1[\ ]]$. For instance let us consider case (1):

$$
\begin{aligned}
V{:}\kappa(E_1[[\ ]N]) &\equiv V{:}\lambda m.\underline{N}(\lambda n.mn\kappa(E_1[\ ])) \\
&\equiv (\lambda m.\underline{N}(\lambda n.mn\kappa(E_1[\ ])))\psi(V) \\
&\to \underline{N}(\lambda n.\psi(V)n\kappa(E_1[\ ])) \\
&\to^+ N{:}\lambda n.\psi(V)n\kappa(E_1[\ ])) &\text{(by lemma 8.5.11)} \\
&\equiv VN{:}\kappa(E_1[\ ]) \\
&\equiv E_1[VN]{:}id &\text{(by lemma 8.5.12)} \\
&= E[V]{:}id \, . &\square
\end{aligned}
$$

**Theorem 8.5.14 (adequacy of CPS translation)** *Suppose* $\vdash_C M : num$, *where $M$ does not contain control operators. Then* $M \to^* n$ *iff* $\underline{M}id \to^* n$ .

PROOF. ($\Rightarrow$) Suppose $M \to^* n$. By lemma 8.5.11: $\underline{M}id \to^* M{:}id$. We show $M \to M'$ implies $M{:}id \to^+ M'{:}id$.

$$
\begin{aligned}
E[(\lambda x.M)V]{:}id &\equiv (\lambda x.M)V{:}\kappa(E) &\text{(by lemma 8.5.12)} \\
&\equiv (\lambda x.\underline{M})\psi(V)\kappa(E) \\
&\to \underline{M[V/x]}\kappa(E) &\text{(by lemma 8.5.9)} \\
&\to^+ M[V/x]{:}\kappa(E) &\text{(by lemma 8.5.11)} \\
&\begin{cases} \to^* E[M[V/x]]{:}id &\text{if } M[V/x] \text{ is a value (by lemma 8.5.13)} \\ \equiv E[M[V/x]]{:}id &\text{otherwise (by lemma 8.5.12) .} \end{cases}
\end{aligned}
$$

($\Leftarrow$) By strong normalization of $\beta$-reduction, $M \to^* m$ for some numeral $m$, hence by ($\Rightarrow$) $\underline{M}id \to^* m$. On the other hand, by hypothesis $\underline{M}id \to^* n$, and by confluence $n = m$. $\qquad \square$

**Exercise 8.5.15** *Given a program $M$ show that when following a call-by-name evaluation of $M{:}id$ all redexes are actually call-by-value redexes, that is, the right hand side of the redex is always a value. This fact is used in [Plo75] to simulate call-by-value reduction in a call-by-name $\lambda$-calculus.*

$$
\begin{array}{lcl}
(x[e], s) & \rightarrow & (e(x), s) \\
((MN)[e], s) & \rightarrow & (M[e], N[e] : s) \\
(\lambda x.M[e], c : s) & \rightarrow & (M[e[c/x]], s) \\
(\mathcal{C}M[e], s) & \rightarrow & (M[e], ret(s)) \\
(\mathcal{A}M[e], s) & \rightarrow & (M[e], \_) \\
(ret(s), c : s') & \rightarrow & (c, s)
\end{array}
$$

Figure 8.17: Call-by-name environment machine handling control operators

---

**Environment machines and control operators.** Environment machines provide a simple implementation of control operators. The stack of an environment machine corresponds to the current evaluation context. The implementation of control operators then amounts to the introduction of operations that allow us to manipulate the stack as a whole. To this end we introduce an operator $ret$ that *retracts* a stack into a closure. Roughly, if the stack $s$ corresponds to the evaluation context $E$ then the closure $ret(s)$ corresponds to the term $\lambda x.\mathcal{A}E[x]$. We consider first the situation for call-by-name. The syntactic entities are defined as follows (note that the collection of closures is enlarged (cf. section 8.3) to include terms of the shape $ret(s)$).

$$
\begin{array}{lll}
\text{Terms} & M ::= v \mid \lambda v.M \mid MM \mid \mathcal{C}M \mid \mathcal{A}M \\
\text{Environments} & e : Var \rightharpoonup Closures \\
\text{Closures} & c ::= M[e] \mid ret(s) \\
\text{Stack} & s \equiv c_1 : \ldots : c_n \ .
\end{array}
$$

The corresponding machine is described in figure 8.17, that extends figure 8.9. The notation $\_$ stands for the empty stack.

The formalization for call-by-value is slightly more complicated. Value closures and stack are redefined as follows (as in section 8.3 $m$ stands for a marker $l$ or $r$):

$$
\begin{array}{lll}
\text{Value Closures} & vc ::= (\lambda v.M)[e] \mid ret(s) \\
\text{Stack} & s \equiv m_1 : c_1 \ldots m_n : c_n \ .
\end{array}
$$

The corresponding machine is described in figure 8.18 that extends figure 8.10. The last rule deserves some explanation: if $ret(s)$ corresponds to $\lambda x.\mathcal{A}E[x]$, $vc$ corresponds to $V$, and $s'$ corresponds to $E'$, then the rule implements the reduction:

$$
E'[(\lambda x.\mathcal{A}E[x])V] \rightarrow E'[\mathcal{A}E[V]] \rightarrow E[V] \ .
$$

It is possible to relate environment machines and CPS interpretations [LRS94]. We give a hint of the connection. Consider the following system of domain equations where $D$ is the domain of interpretation of closures, that is, terms with an environment $e \in Env$, $C$ is the domain of continuations with generic element $k$,

$$\begin{aligned}
(x[e], s) &\rightarrow (e(x), s) \\
((MN)[e], s) &\rightarrow (M[e], r : N[e] : s) \\
(vc, r : c : s) &\rightarrow (c, l : vc : s) \\
(vc, l : \lambda x.M[e] : s) &\rightarrow (M[e[vc/x]], s) \\
(CM[e], s) &\rightarrow (M[e], r : ret(s)) \\
(AM[e], s) &\rightarrow (M[e], \_) \\
(vc, l : ret(s) : s') &\rightarrow (vc, s)
\end{aligned}$$

Figure 8.18: Call-by-value environment machine handling control operators

and $R$ represents a domain of results:

$$\begin{cases}
D &= C \rightarrow R \\
C &= D \times C \quad k \in C \\
Env &= Var \rightarrow D \quad e \in Env \ .
\end{cases}$$

We interpret the terms as follows, where *stop* is an arbitrary but fixed element in $C$, $ret(k) = \lambda(c, k').ck$, and $[\![M]\!] . Env \rightarrow D$.

$$\begin{aligned}
[\![x]\!] e\, k &= e(x)k \\
[\![MN]\!] e\, k &= [\![M]\!] e \langle [\![N]\!] e, k \rangle \\
[\![\lambda x.M]\!] e \langle d, k \rangle &= [\![M]\!] e[d/x]\, k \\
[\![CM]\!] e\, k &= [\![M]\!] e \langle ret(k), stop \rangle \\
[\![AM]\!] e\, k &= [\![M]\!] e\, stop \ .
\end{aligned}$$

Note that in the interpretation we work up to isomorphism. If we regard the continuation $k$ as representing the stack $s$ and $\langle ret(k), stop \rangle$ as representing $ret(s)$ then this interpretation follows exactly the pattern of the call-by-name machine described in figure 8.17.

We remark that in the presentation of the $\lambda_C$-calculus, the domain of results $R$ is represented by *num* and the *stop* continuation is represented by *id*.

**Exercise\* 8.5.16** *Define a CPS interpretation for call-by-value which corresponds to the machine described in figure 8.18.*

# 9

# Powerdomains

In example 8.1.1 we have presented a monad of non-deterministic computations which is based on the finite powerset. We seek an analogy of this construction in the framework of domain theory. To this end, we develop in section 9.1 the *convex, lower, and upper powerdomains* in categories of algebraic cpo's [Plo76, Smy78]. In order to relate these constructions to the semantics of *non-deterministic* and *concurrent* computation we introduce in section 9.2 Milner's CCS [Mil89], a simple calculus of processes interacting by *rendezvous* synchronization on communication channels. We present an operational semantics for CCS based on the notion of *bisimulation*. Finally, in section 9.3 we give a fully abstract interpretation of CCS in a domain obtained from the solution of an equation involving the convex powerdomain [Abr91a].

## 9.1   Monads of powerdomains

We look for a construction in domain theory which can play the role of the finite (or finitary) subsets in the category of sets. The need for this development clearly arises when combining recursion with non-determinism. One complication is that, in the context of domain theory, there are several possible constructions which address this problem. Their relevance might depend on the specific application one is considering. In the following we concentrate on three *powerdomains* which rely on the notion of *semi-lattice*.

**Definition 9.1.1** *A semi-lattice is a set with a binary operation, say* $*$, *that is associative, commutative, and absorptive, that is:*

$$(x * y) * z = x * (y * z), \quad x * y = y * x, \quad x * x = x .$$

From our perspective we regard the binary operation of a semi-lattice as a loose generalization of the union operation on powersets. We seek a method for freely generating this algebraic structure from a domain. We illustrate the construction for preorders and then extend it to algebraic cpo's. Let us consider semi-lattices whose carrier is a preorder.

**Definition 9.1.2** *A preordered semi-lattice is a structure* $(P, \leq, *)$ *where* $(P, \leq)$ *is a preorder (called the carrier),* $(P, *)$ *is a semi-lattice, and the semi-lattice* *operation is monotonic, that is $x \leq x'$ and $y \leq y'$ implies $x * y \leq x' * y'$. Moreover, we say that a preordered semi-lattice $(P, \leq, *)$ is a* join *preordered semi-lattice if it satisfies $x \leq x * y$, and a* meet *preordered semi-lattice if it satisfies $x * y \leq x$.*

Incidentally, we note in the following exercise that every semi-lattice gives rise to a poset with specific properties.

**Exercise 9.1.3** *Given a semi-lattice $(P, *)$ define $x \leq_* y$ iff $x * y = y$. Show that $(P, \leq_*)$ is a poset with lub's of pairs. Exhibit a bijective correspondence between semi-lattices and posets with lub's of pairs.*

However, we are looking in the other direction: we want to build a semi-lattice out of a poset. We define the category in which we can perform this construction.

**Definition 9.1.4** *We denote with* **SP** *the category of preordered semi-lattices where morphisms are monotonic functions $f : (P, \leq) \rightarrow (P', \leq')$ such that $f(x * y) = f(x) *' f(y)$. Let* **JSP** *(MSP) be the full subcategory of* **SP** *composed of join (meet) preordered semi-lattices.*

The category **SP** has a subcategory of semi-lattices whose carriers are algebraic cpo's with a continuous operation $*$, and whose morphisms are continuous.

**Definition 9.1.5** *We denote with* **SAcpo** *the category of preordered semi-lattices $(P, \leq, *)$ such that $(P, \leq)$ is an algebraic cpo, the operation $*$ is continuous, and a morphism $f : (P, \leq, *) \rightarrow (P', \leq', *')$ is a continuous function $f : (P, \leq) \rightarrow (P', \leq')$ such that $f(x * y) = f(x) *' f(y)$. Let* **JSAcpo** *(MSAcpo) be the full subcategory of* **SAcpo** *composed of join (meet) preordered semi-lattices.*

We show that given an algebraic cpo there is a freely generated semi-lattice in the category **SAcpo**. In view of the technique of ideal completion (cf. proposition 1.1.21) this problem can be actually decomposed in the problem of freely generating a semi-lattice in the category **SP**, and then completing it to a semi-lattice in the category **SAcpo**. So, let us consider the situation for preorders first. We fix some notation. Let $\mathcal{P}_{fin}^+(X)$ denote the set of the *non-empty* finite subsets of $X$.

- **P** is the category of preorders and monotonic maps.

- *Forget* : **SP** $\rightarrow$ **P** is the functor that forgets the semi-lattice structure.

**Theorem 9.1.6** *The functor Forget* : **SP** $\rightarrow$ **P** *has a left adjoint Free* : **P** $\rightarrow$ **SP** *that is defined as:*

$$Free(P) = (\mathcal{P}_{fin}^+(P), \leq_c, \cup) \quad Free(f)(X) = f(X),$$

*where the semi-lattice operation is the set theoretical union, and the so-called* convex *preorder is defined as:*

$$X \leq_c Y \quad \text{iff} \quad \forall x \in X \; \exists y \in Y \; (x \leq y) \text{ and } \forall y \in Y \; \exists x \in X \; (x \leq y).$$

PROOF. The natural transformation $\tau_{P,S} : \mathbf{P}[P, Forget(S)] \to \mathbf{SP}[Free(P), S]$ is defined as:

$$\tau_{P,S}(f)(X) = f(x_1) * \cdots * f(x_n) \, ,$$

where $X = \{x_1, \ldots, x_n\} \in \mathcal{P}_{fin}^+(P)$ and $*$ is the binary operation in $S$. The inverse is defined as $\tau'_{P,S}(h)(p) = h(\{p\})$. We have to verify that these morphisms live in the respective categories.

- $\tau_{P,S}(f)$ is monotonic. Suppose $\{x_1, \ldots, x_n\} = X \leq_c Y = \{y_1, \ldots, y_m\}$. By the definition of the convex preorder we can find two multisets $X' = \{\!|w_1, \ldots, w_l|\!\}$ and $Y' = \{\!|z_1, \ldots, z_l|\!\}$ in which the same elements occur, respectively, as in $X$ and $Y$ and such that $w_i \leq z_i$, $i = 1, \ldots, l$. By monotonicity of $f$, and of the binary operation in $S$, we have:

$$f(w_1) * \cdots * f(w_l) \leq_S f(z_1) * \cdots * f(z_l) \, ,$$

and by absorption:

$$\tau_{P,S}(f)(X) = f(w_1) * \cdots * f(w_l) \qquad \tau_{P,S}(f)(Y) = f(z_1) * \cdots * f(z_l) \, .$$

- $\tau_{P,S}(f)$ is a morphism in $\mathbf{SP}$. This is immediate by associativity and absorption. We leave to the reader the verification that $\tau'_{P,S}$ is well defined as well as the check of the naturality of $\tau$.                                                                          □

**Remark 9.1.7** *The adjunction described in theorem 9.1.6 canonically induces (cf. theorem A2.8.7) a convex monad $(P_c, \{\_\}, \bigcup)$, where:*

$$P_c(D) = (\mathcal{P}_{fin}^+(D), \leq_c)$$
$$\{\_\} : D \to P_c(D) \qquad\qquad \{\_\}(d) = \{d\}$$
$$\bigcup : P_c(P_c(D)) \to P_c(D) \qquad \bigcup\{x_1, \ldots, x_m\} = x_1 \cup \cdots \cup x_m \, .$$

Theorem 9.1.6 can be adapted to join and meet preordered semi-lattices by following the same proof schema.

**Theorem 9.1.8** *The forgetful functors $Forget : \mathbf{JSP} \to \mathbf{P}$ and $Forget : \mathbf{MSP} \to \mathbf{P}$ have left adjoints $Free_{\mathbf{JSP}} : \mathbf{P} \to \mathbf{JSP}$ and $Free_{\mathbf{MSP}} : \mathbf{P} \to \mathbf{MSP}$, respectively, defined as:*

$$
\begin{aligned}
Free_{\mathbf{JSP}}(P) &= (\mathcal{P}_{fin}^+(P), \leq_l, \cup) \\
Free_{\mathbf{MSP}}(P) &= (\mathcal{P}_{fin}^+(P), \leq_u, \cup) \\
Free_{\mathbf{JSP}}(f)(X) &= Free_{\mathbf{MSP}}(f)(X) = f(X) \, ,
\end{aligned}
$$

*where the semi-lattice operation is the set theoretical union, and the so-called lower and upper preorders are defined as:*[1]

$$X \leq_l Y \quad \text{iff} \quad \forall x \in X \; \exists y \in Y \; (x \leq y)$$
$$X \leq_u Y \quad \text{iff} \quad \forall y \in Y \; \exists x \in X \; (x \leq y) \, .$$

---

[1]Observe the combination of the terminologies for semi-lattices and preorders: the lower preorder occurs with join preordered semi-lattices, and the upper preorder occurs with meet preordered semi-lattices. Note that $X \leq_c Y$ iff $X \leq_l Y$ and $X \leq_u Y$.

**Example 9.1.9** *We consider the poset* $\mathbf{O} = \{\bot, \top\}$ *where as usual* $\bot < \top$. *We suppose that the semantics of a non-deterministic program is an element of* $\mathcal{P}_{fin}^+(\mathbf{O}) = \{\{\bot\}, \{\top\}, \{\bot, \top\}\}$, $\bot$ *expressing divergence and* $\top$ *convergence. The convex, lower, and upper preorders induce three distinct preorders on* $\mathcal{P}_{fin}^+(\mathbf{O})$. *In the convex preorder* $\{\bot\} <_c \{\bot, \top\} <_c \{\top\}$, *in the lower preorder* $\{\bot, \top\} = \{\top\}$, *and in the upper preorder* $\{\bot\} = \{\bot, \top\}$. *In this context, the lower preorder can be associated with partial correctness assertions, as it compares the outcomes of a program neglecting divergence, whereas the upper preorder can be associated with total correctness assertions, as it collapses programs that may diverge. The convex preorder is the most discriminating, as it compares computations with respect to both partial and total correctness assertions.*

Let us see how theorem 9.1.6 can be extended to the category **Acpo** of algebraic cpo's and continuous functions via the ideal completion.

- There is a functor *Forget* : **SAcpo** → **Acpo**.

- Let *Ide* : **P** → **Acpo** be the ideal completion from preorders to algebraic cpo's which is left adjoint to the relative forgetful functor (cf. proposition 1.1.21). Similarly, one can define a functor from **SP** to **SAcpo**, which makes the ideal completion of the semi-lattice and extends the monotonic binary operation to a continuous one.

**Definition 9.1.10** *Let D be an algebraic cpo and let x stand for c, l, or u. Then we define a function* $P_x[\_] : \mathbf{Acpo} \to \mathbf{Acpo}$ *as follows:*[2]

$$P_x[D] = Ide(\mathcal{P}_{fin}^+(\mathcal{K}(D)), \leq_x) .$$

**Proposition 9.1.11** (1) *If D is finite then* $P_c[D]$ *can be characterized as the collection of convex subsets with the convex partial order. Namely, we have* $(\{Con(u) \mid u \in \mathcal{P}_{fin}^+(D)\}, \leq_c)$, *where* $Con(u) = \{d \mid \exists d', d'' \in u \ (d' \leq d \leq d'')\}$.

(2) *For the flat domain* $\omega_\bot$ *the order* $P_c[\omega_\bot]$ *is isomorphic to the following set with the convex preorder,* $\{u \mid u \subset \mathcal{P}_{fin}^+(\omega)\} \cup \{u \cup \{\bot\} \mid u \subseteq \omega\}$.

PROOF HINT. (1) This follows from the observation that $\mathcal{K}(D) = D$ and the fact that the ideal completion of a finite set does not add any limit point.

(2) Left as an exercise. Note that every computation with a countable collection of results may also diverge. □

**Exercise 9.1.12** *Characterize* $P_x[D]$ *when x equals u or l and D is finite or* $\omega_\bot$.

The function $P_c[\_]$ can be extended to a functor which is left adjoint to the forgetful functor.

**Proposition 9.1.13** *There is a left adjoint Free to the forgetful functor Forget :* **SAcpo** → **Acpo**.

---

[2]Note the difference between, say, $P_c\{\_\}$ as defined in remark 9.1.7, and $P_c[\_]$ as defined here.

PROOF HINT. We define $Free(D) = P_c[D]$ (cf. definition 9.1.10). Given $f : D \rightarrow E$, we define $Free(f)$ on the principal ideals by:

$$Free(f)(\downarrow \{d_1, \ldots, d_m\}) = \{u \in \mathcal{P}_{fin}^+(\mathcal{K}(E)) \mid u \leq_c \{fd_1, \ldots, fd_m\}\} .$$

We note that this is an ideal, and that $Free(f)$ can be extended canonically to $P_c[D]$. □

**Exercise 9.1.14** *Prove the analogous of proposition 9.1.13 for the categories* **JSAcpo** *and* **MSAcpo**.

**Exercise 9.1.15** *Show that the category of Scott domains is closed under the lower and upper powerdomains constructions. Hint: It is enough to prove that every pair of compact elements which is bounded has a lub. On the other hand, show that the category of Scott domains is not closed under the convex powerdomain construction (this motivated the introduction of bifinite domains [Plo76]). Hint: Consider the domain* $\mathbf{T}^2$ *where* $\mathbf{T} = \{\bot, tt, ff\}$.

**Exercise 9.1.16** *Let D be a bifinite domain and let* $\{p_i\}_{i \in I}$ *be the associated directed set of finite projections such that* $\bigvee_{i \in I} p_i = id_D$. *Show that* $\bigvee_{i \in I} P_c[p_i] = P_c[id]$. *Conclude that bifinite domains are closed under the convex powerdomain. Extend this result to the lower and upper powerdomains.*

# 9.2   CCS

The semantics of the programming languages considered so far associates with every input a set of output values. For instance, a finite set if the computation is non-deterministic but finitely branching (cf. example 8.1.1(2)). On the other hand, system applications often require the design of programs which have to interact repeatedly with their environment (e.g., other programs, physical devices, etc.). In this case the specification of a program as an input-output relation is not adequate. In order to specify the ability of a program to perform a certain action it is useful to introduce the simple notion of labelled transition system.

**Definition 9.2.1** *A labelled transition system (lts) is triple of sets* $(Pr, Act, \rightarrow)$ *where* $\rightarrow \subseteq Pr \times Act \times Pr$.

We have adapted our notation to a process calculus to be introduced next, $Pr$ stands for the collection of *processes* and $Act$ for the collection of *actions*. We write $p \xrightarrow{\alpha} q$ for $(p, \alpha, q) \in \rightarrow$, to be read as $p$ *makes an action* $\alpha$ *and becomes* $q$.

**Definition 9.2.2** *An lts is said to be* image finite *if, for all* $p \in Pr$, $\alpha \in Act$, *the set* $\{p' \mid p \xrightarrow{\alpha} p'\}$ *is finite. An image finite lts can be represented as a function* $\rightarrow: Pr \times Act \rightarrow \mathcal{P}_{fin}(Pr)$.

Next we present (a fragment of) Milner's Calculus of Communicating Systems (CCS) [Mil89]. CCS is a model of computation in which a set of *agents* interact by *rendezvous* synchronization on communication channels (syntactically one can

Process variables $V ::= X, Y, Z, \ldots$
Processes $\quad P ::= 0 \mid V \mid a.P \mid P + P \mid P \mid P \mid P \backslash a \mid fixV.P$

Figure 9.1: Syntax of CCS

think of an agent as a sequential unit of computation, that is as a process that cannot be decomposed in the parallel composition of two or more processes).

In general several agents can compete for the reception or the transmission on a certain channel, however each accomplished communication involves just one sending and one receiving agent. Moreover any agent may attempt at the same time a communication on several channels (a non-deterministic sum is used for this purpose).

In CCS, communication is pure synchronization; no data are exchanged between the sender and the receiver. Therefore, it is not actually necessary to distinguish between input and output. All we need to know is when one of two interactions is the dual of the other. This idea can be formalized as follows. Let $L$ be a *finite* collection of labels (we make this hypothesis to simplify the interpretation described in section 9.3). Each label $l \in L$ has a complement $\bar{l}$ which belongs to $\bar{L} = \{\bar{l} \mid l \in L\}$. The overline symbol can be understood as a special marker that one adds to an element of $L$. The marker is chosen so that $L$ and $\bar{L}$ are disjoint.

We denote with $a, b, \ldots$ generic elements in $L \cup \bar{L}$. The complement operation is extended to $\bar{L}$ by making it *involutive*, that is $\bar{\bar{a}} = a$. Finally we define the collection of actions $Act = L \cup \bar{L} \cup \{\tau\}$, where $\tau \notin L \cup \bar{L}$. We denote with $\alpha, \beta, \ldots$ generic elements in $Act$.

The actions $a, \bar{a}$ may be understood as complementary input/output synchronization operations on a channel. The action $\tau$ is an *internal action* in the sense that a process may perform it without the cooperation of the environment.

In figure 9.1, we define a calculus of processes which includes basic combinators for termination, sequentialization, non-deterministic sum, parallel composition, and restriction.

A process is called well-formed if it is: (i) closed, that is all process variables are in the scope of a *fix* operator, and (ii) guarded, that is all (bound) process variables are preceded by a prefix, for instance $fixX.a.X$ is guarded whereas $fixY.(fixX.a.X) + Y$ is not. In the following we always assume that processes are well-formed, these are the objects for which an operational semantics is defined. The intuitive operational behaviour of the process operators is as follows. 0 is the terminated process which can perform no action. $a.P$ is the *prefixing* of $a$ to $P$, that is, $a.P$ performs the action $a$ and becomes $P$. $P + P'$ is the non-deterministic *choice* (sum) between the execution of $P$ and that of $P'$. The choice operator presented here is very convenient in the development of an *algebra of processes*. On the other hand its implementation on a distributed architecture requires sophis-

$$(prefix) \quad \frac{}{\alpha.P \xrightarrow{\alpha} P} \qquad\qquad (sum) \quad \frac{P_1 \xrightarrow{\alpha} P_1'}{P_1 + P_2 \xrightarrow{\alpha} P_1'}$$

$$(comp) \quad \frac{P_1 \xrightarrow{\alpha} P_1'}{P_1 \mid P_2 \xrightarrow{\alpha} P_1' \mid P_2} \qquad (sync) \quad \frac{P_1 \xrightarrow{a} P_1' \quad P_2 \xrightarrow{\bar{a}} P_2'}{P_1 \mid P_2 \xrightarrow{\tau} P_1' \mid P_2'}$$

$$(res) \quad \frac{P \xrightarrow{\alpha} P' \quad \alpha \notin \{a, \bar{a}\}}{P\backslash a \xrightarrow{\alpha} P'\backslash a} \qquad (fix) \quad \frac{P[fixX.P/X] \xrightarrow{\alpha} P'}{fixX.P \xrightarrow{\alpha} P'}$$

Figure 9.2: Labelled transition system for CCS

ticated and expensive protocols. For this reason most parallel languages adopt a restricted form of non-deterministic choice. $P \mid P'$ is the *parallel composition* of $P$ and $P'$. $P\backslash a$ is the process $P$ where the channel $a$ has become private to $P$. This operation is called *restriction*. Finally, *fix* is the least fixpoint operator with the usual unfolding computation rule.

We define next an lts on processes. The intuitive interpretation of the judgment $P \xrightarrow{\alpha} P'$ is the following:

- If $\alpha \equiv \tau$ then $P$ may reduce to $P'$ by means of an internal autonomous communication.

- If $\alpha \equiv a \in L \cup \overline{L}$ then $P$ may reduce to $P'$ provided the environment supplies a dual action $\bar{a}$.

The definition of the lts proceeds non-deterministically by analysis of the process expression structure. The rules are displayed in figure 9.2. The rules (*sum*) and (*comp*) have a symmetric version which is omitted. Given a process $P$ one may repeatedly apply the derivation rules above and build a possibly infinite tree whose edges are labelled by actions.

**Exercise 9.2.3** *(1) Show that any process without a fix operator generates a finite labelled tree. (2) Verify that any CCS process generates an image finite lts. (3) Consider the non-guarded process $P \equiv fixX.((X.0 + a.0) \mid b.0)$. Verify $P \xrightarrow{a} 0 \mid b.0 \mid \cdots \mid b.0$, for an arbitrary number of $b.0$'s. Conclude that CCS with unguarded recursive definitions is not image finite.*

The tree representation is still too concrete to provide a reasonable semantics even for finite CCS processes built out of prefixing and sum. In other words the sum operator of CCS should form a semi-lattice (associative, commutative, and absorptive) with 0 as identity. For processes generating a finite tree, it is possible to build a canonical set theoretical representation. We define inductively the 'synchronization trees' $ST$:

$$ST_0 = \emptyset \quad ST_{n+1} = \mathcal{P}_{fin}(Act \times ST_n) \quad ST = \bigcup\{ST_n \mid n < \omega\} \ .$$

If $P$ generates a finite labelled tree then let $[\![P]\!] = \{(\alpha, [\![P']\!]) \mid P \xrightarrow{\alpha} P'\} \in ST$. For instance one can compute:

$$[\![a.0 \mid \bar{a}.0]\!] = \{(a, \{(\bar{a}, \emptyset)\}), (\tau, \emptyset), (\bar{a}, \{(a, \emptyset)\})\} \ .$$

**Exercise 9.2.4** *Verify that the previous interpretation is well-defined for processes generating a finite labelled tree and that it satisfies the semi-lattice equations.*

There are serious difficulties in extending this naive set theoretical interpretation to infinite processes. For instance one should have:

$$[\![fixX.a.X]\!] = \{(a, \{(a, \{(a, \ldots$$

This seems to ask for the construction of a set $A$ such that $A = \{(a, A)\}$. Assuming the standard representation of an ordered pair $(x, y)$ as $\{x, \{x, y\}\}$ we note that this set is *not well-founded* with respect to the *belongs to* relation as $A \in \{a, A\} \in A$. This contradicts the foundation axiom which is often added to, say, Zermelo-Fraenkel set theory (see, e.g., [Jec78]).

On the other hand it is possible to remove the foundation axiom and develop a non-standard set theory with an *anti-foundation axiom* which assumes the existence of sets like $A$ (see in particular [Acz88] for the development of the connections with process calculi). In section 9.3, we will take a different approach which pursues the construction of a set theoretical structure in domain theory relying on the *convex powerdomain*. The initial idea is to associate with $[\![fixX.a.X]\!]$ the lub of elements of the shape $\{(a, \{(a, \ldots, \{(a, \bot)\} \ldots)\})\}$, modulo a suitable interpretation of the set theoretical notation.

In the following we develop the operational semantics of CCS. To this end we introduce the notion of *bisimulation* [Par81] which is a popular notion of equivalence on lts's. Let $(Pr, Act, \rightarrow)$ be an lts. We define an equivalence relation over $Pr$ that can be characterized as the greatest element of a collection of relations known as *bisimulations* or, equivalently, as the greatest fixpoint of a certain monotonic operator defined on the powerset of $Pr \times Pr$.

**Definition 9.2.5 (operator $\mathcal{F}$)** *Let $(Pr, Act, \rightarrow)$ be a given lts. We define $\mathcal{F} : \mathcal{P}(Pr \times Pr) \rightarrow \mathcal{P}(Pr \times Pr)$ as:*

$$\mathcal{F}(X) = \ \{(p, q) \mid \ \forall p', \alpha \ (p \xrightarrow{\alpha} p' \Rightarrow \exists q' \ (q \xrightarrow{\alpha} q' \ and \ (p', q') \in X)) \ and$$
$$\forall q', \alpha \ (q \xrightarrow{\alpha} q' \Rightarrow \exists p' \ (p \xrightarrow{\alpha} p' \ and \ (p', q') \in X))\} \ .$$

**Definition 9.2.6** *The operator $\mathcal{F}$ is iterated as follows:*

$$\mathcal{F}^0 = Pr \times Pr \quad \mathcal{F}^{\kappa+1} = \mathcal{F}(\mathcal{F}^\kappa)$$
$$\mathcal{F}^\lambda = \bigcap_{\kappa < \lambda} \mathcal{F}^\kappa \quad for \ \lambda \ limit \ ordinal \ .$$

**Proposition 9.2.7** *The operator $\mathcal{F}$ is a monotonic operator over $\mathcal{P}(Pr \times Pr)$, that is $S \subseteq S' \ \Rightarrow \ \mathcal{F}(S) \subseteq \mathcal{F}(S')$.*

PROOF HINT. In the definition 9.2.5, the relation $X$ occurs positively. □

It follows from exercise 1.1.9 that the operator $\mathcal{F}$ has a greatest fixpoint (gfp), where $gfp(\mathcal{F}) = \bigcap_{\kappa < \mu} \mathcal{F}^\kappa$, for some ordinal $\mu$.

**Proposition 9.2.8** *If the lts is image finite then the operator $\mathcal{F}$ preserves codirected sets, in particular $gfp(\mathcal{F}) = \bigcap_{k<\omega} \mathcal{F}^k$.*

PROOF. Suppose $\{S_i\}_{i\in I}$ is a codirected set of relations over $Pr$. The interesting point is to show:

$$\bigcap_{i\in I} \mathcal{F}(S_i) \subseteq \mathcal{F}(\bigcap_{i\in I} S_i) \ .$$

Suppose $\forall i \in I$ $(p\,\mathcal{F}(S_i)\,q)$ and $p \overset{\alpha}{\to} p'$. Let $Q = \{q' \mid q \overset{\alpha}{\to} q'\}$, which is finite. By hypothesis,

$$\forall i \in I \ \exists q' \in Q \ (q \overset{\alpha}{\to} q' \text{ and } p'\,S_i\,q') \ . \tag{9.1}$$

We claim $\exists q' \in Q \ \forall i \in I \ (p'\,S_i\,q')$. By contradiction, suppose that $\forall q' \in Q \ \exists i \in I \ ((p',q') \notin S_i)$. Since $\{S_i\}_{i\in I}$ is a codirected set, $\exists k \in I \ \forall q' \in Q \ ((p',q') \notin S_k)$, contradicting 9.1. □

**Definition 9.2.9 (bisimulation)** *Let $(Pr, Act, \to)$ be a given lts. A binary relation $S \subseteq Pr \times Pr$ is a bisimulation if $S \subseteq \mathcal{F}(S)$.*

**Exercise 9.2.10** *Show that: (i) the empty and identity relations are bisimulations, (ii) bisimulations are closed under inverse, composition, and arbitrary unions, and (iii) there is a greatest bisimulation (cf. exercise 1.1.9). Verify that bisimulations are not closed under (finite) intersection.*

**Definition 9.2.11** *Let $Pr$ be the collection of CCS processes. Let $\mathcal{F}$ be as in definition 9.2.5. We denote with $\sim$ the greatest CCS bisimulation and we set $\sim^\kappa = \mathcal{F}^\kappa$.*

**Exercise 9.2.12** *Show for CCS that $\sim = \sim^\omega$. Hint: Apply exercise 9.2.3 and proposition 9.2.8.*

**Exercise 9.2.13** *Prove that $\sim$ is a congruence for prefixing, sum, parallel composition, and restriction. Hint: To prove that $P \sim Q$ it is enough to find a bisimulation $S$ such that $P\,S\,Q$. Let $[Pr]$ be the collection of equivalence classes generated by the greatest bisimulation $\sim$ on the set of CCS processes. Extend the operations $+$ and $\mid$ to $[Pr]$ and prove that $([Pr], +, [0])$ is a semi-lattice with $[0]$ as identity, and that $([Pr], \mid, [0])$ is a commutative monoid.*

**Exercise\* 9.2.14** *Suppose that $P, Q$ generate finite labelled trees, so that the set theoretical representations as synchronization trees are defined. Show that the synchronization trees are equal iff the two processes are bisimilar. Hint: Adapt the proof presented in the next section 9.3.*

The previous exercises suggest that bisimulation equivalence captures many reasonable process equivalences. However, as stated it is still unsatisfactory as the internal action $\tau$ and an input-output action on a channel are treated in the same way. This implies that for instance, the process $\tau.\tau.a.0$ is not bisimilar to the process $\tau.a.0$. One needs to abstract to some extent from the internal actions. A standard approach to this problem, is to consider a *weak* labelled transition system in which any action (in the sense of the lts defined in figure 9.2) can be preceded and followed by an arbitrary number of internal $\tau$-actions.

**Definition 9.2.15** *Weak labelled reduction, say* $\overset{a}{\Rightarrow}$, *is a relation over CCS processes which is defined as follows:*

$$P \overset{a}{\Rightarrow} P' \quad \text{iff} \quad \exists Q, Q' \ \ P(\overset{\tau}{\rightarrow})^*Q \overset{a}{\rightarrow} Q'(\overset{\tau}{\rightarrow})^*P'$$
$$P \overset{\tau}{\Rightarrow} P' \quad \text{iff} \quad P(\overset{\tau}{\rightarrow})^*P' \ .$$

Weak bisimulation *is the greatest bisimulation relation with respect to the lts* $(Pr, Act, \Rightarrow)$.

The properties of weak bisimulation with respect to CCS operators are described in [Mil89]. We will meet this equivalence again in chapter 16, for the time being we just observe some basic properties.

**Exercise 9.2.16** *Verify that the following equations hold for weak bisimulation:*

$$\alpha.\tau.P = \alpha.P \quad P + \tau.P = \tau.P \quad \alpha.(P + \tau.Q) + \alpha.Q = \alpha.(P + \tau.Q) \ .$$

*More difficult: using these equations give an equational presentation of weak bisimulation for processes built with 0, prefix, and sum.*

## 9.3  Interpretation of CCS

We define an interpretation of CCS in the bifinite domain $D$ which is the initial solution of the domain equation:

$$D = P_c[(Act \times D)_\perp] + 1_\perp \ , \tag{9.2}$$

where $+$ is the coalesced sum (cf. definition 1.4.23), $(\ )_\perp$ is the lifting (cf. definition 1.4.16), and 1 is the one point cpo. The role of the adjoined element $1_\perp$ is to represent the terminated process 0 (cf. [Abr91b]). We denote with $F$ the functor associated with $P_c[(Act \times \_)_\perp] + 1_\perp$.

We will show that the related interpretation captures bisimulation (a full abstraction result). To this end, we will introduce a notion of *syntactic approximation* (definition 9.3.6). A syntactic approximation plays a role similar to that of finite Böhm trees in the $\lambda$-calculus (cf. definition 2.3.1): it provides an approximate description of the operational behaviour of a process. It turns out that syntactic approximations are interpreted in the domain $D$ by compact elements. The key lemma 9.3.13 relates syntactic and semantic approximations. Full abstraction is then obtained by going to the limit.

The existence of an initial solution to equation 9.2 can be proven by the technique of section 7.1. However, in order to relate denotational and operational semantics of CCS it is useful to take a closer look at the structure of $D$. The domain $D$ is the $\omega$-colimit in **Bif**$^{ip}$ of the $\omega$-chain $\{F^n(1), F^n(f_0)\}_{n\in\omega}$ where the morphism $f_0 : 1 \to F(1)$ is uniquely determined in **Bif**$^{ip}$ (it is the constant function $\perp$, cf. proposition 7.1.9). We note that, for each $n \in \omega$, the domain $F^n(1)$ is finite. Therefore the ideal completion has no effect (cf. proposition 9.1.11(1)), and we have that $F^{n+1}(1) \cong (P_{fin}^+((Act \times F^n(1))_\perp) + 1_\perp, \leq_c)$. Every compact element in $D$ can be regarded as an element in $F^n(1)$, for some $n \in \omega$, and, vice versa, every element in $F^n(1)$ can be regarded as a compact element in $D$. It is actually convenient to build inductively the collection of compact elements.

**Definition 9.3.1 (compacts)** *The sets $K_n$, for $n \in \omega$, are the least sets such that:*

$$\{\bot\} \in K_0 \qquad\qquad \emptyset \in K_{n+1}$$

$$\frac{\alpha_i \in Act, d_i \in K_n, m \geq 1}{\{(\alpha_1, d_1), \ldots, (\alpha_m, d_m)\} \in K_{n+1}} \qquad \frac{\alpha_i \in Act, d_i \in K_n, m \geq 0}{\{\bot\} \cup \{(\alpha_1, d_1), \ldots, (\alpha_m, d_m)\} \in K_{n+1}} .$$

**Proposition 9.3.2** *For any $n \in \omega$, (1) $K_n \subseteq K_{n+1}$, and (2) if $d, d' \in K_n$ then $d \cup d' \in K_n$.*

PROOF HINT. By induction on $n$, e.g., suppose $d = \{(\alpha_1, d_1), \ldots, (\alpha_m, d_m)\} \in K_n$ because $m \geq 1$, $\alpha_i \in Act$, and $d_i \in K_{n-1}$. Then, by induction hypothesis, $d_i \in K_n$, and we can conclude $d \in K_{n+1}$. $\qquad\qquad\square$

It is easy to verify that elements in $K_n$ are in bijective correspondence with elements in $F^n(1)$ ($\{\bot\}$ is the least element, and $\emptyset$ plays the role of the adjoined element in equation 9.2). The bijection becomes an order-isomorphism when the elements in $K = \bigcup_{n \in \omega} K_n$ are ordered as follows.

**Definition 9.3.3 (order)** *Let $\leq$ be the least relation on $K$ such that $(U, V$ can be empty):*

$$\frac{\forall u \in U \ \exists v \in V \ (\alpha_u = \alpha'_v \text{ and } d_u \leq d'_v) \quad \forall v \in V \ \exists u \in U \ (\alpha_u = \alpha'_v \text{ and } d_u \leq d'_v)}{\{(\alpha_u, d_u) \mid u \in U\} \leq \{(\alpha'_v, d'_v) \mid v \in V\}}$$

$$\frac{\forall u \in U \ \exists v \in V \ (\alpha_u = \alpha'_v \text{ and } d_u \leq d'_v)}{\{\bot\} \cup \{(\alpha_u, d_u) \mid u \in U\} \leq \{(\alpha'_v, d'_v) \mid v \in V\}}$$

$$\frac{\forall u \in U \ \exists v \in V \ (\alpha_u = \alpha'_v \text{ and } d_u \leq d'_v)}{\{\bot\} \cup \{(\alpha_u, d_u) \mid u \in U\} \leq \{\bot\} \cup \{(\alpha'_v, d'_v) \mid v \in V\}} .$$

Note that in the second and third rules the smaller set contains $\bot$, and so we need to check only half of the definition of convex preorder (cf. theorem 9.1.6). We remark the following properties of the order.

**Exercise 9.3.4** *Prove that if $d \leq d'$ then $\exists n, m \ d \in K_n, \ d' \in K_m$ and $n \leq m$. In particular $K_n$ is downward closed. Moreover, show that if $e \leq \{(\alpha, d)\}$ and $e \in K_{n+1}$ then $\exists d' \in K_n \ (d' \leq d$ and $e \leq \{(\alpha, d')\})$. Hint: Take as $d'$ the projection of $d$ on $K_n$.*

Thus, we have obtained an explicit description of the compact elements. We can assume $D = Ide(K, \leq)$ with the inclusion order, and $\mathcal{K}(D) = \{\downarrow d \mid d \in K\}$. We denote with $I, J$ elements in $D$. We can explicitly define a chain $\{p_n\}_{n \in \omega}$ of image finite projections on $D$ by (cf. section 7.4):

$$p_n(I) = I \cap K_n . \tag{9.3}$$

In figure 9.3 we define inductively on $K$ monotonic functions corresponding to the CCS operators. Of course, these functions can be canonically extended to

$$
\begin{aligned}
Nil \in K && Nil &= \emptyset \\
Pre_\alpha : K \to K && Pre_\alpha(d) &= \{(\alpha, d)\} \\
Sum : K^2 \to K && Sum(d, d') &= d \cup d'
\end{aligned}
$$

$$
\begin{aligned}
&Res_a : K \to K \\
&Res_a(\{\bot\}) && = \{\bot\} \\
&Res_a(\emptyset) && = \emptyset \\
&Res_a(\{(\alpha_u, d_u) \mid u \in U\}) && = \{(\alpha_u, Res_a(d_u)) \mid u \in U, \alpha_u \notin \{a, \bar{a}\}\} \quad (U \neq \emptyset) \\
&Res_a(\{\bot\} \cup \{(\alpha_u, d_u) \mid u \in U\}) && = \{\bot\} \cup \{(\alpha_u, Res_a(d_u)) \mid u \in U, \alpha_u \notin \{a, \bar{a}\}\}
\end{aligned}
$$

$$
\begin{aligned}
&Par : K^2 \to K \\
&Par(\{\bot\}, d) = Par(d, \{\bot\}) && = \{\bot\} \\
&Par(\emptyset, d) = Par(d, \emptyset) && = d \\
&Par(\{(\alpha, d)\}, \{(\alpha', d')\}) && = 
\begin{cases}
\{(\alpha, Par(d, \{(\alpha', d')\}))\} \cup \\
\{(\alpha', Par(\{(\alpha, d)\}, d'))\} \cup \\
\{(\tau, Par(d, d')) \mid \alpha = \overline{\alpha'} \in L \cup \overline{L}\}
\end{cases} \\
&Par(\{d_u \mid u \in U\}, \{d_v \mid v \in V\}) && = \bigcup_{u \in U, v \in V} Par(d_u, d_v) \quad (\sharp U + \sharp V \geq 3, \ \sharp U, \sharp V \geq 1)
\end{aligned}
$$

Figure 9.3: Interpretation of CCS operators on compact elements

---

continuous functions on $D$. In general, given $f : K^n \to K$ we define $\hat{f} : D^n \to D$ as:

$$
\hat{f}(I_1, \ldots, I_n) = \bigcup \{\downarrow f(d_1, \ldots, d_n) \mid d_j \in I_j, j = 1, \ldots, n\} . \tag{9.4}
$$

Next we define a notion of a *syntactic approximation* of a process. Syntactic approximations can be analysed by finite means both at the syntactic level (proposition 9.3.8), and at the semantic level (definition 9.3.9). A syntactic approximation is a process built with 0, prefix, sum and a new constant $\bot$. The notion of labelled transition system and bisimulation for this extended calculus are left unchanged. Hence $\bot$ behaves as 0, operationally. (The denotations of $\bot$ and 0 will be different however, cf. definition 9.3.9 and remark 9.3.15.)

**Definition 9.3.5** *We define inductively a collection of normal forms $\mathcal{N}_k$:*

$$
\frac{}{\bot \in \mathcal{N}_0} \qquad \frac{\forall u \in V \ (N_u \in \mathcal{N}_k) \quad \sharp U < \omega}{\Sigma_{u \in U} \alpha_u.N_u \in \mathcal{N}_{k+1}} .
$$

*Note that $\bot \notin \mathcal{N}_{k+1}$. If $U = \{1, \ldots, n\}$ then $\Sigma_{u \in U} \alpha_u.N_u$ is a shorthand for $\alpha_1.N_1 + \cdots + \alpha_n.N_n$. Conventionally, 0 stands for the empty sum. Hence, $0 \in \mathcal{N}_{k+1}$. We consider terms up to associativity and commutativity of the sum, hence the order of the summands is immaterial.*

**Definition 9.3.6 (syntactic approximation)** *For any process $P$, we define a $k^{th}$ approximation $(P)_k \in \mathcal{N}_k$ as follows:*

$$
\begin{aligned}
(P)_0 &= \bot & (0)_{k+1} &= 0 \\
(\alpha.P)_{k+1} &= \alpha.(P)_k & (P + P')_{k+1} &= (P)_{k+1} + (P')_{k+1} \\
(fixX.P)_{k+1} &= ([fixX.P/X]P)_{k+1}
\end{aligned}
$$

$$\frac{(P)_{k+1} = \Sigma_{u \in U} \alpha_u.P_u}{(P \backslash a)_{k+1} = \Sigma \{\alpha_u.(P_u \backslash a)_k \mid u \in U, \alpha_u \notin \{a, \bar{a}\}\}}$$

$$\frac{(P)_{k+1} = \Sigma_{u \in U} \alpha_u.N_u \quad (P')_{k+1} = \Sigma_{v \in V} \beta_v.N'_v}{(P \mid P')_{k+1} = \begin{cases} \Sigma_{u \in U} \alpha_u.(N_u \mid \Sigma_{v \in V} \beta_v.N'_v)_k + \\ \Sigma_{v \in V} \beta_v.(\Sigma_{u \in U} \alpha_u.N_u \mid N'_v)_k + \\ \Sigma \{\tau.(N_u \mid N'_v)_k \mid u \in U, \ v \in V, \alpha_u = \overline{\beta_v}\} \end{cases}}$$

To show that the definition is well-founded we define a measure *nfix* on processes that counts the number of nested *fix*'s at top level:

$$nfix(0) = nfix(X) = nfix(\alpha.P) = 0$$
$$nfix(P \backslash a) = nfix(P)$$
$$nfix(P \mid P') = nfix(P + P') = max\{nfix(P), nfix(P')\}$$
$$nfix(fixX.P) = 1 + nfix(P) .$$

By the hypothesis that recursive definitions are guarded we have $nfix(fixX.P) = 1 + nfix(P[fixX.P/X])$.

**Exercise 9.3.7** *Prove that the definition of* $(\_)_k$ *is well-founded. Hint: Proceed by induction on* $(k, nfix(P), P)$.

**Proposition 9.3.8** *Let* $P, Q$ *be processes. Then:*

$$P \sim Q \ \text{iff} \ \forall k \in \omega \ ((P)_k \sim^k (Q)_k) .$$

PROOF. First, we observe that for any process $P$:

$$(P)_0 = \bot \in \mathcal{N}_0$$
$$(P)_{k+1} = \Sigma \{\alpha.(P')_k \mid P \xrightarrow{\alpha} P'\} \in \mathcal{N}_{k+1} .$$

From this we derive that for any process $P$, and for any $k \in \omega$, $(P)_k \sim^k P$. Combining with proposition 9.2.8 and using the transitivity of the relation $\sim^k$ we can conclude that:

$$P \sim Q \ \text{iff} \ \forall k \in \omega \ (P \sim^k Q) \ \text{iff} \ \forall k \in \omega \ ((P)_k \sim^k (Q)_k) .$$

$\square$

**Definition 9.3.9** *We define an interpretation in* $K$ *of the normal forms (with reference to the operators in figure 9.3):*

$$[\bot]^K = \{\bot\} \qquad\qquad [0]^K = \emptyset$$
$$[\alpha.N]^K = Pre_\alpha([N]^K) \qquad [N + N']^K = Sum([N]^K, [N']^K) .$$

**Proposition 9.3.10** *Let* $N, N' \in \mathcal{N}_n$ *be normal forms, for* $n \in \omega$. *Then the following properties hold:*

(1) $[N]^K \in K_n$.

(2) $N \sim^n N'$ *iff* $[N]^K = [N']^K$.

PROOF HINT. By induction on $n$. For instance, we consider a case of (2). Let $N = \Sigma_{u \in U} \alpha_u.N_u$ and $N' = \Sigma_{v \in V} \alpha_v.N'_v$ be in $\mathcal{N}_{n+1}$. Then:

$$\llbracket N \rrbracket^K = \{(\alpha_u, \llbracket N_u \rrbracket^K) \mid u \in U\} \text{ and } \llbracket N' \rrbracket^K = \{(\alpha_v, \llbracket N'_v \rrbracket^K) \mid v \in V\} \ .$$

If $N \sim^{n+1} N'$, then:

$$\forall u \in U \ \exists v \in V \ (\alpha_u = \alpha_v \text{ and } N_u \sim^n N'_v)$$
$$\forall v \in V \ \exists u \in U \ (\alpha_u = \alpha_v \text{ and } N_u \sim^n N'_v) \ .$$

By induction hypothesis, this is rewritten as:

$$\forall u \in U \ \exists v \in V \ (\alpha_u = \alpha_v \text{ and } \llbracket N_u \rrbracket^K = \llbracket N'_v \rrbracket^K)$$
$$\forall v \in V \ \exists u \in U \ (\alpha_u = \alpha_v \text{ and } \llbracket N_u \rrbracket^K = \llbracket N'_v \rrbracket^K) \ ,$$

which implies $\llbracket N \rrbracket^K = \llbracket N' \rrbracket^K$. A similar argument shows that $\llbracket N \rrbracket^K = \llbracket N' \rrbracket^K$ implies $N \sim^{n+1} N'$. □

The interpretation of normal forms is canonically lifted to all processes, by taking the continuous extensions (cf. equation 9.4) of the functions defined in figure 9.3, and interpreting $fix$ as the least fixpoint. This is spelled out in the following definition.

**Definition 9.3.11 (interpretation)** *Let $V$ be the collection of process variables, and let $\rho : V \to D$ be an environment. We interpret a process $P$ in the environment $\rho$ as follows (we have $\llbracket P \rrbracket \rho \in D$):*

$$
\begin{aligned}
\llbracket 0 \rrbracket \rho &= \downarrow(\emptyset) \\
\llbracket \alpha.P \rrbracket \rho &= \bigcup \{\downarrow (Pre_\alpha(d)) \mid d \in \llbracket P \rrbracket \rho\} \\
\llbracket P + P' \rrbracket \rho &= \bigcup \{\downarrow (Sum(d, d')) \mid d \in \llbracket P \rrbracket \rho, d' \in \llbracket P' \rrbracket \rho\} \\
\llbracket P\backslash a \rrbracket \rho &= \bigcup \{\downarrow (Res_a(d)) \mid d \in \llbracket P \rrbracket \rho\} \\
\llbracket P \mid P' \rrbracket \rho &= \bigcup \{\downarrow (Par(d, d')) \mid d \in \llbracket P \rrbracket \rho, d' \in \llbracket P' \rrbracket \rho\} \\
\llbracket fix X.P \rrbracket \rho &= \bigcup_{n \in \omega} I_n \text{ with } I_0 = \downarrow(\{\bot\}), I_{n+1} = \llbracket P \rrbracket \rho[I_n/X] \\
\llbracket X \rrbracket \rho &= \rho(X) \ .
\end{aligned}
$$

**Exercise 9.3.12** *Prove that the function $\lambda d.\llbracket P \rrbracket \rho[d/X]$ is continuous.*

**Lemma 9.3.13 (approximation)** *For any process $P$, $n \in \omega$,*

$$p_n(\llbracket P \rrbracket) = \llbracket (P)_n \rrbracket \ .$$

PROOF HINT. Recall that $p_n(\llbracket P \rrbracket) = \llbracket P \rrbracket \cap K_n$. We prove the statement by induction on $(n, nfix(P), P)$. We consider a few significant cases using the properties stated in exercise 9.3.4.

$(\alpha.P)$ We compute:

$$
\begin{aligned}
\llbracket \alpha.P \rrbracket \cap K_{n+1} &= \bigcup \{\downarrow (\{(\alpha, d)\}) \mid d \in \llbracket P \rrbracket\} \cap K_{n+1} \\
&= \bigcup \{\downarrow (\{(\alpha, d)\}) \mid d \in \llbracket P \rrbracket \cap K_n\} \\
&= \bigcup \{\downarrow (\{(\alpha, d)\}) \mid d \leq \llbracket (P)_n \rrbracket^K\} \\
&= \downarrow (\{(\alpha, \llbracket (P)_n \rrbracket^K)\}) \\
&= \downarrow (\llbracket (\alpha.P)_{n+1} \rrbracket^K) \ .
\end{aligned}
$$

$(fixX.P)$  A direct application of the induction hypothesis:

$$\begin{aligned}
[\![fixX.P]\!] \cap K_{n+1} &= [\![P[fixX.P/X]\!]\!] \cap K_{n+1} \\
&= \downarrow ([\![(P[fixX.P/X])_{n+1}]\!]^K) \\
&= \downarrow ([\![(fixX.P)_{n+1}]\!]^K) .
\end{aligned}$$

$(P \mid P')$  We have:

$$\begin{aligned}
[\![P \mid P']\!] \cap K_{n+1} &= \bigcup\{\downarrow (Par(d,d')) \mid d \in [\![P]\!], d' \in [\![P']\!]\} \cap K_{n+1} \\
&= \bigcup\{\downarrow (Par(d,d')) \mid d \in [\![P]\!] \cap K_{n+1}, d' \in [\![P']\!] \cap K_{n+1}\} \cap K_{n+1} \\
&= \bigcup\{\downarrow (Par(d,d')) \mid d \leq [\![(P)_{n+1}]\!]^K, d' \leq [\![(P')_{n+1}]\!]^K\} \cap K_{n+1} \\
&= \downarrow (Par([\![(P)_{n+1}]\!]^K, [\![(P')_{n+1}]\!]^K)) \cap K_{n+1} \\
&= \downarrow ([\![(P \mid P')_{n+1}]\!]^K) .
\end{aligned}$$

To justify the last equation, suppose, e.g., $\alpha = \overline{\alpha'}$, and:

$$\begin{aligned}
(P)_{n+1} = \alpha.N \quad & [\![\alpha.N]\!]^K = \{(\alpha, [\![N]\!]^K)\} = \{(\alpha, d)\} \\
(P')_{n+1} = \alpha'.N' \quad & [\![\alpha.N']\!]^K = \{(\alpha', [\![N']\!]^K)\} = \{(\alpha', d')\} .
\end{aligned}$$

Then we have:

$$\begin{aligned}
&Par([\![(P)_{n+1}]\!]^K, [\![(P')_{n+1}]\!]^K) \\
&= Par(\{(\alpha, d)\}, \{(\alpha', d')\}) \\
&= \{(\alpha, Par(d, \{(\alpha', d')\})), (\alpha', Par(\{(\alpha, d)\}, d')), (\tau, Par(d, d'))\}
\end{aligned}$$

$$\begin{aligned}
&[\![(P \mid P')_{n+1}]\!]^K \\
&= [\![\alpha.(N \mid \alpha'.N')_n + \alpha'.(\alpha.N \mid N')_n + \tau.(N \mid N)_n]\!]^K \\
&= \{(\alpha, [\![(N \mid \alpha'.N')_n]\!]^K), (\alpha', [\![(\alpha.N \mid N')_n]\!]^K), (\tau, [\![(N \mid \alpha'.N')_n]\!]^K)\} .
\end{aligned}$$

We can then apply an inductive argument to show, say:

$$\downarrow ([\![(N \mid \alpha'.N')_n]\!]^K) = \downarrow (Par(d, \{(\alpha', d')\})) \cap K_n . \qquad \square$$

**Theorem 9.3.14 (full abstraction)** *Let $P, Q$ be CCS processes. Then:*

$$P \sim Q \quad \text{iff} \quad [\![P]\!] = [\![Q]\!] .$$

PROOF. We observe:

| | |
|---|---|
| $P \sim Q$ iff $\forall k \in \omega \ ((P)_k \sim^k (Q)_k)$ | (by proposition 9.3.8) |
| $\forall k \in \omega \ ((P)_k \sim^k (Q)_k)$ iff $\forall k \in \omega \ [\![(P)_k]\!] = [\![(Q)_k]\!]$ | (by proposition 9.3.10) |
| $\forall k \in \omega \ [\![(P)_k]\!] = p_k([\![P]\!])$ | (by lemma 9.3.13) |
| $[\![P]\!] = [\![Q]\!]$ iff $\forall k \in \omega \ (p_k([\![P]\!]) = p_k([\![Q]\!]))$ | (since $\bigvee_{k \in \omega} p_k = id$) . $\square$ |

**Remark 9.3.15** (1) *Not all compact elements in $D$ are definable by a CCS process, in particular $\perp$ is not definable. Suppose we add to the CCS processes a process $\Omega = fixX.X$ whose denotation is $\perp$. Then full abstraction fails. For instance we would have $a.0 + \Omega \sim a.0$, whereas $[\![a.0 + \perp]\!] \neq [\![a.0]\!]$. The point is that in the operational semantics, we do not distinguish between a process which is terminated like 0 and a process which diverges like $\Omega$. However, it is possible to refine the bisimulation relation so as to take diverging processes into account (cf. [Abr91b]) and fit the denotational semantics.*

(2) *At the time of writing, the denotational framework described here has not been adapted in a satisfying way to capture weak bisimulation.*

# 10

# Stone duality

We introduce a fundamental duality that arises in topology from the consideration of points versus open sets. A lot of work in topology can be done by working at the level of open sets only. This subject is called the pointless topology, and can be studied in [Joh82]. It leads generally to formulations and proofs of a more constructive nature than the ones 'with points'. For the purpose of computer science, this duality is quite suggestive: points correspond to programs, and open sets to program properties. The investigation of Stone duality for domains has been pioneered by Martin-Löf [ML83] and by Smyth [Smy83b]. The work on intersection types, particularly in relation with the $D^\infty$ models, as exposed in chapter 3, appears as an even earlier precursor. We also recommend [Vic89], which offers a computer science oriented introduction to Stone duality.

In section 10.1, we introduce locales, and Stone duality in its most abstract form. In sections 10.2 and 10.4, we specialize the construction to various categories of dcpo's and continuous functions, most notably those of Scott domains and of profinite dcpo's (cf. definition 5.2.2). On the way, in section 10.3, we prove Stone's theorem: every Boolean algebra is order-isomorphic to an algebra of subsets of some set $X$, closed under set theoretical intersection, union, and complementation. The proof of Stone's theorem involves a form of the axiom of choice (Zorn's lemma), used in the proof of an important technical lemma known as Scott open filter theorem. In contrast, dualities for various categories of algebraic dcpo's can be proved straightforwardly, as a specialization of a simple duality, which we call the basic domain duality. Once the dualities are laid down, we can present the domain constructions 'logically', by means of formulas representing the compact open sets. This programme, which has been carried out quite thoroughly by Abramsky, is sketched in sections 10.5 and 10.6.

We recall that a lattice is a poset with all finite lub's and glb's, that a complete lattice is a poset with all lub's and glb's, that a distributive lattice is a lattice $X$ where $x \wedge (y \vee z) = (x \wedge y) \vee (x \wedge z)$ for all $x, y, z \in X$, and finally that a Boolean algebra is a distributive lattice $B$ in which every element $x$ has a (unique) complement $\neg x$ characterized by $x \wedge (\neg x) = 0$ and $x \vee (\neg x) = 1$ (where $0, 1$ denote the bottom and top element of $B$). We write **Top** to denote the category of topological spaces and continuous functions.

# 10.1  Topological spaces and locales

If we abstract away from the order theoretical properties of the open sets of a topology, we arrive at the following definition.

**Definition 10.1.1 (locale)** *A locale, or a frame, is an ordered set* $(A, \leq)$ *satisfying the following properties:*

(1) *Every finite subset of $A$ has a greatest lower bound.*

(2) *Every subset of $A$ has a least upper bound.*

(3) *The following infinite distributivity property holds, for any $x \in A$ and $Y \subseteq A$:*

$$x \wedge \left( \bigvee Y \right) = \bigvee \{ x \wedge y \mid y \in Y \} \, .$$

In particular, there is a minimum (the empty lub) and a maximum (the empty glb). For any topological space $(X, \Omega X)$, the collection $\Omega X$, ordered by inclusion, is a locale. The elements of a locale will be often called open sets, even if the locale does not arise as a topology. We make some remarks about this definition:

• Condition (1) is implied by condition (2), which in fact implies that all glb's exist. But the maps we consider being those which preserve finite glb's and arbitrary lub's, it is natural to put condition (1) explicitly in the definition of a locale.

• Locales are equivalently defined as complete Heyting algebras, where a complete Heyting algebra is a complete lattice which viewed as a partial order is cartesian closed (cf. definition 4.2.3 and proposition A2.5.3).

**Definition 10.1.2 (frames/locales)** *The category* **Frm** *of frames is the category whose objects are locales, and whose morphisms are the functions preserving finite glb's and all lub's. The category* **Loc** *of locales is defined as* **Frm**$^{op}$. *Locales and frames are named such according to which category is meant.*

Since we develop the theory of locales as an abstraction of the situation with topological spaces, it is natural to focus on **Loc**: for any continuous function $f : (X, \Omega X) \to (Y, \Omega Y)$, the function $f^{-1}$ is a locale morphism from $\Omega X$ to $\Omega Y$.

**Definition 10.1.3** *The functor* $\Omega :$ **Top** $\to$ **Loc**, *called the localization functor, is defined by:*

$$\Omega(X, \Omega X) = \Omega X \qquad \Omega(f) = f^{-1}.$$

The flat domain $\mathbf{O} = \{\bot, \top\}$ (cf. example 1.1.6) lives both in **Top** (endowed with its Scott topology $\{\emptyset, \{\top\}, \{\bot, \top\}\}$, cf. section 1.2) and in **Loc**, and plays a remarkable role in each of these categories:

**Top** : For any topological space $(X, \Omega X)$, the open sets in $\Omega X$ are in one-to-one correspondence with the continuous functions from $(X, \Omega X)$ to $\mathbf{O}$.

**Loc** : The locale $\mathbf{O}$ is terminal in **Loc**: let $(A, \leq)$ be a locale, and $f : A \to \{\bot, \top\}$ be a locale morphism. Then $f(\bot) = \bot$ and $f(\top) = \top$, since the minimum and maximum elements must be preserved.

The fact that $\mathbf{O}$ is terminal in $\mathbf{Loc}$ suggests a way to recover a topological space out of a locale. We shall define points of a locale $A$ to be locale morphisms $g : \{\bot, \top\} \to A$. One may approach the reconstruction of points from open sets in a perhaps more informative way by analyzing the situation of the locale $\Omega X$ of some topological space $X$. If we try to recover a point $x$ out of the locale $\Omega X$, the simplest idea is to collect all the open sets that contain it. The fact that the mapping $x \mapsto \{U \mid x \in U\}$ is injective is exactly the property of the topology to be $T_0$. Any set $F = \{U \mid x \in U\}$ ($x$ fixed) has the following properties:

(1) It is closed under finite intersection.

(2) It is upward closed.

(3) If $P \subseteq \Omega X$ and $\bigcup P \in F$, then $U \in F$ for some $U$ in $P$.

The first two conditions are those defining filters (cf. chapter 3). We abstract the three properties together in the following definition.

**Definition 10.1.4 ((completely coprime) filter)** *Let $A$ be a partial order. A filter over $A$ is an ideal over $A^{op}$, that is, a non-empty subset $F$ such that:*

*(1) If $x \in F$ and $x \leq y$, then $y \in F$.*

*(2) $\forall x, y \in F \ \exists z \in F \ z \leq x, y$.*

*Clearly, in a lower semi-lattice, and in presence of condition (1), condition (2) can be rephrased as (cf. definition 3.3.8):*

*(2') $\forall x, y \in F \ x \wedge y \in F$.*

*A filter $F$ in (a complete lattice) $A$ is called completely coprime if*

*(3) $\forall Y \subseteq A \ (\bigvee Y \in F \ \Rightarrow \ \exists y \in Y \ y \in F)$ .*

*We consider two restrictions of condition (3) (in a lattice, in a dcpo, respectively):*

*(3') $\forall Y \subseteq_{fin} A \ (\bigvee Y \in F \ \Rightarrow \ \exists y \in Y \ y \in F)$ .*

*(3'') $\forall Y \subseteq_{dir} A \ (\bigvee Y \in F \ \Rightarrow \ \exists y \in Y \ y \in F)$ .*

*A filter satisfying (3') is called coprime, and a filter satisfying (3'') is called a Scott open filter (indeed, (3'') is the familiar condition defining Scott open sets, cf. definition 1.2.1). We write:*

- *$\mathcal{F}(A)$ for the set of filters of $A$,*

- *$Spec(A)$ for the set of coprime filters of $A$,*

- *$Pt(A)$ for the set of completely coprime filters of $A$.*

*All these sets are ordered by inclusion.*

Remark that if $\bot = \bigvee \emptyset \in F$, then $F$ is not coprime. In particular, coprime filters are proper subsets.

Here is a third presentation of the same notion. The complement $G$ of a completely coprime filter $F$ is clearly downward closed, and is closed under arbitrary lub's. In particular $G = \downarrow (\bigvee G)$, and we have, by conditions (1) and (2):

$$\bigwedge P \leq \bigvee G \ (P \ finite) \ \Rightarrow \ \exists p \in P \ p \leq \bigvee G \ .$$

**Definition 10.1.5 ((co)prime)** *Let* $(X, \leq)$ *be a partial order. An element* $x$ *of* $X$ *is called prime if*

$$\forall P \subseteq_{fin} X \ (\bigwedge P \text{ exists and } \bigwedge P \leq x) \Rightarrow \exists p \in P \ p \leq x \ .$$

*Dually, a coprime element is an element* $y$ *such that for any finite* $Q \subseteq X$*, if* $\bigvee P$ *exists and* $x \leq \bigvee Q$*, then* $x \leq q$ *for some* $q \in Q$*.*

Notice that a prime element cannot be $\top$ $(= \bigwedge \emptyset)$. Dually, the minimum, if it exists, is not coprime.

**Exercise 10.1.6** *Show that if* $(X, \leq)$ *is a distributive lattice then* $z \in X$ *is coprime iff it is* irreducible*, i.e.,* $z = x \vee y$ *always implies* $x = z$ *or* $y = z$*.*

Thus the complements of completely coprime filters are exactly the sets of the form $\downarrow q$, where $q$ is prime, and there is a one-to-one correspondence between prime open sets and completely coprime filters. The following proposition summarizes the discussion.

**Proposition 10.1.7 (points)** *The following are three equivalent definitions of the set* $Pt(A)$ *of points a locale* $A$*:*

(1) *Locale morphisms from* $\mathbf{O}$ *to* $A$*.*

(2) *Completely coprime filters of* $A$*.*

(3) *Prime elements of* $A$*.*

*For* $x \in Pt(A)$ *and* $p \in A$ *we write* $x \models p$ *to mean* $x(p) = \top$*,* $p \in x$*, or* $p \not\leq x$*, depending on how points are defined. The most standard view is* $p \in x$ *(completely coprime filters).*

We have further to endow the set of points of a locale $A$ with a topology.

**Proposition 10.1.8** *For any locale* $A$*, the collection* $\{U_p\}_{p \in A}$ *defined by* $U_p = \{x \mid x \models p\}$ *is a topology over* $Pt(A)$*. This topology, being the image of* $p \mapsto \{x \mid x \models p\}$*, is called the image topology.*

PROOF. We have $U_p \cap U_q = U_{p \wedge q}$, and $\bigcup \{U_p \mid p \in B\} = U_{\bigvee B}$ for any $B \subseteq A$. □

The following result states that we did the right construction to get a topological space out of a locale. We call spatialization, or $Pt$, the operation that takes a locale to its set of points with the image topology.

**Proposition 10.1.9** $(\Omega \dashv Pt)$ *The spatialization* $A \mapsto Pt(A)$ *provides a right adjoint to the localization functor* $\Omega$ *(cf. definition 10.1.3). The counity at* $A$ *is the map* $p \mapsto \{x \mid x \models p\}$ *(in* **Loc***), and the unity is the map* $x \mapsto \{U \mid x \in U\}$ *(in* **Top***).*

PROOF HINT. Take as inverses:

$$f \mapsto (p \mapsto f^{-1}(\{y \mid y \models p\})) \quad (f : X \to Pt(B) \text{ (in } \mathbf{Top}), p \in B)$$
$$g \mapsto (x \mapsto \{p \mid x \in g(p)\}) \quad (g : \Omega X \to B \text{ (in } \mathbf{Loc}), x \in X) \ . \qquad \square$$

**Proposition 10.1.10 (basic duality)** *The adjunction* $\Omega \dashv Pt$ *cuts down to an equivalence, called the basic duality, between the categories of* spatial *locales and of* sober *spaces, which are the locales at which the counity is iso and the topological spaces at which the unity is iso, respectively.*

PROOF. Cf. exercise A2.6.4. □

We shall restrict the basic duality to some full subcategories of topological spaces and locales.

The following is an intrinsic description of sober spaces. We recall that the closure $\overline{A}$ of a subset $A$ is the smallest closed subset containing it.

**Proposition 10.1.11 (sober-irreducible)** *Let* $(X, \Omega X)$ *be a* $T_0$-*space. The following are equivalent:*

(1) $(X, \Omega X)$ *is sober.*

(2) *Each irreducible closed set (cf. exercise 10.1.6) is of the form* $\overline{\{x\}}$.

(3) *Each prime open set is of the form* $X \backslash \overline{\{x\}}$ *for some* $x$.

PROOF. Looking at the unity of the adjunction, sober means: 'all the completely coprime filters are of the form $\{U \mid x \in U\}$'. By proposition 10.1.7, this can be reformulated as: 'all the prime open sets are of the form $\bigcup \{U \mid x \notin U\}$', which is the complement of $\overline{\{x\}}$. □

**Remark 10.1.12** *Any set of the form* $\overline{\{x\}}$ *is irreducible, so that in sober spaces, the irreducible closed sets are exactly those of the form* $\overline{\{x\}}$ *for some* $x$.

By definition of spatiality, a locale $A$ is spatial if and only if, for all $a, b \in A$:

$$(\forall x \in Pt(A) \quad x \models a \Rightarrow x \models b) \Rightarrow a \leq b,$$

or equivalently: $a \nleq b \Rightarrow \exists x \in Pt(A) \quad x \models a$ and $x \not\models b$. Actually, it is enough to find a Scott open filter $F$ such that $a \in F$ and $b \notin F$. But a form of the axiom of choice is needed to prove this.

**Theorem 10.1.13 (Scott open filter)** *Let* $A$ *be a locale. The following properties hold:*

(1) *For every Scott open filter* $F$, *we have* $\bigcap \{x \in Pt(A) \mid F \subseteq x\} = F$.

(2) $A$ *is spatial iff for all* $a, b \in A$ *such that* $a \nleq b$ *there exists a Scott open filter* $F$ *such that* $a \in F$ *and* $b \notin F$.

PROOF. (1) The direction $\supseteq$ is obvious. We prove $\subseteq$ by contraposition. Suppose $a \notin F$. We want to find an $x$ such that $F \subseteq x$ and $a \notin x$. We claim that there exists a prime open set $p$ such that $p \notin F$ and $a \leq p$. Then we can take $x = \{c \mid c \nleq p\}$. Consider the set $P$ of open sets $b$ such that $b \notin F$ and $a \leq b$. It contains $a$, and every chain of $P$ has an upper bound in $P$ (actually the lub of any directed subset of $P$ is in $P$, because $F$ is Scott open). By Zorn's lemma, $P$ contains a maximal element $q$. We show that $q$ is prime. Suppose that $S$ is a finite set of open sets, and that $b \not\leq q$ for each $b$ in $S$. Then $b \vee q$ is larger than $q$, and thus belongs to $F$, by maximality of $q$. Since $F$ is a filter, it also contains $\bigwedge \{b \vee q \mid b \in S\} = (\bigwedge S) \vee q$, which is therefore larger than $q$, by maximality of $q$. Hence $\bigwedge S \not\leq q$, $q$ is prime, and the claim follows.

(2) One direction follows obviously from the fact that a point is *a fortiori* a Scott open filter. Conversely, if $a \in F$ and $b \notin F$, by (1) there exists a point $x$ such that $F \subseteq x$ and $b \notin x$. Then $x$ fits since $a \in F$ and $F \subseteq x$ imply $a \in x$. □

We shall not use theorem 10.1.13 for the Stone dualities of domains. But it is important for Stone's theorem (section 10.3).

We now exhibit examples of sober spaces. We recall that a $T_2$ space, or Hausdorff space, is a topological space such that any distinct points may be separated by disjoint open sets.

**Proposition 10.1.14** *$T_2$-spaces are sober.*

PROOF. Let $W$ be a prime open set; in particular its complement is non-empty. Suppose that two distinct elements $x, y$ are in the complement, and take disjoint $U, V$ containing $x, y$ respectively. Then $U \cap V$, being empty, is *a fortiori* contained in $W$, but neither $U$ nor $V$ are, contradicting primeness of $W$. Thus a prime open set $W$ is necessarily the complement of a singleton $\{x\}$. We conclude by proposition 10.1.11 (in a $T_1$-space, $\{x\} = \overline{\{x\}}$). □

In exercise 1.2.6 we have anticipated that algebraic dcpo's are sober. This provides an example of a non-$T_2$ (even non-$T_1$, cf. chapter 1) sober space. Actually, more generally, continuous dcpo's (cf. definition 5.1.1) are sober. Before proving this, we exhibit a friendlier presentation of $\overline{\{x\}}$ in suitable topologies on partial orders.

**Proposition 10.1.15** *Given a poset $X$, and a topology $\Omega$ over $X$, the following are equivalent:*

(1) $\forall x \in X \; \overline{\{x\}} = \downarrow x$,

(2) *weak* $\subseteq \Omega \subseteq$ *Alexandrov*,

(3) $\leq_\Omega = \leq$,

*where the weak topology is given by the basis $\{X \backslash (\downarrow x) \mid x \in X\}$, and where $\leq_\Omega$ is the specialization ordering defined by $\Omega$.*[1]

PROOF. (2) $\Rightarrow$ (1) If $x \in A$ ($A$ closed), then $\downarrow x \subseteq A$, since $\Omega \subseteq$ *Alexandrov*. Moreover $\downarrow x$ is closed, since *weak* $\subseteq \Omega$. Hence $\overline{\{x\}} = \downarrow x$.

(1) $\Rightarrow$ (2) If $\overline{\{x\}} = \downarrow x$, then *a fortiori* $\downarrow x$ is closed, hence *weak* $\subseteq \Omega$. If $A$ is closed and $x \in A$, then $\overline{\{x\}} \subseteq A$, hence $\Omega \subseteq$ *Alexandrov*.

(2) $\Leftrightarrow$ (3) We have:

---

[1] We refer to section 1.2 for the definition of Alexandrov topology and of the specialization ordering.

- $\leq\; \subseteq\; \leq_\Omega \Leftrightarrow (x \in U, x \leq y \Rightarrow y \in U) \Leftrightarrow \Omega \subseteq Alexandrov.$

- $(weak \subseteq \Omega) \Rightarrow (\leq_\Omega \subseteq \leq)$. Suppose $x \nleq y$. Then $X\backslash(\downarrow y)$ is an open set containing $x$ but not $y$, hence $x \nleq_\Omega y$.

- $(\leq_\Omega \subseteq \leq$ and $\Omega \subseteq Alexandrov) \Rightarrow (weak \subseteq \Omega)$. We have to prove that any $X\backslash(\downarrow x)$ is in $\Omega$. Pick $y \in X\backslash(\downarrow x)$, i.e., $y \nleq x$. Then $\leq_\Omega \subseteq \leq$ implies that there exists an open set $U_y$ such that $y \in U_y$ and $x \notin U_y$. Since $\Omega \subseteq Alexandrov$ implies $z \notin U_y$ for all $z \leq x$, we have $U_y \subseteq X\backslash(\downarrow x)$. It follows that $X\backslash(\downarrow x)$ is open.$\square$

Proposition 10.1.15 applies in particular to the Scott topology $\tau_S$, since $weak \subseteq \tau_S$ (cf. exercise 1.2.2) and since $\tau_S \subseteq Alexandrov$ by definition.

**Proposition 10.1.16** *The Scott topology for a continuous dcpo is sober.*

PROOF. Let $A$ be closed irreducible, and consider $B = \bigcup_{a\in A} \Downarrow a$, (cf. definition 5.1.1). We first prove that $B$ is directed. Suppose not: let $d, d' \in B$ such that there exists no $a \in A$ and $d'' \ll a$ such that $d, d' \leq d''$. We claim:

$$(\Uparrow d) \cap (\Uparrow d') \cap A = \emptyset .$$

Indeed, suppose $d, d' \ll a$ for some $a \in A$. Then by directedness of $\Downarrow a$ there would exist $d'' \ll a$ such that $d, d' \leq d''$, contradicting our assumption about $d, d'$. This proves the claim, which we rephrase as:

$$A \subseteq (D\backslash(\Uparrow d)) \cup (D\backslash(\Uparrow d')) .$$

But this contradicts the irreducibility of $A$, since $\Uparrow d$ and $\Uparrow d'$ are open (see exercise 5.1.14), and since $d, d' \in B$ can be rephrased as:

$$A \cap (\Uparrow d) \neq \emptyset \text{ and } A \cap (\Uparrow d') \neq \emptyset .$$

Hence $B$ is directed. Since closed sets are closed downwards, we have $B \subseteq A$. Hence $\bigvee B \in A$ since $A$ is closed. We show that $\bigvee B$ is an upper bound of $A$: this follows immediately from the definition of continuous dcpo: if $a \in A$, then $a = \bigvee \Downarrow a \leq \bigvee B$. Therefore $A =\downarrow (\bigvee B) = \overline{\{\bigvee B\}}$.  $\square$

Scott topologies are not always sober.

**Proposition 10.1.17 (Johnstone)** *Consider* $\omega \cup \{\infty\}$, *ordered by:* $n \leq n'$ *iff* $n \leq n'$ *in* $\omega$ *or* $n' = \infty$. *Consider the following partial order on the set* $D = \omega \times (\omega \cup \{\infty\})$:

$$(m, n) \leq (m', n') \quad \text{iff} \quad (m = m' \text{ and } n \leq n') \text{ or } (n' = \infty \text{ and } n \leq m') .$$

*This forms a dcpo. Its Scott topology is not sober.*

PROOF. We first check that we have a dcpo. We claim that any element $(m, \infty)$ is maximal. Let $(m, \infty) \leq (m', n')$: if $m = m'$ and $\infty \leq n'$, then $\infty = n'$, while the other alternative ($n' = \infty$ and $\infty \leq m'$) cannot arise because $m'$ ranges over

$\omega$. In particular, there is no maximum element, since the elements $(m, \infty)$ are comparable only when they are equal.

Let $\Delta$ be directed. If it contains some $(m, \infty)$, then it has a maximum. Otherwise let $(m', n')$, $(m'', n'')$ be two elements of $\Delta$: a common upper bound in $\Delta$ can only be of the form $(m''', n''')$, with $m'''' = m' = m''$. Hence $\Delta = \{m\} \times \Delta'$, for some $m$ and some $\Delta' \subseteq_{dir} \omega$. It is then obvious that $\Delta$ has a lub.

Next we observe that a non-empty Scott open set contains all elements $(p, \infty)$, for $p$ sufficiently large. Indeed, if $(m, n) \in U$, then $p \geq n \Rightarrow (m, n) \leq (p, \infty)$. In particular, any finite intersection of non-empty open sets is non empty. In other words $\emptyset$ is a prime open set, or, equivalently, the whole space $\omega \times (\omega \cup \{\infty\})$ is irreducible. By proposition 10.1.15, we should have $D = \downarrow x$ for some $x$, but we have seen that $D$ has no maximum. $\square$

Nevertheless, sober spaces have something to do with Scott topology.

**Proposition 10.1.18** *The specialization order of any sober space $(X, \Omega)$ forms a dcpo, whose Scott topology contains $\Omega$.*

PROOF. Let $S$ be $\leq_\Omega$-directed. We show that its closure $\overline{S}$ is irreducible. Let $\overline{S} = F_1 \cup F_2$, and suppose $S \not\subseteq F_1$ and $S \not\subseteq F_1$. Let $x \in S \backslash F_1$ and $y \in S \backslash F_2$, and let $z \geq_\Omega x, y$ in $S$. Since $S \subseteq F_1 \cup F_2$, we have, say, $z \in F_1$. Then $x \in F_1$ by definition of $\leq_\Omega$: contradiction. Therefore $\overline{S} = \overline{\{y\}}$ for some $y$.

- $y$ is an upper bound. Pick $s \in S$ and suppose $y \notin U$. Then $\overline{S} = \overline{\{y\}} \subseteq X \backslash U$, and *a fortiori* $s \notin U$. Hence $s \leq_\Omega y$.

The rest of the statement follows from the following claim:

For any open set $U$, if $S \cap U = \emptyset$, then $y \notin U$ .

Indeed, $S \cap U = \emptyset$ implies $\overline{S} \cap U = \emptyset$, and *a fortiori* $y \notin U$.

- $y$ is the least upper bound. Let $z$ be an upper bound of $S$, and suppose $z \notin U$. Then $S \cap U = \emptyset$ by definition of $\leq_\Omega$, and $y \notin U$ follows by the claim.

- Any open set is Scott open. By the claim, since we now know that $y = \bigvee S$. $\square$

**Exercise 10.1.19** *Show that the statement of proposition 10.1.17 can actually be strengthened by replacing 'Its Scott topology is not sober' by: 'There is no sober topology whose specialization order is the order of $D$'. Hint: Use proposition 10.1.18.*

We end the section by mentioning another characterization of sobriety and spatiality, obtained by exploiting the fact that in the adjunction $\Omega \dashv Pt$ the counity is mono (by definition of the topology on $Pt(A)$, the map $p \mapsto \{x \mid x \models p\}$ is surjective, hence, as a locale morphism, is a mono).

**Proposition 10.1.20** *Spatial locales and sober spaces are those topological spaces which are isomorphic to $\Omega X$ for some topological space $X$, and to $Pt(A)$ for some locale $A$, respectively.*

PROOF. By application of lemma A2.6.6 to the adjunction $\Omega \dashv Pt$. $\square$

# 10.2    The duality for algebraic dcpo's

We recall that in algebraic dcpo's the basic Scott open sets have the form $\uparrow a$ ($a$ compact), and have the remarkable property that if $\uparrow a \subseteq \bigcup_i U_i$, then $\uparrow a \subseteq U_i$ for some $i$. This motivates the following definition.

**Definition 10.2.1 (coprime algebraic)** *Let $(A, \leq)$ be a partial order. A compact coprime element is an element $a$ such that, for all $B \subseteq A$, if $\bigvee B$ exists and $a \leq \bigvee B$, then $a \leq b$ for some $b \in B$. A poset $(D, \leq)$ is called coprime algebraic if each element of $D$ is the lub of the compact coprime elements it dominates. We write $\mathcal{C}(D)$ for the set of compact coprime elements of $D$.*

**Remark 10.2.2** *In definition 10.2.1, we do not specify under which lub's we assume $A$ to be closed. In this chapter we are concerned with complete lattices, and in chapter 12, we shall have to do with bounded complete coprime algebraic cpo's.*

**Exercise 10.2.3** *Let $D$ be a partial order in which all finite bounded lub's exist. (1) Show that $D$ is coprime algebraic iff it is algebraic and satisfies the following decomposition property: every compact element is a finite lub of compact coprime elements (cf. exercise 1.4.10). (2) Show that under the finite bounded lub's assumption 'compact coprime' is the same as 'compact and coprime'.*

**Lemma 10.2.4 (lower-set completion)** *A complete lattice $D$ is coprime algebraic iff it is isomorphic to the lower set completion of some partial order $(X, \leq)$, defined as $Dcl(X) = \{Y \subseteq X \mid Y \text{ is a lower subset}\}$ ('lower' is synonymous of 'downward closed'), and we have then $D \cong Dcl(\mathcal{C}(D))$. In particular, a coprime algebraic partial order is a (spatial) locale, since $Dcl(X)$ is Alexandrov's topology over $(X, \geq)$.*

PROOF. Like the proof of proposition 1.1.21.                                    □

**Lemma 10.2.5** *Let $A$ be a coprime algebraic locale. The points of $A$ are in one-to-one correspondence with the filters over the set $\mathcal{C}(A)$ of compact coprime elements of $A$.*

PROOF. The inverses are $G \mapsto \uparrow G$ and $F \mapsto \{x \in F \mid x \text{ compact coprime}\}$.    □

**Proposition 10.2.6 (duality – algebraic dcpo's)** *The basic duality cuts down to an equivalence between the category **Adcpo** of algebraic dcpo's and continuous functions, and the category of locales arising as lower set completion of some partial order.*

PROOF. By lemma 10.2.4, any coprime algebraic locale is spatial. By proposition 1.1.21, any algebraic dcpo is isomorphic to $Ide(X)$ for some partial order $(X, \leq)$. By lemma 10.2.5 we have:

$$Ide(X) = \mathcal{F}(X^{op}) \cong Pt(Dcl(X^{op})) \,.$$

(We omit the proof that the topology induced by $Pt$ on $Ide(X)$ is the Scott topology.) Therefore, up to isomorphism, the class of algebraic dcpo's is the image under $Pt$ of the class of coprime algebraic locales. The statement then follows (cf. exercise A2.6.5).                                                                                                           $\Box$

We call the duality algebraic dcpo's/coprime algebraic locales the *basic domain duality*. The key to this duality is that both terms of the duality have a common reference, namely the set $\mathcal{C}(A)$ of compact coprime elements on the localic side, the set $\mathcal{K}(D)$ of compact elements on the spatial side, with opposite orders:

$$(\mathcal{K}(D), \leq) \cong (\mathcal{C}(A), \geq) .$$

We shall obtain other dualities for various kinds of domains as restrictions of the basic domain duality, through the following meta-lemma.

**Lemma 10.2.7** *If $(S)$ is a property of algebraic dcpo's and $(L)$ is a property of locales such that any algebraic dcpo satisfies $(S)$ iff its Scott topology satisfies $(L)$, then the basic domain duality cuts down to a duality between the category of algebraic dcpo's satisfying $(S)$ and the category of coprime algebraic locales satisfying $(L)$.*

PROOF. Cf. exercise A2.6.5.                                                                    $\Box$

Here are two examples of the use of lemma 10.2.7.

**Proposition 10.2.8 (duality – algebraic cpo's)** *The basic domain duality restricts to an equivalence between the category* **Acpo** *of algebraic cpo's and continuous functions, and the category of locales arising as lower set completion of a partial order having a largest element.*

PROOF. By lemma 10.2.7, with 'has a minimum element' and 'has a maximum compact coprime element' for $(S)$ and $(L)$, respectively. If $D$ satisfies $(S)$, then $\uparrow \bot$ fits. If $\uparrow x$ is the maximum compact coprime element of $\Omega D$, then $\uparrow y \subseteq \uparrow x$ for any other compact coprime element, i.e., $x$ is minimum.                                  $\Box$

**Proposition 10.2.9 (duality – Scott domains)** *The basic domain duality cuts down to an equivalence between the category of Scott domains (cf. definition 1.4.9) and continuous functions, and the category of locales arising as lower set completion of a conditional lower semi-lattice (i.e., a poset in which every finite lower bounded subset has a glb).*

PROOF. We take 'has a minimum element and binary compatible lub's' and 'compact coprime elements form a conditional lower semi-lattice' as $(S)$ and $(L)$, respectively, and we notice that $x \vee y$ exists iff $\uparrow x, \uparrow y$ have a glb.          $\Box$

The following gives an alternative characterization of the locales arising as lower set completion of a conditional lower semi-lattice.

**Proposition 10.2.10** *The following conditions are equivalent for a coprime algebraic locale A:*

(1) *A is isomorphic to the lower set completion of a conditional lower semi-lattice.*

(2) *Finite glb's of compact elements are compact and any finite glb of compact coprime elements is coprime or $\perp$.*

PROOF. By proposition 10.2.4, (1) can be replaced by:

(1') *The compact coprime elements of A form a conditional lower semi-lattice.*

Also, since all lub's exist in $A$, glb's also exist and are defined by (for any $P$):

$$\bigwedge P = \bigvee\{x \mid \forall p \in P \; x \leq p\} = \bigvee\{q \mid q \text{ compact coprime and } \forall p \in P \; q \leq p\} \, .$$

Now, consider a finite set $P$ of compact coprime elements. There are two cases:

(a) $P$ has no compact coprime lower bound: then $\bigwedge P = \bigvee \emptyset = \perp$.

(b) $P$ has a compact coprime lower bound: then $\bigwedge P \neq \perp$.

(1') $\Rightarrow$ (2) We already know that $A$ is a locale; *a fortiori* it is distributive. Let $d = a_1 \vee \cdots \vee a_m$ and $e = b_1 \vee \cdots \vee b_n$ be two compact elements, expressed as finite lub's of compact coprime elements (cf. exercise 10.2.3). Then $d \wedge e = \bigvee_{i,j}(a_i \wedge b_j)$. It is enough to check that each $a_i \wedge b_j$ is compact. If $\{a_i, b_j\}$ has no compact coprime lower bound, then $a_i \wedge b_j = \perp$, which is compact. Otherwise, $a_i \wedge b_j$ is compact by (1'). We have shown that finite non-empty glb's of compact elements are compact. By (1'), the empty glb is compact coprime, hence is *a fortiori* compact. Consider now a finite set $P$ of compact coprime elements. Then either $\bigwedge P = \perp$ (case (a)), or $\bigwedge P$ is compact coprime, by the assumption (1') (case (b)).

(2) $\Rightarrow$ (1') We have to prove that, in case (b), $\bigwedge P$ is compact and coprime. It is compact by the first part of (2). By the second part of (2), $\bigwedge P$ is either coprime or $\perp$. Since (b) implies $\bigwedge P \neq \perp$, $\bigwedge P$ is coprime. $\square$

**Information Systems.** An alternative description of Scott domains is obtained by starting, not from a conditional upper semi-lattice, but from a partial order equipped with a weaker structure, which we first motivate. Let $A$ be a conditional upper semi-lattice. Let $I_1, I_2, I \in Ide(A)$ be such that $I_1, I_2 \subseteq I$. Then the lub of $I_1, I_2$ is given by the following formula:

$$I_1 \vee I_2 = \{a \mid a \leq \bigvee X \text{ for some } X \subseteq_{fin} I_1 \cup I_2\} \, .$$

This suggests that we consider the collection of the finite bounded subsets $X$ of $A$, and the pairs $(X, a)$ with the property $a \leq \bigvee X$. It turns out that we actually do not need to be so specific about this structure. It is enough to have a distinguished collection $Con$ of finite subsets over which $X$ ranges, and an 'entailment' relation $\vdash$ consisting of pairs $(X, a)$. This view leads us to Scott's notion of information system [Sco82], whose axioms we shall discover progressively.

Given a partial order $A$ of tokens, a set $Con$ of finite subsets of $A$, and a relation $\vdash \subseteq Con \times A$, we construct a 'completion' whose elements are the non-empty subsets $x \in A$ which satisfy:

(1)  $X \subseteq_{fin} x \Rightarrow X \in Con$.

(2)  $(X \subseteq_{fin} x$ and $X \vdash a) \Rightarrow a \in x$.

If $A$ is a conditional upper semi-lattice, if $Con$ is the boundedness predicate and $X \vdash a$ is defined by $a \leq \bigvee X$, then it is easily checked that conditions (1) and (2) together characterize the ideals of $A$ (notice that (1) is weaker than directedness, and (2) is stronger than downward closedness). We check that a directed union $\Delta$ of elements is an element: if $X \subseteq_{fin} \bigcup \Delta$, then $X \subseteq_{fin} x$ for some $x \in \Delta$ (by directedness), and (1) and (2) for $\bigcup \Delta$ follow from (1) and (2) applied to $x$.

Candidates for the compact elements are the elements of the form $\overline{X} = \{a \mid X \vdash a\}$. The sets $\overline{X}$ are not necessarily finite, but can be considered finitely generated from $X$. We expect that $X \subseteq \overline{X}$ and that $\overline{X}$ is an element (which by construction is the smallest containing $X$). This is easily proved thanks to the following axioms:

- (A)  $(X \in Con$ and $a \in X) \Rightarrow X \vdash a$,
- (B)  $X \subseteq Y \in Con \Rightarrow X \in Con$,
- (C)  $X \vdash a \Rightarrow X \cup \{a\} \in Con$,
- (D)  $(\{a_1, \ldots, a_n\} \vdash a$ and $X \vdash a_1, \ldots, X \vdash a_n) \Rightarrow X \vdash a$.

Axiom (D) is exactly condition (2) for $\overline{X}$. As for (1), we check, say, that if $a_1, a_2 \in \overline{X}$, then $\{a_1, a_2\} \in Con$. First, an easy consequence of (A) and (D) is:

$$(X \subseteq Y \in Con \text{ and } X \vdash a) \Rightarrow Y \vdash a .$$

Applying this to $X$, $X \cup \{a_1\}$ (which is in $Con$ by (C)) and $a_2$, we obtain $X \cup \{a_1\} \vdash a_2$, and deduce $\{a_1, a_2\} \in Con$ by (A) and (B).

Consider an element $x$ and $\{\overline{X} \mid \overline{X} \subseteq x\} = \{\overline{X} \mid X \subseteq x\}$. This set is directed, since if $X_1, X_2 \subseteq x$, then $X_1 \cup X_2 \subseteq x$ and $\overline{X_1}, \overline{X_2} \subseteq \overline{X_1 \cup X_2}$. We have $x = \bigcup\{\overline{X} \mid \overline{X} \subseteq x\}$ thanks to the following axiom:

- (E)  $\forall a \in A \ \{a\} \in Con$.

We are left to show that $\overline{X}$ is compact. This follows easily from: $\overline{X} \subseteq x$ iff $X \subseteq x$. Finally, we address bounded completeness. If $x_1, x_2 \subseteq x$, then:

$$x_1 \vee x_2 = \{a \mid \exists X \subseteq x_1 \cup x_2 \ X \vdash a\} .$$

**Definition 10.2.11** *An information system is a structure* $(A, Con, \vdash)$ *satisfying the above axioms (A), (B), (C), (D), and (E), and we write* $D(A, Con, \vdash)$ *for the set of elements of* $(A, Con, \vdash)$ *ordered by inclusion.*

**Theorem 10.2.12** *The class of all bounded complete algebraic dcpo's is the class of partial orders which are isomorphic to* $D(A, Con, \vdash)$, *for some information system.*

PROOF. We have done most of the work to establish that $D(A, Con, \vdash)$ is algebraic and bounded complete. Conversely, given $D$, we take the 'intended' interpretation discussed above: $A = \mathcal{K}(D)$, $X \in Con$ iff $X$ has an upper bound, and $X \vdash d$ iff $d \leq \bigvee X$.  □

Theorem 10.2.12 is an example of a representation theorem, relating abstract order theoretical structures (Scott domains) with more concrete ones (information systems). Event structures, concrete data structures, considered in sections 12.3, 14.2, respectively, will provide other examples of representation theorems.

**Exercise 10.2.13** *In our treatment, we have not included the axiomatization of the minimum element. Show that this can be done by means of a special token (which Scott has called* △ *).*

Information systems allow for an attractive characterization of injection-projection pairs, in the line of proposition 3.1.6 and exercise 3.1.7.

**Exercise 10.2.14** *(1) Show that, for any two bounded complete algebraic dcpo's $D, D'$, there exists an injection-projection pair between $D$ and $D'$ iff there exist two information systems $(A, Con, \vdash)$ and $(A', Con', \vdash')$ representing $D$ and $D'$ (i.e., such that $D, D'$ are isomorphic to $D(A, Con, \vdash)$, $D(A', Con', \vdash')$, respectively), and such that:*

$$A \subseteq A' \quad Con = Con' \cap A \quad \vdash = \vdash' \cap (Con \times A). \tag{10.1}$$

*(2) Use this concrete representation to solve domain equations. Hints: By 10.1, we are given a (complete) partial order on information systems, and one checks that the usual domain constructions (cf. example 7.1.16) are continuous when viewed as acting on information systems. If one cares about the largeness of the class of information systems, then one can fix a set of tokens $B$ closed under suitable constructions, and work within the set of information systems $(A, Con, \vdash)$ such that $A \subseteq B$.*

Finally, we briefly hint at the fact that information systems are connected to a new subject called formal topology, that aims at providing a constructive framework for the formalization of topological proofs. In formal topology, (compact coprime) open sets are not manipulated directly: rather, one plays with *presentations* of them (see also section 13.5). In the present setting, an element $X$ of the set $Con$ associated with a Scott domain $D$ stands for a presentation of the compact coprime $\uparrow \bigvee X$, (and $X \vdash a$ reads as $(\uparrow \bigvee X) \subseteq (\uparrow a)$). We refer to [SVV96] for such an account of Scott domains.

# 10.3   Stone spaces *

In this section, we focus on algebraicity on the localic side, and prove Stone's theorem. The 'algebraic cpo line' (section 10.2) and the 'algebraic locale line' will be related when addressing Stone duality for profinite dcpo's (section 10.4).

**Proposition 10.3.1** *Algebraic locales, i.e., locales which viewed as cpo's are algebraic, are spatial.*

PROOF. Let $a \not\leq b$. By theorem 10.1.13, it is enough to find a Scott open filter $F$ such that $a \in F$ and $b \notin F$. By algebraicity, we can find a compact $d$ such that $d \leq a$ and $d \not\leq b$. Then the filter $F = \uparrow d$ is Scott open and fits. □

**Proposition 10.3.2** (1) *The ideal completions of upper semi-lattices are the algebraic complete lattices (i.e., the algebraic cpo's with all lub's).*

(2) *The ideal completions of lattices are the algebraic complete lattices whose compact elements are closed under finite glb's.*

(3) *The ideal completions of distributive lattices are the algebraic locales whose compact elements are closed under finite glb's.*

PROOF. (1) Let $A$ be an algebraic complete lattice. Then $\mathcal{K}(A)$ is an upper semi-lattice, since the lub of a finite set of compact elements is always compact (cf. exercise 1.1.11). Conversely, it is enough to define binary lub's, since the existence of directed and binary lub's implies the existence of all lub's. Define $a \vee b = \bigvee \{ d \vee e \mid d, e \in \mathcal{K}(A), d \leq a$ and $e \leq b \}$.

(2) Obvious.

(3) Let $X$ be a distributive lattice. We show that $A = Ide(X)$ satisfies the infinite distributivity law of definition 10.1.1(3). We have, for ideals:

$$I \wedge J \;=\; \{ z \mid \exists a \in I, b \in J \;\; z \leq a \wedge b \}$$
$$\textstyle\bigvee_{i \in I} I_i \;=\; \{ z \mid \exists i_1, \ldots, i_n, a_1 \in I_1, \ldots, a_n \in I_n \;\; z \leq a_1 \vee \cdots \vee a_n \} \, .$$

Hence, if $z \in J \wedge (\bigvee_{i \in I} I_i)$, then $z \leq a \wedge (a_1 \vee \cdots \vee a_n)$ for some $a \in J$ and $a_1 \in I_{i_1}, \ldots, a_n \in I_{i_n}$, hence $z \leq (a \wedge a_1) \vee \cdots \vee (a \wedge a_n)$ by distributivity of $X$, and $z \in \bigvee_{i \in I} (J \wedge I_i)$. $\square$

**Definition 10.3.3 (coherent locale)** *Locales arising as ideal completions of distributive lattices are called coherent (or spectral). A topological space is called coherent if its topology is coherent.*

In particular, coherent topological spaces are compact (the total space is the empty glb).

**Proposition 10.3.4 (duality – coherent)** *The basic duality cuts down to an equivalence between the category of coherent topological spaces and the category of coherent locales.*

PROOF. Coherent locales are *a fortiori* algebraic locales, hence they are spatial by proposition 10.3.1 (note that this is where we make use of the Scott open filter theorem, and hence of Zorn's lemma). The statement follows (cf. exercise A2.6.5). $\square$

It is then possible to combine the correspondences:

$$\text{coherent spaces} \;\leftrightarrow\; \text{coherent locales} \;\leftrightarrow\; \text{distributive lattices.}$$

However, these correspondences do not extend to dualities of the respective 'natural' categories of continuous functions, locale morphisms, and **DLat**$^{op}$ morphisms, where **DLat** is the category of distributive lattices and lattice morphisms. The reason is that a locale morphism does not map compact elements to compact elements in general. However, this will be true of Stone spaces.

As for coprime algebraic locales, the points of a coherent locale enjoy a simple characterization.

**Lemma 10.3.5** *Let $A$ be a coherent locale. Then the points of $A$ are in one-to-one correspondence with the coprime filters over $\mathcal{K}(A)$:*

$$Spec(\mathcal{K}(A)) = Pt(A) .$$

PROOF. The inverse mappings are: $G \mapsto \uparrow G$ and $F \mapsto \{x \in F \mid x \text{ compact}\}$. We check only that $\uparrow G$ is coprime. Let $x \vee y \in \uparrow G$. Let $g \in G$ be such that $g \leq x \vee y$. Since $A$ is algebraic and since $G$ is completely coprime, we may assume that $g$ is compact. We can write:

$$x \vee y = (\bigvee\{d \mid d \leq x\}) \vee (\bigvee\{e \mid e \leq x\}) = \bigvee\{d \vee e \mid d \leq x, e \leq x\} .$$

By compactness, there exist $d, e \in \mathcal{K}(A)$ such that $d \leq x$, $e \leq x$, and $g \leq d \vee e$. Hence $d \vee e \in G$, and we have $d \in G$ or $e \in G$ by coprimeness of $G$, implying $x \in \uparrow G$ or $y \in \uparrow G$. □

**Remark 10.3.6** *The following table compares lemmas 10.2.5 and 10.3.5:*

| | | |
|---|---|---|
| $\mathcal{F}(\mathcal{C}(A)) \cong Pt(A)$ | *filter* | *lower set completion* |
| $Spec(\mathcal{K}(A)) \cong Pt(A)$ | *coprime filter* | *ideal completion* . |

We move on to Stone spaces. There are several equivalent definitions of Stone spaces [Joh82]. We choose the one which serves to prove the duality.

**Definition 10.3.7 (Stone space)** *A Stone space is a $T_2$-space whose topology is coherent.*

**Proposition 10.3.8 (duality – Stone)** *The Stone spaces are the topological spaces whose topology is isomorphic to the ideal completion of a Boolean algebra. The following three categories are equivalent:*

(1) *Stone spaces and continuous functions.*

(2) *The category of locales arising as ideal completions of Boolean algebras.*

(3) $\mathbf{Bool}^{op}$, *where $\mathbf{Bool}$ is the category of Boolean algebras and lattice morphisms, that is, the functions preserving finite glb's and lub's.*

PROOF. Let $(X, \Omega X)$ be a Stone space. We show that $\mathcal{K}(\Omega X)$ is Boolean. In $T_2$-spaces, compact subsets are closed,[2] and hence the compact subsets are the closed subsets. Hence the compact open subsets are the closed open subsets, which are closed under set theoretical complementation.

Conversely, let $B$ be a Boolean algebra. We show that $Pt(Ide(B))$ is a $T_2$-space. Consider two distinct coprime filters $G_1, G_2$ of $B$. Combining proposition 10.1.8 and lemma 10.3.5, the open sets of $Pt(Ide(B))$ are the sets $U_b = \{G \mid b \in (\uparrow G)\}$. We look for $b_1, b_2$ in $B$ such that $G_1 \in U_{b_1}$, $G_2 \in U_{b_2}$ and $U_{b_1} \cap U_{b_2} = \emptyset$.

- $G_1 \in U_{b_1}$, $G_2 \in U_{b_2}$. Since $G_1 \neq G_2$, we can pick, say, $b_1 \in G_1 \backslash G_2$. We have, setting $b_2 = \neg b_1$:

$$\begin{aligned} b_1 \vee b_2 = 1 &\Rightarrow b_1 \vee b_2 \in G_2 && (G_2 \text{ filter}) \\ &\Rightarrow b_1 \in G_2 \text{ or } b_2 \in G_2 && (\text{coprimeness}) \\ &\Rightarrow b_2 \in G_2 && (b_1 \notin G_2) . \end{aligned}$$

---

[2] This is a basic property of Hausdorff spaces. Hint: Fix a point in the complement of the closed set $K$, and generate a covering of $K$ by picking for each $y \in K$ open sets $U_{xy}$ and $V_{xy}$ separating $x$ and $y$.

*A fortiori*, $b_1 \in G_1, b_2 \in G_2$ imply $G_1 \in U_{b_1}$, $G_2 \in U_{b_2}$.

- $U_{b_1} \cap U_{b_2} = \emptyset$. Suppose not, and let $G$ be such that $b_1 \in (\uparrow G)$ and $b_2 \in (\uparrow G)$. We have:

$$b_1 \wedge b_2 = 0 \;\Rightarrow\; 0 \in \uparrow G \quad (\uparrow G \text{ is a filter})$$
$$\Rightarrow\; 0 \in G \quad (\text{definition of } \uparrow G)$$
$$\Rightarrow\; G = B \quad (G \text{ is a filter}) .$$

But $G = B$ contradicts the coprimeness of $G$.

The categories (1) and (2) are equivalent by restriction of the basic duality. The equivalence between categories (2) and (3) is a consequence of the following claim: the morphisms of category (2) map compact elements to compact elements. The claim is proved easily by taking advantage of spatiality and of the duality (1)/(2). We have seen that the compact open sets are the closed open sets. The claim then follows from the observation that for any continuous function $f$ in **Top**, $f^{-1}$ maps closed subsets to closed subsets. □

# 10.4  Stone duality for profinite dcpo's *

In order to relate propositions 10.2.6 and 10.3.4, we have to understand under which conditions the Scott topology of an algebraic dcpo is coherent.

**Proposition 10.4.1** *The following properties are equivalent for an algebraic dcpo D:*

(1) *D is coherent as a topological space.*

(2) $\forall X \subseteq_{fin} \mathcal{K}(D) \;\; \exists Y \subseteq_{fin} \mathcal{K}(D) \;\; \bigcap_{x \in X}(\uparrow x) = \bigcup_{y \in Y}(\uparrow y)$.

(3) $\mathcal{K}(D) \models M$ *(cf. definition 5.2.6).*

PROOF. Recall from the proof of proposition 10.2.6 that the compact coprime elements of the Scott topology $\Omega$ of $D$ are the sets $\uparrow d$, with $d \in \mathcal{K}(D)$. Therefore, the compact elements of $\Omega$ are the finite unions $\uparrow d_1 \cup \cdots \cup \uparrow d_m$.

(1) $\Leftrightarrow$ (2)  Since property (2) says that the intersection of the compact elements $\uparrow x$ is compact, it clearly holds if $D$ is coherent. Conversely, we have to extend property (2) to a finite intersection of compact elements, say, a binary one. This follows obviously from the observation that such an intersection $(\uparrow d_1 \cup \cdots \cup \uparrow d_m) \cap (\uparrow e_1 \cup \cdots \cup \uparrow e_n)$ is a union of sets $(\uparrow d_i) \cap (\uparrow e_j)$.

(2) $\Rightarrow$ (3)  Let $X \subseteq_{fin} \mathcal{K}(D)$. Then $UB(X) = \bigcap_{x \in X}(\uparrow x)$. Let $Y$ be as in statement (2). Then $MUB(X)$ is the set of minimal elements of $Y$, and hence is *a fortiori* finite.

(3) $\Rightarrow$ (2)  This is obvious, taking $Y = MUB(X)$. □

**Definition 10.4.2 (coherent algebraizing)** *A coherent locale is called coherent algebraizing*[3] *if it is coprime algebraic.*

**Proposition 10.4.3 (duality – algebraic + M)** *The basic domain duality cuts down to an equivalence between the category of algebraic dcpo's whose basis satisfies M and the category of coherent algebraizing locales.*

---

[3]A more standard terminology for this is 'coherent algebraic'. We prefer to use 'algebraizing', to stress that one refers to the algebraicity of the Stone dual cpo, rather than to the algebraicity of the locale (which is also relevant and is part of the definition of 'coherent').

PROOF. The statement follows from proposition 10.4.1: we apply lemma 10.2.7 with 'has a minimum element and the basis satisfies $M$' and 'coherent' for $(S)$ and $(L)$, respectively. □

We move on to the duality for profinite dcpo's (the last we shall consider).

**Lemma 10.4.4** *An algebraic dcpo $D$ is profinite iff*

$$\forall X \subseteq_{fin} \mathcal{K}(D) \ \exists Y \subseteq_{fin} \mathcal{K}(D)$$
$$X \subseteq Y \ and \ (\forall Z \subseteq Y \ \exists Z_1 \subseteq Y \ \bigcap_{x \in Z}(\uparrow x) = \bigcup_{y \in Z_1}(\uparrow y)) \ .$$

PROOF. The equivalence can be rephrased as follows (cf. the proof of proposition 10.4.1): $D$ is bifinite iff

$$\forall X \subseteq_{fin} \mathcal{K}(D) \ \exists Y \subseteq_{fin} \mathcal{K}(D)$$
$$X \subseteq Y \ and \ (\forall Z \subseteq Y \ MUB(Z) \subseteq Y \ and \ MUB(Z) \ is \ complete) \ ,$$

while, by definition, $D$ profinite means: $\forall X \subseteq_{fin} \mathcal{K}(D) \ U^{\infty}(X)$ is finite.

($\Rightarrow$) Take $Y = U^{\infty}(X)$.

($\Leftarrow$) By induction on $n$, we obtain $U^n(X) \subseteq Y$ for all $n$, and since $Y$ is finite the sequence $\{U^n(X)\}_{n \geq 0}$ becomes stationary. □

**Proposition 10.4.5 (duality – profinite)** *The basic domain duality cuts down to an equivalence between the category of profinite dcpo's and the category of coherent algebraizing locales $A$ satisfying the following property:*

$$(\wedge \vee - clos) \quad \begin{cases} \forall X \subseteq_{fin} \mathcal{C}(A) \ \exists Y \subseteq_{fin} \mathcal{C}(A) \\ X \subseteq Y \ and \ (\forall Z \subseteq Y \ \exists Z_1 \subseteq Y \ \bigwedge Z = \bigvee Z_1) \ . \end{cases}$$

PROOF. The statement follows from lemma 10.4.4: we apply lemma 10.2.7 with 'profinite' and the property of the statement as $(S)$ and $(L)$, respectively. □

In figure 10.1, we summarize the dualities for domains that we have proved in this chapter. The second and the third presentations of 'coherent algebraizing' correspond to what we needed to add to 'coherent' and to 'algebraizing', respectively (cf. exercise 10.2.3). The last equality in the figure is based on proposition 10.2.10, which allows us to present the duality for Scott domains as a cut down version of the duality corresponding to coherent algebraizing locales. In the figure, say, 'compact' stands for 'compact element'.

There are of course other dualities, among which is the one for bifinite domains. We recall that a bifinite domain is a profinite dcpo that has a ⊥. Thus the duality for bifinite domains is obtained by combining propositions 10.2.8 and 10.4.5. In full, the basic domain duality cuts down to an equivalence between the category of bifinite domains and the category of coherent algebraizing locales $A$ satisfying $(\wedge \vee - clos)$ and such that there exists a maximum compact coprime element.

(1)  sober spaces / spatial locales

(2)  algebraic dcpo's / coprime algebraic locales

(3)  coherent spaces / coherent locales

(4)  algebraic dcpo's whose basis satisfies $M$ / coherent algebraizing locales

(5)  profinite dcpo's / coherent algebraizing locales satisfying $(\wedge \vee - clos)$

(6)  Scott domains / $\left\{ \begin{array}{l} \text{coprime algebraic locales where} \\ \text{compact coprimes form a conditional lower semi-lattice} \end{array} \right.$

with: $(1) \supset (2), (3) \supset (4) \supset (5) \supset (6)$

coprime algebraic  =  lower set completion of a partial order

coherent  =  ideal completion of a distributive lattice
        =  algebraic locale + closure of compacts under finite glb's

coherent algebraizing  =  coherent + coprime algebraic
        =  $\left\{ \begin{array}{l} \text{ideal completion of a distributive lattice+} \\ \text{every compact is a finite lub of compact coprimes} \end{array} \right.$
        =  $\left\{ \begin{array}{l} \text{coprime algebraic locale+} \\ \text{closure of compacts under finite glb's} \end{array} \right.$

$\left. \begin{array}{l} \text{coprime algebraic + compact coprimes} \\ \text{form a conditional lower semi-lattice} \end{array} \right\} = \left\{ \begin{array}{l} \text{coherent algebraizing+} \\ \text{glb's of compact coprimes} \\ \text{are coprime or } \bot \end{array} \right.$

Figure 10.1: Summary of dualities

---

# 10.5   Scott domains in logical form *

We present domains via their compact open sets, constructed as (equivalence classes of) formulas. Abramsky has called this 'domains in logical form' [Abr91b]. Through such presentations, fruitful connections can be established with program logics and axiomatic semantics such as Hoare logic. We refer to [Bon96] for recent work in this direction.

As a first step, we show how to present the compact open sets of $D \to E$ in terms of the compact open sets of $D$ and $E$. When we write $\Omega D$, we mean the Scott topology on $D$.

**Proposition 10.5.1** *If $D$ and $E$ are algebraic cpo's such that $D \to E$ is algebraic and its basis satisfies $M$, then:*

(1) *For any $U \in \mathcal{K}(\Omega D)$ and $V \in \mathcal{K}(\Omega E)$, the following set is compact:*

$$U \to V = \{f : D \to E \mid f(U) \subseteq V\},$$

and if $U$ and $V$ are compact coprime, then $U \to V$ is compact coprime.

(2) Any compact open set of $D \to E$ is a finite union of finite intersections of such sets $U \to V$, where $U, V$ are, moreover, coprime.

PROOF. (1) Let $U = (\uparrow d_1) \cup \cdots \cup (\uparrow d_m)$ and $V = (\uparrow e_1) \cup \cdots \cup (\uparrow e_n)$. The definition of $U \to V$ can be reformulated as:

$$
\begin{aligned}
U \to V &= \{f : D \to E \mid \forall i \; \exists j \; f(d_i) \geq e_j\} \\
&= \bigcap_i (\bigcup_j (\uparrow (d_i \to e_j))) \,.
\end{aligned}
$$

Each $\uparrow (d_i \to e_j)$ is compact coprime, therefore each $\bigcup_j (\uparrow (d_i \to e_j))$ is compact; the conclusion follows by propositions 10.4.1 and 10.3.2. In particular, if $m = n = 1$, then $U \to V = \uparrow (d_1 \to e_1)$ is compact coprime.

(2) The compact open sets of $D \to E$ are the subsets of the form $\uparrow f^1 \cup \cdots \cup \uparrow f^p$ where each $f^i$ is compact, hence is of the form $(d^1 \to e^1) \vee \cdots \vee (d^q \to e^q)$, that is:

$$
\uparrow f^i = (\uparrow (d^1 \to e^1)) \cap \cdots \cap (\uparrow (d^q \to e^q)) \,.
$$

Then the conclusion follows from the observation that $(\uparrow d) \to (\uparrow e) = \uparrow (d \to e)$, for any compact $d, e$. □

A second step consists in constructing a logical theory based on these sets $U \to V$, now considered as (atomic) formulas. We seek a complete theory in the sense that if two different formulas $u, v$ present two open sets $[\![u]\!], [\![v]\!]$ such that $[\![u]\!] \subseteq [\![v]\!]$, then $u \leq v$ is provable.

**Proposition 10.5.2** Let $D, E$ be Scott domains. Then the set of compact open sets of $D \to E$ is order-isomorphic to the partial order associated with a preorder $\Phi$ defined as follows. The elements of $\Phi$ are formulas defined by:

$$
\frac{U \in \mathcal{K}(\Omega D) \;\; V \in \mathcal{K}(\Omega E)}{U \to V \in \Phi} \qquad \frac{\forall i \in I \; u_i \in \Phi \; (I \; finite)}{\bigwedge_{i \in I} u_i \in \Phi} \qquad \frac{\forall i \in I \; u_i \in \Phi \; (I \; finite)}{\bigvee_{i \in I} u_i \in \Phi} \quad,
$$

and the preorder is the least preorder closed under the following rules (where $=$ stands for the equivalence associated with the preorder):

$$
u \leq u \qquad \frac{u \leq v \quad v \leq w}{u \leq w} \qquad u \wedge (v \vee w) \leq (u \wedge v) \vee (u \wedge w)
$$

$$
\frac{\forall i \in I \; u_i \leq v \quad (I \; finite)}{\bigvee_{i \in I} u_i \leq v} \qquad u_i \leq \bigvee_{i \in I} u_i
$$

$$
\frac{\forall i \in I \; u \leq v_i \quad (I \; finite)}{u \leq \bigwedge_{i \in I} v_i} \qquad \bigwedge_{i \in I} v_i \leq v_i
$$

$$
\frac{U' \subseteq U \quad V \subseteq V'}{U \to V \leq U' \to V'} \qquad U \to (\bigcap_{i \in I} V_i) = \bigwedge_{i \in I}(U \to V_i)
$$

$$
(\bigcup_{i \in I} U_i) \to V = \bigwedge_{i \in I}(U_i \to V) \qquad \frac{U \in \mathcal{C}(\Omega D)}{U \to (\bigcup_{i \in I} V_i) = \bigvee_{i \in I}(U \to V_i)} \quad,
$$

*where capital letters range over compact open sets and small letters range over formulas.*

PROOF. Proposition 10.5.1 gives us a surjection $[\![\_]\!]$ from $\Phi$ to $\Omega(D \to E)$ (interpreting $\wedge, \vee$ as $\cap, \cup$). The soundness of the rules defining the preorder is easy to check, and implies that the surjection is monotonic. All we have to do is to prove completeness: if $[\![u]\!] \leq [\![v]\!]$, then $u \leq v$ is provable. Using distributivity and the last two rules in the statement, we see that any formula $u$ is provably equal to a finite disjunction of formulas of the form $\bigwedge_{i \in I}(U_i \to V_i)$, where the $U_i$'s and the $V_i$'s are compact coprime. Each $U_i \to V_i$ is compact coprime, by proposition 10.5.1. Hence, by proposition 10.2.10, $[\![\bigwedge_{i \in I}(U_i \to V_i)]\!] = \bigcap_{i \in I}(U_i \to V_i)$ is either coprime or $\emptyset$. The proof goes through two claims.

**Claim 1.** If the $U_i$'s and $V_i$'s are coprime and $\bigcap_{i \in I}(U_i \to V_i) = \emptyset$, then $\bigwedge_{i \in I}(U_i \to V_i) = 0 \ (= \bigvee \emptyset)$ is provable.

Since $U_i, V_i$ are coprime, we can write $U_i = \uparrow d_i$, $V_i = \uparrow e_i$, and $U_i \to V_i = \uparrow (d_i \to e_i)$. Therefore, $\bigcap_{i \in I}(U_i \to V_i) \neq \emptyset$ iff $\{d_i \to e_i \mid i \in I\}$ has an upper bound iff $\{d_i \to e_i \mid i \in I\}$ has a lub iff

$$\forall J \subseteq I \ \{d_j \mid j \in J\} \text{ has an upper bound} \Rightarrow \{e_j \mid j \in J\} \text{ has an upper bound.}$$

Hence $\bigcap_{i \in I}(U_i \to V_i) = \emptyset$ iff there exists $J \subseteq I$ such that $\bigcap_{j \in J} U_j \neq \emptyset$ (hence is coprime, by proposition 10.2.10) and $\bigcap_{j \in J} V_j = \emptyset$. Now the claim is proved as follows:

$$\bigwedge_{i \in I}(U_i \to V_i) \leq \bigwedge_{j \in J}(U_j \to V_j) \leq \bigwedge_{j \in J}((\bigcap_{j \in J} U_j) \to V_j) = (\bigcap_{j \in J} U_j) \to (\bigcap_{j \in J} V_j) \, .$$

The last formula can be written $(\bigcap_{j \in J} U_j) \to (\bigcup \emptyset)$, and since $\bigcap_{j \in J} U_j$ is coprime, we have $(\bigcap_{j \in J} U_j) \to (\bigcap_{j \in J} V_j) = \bigvee \emptyset$ (by the last rule). By claim 1, we can eliminate the conjunctions $\bigwedge_{i \in I}(U_i \to V_i)$ such that $\bigcap_{i \in I}(U_i \to V_i) = \emptyset$. Call $u', v'$ the resulting $u' = u'_1 \vee \cdots \vee u'_m = u$ and $v' = v'_1 \vee \cdots \vee v'_n = v$. Then we can write $[\![u'_1]\!] = \uparrow f_1, \ldots,$ $[\![u'_m]\!] = \uparrow f_m$, $[\![v'_1]\!] = \uparrow g_1, \ldots, [\![v'_n]\!] = \uparrow g_n$, and:

$$
\begin{aligned}
[\![u]\!] \leq [\![v]\!] \ &\Leftrightarrow \ [\![u']\!] \leq [\![v']\!] \ \ \Leftrightarrow \ \forall p \ \uparrow f_p \subseteq [\![v']\!] \\
&\Leftrightarrow \ \forall p \ f_p \in [\![v']\!] \ \ \Leftrightarrow \ \forall p \ \exists q \ f_p \geq g_q \ \Leftrightarrow \ \forall p \ \exists q \ [\![u'_p]\!] \leq [\![v'_q]\!] \, ,
\end{aligned}
$$

which brings us to the following second claim.

**Claim 2 (coprime completeness).** If $u', v'$ both have the form $\bigwedge_{i \in I}(U_i \to V_i)$, with the $U_i$'s and $V_i$'s coprime, if $[\![u']\!] \leq [\![v']\!]$, and if $[\![u']\!], [\![v']\!]$ are coprime, then $u' \leq v'$ is provable.

By the definition of $\bigwedge$, we can assume that $v'$ is reduced to one conjunct: $v' = U \to V = \uparrow (d \to e)$. Then, setting $u' = \bigwedge_{i \in I}(U_i \to V_i)$, and $U_i = \uparrow d_i$, $V_i = \uparrow e_i$ for all $i$, the assumption $[\![u']\!] \leq [\![v']\!]$ reads as $d \to e \leq \bigvee_{i \in I}(d_i \to e_i)$, or, equivalently:

$$e \leq (\bigvee_{i \in I}(d_i \to e_i))(d) = \bigvee\{e_j \mid d_j \leq d\} \, .$$

Setting $J = \{j \mid d_j \leq d\}$, we have: $U \subseteq \bigcap_{j \in J} U_j$ and $\bigcap_{j \in J} V_j \subseteq V$. Then:

$$\bigwedge_{i \in I}(U_i \to V_i) \leq (\bigcap_{j \in J} U_j) \to (\bigcap_{j \in J} V_j) \leq U \to V \, .$$

$$\frac{U \in \mathcal{K}(\Omega D_{\kappa_i})}{U \in \Phi(\kappa_i)} \qquad\qquad \frac{u \in \Phi(\sigma) \quad v \in \Phi(\tau)}{u \to v \in \Phi(\sigma \to \tau)}$$

$$\frac{\forall i \in I \;\; u_i \in \Phi(\sigma) \quad (I \text{ finite})}{\bigwedge_{i \in I} u_i \in \Phi(\sigma)} \qquad\qquad \frac{\forall i \in I \;\; u_i \in \Phi(\sigma) \quad (I \text{ finite})}{\bigvee_{i \in I} u_i \in \Phi(\sigma)}$$

Figure 10.2: Domain logic: formulas

We now complete the proof of completeness:

$$[\![u]\!] \leq [\![v]\!] \;\Rightarrow\; \forall p \;\exists q \;\; [\![u_p']\!] \leq [\![v_q']\!] \qquad\qquad \Rightarrow\; \forall p \;\exists q \;\; u_p' \leq v_q'$$
$$\Rightarrow\; u' = \bigvee\nolimits_{k=1,\dots,m} u_k' \leq \bigvee\nolimits_{l=1,\dots,n} u_l' = v' \;\Rightarrow\; u = u' \leq v' = v \;. \qquad \square$$

The last step consists in further 'syntaxizing' domains, by defining a language of formulas, not only for $\mathcal{K}(\Omega(D \to E))$, but also for $\mathcal{K}(\Omega D)$, $\mathcal{K}(\Omega E)$, and more generally for all types. Since the axioms used to describe $\mathcal{K}(\Omega(D \to E))$ involve coprimeness at the lower types, the coprimeness predicate has to be axiomatized as well.

**Definition 10.5.3** *Let* $\{\kappa_1, \dots, \kappa_n\}$ *be a fixed collection of basic types, and let* $D_{\kappa_1}, \dots,$ *$D_{\kappa_n}$ be fixed Scott domains associated with* $\kappa_1, \dots, \kappa_n$. *Consider:*

* *The following collection of types:*

$$\sigma ::= \kappa_1 \mid \cdots \mid \kappa_n \mid \sigma \to \sigma \;.$$

* *The formal system for deriving formula judgments of the form* $u \in \Phi(\sigma)$*, given in figure 10.2. We write* $\bigwedge \emptyset = 1$ *and* $\bigvee \emptyset = 0$.

* *The formal system for deriving two kinds of judgments:*

$$u \leq v \quad (\text{with } u = v \text{ standing for}: (u \leq v \text{ and } v \leq u))$$
$$C(u) \quad (\text{`}u \text{ is coprime'}) ,$$

*given in figure 10.3. The axiom* $C(1)$ *corresponds to the requirement that the associated domain has a* $\bot$ *(cf. proposition 10.2.8). The rule* $(C \to Scott)$ *axiomatizes the characterization of the compact elements of function spaces given in theorem 1.4.12.*

* *The 'type' system given in figure 10.4, whose judgments have the form* $\Gamma \vdash M : u$*, where* $M$ *is a* $\lambda$*-term and* $\Gamma$ *is a set consisting of distinct pairs* $x : v$. *We suppose that all the free variables of* $M$ *are declared in* $\Gamma$*, and* $\Delta \leq \Gamma$ *means:* $\Delta = \{x_1 : u_1, \dots, x_n : u_n\}$, $\Gamma = \{x_1 : v_1, \dots, x_n : v_n\}$, *and* $u_i \leq v_i$ *for all* $i$.

*The denotational semantics of types and of simply typed* $\lambda$*-terms are defined as in chapter 4:* $[\![\sigma \to \tau]\!] = [\![\sigma]\!] \to [\![\tau]\!]$*, etc. The meaning of the formulas of* $\Phi(\sigma)$*, for all* $\sigma$*, is given in figure 10.5. Validity of the three kinds of judgments is defined in figure 10.6.*

The following properties can be verified:

* If $u \leq v$ is provable, then it must be the case that $u \in \Phi(\sigma)$ and $v \in \Phi(\sigma)$, for some $\sigma$.

* If $x_1 : u_1, \dots, x_n : u_n \vdash M : u$ then $u_1 \in \Phi(\sigma_1), \dots, u_n \in \Phi(\sigma_n), u \in \Phi(\sigma)$, and $x_1 : \sigma_1, \dots, x_n : \sigma_n \vdash M : \sigma$, for some $\sigma_1, \dots, \sigma_n, \sigma$.

$$u \leq u \qquad \frac{u \leq v \quad v \leq w}{u \leq w} \qquad\qquad u \wedge (v \vee w) \leq (u \wedge v) \vee (u \wedge w)$$

$$\frac{\forall i \in I \; u_i \leq v \quad (I \text{ finite})}{\bigvee_{i \in I} u_i \leq v} \qquad\qquad u_i \leq \bigvee_{i \in I} u_i$$

$$\frac{\forall i \in I \; u \leq v_i \quad (I \text{ finite})}{u \leq \bigwedge_{i \in I} v_i} \qquad\qquad \bigwedge_{i \in I} v_i \leq v_i$$

$$\frac{U, V \in \mathcal{K}(\Omega D_{\kappa_i}) \quad U \subseteq V}{U \leq V} \qquad\qquad \frac{u' \leq u \quad v \leq v'}{u \rightarrow v \leq u' \rightarrow v'}$$

$$u \rightarrow (\bigwedge_{i \in I} v_i) = \bigwedge_{i \in I} (u \rightarrow v_i) \qquad\qquad (\bigvee_{i \in I} u_i) \rightarrow v = \bigwedge_{i \in I} (u_i \rightarrow v)$$

$$C(1) \qquad\qquad\qquad \frac{C(u)}{u \rightarrow (\bigvee_{i \in I} v_i) = \bigvee_{i \in I} (u \rightarrow v_i)}$$

$$\frac{U \in \mathcal{C}(\Omega D_{\kappa_i})}{C(U)} \qquad\qquad \frac{C(u) \quad u = v}{C(v)}$$

$$(C \rightarrow Scott) \quad \frac{\forall i \in I \; C(u_i) \text{ and } C(v_i) \; \forall J \subseteq I \; (\bigwedge_{j \in J} v_j = 0 \Rightarrow \bigwedge_{j \in J} u_j = 0)}{C(\bigwedge_{i \in I} (u_i \rightarrow v_i))}$$

Figure 10.3: Domain Logic: entailment and coprimeness judgments

$$\frac{x : u \in \Gamma}{\Gamma \vdash x : u} \qquad\qquad \frac{\Gamma \vdash M : u \quad \Delta \leq \Gamma \quad u \leq v}{\Delta \vdash M : v}$$

$$\frac{\Gamma \vdash M : u \rightarrow v \quad \Gamma \vdash N : u}{\Gamma \vdash MN : v} \qquad\qquad \frac{\Gamma, x : u \vdash M : v}{\Gamma \vdash \lambda x.M : u \rightarrow v}$$

$$\frac{\forall i \in I \; \Gamma, x : u_i \vdash M : v \quad (I \text{ finite})}{\Gamma, x : \bigvee_{i \in I} u_i \vdash M : v} \qquad\qquad \frac{\forall i \in I \; \Gamma \vdash M : u_i \quad (I \text{ finite})}{\Gamma \vdash M : \bigwedge_{i \in I} u_i}$$

Figure 10.4: Domain logic: typing judgments

$$[\![ U ]\!] \quad = \quad U \qquad\qquad [\![ u \to v ]\!] \quad = \quad [\![ u ]\!] \to [\![ v ]\!]$$
$$[\![ \bigwedge_{i \in I} u_i ]\!] \quad = \quad \bigcap_{i \in I} [\![ u_i ]\!] \qquad [\![ \bigvee_{i \in I} u_i ]\!] \quad = \quad \bigcup_{i \in I} [\![ u_i ]\!]$$

Figure 10.5: Semantics of formulas

| | | |
|---|---|---|
| $\models u \leq v$ | iff | $[\![ u ]\!] \leq [\![ v ]\!]$ |
| $\models C(u)$ | iff | $[\![ u ]\!]$ is coprime |
| $x_1 : u_1, \ldots, x_n : u_n \models M : u$ | iff | $\forall \rho \; ((\forall i \; \rho(x_i) \in [\![ u_i ]\!]) \Rightarrow [\![ M ]\!] \rho \in [\![ u ]\!])$ |

Figure 10.6: Semantics of judgments

**Theorem 10.5.4** *The following properties hold:*

(1) $u < v$ *is provable iff* $\models u \leq v$.

(2) $C(u)$ *is provable iff* $\models C(u)$.

(3) $\Gamma \vdash M : u$ *iff* $\Gamma \models M : u$.

PROOF HINT. (1) and (2) have been already proved in substance in proposition 10.5.2. (3) is proved via a coprime completeness claim (cf. proposition 10.5.2). For a $u$ such that $[\![ u ]\!]$ is coprime, i.e., $[\![ u ]\!] = \uparrow d$ for some compact $d$, $[\![ M ]\!] \rho \in [\![ u ]\!]$ reads $d \leq [\![ M ]\!] \rho$. Then the coprime completeness claim follows from the following almost obvious equivalences:

$$d \leq [\![ MN ]\!] \rho \quad \text{iff} \quad \exists e \; (d \to e) \leq [\![ M ]\!] \rho \text{ and } e \leq [\![ N ]\!] \rho \quad \text{(by continuity)}$$
$$(d \to e) \leq [\![ \lambda x.M ]\!] \rho \quad \text{iff} \quad e \leq [\![ M ]\!] \rho[d/x] \qquad\qquad \text{(by definition of } d \to e) . \quad \square$$

# 10.6   Bifinite domains in logical form *

We sketch how the logical treatment just given for Scott domains can be adapted to bifinite domains.

**Definition 10.6.1 (Gunter joinable)** *Let $D, E$ be algebraic cpo's. A finite subset $\gamma \subseteq \mathcal{K}(D) \times \mathcal{K}(E)$ is called Gunter joinable if*

$$\forall d_0 \in \mathcal{K}(D) \; \{(d, e) \in \gamma \mid d \leq d_0\} \text{ is non-empty and has a maximum in } \gamma .$$

*Any Gunter joinable set $\gamma$ induces a function $\mathcal{G}(\gamma)$ defined by:*

$$\mathcal{G}(\gamma)(x) = \max\{e \mid \exists d \; (d, e) \in \gamma \text{ and } d \leq x\} .$$

We note that $\mathcal{G}(\gamma)(x)$ is well-defined: we get successively that $\{(d, e) \in \gamma \mid d \leq x\}$ is non-empty (by picking any approximant of $x$) and equal to $\{(d, e) \in \gamma \mid d \leq d_0\}$, for some approximant $d_0$ of $x$ (by finiteness).

**Lemma 10.6.2** *If $\gamma$, $\gamma'$ are Gunter joinable, then:*

(1) $\mathcal{G}(\gamma) = \bigvee\{d \to e \mid (d, e) \in \gamma\}$.

(2) $d' \to e' \le \mathcal{G}(\gamma) \Leftrightarrow \exists d, e \ (d \le d', e' \le e \text{ and } (d, e) \in \gamma)$.

(3) $\mathcal{G}(\gamma) \le \mathcal{G}(\gamma') \Leftrightarrow \forall (d', e') \in \gamma' \ \exists d, e \ d \le d', e' \le e \text{ and } (d, e) \in \gamma$.

PROOF. (1) Follows from the following remark: by definition of $\mathcal{G}(\gamma)$, for all $x$, $\mathcal{G}(\gamma)(x) = (d \to e)(x)$ for some $(d, e) \in \gamma$.

(2) First recall that $d' \to e' \le \mathcal{G}(\gamma)$ can be reformulated as $e' \le \mathcal{G}(\gamma)(d')$.

($\Leftarrow$) Then $d' \to e' \le d \to e$, and *a fortiori* $d' \to e' \le \mathcal{G}(\gamma)$.

($\Rightarrow$) By definition of $\mathcal{G}(\gamma)$, $\mathcal{G}(\gamma)(d') = e$ for some $(d, e) \in \gamma$ with $d \le d'$.

(3) Obvious consequence of (2).                                                   □

**Proposition 10.6.3** *If $D, E$ are bifinite, then:*

$$\mathcal{K}(D \to E) = \{\mathcal{G}(\gamma) \mid \gamma \text{ is Gunter joinable}\} .$$

PROOF. Clearly, each $\mathcal{G}(\gamma)$, as a finite lub of step functions, is compact. Conversely, we know from proposition 5.2.4 that the compact elements of $D \to E$ have the form $r(f)$, where $f : D \to E$ is a continuous function, and $r$ is a finite projection defined from two finite projections $p : D \to D$ and $q : E \to E$ by $r(f)(x) = q(f(p(x)))$. We have to find a $\gamma$ such that $r(f) = \mathcal{G}(\gamma)$. We claim that the following does the job:

$$\gamma = \{(p(y), q(f(p(y)))) \mid y \in D\} .$$

- $\gamma$ is finite. By the finiteness of the range of $p$.

- $\gamma$ is Gunter joinable. Let $x \in D$. We have:

$$p(x) = \max\{p(y) \mid y \in D \text{ and } p(y) \le x\} .$$

Then obviously $(p(x), q(f(p(x))))$ is the maximum of $\{(d, e) \in \gamma \mid d \le x\}$.

- $r(f) = \mathcal{G}(\gamma)$. We have:

$$
\begin{aligned}
r(f)(x) &= q(f(p(x))) &&\text{(by definition of } r) \\
\mathcal{G}(\gamma)(x) &= q(f(p(x))) &&\text{(by definition of } \mathcal{G}(\gamma)) .
\end{aligned}
$$
                                                                                  □

The following equivalent formulation of Gunter joinable subsets is due to Abramsky, and is more easy to capture in logical form.

**Proposition 10.6.4** *Let $\{(d_i, e_i) \mid i \in I\} \subseteq \mathcal{K}(D) \times \mathcal{K}(E)$ be finite. Then $\{(d_i, e_i) \mid i \in I\}$ is Gunter joinable iff*

$$\forall J \subseteq I \ \exists K \subseteq I \ MUB(\{d_j \mid j \in J\}) = \{d_k \mid k \in K\} \text{ and } \forall j \in J, k \in K \ e_j \le e_k .$$

PROOF. ($\Rightarrow$) Let $m \in MUB(\{d_j \mid j \in J\})$, and let $(d_k, e_k) = \max\{(d_i, e_i) \mid d_i \le m\}$. We claim: $m = d_k$. Since $d_k \le m$ by definition, it is enough to show that $d_k \in UB(\{d_j \mid j \in J\})$, which follows from the obvious inclusion $\{d_j \mid j \in J\} \subseteq \{(d_i, e_i) \mid d_i \le m\}$. This inclusion also implies $\forall j \in J \ e_j \le e_k$.

($\Leftarrow$) First, applying the statement to $I = \emptyset$, we obtain that $MUB(\emptyset) \subseteq \{d_i \mid i \in I\}$. Let $d \in \mathcal{K}(D)$, let $J = \{j \mid d_j \le d\}$ and let $K$ be as in the statement. We first observe that $J$ is non-empty (pick a minimal element below $d$). By property $M$, there exists $k \in K$ such that $d_k \ge d$. But then $k \in J$ by definition of $J$, and since $d_k$ is both an upper bound and an element of $\{d_j \mid j \in J\}$, it is a maximum of this set. Moreover, since $e_j \le e_k$, for all $j \in J$, we have that $(d_k, e_k)$ is the desired maximum.       □

**Exercise* 10.6.5** *Show that the statement of theorem 10.5.4 remains true after the following two changes in definition 10.5.3: (1) $D_{\kappa_1}, \ldots, D_{\kappa_n}$ are now fixed bifinite domains. (2) Axiom $(C \rightarrow Scott)$ of definition 10.5.3 is replaced by the following axiom:*

$$(C \rightarrow bifinite) \quad \frac{\forall i \in I \;\; C(u_i) \; and \; C(v_i) \qquad \forall J \subseteq I \;\; \exists K \subseteq I \;\; \bigwedge_{j \in J} u_j = \bigvee_{k \in K} u_k \; and \; \forall j \in J, k \in K \;\; v_j \leq v_k}{C(\bigwedge_{i \in I}(u_i \rightarrow v_i))} \;\;.$$

*Hints: The principal difficulty is to make sure that any u can be written as a disjunction of formulas of the form $\bigwedge_{i \in I}(u_i \rightarrow v_i)$ where the $u_i$'s and the $v_i$'s satisfy the conditions of rule $(C \rightarrow bifinite)$. Remove faulty disjunctions and replace them by disjunctions of conjunctions. Design a terminating strategy for this.*

We end this chapter with a few remarks.

• Nothing prevents us to carry out the same program for profinite dcpo's. It fits even better there, since the duality is more natural for profinite dcpo's (cf. section 10.4). The only 'obstacle' is that we make use of $\perp$ in the definition of the step function $d \rightarrow e$ But actually, any minimal point below $e$ (such a point exists by property $M$ applied to $\emptyset$, cf. section 5.4) does the job.

**Exercise* 10.6.6** *Define a notion of step function for profinite dcpo's, and adapt the results of this section to profinite dcpo's.*

• One may go further (as done in [Abr91b]) in the logical presentation of domains by removing the basic types and by introducing domains from scratch using liftings to get off the ground (cf. remark 3.4.11 and exercise 7.1.23).

• The reader may wonder why we introduced a disjunction in sections 10.5 and 10.6 while intersection types sufficed to our purposes in chapter 3. The answer is twofold. First, as the following exercise suggests, part of Abramsky's program could be carried out with intersection types only. The presentation would then rely on compact co-prime elements and filters rather than compact elements and coprime filters (cf. remark 10.3.6). (The reader should in this respect place theorem 10.5.4(1) and (3) in perspective with theorem 3.4.8 and exercise 3.3.14.) On the other hand, disjunction types are natural if one wants to emphasize the topological aspects of the domains described, since compact open sets are more well-understood mathematical objects than compact coprime open sets.

**Exercise* 10.6.7** *Design a 'simply-typed' version of intersection types built over a set of atoms consisting of the compact open sets of the basic types, and adapt theorem 10.5.4 to this setting. Hints: Now intersection types are type-constrained, e.g. $U \wedge V$ is well-formed only is $U$ and $V$ are open sets of the same basic domain $D_{\kappa_i}$, and then $U \wedge V \in \Phi(\kappa_i)$. Also, in order to deal with cpo's that do not have a top element, one needs to introduce a type corresponding to the emtpy open set (think of $(\uparrow d) \cap (\uparrow e)$ when $d \not\leq e$).*

# 11
## Dependent and second order types

The main goal of this chapter is to introduce $\lambda$-calculi with *dependent* and *second order* types, to discuss their interpretation in the framework of traditional domain theory (chapter 15 will mention another approach based on realizability), and to present some of their relevant syntactic properties.

Calculi with dependent and second order types are rather complex syntactic objects. In order to master some of their complexity let us start with a discussion from a semantic viewpoint. Let $\mathbf{T}$ be a category whose objects are regarded as types. The category $\mathbf{T}$ contains atomic types like the singleton type 1, the type *nat* representing natural numbers, and the type *bool* representing boolean values. The collection $\mathbf{T}$ is also closed with respect to certain data type constructions. For example, if $A$ and $B$ are types then we can form new types such as a *product type* $A \times B$, a *sum type* $A + B$, and an *exponent type* $A \to B$.

In first approximation, a *dependent type* is a family of types indexed over another type $A$. We represent such a family as a transformation $F$ from $A$ into the collection of types $\mathbf{T}$, say $F : A \to \mathbf{T}$. As an example of dependent type we can think of a family *Prod.bool* : $nat \to \mathbf{T}$ that given a number $n$ returns the type $bool \times \cdots \times bool$ ($n$ times).

If the family $F$ is indexed over the collection of all types $\mathbf{T}$, say $F : \mathbf{T} \to \mathbf{T}$, then we are in the realm of *second order types*. As an example of a second order type we can think of a family *Fun* : $\mathbf{T} \to \mathbf{T}$ that given a type $A$ returns the type $A \to A$ of functions over $A$.

If types, and the collection of types $\mathbf{T}$, can be seen as categories then we can think of dependent and second order types as functors. Let us warn the reader that in this preliminary discussion we are considering a simplified situation. In general we want to combine dependent and second order types. For example, we may consider the family *Poly.Prod* : $\mathbf{T} \times nat \to \mathbf{T}$ that takes a type $A$, a number $n$, and returns the type $A \times \cdots \times A$ ($n$ times).

Probably the most familiar examples of dependent and second order types arise in logic. If $\phi(x)$ is a formula depending on the variable $x$ then we can think of $\phi(x)$ as a family of propositions indexed over the universe of terms $U$, say $\phi : U \to Prop$. This is a dependent type. On the other hand, if we consider a formula $\phi(X)$, parametric in a formula variable $X$ then we can think of $\phi(X)$ as a family of propositions indexed over the universe of propositions, say $\phi : Prop \to Prop$. This is a second order type. If we allow quantifications over variables we can form the formulas $\forall x.\phi$, and $\exists x.\phi$. This is the realm of first order logic. If moreover we allow quantifications over formula variables we can form the formulas $\forall X.\phi$, and $\exists X.\phi$, and we are in the realm of second order logic.

Dependent types also appear in several type systems (or generalized logics) such as DeBruijn's Automath [dB80], Martin-Löf's Type Theory [ML84], and Edinburgh LF [HHP93]. Second order types appear in a rather pure form in Girard's system F [Gir72] (which is equivalent to a system of natural deduction for minimal, implicative, propositional second order logic), they also appear, for instance, in the Calculus of Constructions [CH88] but there they are combined with dependent types and more.

Let us now look at the interpretation. Given a family $A : U \to Prop$ we can obtain two new propositions $\forall_U A$, and $\exists_U A$, where we understand $\forall_U$ as a meet or a product, and $\exists_U$ as a join or a sum. In general, given a family of types $F : \mathbf{I} \to \mathbf{T}$ indexed over a category $\mathbf{I}$ we are interested in building two new types that we may denote, respectively, with $\Pi_\mathbf{I} F$ and $\Sigma_\mathbf{I} F$, and that correspond, respectively, to the product and the sum of the family $F$.

Relying on this informal discussion, we can summarize the contents of this chapter as follows. The main problem considered in section 11.1 is to provide a concrete domain theoretical interpretation of the constructions sketched above. In particular, we build a category of domains that is 'closed' under (certain) indexed products, and (certain) indexed sums. The first simple idea is to interpret types as domains of a given category $\mathbf{C}$, and the collection of types as the related category $\mathbf{C}^{ip}$ of injection-projection pairs. What then is a dependent type $F$ indexed over some domain $D$? Since every preorder can be seen as a category, it is natural to ask that $F$ be a functor from $D$ to $\mathbf{C}^{ip}$. Analogously a second order type will be seen as an endo-functor over $\mathbf{C}^{ip}$. However this will not suffice, for instance we will need that the family $F$ preserves directed colimits, namely it is *cocontinuous*.

In section 11.2 we provide a syntactic formalization of the semantic ideas sketched above. To this end we introduce a calculus of dependent and second order types and discuss some of its basic properties. We call this calculus $\lambda P2$-calculus, following a classification proposed in [Bar91a] (the '$P$' stands for positive logic and the '2' for second order). We also briefly discuss an interpretation of the $\lambda P2$-calculus which relies on the domain theoretical constructions introduced in section 11.1. The interpretation is presented in a set theoretical notation, a general categorical treatment would require an amount of category theoretical background that goes beyond our goals. In this respect let us mention [AL91] which contains a rather complete analysis of the categorical structure needed to interpret second order types from the viewpoint of *indexed category theory* and *internal category theory*. Several approaches to the categorical semantics of dependent types have been considered, we refer to [Ehr88, JMS91] for accounts based on fibrations.

In section 11.3 we describe another interpretation of type theories based on the idea that *types denote retractions*. In this respect we take two different but related approaches. First, we further develop the properties of the domain of finitary projections studied in section 7.4. In particular we show how to represent dependent and second order types in this structure. It turns out that certain 'size problems' encountered in the domain constructions described in section 11.1 can be avoided in this context. Second, we present an extension of the $\lambda\beta$-calculus called $\lambda\beta p$-calculus in which '$p$' is a constant that denotes the *retraction of all retractions*. We define a simple, adequate translation of the $\lambda P2$-calculus in the $\lambda\beta p$-calculus.

The $\lambda P2$-calculus can be seen as the combination of two systems of independent interest: the system LF of dependent types and the system F of second order types. We reserve the sections 11.4 and 11.5 to a careful presentation of the syntactic properties of these two systems, the main result being that both systems enjoy the strong normalization property (this property is enjoyed by the $\lambda P2$-calculus as well and can be proved by combining the techniques for system F and system LF). We also discuss two interesting applications that illustrate the expressive power of these systems: (1) The system LF has been proposed as a tool for the encoding of certain recurring aspects of logical systems such as $\alpha$-conversion and substitution. We illustrate this principle by presenting an adequate and faithful representation of first order classical logic in LF. (2) The system F can represent a large variety of inductively defined structures and functions defined on them by *iteration*.

# 11.1   Domain theoretical constructions

In set theory we may represent a family of sets as a function $F : X \to \mathbf{Set}$. More precisely, we consider a graph given as $\{(x, Fx)\}_{x \in X}$. In this way we do not have to speak about the *class* of sets. We formulate some basic constructions that will be suitably abstracted in the sequel. In the first place we can build the (disjoint) sum of the sets in the family as:

$$\Sigma_X F = \{(x, y) \mid x \in X \text{ and } y \in Fx\} \; .$$

Observe that there is a projection morphism $p : \Sigma_X F \to X$ that is defined as $p(x, y) = x$. On the other hand we can build a product of the sets in the family as:

$$\Pi_X F = \{f : X \to \bigcup_{x \in X} Fx \mid \forall x \in X \; (fx \in Fx)\} \; .$$

There is another way to write $\Pi_X F$ using the notion of a *section* of the projection morphism $p : \Sigma_X F \to X$ (the weakness of this method is that it requires the existence of $\Sigma_X F$). A section is a morphism $s : X \to \Sigma_X F$ such that $p \circ s = id_X$, in other words for any $x \in X$ the section $s$ picks up an element in $Fx$. It is then clear that the collection of sections of $p$ is in bijective correspondence with $\Pi_X F$.

**Exercise 11.1.1** *Verify that the definitions of $\Sigma_X F$ and $\Pi_X F$ can be completed so as to obtain the sum (or coproduct) and product of the objects in the family in the category of sets.*

**Exercise 11.1.2** *Suppose that the family $F : X \to \mathbf{Set}$ is constant, say $F(x) = Y$ for each $x$ in $X$. Then verify that $\Sigma_X F \cong X \times Y$, and $\Pi_X F \cong X \to Y$.*

**Exercise 11.1.3** *Show that every small category* **C** *with arbitrary products is a poset (this is an observation of Freyd). Hint: We recall that a category is small if the collection of its morphisms is a set. Given two distinct morphisms* $f, g : a \to b$ *in* **C** *consider products of the form* $\Pi_I b$. *The cardinality of* $\mathbf{C}[a, \Pi_I b]$ *exceeds that of* $Mor_\mathbf{C}$ *when* $I$ *is big enough.*

**Remark 11.1.4** *Observe that in the definition of* $\Sigma_X F$ *and* $\Pi_X F$ *it is important that* $X$ *is a set, so that the graph of* $F$ *is again a set, and so are* $\Sigma_X F$ *and* $\Pi_X F$. *This observation is a prelude to the problem we will find when dealing with second order types. In the interpretation suggested above neither the graph of a family* $F : \mathbf{Set} \to \mathbf{Set}$ *nor* $\Sigma_{\mathbf{Set}} F$ *and* $\Pi_{\mathbf{Set}} F$ *turn out to be sets!*

In the following we generalize the ideas sketched above to a categorical setting. Given a functor $F : \mathbf{X} \to \mathbf{Cat}$, the category $\Sigma_\mathbf{X} F$ provides the interpretation of the sum. On the other hand, the product is represented by the category of *sections*, say $\Pi_\mathbf{X} F$, of the *fibration* $p : \Sigma_\mathbf{X} F \to \mathbf{X}$ that projects $\Sigma_\mathbf{X} F$ onto $\mathbf{X}$. A section $s$ of $p$ is a functor $s : \mathbf{X} \to \Sigma_\mathbf{X} F$ such that $p \circ s = id_\mathbf{X}$.

**Dependent types in Cat.** Let $F : \mathbf{X} \to \mathbf{Cat}$ be a functor where $\mathbf{X}$ is a small category, we define the categories $\Sigma_\mathbf{X} F, \Pi_\mathbf{X} F$, and the functor $p : \Sigma_\mathbf{X} F \to \mathbf{X}$ as follows:

$$
\begin{aligned}
\Sigma_\mathbf{X} F &= \{(x, y) \mid x \in \mathbf{X}, y \in Fx\} \\
\Sigma_\mathbf{X} F[(x, y), (x', y')] &= \{(f, \alpha) \mid f : x \to x', \alpha : F(f)(y) \to y'\} \\
id_{(x,y)} &= (id_x, id_y) \\
(g, \beta) \circ (f, \alpha) &= (g \circ f, \beta \circ (Fg)(\alpha)) \,.
\end{aligned}
$$

The category $\Sigma_\mathbf{X} F$ is often called the *Grothendieck category*. The functor $p : \Sigma_\mathbf{X} F \to \mathbf{X}$ is defined as: $p(x, y) = x$, $p(f, \alpha) = f$. The category $\Pi_\mathbf{X} F$ is defined as:

$$
\begin{aligned}
\Pi_\mathbf{X} F &= \{s : \mathbf{X} \to \Sigma_\mathbf{X} F \mid p \circ s = id_\mathbf{X}\} \\
\Pi_\mathbf{X} F[s, s'] &= \{\nu : s \to s' \mid \nu \text{ is a } \textit{cartesian} \text{ natural transformation}\} \,,
\end{aligned}
$$

where a *cartesian* natural transformation $\nu : s \to s'$ is a natural transformation determined by a family $\{(id_x, \gamma_x)\}_{x \in X}$ with $s(x) = (x, y)$, $s'(x) = (x, z)$, and $\gamma_x : y \to z$ (so the first component of the transformation is constrained to be the identity). Observe that for a section $s$ we have $s(x) = (x, y)$, for all $x \in \mathbf{X}$, and $s(f) = (f, \alpha)$, for all $f \in Mor_\mathbf{X}$.

The next issue concerns the specialization of these definitions to the categories of cpo's and Scott domains. The problem is to determine suitable continuity conditions so that the constructions of sum and product return a 'domain', say an algebraic cpo. It turns out that everything works smoothly for dependent types. On the other hand second order types give some problems.

(1) The sum of a second order type is not in general a domain.

(2) The product of a second order type is only equivalent, as a category, to a domain.

(3) Bifinite domains are not closed under the product construction (this motivates our shift towards Scott domains).

**Dependent types in Cpo.** We refine the construction above to the case where $F : D \rightarrow \mathbf{Cpo}^{ip}$ is a functor, $D$ is a cpo, and $\mathbf{Cpo}^{ip}$ is the category of cpo's and injection-projection pairs. In other terms $\mathbf{X}$ becomes a poset category $D$ and the codomain of the functor is $\mathbf{Cpo}^{ip}$. By convention, if $d \leq d'$ in $D$ then we also denote with $d \leq d'$ the unique morphism from $d$ to $d'$ in the poset category $D$. If $f : D \rightarrow E$ is a morphism in $\mathbf{Cpo}^{ip}$ then we denote with $f^+$ the injection and with $f^-$ the projection.

**Proposition 11.1.5 (dependent sum in $\mathbf{Cpo}^{ip}$)** *Let $D$ be a cpo and $F : D \rightarrow \mathbf{Cpo}^{ip}$ be a functor, then the following is a cpo:*

$$\Sigma_D F = \{(d, e) \mid d \in D, e \in Fd\}, \ \textit{ordered by}$$
$$(d, e) \leq_\Sigma (d', e') \ \textit{iff} \ d \leq_D d' \ \textit{and} \ F(d \leq d')^+(e) \leq_{Fd'} e' \ .$$

PROOF. By proposition 3.1.5, the category $\mathbf{Cpo}^{ip}$ is the same as the category where a morphism is the injection component of an injection-projection pair. The latter is a subcategory of $\mathbf{Cat}$. It is immediate to verify that $(\Sigma_D F, \leq_\Sigma)$ is a poset with least element $(\bot_D, \bot_{F(\bot_D)})$.

Next let $X = \{(d_i, e_i)\}_{i \in I}$ be directed in $\Sigma_D F$. Set for $d = \bigvee_{i \in I} d_i$:

$$\bigvee X = (d, \bigvee_{i \in I} F(d_i \leq d)^+(e_i)) \ .$$

We claim that this is well defined and the lub of $X$ in $\Sigma_D F$.

- $\{F(d_i \leq d)^+(e_i)\}_{i \in I}$ is directed. Since $X$ is directed:

$$\forall i, j \ \exists k \ (d_i \leq d_k, \ d_j \leq d_k, \ F(d_i \leq d_k)^+(e_i) \leq e_k, \ F(d_j \leq d_k)^+(e_j) \leq e_k) \ .$$

Hence $F(d_i \leq d)^+(e_i) = F(d_k \leq d)^+ \circ F(d_i \leq d_k)^+(e_i) \leq F(d_k \leq d)^+(e_k)$, and similarly for $j$.

- $\bigvee X$ is an upper bound for $X$. Immediate, by definition.

- $\bigvee X$ is the lub. If $(d', e')$ is an upper bound for $X$ then it is clear that $d \leq d'$. Next we observe:

$$F(d \leq d')^+(\bigvee_{i \in I} F(d_i \leq d)^+(e_i)) \ = \ \bigvee_{i \in I} F(d \leq d')^+(F(d_i \leq d)^+(e_i))$$
$$= \ \bigvee_{i \in I} (F(d_i \leq d')^+(e_i)) \leq e' \ . \qquad \square$$

**Exercise 11.1.6** *Verify that the definition of $\Sigma_D F$ is an instance of the definition in* **Cat***.*

**Proposition 11.1.7 (dependent product in $\mathbf{Cpo}^{ip}$)** *Let $D$ be a cpo and $F : D \rightarrow \mathbf{Cpo}^{ip}$ be a functor, then the following is a cpo with the pointwise order induced by the space $D \rightarrow \Sigma_D F$ (we use the notation $[\Pi_D F]$ to distinguish this product from the general product construction described above for* **Cat***):*

$$[\Pi_D F] = \{s : D \rightarrow \Sigma_D F \mid s \ \textit{cocontinuous}, \ p \circ s = id_D\} \ .$$

PROOF. We observe that $p : \Sigma_D F \to D$ is continuous as for any $\{(d_i, e_i)\}_{i \in I}$ directed set in $\Sigma_D F$ we have, taking $d = \bigvee_{i \in I} d_i$:

$$
\begin{aligned}
p(\textstyle\bigvee_{i \in I}(d_i, e_i)) &= p(\textstyle\bigvee_{i \in I} d_i, \bigvee_{i \in I} F(d_i \leq d)^+(e_i)) \\
&= \textstyle\bigvee_{i \in I} d_i = \bigvee_{i \in I} p(d_i, e_i) \ .
\end{aligned}
$$

We can also define a least section as $s(d) = (d, \perp_{Fd})$. Next we remark that for any directed set $\{s_i\}_{i \in I}$ in $[\Pi_D F]$ we have, for any $d \in D$:

$$
p \circ (\bigvee_{i \in I} s_i)(d) = p(\bigvee_{i \in I} s_i(d)) = \bigvee_{i \in I} p(s_i(d)) = d \ .
$$

Hence the lub of a directed set of sections exists and it is the same as the lub in $D \to \Sigma_D F$. $\qquad\square$

We give an equivalent definition of cocontinuous section.

**Definition 11.1.8** *Let $D$ be a cpo and $F : D \to \mathbf{Cpo}^{ip}$ be a functor. Consider $f : D \to \bigcup_{d \in D} Fd$ such that $fd \in Fd$, for each $d \in D$. We say that $f$ is cocontinuous if $F(d \leq d')^+(fd) \leq fd'$, and for any $\{d_i\}_{i \in I}$ directed in $D$, such that $\bigvee_{i \in I} d_i = d$,*

$$
f(d) = \bigvee_{i \in I} F(d_i \leq d)^+(f(d_i)) \ .
$$

Clearly $[\Pi_D F]$ is isomorphic to:

$$
\{f : D \to \bigcup_{d \in D} Fd \mid \forall d \ (fd \in Fd) \text{ and } f \text{ is cocontinuous}\},
$$

ordered by $f \leq g$ iff $\forall d \in D \ (fd \leq_{Fd} gd)$.

**Dependent types in Scott domains.** We denote with $\mathbf{S}$ (S for Scott) the category of algebraic, bounded complete cpo's (Scott domains for short, cf. definition 1.4.9). The following hypotheses suffice to guarantee that the constructions defined above return Scott domains:

- The domain of the family is a Scott domain.

- The codomain of the family is the category $\mathbf{S}^{ip}$ of Scott domains and injection-projection pairs.

- Less obviously, the functor $F$ is *cocontinuous* in a sense which we define next.

**Definition 11.1.9 (directed colimits)** *A* directed diagram *is a diagram indexed over a directed set. We say that a category has* directed colimits *if it has colimits of directed diagrams. We say that a functor is* cocontinuous *if it preserves colimits of directed diagrams (cf. proposition 7.1.3).*

Applying the theory developed in section 7.1 it is easy to derive the following properties.

**Proposition 11.1.10** (1) *The category* $\mathbf{S}^{ip}$ *has directed colimits.*

(2) *Given a Scott domain $D$ and a functor $F : D \to \mathbf{S}^{ip}$, $F$ is cocontinuous iff for any $\{d_i\}_{i \in I}$ directed in $D$ such that $\bigvee_{i \in I} d_i = d$,*

$$\bigvee_{i \in I} F(d_i \le d)^+ \circ F(d_i \le d)^- = id_{Fd} \ .$$

(3) *A functor $F : \mathbf{S}^{ip} \to \mathbf{S}^{ip}$ is cocontinuous iff for any Scott domain $D$ and any directed set $\{p_i\}_{i \in I}$ of projections over $D$,*

$$\bigvee_{i \in I} p_i = id_D \quad \Rightarrow \quad \bigvee_{i \in I} F(p_i) = id_{FD} \ .$$

**Proposition 11.1.11 (dependent sum and product in Scott domains)** *Let $D$ be a Scott domain and $F : D \to \mathbf{S}^{ip}$ be a cocontinuous functor, then the cpo's $\Sigma_D F$ and $[\Pi_D F]$ are Scott domains.*

PROOF. • $\Sigma_D F$ is bounded complete. Let $X = \{(d_i, e_i)\}_{i \in I}$ be bounded in $\Sigma_D F$ by $(d', e')$. Then: (i) $\{d_i\}_{i \in I}$ is bounded in $D$ by $d'$ and therefore $\exists \bigvee_{i \in I} d_i = d$. (ii) Moreover $\{F(d_i \le d)^+(e_i)\}_{i \in I}$ is bounded by $F(d \le d')^-(e')$ as:

$$F(d_i \le d')^+(e_i) = F(d \le d')^+ F(d_i \le d)^+(e_i) \le e' \Rightarrow$$
$$F(d_i \le d)^+(e_i) \le F(d \le d')^-(e') \ .$$

Hence we set $e = \bigvee_{i \in I} F(d_i \le d)^+(e_i)$. It is immediate to check that $(d, e)$ is the lub.

• $\Sigma_D F$ is algebraic. We claim:

(1) $\mathcal{K}(\Sigma_D F) \supseteq \{(d, e) \mid d \in \mathcal{K}(D) \text{ and } e \in \mathcal{K}(Fd)\} = K.$

(2) For any $(d, e) \in \Sigma_D F$, $\downarrow (d, e) \cap K$ is directed with lub $(d, e)$.

Proof of (1). Let $d' \in \mathcal{K}(D)$, $e' \in \mathcal{K}(Fd')$, and $X = \{(d_i, e_i)\}_{i \in I}$ be directed in $\Sigma_D F$ with $d' \le \bigvee_{i \in I} d_i = d$, and $F(d' \le d)^+(e') \le \bigvee_{i \in I} F(d_i \le d)^+(e_i)$. By hypothesis, $d'$ and $e'$ are compact. $F(d' \le d)^+(e')$ is also compact (by proposition 3.1.6), hence we can find $j$ such that $d' \le d_j$, $F(d' \le d)^+(e') \le F(d_j \le d)^+(e_j)$, that implies $F(d' \le d_j)^+(e') \le e_j$. That is $(d', e') \le (d_j, e_j)$. Hence $(d', e') \in \mathcal{K}(\Sigma_D F)$.

Proof of (2). The set is directed because $\Sigma_D F$ is bounded complete. Given $(d, e)$ we consider:

(i) $\{d_i\}_{i \in I} \subseteq \mathcal{K}(D)$ directed such that $\bigvee_{i \in I} d_i = d$, and

(ii) $\forall i \in I$ $\{e_{i,j}\}_{j \in J_i} \subseteq \mathcal{K}(Fd_i)$ directed such that $\bigvee_{j \in J_i} e_{i,j} = F(d_i \le d)^-(e)$.

Then the following equations hold (the last one by cocontinuity of $F$):

$$
\begin{aligned}
\bigvee_{i \in I, j \in J_i} (d_i, e_{ij}) &= (d, \bigvee_{i \in I, j \in J_i} F(d_i \le d)^+(e_{i,j})) \\
&= (d, \bigvee_{i \in I} F(d_i \le d)^+(\bigvee_{j \in J_i} e_{i,j})) \\
&= (d, \bigvee_{i \in I} F(d_i \le d)^+ F(d_i \le d)^-(e)) = (d, e) \ .
\end{aligned}
$$

• $[\Pi_D F]$ is bounded complete. Suppose $\{s_i\}_{i \in I}$ is a bounded set in $[\Pi_D F]$. Since bounded completeness is preserved by exponentiation we can compute $\bigvee_{i \in I} s_i$ in $D \to \Sigma_D F$. It remains to observe that $p \circ (\bigvee_{i \in I} s_i) = id_D$, as in the proof of proposition 11.1.7.

• $[\Pi_D F]$ is algebraic. We consider the step sections (cf. lemma 1.4.8) $[d, e]$ for $d \in \mathcal{K}(D)$, $e \in \mathcal{K}(Fd)$, defined as:

$$[d, e](x) = \begin{cases} (x, F(d \leq x)^+(e)) & \text{if } d \leq x \\ (x, \perp_{Fx}) & \text{otherwise .} \end{cases}$$

One can verify that $[d, e]$ is compact in $[\Pi_D F]$. It remains to observe that for any $s \in [\Pi_D F]$, $\bigvee\{[d, e] \mid [d, e] \leq s\} = s$. □

**Second order types in Scott domains.** We look for an interpretation of second order types as domains. Suppose that $F : \mathbf{S}^{ip} \to \mathbf{S}^{ip}$ is a cocontinuous functor. Then, as an instance of the general categorical construction, we can form the category $\Sigma_{\mathbf{S}^{ip}} F$. It is easily verified that $\Sigma_{\mathbf{S}^{ip}} F$ does not need to be a preorder as there can be several injection-projection pairs between two domains. We therefore concentrate our efforts on products. To this end we spell out the notion of cocontinuous section which is similar to definition 11.1.8.

**Definition 11.1.12** *Let $F : \mathbf{S}^{ip} \to \mathbf{S}^{ip}$ be a cocontinuous functor. A cocontinuous section $s$ is a family $\{s(D)\}_{D \in \mathbf{S}^{ip}}$, where $s(D) \in F(D)$, and such that:*

$$f : D \to E \text{ in } \mathbf{S}^{ip} \quad \Rightarrow \quad F(f)^+(s(D)) \leq s(E) , \tag{11.1}$$

*and for any $D \in \mathbf{S}^{ip}$ for any $\{f_i : D_i \to D\}_{i \in I}$ such that $\{f_i^+ \circ f_i^-\}_{i \in I}$ is directed we have:*

$$\bigvee_{i \in I}(f_i^+ \circ f_i^-) = id_D \quad \Rightarrow \quad s(D) = \bigvee_{i \in I}(F f_i)^+(s(D_i)) . \tag{11.2}$$

Let $[\Pi_{\mathbf{S}}^{ip} F]$ be the collection of cocontinuous sections with the pointwise partial order:

$$s \leq s' \text{ iff } \forall D \in \mathbf{S}^{ip} \ (s(D) \leq s'(D)) .$$

The problem with this partial order is that the (graphs of) cocontinuous sections are not sets, hence a fortiori $[\Pi_{\mathbf{S}^{ip}} F]$ cannot be a Scott domain. However there is a way out of this foundational problem, namely it is possible to build a Scott domain which is order isomorphic to $[\Pi_{\mathbf{S}^{ip}} F]$. To this end we observe that the compact objects (cf. definition 7.3.3) in $\mathbf{S}^{ip}$ are the finite bounded complete cpo's, and that there is an enumeration $S_o = \{C_i\}_{i \in \omega}$ up to order-isomorphism of the compact objects. We define $[\Pi_{\mathbf{S}_o^{ip}} F]$ as the collection of sections $\{s(D)\}_{D \in \mathbf{S}_o^{ip}}$ such that:

$$s : D \to E \text{ in } \mathbf{S}_o^{ip} \quad \Rightarrow \quad F(f)^+(s(D)) \leq s(E) . \tag{11.3}$$

This is the monotonicity condition 11.1 in definition 11.1.12 restricted to the subcategory $\mathbf{S}_o^{ip}$ (there is no limit condition, as $\mathbf{S}_o^{ip}$ is made up of compact objects). We observe that $[\Pi_{\mathbf{S}_o^{ip}} F]$ with the pointwise order is a poset. The following theorem is due to [Coq89], after [Gir86]. The basic remark is that a cocontinuous section is determined by its behaviour on $\mathbf{S}_o^{ip}$.

**Theorem 11.1.13 (second order product)** *Let* $F : \mathbf{S}^{ip} \to \mathbf{S}^{ip}$ *be a cocontinuous functor. Then the following properties hold:*

(1) $[\Pi_{\mathbf{S}^{ip}} F]$ *is order isomorphic to* $[\Pi_{\mathbf{S}^{ip}_o} F]$.

(2) *The poset* $[\Pi_{\mathbf{S}^{ip}_o} F]$ *is a Scott-domain.*

PROOF HINT. (1) Any cocontinuous section $s \in [\Pi_{\mathbf{S}^{ip}} F]$ determines by restriction a section $res(s) \in [\Pi_{\mathbf{S}^{ip}_o} F]$. Vice versa, given a section $s \in [\Pi_{\mathbf{S}^{ip}_o} F]$ we define its extension $ext(s)$, as follows:

$$ext(s)(E) = \bigvee\{(Ff)^+(s(D)) \mid D \in \mathbf{S}^{ip}_o \text{ and } f : D \to E \text{ in } \mathbf{S}^{ip}\} . \qquad (11.4)$$

Given $f_0 : D_0 \to E$, $f_1 : D_1 \to E$ we can find $D' \in \mathbf{S}^{ip}_o$ and $g_0 : D_0 \to D'$, $g_1 : D_1 \to D'$, $g : D' \to E$ such that $g \circ g_0 = f_0$ and $g \circ g_1 = f_1$. Hence the set $\{(Ff)^+(s(D)) \mid D \in \mathbf{S}^{ip}_o \text{ and } f : D \to E \text{ in } \mathbf{S}^{ip}\}$ is directed. The section $ext(s)$ satisfies condition 11.1 because given $g : E \to E'$ we compute:

$$
\begin{aligned}
(Fg)^+(ext(s)(E)) &= (Fg)^+(\bigvee\{(Ff)^+(s(D)) \mid D \in \mathbf{S}^{ip}_o \text{ and } f : D \to E\}) \\
&= \bigvee\{F(g \circ f)^+(s(D)) \mid D \in \mathbf{S}^{ip}_o \text{ and } f : D \to E\} \\
&\leq \bigvee\{F(h)^+(s(D)) \mid D \in \mathbf{S}^{ip}_o \text{ and } h : D \to E'\} = ext(s)(E') .
\end{aligned}
$$

With reference to condition 11.2 we need to check that:

$$ext(s)(D) \leq \bigvee_{i \in I}(Ff_i)^+(ext(s)(D_i))$$

(the other inequality follows by condition 11.1). According to the definition of $ext$ consider $D' \in \mathbf{S}^{ip}_o$ and $f : D' \to D$. Since $\mathbf{S}^{ip}$ is almost an algebroidal category (cf. exercise 7.3.9), we can find $j \in I$ and $h : D' \to D_j$ such that $f_j \circ h = f$. Then:

$$
\begin{aligned}
F(f)^+(s(D')) &= F(f_j \circ h)^+(s(D')) \\
&= F(f_j)^+((Fh)^+(s(D'))) \leq F(f_j)^+(ext(s(D_j))) .
\end{aligned}
$$

It is easily checked that $res$ and $ext$ are monotonic. We observe that $s(D) = ext(s)(D)$ if $D \in \mathbf{S}^{ip}_o$. To show $res(ext(s)) \leq s$, consider the identity on $D$, and to prove $res(ext(s)) \geq s$ use condition 11.1.

To prove $ext(res(s)) = s$ we compute, applying condition 11.2 to $s$:

$$
\begin{aligned}
ext(res(s))(D) &= \bigvee\{(Ff)^+((res(s))(D')) \mid D' \in \mathbf{S}^{ip}_o \text{ and } f : D' \to D\} \\
&= \bigvee\{(Ff)^+(s(D')) \mid D' \in \mathbf{S}^{ip}_o \text{ and } f : D' \to D\} = s(D) .
\end{aligned}
$$

(2) The least element is the section $\{\perp_D\}_{D \in \mathbf{S}^{ip}_o}$. The lub $s$ of a directed set $\{s_i\}_{i \in I}$ is defined as $s(D) = \bigvee_{i \in I} s_i(D)$. Bounded completeness is left to the reader. To show algebraicity, we define for $D \in \mathbf{S}^{ip}_o$ and $e \in \mathcal{K}(FD)$ the section:

$$[D, e](D') = \bigvee\{(Ff)^+(e) \mid f : D \to D' \text{ in } \mathbf{S}^{ip}\} . \qquad (11.5)$$

Compact elements are the existing finite lub's of sections with the shape 11.5. □

Hence, although $[\Pi_{\mathbf{S}^{ip}} F]$ is not a poset because its elements are classes, it is nevertheless order-isomorphic to a Scott domain $[\Pi_{\mathbf{S}^{ip}_o} F]$. Figure 11.1 summarizes our results on the closure properties of the $\Sigma$ and $\Pi$ constructions in the categories $\mathbf{Cpo}^{ip}$ and $\mathbf{S}^{ip}$.

$F : D \to \mathbf{Cpo}^{ip}$, $F$ functor, $D$ cpo     $\Rightarrow \Sigma_D F$, $[\Pi_D F]$ cpo's

$F : D \to \mathbf{S}^{ip}$, $F$ cocont., $D$ Scott domain     $\Rightarrow \Sigma_D F$, $[\Pi_D F]$ Scott domains

$F : \mathbf{S}^{ip} \to \mathbf{S}^{ip}$, $F$ cocont.     $\Rightarrow [\Pi_{\mathbf{S}^{ip}} F] \cong [\Pi_{\mathbf{S}_o^{ip}} F]$ Scott domain

Figure 11.1: Dependent and second order types in $\mathbf{Cpo}^{ip}$ and $\mathbf{S}^{ip}$

**Exercise 11.1.14** *Consider the identity functor* $Id : \mathbf{S}^{ip} \to \mathbf{S}^{ip}$. *Prove that* $[\Pi_{\mathbf{S}^{ip}} Id]$ *is the cpo with one element. Hint: Let* $s$ *be a cocontinuous section and* $D$ *a Scott domain. Then there are two standard embeddings,* $in_l$ *and* $in_r$, *of* $D$ *in* $D + D$, *where* $+$ *is the coalesced sum. The condition on sections requires that* $s(D + D) = in_l(s(D)) = in_r(s(D))$, *but this forces* $s(D) = \perp_D$.

**Remark 11.1.15** (1) *Exercise 11.1.14 hints at the fact that cocontinuous sections satisfy certain* uniformity conditions, *namely the choice of the elements has to be invariant with respect to certain embeddings. In practice syntactically definable functors are 'very' uniform so we can look for even stronger uniformity conditions in the model. Here is one that arises in the* stable case *(see chapter 12 and [Gir86]) and that leads to a 'smaller' interpretation of certain types (for a suitable category* **C***).*

$$h : D \to E \text{ in } \mathbf{C}^{ip} \Rightarrow s(D) = (F(h))^-(s(E)) . \tag{11.6}$$

*This condition implies the standard condition in the continuous case. In the stable case one considers stable* injection projection pairs *(cf. section 12.4) and the sections s are such that for all D, s(D) is stable.*

(2) *It can be proved that bifinite domains are not closed with respect to the* $[\Pi_{\mathbf{Bif}} F]$ *construction (see [Jun90]). The basic problem arises from the observation that* $\mathbf{S}_o^{ip}$ *does not need to satisfy property M (cf. definition 5.2.6).*

The following two exercises require the knowledge of stability theory and of coherence spaces (chapters 12 and 13). The first exercise witnesses the difference between the stable and the continuous interpretation. The second presents the uniformity condition as a requirement of stability.

**Exercise 11.1.16** *(1) Show that, in the stable setting just described, the interpretation of* $\forall t.t \to t$ *is (isomorphic to)* **O**. *(2) In contrast, show that in the continuous setting the interpretation of* $\forall t.t \to t$ *is infinite. Hints: For (1), consider a section s. Show that if* $(x, e) \in trace(s(E, \subset))$, *then* $x \subseteq \{e\}$; *make use of two injections from* $E$ *into* $E \cup e'$, *where* $e'$ *is coherent with all the events of* $x$. *Show that* $x \neq \perp$ *with a similar method (e' being now incoherent with e). Show that if s is not* $\perp$ *for all D, then* $s(\{e\}, \subset) = id$, *and hence* $s(D)$ *is the identity everywhere. For (2), consider the (non-stable) functions defined by* $s(D)(x) = x$ *if* $x$ *bounds at least* $n$ *compact elements of* $D$, *and* $s(D)(x) = \perp$ *otherwise.*

**Exercise 11.1.17 (Moggi)** *Let $s$ be a section satisfying the condition in the proof of theorem 11.1.13 and consisting of stable functions. Show that $s$ satisfies the uniformity condition 11.6 iff $s$, viewed as a functor in the Grothendieck category, preserves pullbacks. Hints: (1) Show that $f : (D, x) \rightarrow (D', x')$ and $f' : (D, x) \rightarrow (D', x'')$ form the limit cone of a pullback diagram in the Grothendieck category iff $x = F(f)^{-}(x') \wedge F(f')^{-}(x'')$. (2) Show that for any stable injection-projection pair $f : D \rightarrow D'$, the pair of $f$ and $f$ forms the limit cone of a pullback diagram.*

## 11.2  Dependent and second order types

We introduce the typing rules of the $\lambda P2$-calculus, a $\lambda$-calculus with dependent and second order types. We restrict our attention to the introduction and elimination rules for products. The syntactic categories of the $\lambda P2$-calculus are presented as follows.

| | |
|---|---|
| Variables | $v ::= x \mid y \mid \ldots$ |
| Contexts | $\Gamma ::= \emptyset \mid \Gamma, v : \sigma \mid \Gamma, v : K$ |
| Kinds | $K ::= tp \mid \Pi v : \sigma.K$ |
| Type Families | $\sigma ::= v \mid \Pi v : \sigma.\sigma \mid \Pi v : tp.\sigma \mid \lambda v : \sigma.\sigma \mid \sigma M$ |
| Objects | $M ::= v \mid \lambda v : \sigma.M \mid \lambda v : tp.M \mid MM \mid M\sigma$ . |

Contexts, type families, and objects generalize the syntactic categories we have already defined in the simply typed case (cf. chapter 4). *Kinds* form a new syntactic category, which is used to classify type families, so, intuitively, kinds are the 'types of types'. The basic kind is $tp$ which represents the collection of all types. More complex kinds are built using the $\Pi$ construction and are employed to classify functions from types to the collection of types (type families). The formal system is based on the following *judgments*.

| | |
|---|---|
| Well-formed kind | $\Gamma \vdash K : kd$ |
| Well-formed type family | $\Gamma \vdash \sigma : K$ |
| Well-formed object | $\Gamma \vdash M : \sigma$ . |

The formal rules are displayed in figure 11.2. In the following we will use $A, B, \ldots$ as meta-symbols ranging over objects, type families, kinds, and a special constant $kd$ which is introduced here just to have a uniform notation.

A type is a well-formed type family of kind $tp$. We point-out some properties of the formal system. In a well-formed object $\Gamma \vdash M : \sigma$, $\sigma$ is a type. A well-formed context has always the shape $x_1 : A_1, \ldots, x_n : A_n$ where $A_i$ is either a kind or a type. Note that $A_i$ might actually depend on the previous variables. Syntactically this entails that the rule of exchange of premises is not derivable in the system; the order of hypotheses is important. Semantically we remark that a context cannot be simply interpreted as a product. We will see next that the product is replaced by the Grothendieck category (which generalizes the product, cf. exercise 11.1.2).

The formation rules for kinds are directly related to those for contexts, indeed we use $\Gamma \vdash tp : kd$ to state that the context $\Gamma$ is well-formed. One can consider a slightly less synthetic presentation in which one adds a fourth judgment, say $\Gamma \vdash ok$, which asserts the well-formation of contexts.

We remark that not all premises in the context can be $\lambda$-abstracted. In particular, type families cannot be abstracted with respect to kinds, and objects can be abstracted only with respect to types and the kind *tp*. By convention we abbreviate $\Pi x : A.B$ with $A \to B$, whenever $x \notin FV(B)$.

In the $\lambda P2$-calculus it is not possible to type a *closed* type family

$$\lambda x : \sigma.\tau : \Pi x : \sigma.tp$$

in such a way that $\tau$ actually depends on $x$. In the applications (e.g., see section 11.4) we enrich the calculus with constants such as $Prod.bool : nat \to tp$.

Finally, we note that the rules $(tp.\Pi_I)$ and $(tp.\Pi_E)$ for type families follow the same pattern of the rules $(\Pi_I)$ and $(\Pi_E)$ for objects.

Kinds and types are assigned to type families and objects, respectively, modulo $\beta$-conversion (rules $(tp.Eq)$ and $(Eq)$). Formally, we define the relation $=$ as the symmetric and transitive closure of a relation of *parallel* $\beta$-reduction which is specified in figure 11.3. This is a suitable variation over the notion of parallel $\beta$-reduction that we have defined in figure 2.5 to prove the confluence of the untyped $\lambda\beta$-calculus. Note that the definition of the reduction relation does not rely on the typability of the terms. Indeed this is not necessary to obtain confluence as stated in the following.

**Proposition 11.2.1 (confluence)** *If $A \Rightarrow A'$ and $A \Rightarrow A''$ then there is $B$ such that $A' \Rightarrow B$ and $A'' \Rightarrow B$.*

PROOF HINT. Show that if $A \Rightarrow A'$ and $B \Rightarrow B'$ then $A[B/x] \Rightarrow A'[B'/x]$. □

We state three useful properties of the $\lambda P2$-calculus. We omit the proofs which go by simple inductions on the length of the proof and the structure of the terms.

**Proposition 11.2.2** *The following properties hold:*

| | |
|---|---|
| *Type uniqueness* | $\Gamma \vdash A : B, \ \Gamma \vdash A : B' \ \Rightarrow \ B = B'.$ |
| *Abstraction typing* | $\Gamma \vdash \lambda x : A.A' : \Pi x : B.C \ \Rightarrow \ \Gamma, x : A \vdash A' : C \text{ and } A=B.$ |
| *Subject reduction* | $\Gamma \vdash A : B, \ A \Rightarrow A' \ \Rightarrow \ \Gamma \vdash A' : B.$ |

Let us briefly discuss two relevant extensions of the $\lambda P2$-calculus:

• When embedding logics or data structures in the $\lambda P2$-calculus it is often useful to include $\eta$-conversion as well (cf. sections 11.4 and 11.5):

$$(\eta) \quad \lambda x : A.(Bx) = B \quad x \notin FV(B) . \tag{11.7}$$

The system with $\beta\eta$-conversion is still confluent and strongly normalizing but the proof of this fact is considerably harder than the one for $\beta$-conversion. A basic problem is that *confluence cannot be proved without appealing to typing*. Consider:

$$N \equiv \lambda x : \sigma.(\lambda y : \tau.M)x \quad x \notin FV(M)$$
$$N \to_\beta \lambda x : \sigma.M[x/y] \quad N \to_\eta \lambda y : \tau.M .$$

$$(K.\emptyset) \quad \frac{}{\emptyset \vdash tp : kd} \qquad\qquad (K.kd) \quad \frac{\Gamma \vdash K : kd \quad x \notin dom(\Gamma)}{\Gamma, x : K \vdash tp : kd}$$

$$(K.tp) \quad \frac{\Gamma \vdash \sigma : tp \quad x \notin dom(\Gamma)}{\Gamma, x : \sigma \vdash tp : kd} \qquad (K.\Pi) \quad \frac{\Gamma, x : \sigma \vdash K : kd \quad \Gamma \vdash \sigma : tp}{\Gamma \vdash \Pi x : \sigma.K : kd}$$

Well-formed kind

$$(tp.Asmp) \quad \frac{x : K \in \Gamma \quad \Gamma \vdash tp : kd}{\Gamma \vdash x : K} \qquad (tp.Eq) \quad \frac{\Gamma \vdash \sigma : K \quad \Gamma \vdash K' : kd \quad K = K'}{\Gamma \vdash \sigma : K'}$$

$$(tp.\Pi) \quad \frac{\Gamma, x : \sigma \vdash \tau : tp \quad \Gamma \vdash \sigma : tp}{\Gamma \vdash \Pi x : \sigma.\tau : tp} \qquad (tp.\Pi^2) \quad \frac{\Gamma, x : tp \vdash \tau : tp}{\Gamma \vdash \Pi x : tp.\tau : tp}$$

$$(tp.\Pi_I) \quad \frac{\Gamma, x : \sigma \vdash \tau : K \quad \Gamma \vdash \sigma : tp}{\Gamma \vdash \lambda x : \sigma.\tau : \Pi x : \sigma.K} \qquad (tp.\Pi_E) \quad \frac{\Gamma \vdash \tau : \Pi x : \sigma.K \quad \Gamma \vdash M : \sigma}{\Gamma \vdash \tau M : K[M/x]}$$

Well-formed type family

$$(Asmp) \quad \frac{x : \sigma \in \Gamma \quad \Gamma \vdash tp : kd}{\Gamma \vdash x : \sigma} \qquad (Eq) \quad \frac{\Gamma \vdash M : \sigma \quad \Gamma \vdash \tau : tp \quad \sigma = \tau}{\Gamma \vdash M : \tau}$$

$$(\Pi_I) \quad \frac{\Gamma, x : \sigma \vdash M : \tau \quad \Gamma \vdash \sigma : tp}{\Gamma \vdash \lambda x : \sigma.M : \Pi x : \sigma.\tau} \qquad (\Pi_E) \quad \frac{\Gamma \vdash M : \Pi x : \sigma.\tau \quad \Gamma \vdash N : \sigma}{\Gamma \vdash MN : \tau[N/x]}$$

$$(\Pi_I^2) \quad \frac{\Gamma, x : tp \vdash M : \tau}{\Gamma \vdash \lambda x : tp.M : \Pi x : tp.\tau} \qquad (\Pi_E^2) \quad \frac{\Gamma \vdash M : \Pi x : tp.\tau \quad \Gamma \vdash \sigma : tp}{\Gamma \vdash M\sigma : \tau[\sigma/x]}$$

Well-formed object

Figure 11.2: Typing rules for the $\lambda P2$-calculus

$$\frac{A \Rightarrow A' \quad B \Rightarrow B'}{(\lambda x : C.A)B \Rightarrow A'[B'/x]} \qquad \frac{A \Rightarrow A' \quad B \Rightarrow B'}{AB \Rightarrow A'B'}$$

$$\frac{A \Rightarrow A' \quad B \Rightarrow B'}{\lambda x : A.B \Rightarrow \lambda x : A'.B'} \qquad \frac{A \Rightarrow A' \quad B \Rightarrow B'}{\Pi x : A.B \Rightarrow \Pi x : A'.B'}$$

$$\frac{}{A \Rightarrow A} \qquad \frac{A \Rightarrow C \quad B \Rightarrow C}{A = B}$$

Figure 11.3: Parallel $\beta$-reduction and equality for the $\lambda P2$-calculus

It is not possible to close the diagram unless $\sigma$ and $\tau$ are convertible. Confluence is proven by appealing to judgments of the shape $\Gamma \vdash \sigma = \tau : K$.

- The following rules can be used to formalize the $\Sigma$-construction on dependent types. The constructor $\langle -, - \rangle$ and destructors $fst, snd$ generalize the familiar operators associated with the cartesian product.

$$(tp.\Sigma) \quad \frac{\Gamma, x : \sigma \vdash \tau : tp \quad \Gamma \vdash \sigma : tp}{\Gamma \vdash \Sigma x : \sigma.\tau : tp} \qquad (\Sigma_I) \quad \frac{\Gamma \vdash M : \sigma \quad \Gamma, x : \sigma \vdash N : \tau}{\Gamma \vdash \langle M, N[M/x] \rangle : \Sigma x : \sigma.\tau}$$

$$(\Sigma_{E_1}) \quad \frac{\Gamma \vdash M : \Sigma x : \sigma.\tau}{\Gamma \vdash fst\, M : \sigma} \qquad (\Sigma_{E_2}) \quad \frac{\Gamma \vdash M : \Sigma x : \sigma.\tau}{\Gamma \vdash snd\, M : \tau[fst M/x]} \ .$$

**Interpretation in Scott domains.** We interpret the $\lambda P2$-calculus in the category of Scott domains and injection-projection pairs by appealing to the constructions introduced in section 11.1. The interpretation is given in a naive set theoretical style, our goal being to suggest how the sum and product constructions can be used in an interpretation.

In first approximation the interpretation of a context $\Gamma$ such that $\Gamma \vdash tp$ : $kd$, is a category, say $[\![\Gamma]\!]$, the interpretation of $tp$ is the category $\mathbf{S}^{ip}$ of Scott domains and injection-projection pairs, the interpretation of a type, $\Gamma \vdash \sigma : tp$, is a functor $F = [\![\Gamma \vdash \sigma : tp]\!]$ from $[\![\Gamma]\!]$ to $\mathbf{S}^{ip}$, and the interpretation of a term, $\Gamma \vdash M : \sigma$, is a section of the Grothendieck fibration $p : \Sigma_{[\![\Gamma]\!]} F \to [\![\Gamma]\!]$. Note that the interpretations are interdependent, and they are defined in figure 11.4 by induction on the derivation of the judgment. We use a set theoretical style, in a rigorous approach we should make sure that the defined objects exist in the domain theoretical model. Another aspect which we ignore is the soundness of the equality rules. Indeed, one should verify that $\beta$-reduction is adequately modelled ([CGW88] carries on this verification for second order types).

We start with the trivial category $\mathbf{1}$, and we use the Grothendieck category to extend the context. The interpretation of a kind judgment is a functor from the context interpretation to **Cat**. We define the interpretation parametrically on $y \in [\![\Gamma]\!]$. Given a variable, say $x$, occurring in the well-formed context $\Gamma$ we write $y_x$ for the projection of the $x$-th component of the vector $y \in [\![\Gamma]\!]$.

**Exercise 11.2.3** *Extend the interpretation to handle the rules for dependent sum stated above.*

# 11.3 Types as retractions *

We study two interpretations of types as (particular) retractions. In the first, we develop the properties of finitary projections (cf. chapter 7) towards the interpretation of dependent and second order types. In the second, we present a purely syntactic interpretation of the $\lambda P2$-calculus in the $\lambda \beta p$-calculus, which is a $\lambda$-calculus enriched with a constant $p$ that plays the role of a retraction of all retractions.

In section 7.4, we have discussed how to represent countably based Scott domains as finitary projections over a universal domain $U$. In the following we briefly describe

$$
\begin{aligned}
(K.\emptyset) && [\![\emptyset]\!] &= 1 \\
(K.kd) && [\![\Gamma, x : K]\!] &= \Sigma_{[\![\Gamma]\!]}[\![\Gamma \vdash K : kd]\!] \\
(K.tp) && [\![\Gamma, x : \sigma]\!] &= \Sigma_{[\![\Gamma]\!]}[\![\Gamma \vdash \sigma : tp]\!]
\end{aligned}
$$

Context interpretation

$$
\begin{aligned}
(K.\emptyset, kd, tp) && [\![\Gamma \vdash tp : kd]\!](y) &= \mathbf{S}^{ip} \\
(K.\Pi) && [\![\Gamma \vdash \Pi x : \sigma.K : kd]\!](y) &= [\Pi_{Gy}\lambda y'.F(y, y')] \\
&&& \text{where: } Gy = [\![\Gamma \vdash \sigma : tp]\!](y) \\
&&& \text{and } F(y, y') = [\![\Gamma, x : \sigma \vdash K : kd]\!](y, y')
\end{aligned}
$$

Kind interpretation

$$
\begin{aligned}
(tp.Asmp) && [\![\Gamma \vdash x : K]\!](y) &= y_x \\
(tp.\Pi) && [\![\Gamma \vdash \Pi x : \sigma.\tau : tp]\!](y) &= [\Pi_{Gy}\lambda y'.F(y, y')] \\
&&& \text{where: } Gy = [\![\Gamma \vdash \sigma : tp]\!](y) \\
&&& \text{and } F(y, y') = [\![\Gamma, x : \sigma \vdash \tau : tp]\!](y, y') \\
(tp.\Pi^2) && [\![\Gamma \vdash \Pi x : tp.\tau : tp]\!](y) &= [\Pi_{\mathbf{S}^{ip}}\lambda y'.F(y, y')] \\
&&& \text{where: } F(y, y') = [\![\Gamma, x : tp \vdash \tau : tp]\!](y, y') \\
(tp.\Pi_I) && [\![\Gamma \vdash \lambda x : \sigma.\tau : \Pi x : \sigma.K]\!](y) &= \lambda y' \in Gy.([\![\Gamma, x : \sigma \vdash \tau : K]\!])(y, y') \\
&&& \text{where: } Gy = [\![\Gamma \vdash \sigma : tp]\!](y) \\
(tp.\Pi_E) && [\![\Gamma \vdash \tau M : K[M/x]]\!](y) &= ([\![\Gamma \vdash \tau : \Pi x : \sigma.K]\!](y))([\![\Gamma \vdash M : \sigma]\!](y))
\end{aligned}
$$

Type family interpretation

$$
\begin{aligned}
(Asmp) && [\![\Gamma \vdash x : \sigma]\!](y) &= y_x \\
(\Pi_I) && [\![\Gamma \vdash \lambda x : \sigma.M : \Pi x : \sigma.\tau]\!](y) &= \lambda y' \in Gy.([\![\Gamma, x : \sigma \vdash M : \tau]\!])(y, y') \\
&&& \text{where: } Gy = [\![\Gamma \vdash \sigma : tp]\!](y) \\
(\Pi_E) && [\![\Gamma \vdash MN : \tau[N/x]]\!](y) &= ([\![\Gamma \vdash M : \Pi x : \sigma.\tau]\!](y))([\![\Gamma \vdash N : \sigma]\!](y)) \\
(\Pi_I^2) && [\![\Gamma \vdash \lambda x : tp.M : \Pi x : tp.\tau]\!](y) &= \lambda y' \in \mathbf{S}^{ip}.([\![\Gamma, x : tp \vdash M : \tau]\!])(y, y') \\
(\Pi_E^2) && [\![\Gamma \vdash M\sigma : \tau[\sigma/x]]\!](y) &= ([\![\Gamma \vdash M : \Pi x : tp.\tau]\!](y))([\![\Gamma \vdash \sigma : tp]\!](y))
\end{aligned}
$$

Object interpretation

Figure 11.4: Interpretation of the $\lambda P2$-calculus in $\mathbf{S}^{ip}$

the construction of the operators $\Sigma$ and $\Pi$ in this framework (see [ABL86]). Suppose that $U$ is a Scott domain such that:

$$U \times U \trianglelefteq U \quad \text{via } (\lambda(u, u').\langle u, u' \rangle, \lambda u.((\mathit{fst}\, u), (\mathit{snd}\, u))) : U \times U \to U$$
$$(U \to U) \trianglelefteq U \quad \text{via } (i, j) : (U \to U) \to U .$$

We also know that (see exercise 7.4.8):

$$FP(U) \trianglelefteq (U \to U) \quad \text{via } (id_{FP(U)}, \pi) .$$

We set $\underline{\pi} = i \circ \pi \circ j \in FP(U)$. We define:

- A projection $p \in FP(U)$ that represents the domain $im(p)$.

- A function $f : U \to U$ such that $f = \underline{\pi} \circ f \circ p$ represents a cocontinuous functor $F$ from the domain $im(p)$ to the category $\mathbf{S}^{ip}$, where $F(d) = im(j(fd))$ and $F(d \le d') = (id, j(f(d))_{|im(j(fd'))})$.

It has already been remarked in 7.4.10 that $FP(U)$ and $\mathbf{S}^{ip}$ (more precisely, the sub-category of countably based domains) are not equivalent categories as $FP(U)$ is just a poset. As a matter of fact we get a different model of the $\lambda P2$-calculus where, in particular, one can interpret the second order $\Sigma$-construction as a domain.

**Definition 11.3.1** ($\Sigma$ and $\Pi$ constructions in $FP(U)$) *Let $p \in FP(U)$, and $f : U \to U$ be such that $f = \underline{\pi} \circ f \circ p$. We define:*

$$\Sigma_p f = \lambda u.\langle p(\mathit{fst}\, u), (f(\mathit{fst}\, u))(\mathit{snd}\, u)\rangle : U \to U$$
$$\Pi_p f = \lambda u.i(\lambda x.j(fx)((ju)(px))) : U \to U .$$

**Exercise 11.3.2** *Show that under the hypotheses of definition 11.3.1, $\Sigma_p f, \Pi_p f \in FP(U)$.*

When $f : im(p) \to \mathbf{S}^{ip}$ is regarded as a functor, the sum and product constructions defined in propositions 11.1.5 and 11.1.7, respectively, apply. In particular we have:

$$\Sigma_{im(p)} f = \{(d, e) \mid pd = d \text{ and } (fd)e = e\}$$
$$[\Pi_{im(p)} f] = \{\phi : U \to U \mid \phi \circ p = \phi \text{ and } \forall d\ ((fd)(\phi d) = \phi d)\} .$$

We can then show that $\Sigma_p f$ and $\Pi_p f$ are finitary projections representing the 'right' domains.

**Exercise 11.3.3** *Show that under the hypotheses of definition 11.3.1 the following iso-morphism holds: $im(\Sigma_p f) \cong \Sigma_{im(p)} f$ and $im(\Pi_p f) \cong [\Pi_{im(p)} f]$.*

**Exercise 11.3.4** *Compute $\Pi_{\underline{\pi}} Id$. Compare the corresponding domain with the one obtained in exercise 11.1.14.*

**Exercise 11.3.5** *Consider the formal system for the $\lambda P2$-calculus with the identifica-tion $tp \equiv kd$. This system has been shown to be logically inconsistent by Girard (all types are inhabited). However, not all terms are equated. To prove this fact propose an interpretation of the calculus in the domain of finitary projection. Hint: The finitary projection $\underline{\pi}$ represents the type of all types (see [ABL86]).*

$$(p_1) \ \overline{\overline{(px) \circ (px) = px}} \qquad (p_2) \ \overline{\overline{pp = p}} \qquad (p_3) \ \frac{M \circ M = M}{pM = M}$$

Figure 11.5: Additional rules for the $\lambda\beta p$-calculus

$$\langle kd \rangle \ = \ p \qquad \langle tp \rangle \ = \ p$$
$$\langle x \rangle \ = \ x \qquad \langle AB \rangle \ = \ \langle A \rangle \langle B \rangle$$

$$\langle \Pi x : A.B \rangle \ = \ \lambda z.\lambda t.(\lambda x.\langle B \rangle)(\langle A \rangle t)(z(\langle A \rangle t)) \quad z, t \notin FV(A) \cup FV(B)$$
$$\langle \lambda x : A.B \rangle \ = \ (\lambda x.\langle B \rangle) \circ \langle A \rangle$$

Suppose: $\Gamma_i \equiv x_1 : A_1, \ldots, x_i : A_i, \ i = 1, \ldots, n, \ \Gamma = \Gamma_n$.
$$\langle A \rangle^\Gamma \ = \ \langle A \rangle [P_1/x_1, \ldots, P_n/x_n].$$
$$P_{i+1} \ = \ \langle A_{i+1} \rangle^{\Gamma_i} x_i$$
$$P_1 \ = \ \langle A_1 \rangle x_1$$

Figure 11.6: Translation of the $\lambda P2$-calculus into the $\lambda\beta p$-calculus

We now turn to the syntactic approach. We present an extension of the untyped $\lambda\beta$-calculus with a constant $p$ whose properties are displayed in figure 11.5 (by convention, let $P \circ Q$ stand for $\lambda x.P(Qx)$, with $x$ fresh). The intention is to let $p$ denote the retraction of all retractions. On this basis, $(p_1)$ states that elements in the image of $p$ are retractions, $(p_2)$ entails that $p$ is a retraction as $p \circ p = pp \circ pp = pp = p$, and $(p_3)$ states that all retractions are in the image of $p$.

We want to show that: (i) every model of the $\lambda\beta p$-calculus is also a model of the $\lambda P2$-calculus, and (ii) there are models of the $\lambda\beta p$-calculus. Point (ii) is a corollary of theorem 12.4.16. In particular, every reflexive object in the category of bifinite (stable) domains and stable morphisms (there are plenty of them) can be canonically extended to a model of the $\lambda\beta p$-calculus (cf. exercise 12.4.17).

We remark that the finitary projection model presented above, although based on similar ideas, does not provide a model of the $\lambda\beta p$-calculus if we interpret (as it is natural) $p$ as the projection $\pi$. The problem is that the rule $(p_3)$ requires that *every* retraction is in $\pi$'s image (a similar problem would arise in models based on finitary retractions).

In order to address point (i), we exhibit a syntactic translation of the $\lambda P2$-calculus into the $\lambda\beta p$-calculus which preserves equality. By combining (i) and (ii) we can conclude that every model of the $\lambda\beta$-calculus based on bifinite stable domains, canonically provides a (non-trivial) interpretation of the $\lambda P2$-calculus.

Let us give some intuition for the interpretation. A type or a kind is represented as a retraction, say $r$. An object $d$ has type $r$ if $d = r(d)$. When interpreting the $\lambda$-abstraction $\lambda x : A.B$ the retraction $\langle A \rangle$ is used to coerce the argument to the right type. A similar game is played in the interpretation of $\Pi x : A.B$ which resembles $\Pi_p f$ in definition 11.3.1. Note that if $x \notin FV(B)$ then $\langle \Pi x : A.B \rangle = \lambda z.\langle B \rangle \circ z \circ \langle A \rangle$, which is the way to build a functional space in the Karoubi envelope (cf. definition 4.6.9). Another special case is when $A \equiv tp$, then we obtain $\lambda t.\lambda z.\langle B \rangle[pt/x](z(pt))$. Here the type of the result '$\langle B \rangle[pt/x]$' depends on the input type '$pt$'. The translation is defined in figure 11.6; it respects typing and reduction as stated in the following.

**Proposition 11.3.6** (1) *If* $\Gamma \vdash A : B$ *then* $\langle A \rangle^\Gamma =_{\beta p} \langle B \rangle^\Gamma \langle A \rangle^\Gamma$.

(2) *If* $\Gamma \vdash A : B$ *and* $A \Rightarrow B$ *then* $\langle A \rangle^\Gamma =_{\beta p} \langle B \rangle^\Gamma$.

PROOF. In the first place we observe that $\langle A[B/x] \rangle^\Gamma =_{\beta p} \langle A \rangle^\Gamma [\langle B \rangle^\Gamma / x]$. Next we prove the two statements simultaneously by induction on the length of the typing proof. We consider some significant cases.

$(K.\emptyset)$ We apply axiom $(p_2)$.

$(K.\Pi)$ Let $Q \equiv \langle \Pi x : \sigma.K \rangle^\Gamma$. We prove $pQ =_{\beta p} Q$ by showing $Q \circ Q =_{\beta p} Q$. To this end we expand the left hand side of the equation and apply the inductive hypotheses: $p\langle K \rangle^{\Gamma, x:\sigma} =_{\beta p} \langle K \rangle^{\Gamma, x:\sigma}$ and $p\langle \sigma \rangle^\Gamma =_{\beta p} \langle \sigma \rangle^\Gamma$.

$(tp.Asmp)$ There is $\Gamma'$ contained in $\Gamma$ such that $\Gamma' \vdash K : kd$ and $\langle K \rangle^{\Gamma'} =_{\beta p} \langle K \rangle^\Gamma$. Then by induction hypothesis we know $p\langle K \rangle^\Gamma =_{\beta p} \langle K \rangle^\Gamma$. We conclude observing that $\langle x \rangle^\Gamma =_{\beta p} \langle K \rangle^\Gamma x$, since $x : K \in \Gamma$.

$(tp.Eq)$ There are shorter proofs of $\Gamma \vdash K : kd$ and $\Gamma \vdash K' : kd$. By confluence we know that $K$ and $K'$ have a common reduct. By applying the second part of the statement above we can conclude that $\langle K \rangle^\Gamma =_{\beta p} \langle K' \rangle^\Gamma$. By inductive hypothesis we know $\langle K \rangle^\Gamma \langle \sigma \rangle^\Gamma =_{\beta p} \langle \sigma \rangle^\Gamma$. Combining with the previous equation we get the desired result.

$(tp.\Pi_I)$ We expand the definitions as in the $(K.\Pi)$ case.

$(\Pi_E)$ We observe:

$$
\begin{aligned}
\langle MN \rangle^\Gamma &= {}_{\beta p}(\langle \Pi x : \sigma.\tau \rangle^\Gamma \langle M \rangle^\Gamma)(\langle N \rangle^\Gamma) \\
&= {}_{\beta p}(\langle \tau \rangle^\Gamma [\langle \sigma \rangle^\Gamma \langle N \rangle^\Gamma / x])(\langle M \rangle^\Gamma (\langle \sigma \rangle^\Gamma \langle N \rangle^\Gamma)) \\
&= {}_{\beta p}\langle \tau[N/x] \rangle^\Gamma (\langle M \rangle^\Gamma \langle N \rangle^\Gamma) \, .
\end{aligned}
$$

For the second part of the statement we proceed by induction on the typing and the derivation of a $\beta$-reduction. For instance consider the case $(\lambda x : A.B)C \rightarrow B[C/x]$. If $(\lambda x : A.B)C$ is typable in a context $\Gamma$ then we can find a shorter proof that $\Gamma \vdash C : A$. By (1) we know $\langle A \rangle^\Gamma \langle C \rangle^\Gamma =_{\beta p} \langle C \rangle^\Gamma$. Hence we can compute $\langle (\lambda x : A.B)C \rangle^\Gamma =_{\beta p} (\lambda x.\langle B \rangle^\Gamma)(\langle A \rangle^\Gamma \langle C \rangle^\Gamma)$; which is convertible to $\langle B \rangle^\Gamma [\langle C \rangle^\Gamma / x] = \langle B[C/x] \rangle^\Gamma$. $\square$

# 11.4 System LF

The system LF corresponds to the fragment of the $\lambda P2$-calculus in which we drop second order types. Formally one has to remove the following rules: $(tp.\Pi^2)$, $(\Pi_I^2)$, and $(\Pi_E^2)$.

A large variety of logical systems can be faithfully encoded in LF [AHMP95]. We will highlight some features of this approach by studying the encoding of a Hilbert style presentation of classical first order logic with equality and arithmetic operators. Dependent products play a central role in this encoding. From this one may conclude that dependent products are more 'expressive' than simple types.[1] On the other hand from the view point of the length of the normalization procedure dependent types do not add any complexity. As a matter of fact we show that the strong normalization of system LF can be deduced from the strong normalization of the simply typed $\lambda$-calculus via a simple translation.[2]

**Remark 11.4.1** *Kinds, type families, and objects in $\beta$-normal form have the following shapes where recursively the subterms are in $\beta$-normal form:*

> Kind          $\Pi x_1 : \sigma_1 \ldots \Pi x_n : \sigma_n.tp$
>
> Type family   $\lambda x_1 : \sigma_1 \ldots \lambda x_n : \sigma_n.\Pi y_1 : \tau_1 \ldots y_m : \tau_m.x M_1 \ldots M_k$
>
> Object        $\lambda x_1 : \sigma_1 \ldots \lambda x_n : \sigma_n.x M_1 \ldots M_k$ .

In order to define precise encodings of logics in LF it is useful to introduce the notion of *canonical* form. Roughly a term is in canonical form if it is in $\beta$ normal form and $\eta$-expansion is performed as much as possible. Canonical forms can be regarded as a way to avoid the problematic introduction of full $\beta\eta$-conversion.

**Definition 11.4.2** *The* arity *of a type or kind is the number of $\Pi$'s in the prefix of its $\beta$-normal form. Let $\Gamma \vdash A : B$ be a derivable judgment. The arity of a variable occurring in $A$ or $B$ is the arity of its type or kind.*

**Definition 11.4.3** *Let $\Gamma \vdash A : B$ be a derivable judgment. The term $A$ is in* canonical form *if it is in $\beta$-normal form and all variable occurrences in $A$ are fully applied, where we say that a variable occurrence is* fully applied *if it is applied to a number of arguments equal to the variable's arity.*

In figure 11.7 we give a presentation of classical first order logic (FOL) with equality and arithmetic operators. In figure 11.8 we encode the language in the system LF. To this end we build a context $\Gamma_{FOL}^{syn}$ (*syn* for syntax) composed of:

• The declaration of two new types $\iota, o$ corresponding to the collection of individuals and formulas, respectively.

• The declaration of objects $\hat{0}, \hat{s}$ corresponding to the arithmetic operators and objects $\hat{=}, \hat{\supset}, \hat{\neg}, \hat{\forall}$ corresponding to the logical operators (to increase readability we use an infix notation for $\hat{=}$ and $\hat{\supset}$).

Next we define a function $\lceil \_ \rceil$ that translates terms into objects of type $\iota$ and formulas into objects of type $o$. Note in particular that:

• Variables are identified with the variables of system LF.

• $\lambda$-abstraction is used to encode the quantifier $\forall$.

---

[1] It is known that the validity of a sentence is a decidable problem for propositional logic and an undecidable one for first order logic. Dependent types can be connected to predicate logic in the same way as simple types were connected to propositional logic in section 4.1.

[2] From a logical view point this relates to the well-known fact that the cut-elimination procedures in propositional and first order logic have the same complexity.

$$\text{Terms} \quad t ::= x \mid 0 \mid s(t)$$
$$\text{Formulas} \quad \phi ::= t = t \mid \neg\phi \mid \phi \supset \phi \mid \forall x.\phi$$

$(eq_1)$ $\dfrac{}{t = t}$

$(eq_2)$ $\dfrac{t = t'}{t' = t}$

$(eq_3)$ $\dfrac{t = t' \quad t' = t''}{t = t''}$

$(eq_4)$ $\dfrac{t = t'}{\phi[t/x] = \phi[t'/x]}$

$(pp_1)$ $\dfrac{}{\phi \supset (\psi \supset \phi)}$

$(pp_2)$ $\dfrac{}{(\phi \supset (\psi \supset \chi)) \supset ((\phi \supset \psi) \supset (\phi \supset \chi))}$

$(pp_3)$ $\dfrac{}{(\neg\phi \supset \neg\psi) \supset (\psi \supset \phi)}$

$(mp)$ $\dfrac{\phi \supset \psi \quad \phi}{\psi}$

$(pc_1)$ $\dfrac{\phi}{\forall x.\phi}$

$(pc_2)$ $\dfrac{\forall x.\phi}{\phi[t/x]}$

Figure 11.7: First order logic with equality and arithmetical constants

$$\Gamma^{syn}_{FOL} \left\{ \begin{array}{ll} \text{Constant types} & \iota, o : Tp \\ \text{Constant terms} & \hat{0} : \iota \qquad\qquad \hat{s} : \iota \to \iota \\ & \hat{=} : \iota \to \iota \to o \quad \hat{\supset} : o \to o \to o \\ & \hat{\neg} : o \to o \qquad \hat{\forall} : (\iota \to o) \to o \end{array} \right.$$

$$
\begin{array}{llll}
\lceil x \rceil & = & x & \qquad \lceil 0 \rceil & = & \hat{0} \\
\lceil s(t) \rceil & = & \hat{s}\lceil t \rceil \\
\lceil t = t' \rceil & = & \lceil t \rceil \hat{=} \lceil t' \rceil & \qquad \lceil \neg t \rceil & = & \hat{\neg}\lceil t \rceil \\
\lceil \phi \supset \phi' \rceil & = & \lceil \phi \rceil \hat{\supset} \lceil \phi' \rceil & \qquad \lceil \forall x.\phi \rceil & = & \hat{\forall}(\lambda x : \iota.\lceil \phi \rceil)
\end{array}
$$

Figure 11.8: Coding FOL language in LF

Judgment          $T : o \to tp$

Rules          $\Gamma^{rl}_{FOL}$          $\begin{cases} eq_1 : \Pi x : i.T(x \hat{=} x) \\ eq_2 : \Pi x, y : i.(T(x \hat{=} y) \to T(y \hat{=} x)) \\ eq_3 : \Pi x, y, z : i.(T(x \hat{=} y) \to T(y \hat{=} z) \to T(x \hat{=} z)) \\ eq_4 : \Pi f : \iota \to o.\Pi x, y : i.(T(x \hat{=} y) \to T((fx) \hat{=} (fy))) \\ pp_1 : \Pi f, g : o.T(f \hat{\supset} g \hat{\supset} h) \\ pp_2 : \Pi f, g, h : o.T((f \hat{\supset} (g \hat{\supset} h)) \hat{\supset} ((f \hat{\supset} g) \hat{\supset} (f \supset h))) \\ pp_3 : \Pi f, g : o.T((\hat{\neg} f \hat{\supset} \hat{\neg} g) \hat{\supset} (g \hat{\supset} f)) \\ mp : \Pi f, g : o.T(f \hat{\supset} g) \to T(f) \to T(g) \\ pc_1 : \Pi F : \iota \to o.(\Pi x : \iota.T(Fx)) \to T(\hat{\forall} F) \\ pc_2 : \Pi F : \iota \to o.\Pi x : \iota.T(\hat{\forall} F) \to T(Fx) \end{cases}$

Figure 11.9: Coding FOL proof rules in LF

Hence, the substitution and $\alpha$-renaming available in the meta-theory LF, are used to represent the corresponding notions in first order logic.

The correspondence between the language of FOL and its encoding in LF is quite good.

**Proposition 11.4.4** *There is a bijective correspondence between terms and formulas having free variables in $x_1, \ldots, x_n$, and terms $M$ in canonical form such that $\Gamma^{syn}_{FOL}, x_1 : \iota, \ldots, x_n : \iota \vdash M : \iota$ and $\Gamma^{syn}_{FOL}, x_1 : \iota, \ldots, x_n : \iota \vdash M : o$, respectively.*

A second task concerns the encoding of the proof rules. The complete definition is displayed in figure 11.9. The basic judgment in FOL is that a formula holds, say $\vdash \phi$. Correspondingly, we introduce a *dependent type* $T : o \to tp$ (this is the point where dependent types do play a role!). We also define a context $\Gamma^{rl}_{FOL}$ (*rl* for rule) where we declare constants corresponding to the rules of first order logic (cf. figure 11.7). We note that the rule $(tp.\Pi_E)$ is used to type the proof encodings.

The typing of the constants ensures that objects of type $T(\lceil \phi \rceil)$ relate to proofs of the formula $\phi$. The property of the proof encoding can be stated as follows.[3]

**Proposition 11.4.5** *There is a bijective correspondence between proofs of a formula $\phi$ from the assumptions $\phi_1, \ldots, \phi_m$ and with free variables $x_1, \ldots, x_n$, and terms $M$ in canonical form such that:*

$$\Gamma^{syn}_{FOL}, \Gamma^{rl}_{FOL}, x_1 : \iota, \ldots, x_n : \iota, y_1 : T(\lceil \phi_1 \rceil), \ldots, y_m : T(\lceil \phi_m \rceil) \vdash M : T(\lceil \phi \rceil) .$$

For instance, to the proof

$$\frac{x = x}{\forall x.(x = x)} \quad ,$$

we associate the term $pc_1(\lambda x : \iota. \hat{=} xx)(eq_1)$.

---

[3]Detailed proofs for propositions 11.4.4 and 11.4.5 can be found in [HHP93].

$$
\begin{aligned}
t(tp) &= o & t(x) &= o \\
t(\Pi x : A.B) &= t(A) \rightarrow t(B) \quad & t(\lambda x : A.B) &= t(B) \\
t(AB) &= t(A)
\end{aligned}
$$

$$
\begin{aligned}
|x| &= x & |\Pi x : A.B| &= \pi |A| (\lambda x : t(A).|B|) \\
|AB| &= |A||B| & |\lambda x : A.B| &= (\lambda y : o.\lambda x : t(A).|B|)|A| \quad (y \text{ fresh})
\end{aligned}
$$

Figure 11.10: Translation of LF in the simply typed $\lambda$-calculus

**Strong normalization for LF.** Next we turn to the strong normalization problem for the system LF. This is proven via a translation into the simply typed $\lambda$-calculus which is specified in figure 11.10. The function $t$ applies to kinds and type families whereas the function $|_-|$ applies to type families and objects. The function $t$ forgets the type dependency by replacing every variable by the basic type $o$ and ignoring the argument of a type family. The function $|_-|$ reflects all possible reductions of the LF term. Note in particular that in $|\Pi x : A.B|$ and $|\lambda x : A.B|$ we take into account the reductions of $A$ (this would fail if we translated $\lambda x : A.B$ simply as $\lambda x : t(A).|B|$).

In order to translate terms of the shape $\Pi x : A.B$ we suppose that the simply typed $\lambda$-calculus is enriched with a family of constants $\pi$ having type $o \rightarrow (t(A) \rightarrow o) \rightarrow o$. In the first place, we observe some syntactic properties of these translations.

**Lemma 11.4.6** *If $M$ is an object then the following properties hold:*

(1) $t(A[M/x]) \equiv t(A)$.

(2) $|A[M/x]| \equiv |A|[|M|/x]$.

PROOF HINT. By induction on the structure of $A$.                    □

**Lemma 11.4.7** *If $\Gamma \vdash A : B$ and $A \Rightarrow A'$, where $A$ is a kind or a type family, then $t(A) \equiv t(A')$.*

PROOF. By induction on the proof of the reduction. In the basic case $(\lambda x : A.B)C \rightarrow B[C/x]$ we use the fact that, by the typability hypothesis, $C$ is an object.                    □

The translations $t$ and $|_-|$ preserve typing.

**Proposition 11.4.8** *If $\Gamma \vdash A : B$ in LF and $B \neq kd$ then $t(\Gamma) \vdash |A| : t(B)$ in the simply typed $\lambda$-calculus, where $t(x_1 : A_1, \ldots, x_n : A_n) \equiv x_1 : t(A_1), \ldots, x_n : t(A_n)$.*

PROOF HINT. By induction on the length of the proof.                    □

Finally we can show that the translation reflects reductions, which, by the strong normalization of the simply typed $\lambda$-calculus, implies immediately the strong normalization of system LF.

**Theorem 11.4.9** *If* $\Gamma \vdash A : B$, $B \neq kd$, $A \Rightarrow A'$, *and in the reduction* $A \Rightarrow A'$ *we find at least one $\beta$-reduction, then* $|A| \to_\beta^+ |A'|$.

PROOF. By induction on the derivation of $A \Rightarrow A'$. We consider two cases. Suppose we derive $(\lambda x : A.B)C \Rightarrow B'[C'/x]$ from $B \Rightarrow B'$ and $C \Rightarrow C'$. Then:

$$
\begin{aligned}
|(\lambda x : A.B)C| &= ((\lambda y : o.\lambda x : t(A).|B|)|A|)|C| \\
&\to (\lambda x : t(A).|B|)|C| \\
&\to^* (\lambda x : t(A).|B'|)|C'| &\text{(by induction hypothesis)} \\
&\to |B'|[|C'|/x] = |B'[C'/x]| &\text{(by lemma 11.4.6)}.
\end{aligned}
$$

Suppose we derive $(\lambda x : A.B) \Rightarrow (\lambda x : A'.B')$ from $A \Rightarrow A'$ and $B \Rightarrow B'$. Then:

$$
\begin{aligned}
|\lambda x : A.B| &= (\lambda y : o.\lambda x : t(A).|B|)|A| \\
&\to^* (\lambda y : o.\lambda x : t(A).|B'|)|A'| &\text{(by induction hypothesis)} \\
&= (\lambda y : o.\lambda x : t(A').|B'|)|A'| &\text{(by lemma 11.4.7)} \\
&= |\lambda x : A'.B'|. &\square
\end{aligned}
$$

**Remark 11.4.10** *A consequence of confluence and strong normalization is that it is decidable if a judgment is derivable in the system LF.*

# 11.5   System F

System F is the fragment of the $\lambda P2$-calculus where dependent types and type families are removed. Formally we eliminate the rules: $(K.\Pi)$, $(tp.\Pi_I)$, and $(tp.\Pi_E)$. With these restrictions, the only kind is $tp$, types cannot depend on objects, and the equality rules $(tp.Eq)$ and $(Eq)$ can be dispensed with, as type equality becomes $\alpha$-conversion. Note that in the type $\Pi x : \sigma.\tau$, the type $\tau$ never depends on $x$ and therefore we can simply write $\sigma \to \tau$.

We introduce a notation to distinguish between type variables (i.e., variables of type $tp$) and term variables (i.e., variables of type $\sigma$, where $\sigma$ has kind $tp$): we denote the former with $t, s, \ldots$ and the latter with $x, y, \ldots$ Then the rules for the context formation are redundant. Namely we can simply represent a context as a list $x_1 : \sigma_1, \ldots, x_n : \sigma_n$ (as in the simply typed $\lambda$-calculus), where the types $\sigma_i$ may depend on type variables.

According to these remarks, we give a more compact presentation of system F. Terms and types are defined as follows:

$$
\begin{aligned}
\text{Types} \quad tv &::= t \mid s \mid \ldots \\
\sigma &::= tv \mid \sigma \to \sigma \mid \forall tv.\sigma \\
\text{Terms} \quad v &::= x \mid y \mid \ldots \\
M &::= v \mid \lambda v : \sigma.M \mid MM \mid \lambda tv.M \mid M\sigma.
\end{aligned}
$$

Note that the type of all types is never explicitly mentioned. $\forall t \ldots$ is an abbreviation for $\Pi t : tp \ldots$ and $\lambda t \ldots$ is an abbreviation for $\lambda t : tp \ldots$

$$(Asmp) \quad \frac{x : \sigma \in \Gamma}{\Gamma \vdash x : \sigma}$$

$$(\to_I) \quad \frac{\Gamma, x : \sigma \vdash M : \tau}{\Gamma \vdash \lambda x : \sigma.M : \sigma \to \tau} \qquad (\to_E) \quad \frac{\Gamma \vdash M : \sigma \to \tau \quad \Gamma \vdash N : \sigma}{\Gamma \vdash MN : \tau}$$

$$(\forall_I) \quad \frac{\Gamma \vdash M : \sigma \quad t \notin FV_t(\Gamma)}{\Gamma \vdash \lambda t.M : \forall t.\sigma} \qquad (\forall_E) \quad \frac{\Gamma \vdash M : \forall t.\sigma}{\Gamma \vdash M\tau : \sigma[\tau/t]}$$

Figure 11.11: Typing rules for system F

A context $\Gamma$ is a list $x_1 : \sigma_1, \dots, x_n : \sigma_n$, so the type variables declarations are left implicit. We denote with $FV_t(\Gamma)$ the collection of type variables that occur free in types occurring in $\Gamma$. Derivable typing judgments are specified in figure 11.11. *Mutatis mutandis*, the system is equivalent to the restriction of the one presented in section 11.2.

**Exercise 11.5.1** *Show that in system F $\beta\eta$-reduction is locally confluent on well-typed terms.*

The system F was introduced by Girard [Gir72] as a tool for the study of the cut-elimination procedure in second order arithmetic ($PA_2$), more precisely the normalization of system F implies the termination of the cut-elimination procedure in $PA_2$. By relying on this strong connection between system F and $PA_2$ it was proven that all functions that can be shown to be total in $PA_2$ are *representable* in system F. This is a huge collection of total recursive functions that goes well beyond the primitive recursive functions. System F was later rediscovered by Reynolds [Rey74] as a concise calculus of *type parametric* functions. In this section we illustrate the rich type structure of system F by presenting a systematic method to code finite *free algebras* and *iterative functions* defined on them.

In the following an algebra $S$ is a sort $S$ equipped with a tuple of constructors:

$$f_i^{n_i} : \underbrace{S \times \cdots \times S}_{n_i \; times} \to S \text{ for } i = 1, \dots, k, k \geq 0, n_i \geq 0 \;.$$

We inductively define a collection of total computable functions over the set $T_S$ of *ground terms* of the algebra (that is, the terms built from the constructors only, without variables) as follows.

**Definition 11.5.2** *The collection of* iterative *functions* $f : T_S^n \to T_S$ *over an algebra $S$ is the smallest set such that:*

- *The basic functions $f_i^{n_i}$, constant functions, and projection functions are iterative functions.*

$$\text{Given:} \quad S, f_i^{n_i} : \underbrace{T_S \times \cdots \times T_S}_{n_i \text{ times}} \to T_S, i = 1, \ldots, k$$

$$\text{let:} \quad \sigma \equiv \forall t.\tau_1 \to \cdots \to \tau_k \to t$$

$$\text{where:} \quad \tau_i \equiv \underbrace{t \to \cdots \to t}_{n_i \text{ times}} \to t$$

$$\underline{f_i^n(a_1, \ldots, a_n)} = \lambda t.\lambda x_1 : \tau_1 \ldots \lambda x_k : \tau_k.x_i(\underline{a_1}t\vec{x}) \cdots (\underline{a_n}t\vec{x})$$

Figure 11.12: Coding algebras in system F

- *The set is closed under composition.* If $f_1 : T_S^m \to T_S, \ldots, f_n : T_S^m \to T_S$, and $g : T_S^n \to T_S$ *are iterative then* $\lambda \vec{x}.g(f_1(\vec{x}), \ldots, f_n(\vec{x}))$ *is iterative.*

- *The set is closed under iteration.* If $h_i : T_S^{n_i+m} \to T_S$ *are iterative functions for* $i = 1, \ldots, k$ *then the function* $f : T_S^{m+1} \to T_S$ *defined by the following equations is iterative.*

$$f(\vec{x}, f_i(\vec{y})) = h_i(\vec{x}, f(\vec{x}, y_1), \ldots, f(\vec{x}, y_{n_i})) \quad i = 1, \ldots, k .$$

Iterative definitions generalize primitive recursive definitions (cf. appendix 1) to arbitrary algebras. The basic idea is to define a function by induction on the structure of a ground term, hence we have an equation for every function of the algebra.

**Exercise 11.5.3** *Consider the algebra of natural numbers* $(\omega, s^1, 0^0)$. *Show that the iterative functions coincide with the primitive recursive ones. Hint: The definitions by primitive recursion are apparently more general but they can be simulated using pairing and projections.*

In figure 11.12 we associate with an algebra $S$ a type $\sigma$ of system F, and with a ground term $a$ of the algebra a closed term $\underline{a}$ of system F of type $\sigma$.

**Example 11.5.4** *If we apply the coding method to the algebra of natural numbers defined in exercise 11.5.3 we obtain the type* $\forall t.(t \to t) \to (t \to t)$. *The term* $s(\cdots(s0)\cdots)$ *can be represented by the term* $\lambda t.\lambda f : t \to t.\lambda x : t.f(\cdots(fx)\cdots)$, *which is known as a Church numeral.*

**Exercise 11.5.5** *Make explicit the coding of the following algebras: the algebra with no operation, the algebra with two 0-ary operations, the algebra of binary trees* $(T, nil^0, bin^2)$.

**Proposition 11.5.6** *There is a bijective correspondence between the ground terms of the algebra* $S$ *and the closed terms of system F of type* $\sigma$ *modulo* $\beta\eta$-*conversion.*

PROOF. Let $M$ be a closed term of system F in $\beta$-normal form of type $\sigma$, where $\sigma$ is defined according to figure 11.12 (the existence of the $\beta$-normal form is proved next in theorem 11.5.18). Then $M$ has to have the shape:

$$M \equiv \lambda t.\lambda x_1 : \tau_1 \ldots \lambda x_i : \tau_i.M' \quad i \leq k .$$

If $i < k$ and $M'$ is not a $\lambda$-abstraction then $M'$ has the shape $(\cdots(x_j M_1)\cdots M_h)$ and so we can $\eta$-expand $M'$ without introducing a $\beta$-redex. By iterated $\eta$-expansions we arrive at a term in $\beta$ normal form of the shape:

$$\lambda t.\lambda x_1 : \tau_1 \ldots \lambda x_k : \tau_k.M'',$$

where $M''$ has type $t$, it is in $\beta$ normal form, and may include free variables $x_1, \ldots, x_k$. We note that the types of the variables $x_i$ do not contain second order quantifications. We claim that $M''$ cannot contain a $\lambda$-abstraction:

- A $\lambda$-abstraction on the left of an application would contradict the hypothesis that $M$ is in $\beta$ normal form.

- A $\lambda$-abstraction on the right of an application is incompatible with the 'first order' types of the variables $\tau_i$.

We have shown that a closed term of type $\sigma$ is determined up to $\beta\eta$ conversion by a term $M''$ which is a well-typed combination of the variables $x_i$, for $i = 1, \ldots, k$. Since each variable corresponds to a constructor of the algebra we can conclude that there is a unique ground term of the algebra which corresponds to $M''$. $\square$

Having fixed the representation of ground terms of the algebra, let us turn to the representation of functions.

**Definition 11.5.7** *A function $f : T_S^n \to T_S$ is representable (with respect to the coding defined in figure 11.12) if there is a closed term $M : \sigma^n \to \sigma$, such that for any ground term $\vec{a}$, $M\underline{\vec{a}} =_{\beta\eta} \underline{f(\vec{a})}$.*

**Proposition 11.5.8** *All iterative functions over an algebra $S$ are representable.*

PROOF. We proceed by induction on the definition of iterative function. The only non-trivial case is iteration. Let $h_i : T_S^{n_i+m} \to T_S$ be iterative functions for $i = 1, \ldots, k$, and the function $f : T_S^{m+1} \to T_S$ be defined by:

$$f(\vec{x}, f_i(\vec{y})) = h_i(\vec{x}, f(\vec{x}, y_1), \ldots, f(\vec{x}, y_{n_i})) \quad i = 1, \ldots, k , \tag{11.8}$$

where $\vec{x} \equiv x_1, \ldots, x_m$. We represent $f$ with the function:

$$\underline{f} \equiv \lambda x_1 : \sigma. \ldots . \lambda x_m : \sigma.\lambda x : \sigma.x\sigma(\underline{h_1}\vec{x}) \cdots (\underline{h_k}\vec{x}) ,$$

where we know inductively that $\underline{h_i}$ represents $h_i$. Note that iteration is already built into the representation of the data. We prove by induction on the structure of a ground term $a$ that for any vector of ground terms $\vec{b}$, $\underline{f}\,\underline{\vec{b}}\,\underline{a} =_{\beta\eta} \underline{f(\vec{b}, a)}$.

- If $a \equiv f_i^0$ then $\underline{f}\,\underline{\vec{b}}\,\underline{f_i^0} \to^* \underline{f_i^0}\sigma(\underline{h_1}\underline{\vec{b}}) \cdots (\underline{h_k}\underline{\vec{b}}) \to^* \underline{h_i}\underline{\vec{b}} = \underline{h_i(\vec{b})}$, the last step holds by induction hypothesis on $\underline{h_i}$.

- If $a \equiv f_i^n(a_1, \ldots, a_n)$ then by induction hypothesis on $h_i$:

$$f(\vec{b}, f_i(a_1, \ldots, a_n)) = h_i(\vec{b}, f(\vec{b}, a_1), \ldots, f(\vec{b}, a_n)) = \underline{h_i}\ \underline{\vec{b}}\ f(\vec{b}, a_1) \cdots f(\vec{b}, a_n) \ .$$

On the other hand we compute:

$$\begin{aligned}
&\underline{f}\ \underline{\vec{b}}\ f_i^n(a_1, \ldots, a_n) \\
&\to f_i^n(a_1, \ldots, a_n)\sigma(\underline{h_1}\ \underline{\vec{b}}) \cdots (\underline{h_k}\ \underline{\vec{b}}) \\
&\to (\underline{h_i}\ \underline{\vec{b}})(\underline{a_1}\sigma(\underline{h_1}\ \underline{\vec{b}}) \cdots (\underline{h_k}\ \underline{\vec{b}})) \cdots (\underline{a_n}\sigma(\underline{h_1}\ \underline{\vec{b}}) \cdots (\underline{h_k}\ \underline{\vec{b}})) \ .
\end{aligned}$$

and we observe that by induction hypothesis on $a$:

$$f(\vec{b}, a_i) = \underline{f}\underline{\vec{b}}\underline{a_i} = \underline{a_i}\sigma(\underline{h_1}\underline{\vec{b}}) \cdots (\underline{h_k}\underline{\vec{b}})) \ .$$

Hence $\underline{f}\ \underline{\vec{b}}\ f_i^n(a_1, \ldots, a_n) \to^* \underline{h_i}\ \underline{\vec{b}}\ f(\vec{b}, a_1) \cdots f(\vec{b}, a_n) = f(\vec{b}, f_i(a_1, \ldots, a_n))$. $\qquad\square$

**Exercise 11.5.9** *Consider the case of algebras which are defined parametrically with respect to a collection of data. For instance $List(D)$ is the algebra of lists whose elements belong to the set $D$. This algebra is equipped with the constructors $nil : List(D)$ and $cons : D \times List(D) \to D$. Define iterative functions over $List(D)$ and show that these functions can be represented in system F for a suitable embedding of the closed terms in system F. Hint: The sort $List(D)$ is coded by the type $\forall t.t \to (t \to r \to t) \to t$, where $r$ is a type variable, and generic elements in $List(D)$ are represented by (free) variables of type $r$.*

In system F it is also possible to give *weak* representations of common type constructors. We explain the weakness of the representation in the following example concerning products.

**Example 11.5.10** *For $\sigma, \tau$ types of system F define:*

$$\sigma \underline{\times} \tau \equiv \forall t.(\sigma \to \tau \to t) \to t \ .$$

*Pairing and projections terms can be defined as follows:*

$$\begin{aligned}
\langle M, N \rangle &= \lambda t.\lambda f : \sigma \to \tau \to t.fMN \\
\pi_1 M &= M\sigma(\lambda x : \sigma.\lambda y : \tau.x) \\
\pi_2 M &= M\tau(\lambda x : \sigma.\lambda y : \tau.y) \ .
\end{aligned}$$

*Note that $\pi_i\langle M_1, M_2 \rangle =_{\beta\eta} M_i$ but pairing is not surjective, i.e., $\langle \pi_1 M, \pi_2 M \rangle \neq_{\beta\eta} M$.*

It is possible to prove surjective pairing by making use of relational techniques, much in the spirit of the techniques used in section 7.2 to handle recursively defined predicates. The idea of relational parametricity goes back to Reynolds [Rey83], and its use for proving properties like the one at hand has been advocated by Wadler [Wad89]. In Reynolds' approach, a polymorphic type $\tau$ is associated with a transformation $F$ mapping types to types and relations (not only injection-projection pairs, as considered in section 11.1) to relations, in such a way that if $R$ is an $n$-ary relation between, say, three types $\sigma_1, \sigma_2, \sigma_3$, and if $M$ is a term of type $\tau$, then $(M\sigma_1, M\sigma_2, M\sigma_3) \in F(R)$, i.e., $M$ is invariant under (logical) relations, using the terminology of section 4.5.

We apply this principle of parametricity to give an informal proof of the surjective pairing for the encoding of products given in example 11.5.10. Assuming $\eta$-rules, we have to prove, for all $t$ and $k : \sigma \to \tau \to t$ and for all $M : \sigma\underline{\times}\tau$, that

$$Mtk \quad \text{and} \quad \langle \pi_1 M, \pi_2 M\rangle tk =_\beta k(M\sigma(\lambda x : \sigma.\lambda y : \tau.x))(M\tau(\lambda x : \sigma.\lambda y : \tau.y))$$

are equal. On the other hand, considering $k$ as a relation $\langle k \rangle$ between $\sigma$, $\tau$ and $t$, we have that $(M\sigma, M\tau, Mt) \in F(\langle k \rangle)$, where $F$ is the transformation associated with $\sigma\underline{\times}\tau$. But $F(\langle k \rangle)$ is obtained by replacing $t$ with $\langle k \rangle$ in the definition of $\sigma\underline{\times}\tau$, i.e., $F(\langle k \rangle) = (\sigma \to \tau \to \langle k \rangle) \to \langle k \rangle$, where $\sigma$ and $\tau$ are now meant as identity relations, and where $\to$ is (the ternary version of) the operation on relations given in definition 4.5.1. The rest is a simple exercise with the definition of $\to$. One verifies:

$$((\lambda x : \sigma.\lambda y : \tau.x), (\lambda x : \sigma.\lambda y : \tau.y), k) \in \sigma \to \tau \to \langle k \rangle ,$$

which implies:

$$(M\sigma(\lambda x : \sigma.\lambda y : \tau.x) , \ M\tau(\lambda x : \sigma.\lambda y : \tau.y), Mtk) \in \langle k \rangle ,$$

which is exactly saying that $Mtk$ is equal to $\langle \pi_1 M, \pi_2 M\rangle tk$. Formal systems for this sort of reasoning have been proposed in [ACC93] and [PA93].

**Exercise 11.5.11** *Study the properties of the following codings of sum and existential:*

$$\sigma + \tau \quad as \quad \forall t.(\sigma \to t) \to (\tau \to t) \to t$$
$$\exists t.\sigma \quad as \quad \forall s.(\forall t.\sigma \to s) \to s .$$

We conclude by proving the core of Girard's celebrated result: all terms typable in system F strongly normalize. The proof is based on the notion of *reducibility candidate* which is a variant of the notion of $\mathcal{N}$-saturated set considered in definition 3.5.14 (yet other variants occur in the adequacy proofs of sections 6.3 and 8.2). In order to make notation lighter we will work with untyped terms obtained from the *erasure* of well-typed terms.

**Definition 11.5.12** *The* erasure *function* er *takes a typed term and returns an untyped $\lambda$-term. It is defined by induction on the structure of the term as follows:*

$$er(x) = x \qquad er(\lambda x : \sigma.M) = \lambda x.er(M) \quad er(MN) = er(M)er(N)$$
$$er(\lambda t.M) = er(M) \quad er(M\tau) = er(M) .$$

In system F we distinguish two flavours of $\beta$-reduction: the one involving a redex $(\lambda x : \sigma.M)N$ which we call simply $\beta$ and the one involving a redex $(\lambda t.M)\sigma$ which we call $\beta_t$. Erasing type information we eliminate reductions of the shape $(\lambda t.M)\sigma \to M[\sigma/t]$, however this does not affect the strong normalization property as shown in the following.

**Proposition 11.5.13** *Let $M$ be a well-typed term in system F. Then:*

(1) *If $M \to_\beta N$ then $er(M) \to_\beta er(N)$.*

(2) *If $M \to_{\beta_t} N$ then $er(M) \equiv er(N)$.*

(3) *If $M$ diverges then $er(M)$ diverges.*

PROOF. We leave (1-2) to the reader. For (3), we observe that sequences of $\beta_t$-reductions always terminate as the size of the term shrinks. Hence we can extract an infinite reduction of $er(M)$ from an infinite reduction of $M$. □

**Definition 11.5.14 (reducibility candidate)** *Let SN be the collection of untyped $\lambda\beta$-strongly normalizable terms. A set $X$ of $\lambda$-terms is a reducibility candidate if:*

(1) $P[Q/x]Q_1, \ldots, Q_n \in X$ *and* $Q \in SN$ *implies* $(\lambda x.P)QQ_1, \ldots, Q_n \in X$.

(2) $Q_i \in SN$, $i = 1, \ldots, n$, $n \geq 0$ *implies* $xQ_1, \ldots, Q_n \in X$.

(3) $X \subseteq SN$.

*We denote with $RC$ the collection of reducibility candidates and we abbreviate $Q_1, \ldots, Q_n$ with $\vec{Q}$.*

**Proposition 11.5.15** *(1) The set SN is a reducibility candidate.*

*(2) If $X \in RC$ then $X \neq \emptyset$.*

*(3) The collection $RC$ is closed under arbitrary intersections.*

*(4) If $X, Y \in RC$ then the following set is a reducibility candidate:*

$$X \to Y = \{M \mid \forall N \in X \ (MN \in Y)\} .$$

PROOF. (1) We observe that $P[Q/x]\vec{Q} \in SN$ and $Q \in SN$ implies $(\lambda x.P)Q\vec{Q} \in SN$. Proceed by induction on

$$depth(P) + depth(Q) + depth(Q_1) + \cdots + depth(Q_n),$$

where $depth(P)$ is the length of the longest reduction sequence from $P$ (cf. definition 2.2.2).

(2) By definition $x \in X$.

(3) Immediate.

(4) Here we see the use the saturation condition (cf. proposition 3.5.15). □

**Definition 11.5.16** *Given a type environment $\eta : Tvar \to RC$ we interpret types as follows:*

$$
\begin{aligned}
[\![t]\!]\eta &= \eta(t) \\
[\![\sigma \to \tau]\!]\eta &= [\![\sigma]\!]\eta \to [\![\tau]\!]\eta \\
[\![\forall t.\sigma]\!]\eta &= \bigcap_{X \in RC}[\![\sigma]\!]\eta[X/t] .
\end{aligned}
$$

The following lemma can be regarded as a syntactic version of the fundamental lemma of (unary) logical relations (cf. 4.5.3).

**Lemma 11.5.17** *Let $\eta$ be a type environment $\eta$, and $x_1 : \sigma_1, \ldots, x_n : \sigma_n \vdash M : \tau$ a derivable judgment. Then, if $P_i \in [\![\sigma_i]\!]\eta$, for $i = 1, \ldots, n$ then $er(M)[P_1/x_1, \ldots, P_n/x_n] \in [\![\tau]\!]\eta$.*

PROOF. We abbreviate $[P_1/x_1, \ldots, P_n/x_n]$ with $[\vec{P}/\vec{x}]$. We proceed by induction on the length of the typing proof as in the lemma 3.5.16. We just consider the two new cases.

($\forall_I$) We have to show $er(M)[\vec{P}/\vec{x}] \in \bigcap_{X \in RC} [\![\tau]\!]\eta[X/t]$. By the side condition on the typing rule we know $[\![\sigma_i]\!]\eta = [\![\sigma_i]\!]\eta[X/t]$, for an arbitrary $X \in RC$. By inductive hypothesis $er(M)[\vec{P}/\vec{x}] \in [\![\tau]\!]\eta[X/t]$, for an arbitrary $X \in RC$.

($\forall_E$) We have to show $er(M)[\vec{P}/\vec{x}] \in [\![\tau]\!]\eta[[\![\sigma]\!]\eta/t]$. By inductive hypothesis $er(M)[\vec{P}/\vec{x}] \in \bigcap_{X \in RC} [\![\tau]\!]\eta[X/t]$. Choose $X = [\![\sigma]\!]\eta$.  □

**Theorem 11.5.18 (strong normalization of system F)** *If $\Gamma \vdash M : \sigma$ in system F, then $M$ is strongly normalizing.*

PROOF. We note that $\forall \sigma, \eta, x$ $(x \in [\![\sigma]\!]\eta)$. Then we apply lemma 11.5.17 with $P_i \equiv x_i$, and derive that $er(M) \in [\![\tau]\!]\eta \subseteq SN$. By proposition 11.5.13(3), we conclude that $M$ is strongly normalizing.  □

**Exercise 11.5.19** *We say that a term is neutral if it does not start with a $\lambda$-abstraction. The collection $RC'$ (cf. [GLT89]) is given by the sets $X$ of strongly normalizing terms satisfying the following conditions:*

(1) *$M \in X$ and $M \to_\beta M'$ implies $M' \in X$.*

(2) *$M$ neutral and $\forall M'$ $(M \to_\beta M' \Rightarrow M' \in X)$ implies $M \in X$.*

*Carry on the strong normalization proof using the collection $RC'$.*

**Exercise 11.5.20** *Extend the strong normalization results for system F to $\beta\eta$-reduction, where the $\eta$ rule for type abstraction is: $\lambda t.Mt \to M$ $t \notin FV(M)$.*

**Exercise 11.5.21** *Prove that $\eta$-expansion in system F does not normalize. Hint: Consider the term $\lambda x : \forall t.t.x$.*

**Remark 11.5.22** *It is possible to reduce the strong normalization of the $\lambda P2$-calculus to the strong normalization of system F by a translation technique that generalizes the one employed in section 11.4 for the system LF [GN91].*

# 12
# Stability

The theory of stable functions is originally due to Berry [Ber78]. It has been rediscovered by Girard [Gir86] as a semantic counterpart of his theory of dilators. Similar ideas were also developed independently and with purely mathematical motivations by Diers (see [Tay90a] for references).

Berry discovered stability in his study of sequential computation (cf. theorem 2.4) and of the full abstraction problem for PCF (cf. section 6.4). His intuitions are drawn from an operational perspective, where one is concerned, not only with the input-output behaviour of procedures, but also with questions such as: 'which amount of the input is actually explored by the procedure before it produces an output'. In Girard's work, stable functions arose in a construction of a model of system F (see chapter 11); soon after, his work on stability paved the way to linear logic, which is the subject of chapter 13.

In section 12.1, we introduce the conditionally multiplicative functions, which are the continuous functions preserving binary compatible glb's. In section 12.2, we introduce the stable functions, focusing on minimal points and traces. Stability and conditional multiplicativity are different in general, but are equivalent under a well-foundedness assumption. They both lead to cartesian closed categories. The ordering on function spaces is not the pointwise ordering, but a new ordering, called the stable ordering.

We next develop the theory on algebraic cpo's, as in chapter 5. In Section 12.3, we introduce Berry's dI-domains, which are Scott domains satisfying two additional axioms. The dI-domains can also be presented concretely in terms of so-called (stable) event structures, that specify how data can be built out of elementary pieces of information called events. We show that dI-domains and stable functions form a cartesian closed category. Girard's coherence spaces (which will be investigated in section 13.1) are examples of dI-domains. In section 12.4, we discuss the stable version of bifiniteness. Within the stable bifinite framework a remarkably simple theory of retractions can be developed.

In section 12.5, we build another cartesian closed category of stable functions, based on a characterization of stable functions by the preservation of connected glb's. This category involves certain L-domains satisfying a strong distributivity axiom, which are investigated in section 12.6.

This chapter is based on [Ber78] (sections 12.1, 12.2, 12.3), [Win80] (section 12.3), [Tay90a] (sections 12.5 and 12.6), and [Ama91a] (section 12.4). Figure

(A) Example (A) of figure 5.2 is a meet cpo which is not bounded complete.

(B) $\{\perp, a, b, c, d, e\}$ , ordered as follows:

$$\perp \text{ minimum} \quad a \leq c, d \quad b \leq c, d \quad c, d \leq e,$$

is not a meet cpo (condition (1) of definition 12.1.1 is violated).

(C) The cpo $\omega_\perp \cup \{a, b\}$ of example 1.1.13(4) fails to be a meet cpo (condition (2) of definition 12.1.1 is violated).

Figure 12.1: Meet cpo structure: example, and counter-examples

12.3 summarizes the cartesian closed categories described in the chapter (see also exercise 12.6.7).

# 12.1   Conditionally multiplicative functions

In this section, we focus on functions preserving the compatible binary glb's. We therefore work with cpo's which have such glb's. Moreover, this partial glb operation is required to be continuous. This condition ensures that function spaces are cpo's (ordered by the stable ordering).

**Definition 12.1.1 (meet cpo)** *A cpo* $(D, \leq)$ *is called a meet cpo if*

(1) $\forall x, y \ (x \uparrow y \Rightarrow x \wedge y \ exists)$.

(2) $\forall x \ \forall \Delta \subseteq_{dir} D \ (x \uparrow (\bigvee \Delta) \Rightarrow x \wedge (\bigvee \Delta) = \bigvee \{x \wedge \delta \mid \delta \in \Delta\})$.

Some (counter-) examples are given in figure 12.1. The hypothesis in condition (2) of definition 12.1.1 can be relaxed. Moreover, it comes for free in an algebraic cpo.

**Lemma 12.1.2** (1) *In a meet cpo, whenever* $x \wedge (\bigvee \Delta)$ *exists, then the distributivity equality* $x \wedge (\bigvee \Delta) = \bigvee \{x \wedge \delta \mid \delta \in \Delta\}$ *holds.*

(2) *An algebraic cpo is a meet cpo iff condition (1) of definition 12.1.1 holds.*

PROOF. (1) We apply condition (2) with $x \wedge (\bigvee \Delta)$ in place of $x$:

$$(x \wedge (\bigvee \Delta)) \wedge (\bigvee \Delta) = \bigvee \{(x \wedge (\bigvee \Delta)) \wedge \delta \mid \delta \in \Delta\} = \bigvee \{x \wedge \delta \mid \delta \in \Delta\} \ .$$

(2)   To check $x \wedge (\bigvee \Delta) \leq \bigvee \{x \wedge \delta \mid \delta \in \Delta\}$, it is enough to check that every compact element $e$ such that $e \leq x \wedge (\bigvee \Delta)$ is also such that $e \leq \bigvee \{x \wedge \delta \mid \delta \in \Delta\}$, which is clear since, by the definition of compact elements, $e \leq \bigvee \Delta$ implies $e \leq \delta$ for some $\delta \in \Delta$. □

Two immediate consequences of lemma 12.1.2 are that:

- in bounded complete meet cpo's, the glb function is defined everywhere and is continuous;

- Scott domains are meet cpo's.

**Definition 12.1.3 (conditionally multiplicative)** *Let $D$ and $D'$ be meet cpo's. A function $f : D \to D'$ is called conditionally multiplicative, or cm for short if*

$$\forall x, y \in D \ \ x \uparrow y \Rightarrow f(x \wedge y) = f(x) \wedge f(y) \ .$$

*We write $D \to_{cm} D'$ for the set of cm functions from $D$ to $D'$.*

The function *por* considered in section 6.4 is an example of a continuous functions that is not cm:

$$por(\bot, tt) \wedge por(tt, \bot) = tt \neq \bot = por(\bot, \bot) \ .$$

The following function from $\mathbf{B}_\bot^3$ to $\mathbf{O}$ due to Berry (and independently to Kleene, see section 14.1) is a stable function:[1]

$$BK(x, y, z) = \begin{cases} \top & \text{if } x = tt \text{ and } y = ff \\ \top & \text{if } x = ff \text{ and } z = tt \\ \top & \text{if } y = tt \text{ and } z = ff \\ \bot & \text{otherwise} \ . \end{cases}$$

The simplest way to verify that this function is stable is by checking that its minimal points, i.e., the minimal elements $(x, y, z)$ of $\mathbf{B}_\bot^3$ such that $BK(x, y, z) = \top$ (see definition 12.2.1), are pairwise incompatible. Indeed, if

$$(x_1, y_1, z_1) \uparrow (x_2, y_2, z_2), BK(x_1, y_1, z_1) = \top, \text{ and } BK(x_2, y_2, z_2) = \top,$$

then $(x_1, y_1, z_1)$ and $(x_2, y_2, z_2)$ dominate the same minimal point $(x, y, z)$ by the incompatibility of distinct minimal points, hence $(x, y, z) \leq (x_1, y_1, z_1) \wedge (x_2, y_2, z_2)$, and:

$$BK((x_1, y_1, z_1) \wedge (x_2, y_2, z_2)) = \top = BK(x_1, y_1, z_1) \wedge BK(x_2, y_2, z_2) \ .$$

The main difficulty in getting a cartesian closed category of cm functions resides in making the evaluation morphism *ev* stable. The pointwise ordering $\leq_{ext}$ on functions (cf. definition 1.4.4) does not work. Consider the identity function *id* and the constant function $\top = \lambda x.\top$, both in $\mathbf{O} \to_{cm} \mathbf{O}$. Then $id \leq_{ext} \top$, so that if *ev* were to be stable, we should have $ev(id, \bot) = ev(id, \top) \wedge ev(\top, \bot)$. But in fact:

$$ev(id, \top) \wedge ev(\top, \bot) = \top \wedge \top \neq \bot = ev(id, \bot) \ .$$

To overcome the difficulty, Berry defined the stable ordering $\leq_{st}$. His definition directly stems from the goal of making *ev* cm, as follows. Suppose $f \leq_{st} g$ and $x \leq y$. Then we must have:

$$f(x) = ev(f \wedge g, y \wedge x) = ev(f, y) \wedge ev(g, x) = f(y) \wedge g(x) \ .$$

---

[1]Another name that is used for this function is *gustave*.

**Definition 12.1.4 (stable ordering (cm))** *Let $D$ and $D'$ be two meet cpo's, and $f, g : D \to_{cm} D'$. We define $f \leq_{st} g$ by:*

$$\forall x, y \ (x \leq y \Rightarrow f(x) = f(y) \wedge g(x)) \ .$$

*In particular, if $f \leq_{st} g$, then $f \leq_{ext} g$ (take $x = y$). (From now on, to avoid ambiguities, we use $\leq_{ext}$ for the pointwise ordering.) We write $f \uparrow_{st} g$, $f \uparrow_{ext} g$ if $f, g$ are compatible with respect to $\leq_{st}, \leq_{ext}$, respectively.*

**Lemma 12.1.5** *The relation $\leq_{st}$ of definition 12.1.4 is a partial order.*

PROOF. Reflexivity is obvious. For the transitivity, assume $f \leq_{st} f'$, $f' \leq_{st} f''$, and $x \leq y$:

$$f(x) = f(y) \wedge f'(x) = f(y) \wedge f'(y) \wedge f''(x) = f(y) \wedge f''(x) \ .$$

Antisymmetry follows from the antisymmetry of $\leq_{ext}$. □

**Exercise 12.1.6** *Let $D, D'$ be meet cpo's and $f, g : D \to_{cm} D'$. (1) Show that $f \leq_{st} g$ iff*

$$f \leq_{ext} g \text{ and } \forall x, y \ (x \uparrow y \Rightarrow f(x) \wedge g(y) = f(y) \wedge g(x)) \ .$$

*(2) Show that if $f \uparrow_{st} g$, then:*

$$\forall x, y \ (x \uparrow y \Rightarrow f(x) \wedge g(y) = f(y) \wedge g(x)) \ .$$

*(3) Conversely, assuming that $D'$ is a distributive meet cpo (see definition 12.1.12), show that if*

$$f \uparrow_{ext} g \text{ and } (\forall x, y \ (x \uparrow y \Rightarrow f(x) \wedge g(y) = f(y) \wedge g(x))),$$

*then $f \uparrow_{st} g$. Hint: One uses the information in the assumption to show that the pointwise lub of $f, g$ is their lub in the stable ordering, see the proof of theorem 12.1.14.*

**Exercise 12.1.7** *Show that if $f \leq_{ext} g \leq_{st} h$ and $f \leq_{st} h$, then $f \leq_{st} g$.*

**Exercise 12.1.8** *Let $f, g : D \to E$, with $f$ continuous, $g$ cm, and $f \leq_{st} g$. Show that $f$ is cm.*

**Theorem 12.1.9 (cm – CCC)** *The category of meet cpo's and conditionally multiplicative functions is a cpo-enriched CCC (cf. definition 6.1.1).*

PROOF. The verification that the composition of two cm functions is cm is immediate. As for the cpo-enriched CCC structure, we content ourselves with the verifications that $D \to_{cm} D'$, ordered by the stable ordering, is a meet cpo, and that the evaluation morphism $ev$ is cm.[2]

Directed lub's and binary compatible glb's are defined pointwise (and therefore the continuity property of $\wedge$ comes for free). Let $H \subseteq_{dir} (D \to_{cm} D')$, and define $h$ by $h(x) = \bigvee \{f(x) \mid f \in H\}$.

---

[2]In all the CCC's presented in this chapter, the pairing and currying are the set theoretical ones (cf. exercises 4.2.11 and 4.2.12). We have written one of the proofs (theorem 12.2.8) in full detail.

- $h$ is cm.

$$h(x) \wedge h(y) = (\bigvee_{f \in H} f(x)) \wedge (\bigvee_{f \in H} f(y)) = \bigvee \{f(x) \wedge g(y) \mid f, g \in H\} .$$

We conclude by observing that $f(x) \wedge g(y) \leq k(x) \wedge k(y) = k(x \wedge y)$ if $k$ is an upper bound of $f, g$ in $H$.

- $h$ is an upper bound of $H$. Let $f_0 \in H$ and $x \leq y$:

$$f_0(y) \wedge h(x) = \bigvee \{f_0(y) \wedge f(x) \mid f \in H\} = \bigvee \{f_0(x) \wedge f(y) \mid f \in H\} = f_0(x) \wedge h(y) .$$

A similar argument shows that $h$ is the least upper bound of $H$ in the stable ordering.

If $f \uparrow_{st} g$, we define $f \wedge g$ by $(f \wedge g)(x) = f(x) \wedge g(x)$. We check $f \wedge g \leq_{st} f$. Let $x \leq y$:

$$\begin{aligned}
(f \wedge g)(y) \wedge f(x) &= g(y) \wedge f(x) \\
&= g(x) \wedge f(y) && \text{(cf. exercise 12.1.6)} \\
&= g(y) \wedge f(x) \wedge g(x) \wedge f(y) \\
&= f(x) \wedge g(x) .
\end{aligned}$$

Suppose $k \leq_{st} f, g$. We show $k \leq_{st} f \wedge g$. Let $x \leq y$:

$$(f \wedge g)(x) \wedge k(y) = f(x) \wedge (g(x) \wedge k(y)) = f(x) \wedge k(x) = k(x) .$$

The stability of $ev$ follows from the definition of the stable ordering:

$$\begin{aligned}
ev(f, x) \wedge ev(g, y) &= f(x) \wedge g(y) &&= f(y) \wedge g(x) \\
&= f(x) \wedge f(y) \wedge g(x) \wedge g(y) &&= ev(f \wedge g, x \wedge y) . \qquad \square
\end{aligned}$$

**Exercise 12.1.10** *Show that the following combination of pullbacks (where $(h, z)$ is an upper bound of $(f, x), (g, y)$), borrowed from [Tay90a], offers an attractive picture of the proof that $ev$ is cm:*

$$\begin{array}{ccccc}
(f \wedge g)(x \wedge y) & \to & (f \wedge g)(x) & \to & f(x) \\
\downarrow & (f \wedge g \text{ stable}) & \downarrow & (f \wedge g \leq_{st} f) & \downarrow \\
(f \wedge g)(y) & \to & (f \wedge g)(z) & \to & f(z) \\
\downarrow & (f \wedge g \leq_{st} g) & \downarrow & (\text{definition}) & \downarrow \\
g(y) & \to & g(z) & \to & h(z) .
\end{array}$$

**Exercise 12.1.11** *Show that the composition operation on meet cpo's is cm.*

If we assume bounded completeness of the domains, we are led to introduce distributivity to maintain cartesian closure.

**Definition 12.1.12 (distributive cpo)** *A cpo is called distributive if it is bounded complete and satisfies:*

$$\forall x, y, z \ \{x, y, z\} \ \text{bounded} \ \Rightarrow \ x \wedge (y \vee z) = (x \wedge y) \vee (x \wedge z) .$$

**Example 12.1.13** *The following are basic examples of non-distributive finite lattices.*

*(A)* $\{\bot, a, b, c, d\}$, *ordered as follows:*

$$\bot \ minimum \quad a, b, c \leq d \ .$$

*(B)* $\{\bot, a, b, c, d\}$, *ordered as follows:*

$$\bot \ minimum \quad a \leq d \quad b \leq c \leq d \ .$$

*Notice that any flat cpo is (vacuously) distributive.*

**Theorem 12.1.14** *The category of distributive meet cpo's and cm functions is a cpo-enriched CCC.*

PROOF. Let $f \uparrow_{st} g$. We show that $f \vee g$ defined pointwise is also the stable lub of $f, g$. Let $h(x) = f(x) \vee g(x)$.

- $h$ is stable.

$$
\begin{aligned}
h(x) \wedge h(y) &= (f(x) \vee g(x)) \wedge (f(y) \vee g(y)) \\
&= (f(x) \wedge f(y)) \vee (g(x) \wedge g(y)) \vee (f(x) \wedge g(y)) \vee (g(x) \wedge f(y)) \\
&= (f(x) \wedge f(y)) \vee (g(x) \wedge g(y)) \\
&= h(x \wedge y) \ ,
\end{aligned}
$$

using distributivity and observing that $f(x) \wedge g(y) = g(x) \wedge f(y) \leq f(x) \wedge f(y)$.

- $h$ is a stable upper bound. Let $x \leq y$. We have:

$$h(x) \wedge f(y) = (f(x) \wedge f(y)) \vee (g(x) \wedge f(y)) = f(x) \vee (f(x) \wedge g(y)) = f(x) \ .$$

- $h$ is the stable lub. Let $f, g \leq_{st} k$ and $x \leq y$. We have:

$$k(x) \wedge h(y) = (k(x) \wedge f(y)) \vee (k(x) \wedge g(y)) = f(x) \vee g(x) = h(x) \ . \qquad \square$$

## 12.2 Stable functions

Stable functions can be defined on arbitrary cpo's. Their definition brings us closer to an operational intuition.

**Definition 12.2.1 (stable)** *Let $D$ and $D'$ be cpo's. A function $f : D \to D'$ is called stable if it is continuous and if, for any $x \in D$, $x' \in D'$ such that $x' \leq f(x)$:*

$$\exists x_0 \leq x \ (x' \leq f(x_0) \ and \ (\forall y \leq x \ (x' \leq f(y) \Rightarrow x_0 \leq y))) \ .$$

*This uniquely determined $x_0$ is written $m(f, x, x')$, and is called a minimal point of $f$ (relative to $x'$). We write $D \to_{st} D'$ for the set of stable functions from $D$ to $D'$. The following set is called the trace of $f$:*

$$trace(f) = \{(x, x') \in D \times D' \mid x' \leq f(x) \ and \ x = m(f, x, x')\} \ .$$

*The function $m(f, \_, \_)$ is called the multi-adjoint of $f$ (the situation $x' \leq f(y)$ versus $m(f, x, x') \leq y$ is reminiscent of an adjunction).*

In computational terms, $m(f, x, x')$ represents the amount of $x$ which is 'read' by $f$ in order to 'write' (at least) $x'$. Stable functions can also be described by glb preservation properties, as we now explain.

**Proposition 12.2.2** (1) *Let $D$ and $D'$ be cpo's, and let $f : D \to_{st} D'$. Then for any bounded $X \subseteq D$ such that $\bigwedge X$ exists, $f(\bigwedge X) = \bigwedge f(X)$.*

(2) *Conversely, if $D$ and $D'$ have all non-empty bounded glb's, then a continuous function preserving all such glb's is stable.*

PROOF. (1) $f(\bigwedge X)$ is a lower bound of $f(X)$ by monotonicity. Suppose that $z' \leq f(X)$. Let $y \geq X$. Then $z' \leq f(y)$. Let $z_0 = m(f, y, z')$. Pick $x \in X$. Then $z_0 \leq x$ by the minimality of $z_0$. Hence $z_0 \leq \bigwedge X$, which implies $z' \leq f(\bigwedge X)$, since $z' \leq f(z_0)$. Hence $f(\bigwedge X)$ is the glb of $f(X)$.

(2) Let $y \leq f(x)$. Consider $z_0 = \bigwedge\{z \mid z \leq x \text{ and } y \leq f(z)\}$. We claim that $z_0$ is $m(f, x, y)$. This amounts to showing $y \leq f(z_0)$, which holds since:

$$f(z_0) = \bigwedge\{f(z) \mid z \leq x \text{ and } y \leq f(z)\} .$$

$\square$

In section 12.5, we shall see that stable functions preserve even more glb's (the connected ones, provided they exist). Meanwhile, going from 'more' to 'less', stable functions on meet cpo's are *a fortiori* conditionally multiplicative, by proposition 12.2.2. Berry has provided the following example of a cm, non stable function. Let:

$$D = \omega \cup \{\bot\} \text{ with } \bot \leq \cdots \leq n \leq \cdots \leq 1 \leq 0 .$$

Let $f : D \to \mathbf{O}$ be defined by: $f(\bot) = \bot$, $f(n) = \top$. Then $f$ is cm, but $m(f, 0, \top)$ does not exist. If we prevent the existence of infinite descending chains, then cm and stable are equivalent notions.

**Lemma 12.2.3** *Let $D, D'$ be cpo's and let $f : D \to_{st} D'$. The following properties hold:*

(1) *If $\Delta' \subseteq_{dir} D'$, and if $\bigvee \Delta' \leq f(x)$, then:*

$$m(f, x, \bigvee \Delta') = \bigvee\{m(f, x, \delta') \mid \delta' \in \Delta'\} .$$

(2) *If $D$ and $D'$ are bounded complete, and if $x_1' \leq f(x)$ and $x_2' \leq f(x)$, then:*

$$m(f, x, x_1' \vee x_2') = m(f, x, x_1') \vee m(f, x, x_2') .$$

(3) *If $D$ and $D'$ are algebraic, then $f : D \to D'$ is stable iff for any compact $d \in \mathcal{K}(D)$, $d' \in \mathcal{K}(D')$, such that $d' \leq f(d)$, $m(f, d, d')$ exists.*

PROOF. We only prove (3). Let $x \in D$, $x' \in D'$, not necessarily compact. We have:

$$m(f, x, x') = \bigvee\{m(f, x, d') \mid d' \text{ compact and } d' \leq x'\} \quad \text{(by (1))}$$
$$m(f, x, d') = m(f, d, d') \text{ for some } d \qquad\qquad \text{(by continuity)} .$$ $\square$

**Proposition 12.2.4** *If $D$ and $D'$ are algebraic meet cpo's, and if $\mathcal{K}(D)$ is well-founded, then $f : D \to D'$ is stable iff it is cm.*

PROOF. Let $f$ be cm. By lemma 12.2.3, it is enough to consider $d' \leq f(d)$, with $d, d'$ compact. If $d$ is not minimum with that property, then for some compact $d_1 \leq x$ we have $d' \leq f(d_1)$ and $d \not\leq d_1$. Hence $d' \leq f(d) \wedge f(d_1) = f(d \wedge d_1)$. In this way we construct a strictly decreasing chain $d > d \wedge d_1 > \cdots$ that must eventually end with $e$ satisfying the definition of $m(f, x, d')$. □

The stable ordering between stable functions can be defined in terms of minimal points.

**Definition 12.2.5 (stable ordering (stable))** *Let $D$, $D'$ be cpo's, and $f, g : D \to_{st} D'$. We write $f \leq_{st} g$ iff*

$$f \leq_{ext} g \text{ and } \forall x, x' \ (x' \leq f(x) \Rightarrow m(f, x, x') = m(g, x, x')) \,.$$

*Equivalently, $\leq_{st}$ can be defined by the inclusion of traces:*

$$f \leq_{st} g \quad \text{iff} \quad trace(f) \subseteq trace(g) \,.$$

*It is immediate that $\leq_{st}$ is a partial order, called the stable ordering.*

**Exercise 12.2.6** *Show that the stable ordering can be equivalently defined as follows: $f \leq_{st} g$ iff $(f \leq_{ext} g$ and $\forall x, x' \ (x' \leq f(x) \Rightarrow \forall y \leq x \ (x' \leq g(y) \Rightarrow x' \leq f(y))))$.*

The next lemma shows that the stable ordering just defined coincides with the stable ordering on the underlying cm functions.

**Lemma 12.2.7** *Let $D$ and $D'$ be two cpo's, and $f, g : D \to_{st} D'$. The following equivalence holds:*

$$f \leq_{st} g \Leftrightarrow \forall x, y \ (x \leq y \Rightarrow f(x) = f(y) \wedge g(x))$$

*(in particular, the glb's $f(y) \wedge g(x)$ exist).*

PROOF. ($\Rightarrow$) $f(x)$ is a lower bound of $\{f(y), g(x)\}$. If $z' \leq f(y)$ and $z' \leq g(x)$, then:

$$\begin{aligned} m(g, y, z') &= m(f, y, z') \quad \text{(since } z' \leq f(y) \text{ and } f \leq_{st} g) \\ m(g, y, z') &\leq x \quad \text{(since } z' \leq g(x)) \,. \end{aligned}$$

Hence $m(f, y, z') \leq x$, and $z' \leq f(x)$.

($\Leftarrow$) In particular, taking $x = y$, we get $f \leq_{ext} g$, hence $m(g, z, z') \leq m(f, z, z')$, for $z' \leq f(z)$. On the other hand, for any $z_1 \leq z$, $z' \leq g(z_1)$ implies $z' \leq f(z) \wedge g(z_1) = f(z_1)$, which shows $m(f, z, z') \leq m(g, z, z')$. □

**Theorem 12.2.8 (stable – CCC)** *The category of distributive meet cpo's and stable functions is a cpo-enriched CCC.*

PROOF. First of all, we need to check that the composition of two stable functions is stable. Let $f : D \to_{st} D'$ and $f' : D' \to_{st} D''$, and let $x'' \leq f'(f(x))$. Then we claim:

$$m(f' \circ f, x, x'') = m(f, x, m(f', f(x), x'')) .$$

Indeed, for $y \leq x$, we have: $m(f', f(x), x'') \leq f(y)$ iff $x'' \leq f'(f(y))$. We leave the reader check that the set theoretical product, with the componentwise ordering and the usual projections and pairing, is a categorical product. Notice that for $f : D \to_{st} D'$, $g : D \to_{st} D''$:

$$m(\langle f, g \rangle, x, (x', x'')) = m(f, x, x') \vee m(g, x, x'') .$$

We check in detail that $D \to_{st} D'$ is a categorical exponent. We first show that $D \to_{st} D'$ is a cpo. Let $H \subseteq_{dir} D \to_{st} D'$. Then *a fortiori* $H$ is directed for $\leq_{ext}$. Consider $h$ defined by $h(x) = \bigvee\{f(x) \mid f \in H\}$. We check that $h$ is stable by showing $m(h, x, x') = \bigvee_{f \in H} m(f, x, x' \wedge f(x))$, for all $x, x'$ such that $x' \leq h(x)$. Let $y \leq x$. We have, using the continuity of glb's:

$$m(h, x, x') \leq y \Leftrightarrow x' \leq h(y) \Leftrightarrow \bigvee_{f \in H} (x' \wedge f(y)) = x' .$$

On the other hand we have:

$$\bigvee_{f \in H} m(f, x, x' \wedge f(x)) \leq y \Leftrightarrow \forall f \in H \ x' \wedge f(x) \leq f(y),$$

which can be rephrased as: $\forall f \in H \ x' \wedge f(x) = x' \wedge f(y)$. Thus we are left to show:

$$\forall f \in H \ (x' \wedge f(x) = x' \wedge f(y) \Leftrightarrow \bigvee_{f \in H} (x' \wedge f(y)) = x') .$$

$(\Rightarrow)$ $\bigvee_{f \in H}(x' \wedge f(y)) = \bigvee_{f \in H}(x' \wedge f(x)) = x' \wedge h(x) = x'$.

$(\Leftarrow)$ Let $f_0 \in H$. We have (cf. exercise 12.1.6):

$$\begin{aligned} x' \wedge f_0(x) &= \bigvee_{f \in H}(x' \wedge f(y) \wedge f_0(x)) &= \bigvee_{f \in H}(x' \wedge f(x) \wedge f_0(y)) \\ &= x' \wedge f_0(y) \wedge h(x) &= x' \wedge f_0(y) . \end{aligned}$$

Hence $h$ is stable. Next we show: $\forall f \in H \ f \leq_{st} h$. Let $f \in H$ and $x' \leq f(x)$. Since $f \leq_{ext} h$, we have $m(h, x, x') \leq m(f, x, x')$. On the other hand, since $m(h, x, x') = \bigvee_{f \in H} m(f, x, x' \wedge f(x))$, we have:

$$m(f, x, x') = m(f, x, x' \wedge f(x)) \leq m(h, x, x') .$$

Let $k$ be an upper bound of $H$ in the stable order. We show $h \leq_{st} k$:

$$m(h, x, x') = \bigvee_{f \in H} m(f, x, x' \wedge f(x)) = \bigvee_{f \in H} m(k, x, x' \wedge f(x)) = m(k, x, x') .$$

This completes the proof that $D \to_{st} D'$ is a cpo.

Binary compatible glb's exist, and are defined pointwise: for $f, g \leq_{st} h$, define $k(x) = f(x) \wedge g(x)$. This is a continuous function by continuity of the glb operation. Let $x' \leq k(x)$, and $y \leq x$. Then we have:

$$x' \leq k(y) \quad \Leftrightarrow \quad (m(f, x, x') \leq y \text{ and } m(g, x, x') \leq y) \quad \Leftrightarrow \quad m(h, x, x') \leq y,$$

since $m(f, x, x')$ and $m(g, x, x')$ are both equal to $m(h, x, x')$ by assumption. Hence $m(k, x, x') = m(h, x, x')$. Thus $k$ is stable, $k \leq_{st} f$, and $k \leq_{st} g$. Finally, suppose $k' \leq_{st} f, g$ and $x' \leq k'(x)$. Then $m(k', x, x') = m(f, x, x') = m(g, x, x')$, hence $m(k', x, x') = m(k, x, x')$. This completes the proof that $k = f \wedge g$ (with respect to the stable ordering). The continuity property $f \wedge (\bigvee H) = \bigvee_{h \in H} (f \wedge h)$ follows from the fact that the operations are defined pointwise.

Binary compatible lub's exist too. Suppose $f, g \leq_{st} h$, and define $k(x) = f(x) \vee g(x)$. The proof that $k$ is stable and is the lub of $f, g$ in the stable ordering is completely similar to the proof of directed completeness $D \to_{st} D'$. One replaces everywhere uses of the continuity of the glb operation by uses of its distributivity. The distributivity equation follows from the fact that the operations are defined pointwise. Thus we have proved that $D \to_{st} D'$ is a distributive meet cpo.

We now prove that $ev$ is stable. Consider $(f, x)$ and $x'$ such that $x' \leq f(x) = ev(f, x)$. We show that $m(ev, (f, x), x') = (g, z)$, where $z = m(f, x, x')$ and $g = \lambda y.(x' \wedge f(y \wedge z))$. (By bounded completeness, all binary glb's exist, thus $g$ is well-defined and continuous, cf. lemma 12.1.2.) First, $z \leq x$ by definition. We check $g \leq_{st} f$. We have (for $y \leq y_1$):

$$g(y_1) \wedge f(y) = x' \wedge f(y_1 \wedge z) \wedge f(y) = x' \wedge f(y_1 \wedge z \wedge y) = g(y).$$

Second, we check $x' \leq g(z)$. We actually even have $x' = g(z)$:

$$g(z) = x' \wedge f(z \wedge z) = x' \wedge f(z) = x'.$$

Finally, let $(f_1, x_1) \leq (f, x)$ be such that $x' \leq f_1(x_1)$. Then a fortiori $x' \leq f(x_1)$, hence $z \leq x_1$. Next we show $g \leq_{ext} f_1$:

$$
\begin{aligned}
g(y) \wedge f_1(y) &= x' \wedge (f(y \wedge z) \wedge f_1(y)) &&= x' \wedge f_1(y \wedge z) \\
&= x' \wedge f_1(y \wedge z) \wedge f(x_1) &&= x' \wedge (f(y \wedge z) \wedge f_1(x_1)) \\
&= (x' \wedge f_1(x_1)) \wedge f(y \wedge z) &&= g(y).
\end{aligned}
$$

We prove $g \leq_{st} f_1$. Let $y \leq y_1$:

$$
\begin{aligned}
g(y_1) \wedge f_1(y) &= x' \wedge f(y_1 \wedge z) \wedge f_1(y) &&= x' \wedge f_1(y_1 \wedge z) \wedge f(y) \\
&\leq x' \wedge f(y_1 \wedge z) \wedge f(y) &&= g(y).
\end{aligned}
$$

This completes the proof that $m(ev, (f, x), x') = (g, z)$, and hence that $ev$ is stable.

Next we show that $\Lambda(f)(x)$ is stable. Let $m(f, (x, x'), x'') = (y, y')$. We show that $m(\Lambda(f)(x), x', x'') = y'$. Since $(y, y') \leq (x, y')$, we have $x'' \leq f(x, y')$, that is, $x'' \leq \Lambda(f)(x)(y')$. If $z' \leq x'$ and $x'' \leq \Lambda(f)(x)(z')$, then $(y, y') \leq (x, z')$, and in particular $y' \leq z'$. This proves the stability of $\Lambda(f)(x)$, and also that $\Lambda(f)$ is monotonic: if $x \leq x_1$, then:

$$m(\Lambda(f)(x), x', x'') = m(\Lambda(f)(x_1), x', x'') = y'.$$

Finally, we check that $\Lambda(f)$ is stable. We show, for $g \leq_{st} \Lambda(f)(x)$:

$$m(\Lambda(f), x, g) = \bigwedge T \quad \text{where } T = \{y \mid y \leq x \text{ and } g \leq_{st} \Lambda(f)(y)\} .$$

We have to check that $g \leq_{st} \Lambda(f)(\bigwedge T)$. For any $x'$, since $g(x') \leq f(y, x')$ for any $y \in T$, we have by stability (cf. proposition 12.2.2):

$$g(x') \leq \bigwedge_{y \in T} f(y, x') = f(\bigwedge T, x'),$$

i.e., $g \leq_{ext} \Lambda(f)(\bigwedge T)$. By exercise 12.1.7, $g \leq_{st} \Lambda(f)(x)$ and $\Lambda(f)(\bigwedge T) \leq_{st} \Lambda(f)(x)$ imply $g \leq_{st} \Lambda(f)(\bigwedge T)$. Thus we have established the CCC structure.

Finally, we check that $\Lambda$ is monotonic. Suppose $f \leq_{st} g$. We first show $\Lambda(f) \leq_{ext} \Lambda(g)$, i.e., $\forall x \; \Lambda(f)(x) \leq_{st} \Lambda(g)(x)$. Recall that $m(\Lambda(f)(x), x', x'') = y'$, where $y'$ is the second component of $m(f, (x, x'), x'')$. Since $f \leq_{st} g$, we have $m(g, (x, x'), x'') = m(f, (x, x'), x'')$. Hence:

$$m(\Lambda(f)(x), x', x'') = m(\Lambda(g)(x), x', x'') .$$

Next, suppose $y \leq x$. We have to check $\Lambda(f)(y) = \Lambda(f)(x) \wedge \Lambda(g)(y)$. By the pointwise definition of binary compatible glb's, this amounts to $f(y, x') = f(x, x') \wedge g(y, x')$, for all $x'$, which holds since $f \leq_{st} g$. □

**Remark 12.2.9** *Notice the use of the distributivity assumption in theorem 12.2.8: bounded completeness comes in to get products, and distributivity comes in to show that binary compatible lub's are stable. The situation was different in section 12.1: we have obtained a cartesian closed category of cm functions without assuming distributivity (and a full cartesian closed subcategory of distributive meet cpo's).*

**Exercise 12.2.10 (trace factorization [Tay90b])** *Show that* trace$(f)$, *ordered by the induced componentwise order, is a cpo. Consider the following functions:*

$$
\begin{aligned}
\pi &: trace(f) \to D & \pi(x, x') &= x \\
\pi' &: trace(f) \to D' & \pi'(x, x') &= x' \\
h &: D \to trace(f) & h(x) &= \{(m(f, x, f(x)), f(x)) \mid x \in D\} .
\end{aligned}
$$

*(1) Show that* $\pi \dashv h$, *i.e.,* $(x_1, y_1) \leq h(x) \Leftrightarrow x_1 \leq x$. *(2) A monotonic function* $f : X \to Y$ *between two partial orders is called a fibration if for any pair* $(x, y)$ *such that* $y \leq f(x)$, *there exists an element* $\omega(f, x, y)$ *of* $X$ *such that:*

$$
\begin{aligned}
(\Phi_0) \quad & \omega(f, x, y) \leq x \\
(\Phi_1) \quad & f(\omega(f, x, y)) = y \\
(\Phi_2) \quad & \forall z \leq x \; (f(z) \leq y \Rightarrow z \leq \omega(f, x, y)) .
\end{aligned}
$$

*Show that* $\pi' : trace(f) \to D'$ *is a fibration, and that, moreover,* $\omega(f, \_, \_)$ *is the multi-adjoint of* $\pi'$. *(3) Show that such a fibration, called a stable fibration, can be equivalently defined as a fibration (with* $\omega$*) which is stable (with a multi-adjoint* $m$*) and is such that all fibers are groupoids, i.e., all subsets* $f^{-1}(x)$ *consist of non comparable points. (4) Show that the sets*

$$
\begin{aligned}
\mathcal{M} \quad & \textit{of functions with a left adjoint and} \\
\mathcal{E} \quad & \textit{of stable fibrations}
\end{aligned}
$$

*form a factorization system for stable functions, by which we mean:*

(a) *Any stable function $f$ factorizes as $f = \pi' \circ h$, with $h \in \mathcal{M}$ and $\pi' \in \mathcal{E}$.*

(b) *$\mathcal{M}$ and $\mathcal{E}$ contain the order-isomorphisms and are closed under composition with order-isomorphisms.*

(c) *For every commuting square $g \circ h = l \circ f$ where $h \in \mathcal{M}$ and $l \in \mathcal{E}$, there exists a unique stable $\phi$ (called a diagonal fill-in) such that $l \circ \phi = g$ and $\phi \circ h \leq f$. (The unique diagonal fill-in property allows us to show the uniqueness of the $\mathcal{E}$-$\mathcal{M}$ factorization.)*

**Exercise 12.2.11** *Show that the category of cpo's and stable functions is not cartesian. Hints: Consider example (B) in figure 12.1. Call this domain $D$ and define a pair of functions $f : D \to \mathbf{O}$ and $g : D \to \mathbf{O}$ such that the pairing fails to be stable.*

**Exercise\* 12.2.12** *Develop a theory of stable, partial functions by analogy with the continuous case. Discuss lifting and sum in this framework.*

# 12.3 dI-domains and event structures

We now address algebraicity. In continuous domain theory, the compact functions are finite lub's of step functions $d \to e$ (cf. proposition 1.4.8). Step functions are stable, but they do not serve as approximations of functions as in the continuous case. In the continuous case, one simply has $(d \to e) \leq_{ext} f$ iff $e \leq f(d)$. However it is not true in general that $e \leq f(d)$ (or even $m(f, d, e) = d$) implies $(d \to e) \leq_{st} f$. The point is that for $e_1 < e$, one may have $m(f, d, e_1) < d$, which precludes $(d \to e) \leq_{st} f$, since $m(d \to e, d, e_1) = d$. This suggests that we 'saturate' our candidate $d \to e$ by forming a lub $(d \to e) \vee \cdots \vee (d_i \to e_i) \vee \cdots$, with $e_i < e$ and $d_i = m(f, d, e_i)$. The following property $I$, which may be read as 'finite is really finite', ensures the finiteness of this saturation process. (These considerations are for heuristic purposes only: the proof of cartesian closure does not use step functions.)

**Definition 12.3.1 (dI-domain)** *Let $D$ be an algebraic cpo. Property $I$ is defined as follows:*

(I) *Each compact element dominates finitely many elements.*

*An algebraic distributive cpo satisfying property $I$ is called a dI-domain.*

**Exercise 12.3.2** *Show that an algebraic domain satisfies $I$ iff each compact element dominates finitely many compact elements. Hint: For any $y \leq x$ the approximants of $y$ are also approximants of $x$, hence are finitely many.*

Clearly, property $I$ implies well-foundedness of $\mathcal{K}(D)$, hence under the assumption that property $I$ is satisfied stable functions are the same as cm functions (by proposition 12.2.4).

The dI-domains are due to Berry, who showed that they form a cartesian closed category. We take a concrete approach, based on event structures. An event structure can be perceived as a specification of how to build data out of distinct discrete pieces, or events, respecting consistency and causality requirements. These intuitions come from the theory of concurrency, and, indeed, event structures have been investigated in connection with Petri nets. Winskel [Win80, Win86] noticed that they could be used for domain theory, and this is what concerns us here. Any event structure generates a cpo, and dI-domains are recast from a subclass of event structures satisfying an axiom corresponding to distributivity.

**Definition 12.3.3 (event structure)** *An event structure* $(E, Con, \vdash)$ *(also called* $E$ *for short) is given by:*

- *a set* $E$ *whose elements are called* events,

- *a non-empty predicate* $Con \subseteq \mathcal{P}_{fin}(E)$, *called* consistency, *satisfying:*

$$(\subseteq Con) \quad (X \in Con \text{ and } Y \subseteq X) \Rightarrow Y \in Con \;,$$

- *a relation* $\vdash \subseteq Con \times E$, *called the* enabling *relation; if* $X \vdash e$, *we say that* $X$ *is an enabling of* $e$.

*Enablings serve to define proofs of events. A proof of an event* $e$ *is a set of events defined recursively as follows. If* $\vdash e$, *then* $e$ *has an empty proof. If* $t_1, \dots, t_n$ *are proofs of* $e_1, \dots, e_n$, *and if* $\{e_1, \dots, e_n\} \vdash e$, *then* $t_1 \cup \{e_1\} \cup \cdots \cup t_n \cup \{e_n\}$ *is a proof of* $e$.

*A state (or configuration) is a subset* $x$ *of* $E$ *which is:*

- consistent, *that is,* $\forall X \subseteq_{fin} x \; X \in Con$,

- safe, *that is, for any* $e \in x$, $x$ *contains a proof of* $e$.

*We write* $D(E, Con, \vdash)$ *for the collection of states of* $E$, *ordered by inclusion.*

*An event structure is called* stable *if for any state* $x$, *for any* $X, Y$, *and* $e$ *such that* $e \in x$, $X \subseteq_{fin} x$, $Y \subseteq_{fin} x$, *then* $(X \vdash e \text{ and } Y \vdash e \Rightarrow X = Y)$.

*A partial order is called a (stable)* event domain *if it is generated by some (stable) event structure, i.e., if it is isomorphic to* $D(E, Con, \vdash)$ *for some (stable) event structure* $(E, Con, \vdash)$.

The stability condition on event structures allows us to define the glb of two compatible states as their set theoretical intersection.

**Proposition 12.3.4** *Event domains are Scott domains satisfying property* $I$. *The minimum element is the empty state which is indifferently written* $\perp$ *or* $\emptyset$. *Stable event domains are dI-domains.*

PROOF. Let $E$ be an event structure. We first show that $D(E, Con, \vdash)$ ($D$ for short) is a bounded complete cpo. Let $\Delta$ be a directed set of states, and consider its set theoretical union $x$. We prove that $x$ is a state. Let $X \subseteq_{fin} x$. Then, by directedness, $X \subseteq_{fin} \delta$ for some $\delta \in \Delta$. Hence $X \in Con$. Safety is obvious for a union. Let now $x, y, z$ be states such that $x, y \leq z$. The set theoretical union of $x$ and $y$ is again a state, by the same argument. The algebraicity of $D$ follows from the observation that finite states are compact, and that every state $x$ is the union of the proofs of the events $e \in x$. Moreover the compact states are exactly the finite ones, from which property $I$ follows.

Let us now assume that $E$ is stable. Distributivity follows from the set theoretical distributivity of intersection over union. □

We shall see that in fact dI-domains and stable event domains are the same (proposition 12.3.10).

**Example 12.3.5** *Consider* $E = \{e_1, e_2, e_3\}$, $Con = \mathcal{P}(E)$ *and* $\vdash$ *given by:*

$$\vdash e_1 \qquad \vdash e_2 \qquad e_1 \vdash e_3 \qquad e_2 \vdash e_3 \ .$$

*Then* $(E, Con, \vdash)$ *is an event structure that is not stable (consider* $\{e_1, e_2, e_3\}$*).*

As a motivation for the notions of consistency predicate and enabling, consider a stable function $f$, viewed as a state (anticipating theorem 12.3.6 and remark 12.3.7).

• If $(d_1, e_1'), (d_2, e_2') \in trace(f)$ and if $d_1, d_2 \leq d$, then $e_1', e_2' \leq f(d)$. Therefore $\{(d_1, e_1'), (d_2, e_2')\}$ should not be consistent if $d_1 \uparrow d_2$ and $e_1' \not\uparrow e_2'$.

• If $(d_1, e'), (d_2, e') \in trace(f)$ (with $d_1 \neq d_2$), then $d_1 \not\uparrow d_2$ by definition of a stable function. Therefore $\{(d_1, e_1'), (d_2, e_2')\}$ should not be consistent if $d_1 \uparrow d_2$, $d_1 \neq d_2$, and $e_1' = e_2'$.

• Let $(d, e') \in trace(f)$ and $e_1' < e'$. Then $e_1' \leq f(d)$ implies $(m(f, d, e_1'), e_1') \in trace(f)$ (cf. the discussion on step functions at the beginning of the section), and $(m(f, d, e_1'), e_1')$ should occur in the proof of $(d, e')$ in $trace(f)$.

**Theorem 12.3.6 (dI-domains – CCC)** *The category* **dI-Dom** *of stable event domains and stable functions is a cpo-enriched CCC.*[3]

PROOF. We only give the construction of the product and exponent objects. Specifically, given $E$ and $E'$, we construct $E \times E'$ and $E \to E'$ in such a way that $D(E \times E')$ is the product of $D(E)$ and $D(E')$ in **Poset**, and that $D(E \to E') = D(E) \to_{st} D(E')$. We define $E \times E'$ as follows:

• The collection of events is the disjoint union of $E$ and $E'$.

• Consistency is defined componentwise: $X$ is consistent iff both $X \cap E$ and $X \cap E'$ are consistent.

• The enabling relation is the disjoint union of the component enabling relations.

We define $E \to E'$ as follows:

• Events are pairs $(x, e')$ where $x$ is a finite state of $E$, and $e' \in E'$.

• A finite set $\{(x_i, e_i') \mid i \in I\}$ is consistent iff

$$\forall J \subseteq I \ \{x_j \mid j \in J\} \text{ bounded} \Rightarrow \{e_j' \mid j \in J\} \in Con, \text{ and}$$
$$\forall i, j \ e_i' = e_j' \Rightarrow (x_i = x_j \text{ or } x_i \not\uparrow x_j).$$

---

[3]The name will be justified by proposition 12.3.10.

- $\{(x_i, e'_i) \mid i \in I\} \vdash (x, e')$ iff $\forall i \; x_i \subseteq x$ and $\{e'_i \mid i \in I\} \vdash e'$.

Axiom ($\subseteq Con$) is trivially satisfied. We show that there is an order-isomorphism between $D(E) \to_{st} D(E')$ ordered by the stable ordering and $D(E \to E')$ ordered by inclusion. With $f : D(E) \to_{st} D(E')$ we associate:

$$trace(f) = \{(x, e') \mid e' \in f(x) \text{ and } (y \leq x \Rightarrow e' \notin f(y))\} \;.$$

We show that $trace(f)$ is a state. Consider $\{(x_i, e'_i) \mid i \in I\} \subseteq trace(f)$ and $J \subseteq I$ such that $\{x_j \mid j \in J\}$ has a bound $x$. Then $\{e'_j \mid j \in J\} \subseteq f(x)$, hence is consistent. The second condition follows from the definition of stable function (see remark 12.3.7). As for safety, consider $(x, e') \in trace(f)$ and a proof of $e'$ in $f(x)$. We can attach to any $e'_1$ in this proof the minimal point under $x$ where $f$ reaches $e'_1$. In this way we obtain a proof of $(x, e')$ in $trace(f)$.

That $f \leq_{st} g$ is equivalent to $trace(f) \subseteq trace(g)$ is just the definition of the stable ordering (cf. definition 12.2.5). The converse transformation is defined as follows. Given a state $z$ of $E \to E'$, we define:

$$fun(z)(x) = \{e' \mid \exists y \; (y, e') \in z \text{ and } y \subseteq x\} \;.$$

We first have to check that $fun(z)(x)$ is a state. Its consistency follows from the first condition in the definition of higher order consistency. Its safety follows from the safety of $z$, noticing that all the events in a proof of $(y, e') \in z$ have the form $(y_1, e'_1)$, with $y_1 \leq y$. The function $fun(z)$ is continuous by definition (notice that the $y$ in the right hand side is finite). As for the stability, suppose that $y_1$ and $y_2$ are minimal under $x$ relative to $e'$. Then by the definition of $fun(z)$, it must be the case that $(y_1, e'), (y_2, e') \in z$, hence $y_1 = y_2$ by the definition of higher order consistency.

Finally, it is easy to check that $trace$ and $fun$ are inverse bijections. We also omit the verification that $E \times E'$ and $E \to E'$ are stable. $\square$

**Remark 12.3.7** *The definition of trace used in the proof of theorem 12.3.6 is a variation of the one given in definition 12.2.1. It exploits the fact that in a stable event domain, a function $f$ is stable if and only if, whenever $e' \in f(x)$, there exists a minimum $x_0 \leq x$ such that $e' \in f(x_0)$. (The stability condition ensures that there exists $x' \leq f(x)$ such that $e' \in f(y) \Leftrightarrow x' \leq f(y)$, for all $y \leq x$.)*

What we lack at this point are representation theorems, in the style of theorem 10.2.12, giving an abstract order theoretical characterization of event domains and stable event domains. Droste [Dro89] has provided a representation theorem for event domains (adapted from [Win80]). We present this material in the form of an exercise, which relies on the following definition.

**Definition 12.3.8** *In a partial order, a prime interval is defined as a pair of elements $x, y$ such that $x \prec y$, i.e., $x < y$ and $\not\exists z \; x < z < y$.*

Prime intervals capture the intuition of an event as a discrete increment.

**Exercise\* 12.3.9** *Show that the event domains are the algebraic cpo's which satisfy I as well as the following two axioms on compact elements:*

(C) $(x \prec y, x \prec z, y \neq z, y \uparrow z) \Rightarrow (y \lor z \text{ exists}, y \prec y \lor z, z \prec y \lor z)$

(S) $[x, x'] \bowtie [y, y'], x \leq y \Rightarrow x' \leq y'$ .

*In axiom (S), $[x, x']$ stands for a prime interval, and $\bowtie$ stands for the reflexive, symmetric and transitive closure of the relation $[x, y] \prec [z, y \lor z]$ (where $x, y, z$ satisfy the assumptions of (C)). The idea is to take as events the equivalence classes of prime intervals. Hints: If $x, y$ are compact and $x \leq y$, there exists $x = z_0 \prec \cdots \prec z_n \prec y$. Such a sequence is called a chain from $x$ to $y$. If $z_0, \ldots, z_m$ and $z'_0, \ldots, z'_{n'}$ are two chains from $x$ to $y$, then for any equivalence class $e$ of prime intervals $\sharp\{i \mid [z_i, z_{i+1}] \in e\} = \sharp\{j \mid [z'_j, z'_{j+1}] \in e\}$. Show the following implication: $x \prec x' \leq y \prec y' \Rightarrow \neg([x, x'] \bowtie [y, y'])$.*

If distributivity is assumed, then the characterization is much simpler: the stable event domains are exactly dI-domains.

**Proposition 12.3.10** *The following classes of cpo's coincide:*

(1) *stable event domains.*

(2) *dI-domains.*

(3) *coprime algebraic Scott domains (cf. definition 10.2.1) satisfying I.*

PROOF. (1) $\Rightarrow$ (2) This is the second statement of proposition 12.3.4.

(2) $\Rightarrow$ (3) Let $D$ be a dI-domain. We use the characterization given in exercise 10.2.3, and show that the compact elements of $D$ are finite lub's of compact coprime elements. We follow a proof of Zhang [Zha91]. We first claim:

**Claim.** The compact coprime elements are those compact elements that cover exactly one element.

To prove the claim, we notice that by property $I$, for any compact $d$, $\{e \mid e \prec d\}$ is finite, and if $d_1 \prec d$, $d_2 \prec d$ and $d_1 \neq d_2$, then we must have $d_1 \lor d_2 = d$, and hence $d$ is not coprime. Conversely, if $d$ covers exactly one element $d_1$, let $d \leq \bigvee X$ for a finite bounded $X$. By distributivity we get $d = \bigvee\{d \land x \mid x \in X\}$. Pick $x \in X$. If $d \land x \neq d$, by property $I$ we can find an element covered by $d$ above $d \land x$, which by assumption means $d \land x \leq d_1$. Hence at least one $d \land x$ must be such that $d \land x = d$ (and hence $d$ is coprime) as otherwise we would have $d = \bigvee\{d \land x \mid x \in X\} \leq d_1$.

Now we show that any compact $d \neq \bot$ is a lub of finitely many compact coprime elements. Consider the tree rooted at $d$ formed by taking as sons of the root all the distinct elements $d_1, \ldots, d_n$ covered by $d$ if there are at least two such elements, and continuing in this way recursively. Notice that $d_i \neq \bot$ for all $i$, otherwise we would have $d_i = \bot < d_j < d$ (picking $j \neq i$), contradicting $d_i \prec d$. Hence $d$ is the lub of all the leaves of the tree, which are coprime since they cover exactly one element.

(3) $\Rightarrow$ (1) Let $D$ be as in (3). We define $(E, \leq, \vdash)$ as follows.

- $E$ consists of the compact coprime elements of $D$,

- *Con* consists of the finite bounded subsets of $E$,

- $\{e_1 \mid e_1 \prec e\} \vdash d$, for any $e \in E$.

This is clearly an event structure, and the uniqueness of enablings makes it *a fortiori* stable. We show that $D$ is order-isomorphic to $D(E, Con, \vdash)$. To $x \in D$ we associate $g(x) = \{e \mid e$ compact coprime and $e \leq x\}$, which is consistent since it is bounded, and is safe since by property $I$ any event has a unique finite proof. Conversely, to any state $y \in D(E, Con, \vdash)$ we associate $\bigvee y$ which exists by bounded completeness. The composition $(\bigvee \circ g)$ is the identity of $D$ by definition of coprime-algebraicity. If $e' \leq \bigvee y$, then $e' \leq e$ for some $e \in y$ since $e'$ is compact coprime. Then, by the definition of enabling, $e'$ occurs in the proof of $e$ and is therefore in $y$ by safety. Hence $(g \circ \bigvee)$ is the identity on $D(E, Con, \vdash)$. $\square$

Girard has considered special classes of stable event structures: qualitative domains and coherence spaces.

**Definition 12.3.11 (qualitative domain)** *Event domains all of whose events are initial, i.e., where all enablings are empty, are called qualitative domains. (In a qualitative domain $E$, we thus have $Con = \mathcal{K}(D(E))$.)*

If moreover *Con* is specified by means of a reflexive and symmetric relation $\subset$, i.e., $(X \in Con \Leftrightarrow \forall e_1, e_2 \in X \; e_1 \subset e_2)$, then $E$ is called a coherence space (see definition 13.1.1). Coherence spaces will be discussed at length in section 13.1.

**Exercise 12.3.12** *Show that the qualitative domains are the dI-domains in which the compact coprime elements $p$ are atomic, i.e., $\bot \prec p$.*

**Exercise 12.3.13** *Show that the category of qualitative domains and stable functions is a cpo-enriched CCC.*

**Exercise 12.3.14** *Show that the dI-domains are the distributive cpo's such that the finite stable projections (see definition 12.4.2) form a directed set (with respect to the stable ordering) which has as lub the identity. Use this characterization to show that the category of dI-domains and stable functions is cartesian closed (this is Berry's original proof). Hints: Consider the projections defined by $p_X(x) = \bigvee \{d \wedge x \mid d \in X\}$, for each $X \subseteq_{fin} \mathcal{K}(D)$; proceed as in the proof of proposition 5.2.4.*

**Exercise 12.3.15 (stable neighborhoods [Zha91])** *Let $D$ be an $\omega$-algebraic meet cpo satisfying property I. (1) Characterize $\{f^{-1}(\top) \mid f : D \to_{st} \mathbf{O}\}$. (2) Such sets are called stable neighborhoods. Prove that they are closed under intersection but not under union. (3) Show that there is no topology for which the stable functions are exactly the continuous ones. Hint: Consider the stable functions from $\mathbf{O} \times \mathbf{O}$ to $\mathbf{O}$. There are four possible choices of a topology for $\mathbf{O}$; show that for each choice the sets of stable and continuous functions do not coincide. (4) Characterize stable functions as those functions that preserve stable neighborhoods by inverse image.*

**Exercise 12.3.16** *Show that property I may not be preserved by the function space construction with the pointwise ordering. Hints: Take $(\omega_\bot \to \mathbf{O}) \to \mathbf{O}$, define $f_n(x) = \top$ iff $\bot \neq x \leq n$, and consider the step functions $f_n \to \top$.*

**Exercise 12.3.17** *(1) If $D$ is a complete $\omega$-algebraic lattice with property $I$, show: $(D \to_{st} \mathbf{O}) \cong \mathcal{K}(D)$ , with the flat ordering on $\mathcal{K}(D)$. (2) On the other hand, given a flat cpo $E_\perp$, show: $(E_\perp \to_{st} \mathbf{O}) \cong (\mathcal{P}(E), \subseteq) + \mathbf{O}$, where $+$ is the coalesced sum (cf. definition 1.4.23).*

# 12.4 Stable bifinite domains *

We investigate the stable version of bifiniteness. Stable projections are better behaved than the continuous ones. Stable bifinite domains enjoy a characterization similar to that for bifinite domains (cf. theorem 5.2.7). They lend themselves to a simple theory of retractions. In particular, there is a retraction of all retractions. Also, there exists a universal stable bifinite domain.

**Proposition 12.4.1** *Let $D$ be a meet cpo, and let $p, q : D \to_{st} D$ be such that $p, q \leq_{st} id_D$. Then:*

(1) $p \circ q = p \wedge q$.

(2) *$p$ is a projection.*

(3) *$im(p)$ is downward closed.*

PROOF. (1) Remark first that since $p$ and $q$ are bounded their glb exists. Next observe:

$$qx \leq x \Rightarrow p(q(x)) = p(x) \wedge q(x) = (p \wedge q)(x) .$$

(2) For $p = q$ we obtain from (1): $p(p(x)) = p(x) \wedge p(x) = p(x)$.

(3) $x \leq py \Rightarrow p(x) = p(p(y)) \wedge x = p(y) \wedge x = x$ □

Proposition 12.4.1 justifies the following definition.

**Definition 12.4.2 (stable projection)** *Let $D$ be a meet cpo. A stable function $p : D \to_{st} D$ such that $p \leq_{st} id_D$ is called a stable projection. If moreover $im(p)$ is finite, $p$ is called finite. A stable injection-projection pair, or rigid embedding, is an injection-projection pair whose projection component is a stable projection.*

Now we define stable bifinite domains (cf. definition 5.2.2).

**Definition 12.4.3 (stable bifinite)** *A meet cpo $D$ is called a stable bifinite domain if the finite stable projections $p : D \to_{st} D$ form a directed set which has as lub the identity (in the stable ordering). We call $\mathbf{Bif}_\wedge$ the category of stable bifinite domains and stable functions. If id is actually the stable lub of an ascending sequence $\{p_n\}_{n \in \omega}$ of finite projections, then we say that $D$ is a stable $\omega$-bifinite domain. We denote with $\omega\mathbf{Bif}_\wedge$ the full subcategory of stable $\omega$-bifinite domains.*

**Proposition 12.4.4 (stable bifinites – CCC)** *(1) Stable bifinite domains are algebraic and satisfy property $I$. The compact elements are those of the form $p(x)$, where $p$ is a finite stable projection.*

*(2) The categories $\mathbf{Bif}_\wedge$ and $\omega\mathbf{Bif}_\wedge$ are cartesian closed.*

PROOF. We only detail what is specific to the stable case.

(1)  The satisfaction of $I$ follows from proposition 12.4.1(3).

(2)  All we have to do is to check that if $p, q$ are finite stable projections, then both $p \times q \leq_{st} id$ and $r = \lambda f x. q(f(p(x))) \leq_{st} id$.

- $(x, y) \leq (x', y') \Rightarrow (p(x), q(y)) = (p(x') \wedge x, q(y') \wedge y) = (p(x'), q(y')) \wedge (x, y)$.

- We have to show that $f \leq_{st} g$ implies $r(f) = r(g) \wedge f$, that is, for all $x$:

$$q(f(p(x))) = q(g(p(x))) \wedge f(x) .$$

We set $\alpha(d) = q(f(p(d)))$ and $\beta(d) = q(g(p(d))) \wedge f(d)$. Observe:

$$f(p(x)) \leq g(x), q \leq_{st} id \;\;\Rightarrow\;\; q(f(p(x))) = q(g(x)) \wedge f(p(x))$$
$$p(x) \leq x, f \leq_{st} g \;\;\Rightarrow\;\; f(p(x)) = f(x) \wedge g(p(x))$$
$$g(p(x)) \leq g(x), q \leq_{st} id \;\;\Rightarrow\;\; q(g(p(x))) = q(g(x)) \wedge g(p(x)) .$$

Therefore, we have, as required:

$$q(f(p(x))) = q(g(x)) \wedge f(p(x)) = q(g(x)) \wedge f(x) \wedge g(p(x)) = q(g(p(x))) \wedge f(x) .$$

The rest of the proof is a straightforward adaptation of the proof of proposition 5.2.4.□

**Characterization of stable bifinite domains.**  The main result here is a characterization of the objects in **Bif**$_\wedge$. Roughly they are algebraic meet cpo's satisfying a combination of properties $M^\infty$ (cf. theorem 5.2.7) and $I$ that we call $(MI)^\infty$. It is convenient to decompose property $I$ into simpler properties.

**Definition 12.4.5** *Let $D$ be a cpo. We define the three properties $I_1, I_2$, and $I_3$ as follows:*

$(I_1)$  *Every decreasing sequence of compact elements is finite:*

$$(\{d_n\}_{n \in \omega} \subseteq \mathcal{K}(D) \text{ and } \forall n \in \omega \; d_n \geq d_{n+1}) \Rightarrow \{d_n\}_{n \in \omega} \text{ is finite} .$$

$(I_2)$  *Every increasing sequence of compact elements under a compact element is finite:*

$$(\{d\} \cup \{d_n\}_{n \in \omega} \subseteq \mathcal{K}(D) \text{ and } \forall n \in \omega \; d_n \leq d_{n+1} \leq d) \Rightarrow \{d_n\}_{n \in \omega} \text{ finite} .$$

$(I_3)$  *The immediate predecessors of a compact element are of finite number:*

$$d \in \mathcal{K}(D) \Rightarrow pred(d) \text{ is finite,}$$

*where $pred(d) = \{e \in D \mid e \prec d\}$.*

**Proposition 12.4.6** *Let $D$ be an algebraic cpo. Then it has property $I$ iff it has properties $I_1$, $I_2$, and $I_3$.*

PROOF. ($\Rightarrow$) Note that the sets involved in $I_1, I_2$ and $I_3$ are each contained in some $\downarrow d$ (where $d$ is an appropriately chosen compact element).

($\Leftarrow$) Let $d \in \mathcal{K}(D)$. First we claim that $\downarrow d \subseteq \mathcal{K}(D)$. Suppose there is a non compact element $x$ under $d$, then $(\downarrow x) \cap \mathcal{K}(D)$ is directed since $D$ is an algebraic cpo, and

(A) $I_1$ fails for $\{\bot\} \cup \underline{\omega}$, with $\underline{\omega} = \{\underline{n} \mid n \in \omega\}$, ordered as follows:

$$\bot \text{ minimum} \quad (\underline{m} \leq \underline{n} \text{ iff } n \leq m) .$$

(B) $I_2$ fails for $\omega \cup \{\infty, a\}$, ordered as follows:

$$x \leq y \text{ iff } y = a \text{ or } (y = \infty \text{ and } x \in \omega \cup \{\infty\}) \text{ or } (x, y \in \omega \text{ and } x \leq y) .$$

(C) $I_3$ fails for $\omega \cup \{\bot, a\}$, ordered as follows:

$$\forall n \in \omega \ \bot \leq n \leq a .$$

Figure 12.2: Failure of property $I$

$\bigvee((\downarrow x) \cap \mathcal{K}(D)) = x$. So we can build an infinite strictly ascending chain under $d$, contradicting $I_2$. Property $I_2$ also implies that $pred(d)$ is complete in the sense that:

$$e < d \Rightarrow \exists e' \in pred(d) \ e \leq e' < d .$$

Otherwise we can again build a strictly growing chain under $d$. By this latter property and by $I_1$, we can display (with repetitions) the elements of $\downarrow d$ as a tree, where, for all $e \leq d$, the elements of $pred(e)$ are immediately below $e$. This tree has:

$$\begin{array}{ll} \text{only finite branches} & \text{(by property } I_1) \\ \text{finite branching} & \text{(by property } I_3) . \end{array}$$

Hence (by the contrapositive of König's lemma) the tree is finite, and *a fortiori* $\downarrow d$ is finite. $\qquad\qquad\qquad\square$

Figure 12.2 presents typical situations where property $I$ fails.

**Lemma 12.4.7** (1) *If $D$ is an algebraic cpo satisfying property $I_1$, then $\mathcal{K}(D) \models m$ (cf. definition 5.2.6).*

(2) *If $D$ is an algebraic meet cpo such that $\mathcal{K}(D) \models m$, then $D$ is an L-domain (cf. definition 5.2.11).*

(3) *Stable bifinite domains are L-domains.*

PROOF. (1) Let $X \subseteq_{fin} \mathcal{K}(D)$. Given any upper bound $y$ of $X$, there exists by algebraicity a compact $d \leq y$ that is also an upper bound for $X$. By the property $I_1$ there exists $e \in \mathcal{K}(D)$ such that $e \leq d$ and $e \in MUB(X)$. Otherwise we could build an infinite decreasing chain under $d$.

(2) Let $A \subseteq \mathcal{K}(D)$ and $x \in UB(A)$, and suppose $y_1, y_2 \leq x$ and $y_1, y_2 \in MUB(A)$. Then $y_1 \wedge y_2 \in MUB(A)$, which forces $y_1 = y_2$. We then conclude by exercise 5.2.13(2).

(3) This follows immediately from (1) and (2), since stable bifinite domains are algebraic and satisfy property $I$ by proposition 12.4.4. $\qquad\qquad\qquad\square$

As a consequence, the operator $U$ (cf. theorem 5.2.7) is idempotent for stable bifinite domains (cf. proposition 5.2.14). This indicates that a more liberal operator than $U$ has to be introduced in order to characterize stable bifiniteness in a way similar to the characterization of bifiniteness. We have already exploited the fact that images of projections are downward closed. This should motivate the following definition.

**Definition 12.4.8 (property** $(MI)^\infty$ **)** *Let $(P, \leq)$ be a poset, and let $X \subseteq_{fin} P$. We set $U\!\downarrow (X) = U(\downarrow (X))$. Let $(U\!\downarrow)^\infty(X) = \bigcup_{n\in\omega}(U\!\downarrow)^n(X)$. If $D$ is an algebraic meet cpo, then we say that $\mathcal{K}(D)$ has property $(MI)^\infty$ if*

$$\forall X \subseteq_{fin} \mathcal{K}(D) \ (U\!\downarrow)^\infty(X) \text{ is finite}.$$

Let $D$ be an algebraic meet cpo. If $\mathcal{K}(D) \models (MI)^\infty$, then property $I$ holds and $\mathcal{K}(D) \models M$, as if $d, e \in \mathcal{K}(D)$ then:

$$\downarrow d \subseteq (U\!\downarrow)^\infty(\{d\}) \quad \text{and} \quad U(\{d, e\}) \subseteq (U\!\downarrow)^\infty(\{d, e\}).$$

The converse does not hold: see example 12.4.12.

**Theorem 12.4.9** *A cpo $D$ is a stable bifinite domain iff $D$ is an algebraic meet cpo such that $\mathcal{K}(D) \models (MI)^\infty$.*

PROOF HINT. ($\Rightarrow$) If $X \subseteq_{fin} \mathcal{K}(D)$, then $X \subseteq p(D)$ for some finite stable projection. The argument in the proof of theorem 5.2.7 yields not only $U(X) \subseteq p(D)$, but also $(U\!\downarrow)(X) \subseteq p(D)$.

($\Leftarrow$) Let $A \subseteq_{fin} \mathcal{K}(D)$, and consider $p_A$ defined by $p_A(y) = \bigvee((U\!\downarrow)^\infty(A) \cap (\downarrow y))$. Notice the use of the $(U\!\downarrow)$ operator, instead of $U$. The fact that $B = (U\!\downarrow)^\infty(A)$ is downward closed serves in establishing that $p_A \leq_{st} id$, that $(A \subseteq B \Rightarrow p_A \leq_{st} p_B)$, and that $p_A$ is stable. We only check $p_A \leq_{st} id$. Let $x \leq y$. We check $p_A(y) \wedge x \leq p_A(x)$. Since $p_A(D) = (U\!\downarrow)^\infty(A)$ is downward closed, we have $p_A(y) \wedge x \in (U\!\downarrow)^\infty(A)$, hence $p_A(y) \wedge x \leq p_A(x)$ by definition of $p_A$.                                                                    $\square$

**Exercise 12.4.10** *Show that any event domain is a stable bifinite domain. Hints: In a Scott domain, all glb's exist, and $U(X) = \{\bigvee Y \mid Y \subseteq_{fin} X \text{ and } Y \text{ bounded}\}$, for all finite $X$. Show that $(U\!\downarrow)^\infty(X) \subseteq \bigcup X$, for any $n$.*

We now list without proof some results from [Ama91a] towards the goal of a Smyth like theorem: is $\omega\mathbf{Bif}_\wedge$ the maximum cartesian closed full subcategory of $\omega$-algebraic meet cpo's and stable functions?[4] It turns out that properties $M$, $I_1$, and $I_2$ are necessary to enforce the $\omega$-algebraicity of function spaces. One can also show that property $I_3$ is necessary under a rather mild hypothesis. The necessity of property $(MI)^\infty$ is still open. In the first place, a stable version of theorem 5.2.17 holds: in any full subcategory of algebraic meet cpo's, if the terminal object, the product and the exponent exist, then they coincide up to isomorphism with the ones defined in $\mathbf{Cpo}_\wedge$. The proof is basically the same as in the continuous case. Here is a summary of the results in [Ama91a]

- If $D$ and $D \to_{st} D$ are $\omega$-algebraic meet cpo's, then $D \models M$ and $D$ has properties $I_1$ and $I_2$.

---

[4]Zhang has answered positively the similar question obtained by replacing $\omega$-algebraic meet cpo's by $\omega$-algebraic Scott domains and $\omega\mathbf{Bif}_\wedge$ by the full subcategory of $\omega$-algebraic dI-domains [Zha95].

- If $D$ and $D \to_{st} D$ are $\omega$-algebraic meet cpo's and, for each $d \in \mathcal{K}(D)$, $(\downarrow d) \to_{st} (\downarrow d)$ is an $\omega$-algebraic meet cpo, then $D$ has property $I_3$.

The following properties serve as stepping stones in the proof. If $D$ and $D \to_{st} D$ are $\omega$-algebraic meet cpo's, then:

(1) If $x \in D$, then $\downarrow x$ is an $\omega$-algebraic lattice.

(2) If $d \in \mathcal{K}(D)$ and $\downarrow d$ is distributive, then $\downarrow d$ is finite.

(3) If $\downarrow d$ is distributive for each $d \in \mathcal{K}(D)$, then $D$ has property $I$.

The following exercise, taken from [Ber79] illustrates the necessity of $I_2$.

**Exercise 12.4.11** *Let $D$ be example (B) from figure 12.2. Show that $D \to_{st} D$ is not $\omega$-algebraic. Hints: Observe that $(D \to_{st} D) = (D \to_{cm} D) = (D \to_{cont} D)$. Show that, for any $h, k$, if $(h(a) = a$, $k(a) = a$ and $h \uparrow_{st} k$, then $h = k$. Show that any continuous function $h$ such that $h(a) = a$ is compact.*

The following exercise shows that $M+I$ does not imply $(MI)^\infty$ and that compactness may differ from finiteness.

**Exercise 12.4.12** *Let $D = \{\bot\} \cup \omega_B \cup \omega_T$ where $\omega_B = \{n_B \mid n \in \omega\}$ and $\omega_T = \{n_T \mid n \in \omega\}$, ordered as follows:*

$$\bot \text{ is the minimum} \quad n_B \le n_T, (n+1)_T \ (n \ge 0) \quad n_B \le (n-1)_T \ (n \ge 1) \ .$$

*(1) Show that $(U\downarrow)^\infty(\{i_T\}) = D$ (for any $i$) (and therefore that $D$ is not a stable bifinite domain, by theorem 12.4.9). Hint: Notice that $(i+1)_T \in U\downarrow (\{i_T\})$. (2) Show that $id_D$ (whose trace is clearly infinite) is a compact element of $D \to_{st} D$. Hint: Prove that $(f =_k id, f \le_{st} id \Rightarrow f =_{k+1} id)$, where $f =_k id$ stands for $(\forall i \le k \ f(i_B) = i_B$ and $f(i_T) = i_T)$.*

**A retraction of all retractions.** Scott [Sco80] has shown that the collection of finitary retractions (cf. definition 7.4.5) over a bounded complete algebraic cpo $D$ is the image of a finitary retraction over the space $D \to_{cont} D$ of continuous functions. In the stable case Berardi [Ber91] was apparently the first to observe that when working over dI-domains the image of a stable retraction is still a dI-domain, i.e., that any stable retraction is finitary. It was then possible to adapt Scott's technique to show that the set of retractions over a dI-domain is itself the (image of a) retraction. We shall give the corresponding of Berardi's result for stable bifinite domains. The proof exploits the fact that stable bifinite domains can be described as directed colimits of stable projections. A retraction of all retractions serves to provide a model for a type theory with a type of all types (see exercise 11.3.5).

**Proposition 12.4.13** *Let $D$ be a stable bifinite domain and $r$ be a stable retraction over $D$. Then $r(D)$ is a stable bifinite domain.*

PROOF. Let $p : D \to_{st} D$ be a finite projection. Define $q = r \circ p \circ r$. Then $im(q)$ is finite and $q \le_{st} r \circ id \circ r = r$. Moreover, since the lub of the $p$'s is $id$, the lub of the $q$'s is $r$. □

We give a simple proof of the fact that the collection $Ret(D)$ of the stable retractions over a stable bifinite domain $D$ is a retract of its functional space $D \to_{st} D$. The keystone of the construction is to observe that given $f : D \to_{st} D$, with $im(f)$ finite, there is a natural way to associate to $f$ a retraction, namely iterate $f$ a finite number of times. First we recall a simple combinatorial fact.

**Lemma 12.4.14** *Let $X$ be a set and let $f : X \to X$, with $im(f)$ finite. Then $\sharp\{f^k \mid k \geq 1\} \cap Ret(X) = 1$.*

PROOF. First observe $\forall k \geq 1$ $im(f^{k+1}) \subseteq im(f^k)$. Since $im(f)$ is finite, there exists $h$ such that $im(f^{h+1}) = im(f^h)$. In particular, any $h \geq \sharp im(f)$ is such that $im(f^{h+1}) = im(f^h)$. The restriction of $f$ to $im(f^h)$ is a permutation (being a surjection from $im(f^k)$ onto itself). Let $n = \sharp im(f^h)$: then $(f^h)^{n!}$ is the identity on $im(f^h)$, and therefore is a retraction over $X$. As for the uniqueness observe that if $f^i \circ f^i = f^i$ and $f^j \circ f^j = f^j$ for $i, j \geq 1$ then $f^i = f^{ij} = f^j$. $\qquad\square$

**Lemma 12.4.15** *Let $D$ be a stable bifinite domain. Then the following property holds, for any $f : D \to_{st} D$ and any finite stable projection:*

$$\sharp\{(f \circ p \circ f)^k \mid k \geq 1\} \cap Ret(D) = 1 .$$

PROOF. The finiteness of $im(p)$ implies the finiteness of $im(f \circ p \circ f) \subseteq f(im(p \circ f))$, and the conclusion then follows from lemma 12.4.14. $\qquad\square$

**Theorem 12.4.16** *Given a stable bifinite domain $D$, the collection $Ret(D)$ of stable retractions is a stable retract of the functional space $D \to_{st} D$.*

PROOF. First, it is easily shown that if $D$ is a meet cpo, then $Ret(D)$ is a meet cpo, with the order induced by $D \to_{st} D$ (the proof is similar to the one of proposition 7.4.5). We write:

$$f_p = f \circ p \circ f \qquad k_p = (\sharp im(p))(\sharp im(p)!) .$$

We have $f_p^{k_p} \in Ret(D)$. Indeed, using the notation of lemma 12.4.15, and setting $h = \sharp im(p)$, we note that $\sharp im(p)!$ is a multiple of $n! = \sharp im(f^h)!$, hence $(f^h)^{\sharp im(p)!}$ is the identity on $im(f^h)$ since $(f^h)^{n!}$ is. Note that $k_p$ is independent from $f$. The crucial remark is that:

$$r \in Ret(D) \Rightarrow r_p \in Ret(D),$$

because by the definition of stable order, for any $x$:

$$r_p \leq_{st} r \circ r = r, r_p(x) \leq r(x) \Rightarrow r_p(r_p(x)) = r_p(r(x)) \wedge r(r_p(x)) = r_p(x) .$$

Notice that the form of $f_p$ has been precisely chosen to have $r_p(r(x)) = r_p(x)$ and $r(r_p(x)) = r_p(x)$. We define $\rho : (D \to_{st} D) \to_{st} Ret(D)$ as follows:

$$\rho(f) = \bigvee_{p \leq_{st} id} (f_p)^{k_p} .$$

We check that this definition is correct. First, we observe, for $p \leq_{st} q$:

$$(f_p)^{k_p} = (f_p)^{k_p k_q} \leq_{st} (f_q)^{k_p k_q} = (f_q)^{k_q} .$$

It follows that $\{(f_p)^{k_p} \mid p \leq_{st} id\}$ is directed. Hence $\rho(f)$ is defined and is a retraction, since the lub of a directed set of retractions is a retraction. Also, $\rho$ is a retraction, because:

$$r \in Ret(D) \Rightarrow \rho(r) = \bigvee_{p \leq_{st} id} (r_p)^{k_p} = \bigvee_{p \leq_{st} id} r_p = r \circ r = r .$$

Next we show that $\rho$ preserves binary compatible glb's. Suppose $f, g \leq_{st} h$. Since the composition operation is cm (cf. exercise 12.1.11), we have:

$$
\begin{aligned}
\rho(f \wedge g) &= \bigvee_{p \leq_{st} id}((f \wedge g)_p)^{k_p} &= \bigvee_{p \leq_{st} id}(f_p \wedge g_p)^{k_p} \\
&= \bigvee_{p \leq_{st} id}(f_p)^{k_p} \wedge (g_p)^{k_p} &= (\bigvee_{p \leq_{st} id}(f_p)^{k_p}) \wedge (\bigvee_{p \leq_{st} id}(g_p)^{k_p}) \\
&= \rho(f) \wedge \rho(g) .
\end{aligned}
$$

It remains to show that $\rho$ preserves directed sets. Let $H$ be a directed set in $D \to_{st} D$. We have:

$$(\bigvee H)_p = (\bigvee H) \circ p \circ (\bigvee H) = \bigvee_{h \in H}(h \circ p \circ h) = \bigvee_{h \in H} h_p$$
$$(\bigvee_{h \in H} h_p)^{k_p} = \bigvee_{h \in H}(h_p)^{k_p} .$$

Hence:

$$\rho(\bigvee H) = \bigvee_{p \leq_{st} id}((\bigvee H)_p)^{k_p} = \bigvee_{p \leq_{st} id} \bigvee_{h \in H}(h_p)^{k_p} = \bigvee_{h \in H} \bigvee_{p \leq_{st} id}(h_p)^{k_p} = \bigvee_{h \in H} \rho(h) . \qquad \square$$

**Exercise 12.4.17** *Show that every reflexive object in the category of stable bifinites and stable morphisms provides a model for the $\lambda\beta p$-calculus of section 11.3.*

**Exercise 12.4.18** *Show that if $D$ is a stable bifinite domain, then $Prj(D) = \downarrow id_D$ is a stable bifinite domain and a lattice.*

**Exercise 12.4.19** *Show that the identity is always a maximal element in the stable ordering. In particular, the only stable closure (cf. definition 7.4.5) is the identity.*

**Exercise 12.4.20** *Let $D$ be the cpo of example 12.1(A). Show that it is not the case that $Prj(D)$ is (the image of) a projection of $D \to_{st} D$. (cf. exercise 7.4.8).*

We end the section with a brief account of universality in the stable bifinite framework [DR93].

**Proposition 12.4.21** *Let $\omega\mathbf{Bif}_\wedge{}^{ip_s}$ be the category whose objects are the stable $\omega$-bifinite domains and whose arrows are the stable injection-projection pairs (notation: $(i,j) : D \to_{ip_s} D'$). The following properties hold:*

*(1) $\omega\mathbf{Bif}_\wedge{}^{ip_s}$ is an $\omega$-algebroidal category and the collection of compact objects has the amalgamation property.*

*(2) $\omega\mathbf{Bif}_\wedge{}^{ip_s}$ has a universal homogeneous object.*

PROOF HINT. (1) The proof follows the same pattern as in the continuous case. Let us just show that $\omega\mathbf{Bif}_\wedge{}^{ip_s}$ has the amalgamation property. Consider three finite posets $(E, \leq), (D_1, \leq_1), (D_2, \leq_2)$ with functions $(h_i^+, h_i^-) : E \to_{ip_s} D_i$, $(i \in \{1, 2\})$. Without loss of generality we may assume $E = D_1 \cap D_2$. Then:

$$\forall e, e' \in E \quad e \leq e' \Leftrightarrow (e \leq_1 e' \text{ and } e \leq_2 e') .$$

Now we define the amalgam as $F = E \cup (D_1 \backslash E) \cup (D_2 \backslash E)$. It is helpful to recall that $E$ is downward closed in $D_i$, so we define:

$$f \leq_F f' \Leftrightarrow \exists i \in \{1, 2\} \; f, f' \in D_i \text{ and } f \leq_i f' .$$

The morphisms $(k_i^+, k_i^-) : D_i \to_{ip_s} F$ $(i \in \{1, 2\})$ are defined exactly as in the proof of proposition 7.3.8.

(2) By theorem 7.3.10. $\qquad \square$

**Exercise 12.4.22** *Prove that $\mathbf{Cpo}_\wedge$ has limits of $\omega^{op}$-diagrams. Study the representation problem of the functors over $\omega\mathbf{Bif}_\wedge{}^{ip_s}$ as stable functions over $Prj(U)$, where $U$ is some universal (homogeneous) domain (cf. section 7.4). Show that product and exponent are representable.*

# 12.5   Connected glb's *

Following Taylor [Tay90a], we focus on a characterization of stable functions by the property of preservation of all connected glb's. This leads to another cartesian closed category of stable functions, whose objects are dcpo's that have all connected glb's and and are such that these glb's distribute over directed lub's.

First we introduce the notions of connected set and of connected meet cpo, which are related to those of L-domain and of continuous dcpo investigated in chapter 5.

**Definition 12.5.1 (connected)** *Let $X$ be a partial order. We say that $Y \subseteq X$ is connected if for any two points $x, y$ of $Y$ there exists a zigzag between them in $Y$, that is, $x = z_0 \star z_1 \star \cdots \star z_n = y$, where $\star$ stands for $\leq$ or $\geq$, and where $z_i \in Y$ for all $i$.*

The notion of zigzag induces a natural equivalence relation over any subset $Y \subseteq X$: for $x, y$ in $Y$, write $x \approx y$ if there exists a zigzag from $x$ to $y$ in $Y$. The equivalence classes for this relation can be seen as the disjoint connected components of $Y$.

**Exercise 12.5.2** *(1) Show that the order theoretical connectedness defined above coincides with topological connectedness with respect to Alexandrov topology or Scott topology (cf. section 1.2). (Recall that $X$ is called connected if, for any open sets $U, V$, $Y \subseteq U \cup V \Rightarrow U \cap V \neq \emptyset$.). Show that these topologies are locally connected, i.e., every open set is a disjoint union of connected open sets.*

**Lemma 12.5.3** *A partial order $X$ has compatible binary glb's iff any zigzag, viewed as a collection of points, has a glb.*

PROOF. By induction on the length of the zigzag, in the notation of definition 12.5.1. If the last $\star$ is $\leq$, then clearly $z_0 \wedge \cdots \wedge z_n = z_0 \wedge \cdots \wedge z_{n-1}$; if it is $\geq$, then $z_0 \wedge \cdots \wedge z_{n-1}$ and $z_n$ both have $z_{n-1}$ as an upper bound, hence $z_0 \wedge \cdots \wedge z_n = (z_0 \wedge \cdots \wedge z_{n-1}) \wedge z_n$ exists. □

**Definition 12.5.4** *In a partial order $X$, a multilub of a subset $Y \subseteq X$ is a set $J$ of upper bounds of $Y$ that is multiversal, i.e., such that any upper bound $x$ of $Y$ dominates a unique element of $J$.*

**Proposition 12.5.5** *For a partial order, the following properties are equivalent:*

(1) *All compatible binary glb's and codirected glb's exist.*

(2) *All connected glb's exist.*

(3) *All $\downarrow x$'s have all glb's.*

(4) *All $\downarrow x$'s have all lub's.*

(5) *All subsets have multilub's.*

*We call such partial orders L partial orders.*

PROOF. (1) $\Rightarrow$ (2) Let $Y \subseteq X$ be connected. Let $Z$ be the set of the glb's of all finite zigzags in $Y$ ($Z$ is well-defined by lemma 12.5.3). Clearly, if $Z$ has a glb, then its glb is also the glb of $Y$. Thus it is enough to show that $Z$ is codirected. Let $z_0 \wedge \cdots \wedge z_n \in Z$ and $z_0' \wedge \cdots \wedge z_{n'}' \in Z$. Then by connectedness one may build a zigzag between $z_n$ and $z_0'$. Then the glb of the zigzag obtained by joining the three zigzags is in $Z$ and is a lower bound of $z_0 \wedge \cdots \wedge z_n$ and $z_0' \wedge \cdots \wedge z_{n'}'$.

(2) $\Rightarrow$ (3)  Let $Y \subseteq \downarrow x$. Then $Y \cup \{x\}$ is connected, hence has a glb in $X$, which is the same as the glb of $Y$ (this includes the limit case $Y = \emptyset$).

(3) $\Rightarrow$ (1)  Let $x_1, x_2$ be a bounded pair. Its glb exists in $\downarrow x$, for any upper bound $x$ of $x_1, x_2$, and is their glb in $X$. For codirected glb's, notice that if $Y$ is codirected, and $x \in Y$, then $Y$ and $Y \cap \downarrow x$ have the same glb if any.

(3) $\Leftrightarrow$ (4)  For a partial order, having all glb's is equivalent to having all lub's.

(4) $\Rightarrow$ (5)  Let $Y \subseteq X$. Consider the collection $Z$ of all upper bounds of $Y$. We form the set $J = \{\bigvee^z Y \mid z \in Z\}$, where $\bigvee^z$ denotes a lub taken in $\downarrow z$. Clearly, this is a set of upper bounds of $Y$, and by construction every upper bound $z \in Z$ of $Z$ dominates $\bigvee^z Y \in J$. We are left to show the uniqueness: if $z \geq \bigvee^{z_1} Y$, then $\bigvee^{z_1} Y \geq \bigvee^z Y$ since $\bigvee^{z_1} Y$ is an upper bound of $Y$ in $\downarrow z$. Next, $z_1 \geq \bigvee^z Y$ follows, since $z_1 \geq \bigvee^{z_1} Y$. Finally we have $\bigvee^z Y \geq \bigvee^{z_1} Y$ (whence the uniqueness), since $\bigvee^z Y$ is an upper bound of $Y$ in $\downarrow z_1$.

(5) $\Rightarrow$ (4)  Obvious.                                                                    $\square$

The L partial orders that are cpo's are the same thing as L-domains (cf. definition 5.2.11).

**Exercise 12.5.6** *(1) Show that a cpo is an L partial order iff all its finite subsets have multilub's. Hint: Use characterization (5) of proposition 12.5.5. (2) Show that, relaxing the finiteness assumption, proposition 5.2.14 provides a sixth characterization of L partial orders.*

**Proposition 12.5.7** (1) *Let $D$ and $D'$ be cpo's, and lef $f : D \to D'$ be stable. Then for any connected $X \subseteq D$ such that $\bigwedge X$ exists, $f(\bigwedge X) = \bigwedge f(X)$.*

(2) *If all connected glb's exist, the stable functions are exactly the continuous functions preserving connected glb's.*

PROOF. (1)  $f(\bigwedge X)$ is a lower bound of $f(X)$ by monotonicity. Suppose that $z' \leq f(X)$. We show that all $m(f, x, z')$'s are equal, for $x$ ranging over $X$. This follows obviously from the fact that for two comparable $x_1, x_2$, we have $m(f, x_1, z') = m(f, x_2, z')$. Let $z$ stand for this common value. Then we have $z < \bigwedge X$ and $z' \leq f(z)$. Therefore $z' \leq f(\bigwedge X)$.

(2)  This follows from proposition 12.2.2, observing that the preservation of the glb of a bounded set $M$ can be rephrased as the preservation of the glb of the connected set $M \cup \{x\}$, where $x$ is an upper bound of $M$.                                                $\square$

To get cartesian closure, similarly to the cm case, a property of distributivity (or continuity of glb's) is required, namely that connected glb's distribute over directed lub's. Equivalently, the domains are required to be continuous L-domains (see section 12.6).

**Definition 12.5.8 (connected meet cpo)** *A connected meet cpo is a cpo which is an L partial order such that connected glb's distribute over directed lub's, that is, if $\{\Delta_j\}_{j \in J}$ is an indexed collection of directed sets, and if $\{\bigvee \Delta_j \mid j \in J\}$ is connected, then:*

$$\bigwedge_{j \in J} \left(\bigvee \Delta_j\right) = \bigvee \left\{ \bigwedge_{j \in J} x_j \mid \{x_j\}_{j \in J} \in \Pi_{j \in J} \Delta_j \right\} .$$

**Remark 12.5.9** *Notice that the glb's $\bigwedge_{j \in J} x_j$ exist, because $\{x_j\}_{j \in J} \cup \{\bigvee \Delta_j \mid j \in J\}$ is connected.*

**Theorem 12.5.10 (continuous L-domains – CCC)** *The category* **CLDom** *of connected meet cpo's and stable functions is a cpo-enriched CCC.*[5]

PROOF. The composition of two stable functions is stable, because a monotonic function maps connected sets to connected sets. As for cm functions and stable functions, directed lub's and binary compatible glb's of stable functions are defined pointwise.

Let $H \subseteq_{dir} D \to_{st} D'$. The lub of $H$ is $h$ defined by $h(x) = \bigvee \{f(x) \mid f \in H\}$. We check that $h$ is stable. Let $X = \{x_i \mid i \in I\}$ be connected:

$$
\begin{aligned}
h(\bigwedge X) &= \bigvee_{f \in H} (f(\bigwedge X)) \\
\bigwedge_{i \in I} h(x_i) &= \bigwedge_{i \in I} (\bigvee_{f \in H} f(x_i)) = \bigvee \{\bigwedge_{i \in I} f_i(x_i) \mid \{f_i\}_{i \in I} \in \Pi_{i \in I} H\} \,.
\end{aligned}
$$

The distributivity gives us too many glb's: we are only interested in the families $\{f_i\}$ which are constant. We cannot use the same argument as in the cm case, because we do not have an upper bound available for a family like $\{f_i\}$. We claim:

$$
\bigwedge_{i \in I} f_i(x_i) = \bigwedge \{f_i(x_j) \mid i, j \in I\} \quad (= \bigwedge_{i \in I} f_i(\bigwedge X)) \,.
$$

The claim can be reformulated as $\forall i, j \; \bigwedge_{i \in I} f_i(x_i) \leq f_i(x_j)$. For fixed $i$, we prove the inequality $\bigwedge_{i \in I} f_i(x_i) \leq f_i(x_j)$ by induction on the length of the zigzag from $x_i$ to $x_j$. Let $x_k$ be the point preceding $x_j$ in the zigzag. Thus by induction $\bigwedge_{i \in I} f_i(x_i) \leq f_i(x_k)$. There are two cases:

- $x_k \leq x_j$. $\bigwedge_{i \in I} f_i(x_i) \leq f_i(x_j)$ follows obviously by monotonicity.

- $x_j \leq x_k$. Let $f \in H$ be such that $f_i, f_j \leq f$. We have:

$$
f_i(x_j) = f_i(x_k) \wedge f(x_j) \geq f_i(x_k) \wedge f_j(x_j) \,.
$$

  Using induction, we get:

$$
\bigwedge_{i \in I} f_i(x_i) \leq f_i(x_k) \wedge f_j(x_j) \leq f_i(x_j) \,.
$$

Turning back to the stability of $h$, we are left to show:

$$
\bigvee_{f \in H} (f(\bigwedge X)) = \bigvee \{\bigwedge_{i \in I} f_i(\bigwedge X) \mid \{f_i\}_{i \in I} \in \Pi_{i \in I} H\} \,.
$$

($\leq$) Take the constant family $f$.

($\geq$) $\bigwedge_{i \in I} f_i(\bigwedge X) \leq \bigvee_{i \in I} f_i(\bigwedge X) \leq \bigvee_{f \in H} (f(\bigwedge X))$.

Let $K$ be a connected subset of $D \to_{st} D$. Its glb $k$ is defined by $k(x) = \bigwedge_{f \in K} f(x)$.

- $k$ is stable. The preservation of glb's is obvious, but the continuity requires a proof, which is somewhat dual to the proof of stability of $\bigvee H$. We write $K = \{f_i \mid i \in I\}$.

$$
\begin{aligned}
k(\bigvee \Delta) &= \bigwedge_{i \in I} (\bigvee f_i(\Delta)) = \bigvee \{\bigwedge_{i \in I} f_i(\delta_i) \mid \{\delta_i\}_{i \in I} \in \Pi_{i \in I} \Delta\} \\
\bigvee k(\Delta) &= \bigvee_{\delta \in \Delta} k(\delta) \,.
\end{aligned}
$$

---

[5]The name will be justified by theorem 12.6.6.

We claim:

$$\bigwedge_{i\in I} f_i(\delta_i) = \bigwedge\{f_j(\delta_i) \mid i,j \in I\} \quad (= \bigwedge_{i\in I} k(\delta_i)) \ .$$

The claim can be reformulated as $\forall i,j \ \bigwedge_{i\in I} f_i(\delta_i) \le f_j(\delta_i)$. For fixed $i$, we prove the inequality $\bigwedge_{i\in I} f_i(\delta_i) \le f_j(\delta_i)$ by induction on the length of the zigzag from $f_i$ to $f_j$. Let $f_k$ be the point preceding $f_j$ in the zigzag. Thus by induction $\bigwedge_{i\in I} f_i(\delta_i) \le f_k(\delta_i)$. There are two cases:

- $f_k \le f_j$. $\bigwedge_{i\in I} f_i(\delta_i) \le f_j(\delta_i)$ follows obviously by monotonicity.

- $f_j \le f_k$. Let $\delta \in \Delta$ such that $\delta_i, \delta_j \le \delta$. We have:

$$f_j(\delta_i) = f_k(\delta_i) \wedge f_j(\delta) \ge f_k(\delta_i) \wedge f_j(\delta_j) \ .$$

  Using induction, we get:

$$\bigwedge_{i\in I} f_i(\delta_i) \le f_k(\delta_i) \wedge f_j(\delta_j) \le f_j(\delta_i) \ .$$

Turning back to the continuity of $k$, we are left to show:

$$\bigvee_{\delta\in\Delta} k(\delta) = \bigvee\{\bigwedge_{i\in I} k(\delta_i) \mid \{\delta_i\}_{i\in I} \in \Pi_{i\in I}\Delta\} \ .$$

$(\le)$ Take the constant family $\delta$.

$(\ge)$ $\bigwedge_{i\in I} k(\delta_i) \le \bigvee_{i\in I} k(\delta_i) \le \bigvee_{\delta\in\Delta} k(\delta)$.

- $k$ is a lower bound of $K$. Let $x \le y$, and let $f_0 \in K$. We have to prove that $z \le f_0(x), k(y)$ implies $z \le k(x)$, i.e., $z \le f_1(x)$ for all $f_1 \in K$. It is enough to check this for $f_0 \le_{st} f_1$ or $f_1 \le_{st} f_0$:

  - $f_0 \le_{st} f_1$. Then *a fortiori* $f_0 \le_{ext} f_1$, hence $z \le f_0(x) \le f_1(x)$.

  - $f_1 \le_{st} f_0$. Then *a fortiori* $z \le f_0(x), f_1(y)$, hence $z \le f_0(x) \wedge f_1(y) = f_1(x)$.

- $k$ is the greatest lower bound of $K$. Suppose $k_1 \le_{st} K$. We show $k_1 \le_{st} k$. Let $x \le y$, and let $f_0 \in K$: $k(x) \wedge k_1(y) = k(x) \wedge (f_0(x) \wedge k_1(y)) = k(x) \wedge k_1(x) = k_1(x)$. $\square$

Summarizing, in section 12.2 and in this section, we have obtained cartesian closure for two categories of stable functions exploiting two different sorts of distributivity: the (compatible) distributivity of binary glb's over binary lub's, and the distributivity of connected glb's over directed lub's, respectively. The proof techniques are quite different too, since Berry's proof uses the definition of stability through minimal points, while in Taylor's category the techniques used for meet cpo's and cm functions are extended to connected glb's.

**Exercise 12.5.11** *Show that a dI-domain satisfies the distributivity of connected glb's over directed lub's. Hint: Go through stable event structures.*

# 12.6   Continuous L-domains *

In this section, we show that connected meet cpo's can be alternatively presented as continuous L-domains. We call a continuous lattice a partial order which is both a complete lattice and a continuous cpo (cf. definition 5.1.1). We first investigate some properties of continuous lattices. Recall the adjoint functor theorem in the poset case (cf. example A2.5.3): if $X, Y$ are partial orders which have all glb's (i.e., are complete lattices), a monotonic function $f : X \to Y$ has a left adjoint iff $f : X \to Y$ preserves all glb's. The adjoint is defined by $g(y) = \bigwedge \{ z \mid y \leq f(z) \}$.

**Remark 12.6.1** *The complete lattice assumption can be weakened to the requirement that the glb's of the form $\bigwedge \{ z \mid y \leq f(z) \}$ exist. (They are the ones involved in the proof.)*

**Remark 12.6.2** *Stable functions do not preserve enough glb's to have a left adjoint: the set $\{ z \mid y \leq f(z) \}$ is not bounded in general, nor connected. But stable functions preserve enough glb's to be characterized as having a multi-adjoint (cf. definition 12.2.1). Indeed, the proof of proposition 12.2.2 is a variation of the proof of the (poset version of) the adjoint functor theorem.*

We shall apply the adjoint functor theorem to (subclasses of) continuous dcpo's. First we characterize continuous dcpo's by an adjunction property.

**Proposition 12.6.3** *A dcpo $D$ is continuous iff $\bigvee : Ide(D) \to D$ has a left adjoint.*

PROOF. ($\Leftarrow$) Call $g$ the left adjoint of $\bigvee$. For any ideal $I$ and any $x$ we have: $x \leq \bigvee I$ iff $g(x) \subseteq I$. We show that $g(x) = {\Downarrow}(x)$.

• $g(x) \subseteq {\Downarrow}(x)$. If $y \in g(x)$, then for any ideal $I$ such that $x \leq \bigvee I$ we have $y \in I$. Hence for any directed $\Delta$ such that $x \leq \bigvee \Delta$, we have $y \leq \delta$ for some $\delta \in \Delta$, which means exactly $y \ll x$.

• ${\Downarrow}(x) \subseteq g(x)$. We have $x \leq \bigvee g(x)$ by adjointness. Hence if $y \ll x$, we have $y \in g(x)$ by definition of $\ll$ and of ideal.

Thus ${\Downarrow}(x) = g(x)$ is directed, and $x = \bigvee({\Downarrow}(x))$ since $x$ dominates ${\Downarrow}(x)$.

($\Rightarrow$) Obvious.                                                                        □

**Proposition 12.6.4** *A complete lattice $D$ is continuous iff arbitrary glb's distribute over directed lub's, that is, if $\{\Delta_j\}_{j \in J}$ is an indexed collection of directed sets, then:*

$$\bigwedge_{j \in J} \left( \bigvee \Delta_j \right) = \bigvee \left\{ \bigwedge_{j \in J} x_j \mid \{x_j\}_{j \in J} \in \Pi_{j \in J} \Delta_j \right\}.$$

PROOF. We first show that ideals are closed under intersection. Let $\{I_j\}_{j \in J}$ be a collection of ideals. Take $x_1, x_2 \in \bigcap_{j \in J} I_j$. In each $I_j$ we can pick $y_j \geq x_1, x_2$. Then $\bigwedge_{j \in J} y_j$ is an upper bound for $x_1, x_2$ in $\bigcap_{j \in J} I_j$.

By proposition 12.6.3 and by the adjoint functor theorem, $D$ is continuous iff $\bigvee$ preserves the intersection of ideals. Hence $D$ is continuous iff

$$\bigvee \bigcap_{j \in J} I_j = \bigwedge_{j \in J} \left( \bigvee I_j \right) \quad \text{for any } \{I_j\}_{j \in J},$$

(1)  meet cpo's and cm functions

(1′)  distributive meet cpo's and cm functions

(2)  distributive meet cpo's and stable functions

(3)  connected meet cpo's (= continuous L-domains) and stable functions

$$\text{Domains satisfying } I \quad (\text{stable} = \text{cm})$$

(4)  stable bifinite domains axiomatized via:

- finite stable projections
- property $(MI)^\infty$

(5)  dI-domains axiomatized via:

- $d, I$ (abstract)
- coprime algebraic $+$ $I$ (abstract)
- bounded complete $+$ finite projections (abstract) (cf. exercise 12.3.14)
- stable event structures (concrete)

(6)  qualitative domains

(7)  coherence spaces

$$(7) \subseteq (6) \subseteq (5) \subseteq \begin{cases} (4) \subseteq (1) & (\text{cf. exercise 12.4.10}) \\ (2) \subseteq (1') \subseteq (1) & \\ (3) & (\text{cf. exercise 12.5.11}) \end{cases}$$

Figure 12.3: CCC's of stable and cm functions

which is equivalent to the equality of the statement since $\downarrow \{\bigwedge_{j\in J} x_j \mid \{x_J\}_{j\in J} \in \Pi_{j\in J}\Delta_j\} = \bigcap_{j\in J} \downarrow (\Delta_j)$.    □

We can require less glb's. Indeed, connectedness suffices to make the above proof work. We now adapt proposition 12.6.4 to L-domains.

**Lemma 12.6.5** *Let $D$ be an L-domain. If $\{I_j\}_{j\in J}$ is an indexed collection of ideals of $D$, and if $\{\bigvee I_j \mid j \in J\}$ is connected, then $\bigcap_{j\in J} I_j$ is an ideal.*

PROOF. Take $x_1, x_2 \in \bigcap_{j\in J} I_j$, and pick $y_j \geq x_1, x_2$ in each $I_j$. Then $\bigwedge_{j\in J} y_j$ exists (cf. remark 12.5.9) and is a bound for $x_1, x_2$ in $\bigcap_{j\in J} I_j$.    □

**Theorem 12.6.6** *An L-domain $D$ is continuous iff it is a connected meet cpo.*

PROOF. We adapt the proof of proposition 12.6.4. We know that $D$ is continuous iff $\bigvee$ preserves the intersection of ideals, provided 'enough' of these intersections exist: by remark 12.6.1, it suffices to check that $\{I \mid y \leq \bigvee I\}$ satisfies the conditions of lemma 12.6.5, i.e., that $Y = \{\bigvee I \mid y \leq \bigvee I\}$ is connected. This is immediate, since $y = \bigvee(\downarrow y) \in Y$ implies $\downarrow y \in \{I \mid y \leq \bigvee I\}$, from which the connectedness of $\{\bigvee I \mid y \leq \bigvee I\}$ follows. Therefore $D$ is continuous iff $\bigvee(\bigcap_{j \in J} I_j) = \bigwedge_{j \in J}(\bigvee I_j)$ for any collection $\{I_j\}_{j \in J}$ of ideals such that $\{\bigvee I_j \mid j \in J\}$ is connected. This is equivalent to the following property for any collection of directed sets $\Delta_j$ such that $\{\bigvee \Delta_j \mid j \in J\}$ is connected:

$$\bigvee \{\bigwedge_{j \in J} x_j \mid \{x_j\}_{j \in J} \in \Pi_{j \in J} \Delta_j\} = \bigwedge_{j \in J}(\bigvee \Delta_j) \,. \qquad \square$$

**Exercise\* 12.6.7** *(1) Show that the inclusions at the bottom of figure 12.3 are all strict. (2) Show that the categories (2), (3), and (4) of that figure are not related by inclusion.*

# 13
# Towards linear logic

Girard's linear logic [Gir87] is an extension of propositional logic with new connectives providing a logical treatment of resource control. As a first hint, consider the linear $\lambda$-terms, which are the $\lambda$-terms defined with the following restriction: when an abstraction $\lambda x.M$ is formed, then $x$ occurs exactly once in $M$. Linear $\lambda$-terms are normalized in linear time, that is, the number of reduction steps to their normal form is proportional to their size: a linear $\beta$-redex $(\lambda x.M)N$ involves no duplication of the argument $N$. Thus all the complexity of normalization comes from non-linearity.

Linear logic pushes the limits of constructivity much beyond intuitionistic logic. A proper proof theoretical introduction to linear logic is beyond the scope of this book. In this chapter, we content ourselves with a semantic introduction. By doing so, we actually follow the historical thread: the connectives of linear logic arose from the consideration of (a particularly simple version of) the stable model.

In section 13.1, we examine stable functions between coherence spaces, and discover two decompositions. First the function space $E \to E'$ is isomorphic to a space $(!E) {\multimap} E'$, where $\multimap$ constructs the space of linear functions, and where ! is a constructor which allows reuse of data. Intuitively, linear functions, like linear terms, can use their input only once. On the other hand, the explicit declaration of reusability, !, allows us to recover all functions and terms. The second decomposition is the linear version of the classical definition of implication: $E {\multimap} E'$ is the same as $E^{\perp} \wp E'$, where $^{\perp}$ is the negation of linear logic and where $\wp$ is a disjunction connective (due to resource sensitiveness, there are two different conjunctions and two different disjunctions in linear logic).

In section 13.2, we introduce the categorical material needed to express the properties of the new connectives. We introduce a sequent calculus for linear logic, and we sketch its categorical interpretation.

In the rest of the chapter, we investigate other models in which linear logic can be interpreted. In section 13.3, we present Bucciarelli-Ehrhard's notion of strong stability and Ehrhard's model of hypercoherences [BE94, Ehr93]. Strongly stable functions provide an extensional (although not an order-extensional) model whose morphisms at the first order types are the sequential functions (cf. section 6.5). A non-extensional treatment of sequentiality, where morphisms at all orders are explicitly sequential, and in which a part of linear logic can also be interpreted, is offered in chapter 14. In section 13.4, we present the model of bistructures, which combines the stable order of chapter 12 and the pointwise order of chapter 1 in an intriguing way [CPW96]. Finally, in section 13.5, we show that Scott continuous functions also lend themselves to a linear decomposition based on the idea of presentations of (Scott) topologies [Lam94].

Summarizing, linear logic cuts across most of the flavours of domain theory met in this book: continuity, stability, and sequentiality.

# 13.1   Coherence spaces

Coherence spaces offer an extremely simple framework for stability. They were briefly mentioned in section 12.3.

**Definition 13.1.1 (coherence space)** *A coherence space* $(E, \bigcirc)$ *(E for short) is given by a set $E$ of events, or tokens, and by a binary reflexive and symmetric relation $\bigcirc$ over $E$. $E$ is called the* web *of* $(E, \bigcirc)$. *A state (or clique) of $E$ is a set $x$ of events satisfying the following consistency condition:*

$$\forall e_1, e_2 \in x \ \ e_1 \bigcirc e_2.$$

*We denote with $D(E)$ the set of states of $E$, ordered by inclusion. If $(E, \bigcirc)$ is a coherence space, its* incoherence[1] *is the relation $\asymp$ defined by:*

$$e_1 \asymp e_2 \Leftrightarrow \neg(e_1 \bigcirc e_2) \text{ or } e_1 = e_2.$$

Clearly, coherence can be recovered from incoherence:

$$e_1 \bigcirc e_2 \Leftrightarrow \neg(e_1 \asymp e_2) \text{ or } e_1 = e_2.$$

Since a coherence space $E$ is a special case of event structure (cf. definition 12.3.11), we already know from proposition 12.3.4 that $D(E)$ is a dI-domain whose compact elements are the finite states, whose minimum is $\bot = \emptyset$, and whose bounded lub's are set unions.

**Definition 13.1.2** *We call* **Coh** *the category whose objects are coherence spaces and whose homsets are the stable functions:*

$$\mathbf{Coh}[E, E'] = D(E) \to_{st} D(E').$$

**Proposition 13.1.3** *The category* **Coh** *is cartesian closed.*

PROOF. The category **Coh** can be viewed as a full subcategory of the category of dI-domains, and the following constructions show that the terminal dI-domain is a coherence space, and that the products and the exponents of coherence spaces are coherence spaces.

- $1 = (\emptyset, \emptyset)$.

---

[1]Notice that the incoherence is not the complement of the coherence, since the coherence and the incoherence are both reflexive.

• The events of $E \times E'$ are either $e.1$, with $e \in E$, or $e'.2$, with $e' \in E'$ (using an explicit notation for disjoint unions), and the coherence is:

$$(e_1.i) \frown (e_2.j) \Leftrightarrow i \neq j \text{ or } (i = j \text{ and } e_1 \frown e_2).$$

• The events of $E \to E'$ are pairs $(x, e')$, where $x$ is a finite state of $E$ and where $e' \in E'$, and the coherence is:

$$(x_1, e_1') \frown (x_2, e_2') \Leftrightarrow (x_1 \uparrow x_2 \Rightarrow (e_1' \frown e_2' \text{ and } (x_1 \neq x_2 \Rightarrow e_1' \neq e_2'))).$$

The proposition then follows as a corollary of theorem 12.3.6.    □

The key observation that served as a starting point to linear logic is the following: the dissymmetry in the pairs (state,event) indicates that $\to$ should not be taken as primitive. Instead, Girard proposed a unary constructor ! and a binary constructor $\multimap$ such that $E \to E' = (!E) \multimap E'$.

**Definition 13.1.4 (linear exponent – coherence spaces)** *The linear exponent $E \multimap E'$ of two coherence spaces $E$ and $E'$ is the coherence space whose events are the pairs $(e, e')$ where $e \in E$ and $e' \in E'$, and whose coherence is given by:*

$$(e_1, e_1') \frown (e_2, e_2') \Leftrightarrow (e_1 \frown e_2 \Rightarrow (e_1' \frown e_2' \text{ and } (e_1 \neq e_2 \Rightarrow e_1' \neq e_2'))).$$

**Lemma 13.1.5** *In $E \multimap E'$, the following equivalences hold (and thus may alternatively serve as the definition of coherence):*

(1)  $(e_1, e_1') \frown (e_2, e_2') \;\Leftrightarrow\; (e_1 \frown e_2 \Rightarrow e_1' \frown e_2') \text{ and } (e_1' \asymp e_2' \Rightarrow e_1 \asymp e_2)$
(2)  $(e_1, e_1') \asymp (e_2, e_2') \;\Leftrightarrow\; e_1 \frown e_2 \text{ and } e_1' \asymp e_2'$.

PROOF. The equivalence (1) is clearly a rephrasing of the equivalence given in definition 13.1.4 (turning $(e_1' \asymp e_2' \Rightarrow e_1 \asymp e_2)$ into $\neg(e_1 \asymp e_2) \Rightarrow \neg(e_1' \asymp e_2')$). We next show that (2) is equivalent to (1). We have, by successive simple boolean manipulations:

$$\neg((e_1 \frown e_2 \Rightarrow e_1' \frown e_2') \text{ and } (e_1' \asymp e_2' \Rightarrow e_1 \asymp e_2))$$
$$\Leftrightarrow (e_1 \frown e_2 \text{ and } \neg(e_1' \frown e_2')) \text{ or } (e_1' \asymp e_2' \text{ and } \neg(e_1 \asymp e_2))$$
$$\Leftrightarrow e_1 \frown e_2 \text{ and } (\neg(e_1' \frown e_2') \text{ or } (e_1' \asymp e_2' \text{ and } \neg(e_1 \asymp e_2)))$$
$$\Leftrightarrow e_1 \frown e_2 \text{ and } e_1' \asymp e_2' \text{ and } (\neg(e_1' \frown e_2') \text{ or } \neg(e_1 \asymp e_2)).$$

We next observe:

$$e_1 \frown e_2 \text{ and } e_1' \asymp e_2' \Rightarrow ((e_1, e_1') = (e_2, e_2') \text{ or } \neg(e_1' \frown e_2') \text{ or } \neg(e_1 \asymp e_2)),$$

which we use as follows:

$$(e_1, e_1') \asymp (e_2, e_2') \;\Leftrightarrow\; (e_1, e_1') = (e_2, e_2') \text{ or } \neg((e_1, e_1') \frown (e_2, e_2'))$$
$$\Leftrightarrow \begin{cases} (e_1, e_1') = (e_2, e_2') \text{ or} \\ (e_1 \frown e_2 \text{ and } e_1' \asymp e_2' \text{ and } (\neg(e_1' \frown e_2') \text{ or } \neg(e_1 \asymp e_2))) \end{cases}$$
$$\Leftrightarrow e_1 \frown e_2 \text{ and } e_1' \asymp e_2'.$$    □

The states of $E \multimap E'$ are in one-to-one correspondence with the linear functions from $D(E)$ to $D(E')$, which we define next.

**Definition 13.1.6 (additive function)** *Let $D, D'$ be two bounded complete cpo's. A continuous function $f : D \to D'$ is called additive if*

$$f(\bot) = \bot \quad \text{and} \quad (\forall x, y \ (x \uparrow y \Rightarrow f(x \vee y) = f(x) \vee f(y))) \ .$$

**Definition 13.1.7 (linear function)** *Let $(E, \bigcirc)$ and $(E', \bigcirc)$ be two coherence spaces. A stable and additive function $f : D(E) \to D(E')$ is called linear. We write $D(E) \to_{lin} D(E')$ for the set of linear functions from $D(E)$ to $D(E')$.*

**Proposition 13.1.8** *Let $E$ and $E'$ be coherence spaces. A stable function $f : D(E) \to D(E')$ is linear if and only its trace (cf. theorem 12.3.6) consists of pairs of the form $(\{e\}, e')$. Hence we freely write, for a linear function:*

$$trace(f) = \{(e, e') \mid e' \in f(\{e\})\}.$$

*Moreover, trace is an order-isomorphism from $D(E) \to_{lin} D(E')$ (ordered by the stable order) to $D(E \multimap E')$ (ordered by inclusion).*

PROOF. ($\Rightarrow$) Let $f$ be linear, and let $(x, e') \in trace(f)$, and suppose that $x$ is not a singleton. If $x = \bot$, then $e' \in f(\bot)$, and this violates $f(\bot) = \bot$. Otherwise, since in a coherence space any subset of a state is a state, $x$ can be written as $x_1 \cup x_2$, with $x_1, x_2 < x$. Then $e' \notin f(x_1)$ and $e' \notin f(x_2)$ by definition of a trace, therefore $e' \notin f(x_1) \cup f(x_2) = f(x_1) \vee f(x_2)$, violating $f(x) = f(x_1 \vee x_2) = f(x_1) \vee f(x_2)$.

($\Leftarrow$) Suppose that $f(\bot) \neq \bot$, and let $e' \in f(\bot)$. Then $(\bot, e') \in trace(f)$ by definition of a trace, violating the assumption on $trace(f)$. Suppose that $x_1 \uparrow x_2$, and let $e' \in f(x_1 \cup x_2)$. Then there exists $(\{e\}, e') \in trace(f)$ such that $\{e\} \subseteq (x_1 \cup x_2)$, which obviously implies $\{e\} \subseteq x_1$ or $\{e\} \subseteq x_2$, and therefore $e' \in f(x_1)$ or $e' \in f(x_2)$.

Finally, the isomorphism $D(E) \to_{lin} D(E') \cong D(E \multimap E')$ follows from the observation that a set $\phi$ of pairs $(e, e')$ is a state of $E \multimap E'$ iff $\{(\{e\}, e') \mid (e, e') \in \phi\}$ is a state of $E \to E'$. □

**Remark 13.1.9** *A computational interpretation of the characterization of a linear function $f$ given in proposition 13.1.8 can be given as follows. In order to produce an atomic piece of output $e'$, $f$ needs to build, or explore, or consume an atomic piece of input $e$. In contrast, if $(x, e')$ is in the trace of a stable function $f$ and if $x$ is not a singleton, then $f$ needs to look at $x$ 'more than once', specifically $\sharp x$ times, before it can produce $e'$. In this framework, events can be viewed as units of resource consumption (see remark 14.3.22 for a different flavour of resource counting).*

**Proposition 13.1.10** *The composition of two linear functions $f$ and $g$ is linear, and its trace is the relation composition of $trace(f)$ and $trace(g)$.*

PROOF. Let, say, $f : D(E) \to D(E')$ and $g : D(E') \to D(E'')$. The first part of the statement is obvious using the characterization of linearity by lub and meet preservation properties. We show $trace(g \circ f) \subseteq trace(g) \circ trace(f)$. Let $(e, e'') \in trace(g \circ f)$. By linearity, there exists $e'$ such that $(e', e'') \in trace(g)$

and $e' \in f(\{e\})$ (that is, $(e, e') \in trace(f)$). We now show $trace(g) \circ trace(f) \subseteq trace(g \circ f)$. Let $(e, e') \in trace(f)$ and $(e', e'') \in trace(g)$. Since $e' \leq f(\{e\})$ and $e'' \leq g(\{e'\})$, we have $e'' \leq g(f(\{e\}))$, that is, $(e, e'') \in trace(g \circ f)$. □

This characterization of the composition of linear functions by trace composition holds in general for dI-domains.

**Exercise 13.1.11** *Show the dI-domain version of proposition 13.1.10. Hint: Traces then consist of pairs of compact coprime elements.*

**Definition 13.1.12** *The category* **Coh**$_l$ *is the category whose objects are coherence spaces, and whose morphisms are the linear functions:*

$$\text{Coh}_l[E, E'] = D(E) \to_{lin} D(E').$$

**Proposition 13.1.13** *The category* **Coh**$_l$ *is cartesian. The terminal object and the products are those of* **Coh***.*

PROOF HINT. The projection functions are linear, and the pairing of two linear functions is linear. □

**Definition 13.1.14 (exponential – coherence spaces)** *Let* $(E, \bigcirc)$ *be a coherence space. The exponential* $!E$ *(pronounce 'of course $E$', or 'bang $E$') is the coherence space whose events are the finite states of $E$, and whose coherence is given by* $(x_1 \bigcirc x_2 \Leftrightarrow x_1 \uparrow x_2)$*.*

**Proposition 13.1.15** *The operation* ! *extends to a functor* ! : **Coh** $\to$ **Coh**$_l$ *which is left adjoint to the inclusion functor* $\subseteq$ : **Coh**$_l$ $\to$ **Coh***.*

PROOF HINT. The natural bijections between **Coh**$[E, E']$ and **Coh**$_l[!E, E']$ are induced by the interpretation of $x$ in a pair $(x, e')$ as either a finite state of $E$ or an event of $!E$, respectively. □

**Remark 13.1.16** *The finite states of $D(!E)$ can be seen as presentations of the states of $E$, via the lub operation associating $\bigvee X$ with $X = \{x_1, \ldots, x_n\}$. There are two presentations of $\perp$: $\emptyset$, and $\{\perp\}$. It follows that $D(!E)$ contains a lifting of $D(E)$ (cf. definition 1.4.16).[2] Hence the adjunction* ! $\dashv \subseteq$ *is somewhat similar to the adjunction relating* **Scpo** *and* **Cpo** *(cf. proposition 1.4.20).*

The second equivalence of the statement of lemma 13.1.5 naturally suggests a further decomposition of $E \multimap E'$ as $E^\perp \wp E'$, where the new constructors $^\perp$ and $\wp$ are defined as follows.

**Definition 13.1.17 (linear negation – coherence spaces)** *The linear negation $E^\perp$ (pronounce '$E$ perp') of a coherence space $(E, \bigcirc)$ is defined as $E^\perp = (E, \asymp)$.*

---

[2]Actually, this containment is strict. For example, !**O** is isomorphic to **O** $\times$ **O**, which has four elements, while $(\mathbf{O})_\perp$ has three elements and is not a coherence space.

**Definition 13.1.18 (par – coherence spaces)** *Let $E$, $E'$ be coherence spaces. Their multiplicative disjunction $E \wp E'$ (pronounce 'E par E'') is the coherence space whose events are pairs $(e, e')$ where $e \in E$ and $e' \in E'$, and whose incoherence is given by:*

$$(e_1, e_1') \frown (e_2, e_2') \Leftrightarrow (e_1 \frown e_2 \text{ and } e_1' \frown e_2').$$

Other connectives can be defined by De Morgan duality. The dual of $\times$ is another disjunction $\oplus$, called additive. The dual of 1 is written 0. The dual of ! is written ? and called 'why not'. The dual of $\wp$ is the tensor product, whose direct definition, dictated by $(E \otimes E')^\perp = E^\perp \wp E'^\perp$, is as follows.

**Definition 13.1.19 (tensor – coherence spaces)** *The tensor product (or multiplicative conjunction) $E \otimes E'$ of two coherence spaces $E$ and $E'$ is the coherence space whose events are pairs $(e, e')$ where $e \in E$ and $e' \in E'$, and whose coherence is given by:*

$$(e_1, e_1') \smallfrown (e_2, e_2') \Leftrightarrow (e_1 \smallfrown e_2 \text{ and } e_1' \smallfrown e_2').$$

Finally, there is a connective called the tensor unit:

$$I = (\{*\}, id).$$

The dual of $I$ is written $\perp$. These connectives obey some categorical constructions, which ensure that they allow us to interpret linear logic. Some of them have been already discussed in this section (propositions 13.1.3 and 13.1.15). The rest will be completed in the next section.

**Exercise 13.1.20** *(1) Let $(E, \smallfrown)$ and $(E', \smallfrown')$ be two coherence spaces. We say that $(E, \smallfrown)$ is rigidly included in $(E', \smallfrown')$ (and we write $(E, \smallfrown) \subseteq (E', \smallfrown')$) if $\smallfrown = \smallfrown' \cap (E \times E)$. Show that $(id, \lambda x'.x' \cap E)$ is a rigid embedding from $D(E)$ to $D(E')$ (cf. definition 12.4.2). (2) Conversely, given coherence spaces $(E, \smallfrown)$ and $(E', \smallfrown')$ and a rigid embedding $(\phi, \psi)$ from $D(E)$ to $D(E')$, show that there exist two coherence spaces $(E_1, \smallfrown_1)$ and $(E_1', \smallfrown_1')$ such that:*

$$D(E) \cong D(E_1) \quad D(E') \cong D(E_1') \quad (E_1, \smallfrown_1) \subseteq (E_1', \smallfrown_1') .$$

*(3) Exploit this correspondence to solve some domain equations in the framework of coherence spaces (cf. exercises 10.2.14 and 13.1.21).*

**Exercise\* 13.1.21** *The goal of this exercise, based on [Zha97], is to propose the construction of a universal homogeneous object (cf. section 7.3) in the category of coherence spaces (with a denumerable set of events) and rigid embeddings. (1) Consider the following coherence space $(E_u, \smallfrown_u)$, where $E_u = \{0, 1\}^*$ (the words over $0, 1$), and where $\smallfrown_1$ is the symmetric closure of the following relation $R$:*

$$a_1 \cdots a_m \, R \, b_1 \cdots b_n \Leftrightarrow m < n \text{ and } b_{m+1} = 1 .$$

*Show that $(E_u, \smallfrown_u)$ is universal (cf. definition 7.3.6). Hint: Given a coherence space $(E, \smallfrown)$ with $E$ finite, define an injection $i$ from $E = \{e_1, \ldots, e_n, \ldots\}$ to $E_u$ by setting $i(e_n) = a_1 \cdots a_{n-1}$ where $a_j = 1$ iff $e_i \smallfrown e_j$. (2) Show that $(E_u, \smallfrown_u)$ is not homogeneous. Hint: Consider the coherence space $(\{e_1, e_2, e_3\}, \smallfrown)$ where $\smallfrown$ is given by $e_1 \smallfrown e_2$. (3)*

*Show that the following coherence space* $(E_{uh}, \subset_{uh})$ *is universal and homogeneous. The web* $E_{uh}$ *is built by levels as follows. There is one event* $e_{11}$ *at level 1. Let* $E_{uh}^n$ *be the set of events constructed so far when construction at level* $n$ *has been completed. Then level* $n + 1$ *is constructed by adjoining* $m$ *new events* $e_{(n+1)1}, \cdots e_{(n+1)m}$, *with* $\mathcal{P}(E_{uh}^n) = \{X_1, \ldots, X_m\}$ *and* $\{e \in E_{uh}^n \mid e \subset e_{(n+1)i}\} = X_i$, *for all* $i \leq m$. *Hint: The key stepping stone is to show that if* $(E, \subset)$ *and* $(E_1, \subset_1)$ *are finite, isomorphic, and rigidly included in* $(E_{uh}, \subset_{uh})$, *and if* $e \in E_{uh} \backslash E$, *then there exists* $e_1 \in E_{uh} \backslash E_1$ *such that* $(E \cup \{e\}, \subset)$ *and* $E_1 \cup \{e_1\}, \subset_1)$ *are finite, isomorphic, and rigidly included in* $(E_{uh}, \subset_{uh})$.

# 13.2 Categorical interpretation of linear logic

In this section, we start with a sketchy introduction to linear logic. We then introduce a few categorical notions, culminating in the notion of $*_l$-autonomous category (definition 13.2.12). We show that $\mathbf{Coh}_l$ (cf. section 13.1) provides an example of $*_l$-autonomous category (proposition 13.2.20), and give evidence of how linear logic proofs can be interpreted in any $*_l$-autonomous category.

The connectives introduced in section 13.1 fall into three groups, which Girard has named as follows:

(multiplicatives)    $I, \bot, \otimes, \wp$, and linear negation
(additives)         $1, 0, \times, \oplus$
(exponentials)    $!, ?$ .

In figure 13.2, we present a sequent calculus for linear logic. A much better presentation of the proofs of linear logic is by means of certain graphs called proof nets, which forget some irrelevant details of syntax, and are the gate to a geometric understanding of logic and computation. This goes beyond the scope of this book. We simply refer to [Gir87] and [Dan90], and mention that sequential algorithms introduced in chapter 14 are in the same spirit. The sequents of figure 13.2 are of the form $\vdash \Gamma$, where $\Gamma$ is a list of formulas, possibly with repetitions. In the rule (*Exchange*), $\sigma(\Gamma)$ means any permutation of the list $\Gamma$. Here are brief comments on this proof system:

- There are no weakening and contraction rules. Weakening allows us to add assumptions to a sequent, contraction allows us to identify repeated assumptions with a single assumption. They express the two aspects of non-linearity (cf. definition 13.1.7): weakening allows non-strictness, while contraction allows repeated use of resources.

- The rule ($\otimes$) expresses a splitting of resources: $\Gamma$ for $A$, and $\Delta$ for $B$. Multiplicative connectives correspond to a form of parallelism without communication. The corresponding categorical notion is that of monoidal category, introduced below.

- The rule ($\times$) expresses sharing of resources: $\Gamma$ is used both by $A$ and $B$. The corresponding categorical construction is the product.

- The exponential rules regulate the explicit reusability of resources. Rule (*Promotion*) says that a formula proved under reusable assumptions is itself

## LOGICAL RULES

$$(\text{Axiom}) \quad \dfrac{}{\vdash A, A^{\perp}} \qquad (\text{Cut}) \quad \dfrac{\vdash A, \Gamma \quad \vdash A^{\perp}, \Delta}{\vdash \Gamma, \Delta} \qquad (\text{Exchange}) \quad \dfrac{\vdash \Gamma}{\vdash \sigma(\Gamma)}$$

## MULTIPLICATIVES

$$(I) \quad \vdash I \qquad\qquad\qquad (\perp) \quad \dfrac{\vdash \Gamma}{\vdash \perp, \Gamma}$$

$$(\otimes) \quad \dfrac{\vdash A, \Gamma \quad \vdash B, \Delta}{\vdash A \otimes B, \Gamma, \Delta} \qquad (\wp) \quad \dfrac{\vdash A, B, \Gamma}{\vdash A \wp B, \Gamma}$$

## ADDITIVES

$$(1) \quad \vdash 1, \Gamma \qquad (\times) \quad \dfrac{\vdash A, \Gamma \quad \vdash B, \Gamma}{\vdash A \times B, \Gamma} \qquad (\oplus) \quad \dfrac{\vdash A, \Gamma}{\vdash A \oplus B, \Gamma} \quad \dfrac{\vdash B, \Gamma}{\vdash A \oplus B, \Gamma}$$

## EXPONENTIALS

$$(\text{Promotion}) \quad \dfrac{\vdash A, ?B_1, \ldots, ?B_n}{\vdash !A, ?B_1, \ldots, ?B_n} \qquad (\text{Dereliction}) \quad \dfrac{\vdash A, \Gamma}{\vdash ?A, \Gamma}$$

$$(\text{Contraction}) \quad \dfrac{\vdash ?A, ?A, \Gamma}{\vdash ?A, \Gamma} \qquad (\text{Weakening}) \quad \dfrac{\vdash \Gamma}{\vdash ?A, \Gamma}$$

Figure 13.1: Sequent calculus for linear logic

---

reusable. Rule (*Dereliction*) says that a resource that can be used once is a resource which can be used $n$ times, for some $n$. Since $n$ can in particular be 0, some information is lost when this rule is applied. Rules (*Contraction*) and (*Weakening*) say that reusable data can be duplicated.

We now sketch the categorical interpretation of the formulas and proofs of linear logic. We first introduce a few categorical notions, building upon the structure of monoidal category [ML71, Bar91b].

**Definition 13.2.1 (monoidal)** *A monoidal category is a category* **C** *equipped with:*

- *a functor* $\otimes : \mathbf{C} \times \mathbf{C} \to \mathbf{C}$, *called the* tensor product,

- *a distinguished object* $I$, *called the* tensor unit, *and*

- *natural isomorphisms, also called the canonical isomorphisms:*

$$\alpha : A \otimes (B \otimes C) \to (A \otimes B) \otimes C$$
$$\iota_l : I \otimes A \to A$$
$$\iota_r : A \otimes I \to A \,,$$

*satisfying the following two so-called coherence equations:*

$$(\alpha - \alpha) \quad \alpha \circ \alpha \quad = \quad (\alpha \otimes id) \circ \alpha \circ (id \otimes \alpha)$$
$$(\alpha - \iota) \quad (\iota_r \otimes id) \circ \alpha \quad = \quad id \otimes \iota_l \,.$$

Where do the two coherence equations of definition 13.2.1 come from? As observed by Huet (unpublished), a good answer comes from rewriting theory (a subject that did not exist when monoidal categories were defined by Mac Lane in the early sixties). Consider the domains and codomains of the canonical isomorphisms and of the equated arrows as the left and right hand sides of rewriting rules and rewriting sequences, respectively:

$$
\begin{array}{llll}
(\alpha) & A \otimes (B \otimes C) & \to & (A \otimes B) \otimes C \\
(\iota_l) & I \otimes A & \to & A \\
(\iota_r) & A \otimes I & \to & A
\end{array}
$$

$$
\begin{array}{llll}
(\alpha - \alpha) & A \otimes (B \otimes (C \otimes D)) & \to^* & ((A \otimes B) \otimes C) \otimes D \\
(\alpha - \iota) & A \otimes (B \otimes I) & \to^* & A \otimes B \,.
\end{array}
$$

Then the two coherence equations correspond to equating different reduction sequences: $\alpha \circ \alpha$ encodes

$$A \otimes (B \otimes (C \otimes D)) \to (A \otimes B) \otimes (C \otimes D) \to ((A \otimes B) \otimes C) \otimes D,$$

while $(\alpha \otimes id) \circ \alpha \circ (id \otimes \alpha)$ encodes

$$A \otimes (B \otimes (C \otimes D)) \to A \otimes ((B \otimes C) \otimes D) \to^* ((A \otimes B) \otimes C) \otimes D.$$

Similarly, the two sides of the second equation encode

$$A \otimes (I \otimes B) \to (A \otimes I) \otimes B \to A \otimes B$$
$$A \otimes (I \otimes B) \to A \otimes B \,.$$

These pairs of derivations form local confluence diagrams for the rewriting system on objects induced by $(\alpha), (\iota_l)$, and $(\iota_r)$. We pursue this interpretation in exercise 13.2.2, which assumes familiarity with basic rewriting theory.

**Exercise 13.2.2 (coherence – monoidal)** *(1) Find all the critical pairs of the rewriting system on objects underlying $\alpha, \iota_l$, and $\iota_r$, and show that the corresponding equations between canonical isomorphisms are derivable from the two equations given in definition 13.2.1. Hint: There are three other critical pairs; exploit the fact that $\alpha, \iota_l$, and $\iota_r$ are isos. (2) Prove the so-called coherence theorem for monoidal categories: every two canonical morphisms (that is, terms over the signature $\{\circ, id, \otimes, \alpha, \alpha^{-1}, \iota_l, \iota_l^{-1}, \iota_r, \iota_r^{-1}\}$) with the same domain and codomain are equal. Hint: Remove first $\alpha^{-1}, \iota_l^{-1}$, and $\iota_r^{-1}$, and proceed as in the proof of the Knuth-Bendix theorem (confluence of critical pairs implies local confluence) [HO80].*

**Definition 13.2.3 (symmetric monoidal)** *A symmetric monoidal category is a monoidal category together with an additional canonical isomorphism* $\gamma : A \otimes B \to B \otimes A$ *satisfying:*

$$(\gamma - \gamma) \quad \gamma \circ \gamma \quad = \quad id$$
$$(\alpha - \gamma) \quad \alpha \circ \gamma \circ \alpha \quad = \quad (\gamma \otimes id) \circ \alpha \circ (id \otimes \gamma)\,.$$

The coherence theorem still holds in the symmetric monoidal case, but needs more care: clearly we do not want to identify $\gamma : A \otimes A \to A \otimes A$ and $id : A \otimes A \to A \otimes A$. Category theorists exclude this by speaking, not of terms, but of natural transformations:

$$\gamma : (\lambda(A,B).A \otimes B) \to (\lambda(A,B).B \otimes A) \quad id : (\lambda(A,B).A \otimes B) \to (\lambda(A,B).A \otimes B).$$

do not have the same codomain. A more elementary point of view is to restrict attention to linear terms for objects.

**Exercise* 13.2.4 (coherence – symmetric monoidal)** *Show that, in a symmetric monoidal category, any two canonical natural transformations between the same functors are equal. Hints: Use monoidal coherence, and the following presentation of the symmetric group by means of the transpositions* $\sigma_i$ *which permute two successive elements* $i$ *and* $i + 1$:

$$\sigma_i \circ \sigma_i = id \quad \sigma_i \circ \sigma_j = \sigma_j \circ \sigma_i \ (j - i > 1) \quad \sigma_i \circ \sigma_{i+1} \circ \sigma_i = \sigma_{i+1} \circ \sigma_i \circ \sigma_{i+1}.$$

**Definition 13.2.5 (monoidal closed)** *A monoidal closed category is a monoidal category* **C** *such that for any object* $A$ *the functor* $\lambda C.(C \otimes A)$ *has a right adjoint, written* $\lambda B.(A \multimap B)$. *In other words, for every objects* $A, B$, *there exists an object* $A \multimap B$, *called the* linear exponent, *and natural bijections (for all* $C$):

$$\Lambda_l : \mathbf{C}[C \otimes A, B] \to \mathbf{C}[C, A \multimap B].$$

*We write* $ev_l = \Lambda_l^{-1}(id)$.

Notice that there are no accompanying additional coherence equations for monoidal categories. This comes from the difference in nature between the constructions $\otimes$ and $\multimap$: the latter is given together with a universal construction (an adjunction), while the first is just a functor with some associated isomorphisms. This difference is often referred to as the difference between 'additional structure' ($\otimes$) and 'property' ($\multimap$). The notion of dualizing object, introduced next, is 'additional structure'.

**Definition 13.2.6 (*-autonomous)** *A symmetric monoidal closed category* **C** *is called *-autonomous if it has a distinguished object* $\perp$, *called a* dualizing object, *such that for any* $A$ *the morphisms*

$$\Lambda_l(ev_l \circ \gamma) : \mathbf{C}[A, (A \multimap \perp) \multimap \perp],$$

*called canonical, have an inverse. If no ambiguity can arise, we write* $A^{\perp}$ *for* $A \multimap \perp$, *and* $A^{\perp\perp}$ *for* $(A^{\perp})^{\perp}$.

**Proposition 13.2.7** *Let* $\mathbf{C}$ *be a* $*$-*autonomous category.*

(1) *There exists a natural bijection between* $\mathbf{C}[A, B]$ *and* $\mathbf{C}[B^{\perp}, A^{\perp}]$.

(2) *There exists a natural isomorphism* $(A\multimap B)^{\perp} \cong A \otimes B^{\perp}$.

(3) *There exists a natural isomorphism* $I \cong \perp^{\perp}$.

PROOF HINT. (1) By functoriality of $\multimap$, with every $f : A \to B$ we can associate $(f\multimap\perp) : B^{\perp} \to A^{\perp}$. In the other direction, starting from $g : B^{\perp} \to A^{\perp}$, we arrive at $(g\multimap\perp) : A^{\perp\perp} \to B^{\perp\perp}$, which up to natural isomorphism is in $\mathbf{C}[A, B]$.

(2) In one direction, by associativity, and using $ev_l$ twice, we get a morphism from $(A \otimes B^{\perp}) \otimes (A\multimap B)$ to $\perp$. In the other direction, we take the image of $id_{A\multimap B}$ through the following chain of transformations:

$$
\begin{aligned}
\mathbf{C}[(A\multimap B)^{\perp}, A \otimes B^{\perp}] &\cong \mathbf{C}[(A \otimes B^{\perp})^{\perp}, (A\multimap B)^{\perp\perp}] &&\text{(by (1))} \\
&\cong \mathbf{C}[(A \otimes B^{\perp})^{\perp}, A\multimap B] &&(\perp \text{ is dualizing)} \\
&\cong \mathbf{C}[A\multimap B^{\perp\perp}, A\multimap B] &&(\mathbf{C} \text{ is closed}) \\
&\cong \mathbf{C}[A\multimap B, A\multimap B] &&(\perp \text{ is dualizing}) .
\end{aligned}
$$

(3) We proceed similarly, using $id \circ \iota_l : I \otimes \perp \to \perp$ and $ev_l \circ \iota_r^{-1} : I^{\perp} \to \perp$. $\quad\square$

Part (3) of proposition 13.2.7 shows in retrospective that the name $\perp$ for the dualizing object is deserved: we can indeed understand it as the multiplicative false. Often, the linear negation comes first in the semantics. The following approach is thus helpful.

**Proposition 13.2.8** *Suppose that* $\mathbf{C}$ *is a symmetric monoidal category, and that* $(\_)^{\perp} : \mathbf{C}^{op} \to \mathbf{C}$ *is a functor (which we shall call the dualizing functor) which is given together with:*

(1) *A natural isomorphism* $A \cong A^{\perp\perp}$.

(2) *A natural bijection* $\mathbf{C}[I, (A \otimes B^{\perp})^{\perp}] \cong \mathbf{C}[A, B]$.

*Then* $\mathbf{C}$ *is monoidal closed, with* $\multimap$ *defined by* $A\multimap B = (A \otimes B^{\perp})^{\perp}$.

PROOF. We have:

$$
\begin{aligned}
\mathbf{C}[A, B\multimap C] &= \mathbf{C}[A, (B \otimes C^{\perp})^{\perp}] &&\text{(by definition)} \\
&\cong \mathbf{C}[I, (A \otimes (B \otimes C^{\perp})^{\perp\perp})^{\perp}] &&\text{(by (2))} \\
&\cong \mathbf{C}[I, (A \otimes (B \otimes C^{\perp}))^{\perp}] &&\text{(by (1))} \\
&\cong \mathbf{C}[I, ((A \otimes B) \otimes C^{\perp})^{\perp}] &&\text{(by associativity)} \\
&\cong \mathbf{C}[A \otimes B, C] &&\text{(by (2)) .} \quad\square
\end{aligned}
$$

**Remark 13.2.9** *The above data are close to ensuring that* $\mathbf{C}$ *is* $*$-*autonomous. Indeed, from* $A \cong A^{\perp\perp}$ *and*

$$
A\multimap I^{\perp} = (A \otimes I^{\perp\perp})^{\perp} \cong (A \otimes I)^{\perp} \cong A^{\perp},
$$

*we obtain* $A \cong (A\multimap I^{\perp})\multimap I^{\perp}$. *However, one would need to impose tedious coherence axioms relating the natural isomorphisms and bijections of proposition*

*13.2.8, in order to ensure that this isomorphism is indeed the one obtained by twisting and currying the evaluation morphism. One such condition is that the composition of isomorphisms*

$$C[A, B] \cong C[I, (A \otimes B^\perp)^\perp] \cong C[I, (B^\perp \otimes A)^\perp] \cong C[I, (B^\perp \otimes A^{\perp\perp})^\perp] \cong C[B^\perp, A^\perp]$$

*has to be the action of the functor $\perp$ on $C[A, B]$.*

The last ingredient we need is the notion of comonad, which is dual to that of monad (cf. definition A2.8.1).

**Definition 13.2.10 (comonad)** *A comonad over a category $C$ is a triple $(T, \epsilon, \delta)$ where $T : C \to C$ is a functor, $\epsilon : T \to id_C$, $\delta : T \to T^2$ are natural transformations, and the following equations hold:*

$$\epsilon_{TA} \circ \delta_A = id_{TA} \quad T\epsilon_A \circ \delta_A = id_{TA} \quad \delta_{TA} \circ \delta_A = T\delta_A \circ \delta_A.$$

*The following derived operation is useful. For all $f : TA \to B$, one constructs $\kappa(f) : TA \to TB$ as follows:*

$$\kappa(f) = Tf \circ \delta.$$

*We define the co-Kleisli category $cK_T$ (often simply called the Kleisli category) as follows. The objects of $cK_T$ are the objects of $C$, and for any $A, B$:*

$$cK_T[A, B] = C[TA, B].$$

*The identity morphisms are given by $\epsilon$, and composition $\circ_{cK}$ is defined by:*

$$g \circ_{cK} f = g \circ \kappa(f).$$

As with monads, every adjunction induces a comonad.

**Proposition 13.2.11** *Every adjunction $(F, G, \eta, \epsilon)$, where $F : C \to C'$ and $G : C' \to C$, induces a comonad $(F \circ G, \epsilon, \delta)$ on $C'$, where $\epsilon$ is the counit of the adjunction, and where $\delta = F\eta G$, i.e., $\delta_B = F(\eta_{GB})$ (for all $B$). The Kleisli category associated with the comonad is equivalent to the full subcategory of $C$ whose objects are in the image of $G$.*

We follow [Bar91b, See89] in our definition of a category allowing us to interpret linear logic. Recently, it was pointed out by Bierman that Seely's definition does not validate all the proof reduction rules one would wish for. He proposed a satisfactory definition of a model of intuitionistic linear logic. We refer to [Bie95] for details (see also remark 13.2.22). Here we stick to Seely's style of definition, which is simpler and good enough for introductory purposes.

**Definition 13.2.12 ($*_l$-autonomous category)** *A $*_l$-autonomous category is a structure consisting of the following data:*

(1) *A $*$-autonomous category $C_l$ which is at the same time cartesian.*

(2) *A comonad $(!, \epsilon, \delta)$ over $C_l$, called the exponential, together with two natural isomorphisms:*

$$!(A \times B) \cong (!A) \otimes (!B) \quad !1 \cong I.$$

**Remark 13.2.13** *If $C_l$ is a symmetric monoidal closed category that is not equipped with a dualizing object but has the rest of the structure of a $*_l$-autonomous category, then we can still interpret in it the connectives $-\circ, I, \otimes, 1, \times, !$ that constitute intuitionistic linear logic.*

**Remark 13.2.14** *It is often the case that the comonad $!$ is defined via an adjunction $F \dashv G$ between two functors $F : C \to C_l$ and $G : C_l \to C$. By proposition 13.2.11, if each object of $C$ is isomorphic to some object in the image of $G$, then the Kleisli category associated with the comonad is equivalent to $C$. This is a fortiori the case when $G$ is the (surjective) identity on objects, as in the stable model.*

We examine some consequences of our definition of $*_l$-autonomous category.

**Proposition 13.2.15** *If $C_l$ is a $*_l$-autonomous category, then the associated co-Kleisli (Kleisli for short) category, which we denote $C$, is cartesian closed.*

PROOF. As product on objects and as pairing of arrows we take the product on objects and the pairing of arrows of $C_l$. As projections we take $\pi_1 \circ \epsilon$ and $\pi_2 \circ \epsilon$. We check one commutation diagram:

$$(\pi_1 \circ \epsilon) \circ_{cK} \langle f, f' \rangle = \pi_1 \circ (\epsilon \circ \kappa(\langle f, f' \rangle))$$
$$= \pi_1 \circ \langle f, f' \rangle = f .$$

Next we define $A \to B = (!A)-\circ B$. The natural bijections are obtained via the following chain (recall that we write $C$ for the Kleisli category):

$$C[A \times B, C] = C_l[!(A \times B), C] \cong C_l[(!A) \otimes (!B), C]$$
$$\cong C_l[!A, (!B)-\circ C] = C_l[!A, B \to C]$$
$$= C[A, B \to C] . \qquad \square$$

Conversely, the first of the natural isomorphisms of definition 13.2.12 is implied by the CCC structure of the Kleisli category.

**Proposition 13.2.10** *Let $C_l$ be a $*$-autonomous category which is at the same time cartesian, and which is equipped with a comonad $(!, \epsilon, \delta)$ such that the associated Kleisli category $C$ is cartesian closed. Then there exists a natural isomorphism from $(!A) \otimes (!B)$ to $!(A \times B)$.*

PROOF. Note first that the assumptions of the statement are slightly redundant since we have already seen that the cartesian structure on the Kleisli category is implied. Consider the following chain of transformations:

$$C_l[!(A \times B), !(A \times B)] = C[A \times B, !(A \times B)]$$
$$\cong C[A, B \to !(A \times B)]$$
$$= C_l[!A, (!B)-\circ !(A \times B)]$$
$$\cong C_l[(!A) \otimes (!B), !(A \times B)] .$$

We obtain the desired arrow from $(!A) \otimes (!B)$ to $!(A \times B)$ as the image of $id : !(A \times B) \to !(A \times B)$. The arrow in the other direction is constructed similarly. $\square$

Another implied structure is that each object of the form $!A$ is endowed with the structure of a comonoid: there are two arrows

$$e : !A \to I \qquad d : !A \to (!A) \otimes (!A)$$

satisfying the three (categorical versions of the) comonoid laws (see exercise 13.2.17). These arrows are constructed as follows:

$$e \cong !(!_A) \qquad (\text{where } !_A : A \to 1)$$
$$d \cong !(\langle id, id \rangle),$$

where $\cong$ is to be read as 'composition with the isomorphisms $!1 \cong I$ and $!(A \times A) \cong (!A) \otimes (!A)$'.

**Exercise 13.2.17** *Let $d$ and $e$ be as just defined. Show that the following equations are satisfied:*

$$\iota_l \circ (e \otimes id) \circ d = id \qquad \iota_r \circ (id \otimes e) \circ d = id$$
$$\alpha \circ (id \otimes d) \circ d = (d \otimes id) \circ d \qquad \gamma \circ d = d.$$

This implicit comonoid structure may serve as a guide in constructing a $*_l$-autonomous category. Some authors have even insisted that $!$ should be a free comonoid construction. We content ourselves with the following exercise and remark.

**Exercise 13.2.18** *Show that, for any symmetric monoidal category $\mathbf{C}_l$, the category $\mathbf{Com}(\mathbf{C}_l)$ whose objects are comonoids $(A, d, e)$ over $\mathbf{C}_l$ and whose morphisms are comonoid morphisms (i.e., morphisms of $\mathbf{C}_l$ which commute with $d, e$ in the obvious sense) is cartesian, and that the forgetful functor $U : \mathbf{Com}(\mathbf{C}_l) \to \mathbf{C}_l$ maps products to tensor products.*

**Remark 13.2.19** *Exercise 13.2.18 suggests a 'recipe' for constructing a $*_l$-autonomous category out of a cartesian and $*$-autonomous category $\mathbf{C}_l$.*

• *Focus on an appropriate (full) subcategory $\mathbf{C}$ of $\mathbf{Com}(\mathbf{C}_l)$ which has the same products as $\mathbf{Com}(\mathbf{C}_l)$.*

• *Construct an adjunction of the form $U \vdash G$ between $\mathbf{C}$ and $\mathbf{Com}(\mathbf{C}_l)$, where $U$ is the restriction of the forgetful functor to $\mathbf{C}$.*

*Then, setting $! = U \circ G$, the natural isomorphism $!(A \times B) \cong (!A) \otimes (!B)$ comes for free:*

$$G(A \times B) \cong G(A) \times G(B) \qquad \text{(right adjoints preserve limits)}$$
$$U(G(A) \times G(B)) = (U(G(A)) \otimes (U(G(B))) \qquad \text{(cf. exercise 13.2.18)}.$$

We next complete the work of section 13.1 and show that coherence spaces form a $*_l$-autonomous category.

**Proposition 13.2.20** *The category $\mathbf{Coh}_l$ together with the comonad on $\mathbf{Coh}_l$ induced by the adjunction $! \dashv \subseteq$ is a $*_l$-autonomous category whose Kleisli category is equivalent to $\mathbf{Coh}$.*

PROOF. For the symmetric monoidal structure, we just notice that at the level of events the canonical isomorphisms are given by:

$$((e,e'),e'') \leftrightarrow (e,(e',e'')) \quad (e,*) \leftrightarrow e \quad (*,e) \leftrightarrow e \quad (e,e') \leftrightarrow (e',e) .$$

There is a natural bijection $\mathbf{Coh}_l[I,E] \cong D(E)$, since $(*,e_1) \frown (*,e_2)$ boils down to $e_1 \frown e_2$. Hence we have:

$$\begin{aligned} \mathbf{Coh}_l[I,(E \otimes E'^{\perp})^{\perp}] &\cong D(E \otimes E'^{\perp})^{\perp}) \\ &= D(E \multimap E') \\ &\cong \mathbf{Coh}_l[E,E'] \quad \text{(by proposition 13.1.8)} . \end{aligned}$$

Then the closed structure follows from proposition 13.2.8.

To see that $\mathbf{Coh}_l$ is $*$-autonomous, we set $\perp = I^{\perp} (= I)$, and we observe the trace of $\Lambda_l(ev_l \circ \gamma) : A \to (A \multimap \perp) \multimap \perp$, which is $\{(e,((e,*),*)) \mid e \in E\}$. It has as inverse the function whose trace is $\{(((e,*),*),e) \mid e \in E\}$.

That $\mathbf{Coh}$ is equivalent to the Kleisli category follows from remark 13.2.14. We are left to verify the two natural isomorphisms. The first one holds by proposition 13.2.16. For the second one, notice that $D(1)$ is a singleton. □

**Exercise 13.2.21** *Show that the transformations $\epsilon$ and $\delta$ associated with the comonad $! \circ \subseteq$ on $\mathbf{Coh}_l$ are the following functions:*

$$\epsilon(X) = \{c \mid \{c\} \in X\} \quad \delta(X) = \{Y \mid \bigcup Y \in X\} .$$

**Interpretation of linear logic proofs.** Finally, we sketch the interpretation of the sequents of linear logic in a $*_l$-autonomous category $\mathbf{C}_l$. A proof of a sequent $\vdash A_1, \ldots, A_n$ is interpreted by a morphism $f : I \to (A_1 \wp \ldots \wp A_n)$ (confusing the formulas with their interpretations as objects of $\mathbf{C}_l$). The rules are interpreted as follows:

$(I)$ $\vdash I$ is interpreted by $id : I \to I$.

$(\perp)$ Obvious, since $\perp$ is the dual of $I$ (cf. proposition 13.2.7).

$(\otimes)$ If $f : I \to (A \wp \Gamma)$ and $g : I \to (B \wp \Delta)$, then by the isomorphisms $A \wp \Gamma \cong \Gamma \wp A \cong \Gamma^{\perp} \multimap A$ (and similarly $B \wp \Delta \cong \Delta^{\perp} \multimap B$) and by uncurrying, we can consider $f : \Gamma^{\perp} \to A$ and $g : \Delta^{\perp} \to B$. Then we form $f \otimes g : \Gamma^{\perp} \otimes \Delta^{\perp} \to A \otimes B$ which by similar manipulations can be considered as a morphism from $I$ to $(A \otimes B) \wp (\Gamma^{\perp} \otimes \Delta^{\perp})^{\perp} \cong (A \otimes B) \wp (\Gamma \wp \Delta)$.

$(\wp)$ Obvious by associativity of $\wp$.

$(Axiom)$ Since $A \wp A^{\perp} \cong A \multimap A$, we interpret $\vdash A, A^{\perp}$ by the currying of the identity considered as from $I \otimes A$ to $A$.

$(Cut)$ Similar to $(\otimes)$: from $f : I \to (A \wp \Gamma)$ and $g : I \to (A^{\perp} \wp \Delta)$ we get $ev_l \circ \gamma \circ (f \otimes g) : \Gamma^{\perp} \otimes \Delta^{\perp} \to \perp$, which we can read as a morphism from $I$ to $(\Gamma \wp \Delta) \wp \perp \cong \Gamma \wp \Delta$.

$(Exchange)$ By associativity and commutativity.

$(1)$ Interpreting $\vdash 1 \wp \Gamma$ amounts to giving an arrow from $\Gamma^{\perp}$ to 1. Since 1 is terminal, we take the unique such arrow.

($\times$)  The pairing of $f : I \to (A \wp \Gamma)$ and $g : I \to (B \wp \Gamma)$ yields $\langle f, g \rangle : \Gamma^{\perp} \to (A \times B)$.

($\oplus$)  Given $f : I \to (A \wp \Gamma)$, we build $f \circ \pi_1 : A^{\perp} \times B^{\perp} \to \Gamma$, which we can consider as a morphism from $I$ to $(A \oplus B) \wp \Gamma$.

(*Dereliction*)  Given $f : I \to (A \wp \Gamma)$, we build $f \circ \epsilon : !(A^{\perp}) \to \Gamma$, where $\epsilon$ is the first natural transformation of the comonad.

(*Weakening*)  For this case and the following one, we use the comonoid structure induced on $!A$. Let $f : I \to \Gamma$. Then we can consider that $f \circ e = !(A^{\perp}) \to \Gamma$ is a proof of $\vdash ?A, \Gamma$.

(*Contraction*)  This case is similar to the case (*Weakening*), replacing $e$ by $d$.

(*Promotion*)  Let $f : I \to (A \wp ?B_1 \wp \ldots \wp ?B_n)$, which we can consider as an arrow from $!(B_1^{\perp} \times \ldots \times B_n^{\perp})$ to $A$. Here we have made an essential use of the natural isomorphisms required in the definition of $*_l$-autonomous category. Then we can consider $\kappa(f) : !(B_1^{\perp} \times \ldots \times B_n^{\perp}) \to !A$ as a proof of $\vdash !A, ?B_1, \ldots, ?B_n$.

**Remark 13.2.22**  (1)  *Proposition 13.2.16 deals only with the first natural isomorphism of the definition of $*_l$-autonomous category. It would be more agreeable to have the other natural isomorphism $!1 \cong I$ implied as well. However, the categorical structure considered here is not rich enough to provide us with an arrow from $I$ to $!1$.*

(2)  *The interpretation given above for the rule (Promotion) makes use of products. This is a bit odd since linear logic without additive connectives, but with exponentials, is interesting enough.*

*These anomalies are repaired in the setting of [Bie95].*

**Remark 13.2.23**  *In some models, like the sequential model presented in chapter 14, the terminal object is the unit. Then we can define projections $\pi_1 : A \otimes B \to A$ and $\pi_2 : A \otimes B \to B$ as follows. One goes, say, from $A \otimes B$ to $A \otimes 1$ (using the fact that 1 is terminal) and then to $A$ by a coherent isomorphism. A consequence is that the usual weakening rule*

$$\frac{\vdash \Gamma}{\vdash A, \Gamma}$$

*is valid. Indeed, given $f : I \to \Gamma$, we build $f \circ \pi_1 : I \otimes A^{\perp} \to \Gamma$. Intuitionistic linear logic (cf. remark 13.2.13) plus weakening is called the intuitionistic affine logic.*

## 13.3  Hypercoherences and strong stability *

In this section, we investigate Ehrhard's hypercoherences [Ehr93]. The theory as presented here starts as a variation on the theme of coherence spaces. A hypercoherence is given by a set $E$ of events, and a collection $\Gamma$ of non-empty finite subsets of events in place of a coherence relation. A key point is that $\Gamma$ need not be downward closed, which makes these structures differ quite radically from, say, qualitative domains (cf. definition 12.3.11). The morphisms between hypercoherences, called the (linear and) strongly stable functions, are closely related to sequential functions (cf. section 6.5) and sequential algorithms (see the remarks at the end of section 14.3). The basic connection with sequentiality is established through theorem 13.3.18, which states that strongly stable functions coincide with sequential functions at first order types.

We first define hypercoherences. Then we introduce the exponent of two hypercoherences, leading to a simple concrete definition of morphism. We define a linear category of hypercoherences and show that it is cartesian. We pause to show the connection with sequential functions, and then complete the construction of the $*_l$-autonomous category of hypercoherences.

**Definition 13.3.1 (hypercoherence)** *A hypercoherence is a pair* $(E, \Gamma)$, *where* $E$ *is a set, called the web of* $E$, *and where* $\Gamma$ *is a subset of* $\mathcal{P}_{fin}^{+}(E)$, *called the* atomic coherence *(or simply coherence), such that for any* $a \in E$, $\{a\} \in \Gamma$. *We write* $\Gamma^{*} = \{u \in \Gamma \mid \sharp u > 1\}$, *and call* $\Gamma^{*}$ *the strict atomic coherence. If needed from the context, we write* $\Gamma = \Gamma(E)$. *A hypercoherence is called a* hereditary *if*

$$\forall u \in \Gamma, v \ (v \subseteq u \ and \ v \neq \emptyset) \Rightarrow v \in \Gamma .$$

*A state of a hypercoherence* $(E, \Gamma)$ *is a set* $x \subseteq E$ *such that:*

$$\forall u \subseteq_{fin}^{*} x \ u \in \Gamma,$$

*where* $u \subseteq_{fin}^{*} x$ *means that* $u$ *is a finite and non-empty subset of* $x$. *We call* $D(E)$ *the set of states of* $E$, *ordered by inclusion.*

**Proposition 13.3.2** *Let* $(E, \Gamma)$ *be a hypercoherence. The poset* $D(E)$, *ordered by inclusion, is a qualitative domain (cf. definition 12.3.11), whose compact elements are the finite states.*

PROOF. We observe that singletons are states, and that the definition of state enforces that $(u \in \mathcal{K}(D(E))$ and $v \subseteq u)$ imply $v \in \mathcal{K}(D(E))$. □

**Remark 13.3.3** *Since any qualitative domain can be obviously viewed as a hereditary hypercoherence, we can say in view of proposition 13.3.2 that qualitative domains and hereditary hypercoherences are the same (see proposition 13.3.13). But of course there are more hypercoherences than those arising naturally from qualitative domains (see in particular definition 13.3.16).*

The atomic coherence also gives rise to a collection of distinguished sets of states, enjoying some interesting closure properties. They will allow us to get a more abstract view of the morphisms of the hypercoherence model, in the same way as linear or stable functions are more abstract than their representing traces. We need a technical definition.

**Definition 13.3.4 (multisection)** *Let* $E$ *be a set, and let* $u \subseteq E$ *and* $A \subseteq \mathcal{P}(E)$. *We write* $u \triangleleft A$, *and say that* $u$ *is a multisection of* $A$, *iff*

$$(\forall e \in u \ \exists x \in A \ e \in x) \quad and \quad (\forall x \in A \ \exists e \in u \ e \in x).$$

**Remark 13.3.5** *If both* $u$ *and* $A$ *are finite,* $u \triangleleft A$ *holds exactly when we can find a list of pairs* $(e_1, x_1), \ldots, (e_n, x_n)$ *such that* $e_i \in x_i$ *for all* $i$, *and:*

$$u = \{e_i \mid 1 \leq i \leq n\} \quad A = \{x_i \mid 1 \leq i \leq n\}.$$

**Definition 13.3.6 (state coherence)** *Let* $(E, \Gamma)$ *be a hypercoherence. We define a set* $C(E) \subseteq \mathcal{P}^+_{fin}(D(E))$, *called the state coherence of* $(E, \Gamma)$, *as follows:*

$$C(E) = \{A \subseteq^*_{fin} D(E) \mid \forall u \subseteq^*_{fin} E \ u \lhd A \Rightarrow u \in \Gamma\}.$$

We recall the convex ordering from theorem 9.1.6. Given a partial order $D$ and two subsets $B, A$ of $D$, we write $B \leq_c A$ for

$$(\forall y \in B \ \exists x \in A \ y \leq x) \quad \text{and} \quad (\forall x \in A \ \exists y \in B \ y \leq x).$$

(Notice that this obeys the same pattern as the definition of $\lhd$.)

**Lemma 13.3.7** *Let* $(E, \Gamma)$ *be a hypercoherence. The state coherence* $C(E)$ *satisfies the following properties:*

(1) *If* $x \in D(E)$, *then* $\{x\} \in C(E)$.

(2) *If* $A \in C(E)$ *and* $B \leq_c A$, *then* $B \in C(E)$.

(3) *If* $A \subseteq^*_{fin} D(E)$ *has an upper bound in* $D(E)$, *then* $A \in C(E)$.

(4) *If* $A \subseteq^*_{fin} D(E)$ *and* $\emptyset \in A$, *then* $A \in C(E)$.

PROOF. (1) If $u \lhd \{x\}$, then half of the definition of $\lhd$ says $u \subseteq x$, and $u \in \Gamma$ then follows by definition of a state.

(2) Let $A \in C(E)$, $B \leq_c A$, and $u \lhd B$. It follows from the definitions of $\leq_c$ and $\lhd$ that $u \lhd A$, and from $A \in C(E)$ that $u \in \Gamma$.

(3) This follows from (1) and (2), since we can express that $A$ has an upper bound $z$ as $A \leq_c \{z\}$.

(4) If $\emptyset \in A$, then we cannot find a $u$ such that $u \lhd A$, and the condition characterizing $A \in C(E)$ holds vacuously. □

**Lemma 13.3.8** *If* $(E, \Gamma)$ *is a hereditary hypercoherence, then:*

$$A \in C(E) \quad \Leftrightarrow \quad (\emptyset \in A) \text{ or } (A \text{ is bounded}).$$

PROOF. The direction ($\Leftarrow$) holds in any hypercoherence, by lemma 13.3.7. Suppose conversely that $A \in C(E)$, $\emptyset \notin A$, and $A$ is not bounded , i.e. $\bigcup A$ is not a state. Then there exists $u \subseteq^*_{fin} \bigcup A$ which is not in the atomic coherence $\Gamma$. Let $v$ be such that $u \subseteq v$ and $v \lhd A$ (such a $v$ exists, since $\emptyset \notin A$). We reach a contradiction as follows:

$$v \in \Gamma \quad \text{(by definition of the state coherence)}$$
$$u \in \Gamma \quad \text{(by heredity)} .$$

□

**Definition 13.3.9 (strongly stable)** *Let* $(E, \Gamma)$ *and* $(E', \Gamma')$ *be hypercoherences. A continuous function* $f : D(E) \to D(E')$ *is called strongly stable from* $(E, \Gamma)$ *to* $(E', \Gamma')$ *if*

$$\forall A \in C(E) \ (f(A) \in C(E') \text{ and } f(\bigwedge A) = \bigwedge f(A)).$$

*We call* **HCoh** *the category of hypercoherences and strongly stable functions.*

Strongly stable functions are to form (up to equivalence) the Kleisli category of our model. We turn to the definition of a cartesian linear category.

**Definition 13.3.10 (linear exponent – hypercoherences)** *Given two hypercoherences* $(E, \Gamma)$, $(E', \Gamma')$, *the linear exponent* $E \multimap E'$ *is the hypercoherence whose events are the pairs* $(e, e')$ *where* $e \in E$ *and* $e' \in E'$, *and whose atomic coherence consists of the finite non-empty* $w$'s *such that:*

$$\pi_1(w) \in \Gamma \Rightarrow (\pi_2(w) \in \Gamma' \text{ and } (\sharp\pi_2(w) = 1 \Rightarrow \sharp\pi_1(w) = 1)),$$

*where* $\pi_1$, $\pi_2$ *are projection functions, i.e., say,* $\pi_1(w) = \{e \mid \exists e' \ (e, e') \in w\}$.

**Definition 13.3.11** *The category* $\mathbf{HCoh}_l$ *is the category whose objects are hypercoherences, and whose morphisms are given by:*

$$\mathbf{HCoh}_l[E, E'] = D(E \multimap E'),$$

*for all* $E, E'$, *with identity relations and relation composition as identities and composition.*

**Proposition 13.3.12** *The data of definition 13.3.11 indeed define a category.*

PROOF. The only non-obvious property to check is that the relation composition of two states is a state. Suppose thus that $(E, \Gamma)$, $(E', \Gamma')$, and $(E'', \Gamma'')$ are given, as well as $\phi \in D(E \multimap E')$ and $\phi' \in D(E' \multimap E'')$. We first claim that if $(e, e'') \in \phi' \circ \phi$, then there exists a unique $e' \in E'$ such that $(e, e') \in \phi$ and $(e', e'') \in \phi'$. Let $w'$ be a finite non-empty subset of $W' = \{e' \mid (e, e') \in \phi \text{ and } (e', e'') \in \phi'\}$ $(e, e''$ fixed). Considering $\{(e, e') \mid e' \in w'\}$, we obtain that $w' \in \Gamma'$ since $\{e\} \in \Gamma$. Then, considering $\{(c', c'') \mid c' \subset w'\}$, we get $\sharp w' = 1$ since $\sharp\{c''\} = 1$. Therefore $W'$ is also a singleton. Now let $w$ be a finite non-empty subset of $\phi' \circ \phi$ such that $\pi_1(w) \in \Gamma$. Consider:

$$
\begin{aligned}
u &= \{(e, e') \in \phi \mid \exists e'' \ (e', e'') \in \phi' \text{ and } (e, e'') \in w\} \\
v &= \{(e', e'') \in \phi' \mid \exists e \ (e, e') \in \phi \text{ and } (e, e'') \in w\}.
\end{aligned}
$$

The claim implies that $u$ and $v$ are finite. We have $\pi_1(u) = \pi_1(w)$ by definition of $u$ and of $\phi' \circ \phi$. It follows that $\pi_2(u) \in \Gamma'$ since we have assumed $\pi_1(w) \in \Gamma$. But $\pi_2(u) = \pi_1(v)$, hence $\pi_2(w) = \pi_2(v) \in \Gamma''$. If, furthermore, $\sharp\pi_2(w) = 1$, then $\sharp\pi_1(v) = 1 = \sharp\pi_2(u)$, and $\sharp\pi_1(u) = 1 = \sharp\pi_1(w)$. □

**Proposition 13.3.13** (1) *The category* $\mathbf{HCoh}_l$ *is equivalent to the category of hypercoherences and linear and strongly stable functions.*[3]

(2) *The full subcategory of* $\mathbf{HCoh}_l$ *whose objects are the hereditary hypercoherences is equivalent to the category of qualitative domains and linear functions.*

PROOF. (1) This is proved as in the stable case (cf. proposition 13.1.8).

(2) We have already observed (remark 13.3.3) that at the level of objects qualitative domains are the same as hereditary hypercoherences. Suppose that $(E, \Gamma)$ and $(E', \Gamma')$ are hereditary hypercoherences. We show that $f : D(E) \to D(E')$ is linear and strongly stable iff it is linear. We only have to check that (under the hereditarity assumptions) 'linear implies strongly stable'. If $f$ is linear and $A \in \mathcal{C}(E)$, there are two cases, by lemma 13.3.8:

- $\emptyset \in A$. Then, by linearity, $\emptyset \in f(A)$ (hence $f(A) \in \mathcal{C}(E')$), and:

$$f(\bigwedge A) = f(\emptyset) = \emptyset = \bigwedge f(A).$$

- $A$ is bounded. Then $f(A)$ is bounded, and $f(\bigwedge A) = \bigwedge f(A)$ by stability. □

---

[3]Notice that this is slightly redundant, since the preservation of bounded glb's, which is part of our definition of linear function (cf. definition 13.1.7) is a consequence of strong stability.

**Proposition 13.3.14 (product – hypercoherences)** *The category* $\mathbf{HCoh}_l$ *is cartesian. If* $(E,\Gamma)$ *and* $(E',\Gamma')$ *are hypercoherences, their product* $E \times E'$ *is defined as follows:*

- *Events are either* $e.1$ *where* $e \in E$ *or* $e'.2$ *where* $e' \in E'$.

- *The atomic coherence consists of the (finite non-empty) subsets* $w$ *such that:*

$$(w\lceil_E = \emptyset \Rightarrow w\lceil_{E'} \in \Gamma') \text{ and } (w\lceil_{E'} = \emptyset \Rightarrow w\lceil_E \in \Gamma),$$

*where, say,* $w\lceil_E = \{e \mid e.1 \in w\}$. *We have:*

$$
\begin{aligned}
D(E \times E') &\cong D(E) \times D(E') \\
A \in \mathcal{C}(E \times E') &\Leftrightarrow (A\lceil_E \in \mathcal{C}(E) \text{ and } A\lceil_{E'} \in \mathcal{C}(E')),
\end{aligned}
$$

*where, say,* $A\lceil_E = \{x\lceil_E \mid x \in A\}$. *The terminal object is the empty hypercoherence.*

PROOF. The projection morphisms and pairing are given by:

$$
\begin{aligned}
\pi_1 &= \{(e.1, e) \mid e \in E\} \\
\pi_2 &= \{(e'.2, e') \mid e' \in E'\} \\
\langle \phi, \phi' \rangle &= \{(e'', e.1) \mid (e'', e) \in \phi\} \cup \{(e'', e'.2) \mid (e'', e') \in \phi'\}.
\end{aligned}
$$

The only point which requires care is the verification that $\langle \phi, \phi' \rangle$ is a morphism. Let $w \subseteq^*_{fin} \langle \phi, \phi' \rangle$ be such that $\pi_1(w) \in \Gamma''$. Notice that, in order to tell something about $\pi_2(w)\lceil_E$, we are led to consider $w_E = \{(e'', e) \mid (e'', e.1) \in w\}$. If $\pi_1(w_E)$ is a strict subset of $\pi_1(w)$, we don't know whether $\pi_1(w_E)$ is in the atomic coherence of $E$, unless $(E,\Gamma)$ is hereditary (see remark 13.3.15). These considerations should help to understand the definition of $\Gamma(E \times E')$. Indeed, all we have to check is that if $\pi_2(w)\lceil_{E'} = \emptyset$ then $\pi_2(w)\lceil_E \in \Gamma$ (the other implication being proved similarly). The assumption $\pi_2(w)\lceil_{E'} = \emptyset$ implies $w = w_E$, and:

$$
\begin{aligned}
\pi_1(w_E) &\in \Gamma'' &&(\text{since } \pi_1(w) \in \Gamma'') \\
\pi_2(w)\lceil_E &= \pi_2(w_E) \in \Gamma &&(\text{since } w_E \subseteq^*_{fin} \phi).
\end{aligned}
$$

If moreover $\sharp \pi_2(w) = 1$, then, say, $\pi_2(w) = \{e.1\}$, hence $\pi_2(w_E) = \{e\}$, which entails $\sharp \pi_1(w_E) = 1$, and $\sharp \pi_1(w) = 1$ since $\pi_2(w) = \{e.1\}$ a fortiori implies $\pi_2(w)\lceil_{E'} = \emptyset$.

We show that $\lambda x.(x\lceil_E, x\lceil_{E'})$ defines a bijection (actually an order-isomorphism) from $D(E \times E')$ to $D(E) \times D(E')$. All what we have to do is to show that this mapping and its inverse indeed have $D(E) \times D(E')$ and $D(E \times E')$ as codomains, respectively. This follows easily from the following observation (and from the similar observation relative to $E'$):

$$\forall u \subseteq^*_{fin} x\lceil_E \quad (u \in \Gamma \Leftrightarrow \{e.1 \mid e \in u\} \in \Gamma(E \times E')).$$

The same observation serves to prove the characterization of $\mathcal{C}(E \times E')$, since in order to check that $A \in \mathcal{C}(E \times E')$, we need only to consider $u$'s such that either $u\lceil_E = \emptyset$ or $u\lceil_{E'} = \emptyset$. $\qquad\square$

**Remark 13.3.15** *The cartesian product of two hereditary hypercoherences is not hereditary in general. Indeed, given any finite* $u \subseteq E$ *and* $u' \subseteq E'$, *where, say,* $u \notin \Gamma(E)$, *we have* $\{e.1 \mid e \in u\} \cup \{e'.2 \mid e' \in u'\} \in \Gamma(E \times E')$ *as soon as both* $u$ *and* $u'$ *are non-empty, but* $\{e.1 \mid e \in u\} \notin \Gamma(E \times E')$. *(See also proposition 13.3.17.)*

*The full subcategory of hereditary hypercoherences, being equivalent to that of qualitative domains, has a product, though, which is given by the same set of events, but a different atomic coherence, consisting of the* $w$ *'s such that:*

$$w\lceil_E \in \Gamma \text{ and } w\lceil_{E'} \in \Gamma'.$$

The product structure on $\mathbf{HCoh}_l$ gives rise to an interesting class of hypercoherences, which are the key to the link between sequentiality and strong stability, and which are therefore at the root of the theory of hypercoherences and strong stability. Coherence spaces $(E, \bigcirc)$ are special qualitative domains, and can therefore be seen as hereditary hypercoherences. But they can also be endowed with another hypercoherence structure, which we define next.

**Definition 13.3.16** (1) *Let* $(E, \bigcirc)$ *be a coherence space. It induces a hypercoherence* $(E, \Gamma_L)$, *called the* linear hypercoherence, *where:*

$$\Gamma_L^* = \{u \subseteq_{fin}^* E \mid \exists e_1, e_2 \in u \ (e_1 \neq e_2 \ and \ e_1 \bigcirc e_2)\}.$$

(2) *Let* $X$ *be a set. The hereditary hypercoherence* $X_\perp = (X, \{\{x\} \mid x \in X\})$ *is called the* flat hypercoherence *associated to* $X$. *Clearly,* $D(X_\perp) = X_\perp$, *whence the name and the notation (cf. example 1.1.6).*

**Proposition 13.3.17** *Let* $E_1, \ldots, E_n$ *be flat hypercoherences. Let* $E$ *be the product of* $E_1, \ldots, E_n$ *in the category of coherence spaces. Then* $(E, \Gamma_L)$ *is the product of* $E_1, \ldots, E_n$ *in* $\mathbf{HCoh}_l$.

PROOF. Consider a product of, say, three flat hypercoherences $E_1$, $E_2$, and $E_3$. By definition, the product hypercoherence consists of those $w$'s such that:

$$(w_1 \neq \emptyset \ \text{or} \ w_2 \neq \emptyset \ \text{or} \ \sharp w_3 = 1) \ \text{and}$$
$$(w_1 \neq \emptyset \ \text{or} \ w_3 \neq \emptyset \ \text{or} \ \sharp w_2 = 1) \ \text{and}$$
$$(w_2 \neq \emptyset \ \text{or} \ w_3 \neq \emptyset \ \text{or} \ \sharp w_1 = 1) ,$$

writing $w_i$ for $w \lceil_{E_i}$. Under the assumption $\sharp w > 1$, we have, say:

$$(w_1 \neq \emptyset \ \text{or} \ w_2 \neq \emptyset \ \text{or} \ \sharp w_3 = 1) \quad \Rightarrow \quad (w_1 \neq \emptyset \ \text{or} \ w_2 \neq \emptyset) ,$$

hence the strict coherence of the product consists of the $w$'s such that:

$$(w_1 \neq \emptyset \ \text{or} \ w_2 \neq \emptyset) \ \text{and}$$
$$(w_1 \neq \emptyset \ \text{or} \ w_3 \neq \emptyset) \ \text{and}$$
$$(w_2 \neq \emptyset \ \text{or} \ w_3 \neq \emptyset) ,$$

or (generalizing from 3 to $n$):

$$\exists i, j \leq n \ i \neq j \ \text{and} \ (w_i \neq \emptyset \ \text{and} \ w_j \neq \emptyset),$$

which by proposition 13.1.3 and by definition is the linear coherence on $E$.  $\square$

We have now all the ingredients to show where strong stability comes from.

**Theorem 13.3.18** *Suppose that* $E_1, \ldots, E_n, E$ *are flat hypercoherences. A function* $f :$ $D(E_1) \times \cdots \times D(E_n) \to D(E)$ *is sequential iff it is strongly stable from* $(E_1 \times \cdots \times E_n, \Gamma_L)$ *to* $E$.

PROOF. By proposition 13.3.17, $(E_1 \times \cdots \times E_n, \Gamma_L)$ is the product $E_1 \times \cdots \times E_n$ in $\mathbf{HCoh}_l$. Hence, by proposition 13.3.14:

$$A \in \mathcal{C}_L \Leftrightarrow \forall i \in \{1, \ldots, n\} \ A \lceil_{E_i} \in \mathcal{C}(E_i),$$

where $\mathcal{C}_L$ is the state coherence associated with $\Gamma_L$. If $A = \{x_1, \ldots, x_k\}$ and $x_j = (x_{1j}, \ldots, x_{nj})$ for all $j \leq k$, then by lemma 13.3.8 we can rephrase this as:

$$\{x_1, \ldots, x_k\} \in \mathcal{C}_L$$
$$\Leftrightarrow \quad \forall i \in \{1, \ldots, n\} \ (\exists j \leq k \ x_{ij} = \bot) \text{ or } (x_{i1} = \cdots = x_{ik} \neq \bot).$$

On the other hand, by theorem 6.5.4, $f$ is sequential iff it is invariant under the relations $S_{k+1}$ defined by:

$$(x_1, \ldots, x_{k+1}) \in S_{k+1} \quad \Leftrightarrow \quad (\exists j \leq k \ x_j = \bot) \text{ or } (x_1 = \ldots = x_{k+1} \neq \bot).$$

The conclusion then follows from the following easy observations:

- $(x_{i1}, \ldots, x_{i(k+1)}) \in S_{k+1}$ may be rephrased as $(x_{i1}, \ldots, x_{ik}) \in \mathcal{C}(E_i)$ and $\bigwedge_{1 \leq j \leq k} x_{ij} \leq x_{i(k+1)}$, hence:

$$(x_1, \ldots, x_{k+1}) \in S_{k+1}^n \Leftrightarrow (x_1, \ldots, x_k) \in \mathcal{C}_L \text{ and } \bigwedge_{1 \leq j \leq k} x_j \leq x_{k+1}.$$

- $f(\bigwedge A) = \bigwedge f(A)$ can be rephrased as $\forall x \ \bigwedge f(A) \leq \bigwedge A \Rightarrow f(x) \leq x$. $\quad\square$

We now continue the investigation of $\mathbf{HCoh}_l$ and show that it can be turned into a $*_l$-autonomous category.

**Lemma 13.3.19** *In $E \multimap E' = E''$, the following equivalences hold (and thus may alternatively serve as the definition of atomic coherence):*

(1) $w \in \Gamma'' \quad \Leftrightarrow \quad (\pi_1(w) \in \Gamma \Rightarrow \pi_2(w) \in \Gamma') \text{ and } (\pi_1(w) \in \Gamma^* \Rightarrow \pi_2(w) \in \Gamma'^*)$
(2) $w \in \Gamma''^* \quad \Leftrightarrow \quad \pi_1(w) \notin \Gamma \text{ or } \pi_2(w) \in \Gamma'^*$.

PROOF. The equivalence (1) is just a rephrasing of the equivalence given in definition 13.3.10. By Boolean manipulations, we get successively:

right hand side of (1)

$$\Leftrightarrow \quad \left\{ \begin{array}{l} (\pi_1(w) \notin \Gamma \text{ and } (\pi_1(w) \notin \Gamma^* \text{ or } \pi_2(w) \in \Gamma'^*)) \text{ or} \\ (\pi_2(w) \in \Gamma' \text{ and } (\pi_1(w) \notin \Gamma^* \text{ or } \pi_2(w) \in \Gamma'^*)) \end{array} \right.$$

$$\Leftrightarrow \quad \pi_1(w) \notin \Gamma \text{ or } \pi_2(w) \in \Gamma'^* \text{ or } (\pi_2(w) \in \Gamma' \text{ and } \pi_1(w) \notin \Gamma^*).$$

Now we suppose that $\sharp w > 1$. Then either $\sharp \pi_1(w) > 1$ or $\sharp \pi_2(w) > 1$. If $\sharp \pi_2(w) > 1$, then $\pi_2(w) \in \Gamma'$ is the same as $\pi_2(w) \in \Gamma'^*$. Similarly, if $\sharp \pi_2(w) > 1$, then $\pi_1(w) \notin \Gamma^*$ is the same as $\pi_1(w) \notin \Gamma$, Hence, under the assumption $\sharp w > 1$:

$$(\pi_2(w) \in \Gamma' \text{ and } \pi_1(w) \notin \Gamma^*) \Rightarrow (\pi_1(w) \notin \Gamma \text{ or } \pi_2(w) \in \Gamma'^*),$$

and the right hand side of (1) boils down to the right hand side of (2), which completes the proof. $\quad\square$

As in the stable case, the equivalence (2) of lemma 13.3.19 directly suggests a definition of tensor product and of linear negation.

**Definition 13.3.20 (tensor – hypercoherences)** *Let $(E, \Gamma)$ and $(E', \Gamma')$ be hypercoherences. Their tensor product $E \otimes E'$ is the hypercoherence whose web is $E \times E'$, and whose atomic coherence consists of the non-empty finite $w$'s such that $\pi_1(w) \in \Gamma$ and $\pi_2(w) \in \Gamma$.*

**Definition 13.3.21 (linear negation – hypercoherences)** *Let $(E, \Gamma)$ be a hypercoherence. The linear negation $E^\perp$ of $E$ is the hypercoherence whose web is $E$, and whose atomic coherence is $\mathcal{P}_{fin}^+(E)\backslash\Gamma^*$. Or, alternatively, $u \in \Gamma^*(E^\perp)$ iff $u \notin \Gamma(E)$.*

**Proposition 13.3.22** *The category $\mathbf{HCoh}_l$ is $*$-autonomous. Its unit is the unique hypercoherence whose web is the singleton $\{*\}$.*

PROOF. The proof is a straightforward adaptation of the proof of proposition 13.2.20. We even have $D((E \otimes E'^\perp)^\perp) = \mathbf{HCoh}_l[E, E']$.  $\square$

**Definition 13.3.23 (exponential – hypercoherences)** *Let $(E, \Gamma)$ be a hypercoherence. The exponential $!E$ is the hypercoherence whose events are the finite states of $E$ and whose atomic coherence is the state coherence of $E$.*

**Proposition 13.3.24** *The operation $!$ extends to a functor $! : \mathbf{HCoh} \to \mathbf{HCoh}_l$ which is left adjoint to the inclusion functor $\subseteq : \mathbf{HCoh}_l \to \mathbf{HCoh}$ defined as follows:*

$$\subseteq (E, \Gamma) = (E, \Gamma) \quad \subseteq (\phi) = fun(\phi) \ ,$$

*where $fun(\phi)(x) = \{e' \mid \exists e \ (e, e') \in \phi \text{ and } e \in x\}$.*

PROOF. We exhibit inverse bijections between $D(!E \multimap E')$ and $\mathbf{HCoh}[E, E']$. Given a strongly stable function $f$, we define:

$$trace(f) = \{(x, e') \mid e' \in f(x) \text{ and } (\forall y < x \ e' \notin f(x))\}.$$

Conversely, given $\phi \in D(!E \multimap E')$, we define:

$$fun(\phi)(x) = \{e' \mid \exists y \ (y, e') \in \phi \text{ and } y \subseteq x\}.$$

This definition of $fun$ extends that given in the statement, up to the identification of events $e$ with singletons $\{e\}$. Therefore, the subsequent proof also establishes that $\subseteq$ is well-defined. That $trace$ and $fun$ are inverses is proved exactly as in theorem 12.3.6. We prove that $trace$ and $fun$ are well-defined:

• $trace(f)$ is a state. Let $w_0 \subseteq_{fin}^* trace(f)$, and suppose that $\pi_1(w_0) \in \Gamma(!E) = \mathcal{C}(E)$. By definition of $trace$, $\pi_2(w_0) \vartriangleleft f(\pi_1(w_0))$. Hence $\pi_2(w_0) \in \Gamma'$, since $f(\pi_1(w_0)) \in \mathcal{C}(E')$. If, moreover, $\pi_2(w_0) = \{e'\}$, then $e' \in \bigwedge f(\pi_1(w_0)) = f(\bigwedge \pi_1(w_0))$. Let $z \leq \bigwedge \pi_1(w_0)$ be such that $(z, e') \in trace(f)$. Then, by minimality, $z$ is equal to each of the elements of $\pi_1(w_0)$.

• $fun(\phi)$ is strongly stable. First of all, we have to check that $fun(\phi)(x) \in D(E')$, for any finite $x \in D(E)$. Let $v_1 \subseteq_{fin}^* fun(\phi)(x)$. Let $w_1 = \{(z, e') \in \phi \mid z \subseteq x \text{ and } e' \in v_1\}$. By definition, $w_1$ is finite and non-empty. Hence $w_1 \in \Gamma(E \multimap E')$. We have $\pi_1(w_1) \in \Gamma(!E)$ since $\pi_1(w_1)$ is bounded. Hence $v_1 = \pi_2(w_1) \in \Gamma'$. Next we prove that $fun(\phi)$ is strongly stable. Let $A \in \mathcal{C}(E)$, and let $v_2 \vartriangleleft fun(\phi)(A)$. Let:

$$w_2 = \{(z, e') \in \phi \mid e' \in v_2 \text{ and } z \subseteq y \text{ for some } y \in A\},$$

and let $x \in A$. Since $v_2 \vartriangleleft fun(\phi)(A)$, there exists $e' \in v_2$ such that $e' \in fun(\phi)(x)$. Hence there exists $z \in \pi_1(w_2)$ such that $z \subseteq x$, by definition of $fun(\phi)$ and $w_2$. It follows that $\pi_1(w_2) \leq_c A$. Hence $\pi_1(w_2) \in \mathcal{C}(E)$ by lemma 13.3.7. This entails $v_2 = \pi_2(w_2) \in \Gamma'$. Hence $fun(\phi)(A) \in \mathcal{C}(E')$. Moreover, we show that $\bigwedge fun(\phi)(A) \leq fun(\phi)(\bigwedge A)$. Let $e' \in \bigwedge fun(\phi)(A)$, i.e., $\{e'\} \vartriangleleft fun(\phi)(A)$. Then, instantiating $v_2$ above as $v_2 = \{e'\}$ (and the corresponding $w_2$), we have $\sharp\pi_1(w_2) = 1$, since $\sharp\pi_2(w_2) = \sharp\{e'\} = 1$. Let $\pi_1(w_2) = \{x\}$. Then $x \leq A$ by definition of $w_2$, hence $e' \in fun(\phi)(x) \subseteq fun(\phi)(\bigwedge A)$. $\square$

**Proposition 13.3.25** *The category* $\mathbf{HCoh}_l$, *together with the comonad induced by the adjunction of proposition 13.3.24, is a* $*_l$*-autonomous category.*

PROOF. We are left to check the natural isomorphisms. The isomorphism $!1 \cong I$ is immediate as with coherence spaces. We check $!(E \times E') \cong (!E) \otimes (!E')$ (notice that we did not prove that $\mathbf{HCoh}$ is cartesian closed: this will rather follow as a corollary, cf. proposition 13.2.15). We have:

$$
\begin{aligned}
!(E \times E') &= \mathcal{K}(D(E \times E')) \\
&\cong \mathcal{K}(D(E) \times D(E')) \\
&= \mathcal{K}(D(E)) \times \mathcal{K}(D(E')) \\
&= !E \times !E' \\
&= (!E) \otimes (!E')
\end{aligned}
$$

and

$$
\begin{aligned}
A \in \Gamma(!(E \times E')) \;&\Leftrightarrow\; A \in \mathcal{C}(E \times E') \\
&\Leftrightarrow\; (A\lceil_E \in \mathcal{C}(E) \text{ and } A\lceil_{E'} \in \mathcal{C}(E')) \;\text{(by proposition 13.3.14)} \\
&\Leftrightarrow\; \{(z\lceil_E, z\lceil_{E'}) \mid z \in A\} \in \Gamma((!E) \otimes (!E')) \,.
\end{aligned}
$$

The inverse of $A \mapsto \{(z\lceil_E, z\lceil_{E'}) \mid z \in A\}$ is $B \mapsto \{x.1 \cup x'.2 \mid (x, x') \in B\}$. □

## 13.4 Bistructures *

Berry [Ber79] combined the stable approach and the continuous approach to domains by defining bidomains, which maintain extensionality and stability together, and thus offer an order-extensional account of stability (cf. sections 6.3 and 6.4). Berry's hope was to get 'closer' to the (order-extensional) fully abstract model of PCF (cf. section 6.4); we refer the reader to the discussion preceding exercise 14.3.51 in the next chapter.

Berry's work was then revisited by Winskel, resulting in a theory of stable event structures [Win80]. The account offered here, based on [CPW96] is informed by linear logic (which was not available at the time). We present an intriguing model of linear logic in which the linear negation is modelled, roughly speaking, by the reversal of the roles of two order relations, one connected with the stable ordering, the other with the extensional ordering.

We build on coherence spaces (cf. section 13.1). Let $E$ and $E'$ be two coherence spaces. Recall that the structure $E \to E'$ has as events the pairs $(x, e')$ of a finite state of $E$ and an event of $E'$, that these events, when put together to form a higher order state $\phi$, describe the minimal points of the function represented by $\phi$, and that the inclusion of states naturally corresponds to the stable ordering. In $E \to E'$, there arises a natural order between events, which is inspired by contravariance:

$$
(x_1, e_1') \leq^L (x, e') \;\Leftrightarrow\; (x \subseteq x_1 \text{ and } e_1' = e').
$$

The superscript $^L$ will be explained later. The order $\leq^L$ allows us to describe the pointwise order between stable functions, at the level of traces.

**Definition 13.4.1** *Let* $E$ *and* $E'$ *be two coherence spaces. We define a partial order* $\sqsubseteq$ *on* $D(E \to E')$ *by* $\phi \sqsubseteq \psi \Leftrightarrow (\forall (x, e') \in \phi \; \exists x' \subseteq x \; (x', e') \in \psi)$. *(Notice that, given* $(x, e')$ *the* $x'$ *is unique.) Equivalently:*

$$
\phi \sqsubseteq \psi \;\Leftrightarrow\; \forall e'' \in \phi \; \exists e_1'' \; (e'' \leq^L e_1'' \text{ and } e_1'' \in \psi).
$$

**Proposition 13.4.2** *Let $E$ and $E'$ be coherence spaces, and $f, g : D(E) \to_{st} D(E')$. Then the following equivalence holds: $f \leq_{ext} g \Leftrightarrow trace(f) \sqsubseteq trace(g)$.*

We shall see (lemma 13.4.12) that $\phi \sqsubseteq \psi$ can be factored as $\phi \sqsubseteq^L \chi \subseteq \psi$, where $\phi \sqsubseteq^L \chi$ means: $\phi \sqsubseteq \chi$ and $\chi$ is minimal with respect to the inclusion (i.e., to the stable ordering) among all $\chi'$ such that $\phi \sqsubseteq \chi'$ ($\chi$ is the part of $\psi$ used to verify $\phi \sqsubseteq \psi$).

Next we want to force stable functionals to be order extensional, that is, we want to retain only functionals $H$ such that $\forall \phi, \psi$ ($\phi \sqsubseteq \psi \Rightarrow H(\phi) \leq H(\psi)$) (where we freely confuse functions with their traces), which, by the definition of $\sqsubseteq^L$, can be rephrased as:

$$\forall \phi, \psi \ (\phi \sqsubseteq^L \psi \Rightarrow H(\phi) \leq H(\psi)).$$

Suppose that $(\phi, e') \in H$. Then we must have $e' \in H(\psi)$, i.e., there must exist $(\psi_1, e') \in H$ such that $\psi_1 \subseteq \psi$. Therefore we ask for the following condition:

$$\forall e''' \in H \ \forall e_1''' \ (e_1''' \leq^R e''' \Rightarrow \exists e_2''' \in H \ e_1''' \leq^L e_2'''),$$

where the order $\leq^R$ is defined by:

$$(\psi, e_1') \leq^R (\phi, e') \Leftrightarrow (\phi \sqsubseteq^L \psi \text{ and } e_1' = e').$$

Summarizing, we have introduced (instances of) two orderings $\leq^L$ and $\leq^R$ on events. The first ordering allows us to describe the extensional ordering on functions, and the two orderings are used to capture the preservation of the extensional ordering between functionals.

**Definition 13.4.3 (bistructure)** *A bistructure $(E, \bigcirc, \leq^L, \leq^R)$ (or $E$ for short) is given by a set $E$ of events, by a reflexive and symmetric binary relation $\bigcirc$ on $E$, called the coherence relation, and by partial orders $\leq^L$ and $\leq^R$, satisfying the following axioms.*

$(B_1)$ $\forall e_1, e_2 \in E$ $(e_1 \downarrow^L e_2 \Rightarrow e_1 \asymp e_2)$

*where $e_1 \downarrow^L e_2$ means $\exists e \in E$ ($e \leq^L e_1$ and $e \leq^L e_2$), and where $e_1 \asymp e_2$ means $\neg(e_1 \bigcirc e_2)$ or $e_1 = e_2$ (cf. section 13.1).*

$(B_2)$ $\forall e_1, e_2 \in E$ $(e_1 \uparrow^R e_2 \Rightarrow e_1 \bigcirc e_2)$

*where $\uparrow$ is upward compatibility with respect to $\leq^R$.*

$(B_3)$ $\forall e_1, e_2 \in E$ $(e_1 \leq e_2 \Rightarrow (\exists c \in E \ c_1 \leq^L c \leq^R c_2))$

*where $\leq = (\leq^L \cup \leq^R)^*$.*

$(B_4)$ *The relation $\preceq = (\geq^L \cup \leq^R)^*$ is a partial order.*

$(B_5)$ $\forall e \in E$ $\{e' \in E \mid e' \preceq e\}$ *is finite.*

**Remark 13.4.4** *In the presence of axiom $(B_5)$, which is the bistructure version of axiom I, axiom $(B_4)$ is equivalent to requiring the non-existence of infinite sequences $\{e_n\}_{n<\omega}$ such that for all $n$ $e_{n+1} \prec e_n$, where $e \prec e'$ means $e \preceq e'$ and $e \neq e'$.*

The axioms of bistructures are strong enough to imply the uniqueness of the decomposition of $\leq = (\leq^L \cup \leq^R)^*$, and that $\leq$ is a partial order.

**Lemma 13.4.5** *Let $E$ be a bistructure. For all $e_1, e_2 \in E$, the following properties hold:*

(1) $(e_1 \downarrow^L e_2 \text{ and } e_1 \uparrow^R e_2) \Rightarrow e_1 = e_2$.

(2) $e_1 \leq e_2 \Rightarrow \exists! e \ (e_1 \leq^L e \leq^R e_2)$ .

PROOF. (1) If $e_1 \downarrow^L e_2$ and $e_1 \uparrow^R e_2$, then $e_1 \asymp e_2$ and $e_1 \subset\!\!\!\supset e_2$, which implies $e_1 = e_2$ by definition of $\asymp$.

(2) Suppose that $e_1 \leq^L e \leq^R e_2$ and $e_1 \leq^L e' \leq^R e_2$. Then $e \downarrow^L e'$ and $e \uparrow^R e'$, therefore $e = e'$ by (1).                                                                                  □

**Lemma 13.4.6** *The relation* $\leq = (\leq^L \cup \leq^R)^*$ *of definition 13.4.3 is a partial order.*

PROOF. We only have to prove that $\leq$ is antisymmetric. Suppose $e \leq e' \leq e$, and let $\epsilon, \epsilon'$ be such that $e \leq^L \epsilon' \leq^R e'$ and $e' \leq^L \epsilon \leq^R e$. We factor $e \leq \epsilon$: for some $\epsilon''$, $e \leq^L \epsilon'' \leq^R \epsilon$. Since $e \leq^L \epsilon'' \leq^R e$, we get:

$$\epsilon'' = e \quad \text{(by lemma 13.4.5)}$$
$$\epsilon = e \quad \text{(by the antisymmetry of } \leq^R\text{)} .$$

We then have $e' \leq^L \epsilon = e \leq^L \epsilon' \leq^R e'$, and:

$$\epsilon' = e' \quad \text{(by lemma 13.4.5)}$$
$$e = e' \quad \text{(by the antisymmetry of } \leq^L\text{)} .$$                                      □

We next define states of bistructures.

**Definition 13.4.7** *Let* $E = (E, \subset\!\!\!\supset, \leq^L, \leq^R)$ *be a bistructure. A state of* $E$ *is a subset* $x$ *of* $E$ *satisfying the following two conditions:*

*(consistency)* $\quad \forall e_1, e_2 \in x \ (e_1 \subset\!\!\!\supset e_2)$
*(extensionality)* $\quad \forall e \in x \ \forall e_1 \leq^R e \ \exists e_2 \ (e_1 \leq^L e_2 \text{ and } e_2 \in x) .$

*(The condition of extensionality is called the securedness condition in [CPW96].) We write* $(D(E), \sqsubseteq, \sqsubseteq^R)$ *for the collection of states of* $E$, *equipped with two orders* $\sqsubseteq^R$ *and* $\sqsubseteq$, *which are called the stable order and the extensional order, respectively, and which are defined as follows:*

- $\sqsubseteq^R$ *is the set theoretical inclusion,*

- $x \sqsubseteq y \Leftrightarrow \forall e \in x \ \exists e_1 \in y \ (e \leq^L e_1) .$

*Observe that axiom* $(B_1)$ *enforces the uniqueness of* $e_2$ *in the extensionality condition of states, and of* $e_1$ *in the definition of* $\sqsubseteq$. *We also define a third relation* $\sqsubseteq^L$ *between states by:*

$$x \sqsubseteq^L y \Leftrightarrow x \sqsubseteq y \text{ and } (\forall y_1 \in D(E) \ (x \sqsubseteq y_1 \text{ and } y_1 \sqsubseteq^R y) \Rightarrow y_1 = y).$$

We shall next examine some properties of the three relations $\sqsubseteq^R$, $\sqsubseteq$, and $\sqsubseteq^L$.

**Lemma 13.4.8** *Let* $E$ *be a bistructure, and let* $x \in D(E)$. *If* $e$ *is in the* $\leq$ *downward closure of* $x$, *then it is in the* $\leq^L$ *downward closure of* $x$.

PROOF. Let $e_1 \in x$ be such that $e \leq e_1$:

$$\exists e_2 \ e \leq^L e_2 \leq^R e_1 \quad \text{(by factorization)}$$
$$\exists e_3 \in x \ e_2 \leq^L e_3 \quad \text{(by extensionality)} .$$

Then $e \leq^L e_3$, which proves the statement.                                          □

**Lemma 13.4.9** *Let $\sqsubseteq^R$ and $\sqsubseteq$ be as in definition 13.4.7.*

(1) *If $x, y \in D(E)$, if $x \uparrow^R y$ (i.e., $\exists z \in D(E)$  $x \sqsubseteq^R z$ and $y \sqsubseteq^R z$), if $e_1 \in x$  $e_2 \in y$ and if $e_1 \downarrow^L e_2$, then $e_1 = e_2$.*

(2) *For all $x, y \in D(E)$, the following implication holds:*

$$(x \sqsubseteq y \text{ and } y \sqsubseteq^R x) \Rightarrow x = y.$$

PROOF. (1) Let $x$ be such that $x \sqsubseteq^R z$ and $y \sqsubseteq^R z$. Then $e_1, e_2 \in z$, hence $e_1 \frown e_2$. On the other hand, we have $e_1 \frown e_2$ by $(B_1)$. Hence $e_1 = e_2$.

(2) Let $e \in x$, and let $e_1 \in y$ be such that $e \leq^L e_1$. Then, by (1) applied to $x, y, e, e_1$, we have $e = e_1 \in y$. Hence $y \sqsubseteq^R x$, and the conclusion follows.          □

We mention the following two consequences of lemma 13.4.9:

- If $x$ is a configuration and $e \in x$, then $e$ is $\leq^L$-maximal in $x$.

- If $x \uparrow^R y$, then the set intersection $x \cap y$ is the glb of $x$ and $y$ with respect to both $\sqsubseteq^R$ and $\sqsubseteq$.

**Definition 13.4.10** *Let $E$ be a bistructure, and let $x \in D(E)$. We write $\preceq_x$ for the reflexive and transitive closure of the following relation $\preceq_x^1$ between events of $x$:*

$$e_1 \preceq_x^1 e_2 \iff (e_1, e_2 \in x \text{ and } \exists e \ e_1 \geq^L e \leq^R e_2) \,.$$

**Lemma 13.4.11** *Let $E$ be a bistructure, let $x, y \in D(E)$ and $e_2 \in E$ such that $x \uparrow^R y$ and $e_2 \in x \cap y$. Then the following equivalence holds, for any $e_1 \in E$:*

$$e_1 \preceq_x e_2 \iff e_1 \preceq_y e_2.$$

PROOF. It is clearly enough to show ($\Rightarrow$) for the one step relation $\preceq_x^1$. Thus let $e$ be such that $e_1 \geq^L e \leq^R e_2$. By extensionality of $y$, and since $e_2 \in y$, there exists $e_1' \in y$ such that $e \leq^L e_1'$. Then we get $e_1' = e_1$ (and hence $e_1 = e_1' \preceq_y e_2$) by lemma 13.4.9(1) applied to $x, y, e_1, e_1'$.          □

**Lemma 13.4.12** *Let $\sqsubseteq^R, \sqsubseteq,$ and $\sqsubseteq^L$ be as in definition 13.4.7. The following properties hold.*

(1) *$\sqsubseteq$ is $(\sqsubseteq^L \cup \sqsubseteq^R)^*$, and $\sqsubseteq^L, \sqsubseteq^R$ satisfy $(B_3)$.*

(2) *For all states $x, y$: $x \sqsubseteq^L y \iff (x \sqsubseteq y \text{ and } \forall e \in y \ \exists e_0 \in x, e_1 \in y \ e \preceq_y e_1 \geq^L e_0)$.*

(3) *$\sqsubseteq^L$ is a partial order.*

PROOF. (1) Let $x \sqsubseteq y$. The subset $\{e_1 \in y \mid \exists e_0 \in x \ e_0 \leq^L e_1\}$ represents the part of $y$ actually used to check $x \sqsubseteq y$. But we have to close this subset to make it extensional. Thus define:

$$y_1 = \{e \in y \mid \exists e_0 \in x, e_1 \in y, e \preceq_y e_1 \geq^L e_0\}.$$

As a subset of $y$, $y_1$ is consistent. By construction, $y_1$ satisfies the following property: if $e \in y_1$ and $e' \preceq_y e$, then $e' \in y_1$. If $e \in y_1$ and $e_1 \leq^R e$, since $y$ is extensional, there exists $e_2 \in y$ such that $e_1 \leq^L e_2$, and $e_2 \in y_1$ by construction. Thus $y_1$ is a state. We show $x \sqsubseteq^L y_1$. Suppose that $x \sqsubseteq y_1' \sqsubseteq^R y_1$, and let $e \in y_1$. By construction let $e_0 \in x$ and $e_1 \in y$ be such that $e \preceq_y e_1 \geq^L e_0$. Since $x \sqsubseteq y_1'$, $e_0 \leq^L e_1'$ for some $e_1' \in y_1'$. Applying lemma 13.4.9(1) to $y, y_1', e_1, e_1'$, we get $e_1 = e_1'$, hence $e_1 \in y_1'$, which implies

$e \in y_1'$ by lemma 13.4.11. Therefore $y_1 \sqsubseteq^R y_1'$, which completes the proof of $x \sqsubseteq^L y_1$. The decomposition $x \sqsubseteq^L y_1 \sqsubseteq^R y$ shows that $\sqsubseteq$ is contained in $(\sqsubseteq^L \cup \sqsubseteq^R)^*$. The converse inclusion is obvious.

(2) This follows immediately from the proof of (1).

(3) The reflexivity and the antisymmetry follow from $(\sqsubseteq^L) \subseteq (\sqsubseteq)$. Let $x \sqsubseteq^L y' \sqsubseteq^L y$, and let $e \in y$. By (2), there exist $e_0 \in y', e_1 \in y$ and $e_0' \in x, e_1' \in y'$ such that $e \preceq_y e_1 \geq^L e_0$ and $e' \preceq_x e_1' \geq^L e_0'$, or in full:

$$e_0 \leq^L e_1 \geq^R e_2 \leq^L \cdots \leq^L e_{2i+1} = e \qquad e_{2j+1} \in y \text{ for all } 0 \leq j \leq i$$
$$e_0' \leq^L e_1' \geq^R e_2' \leq^L \cdots \leq^L e_{2i'+1}' = e_0 \qquad e_{2j+1}' \in y' \text{ for all } 0 \leq j \leq i' .$$

Since $y' \sqsubseteq y$ and $e_1' \in y'$, there exists $e_1''$ such that $e_1' \leq^L e_1''$ and $e_1'' \in y$. Since $e_2' \leq^R e_1' \leq^L e_1''$, there exists $e_2''$ such that $e_2' \leq^L e_2'' \leq^R e_1''$, by factorization. Since $y$ is extensional, there exists $e_3'' \in y$ such that $e_2'' \leq^L e_3''$. In order to continue this lifting of the $e_i'$'s relative to $y'$ to a sequence of $e_i''$'s relative to $y$, we have to make sure that $e_3' \leq^L e_3''$:

$$e_3' \leq^L e_3''' \in y \text{ for some } e_3''' \in y \qquad \text{(since } y' \sqsubseteq y)$$
$$e_3''' = e_3'' \qquad \text{(since } e_2' \leq^L e_3'', e_2' \leq^L e_3''', \text{ and } e_3'', e_3''' \in y) .$$

Continuing in this way, we get:

$$e_0' \leq^L e_1'' \geq^R e_2'' \leq^L \cdots \leq^L e_{2i'+1}'' = e_1 \geq^R e_2 \leq^L \cdots \leq^L e_{2i+1} = e,$$

where $e_{2i'+1}'' = e_1$ follows by lemma 13.4.9(1) applied to $y, y, e_{2i'+1}'', e_1$. Since $e_{2j+1} \in y$ for all $0 \leq j \leq i$ and $e_{2j+1}'' \in y$ for all $0 \leq j \leq i'$, by (2), we conclude that $x \sqsubseteq^L y$. $\square$

We explore some of the finiteness and completeness properties of the two orders $\sqsubseteq$ and $\sqsubseteq^R$.

**Lemma 13.4.13** *Let $E$ be a bistructure, let $e \in x \in D(E)$. Then there exists a finite state $[e]_x$ such that $e \in [e]_x \sqsubseteq^R x$ and $(\forall y \in D(E)) (e \in y \sqsubseteq^R x) \Rightarrow ([e]_x \sqsubseteq^R y)$.*

PROOF. We define $[e]_x$ as follows (cf. lemma 13.4.12):

$$[e]_x = \{e' \in x \mid e' \preceq_x e\}.$$

The finiteness of $[e]_x$ follows from axiom $(B_5)$. The rest of the statement is an immediate consequence of lemma 13.4.11. $\square$

**Proposition 13.4.14** *Let $E$ be a bistructure. The following properties hold.*

(1) *All $\sqsubseteq$ directed lub's, $\sqsubseteq^R$ directed lub's, and $\sqsubseteq^R$ bounded lub's exist in $(D(E), \sqsubseteq, \sqsubseteq^R)$.*

(2) *The $\sqsubseteq$ and $\sqsubseteq^R$ lub's of $\sqsubseteq^R$ directed sets coincide.*

(3) *A state is $\sqsubseteq$ compact iff it is $\sqsubseteq^R$ compact iff it is finite, and $(D(E), \sqsubseteq^R)$ and $(D(E), \sqsubseteq)$ are $\omega$-algebraic cpo's.*

(4) *$(D(E), \sqsubseteq^R)$ is a dI-domain whose compact coprime elements are the states of the form $[e]_x$.*

PROOF. (1) Let $\Delta$ be $\sqsubseteq$ directed. We show that the $\sqsubseteq$ lub of $\Delta$ is:

$$z = \{e \in \bigcup \Delta \mid e \text{ is } \leq^L \text{ maximal in } \bigcup \Delta\} \,.$$

We first check that $z$ is a state. If $e_1, e_2 \in z$, then $e_1 \in \delta_1$, $e_2 \in \delta_2$ for some $\delta_1, \delta_2 \in \Delta$. Let $\delta \in \Delta$ be such that $\delta_1, \delta_2 \sqsubseteq \delta$. Then by definition of $z$ and $\sqsubseteq$, it follows that $e_1, e_2 \in \delta$. Therefore $e_1 \mathbin{\frown\!\!\!\smile} e_2$. If $e \in z$ and $e_1 \leq^R e$, let $\delta \in \Delta$ be such that $e \in \delta$. By extensionality of $\delta$, there exists $e_2 \in \delta$ such that $e_1 \leq^L e_2$. By definition of $z$ and by $(B_4)$ and $(B_5)$ (cf. remark 13.4.4), we can find $e_3 \in z$ such that $e_2 \leq^L e_3$. Hence $z$ is a state. It is obvious from the definition of $z$ that $\delta \sqsubseteq z$ holds for any $\delta \in \Delta$, and that if $z_1$ is an $\sqsubseteq$ upper bound of $\Delta$ then $z \sqsubseteq z_1$.

The $\sqsubseteq^R$ bounded lub's exist: if $X \subseteq D(E)$ and if $x$ is an $\sqsubseteq^R$ upper bound of $X$, then $\bigcup X$ is consistent as a subset of $x$ and extensional as a union of extensional sets of events. Similarly, the lub of a $\sqsubseteq^R$ directed set $\Delta$ is $\bigcup \Delta$.

(2) Let $\Delta$ be $\sqsubseteq^R$ directed (and hence *a fortiori* $\sqsubseteq$ directed). We prove that $\sqcup \Delta = \sqcup^R \Delta$ (where $\sqcup^R$ and $\sqcup$ are relative to $\sqsubseteq^R$ and $\sqsubseteq$, respectively). We have to show that any $e \in \bigcup \Delta$ is $\leq^L$ maximal. Suppose there exists $e_1 \in \bigcup \Delta$ such that $e \leq^L e_1$. Then, applying lemma 13.4.9(1) to $\bigcup \Delta, \bigcup \Delta, e, e_1$, we get $e = e_1$.

(3) We decompose the proof into three implications:

- $x$ is finite $\Rightarrow x$ is $\sqsubseteq$ compact. Let $\{e_1, \ldots, e_n\} \sqsubseteq \sqcup \Delta$. There exist $e'_1, \ldots, e'_n \in \sqcup \Delta$ such that $e_i \leq^L e'_i$ for all $i$. Let $\delta_1, \ldots, \delta_n \in \Delta$ such that $e'_i \in \delta_i$ for all $i$, and let $\delta \in \Delta$ be such that $\delta_i \sqsubseteq \delta$ for all $i$. Then by the $\leq^L$ maximality of $e'_1, \ldots, e'_n$ we get $e'_i \in \delta$ for all $i$. Hence $\{e_1, \ldots, e_n\} \sqsubseteq \delta$.

- $x$ is $\sqsubseteq$ compact $\Rightarrow x$ is $\sqsubseteq^R$ compact. If $x \sqsubseteq^R \sqcup^R \Delta$, then *a fortiori* $x \sqsubseteq \sqcup \Delta$, therefore $x \sqsubseteq \delta$ for some $\delta \in \Delta$. We show that actually $x \sqsubseteq^R \delta$ holds. Let $e \in x$, and let $e_1 \in \delta$ such that $e \leq^L e_1$. Then we get $e = e_1$ by lemma 13.4.9(1) applied to $x, \delta, e, e_1$.

- $x$ is $\sqsubseteq^R$ compact $\Rightarrow x$ is finite. We claim that $\{y \mid y \text{ finite and } y \sqsubseteq^R z\}$ is $\sqsubseteq^R$ directed and has $z$ as lub, for any $z$. The directedness is obvious. We have to check that $z \sqsubseteq^R \sqcup^R \{y \mid y \text{ finite and } y \sqsubseteq^R z\}$, that is, for all $e \in z$, there exists a finite $y$ such that $y \sqsubseteq^R z$ and $e \in y$. The state $[e]_x$ (cf. lemma 13.4.13) does the job.

(4) Recall that dI-domains are the same as coprime algebraic Scott domains (cf. proposition 12.3.10). Consider a configuration $[e]_x$. If $[e]_x \sqsubseteq^R \sqcup^R Y = \bigcup Y$, then $e \in y$ for some $y$ in $Y$. Since $[e]_x \uparrow^R y$, we infer that $[e]_x \subseteq y$, by lemma 13.4.11. Conversely, every compact coprime element is of this form, since for any state $x$ we have $x = \bigcup\{[e]_x \mid e \in x\}$. □

We define a monoidal closed category of bistructures.

**Definition 13.4.15 (linear exponent – bistructures)** *Let $E$ and $E'$ be two bistructures. The linear exponent bistructure $E \multimap E'$ is defined as follows:*

- *events are pairs $(e, e')$ where $e \in E$ and $e' \in E'$,*
- *$(e_1, e'_1) \mathbin{\smile\!\!\!\frown} (e_2, e'_2) \Leftrightarrow e_1 \mathbin{\frown\!\!\!\smile} e_2$ and $e'_1 \mathbin{\smile\!\!\!\frown} e'_2$,*
- *$(e_1, e'_1) \leq^L (e, e') \Leftrightarrow e \leq^R e_1$ and $e'_1 \leq^L e'$,*
- *$(e_1, e'_1) \leq^R (e, e') \Leftrightarrow e \leq^L e_1$ and $e'_1 \leq^R e'$.*

As for coherence spaces, the coherence in the linear exponent can be defined by either of the following equivalences (cf. lemma 13.1.5):

$$\begin{aligned}
(e_1, e'_1) \mathbin{\frown\!\!\!\smile} (e_2, e'_2) &\Leftrightarrow (e_1 \mathbin{\frown\!\!\!\smile} e_2 \Rightarrow (e'_1 \mathbin{\frown\!\!\!\smile} e'_2 \text{ and } (e_1 \neq e_2 \Rightarrow e'_1 \neq e'_2))) \\
(e_1, e'_1) \mathbin{\frown\!\!\!\smile} (e_2, e'_2) &\Leftrightarrow (e_1 \mathbin{\frown\!\!\!\smile} e_2 \Rightarrow e'_1 \mathbin{\frown\!\!\!\smile} e'_2) \text{ and } (e'_1 \mathbin{\smile\!\!\!\frown} e'_2 \Rightarrow e_1 \mathbin{\smile\!\!\!\frown} e_2) \,.
\end{aligned}$$

The definition of linear exponent suggests what the linear negation should be, and what the connective $\wp$ should be. We shall define these connectives right away, and prove that they are correctly defined. The correctness of the definition of $E \multimap E'$ will then follow.

**Definition 13.4.16 (linear negation – bistructures)** *The linear negation $E^{\perp}$ of a bistructure $(E, \subset, \leq^L, \leq^R)$ is defined by:*

$$E^{\perp} = (E, \asymp, \geq^R, \geq^L).$$

**Proposition 13.4.17** $E^{\perp}$ *is a well-defined bistructure.*

PROOF. We add subscripts that make clear to which bistructures we refer. We have:

$$e_1 \downarrow^L_{E^{\perp}} e_2 \Leftrightarrow e_1 \uparrow^R_E e_2 \Rightarrow e_1 \subset_E e_2 \Leftrightarrow e_1 \asymp_{E^{\perp}} e_2,$$

and similarly for $(B_2)$. The satisfaction of $(B_3)$ to $(B_5)$ follows from:

$$(\leq^L_{E^{\perp}} \cup \leq^R_{E^{\perp}} = \geq^R \cup \geq^L) \quad \text{and} \quad (\geq^L_{E^{\perp}} \cup \leq^R_{E^{\perp}} = \leq^R \cup \geq^L). \qquad \square$$

**Definition 13.4.18 (par – bistructures)** *Let $E$ and $E'$ be two bistructures. The bistructure $E \wp E'$ is defined as follows:*

- *events are pairs $(e, e')$ where $e \in E$ and $e' \in E'$,*
- *$(e_1, e'_1) \asymp (e_2, e'_2) \Leftrightarrow e_1 \asymp e_2$ and $e'_1 \asymp e'_2$,*
- *$(e_1, e'_1) \leq^L (e, e') \Leftrightarrow e_1 \leq^L e$ and $e'_1 \leq^L e'$,*
- *$(e_1, e'_1) \leq^R (e, e') \Leftrightarrow e_1 \leq^R e$ and $e'_1 \leq^R e'$.*

**Proposition 13.4.19** $E \wp E'$ *is a well-defined bistructure.*

PROOF. $(B_1)$ Let $(e_1, e'_1) \downarrow^L (e, e')$. We have $e_1 \asymp e$ from $e_1 \downarrow^L e$ and $e'_1 \asymp e'$ from $e'_1 \downarrow^L e'$.

$(B_2)$ Let $(e_1, e'_1) \uparrow^R (e, e')$, and suppose $(e_1, e'_1) \asymp (e, e')$. As in the previous case, we have $e_1 \subset e$ and $e'_1 \subset e'$, which, combined with the definition of $(e_1, e'_1) \asymp (e, e')$, gives $e_1 = e$ and $e'_1 = e'$.

The other axioms follow from the componentwise definition of the orders. $\square$

**Proposition 13.4.20** *Let $E$, $E'$, and $E''$ be bistructures, let $\phi \in D(E \multimap E')$ and $\psi \in D(E' \multimap E'')$. The graph composition $\psi \circ \phi$ of $\phi$ and $\psi$ is a state of $E \multimap E''$.*

PROOF. Let $(e_1, e''_1), (e_2, e''_2) \in \psi \circ \phi$, and let $e'_1, e'_2 \in E'$ be such that:

$$(e_1, e'_1) \in \phi \quad (e'_1, e''_1) \in \psi \quad (e_2, e'_2) \in \phi \quad (e'_2, e''_2) \in \psi.$$

Suppose $e_1 \subset e_2$. Since $(e_1, e'_1), (e_2, e'_2) \in \phi$ we have $e'_1 \subset e'_2$. Since $(e'_1, e''_1), (e'_2, e''_2) \in \psi$, we have $e''_1 \subset e''_2$. Similarly, $e''_1 \asymp e''_2$ implies $e_1 \asymp e_2$. Thus $\psi \circ \phi$ is consistent.

We now check that $\psi \circ \phi$ is extensional. Let $(e, e'') \in \psi \circ \phi$, and $(e_1, e''_1) \leq^R (e, e'')$. Thus $e \leq^L e_1$ and $e''_1 \leq^R e''$, and there exists $e'$ such that $(e, e') \in \phi$ and $(e', e'') \in \psi$. By extensionality of $\phi$, and since $(e_1, e') \leq^R (e, e')$, there exists $(e_2, e'_2) \in \phi$ such that $(e_1, e') \leq^L (e_2, e'_2)$, that is, $e_2 \leq^R e_1$ and $e' \leq^L e'_2$. By extensionality of $\psi$, and since

$(e_2', e_1'') \leq^R (e', e'')$, there exists $(e_3', e_3'') \in \psi$ such that $e_3' \leq^R e_2'$ and $e_1'' \leq^L e_3''$. By extensionality of $\phi$, and since $(e_2, e_3') \leq^R (e_2, e_2')$, there exists $(e_4, e_4') \in \phi$ such that $e_4 \leq^R e_2$ and $e_3' \leq^L e_4'$. In this way we build sequences such that:

$$e \leq^L e_1 \geq^R e_2 \geq^R e_4 \geq^R \cdots \quad (e, e'), (e_2, e_2'), (e_4, e_4'), \ldots \in \phi$$
$$e' \leq^L e_2' \geq^R e_3' \leq^L e_4' \geq^R \cdots$$
$$e'' \geq^R e_1'' \leq^L e_3'' \leq^L \cdots \quad (e', e''), (e_3', e_3''), \ldots \in \psi.$$

By axiom $(B_4)$, the sequence $\{e_n'\}_{n<\omega}$ becomes stationary. Let $i$ be such that $e_{2i}' = e_{2i+1}'$. Then we have:

$$(e_{2i}, e_{2i+1}'') \in \psi \circ \phi \quad \text{(since by construction } (e_{2i}, e_{2i}') \in \phi \text{ and } (e_{2i+1}', e_{2i+1}'') \in \psi)$$
$$(e_1, e_1'') \leq^L (e_{2i}, e_{2i+1}'') \quad \text{(since by construction } e_1 \geq^R e_{2i} \text{ and } e_1'' \leq^L e_{2i+1}'').$$ □

Thus we have all the ingredients to define a linear category of bistructures.

**Definition 13.4.21** *We define the category $\mathbf{BS}_l$ as follows: objects are bistructures, and for any $E, E'$, we set $\mathbf{BS}_l[E, E'] = D(E \multimap E')$. Composition is relation composition, and the identities are the identity relations: $id_E = \{(e, e) \mid e \in E\}$.*

**Remark 13.4.22** *The morphisms of $\mathbf{BS}_l$, unlike in the case of coherence spaces and of hypercoherences, do not enjoy a simple abstract characterization as 'linear and exten-sional functions'. In coherence spaces, events are in one to one correspondence with the compact coprime states, which are singletons $\{e\}$. In the present framework, $\{e\}$ has no reason to be extensional in general, and there may be several ways to extend $\{e\}$ into a minimal state. These considerations should explain why we have chosen to concentrate on a concrete description of the morphisms of $\mathbf{BS}_l$.*

Next we define a tensor product. Its definition is dictated by (and its correctness follows from) the equation $(E \otimes E')^\perp = E^\perp \wp E'^\perp$.

**Definition 13.4.23 (tensor – bistructures)** *Let $E$ and $E'$ be two bistructures. The bistructure $E \wp E'$ is defined as follows:*

- *events are pairs $(e, e')$ where $e \in E$ and $e' \in E'$,*

- *$(e_1, e_1') \mathrel{\subset\!\!\!\!\supset} (e_2, e_2') \Leftrightarrow e_1 \mathrel{\subset\!\!\!\!\supset} e_2$ and $e_1' \mathrel{\subset\!\!\!\!\supset} e_2'$,*

- *$(e_1, e_1') \leq^L (e, e') \Leftrightarrow e_1 \leq^L e$ and $e_1' \leq^L e'$,*

- *$(e_1, e_1') \leq^R (e, e') \Leftrightarrow e_1 \leq^R e$ and $e_1' \leq^R e'$.*

*The operation $\otimes$ is extended to a functor as follows. Let $\phi \in D(E_1 \multimap E_1')$ and $\psi \in D(E_2 \multimap E_2')$, and set $\phi \otimes \psi = \{((e_1, e_2), (e_1', e_2')) \mid (e_1, e_1') \in \phi \text{ and } (e_2, e_2') \in \psi\}$.*

**Theorem 13.4.24** *The category $\mathbf{BS}_l$ is $*$-autonomous. The unit is defined by $I = (\{*\}, id, id, id)$.*

PROOF. The proof is a straightforward extension of the proof that $\mathbf{Coh}_l$ is $*$-autonomous (proposition 13.2.20). We have, say:

$$((e_1, e_1'), e_1'') \leq^L_{E \otimes E' \multimap E''} ((e_2, e_2'), e_2'') \Leftrightarrow e_2 \leq^R_E e_1 \text{ and } e_1' \leq^R_{E'} e_2' \text{ and } e_1'' \leq^R_{E''} e_2''$$
$$\Leftrightarrow (e_1, (e_1', e_1'')) \leq^R_{E \multimap (E' \multimap E'')} (e_2, (e_2', e_2'')).$$ □

**Remark 13.4.25** *Like in the coherence model, we have $I^\perp = I$.*

We now define a related cartesian closed category of order-extensional stable functions.

**Definition 13.4.26** *We define the category* **BS** *as follows: objects are bistructures; and for any $E, E'$,* **BS**$[E, E']$ *consists of the functions from $D(E)$ to $D(E')$ which are $\sqsubseteq^R$ stable and $\sqsubseteq$ monotonic.*

We did not require $\sqsubseteq$ continuity in definition 13.4.26, because it is an implied property.

**Lemma 13.4.27** *Let $E$ and $E'$ be bistructures. If $f : D(E) \to D(E')$ is $\sqsubseteq^R$ continuous and $\sqsubseteq$ monotonic, then it is also $\sqsubseteq$ continuous.*

PROOF. Let $\{e_1, \ldots, e_n\} \sqsubseteq f(x)$. There exist $e'_1, \ldots, e'_n \in f(x)$ such that $e_i \leq^L e'_i$ for all $i$. By $\sqsubseteq^R$ continuity, there exists a finite $x_1 \sqsubseteq^R x$ such that $e'_1, \ldots, e'_n \in f(x_1)$, hence $\{e_1, \ldots, e_n\} \sqsubseteq f(x_1)$.                    □

**Definition 13.4.28 (product – bistructures)** *Let $E$ and $E'$ be two bistructures. The bistructure $E \times E'$ is defined as follows:*

- *events are either $e.1$ where $e \in E$ or $e'.2$ where $e' \in E'$,*

- $(e_1.i) \supset (e_2.j) \Leftrightarrow i = j$ *and* $e_1 \supset e_2$,

- $(e_1.i) \leq^L (e_2.j) \Leftrightarrow i = j$ *and* $e_1 \leq^L e_2$,

- $(e_1.i) \leq^R (e_2.j) \Leftrightarrow i = j$ *and* $e_1 \leq^R e_2$.

**Proposition 13.4.29** *The category* **BS**$_l$ *is cartesian. The terminal object is $1 = (\emptyset, \emptyset, \emptyset, \emptyset)$.*

We now relate the categories **BS**$_l$ and **BS** through an adjunction that corresponds to the fundamental decomposition $E \to E' = (!E) \multimap E'$. We define an 'inclusion' functor $\subseteq : \mathbf{BS}_l \to \mathbf{BS}$ as follows.

**Definition 13.4.30** *We set:*

$$\subseteq (E) = E \qquad \subseteq (\phi)(x) = \{e' \mid \exists e \in x \ (e, e') \in \phi\}.$$

**Proposition 13.4.31** *The data of definition 13.4.30 define a functor from* **BS**$_l$ *to* **BS**.

PROOF HINT. To check that $\subseteq (\phi)$ is $\sqsubseteq$ monotonic, we use a technique similar to the one used in the proof of proposition 13.4.20 (application is a special case of composition).□

The following connective ! allows us to go the other way around, from **BS** to **BS**$_l$.

**Definition 13.4.32 (exponential – bistructures)** *Let $E$ be a bistructure. The bistructure $!E$ is defined as follows:*

- *the events are the finite states of $E$,*

- $x_1 \supset x_2 \Leftrightarrow x_1 \uparrow^R x_2$,

- $\leq^L$ *is* $\sqsubseteq^L$,

- $\leq^R$ *is* $\sqsubseteq^R$.

**Proposition 13.4.33** *!E is a well-defined bistructure.*

PROOF. Obviously, $\sqsubseteq^R$ is a partial order. By lemma 13.4.12, $\sqsubseteq^L$ is a partial order and $(B_3)$ holds. And $(B_2)$ holds *a fortiori*, by definition of $\frown$.

$(B_1)$ By the definition of $\frown_{!E}$ we can rephrase $(B_1)$ as:

$$(x_1 \downarrow^L x_2 \text{ and } x_1 \uparrow^R x_2) \Rightarrow x_1 = x_2.$$

Let $x_3 \sqsubseteq^L x_1, x_2$, and let $e \in x_1$. Let $e_0 \in x_3$ and $e_1 \in x_1$ be such that $e \preceq_{x_1} e_1 \geq^L e_0$. Exploiting $x_3 \sqsubseteq x_2$ and $x_1 \uparrow^R x_2$ and using lemma 13.4.9(1), we get $e_1 \in x_2$, and $e \in x_2$ then follows by lemma 13.4.11. This completes the proof of $x_1 \sqsubseteq^R x_2$. The converse inclusion is proved symmetrically, exploiting $x_3 \sqsubseteq^L x_2$ and $x_3 \sqsubseteq x_1$.

$(B_4)$ We show that $(\sqsupseteq^L \cup \sqsubseteq^R)^*$ is antisymmetric. Since $\sqsubseteq^R$ and $\sqsupseteq^L$ are both partial orders, it is enough to consider a sequence $x_0 \sqsubseteq^R x_0' \sqsupseteq^L x_1 \cdots x_{n-1}' \sqsupseteq^L x_n = x_0$ and prove that $x_0 = x_0' = x_1 = \cdots = x_{n-1}' = x_n$. The proof goes through two claims.

**Claim 1.** The set theoretical intersection $X = \bigcap_{i=1\cdots n} x_i$ is a state.

Clearly, $X$ is consistent as a subset of, say, $x_0$. Let $e \in X$ and $e_1 \leq^R e$. Since $e \in x_i$, there exists $e_1^i \in x_i$ such that $e_1 \leq^L e_1^i$, for all $i \geq 1$. Since $x_i \sqsubseteq x_{i-1}'$, there exists $e_1'^i \in x_{i-1}'$ such that $e_1^i \leq^L e_1'^i$, for all $i \geq 1$. We now make two applications of lemma 13.4.9(1):

- From $e_1 \leq^L e_1'^i$, $e_1 \leq^L e_1^{i-1}$ and $x_{i-1} \sqsubseteq^R x_{i-1}'$ we conclude $e_1'^i = e_1^{i-1}$, therefore $e_1^{i-1} \geq^L e_1^i$.

- From $e_1 \leq^L e_1^0$, $e_1 \leq^L e_1^n$ and $x_0 = x_n$, we obtain $e_1^0 = e_1^n$.

Since $\leq^L$ is a partial order, we get $e_1^0 = \cdots = e_1^i = \cdots = e_1^n$, hence $e_1^0 \in X$, which completes the proof of the claim.

**Claim 2.** $x_i' \sqsubseteq^R X$, for all $i$.

Since we have a cycle from $x_0$ to $x_n$, any index $i$ can be brought to head position by a circular permutation. Hence it is enough to show $x_0' \sqsubseteq^R X$. Let $e_0 \in x_0'$. By lemma 13.4.12, we can find $e_0' \in x_0'$ and $e_1 \in x_1$ such that $e_0 \preceq_{x_0'} e_0' \geq^L e_1$. We continue in this way and find:

$$e_1' \in x_1', e_2 \in x_2 \qquad \text{such that } e_1 \preceq_{x_1'} e_1' \geq^L e_2$$
$$\cdots$$
$$e_{n-1}' \in x_{n-1}', e_n \in x_n = x_0 \quad \text{such that } e_{n-1} \preceq_{x_{n-1}'} e_{n-1}' \geq^L e_n \ .$$

In particular, we have $e_i \preceq e_{i+1}$, for all $i$. We continue round the clock, generating $e_{n+i} \in x_i$, $e_{2n+i} \in x_i, \ldots, e_{kn+i} \in x_i$. Since $x_i$ is finite, there exist $k_1, k_2$ for which $e_{k_1 n} = e_{k_2 n} \in x_0$. By the antisymmetry of $\preceq$ (in $E$), we obtain:

$$e_{k_1 n} = e_{k_1 n+1} = \cdots = e_{(k_1+1)n} = \cdots = e_{k_2 n}.$$

Therefore $e_{k_1 n} \in X$, since $e_{k_1 n+i} \in x_i$ for all $i$. Our next goal is to carry this back to $e_0$, and show $e_0 \in X$. Suppose that we have proved $e_m \in X$. We have:

$$e_m = e_{m-1}' \quad \text{(by lemma 13.4.9(1) applied to } X, x_{m-1}', e_m, e_{m-1}')$$
$$e_{m-1} \in X \quad \text{(by lemma 13.4.11 applied to } x_{m-1}', X, e_{m_1}', e_{m-1}) \ .$$

Finally, we arrive at $e_0 \in X$.

We can now prove $(B_4)$. From $x_0 \sqsubseteq^R x_0' \sqsubseteq^R X \sqsubseteq^R x_0$ we get $x_0 = x_0' = X$. From $x_0' \sqsupseteq^L x_1$ and $x_0' = X \sqsubseteq^R x_1$ we get $x_0' = x_1$ by lemma 13.4.9(2), and, progressively, $x_0 = x_0' = x_1 = \cdots = x_{n-1}' = x_n$ (using $x_0' \sqsubseteq^R X$), as desired.

$(B_5)$ Let $x$ be a finite state. Let $\bar{x} = \{e \mid \exists e_0 \in x \ e \preceq e_0\}$. This set is finite. By lemma 13.4.12, any $y$ such that $y \ (\sqsupseteq^L \cup \sqsubseteq^R)^* \ x$ is a subset of $\bar{x}$, and $(B_5)$ follows.             □

**Lemma 13.4.34** *Let $E$ and $E'$ be bistructures. A function $f : D(E) \to D(E')$ is $\sqsubseteq^R$ continuous iff, for any $e'$ and $x$, $e' \in f(x)$ implies $e' \in f(y)$ for some finite $y \sqsubseteq^R x$.*

PROOF. If $f$ is continuous and $e' \in f(x)$, then $[e']_{f(x)} \sqsubseteq^R f(x)$ (cf. lemma 13.4.13), and by continuity there exists a finite $x_1$ such that $[e']_{f(x)} \sqsubseteq^R f(x_1)$, hence *a fortiori* $e' \in f(x_1)$. Conversely, let $\{e_1', \ldots, e_n'\} \sqsubseteq^R f(x)$. Then let $x_1, \ldots, x_n$ be such that $x_i \sqsubseteq_{fin} x$ and $e_i' \in f(x_i)$ for all $i$. Then $\bigcup_{i=1\cdots n} x_i$ is a finite state, and $\{e_1, \ldots, e_n\} \sqsubseteq^R f(\bigcup_{i=1\cdots n} x_i)$.             □

**Theorem 13.4.35** *The operation ! extends to a functor ! : **BS** $\to$ **BS**$_l$ which is left adjoint to $\sqsubseteq$.*

PROOF. The correspondences between states of $!E \multimap E'$ and the stable and order-extensional functions are as follows:

$$f \mapsto trace(f) = \{(x, e') \mid e' \in f(x) \text{ and } (y \sqsubseteq^R x \text{ and } e' \in f(y) \Rightarrow y = x)\}$$
$$\phi \mapsto fun(\phi)(z) = \{e' \mid \exists y \sqsubseteq^R z \ (y, e') \in \phi\} \, .$$

We show that $trace(f)$ is a state. It is a set of events of $!E \multimap E'$ by lemma 13.4.34. Let $(x_1, e_1'), (x_2, e_2') \in trace(f)$ with $x_1 \subset x_2$, i.e., $x_1 \uparrow^R x_2$. Let $x$ be such that $x_1, x_2 \leq^R x$. Then $e_1' \subset e_2'$, since $e_1', e_2' \in f(x)$. Suppose, moreover, that $e_1' = e_2'$. Then $x_1 = x_2$, by stability. This completes the proof of consistency. Let $(x, e') \in trace(f)$ and $(x_1, e_1') \leq^R (x, e')$. We look for $(x_2, e_2') \in trace(f)$ such that $(x_1, e_1') \leq^L (x_2, e_2')$. From $e' \in f(x)$ we get that $e'$ is in the $\leq$ downward closure of $f(x_1)$ by $\sqsubseteq$ monotonicity. By lemma 13.4.8, $e_2' \in f(x_1)$ for some $e_2' \geq^L e_1'$, since $e_1' \leq^R e'$. Therefore, by the definition of the trace, $(x_2, e_2') \in trace(f)$ for some $x_2 \sqsubseteq^R x_1$. This pair fits, and this completes the proof of extensionality.

In the other direction, the $\sqsubseteq^R$ stability of $fun(\phi)$ is obvious from the definition of $fun$ and the consistency of $\phi$. We check that $fun(\phi)$ is $\sqsubseteq$ monotonic. Let $y \sqsubseteq z$, and let $e' \in fun(\phi)(y)$. Let $x_1 \sqsubseteq^R y$ be such that $(x_1, e') \in \phi$. Let $x_2$ be such that $x_1 \sqsubseteq^L x_2 \sqsubseteq^R z$. Since $(x_2, e') \sqsubseteq^R (x_1, e')$, by extensionality there exists $(x_3, e_3') \in \phi$ such that $(x_2, e') \sqsubseteq^L (x_3, e_3')$. We have $e' \leq^L e_3'$, and $e_3' \in f(z)$ since $e_3' \in f(x_3)$ and $x_3 \sqsubseteq^R z$.             □

The required isomorphisms relating additives and multiplicatives are as follows:

- $!1 \cong I$. The only state of 1 is $\emptyset$, which corresponds to the unique event $*$ of $I$.

- $!(A \times B) \cong (!A) \otimes (!B)$. By the definition of product, $x$ is a state of $E \times E'$ iff $x_1 = \{e \in E \mid (e.1) \in x\}$ and $x_2 = \{e \in E \mid (e.2) \in x\}$ are states of $E, E'$ and $x = x_1 \cup x_2$. This establishes a bijective correspondence $x \leftrightarrow (x_1, x_2)$ between the events of $!(A \times B)$ and those of $(!A) \otimes (!B)$.

Altogether, we have constructed a $*_l$-autonomous category of bistructures. We could have carried the same constructions over hypercoherences, as the following exercise shows.

**Exercise\* 13.4.36** *Adapt the constructions and the results of this section to the setting of hypercoherences, replacing bistructures $(E, \bigcirc, \leq^L, \leq^R)$ by structures of the form $(E, \Gamma, \leq^L, \leq^R)$, and replacing axioms $(B_1)$ and $(B_2)$ by the following axioms:*

$$(u \in \Gamma \text{ and } u \text{ has a } \leq^l \text{ lower bound}) \Rightarrow \natural u = 1$$
$$(u \text{ has a } \leq^R \text{ upper bound}) \Rightarrow u \in \Gamma .$$

# 13.5    Chu spaces and continuity \*

The Chu construction (see [Bar78, Bar91b]) allows us to construct a \*-autonomous category out of a monoidal category with finite limits. Here we present the construction over the category of sets, which is enough for our purposes.

By imposing some order theoretical axioms, we arrive at the notion of a casuistry (definition 13.5.13). Roughly speaking, a casuistry is a dcpo together with a choice of an appropriate collection of Scott open sets. A linear morphism between two casuistries is a function whose inverse image maps chosen open sets back to chosen open sets. For any continuous function $f$, the inverse image $f^{-1}(U)$ of a chosen open set $U$ is open, but is not necessarily a chosen open set. An exponential construction allows to fill the gap between the morphisms of casuistries and the continuous functions (proposition 13.5.19). The material of this section is based on [Lam94].

**Definition 13.5.1 (Chu space)** *Let $K$ be a set. A Chu space over $K$ (Chu space for short) is a triple $\mathbf{A} = (A_*, A^*, \langle\ ,\ \rangle)$, where $A_*$ and $A^*$ are sets and where $\langle\_,\_\rangle$ is a function from $A_* \times A^*$ to $K$, called the* agreement *function. A morphism $\mathbf{f} : \mathbf{A} \to \mathbf{B}$ of Chu spaces is a pair $(f_*, f^*)$ of functions, where $f_* : A_* \to B_*$ and $f^* : B^* \to A^*$, satisfying, for all $x \in A_*, \beta \in B^*$:*

$$(^*_*) \quad \langle f_*(x), \beta \rangle = \langle x, f^*(\beta) \rangle.$$

*The mapping $\langle\_,\_\rangle$ can be equivalently presented as a function $l_A : A_* \to (A^* \to K)$ or a function $r_A : A^* \to (A_* \to K)$. If $l_A$ (l for short) is injective, we say that $\mathbf{A}$ is* left separated, *and symmetrically, if $r_A$ (r for short) is injective, we say that $\mathbf{A}$ is* right separated. *A* separated *Chu space is a Chu space which is both left and right separated. We write $\mathbf{Chu}$ for the category of Chu spaces, and $\mathbf{Chu}_s$ for the full subcategory of separated Chu spaces.*

*There are two obvious forgetful functors $_*$ and $^*$ (covariant and contravariant, respectively) from $\mathbf{Chu}$ to the category of sets:*

$$\mathbf{A}_* = A_* \quad (f_*, f^*)_* = f_*$$
$$\mathbf{A}^* = A^* \quad (f_*, f^*)^* = f^* .$$

**Lemma 13.5.2** *The following are equivalent formulations of $(^*_*)$:*

$$(^*_{*l}) \quad l_B(f_*(x)) = l_A(x) \circ f^*$$
$$(^*_{*r}) \quad r_A(f^*(\beta)) = r_B(\beta) \circ f_* .$$

**Lemma 13.5.3** *Every right separated Chu space is isomorphic to a Chu space $\mathbf{A}$ where $A^*$ is a set of functions from $A_*$ to $K$, and where $\langle x, f \rangle = f(x)$. If, moreover, $K = \{\bot, \top\}$, every right separated Chu space is isomorphic to a right strict Chu space, where a right strict Chu space is a Chu space $\mathbf{A}$ such that $A^*$ is a set of subsets of $A_*$ and where agreement is membership. Left strict separated Chu spaces are defined similarly.*

**Example 13.5.4** *Every topological space* $(X, \Omega)$ *is a right strict Chu space. It is left separated exactly when it is* $T_0$ *(cf. section 1.2). Moreover, the morphisms between topological spaces viewed as Chu spaces are exactly the continuous functions (see lemma 13.5.5), so that topological spaces and continuous functions may be considered a full subcategory of* $\mathbf{Chu}_s$.

**Lemma 13.5.5** *A morphism of right separated Chu spaces* $\mathbf{A}$ *and* $\mathbf{B}$ *is equivalently defined as a function* $f_* : A_* \to B_*$ *such that:*

$$\forall \beta \in B^* \ \exists \alpha \in A^* \ r(\beta) \circ f_* = r(\alpha).$$

*If moreover* $\mathbf{A}$ *and* $\mathbf{B}$ *are right strict, this condition boils down to:*

$$\forall \beta \in B^* \ f^{-1}(\beta) \in A^*.$$

PROOF. Let $(f_*, f^*)$ be a morphism. Then $f_*$ satisfies the condition of the statement by $\binom{*}{*r}$. Conversely, the injectivity of $r$ guarantees the uniqueness of $\alpha$, hence the formula of the statement defines a function $f^* : B^* \to A^*$. □

**Lemma 13.5.6** *Let* $\mathbf{A}$ *and* $\mathbf{B}$ *be Chu spaces, and suppose that* $\mathbf{A}$ *is right separated and that* $\mathbf{B}$ *is left separated. Then a morphism from* $\mathbf{A}$ *to* $\mathbf{B}$ *is equivalently defined as a function* $h : A_* \times B^* \to K$ *whose curryings factor through* $l_B$ *and* $r_A$, *respectively.*

PROOF. Let $(f_*, f^*)$ be a morphism. Then the required $h$ is defined by:

$$h(x, \beta) = \langle f_*(x), \beta \rangle = \langle x, f^*(\beta) \rangle,$$

and the factorizations are given by $\binom{*}{*l}$ and $\binom{*}{*r}$, respectively. Conversely, the two factorizations determine two functions $f_* : A_* \to B_*$ and $f^* : B^* \to A^*$, and $\binom{*}{*}$ holds by construction. □

**Definition 13.5.7 (tensor – Chu spaces)** *Let* $\mathbf{A}$ *and* $\mathbf{A}'$ *be two Chu spaces. Their tensor product* $\mathbf{A} \otimes \mathbf{A}'$ *is defined as follows:*

- $(\mathbf{A} \otimes \mathbf{A}')_* = A_* \times A'_*$.

- $(\mathbf{A} \otimes \mathbf{A}')^*$ *consists of the pairs of functions* $(f, g)$, *with* $f : A_* \to A'^*$ *and* $g : A'_* \to A^*$, *which satisfy* $\langle x, g(x') \rangle = \langle x', f(x) \rangle$, *for all* $x \in A_*, x' \in A'_*$.

- $\langle (x, x'), (f, g) \rangle = \langle x, g(x') \rangle = \langle x', f(x) \rangle$.

**Definition 13.5.8 (linear negation – Chu spaces)** *The linear negation of a Chu space is defined as follows (where* $\gamma$ *is as in definition 13.2.3):*

$$(A_*, A^*, \langle \_, \_ \rangle)^\perp = (A^*, A_*, \langle \_, \_ \rangle \circ \gamma).$$

**Proposition 13.5.9** (1) *The category* $\mathbf{Chu}$ *is* $*$-*autonomous. The tensor product is as given in definition 13.5.7, the unit is* $I = (\{*\}, K, \pi_2)$ *and the dualizing object is* $\perp = (K, \{*\}, \pi_1)$.

(2) *There exists a natural bijection* $\mathbf{Chu}[I, \mathbf{A}] \cong A_*$.

PROOF. For the symmetric monoidal structure, we just check that $\mathbf{A} \otimes I \cong \mathbf{A}$. The $*$ component of $\mathbf{A} \otimes I$ is $A_* \times \{*\}$, which is $A_*$ up to natural bijection. An element of the $*$ component of $\mathbf{A} \otimes I$ can be considered as a pair of a function $f : A_* \to K$ and an element $\alpha \in A^*$. Looking at the condition linking $f$ and $\alpha$, we see that it boils down to the definition of $f$ as $\lambda x.\langle x, \alpha \rangle$.

By a similar reasoning, we get (2). To establish the closed structure, we rely on proposition 13.2.8. The dualizing functor is given by definition 13.5.8. The required isomorphisms $\mathbf{A}^{\perp\perp} \cong \mathbf{A}$ are actually identities. We verify the bijections:

$$\mathbf{Chu}[I, (\mathbf{A} \otimes \mathbf{B}^{\perp})^{\perp}] \cong \mathbf{Chu}[\mathbf{A}, \mathbf{B}].$$

Let $\mathbf{f} : \mathbf{A} \to \mathbf{B}$:

$$\mathbf{f} \in (\mathbf{A} \otimes \mathbf{B}^{\perp})^* \quad \text{(by the definition of } \otimes\text{)}$$
$$\mathbf{f} \in (\mathbf{A} \otimes \mathbf{B}^{\perp})^{\perp}_* \quad \text{(by the definition of } {}^{\perp}\text{)}\,.$$

We conclude by using (2). To see that **Chu** is $*$-autonomous, we proceed essentially as in proposition 13.2.20: the canonical morphism from $\mathbf{A}$ to $(\mathbf{A} \multimap \perp) \multimap \perp$ is the identity modulo identifications similar to those used above for proving $\mathbf{A} \otimes I \cong \mathbf{A}$. $\quad\square$

**Lemma 13.5.10 (slice condition)** *The tensor product of two right separated Chu spaces* $\mathbf{A}$ *and* $\mathbf{A}'$ *is right separated, and can be reformulated as follows:*

- $(\mathbf{A} \otimes \mathbf{A}')_* = A_* \times A'_*.$

- $(\mathbf{A} \otimes \mathbf{A}')^*$ *consists of the functions* $h : A_* \times A'_* \to K$ *whose curryings factor through* $A^*$ *and* $A'^*$, *that is such that, for some* $f$ *and* $g$:

$$\Lambda(h) = r_{A'} \circ f \qquad \Lambda(h \circ \gamma) = r_A \circ g\,.$$

- $\langle (x, x'), h \rangle = h(x, x').$

*If moreover* $\mathbf{A}$ *and* $\mathbf{A}'$ *are right strict, then the reformulation says that* $(\mathbf{A} \otimes \mathbf{A}')^*$ *consists of the subsets* $U$ *of* $A_* \times A'_*$ *satisfying the following condition, called the slice condition:*

$$(\forall x \in A_* \ \{x' \mid (x, x') \in U\} \in A'^*) \quad \text{and} \quad (\forall x' \in A'_* \ \{x \mid (x, x') \in U\} \in A^*).$$

PROOF. By definition of ${}^{\perp}$ and by proposition 13.5.9, an element of $(\mathbf{A} \otimes \mathbf{B})^*$ can be described as a morphism of $\mathbf{Chu}[\mathbf{A}, \mathbf{B}^{\perp}]$. The conclusion then follows from lemma 13.5.6. $\quad\square$

Unlike right separation, left separation has to be forced upon the tensor product structure.

**Lemma 13.5.11** *With every Chu space* $\mathbf{A}$ *we associate a left separated Chu space* $\mathbf{A}_l$ *as follows:*

- $(A_l)^* = A^*.$

- $(A_l)_* = A_*/\approx$, *where* $\approx$ *is the equivalence relation defined by:*

$$x_1 \approx x_2 \Leftrightarrow \forall \alpha \in A^* \ \langle x_1, \alpha \rangle = \langle x_2, \alpha \rangle.$$

- $\langle [x], \alpha \rangle = \langle x, \alpha \rangle.$

*If moreover* $\mathbf{A}$ *is right separated, then* $\mathbf{A}_l$ *is separated. There is a symmetric construction* $\mathbf{A}_r$ *which forces right separation.*

**Proposition 13.5.12** *The statement of proposition 13.5.9 holds true replacing* **Chu** *by* **Chu**$_s$ *and redefining the tensor product as* $\mathbf{A} \otimes_s \mathbf{B} = (\mathbf{A} \otimes \mathbf{B})_l$. *(We shall omit the subscript in* $\otimes_s$ *if no ambiguity can arise.)*

PROOF. The proof is by a straightforward adaptation of the proof of proposition 13.5.9. Notice that $\mathbf{f} : \mathbf{A} \to \mathbf{B}$ reads as $\mathbf{f} \in (\mathbf{A} \otimes_s \mathbf{B}^\perp)^*$ since $(\mathbf{A} \otimes_s \mathbf{B}^\perp)^* = (\mathbf{A} \otimes \mathbf{B}^\perp)^*$.  □

Our last step consists in adding directed lub's, more precisely directed unions. From now on, we assume that $K = \{\perp, \top\}$, and freely confuse a function $h$ into $K$ with the set it is the characteristic function of.

**Definition 13.5.13 (casuistry)** *A casuistry is a separated Chu space* $\mathbf{A}$ *such that both* $A_*$ *and* $A^*$ *are dcpo's under the induced orders defined by:*

$$x \leq x' \Leftrightarrow l(x) \subseteq l(x') \quad (\text{for all } x, x' \in A_*)$$

*(and symmetrically for* $A^*$*), and moreover* $l(\bigvee \Delta) = \bigcup l(\Delta)$ *for any* $\Delta \subseteq_{dir} A_*$, *and similarly for* $r$. *We call* **Cas** *the full subcategory of* **Chu**$_s$ *whose objects are casuistries.*

**Exercise 13.5.14** *Given a right strict Chu space* $\mathbf{A}$, *we say that* $x \in A_*$ *is empty if* $\forall U \in A^*$ $x \notin U$. *Consider now two casuistries* $\mathbf{A}$ *and* $\mathbf{B}$. *Show that, for any* $[x, y] \in (\mathbf{A} \otimes_s \mathbf{B})_*$:

$$[x, y] = \begin{cases} \{(x, y)\} & \text{if neither } x \text{ nor } y \text{ are empty} \\ \text{the empty element of } (\mathbf{A} \otimes_s \mathbf{B})_* & \text{otherwise} . \end{cases}$$

**Lemma 13.5.15** *A topological space* $(X, \Omega)$ *viewed as a Chu space is a casuistry iff its topology is* $T_0$, *its specialization order is a dcpo, and every open set is Scott open.*

PROOF. A topology is *a fortiori* closed under directed unions. Thus the requirement concerns $X$. Notice that $l(\bigvee \Delta) = \bigcup l(\Delta)$ reads as:

$$\forall U \in \Omega \ \bigvee \Delta \in U \Leftrightarrow (\exists \delta \in \Delta \ \delta \in U) .$$

□

**Lemma 13.5.16** *All morphisms between casuistries preserve directed lub's.*

PROOF. It is enough to check $l(f(\bigvee \Delta)) \subseteq \bigcup l(f(\Delta))$. We have:

$$
\begin{aligned}
l(f(\bigvee \Delta)) &= \{U \mid f(\bigvee \Delta) \in U\} \\
&= \{U \mid \bigvee \Delta \in f^{-1}(U)\} ,
\end{aligned}
$$

and we conclude by exploiting the fact that $f^{-1}(U)$ is Scott open.  □

**Proposition 13.5.17** *The category* **Cas** *is* *-autonomous, and all the constructions are the restrictions of the constructions on* **Chu**$_s$. *Lub's in* $(\mathbf{A} \otimes_s \mathbf{B})_*$ *are coordinatewise.*

PROOF. Let $\mathbf{A}$ and $\mathbf{B}$ be casuistries. We sketch the proof that $\mathbf{A} \otimes_s \mathbf{B}$ is a casuistry. Consider a directed subset $\Delta$ of $(\mathbf{A} \otimes_s \mathbf{B})^* = (\mathbf{A} \otimes \mathbf{B})^*$. The reason why $\bigcup \Delta$ satisfies the slice conditions (cf. lemma 13.5.10) is that a slice of a directed union is a directed union of slices. Consider now a directed subset $\Delta$ of $(\mathbf{A} \otimes_s \mathbf{B})_*$. Without loss of generality, we can assume that the empty element is not in $\Delta$, hence (cf. exercise 13.5.14) that $\Delta \subseteq A_* \times B_*$. We claim:

$$l(\bigvee \pi_1(\Delta), \bigvee \pi_2(\Delta)) = \bigcup l(\Delta).$$

The direction $\supseteq$ is an immediate consequence of pointwise monotonicity, i.e.:

$$(x_1 \leq x_2 \text{ and } y_1 \leq y_2) \Rightarrow l(x_1, y_1) \subseteq l(x_2, y_2) \,,$$

which we establish as follows. If $(x_1, y_1) \in U$, then $x_1 \in \{x \mid (x, y_1) \in U\}$. Hence:

$$x_2 \in \{x \mid (x, y_1) \in U\} \text{ since } \{x \mid (x, y_1) \in U\} \text{ is open and } x_1 \leq x_2.$$

We have obtained $(x_2, y_1) \in U$, from which we obtain $(x_2, y_2) \in U$ by a similar reasoning, now using the slice $\{y \mid (x_2, y) \in U\}$. The direction $\subseteq$ is proved similarly, making use of the fact that the slices are Scott open by definition of casuistries. □

**Proposition 13.5.18** *The categories* **Chu**, **Chu**$_s$, *and* **Cas** *are cartesian. The terminal object is* $(\{*\}, \emptyset)$ *(with vacuous* $\langle \_, \_ \rangle$*). The product in* **Chu** *is given by:*

$$(A \times A')_* = A_* \times A'_*$$
$$(A \times A')^* = A^* + A'^*$$
$$\langle (x, x'), \alpha \rangle = \begin{cases} \langle x, \alpha \rangle & \text{if } \alpha \in A^* \\ \langle x', \alpha \rangle & \text{if } \alpha \in A'^* \,. \end{cases}$$

*In* **Chu**$_s$, *and* **Cas**, *right separation has to be forced (cf. lemma 13.5.11), and the product* $\times_s$ *(or* $\times$ *if no ambiguity can arise) is given by:*

$$A \times_s A' = (A \times A')_r.$$

*(cf. lemma 13.5.11). If $A$ and $A'$ are right strict, then we can reformulate their product (in* **Chu**$_s$, *and* **Cas***) as follows:*

$$(A \times A')_* = A_* \times A'_*$$
$$(A \times A')^* = \{U \times A' \mid U \in A^*\} \cup \{A \times U' \mid U' \in A^*\} \,.$$

*The order induced on $A_* \times A'_*$ is the pointwise ordering.*

PROOF. We only show that 1 is terminal, and that the induced order on products is pointwise. By the vacuity of $1^*$, being a morphism into 1 amounts to being a function to $1_* = \{*\}$. Suppose that $(x, x') \leq (y, y')$, and that $x \in U$. Then $(x, x') \in U \times A' \in (A \times A')^*$. Hence $(y, y') \in U \times A'$, i.e., $y \in U$. Similarly we get $x' \leq y'$. The converse direction is proved similarly. □

Finally, we define an adjunction between the category of casuistries and the category of dcpo's.

**Proposition 13.5.19** *Consider the two following functors* $\subseteq$: **Dcpo** $\to$ **Cas** *and* ! : **Cas** $\to$ **Dcpo**, *defined as follows:*

$$\subseteq (D, \leq) = (D, \tau_S(D), \in) \qquad \subseteq (f) = f$$
$$!(X_*, X^*, \langle \_, \_ \rangle) = (X_*, \leq) \qquad !(f) = f \,,$$

*where $\tau_S(D)$ denotes Scott topology (cf. definition 1.2.1), and where $\leq$ in the second line is the induced ordering (cf. definition 13.5.13). Then $\subseteq \dashv !$. Moreover, the induced comonad $\subseteq \circ !$, written simply !, satisfies the isomorphisms of definition 13.2.12, i.e., casuistries together with ! form a $*_l$-autonomous category, whose Kleisli category is equivalent to the category* **Dcpo**.

PROOF. To establish $\subseteq \dashv \,!$, we have to prove that, given $(D, \leq)$ and $(X_*, X^*, \in)$, a function $f : D \rightarrow X_*$ is a Chu morphism from $(D, \tau_S(D), \in)$ to $(X_*, X^*, \in)$ iff it is a directed lub preserving function from $(D, \leq)$ to $(X_*, \leq)$. If $f$ is a Chu morphism, then it preserves directed lub's with respect to the induced orders by lemma 13.5.16. But (cf. lemma 1.2.3) the induced, or specialized, order of a Scott topology is the original order, i.e., $! \circ \subseteq = id$. Hence $f$ preserves the lub's with respect to the order $\leq$ of $D$. If $f$ preserves directed lub's, then it is continuous with respect to the Scott topologies, and *a fortiori* it is a Chu morphism from $(D, \tau_S(D), \in)$ to $(X_*, X^*, \in)$, since $X^* \subseteq \tau_S(X_*)$ by proposition 13.5.15.

We already observed that $! \circ \subseteq = id$, hence *a fortiori* $!$ is surjective on objects. As a consequence (cf. remark 13.2.14), the Kleisli category is equivalent to **Dcpo**, and thus is cartesian closed, which in turn entails the isomorphisms $!(\mathbf{A} \times \mathbf{B}) \cong (!\mathbf{A}) \otimes (!\mathbf{B})$, by proposition 13.2.16. We are left to show $!1 \cong I$. Recall that $I$, formulated as a right strict Chu space, is $(\{*\}, \{\emptyset, \{*\}\})$. We have:

$$I_* = (!1)_* \quad \text{and} \quad I^* \text{ is the Scott topology over } \{*\}.$$

$\square$

**Remark 13.5.20** *We have expressed the comonad for the stable model and for the hypercoherence model via an adjunction of the form* $! \dashv \subseteq$*, while we just presented a continuous model via an adjunction of the form* $\subseteq \dashv \,!$*. One should not take that too seriously. In each situation, we have called* $\subseteq$ *the obvious inclusion at hand. But both the stable* $\subseteq$ *and the continuous* $!$ *are faithful functors: in particular, morphisms in* **Cas** *can be considered as special Scott-continuous functions (those mapping (chosen) open sets to chosen open sets).*

A more liberal $!$ (leading to a larger Kleisli category), also taken from [Lam94], is described in exercise 13.5.21.

**Exercise 13.5.21** *Call a topological space* $(X, \Omega)$ *anti-separated if, whenever a subset* $U$ *of* $X \times X$ *satisfies the slice condition (cf. lemma 13.5.10), then* $\{x \mid (x, x) \in U\} \in \Omega$*. Show that* **Dcpo** *is a full subcategory of the category* $\Delta$**Cas** *of anti-separated topological spaces that moreover viewed as Chu spaces are casuistries. Show that* **Cas** *together with the following definition of* $!$ *yields a* $*_l$*-autonomous category whose Kleisli category is equivalent to* $\Delta$**Cas***:*

$$!\mathbf{A} = \text{the smallest anti-separated topology on } A_* \text{ containing } A^*.$$

*Hints: The anti-separation condition says that the diagonal function* $\lambda x.(x, x)$ *is continuous from* $X$ *(viewed as a separated Chu space) to* $X \otimes X$*. Follow the guidelines of remark 13.2.19. In order to prove* $U \dashv \,!$*, give an inductive definition of* $!(\mathbf{A})^*$*.*

# 14
# Sequentiality

This chapter is devoted to the semantics of sequentiality. At first order, the notion of sequential function is well-understood, as summarized in theorem 6.5.4. At higher orders, the situation is not as simple. Building on theorem 13.3.18, Ehrhard and Bucciarelli have developped a model of strongly stable functions, which we have described in section 13.3. But in the strongly stable model an explicit reference to a concept of sequentiality is lost at higher orders. Here there is an intrinsic difficulty: there does not exist a cartesian closed category of sequential (set theoretical) functions (see theorem 14.1.12). Berry suggested that replacing functions by morphisms of a more concrete nature, and retaining information on the order in which the input is explored in order to produce a given part of the output, could be a way to develop a theory of higher order sequentiality. This intuition gave birth to the model of sequential algorithms of Berry and Curien, which is described in this chapter [BC82, BC85].

In section 14.1, we introduce Kahn and Plotkin's (filiform and stable) concrete data structures and sequential functions between concrete data structures [KP93]. This definition generalizes Vuillemin's definition 6.5.1. A concrete data structure consists of cells that can be filled with a value, much like a PASCAL record field can be given a value. A concrete data structure generates a cpo of states, which are sets of pairs (cell, value), also called events (cf. section 12.3). Cells generalize the notion of argument position that plays a central role in Vuillemin's definition of sequential function. Kahn-Plotkin's definition of sequential function is based on cells, and reads roughly as follows: for a given input $x$ and output cell $c'$, if $c'$ is filled in $f(y)$ for some $y \geq x$, i.e., if $(c', v') \in f(y)$ for some $v'$, then there exists a cell $c$, depending on $x$ and $c'$ only, such that $c$ is filled in all such $y$. In other words, it is necessary to compute the value of $c$ in order to fill $c'$. Such a cell $c$ is called a sequentiality index at $(x, c')$. The category of sequential functions on concrete data structures is cartesian, but not cartesian closed.

In section 14.2, we define sequential algorithms on concrete data structures. They can be presented in different ways. We first define an exponent concrete data structure, whose states are called sequential algorithms. The notion of abstract algorithm provides a more intuitive presentation. An abstract algorithm is a partial function that maps a pair of a (finite) input state $x$ and an output cell $c'$ to either an output value $v'$ (if $(c', v') \in f(x)$) or to an input cell $c$, where $c$ is a sequentiality index at $(x, c')$. Hence sequential algorithms involve an explicit choice of sequentiality indices. Many functions admit more than one sequentiality index for a given pair $(x, c')$. For example, adding two numbers requires computing these two numbers. In the model of sequential algorithms, there exist *two* addition algorithms, one of which computes the first argument then the second before adding them, while the other scans its input in the converse order. We show that sequential algorithms form a category called **Algo**. Due to the concrete nature of the morphisms, it takes some time until we can recognize the structure of a category. A third presentation of sequential algorithms as functions between domains containing error values is given in section 14.4.

In section 14.3, we present a linear decomposition of the category of sequential algorithms. We define symmetric algorithms, which are pairs of sequential functions, mapping input values to output values, and output exploration trees to input exploration trees, respectively. It is convenient to work with sequential data structures, which are a more symmetric reformulation of (filiform and stable) concrete data structures. Sequential data structures and symmetric algorithms are the objects and morphisms of a symmetric monoidal closed category called **Algo**$_l$, which is related to the category of sequential algorithms through an adjunction. The category **Algo**$_l$ is also cartesian. Moreover, the unit is terminal. Due to this last property, our decomposition is actually an affine decomposition (cf. remark 13.2.23). The category of symmetric algorithms is a full subcategory of a category of games considered by Lamarche [Lam92b]. Related categories are studied in [Bla72, Bla92, AJ92].

In section 14.4, we investigate an extension of PCF with a control operator *catch* (cf. section 8.5). The extended language enables the programmer to observe and exploit the evaluation order of arguments to procedures. Sequential algorithms can make such distinctions too, e.g., one can write a sequential algorithm that returns *tt* and *ff* when applied to the left addition algorithm and the right addition algorithm, respectively (see exercise 14.2.15). As a matter of fact, we show that the model of sequential algorithms is fully abstract for this extension of PCF.

# 14.1    Sequential functions

First we define the concrete data structures (cds's). We give some examples of cds's, and define the product of two cds's. We then define Kahn-Plotkin sequential functions [KP93], which generalize the first order sequential functions of definition 6.5.1. The category of cds's and sequential functions is cartesian but not cartesian closed (theorem 14.1.12).

**Definition 14.1.1** *A concrete data structure (or cds)* $\mathbf{M} = (C, V, E, \vdash)$ *is given by three sets* $C$, $V$, *and* $E$ *of cells, values, and events, such that:*

$$E \subseteq C \times V \quad \text{and} \quad \forall c \in C \ \exists v \in V \ (c, v) \in E \ ,$$

*and a relation* $\vdash$ *between finite parts of* $E$ *and elements of* $C$, *called the* enabling *relation. We write simply* $e_1, \ldots, e_n \vdash c$ *for* $\{e_1, \ldots, e_n\} \vdash c$. *A cell* $c$ *such that* $\vdash c$ *is called* initial.

*Proofs of cells c are sets of events defined recursively as follows: If c is initial, then it has an empty proof. If $(c_1, v_1), \ldots, (c_n, v_n) \vdash c$, and if $p_1, \ldots, p_n$ are proofs of $c_1, \ldots, c_n$, then $p_1 \cup \{(c_1, v_1)\} \cup \cdots \cup p_n \cup \{(c_n, v_n)\}$ is a proof of c.*

*A state is a subset $x$ of $E$ such that:*

(1) $(c, v_1), (c, v_2) \in x \Rightarrow v_1 = v_2$.

(2) *If $(c, v) \in x$, then $x$ contains a proof of c.*

*The conditions (1) and (2) are called consistency and safety, respectively. The set of states of a cds $\mathbf{M}$, ordered by set inclusion, is a partial order denoted by $(D(\mathbf{M}), \leq)$ (or $(D(\mathbf{M}), \subseteq)$). If $D$ is isomorphic to $D(\mathbf{M})$, we say that $\mathbf{M}$ generates $D$.*

**Definition 14.1.2** *Let $\mathbf{M} = (C, V, E, \vdash)$ be a cds.*

(1) $\mathbf{M}$ *is called* well-founded *if the reflexive closure of the relation $\ll$ defined on $C$ by*

$$c_1 \ll c \text{ iff some enabling of } c \text{ contains an event } (c_1, v)$$

*is well-founded, that is, there is no infinite sequence $\{c_n\}_{n \geq 0}$ such that $\cdots c_{n+1} < < c_n \ll \cdots c_0$.*

(2) $\mathbf{M}$ *is called* stable *if for any state $x$ and any cell $c$ enabled in $x$, if $X \vdash c$, $X' \vdash c$, and $X, X' \subseteq x$, then $X = X'$.*

(3) $\mathbf{M}$ *is called* filiform *if all its enablings contain at most one event.*

**Remark 14.1.3** *Well-foundedness allows us to reformulate the safety condition as a local condition:*

(2′) *If $(c, v) \in x$, then $x$ contains an enabling $\{e_1, \ldots, e_n\}$ of c.*

**Remark 14.1.4** *Almost all the constructions of sections 14.1 and 14.2 go through for well-founded and stable cds's that are not necessarily filiform. But it simplifies notation to work with filiform cds's. In particular, in a filiform cds, a proof of a cell boils down to a sequence $(c_1, v_1), \ldots, (c_n, v_n)$ such that $(c_i, v_i) \vdash c_{i+1}$ for all $i$. Filiform cds's are in any case enough for our purposes. Hence we shall assume hereafter that cds's are well-founded, stable, and filiform, while making it explicit when 'stable', or 'filiform', are essential.*

**Definition 14.1.5** *Let $x$ be a set of events of a cds. A cell $c$ is called:*

• filled *(with $v$) in $x$ iff $(c, v) \in x$,*

• enabled *in $x$ iff $x$ contains an enabling of c,*

• accessible *from $x$ iff it is enabled, but not filled in $x$.*

*We denote by $F(x)$, $E(x)$, and $A(x)$ the sets of cells which are filled, enabled, and accessible in or from $x$, respectively. We write:*

$$x <_c y \quad \text{if } c \in A(x), c \in F(y) \text{ and } x < y$$
$$x \prec_c y \quad \text{if } x <_c y \text{ and } x \prec y \text{ (cf. definition 12.3.8)}.$$

**Proposition 14.1.6** (1) *Let* M *be a cds. The partial order* $(D(\mathbf{M}), \leq)$ *is a Scott domain whose compact elements are the finite states. Upper bounded lub's are set theoretical unions.*

(2) *If* M *is stable, then* $(D(\mathbf{M}), \leq)$ *is a dI-domain. For any upper bounded set* $X$ *of states of* M, *the set theoretical intersection* $\bigcap X$ *is a state of* M, *and hence is the glb of* $X$ *in* $D(\mathbf{M})$.

PROOF. We only check the last part of the statement. Let $z$ be an upper bound of $X$, and $c \in F(\bigcap X)$. By stability, $c$ has the same proof in all the elements of $X$, namely the proof of $c$ in $z$. $\square$

**Example 14.1.7** (1) *Flat cpo's. The flat cpo* $X_\perp$ *is generated by the following cds, which we denote by* $X_\perp$ *to avoid useless inflation of notation:*

$$X_\perp = (\{?\}, X, \{?\} \times X, \{\vdash?\}).$$

(2) *The following cds* **LAMBDA** $= (C, V, E, \vdash)$ *generates the (possibly infinite) terms of the untyped $\lambda$-calculus with constants, including $\Omega$ (cf. definition 2.3.1) (the typed case is similar):*

$$C = \{0, 1, 2\}^* \quad V = \{\cdot\} \cup \{x, \lambda x \mid x \in Var\} \cup Cons \quad E = C \times V$$
$$\vdash \epsilon \quad (u, \lambda x) \vdash u0 \quad (u, \cdot) \vdash u1, u2,$$

*where Var is the set of variables and Cons is the set of constants. For example, the term* $t = (\lambda x.y)x$ *is represented by* $\{(\epsilon, \cdot), (1, \lambda x)), (10, y), (2, x)\}$. *Here cells are occurrences, cf. definition 2.1.4.*

Products of cds's are obtained by putting the component structures side by side, and by renaming the cells in each cds to avoid confusion.

**Definition 14.1.8** *Let* M *and* M′ *be two cds's. We define the product* M × M′ $= (C, V, E, \vdash)$ *of* M *and* M′ *by:*

- $C = \{c.1 \mid c \in C_{\mathbf{M}}\} \cup \{c'.2 \mid c' \in C_{\mathbf{M'}}\}$,
- $V = V_{\mathbf{M}} \cup V_{\mathbf{M'}}$,
- $E = \{(c.1, v) \mid (c, v) \in E_{\mathbf{M}}\} \cup \{(c'.2, v') \mid (c', v') \in E_{\mathbf{M'}}\}$,
- $(c_1.1, v_1) \vdash c.1 \Leftrightarrow (c_1, v_1) \vdash c$ *(and similarly for* M′*).*

Clearly, M × M′ generates $D(\mathbf{M}) \times D(\mathbf{M'})$ (the ordered set theoretical product).

**Definition 14.1.9 (sequential function (Kahn-Plotkin))** *Let* M *and* M′ *be two cds's. A continuous function* $f : D(\mathbf{M}) \to D(\mathbf{M'})$ *is called sequential at* $x$ *if for any* $c' \in A(f(x))$ *one of the following properties hold:*

(1) $\forall y \geq x \; c' \notin F(f(y))$.

(2) $\exists c \in A(x) \; \forall y > x \; (f(x) <_{c'} f(y) \Rightarrow x <_c y)$.

*A cell $c$ satisfying condition (2) is called a* sequentiality index *of $f$ at* $(x, c')$. *The index is called strict if (1) does not hold. If (1) holds, then any cell $c$ in $A(x)$ is a (vacuous) sequentiality index. The function $f$ is called sequential from* M *to* M′ *if it is sequential at all points. We denote by* M $\to_{seq}$ M′ *the set of these functions. A sequential function is called* strongly sequential *if, for any cell $c'$ and any state $x$ where it has a strict index, this index is unique.*

Examples of sequential functions are given in lemma 14.1.10 and in exercises 14.1.14, 14.1.16, and 2.4.4. The concrete data structures and the sequential functions form a cartesian category.

**Lemma 14.1.10** (1) *The identity functions, the first and second projection functions, and the constant functions are strongly sequential; the composition and the pairing of two sequential functions is sequential.*

(2) *If* $\mathbf{M}$ *and* $\mathbf{M}'$ *are cds's and* $f : D(\mathbf{M}) \to D(\mathbf{M}')$ *is an order-isomorphism, then* $f$ *is sequential.*

The sequential functions are stable, but not conversely. The counter-example given in the proof of the next proposition is due to Kleene and Berry, independently.

**Proposition 14.1.11** *Let* $\mathbf{M}$ *and* $\mathbf{M}'$ *be two cds's. The following properties hold.*

(1) *Sequential functions from* $\mathbf{M}$ *to* $\mathbf{M}'$ *are stable.*

(2) *If* $g$ *is sequential, if* $f$ *is continuous, and if* $f \leq_{st} g$, *then* $f$ *is sequential, and for any* $x$ *and* $c' \in A(f(x))$, *if* $f$ *has a strict index at* $x$, *then* $c' \in A(g(x))$, *and any index of* $g$ *at* $x$ *for* $c'$ *is also an index of* $f$ *at* $x$ *for* $c'$.

(3) *There exist stable functions that are not sequential.*

PROOF. (1) If $x \uparrow y$ and $g(x \wedge y) < g(x) \wedge g(y)$, then $g(x \wedge y) <_{c'} g(x) \wedge g(y)$, for some $c'$. Let $c$ be a sequentiality index at $(x \wedge y, c')$. Then $x \wedge y <_c x$ and $x \wedge y <_c y$. Let $v$ and $w$ be such that $(c, v) \in x$ and $(c, w) \in y$. Let $z$ be an upper bound of $x, y$. By consistency of $z$ we have $v = w$, which in turn implies $c \in F(x \wedge y)$ by stability (cf. proposition 14.1.6). This contradicts $c \in A(x \wedge y)$. Hence $g$ is stable.

(2) Let $f$ be such that $f \leq_{st} g$, and let $c' \in A(f(x))$. If $c' \in F(g(x))$, then $c' \in A(f(y))$ for all $y \geq x$, since $F(f(x)) = F(f(y)) \cap F(g(x))$. If $c' \in A(g(x))$, $x \leq y$ and $f(x) <_{c'} f(y)$, then *a fortiori* $g(x) <_{c'} g(y)$, and $x <_c y$, where $c$ is a (strict) index of $g$ at $(x, c')$. Hence $f$ is sequential, and $c$ is a strict index of $f$ at $(x, c')$.

(3) Let $BK$ be the following stable function from $(\mathbf{B}_\perp)^3$ to $\mathbf{O}$ (cf. section 12.1):

$$BK(x, y, z) = \begin{cases} \top & \text{if } x = tt \text{ and } y = \mathit{ff} \\ \top & \text{if } x = \mathit{ff} \text{ and } z = tt \\ \top & \text{if } y = tt \text{ and } z = \mathit{ff} \\ \perp & \text{otherwise .} \end{cases}$$

One checks easily that $BK$ has no index at $\perp$ for ?. □

We now show that the category of cds's and sequential functions is not cartesian closed.

**Theorem 14.1.12** *The category* **Seq** *of cds's and sequential functions is not cartesian closed.*

PROOF. The following simple proof is due to Ehrhard [Ehr96]. (The original proof [Cur86] was similar to the proof of proposition 5.2.17). First we observe that if a category $C$ has enough points, (cf. definition 4.5.4), then the products, projections and pairings are the set theoretical ones. Also, we can assume $C[A, B] = D(A \to B)$ and that application and currying are the set theoretical ones (due to the bijection between $C[1, A \to B]$ and $C[A, B]$). We assume that $\mathbf{Seq}$ is cartesian closed. The proof by contradiction goes through successive claims.

(1) For any $\mathbf{M}$, $\mathbf{M}'$, the minimum of $D(\mathbf{M} \to \mathbf{M}')$ is $\lambda y.\bot$. To establish $\lambda y.\bot \leq_{st} f$ ($f$ fixed and arbitrary), consider $g : \mathbf{O} \times D(\mathbf{M}) \to D(\mathbf{M}')$, defined by:

$$g(x, y) = \begin{cases} \bot & \text{if } x = \bot \\ f(y) & \text{if } x \neq \bot. \end{cases}$$

The function $g$ is sequential, and therefore is a morphism of $\mathbf{Seq}$. Hence we can consider $\Lambda(g)$, which is *a fortiori* monotonic:

$$\lambda y.\bot = \Lambda(g)(\bot) \leq_{st} \Lambda(g)(\top) = f.$$

(2) For any $\mathbf{M}$, there exists an (initial) cell $c$ in $\mathbf{M} \to \mathbf{O}$ such that:

$$\forall f \in D(\mathbf{M} \to \mathbf{O}) \ (f \neq \lambda y.\bot \Rightarrow c \in F(f)).$$

Indeed, the set theoretical application, being the evaluation morphism, is sequential. It is non-strict in its second argument ($ev(f, \bot) = f(\bot) \neq \bot$ for, say, any constant function different from $\lambda y.\bot$). Hence $ev$ has a sequentiality index of the form $c.1$ at $((\bot, \bot), ?)$. Then let $f \in D(\mathbf{M} \to \mathbf{O})$ be such that $f \neq \lambda y.\bot$, i.e., $? \in F(ev(f, z)) = F(f(z))$ for some $z$. By sequentiality we get $c \in F(f)$.

(3) Finally, consider the following form $h$ of the conditional function from $\mathbf{O}^2 \times \mathbf{B}_\bot$ to $\mathbf{O}$:

$$h((x, y), z) = \begin{cases} \bot & \text{if } z = \bot \\ x & \text{if } z = tt \\ y & \text{if } z = ff. \end{cases}$$

Then we have:

$$\Lambda(h)(\bot, \bot) = \lambda z.\bot \quad \Lambda(h)(\top, \bot) \neq \lambda z.\bot \quad \Lambda(h)(\bot, \top) \neq \lambda z.\bot,$$

from which we derive:

$$c \notin F(\Lambda(h)(\bot, \bot)) \qquad \qquad \text{(by claim 1)}$$
$$c \in F(\Lambda(h)(\top, \bot)) \text{ and } c \in F(\Lambda(h)(\bot, \top)) \quad \text{(by claim 2)}.$$

But this contradicts the sequentiality of $\Lambda(h)$.                              □

**Exercise 14.1.13** *Show that the restriction of any stable function to a principal ideal* $\downarrow x$ *is sequential.*

**Exercise 14.1.14** *Let* $\mathbf{M}$ *and* $\mathbf{M}'$ *be two cds's and let* $(\phi, \psi)$ *be a rigid embedding from* $D(\mathbf{M})$ *to* $D(\mathbf{M}')$ *(cf. definition 12.4.2). Show that* $\phi$ *and* $\psi$ *are strongly sequential.*

**Exercise 14.1.15** *(1) We say that a cds* $\mathbf{M} = (C, V, E, \vdash)$ *is included in a cds* $\mathbf{M'} = (C', V', E', \vdash')$ *(and we write* $\mathbf{M} \subseteq \mathbf{M'}$*) if*

$$C \subseteq C' \qquad V \subseteq V' \qquad E \subseteq E' \qquad \vdash \subseteq \vdash' \ .$$

*Show that* $(id, \lambda x'.x' \cap E)$ *is a rigid embedding from* $D(\mathbf{M})$ *to* $D(\mathbf{M'})$*. (2) Conversely, given* $D, D'$*, each generated by some cds, and a rigid embedding* $(\phi, \psi)$ *from* $D$ *to* $D'$*, show that there exist two cds's* $\mathbf{M}$ *and* $\mathbf{M'}$ *such that:*

$$D \cong D(\mathbf{M}) \qquad D' \cong D(\mathbf{M'}) \qquad \mathbf{M} \subseteq \mathbf{M'} \ .$$

*(3) Show that this correspondence goes through for the strengthened notion of inclusion where one moreover imposes* $(X \vdash' c \Rightarrow X \vdash c)$ *(cf. the notion of rigid inclusion in exercise 13.1.20). (4) Exploit the correspondence to solve some domain equations in the framework of cds's (cf. exercise 10.2.14).*

**Exercise 14.1.16** *Define a cds* **BÖHM** *of Böhm trees, and show that theorem 2.4.3 reads as: BT is sequential from* **LAMBDA** *to* **BÖHM***.*

The following exercise justifies the terminology of stable cds.

**Exercise 14.1.17** *Let* $\mathbf{M}$ *be a cds. (1) Show that the functions* $\underline{c} : D(\mathbf{M}) \to D(\mathbf{O})$ *defined by* $\underline{c}(x) = \top$ *iff* $c \in F(x)$ *are additive (cf. definition 13.1.6). (2) Show that* $\mathbf{M}$ *is stable iff the functions* $\underline{c}$ *are stable. (3) Show that if* $\mathbf{M}$ *is stable and filiform, then it is sequential, by which we mean that the functions* $\underline{c}$ *are sequential.*

# 14.2 Sequential algorithms

A sequential function having at a given point more than one sequentiality index may be computed in different ways according to the order in which these indices are explored. For example, the addition function on $\omega_\perp \times \omega_\perp$ has ?.1 and ?.2 as sequentiality indices at $\perp$. The left addition computes ?.1, then ?.2, whereas the right addition does the same computations in the inverse order. The sequential algorithms formalize these ideas. For all cds's $\mathbf{M}$ and $\mathbf{M'}$, we define an exponent cds $\mathbf{M} \to \mathbf{M'}$, whose states are called the sequential algorithms from $\mathbf{M}$ to $\mathbf{M'}$. We give an abstract characterization of a sequential algorithm by a function describing both its input-output behaviour and its computation strategy. The characterization serves to define the composition of sequential algorithms.

**Definition 14.2.1 (exponent cds)** *If* $\mathbf{M}$*,* $\mathbf{M'}$ *are two cds's, the cds* $\mathbf{M} \to \mathbf{M'}$ *is defined as follows:*

- *If* $x$ *is a finite state of* $\mathbf{M}$*, and if* $c'$ *is a cell of* $\mathbf{M'}$*, then* $xc'$ *is a cell of* $\mathbf{M} \to \mathbf{M'}$*.*

- *The values and the events are of two types, called 'valof' and 'output', respectively:*

– *If* $c$ *is a cell of* $\mathbf{M}$*, then valof* $c$ *is a value of* $\mathbf{M} \to \mathbf{M'}$*, and* $(xc', valof\ c)$ *is an event of* $\mathbf{M} \to \mathbf{M'}$ *iff* $c$ *is accessible from* $x$*;*

– *if* $v'$ *is a value of* $\mathbf{M'}$*, then output* $v'$ *is a value of* $\mathbf{M} \to \mathbf{M'}$*, and* $(xc', output\ v')$ *is an event of* $\mathbf{M} \to \mathbf{M'}$ *iff* $(c', v')$ *is an event of* $\mathbf{M'}$*.*

- The enablings are also of two types:

$$(yc', valof\ c) \vdash xc' \qquad iff \quad y \prec_c x \qquad\qquad\qquad ('valof')$$
$$(x_1c_1', output\ v_1') \vdash xc' \quad iff \quad x = x_1\ and\ (c_1', v_1') \vdash c' \quad ('output')\ .$$

A state of $\mathbf{M} \to \mathbf{M}'$ is called a sequential algorithm, or simply an algorithm. If $a$ and $x$ are states of $\mathbf{M} \to \mathbf{M}'$ and $\mathbf{M}$, respectively, we write:

$$a{\cdot}x = \{(c', v') \mid \exists y \leq x\ (yc', output\ v') \in a\}.$$

The function $\lambda x.(a{\cdot}x)$ is called the input-output function computed by $a$.

**Example 14.2.2** (1)  The left addition algorithm $ADD_l : \omega_\perp \times \omega_\perp \to \omega_\perp$ consists of the following events:

$$(\emptyset?, valof\ ?.1)$$
$$(\{(?.1, i)\}?, valof\ ?.2) \qquad\qquad (i \in \omega)$$
$$(\{(?.1, i), (?.2, j)\}?, output\ i + j) \quad (i, j \in \omega)\ .$$

The right addition algorithm $ADD_r$ is defined similarly.

(2)  There are four different disjunction algorithms from $\mathbf{B}_\perp \times \mathbf{B}_\perp$ to $\mathbf{B}_\perp$. The two algorithms $OR_{sl}$ and $OR_{sr}$ compute the disjunction function that is strict in both its arguments; they are similar to $ADD_l$ and $ADD_r$. The two algorithms $OR_l$ and $OR_r$ compute the left and right disjunction functions that are strict in one of their arguments only, respectively. The four algorithms are described in figure 14.1. In this figure, $OR$ is the usual interpretation of disjunction over $\mathbf{B} = \{tt, ff\}$.

**Lemma 14.2.3** Let $\mathbf{M}$ and $\mathbf{M}'$ be two cds's. If $\mathbf{M}'$ is well-founded (filiform), then $\mathbf{M} \to \mathbf{M}'$ is well-founded (filiform).

PROOF. We observe that if $xc' \ll yd'$, then $x < y$ (with $y$ finite) or $c' \ll d'$.  □

The stability condition is essential to ensure that $\lambda x.(a{\cdot}x)$ is a function from $D(\mathbf{M})$ to $D(\mathbf{M}')$. The following example shows that this is not true in general. Let:

$$\mathbf{M} = (\{c\}, \{v\}, \{(c, v)\}, \vdash)$$
$$\text{with } \vdash c$$
$$\mathbf{M}' = (\{c_1', c_2', c_3'\}, \{1, 2\}, \{(c_i', j) \mid 1 \leq i \leq 3 \text{ and } 1 \leq j \leq 2\}, \vdash)$$
$$\text{with } \vdash c_1' \quad \vdash c_2' \quad (c_1', 1) \vdash c_3' \quad (c_2', 1) \vdash c_3'\ ,$$

where $\mathbf{M}'$ is not stable, since $c_3'$ has two enablings in $\{(c_1', 1), (c_2', 1)\}$. We choose $a$ and $x$ as follows:

$$a = \{(\perp c_1', output\ 1), (\perp c_2', valof\ c), (\{(c, v)\}c_2', output\ 1),$$
$$\qquad (\perp c_3', output\ 1), (\{(c, v)\}c_3', output\ 2)\}$$
$$x = \{c, v\}\ .$$

Then $a$ and $x$ are states of $\mathbf{M} \to \mathbf{M}'$ and $\mathbf{M}$, respectively, but $a{\cdot}x$ is not a state of $\mathbf{M}'$, since it contains both $(c_3', 1)$ and $(c_3', 2)$.

The following is a key technical proposition.

$$OR_{sl} = \begin{array}{ll} (\emptyset?, valof\ ?.1) & \\ (\{(?.1, i)\}?, valof\ ?.2) & (i \in \mathbf{B}) \\ (\{(?.1, i), (?.2, j)\}?, output\ OR(i, j)) & (i, j \in \mathbf{B}) \end{array}$$

$$OR_{sr} = \begin{array}{ll} (\emptyset?, valof\ ?.2) & \\ (\{(?.2, i)\}?, valof\ ?.1) & (i \in \mathbf{B}) \\ (\{(?.2, i), (?.1, j)\}?, output\ OR(j, i)) & (i, j \in \mathbf{B}) \end{array}$$

$$OR_l = \begin{array}{ll} (\emptyset?, valof\ ?.1) & \\ (\{(?.1, tt)\}?, output\ tt) & \\ (\{(?.1, f\!\!f)\}?, valof\ ?.2) & \\ (\{(?.1, f\!\!f), (?.2, j)\}?, output\ j) & (j \in \mathbf{B}) \end{array}$$

$$OR_r = \begin{array}{ll} (\emptyset?, valof\ ?.2) & \\ (\{(?.2, tt)\}?, output\ tt) & \\ (\{(?.2, f\!\!f)\}?, valof\ ?.1) & \\ (\{(?.2, f\!\!f), (?.1, j)\}?, output\ j) & (j \in \mathbf{B}) \end{array}$$

Figure 14.1: The four disjunction algorithms

**Proposition 14.2.4** *Let* $\mathbf{M}$ *and* $\mathbf{M}'$ *be cds's, and let* $a$ *be a state of* $\mathbf{M} \to \mathbf{M}'$. *The following properties hold:*

(1) *If* $(xc', u), (zc', w) \in a$ *and* $x \uparrow z$, *then* $x \leq z$ *or* $z \leq x$; *if* $x < z$, *there exists a chain*

$$x = y_0 \prec_{c_0} y_1 \cdots y_{n-1} \prec_{c_{n-1}} y_n = z$$

*such that* $\forall i < n\ (y_i c', valof\ c_i) \in a$. *If* $u$ *and* $w$ *are of type 'output', then* $x = z$.

(2) *The set* $a \cdot x$ *is a state of* $\mathbf{M}'$, *for all* $x \in D(\mathbf{M})$.

(3) *For all* $xc' \in F(a)$, $xc'$ *has only one enabling in* $a$; *hence* $\mathbf{M} \to \mathbf{M}'$ *is stable.*

(4) *The function* $\lambda x.(a \cdot x)$ *is stable.*

PROOF. We prove (1), (2) and (3) together, by induction on $c'$. At each induction step we prove $(2')$, (1), and (3), where $(2')$ is the following property:

$(2')$ The set $(a \cdot x)_{c'} = \{(d', v') \mid \exists y \leq x\ (yd', output\ v') \in a\ \text{and}\ d' \ll^+ c'\}$ is a state, for all $x \in D(\mathbf{M})$.

Property (2) is indeed a consequence of (1) and $(2')$: by $(2')$, the set $a \cdot x$ is safe, and, by (1), it is consistent.

$(2')$ Let $x$ be a state of $\mathbf{M}$, and let $d' \in F((a \cdot x)_{c'})$. Then, by definition, $\exists y \leq x\ yd' \in F(a)$. By analyzing a proof of $yd'$ in $a$, we check easily that $d'$ is enabled in $(a \cdot x)_{c'}$. Suppose $(d', v_1'), (d', v_2') \in (a \cdot x)_{c'}$. Then:

$$\exists y_1, y_2 \leq x\ (y_1 d', output\ v_1'), (y_2 d', output\ v_2') \in a,$$

whence we derive $y_1 = y_2$ by induction hypothesis (1), and $v_1' = v_2'$ by consistency of $a$. Hence $(a{\cdot}x)_{c'}$ is a state.

(1) We first remark that the last assertion of (1) follows from the others, since if $x \neq z$, then the existence of a chain between $x$ and $y$ as described in the statement entails that $u$ or $w$ is of type 'valof'. Let $s$ and $t$ be two proofs of $xc'$ and $zc'$ in $a$, respectively; here is the detail of $s$ until the first enabling of type 'output' is met:

$$(x_0 c'^1, output\ v'^1), (x_0 c', u_0), (x_1 c', valof\ c_1), \ldots, (x_{k-1} c', valof\ c_{k-1}), (xc', u)\ .$$

The following properties hold, by definition of the enablings of $\mathbf{M} \to \mathbf{M}'$:

- If $k = 0$, then $u_0 = u$. If $k > 0$, then $\exists c_0\ u_0 = valof\ c_0$, and $\forall i < k\ x_i \prec_{c_i} x_{i+1}$ (we write $x = x_k$).

- $(c'^1, v'^1) \vdash c'$.

Similar properties hold in $t$, replacing $x, x_0, \ldots, x_k, u_0, c_0, \ldots, c_{k-1}, c'^1, v'^1$ by:

$$z, z_0, \ldots, z_m, w_0, d_0, \ldots, d_{m-1}, c'^2, v'^2.$$

First we prove that $x_0 = z_0$. Let $y$ be such that $x, z \leq y$. The set $(a{\cdot}y)_{c'}$, which is a state by induction hypothesis (2'), contains $(c'^1, v'^1)$ and $(c'^2, v'^2)$, which are two enablings of $c'$. We have:

$c'^1 = c'^2$ (since $\mathbf{M}'$ is stable),

$x_0 = z_0$ (by the induction hypothesis (1)),

$u_0 = w_0$ (by consistency of $a$).

Property (1) clearly holds if $m = 0$ or $k = 0$. Hence we may suppose $k, m \neq 0$ and $k \leq m$ (by symmetry). We show by induction on $i$ that $x_i = z_i$ if $i \leq k$. Using the induction hypothesis we may rewrite $x_{i-1} \prec_{c_{i-1}} x_i$ as $z_{i-1} \prec_{d_{i-1}} x_i$ (note that $c_{i-1} = d_{i-1}$ by consistency of $a$). As we also have $z_{i-1} \prec_{d_{i-1}} z_i$ and $x_i \uparrow z_i$, we derive $x_i = z_i$. If $k < m$, the chain $x = z_k \prec_{d_k} z_{k+1} \prec \cdots \prec_{d_{m-1}} z$ has the property stated in (1). If $k = m$, then $x = z$.

(3) We exploit the proof of (1): if we start with the assumption that $x = z$, then the part of the proof $s$ which we have displayed coincides with the corresponding part of the proof $t$; in particular, $xc'$ has the same enabling in both proofs. Hence $xc'$ has only one enabling in $a$.

(4) Finally, we prove that $\lambda x.(a{\cdot}x)$ is stable. We first check continuity. Let $\Delta$ be directed, let $(c', v') \in a{\cdot}(\bigvee \Delta)$, and let $x \leq \bigvee \Delta$ be such that $(xc', output\ v') \in a$. Since $x$ is finite, $\exists y \in \Delta\ x \leq y$. Hence $(c', v') \in a{\cdot}y$. As for the stability, let $x \uparrow y$, and let $c' \in F(a{\cdot}x) \cap F(a{\cdot}y)$. Then, by (1) there exists $z \leq x, y$ and $v'$ such that $(zc', output\ v') \in a$; hence $(c', v') \in a{\cdot}(x \wedge y)$. □

Now we present an abstract characterization of sequential algorithms. Intuitively, if a sequential algorithm $a$ contains $(xc', u)$, information on the computation of $a$ at $x$ is given: if $u = output\ v'$, then $a{\cdot}x$ contains $(c', v')$; if $u = valof\ c$, then the contents of $c$ must be computed in order to fill $c'$ (we show in proposition 14.2.9 that the function computed by $a$ is indeed sequential). These informations remain true at $y > x$, supposing in the second case that $c$ is still not filled in $y$. The 'indications' given by $a$ are not limited to cells filled in $a$. For example $ADD_l$ 'indicates' $valof\ ?.1$ at $\{(?.2, 0)\}$ as well as at $\perp$. The following definition and proposition formalize these ideas.

**Definition 14.2.5 (abstract algorithm)** *Let* $\mathbf{M}$ *and* $\mathbf{M}'$ *be cds's. An abstract algorithm from* $\mathbf{M}$ *to* $\mathbf{M}'$ *is a partial function* $f : C_{\mathbf{M} \to \mathbf{M}'} \rightharpoonup V_{\mathbf{M} \to \mathbf{M}'}$ *satisfying the following axioms:*

$(A_1)$ *If* $f(xc') = u$, *then* $(xc', u) \in E_{\mathbf{M} \to \mathbf{M}'}$.

$(A_2)$ *If* $f(xc') = u$, $x \leq y$ *and* $(yc', u) \in E_{\mathbf{M} \to \mathbf{M}'}$, *then* $f(yc') = u$.

$(A_3)$ *Let* $f \cdot y = \{(c', v') \mid f(yc') = output\ v'\}$. *Then:*

$$f(yc') \downarrow\ \Rightarrow (c' \in E(f \cdot y)\ and\ (z \leq y\ and\ c' \in E(f \cdot z) \Rightarrow f(zc') \downarrow)).$$

*We write* $f(xc') = \omega$ *if* $f$ *is not defined at* $xc'$. *Whenever we write* $u$, *we mean* $u \in V_{\mathbf{M} \to \mathbf{M}'}$ *and* $u \neq \omega$. *An easy consequence of* $(A_3)$ *is that* $f \cdot z$ *is a state. We denote by* $(\mathcal{A}(\mathbf{M}, \mathbf{M}'), \leq)$ *the set of abstract algorithms from* $\mathbf{M}$ *to* $\mathbf{M}'$, *ordered as follows:*

$$f \leq f'\ \ iff\ \ (f(xc') = u \Rightarrow f'(xc') = u).$$

It will be convenient (when defining the composition of algorithms) to extend an abstract algorithm $f$ to a partial function from $D(\mathbf{M}) \times \mathbf{C}'$ to $V_{\mathbf{M} \to \mathbf{M}'}$. We keep the same name $f$ for the extended function:

$$f(xc') = u\ \ \text{iff}\ \ \begin{cases} f(yc') = u \text{ for some finite } y \leq x \text{ and} \\ \text{either } (u = valof\ c \text{ and } c \in A(x)) \text{ or } u = output\ v'\ . \end{cases}$$

**Exercise 14.2.6** *Show that an abstract algorithm between two cds's* $\mathbf{M}$ *and* $\mathbf{M}'$ *may be axiomatized as a partial function from* $D(\mathbf{M}) \times \mathbf{C}'$ *to* $V_{\mathbf{M} \to \mathbf{M}'}$ *which satisfies the following axiom in addition to the axioms* $(A_1)$, $(A_2)$, *and* $(A_3)$:

$(A0)$ *If* $f(xc') = u$, *then* $f(yc') = u$, *for some finite* $y \leq x$.

The abstract algorithms may be viewed as pairs $(\lambda x.(f \cdot x), i)$ where $i$, which may be called a computation strategy, is the function defined by 'restricting' $f$ to its control aspects, that is, $i(xc') = c$ iff $f(xc') = valof\ c$.

**Exercise 14.2.7** *Show that an abstract algorithm from a cds* $\mathbf{M}$ *to a cds* $\mathbf{M}'$ *may equivalently be defined as a pair of a sequential function* $f$ *from* $\mathbf{M}$ *to* $\mathbf{M}'$, *and of a computation strategy* $i$ *for it, which is a partial function* $i : D(\mathbf{M}) \times \mathbf{C}' \rightharpoonup \mathbf{C}$ *that satisfies the following axioms:*

(1) *If* $i(xc') = c$, *then* $c \in A(x)$ *and* $c' \in A(f(x))$.

(2) *If* $i(xc') = c$, *then* $i(yc') = c$ *for some finite* $y \leq x$.

(3) *If* $c' \in A(f(x))$ *and* $c' \in F(f(y))$ *for some* $y \geq x$ *then* $i(xc')$ *is defined and is a sequentiality index for* $f$ *at* $(x, c')$.

(4) *If* $i(xc') = c$, *if* $x \leq y$ *and* $c \in A(y)$, *then* $i(yc') = c$.

(5) *If* $i(xc') = c$ *and* $y \leq x$ *is such that* $c' \in A(f(y))$, *then* $i(yc')$ *is defined.*

The next theorem relates the abstract algorithms with the states of the exponent cds's.

**Proposition 14.2.8** *Let* $\mathbf{M}$ *and* $\mathbf{M}'$ *be cds's. Let* $a$ *be a state of* $\mathbf{M} \rightarrow \mathbf{M}'$. *Let* $a^+ : C_{\mathbf{M} \rightarrow \mathbf{M}'} \rightharpoonup V_{\mathbf{M} \rightarrow \mathbf{M}'}$ *be given by:*

$$a^+(xc') = u \quad \text{iff} \quad \exists y \leq x \ (yc', u) \in a \ \text{and} \ (xc', u) \in E_{\mathbf{M} \rightarrow \mathbf{M}'}.$$

*Let* $f \in \mathcal{A}(\mathbf{M}, \mathbf{M}')$. *We set:*

$$f^- = \{(xc', u) \mid f(xc') = u \ \text{and} \ (y < x \Rightarrow f(yc') \neq u)\}.$$

*The following properties hold:*

(1) *For all* $a \in D(\mathbf{M} \rightarrow \mathbf{M}')$, $a^+$ *is an abstract algorithm from* $\mathbf{M}$ *to* $\mathbf{M}'$.

(2) *For all* $f \in \mathcal{A}(\mathbf{M}, \mathbf{M}')$, $f^-$ *is a state of* $\mathbf{M} \rightarrow \mathbf{M}'$.

(3) $(\_)^+$ *is an isomorphism from* $(D(\mathbf{M} \rightarrow \mathbf{M}'), \leq)$ *onto* $(\mathcal{A}(\mathbf{M}, \mathbf{M}'), \leq)$, *and has* $(\_)^-$ *as inverse; if* $f, f' \in \mathcal{A}(\mathbf{M}, \mathbf{M}')$ *and* $f \leq f'$, *then* $(\lambda x.(f \bullet x)) \leq_{st} (\lambda x.(f' \bullet x))$.

PROOF. (1) Let $a$ be a state of $\mathbf{M} \rightarrow \mathbf{M}'$. Clearly, $a^+$ satisfies $(A_1)$ and $(A_2)$ by definition. Suppose $a^+(yc') = u$; then $\exists x \leq y \ (xc', u) \in a$. Let $s$ be a proof of $xc'$ in $a$, with the notation of the proof of proposition 14.2.4. Since $(c'^1, v'^1) \in a \bullet x$, we have $c' \in E(a \bullet x)$. Clearly, $a \bullet x = a^+ \bullet x \leq a^+ \bullet y$ (if $(xc', \text{output } v')$ is an event of $\mathbf{M} \rightarrow \mathbf{M}'$, so is $(yc', \text{output } v')$); hence $c' \in E(a^+ \bullet y)$. Suppose $z \leq y$ and $c' \in E(a^+ \bullet z)$. As $a^+ \bullet z = a \bullet z \uparrow a \bullet x$, $c'$ has the same enabling in $a \bullet x$ and $a \bullet z$. So, by definition of $a \bullet z$:

$$\exists z_0 \leq z \ (z_0 c'^1, \text{output } v'^1) \in a.$$

By proposition 14.2.4, we get $z_0 = x_0$, whence we derive $x_0 \leq z$. Let $i$ be maximum such that $x_i \leq z$. We prove $a^+(zc') = a^+(x_i c')$, hence a fortiori $a^+(zc') \neq \omega$ (we have $a^+(x_i c') \neq \omega$, since $x_i c' \in F(a)$). If $i = k$ and $u$ is of type 'output' then $(zc', u)$ is an event of $\mathbf{M} \rightarrow \mathbf{M}'$, hence $f(zc') = f(xc')$ is defined. Otherwise, we claim that $(zc', \text{valof } c_i)$ is an event, that is, $c_i \in A(z)$ (if $i = k$ and $u$ is of type 'valof' we write $u = \text{valof } c_k$). First, $c_i \in E(z)$, since $c_i \in A(x_i) \subseteq E(x_i) \subseteq E(z)$. Suppose $c_i \in F(z)$. We distinguish two cases:

• $i < k$. Then $x_{i+1} \leq z$, since $x_i \prec_{c_i} x_{i+1}$ and $x_{i+1} \uparrow z$. This contradicts the maximality of $i$.

• $i = k$. Then $a^+(yc') = \text{valof } c_k$ implies $(yc', \text{valof } c_k) \in E_{\mathbf{M} \rightarrow \mathbf{M}'}$, which implies $c_k \in A(y)$. This contradicts $c_k \in F(z) \subseteq F(y)$.

This proves the claim, which implies that $f(zc')$ is defined (and equal to $f(x_i c')$).

(2) Let $f$ be an abstract algorithm from $\mathbf{M}$ to $\mathbf{M}'$. We prove that $f^-$ is a state of $\mathbf{M} \rightarrow \mathbf{M}'$. It is consistent by definition, since $(xc', u) \in f^- \Rightarrow f(xc') = u$. We prove by induction on $c'$ that

$$f^- \backslash c' = \{(yd', w) \in f^- \mid d' \ll^* c'\}$$

is safe, which will imply the safety of $f^-$. If $(xc', u) \in f^-$, then by $(A_3)$ $f \cdot x$ contains an enabling $(c'^1, v'^1)$ of $c'$. Let $x_0 \leq x$ be minimal such that $f(x_0 c'^1) = output\ v'^1$, that is, $(x_0 c'^1, output\ v'^1) \in f^-$. We construct a chain

$$x_0 \prec_{c_0} x_1 \prec \cdots \prec x_{k-1} \prec_{c_{k-1}} x_k = x$$

as follows. Suppose that we have built the chain up to $i$, with $x_i < x$. Then we define $c_i$ by $f(x_i c') = valof\ c_i$ $(f(x_i c') \neq \omega$ by $(A_3)$, and is not of type 'output' by minimality of $x$). Then $x_i <_{c_i} x$, since $f(xc') = f(x_i c')$ would again contradict the minimality of $x$; we choose $x_{i+1}$ characterized by $x_i \prec_{c_i} x_{i+1} \leq x$. We show by induction:

$$\forall i < k \ \ (x_i c', valof\ c_i) \in f^-,$$

which together with the induction hypothesis will establish the safety of $f^- \backslash c'$. Suppose that there exists $z < x_i$ such that $f(zc') = valof\ c_i$. By $(A_3)$ again, $f^-$ would contain $(z_0 c'^2, output\ v'^2)$ such that $(c'^2, v'^2) \vdash c'$. By induction, we may suppose that $a = f^- \backslash c'^1 \cup f^- \backslash c'^2$ is safe; it is actually a state (consistency follows from $a \subseteq f^-$). Hence $a \cdot x$ is a state by proposition 14.2.4, whence we derive $c'^1 = c'^2$ by stability and $x_0 = z_0$ by proposition 14.2.4, which implies $x_0 \leq z$. Let $j$ be maximum $\leq i$ such that $x_j \leq z$. We have:

$$\begin{aligned} &j < i &&\text{(since } z < x_i) \\ &f(zc') = valof\ c_j &&\text{(by maximality of } j) \\ &c_j = c_i &&\text{(since } f(zc') = f(x_i c')) \,. \end{aligned}$$

But $c_i \in F(x_i)$ and $c_i \in A(x_i)$ by construction, contradicting $c_j = c_i$. This shows $(x_i c', valof\ c_i) \in f^-$, and ends the proof of (2).

(3) Let $a, a' \in \mathbf{M} \to \mathbf{M}'$. Clearly $(a^+)^- \subseteq a$. Reciprocally, if $(xc', u), (zc', w) \in a$ and $x < z$, we have $u \neq w$, since $u$ is $valof\ c$ for some $c \in F(z)$. It follows easily that $a \subseteq (a^+)^-$. If $a \leq a'$, then $a^+ \leq a'^+$ is an immediate consequence of the definition of $(\_)^+$. Let $f, f' \in \mathcal{A}(\mathbf{M}, \mathbf{M}')$. One checks easily that $f \subseteq (f^-)^+$ by $(A_1)$, and that $(f^-)^+ \subseteq f$ by $(A_2)$. Let $f \leq_{st} f'$. We first prove the last assertion of (3). If $x, y \in D(\mathbf{M})$ and $y \leq x$, we have to prove $(f \cdot x) \wedge (f' \cdot y) \subseteq f \cdot y$, that is, for any $c'$:

$$(f(xc') = output\ v' \text{ and } f'(yc') = output\ v') \Rightarrow f(yc') = output\ v'.$$

We proceed by induction on $c'$. Since $f \leq_{st} f'$, we only have to prove $f(yc') \neq \omega$, and hence to show $c' \in E(f \cdot y)$. As $f \cdot x \leq f' \cdot x$ and $f' \cdot y \leq f' \cdot x$, $c'$ has the same enabling $(c'^1, v'^1)$ in $f \cdot x$ and $f' \cdot y$. Hence $f(xc'^1) = f'(yc'^1) = output\ v'^1$, whence we derive by induction $f(yc'^1) = output\ v'^1$, proving $c' \in E(f \cdot y)$.

Finally, we prove $f^- \leq f'^-$. Suppose $(xc', u) \in f^-$. Then $f'(xc') = f(xc') = u$. Suppose $f'(yc') = u$ for some $y < x$. Then $c' \in E(f' \cdot y)$. As we also have $c' \in E(f \cdot x)$, we obtain $c' \in E(f \cdot y)$ by what has just been proved. Hence $f(yc') \neq \omega$, implying $f(yc') = f'(yc') = u$ and contradicting the minimality of $x$. $\qquad \square$

We now relate abstract algorithms to sequential functions.

**Proposition 14.2.9** *Let* $M$ *and* $M'$ *be cds's. If* $a, a' \in D(M \to M')$, *we write:*

$$a =_{ext} a' \quad \textit{iff} \quad (\forall\, x \in D(M))\ a{\cdot}x = a'{\cdot}x).$$

*The partial orders* $(D(M \to M')/=_{ext}, \leq /=_{ext})$ *and* $(M \to_{seq} M', \leq_{st})$ *are isomorphic; in particular, for any* $a \in D(M \to M')$, $\lambda x.(a{\cdot}x)$ *is sequential.*

PROOF. First we prove that if $a \in D(M \to M')$, then $\lambda x.(a{\cdot}x)$ is sequential. If $c' \in A(a{\cdot}x)$ and if there exist $y > x$ and $v'$ such that $(c', v') \in a{\cdot}y$, then $a^+(yc') = output\ v'$, and by $(A_3)$ $a^+(xc') = u \neq \omega$. Specifically:

$u$ has the form *valof* $c$    (since $c' \in A(a{\cdot}x)$)

$c \in F(y)$               (by $(A_2)$)

$c \in A(x)$               (by $(A_1)$) .

Hence $\lambda x.(a{\cdot}x)$ is sequential and has $c$ as index at $(x, c')$. By proposition 14.2.8:

$$\forall a \leq a' \in D(M \to M')\ (\lambda x.(a{\cdot}x) = a^+{\cdot}x) \leq_{st} (\lambda x.(a'{\cdot}x) = a'^+{\cdot}x).$$

So we only have to prove, for all $g, g' \in M \to_{seq} M'$ such that $g \leq_{st} g'$:

$$\exists\, a, a' \in D(M \to M')\ (g = (\lambda x.(a{\cdot}x)), g' = (\lambda x.(a'{\cdot}x))\ \text{and}\ a \leq a').$$

We build $a$ and $a'$ progressively. For any cell $c'$, we define sets $X^n_{g',c'}$ (for all $n \geq 0$) and a function $V_{g',c'}$ as follows, by induction on $n$:

- $X^0_{g',c'} = \{x \in m_e(g', c') \mid \exists\, z \geq x\ c' \in F(g'(z))\}$, where $m_e(g', c')$ is the set of the minimal $x$'s such that $c' \in E(g'(x))$.

- For all $x \in X^n_{g',c'}$:

− $V_{g',c'}(x) = valof\ c$ if $c' \in A(g'(x))$ and if $c$ is an arbitrarily chosen sequentiality index of $g'$ at $(x, c')$;

− $V_{g',c'}(x) = output\ v'$ if $(c', v') \in g'(x)$.

- $X^{n+1}_{g',c'}$ is the smallest set such that, for all $x \in X^n_{g',c'}, y \in D(M)$:

$$(V_{g',c'}(x) = valof\ c, x \prec_c y, (\exists\, z \geq y\ c' \in F(g'(z)))) \Rightarrow y \in X^{n+1}_{g',c'}.$$

It is easy to establish the following properties by induction:

$$\forall\, x, x' \in X^n_{g',c'}\ (x = x'\ \text{or}\ x \uparrow x') \quad \text{(for all } n)$$
$$\forall\, x \in X^n_{g',c'}\ \exists\, y \in X^m_{g',c'}\ y < x \quad \text{(for all } m, n \text{ such that } m < n) .$$

As a consequence, $X^n_{g',c'} \cap X^m_{g',c'} = \emptyset$, for any $n, m$ such that $n \neq m$. Thus the definition of $V_{g',c'}$ is unambiguous. Let $X_{g',c'} = \bigcup \{X^n_{g',c'} \mid n \geq 0\}$. We define likewise $X_{g,c'}$, $V_{g,c'}$ such that $X_{g',c'}$ contains $X_{g,c'}$ and $V_{g,c'}$ is the restriction of $V_{g',c'}$ to $X_{g,c'}$ (this may be done by proposition 14.1.11). Let:

$$a' = \bigcup \{(xc', V_{g',c'}(x)) \mid c' \in C', x \in X_{g',c'}\} .$$

We define likewise $a$. By construction, $a$ and $a'$ are consistent, and $a \leq a'$. We check that $a'$ is safe. This is clear by construction for an event $(xc', V_{g',c'}(x))$

where $x \in X^n_{g',c'}$ and $n > 0$. If $n = 0$, then by construction $x \in m_e(g', c')$, hence $x$ is minimal such that $d' \in F(g'(x))$, for some $d' \ll c'$. Then safety follows from the fact that by construction $X_{g',c'}$ contains all minimal points $z$ such that $d' \in g'(z)$, for all $d' \in C'$. Finally, it is evident by construction that $(c', v') \in g'(x)$ iff $(c', v') \in a' \cdot x$. The same arguments can be applied to $a$. $\qquad\square$

We next define the composition of sequential algorithms, using their abstract characterization. We first discuss the composition of sequential algorithms informally. If $a$ and $a'$ are algorithms from $\mathbf{M}$ to $\mathbf{M}'$ and from $\mathbf{M}'$ to $\mathbf{M}''$, respectively, then the input-output function of $a' \circ a$ should be the composition of the input-output functions of $a$ and $a'$, that is, for any state $x$ of $\mathbf{M}$:

$$(a' \circ a) \cdot x = a' \cdot (a \cdot x).$$

How can this equation help in the characterization of the events of $a' \circ a$? By definition of the operator $\cdot$ we obtain:

$$\exists z \leq x \ (zc'', output\ v'') \in a' \circ a \Leftrightarrow \exists z' \leq a \cdot x \ (z'c'', output\ v'') \in a'.$$

This equivalence allows us to describe events that are 'almost' in $a' \circ a$. Using the notation of proposition 14.2.8, we get:

$$(a' \circ a)^+(xc'') = output\ v'' \quad \text{iff} \quad a'^+((a \cdot x)c'') = output\ v''.$$

The equation does not characterize events belonging to $a' \circ a$, but events where $(a' \circ a)^+$ is defined. Hence it seems natural to define the composition of sequential algorithms using their abstract characterization.

What about the computation strategy of $a' \circ a$? The definition of sequential functions suggests an output-directed computation: 'in order to compute $c'$, the index $c$ has to be computed'. Hence it is natural to compose strategies in the following way: if $a'$ indicates *valof* $c'$ at $a \cdot x$ for $c''$, and if $a$ indicates *valof* $c$ at $x$ for $c'$, then $a' \circ a$ indicates *valof* $c$ at $x$ for $c''$, which is summarized by the following equivalence:

$$(a' \circ a)^+(xc'') = valof\ c \quad \text{iff} \quad \begin{cases} a'^+((a \cdot x)c'') = valof\ c' \text{ and} \\ a^+(xc') = valof\ c \,. \end{cases}$$

The next proposition shows that these equivalences indeed define an abstract algorithm.

**Proposition 14.2.10** *Let* $\mathbf{M}$, $\mathbf{M}'$ *and* $\mathbf{M}''$ *be cds's, and let* $a$ *and* $a'$ *be two states of* $\mathbf{M} \to \mathbf{M}'$ *and* $\mathbf{M}' \to \mathbf{M}''$, *respectively. The function* $f : C_{\mathbf{M} \to \mathbf{M}''} \rightharpoonup V_{\mathbf{M} \to \mathbf{M}''}$, *defined as follows, is an abstract algorithm from* $\mathbf{M}$ *to* $\mathbf{M}''$:

$$f(xc'') = \begin{cases} output\ v'' & \text{if } a'^+((a \cdot x)c'') = output\ v'' \\ \\ valof\ c & \text{if } \begin{cases} a'^+((a \cdot x)c'') = valof\ c' \text{ and} \\ a^+(xc') = valof\ c \,. \end{cases} \end{cases}$$

PROOF. First we remark that the definition of $f$ involves $a'^+((a \bullet x)c'')$, where $a \bullet x$ is not necessarily finite. This makes sense, since we have seen that an abstract algorithm can be extended to (a subset of) $D(\mathbf{M}) \times \mathbf{C}'$ (cf. exercise 14.2.6).

$(A_1), (A_2)$ If $f(xc'') = output\ v''$ and $x \leq y$, then $(xc'', output\ v'')$ is an event, since it follows from the definition of $a'^+$ that $(c'', v'') \in E_{\mathbf{M}''}$, and:

$$a \bullet x \leq a \bullet y \Rightarrow a'^+((a \bullet y)c'') = output\ v'' = f(yc'').$$

If $f(xc'') = valof\ c$, $x \leq y$ and $c \in A(y)$, then $a'^+((a \bullet x)c'') = valof\ c'$ and $a^+(xc') = valof\ c$; hence $c \in A(x)$, since $(xc', valof\ c)$ is an event. Also, $c \in A(y)$ implies $a^+(yc') = valof\ c$. In particular, $c' \notin F(a \bullet y)$, hence $c' \in A(a \bullet y)$ by $(A_3)$ applied to $a^+$. Then we obtain $a'^+((a \bullet y)c'') = valof\ c'$ by $(A_2)$ applied to $a'^+$, which yields $f(yc'') = valof\ c$.

$(A_3)$ If $f(yc'') \neq \omega$, then $a'^+((a \bullet y)c'') \neq \omega$. Hence $c'' \in E(f \bullet y)$, since it is easily checked that $f \bullet y = a' \bullet (a \bullet y)$ . Moreover if $z \leq y$ and $c'' \in E(f \bullet z)$, then $a \bullet z \leq a \bullet y$ and $c'' \in E(a'\bullet(a \bullet z))$, whence we derive $a'^+((a \bullet z)c'') \neq \omega$ by $(A_3)$ applied to $a'^+$. If $a'^+((a \bullet z)c'') = output\ v''$, then $f(zc'') = output\ v''$ by definition. If $a'^+((a \bullet z)c'') = valof\ c'$, then $c' \in A(a \bullet z) \subseteq E(a \bullet z)$. We show $a^+(yc') \neq \omega$. There are two cases:

(1) $c' \in F(a \bullet y)$. Then $a^+(yc') \neq \omega$ by definition of $a \bullet y$.

(2) $c' \in A(a \bullet y)$. Then $a'^+((a \bullet y)c'') = valof\ c'$ by $(A_2)$ applied to $a'^+$, which forces $a^+(yc') = valof\ c$, for some $c$, since $f(yc') \neq \omega$.

In both cases, $a^+(yc') \neq \omega$, hence $a^+(zc') \neq \omega$ by $(A_3)$ applied to $a^+$; moreover $a^+(zc')$ is of type 'valof', since the contrary would imply $c' \in F(a \bullet z)$. Hence $f(zc'') \neq \omega$. □

**Theorem 14.2.11** *Cds's and sequential algorithms form a category. Let $a$, $a'$, and $f$ be as in proposition 14.2.10. We define the composition $a' \circ a$ of $a'$ and $a$ by the following equation:*

$$a' \circ a = f^-.$$

*For any cds $\mathbf{M}$ there exists a unique algorithm id such that $\lambda x.(id \bullet x)$ is the identity function. It is characterized by:*

$$id^+(xc) = output\ v \quad iff \quad (c, v) \in x$$
$$id^+(xc) = valof\ c \quad iff \quad c \in A(x) .$$

In particular, the input-output function of $a' \circ a$ is the composition of the input-output functions of $a$ and $a'$. We call **Algo** the category of cds's and sequential algorithms.

**Exercise 14.2.12** *Let $\mathbf{M}$ and $\mathbf{M}'$ be cds's. Show that a function $f : D(\mathbf{M}) \to D(\mathbf{M}')$ is sequential if and only if it is continuous and sequential at any compact point. Hint: Use proposition 14.2.9.*

**Exercise 14.2.13** *Let $\mathbf{M}$ and $\mathbf{M}'$ be cds's, and let $f$ be a strongly sequential function. Show that there exists a minimum algorithm $a$ such that $f = \lambda x.(a \bullet x)$.*

**Exercise 14.2.14** *Let* $\mathbf{M}$ *and* $\mathbf{M}'$ *be two (well-founded and stable) sequential cds's. Show that* $\mathbf{M} \times \mathbf{M}'$ *and* $\mathbf{M} \to \mathbf{M}'$ *are sequential (cf. exercise 14.1.17).*

**Exercise 14.2.15** *Write a sequential algorithm* $Add\_Tester : (\omega_\perp \times \omega_\perp \to \omega_\perp) \to \mathbf{B}_\perp$ *such that* $Add\_Tester \bullet ADD_l = \{(?, tt)\}$ *and* $Add\_Tester \bullet ADD_r = \{(?, ff)\}$ *(cf. example 14.2.2).*

We end the section with an exercise based on [Col89, Coq92]: primitive recursive definitions give rise to sequential algorithms in a natural way, and moreover exhibit a particular behaviour called the ultimate obstination.

**Exercise\* 14.2.16** *We use the domain* $\omega_L$ *of lazy natural numbers defined in exercise 7.1.22. We define primitive recursive (or pr.r.) functions from* $(\omega_L)^n$ *to* $\omega_L$ *as follows (cf. theorem A1.1.1): (i)* $\lambda\vec{x}.0$ *is pr.r., (ii) the successor function defined by* $f(x) = S(x)$ *and* $f(S^\omega(\perp)) = S^\omega(\perp)$ *is pr.r., (iii) the projection functions* $\pi_i^n : (\omega_L)^n \to \omega_L$ *are pr.r., (iv) if* $f$ *is pr.r. of arity* $n$ *and if* $g_1, \dots, g_n$ *are pr.r. of arity* $m$ *then* $h = f \circ \langle \vec{g} \rangle$ *is pr.r. of arity* $m$, *(v) if* $g, h$ *are pr.r. of arities* $n, n+2$, *respectively, then the following* $f = rec(g, h)$ *is pr.r.:*

$$f(\perp, \vec{y}) = \perp \quad f(0, \vec{y}) = g(\vec{y}) \quad f(S(x), \vec{y}) = h(x, f(x, \vec{y}), \vec{y}) \ .$$

*(1) Write pr.r. definitions for the left and right addition functions* $add_g$ *and* $add_d$; *compute* $add_g(S^m(\perp), S^n(\perp))$ *and* $add_d(S^m(\perp), S^n(\perp))$ *(the 'intensional behaviour' of* $add_g$, $add_d$*). (2) Show that* $\omega_L$ *is generated by the cds* $\mathbf{M} = (\{c_i \mid i \in \omega\}, \{0, S\}, E, \vdash)$, *where* $E = \{c_i \mid i \in \omega\} \times \{0, S\}$ *and where* $(c_i, S) \vdash c_{i+1}$ *(for all* $i$*). (3) Show that the pr.r. functions are sequential; more precisely, associate a sequential algorithm with each pr.r. definition. (4) Using only the fact that pr.r. functions are stable, show that if* $f$ *is pr.r. of arity* $n$ *and if* $f(\vec{x}) = S^\omega(\perp)$, *then there exists (i)* $\vec{d} \le \vec{x}$, *(ii)* $i$ *such that* $1 \le i \le n$, *and (iii) a monotonic function* $\phi : \omega \to \omega$ *(with the standard ordering* $0 \le 1 \le \cdots$*) such that* $d_1, \dots, d_n$ *are finite,* $x_i = S^\omega(\perp)$, *and:*

$$f(\vec{z}) = S^{\phi(n_i)}(\perp) \text{ for all } \vec{z} \text{ such that } \vec{d} \le \vec{z} \le \vec{x} \text{ and } z_i = S^{n_i}(\perp) \ ,$$

*i.e., '*$f$ *has eventually constantly the sequentiality index* $i$*'. Hints: The interesting case is:* $f = rec(g, h)$, $\vec{x} = (S^\omega(\perp), \vec{y})$, *and* $h$ *has the sequentiality index* $2$ *at* $(S^\omega(\perp), S^\omega(\perp), \vec{y})$. *By induction let* $m_0, n_0, \vec{d}$ *and* $\phi$ *be such that if* $m_0 \le m, n_0 \le n$ *and* $\vec{d} \le \vec{z} \le \vec{y}$ *then* $f(S^m(\perp), S^n(\perp), \vec{z}) = S^{\phi(n)}(\perp)$. *Note that in particular:* $f(S^m(\perp), S^n(\perp), \vec{d}) = f(S^m(\perp), S^n(\perp), \vec{z})$. *Prove by induction on* $m$ *that:*

$$f(S^m(\perp), \vec{d}) = f(S^m(\perp), \vec{z}) \text{ for all } \vec{z} \text{ such that } \vec{d} \le \vec{z} \le \vec{y} \ .$$

*Then show by induction on* $k \ge 0$ *that:*

$$f(S^{m_0+k}(\perp), \vec{z}) = S^{\phi^k(N)}(\perp) \text{ for all } \vec{z} \text{ such that } \vec{d} \le \vec{z} \le \vec{y},$$

*where* $N$ *is such that* $f(S^{m_0}(\perp), \vec{d}) = S^N(\perp)$, *and where* $m_0, \vec{d}$ *have been chosen such that* $n_0 \le N$. *(5) Give an alternative proof of statement (4) using the sequential algorithms* $[\![f]\!]$ *associated with the pr.r. definitions (cf. (3)). Hint: Define sets* $X_i(f)$ *by* $v \in X_i(f)$ *iff* $[\![f]\!]$ *'indicates' a cell of the form* $c_j.i$ *at* $v$, *and show, for* $f = rec(g, h)$:

$$(S^k(\perp), f(S^k(\perp), v), v) \in X_2(h) \Rightarrow (\forall l \le k+1 \ (S^l(\perp), v) \in X_1(f)) \ .$$

# 14.3   Algorithms as strategies *

We first define sequential data structures, which enhance the implicit symmetry between events and enablings in a filiform cds. Then we define the affine exponent $S \multimap S'$ of two sequential data structures $S$ and $S'$. The states of $S \multimap S'$ are called affine algorithms. Like sequential algorithms, affine algorithms can be presented abstractly (definition 14.3.29). The abstract affine algorithms are called symmetric algorithms. A symmetric algorithm is a pair $(f, g)$ of a function $f$ from input strategies to output strategies, and of a partial function $g$ from output counter-strategies to input counter-strategies.

The composition of two affine algorithms can be defined either abstractly (proposition 14.3.34) or concretely (proposition 14.3.38). The concrete description serves to establish the monoidal closed structure of the category of affine algorithms, while the abstract characterization serves to define a functor **cds** from the category of sequential data structures and affine algorithms to the category of concrete data structures and sequential algorithms. Finally, we show that **cds** has a left adjoint (theorem 14.3.48), which together with the affine exponent yields a decomposition of the exponent of **Algo**.

**Definition 14.3.1** *A* sequential data structure *(sds for short)* $S = (C, V, P)$ *is given by two sets $C$ and $V$ of cells and values, which are assumed disjoint, and by a collection $P$ of non-empty words $p$ of the form:*

$$c_1 v_1 \cdots c_n v_n \quad \text{or} \quad c_1 v_1 \cdots c_{n-1} v_{n-1} c_n \,,$$

*where $c_i \in C$ and $v_i \in V$ for all $i$. Thus any $p \in P$ is alternating and starts with a cell. Moreover, it is assumed that $P$ is closed under non-empty prefixes. We call the elements of $P$* positions *of* $S$*. We call* move *any element of $M = C \cup V$. We use $m$ to denote a move. A position ending with a value is called a* response*, and a position ending with a cell is called a* query*. We use $p$ (or $s$, or $t$), $q$, and $r$, to range over positions, queries, and responses, respectively. We denote by $Q$ and $R$ the sets of queries and responses, respectively.*

*A* strategy *of* $S$ *is a subset $x$ of $R$ that is closed under response prefixes and binary non-empty glb's:*

$$r_1, r_2 \in x, r_1 \wedge r_2 \neq \epsilon \;\; \Rightarrow \;\; r_1 \wedge r_2 \in x \,,$$

*where $\epsilon$ denotes the empty word. A* counter-strategy *is a non-empty subset of $Q$ that is closed under query prefixes and under binary glb's. We use $x, y, \ldots$ and $\alpha, \beta, \ldots$ to range over strategies and counter-strategies, respectively.*

*Both sets of strategies and of counter-strategies are ordered by inclusion. They are denoted by $D(S)$ and $D^{\perp}(S)$, respectively. Notice that $D(S)$ has always a minimum element (the empty strategy, written $\emptyset$ or $\perp$), while $D^{\perp}(S)$ has no minimum element in general. If a partial order is isomorphic to some $D(S)$, it is called an sds domain generated by* $S$*.*

Among the strategies are the sets of response prefixes of a response $r$. By abuse of notation we still call $r$ the resulting strategy. It is easy to see that those $r$'s are exactly the compact coprime elements of $D(S)$ (cf. definition 10.2.1).

We adapt the terminology of definition 14.1.5 to sds's.

**Definition 14.3.2** *Let* S *be an sds and let $x$ be a strategy of* S*:*

• *If $qv \in x$ for some $v$, we write $q \in F(x)$ ($q$ is filled in $x$).*

- *If $r \in x$ and $q = rc$ for some $c$, we say that $q$ is enabled in $x$.*

- *If $q$ is enabled in $x$ but $q \notin F(x)$, we write $q \in A(x)$ ($q$ is accessible from $x$).*

*Likewise we define $r \in F(\alpha), r \in A(\alpha)$ for a response $r$ and a counter-strategy $\alpha$.*

Sds's and (filiform) cds's are essentially the same notion, as shown in proposition 14.3.3, lemma 14.3.5, and exercise 14.3.7.

**Proposition 14.3.3** *Let* $\mathbf{S} = (C, V, P)$ *be an sds, and let $Q$ and $R$ be the associated sets of queries and responses. Let* $\mathbf{cds(S)} = (Q, R, E, \vdash)$, *with*

$$E = \{(q, qv) \mid qv \in P\} \quad \vdash c \ \ if \, c \in C \cap P \quad (q, qv) \vdash qvc \ \ if \, qvc \in P.$$

*Then* $\mathbf{cds(S)}$ *is a filiform cds and $D(cds(\mathbf{S}))$ is isomorphic to $D(\mathbf{S})$.*

PROOF. With a strategy $x$ of $\mathbf{S}$, we associate $\mathbf{cds}(x) = \{(q, qv) \mid qv \in x\}$, which is consistent and safe by the definition of a strategy. More precisely, consistency follows from the closure under glb's, and safety follows from the closure under prefixes. This transformation is clearly bijective. □

**Proposition 14.3.4** *If* $\mathbf{S}$ *is an sds, then $D(\mathbf{S})$ is a dI-domain, whose compact elements are the finite strategies. $D^{\perp}(\mathbf{S})$ enjoys the same properties (except for the existence of a minimum element). Upper bounded lub's and upper bounded glb's are set theoretical unions and intersections.*

PROOF. The proof is similar to the proof of proposition 14.1.6. (The first part of the statement is a consequence of propositions 14.1.6 and 14.3.3.) □

**Lemma 14.3.5** *Let* $\mathbf{M}$ *be a well-founded, stable, and filiform cds. For any cell $c$ and any two distinct proofs $t_1$ and $t_2$ of $c$, there exist $s, d, v_1, v_2$ such that $v_1 \neq v_2$, $s, (d, v_1)$ is a prefix of $t_1$ and $s, (d, v_2)$ is a prefix of $t_2$.*

PROOF. We proceed by induction on $c$. We observe:

$t_1 \cup t_2$ is safe                    (by construction)
$t_1 \cup t_2$ is not a state          (by stability)
no cell is repeated along $t_1$, nor along $t_2$    (by well-foundedness) .

These observations entail that $(d, w_1) \in t_1$ and $(d, w_2) \in t_2$ for some cell $d \ll^+ c$ and for some distinct $w_1$ and $w_2$. If the proofs of $d$ in $t_1$ and $t_2$ are distinct, the conclusion follows by applying induction to $d$. If the proofs are the same, then the conclusion follows right away. □

**Remark 14.3.6** *Conversely, the property stated in lemma 14.3.5 implies that* $\mathbf{M}$ *is stable, hence we could have used it to define the notion of stable (filiform) cds.*

**Exercise 14.3.7** *Let* $\mathbf{M} = (C, V, E, \vdash)$ *be a well-founded, stable, and filiform cds. Show that* $\mathbf{sds(M)} = (C, V, P)$, *where*

$$P = \{c_1 v_1 \cdots c_n v_n c \mid (c_1, v_1), \ldots, (c_n, v_n) \text{ is a proof of } c\} \cup$$
$$\{rcv \mid rc \in P \text{ and } (c, v) \in E\}$$

*is an sds such that $D(sds(\mathbf{M}))$ and $D(\mathbf{M})$ are isomorphic. Hint: Use lemma 14.3.5.*

**Example 14.3.8** (1) *Flat cpo's. In the setting of sds's:*

$$X_\perp = (\{?\}, X, \{?\} \cup \{?v \mid v \in X\}).$$

(2) *The following generates* $\mathbf{B}_\perp^2$ *(see definition 14.3.43 for the general case):*

$$(\{?.1, ?.2\}, \{tt, ff\}, \{?.1, ?.2\} \cup \{(?.1)tt, (?.1)ff, (?.2)tt, (?.2)ff\}).$$

(3) *An sds generating the partial terms over a signature, say,* $\Sigma = \{a^0, f^1, g^2\}$, *where the superscripts indicate the arities, is given as follows:* $C = \{?, 1, 2\}$, $V = \Sigma$, *and* $P$ *consists of the positions respecting the arities: the positions ending with* $a$ *are maximal, the positions ending with* $f$ *can only be followed by 1, and the positions ending with* $g$ *can be followed by 1 or 2. All the positions start with* ? *(which serves only for that purpose). For example, the strategy representing* $g(a, f(a))$ *is:*

$$\{?g, ?g1a, ?g2f, ?g2f1a\}.$$

*Here is a counter-strategy:*

$$\{?, ?f1, ?f1f1, ?f1g2, ?g1\}.$$

The counter-strategy of example 14.3.8 (3) can be read as an exploration tree, or a pattern. The root is investigated first; if the function symbol found at the root is $g$, then its left son is investigated next; otherwise, if the function symbol found at the root is $f$, then its son is investigated next, and the investigation goes further if the symbol found at node 1 is either $f$ or $g$.

A more geometric reading of the definitions of sds, strategy and counter-strategy is the following:

- An sds is a labelled forest, where the ancestor relation alternates cells and values, and where the roots are labelled by cells.

- A strategy is a sub-forest which is allowed to branch only at values.

- A counter-strategy $\alpha$ is a non-empty subtree (if it contained $c_1$ and $c_2$ as positions of length 1, they should contain their glb, which is $\epsilon$, contradicting $\alpha \subseteq P$) which is allowed to branch only at cells.

The pairs cell–value, query–response, and strategy–counter-strategy give to sds's a flavour of symmetry. These pairs are related to other important dualities in programming: input–output, constructor–destructor (cf. example 14.3.8(3)). It is thus tempting to consider the counter-strategies of an sds **S** as the strategies of a dual structure **S**$^\perp$ whose cells are the values of **S** and whose values are the cells of **S**. However, the structure obtained in this way is not an sds anymore, since positions now start with a value. We refer to [Lam92a] for an elaboration of a theory of sds's with polarities, where both **S** and **S**$^\perp$ can live (see also exercises 14.3.23 and 14.3.40).

**Sequential data structures as games.** An sds can be considered as a game between two persons, the *opponent* and the *player*. The values are the player's moves, and the cells are the opponent's moves. A player's strategy consists in having ready answers for (some of) the (sequences of) opponent's moves. Counter-strategies are opponent's strategies. The following definition and proposition make the analogy more precise.

**Definition 14.3.9 (play)** *Let* S *be an sds,* $x$ *be a strategy and* $\alpha$ *be a counter-strategy of* S, *one of which is finite. We define* $x \mid \alpha$, *called a* play, *as the set of positions* $p$ *which are such that all the response prefixes of* $p$ *are in* $x$ *and all the query prefixes of* $p$ *are in* $\alpha$.

**Proposition 14.3.10** *Given* $x$ *and* $\alpha$ *as in definition 14.3.9, the play* $x \mid \alpha$ *is non-empty and totally ordered, and can be confused with its maximum element, which is uniquely characterized as follows:*

$x \mid \alpha$ *is the unique element of* $x \cap A(\alpha)$    *if* $x \mid \alpha$ *is a response*
$x \mid \alpha$ *is the unique element of* $\alpha \cap A(x)$    *if* $x \mid \alpha$ *is a query* .

PROOF. A counter-strategy is non-empty by definition, and contains a (unique) query $c$ of length 1, which is also in $x \mid \alpha$ by definition of a play. Suppose that $p_1, p_2 \in x \mid \alpha$. We show that $p_1$ and $p_2$ are comparable, by contradiction. Thus suppose $p_1 \wedge p_2 < p_1$ and $p_1 \wedge p_2 < p_2$. Let $q_1$ be the largest query prefix of $p_1$, let $r_1$ be the largest prefix of $p_1$ which is either a response or $\epsilon$, and let $q_2$ and $r_2$ be defined similarly. We show:

$$p_1 \wedge p_2 = q_1 \wedge q_2 = r_1 \wedge r_2.$$

The inequality $q_1 \wedge q_2 \leq p_1 \wedge p_2$ follows by the monotonicity of $\wedge$. For the other direction, we remark that by the maximality of $q_1$, $p_1 \wedge p_2 < p_1$ implies $p_1 \wedge p_2 \leq q_1$; and, similarly, we deduce $p_1 \wedge p_2 \leq q_2$, which completes the proof of $p_1 \wedge p_2 \leq q_1 \wedge q_2$. The equality $p_1 \wedge p_2 = r_1 \wedge r_2$ is proved similarly. But by definition of a strategy and of a counter-strategy, $q_1 \wedge q_2$ is a query, and $r_1 \wedge r_2$ is either a response or $\epsilon$. The equalities just proven imply that $p_1 \wedge p_2$ is of both odd and even length: contradiction. Thus $x \mid \alpha$ is totally ordered. It has a maximum element, since the finiteness of $x$ or $\alpha$ implies finiteness of $x \mid \alpha$.

To prove the rest of the statement, we first observe that $x \cap A(\alpha) \subseteq x \mid \alpha$ and $\alpha \cap A(x) \subseteq x \mid \alpha$, by definition of $x \mid \alpha$. We next show that $x \cap A(\alpha)$ and $\alpha \cap A(x)$ have at most one element. If $p_1, p_2 \in x \cap A(\alpha)$, then by the first part of the statement $p_1$ and $p_2$ are comparable, say $p_1 \leq p_2$. But if $p_2 \in A(\alpha)$ and $p_1 < p_2$, then $p_1 \in F(\alpha)$, contradicting the assumption $p_1 \in A(\alpha)$. Hence $p_1 = p_2$. The proof is similar for $\alpha \cap A(x)$. Finally, if $x \mid \alpha$ viewed as a position is a response, then $x \mid \alpha \in x$, $x \mid \alpha$ is enabled in $\alpha$, and the maximality of $x \mid \alpha$ implies that $x \mid \alpha$ is not filled in $\alpha$. Hence $x \mid \alpha \in x \cap A(\alpha)$, i.e., $x \cap A(\alpha) = \{x \mid \alpha\}$. □

**Definition 14.3.11 (winning)** *Let* $x$ *and* $\alpha$ *be as in definition 14.3.9. If* $x \mid \alpha$ *is a response, we say that* $x$ *wins against* $\alpha$, *and we denote this predicate by* $x \triangleleft \alpha$. *If* $x \mid \alpha$ *is a query, we say that* $\alpha$ *wins against* $x$, *and we write* $x \triangleright \alpha$, *thus* $\triangleright$ *is the negation of* $\triangleleft$. *To stress who is the winner, we write:*

$$x \mid \alpha = \begin{cases} x \triangleleft \mid \alpha & \text{when } x \text{ wins} \\ x \mid \triangleright \alpha & \text{when } \alpha \text{ wins} . \end{cases}$$

The position $x \mid \alpha$ formalizes the interplay between the player with strategy $x$ and the opponent with strategy $\alpha$. If $x \mid \alpha$ is a response, then the player wins since he made the last move, and if $x \mid \alpha$ is a query, then the opponent wins. Here is a game theoretical reading of $x \mid \alpha$. At the beginning the opponent makes a move $c$: his strategy determines that move uniquely. Then either the player is unable to move ($x$ contains no position of the form $cv$), or his strategy determines a unique move. The play goes on until one of $x$ or $\alpha$ does not have the provision to answer its opponent's move. As an example, if

$x$ and $\alpha$ are the strategy and counter-strategy of example 14.3.8(3), then $x \mid \alpha = \epsilon g 1 a$, and the player wins.

In the following lemmas, we show some elementary properties of plays and strategies.

**Lemma 14.3.12** *Let* S *be an sds,* $x$ *be a strategy and* $\alpha$ *be a counter-strategy of* S. *The following properties hold:*

(1) *If* $x \triangleleft \alpha$, *then* $(x \triangleleft \mid \alpha) \triangleleft \alpha$.

(2) *If* $x \triangleleft \alpha$ *and* $x \le y$, *then* $y \triangleleft \alpha$ *and* $x \triangleleft \mid \alpha = y \triangleleft \mid \alpha$.

(3) *If* $x \triangleright \alpha$ *and* $y \le x$, *then* $y \triangleright \alpha$.

*Similar implications hold with the assumptions* $x \triangleright \alpha$, $(x \triangleright \alpha$ *and* $\alpha \le \beta)$, *and* $(x \triangleleft \alpha$ *and* $\beta \le \alpha)$, *respectively.*

PROOF. The properties (1) and (2) follow obviously from the characterization of $x \triangleleft \mid \alpha$ as the unique element of $x \cap A(\alpha)$. Property (3) is a consequence of (2) by contraposition. □

**Lemma 14.3.13** *Let* S *be an sds,* $x$ *be a strategy and* $q$ *be a query of* S. *The following implications hold:*

(1) $q \in F(x) \Rightarrow x \triangleleft q$.

(2) $q \in A(x) \Rightarrow x \triangleright q$.

(3) $(q \in F(x), y \le x, y \triangleleft q) \Rightarrow q \in F(y)$.

*Similar implications hold with a counter-strategy and a response of* S.

PROOF. If $q \in F(x)$, then $qv \in x$ for some $v$, hence $qv \in x \cap A(q)$, which means $x \triangleleft q$. If $q \in A(x)$, then $q \in q \cap A(x)$, which means $x \triangleright q$. If $q \in F(x), y \le x$, and $y \triangleleft q$, let $q_1 v_1$ be the unique element of $y \cap A(q)$. In particular, $q_1 \le q$. Suppose $q_1 < q$: then $q_1 v_1 \wedge qv = q_1$, since $q_1 v_1 \not< q$. On the other hand, the glb of $q_1 v_1$ and $qv$, cannot be a query, by definition of a strategy: contradiction.                                    □

The converse of lemma 14.3.13(1) is not true: we may have $x \triangleleft \mid q = q_1 v_1$ and $q > q_1 v_2$, for some $q, v_1, v_2$, with $v_1 \ne v_2$.

**Lemma 14.3.14** *Let* S $= (C, V, P)$ *be an sds,* $x$ *be a strategy and let* $q \in A(x)$. *The following properties hold:*

(1) *For any* $r \in x$, $q \wedge r$ *is* $\epsilon$ *or is a response, and thus, for any* $qv \in P$, $x \cup \{qv\}$ *is a strategy.*

(2) *If* $q_1 \ne q$ *and* $q_1 \in A(x)$, *then* $q_1 \wedge q$ *is a strict prefix of* $q_1$ *and* $q$ *and is* $\epsilon$ *or a response.*

*Similar properties hold with a counter-strategy* $\alpha$ *and a response* $r$ *such that* $r \in A(\alpha)$.

PROOF. We prove only (1). Let $q = r_1 c$. We claim that $q \wedge r \le r_1$. Suppose $q \wedge r \not\le r_1$. Then $q \wedge r = q$ since $q \wedge r \le q = r_1 c$. Hence $q < r$, contradicting $q \in A(x)$. The claim in turn implies $q \wedge r = r_1 \wedge r$. The conclusion follows, since by definition of a strategy $r_1 \wedge r$ is $\epsilon$ or is a response.                                    □

**Lemma 14.3.15** *Let* S *be an sds, and let* $x \in D(\mathrm{S})$ *and* $q \in F(x)$. *Then* $x - q = \{r \in x \mid q \not< r\}$ *is a strategy.*

PROOF. Since $\{r \in R \mid q \not\leq r\}$ is closed under response prefixes, so is $x - q$.  □

**Lemma 14.3.16** *Let* **S** *be an sds. If* $r_1, r_2 \in R$ *and* $r_1 \wedge r_2$ *is* $\epsilon$ *or is a response, then* $\{r \in R \mid r \leq r_1 \text{ or } r \leq r_2\}$ *is a strategy, and is* $r_1 \vee r_2$.

PROOF. The set $\{r \in R \mid r \leq r_1 \text{ or } r \leq r_2\}$ is obviously closed under response prefixes. Pick $r_3, r_4$ in this set. If they are both prefixes of, say, $r_1$, then they are comparable, hence, say, $r_3 \wedge r_4 = r_3$ is a response. Thus we may suppose, say, $r_3 \leq r_1$, $r_3 \not\leq r_2$, $r_4 \leq r_2$, and $r_4 \not\leq r_1$. This entails $r_3 > r_1 \wedge r_2$ and $r_4 > r_1 \wedge r_2$, and therefore $r_3 \wedge r_4 = r_1 \wedge r_2$.  □

**Exercise 14.3.17** *Let* **S** *and* **S**′ *be sds's. Show that a continuous function* $f : D(\mathbf{S}) \rightarrow D(\mathbf{S}')$ *is sequential iff, for any pair* $(x, \alpha') \in \mathcal{K}(D(\mathbf{S})) \times \mathcal{K}(D^{\perp}(\mathbf{S}'))$ *such that* $f(x) \triangleright \alpha'$ *and* $f(z) \triangleleft \alpha'$ *for some* $z \geq x$, *there exists* $\alpha \in \mathcal{K}(D^{\perp}(\mathbf{S}))$, *called a generalized sequentiality index of* $f$ *at* $(x, \alpha')$, *such that* $x \triangleright \alpha$ *and for any* $y \geq x$, $f(y) \triangleleft \alpha'$ *implies* $y \triangleleft \alpha$.

**Affine algorithms.** We next define the affine exponent of two sds's, which will serve to define the morphisms of a category of affine algorithms.

**Definition 14.3.18** *Given sets* $A, B \subseteq \mathcal{A}$, *for any word* $w \in A^*$, *we define* $w\lceil_B$ *as follows:*

$$\epsilon\lceil_B = \epsilon \qquad wm\lceil_B = \begin{cases} w\lceil_B & \text{if } m \in A \backslash B \\ (w\lceil_B)m & \text{if } m \in B . \end{cases}$$

**Definition 14.3.19 (affine exponent – sds)** *Given two sds's* $\mathbf{S} = (C, V, P)$ *and* $\mathbf{S}' = (C', V', P')$, *we define* $\mathbf{S} \multimap \mathbf{S}' = (C'', V'', P'')$ *as follows. The sets* $C''$ *and* $V''$ *are disjoint unions:*

$$\begin{aligned} C'' &= \{\text{request } c' \mid c' \in C'\} \cup \{\text{is } v \mid v \in V\} \\ V'' &= \{\text{output } v' \mid v' \in V'\} \cup \{\text{valof } c \mid c \in C\} . \end{aligned}$$

$P''$ *consists of the alternating positions* $s$ *starting with a request* $c'$, *and which are such that:*

$s\lceil_{\mathbf{S}'} \in P', (s\lceil_{\mathbf{S}} = \epsilon \text{ or } s\lceil_{\mathbf{S}} \in P)$, *and*
$s$ *has no prefix of the form* $s(\text{valof } c)(\text{request } c')$.

*We often omit the tags* request, valof, is, output, *as we have just done in the notation* $s\lceil_{\mathbf{S}} = s\lceil_{C \cup V}$ *(and similarly for* $s\lceil_{\mathbf{S}'}$).

We call affine sequential algorithms *(or affine algorithms) from* **S** *to* **S**′ *the strategies of* $\mathbf{S} \multimap \mathbf{S}'$. *The identity affine algorithm* $id \in D(\mathbf{S} \multimap \mathbf{S}')$ *is defined as follows:*

$$id = \{\text{copycat}(r) \mid r \text{ is a response of } \mathbf{S}\},$$

*where* copycat *is defined as follows:*

$$\begin{aligned} copycat(\epsilon) &= \epsilon \\ copycat(rc) &= copycat(r)(\text{request } c)(\text{valof } c) \\ copycat(qv) &= copycat(q)(\text{is } v)(\text{output } v) . \end{aligned}$$

The word *copycat* used in the description of the identity algorithm has been proposed in [AJ92], and corresponds to a game theoretical understanding: the player always repeats the last move of the opponent.

**Remark 14.3.20** *The definition also implies that $P'$ contains no position of the form* $sv'v$. *Suppose it does: then since* $(sv'v)\lceil_S \in P$, $s$ *contains a prefix* $s_1c$ *such that* $(sv'v)\lceil_S = ((s_1c)\lceil_S)v$. *Let $m$ be the move following $s_1c$ in $sv'$. Then*

$$m \notin V \quad (\text{since } (sv'v)\lceil_S = ((s_1c)\lceil_S)v)$$
$$m \notin C' \quad (\text{by the definition of } S \multimap S').$$

The constraint 'no $scc'$' can be formulated more informally as follows. Thinking of *valof $c$* as a call to a subroutine, the principal routine cannot proceed further until it receives a result $v$ from the subroutine.

**Example 14.3.21** (1) *It should be clear that the following is an affine algorithm which computes the boolean negation function:*

$$\{(request\ ?)(valof\ ?),$$
$$(request\ ?)(valof\ ?)(is\ tt)(output\ f\!f),$$
$$(request\ ?)(valof\ ?)(is\ f\!f)(output\ tt)\}.$$

(2) *On the other hand, the left disjunction function cannot be computed by an affine algorithm. Indeed, attempting to write an sds version of the algorithm $OR_l$ of example 14.2.2 would result in:*

$$\{(request\ ?)(valof\ ?.1),$$
$$(request\ ?)(valof\ ?.1)(is\ tt)(output\ tt),$$
$$(request\ ?)(valof\ ?.1)(is\ f\!f)(valof\ ?.2),$$
$$(request\ ?)(valof\ ?.1)(is\ f\!f)(valof\ ?.2)(is\ tt)(output\ tt),$$
$$(request\ ?)(valof\ ?.1)(is\ f\!f)(valof\ ?.2)(is\ f\!f)(output\ f\!f)\},$$

*which is not a subset of the set of positions of* $(\mathbf{B}_\perp)^2 \multimap \mathbf{B}_\perp$, *because the projections on* $(\mathbf{B}_\perp)^2$ *of the last two sequences of moves are not positions of* $(\mathbf{B}_\perp)^2$.

(3) *Every constant function gives rise to an affine algorithm, whose responses have the form* $(request\ c'_1)(output\ v'_1)\ldots(request\ c'_n)(output\ v'_n)$.

**Remark 14.3.22** *Example 14.3.21(2) suggests the difference between affine and general sequential algorithms. Both kinds of algorithms ask successive queries to their input, and proceed only when they get responses to these queries. An affine algorithm is moreover required to ask these queries monotonically: each new query must be an extension of the previous one. The 'unit' of resource consumption (cf. remark 13.1.9) is thus a sequence of queries/responses that can be arbitrarily large, as long as it builds a position of the input sds. The disjunction algorithms are not affine, because they may have to ask successively the queries $?.1$ and $?.2$, which are not related by the prefix ordering.*

A generic affine algorithm, as represented in figure 14.2, can be viewed as a 'combination' of the following (generic) output strategy and input counter-strategy (or exploration tree):

$$\text{request } c' \text{ valof } c \left\{ \begin{array}{l} \text{is } v_1 \cdots \\ \vdots \\ \text{is } v_i \text{ valof } d \left\{ \begin{array}{l} \vdots \\ \text{is } w \text{ output } v' \left\{ \begin{array}{l} \text{request } c_1' \cdots \\ \vdots \\ \text{request } c_m' \cdots \end{array} \right. \\ \vdots \end{array} \right. \\ \vdots \\ \text{is } v_n \cdots \end{array} \right.$$

Figure 14.2: A generic affine algorithm

An alternative presentation of the affine exponent, due to Lamarche [Lam92b] is given in exercise 14.3.23.

**Exercise 14.3.23** *This exercise is based on a small variant of the presentation of an sds, whose advantage is to give a tree structure rather than a forest structure to the sds's and to strategies. In this variant, a sds is a structure $(C, V \cup \{\bullet\}, P)$ where $\bullet$ is a distinguished element that does not belong to $V$ (nor $C$), and where all positions of $P$ start with $\bullet$ (this being the only place where $\bullet$ can occur). In this setting, strategies have to be non-empty. We say that a move $m \in C \cup (V \cup \{\bullet\})$ has:*

$$\begin{array}{ll} \text{polarity } \bullet & \text{if } m \in V \cup \{\bullet\} \\ \text{polarity } \circ & \text{if } m \in C \,. \end{array}$$

*(1) Establish a precise correspondence between sds's and the present variants of sds's.*
*(2) Based on these variants, construct the affine exponent of two sds's $(C, V \cup \{\bullet\}, P)$ and $(C', V' \cup \{\bullet\}, P')$ along the following lines.*

*(a) The moves of the affine exponent are pairs $(m, m')$ of moves $m \in C \cup V \cup \{\bullet\}$ and $m' \in C' \cup V' \cup \{\bullet\}$ whose polarities are not in the combination $(\circ, \bullet)$.*

*(b) The moves $(m, m')$ of polarity $\circ$ and those of polarity $\bullet$ are as indicated by the following table:*

| $m$ | $m'$ | $(m, m')$ |
|-----|------|-----------|
| $\bullet$ | $\bullet$ | $\bullet$ |
| $\bullet$ | $\circ$ | $\circ$ |
| $\circ$ | $\bullet$ | undefined |
| $\circ$ | $\circ$ | $\bullet$ |

*(c) One moves only on one side at a time: if $(m, m')$ is a move, it is followed by a move of the form $(n, m')$ or $(m, n')$.*

We next state a key technical property.

**Lemma 14.3.24** *Let* $\phi : S \to S'$ *be an affine algorithm between two sds's* S *and* S'. *The following properties hold.*

(1) *The function* $\lambda s.(s\lceil_S, s\lceil_{S'})$ *is an order-isomorphism from* $\phi$ *to its image, ordered componentwise by the prefix ordering.*

(2) *If two elements* $s_1$ *and* $s_2$ *of* $\phi$ *are such that* $(s_1\lceil_S) \wedge (s_2\lceil_S)$ *is either* $\epsilon$ *or is a response, and if* $s_1\lceil_{S'}$ *and* $s_2\lceil_{S'}$ *are comparable, then* $s_1$ *and* $s_2$ *are comparable.*

(3) *If two elements* $s_1$ *and* $s_2$ *of* $\phi$ *are such that* $(s_1\lceil_{S'}) \wedge (s_2\lceil_{S'})$ *is a query, and if* $s_1\lceil_S$ *and* $s_2\lceil_S$ *are comparable, then* $s_1$ *and* $s_2$ *are comparable.*

PROOF. (2) (or (3)) $\Rightarrow$ (1) It is obvious that $\lambda s.(s\lceil_S, s\lceil_{S'})$ is monotonic. Suppose that $s_1\lceil_S \leq s\lceil_S$, $s_1\lceil_{S'} \leq s\lceil_{S'}$, and $s_1 \not\leq s$. Then $s \leq s_1$ by the second part of the statement, and by monotonicity $s\lceil_S \leq s_1\lceil_S$ and $s\lceil_{S'} \leq s_1\lceil_{S'}$. Hence $s_1\lceil_S = s\lceil_S$, $s_1\lceil_{S'} = s\lceil_{S'}$, and $s = s_1$ follows, since $s < s_1$ would imply either $s\lceil_S < s_1\lceil_S$ or $s\lceil_{S'} < s_1\lceil_{S'}$.

(2) Let $t = s_1 \wedge s_2$, which is $\epsilon$ or is a response, since $\phi$ is a strategy. Suppose that $t < s_1$ and $t < s_2$. If $t$ has the form $t_1c$, then $t < s_1$ and $t < s_2$ imply that $tv_1 \leq s_1$ and $tv_2 \leq s_2$ for some $v_1$ and $v_2$, which must be different since $t = s_1 \wedge s_2$: but then $(s_1\lceil_S) \wedge (s_2\lceil_S)$ is a query, contradicting the assumption. If $t$ is $\epsilon$ or has the form $t_1v'$, then $t < s_1$ and $t < s_2$ imply that $tc_1' < s_1$ and $tc_2' < s_2$ for some $c_1'$ and $c_2'$, which must be different since $t = s_1 \wedge s_2$: this contradicts the assumption that $s_1\lceil_{S'}$ and $s_2\lceil_{S'}$ are comparable. Hence $t = s_1$ or $t = s_2$, i.e., $s_1 \leq s_2$ or $s_2 \leq s_1$. The proof of property (3) is similar. □

**Remark 14.3.25** *Any* $(s\lceil_S, s\lceil_{S'})$ *in the image of* $\phi$ *under the mapping* $\lambda s.(s\lceil_S, s\lceil_{S'})$ *is either a pair of responses or a pair of queries. It is a pair of responses iff* $s$ *ends with a value* $v'$; *it is a pair of queries iff* $s$ *ends with a cell* $c$.

There exists a more abstract description of affine algorithms, which we shall come to after some preliminaries.

**Definition 14.3.26 (affine function)** *Let* S *and* S' *be two sds's. We call a function* $f : D(S) \to D(S')$ *affine when it is stable and satisfies the following condition:*

$$r' \in f(x) \Rightarrow (\exists r \in x \ r' \in f(r)).$$

Equivalently, an affine function can be defined as a stable function preserving lub's of pairs of compatible elements. The definition applies also to (partial) functions $g : D^\perp(S') \to D^\perp(S)$.

If a function $f : D(S) \to D(S')$ is affine, then it is natural to adopt the following definition of trace:

$$trace(f) = \{(r, r') \mid r' \leq f(r) \text{ and } (\forall r_0 < r \ r' \not\leq f(r_0))\} \subseteq (R \cup \{\epsilon\}) \times R'$$

(and likewise for $g : D^\perp(S') \to D^\perp(S)$).

**Lemma 14.3.27** *The composition of two affine functions is affine, and its trace is the relation composition of the traces of* $f$ *and* $g$.

PROOF. This is a straightforward variant of (the dI-domain version of) proposition 13.1.10 (cf. exercise 13.1.11). □

**Proposition 14.3.28** *Any affine function* $f$ *between two sds's is strongly sequential.*

PROOF. Let $q' \in A(f(x))$ be such that $r' = q'v' \in f(z)$ for some $v'$ and $z \geq x$. Let $r$ be the unique response such that $(r, r') \in trace(f)$ and $r \in z$. Let $q$ be the unique query such that $q < r$ and $q \in A(x)$. Now consider $z_1 \geq x$ such that $q' \in F(f(z_1))$, and define $r'_1 = q'v'_1, r_1, q_1$ similarly. By lemma 14.3.14(2), if $q_1 \neq q$, then $q_1 \wedge q$ is a strict prefix of $q_1$ and $q$, and is $\epsilon$ or a response. But then $q < r$ and $q_1 < r_1$ imply $q_1 \wedge q = r_1 \wedge r$. Therefore $r_1 \uparrow r$ by lemma 14.3.16, which implies $r'_1 \uparrow r'$ by definition of a trace. Therefore $v'_1 = v'$, hence $r'_1 = r'$, which implies $r_1 = r$ by stability, and $q_1 = q$ by construction. Thus $q$ is a sequentiality index of $f$ at $(x, q')$. Suppose now that $q_1$ is another sequentiality index of $f$ at $(x, q')$. Let $z$ be as above, and consider $z - q$ and $z - q_1$ (cf. lemma 14.3.15). By affinity, $f(z) = f(z - q) \vee f(z - q_1)$, therefore, say, $q' \in F(f(z - q))$, which contradicts the fact that $q$ is a sequentiality index. $\square$

The converse is not true: there are strongly sequential functions that are not affine: the left and the right disjunction functions are examples.

Now we are ready to give an abstract description of affine algorithms.

**Definition 14.3.29 (symmetric algorithm)** *Let* S *and* S' *be two sds's. A symmetric algorithm from* S *to* S' *is a pair*

$$(f : D(\mathbf{S}) \to D(\mathbf{S}'), g : D^\perp(\mathbf{S}') \to D^\perp(\mathbf{S}))$$

*of a function and a partial function that are both continuous and satisfy the following axioms:*

(L) $(x \in D(\mathbf{S}), \alpha' \in \mathcal{K}(D^\perp(\mathbf{S}')), f(x) \triangleleft \alpha') \Rightarrow \begin{cases} x \triangleleft g(\alpha') \text{ and} \\ m(f, x, \alpha') = x \triangleleft \mid g(\alpha') \end{cases}$

(R) $(\alpha' \in D^\perp(\mathbf{S}'), x \in \mathcal{K}(D(\mathbf{S})), x \triangleright g(\alpha')) \Rightarrow \begin{cases} f(x) \triangleright \alpha' \text{ and} \\ m(g, \alpha', x) = f(x) \mid \triangleright \alpha' \end{cases}$,

*where* $m(f, x, \alpha')$ *is the minimum* $y \leq x$ *such that* $f(y) \triangleleft \alpha'$ *($m(g, \alpha', x)$ is defined similarly). We set as a convention, for any* $x$ *and any* $\alpha'$ *such that* $g(\alpha')$ *is undefined:*

$$x \triangleleft g(\alpha') \text{ and } x \triangleleft \mid g(\alpha') = \emptyset.$$

*Thus the conclusion of* (L) *is simply* $m(f, x, \alpha') = \emptyset$ *when* $g(\alpha')$ *is undefined. In contrast, when we write* $x \triangleright g(\alpha')$ *in* (R)*, we assume that* $g(\alpha')$ *is defined. (This convention is consistent with the setting of exercise 14.3.23.) The collection of symmetric algorithms is ordered componentwise by the pointwise ordering:*

$$(f_1, g_1) \leq (f_2, g_2) \text{ iff } ((\forall x\ f_1(x) \leq f_2(x)) \text{ and } (\forall \alpha\ g_1(\alpha) \downarrow \Rightarrow g_1(\alpha) \leq g_2(\alpha))).$$

These axioms enable us, knowing $f$ and $g$, to reconstruct the traces of $f$ and $g$. They also imply that $f$ and $g$ are affine (and hence sequential). Moreover, $g$ allows us to compute the sequentiality indices of $f$, and conversely.

**Proposition 14.3.30** *Let* $f$ *and* $g$ *be as in the previous definition. Then* $f$ *and* $g$ *are affine and satisfy the following two axioms:*

(LS) *If* $x \in D(\mathbf{S})$*,* $\alpha' \in \mathcal{K}(D^\perp(\mathbf{S}'))$*,*$f(x) \triangleright \alpha'$*, and* $f(y) \triangleleft \alpha'$ *for some* $y > x$*, then* $x \triangleright g(\alpha')$*, and* $x \mid \triangleright g(\alpha')$ *is a sequentiality index of* $f$ *at* $(x, \alpha')$*.*

(RS) *If* $\alpha' \in D^\perp(\mathbf{S}')$*,* $x \in \mathcal{K}(D(\mathbf{S}))$*,* $x \triangleleft g(\alpha')$*, and* $x \triangleright g(\beta')$ *for some* $\beta' > \alpha'$*, then* $f(x) \triangleleft \alpha'$*, and* $f(x) \triangleleft \mid \alpha'$ *is a sequentiality index of* $g$ *at* $(\alpha', x)$*.*

PROOF. We only prove that $f$ is affine and that property $(LS)$ holds. The stability of $f$ follows easily from the existence of $m(f, x, \alpha')$ for all $x, \alpha'$ such that $f(x) \triangleleft \alpha'$ (cf. remark 12.3.7). We show that $f$ is affine. Suppose $q'v' \in f(x)$. Then $f(x) \triangleleft q'$. By $(L)$, $x \triangleleft g(q')$ and $f(r) \triangleleft q'$, where $r = x \triangleleft |\, g(q')$. Let $q_1'v_1' = f(r) \triangleleft |\, q'$, and suppose $q_1' < q'$. On one hand $q_1'v_1' \in A(q')$ implies $q_1'v_1' \not\leq q'$. On the other hand:

$$q_1'v_1' \in f(x) \quad \text{since } q_1'v_1' \in f(r) \text{ and } r \leq x$$
$$q_1'v_1' \leq q' \quad \text{since } q'v', q_1'v_1' \in f(x) \,.$$

Hence $q_1' = q'$, and moreover $v_1' = v'$ since $q'v', q_1'v_1' \in f(x)$. We have proved $f(r) \triangleleft |\, q' = q'v'$, and *a fortiori* $q'v' \in f(r)$.

We now prove that Axiom $(L)$ implies property $(LS)$. Suppose $x \in D(\mathbf{S})$, and $\alpha' \in \mathcal{K}(D^\perp(\mathbf{S}'))$, $f(x) \triangleright \alpha'$ and $f(y) \triangleleft \alpha'$ for some $y > x$. By $(L)$, we have $f(r_1) \triangleleft \alpha'$, where $r_1 = y \triangleleft |\, g(\alpha')$, which implies $r_1 \not\subseteq x$ since $f(x) \triangleright \alpha'$. Let $r$ be the largest response prefix of $r_1$ contained in $x$, and let $rc$ be such that $rc < r_1$. We claim that $x \mid \triangleright g(\alpha') = rc$. From $r_1 \in A(g(\alpha'))$ and $rc < r_1$, we get $rc \in g(\alpha')$. We have $r \in x$ by construction, thus $rc$ is enabled in $x$. If $rc$ is filled in $x$, it must be filled with the same value $v$ in $x$ and $r_1$, contradicting the maximality of $r$. Hence $rc \in g(\alpha') \cap A(x)$, which proves the claim. The proof of $(LS)$ is completed by observing that $rc < r_1, r_1 \leq y$ imply $rc \in F(y)$ and that $rc = x \mid \triangleright g(\alpha')$ does not depend on $y$.                                                                   □

A familiar feature of stability is not apparent in definition 14.3.29: the order is not defined by means of the stable ordering (cf. definition 12.1.4). But the stable ordering arises as a derived property.

**Exercise 14.3.31** *Show that if $(f_1, g_1) \leq (f_2, g_2)$ (cf. definition 14.3.29), then $f_1 \leq_{st} f_2$ and $g_1 \leq_{st} g_2$. Hint: To show $f_1 \leq_{st} f_2$, apply $(LS)$ to $(f_1, g_1)$, $(R)$ to $(f_2, g_2)$, and $(LS)$ to $(f_2, g_2)$.*

We show the equivalence between the two presentations of affine algorithms, as strategies, and as pairs $(f, g)$.

**Theorem 14.3.32** *Let $\mathbf{S}$ and $\mathbf{S}'$ be two sds's. Given $\phi \in D(\mathbf{S} \multimap \mathbf{S}')$, we define a pair $(f, g)$ of a function and a partial function as follows:*

$$f(x) = \{r' \mid r' = s\lceil_{\mathbf{S}'} \text{ and } s\lceil_{\mathbf{S}} \in x \text{ for some } s \in \phi\}$$
$$g(\alpha') = \{q \mid q = s\lceil_{\mathbf{S}} \text{ and } s\lceil_{\mathbf{S}'} \in \alpha' \text{ for some } s \in \phi\}.$$

*By convention, if for some $\alpha'$ the right hand side of the definition of $g$ is empty, we interpret this definitional equality as saying that $g(\alpha')$ is undefined.*

*Conversely, given a symmetric algorithm $(f, g)$ from $\mathbf{S}$ to $\mathbf{S}'$, we construct an affine algorithm $\phi \in D(\mathbf{S} \multimap \mathbf{S}')$ as follows. We build the positions $s$ of $\phi$ by induction on the length of $s$:*

- *If $s \in \phi$, if $s\lceil_{\mathbf{S}}$ and $s\lceil_{\mathbf{S}'}$ are responses, and if $q' = (s\lceil_{\mathbf{S}'})c'$ for some $c'$, then:*

  $$sc'c \in \phi \quad \text{if } (s\lceil_{\mathbf{S}})c \in g(q')$$
  $$sc'v' \in \phi \quad \text{if } q'v' \in f(s\lceil_{\mathbf{S}}) \,.$$

- *If $s \in \phi$, if $s\lceil_{\mathbf{S}}$ and $s\lceil_{\mathbf{S}'}$ are queries, and if $r = (s\lceil_{\mathbf{S}})v$ for some $v$, then:*

  $$svc \in \phi \quad \text{if } rc \in g(s\lceil_{\mathbf{S}'})$$
  $$svv' \in \phi \quad \text{if } (s\lceil_{\mathbf{S}'})v' \in f(r) \,.$$

*(The cases in the definition of $\phi$ are mutually exclusive, by (L).)*

These two transformations define an isomorphism between $D(\mathbf{S} \multimap \mathbf{S}')$, ordered by inclusion, and the set of symmetric algorithms from $\mathbf{S}$ to $\mathbf{S}'$, ordered pointwise componentwise.

PROOF HINT. We only check that $(f, g)$ satisfies $(L)$. If $x \in D(\mathbf{S})$, $\alpha' \in \mathcal{K}(D^\perp(\mathbf{S}'))$ and $f(x) \vartriangleleft \alpha'$, let $q'v' = f(x) \vartriangleleft \mid \alpha'$, and let $s \in \phi$ be such that $q'v' = s\lceil_{\mathbf{S}'}$ and $s\lceil_{\mathbf{S}} \in x$. Then $s$ ends with $v'$ (cf. remark 14.3.25). We claim:

(1) $\quad s\lceil_{\mathbf{S}} = x \vartriangleleft \mid g(\alpha') \qquad$ (2) $\quad s\lceil_{\mathbf{S}} = m(f, x, \alpha')$ .

(1) Since $s\lceil_{\mathbf{S}} \in x$, we are left to show $s\lceil_{\mathbf{S}} \in A(g(\alpha'))$. Since $q'v' = f(x) \vartriangleleft \mid \alpha'$, we have $q'v' \in A(\alpha')$, hence $q' \in \alpha'$. We first show that $s\lceil_{\mathbf{S}}$ is enabled in $g(\alpha')$. Let $s\lceil_{\mathbf{S}} = qv$, and let $s_1$ be the least prefix of $s$ such that $s_1\lceil_{\mathbf{S}} = q$. We claim that $s_1\lceil_{\mathbf{S}'} \in \alpha'$. By the definition of $s_1$, and since $s$ ends with $v'$, $s_1$ is a strict prefix of $s$ and $s_1\lceil_{\mathbf{S}'} < s\lceil_{\mathbf{S}'}$. Hence $s_1\lceil_{\mathbf{S}'} \leq q'$, which implies the claim. Since $s_1\lceil_{\mathbf{S}} = q$, the claim implies $q \in g(\alpha')$ by definition of $g$, and that $s\lceil_{\mathbf{S}} = qv$ is enabled in $g(\alpha')$. Suppose now that $s\lceil_{\mathbf{S}}$ is filled in $g(\alpha')$. Then there exist $c$ and $s_2 \in \phi$ such that $(s\lceil_{\mathbf{S}})c = s_2\lceil_{\mathbf{S}}$ and $s_2\lceil_{\mathbf{S}'} \in \alpha'$. By lemma 14.3.14(1) and by lemma 14.3.24(3), $s$ and $s_2$ are comparable. But, since $(s\lceil_{\mathbf{S}})c = s_2\lceil_{\mathbf{S}}$, we cannot have $s_2 \leq s$, and since $s_2\lceil_{\mathbf{S}'} \in \alpha'$ and $s\lceil_{\mathbf{S}'} \in A(\alpha')$, we cannot have $s \leq s_2$: contradiction.

(2) By definition of $f$, we have $s\lceil_{\mathbf{S}'} \in f(s\lceil_{\mathbf{S}})$, hence $f(s\lceil_{\mathbf{S}}) \vartriangleleft \alpha'$. Suppose now that $y \leq x$ and $f(y) \vartriangleleft \alpha'$. By lemma 14.3.12(2), $f(y) \vartriangleleft \mid \alpha' = f(x) \vartriangleleft \mid \alpha'$, thus $q'v' \in f(y)$. Let $s_3 \in \phi$ be such that $q'v' = s_3\lceil_{\mathbf{S}'}$ and $s_3\lceil_{\mathbf{S}} \in y$. By lemma 14.3.24(2), $s$ and $s_3$ are comparable. Since $s$ ends with $v'$ and since $s_3\lceil_{\mathbf{S}'} = s\lceil_{\mathbf{S}'}$, $s_3$ cannot be a proper prefix of $s$. Thus $s \leq s_3$, and this entails $s\lceil_{\mathbf{S}} \in y$ since $s\lceil_{\mathbf{S}} \leq s_3\lceil_{\mathbf{S}}$ and $s_3\lceil_{\mathbf{S}} \in y$. □

The definition of $f$ (the function computed by $\phi$) in theorem 14.3.32 is so compact that it may hide the underlying operational semantics. The application of $\phi$ to a strategy $x$ of $\mathbf{S}$ involves an interplay between $\phi$ and $x$ that is very similar to the situation described in definition 14.3.9. We have already suggested that an affine algorithm 'contains' input counter-strategies. Let $\phi$ be the generic algorithm of figure 14.2, and let $x$ be the following input strategy, represented suggestively as a forest:

$$
\left\{
\begin{array}{l}
c\, v_i \left\{
\begin{array}{l}
d\, w \\
\vdots \\
d_1 \cdots
\end{array}
\right. \\
\vdots \\
c_1 \cdots
\end{array}
\right.
$$

The matching of $\phi$ against $x$ results in the 'play' $cv_i dw$.

We turn to the composition of affine algorithms.

**Definition 14.3.33** *Let $\mathbf{S}$, $\mathbf{S}'$ and $\mathbf{S}''$ be sds's, and let $(f, g)$ and $(f', g')$ be symmetric algorithms from $\mathbf{S}$ to $\mathbf{S}'$ and from $\mathbf{S}'$ to $\mathbf{S}''$. We define their composition $(f'', g'')$ from $\mathbf{S}$ to $\mathbf{S}''$ as follows:*

$$ f'' = f' \circ f \quad and \quad g'' = g \circ g'. $$

**Proposition 14.3.34** *The pair $(f'', g'')$ in definition 14.3.33 indeed defines a symmetric algorithm.*

PROOF. We only check axiom $(L)$. Suppose $f'(f(x))\triangleleft \alpha''$. By $(L)$ applied to $(f', g')$, we have $f(x)\triangleleft g'(\alpha'')$ and $m(f', f(x), \alpha'') = f(x) \triangleleft\mid g'(\alpha'')$. By $(L)$ applied to $(f, g)$, from $f(x)\triangleleft g'(\alpha'')$ we get $x\triangleleft g(g'(\alpha''))$ and $m(f, x, g'(\alpha'')) = x \triangleleft\mid g(g'(\alpha''))$. We set $r = x \triangleleft\mid g(g'(\alpha''))$. We have to prove $m(f' \circ f, x, \alpha'') = r$. Since $m(f, x, g'(\alpha'')) = r$, we have $f(r)\triangleleft g'(\alpha'')$. We claim that $f'(f(r))\triangleleft\alpha''$. Suppose the contrary, that is, $f'(f(r))\triangleright\alpha''$. Then, by $(LS)$ applied to $(f', g')$ at $(f(r), \alpha'')$, we have $f(r)\triangleright g'(\alpha'')$, which contradicts our previous deduction that $f(r)\triangleleft g'(\alpha'')$. Hence the claim holds. We are left to prove that, for any $y \leq x$ such that $f'(f(y))\triangleleft\alpha''$, then $r \leq y$. Since $m(f, x, g'(\alpha'')) = r$, this second claim can be rephrased as $f(y)\triangleleft g'(\alpha'')$. We set $r' = f(x) \triangleleft\mid g'(\alpha'')$. We have:

$$(f(y) \leq f(x), m(f', f(x), \alpha'') = r' \text{ and } f'(f(y))\triangleleft\alpha'') \Rightarrow r' \leq f(y) \ .$$

But $r'\triangleleft g'(\alpha'')$ by definition of $r'$ and by lemma 14.3.12(1), and the conclusion follows by lemma 14.3.12(2).                                                    □

**Definition 14.3.35** *The category* **Algo**$_l$ *is defined as follows. Its objects are the sequential data stuctures and its morphisms are the affine algorithms. If $\phi \in D(\mathbf{S} \multimap \mathbf{S}')$ and $\phi' \in D(\mathbf{S}' \multimap \mathbf{S}'')$, if $(f, g)$ and $(f', g')$ are the symmetric algorithms associated with $\phi$ and $\phi'$, respectively, then $\phi' \circ \phi$ is the affine algorithm $\phi''$ associated with $(f' \circ f, g \circ g')$.*

We interchangeably look at morphisms as affine algorithms or as symmetric algorithms. In particular, there are two descriptions of the identity morphism.

**Exercise 14.3.36** *Show that $(id, id)$ is the symmetric algorithm corresponding to the strategy id described in definition 14.3.19.*

Alternatively, composition can be defined operationally. This idea goes back to [BC85]. The form presented here is close to that given in [AJ92].

**Lemma 14.3.37** *Let $\phi$ and $(f, g)$ be as in the statement of theorem 14.3.32. Then we have the following equalities, where $r, r'$ range over responses and $q, q'$ range over queries:*

(1)   $trace(f) = \{(r, r') \mid r = s\lceil_\mathbf{S} \text{ and } r' = s\lceil_{\mathbf{S}'} \text{ for some } s \in \phi\}$
(2)   $trace(g) = \{(q', q) \mid q' = s\lceil_{\mathbf{S}'} \text{ and } q = s\lceil_\mathbf{S} \text{ for some } s \in \phi\} \ .$

PROOF. (1) If $r = s\lceil_\mathbf{S}$ and $q'v' = r' = s\lceil_{\mathbf{S}'}$, for some $s \in \phi$, then a fortiori $s\lceil_\mathbf{S}\leq r$, thus $r' \in f(r)$. Suppose that $r' \in f(r_1)$ for some $r_1 < r$. Let $s_1 \in \phi$ be such that $r' = s_1\lceil_{\mathbf{S}'}$ and $s_1\lceil_\mathbf{S}\leq r_1$. Then $(s_1\lceil_\mathbf{S}, s_1\lceil_{\mathbf{S}'}) < (s\lceil_\mathbf{S}, s\lceil_{\mathbf{S}'})$, which by lemma 14.3.24 implies $s_1 < s$. By remark 14.3.25, $r' = s\lceil_{\mathbf{S}'}$ implies that $s$ ends with $v'$, and hence $s_1\lceil_{\mathbf{S}'}< s\lceil_{\mathbf{S}'}$, contradicting $r' = s_1\lceil_{\mathbf{S}'}$. Thus $(r, r') \in trace(f)$. Reciprocally, if $(r, r') \in trace(f)$, then let $s \in \phi$ be such that $r' = s\lceil_{\mathbf{S}'}$ and $s\lceil_\mathbf{S}\leq r$. Then, by minimality of $r$, we must have $s\lceil_\mathbf{S}= r$. The proof of (2) is similar.                                    □

**Proposition 14.3.38** *Let $\mathbf{S} = (C, V, P)$, $\mathbf{S}' = (C', V', P')$ and $\mathbf{S}'' = (C'', V'', P'')$ be three sds's. Let $\phi \in D(\mathbf{S} \multimap \mathbf{S}')$, $\phi' \in D(\mathbf{S}' \multimap \mathbf{S}'')$. Then:*

$$\phi' \circ \phi = \{s\lceil_{\mathbf{S}\cup\mathbf{S}''} \mid s \in \mathcal{L}(\mathbf{S}, \mathbf{S}', \mathbf{S}''), s\lceil_{\mathbf{S}\cup\mathbf{S}'}\in \phi, \text{ and } s\lceil_{\mathbf{S}'\cup\mathbf{S}''}\in \phi'\} \ ,$$

*where $\mathcal{L}(\mathbf{S}, \mathbf{S}', \mathbf{S}'')$ denotes the set of words in $(C \cup V \cup C' \cup V' \cup C'' \cup V'')^*$ such that two consecutive symbols are not such that one is in $C \cup V$ and the other is in $C'' \cup V''$.*

PROOF HINT. One verifies easily that this defines a strategy of $\mathbf{S} \multimap \mathbf{S}''$. Then, by lemma 14.3.37, and by the injectivity of $\lambda s.(s\lceil\mathbf{S}, s\lceil\mathbf{S}')$ (lemma 14.3.24), it is enough to check:

$$\{(s\lceil\mathbf{S}, s\lceil\mathbf{S}'') \mid s \in \mathcal{L}(\mathbf{S}, \mathbf{S}', \mathbf{S}''), s\lceil\mathbf{S}\cup\mathbf{S}'\in \phi, \text{ and } s\lceil\mathbf{S}'\cup\mathbf{S}''\in \phi'\} =$$
$$\{(p,p'') \mid p = s_1\lceil\mathbf{S}, s_1\lceil\mathbf{S}' = s_2\lceil\mathbf{S}', \text{ and } p'' = s_2\lceil\mathbf{S}'', \text{ for some } s_1 \in \phi, s_2 \in \phi'\}.$$

Obviously, the left hand side is included in the right hand side, taking $s_1 = s\lceil\mathbf{S}\cup\mathbf{S}'$ and $s_2 = s\lceil\mathbf{S}'\cup\mathbf{S}''$. For the other direction we construct $s$ from $s_1$ and $s_2$ by replacing every $c'v'$ in $s_2$ by the corresponding portion $c'c_1v_1\cdots c_nv_nv'$ of $s_1$. By construction $s \in \mathcal{L}(\mathbf{S}, \mathbf{S}', \mathbf{S}'')$.                                                                                       □

This alternative definition of composition is convenient to establish the symmetric monoidal structure of the category $\mathbf{Algo}_l$.

**Definition 14.3.39 (tensor – sds)** *Let* $\mathbf{S} = (C, V, P)$ *and* $\mathbf{S}' = (C', V', P')$ *be two sds's. We define the sds* $\mathbf{S} \otimes \mathbf{S}' = (C'', V'', P'')$ *as follows. The sets* $C''$ *and* $V''$ *are disjoint unions:*

$$C'' = \{c.1 \mid c \in C\} \cup \{c'.2 \mid c' \in C'\}$$
$$V'' = \{v.1 \mid v \in V\} \cup \{v'.2 \mid v' \in V'\}.$$

$P''$ *consists of the alternating non-empty positions* $s$ *which are such that:*

$s\lceil\mathbf{S}\in P \cup \{\epsilon\}$ *and* $s\lceil\mathbf{S}'\in P' \cup \{\epsilon\}$, *and*
$s$ *has no prefix of the form* $scv'$

*(removing the tags .1 and .2 from* $s\lceil\mathbf{S}$ *and* $s\lceil\mathbf{S}'$ *). Let* $\mathbf{S}_1, \mathbf{S}_2, \mathbf{S}_1', \mathbf{S}_2'$ *be sds's, and let* $\phi_1 \in D(\mathbf{S}_1 \multimap \mathbf{S}_1')$ *and* $\phi_2 \in D(\mathbf{S}_2 \multimap \mathbf{S}_2')$. *We define* $\phi_1 \otimes \phi_2 \in D((\mathbf{S}_1 \otimes \mathbf{S}_2) \multimap (\mathbf{S}_1' \otimes \mathbf{S}_2'))$ *as follows. It consists of the positions of* $(\mathbf{S}_1 \otimes \mathbf{S}_2) \multimap (\mathbf{S}_1' \otimes \mathbf{S}_2')$ *whose projections on* $\mathbf{S}_1 \cup \mathbf{S}_1'$ *and on* $\mathbf{S}_2 \cup \mathbf{S}_2'$ *are in* $\phi_1$ *and in* $\phi_2$, *respectively.*

As for definition 14.3.19, the second constraint in definition 14.3.39 implies that $P''$ contains no position of the form $sc'v$.

**Exercise 14.3.40** *Construct the tensor product along the same lines as in exercise 14.3.23, using the following table of polarities (which is obtained through the encoding of* $\mathbf{S} \otimes \mathbf{S}'$ *as* $(\mathbf{S} \multimap \mathbf{S}'^\perp)^\perp$ *):*

| $m$ | $m'$ | $(m, m')$ |
|:---:|:---:|:---:|
| ● | ● | ● |
| ● | ○ | ○ |
| ○ | ● | ○ |
| ○ | ○ | undefined |

**Proposition 14.3.41** *The data of definition 14.3.39 indeed define a functor which, together with the empty sds* $(\emptyset, \emptyset, \emptyset)$ *as unit, turns* $\mathbf{Algo}_l$ *into a symmetric monoidal category.*

PROOF. The coherent isomorphisms are based on the bijective correspondences which associate, say, a move $m.1$ in $\mathbf{S} \otimes (\mathbf{S}' \otimes \mathbf{S}'')$ to the move $m.1.1$ in $(\mathbf{S} \otimes \mathbf{S}') \otimes \mathbf{S}''$.                □

**Proposition 14.3.42** *The category* $\mathbf{Algo}_l$ *is symmetric monoidal closed.*

PROOF. Loosely, $((\mathbf{S} \otimes \mathbf{S}') \multimap \mathbf{S}'')$ and $\mathbf{S} \multimap (\mathbf{S}' \multimap \mathbf{S}'')$ coincide (up to tags). Given $\phi \in D(\mathbf{S}_1 \multimap \mathbf{S})$ and $\psi \in D(\mathbf{S} \multimap (\mathbf{S}' \multimap \mathbf{S}''))$, in order to turn a position $s$ whose projection on $\mathbf{S}_1 \cup (\mathbf{S}' \multimap \mathbf{S}'')$ is in $\psi \circ \phi$ into a position whose projection on $(\mathbf{S}_1 \otimes \mathbf{S}') \cup \mathbf{S}''$ is in the corresponding composed morphism from $\mathbf{S}_1 \otimes \mathbf{S}'$ to $\mathbf{S}''$, we replace every portion $c'v'$ of $s$ by $c'c'v'v'$ (cf. the description of $id$).                                    □

The category $\mathbf{Algo}_l$ is also cartesian.

**Definition 14.3.43 (product – sds)** *Let* $\mathbf{S} = (C, V, P)$ *and* $\mathbf{S}' = (C', V', P')$ *be two sds's. We define* $\mathbf{S} \times \mathbf{S}' = (C'', V'', P'')$ *as follows:*

- $C''$ *and* $V''$ *are as in definition 14.3.39.*

- $P'' = \{p.1 \mid p \in P\} \cup \{p'.2 \mid p' \in P'\}$ *where* $p.1$ *is a shorthand for the position formed by tagging all the moves of* $p$ *with 1, and similarly for* $p'$.

**Proposition 14.3.44** *The category* $\mathbf{Algo}_l$ *is cartesian. The binary products are as specified in definition 14.3.43, and the terminal object is the empty sds* $(\emptyset, \emptyset, \emptyset)$.

PROOF. It is easily seen that $D(\mathbf{S} \times \mathbf{S}')$ is the set theoretical product of $D(\mathbf{S})$ and $D(\mathbf{S}')$, and that $D^{\perp}(\mathbf{S} \times \mathbf{S}')$ is the disjoint union of $D^{\perp}(\mathbf{S})$ and $D^{\perp}(\mathbf{S}')$. The first projection is the symmetric algorithm $(\pi_1, in_1)$ where $\pi_1$ and $in_1$ are the set theoretical first projection and injection, respectively. Similarly, the second projection is $(\pi_2, in_2)$. If $(f, g) : \mathbf{S} \to \mathbf{S}'$ and $(f', g') : \mathbf{S}' \to \mathbf{S}''$, then $\langle (f, g), (f', g') \rangle$ is defined as $(\langle f, f' \rangle, [g, g'])$, where $\langle \_, \_ \rangle$ and $[\_, \_]$ denote the set theoretical pairing and copairing.                                    □

Thus, in $\mathbf{Algo}_l$, the empty sds is both the unit of the tensor and a terminal object. It is this property that makes $\mathbf{Algo}_l$ a model of intuitionistic affine logic (cf. remark 13.2.23).

Finally, we relate the two categories $\mathbf{Algo}$ and $\mathbf{Algo}_l$ by an adjunction.

**Proposition 14.3.45** *The mapping* cds *from sds's to cds's defined in proposition 14.3.3 extends to a functor* cds : $\mathbf{Algo}_l \to \mathbf{Algo}$ *as follows. Let* $\mathbf{S}$ *and* $\mathbf{S}'$ *be two sds's, and let* $(f, g)$ *be a symmetric algorithm from* $\mathbf{S}$ *to* $\mathbf{S}'$. *We define an abstract algorithm* $cds(f, g) : cds(\mathbf{S}) \to cds(\mathbf{S}')$ *as follows:*

$$cds(f, g)(xq') = \begin{cases} valof\ (x \mid \triangleright g(q')) & if\ x \triangleright g(q') \\ output\ q'v' & if\ q'v' \in f(x), \end{cases}$$

*where we freely confuse* $x \in D(\mathbf{S})$ *with the associated state* $cds(x) \in D(cds(\mathbf{S}))$. *(As in theorem 14.3.32, the cases in the definition of* $cds(f, g)$ *are mutually exclusive.)*

PROOF. We only prove $cds(f' \circ f, g \circ g') = cds(f', g') \circ cds(f, g)$. Given $x$ and $q''$, there are three cases:

- $q''v'' \in f'(f(x))$. Then, obviously:

$$cds(f' \circ f, g \circ g')(xq'') = output\ q''v'' = (cds(f', g') \circ cds(f, g))(xq'').$$

- $x \triangleright g(g'(q''))$. Then $f(x) \triangleright g'(q'')$ by $(R)$. It follows that $cds(f', g')(f(x)q'') = valof\ q'$, where $q' = f(x) \mid \triangleright g'(q'')$. We claim that $x \triangleright g(q')$. Suppose not: since $q' \leq g'(q'')$ and $x \triangleright g(g'(q''))$, this would entail $f(x) \triangleleft q'$ by $(RS)$, which is a contradiction since the contrary holds by definition of $q'$. Then, by the claim, $\mathbf{cds}(f,g)(xq') = valof\ q$, where $q = x\ |\!\triangleright g(q')$. It follows that:

$$\mathbf{cds}(f'\circ f, g\circ g')(xq'') = valof\ q = (\mathbf{cds}(f',g')\circ \mathbf{cds}(f,g))(xq'')\ .$$

- $\mathbf{cds}(f'\circ f, g\circ g')(xq'') = \omega$. In particular $q'' \notin F(f'(f(x)))$, hence $(\mathbf{cds}(f',g')\circ \mathbf{cds}(f,g))(xq'')$ could only be defined if we had:

$$f(x)\triangleright g'(q'')\ \text{and}\ x\triangleright g(f(x)\ |\!\triangleright g'(q''))\ .$$

But then we would have $x\triangleright g(g'(q''))$, contradicting the assumption.  □

We now show that the functor $\mathbf{cds}$ has a left adjoint.

**Definition 14.3.46 (exponential – sds)** *Let* $\mathbf{M} = (C,V,E,\vdash)$ *be a (filiform) cds. The following recursive clauses define a set* $P_!$ *of alternating words over* $C\cup V$:

$$rc \in P_! \quad \textit{if}\ c \in A(state(r))$$
$$rcv \in P_! \quad \textit{if}\ rc \in P_!\ \textit{and}\ state(rcv) \in D(M)\ ,$$

*where* state *is the following function mapping responses (or* $\epsilon$*) of* $P_!$ *to states of* $\mathbf{M}$:

$$state(\epsilon) = \emptyset \quad state(rcv) = state(r)\cup\{(c,v)\}.$$

*The sds* $(C,V,P_!)$ *is called* $!\mathbf{M}$. *We define* $\eta : \mathbf{M} \to \mathbf{cds}(!\mathbf{M})$ *by:*

$$\eta(x(rc)) = \begin{cases} valof\ c & \textit{if}\ state(r) \subseteq x\ \textit{and}\ c \in A(x) \\ output\ (rcv) & \textit{if}\ state(r)\cup\{(c,v)\} \subseteq x\ . \end{cases}$$

*(Hence* $\eta\bullet x = \{r \mid state(r) \subseteq x\}$.)

**Remark 14.3.47** *The reader should compare the definitions of* $\mathbf{sds}(\mathbf{M})$ *(exercise 14.3.7) and of* $!\mathbf{M}$. *In* $\mathbf{sds}(\mathbf{M})$, *the positions are built out of the proofs of the cells of* $\mathbf{M}$, *in* $!\mathbf{M}$, *they encode (safety respecting) enumerations of the events contained in the finite states of* $\mathbf{M}$. *Back to example 14.3.21, it should be now clear that, say,* $OR_l$ *can be considered as an affine algorithm from* $!((\mathbf{B}_\perp)^2)$ *to* $\mathbf{B}_\perp$.

**Theorem 14.3.48** *The transformation* $!$ *described in definition 14.3.46 extends to a functor* $!: \mathbf{Algo} \to \mathbf{Algo}_l$ *which is left adjoint to* $\mathbf{cds}$, *with* $\eta$ *as unity. Moreover, the co-Kleisli category associated to the comonad* $!\circ\mathbf{cds} : \mathbf{Algo}_l \to \mathbf{Algo}_l$ *is equivalent to* $\mathbf{Algo}$. *We shall freely abbreviate* $!\circ\mathbf{cds}$ *as* $!$.

PROOF HINT. Let $a \in D(\mathbf{M} \to \mathbf{cds}(\mathbf{S}'))$. We associate a response of $!\mathbf{M}\multimap\mathbf{S}'$ with each event $(xq',u)$ of $a$ as follows:

- If $xq'$ is enabled in $a$ by $(x_1q',valof\ c_1)$, with $x = x_1\cup\{(c_1,v_1)\}$ for some $v_1$, and if $sc_1$ is the response associated with $(x_1q',valof\ c_1)$, then the response associated with $(xq',u)$ is:

$$sc_1v_1c \quad \text{if}\ u = valof\ c$$
$$sc_1v_1v' \quad \text{if}\ u = output\ (q'v')\ .$$

- If $xq'$ is enabled in $a$ by $(xq_1',output\ (q_1'v_1'))$, with $q' = q_1'v_1'c'$ for some $c'$, and if $sv_1'$ is the response associated with $(xq_1',output\ (q_1'v_1'))$, then the response associated with $(xq',u)$ is:

$sv_1'c'c$    if $u = valof\ c$
$sv_1'c'v'$    if $u = output\ (q'v')$ .

We denote with $\zeta(a)$ the set of responses associated to the events of $a$ in this way. We omit the tedious verification of the two equations:

$$\mathbf{cds}(\zeta(a)) \circ \eta = a \qquad \zeta(\mathbf{cds}(\phi) \circ \eta) = \phi.$$

Roughly, the mapping $\zeta$ makes the proofs of cells explicit, while **cds** 'undoes' the job of $\zeta$ by 'filtering' input states against the positions of $\phi$. The second part of the statement follows from the fact that any object $\mathbf{M}$ of **Algo** is isomorphic to an object of the form $\mathbf{cds}(\mathbf{S})$ (specifically, to $\mathbf{cds}(\mathbf{sds}(\mathbf{M}))$, cf. exercise 14.3.7).    □

**Theorem 14.3.49** *The category* **Algo** *is cartesian closed. There are natural isomorphisms in* **Algo**$_l$ *between* $(!\mathbf{S}) \otimes (!\mathbf{S}')$ *and* $!(\mathbf{S} \times \mathbf{S}')$.

PROOF. The first part of the statement is a consequence of the second part, by proposition 13.2.15. For the second part, notice:

- A cell of $!(\mathbf{S} \times \mathbf{S}')$ is of the form, say, $(c_1.1)(v_1.1) \cdots (c_n.1)$ where $c_1 v_1 \cdots c_n$ is a query of $\mathbf{S}$, while the corresponding cell of $(!\mathbf{S}) \otimes (!\mathbf{S}')$ is $(c_1 v_1 \cdots c_n).1$.

- A position $(!\mathbf{S}) \otimes (!\mathbf{S}')$ encodes a shuffling of safety respecting enumerations of a strategy $x$ of $\mathbf{S}$ and of a strategy $x'$ of $\mathbf{S}'$, which is the same as the encoding of a safety respecting enumeration of $(x, x')$.    □

**Exercise 14.3.50** *Let* $\mathbf{S} = (C, V, P)$ *be an sds, and consider the sds:*

$$\mathbf{S}^\uparrow = (V \cup \{\circ\}, C, \{\circ p \mid p \in P\}) .$$

*Show that this operation extends to a functor from* **Algo**$_l$ *to* **Algo**$_l^{op}$ *which is adjoint to itself.*

We end this section with some remarks and comparisons, and by stating two open problems.

- A more abstract setting for sequential algorithms, into which our theory can be embedded, has been developped by Bucciarelli and Ehrhard [BE93]. They abstract cells as some special predicates (cf. exercise 14.1.17) and they introduce so-called sequential structures of the form $(X_*, X^*)$, where $X_*$ plays the role of $D(\mathbf{M})$, and where $X^*$ is a set of linear functions from $X_*$ to $\mathbf{O}$. Their morphisms are defined in the style of exercise 14.2.7.

- Sequential algorithms bear a striking similarity with the oracles that Kleene has developed in his late works on the semantics of higher order recursion theory. In a series of papers [Kle78, Kle80, Kle82, Kle85], he developed up to rank 3 a theory of unimonotonous functions that are closely related to sequential algorithms (see [Buc93] for a precise correspondence). He lacked synthetic tools to develop a theory at all ranks.

- Sequential algorithms, as well as strongly stable functions (cf. section 13.3), yield standard models of PCF. Indeed, it is easily checked that **Algo** and **HCoh** are cpo-enriched CCC's, and we know from theorem 6.5.4 that the standard interpretations of all first order constants of PCF are sequential and strongly stable. Ehrhard [Ehr96] has proved that the hypercoherence model of PCF is actually the extensional collapse of the model of sequential algorithms (cf. exercise 4.5.6). This quite difficult result relies on the following steps:

(1)   For any hypercoherence $(E, \Gamma)$, any $A \in \mathcal{C}(E)$ and any $n \geq \sharp A$, there exists $G \in \mathcal{C}(\omega_\perp^n)$ and a strongly stable function $g : \omega_\perp^n \to E$ such that $g(G) = A$.

(2)   Every compact element $e$ of the model at any type $\tau$ is 2-PCF-definable, which means that there exists a term $x_1 : \sigma_1, \ldots, x_n : \sigma_n \vdash M : \tau$, with $\sigma_1, \ldots, \sigma_n$ of rank at most 2 (cf. definition 4.5.10), such that $e = [\![M]\!](d_1, \ldots, d_n)$ for some $d_1, \ldots, d_n$.

(3)   The 2-PCF-definability allows us to prove the surjectivity (hence the functionality, cf. section 4.5) of the logical relation between the model of sequential algorithms and the strongly stable model generated by the identity at basic types.

• In section 6.4, we mentioned that the study of sequentiality (and of stability) had been motivated by the full abstraction problem for PCF. What has been achieved in this respect? While sequential algorithms are fully abstract for an extension of PCF with a control operation (see section 14.4), none of the models considered in the previous chapters (stable model, strongly stable model, bistructure model, model of sequential algorithms) is fully abstract for PCF. The non-definable functional described in exercise 4.5.18 exists in all these models.

Even worse, the above models even fail to provide a theory including that of the continuous model (see exercise 14.3.51 [JM94]) That much can be repaired, though: Winskel has adapted the model of bistructures so as to make its theory intermediate between the theory of the continuous model of PCF and that of the fully abstract model [Win94]. Bucciarelli and Ehrhard [BE94] and Bucciarelli [Buc97] have proposed combinations of the stable (or strongly stable) model and the continuous model by means of embeddings and logical relations (cf. lemma 4.5.7), respectively, that also achieve a coarsening of the continuous theory.

**Exercise 14.3.51** *Define a closed term M of PCF whose semantics is a functional that returns tt for a functional argument that returns tt and ff when applied to the left disjunction function and to the right disjunction function, respectively (cf. example 14.2.2(2)). Show that $[\![M]\!] = [\![\lambda y.\Omega]\!]$ in the continuous model and that $[\![M]\!] \neq [\![\lambda y.\Omega]\!]$ in the stable model, in the strongly stable model, in the model of bistructures and in the model of sequential algorithms.*

• We have used a vocabulary of games both in the present section and in section 6.6. The two interpretations carry indeed a lot in common, in particular they draw the attention on a computation-as-interaction paradigm. The main differences between the two kinds of game models are in our opinion the following:

(1)   The 'term model games' of section 6.6 allow us to capture PCF definability exactly, whereas the games associated with sequential algorithms also accommodate operations like *catch* that are not definable in PCF (see section 14.4).

(2)   The two sorts of models differ drastically in size. The type $o \to o$ is interpreted by a finite cds (i.e., a cds with finitely many states) in the model of sequential algorithms, while there are infinitely PCF Böhm trees (and hence infinitely many strategies in the term model games) of that type. This finitary nature of sequential algorithms implies that equality in the model (and hence observational equivalence in the language of section 6.4) is decidable for any type built over $o$, while the term model games do not provide effective tools to tackle observational equivalences.

We already mentioned in section 6.4 the result of Loader that the observational equivalence in (finitary) PCF is undecidable. It indicates that the conflict between (1) and (2) cannot be solved. Game models seem to be bound to be infinitary if the goal is to match PCF exactly.

**Remark 14.3.52** *The two sorts of models correspond to different treatments of the exponential. In the present section, we have mimicked the exponential of coherence spaces (cf. section 13.1), shifting from positions (corresponding to events) to enumerations of positions (corresponding to finite states). The exponential constructions that underly the term game models are of a different nature: they allow repetitions (of positions, or of variables). For example, the terms*

$$\textit{if zero? x then tt else ff} \quad \textit{and}$$
$$\textit{if zero? x then if zero? x then tt else ff else ff}$$

*receive the same interpretation in the model of sequential algorithms, and a different interpretation in the term model games. The exponentials in the term model games can be compared with another exponential for coherence spaces, where the tokens of !E are not the finite states of E but the finite multisets of (coherent) events of E.*

**Exercise\* 14.3.53** *Show that the interpretation function of PCF in* **Algo** *is actually computed by a sequential algorithm (representing PCF terms through a cds, like* **LAMBDA**, *cf. example 14.1.7).*

We mention the following two open problems.

(1) Denoting simply by $[\![\_]\!]$ the 'natural' algorithm that computes the semantic function $[\![\_]\!]$ (cf. exercise 14.3.53) and denoting likewise by $BT$ the minimum algorithm computing $BT$, does the equality (of algorithms) $[\![\_]\!] = [\![\_]\!] \circ BT$ hold? In other words, does the semantic evaluation respect the indications of sequentiality provided by the syntax itself?

(2) If $a$ and $a'$ are two definable algorithms such that $a < a'$, can we find $N$ and $N'$ such that $N < N'$ (in the sense of definition 2.3.1), $a = [\![N]\!]$, and $a' = [\![N']\!]$? In other words, does the order on algorithms reflect the syntactic ordering?

# 14.4  Full abstraction for PCF + *catch* \*

In this section, we extend the language PCF with an operation *catch*, inspired from the constructions 'catch' and 'throw' found in several dialects of LISP. The model of sequential algorithms is fully abstract for this extension of PCF, called SPCF. This stands in sharp contrast with the situation of this model with respect to PCF (cf. section 6.5). The material of this section is adapted from [CF92, CCF94].

**Observing sequential algorithms.** Before defining SPCF, we present a third characterization of sequential algorithms, in addition to the descriptions as states and as abstract algorithms. Although sequential algorithms are not functions in the ordinary sense, it would be useful to be able to compare two algorithms by applying them to (extended) inputs. The explicit consideration of an error element allows this.

**Definition 14.4.1 (observable state)** *We assume once and for all that there exists a reserved, non-empty set Err of error values, which is disjoint from any set V of values of any cds* $\mathbf{M} = (C, V, E, \vdash)$. *We stress this by calling an element of V a proper value.*

*Unless stated otherwise explicitly, we assume that Err is a singleton, and we write Err = {e}.*
*Given a cds* $M = (C, V, E, \vdash)$, *we call an observable state of* $M$ *a set* $x$ *of pairs* $(c, w)$, *where either* $(c, w) \in E$ *or* $w \in Err$, *satisfying the conditions that define a state of a cds. The set of observable states of* $M$ *is denoted* $D_\mathcal{O}(M)$. *Note that states are a fortiori observable states: this may be stressed by calling the states of* $M$ *error free. With each observable state* $x$, *we associate an error-free state* $x_{-e}$ *defined by:*

$$x_{-e} = x \cap E.$$

Notice that enablings are not allowed to contain error values, because the enabling relation is part of the structure of a cds, which we did not change. Thus, in the tree representation of an observable state, error values can occur only at the leaves. As an example, the cds $\omega_\perp$ has (up to isomorphism) $\omega_\perp \cup Err$ as its set of extended states. Next we explain how sequential algorithms act on observable states.

**Definition 14.4.2** *Let* $M$ *and* $M'$ *be two cds's. Every sequential algorithm* $a : M \to M'$ *determines an observable input-output function from* $D_\mathcal{O}(M)$ *to* $D_\mathcal{O}(M')$, *defined by:*

$$a \bullet x = \{(c', output\ v') \mid \exists y \leq x\ (yc', output\ v') \in a\} \cup$$
$$\{(c', e) \mid \exists y \leq x\ (yc', valof\ c) \in a\ and\ (c, e) \in x\}.$$

On error free states, this definition agrees with the definition of $a \bullet x$ given in definition 14.2.1. The second component of the union is only 'active' when the input contains error values, and 'implements' a propagation of these values to the output.

**Lemma 14.4.3** *The function* $\lambda x.(a \bullet x) : D_\mathcal{O}(M) \to D_\mathcal{O}(M')$ *of definition 14.4.2 is well-defined and continuous.*

PROOF. Continuity obviously follows from the definition. We have to show that $a \bullet x$ is (i) consistent, and (ii) safe. We claim that once $c'$ is fixed, then there is at most one $y$ which ensures that $c'$ is filled in $a \bullet x$. Property (i) immediately follows from the claim. We prove the claim by contradiction. There are three cases:

(1) $(y_1 c', output\ v_1'), (y_2 c', output\ v_2') \in a$. Then $y_1 = y_2$ by proposition 14.2.4, contradicting the assumption.

(2) $(y_1 c', output\ v_1') \in a$, $(y_2 c', valof\ c_2) \in a$ and $(c_2, e) \in x$. By proposition 14.2.4, $y_2 < y_1$, and moreover $c_2$ must be filled in $y_1$, and hence in $x$, with a proper value, since $y_1$ is error free. This contradicts the consistency of $x$, since we also assumed $(c_2, e) \in x$.

(3) $(y_1 c', valof\ c_1) \in a$, $(c_1, e) \in x$ and $(y_2 c', valof\ c_2) \in a$, $(c_2, e) \in x$. Then, say, $y_1 < y_2$, and the reasoning is the same as in case 2.

Next we show safety. From the above analysis, it follows that $a \bullet x$ is the disjoint union of $\{(c', output\ v') \mid \exists y \leq x\ (yc', output\ v') \in a\}$ and $\{(c', e) \mid \exists y \leq x\ (yc', valof\ c) \in a\ and\ (c, e) \in x\}$. The first of these sets is $a \bullet (x_{-e})$, which is a state by proposition 14.2.4. If $c'$ is filled in the second set, then by definition $(yc', valof\ c) \in a$ for some $y$, which entails $c' \in A(a \bullet y)$ and $c' \in E(a \bullet x)$. □

The following proposition shows what the consideration of errors is good for.

**Proposition 14.4.4** *Let* $M$ *and* $M'$ *be two cds's. If* $a \bullet x \leq a' \bullet x$ *for all* $x \in D_\mathcal{O}(M)$, *then* $a \leq a'$.

PROOF. The proof is by contradiction. Let $yc'$ be a minimal cell of $M \to M'$ such that $yc'$ is filled in $a$, and is either not filled, or filled with a different value in $a'$. We shall call witness an observable $z$ such that $a.z \not\leq a'.z$. There are two cases:

(1) If $(yc', output\ v') \in a$, then $(c', v') \in a{\scriptstyle\bullet}y$. If $(c', output\ v') \notin a'{\scriptstyle\bullet}y$, then $y$ is a witness. If $(c', output\ v') \in a'{\scriptstyle\bullet}y$, then, since $y$ is error free, there exists $z \leq y$ such that $(zc', output\ v') \in a'$.

(2) If $(yc', valof\ c) \in a$, then $(c', e) \in a{\scriptstyle\bullet}(y \cup \{(c, e)\})$. If $(c', e) \notin a'{\scriptstyle\bullet}(y \cup \{(c, e)\})$, then $y \cup \{(c, e)\}$ is a witness. If $(c', e) \in a'{\scriptstyle\bullet}(y \cup \{(c, e)\})$, then, by definition of the observable input-output function:

$$\exists z \leq y \cup \{(c, e)\} \quad (zc', valof\ c_1) \in a' \text{ and } (c_1, e) \in y \cup \{(c, e)\}.$$

Then $z \leq y$, since $z$ is error free and $z \leq y \cup \{(c, e)\}$. Also, $(c_1, e) \in y \cup \{(c, e)\}$ implies $c_1 = c$, since $y$ is error free.

Both cases 1 and 2 reduce to the situation where $(yc', u) \in a$ and $(zc', u) \in a'$, for some $z \leq y$ and for some $u$. This forces $z < y$, since by assumption $(yc', u) \notin a'$. Also, $(zc', u) \in a$, by the minimality assumption. But the conjunction of $(yc', u) \in a$, $(zc', u) \in a$, and $y < z$ is excluded by proposition 14.2.4, which forces $u = valof\ c$ and $y <_c z$ for some $c$, and precludes $(zc', valof\ c)$ to be an event.                    □

We gather more material in exercises 14.4.6, 14.4.7, and 14.4.8.

**Exercise 14.4.5** *Let* $M$ *be a cds. Let* $a \in D_{\mathcal{O}}(M \to \omega_\perp)$. *Show the following properties, for any cell* $x? \in E(a)$:

(1) $a{\scriptstyle\bullet}x = \{(?, n)\}$          $\Leftrightarrow$   $(x?, output\ n) \in a$
(2) $(a{\scriptstyle\bullet}x = \perp \text{ and } a{\scriptstyle\bullet}(x \cup \{(c, e)\})) = \{(?, e)\})$   $\Leftrightarrow$   $(x?, valof\ c) \in a$
(3) $a{\scriptstyle\bullet}x = \{(?, e)\}$          $\Leftrightarrow$   $(x?, e) \in a$.

*Generalize these properties for* $a \in D_{\mathcal{O}}(M_1 \to \cdots \to M_n \to \omega_\perp)$. *Hint: These properties are variations of proposition 14.2.4.*

**Exercise 14.4.6** *Let* $M$ *and* $M'$ *be two cds's. The observable input-output function of an observable algorithm, that is, of an observable state of* $M \to M'$, *is defined as follows:*

$$
\begin{aligned}
a{\scriptstyle\bullet}x \;=\; & \{(c', output\ v') \mid \exists y \leq x\ (yc', output\ v') \in a\} \cup \\
& \{(c', e) \mid \exists y \leq x\ (yc', e) \in a\} \cup \\
& \{(c', e) \mid \exists y \leq x\ (yc', valof\ c) \in a \text{ and } (c, e) \in x\}.
\end{aligned}
$$

*(Here we do not assume that* Err *is a singleton, and* e *is used to denote a generic element of* Err.*) Show that the statement of proposition 14.4.4 fails for observable algorithms if* Err $= \{e\}$, *and holds if* Err *contains at least two elements. Hint: Consider* $a = \{(\emptyset?, valof\ ?)\}$ *and* $a' = \{(\emptyset?, e)\}$, *between, say, two flat domains.*

**Exercise 14.4.7** *Let* $M$ *and* $M'$ *be two cds's. (1) Show that there exists an order-isomorphism between* $D(M \to M')$ *and the pointwise ordered set of functions* $h$ *from* $D_{\mathcal{O}}(M)$ *to* $D_{\mathcal{O}}(M')$ *which are:*

● *error-sensitive: For any* $x$ *and* $c'$ *such that* $c' \in A(h(x))$ *and* $c' \in F(h(z))$ *for some* $z > x$, *there exists* $c \in A(x)$, *called a sequentiality index, such that:*

$$\forall y > x\ (h(x) <_{c'} h(y) \;\Rightarrow\; x <_c y)$$
$$\forall e \in Err\ h(x \cup \{(c, e)\}) = h(x) \cup \{(c', e)\}\ ;$$

$$\frac{\Gamma \vdash M : \sigma}{\Gamma \vdash catch(M) : \iota} \qquad \overline{\Gamma \vdash e : \iota} \qquad \overline{\Gamma \vdash e : o}$$

Figure 14.3: The additional constants of SPCF and of SPCF($Err$)

---

- error-reflecting: For any $c'$, e and $y$, if $(c', e) \in h(y)$, then $h$ has a sequentiality index $c$ at $(x, c')$ for some $x < y$, and $(c, e) \in y$.

(2) Show that sequentiality indices of error-sensitive functions are unique (for fixed $x$ and $c'$). (3) Show that this isomorphism extends to an isomorphism from $D_{\mathcal{O}}(\mathbf{M} \to \mathbf{M}')$ to the set of pointwise ordered error-sensitive functions from $D_{\mathcal{O}}(\mathbf{M})$ to $D_{\mathcal{O}}(\mathbf{M}')$. Hints: Use proposition 14.4.4. For the surjectivity of the mapping from a to $\lambda x.(a \bullet x)$, proceed as in the proof of proposition 14.2.9.

**Exercise 14.4.8** Show that the category whose objects are cds's and whose arrows are observable algorithms (cf. exercise 14.4.6) is cartesian closed. Hint: Use the characterization given in exercise 14.4.7.

We come now to the proper subject of this section. We extend PCF with a family of unary operators catch at each PCF type $\sigma$. The resulting extended language is called SPCF. Just as in the semantics, it may be convenient to introduce explicit errors in the syntax. We thus occasionally work with SPCF($Err$), which is SPCF plus constants $e \in Err$ of basic type, which are interpreted using error values with the same name. The typing rules for the constants of SPCF and of SPCF($Err$) are summarized in figure 14.3. As for PCF, a program is a closed term of basic type. We also include constants $\Omega$ of basic type, with $[\![\Omega]\!] = \bot$.

As for PCF, we use the same name for the operator catch and for its interpretation in the category **Algo**, i.e., we write:

$$[\![\Gamma \vdash catch(M) : \iota]\!] = catch^\sigma \circ [\![\Gamma \vdash M : \sigma]\!],$$

where the right hand side catch is given in figure 14.4. In this figure, and in the rest of this section, we shall adopt the following conventions:

- $\vec{\bot}?$ denotes the initial cell $\bot \ldots \bot?$ of (the interpretation of) any type.

- We freely switch between curried and uncurried algorithms (for example, in the third line of figure 14.4, $(\vec{\bot}?).i$ is a cell of $\sigma_1 \times \cdots \times \sigma_m$).

The algorithm catch asks its unique argument about the value of its initial cell ('what do you do if you know nothing about your argument?'). If this cell is filled with *output n*, i.e., if the argument is the constant $n$, then catch outputs $m+n$. If instead the argument asks about the initial cell of its $i^{th}$ argument $(0 \le i \le m)$, then catch outputs $i - 1$.

**Operational semantics.** We describe next the operational semantics of SPCF. It is convenient to use *evaluation* contexts (cf. section 8.5). They have a unique hole, where 'the next reduction takes place'. They are declared as follows:

$$E ::= [\,] \mid fE \mid EM \mid catch(\lambda \vec{x}.E),$$

$$catch^{(\sigma_1 \to \cdots \to \sigma_m \to \iota) \to \iota} = \{(\bot?, valof \vec{1}?),$$
$$(\{(\vec{1}?, output\ n)\}?, output\ m + n),\quad (n \in \omega)$$
$$(\{\{(\vec{1}?, valof\ (\vec{1}?).i)\}?, output\ i - 1)\}\quad (1 \le i \le m)$$

Figure 14.4: Interpretation of *catch* in **Algo**

---

$$
\begin{array}{llll}
E[catch(\lambda x_1 \ldots x_m.E[x_i])] & \to & E[i-1] & (i \le m, x_i \text{ free in } E[x_i]) \\
E[catch(\lambda x_1 \ldots x_m.n)] & \to & E[m+n] & \\
E[catch(f)] & \to & E[0] & (f \in \{succ, pred, zero?, cond\}) \\
E[M] & \to & E[N] & (\text{for all the axioms } M \to N \text{ of figure 6.3})
\end{array}
$$

Figure 14.5: Operational semantics for SPCF

---

where $f \in \{succ, pred, zero?, cond\}$ and where $\vec{x}$ abbreviates $x_1 \ldots x_n$ (the intended subscripts may vary). In particular, $n$ may be 0, i.e., $catch(E)$ is an evaluation context. We denote by $E[N]$ the result of filling the hole of $E$ with a term $N$.

The evaluation rules are given in figure 14.5. In addition to those for PCF, there are three axioms for *catch*. The *catch* rules deserve some explanation. The constant *catch* is a so-called control operator. If the argument of *catch* is strict in its *i*th argument, then the value $i - 1$ is returned. If the argument $f$ of *catch* is a constant function, then *catch* returns that constant (plus the arity of $f$, since the outputs $0, \ldots, m - 1$ have a special meaning in this context). The reader may check that $catch(add_l) \to^* 0$ and $catch(add_r) \to^* 1$, where $add_l$ and $add_r$ are the PCF terms denoting the left and right addition algorithms (cf. exercise 6.3.3).

We extend the operational semantics to SPCF($Err$) (cf. figure 14.3) by adding the following rule:

$$E[e] \to e.$$

**Exercise 14.4.9** *Show that the following properties hold: (1) If $E$, $E'$ are evaluation contexts, then $E[E']$ is an evaluation context. (2) If $M \to M' \ne e$, then $E[M] \to E[M']$; if $M \to e$, then $E[M] \to e$.*

**Exercise 14.4.10 (soundness)** *Show that if $M \to M'$, then $[\![M]\!] = [\![M']\!]$.*

**Exercise\* 14.4.11** *Show the following properties.*

(1) *If $M\Omega \cdots \Omega \to^* e$, then $catch(M) \to^* e$.*

(2) *If $catch(M) \to^* e$, then $M\Omega \cdots \Omega \to^* e$.*

(3) *If $M\Omega \cdots \Omega \to^* n$, where $M$ is of type $\sigma_1 \to \cdots \to \sigma_m \to \iota$, then $catch(M) \to^* n + m$.*

(4) If $MQ_1 \cdots Q_m \to^* e$ $(m \geq 1)$, where all $Q_j$'s are $\Omega$, except $Q_i = \lambda \vec{y}.e$, and if $M\Omega \cdots \Omega \to^* e$ does not hold, then $catch(M) \to^* i - 1$.

**Exercise* 14.4.12 (adequacy)** *(1) Let $M$ be an SPCF(Err) program. Show that the following equivalences hold:*

$$[\![M]\!] = n \iff M \to^* n \qquad [\![M]\!] = e \iff M \to^* e .$$

*Hint: Adapt the proof of theorem 6.3.6, and use exercise 14.4.11. (2) Let $M$ be an SPCF program. Show that the following equivalence holds:*

$$[\![M]\!] = n \iff M \to^* n .$$

*Hint: Use (1) and the observation that if $M$ is an SPCF term and $M \to^* n$ in SPCF(Err), then $M \to^* n$ in SPCF.*

**Full abstraction.** We first prove, by a semantic argument, that SPCF is a sequential language (cf. section 6.4).

**Proposition 14.4.13** *If $C$ is an SPCF program context with several holes, if*

$$[\![\vdash C[\Omega, \ldots, \Omega]]\!] = \bot \quad and \quad \exists M_1, \ldots, M_n \; [\![\vdash C[M_1, \ldots, M_n]]\!] \neq \bot,$$

*then there exists an $i$, called a sequentiality index, such that:*

$$\forall N_1, \ldots, N_{i-1}, N_{i+1}, \ldots, N_n \; \begin{cases} [\![\vdash C[N_1, \ldots, N_{i-1}, \Omega, N_{i+1}, \ldots, N_n]]\!] = \bot \\ [\![\vdash C[N_1, \ldots, N_{i-1}, e, N_{i+1}, \ldots, N_n]]\!] = \{(?, e)\} . \end{cases}$$

*(Here, $M_1, \ldots, M_n, N_1, \ldots, N_n$ are ranging over closed SPCF terms.)*

PROOF. Let $a = [\![\vdash \lambda x_1 \cdots x_n.C[x_1, \ldots, x_n]]\!]$. We have, by the validity of $\beta$, for all closed $M_1, \ldots, M_n$:

$$[\![\vdash C[M_1, \ldots, M_n]]\!] = a \bullet [\![\vdash M_1]\!] \bullet \ldots \bullet [\![\vdash M_n]\!].$$

We have:

$$\exists M_1, \ldots, M_n \; [\![\vdash C[M_1, \ldots, M_n]]\!] \neq \bot \implies a \neq \emptyset$$
$$[\![\vdash C[\Omega, \ldots, \Omega]]\!] = \bot \implies \not\exists n \; ((\vec{\bot}?, output\, n) \in a) .$$

Hence $(\vec{\bot}?, valof\,(\vec{\bot}?).i) \in a$ for some $i$, and the conclusion follows by the definition of the composition of sequential algorithms. $\square$

We recall the (semantic formulation of the) full abstraction property, which we want to prove for **Algo** with respect to SPCF:

$$\forall M, N \; ((\forall C \; [\![\vdash C[M]]\!] \leq [\![\vdash C[N]]\!]) \iff [\![M]\!] \leq [\![N]\!]),$$

where $C$ ranges over program contexts. We are used to linking full abstraction and definability, cf. section 6.4, using applicative contexts. However, proposition 6.4.6 applies to an order-extensional model. Fortunately, we can use contexts other than the applicative ones to show full abstraction for SPCF from definability.

**Lemma 14.4.14** *Let $\mathbf{M}$ be a cds, and let $x, y \in D(\mathbf{M})$. If $x \not\leq y$, then there exists a finite sequential algorithm $a : \mathbf{M} \to \omega_\bot$ such that $a \bullet x \not\leq a \bullet y$.*

PROOF. Let $c$ be a minimal cell such that $(c, v) \in F(x)$ and either $c \notin F(x)$ or $c$ is filled in $y$ with a different value. Let $(c_0, v_0), \ldots, (c_n, v_n)$ be the proof of $c$ in $x$. Define:

$$x_0 = \emptyset, \ldots, x_n = x_{n-1} \cup \{(c_{n-1}, v_{n-1})\}, x_{n+1} = x_n \cup \{(c, v)\}.$$

Then we set $a = \{(x_0?, \mathit{valof}\, c_0), \ldots, (x_n?, \mathit{valof}\, c_n), (x_{n+1}?, \mathit{output}\, 1)\}$. We have $(?, 1) \in a{\cdot}x$ and $(?, 1) \notin a{\cdot}y$, hence $a{\cdot}x \not\leq a{\cdot}y$. $\square$

**Theorem 14.4.15 (definability for SPCF)** *Let $\tau$ be a PCF type. Any finite state $d$ of the cds $\mathbf{M}^\tau$ interpreting $\tau$ in* **Algo** *is definable.*

PROOF. Let $B \in \mathcal{K}(D(\mathbf{M}^{\tau_1 \to \cdots \to \tau_k \to \kappa}))$. We take $\kappa = \iota$ without loss of generality. Let

$$\emptyset = B_0 \prec \cdots \prec B^{\alpha-1} \prec_{\vec{b}^\alpha?} B^\alpha \prec \cdots \prec B^\beta = B$$

be a chain from $\emptyset$ to $B$, where $\vec{b}^\alpha?$ is an abbreviation for $b_1^\alpha \ldots b_k^\alpha?$. We shall associate with $B^\alpha$ a term $x_1 : \tau_1, \ldots, x_k : \tau_k \vdash P^\alpha : \iota$, as well as an injection $i^\alpha$ from $A(B^\alpha) \cap F(B)$ into the set of occurrences of $\Omega$ in $P^\alpha$. The construction is by a lexicographic induction on $(rank(\tau), \sharp B)$ (cf. definition 4.5.10).

(Base case) We set $P^\emptyset = \Omega$. The only initial cell of $\mathbf{M}^{\tau_1 \to \cdots \to \tau_k \to \kappa}$ is $\bot?$, and we associate with it the unique occurrence of $\Omega$ in $P^\emptyset$.

(Induction case) Let $P^{\alpha-1} = C^\alpha[\Omega]$, where $C^\alpha$ is the occurrence context corresponding to $i^{\alpha-1}(\vec{b}^\alpha?)$ (cf. proposition 2.1.7). We set $P^\alpha = C^\alpha[R]$, where $R$ is defined next. We distinguish two cases:

(*output*) $(\vec{b}^\alpha?, \mathit{output}\, n) \in B$. Then we set $R = n$.

(*valof*) $(\vec{b}^\alpha?, \mathit{valof}\, c.i) \in B$, for some $c \in A(b_i^\alpha)$. Any cell in $(A(B^{\alpha+1}) \cap F(B)) \setminus A(B^\alpha)$ has the form $b_1 \ldots b_{i-1} b b_{i+1} \ldots b_k?$, where $b = b_i \cup \{(c, u)\}$ for some $u$, and is thus determined by this $u$. Let $\tau_i = \sigma_1 \to \cdots \to \sigma_l \to \iota$ and $c = a_1 \cdots a_l?$. The set $U^\alpha$ of the $u$'s can be decomposed as follows:

$$U^\alpha = \begin{cases} \{\mathit{output}\, n_1, \ldots, \mathit{output}\, n_{q_0}\} \cup \\ \{\mathit{valof}\, c_{11}.1, \ldots, \mathit{valof}\, c_{1q_1}.1\} \cup \cdots \cup \\ \{\mathit{valof}\, c_{j1}.j, \ldots, \mathit{valof}\, c_{jq_j}.j\} \cup \cdots \cup \\ \{\mathit{valof}\, c_{l1}.l, \ldots, \mathit{valof}\, c_{lq_l}.l\}. \end{cases}$$

We further analyze the type $\sigma_j = \rho_1 \to \cdots \to \rho_p \to \kappa$. Let us consider an auxiliary type $\sigma_j' = \rho_1 \to \cdots \to \rho_p \to \kappa \to \cdots \to \kappa$, of $p + q_j$ arguments. Cells (and observable states) can be injected from $\mathbf{M}^{\sigma_j}$ to $\mathbf{M}^{\sigma_j'}$ in the following way: a cell $d = z_1 \ldots z_p?$ becomes $\hat{d} = z_1 \ldots z_p \bot \ldots \bot?$, and an observable state $a$ becomes $\hat{a} = \{(\hat{d}, u) \mid (d, u) \in a\}$. We set:

$$a_j' = \hat{a_j} \cup \{(\widehat{c_{j1}}, \mathit{valof}\, ?.(p+1))\} \cup \ldots \cup \{(\widehat{c_{jq_j}}, \mathit{valof}\, ?.(p+q_j))\}.$$

In particular, if $q_j = 0$, then $a_j' = a_j$. Since $rank(\sigma_j') = rank(\sigma_j) < rank(\tau))$, we can apply induction and get closed terms $M_1', \ldots, M_l'$ defining $a_1', \ldots, a_l'$. We set, for all $j \leq l$:

$$M_j = \lambda z_1 \ldots z_p . M_j' z_1 \ldots z_p y_{j1} \cdots y_{jq_j},$$

where $y_{j1}, \ldots, y_{jq_j}$ are fresh and distinct variables of basic type. Finally we define, using the syntax of section 6.6 ($\vec{y}_j$ stands for $y_{j1} \cdots y_{jq_j}$):

$$R = \mathit{case}\ \mathit{catch}(S)\ [F]\quad \text{where}\quad S = \lambda \vec{y}_1 \cdots \vec{y}_l . x_i M_1 \ldots M_l,$$

and where $F$ is the partial function that places an $\Omega$ at branches matching the elements of $U^\alpha$. More precisely:

$$F(r) = \begin{cases} \Omega & \text{if } r < q_1 + \cdots + q_l \\ \Omega & \text{if } r = q_1 + \cdots + q_l + n_1 \\ \vdots & \\ \Omega & \text{if } r = q_1 + \cdots + q_l + n_{q_0} \\ \text{undefined} & \text{otherwise}. \end{cases}$$

We shall use the following notation:

$$\begin{aligned} &\text{'valof } c_{jm} \cdot j\text{'} \quad \text{for} \quad q_1 + \cdots + q_{j-1} + m - 1 \quad (j \le q_j, m \le q_j) \\ &\text{'output } n_m\text{'} \quad \text{for} \quad q_1 + \cdots + q_l + n_m \quad (m \le q_0). \end{aligned}$$

The proof goes via two successive claims. The definition of $i^\alpha$ for $\alpha > 0$ will be given in the proof of the second claim.

**Claim 1.** Let $c = a_1 \cdots a_l?, n_m \ (m \le q_0)$, and $c_{jm} \ (j \le l, m \le q_j)$ be as above, and let $d_1, \ldots, d_k$ be observable states such that $c \in E(d_i)$. The following properties hold:

(1) $(c, \text{output } n_m) \in d_i \quad\Leftrightarrow\quad (\vec{\perp}?, \text{output } n_m) \in [\![S]\!]{\bullet}(d_1, \ldots, d_k)$

(2) $(c, \text{valof } c_{jm} \cdot j) \in d_i \quad\Leftrightarrow\quad (\vec{\perp}?, \text{valof } y_{jm}) \in [\![S]\!]{\bullet}(d_1, \ldots, d_k)$

(3) $(c, \mathsf{e}) \in d_i \quad\Leftrightarrow\quad (\vec{\perp}?, \mathsf{e}) \in [\![S]\!]{\bullet}(d_1, \ldots, d_k)$,

where *valof* $y_{jm}$ stands for *valof* $?.(q_1 + \cdots + q_{j-1} + m)$.

For all observable states $d_1, \ldots, d_k, e_{11}, \ldots, e_{lq_l}$, we have, by definition of $S$:

$$[\![S]\!]{\bullet}(d_1, \ldots, d_k){\bullet}\vec{e}_1{\bullet}\cdots{\bullet}\vec{e}_l = d_i{\bullet}([\![M_1]\!]{\bullet}\vec{e}_1){\bullet}\cdots{\bullet}([\![M_l]\!]{\bullet}\vec{e}_l).$$

Thus we are led to examine the $[\![M_j]\!]{\bullet}\vec{e}_j$'s. For all observable states $z_1, \ldots, z_p$, we have, by definition of $M_j, M_j'$, and $a_j'$:

$$\begin{aligned} [\![M_j]\!]{\bullet}\vec{e}_j{\bullet}z_1{\bullet}\cdots{\bullet}z_p &= [\![M_j']\!]{\bullet}z_1{\bullet}\cdots{\bullet}z_p{\bullet}\vec{e}_j \\ &= a_j'{\bullet}z_1{\bullet}\cdots{\bullet}z_p{\bullet}\vec{e}_j \\ &= \begin{cases} \{(?, \mathsf{e})\} & \text{if } \exists m \le q_j \ (c_{jm} \le \vec{z} \text{ and } e_{jm} = \{(?, \mathsf{e})\}) \\ a_j{\bullet}z_1{\bullet}\cdots{\bullet}z_p & \text{otherwise}, \end{cases} \end{aligned}$$

where $c_{jm} \le \vec{z}$ is a shorthand for:

$$c_{jm} = z_{1m} \cdots z_{pm}? \text{ and } (z_{1m} \le z_1, \ldots, z_{pm} \le z_p).$$

We single out two consequences of this computation. First, setting $\vec{e}_j = \vec{\perp}$, we get $[\![M_j]\!]{\bullet}\vec{\perp} = a_j$ (by proposition 14.4.4), hence:

$$[\![S]\!]{\bullet}(d_1, \ldots, d_k){\bullet}\vec{\perp}{\bullet}\cdots{\bullet}\vec{\perp} = d_i{\bullet}a_1 \cdots {\bullet}a_l \tag{14.1}$$

Second, if $e_{jm} = \{(?, \mathsf{e})\}$ and $e_{j1} = \cdots = e_{j(m-1)} = e_{j(m+1)} = \cdots e_{jq_j} = \perp$, then:

$$[\![M_j]\!]{\bullet}\vec{e}_j = a_j \cup \{(c_{jm}, \mathsf{e})\}. \tag{14.2}$$

We now prove property (1) of the claim:

$$\begin{aligned} & (\vec{\perp}?, \text{output } n_m) \in [\![S]\!]{\bullet}(d_1, \ldots, d_k) \\ \Leftrightarrow\ & [\![S]\!]{\bullet}(d_1, \ldots, d_k){\bullet}\vec{\perp}{\bullet}\cdots{\bullet}\vec{\perp} = \{(?, n_m)\} \\ \Leftrightarrow\ & d_i{\bullet}a_1 \cdots {\bullet}a_l = \{(?, n_m)\} && \text{(by 14.1)} \\ \Leftrightarrow\ & (c, \text{output } n_m) \in d_i && \text{(by exercise 14.4.5 )}. \end{aligned}$$

Properties (2) and (3) are proved much in the same way, making use of 14.1, 14.2, and exercise 14.4.5.

**Claim 2.** For any $\alpha < \beta$, for any $b_1 \ldots b_k? \in A(B^\alpha) \cap F(B)$ (abbreviated as $\vec{b}?$), for any observable states $d_1, \ldots, d_k$, and for any $x_1 : \tau_1, \ldots, x_k : \tau_k \vdash N : \iota$,

$$[\![C[N]]\!] \bullet (d_1, \ldots, d_k) \;=\; \begin{cases} [\![N]\!] \bullet (d_1, \ldots, d_k) & \text{if } b_i \leq d_i \text{ for all } i \leq k \\ B^\alpha \bullet d_1 \bullet \cdots \bullet d_k & \text{otherwise} \end{cases}$$

where $C$ is the occurrence context associated with $i^\alpha(\vec{b}?)$.

We first show that the statement follows from claim 2. More precisely, applying the claim to $\alpha - 1$, $\vec{b}^\alpha?$ and $C = C^\alpha$, we prove:

$$[\![\lambda x_1 \ldots x_k . P^\alpha]\!] = B^\alpha \,,$$

hence, in particular, $[\![\lambda x_1 \ldots x_k . P^\beta]\!] = B$ (taking $\alpha = \beta$). By proposition 14.4.4 it is enough to show, for all observable $d_1, \ldots, d_k$:

$$[\![C^\alpha[R]]\!] \bullet (d_1, \ldots, d_k) \;=\; B^\alpha \bullet d_1 \bullet \cdots \bullet d_k.$$

We deal only with the case *(valof)* (the case *(output)* is similar and easier). By the claim, $[\![C^\alpha[R]]\!]$ is a combination of $[\![R]\!]$ and $B^{\alpha-1}$. Let us analyse $[\![R]\!]$ and $B^{\alpha-1}$. Since all the case branches of $R$ are $\Omega$'s, we have:

$$[\![R]\!] \bullet (d_1, \ldots, d_k) \neq \bot \Rightarrow [\![catch(S)]\!] \bullet (d_1, \ldots, d_k) = \{(?, \mathsf{e})\} \,.$$

Hence, by claim 1, we get:

$$[\![R]\!] \bullet (d_1, \ldots, d_k) = \begin{cases} \bot & \text{if } (c, \mathsf{e}) \notin d_i \\ \{(?, \mathsf{e})\} & \text{if } (c, \mathsf{e}) \in d_i \,. \end{cases} \tag{14.3}$$

On the other hand, since $B^\alpha = B^{\alpha-1} \cup set(\vec{b}^\alpha?, valof\ c.i)$, we have:

$$B^\alpha \bullet d_1 \bullet \cdots \bullet d_k = \begin{cases} \{(?, \mathsf{e})\} & \text{if } (b_i^\alpha \leq d_i \text{ for all } i \leq k) \text{ and } (c, \mathsf{e}) \in d_i \\ B^{\alpha-1} \bullet d_1 \bullet \cdots \bullet d_k & \text{otherwise} \,. \end{cases}$$

We put these observations together, distinguishing three cases.

(i) $((b_i^\alpha \leq d_i \text{ for all } i \leq k) \text{ and } (c, \mathsf{e}) \notin d_i)$. Then:

$$[\![C^\alpha[R]]\!] \bullet (d_1, \ldots, d_k) = [\![R]\!] \bullet (d_1, \ldots, d_k) = \bot \,.$$

On the other hand:

$$B^\alpha \bullet d_1 \bullet \cdots \bullet d_k = B^{\alpha-1} \bullet d_1 \bullet \cdots \bullet d_k = \bot,$$

since $\vec{b}^\alpha? \in A(B^{\alpha-1})$.

(ii) $((b_i^\alpha \leq d_i \text{ for all } i \leq k) \text{ and } (c, \mathsf{e}) \in d_i)$. Then:

$$[\![C^\alpha[R]]\!] \bullet (d_1, \ldots, d_k) = [\![R]\!] \bullet (d_1, \ldots, d_k) = \{(?, \mathsf{e})\} = B^\alpha \bullet d_1 \bullet \cdots \bullet d_k \,.$$

(iii) Otherwise, we have:

$$[\![C^\alpha[R]]\!] \bullet (d_1, \ldots, d_k) = B^{\alpha-1} \bullet d_1 \bullet \cdots \bullet d_k = B^\alpha \bullet d_1 \bullet \cdots \bullet d_k \,.$$

Hence in all cases, the meanings of $C^\alpha[R]$ and $B^\alpha$ coincide.

We are left to prove claim 2. Consider $\vec{b}? \in A(B^\alpha) \cap F(B)$ (hence, in particular, $\vec{b}? \neq \vec{b}^\alpha?$). There are two cases.

(I) $\vec{b}? \in A(B^{\alpha-1})$. Then we set $i^\alpha(\vec{b}?) = i^{\alpha-1}(\vec{b}?)$. We write $P^{\alpha-1} = D[\Omega][\Omega]_1$, where $D$ is a context with two holes $[\,]$ and $[\,]_1$ occurring each once and corresponding to $\vec{b}^\alpha?$ and $\vec{b}?$, respectively. Let now $d_1, \ldots, d_k$ be observable states. We distinguish three cases.

(A) $(\forall i \leq k \ b_i \leq d_i)$. By induction we have, for all $N$:

$$[D[\Omega][N]_1]\bullet(d_1, \ldots, d_k) = [N]\bullet(d_1, \ldots, d_k). \tag{14.4}$$

In particular, $[D[\Omega][m]_1]\bullet(d_1, \ldots, d_k) = \{(?, m)\}$ ($m$ arbitrary). By induction, we can also suppose that $d_i = [Q_i]$ for some $Q_i$, for all $i$. Let $D' = D[\vec{Q}/\vec{x}]$. Then $[D'[\Omega][m]_1] = \{(?, m)\}$ by what we just noticed. It follows that $[\,]$ is not a sequentiality index. Hence the sequentiality index, which exists by proposition 14.4.13, is $[\,]_1$. In particular:

$$[D[R][\Omega]_1]\bullet(d_1, \ldots, d_k) = \bot. \tag{14.5}$$

We have to prove $[D[R][N]_1]\bullet(d_1, \ldots, d_k) = [N]\bullet(d_1, \ldots, d_k)$, for all $N$. We distinguish two cases.

(a) $[N]\bullet(d_1, \ldots, d_k) \neq \bot$. Then the conclusion follows from 14.4 by monotonicity.

(b) $[N]\bullet(d_1, \ldots, d_k) = \bot$. Then the conclusion boils down to 14.5.

(B) $(\exists j \ b_j \not\leq d_j)$ and $(\forall i \leq k \ b_i^\alpha \leq d_i)$. By induction, we have, for all $L$:

$$[D[L][\Omega]_1]\bullet(d_1, \ldots, d_k) = [L]\bullet(d_1, \ldots, d_k). \tag{14.6}$$

and our goal is to prove $[D[R][N]_1]\bullet(d_1, \ldots, d_k) = B^\alpha\bullet d_1\bullet\cdots\bullet d_k$, for all $N$. We distinguish three cases.

(a) $(\vec{b}^\alpha?, output \ n) \in B^\alpha$. Then $B^\alpha\bullet d_1\bullet\cdots\bullet d_k = \{(?, n)\}$, by the definition of $\bullet$. On the other hand, $[R] = \{(\vec{\perp}?, n)\}$ by construction, and the conclusion then follows from 14.6 by monotonicity.

(b) $(\vec{b}^\alpha?, valof \ c.i) \in B^\alpha$ and $(c, \mathsf{e}) \in d_i$. Then $B^\alpha\bullet d_1\bullet\cdots\bullet d_k = \{(?, \mathsf{e})\}$. On the other hand, by claim 1, we have $[catch(S)]\bullet(d_1, \ldots, d_k) = \{(?, \mathsf{e})\}$, hence $[R]\bullet(d_1, \ldots, d_k) = \{(?, \mathsf{e})\}$. The conclusion follows again from 14.6 by monotonicity.

(c) $(\vec{b}^\alpha?, valof \ c.i) \in B^\alpha$ and $(c, \mathsf{e}) \notin d_i$. Then $B^\alpha\bullet d_1\bullet\cdots\bullet d_k = \bot$. Reasoning as for 14.4 above, we conclude from 14.6 that $[\,]$ is the sequentiality index. Hence, for all $N$:

$$[D[\Omega][N]_1]\bullet(d_1, \ldots, d_k) = \bot. \tag{14.7}$$

The conclusion then follows from 14.3 and 14.7, using the assumption $(c, \mathsf{e}) \notin d_i$.

(C) $(\exists j \ b_j \not\leq d_j)$ and $(\exists j_1 \ b_{j_1}^\alpha \not\leq d_{j_1})$. By induction we have, for all $N$ and $L$:

$$[D[\Omega][N]_1]\bullet(d_1, \ldots, d_k) = B^\alpha\bullet d_1\bullet\cdots\bullet d_k \tag{14.8}$$

$$[D[L][\Omega]_1]\bullet(d_1, \ldots, d_k) = B^\alpha\bullet d_1\bullet\cdots\bullet d_k . \tag{14.9}$$

There are two cases:

(a) $B^\alpha \cdot d_1 \cdot \cdots \cdot d_k \neq \bot$. Then the conclusion follows from 14.8 by monotonicity.

(b) $B^\alpha \cdot d_1 \cdot \cdots \cdot d_k = \bot$. Then since 14.8, 14.9 hold in particular for $N = \mathbf{e}$, $L = \mathbf{e}$, respectively, we conclude that neither $[\ ]$ nor $[\ ]_1$ can be sequentiality indices. Hence the conclusion $[\![D[R][N]]\!] \cdot (d_1, \ldots, d_k) = \bot$ follows, as otherwise there would exist a sequentiality index, by proposition 14.4.13.

(II) $\vec{b}? \notin A(B^{\alpha-1})$. This can only happen if $\vec{b}^\alpha?$ is filled with some *valof c.i* in $B^\alpha$, and if $\vec{b}$ has the following form:

$$b_j = b_j^\alpha \qquad \text{if } j \neq i$$
$$b_i = b_i^\alpha \cup \{(c, u)\} \quad \text{for some } u .$$

By construction, this $u$ is associated with one of the branches of $R$, which we represent by means of a context $R = C_u[\Omega]$. Then we define $i^\alpha(\vec{b}?)$ as the occurrence of $[\ ]$ in $C[C_u]$. We distinguish the same cases as for (I).

(A) $(\forall i \leq k \ b_i \leq d_i)$. Our goal is to show $[\![C[C_u[N]]]\!] \cdot (d_1, \ldots, d_k) = [\![N]\!] \cdot (d_1, \ldots, d_k)$. Since we have *a fortiori* $b_i^\alpha \leq d_i$ for all $i$, we have by induction:

$$[\![C[C_u[N]]]\!] \cdot (d_1, \ldots, d_k) = [\![C_u[N]]\!] \cdot (d_1, \ldots, d_k). \tag{14.10}$$

On the other hand, we have $[\![catch(S)]\!] \cdot (d_1, \ldots, d_k) = \text{'}u\text{'}$ by claim 1, since $(c, u) \in d_i$. By the definition of $C_u$, this implies (for all $N$):

$$[\![C_u[N]]\!] \cdot (d_1, \ldots, d_k) = [\![N]\!] \cdot (d_1, \ldots, d_k). \tag{14.11}$$

Then the conclusion follows from 14.10 and 14.11.

(B) $(\exists j \ b_j \not\leq d_j)$ and $(\forall i \leq k \ b_i^\alpha \leq d_i)$. It follows from these assumptions that $b_i \not\leq d_i$, and that $(c, u) \notin d_i$. We still have 14.10 by induction. Our goal is to show $[\![C[C_u[N]]]\!] \cdot (d_1, \ldots, d_k) = (B^{\alpha-1} \cup \{(\vec{b}^\alpha?, valof\ c.i)\}) \cdot d_1 \cdot \cdots \cdot d_k$, for all $N$. By definition of $\bullet$, we have:

$$(B^{\alpha-1} \cup \{(\vec{b}^\alpha?, valof\ c.i)\}) \cdot d_1 \cdot \cdots \cdot d_k = \begin{cases} \{(?, \mathbf{e})\} & \text{if } (c, \mathbf{e}) \in d_i \\ \bot & \text{otherwise .} \end{cases} \tag{14.12}$$

On the other hand, by the definition of $C_u$, we can have $[\![C_u[N]]\!] \cdot (d_1, \ldots, d_k) \neq \bot$ only if either of the two following properties hold.

(a) $[\![catch(S)]\!] \cdot (d_1, \ldots, d_k) = \text{'}u\text{'}$. This case is impossible by claim 1, since $(c, u) \notin d_i$.

(b) $[\![catch(S)]\!] \cdot (d_1, \ldots, d_k) = \{(?, \mathbf{e})\}$. By claim 1, this happens exactly when $(c, \mathbf{e}) \in d_i$, and then $[\![C_u[N]]\!] \cdot (d_1, \ldots, d_k) = \{(?, \mathbf{e})\}$.

The conclusion follows from this case analysis and from 14.12.

(C) $(\exists j \ b_j \not\leq d_j)$ and $(\exists j_1 \ b_{j_1}^\alpha \not\leq d_{j_1})$. We have, for all $L$:

$$\begin{aligned} [\![C[L]]\!] \cdot (d_1, \ldots, d_k) &= B^{\alpha-1} \cdot d_1 \cdot \cdots \cdot d_k \quad \text{(by induction)} \\ &= B^\alpha \cdot d_1 \cdot \cdots \cdot d_k \quad \text{(since } b_{j_1}^\alpha \not\leq d_{j_1}) . \end{aligned}$$

Then the conclusion follows by instantiating $L$ as $C_u[N]$. $\qquad\qquad \square$

**Theorem 14.4.16 (full abstraction for SPCF)** *The model of sequential algorithms is fully abstract for SPCF.*

PROOF. Let $M$ and $N$ be such that $[\![M]\!] \not\leq [\![N]\!]$. We can assume $M, N$ closed since currying is monotonic. By lemma 14.4.14 and by theorem 14.4.15, there exists an algorithm $a$ defined by a closed term $F$ such that:

$$[\![FM]\!] = (a \bullet [\![M]\!]) \not\leq (a \bullet [\![N]\!]) = [\![FN]\!].$$

The context $C = F[\ ]$ witnesses $M \not\leq_{obs} N$.                                    □

**Exercise 14.4.17** *Adapt the proof of theorem 14.4.15 to show that the model of observable algorithms (cf. exercise 14.4.8) is fully abstract for SPCF(Err).*

**Remark 14.4.18** *In [RK93] a stronger result is proved: the language SPCF is universal for sequential algorithms, i.e., every computable element of the model of sequential algorithms is definable. This should be contrasted with the situation with respect to the continuous model, where Plotkin had to add a first (finitary) parallel constant to achieve the definability of compact elements, and then a second (infinitary) parallel constant to achieve universality [Plo77].*

# 15
## Domains and realizability

Kleene [Kle45] first introduced a realizability interpretation of Heyting arithmetic (*HA*) as a tool for proving its consistency. This interpretation provides a standard link between constructive mathematics (as formalized in *HA*) and classical recursion theory. Moreover, it has the merit of giving a solid mathematical content to the Brouwer-Heyting-Kolmogorov explanation of constructive proofs (see, e.g., [TvD88]).

Let us consider Peano arithmetic formalized in an intuitionistic first-order logic with equality and a signature with symbols 0 for zero, and $s$ for successor (this is also known as Heyting arithmetic *HA*). Let $\mathcal{N}$ be the intended interpretation of the signature over the structure of natural numbers. We write $\mathcal{N} \models t = s$ if the formula $t = s$ is valid in $\mathcal{N}$. We define a realizability binary relation $\Vdash \subseteq \omega \times Form$ between numbers and formulas, by induction on the formulas, as follows:

$$
\begin{aligned}
&n \Vdash \bot && \text{never} \\
&n \Vdash t = s && \text{if } \mathcal{N} \models t = s \\
&n \Vdash \phi \wedge \psi && \text{if } \pi_1 n \Vdash \phi \text{ and } \pi_2 n \Vdash \psi && (1) \\
&n \Vdash \phi \vee \psi && \text{if } (\pi_1 n = 0 \text{ and } \pi_2 n \Vdash \phi) \text{ or } (\pi_1 n = 1 \text{ and } \pi_2 n \Vdash \psi) \\
&n \Vdash \phi \rightarrow \psi && \text{if for each } m \, (m \Vdash \phi \Rightarrow \{n\}m \Vdash \psi) && (2) \\
&n \Vdash \forall x.\phi && \text{if for each } m \, (\{n\}m \downarrow \text{ and } \{n\}m \Vdash \phi[\underline{m}/x]) && (3) \\
&n \Vdash \exists x.\phi && \text{if } \pi_2 n \Vdash \phi[\underline{\pi_1 n}/x] \, ,
\end{aligned}
$$

where: (1) $\pi_1, \pi_2$ are the first and second projections with respect to an injective coding $\langle \_, \_ \rangle : \omega^2 \to \omega$ (cf. appendix 1), (2) $\{n\}m$ is the $n^{th}$ Turing machine applied to the input $m$, (3) $\underline{m}$ is the numeral $s^m 0$. We note that the formula $\bot$ is never realized. $t \downarrow$ denotes the fact that the expression $t$ is defined. Whenever $ts \downarrow$ it is the case that $t \downarrow$ and $s \downarrow$.

Let us turn towards potential applications of this interpretation. To any formula $\phi$ in *HA* we can associate the set $[\![\phi]\!]$ of its realizers $[\![\phi]\!] = \{n \mid n \Vdash \phi\}$. It is easy to prove a soundness theorem saying that any provable formula in *HA* has a non-empty collection of realizers (i.e., it is realizable). The consistency of *HA* is an immediate corollary as $[\![\bot]\!] = \emptyset$. More interestingly, realizability can be used to check the consistency of various extensions of Heyting arithmetic. For instance let us consider the formalization in *HA* of two popular axiom schemata known as the Church Thesis (*CT*) and the Markov Principle (*MP*). In the following $\phi$ is a primitive recursive predicate, i.e., a formula without unbounded quantifications.

- $(CT)$ $\forall n.\exists!m.\phi(n,m) \to \exists k.\forall n.\exists m'.(\phi(n,U(m')) \wedge T(k,n,m'))$

where $U$ is a function and $T$ is a predicate (called the Kleene predicate) such that $k(n) \cong U(\mu m' T(k,n,m'))$ ($\mu$ is the minimalization operator, cf. appendix 1). Intuitively, $U$ is the function which extracts the result from the code of a terminating computation $m'$, and $T(k,n,m')$ holds iff the program $k$ with input $n$ produces a terminating computation $m'$. (Both $U$ and $T$ are primitive recursive.) Church's thesis states that any single-valued relation over the natural numbers that is definable in *HA* is computable by some recursive function. The reason being that from any (constructive) proof of a $\Pi_2^0$ sentence, $\forall n.\exists!m.\phi(n,m)$, we can (effectively) extract an algorithm $k$ that given $n$ finds the $m$ such that $\phi(n,m)$.

- $(MP)$ $(\forall n.(\phi(n) \vee \neg\phi(n)) \wedge \neg\neg\exists n.\phi(n)) \to \exists n.\phi(n)$.

The intuition behind $(MP)$ is the following: if we have a decidable predicate $(\forall n.(\phi(n) \vee \neg\phi(n))$ and an oracle that tells us that such a predicate is non-empty $(\neg\neg\exists n.\phi(n))$ then we can effectively find an element satisfying the predicate simply by enumerating the candidates and checking the predicate on them.

$(CT)$ and $(MP)$ are not provable in *HA* but they can be consistently added to it. This fact, which is not obvious, can be proved by showing that $(CT)$ and $(MP)$ are realized in the Kleene interpretation.

Having provided some historical and technical perspective on realizability we can outline the main theme of this chapter. Our goal is to generalize the Kleene interpretation in two respects: (1) We want to model Type Theories (not just *HA*). (2) We want to interpret Proofs/Programs and not just Propositions/Types. In order to obtain some results in this direction we will concentrate on a special class of 'realizability models'. Two basic features of these models are:

(1) Types can be regarded as *constructive* sets.

(2) There is a distinction between a *typed value* and its *untyped realizers*.

The first feature relates to a general programme known as *synthetic domain theory* (see [Hyl91, LS95, Jun96]) that advocates the construction of a mathematical framework in which data types can be regarded as sets. A number of examples show that classical set theory is not well-suited to this purpose, think of models for recursive functions definitions, untyped $\lambda$-calculus, and polymorphism. On the other hand some promising results have been obtained when working in a universe of *constructive* sets. In particular *realizability* has been the part of constructive mathematics that has been most successful in implementing this plan. Historically this programme was first pushed by Scott and his students McCarty and Rosolini [McC84, Ros86], whose work relates in particular to the effective topos [Hyl82] (but see also [Mul81] for another approach). Related results can be found in [Ama91c, AP90, FMRS92, Pho90, Ama93a]. In a realizability universe the size of function spaces, and dependent and second order products can be surprisingly small. A typical result is the validity of a *Uniformity Principle* which plays an important role in the interpretation of second order quantification as intersection (more on this in section 15.2).

The second feature relates to the way 'constructivity' is built into the realizability model. We rely on a *partial combinatory algebra* (pca) which is an untyped applicative structure satisfying weaker requirements than a $\lambda$-model. We build over a pca, say $D$, a set theoretical universe where every set, say $X$, is equipped with a realizability relation $\Vdash_X \subseteq D \times X$. If $d \Vdash_X x$ then $d$ can be regarded as a realizer of $x$. Morphisms between the 'sets' $(X, \Vdash_X)$ and $(Y, \Vdash_Y)$ are set theoretical functions between $X$ and $Y$ that can be actually realized in the underlying pca in a sense that we will make clear later. In programming practice there is a distinction between the explicitly typed program which is offered to the type checker, and its untyped run time representation which is actually executed. Intuitively the typed terms $\lambda x : nat.x$ and $\lambda x : bool.x$ may well have the same run-time representation, say $\lambda x.x$. This aspect is ignored by the domain theoretical interpretation we have considered so far. In this interpretation $\lambda x : nat.x$ and $\lambda x : bool.x$ live in *different* universes. Realizers can also be regarded as untyped 'implementations' of typed programs. Models based on realizability offer a two-levels view of computation: one at a typed and another at an untyped level. This aspect will be exploited to provide an interpretation of *type assignment* (section 15.3) and *subtyping* systems (section 15.8).

The technical contents of the chapter is organised as follows. In section 15.1 we build a category of $D$-sets over a pca $D$. These are sets equipped with a realizability relation (as described above) and provide a nice generalization of Kleene realizability.

In section 15.2 we interpret system F (cf. section 11.5) in the category of *partial equivalence relations* (per's) which is equivalent to a particularly well behaved subcategory of the category of $D$-sets.

In section 15.3 we exploit the two-levels structure of realizability models to interpret type assignment systems which are formal systems where types are assigned to untyped terms (cf. section 3.5). We prove a completeness theorem by relying on a standard term model construction.

In section 15.4 we study the notion of partiality in the category of partial equivalence relations and obtain in this way a pCCC of per's. We exploit the dominance $\Sigma$ of the pCCC to define an 'intrinsic' preorder on the points of a per. The full subcategory of the per's for which this preorder is a partial order (i.e., antisymmetric) forms a *reflective* subcategory of the category of per's. We refer to these per's as *separated* per's or $\Sigma$per's for short.

In section 15.5 we work with Kleene's pca $(\omega, \bullet)$ and we introduce a subcategory of *complete* separated per's which have lub's of (effectively given) chains. In this framework we prove a variant of the Myhill-Shepherdson theorem (cf. section 1.3) asserting that all realized functions are Scott-continuous. In section 15.6 we study a related category of *extensional* per's.

In section 15.7 we concentrate on a $D_\infty$ $\lambda$-model and identify in this framework a full subcategory of *complete, uniform* per's, where we can solve recursive domain equations up to equality. Finally, in section 15.8 we introduce a theory of subtyping for recursive types and present a sound interpretation in the category of complete uniform per's.

# 15.1 A universe of realizable sets

In the Kleene interpretation the basic *realizability* structure is given by the collection of natural numbers with an operation of partial application of a number, seen as a program, to another number, seen as an input. A convenient generalization of this notion is that of *partial combinatory algebra* (cf. [Bet88]).

**Definition 15.1.1 (partial combinatory algebra)** *A partial combinatory algebra (pca) is a structure* $(D, k, s, \bullet)$ *where* $k, s \in D$, $\bullet : D \times D \rightharpoonup D$, *and* $kxy = x$, $sxy \downarrow$, *and* $sxyz \cong xz(yz)$ *(we abbreviate* $d \bullet e$ *with* $de$ *and* $(D, k, s, \bullet)$ *with* $D$*)*.

In pca's it is possible to simulate $\lambda$-abstraction. Let $D$ be a pca and let $t$ be a closed term over the pca enriched with a constant $d$ for every element $d \in D$. Clearly every term either denotes an element in $D$ or is undefined. Given a term $t$ we define inductively on the structure of $t$, a new term $\lambda^* d.t$ in which the element $d$ is 'abstracted':

$$\begin{aligned}
\lambda^* d.d &= skk \\
\lambda^* d.t &= kt \quad (d \text{ does not occur in } t) \\
\lambda^* d.tt' &= s(\lambda^* d.t)(\lambda^* d.t') \,.
\end{aligned}$$

It is easy to verify that for all $d \in D$, $(\lambda^* d.t)d \cong t$.

**Example 15.1.2** (1) *An important example of a pca is Kleene's* $(\omega, \bullet)$ *where* $\omega$ *is the set of natural numbers and* $n \bullet m$ *is the* $n^{th}$ *Turing machine applied to the input* $m$.

(2) *Another canonical example of a pca is that of a non-trivial domain $D$ that is a retract of its partial function space in* **pDcpo** *(cf. section 1.4), say* $(D \rightharpoonup D) \triangleleft D$, *via the retraction pair* $(i, j)$*. In this case we define* $d \bullet e \cong j(d)(e)$.

Given a pca we have to decide how to interpret formulas and proofs, and more generally types and programs. In the Kleene interpretation, formulas are interpreted as subsets of natural numbers, on the other hand no mention is made of morphisms, hence no obvious interpretation of proofs is available.

The first attempt could consist in interpreting types as subsets of the realizability structure. But in order to have a model of type theory we need at least a CCC, so which are the morphisms? It is clear that, to build an interesting structure, morphisms have to be somehow *realized*. It appears that some structure is missing to get a CCC, for this reason we seek a finer description of types. Rather than identifying types with a collection of realizers we consider a type as a *partial equivalence relation* (per) over the collection of realizers. There is now an obvious notion of morphism that makes the category into a CCC.

Let $A, B, \ldots$ be binary relations over a set $D$. We fix some notation:

$$\begin{aligned}
d \, A \, e & \quad \text{iff} \quad (d, e) \in A & & \text{related elements} \\
[d]_A &= \{e \in D \mid d \, A \, e\} & & \text{equivalence class } (A \text{ per}) \\
[A] &= \{[d]_A \mid d \, A \, d\} & & \text{quotient space } (A \text{ per}) \\
|A| &= \{d \in D \mid d \, A \, d\} & & \text{domain of definition} \\
d : A & \quad \text{iff} \quad d \in |A| & & \text{element in the domain of definition} \,.
\end{aligned}$$

**Definition 15.1.3 (partial equivalence relations)** *Let $D$ be a pca. The category of per's over $D$ ($\mathbf{per}_D$) is defined as follows:*

$$\mathbf{per}_D \quad = \quad \{A \mid A \subseteq D \times D \text{ and } A \text{ is symmetric and transitive}\}$$
$$\mathbf{per}_D[A, B] \quad = \quad \{f : [A] \to [B] \mid \exists \phi \in D \; \forall d \in D \; (d \, A \, d \Rightarrow \phi d \in f([d]_A))\} \;.$$

If $\phi$ is a realizer for the morphism $f : A \to B$, i.e., $\forall d \in D \; (d \, A \, d \Rightarrow \phi d \in f([d]_A))$, we may denote $f$ with $[\phi]_{A \to B}$ (consistently with the definition of exponent in $\mathbf{per}_D$ given in the following theorem).

**Theorem 15.1.4 ($\mathbf{per}_D$ is a CCC)** *The category, $\mathbf{per}_D$ of partial equivalence relations over a pca $D$ is cartesian closed.*

PROOF. Mimicking what is done in the $\lambda$-calculus (cf. theorem 4.6.10), we can define pairing as $\langle d_1, d_2 \rangle \equiv \lambda^* p.(pd_1)d_2$, and projections as $\pi_1 d \equiv dk$ and $\pi_2 d \equiv d(k(skk))$.

• Terminal object. We set $1 = D \times D$. For all $d \in D$ the 'constant function' $\lambda^* e.d$ realizes the unique morphism from a per $A$ into $1$.

• Product. We define for the product per:

$$d (A \times B) e \quad \text{iff} \quad \pi_1 d \, A \, \pi_1 e \text{ and } \pi_2 d \, B \, \pi_2 e \;.$$

It is immediate to verify that pairing and projections in the pca realize the pairing and projections morphisms of the category.

• Exponent. We define for the exponent per:

$$h \, B^A \, k \quad \text{iff} \quad \forall d, e \; (d \, A \, e \Rightarrow hd \, B \, ke) \;.$$

Morphisms can be regarded as equivalence classes. The evaluation is realized by $\lambda^* d.(\pi_1 d)(\pi_2 d)$, the natural isomorphism $\Lambda$ is realized by $\lambda^* \phi.\lambda^* c.\lambda^* a.\phi\langle c, a \rangle$.  □

The following exercises should motivate the shift from subsets of $D$ to per's.

**Exercise 15.1.5** *One can identify the subsets of the realizability structure with those per's that have at most one equivalence class. Show that the full subcategory composed of these per's is cartesian closed, but each object is either initial or terminal.*

**Exercise 15.1.6** *Consider a category of per's over the pca $D$, say $\mathbf{C}$, in which, as above, per's have at most one equivalence class but where morphisms are defined as follows: $\mathbf{C}[A, B] = \{\phi \in D \mid \forall d \in D \; (d \in |A| \Rightarrow \phi d \in |B|)\}$. Show that $\mathbf{C}$ is not cartesian closed.*

**Exercise 15.1.7** *Show that $\mathbf{per}_D$ has all finite limits and colimits.*

Given a pca $D$ we introduce the category of $D$-sets in which we can pin-point a full reflective subcategory of *modest sets*, say $\mathbf{M}_D$, that is equivalent to $\mathbf{per}_D$. The category of $D$-sets intuitively justifies our claim of working in a 'constructive' universe of sets. Formally one can show that $D$-sets form a full subcategory of the *effective topos* [Hyl82].

**Definition 15.1.8** (*D*-set) *A D-set is a pair* $(X, \Vdash_X)$ *where* $X$ *is a set and* $\Vdash_X \subseteq D \times X$ *is an onto realizability relation, that is,* $\forall x \in X \; \exists d \in D \; d \Vdash_X x$. *A morphism of D-sets, say* $f : (X, \Vdash_X) \to (Y, \Vdash_Y)$, *is a function* $f : X \to Y$, *such that:*

$$\exists \phi \in D \; \forall d, x \; (d \Vdash_X x \Rightarrow \phi d \Vdash_Y f(x)) \; .$$

*A D-set* $(X, \Vdash_X)$ *is modest if the relation* $\Vdash_X$ *is single valued, that is,* $d \Vdash_X x$ *and* $d \Vdash_X y$ *implies* $x = y$. *We denote with* **D-set** *the category of D-sets and with* $\mathbf{M}_D$ *the full subcategory of modest sets.*

**Proposition 15.1.9** (1) *The categories* $\mathbf{M}_D$ *and* $\mathbf{per}_D$ *are equivalent.*

(2) *The category* $\mathbf{M}_D$ *is a reflective subcategory of D-set.*

PROOF. (1) To the modest set $(X, \Vdash_X)$ we associate the per $P(X, \Vdash_X)$ defined as:

$$d \, P(X, \Vdash_X) \, e \; \text{ iff } \; \exists x \in X \; (d \Vdash_X x \text{ and } e \Vdash_X x) \; .$$

(2) The basic observation is that if $f : (X, \Vdash_X) \to (Y, \Vdash_Y)$ where $(Y, \Vdash_Y)$ is modest then:

$$d \Vdash_X x \text{ and } d \Vdash_X y \; \Rightarrow \; f(x) = f(y) \; .$$

Indeed, if $f$ is realized by $\phi$ then $\phi d \Vdash_Y f(x)$ and $\phi d \Vdash_Y f(y)$, which forces $f(x) = f(y)$. Let us now describe how to associate a modest set $(Y, \Vdash_Y)$ to a $D$-set $(X, \Vdash_X)$. First we define a relation $R$ over $X$ as:

$$x R y \; \text{ iff } \; \exists d \in D \; (d \Vdash_X x \text{ and } d \Vdash_X y) \; .$$

Let $R^+$ denote the equivalence relation obtained by the transitive closure of $R$. We consider the quotient set $Y = [X]_{R^+}$ equipped with the relation $\Vdash_Y$ defined as follows:

$$d \Vdash_Y [x]_{R^+} \; \text{ iff } \; \exists z \in [x]_{R^+} \; d \Vdash_X z \; .$$

The pair $(Y, \Vdash_Y)$ is the modest set we looked for. We leave to the reader the definition of the natural isomorphism. $\square$

# 15.2 Interpretation of system F

We define an interpretation of system F (cf. section 11.5) in the category of per's. Since $\mathbf{per}_D$ is a CCC we already know how to interpret the simply typed fragment of system F. On the other hand the interpretation of the clauses $(\forall_I)$ and $(\forall_E)$ is more problematic. To overcome this difficulty, we proceed as follows:

(1) We interpret the erasures (cf. definition 11.5.12) of the typed terms in a pca.

(2) We prove that the erasure of a term $M$ of type $\sigma$ is in $|[\![\sigma]\!]|$ (cf. theorem 15.2.2).

(3) We take as the interpretation of the term $M$ of type $\sigma$, the equivalence class in the per $[\![\sigma]\!]$ of the interpretation of the erasure of $M$, say $[\![M]\!] = [\![er(M)]\!]]_{[\![\sigma]\!]}$.

$$[x]\rho = \rho(x)$$
$$[\lambda x.P]\rho = \lambda^* d.[P]\rho[d/x]$$
$$[PQ]\rho = ([P]\rho)([Q]\rho)$$

Figure 15.1: Interpretation of $\lambda$-terms in a pca

**Definition 15.2.1 (type interpretation)** *Let Tvar be the set of type variables. Given a type environment, say $\eta : Tvar \to \mathbf{per}_D$, the interpretation of a type is a per defined by induction as follows:*

$$[t]\eta = \eta(t)$$
$$[\sigma \to \tau]\eta = [\tau]\eta^{[\sigma]\eta}$$
$$[\forall t.\sigma]\eta = \bigcap_{A \in per_D} [\sigma]\eta[A/t] .$$

We note in particular that the second order universal quantification is interpreted by an intersection over all per's. Surprisingly, the intersection can be regarded as a product (cf. proposition 15.2.9).

Let *Var* denote the set of term variables and $\rho : Var \to D$ be an environment. In figure 15.1 we define the interpretation of an untyped $\lambda$-term in the pca $D$.

**Theorem 15.2.2** *Suppose $\Gamma \vdash M : \sigma$ in F, where $\Gamma \equiv x_1 : \sigma_1, \ldots, x_n : \sigma_n$. Then for any type assignment $\eta$, and for any $d_i, e_i$ such that $d_i [\sigma_i]\eta e_i$, for $i = 1, \ldots, n$, we have:*

$$([er(M)][\vec{d}/\vec{x}]) \; ([\sigma]\eta) \; ([er(M)][\vec{e}/\vec{x}]) .$$

PROOF. This is a simple induction on the length of the typing judgment, and can be regarded as yet another variation on the fundamental lemma of logical relations 4.5.3. (*Asmp*) is satisfied by hypothesis. The interpretations for $(\to_I)$ and $(\to_E)$ use the realizers of the natural transformation $\Lambda$ and of the evaluation morphism. The crucial point is $(\forall_I)$ where we use the side condition $t \notin FV_t(\Gamma)$. The case $(\forall_E)$ follows by the interpretation of second order quantification as intersection. $\square$

Given $\Gamma \equiv x_1 : \sigma_1, \ldots, x_n : \sigma_n$ and $\eta$ a type environment, let:

$$[\Gamma]\eta = (\cdots (1 \times [\sigma_1]\eta) \times \cdots \times [\sigma_n]\eta) .$$

The interpretation of a term $\Gamma \vdash M : \sigma$ should be a morphism $f : [\Gamma]\eta \to [\sigma]\eta$. Equivalently, we can determine this morphism by taking the equivalence class of a realizer $\phi$ in the exponent per $([\sigma]\eta)^{[\Gamma]\eta}$. The existence of the realizer $\phi$ follows by theorem 15.2.2. Hence we have the following definition.

**Definition 15.2.3 (typed term interpretation)** *Given a type environment $\eta$, the interpretation of a judgment $\Gamma \vdash M : \sigma$ in system F is defined as follows:*

$$[\Gamma \vdash M : \sigma]\eta = [\lambda^* d.[er(M)][\vec{d_{n,i}}/\vec{x_i}]]_{[\sigma]\eta^{[\Gamma]\eta}} ,$$

*where $d_{n,i} = \pi_2(\pi_1(\cdots \pi_1(d) \cdots))$, with $\pi_1$ iterated $(n - i)$ times.*

**Exercise 15.2.4** *Show that on the simply typed fragment of system F, the interpretation given by the definition 15.2.3 corresponds to the interpretation in the CCC* **per** *according to the equations given in figure 4.4.*

**Exercise 15.2.5** *(1) Show that two terms with the same type and with identical erasures receive the same interpretation in per models. (2) Verify that βη-convertible terms are equated in per models.*

The interpretation in $\mathbf{per}_D$ can be extended to handle dependent types (cf. chapter 11). In the following we outline some results in this direction.

**Definition 15.2.6** *Given a D-set* $\underline{X} = (X, \Vdash_X)$ *and a morphism* $F : \underline{X} \to$ *D-set we define the D-set* $([\Pi_{\underline{X}} F], \Vdash_{\Pi F})$ *as follows (cf. section 11.1):*

$$[\Pi_{\underline{X}} F] = \{ f \in \Pi_X F \mid \exists \phi \in D \ \phi \Vdash_{\Pi F} f \}, \ \text{where}$$
$$\phi \Vdash_{\Pi F} f \ \text{if} \ \forall x \in X \ \forall d \in D \ (d \Vdash_X x \Rightarrow \phi d \Vdash_{F(x)} f(x)) \ .$$

If we look at modest sets as the collection of types then a function $F : X \to \mathbf{M}_D$ can be regarded as a dependent type.

**Exercise 15.2.7** *In the hypotheses of definition 15.2.6, show that if* $F : X \to \mathbf{M}_D$ *then the D-set* $([\Pi_X F], \Vdash_{\Pi F})$ *is modest. Hint: Check that* $\Vdash_{\Pi F}$ *is single valued using the fact that the realizability relations associated to modest sets are single valued.*

The construction defined above can be shown to be a categorical product in a suitable framework.

**Exercise\* 15.2.8** *Define an interpretation of the system LF (cf. section 11.4) in the category of D-sets.*

Finally we hint at the relationship between intersection and product in **per** (we refer to [LM92] for a more extended discussion). Since $\mathbf{M}_D$ is not a small category we consider transformations $F : \mathbf{per}_D \to \mathbf{M}_D$. Moreover we regard the collection of per's as a $D$-set, say $\underline{\mathbf{per}}_D$, by equipping it with the full realizability relation $\underline{\mathbf{per}}_D = (\mathbf{per}_D, D \times \mathbf{per}_D)$.

**Proposition 15.2.9** *Given a function* $F : \underline{\mathbf{per}}_D \to \mathbf{M}_D$, *we have:*

$$([\Pi_{\underline{\mathbf{per}}_D} F], \Vdash_{\Pi F}) \cong \bigcap_{A \in \mathbf{per}_D} P(F(A)) \ ,$$

*where if* $(X, \Vdash_X)$ *is a modest set then* $P(X, \Vdash_X)$ *is the corresponding per, as defined in proposition 15.1.9.*

PROOF HINT. The isomorphism from the product to the intersection is realized by $\lambda^* \phi . \phi d_0$, for some $d_0 \in D$, and its inverse is realized by $\lambda^* d . \lambda^* d' . d$. $\square$

# 15.3    Interpretation of type assignment

We consider the problem of building *complete* formal systems for assigning types
to untyped λ-terms [CF58, BCD83, Hin83]. In chapter 4 we have referred to
this approach as typing à la Curry and we have pointed out its relevance in the
definition of algorithms that reconstruct automatically the type information that
is not explicitly available in the program.

We develop a type assignment system that is parametric with respect to: (1)
a λ-theory $\mathcal{E}$, and (2) a collection of typing hypotheses $B$ on variables and closed
λ-terms. To interpret type assignment we introduce *type structures* which are a
slight variation of per models.

**Definition 15.3.1** *A type frame $\mathcal{T}$ is made up of three components:*

(1)  *A λ-model $(D, \bullet)$ (cf. definition 3.2.2).*

(2)  *A collection $T \subseteq per_D$ closed under exponentiation:*

$$X, Y \in T \ \Rightarrow\ Y^X \in T .$$

(3)  *A collection $[T \to T] \subseteq \mathbf{Set}[T, T]$ closed under intersection:*

$$F \in [T \to T] \ \Rightarrow\ \bigcap_{A \in T} F(A) \in T .$$

Condition (1) is natural since we consider systems to assign types to λ-terms
and not to combinators. Conditions (2) and (3) generalize two properties satisfied
by the per model. Note that in a type frame we can select a proper subset of the
per's. This is instrumental in the construction of a term model, as we can take as
per's the 'definable' ones. The type interpretation defined in 15.2.1 can be easily
adapted to an arbitrary type frame.

**Definition 15.3.2** *The types of system F are interpreted in a type frame $\mathcal{T}$ parametrically with respect to a type environment $\eta : Tvar \to T$ as follows:*

$$
\begin{aligned}
[\![t]\!]\eta &= \eta(t) \\
[\![\sigma \to \tau]\!]\eta &= ([\![\tau]\!]\eta)^{[\![\sigma]\!]\eta} \\
[\![\forall t.\sigma]\!]\eta &= \bigcap_{A \in T}[\![\sigma]\!]\eta[A/t] .
\end{aligned}
$$

*A type frame is a* type structure *whenever the interpretation of intersection is
correct, that is for any $\sigma$, $\lambda A \in T.[\![\sigma]\!]\eta[A/t] \in [T \to T]$ (cf. definition of λ-model
in chapter 3).*

*A type structure has* no empty types *if $\forall A \in T \ (A \neq \emptyset)$.*

**Exercise 15.3.3** *Give an example of type structure without empty types.*

A type free λ-term is interpreted in the λβ-model $(D, \bullet)$ according to the
definition 3.2.2. We recall that the interpretation is parametric in an environment
$\rho$.

**Definition 15.3.4 (basis)** *A basis $B$ is a (possibly infinite) set $\{P_i : \sigma_i\}_{i \in I}$ where
$P_i$ is either a closed untyped λ-term or a variable, and all variables are distinct.*

$$(Asmp) \quad \frac{P : \sigma \in B}{B \vdash P : \sigma} \qquad\qquad (Eq) \quad \frac{B \vdash P' : \sigma \quad P =_{\mathcal{E}} P'}{B \vdash P : \sigma}$$

$$(rmv) \quad \frac{B \cup \{x : \sigma\} \vdash P : \tau \quad x \notin FV(P)}{B \vdash P : \tau} \qquad (weak) \quad \frac{B \vdash P : \sigma \quad B \cup B' \text{ well-formed}}{B \cup B' \vdash P : \sigma}$$

$$(\rightarrow_I) \quad \frac{B \cup \{x : \sigma\} \vdash P : \tau}{B \vdash \lambda x.P : \sigma \rightarrow \tau} \qquad\qquad (\rightarrow_E) \quad \frac{B \vdash P : \sigma \rightarrow \tau \quad B \vdash Q : \sigma}{B \vdash PQ : \tau}$$

$$(\rightarrow_I^\eta) \quad \frac{B \vdash \lambda x.Px : \sigma \rightarrow \tau \quad x \notin FV(P)}{B \vdash P : \sigma \rightarrow \tau}$$

$$(\forall_I) \quad \frac{B \vdash P : \sigma \quad t \notin FV_t(B)}{B \vdash P : \forall t.\sigma} \qquad\qquad (\forall_E) \quad \frac{B \vdash P : \forall t.\sigma}{B \vdash P : \sigma[\tau/t]}$$

Figure 15.2: Type assignment system for second order types

Let us fix an untyped $\lambda$-theory, say $\mathcal{E}$ (cf. section 4.6). We define a system to assign types to untyped $\lambda$-terms assuming a basis $B$ and modulo $\mathcal{E}$. For instance, we may be interested in a system to type terms under a basis $B = \{\lambda x.x : \iota \rightarrow s\}$ and modulo the $(\eta)$ rule. The basis $B$ asserts that every term having type $t$ has also type $s$ and the rule $(\eta)$ forces extensionality.

Given a $\lambda$-theory $\mathcal{E}$ we define in figure 15.2 a type assignment system whose judgments are of the form $B \vdash P : \sigma$, where $B$ is a basis, $P$ is an untyped $\lambda$-term, and $\sigma$ is a type of system F. Note that the rule $(\rightarrow_I^\eta)$ provides an extensionality principle which applies to terms of functional type only (this is weaker than adding the rule $\eta$ to the $\lambda$-theory $\mathcal{E}$). The rule is exploited in the construction of an exponent in the proof of theorem 15.3.9.

**Definition 15.3.5 (interpretation)** *Let $\mathcal{T}$ be a type structure over the $\lambda$-model $D$ and let $Th(D)$ be the $\lambda$-theory induced by $D$ (cf. chapter 4). We write $\mathcal{T} \models \mathcal{E}$ if $\mathcal{E} \subseteq Th(D)$. Given a type structure $\mathcal{T}$ such that $\mathcal{T} \models \mathcal{E}$ we write:*

$$B \models_{\mathcal{T}} P : \sigma \qquad \text{if } \forall \rho : Var \rightarrow D, \eta : Tvar \rightarrow \mathcal{T} \ (\rho, \eta \models B \ \Rightarrow \ \rho, \eta \models P : \sigma)$$
$$\rho, \eta \models P : \sigma \qquad \text{if } [\![P]\!]\rho \in |[\![\sigma]\!]\eta|$$
$$\rho, \eta \models \{P_i : \sigma_i\}_{i \in I} \quad \text{if } \forall i \in I \ (\rho, \eta \models P_i : \sigma_i) \ .$$

*When the type structure is fixed we omit writing $\mathcal{T}$.*

**Proposition 15.3.6 (soundness)** *Let $\mathcal{T}$ be a type structure without empty types such that $\mathcal{T} \models \mathcal{E}$. If $B \vdash P : \sigma$ (modulo $\mathcal{E}$) then $B \models_{\mathcal{T}} P : \sigma$.*

PROOF. The statement is not obvious because of the $(\rightarrow_I)$ rule. Suppose $\sigma, \tau$ are closed. Then we have:

$$x : \sigma \models x : \tau \qquad \text{iff} \qquad |[\![\sigma]\!]| \subseteq |[\![\tau]\!]|$$
$$\models \lambda x.x : \sigma \rightarrow \tau \qquad \text{iff} \qquad [\![\sigma]\!] \subseteq [\![\tau]\!] \ .$$

For this reason, we define a more general notion of satisfaction which depends on two environments:

$$\rho_1, \rho_2, \eta \models P : \sigma \quad \text{if} \quad [\![P]\!]\rho_1 \, [\sigma]\eta \, [\![P]\!]\rho_2 \, .$$

Then we prove the statement with respect to the modified satisfaction relation by induction on the length of the proof.                                                                    □

**Remark 15.3.7** *For a type structure with empty types the rule* $(rmv)$ *is not sound as from an hypothesis which is never realized we can derive everything. For instance we have* $\{x : \forall t.t\} \models_{per} \lambda x.x : \forall t.t$ *and* $\not\models_{per} \lambda x.x : \forall t.t$. *If we eliminate the rule* $(rmv)$ *then the type assignment system is sound for arbitrary type structures.*

The type assignment system in figure 15.2 is sound and *complete* to derive all judgments which are valid in type structures *without* empty types. This result can be extended to arbitrary type structures [Mit88]. In this case one introduces additional rules to reason about types' emptyness. For instance, one may enrich the basis with assertions $empty(\sigma)$ which hold if $\sigma$'s interpretation is empty and then add the following typing rules.

$$\frac{}{\{x : \sigma, empty(\sigma)\} \vdash M : \tau} \qquad \frac{B \cup \{x : \sigma\} \vdash M : \tau \quad B \cup \{empty(\sigma)\} \vdash M : \tau}{B \vdash M : \tau} \, .$$

**Exercise 15.3.8** *Check the soundness of the typing rules above.*

**Theorem 15.3.9 (completeness)** *Let* $\mathcal{E}$ *be a* $\lambda$-*theory and* $B$ *be a basis. It is possible to build a type structure without empty types* $\mathcal{T}_{\mathcal{E},B}$ *over the term* $\lambda\beta$-*model induced by the* $\lambda$-*theory* $\mathcal{E}$ *so that:*

$$B \vdash P : \sigma \quad \text{iff} \quad B \models_{\mathcal{T}_{\mathcal{E},B}} P : \sigma \, .$$

PROOF. The proof can be decomposed in two parts: (1) The proof that we can *conservatively* adjoin to the basis $B$ a countable collection of type assignments $x_i : \sigma_i$, where $i \in \omega$, and $x_i$ is a fresh variable. (2) The construction of a type structure starting from a basis $B'$ containing countably many type assignments $x_i : \sigma_i$.

Proof of (1). Let $\theta$ be an injective substitution from (type) variables to (type) variables such that $Var \backslash cod(\theta)$ and $Tvar \backslash cod(\theta)$ are infinite. We observe that:

$$B \vdash P : \sigma \quad \text{iff} \quad \theta(B \vdash P : \sigma) \, ,$$

where the substitution is distributed componentwise. Given (i) a basis $B$, (ii) an enumeration of the types $\{\sigma_i\}_{i \in \omega}$ where each type occurs countably many times, (iii) an injective substitution $\theta$ as above, and (iv) a sequence $\{x_i\}_{i \in \omega}$ of distinct variables such that $\{x_i\}_{i \in \omega} \cap cod(\theta) = \emptyset$, we define:

$$B' = \{\theta(Q : \sigma) \mid Q : \sigma \in B\} \cup \{x_i : \sigma_i\}_{i \in \omega} \, .$$

The following facts can be easily verified:

- Given a type structure without empty types $\mathcal{T}$ such that $\mathcal{T} \models \mathcal{E}$,

$$B \models_{\mathcal{T}} P : \sigma \quad \text{iff} \quad B' \models_{\mathcal{T}} \theta(P : \sigma) \ .$$

Hint: Since types are non-empty we can canonically extend any $\rho, \eta$ such that $\rho, \eta \models B$ to $\rho', \eta'$ such that $\rho', \eta' \models B'$.

- If $B' \vdash \theta(P : \sigma)$ then $B \vdash P : \sigma$. Hint: Use first compactness (if there is a proof, there is a proof that uses a finite part of the basis) to get a derivation with respect to a finite basis, then use $(rmv)$ to eliminate the remaining adjoined variables.

Proof of (2). Given a basis $B'$ as above, we define a type structure $\mathcal{T}_{\mathcal{E},B}$ without empty types as follows:

(1) Let $D$ be the term $\lambda$-model induced by the $\lambda$-theory $\mathcal{E}$ (cf. section 4.4). Let $[P]$ denote a generic element in $D$, that is the equivalence class of $P$ modulo $\mathcal{E}$.

(2) We consider the collection of per's $T = \{\langle \sigma \rangle \mid \sigma \text{ type}\}$ defined as follows (here and in the following point, we use the fact that we work with a type frame):

$$[P]\langle \sigma \rangle[Q] \quad \text{iff} \quad B' \vdash P : \sigma \text{ and } B' \vdash Q : \sigma \ .$$

(3) As for the type functionals we consider the 'definable' ones:

$$[T \to T] = \{F : T \to T \mid \exists \sigma, t \ F(\langle \tau \rangle) = \langle \sigma[\tau/t] \rangle\} \ .$$

Next we verify that this is a type structure without empty types.

- There are no empty types because $x_i : \sigma \in B'$ (here we use the extension of $B$ to $B'$). Note that it would be enough to show that the type $\forall t.t.$ is inhabited to conclude by $(\forall_E)$ that every type is inhabited.

- Closure under exponentiation amounts to verifying:

$$[P]\langle \sigma \to \tau \rangle[Q] \quad \text{iff} \quad \forall [P'], [Q'] \ ([P']\langle \sigma \rangle[Q'] \Rightarrow [PP']\langle \tau \rangle[QQ']) \ .$$

Hint: The direction $(\Leftarrow)$ follows from the following deduction where $x$ is a fresh variable adjoined to the basis $B$ (the fresh variable exists by the hypothesis that each type occurs infinitely often):

$$\begin{aligned}
B' \vdash x : \sigma &\Rightarrow B' \vdash Px : \tau \\
&\Rightarrow B' \vdash \lambda x.Px : \sigma \to \tau \quad \text{by } (\to_I) \\
&\Rightarrow B' \vdash P : \sigma \to \tau \quad \text{by } (\to_I^\eta) \ .
\end{aligned}$$

- Closure under intersection follows from:

$$[P]\langle \forall t.\sigma \rangle[Q] \quad \text{iff} \quad \forall \tau \ ([P]\langle \sigma[\tau/t] \rangle[Q]) \ .$$

We can now conclude our proof. If $B \vdash P : \sigma$, then $B \models_{\mathcal{T}_{\mathcal{E},B}} P : \sigma$, by soundness. Vice versa, suppose $B \models_{\mathcal{T}_{\mathcal{E},B}} P : \sigma$. Then $B' \models_{\mathcal{T}_{\mathcal{E},B}} \theta(P : \sigma)$. Pick the environment $\rho_o, \eta_o$ defined as:

$$\rho_o(x) = [x] \quad \eta_o(t) = \langle t \rangle \ .$$

One can check $\rho_o, \eta_o \models B'$. From this we know $\rho_o, \eta_o \models \theta(P : \sigma)$ which is the same as $B' \vdash \theta(P : \sigma)$, and we can extract a proof of $B \vdash P : \sigma$. $\quad\square$

# 15.4 Partiality and separation in per

In the following we concentrate on the problem of giving a per interpretation of type theories including *recursion* on terms and types. As usual we are naturally led towards a notion of *complete* partially ordered set. At the same time we want to stay faithful to our goal of regarding data types as particular sets of our realizability universe. Hence we look for a collection of 'sets' on which it is possible to find an *intrinsic order* that is preserved by all set theoretical functions. The method will be that of restricting the attention to *full* subcategories of $\mathbf{per}_D$. Hence, as in the classical approach described in chapter 1 we restrict our attention to certain sets endowed with structure, however, as opposed to that approach, we consider all 'set theoretical' functions and not just the continuous ones. The fact that functions are continuous is a theorem and not an hypothesis.

In chapter 8 we have introduced some basic notions about partial cartesian closed categories (pCCC) and their properties. We recall that every pCCC has an object $\Sigma$, called the dominance, that classifies the admissible subobjects. In a pCCC the morphisms from an object $a$ to the dominance $\Sigma$ play the role of *convergence tests*. These tests induce a preorder $\leq_a$ on the points of an object. The idea of ordering points by tests bears a striking analogy with the one encountered in operational semantics of ordering terms by observations (cf. section 6.4). Following [Ros86] we focus on the full subcategory of separated objects, which are composed of those objects for which $\leq_a$ is antisymmetric.

By convention, we write $x : a$ to indicate that $x$ is a point of $a$, that is, a morphism $x : 1 \to a$. Since we will be dealing with CCC's and pCCC's we confuse points in the objects $a \to b$ and $a \rightharpoonup b$ with morphisms in $\mathbf{C}[a, b]$ and $\mathbf{pC}[a, b]$, respectively. For instance, $f : a \to b$ can be seen both as a morphism from $a$ to $b$ and as a point in $a \to b$. We introduce a convergence predicate, say $\downarrow$, as follows: if $x : a$, $p = [m, f] : a \rightharpoonup b$, with $m : d \to a$, $f : d \to b$ then:

$$p \circ x \downarrow \quad \text{iff} \quad \exists h : 1 \to d \ (m \circ h = x).$$

We write $p : a \rightharpoonup b$ and $p : a \to b_\perp$ interchangeably. When $x$ is a point, we shall often abbreviate $p \circ x$ with $px$.

**Definition 15.4.1 (intrinsic preorder)** *Let* $(\mathbf{C}, \mathcal{M})$ *be a pCCC with dominance* $\Sigma$, *and* $a$ *be an object of* $\mathbf{C}$. *We define a preorder* $\leq_a$, *called intrinsic preorder, on the points of* $a$ *as:*

$$x \leq_a y \quad \text{iff} \quad \forall p : a \to \Sigma \ (p \circ x \downarrow \Rightarrow p \circ y \downarrow).$$

The intuition is that $x$ is less then $y$ in $a$, if every convergence test $p : a \to \Sigma$ that succeeds on $x$ also succeeds on $y$. In the following we also write $p \circ x \leq p \circ y$ for $(p \circ x \downarrow \ \Rightarrow \ p \circ y \downarrow)$.

**Definition 15.4.2 (category of $\Sigma$-objects)** *Given a pCCC* $(\mathbf{C}, M)$ *with dominance* $\Sigma$ *we denote with* $\Sigma\mathbf{C}$ *the full subcategory of* $\mathbf{C}$ *whose objects enjoy the property that the intrinsic preorder is anti-symmetric. An object* $a$ *such that* $\leq_a$ *is a partial order is called a* $\Sigma$-object *or, equivalently, a separated object.*

**Proposition 15.4.3** *Let* $(C, M)$ *be a* $pCCC$ *with dominance* $\Sigma$. *Then:*

(1) *Morphisms preserve the intrinsic preorder.*

(2) $\Sigma$-*objects are closed under subobjects.*

PROOF. (1) Let $f : a \to b$ and $x, y : a$. Suppose $x \leq_a y$, then given any $p : b \to \Sigma$ we have by hypothesis $p \circ f \circ x \leq p \circ f \circ y$, since $p \circ f : a \to \Sigma$. Hence $f \circ x \leq_b f \circ y : b$.

(2) Let $m : a \to b$ be a mono and $b$ be a $\Sigma$-object. If $x$ and $y$ are two distinct points in $a$ then $m \circ x$ and $m \circ y$ are two distinct points in $b$. Hence, since $b$ is a $\Sigma$-object, they are separable by a morphism $p : b \to \Sigma$. Then the morphism $p \circ m$ separates the points $x$ and $y$. □

Partiality is explicitly given in a pca $D$, and by generalizing basic facts of recursion theory (i.e., r.e. sets are exactly the domains of computable functions) it also provides a notion of semi-computable predicate on $D$. We elaborate this point in the following.

**Definition 15.4.4** *Let* $D$ *be a pca, for any* $d \in D$ *let* $dom(d) = \{e \in D \mid de \downarrow\}$. *Then we define a collection of semi-computable predicates on* $D$ *as follows:*

$$\Sigma(D) = \{dom(d) \mid d \in D\} \ .$$

The collection of predicates $\Sigma(D)$ induces a refinement preorder on $D$ defined as (this is the untyped intrinsic preorder):

$$d \leq_D e \text{ iff } \forall W \in \Sigma(D) \ (d \in W \Rightarrow e \in W) \ . \tag{15.1}$$

We observe that the operation of application preserves this preorder:

$$\forall d \in D \ (e \leq_D e' \Rightarrow de \leq_D de') \ .$$

Suppose $\exists d \in D \ \forall e \in D \ de \uparrow$, then $\Sigma(D)$ can be seen as a basis for a topology as:

(1) $\emptyset, D \in \Sigma(D)$, taking respectively the always divergent and always convergent morphism.

(2) If $W, W' \in \Sigma(D)$ then $W \cap W' = dom(\lambda^*d.(\lambda^*x.\lambda^*y.c)(ed)(e'd)) \in \Sigma(D)$, where $c \in D$.

We show that given any per, say $A$, $\Sigma(D)$ induces a collection, say $\Sigma(A)$, of semi-computable predicates on $A$. From this structure it is easy to obtain a family $\mathcal{M}_D$ of admissible monos on $\mathbf{per}_D$ that turns the category into a pCCC.

**Definition 15.4.5** *Let* $A \in \mathbf{per}_D$. *Then we define:*

$$\Sigma(A) = \{B \in \mathbf{per}_D \mid [B] \subseteq [A] \text{ and } \exists W \in \Sigma(D) \ (|A| \cap W = |B|)\} \ .$$

In other words $B$ belongs to $\Sigma(A)$ if the equivalence classes in $B$ form a subset of those in $A$ and there is a set $W \subseteq \Sigma(D)$ that separates $[B]$ from the other equivalence classes in $[A]$.

Note that if $\exists d \in D \ \forall e \in D \ de \uparrow$ then the following properties hold (by applying the related properties of $\Sigma(D)$):

(1)  $\emptyset, A \in \Sigma(A)$.

(2)  If $B, B' \in \Sigma(A)$ then $B'' \in \Sigma(A)$, where $B''$ is the per corresponding to the partial partition $[B] \cap [B']$.

**Definition 15.4.6**  *Define* $\mathcal{M}_D$ *as the following family of monos in* $\mathbf{per}_D$.

$$m : A' \to A \in \mathcal{M}_D(A) \quad \textit{iff} \quad A' \in \Sigma(A) \ \textit{and } m \ \textit{is the inclusion morphism} .$$

Note that the morphism $m$ is realized by the identity. It is easy to check that this collection of monos is indeed admissible. The conditions for identity and composition are clear. Let us consider the case for the pullbacks. Assume $f : A \to B$ and $m : C \to B$ with $\phi$ realizer of $f$ and $|B| \cap dom(\psi) = |C|$. To construct the pullback consider $W' = dom(\lambda^* d.\psi(\phi d))$ and the related admissible subobject of $A$.

The following exercise provides a convenient presentation of the category $(\mathbf{per}_D, \mathcal{M}_D)$.

**Exercise 15.4.7**  *Show that the category* $(\mathbf{per}_D, \mathcal{M}_D)$ *of per's and partial morphisms is equivalent to the category* $\mathbf{pper}_D$ *defined as follows:*

$$
\begin{aligned}
Ob\mathbf{pper}_D \ &= \ Ob\mathbf{per}_D \\
\mathbf{pper}_D[A, B] \ &= \ \{f : [A] \to [B] \mid \exists \phi \in D \ \forall d \\
&\qquad d\,A\,d \Rightarrow ((\phi d \downarrow \Leftrightarrow f([d]_A) \downarrow) \ and \ (\phi d \downarrow \Rightarrow \phi d \in f([d]_A))\} .
\end{aligned}
$$

**Proposition 15.4.8**  *The category* $(\mathbf{per}_D, \mathcal{M}_D)$ *is a pCCC. The partial exponent* $A \rightharpoonup B$ *is defined as:*

$$f \, (A \rightharpoonup B) \, g \quad \textit{iff} \quad \forall d, e \ (d\,A\,e \Rightarrow fd \cong_B ge) ,$$

*where* $\cong_B$ *is Kleene equality relativized to* $B$, *namely* $t \cong_B s$ *iff* $(t \downarrow \ \Leftrightarrow \ s \downarrow)$ *and* $(t \downarrow \ \Rightarrow \ tBs)$.

We remark that the category $\mathbf{per}_D$ has enough points. Taking the terminal object as $1 = D \times D$, the dominance is $\Sigma = 1 \rightharpoonup 1 = \{\perp, \top\}$, where $\perp = \{d \in D \mid \forall e \ (de \uparrow)\}$, and $\top = \{d \in D \mid \forall e \ (de \downarrow)\}$. We can then specialize definition 15.4.2 as follows.

**Definition 15.4.9**  *The category* $\Sigma\mathbf{per}_D$ *is the full subcategory of* $\mathbf{per}_D$ *whose objects are* $\Sigma$-*objects.*

**Remark 15.4.10**  *We observe that if* $d \leq_D d'$ *(cf. 15.1),* $A \in \mathbf{per}_D$, *and* $d, d' \in |A|$ *then a fortiori* $[d]_A \leq_A [d']_A$. *Suppose* $B \in \Sigma(A)$ *and* $[d]_A \in [B]$, *then there is a* $W \in \Sigma(D)$ *such that* $|A| \cap W = |B|$. *But by hypothesis* $d' \in W$ *and therefore* $[d']_A \in [B]$. *This fact corresponds to the intuition that if two elements cannot be separated in the type free universe of the realizability structure* $D$ *then a fortiori they cannot be separated in the typed structure of per's.*

Proposition 15.4.3 can be used to establish some elementary facts about $\Sigma\mathbf{per}_D$. The main result is the following.

**Theorem 15.4.11** *The category $\Sigma\mathbf{per}_D$ is a full reflective subcategory of $\mathbf{per}_D$.*

PROOF. The simple idea for obtaining a $\Sigma\mathrm{per}$ $L_\Sigma(A)$ from the per $A$ is to collapse equivalence classes that cannot be separated by $\Sigma(A)$. Given a per $A$ and the intrinsic preorder $\leq_A$ we define an equivalence relation, $\approx_A$, on $[A]$ as:

$$[d]_A \approx_A [e]_A \quad\text{iff}\quad d, e \in |A| \text{ and } [d]_A \leq_A [e]_A \text{ and } [e]_A \leq_A [d]_A .$$

Let the reflector $L_\Sigma : \mathbf{per}_D \to \Sigma\mathbf{per}_D$ be as follows:

$$d\, L_\Sigma(A)\, e \quad\text{iff}\quad [d]_A \approx_A [e]_A \quad \text{for } A \in \mathbf{per}_D$$
$$L_\Sigma(f)([d]_{L_\Sigma(A)}) = [f([d]_A)]_{\approx_B} \quad \text{for } f : A \to B .$$

We verify that: (1) $L_\Sigma(A)$ is a $\Sigma\mathrm{per}$. Actually it is the least $\Sigma\mathrm{per}$ containing $A$ (as a relation). (2) If $B$ is separated, then $d\, L_\Sigma(A)\, e$ implies $f([d]_A) = f([e]_A)$. From these facts it is easy to exhibit the natural isomorphism of the adjunction. □

The following corollary summarizes our progress. We have managed to build a full subcategory of per's that has the same closure properties of $\mathbf{per}_D$, and moreover has an intrinsic notion of partial order that will turn out to be useful in the interpretation of recursion.

**Corollary 15.4.12** *The category $\Sigma\mathbf{per}_D$ is cartesian closed and it has all limits and colimits of $\mathbf{per}_D$.*

PROOF. The existence of limits and colimits is guaranteed by the reflection. Let us check that $\Sigma\mathbf{per}_D$ is closed under the usual definition of exponent in $\mathbf{per}_D$. Suppose $B \in \Sigma\mathbf{per}_D$ and $f, g : A \to B$. If $f$ and $g$ are distinct, then there is a point $x : A$ such that $fx, gx$ are distinct and, by hypothesis, separable by means of $k : B \to \Sigma$. Then the morphism $\lambda h : A \to B.k(hx)$ separates $f$ and $g$. □

# 15.5 Complete per's

We are interested in finding an analogy of the notion of $\omega$-completeness in a realizability framework. In the first place we need an object $N$ that can play the role of the natural numbers. More precisely a *natural number object* (nno) is a diagram $1 \xrightarrow{0} N \xrightarrow{s} N$ that is initial among all diagrams of the shape: $1 \xrightarrow{x} A \xrightarrow{f} A$. In this section we work over Kleene's pca $(\omega, \bullet)$ and with the related category of per's $\mathbf{per}_\omega$. We define as nno:

$$N = \{\{n\} \mid n \in \omega\} .$$

In particular we shall make use of the fact that for $K = \{n \mid nn \downarrow\}$ and $O = \{K, K^c\}$, $\{K^c\} \notin \Sigma(O)$.

We will concentrate on $(N\text{-})$complete $\Sigma$per's, that is, $\Sigma$per's such that any ascending sequence on them, that is definable as a morphism in the category, has a lub with respect to the intrinsic order.

When restricting the attention to complete $\Sigma$per's it is possible to prove a variant of the Myhill-Shepherdson's theorem (cf. section 1.3) asserting that all morphisms preserve lub's of chains. This will arise as a corollary of the fact that for any per $A$ the elements of $\Sigma(A)$ are Scott opens.

A consequence of this result is that the full subcategory of complete, separated per's can be seen as a sort of pre-O-category in that the morphisms are partially ordered, there are lub's of *definable* chains, and the operation of composition preserves this structure.

When stating the completeness condition for a $\Sigma$per $A$ we will only be interested in the existence of the lub's of the chains, $\chi : N \to A$, that are definable as morphisms from the nno $N$ to $A$.

**Definition 15.5.1** *Let $A$ be a per. We write $\chi : AS(A)$ (AS for ascending sequence) if*
$$\chi : N \to A \text{ and } \forall n : N \ (\chi(n) \leq_A \chi(n+1)) .$$

**Remark 15.5.2** *Observe that whenever we select a subset of the equivalence classes of a (separated) per we can naturally consider it as a (separated) per (for example $AS(A)$, as a subset of $[N \to A]$).*

According to a constructive reading the existence of the lub of every ascending sequence implies the existence of a method to find this lub given a realizer for the sequence. Indeed as soon as we consider the problem of the closure of the collection of $N$-complete objects with respect to the function space constructor it becomes important to have a realizer that uniformly, for every ascending sequence of a given type, computes the lub (we refer to [Pho90] for more information on the closure properties of this category). This motivates the following definition.

**Definition 15.5.3 (complete per)** *A separated per $A$ is complete if*

$$\exists \sigma_A : AS(A) \to A \ \forall \chi : AS(A) \ (\sigma_A(\chi) = \bigvee_A \chi) .$$

*(Thus there is a method $\sigma_A$ to compute the lub in $A$ of every chain $\chi : AS(A)$.)*

If it exists, the morphism $\sigma_A$ is uniquely determined, hence we will simply indicate with $A$ rather than with $(A, \sigma_A)$ a complete separated per.

**Remark 15.5.4** *The category of complete separated per's is non-trivial as every separated object $A$ in which all elements are incomparable is complete (one can define $\sigma_A = \lambda\chi : AS(A).\chi(0)$, where 0 is the zero of the nno, as every ascending sequence is constant).*

**Remark 15.5.5** *The definition of completeness highlights the difference between a classical set theoretical definition (say in a system like $ZF$) and a constructive one. When working in a realizability universe it is a good habit to read definitions and theorems constructively. This approach will not be pursued in this introductory chapter, the problem being that a rigorous exposition requires some background on the internal logic of the effective topos, basically a higher order intuitionistic type theory that includes principles like the countable axiom of choice $(AC_\omega)$, the computability of all the morphisms on natural numbers (Church's Thesis), the Uniformity Principle, and the Markov Principle (see [Hyl82]).*

**Definition 15.5.6** *Let $A$ be a per. A subset $U$ of $[A]$ is a Scott open (cf. definition 1.2.1) and we write $U \in \tau(A)$ iff*

(1) $\forall x, y : A \ (x : U \text{ and } x \leq_A y \Rightarrow y : U)$, *and*

(2) $\forall \chi : AS(A) \ (\exists \bigvee_A \chi : U \Rightarrow \exists n : N \ (\chi n : U))$.

Note that this definition makes sense in any preorder. It is immediate to check that $\tau(A)$ defines a topology over $[A]$. As in the Rice-Shapiro theorem A1.3.1, the following result points out a Scott topological structure on semi-computable predicates.

**Theorem 15.5.7** *If $A$ is a separated, complete per and $U \in \Sigma(A)$ then $U \in \tau(A)$.*

PROOF. The first condition of upward closure follows by the definition of intrinsic order. Take $x : U$ and suppose $x \leq_A y$. Then $y : U$ as:

$$x \leq_A y \text{ iff } \forall U \in \Sigma(A) \ (x : U \Rightarrow y : U) \ .$$

The proof of the second condition takes advantage of the specific recursion theoretical character of the pca $(\omega, \bullet)$, indeed the following argument is a keystone of the theory.

Consider the set $K = \{n \mid (nn) \downarrow\}$ and the per $O = \{K, K^c\}$. We observe $\{K\} \in \Sigma(O)$ and $\{K^c\} \notin \Sigma(O)$. The predicate $(nn) \downarrow_i$ means that the computation $nn$ of the $n^{th}$ machine applied to the input $n$ will stop in at most $i$ steps. This is a decidable predicate.

Now let us proceed by contradiction assuming there is $\chi : AS(A)$ such that:

$$\exists \bigvee_A \chi : U \text{ and } \forall n : N \ \neg(\chi n : U) \ .$$

The crucial idea is to build a function $h : O \to A$ mapping $K$ to $\{\chi n \mid n : N\}$, and $K^c$ to $\bigvee_A \chi$. By the pullback condition we derive the contradiction:

$$h^{-1}(U) = \{K^c\} \in \Sigma(O) \ .$$

For any $n$ we define an ascending sequence $\lambda i.c(n, i) : N \to A$. In the following $\mu k \leq i.(nn) \downarrow_k$ is the least element $k \leq i$ such that $(nn) \downarrow k$.

$$c(n, i) = \begin{cases} \chi i & \text{if } \neg((nn) \downarrow_i) \\ \chi(\mu k \leq i.(nn) \downarrow_k) & \text{otherwise} \end{cases}.$$

We observe that for any given $n$ if $n \in K$ then $\lambda i.c(n, i)$ coincides with the ascending sequence $\chi$ up to the first $k$ such that $(nn) \downarrow_k$ and then becomes definitely constant; on the other hand if $n \in K^c$ then $\lambda i.c(n, i)$ coincides with $\chi$. We note that $\lambda i.c(n, i) : AS(A)$. Using the existence of a morphism $\sigma_A$ that uniformly realizes the lub of ascending sequences we define a morphism $h : O \to A$ such that:

$$h([n]_O) = \sigma_A(\lambda i.c(n, i)) .$$

We have just observed $h([n]_O) = \bigvee_A \chi$ if $n \in K^c$ and $h([n]_O) \in \{\chi n \mid n : N\}$ otherwise, from this we can obtain the desired contradiction. □

**Remark 15.5.8** *For the logically inclined reader we mention that this proof by contradiction can be turned into a* constructive *proof via the Markov Principle.*

**Definition 15.5.9** *Let $A, B$ be separated per's. We say that $f : A \to B$ preserves chains if*

$$\forall \chi : AS(A) \ (\exists \bigvee_A \chi : A \Rightarrow (\exists \bigvee_B f \circ \chi : B \text{ and } f(\bigvee_A \chi) = \bigvee_B f \circ \chi)) .$$

As in the Myhill-Shepherdson theorem 1.3.1(1), we can prove that 'computable' functions are Scott continuous.

**Proposition 15.5.10** *Suppose $A, B$ are complete separated per's. Then any morphism $f : A \to B$ preserves chains and it is Scott continuous.*

PROOF. Consider $\chi : AS(A)$. In order to show $\bigvee_B(f \circ \chi) = f(\bigvee_A \chi)$ we prove that for any upper bound $y : B$ of $f \circ \chi : AS(B)$ we have $f(\bigvee_A \chi) \leq_B y$. We recall that:

$$f(\bigvee_A \chi) \leq_B y \text{ iff } \forall U \in \Sigma(B) \ (f(\bigvee_A \chi) : U \Rightarrow y : U) .$$

Now $U \in \Sigma(B)$ implies, by the pullback condition of admissible domains, $f^{-1}(U) \in \Sigma(A)$, hence by theorem 15.5.7, $f^{-1}(U) \in \tau(A)$. Since $f(\bigvee_A \chi) : U$, we have $\bigvee_A \chi : f^{-1}(U)$, which implies by the definition of open set $\exists n : N \ (\chi n : f^{-1}(U))$. Therefore $\exists n : N \ (f(\chi n) : U)$, and this implies $y : U$.

To show continuity, we take $U \in \tau(B)$ and we consider $f^{-1}(U)$. This is upward closed by the fact that $f$ is monotonic. Moreover, let $\chi : AS(A)$ and suppose $\bigvee_A \chi : f^{-1}(U)$. Then by hypothesis $f(\bigvee_A \chi) = \bigvee_B(f \circ \chi) : U$. Therefore $\exists n : N \ (f(\chi n) : U)$ i.e., $\chi n : f^{-1}(U)$. □

The category of complete separated per's can also be shown to be reflective in $\Sigma$**per** and cartesian closed when appropriately formulated in the internal language of the effective topos [Pho90], however this proof lies outside the realm of our introductive approach to realizability.

# 15.6   Extensional per's *

So far the theory has been developed in a rather synthetic and abstract way. To use the theory in practice it is often useful (if not necessary) to have a *concrete* presentation of the denotational model. For instance we would like to characterize the order on function spaces, to compute lub's explicitly, etc. In the following we introduce a category of *extensional* per's for which we can provide answers to these questions (an even more concrete category based on a different pca will be presented in the next section). The initial idea is to look at per's of the shape $\Sigma^A$. First we need to develop a few notions.

**Definition 15.6.1 ($\Sigma$-linked)**   *A per $A$ is $\Sigma$-linked if for all $x, y \in [A]$,*

$$x \leq_A y \;\Rightarrow\; \exists f : \Sigma \to A \;(f\bot = x \text{ and } f\top = y) \;.$$

We note that if $f\bot = x$ and $f\top = y$ then $x \leq_A y$, by monotonicity. We shall prove in proposition 15.6.10 that all complete separated per's are $\Sigma$-linked, but there are separated per's which are not $\Sigma$-linked. The existence of a counter-example relies on a rather deep recursion theoretical result.

**Definition 15.6.2**   *Let $X, Y \subseteq \omega$ be sets. We say that $X$ is* many-reducible *to $Y$ and write $X \leq_m Y$ if there is a total recursive function $f$ such that:*

$$x \in X \quad \textit{iff} \quad f(x) \in Y \;.$$

The following proposition is due to Post (a proof can be found in [Soa87]).

**Proposition 15.6.3**   *Any r.e. set $X$ is many reducible to the set $K = \{n \mid nn \downarrow\}$. There is an r.e., non-recursive set to which $K$ cannot be many-reduced.*

**Proposition 15.6.4**   *(1)   If $X$ is a r.e. non-recursive set then $A = \{X, X^c\}$ is a separated per where $X^c <_A X$.*

*(2)   The dominance $\Sigma$ is isomorphic to the separated per $\{K, K^c\}$.*

*(3)   There is an r.e., non recursive, set such that $\{X, X^c\}$ is not $\Sigma$-linked.*

PROOF.   (1)   If a partial morphism from $\{X, X^c\}$ to the terminal object converges on $X^c$ and diverges on $X$ then it contradicts the hypothesis that $X$ is not recursive.

(2)   We recall that $\Sigma = \{\bot, \top\}$ where $\bot = \{n \mid \forall m \; nm \uparrow\}$ and $\top = \{n \mid \forall m \; nm \downarrow\}$. From $\Sigma$ to $\{K^c, K\}$ consider the morphism realized by the identity. In the other direction consider the map realized by $\lambda^* n.\lambda^* m.nn$.

(3)   First we observe for $X, Y \subseteq \omega$:

$$X \leq_m Y \quad \text{iff} \quad \exists h : \{X, X^c\} \to \{Y, Y^c\} \;\; \text{mono such that } h(X) = Y \;.$$

Then pick a r.e., non-recursive set $Y$ to which $K$ cannot be many-reduced. The separated per $\{Y, Y^c\}$ is not $\Sigma$-linked, by definition.   □

Hence, we can build two separated per's having the same order as Sierpinski space that are not isomorphic!

**Exercise 15.6.5**   *Show that there is a set $X \subset \omega$ such that $\{X, X^c\}$ is not separated.*

**Definition 15.6.6** *Let $A = \Pi_{i \in I} A_i$ be a product in **per** with projections $\{\pi_i\}_{i \in I}$. We say that $A$ is ordered pointwise if*

$$x \leq_A y \quad \text{iff} \quad \forall i \in I \ (\pi_i \circ x \leq_{A_i} \pi_i \circ y) \ .$$

**Proposition 15.6.7** (1) *The dominance $\Sigma$ is $\Sigma$-linked.*

(2) *Let $A = \Pi_{i \in I} A_i$ be a product of $\Sigma$-linked per's with projections $\{\pi_i\}_{i \in I}$. Then $A$ is ordered pointwise and $\Sigma$-linked.*

(3) *If $A$ is $\Sigma$-linked and $[B] \subseteq [A]$ then $B$ is $\Sigma$-linked and the order on $B$ is the restriction of the order on $A$.*

PROOF. (1) Take the identity function.

(2) Consider $x, y : \Pi_{\in I} A_i$ such that $\forall i \in I \ (\pi_i \circ x \leq_{A_i} \pi_i \circ y)$ ($x$ is pointwise smaller than $y$). By hypothesis:

$$\forall i \in I \ \exists f_i : \Sigma \to A_i \ (f_i \circ \bot = \pi_i \circ x \text{ and } f_i \circ \top = \pi_i \circ y) \ .$$

By definition of product there is a morphism $\langle f_i \rangle : \Sigma \to \Pi_{\in I} A_i$ such that $\pi_i \circ \langle f_i \rangle = f_i$. Then we can derive:

$$\pi_i \circ \langle f_i \rangle \circ \bot = f_i \circ \bot = \pi_i \circ x$$
$$\pi_i \circ \langle f_i \rangle \circ \top = f_i \circ \top = \pi_i \circ y \ .$$

Then $\langle f_i \rangle \circ \bot = x$ and $\langle f_i \rangle \circ \top = y$. Hence $x \leq_A y$ and $A$ is $\Sigma$-linked.

(3) If $x \leq_A y$ then there is a morphism $f : \Sigma \to A$ such that $f(\bot) = x$ and $f(\top) = y$. If $x, y : B$ then $f$ can be restricted to $f' : \Sigma \to B$. By monotonicity it follows $x = f'(\bot) \leq_B f'(\top) = y$, and that $B$ is $\Sigma$-linked provided we prove that $x \leq_B y \Rightarrow x \leq_A y$. Suppose $x \leq_B y$, $f : A \to \Sigma$, and $f(x) = \top$, then $f$ can be restricted to $B$, and by definition of intrinsic ordering $f(y) = \top$. Hence $x \leq_A y$. □

**Definition 15.6.8** *The pointwise order $\leq_{ext}$ on functions $f, g : A \to B$ is defined as:*

$$f \leq_{ext} g \quad \text{iff} \quad \forall x : A \ (f \circ x \leq_B g \circ x) \ .$$

The following theorem provides the basic insight into the structure of $\Sigma^A$.

**Theorem 15.6.9** *Let $A$ be a per. Then the following properties hold:*

(1) *The per $\Sigma^A$ is separated and $\Sigma$-linked.*

(2) *The intrinsic order on $\Sigma^A$ coincides with the pointwise order.*

(3) *The per $\Sigma^A$ is complete.*

PROOF. We start with the construction of a lub. Let $AS^{ext}(\Sigma^A)$ be the collection of functions $\chi : N \to (\Sigma^A)$ such that $\chi(n) \leq_{ext} \chi(n+1)$, that is the collection of ascending sequences with respect to the pointwise order. We define a function $\sigma : AS^{ext}(\Sigma^A) \to \Sigma^A$ (looking at $\Sigma$ as $1 \to 1$ and supposing $p \in |1|$):

$$\sigma(\chi) = \lambda x : A.\lambda z : 1.\text{if } (\exists n \ \chi(n)(x) \downarrow) \text{ then } p \ .$$

It is immediately verified that $\sigma(\chi)$ is the lub of $\chi$ with respect to the pointwise order. Next, suppose $f, g : A \to \Sigma$ and $f \leq_{ext} g$. We take $\Sigma = \{K, K^c\}$ and build $h : \Sigma \to (\Sigma^A)$ such that $h(K) = g$ and $h(K^c) = f$. By proposition 15.6.4(2), this implies that $\Sigma^A$ is $\Sigma$-linked and that the pointwise and intrinsic orders coincide. Consider a family of chains $c(n, i) : A \to \Sigma$ defined as follows (cf. proof theorem 15.5.7):

$$c(n, i)(x) = \begin{cases} g(x) & \text{if } nn \downarrow_i \\ f(x) & \text{otherwise .} \end{cases}$$

We observe that for all $n$, $\lambda i.c(n, i) : AS^{ext}(\Sigma^A)$ and that:

$$\sigma(\lambda i.c(n, i)) = \begin{cases} g & \text{if } n \in K \\ f & \text{if } n \in K^c \text{ .} \end{cases}$$

Then $h = \lambda n.\sigma(\lambda i.c(n, i))$ fits. Finally observe that since pointwise and intrinsic order coincide, the function $\sigma$ proves that $\Sigma^A$ is complete. $\square$

Basically the same proof technique is used to prove the following result.

**Proposition 15.6.10** *If $A$ is a complete and separated per then $A$ is $\Sigma$-linked.*

PROOF. Let $x \leq_A y$ and consider the following family of chains:

$$c(n, i) = \begin{cases} y & \text{if } nn \downarrow_i \\ x & \text{otherwise .} \end{cases}$$

If $n$ is fixed, the ascending sequence $\lambda i.c(n, i)$ is apparently innocuous, as it can take at most two values. However for a general per we do not know how to compute the lub of this sequence. For complete per's we can use $\sigma_A$ to define:

$$h(n) = \sigma_A(\lambda i.c(n, i)) \ .$$

Observe that $h : \{K, K^c\} \to A$ with $h(K) = y$ and $h(K^c) = x$. $\square$

Next we consider a condition stronger than separation and $\Sigma$-linkage which is due to [FMRS92].

**Definition 15.6.11 (extensional per)** *A per $A$ is* extensional *if there is a per $B$ such that $[A] \subseteq [\Sigma^B]$. We denote with* **exper** *the full subcategory of extensional per's.*

**Exercise 15.6.12** *Show that the following is an equivalent definition of extensional per. $A$ is an exper if there is $X \subseteq D$ such that $[A] \subseteq [\Sigma^{Diag(X)}]$, where $Diag(X) = \{(x, x) \mid x \in X\}$. Hint: For $A$ per, $[\Sigma^A] \subseteq [\Sigma^{Diag(|A|)}]$.*

**Proposition 15.6.13** *Let $[A] \subseteq [\Sigma^B]$ be an extensional per. Then:*

(1) *$A$ is separated and $\Sigma$-linked.*

(2) *If $f, g : A$ then $f \leq_A g$ iff $\forall b : B \ (f \circ b \leq_\Sigma g \circ b)$.*

PROOF. (1) Every per $\Sigma^B$ is separated (cf. proof of corollary 15.4.12), and separated per's are closed under subobjects. By theorem 15.6.9, $\Sigma^B$ is $\Sigma$-linked and by proposition 15.6.7, $\Sigma$-linked per's are closed under subobjects obtained by selecting a subset of the quotient space.

(2) By proposition 15.6.7, $f \leq_A g$ iff $f \leq_{\Sigma^B} g$. By theorem 15.6.9, we know that the order on $\Sigma^B$ is pointwise. $\square$

**Theorem 15.6.14** *The category* **exper** *is reflective in the category of separated per's.*

PROOF. We use $A \Rightarrow \Sigma$ as a linear notation for $\Sigma^A$. We already know that every extensional per is separated. We define a reflector $L_{ex} : \Sigma\mathbf{per} \to \mathbf{exper}$ as follows:

$$[L_{ex}(A)] = \{[\lambda^* u.ud]_{(A \Rightarrow \Sigma) \Rightarrow \Sigma} \mid d \in |A|\} .$$

This is an exper as by definition $[L_{ex}(A)] \subseteq [(A \Rightarrow \Sigma) \Rightarrow \Sigma]$. The universal morphism $e_A : A \to L_{ex}(A)$ is the one realized by $\lambda^* d.\lambda^* u.ud$. Intuitively it takes an element $d$ to the collection of its neighbourhoods $\lambda^* u.ud$. By construction $e_A$ is an epi, moreover it is also a mono if $A$ is separated (note that $L_{ex}$ can also work as a reflector from **per** to **exper**).

As a second step, we show that if $B$ is extensional then $e_B : B \to L_{ex}(B)$ is an iso. Suppose $[B] \subseteq [C \Rightarrow \Sigma]$. We take $e_B^{-1} : L_{ex}(B) \to B$ as the morphism realized by $\lambda^* i.\lambda^* c.i(\lambda^* u.uc)$. First one can check that:

$$\lambda^* i.\lambda^* c.i(\lambda^* u.uc) \in |((B \Rightarrow \Sigma) \Rightarrow \Sigma) \Rightarrow (C \Rightarrow \Sigma)| .$$

Since $L_{ex}(B) \subseteq (B \Rightarrow \Sigma) \Rightarrow \Sigma$, we can also 'type' the term as follows:

$$\lambda^* i.\lambda^* c.i(\lambda^* u.uc) \in |L_{ex}(B) \Rightarrow (C \Rightarrow \Sigma)| . \tag{15.2}$$

Looking at the definition of $L_{ex}(B)$ we shall prove

$$\lambda^* i.\lambda^* c.i(\lambda^* u.uc) \in |L_{ex}(B) \Rightarrow B| .$$

Suppose $\theta \, L_{ex}(B) \, \theta'$. Then there is $f \in |B|$ such that

$$\theta \, ((B \Rightarrow \Sigma) \Rightarrow \Sigma) \, \lambda^* v.vf \, ((B \Rightarrow \Sigma) \Rightarrow \Sigma) \, \theta' .$$

We compute:

$$
\begin{aligned}
(\lambda^* i.\lambda^* c.i(\lambda^* u.uc))(\lambda^* v.vf) &= \lambda^* c.(\lambda^* v.vf)(\lambda^* u.uc) \\
&= \lambda^* c.(\lambda^* u.uc)f \\
&= \lambda^* c.fc .
\end{aligned}
$$

From the typing 15.2 we derive:

$$\lambda^* c.\theta(\lambda^* u.uc) \, (C \Rightarrow \Sigma) \, \lambda^* c.fc \, (C \Rightarrow \Sigma) \, \lambda^* c.\theta'(\lambda^* u.uc) .$$

Since $\lambda^* c.fc \, (C \Rightarrow \Sigma) \, f$ and $f \in |B|$, it follows $\lambda^* c.\theta(\lambda^* u.uc) \, B \, \lambda^* c.\theta'(\lambda^* u.uc)$. To show that $e_B^{-1}$ is an iso, we compute the realizers:

$$
\begin{aligned}
(\lambda^* i.\lambda^* c.i(\lambda^* u.uc))(\lambda^* d\lambda^* w.wd)f &= (\lambda^* i.\lambda^* c.i(\lambda^* u.uc))(\lambda^* w.wf) \\
&= \lambda^* c.(\lambda^* w.wf)(\lambda^* u.uc) \\
&= \lambda^* c.fc .
\end{aligned}
$$

Vice versa $(\lambda^* d\lambda^* w.wd)(\lambda^* c.fc) = \lambda^* w.w(\lambda^* c.fc)$.

Next, we complete the construction of the reflector functor. Given $\phi \in |A \Rightarrow B|$, we define $\phi' \in |L_{ex}(A) \Rightarrow L_{ex}(B)|$ as follows:

$$\phi' = \lambda^* i.\lambda^* u.i(\lambda^* a.u(\phi a)) .$$

If $f = [\phi]_{A \Rightarrow B}$ set $L_{ex}(f) = [\phi']_{L_{ex}(A) \Rightarrow L_{ex}(B)}$. Finally, we define for $A \in \Sigma\mathbf{per}$ and $B \in \mathbf{exper}$:

$$
\begin{aligned}
\tau &: \mathbf{per}[A, B] \to \mathbf{per}[L_{ex}(A), B] \quad \tau(f) = e_B^{-1} \circ L_{ex}(f) \\
\tau' &: \mathbf{per}[L_{ex}(A), B] \to \mathbf{per}[A, B] \quad \tau'(g) = g \circ e_A .
\end{aligned}
$$

Computations of the type shown above entail that $\tau$ is a natural isomorphism with inverse $\tau'$.  □

**Theorem 15.6.15** (1) *The categories of extensional per's and complete extensional per's are closed under arbitrary intersections.*

(2) *The category of complete extensional per's (**cexper**) is reflective in **exper**.*

PROOF HINT. (1) If $[A_i] \subseteq [\Sigma^{B_i}]$ for $i \in I$, then $[\bigcap_{i \in I} A_i] \subseteq [\Sigma^{\bigcup_{i \in I} B_i}]$. This shows that **exper** is closed under arbitrary intersections. Note that the fixpoint combinator $\sigma$ defined in the proof of theorem 15.6.9 has a realizer that works uniformly on all ascending sequences. This realizer can be used to prove that $\bigcap_{i \in I} A_i$ is complete if the $A_i$'s are complete.

(2) Suppose $[A] \subseteq [\Sigma^B]$. We define the reflection $L_c(A)$ as the least cexper such that:

$$[A] \subseteq [L_c(A)] \subseteq [\Sigma^B] .$$

(So we add the lub's of ascending sequences in $A$.) If $\phi \Vdash f : A \to A'$ then let $L_c(f)$ be the morphism realized by $\phi$. We adapt the proof of proposition 15.5.10 (realized maps preserve lub's), to show that $L_c(f)$ is well-defined. □

**Exercise 15.6.16** *Show that the category of (complete) extensional per's is cartesian closed.*

To summarize we have proven the following reflections when working over the pca $(\omega, \bullet)$:

$$\textbf{cexper} \subset_> \textbf{exper} \subset_> \Sigma\textbf{per} \subset_> \textbf{per} \subset_> \omega\text{-set} .$$

From left to right: theorem 15.6.15, theorem 15.6.14, theorem 15.4.11, and proposition 15.1.9.

# 15.7 Per's over $D_\infty$ \*

We identify a category of *complete uniform* per's (cuper's), which is a full subcategory of the category of per's when working over a specific $\lambda$-model. Under suitable hypotheses, the quotient space $[A]$ of a cuper is a bifinite domain and domain equations can be solved up to equality. These strong properties will be exploited in the following section 15.8 to model subtyping rules for recursive types.

**Definition 15.7.1** *Let $D$ be the initial solution of the equation*

$$D = (D \to D) + (D \times D)$$

*in the category of cpo's and injection-projection pairs where $+$ is the coalesced sum (cf. example 7.1.16).*

We define $D_0 = \{\bot\}$ and $D_{n+1} = (D_n \to D_n) + (D_n \times D_n)$ with injection-projection pairs $(i_{n\infty}, j_{n\infty}) : D_n \to D$. We remark that $D$ is bifinite. Let $p_n = i_n \circ j_n : D \to D$ (hence $p_n$ is a projection and $im(p_n) = i_n(D_n)$). We note that $in_1 : D \to D \to D$ forms the injection part of an injection-projection pair $(in_1, j_\to)$ (as well as $in_2$, cf. exercise 3.1.3). As usual we define for $d, e \in D$:

$$\langle d, e \rangle = in_2(d, e) \quad de = j_\to(d)(e) \quad d_n = p_n(d) .$$

The application $de$ has the properties required for a pca. We will use the following properties (cf. lemma 3.1.16):

$$\begin{aligned}
\langle d, e \rangle_{n+1} &= \langle d_n, e_n \rangle \\
d_{n+1}e &= d_{n+1}e_n = (de)_n .
\end{aligned}$$

**Exercise 15.7.2** *Prove the properties above following section 3.1.*

In this section $D$ stands for the domain specified in definition 15.7.1. Whenever we speak of a relation we intend by default a binary relation over $D$. For $A \in per_D$ we let $A_n = A \cap (im(p_n) \times im(p_n))$. In order to distinguish indexes from approximants we write indexes in superscript position, e.g., we write $d_n^i = p_n(d^i)$.

**Definition 15.7.3** *A relation $R$ is:*

(1) pointed *if* $\perp_D R \perp_D$.

(2) complete *if for all directed* $X \subseteq A$, $\bigvee X \in A$.[1]

(3) uniform *if* $A \neq \emptyset$ *and* $\forall n \in \omega$ $(d A e \Rightarrow d_n A e_n)$.

A uniform relation is always pointed as $d R e$ implies $\perp = d_0 R e_0 = \perp$. A complete uniform per is called a cuper. The uniformity condition will play an important role in proving that the associated quotient space is algebraic and in solving domain equations.

**Proposition 15.7.4** *The category of complete uniform per's is cartesian closed.*

PROOF HINT. We define the terminal object as $1 = D \times D$. For the product let:

$$d (A_1 \times A_2) e \text{ iff } \pi_i(j_\times(d)) A_i \pi_i(j_\times(e)) \text{ for } i = 1, 2 .$$

The exponent is defined as usual:

$$f B^A g \text{ iff } \forall d, e \ (d A e \Rightarrow f d B g e) .$$

Let us check that $B^A$ is uniform if $A, B$ are. From $\perp B \perp$, $\perp B^A \perp$ follows, since $\forall d \perp d = \perp$. Suppose $f B^A g$ and $d A e$. To show $f_n d B g_n e$ observe:

$$d A e \Rightarrow d_n A e_n \Rightarrow f d_n B g e_n \Rightarrow (f d_n)_n B (g e_n)_n ,$$

and we know $(f d_n)_n = f_{n+1} d$. $\qquad \square$

**Exercise 15.7.5** *Show that cuper's are closed under intersection. Following section 15.2, define an interpretation of system F in cuper's.*

Complete per's (cper's for short) are also closed under arbitrary intersections. Then we can complete a per to a cper as follows.

**Definition 15.7.6 (completion)** *Let $A$ be a per over $D$. The least complete per containing $A$ is defined as:*

$$\underline{A} = \bigcap \{B \mid B \text{ cper and } B \supseteq A\} .$$

In the following we give an inductive characterization of $\underline{A}$.

**Definition 15.7.7** *Let $R$ be a binary relation on $D$. We define:*

$$
\begin{aligned}
Sup(R) &= \{\bigvee X \mid X \text{ directed in } R\} &\text{(directed closure)} \\
TC(R) &= \bigcap \{S \mid S \text{ transitive and } S \supseteq R\} &\text{(transitive closure)} .
\end{aligned}
$$

---

[1] In this section 'complete' has a different meaning than in the previous section.

**Proposition 15.7.8** (1)  *If $R$ is symmetric (pointed) then $Sup(R)$ and $TC(R)$ are symmetric (pointed).*

(2)  *If $A$ is a pointed per then $TC(Sup(A))$ is a pointed per.*

PROOF. Immediate. □

**Definition 15.7.9** *Let $A$ be a pointed per. Define:*

$$
\begin{aligned}
A(0) &= A \\
A(\alpha + 1) &= TC(Sup(A(\alpha))) \\
A(\mu) &= \textstyle\bigcup_{\alpha < \mu} A(\alpha) \qquad (\mu \text{ a limit ordinal}) \ .
\end{aligned}
$$

Let $A$ be a pointed per. Then for cardinality reasons there is some $\beta$ such that $A(\beta) = \underline{A}$. The following lemma points out the effect of the completion process on the function space and on uniformity.

**Lemma 15.7.10** (1)  *If $A$ and $B$ are pointed per's then $B^A \subseteq \underline{B}^{\underline{A}}$.*

(2)  *If $A$ is a uniform per then $\underline{A}$ is a cuper.*

PROOF. (1) By induction on $\alpha$ we show that $B^A \subseteq B(\alpha)^{A(\alpha)}$. The base and limit case are clear. Suppose $f \, B^A \, g$. We distinguish two cases.

• If $d = \bigvee_{i \in I} d^i$ and $e = \bigvee_{i \in I} e^i$, where $\{(d^i, e^i)\}_{i \in I}$ is directed in $A(\alpha)$, then $\{(fd^i, ge^i)\}_{i \in I}$ is directed in $B(\alpha)$ and therefore by continuity of $f$ and $g$:

$$
(fd, ge) = (\bigvee_{i \in I} fd^i, \bigvee_{i \in I} ge^i) \in Sup(B(\alpha)) \ .
$$

• If $d \, TC(Sup(A(\alpha))) \, e$ then we can apply the previous case to each edge of the path connecting $d$ to $e$.

(2) By induction on $\alpha$ we show that $A(\alpha)$ is uniform. The base and limit cases are clear. Suppose $d \, A(\alpha + 1) \, e$. Again we distinguish two cases:

• If $d = \bigvee_{i \in I} d^i$ and $e = \bigvee_{i \in I} e^i$, where $\{(d^i, e^i)\}_{i \in I}$ is directed in $A(\alpha)$, we show $d_n \, Sup(A(\alpha)) \, e_n$ by observing that $(\bigvee_{i \in I} d^i)_n = \bigvee_{i \in I}(d^i)_n$ and $\{((d^i)_n, (e^i)_n)\}_{i \in I}$ is directed in $A(\alpha)$. Hence $Sup(A(\alpha))$ is uniform.

• Suppose $d^1 \, TC(Sup(A(\alpha))) \, d^k$ because $d^1 \, Sup(A(\alpha)) \, d^2 \cdots d^{k-1} \, Sup(A(\alpha)) \, d^k$. Then $(d^1)_n \, Sup(A(\alpha)) \, (d^2)_n \cdots (d^{k-1})_n \, Sup(A(\alpha)) \, (d^k)_n$, as $Sup(A(\alpha))$ is uniform by the previous case. Therefore $(d^1)_n \, TC(Sup(A(\alpha))) \, (d^k)_n$. □

**Exercise 15.7.11** *Show that the category of complete per's is reflective in the category of pointed per's, and that the category of complete uniform per's is reflective in the category of uniform per's.*

The intrinsic preorder $\leq_A$ (cf. definition 15.4.1) on a cuper $A$ induces a preorder on $|A|$ as follows.

**Definition 15.7.12 (induced preorder)** *Let $A$ be a cuper and $d, e \in |A|$. We define:*

$$
d \leq_A e \quad iff \quad [d]_A \leq_A [e]_A \ .
$$

**Exercise 15.7.13** *Show that if $A$ is a complete per then $\leq_A$ is complete.*

In the following we characterize the induced preorder.

**Definition 15.7.14** *Let $A$ be a cuper. Define $\preceq_A = TC(A \cup (\leq_D \cap |A|^2))$.*

**Lemma 15.7.15** *Let $A$ be a cuper. Then $\preceq_A$ is a uniform preorder on $|A|$.*

PROOF. We observe that $A \cup (\leq_D \cap |A|^2)$ is uniform and that transitive closure preserves uniformity (cf. proof of lemma 15.7.10(2)). $\square$

**Lemma 15.7.16** *Let $d \in \mathcal{K}(D)$ be a compact element and let $A$ be a cuper. The following properties hold:*

(1) *The following set is a Scott open: $W(d) = \{e \in D \mid \exists e' \in |A| \ (d \preceq_A e' \leq_D e)\}$.*

(2) *$U(d) = \{[e]_A \mid d \preceq_A e\} \in \Sigma(A)$.*

(3) *$d \preceq_A e$ iff $d \leq_A e$ .*

PROOF. (1) Clearly $W(d)$ is upward closed. Suppose $e = \bigvee_{i \in I} e^i \in W(d)$ for $\{e^i\}_{i \in I}$ directed. From $d \preceq_A e' \leq_D \bigvee_{i \in I} e^i$ we derive:

$$\exists n, j \ (d = d_n \preceq_A e'_n \leq_D (\bigvee_{i \in I} e^i)_n = e^j_n \leq e^j) \ .$$

This follows from the uniformity of $\preceq_A$ and the fact that $im(p_n)$ is finite. We can conclude $e^j \in W(d)$.

(2) It is enough to observe $W(d) \cap |A| = |U(d)|$.

(3) By remark 15.4.10 it follows $d \preceq_A e$ implies $d \leq_A e$. Vice versa, suppose $d \leq_A e$ and *not* $d \preceq_A e$. Build the Scott open $W(d)$ as in (1) and the sub-per $U(d)$ as in (2). Then $[d]_A \in U(d)$ and $[e]_A \notin U(d)$ which contradicts $d \leq_A e$. $\square$

**Theorem 15.7.17** *Let $A$ be a cuper. Then:*

(1) *The induced preorder is the least complete preorder containing $\preceq_A$.*

(2) *The preorder $\leq_A$ is uniform.*

PROOF. We denote with $\preceq_A^c$ the least complete preorder containing $\preceq_A$.

(1) We already know that $\preceq_A \subseteq \leq_A$. Hence $\preceq_A^c \subseteq \leq_A$ since $\leq_A$ is complete. Vice versa, suppose $d \leq_A e$. Then $\forall n \ (d_n \leq_D d \leq_A e)$. So $\forall n \ (d_n \leq_A e)$ and by lemma 15.7.16(3), $\forall n \ (d_n \preceq_A e)$. By completeness $d = \bigvee_{n < \omega} d_n \preceq_A^c e$.

(2) We know from lemma 15.7.15 that $\preceq_A$ is uniform and we can adapt the proof of lemma 15.7.10 to show that the completion process preserves uniformity. $\square$

**Theorem 15.7.18** *Let $A$ be a separated cuper. Then $([A], \leq_A)$ is a bifinite domain.*

PROOF. Clearly $([A], \leq_A)$ is a poset with least element $[\perp]_A$.

• We show that any (infinite) directed set $\{[d^i]_A\}_{i \in I}$ has a lub. Given $J' \subseteq J \subseteq I$ we say that $J'$ is *cofinal* with $J$ if

$$\forall i \in J \ \exists j \in J' \ (d^i \leq_A d^j) \ .$$

Let $X_n = \{e \in D \mid \forall i \in I \; \exists j \in I \; (d^i \leq_A d^j \text{ and } e = d_n^j)\}$, in other words $e \in X_n$ if there is a subset $J$ of $I$, cofinal with $I$, and such that $\forall j \in J \; (e = d_n^j)$. We remark:

- $X_n \subseteq im(p_n) \cap |A|$ is finite since $im(p_n)$ is finite. To show that $X_n \neq \emptyset$, consider $X_n' = \{d_n^i\}_{i \in I} = \{x_1, \ldots, x_k\}$, $(k \geq 1)$. By finiteness and directedness, $X_n'$ has a maximum $x_h$. Let $l \in I$ be such that $x_h = d_n^l$. Now we take $J = \{i \in I \mid d^l \leq_A d^i\}$ which is cofinal with $I$. Moreover $\forall i \in J \; d_n^i = d_n^l = x_h$. Hence $x_h \in X_n$.

- $\forall e \in X_n \; \exists e' \in X_{n+1} \; (e \leq_D e')$. We show this by induction on $n$. If $n = 0$ then $e = \bot$ and every $e'$ will do. If $e \in X_n$ then there is a $J$, cofinal with $I$ such that $J \subseteq I$ and $\forall j \in J \; (d_n^j = e)$. Since $im(p_{n+1})$ is finite there is $J' \subseteq J$ cofinal with $J$ (hence with $I$) and an element $e'$ such that $\forall j \in J' \; (d_{n+1}^j = e')$. Then $e \leq e'$ since $e = d_n^j \leq_D d_{n+1}^j = e'$, and $e' \in X_{n+1}$, by construction.

Hence we can build a sequence $\{e^n\}_{n \in \omega}$ such that $e^n \in X_n$ and $e^n \leq_D e^{n+1}$. By completeness we have $\bigvee_{n \in \omega} e^n \in |A|$. We claim:

$$\bigvee_{i \in I} [d^i]_A = [\bigvee_{n \in \omega} e^n]_A .$$

In the first place we show that $\forall i \in I \; (d^i \leq_A \bigvee_{n \in \omega} e^n)$. By completeness and uniformity it is enough to prove:

$$\forall i \in I \; \forall m \in \omega \; (d_m^i \leq_A \bigvee_{n \in \omega} e^n) .$$

We observe:

$$\forall i \in I \; \forall m \in \omega \; \exists j \in I \; d^i \leq_A d^j \text{ and } d_m^j = e^m .$$

We have $d_m^i \leq_A d_m^j$ by uniformity, and $d_m^j = e^m \leq_D \bigvee e^n$. Finally we note:

$$\forall n \in \omega \; \exists i \in I \; e^n \leq_A d^i ,$$

as $\exists i \; (e^n = d_n^i \leq_D d^i)$. It follows that if $[d]_A$ is an upper bound for $\{[d^i]_A\}_{i \in i}$, then $\bigvee_{n \in \omega} e^n \leq_A d$.

- Next let us prove that the quotient space is $\omega$-algebraic. We claim:

(1) If $d \in \mathcal{K}(D) \cap |A|$ then $[d]_A$ is compact in $([A], \leq_A)$.

Suppose $[d]_A \leq_A \bigvee_{i \in I} [d^i]_A$, for $\{[d^i]_A\}_{i \in I}$ directed. Consider the chain $\{e^n\}_{n \in \omega}$ we have built above. Then $d \leq_A \bigvee_{n \in \omega} e^n$ Hence:

$$\exists m, p, j \; (d = d_m \leq_A (\bigvee_{n \in \omega} e^n)_m = e_m^p \leq_A e^p \leq_A d^j) .$$

(2) $\forall d \in |A| \; ([d]_A = \bigvee_{n \in \omega} [d_n]_A)$.

We observe that $d_n \leq_D d_{n+1}$ implies $d_n \leq_A d_{n+1}$, hence $\{[d_n]_A \mid n \in \omega\}$ is directed. Moreover, if $\forall n \in \omega \; d_n \leq_A e$ then by completeness $\bigvee_{n \in \omega} d_n \leq_A e$.

- To prove that $([A], \leq_A)$ is bifinite we consider the sequence $\{prj^n : A \to A\}_{n \in \omega}$ where $prj^n$ is the function realized by the projection $p_n$.                                    $\square$

**Corollary 15.7.19** *All morphisms in the full subcategory of separated, complete, uniform per's are Scott continuous.*

PROOF. Consider $f : A \to B$ and $\{[d^i]_A\}_{i \in I}$ directed in $[A]$. That $\bigvee_{i \in I} f([d^i]_A)$ exists is guaranteed by the monotonicity of $f$ and theorem 15.7.18. It remains to prove:

$$f(\bigvee_{i \in I} [d^i]_A) \leq_B \bigvee_{i \in I} f([d^i]_A) .$$

Suppose $\phi \Vdash f$ and consider the chain $\{e^n\}_{n \in \omega}$ built in theorem 15.7.18. Then we have $\phi(\bigvee_{n \in \omega} e^n) \cong \bigvee_{n \in \omega} \phi e^n$. Also, since $\forall n \ \exists i \in I \ (e^n \leq_A d^i)$, we have, by monotonicity $\forall n \in \omega \ \exists i \in I \ (\phi e^n \leq_B \phi d^i)$. Hence we can conclude $[\bigvee_{n \in \omega} \phi e^n]_B \leq_B \bigvee_{i \in I} f([d^i]_A)$, by the completeness of $\leq_B$ (cf. exercise 15.7.13). $\square$

Domain equations can be solved in the category of cuper's, by an adaptation of the traditional approach based on injection-projection pairs [AP90]. We follow a more direct path that exposes an interesting metric structure on the space *cuper* of cuper's [Ama91c].

**Definition 15.7.20** *We define a closeness function* $c : cuper^2 \to \omega \cup \{\infty\}$ *as follows:*

$$c(A, B) = \begin{cases} max\{n \mid A_n = B_n\} & \text{if } A \neq B \\ \infty & \text{otherwise} . \end{cases}$$

*The distance* $d : cuper^2 \to R$ *is defined as:*

$$d(A, B) = \begin{cases} 2^{-c(A,B)} & \text{if } A \neq B \\ 0 & \text{otherwise} . \end{cases}$$

We note that $d(A, B) = 0$ iff $A = B$, as $(d, e) \in A \backslash B$ implies $\forall n \ (d_n, e_n) \in A$ by uniformity, and $\exists n \ (d_n, e_n) \notin B$ by completeness. Hence $c(A, B) < \infty$.[2]

**Proposition 15.7.21** (1) *(cuper, d) is a metric space.*

(2) *The space is an* ultra-metric, *that is* $d(A, C) \leq max\{d(A, B), d(B, C)\}$.

(3) *The space is (Cauchy) complete.*

PROOF. The first point is left to the reader. For the second point observe that:

$$(A_n = B_n \text{ and } B_m = C_m) \Rightarrow (A_k = C_k \text{ where } k = min\{n, m\}) .$$

For the third point, let $\{A^i\}_{i < \omega}$ be a Cauchy sequence, that is:

$$\forall \epsilon > 0 \ \exists n_\epsilon \ \exists i, j \geq n_\epsilon \ (d(A^i, A^j) < \epsilon) .$$

We build $A = lim_{i < \omega} A^i$ by stages. We note that:

$$\forall n > 0 \ \exists k_n \ \forall i \geq k_n \ A_n^i \text{ is constant,}$$

as $d(A^i, A^j) < 2^{-n}$ implies $A_n^i = A_n^j$. Let $B^i = A_i^{k_i}$. We choose $k_i \leq k_{i+1}$. Then we observe that $\{B^i\}_{i < \omega}$ is a chain of cuper's with respect to inclusion. Let $B = \bigcup_{i < \omega} B^i$. We claim that $\underline{B} = lim_{i < \omega} A^i$. To this end it is enough to check (cf. definitions 15.7.6 and 15.7.9):

$$\forall i \ \forall \alpha \ B^i = (B(\alpha))_i .$$

---

[2]The ultra-metric considered here resembles the one arising in spaces of infinite labelled trees (see [AN80]).

Hence, suppose $k_n \leq i$, for any $n$. Then $d(\underline{B}, A^i) < 2^{-n}$, as $\underline{B}_n = B^n = A^i_n$. In other terms the completion operation does not add new approximating elements. This can be shown by induction on $\alpha$ (cf. proof lemma 15.7.10). □

An operator $f$ over a metric space $(X, d)$ is *contractive* if there is a constant $c$ such that $0 \leq c < 1$, and:

$$\forall x, y \ d(f(x), f(y)) \leq c \, d(x, y) \ .$$

It turns out that exponent and product type constructors are contractive. It follows that the related recursive type equations have a unique solution in cuper up to equality. This fact is applied in exercise 15.8.5.

**Proposition 15.7.22** *Let $d((A, B), (A', B')) = max\{d(A, A'), d(B, B')\}$. Then:*

(1) $d(B^A, B'^{A'}) \leq (1/2)d((A, B), (A', B'))$.

(2) $d(A \times B, A' \times B') \leq (1/2)d((A, B), (A', B'))$.

PROOF HINT. We note that: $A_k = A'_k$ and $B_k = B'_k \Rightarrow (B^A)_{k+1} = (B'^{A'})_{k+1}$. The factor $(1/2)$ comes from definition 15.7.20 and the properties of the $D_\infty$ models (cf. lemma 3.1.16). □

# 15.8 Interpretation of subtyping *

We present an application of the category of cuper's to the development and interpretation of a theory for the subtyping of recursive types. Let us start with an intuitive explanation of what subtyping is. Various theories of subtyping have been proposed in the literature on software engineering (see, e.g., [Car88, Lis88]). Their principal aim is to support a certain cycle of software development where programs evolve over time as they are restructured and new functionalities are added. Such theories support an incremental design of software systems and establish under which conditions the programmer is allowed to *reuse* previously created modules.

Such reuse may require the introduction of explicit or implicit *coercions* whose effect on the semantics of the program has to be clearly understood by the programmer. A formalization of this concept in the context of *typed languages* can be given in two steps:

- Introduce a relation of subtype denoted by $\leq$. If $\sigma$ and $\tau$ are types, the intuitive interpretation of $\sigma \leq \tau$ (read as $\sigma$ is a subtype of $\tau$) is: every $\sigma$-value can be coerced to a $\tau$-value.

- Specifiy the nature and use of such coercions.

The two basic questions in the design of a typed $\lambda$-calculus with subtypes are whether two types are in the subtype relation, and whether a term has a type.

In the approach to be formalized next we take the view that $\sigma$ is a subtype of $\tau$ if for every term $M$ of type $\sigma$, say $M : \sigma$, and for every possible choice of a run time code $d$ for $M$ (henceforth we will say that $d$ is a realizer for $M$), there is a unique term $N : \tau$ (up to semantic equivalence) that has $d$ among its realizers. Then $N$ is the result of coercing $M$ from the type $\sigma$ to the type $\tau$.

This approach is inspired by model theoretical considerations [BL88] as one can give a precise mathematical meaning to our informal statements in the framework of per models. For the time being let us anticipate the pragmatic consequences of our view of subtyping and coercions:

- Coercions are uniquely determined.

- Coercions do not produce run-time code, hence there is no need for recompilation.

- The specific 'implementation' of a data-type becomes relevant, as subtyping is not invariant under isomorphism. For instance the types $\sigma \times \sigma' \to \tau$ and $\sigma \to (\sigma' \to \tau)$ are isomorphic but they are incomparable with respect to the subtyping relation.

**Definition 15.8.1 (interpretation of subtyping)** *Let $T$ be a type structure (cf. definition 15.3.1). We write $T \models \sigma \leq \tau$ if for all $\eta$, $[\![\sigma]\!]\eta \subseteq [\![\tau]\!]\eta$ (this is the inclusion of per's as relations).*

**Remark 15.8.2** (1) *In the semantic framework developed for type assignment systems in section 15.3 we have that $T \models \sigma \leq \tau$ iff $T \models \lambda x.x : \sigma \to \tau$.*

(2) *Let $A, B$ be per's. If $A \subseteq B$ then there is a (unique) morphism $c : A \to B$ in per that has the identity (formally the combinator skk) among its realizers. We refer to this morphism as the coercion morphism from $A$ to $B$. Incidentally the vice versa also holds: if $c : A \to B$ is a coercion morphism then $A \subseteq B$.*

In order to discuss the impact of this interpretation of subtyping on language design we consider a simply typed $\lambda$-calculus with recursive types, the $\lambda\mu_\leq$-calculus for short. The language of types is defined as follows:

$$tv ::= t \mid s \mid \dots$$
$$\sigma ::= tv \mid \bot \mid \top \mid \sigma \to \tau \mid \mu tv.\sigma .$$

Here $\bot$ and $\top$ are two constant types that denote the least and greatest type in the subtyping relation, respectively. The type $\mu t.\sigma$ is intended to denote the 'least' solution of the equation $t = \sigma(t)$. The language of terms is defined as follows:

$$v ::= x \mid y \mid \dots$$
$$M ::= v \mid \lambda v : \sigma.M \mid MM \mid fold_{\mu tv.\sigma}M \mid unfold_{\mu tv.\sigma}M .$$

Besides the usual rules for the simply typed $\lambda$-calculus we have rules for *folding* and *unfolding* recursive types:

$$\frac{\Gamma \vdash M : \sigma[\mu t.\sigma/t]}{\Gamma \vdash fold_{\mu t.\sigma}M : \mu t.\sigma} \qquad \frac{\Gamma \vdash M : \mu t.\sigma}{\Gamma \vdash unfold_{\mu t.\sigma}M : \sigma[\mu t.\sigma/t]} .$$

Following our informal discussion on subtyping we want to define a formal theory to derive when $\sigma \leq \tau$ and enrich the typing system with the following rule:

$$(Sub) \quad \frac{\Gamma \vdash M : \sigma \quad \sigma \leq \tau}{\Gamma \vdash M : \tau} .$$

We introduce in figure 15.3 a formal theory for deriving subtyping judgments on recursive types. The theory is composed of two groups of rules:

(1) The first group defines the least congruence induced by the rules $(\mu\text{-}\bot)$, $(fold)$, and $(\mu_\downarrow)$. In the $(\mu_\downarrow)$ rule the condition $\sigma \downarrow t$ is read as $t$ is *contractive* in $\sigma$ and means that $\sigma$ can be rewritten by unfolding the recursion into a type of the shape $\sigma_1 \to \sigma_2$. For instance $\mu s.(t \to s) \downarrow t$ because by unfolding $s$ we obtain $t \to (\mu s.(t \to s))$, but $\mu s.t \not\downarrow t$, because by unfolding $s$ we obtain $t$. The rules for type equivalence are inspired

$$(refl) \quad \frac{}{\sigma = \sigma} \qquad\qquad (sym) \quad \frac{\sigma = \tau}{\tau = \sigma}$$

$$(tr) \quad \frac{\sigma = \tau \quad \tau = \rho}{\sigma = \rho} \qquad\qquad (\to_=) \quad \frac{\sigma = \sigma \quad \tau = \tau'}{\sigma \to \tau = \sigma' \to \tau'}$$

$$(\mu_=) \quad \frac{\sigma = \tau}{\mu t.\sigma = \mu t.\tau} \qquad\qquad (\mu\text{-}\bot) \quad \frac{}{\mu t.t = \bot}$$

$$(fold) \quad \frac{}{\mu t.\sigma = \sigma[\mu t.\sigma/t]} \qquad (\mu_\downarrow) \quad \frac{\sigma[\tau/t] = \tau \quad \sigma[\tau'/t] = \tau' \quad \sigma \downarrow t}{\tau = \tau'}$$

Rules for equality

$$(eq) \quad \frac{\sigma = \tau}{\Delta \vdash \sigma \leq \tau} \qquad\qquad (tr) \quad \frac{\Delta \vdash \sigma \leq \tau \quad \Delta \vdash \tau \leq \rho}{\Delta \vdash \sigma \leq \rho}$$

$$(Asmp) \quad \frac{t \leq s \in \Delta}{\Delta \vdash t \leq s}$$

$$(\bot) \quad \frac{}{\Delta \vdash \bot \leq \sigma} \qquad\qquad (\top) \quad \frac{}{\Delta \vdash \sigma \leq \top}$$

$$(\to) \quad \frac{\Delta \vdash \sigma' \leq \sigma \quad \Delta \vdash \tau \leq \tau'}{\Delta \vdash \sigma \to \tau \leq \sigma' \to \tau'} \quad (\mu) \quad \frac{\Delta, t \leq s \vdash \sigma \leq \tau \quad t \notin FV(\tau), \ s \notin FV(\sigma)}{\Delta \vdash \mu t.\sigma \leq \mu s.\tau}$$

Rules for subtyping

Figure 15.3: Subtyping recursive types

by classical results on regular languages (see, e.g., [Sal66]). The $(\mu_\downarrow)$ rule should be regarded as a syntactic version of Banach's theorem (cf. section 15.7).

(2) The second group of rules is used to derive proper inequalities. The basic judgment has the shape $\Delta \vdash \sigma \leq \tau$, where $\Delta \equiv t_1 \leq s_1, \ldots, t_n \leq s_n$, $t_i, s_i$ are type variables, and $n \geq 0$. The rule $(\to)$ resembles the rule $(\to_2)$ introduced for filter models in definition 3.3.1. The intuition for the premise of the rule $(\mu)$ is that the following holds: for all per's $A, B$, if $A \subseteq B$ then $[\![\sigma]\!][A/t] \subseteq [\![\tau]\!][B/s]$.

**Exercise 15.8.3** *Derive the following judgments:*

$$\begin{aligned}
\mu t.(s \to t) &= \mu t.(s \to (s \to t)) \\
\mu t.(t \to (t \to t)) &= \mu t.((t \to t) \to t) \\
\mu s.(\top \to s) &\leq \bot \to (\mu s.(s \to s)) .
\end{aligned}$$

Next we interpret the $\lambda\mu_\leq$-calculus in cuper's.

**Definition 15.8.4** *The type interpretation is parametric in* $\eta : Tvar \to cuper$ *and is defined as follows:*

$$
\begin{aligned}
[\![\perp]\!]\eta &= \{(\perp_D, \perp_D)\} \\
[\![\top]\!]\eta &= D \times D \\
[\![\sigma \to \tau]\!]\eta &= ([\![\tau]\!]\eta)^{[\![\sigma]\!]\eta} \\
[\![\mu t.\sigma]\!]\eta &= Fix(\lambda A.[\![\sigma]\!]\eta[A/t])
\end{aligned}
$$

$$
Fix(f) = \begin{cases}
x & \text{if } f \text{ is contractive and } f(x) = x \\
\{(\perp_D, \perp_D)\} & \text{if } f = id \\
\text{undefined} & \text{otherwise} .
\end{cases}
$$

**Exercise 15.8.5** *Verify that the type interpretation is always defined, that is all definable functions are either contractive (cf. proposition 15.7.22) or the identity.*

**Definition 15.8.6** *We write* $t_1 \leq s_1, \ldots, t_n \leq s_n \models \sigma \leq \tau$ *if for all type environments* $\eta$, *if* $\eta(t_i) \subseteq \eta(s_i)$ *for* $i = 1, \ldots, n$ *then* $[\![\sigma]\!]\eta \subseteq [\![\tau]\!]\eta$.

**Theorem 15.8.7** *If* $\Delta \vdash \sigma \leq \tau$ *then* $\Delta \models \sigma \leq \tau$.

PROOF HINT. By induction on the length of the derivation. We have already observed that rule $(\mu_\downarrow)$ is a syntactic version of Banach's theorem. The only rule that deserves an additional comment is $(\mu)$. If $f$ is contractive or the identity and $C$ is the least cuper then the Cauchy sequence $\{f^n(C)\}_{n<\omega}$ converges to $Fix(f)$ (cf. exercise 1.2.7). Suppose $f, g$ are contractive or the identity, the semantic reading of the rule goes as follows:

$$
\frac{\forall A, B \ (A \subseteq B \Rightarrow f(A) \subseteq g(B))}{Fix(f) \subseteq Fix(g)} .
$$

From the premises we can prove by induction $f^n(C) \subseteq g^n(C)$. From this we can draw the conclusion $Fix(f) \subseteq Fix(g)$. □

**Exercise 15.8.8** *Prove that the following inequality holds in the cuper's interpretation but is not derivable in the system (with an empty context)* $\sigma \to \sigma' \leq \tau \to \top$. *(It is shown in [AC93] that the system extended with the inequality above is complete with respect to a modified interpretation.)*

The *term interpretation* follows the interpretation of system F in the category of per's defined in section 15.2. The constants *fold* and *unfold* are interpreted by the identity, as recursive equations are solved up to equality. More results on this theory of subtyping can be found in [AC93]. Two important points that hint to the practical relevance of the theory sketched above are:

(1) It is decidable if $\emptyset \vdash \sigma \leq \tau$. (The decision algorithm can be made efficient [KPS93].)

(2) There is an algorithm that decides if a term is typable, and if this is the case the algorithm returns the least type that can be assigned to the term.

# 16
# Functions and processes

The functional view of computation finds perhaps its most serious limitation in the analysis of concurrent systems (cf. chapter 9). The challenge is then to cope with the problems offered by concurrent systems while retaining some of the mathematically brilliant ideas and techniques developed in the pure functional setting.

In this chapter we introduce a simple extension of CCS known as $\pi$-calculus. The $\pi$-calculus is a rather minimal calculus whose initial purpose was to represent the notion of name or reference in a concurrent computing setting. It turns out that the $\pi$-calculus allows us for simple encodings of various functional and concurrent models. It can then be used as a privileged tool to understand in which sense functional computation can be embedded in a concurrent model.

Section 16.1 is dedicated to the introduction of some basic theory of the $\pi$-calculus. In section 16.2, we illustrate the expressive power of the $\pi$-calculus by encoding into it a concurrent functional language, called $\lambda_{\|}$-calculus, that can be regarded as the kernel of *concurrent* extensions of the ML programming language such as LCS, CML and Facile where an integration of functional and concurrent programming is attempted. In section 16.3, we study the adequacy of the encoding of the $\lambda_{\|}$-calculus in the $\pi$-calculus.

This chapter presents an operational phenomenon but fails to give a denotational account of it. As this book goes to press, there have been a few attempts in this direction [FMS96, Sta96]. It seems too early to say if they can provide useful insights.

## 16.1 $\pi$-calculus

In chapter 9 we have presented a calculus of processes, CCS, in which interaction arises as *rendezvous* synchronization on communication channels. This computation paradigm is enhanced in the $\pi$-calculus (see [MPW92], after [AZ84, EN86]) by allowing:

- channel names as transmissible values.

- the generation of new channels.

Because of these essential features the development of the $\pi$-calculus theory along the lines known for CCS (labelled transition system and related bisimulation) leads to a series of complications which can be hard to appreciate for a beginner. For this reason we follow a different approach. We present first the $\pi$-calculus as a *programming language*. Technically this means to specify abstractly how a $\pi$-calculus program can be evaluated and to explain how this evaluation can be implemented. Once a reasonably clear implementation model has been sketched we introduce a notion of observation as the capability of a process to *commit* to a certain communication and we derive a notion of *barbed equivalence* on processes.

Barbed equivalence is a natural relation by which two $\pi$-terms can be compared [MS92]. Unfortunately it is difficult to relate two processes using this approach, as we always have to work with arbitrary contexts. This motivates the quest for a characterization of barbed equivalence which is better suited to mechanical verification. Towards this end, we introduce a labelled transition system and a related notion of $\pi$-*bisimulation*. A central result, whose proof we present here, says that $\pi$-bisimulation and barbed equivalence coincide. As an application of this characterization we show the decidability of equivalence for a special class of *finite control* processes.

**The language.** We suppose that there is a countable collection $Ch$ of *channel names* that we denote with $a, b, \ldots$ *Processes* are specified by the following grammar:

$$n \; ::= a \mid b \mid \ldots$$
$$P \; ::= 0 \mid \bar{a}n.P \mid n(n).P \mid \nu n\, P \mid (P \mid P) \mid [n = n]P \mid (\gamma.P + \cdots + \gamma.P) \mid A(\vec{n}) \, .$$

$0$ is the process which is terminated and that can be garbage collected. Usually we omit writing $0$, e.g., $\bar{a}b$ stands for $\bar{a}b.0$.

$\bar{a}b.P$ is the process that sends the channel name $b$ on the channel $a$ and becomes $P$.

$a(b).P$ is the process that receives a channel name, say $c$, on the channel $a$ and becomes $P[b/c]$. The formal parameter $b$ is bound in $P$, in general bound names can be renamed.

$\nu a\, P$ is the process that creates a new name different from all the existing ones and becomes $P$. The name $a$ is bound in $P$. We denote with $FV(P)$ the collection of names occurring free in $P$.

$(P \mid P)$ is the parallel composition of two processes.

$[a = b]P$ is the matching construct. If the match holds then execute $P$ else terminate.

$\gamma_1.P + \cdots + \gamma_n.P$ is a *guarded sum*, where all alternative processes commit on an input/output action. The prefix $\gamma$ is an abbreviation for an input/output guard, i.e., $\gamma ::= \bar{n}n \mid n(n)$. When writing processes, guarded sum has precedence over parallel composition.

We denote with $A, B, \ldots$ agent identifiers. For every agent identifier we assume that there is a unique defining equation $A(a_1, \ldots, a_n) = P$ where all free names in $P$ are included in $\{a_1, \ldots, a_n\}$ and all occurrences of an agent identifier in $P$

$$\overline{(\overline{a}b.P + P') \mid (a(c).Q + Q') \to P \mid Q[b/c]} \qquad \overline{[a = a]P \to P}$$

$$\frac{P \to Q}{D[P] \to D[Q]} \text{ where } D ::= [\,] \mid D \mid P \mid \nu n\, D \qquad \frac{P \equiv P' \quad P' \to Q' \quad Q' \equiv Q}{P \to Q}$$

Figure 16.1: Reduction for the π-calculus

are preceded by an input/output prefix. Note that the equations may be mutually defined, hence a process definition may eventually depend on a *system* of equations. We require that this system is finite.

**Structural congruence and reduction.** The basic computation rule in π-calculus is:

$$\overline{a}b.P \mid a(c).Q \to P \mid Q[b/c] \ . \tag{16.1}$$

Unlabelled reductions like those in rule 16.1 represent internal communications and correspond to the τ-transitions in CCS. The reduction rule 16.1 is not sufficient to represent all possible internal communications. In order to have a greater flexibility we define a relation ≡, called *structural congruence*, which is the smallest congruence on processes generated by the following equations:

- Renaming: $c(a).P \equiv c(b).P[b/a]$ for $b \notin FV(c(a).P)$, and $\nu a\, Q \equiv \nu b\, Q[b/a]$, for $b \notin FV(\nu a\, Q)$. We denote with $\equiv_\alpha$ the congruence that identifies terms differing only by the name of their bound variables.

- Parallel composition is an associative and commutative operator with 0 as identity.

- The order of the guards in the sum is irrelevant. By convention whenever we write $\gamma.P + Q$ we intend that $Q$ denotes the rest of the guard, if there is any.

- Restriction commutations: $\nu a\, P \mid Q \equiv \nu a\,(P \mid Q)$, for $a \notin FV(Q)$.

- Equation unfolding: any agent identifier can be replaced by its definition.

**Remark 16.1.1** *Every term without matching is structurally congruent to a term:*

$$\nu a_1 \ldots \nu a_k\, (Q_1 \mid \cdots \mid Q_m),$$

*where $Q_i$ is a guard, namely $Q_i \equiv \gamma_{i,1}.P_{i,1} + \cdots + \gamma_{i,n_i}.P_{i,n_i}$, for $i = 1, \ldots, m$ and $k, m, n_i \geq 0$ (conventionally take the parallel composition equal to 0 if $m = 0$).*

The reduction relation is presented in figure 16.1. In the first place, the reduction rule 16.1 is generalized in order to take into account guarded sums. Second, it is assumed that rewriting is modulo structural congruence, and third, reduction can be performed in certain contexts $D$ (note that it is not possible to reduce under an input/output guard, a bit like in the weak $\lambda$-calculus where it is not possible to reduce under $\lambda$-abstraction, see section 8.3). There is also a rule taking care of matching. In order to understand the role of the various rules we invite the reader to consider the following examples.

- Channel transmission: a process sends on the channel $b$ a channel name $a$ which allows interaction with a process receiving on $a$.

$$\nu a \, (\nu b \, (\overline{b}a \mid b(c).\overline{c}e) \mid a(d).R') \to^+ \nu a \, \nu b \, R'[e/d] \, . \tag{16.2}$$

- Scope intrusion: when receiving a channel under the scope of a restriction, one has to avoid name clashes (on $a$ in the example).

$$\overline{b}a \mid \nu a \, (b(c).Q \mid S) \to \nu a' \, (Q[a'/a][a/c] \mid S[a'/a]) \quad (a' \text{ fresh }) \, . \tag{16.3}$$

- Scope extrusion: when transmitting a restricted name, the scope of restriction has to be enlarged to the receiving process, this phenomenon is called scope extrusion (in the example $a$ is the extruded name).

$$\nu a \, (\overline{b}a.P \mid R) \mid b(c).Q \to \nu a \, (P \mid R \mid Q[a/c]) \quad (a \notin FV(\nu c \, Q)) \, . \tag{16.4}$$

**Implementation.** In this section we define an abstract machine which addresses two implementation problems: substitution and new name generation. These problems are specific to the $\pi$-calculus as opposed to CCS.

In order to implement substitution we can import the ideas already developed for environment machines (cf. section 8.3), hence reduction is defined on closures which are pairs of code and environment. Name generation requires a new idea. In the reduction rules of the $\pi$-calculus, name generation is treated implicitly via $\alpha$-renaming and structural congruence, in an implementation this is not admissible.

We describe an *abstract* machine as a term rewriting system modulo an associative and commutative operator representing parallel composition. Guarded sum, matching, and agent definitions are omitted in the following discussion. The machine can be extended to deal with these features without particular difficulties.

- *Channels* are represented as strings.

- *Process code* syntax differs from process syntax by the insertion of a commitment operator $\succ$. This operator is used to represent the fact that the evaluation of the prefix is terminated and the process is ready to commit on a communication.

$$C ::= 0 \mid \overline{n}n.C \mid n(n).C \mid \nu n \, C \mid (C \mid C) \mid \overline{n}n \succ C \mid n(n) \succ C \, .$$

- An *environment* $\rho$ is a total function mapping channel names to channel names. Initially the environment is the identity function. The substitution operation is not carried out but it is recorded in the environment. The *actual* value of a channel name is obtained by application of the environment function.

- A *channel generator* is a string in $\{0, 1\}^*$, we denote with $\theta$ a generic string and with $\epsilon$ the empty string. We suppose that there is an injective function $ch : \{0, 1\}^* \to Ch$ such that $Ch \backslash im(ch)$ is infinite.

$$
\begin{aligned}
(0, \rho, \theta) &\rightarrow 1 \\
(C \mid C', \rho, \theta) &\rightarrow (C, \rho, \theta 0) \parallel (C', \rho, \theta 1) \\
(\nu a\, C, \rho, \theta) &\rightarrow (C, \rho[ch(\theta)/a], \theta 0) \\
(\overline{a}b.C, \rho, \theta) &\rightarrow (\overline{a'}b' \succ C, \rho, \theta) \quad (\text{if } \rho(a) = a' \text{ and } \rho(b) = b') \\
(a(b).C, \rho, \theta) &\rightarrow (a'(b) \succ C, \rho, \theta) \quad (\text{if } \rho(a) = a') \\
(\overline{a}b \succ C, \rho, \theta) \parallel (a(c) \succ C', \rho', \theta') &\rightarrow (C, \rho, \theta) \parallel (C', \rho'[b/c], \theta')
\end{aligned}
$$

Figure 16.2: An environment machine for the π-calculus

- A *process descriptor* is a triple $(C, \rho, \theta)$.

- We suppose that there is an associative and commutative operator $\parallel$ on process descriptors having 1 as identity. This is the only structural congruence on which we rely.

- The process $P$ is *compiled* into $(P, id, \epsilon)$. Initially all names in $P$ are distinct from a name $ch(\theta)$, for any $\theta$.

With the conventions above, an environment machine to reduce π-terms is described in figure 16.2 as a finite collection of term rewriting rules.

**Exercise 16.1.2** *Reduce* $(\nu a\,\overline{b}a.a(a).\overline{a}b.0 \mid a(c).\overline{c}d.d(c).0, id, \epsilon)$.

**Exercise\* 16.1.3** *(1) The machine in figure 16.2 solves at once the substitution and the name generation problem. Describe a simpler machine which handles the name generation problem only, leaving substitution as a meta-operation. (2) Formulate a theorem that relates reduction in the π-calculus to reductions in the abstract machine specified in (1).*

There are other implementation problems that relate to concurrent languages in general and that will not be studied here. For instance, we may note that the machine described in figure 16.2 reduces modulo associativity and commutativity. Algebraic manipulations are needed in order to bring in a contiguous position two process descriptors committed on dual communications. Moreover the selection of the term to be reduced next is non-deterministic. In practice we need an efficient and distributed way to perform communications. This task may include:

- The definition of a scheduler to order the jobs' execution on a processor.

- The introduction of data structures to know which process wants to communicate on which channel.

- The execution of non-trivial protocols that guarantee a coherent selection of communications avoiding deadlock (see, e.g., [BS83]).

**Barbed equivalence.** We now turn to the issue of stating when two processes are equivalent. We postulate that what can be observed of a process is its capability of committing (engaging) on an input/output communication on a visible (i.e., non-restricted) channel. From this a notion of process equivalence is derived as follows.

**Definition 16.1.4 (commitment)** *A relation of immediate commitment* $P \downarrow \beta$ *where* $\beta ::= n \mid \bar{n}$ *is defined as follows:*

$$P \downarrow c \quad if \quad P \equiv \nu\vec{c}(c(a).P + P' \mid Q) \quad c \notin \{\vec{c}\}$$
$$P \downarrow \bar{c} \quad if \quad P \equiv \nu\vec{c}(\bar{c}d.P + P' \mid Q) \quad c \notin \{\vec{c}\} \ .$$

*Moreover, define* $\rightarrow^*$ *as the reflexive and transitive closure of the reduction relation* $\rightarrow$. *Then a* weak commitment *relation* $P \downarrow_* \beta$ *is defined as:*

$$P \downarrow_* \beta \ if \ \exists P' \ (P \rightarrow^* P' \quad and \quad P' \downarrow \beta) \ .$$

**Definition 16.1.5 (barbed (bi-)simulation)** *A binary relation* $S$ *between processes is a* (strong) barbed simulation *if* $PSQ$ *implies:*

$$\forall P' \ (P \rightarrow P' \ \Rightarrow \ \exists Q' \ (Q \rightarrow Q' \ and \ P'SQ')) \ and$$
$$\forall \beta \ (P \downarrow \beta \ \Rightarrow \ Q \downarrow \beta) \ .$$

$S$ *is a* barbed bisimulation *if* $S$ *and* $S^{-1}$ *are barbed simulations. The greatest barbed bisimulation is denoted with* $\overset{\bullet}{\sim}$. *By replacing everywhere* $\rightarrow$ *by* $\rightarrow^*$ *and* $\downarrow$ *by* $\downarrow_*$ *one obtains the notion of* weak barbed bisimulation. *The greatest weak barbed bisimulation is denoted with* $\overset{\bullet}{\approx}$.[1]

The relation $\overset{\bullet}{\sim}$ (or $\overset{\bullet}{\approx}$) fails to be a congruence, in particular $P \overset{\bullet}{\sim} P'$ does not imply $P \mid Q \overset{\bullet}{\sim} P' \mid Q$ (already in CCS, $a.b \overset{\bullet}{\sim} a.c$ does *not* imply $a.b \mid \bar{a} \overset{\bullet}{\sim} a.c \mid \bar{a}$). This motivates the introduction of the following definition.

**Definition 16.1.6 (barbed equivalence)** *We define a relation* $\sim$ *of strong barbed equivalence and a relation* $\approx$ *of weak barbed equivalence as follows:*

$$P \sim P' \quad if \quad \forall Q \ (P \mid Q \overset{\bullet}{\sim} P' \mid Q)$$
$$P \approx P' \quad if \quad \forall Q \ (P \mid Q \overset{\bullet}{\approx} P' \mid Q) \ .$$

**Exercise\* 16.1.7** *Which operators of the* $\pi$-calculus preserve $\sim$ and $\approx$? Hint: Theorem 16.1.18 can be helpful as it provides a characterization of strong barbed equivalence.

---

[1] The adjective barbed relates to a pictorial representation of the reductions and commitments of a process. In this representation the commitments are the barbs and the internal reductions are the wires connecting the barbs.

**Labelled transition system.** The aim is to define a labelled transition system (lts) (cf. section 9.2) for the π-calculus which describes not only the computations that a process can perform autonomously (the τ transitions) but also the computations that the process can perform with an appropriate cooperation from the environment.

**Definition 16.1.8 (actions)** *We postulate that a process can perform five kinds of actions* α:

$$\alpha ::= \tau \mid nn \mid \bar{n}n \mid n \mid \bar{n} \ .$$

We can provide the following intuition for the meaning of each action:

- The τ action corresponds to internal reduction as defined in figure 16.1.

- The $cd$ and $\bar{c}d$ actions are complementary and they correspond, respectively, to the input and the output on channel $c$ of a 'global' channel name $d$.

- The $c$ and $\bar{c}$ actions are also complementary and they correspond, respectively, to the input and the output on channel $c$ of a 'new' channel.

The notions of 'global' and 'new' are intended as relative to a given collection of channels which is visible to the environment. To represent this collection we introduce next the notion of context. It is possible to define the lts without referring to contexts as shown later in figure 16.4. At first, we prefer to stick to a more redundant notation which allows for an intuitive explanation of the rules.

**Definition 16.1.9 (context)** *A context* Γ *is a finite, possibly empty, set of channel names. We write* $c_1, \ldots, c_n$ $(n \geq 0)$ *for the set* $\{c_1, \ldots, c_n\}$, *and* Γ, $c$ *for the set* $\Gamma \cup \{c\}$ *where* $c \notin \Gamma$.

To consider a process in a context we write $\Gamma \vdash P$. It is always intended that the context contains all channel names free in $P$. We are now ready to define an lts as an inference system for judgments of the shape $(\Gamma \vdash P) \xrightarrow{\alpha} (\Gamma' \vdash P')$, to be read as the process $P$ in the context $\Gamma$ can make an action $\alpha$ and become $P'$ in the context $\Gamma'$. The actions $\tau$, $cd$ and $\bar{c}d$ leave the context unchanged whereas the actions $c$ and $\bar{c}$ enrich the context with a new channel.

The labelled transition system is presented in figure 16.3. The symmetric version of the rules $(sync)$, $(sync_{ex})$, and $(comp)$ is omitted. The only 'structural rule' is α-renaming. In order to keep the system finitely branching we suppose that the collection of channel names $Ch$ is well-ordered and we let $fst$ be a function that returns the least element in a non-empty set of channel names. In practice we pick the first name that does not occur in the current context (and hence is not free in the process at hand).

The first six rules are the most important, and they can be divided in two groups. The first group is composed of the rules $(out)$, $(in)$, and $(synch)$ and it concerns global names, i.e., names in the context $\Gamma$. The second group is composed of the rules $(out_{ex})$, $(in_{ex})$, and $(synch_{ex})$ and it concerns new names, i.e., names which are *not* in the context $\Gamma$.

To some extent all that matters in the computation of the transitions are the *distinctions* between channel names. In particular note that the choice of the new

$$(out) \quad \frac{}{\Gamma \vdash \bar{c}d.P \xrightarrow{\bar{c}d} \Gamma \vdash P} \qquad (in) \quad \frac{d \in \Gamma}{\Gamma \vdash c(a).P \xrightarrow{cd} \Gamma \vdash P[d/a]}$$

$$(out_{ex}) \quad \frac{\Gamma, c \vdash P \xrightarrow{\bar{d}c} \Gamma, c \vdash P' \quad c = fst(Ch\backslash\Gamma)}{\Gamma \vdash \nu c\,P \xrightarrow{\bar{d}} \Gamma, c \vdash P'} \qquad (in_{ex}) \quad \frac{a = fst(Ch\backslash\Gamma)}{\Gamma \vdash c(a).P \xrightarrow{c} \Gamma, a \vdash P}$$

$$(sync) \quad \frac{\Gamma \vdash P \xrightarrow{\bar{d}c} \Gamma \vdash P' \quad \Gamma \vdash Q \xrightarrow{dc} \Gamma \vdash Q'}{\Gamma \vdash P \mid Q \xrightarrow{\tau} \Gamma \vdash P' \mid Q'}$$

$$(sync_{ex}) \quad \frac{\Gamma \vdash P \xrightarrow{\bar{d}} \Gamma, c \vdash P' \quad \Gamma \vdash Q \xrightarrow{d} \Gamma, c \vdash Q'}{\Gamma \vdash P \mid Q \xrightarrow{\tau} \Gamma \vdash \nu c\,(P' \mid Q')}$$

$$(rename) \quad \frac{P \equiv_\alpha P' \quad \Gamma \vdash P' \xrightarrow{\alpha} \Gamma' \vdash Q' \quad Q' \equiv_\alpha Q}{\Gamma \vdash P \xrightarrow{\alpha} \Gamma' \vdash Q}$$

$$(\nu) \quad \frac{\Gamma, c \vdash P \xrightarrow{\alpha} \Gamma, c, \Gamma' \vdash P' \quad c = fst(Ch\backslash\Gamma) \quad c \text{ not in } \alpha}{\Gamma \vdash \nu c\,P \xrightarrow{\alpha} \Gamma, \Gamma' \vdash \nu c\,P'}$$

$$(comp) \quad \frac{\Gamma \vdash P \xrightarrow{\alpha} \Gamma' \vdash P'}{\Gamma \vdash P \mid Q \xrightarrow{\alpha} \Gamma' \vdash P' \mid Q} \qquad (sum) \quad \frac{\Gamma \vdash \gamma_i.P_i \xrightarrow{\alpha} \Gamma' \vdash P'}{\Gamma \vdash \gamma_1.P_1 + \cdots + \gamma_n.P_n \xrightarrow{\alpha} \Gamma' \vdash P'}$$

$$(match) \quad \frac{}{\Gamma \vdash [c = c]P \xrightarrow{\tau} \Gamma \vdash P} \qquad (fix) \quad \frac{\Gamma \vdash P[\bar{c}/\bar{a}] \xrightarrow{\alpha} \Gamma' \vdash P' \quad A(\bar{a}) = P}{\Gamma \vdash A(\bar{c}) \xrightarrow{\alpha} \Gamma' \vdash P'}$$

Figure 16.3: A labelled transition system for the $\pi$-calculus

names is completely arbitrary. We invite the reader to carry on the following exercise which is useful in the proof of the following propositions.

**Exercise 16.1.10** *(1) Let $\sigma$ be an injective substitution on channel names. Relate transitions of $\Gamma \vdash P$ and $\sigma\Gamma \vdash \sigma P$. (2) Relate the transitions of $\Gamma \vdash P$ and $\Gamma' \vdash P$ for $FV(P) \subseteq \Gamma \subseteq \Gamma'$.*

**Definition 16.1.11** *A binary relation $S$ on processes is a (strong) $\pi$-simulation if whenever $P\,S\,Q$ and $\Gamma = FV(P \mid Q)$ the following holds:*

$$\forall P'\ (\Gamma \vdash P \xrightarrow{\alpha} \Gamma' \vdash P') \ \Rightarrow \ \exists Q'\ (\Gamma \vdash Q \xrightarrow{\alpha} \Gamma' \vdash Q' \text{ and } P'\,S\,Q')\,.$$

*The relation $S$ is a $\pi$-bisimulation if $S$ and $S^{-1}$ are $\pi$-simulations. We denote with $\sim_\pi$ the greatest $\pi$-bisimulation.*

**Definition 16.1.12** *Let $Pr$ be the collection of processes. We define a function $\mathcal{F} : \mathcal{P}(Pr \times Pr) \to \mathcal{P}(Pr \times Pr)$ by $P\,\mathcal{F}(S)\,Q$ if*

$$\forall \alpha, P', \Gamma, \Gamma'\ (\Gamma = FV(P \mid Q) \text{ and } \Gamma \vdash P \xrightarrow{\alpha} \Gamma' \vdash P')$$
$$\Rightarrow \ \exists Q'\ (\Gamma \vdash Q \xrightarrow{\alpha} \Gamma' \vdash Q' \text{ and } P'SQ')\,,$$

*and symmetrically.*

**Exercise 16.1.13** *Let $\sim^0 = Pr^2$, $\sim^{\kappa+1} = \mathcal{F}(\sim^\kappa)$, and $\sim^\lambda = \bigcap_{\kappa<\lambda} \sim^\kappa$, for $\lambda$ limit ordinal. Prove that: (1) $\mathcal{F}$ is monotonic. (2) $S$ is a $\pi$-bisimulation iff $S \subseteq \mathcal{F}(S)$. (3) If $\{X_i\}_{i \in I}$ is a codirected set, then $\mathcal{F}(\bigcap_{i \in I} X_i) = \bigcap_{i \in I} \mathcal{F}(X_i)$. (4) The greatest $\pi$-bisimulation $\sim_\pi$ exists and coincides with $\sim^\omega$ (cf. proposition 9.2.8).*

**Proposition 16.1.14** *Let $\sigma$ be an injective substitution on names. Then for any processes $P, Q$, $P \sim_\pi Q$ iff $\sigma P \sim_\pi \sigma Q$.*

PROOF HINT. We show that the following relation is a $\pi$-bisimulation:

$$\{(P, Q) \mid \exists \sigma \text{ injective on } FV(P \mid Q) \text{ such that } \sigma P \sim_\pi \sigma Q\} . \qquad \square$$

**Exercise 16.1.15** *In the definition of $\pi$-bisimulation we consider transitions with respect to a context $\Gamma = FV(P \mid Q)$. This requirement can be relaxed. Consider a sharpened definition of the functional $\mathcal{F}$, say $\mathcal{F}_\sharp$, where the condition '$\Gamma = FV(P \mid Q)$' is replaced by the condition '$\Gamma \supseteq FV(P \mid Q)$'. Let $\sim_\sharp$ be the greatest fixpoint of the functional $\mathcal{F}_\sharp$. Check that $\sim_\pi = \sim_\sharp$. Hint: $\sim_\pi \subseteq \mathcal{F}_\sharp(\sim_\pi)$.*

**Exercise 16.1.16** *(1) Show that all structurally congruent processes are $\pi$-bisimilar. (2) Which operators preserve $\pi$-bisimulation? Hint: $\pi$-bisimulation is not preserved by the input prefix, that is, $P \sim_\pi Q$ does not imply $a(b).P \sim_\pi a(b).Q$. (3) Define a notion of weak $\pi$-bisimulation (cf. definition 9.2.15).*

We hint at a presentation of the labelled transition system which does not use contexts. We suppose that the actions are redefined as follows:

$$\alpha ::= \tau \mid nn \mid \overline{n}n \mid n(n) \mid \overline{n}(n) .$$

This differs from definition 16.1.8 because the *new* name $b$ that is being received or emitted is explicitly indicated in $a(b), \overline{a}(b)$ (which replace, respectively, the actions $a, \overline{a}$). The name $b$ is bound in these actions. More generally we define the following functions on actions, where $fn$ stands for free names and $bn$ stands for bound names.

$$fn(\tau) = \emptyset \quad fn(\overline{a}(b)) = fn(a(b)) = \{a\} \quad fn(\overline{a}b) = fn(ab) = \{a, b\}$$
$$bn(\tau) = \emptyset \quad bn(\overline{a}(b)) = bn(a(b)) = \{b\} \quad bn(\overline{a}b) = bn(ab) = \emptyset .$$

We set $n(\alpha) = bn(\alpha) \cup fn(\alpha)$. The labelled transition system is defined in figure 16.4, where the symmetric version of the rules $(sync)$, $(sync_{ex})$, and $(comp)$ is omitted. Comparing with the system in figure 16.3 we note that the rules are in bijective correspondence with those of the new system. Name clashes in the new system are avoided by inserting a suitable side condition in the rule $(comp)$. In a sense we trade contexts against side conditions. The definition of bisimulation can be adapted to the lts without contexts as follows.

**Exercise 16.1.17** *Let $Pr$ be the collection of processes. Define an operator $\mathcal{F} : \mathcal{P}(Pr \times Pr) \to \mathcal{P}(Pr \times Pr)$ as:*

$$P \mathcal{F}(S) Q \quad \text{if} \quad \forall P' \; \forall \alpha \; (bn(\alpha) \cap FV(Q) = \emptyset \text{ and } P \xrightarrow{\alpha} P')$$
$$\Rightarrow \exists Q' \; (Q \xrightarrow{\alpha} Q' \text{ and } P' S Q') \text{ (and symmetrically)} ,$$

*where the transitions are computed in the lts defined in figure 16.4. A relation $S$ is a bisimulation if $S \subseteq \mathcal{F}(S)$. Define $\sim_{\pi'} = \bigcup \{S \mid S \subseteq \mathcal{F}(S)\}$. The condition $bn(\alpha) \cap FV(Q) = \emptyset$ is used to avoid name clashes (cf. rule $(comp)$). Show that for all processes $P, Q$, $P \sim_\pi Q$ iff $P \sim_{\pi'} Q$.*

$$(in) \quad \frac{}{a(b).P \xrightarrow{ac} [c/b]P} \qquad\qquad (out) \quad \frac{}{\bar{a}b.P \xrightarrow{\bar{a}b} P}$$

$$(in_{ex}) \quad \frac{}{a(b).P \xrightarrow{a(b)} P} \qquad\qquad (out_{ex}) \quad \frac{P \xrightarrow{\bar{a}b} P' \quad a \neq b}{\nu b\, P \xrightarrow{\bar{a}(b)} P'}$$

$$(sync) \quad \frac{P \xrightarrow{\bar{a}b} P' \quad Q \xrightarrow{ab} Q'}{P \mid Q \xrightarrow{\tau} P' \mid Q'} \qquad (sync_{ex}) \quad \frac{P \xrightarrow{\bar{a}(b)} P' \quad Q \xrightarrow{a(b)} Q'}{P \mid Q \xrightarrow{\tau} \nu b\,(P' \mid Q')}$$

$$(rename) \quad \frac{P \equiv P' \quad P' \xrightarrow{\alpha} Q' \quad Q' \equiv Q}{P \xrightarrow{\alpha} Q} \qquad (\nu) \quad \frac{P \xrightarrow{\alpha} P' \quad a \notin n(\alpha)}{\nu a\, P \xrightarrow{\alpha} \nu a\, P'}$$

$$(comp) \quad \frac{P \xrightarrow{\alpha} P' \quad bn(\alpha) \cap FV(Q) = \emptyset}{P \mid Q \xrightarrow{\alpha} P' \mid Q} \qquad (sum) \quad \frac{\gamma_i.P_i \xrightarrow{\alpha} P'}{\gamma_1.P_1 + \cdots + \gamma_n.P_n \xrightarrow{\alpha} P'}$$

$$(match) \quad \frac{}{[a=a]P \xrightarrow{\tau} P} \qquad (fix) \quad \frac{P[\vec{b}/\vec{a}] \xrightarrow{\alpha} P' \quad A(\vec{a}) = P}{A(\vec{b}) \xrightarrow{\alpha} P'}$$

Figure 16.4: A labelled transition system without contexts

**Characterization of barbed equivalence.** The definition of $\pi$-bisimulation is technically appealing because the check of the equivalence of two processes can be performed 'locally', that is, without referring to an arbitrary parallel context as in the definition of barbed equivalence. On the other hand the definition of $\pi$-bisimulation is quite intensional and clearly contains some arbitrary choices: the actions to be observed, the selection of new names, etc. The following result, first stated in [MS92], shows that strong $\pi$-bisimulation and barbed equivalence are two presentations of the same notion, and it justifies, a posteriori, the choice of the actions specified in definition 16.1.8 (this choice is not obvious, for instance the 'late' $\pi$-bisimulation first studied in [MPW92], which is based on a different treatment of the input action, is strictly stronger than barbed equivalence).

**Theorem 16.1.18** *Strong barbed equivalence and strong $\pi$-bisimulation coincide.*

PROOF. We first outline the proof for a CCS-like calculus following the notation in section 9.2. CCS can be seen as a $\pi$-calculus in which the transmitted names are irrelevant. Formally, we could code $a.P$ as $a(b).P$ and $\bar{a}.P$ as $\nu b\,\bar{a}b.P$, where $b \notin FV(P)$.

- $P \sim_\pi Q \;\Rightarrow\; P \sim Q$. We observe that:

(1) $P \sim_\pi Q \;\Rightarrow\; P \overset{\bullet}{\sim} Q$.

(2) $P \sim_\pi Q \;\Rightarrow\; P \mid R \sim_\pi Q \mid R$, for any $R$.

Hence, $P \sim_\pi Q$ implies $P \mid R \stackrel{\bullet}{\sim} Q \mid R$, for any $R$, that is $P \sim Q$.

- $P \sim Q \Rightarrow P \sim_\pi Q$. This direction is a bit more complicated. We define a collection of tests $R(n, L)$ depending on $n \in \omega$ and a finite set $L$ of channel names, and show by induction on $n$ that:

$$\exists L \; (L \supseteq FV(P \mid Q) \text{ and } (P \mid R(n, L)) \stackrel{\bullet}{\sim} (Q \mid R(n, L))) \Rightarrow P \sim_\pi^n Q.$$

If the property above holds then we can conclude the proof by observing:

$$
\begin{aligned}
P \sim Q &\Rightarrow \forall R \; (P \mid R \stackrel{\bullet}{\sim} Q \mid R) \\
&\Rightarrow \forall n \in \omega \; (P \mid R(n, L) \stackrel{\bullet}{\sim} Q \mid R(n, L)) \quad \text{(with } L = FV(P \mid Q)) \\
&\Rightarrow \forall n \in \omega \; (P \sim_\pi^n Q) \\
&\Rightarrow P \sim_\pi^\omega Q \\
&\Rightarrow P \sim_\pi Q \qquad\qquad\qquad\qquad\qquad\qquad \text{(by exercise 16.1.13) .}
\end{aligned}
$$

We use an internal sum operator $\oplus$ which is a derived n-ary operator defined as follows:

$$P_1 \oplus \cdots \oplus P_n \equiv \nu a \, (a.P_1 \mid \cdots \mid a.P_n \mid \bar{a}) \quad a \notin FV(P_1 \mid \cdots \mid P_n) \, .$$

We note that (up to garbage collection of deadlocked processes) $P_1 \oplus \cdots \oplus P_n \stackrel{\tau}{\to} P_i$ for $i = 1, \ldots, n$. We suppose that the collection of channel names $Ch$ has been partitioned in two infinite well-ordered sets $Ch'$ and $Ch''$ (for instance we put all $Ch'$ before $Ch''$). In the following we have $L \subseteq_{fin} Ch''$. We also assume we have the following sequences of distinct names in $Ch'$:

$$
\begin{aligned}
&\{b_n, b_n' \mid n \in \omega\} \\
&\{c_n^\beta \mid n \in \omega \text{ and } \beta \in \{\tau\} \cup \{a, \bar{a} \mid a \in Ch''\}\} \\
&\{c_n'^\beta \mid n \in \omega \text{ and } \beta \in \{a, \bar{a} \mid a \in Ch''\}\} \, .
\end{aligned}
$$

Commitments on these names permit us to control the execution of the processes $R(n, L)$ which we define by induction on $n \in \omega$ as follows:

$$
\begin{aligned}
R(0, L) &= b_0 \oplus b_0', \quad \text{and for } n > 0 \\
R(n, L) &= b_n \oplus b_n' \oplus \\
&\quad (c_n^\tau \oplus R(n - 1, L)) \oplus \\
&\quad \oplus \{c_n^\alpha \oplus (\alpha.(c_n'^\alpha \oplus R(n - 1, L))) \mid \alpha \in L \cup \overline{L}\} \, .
\end{aligned}
$$

We suppose $n > 0$, $FV(P \mid Q) \subseteq L$, $(P \mid R(n, L)) \stackrel{\bullet}{\sim} (Q \mid R(n, L))$, and $P \stackrel{\alpha}{\to} P'$. We proceed by case analysis on the action $\alpha$ to show that $Q$ can match the action $\alpha$. We observe that the processes $R(n, L)$ can either perform internal reductions (which always cause the loss of a commitment) or offer a communication $\alpha$.

$\alpha \equiv \tau$. Then:

$$(P \mid R(n, L)) \stackrel{\tau}{\to} (P \mid (c_n^\tau \oplus R(n - 1, L))) \, .$$

To match this reduction up to barbed bisimulation we have no choice:

$$(Q \mid R(n, L)) \stackrel{\tau}{\to} (Q \mid (c_n^\tau \oplus R(n - 1, L))) \, .$$

We take two steps on the left hand side:

$$(P \mid (c_n^\tau \oplus R(n-1, L))) \xrightarrow{\tau}^2 (P' \mid R(n-1, L)) \ .$$

Again this has to be matched by:

$$(Q \mid (c_n^\tau \oplus R(n-1, L))) \xrightarrow{\tau}^2 (Q' \mid R(n-1, L)) \ ,$$

with $Q \xrightarrow{\tau} Q'$ (the $c_n^\tau$ has to be removed and $R(n-1, L)$ must not be reduced). Since $P' \mid R(n-1, L) \overset{\bullet}{\sim} Q' \mid R(n-1, L)$, we have by induction $P' \sim_\pi^{n-1} Q'$.

$\alpha \equiv \bar{a}$ (the case $\alpha \equiv a$ is symmetric). We may suppose $a \in L$.

$$(P \mid R(n, L)) \xrightarrow{\tau}^2 (P \mid (c_n^a \oplus a.(c_n'^a \oplus R(n-1, L)))) \ .$$

To match this reduction up to barbed bisimulation we have:

$$(Q \mid R(n, L)) \xrightarrow{\tau}^2 (Q \mid (c_n^a \oplus a.(c_n'^a \oplus R(n-1, L)))) \ .$$

We take three steps on the left hand side:

$$(P \mid (c_n^a \oplus a.(c_n'^a \oplus R(n-1, L)))) \xrightarrow{\tau}^3 (P' \mid R(n-1, L)) \ .$$

Again this has to be matched by:

$$(Q \mid (c_n^a \oplus a.(c_n'^a \oplus R(n-1, L)))) \xrightarrow{\tau}^3 (Q' \mid R(n-1, L)) \ .$$

with $Q \xrightarrow{\bar{a}} Q'$ (note the use of $c_n'^a$). As above, applying the inductive hypothesis, we have $P' \sim_\pi^{n-1} Q'$. Hence, in all cases, if $P \xrightarrow{\alpha} P'$ then $Q \xrightarrow{\alpha} Q'$ and $P' \sim_\pi^{n-1} Q'$, i.e., we have proved $P \sim_\pi^n Q$.

• Next we generalize the definitions in order to deal with the $\pi$-calculus. We assume we have the following sequences of distinct names in $Ch'$:

$$\{b_n, b_n' \mid n \in \omega\}$$
$$\{c_n^\beta \mid n \in \omega \text{ and } \beta \in \{\tau, aa', a, \bar{a}a', \bar{a} \mid a, a' \in Ch''\}\}$$
$$\{c_n'^\beta \mid n \in \omega \text{ and } \beta \in \{aa', a, \bar{a}a', \bar{a} \mid a, a' \in Ch''\}\}$$
$$\{d_n^\beta \mid n \in \omega \text{ and } \beta \in \{a \mid a \in Ch''\}\}$$
$$\{e_n \mid n \in \omega\} \ .$$

The test $R(n, L)$ is defined by induction on $n$ as follows. (When emitting or receiving a name which is not in $L \subseteq FV(P \mid Q)$, we work up to injective substitution to show that $P \sim_\pi^n Q$.)

$R(0, L) = b_0 \oplus b_0'$, and for $n > 0$

$$R(n, L) = b_n \oplus b_n' \oplus$$
$$(c_n^\tau \oplus R(n-1, L)) \oplus$$
$$\oplus \{c_n^{\bar{a}a'} \oplus (\bar{a}a'.(c_n'^{\bar{a}a'} \oplus R(n-1, L))) \mid a, a' \in L\} \oplus$$
$$\oplus \{c_n^{\bar{a}} \oplus \nu a''(\bar{a}a''.(c_n'^{\bar{a}} \oplus R(n-1, L \cup \{a''\}))) \mid a \in L\} \oplus$$
$$\oplus \{c_n^{aa'} \oplus a(a'').(c_n'^{aa'} \oplus ([a'' = a']d_n^{a'} \oplus R(n-1, L))) \mid a, a' \in L\} \oplus$$
$$\oplus \{c_n^a \oplus a(a'').(c_n'^a \oplus (\oplus\{[a'' = a']d_n^{a'} \mid a' \in L\} \oplus e_n \oplus R(n-1, L \cup \{a''\}))) \mid a \in L\} \ .$$

The name $a''$ is fresh, for instance we can pick the first name in the well-ordered set $Ch''\backslash L$. Note the use of matching to compare the identity of the received names. In order to take into account the exchange of new names between the observed process and the test $R(n, L)$, we have to generalize the statement as follows.

$$\exists L, L' \ (L \supseteq FV(P \mid Q), L' \subseteq L \text{ and } \nu L' \, (P \mid R(n, L)) \overset{\bullet}{\sim} \nu L' \, (Q \mid R(n, L)))$$
$$\Rightarrow P \sim_\pi^n Q \, .$$

One can now proceed with an analysis of the possible actions of $P$ mimicking what was done above in the CCS case. □

The proof technique presented here can be extended to the weak case (using the same definitions of $R(n, L)$) as stated in the following exercise.

**Exercise\* 16.1.19** *Show that $P \approx Q$ implies $P \approx_\pi^\omega Q$. Conclude that on image finite labelled transition systems (cf. definition 9.2.3, proposition 9.2.8, and exercise 16.1.13) weak barbed bisimulation coincides with weak $\pi$-bisimulation.*

**Finite control processes.** We restrict our attention to processes which are the parallel composition of a finite number of 'finite control' processes defined by a finite system of recursive equations. The basic restriction that is satisfied by finite control processes is that recursion does not go through parallel composition. This implies that the number of processes running in parallel is bound. Here is a simple example of a process which does not satisfy this restriction:

$$A(c) = c(d).(A(d) \mid A(c)) \, . \tag{16.5}$$

We also suppose that the equations have the following standard form (a standard trick to adhere to this form is to introduce auxiliary agent identifiers):

$$A(c_1, \ldots, c_n) = \delta_1.A_1(\vec{d_1}) + \cdots + \delta_m.A_m(\vec{d_m}) \, , \tag{16.6}$$

where the right hand side of the equation is taken to be 0 if $m = 0$, and $\delta_i$ has the shape $a(b)$ (input), or $\bar{a}b$ (output), or $\bar{d}(c)$ that is an abbreviation for $\nu c \, \bar{d}c$ (bound output).

The parameters $\vec{d_j}$ are drawn from either $c_1, \ldots, c_n$ or the bound variable in the prefix $\delta_j$ (hence the equation has no free parameters). Our main goal is to show that bisimulation is *decidable* for this class of processes (the argument we give is based on [Dam94]). First, let us consider some processes that can be defined in the fragment of the $\pi$-calculus described above.

**Example 16.1.20** (1) *The following process models a (persistent) memory cell (we write with $\overline{in}$ and we read with out):*

$$Mem(a) = in(b).Mem(b) + \overline{out} \, a.Mem(a) \, .$$

(2) *The system $\nu a \, (G(a) \mid F(a))$ is composed of a new name generator $G(a)$ and a process $F(a)$ that forwards one of the last two names received:*

$$\begin{aligned}
G(a) &= \overline{a}(b).G(a) & F(a) &= a(c).F'(a, c) \\
F'(a, c) &= a(d).F''(a, c, d) & F''(a, c, d) &= \overline{a}c.F(a) + \overline{a}d.F(a) \, .
\end{aligned}$$

Note that if we try to compute the synchronization tree (cf. section 9.2) associated with, say, the process $G(a)$ we may end up with an infinite tree in which an infinite number of labels occur. We need some more work to capture the regular behaviour of the process. To fix the ideas suppose that we want to compare two processes $P_1$, $P_2$ consisting of the parallel composition of $n$ processes. Each one of these processes is described by a system of $m$ equations, of the shape 16.6. For the sake of simplicity, we always suppose that each agent identifier $A$ depends on $k$ parameters. Then the process $P_1$ is defined as follows:

$$P_1 \equiv \nu \vec{a} \left( A_{j_1}(\vec{c_1}) \mid \cdots \mid A_{j_n}(\vec{c_n}) \right),$$

where $1 \le j_h \le m$. The element $A_{j_h}(\vec{c_h})$, for $1 \le h \le n$ determines the equation and the parameters being applied at the $h^{th}$ component. Similarly, the process $P_2$ is described by:

$$P_2 \equiv \nu \vec{b} \left( B_{j_1}(\vec{d_1}) \mid \cdots \mid B_{j_n}(\vec{d_n}) \right).$$

The process $P_1$ (or $P_2$) may evolve by labelled transitions into another process of the same shape. Since the system of equations is finite, there is a finite number of combinations of the agent identifiers which can arise. In turn, the agent identifiers may depend on channel names which range over an infinite domain. Note however that we can bound the number of distinct channel names on which a (finite control) process may depend. The insight is then that we can compare the processes $P_1$, $P_2$ according to the rules of bisimulation, by using only a suitably large but *finite* set of channel names. This property leads to the decidability of bisimulation.

**Proposition 16.1.21** *It can be decided if two processes having the structure of $P_1$ and $P_2$ above are bisimilar.*

PROOF. Suppose that we compare $P_1$ and $P_2$ by applying the definition of $\pi$-bisimulation. It is clear that at any moment of the computation each process may depend at most on $nk$ distinct channel names. We may suppose that the free channel names in $P_1$ and $P_2$ form an initial segment in the ordering of the channel names (if this is not the case we can always apply an injective substitution). Moreover we identify the process $\nu c\, P$ with the process $P$ whenever $c \notin FV(P)$. Hence the size of the vectors of restricted channels $\vec{a}$ and $\vec{b}$ is bound.

Next we select a set of channel names $\Delta$ which is the initial segment of the ordered channel names of cardinality $2nk + 1$ (this segment is large enough to contain the free channel names of $P_1$, $P_2$, and to provide a fresh channel). There is a finite number of processes of the shape $P_1$ or $P_2$ which can be written using names in $\Delta$. So we can find $Pr_1 \subseteq_{fin} Pr$ such that $P_1, P_2 \in Pr_1$, and if $\Gamma \vdash P \xrightarrow{\alpha} \Gamma' \vdash P''$ then $P'' \in Pr_1$ up to renaming and elimination of useless restrictions. It follows that:

$$P_1 \sim P_2 \text{ iff } \forall n \in \omega \ (P_1 \sim^n P_2) \text{ iff } \forall n \in \omega \ (P_1(\sim^n \cap (Pr_1 \times Pr_1))P_2).$$

The sequence $Pr_1 \times Pr_1 \supseteq (\sim^1 \cap (Pr_1 \times Pr_1)) \supseteq \cdots$ converges in a finite number of steps since $Pr_1$ is finite. □

**Polyadic π-calculus.** We introduce some additional concepts and notations for the π-calculus. So far we have assumed that each channel may transmit exactly one channel name. In practice it is more handy to have a calculus where tuples of channel names can be transmitted at once. This raises the problem of enforcing some sort discipline on channels, as emitting and receiving processes have to transmit and accept, respectively, a tuple of the same length. A simple sort discipline can be defined as follows. Every channel is supposed to be labelled by its *sort*. Sorts are used to constraint the arity of a channel. A channel of sort $Ch(s_1, \ldots, s_n)$ can carry a tuple $z_1, \ldots, z_n$, where $z_i$ has sort $s_i$, for $i = 1, \ldots, n$. For instance, if $n = 0$ then the channel can be used only for synchronization (as in CCS), and if the sort is $Ch(o)$ then the channel can only transmit some ground data of type $o$.

$$\text{Simple sorts} \quad s ::= o \mid Ch(s_1, \ldots, s_n) \quad (n \geq 0) \ .$$

The syntax for processes is extended in the obvious way:

$$P ::= \overline{n}(n, \ldots, n).P \mid n(n, \ldots, n).P \mid \cdots \ .$$

Well-formed processes have to respect the sort associated with the channel names. For instance, $\overline{a}(b_1, \ldots b_n).P$ is well formed if $P$ is well formed, $Ch(s_1, \ldots, s_n)$ is the sort of $a$, and $s_i$ is the sort of $b_i$, for $i = 1, \ldots, n$. *Mutatis mutandis*, reduction is defined as in figure 16.1. We call the resulting π-calculus *polyadic*.

**Exercise 16.1.22** *(1) Define a translation from the polyadic to the monadic π-calculus. Hint: Consider the translation* $\langle \overline{c}(a_1, \ldots, a_n).P \rangle = \nu b \, \overline{c}b.\overline{b}a_1 \ldots \overline{b}a_n.\langle P \rangle$. *(2) Check that* $\tau$*-reduction is adequately simulated.*

**Replication.** As usual, let $\vec{a}$ stand for $a_1, \ldots, a_n$ $(n \geq 0)$. The process $!(c(\vec{a}).P)$ with free variables $\vec{b}$ stands for a recursively defined process $A(\vec{b})$ satisfying the equation $A(\vec{b}) = c(\vec{a}).(P \mid A(\vec{b}))$, where $\{\vec{a}\} \cap \{\vec{b}\} = \emptyset$. The operator $!$ is traditionally called *replication*.

**Exercise 16.1.23** *Prove that for any process $P$,* $!(c(\vec{a}).P) \sim ((c(\vec{a}).P) \mid !(c(\vec{a}).P))$ *and* $\nu c \, (!(c(\vec{a}).P)) \sim 0$.

These properties will be tacitly used when working with the replication operator. It is also possible to simulate recursive definitions, using the replication operator.

**Exercise 16.1.24** *Given a recursive definition $A(\vec{b}) = P$ where (for simplicity) we suppose that only the agent identifier $A$ occurs in $P$, find a process $P'$ which relies on replication rather than recursion, and which is weakly bisimilar to $A(\vec{c})$. Hint: Let $P''$ be the process where we replace every occurrence of $A(\vec{c'})$ in $P$ with $\overline{d}\vec{c'}.0$, for $d$ fresh (the message $\overline{d}\vec{c'}$ 'calls' the recursive definition). Then consider $P' = \nu d \, (!(d(\vec{b}).P'') \mid \overline{d}\vec{c}.0)$.*

## 16.2　A concurrent functional language

Programming languages that combine functional and concurrent programming, such as LCS [BGG91], CML [Rep91] and Facile [GMP89, TLP+93], are starting to emerge and get applied. These languages are conceived for the programming of reactive systems and distributed systems. A main motivation for using these languages is that they offer integration of different computational paradigms in a clean and well understood programming model that allows formal reasoning about programs' behaviour.

We define a simply typed language, called $\lambda_{\parallel}$, first presented in [ALT95] (and inspired by previous work on the Facile programming language [GMP89, TLP+93, Ama94]), whose three basic ingredients are:

- A call-by-value $\lambda$-calculus extended with the possibility of parallel evaluation of expressions.

- A notion of channel, and primitives to read/write channels in a synchronous way. The communications are performed as side effects of expression evaluation.[2] The $\lambda_{\parallel}$-calculus adopts the communication model of CCS and $\pi$-calculus.

- The possibility of dynamically generating new channels during execution.

The $\lambda_{\parallel}$-calculus should be regarded as a bridge between programming languages such as Facile and CML [Rep91] and theoretical calculi such as the $\pi$-calculus. To this end it includes abstraction and application among its basic primitives. Benefits of having a direct treatment of abstraction and application include: (i) A handy and well-understood functional fragment is available, this simplifies the practice of programming. (ii) The distinction between sequential reduction and inter-process communication makes more efficient implementations possible.

We start by fixing some notation for the $\lambda_{\parallel}$-calculus, ignoring typing issues for the time being. There is a universe of expressions $e, e', \ldots$ inductively generated by the following operators: $\lambda$-abstraction $(\lambda x.e)$, application $(ee')$, the terminated process $0$, parallel composition $(e \mid e')$, restriction $(\nu x\, e)$, output $(e!e')$, and input $(e?)$.[3]

The evaluation of an expression follows a call-by-value order. If the evaluator arrives at an expression of the form $c!v$ or $c?$ (where $c$ is a channel and $v$ is a value) then it is stuck until a synchronization with a parallel expression trying to perform a dual action occurs.

In the $\lambda_{\parallel}$-calculus prefixing can be defined by relying on the call-by-value evaluation order. For instance, we can define $c?y.e$ as $(\lambda y.e)(c?)$, and $c!v.e$ as $(\lambda x.e)(c!v)$, where $x$ is a fresh variable (in particular we write $c!v.0$ for $(\lambda x.0)(c!v)$). All bindings can be understood as either $\lambda$-bindings or $\nu$-bindings.[4]

---

[2]The fact that parallel expressions may synchronize makes the $\lambda_{\parallel}$-calculus more complicated than the $\lambda_{\sqcup}$-calculus considered in section 8.4. As a matter of fact, the join operator can be programmed in the $\pi$-calculus (cf. exercise 16.2.8), which in turn can be regarded as a fragment of the $\lambda_{\parallel}$-calculus.

[3]Do not confuse the prefix, unary replication operator of the $\pi$-calculus with the infix, binary output operator of the $\lambda_{\parallel}$-calculus.

[4]In a slightly different formulation, the $\nu$-binding can be reduced to the $\lambda$-binding, by introducing a constant *new* whose evaluation returns a new name. One then defines $\nu x\, e \equiv$

As a programming example consider the following functional $F$ that takes two functions, evaluates them in parallel on the number 3 and transmits the product of their outputs on a channel $c$ (we suppose to have natural numbers with the relative product operation $\times$):

$$F \equiv \lambda f.\lambda g.\nu y\,(y!(f3).0 \mid y!(g3).0 \mid c!(y? \times y?).0) \ .$$

In order to implement the parallel evaluation of $f3$ and $g3$ a local channel $y$ and two processes $y!(f3).0$ and $y!(g3).0$ are created. Upon termination of the evaluation of, say, $f3$ the value is transmitted to the third process $c!(y? \times y?).0$. When both values are received the product $(f3) \times (g3)$ is computed and sent on the channel $c$. Here is an example of evaluation where we suppose that $f$, $g$ are functions which evaluate to 4, 5 on the argument 3, respectively.

$$
\begin{aligned}
(Ff)g \quad &\rightarrow \quad \nu y\,(y!(f3).0 \mid y!(g3).0 \mid c!(y? \times y?).0) \\
&\rightarrow \quad \nu y\,(y!4.0 \mid y!(g3).0 \mid c!(y? \times y?).0) \\
&\rightarrow \quad \nu y\,(y!(g3).0 \mid c!(4 \times y?).0) \\
&\rightarrow \quad \nu y\,(y!5.0 \mid c!(4 \times y?).0) \qquad\qquad \rightarrow \quad c!(4 \times 5).0 \quad \rightarrow \quad c!20.0 \ .
\end{aligned}
$$

Our first task is to provide the $\lambda_\parallel$-calculus with a natural (operational) notion of equivalence. To this end we define the relations of reduction and commitment and build on top of them the notions of barbed bisimulation and equivalence following what was done in section 16.1 for the $\pi$-calculus.

**A concurrent $\lambda$-calculus.** We formally present the $\lambda_\parallel$-calculus, define its semantics and illustrate its expressive power by some examples.

- Types are partitioned into value types and *one* behaviour type.

$$
\begin{aligned}
\sigma &::= o \mid (\sigma \rightarrow \sigma) \mid Ch(\sigma) \mid (\sigma \rightarrow b) \quad &\text{(value type)} \\
b & &\text{(behaviour type)} \\
\alpha &::= \sigma \mid b \quad &\text{(value or behaviour type)} \ .
\end{aligned}
$$

$o$ is called the ground (or basic) type.

- An infinite supply of variables $x^\sigma, y^\sigma, \ldots$, labelled with their type, is assumed for any value type $\sigma$. We reserve variables $f, g, \ldots$ for functional types $\sigma \rightarrow \alpha$. Moreover, an infinite collection of constants $c^\sigma, d^\sigma, \ldots$ is given where $\sigma$ is either a ground type $o$ or a channel type $Ch(\sigma')$, for some value type $\sigma'$. In particular there is a special constant $*^o$ which we take as the canonical result of the evaluation of expressions which operate by side-effect. We denote with $z, z', \ldots$ variables or constants.

$$
\begin{aligned}
v \ &::= x \mid y \mid \ldots \\
e \ &::= c^\sigma \mid v^\sigma \mid \lambda v^\sigma.e \mid ee \mid e!e \mid e? \mid \nu v^{Ch(\sigma)}\,e \mid 0 \mid (e \mid e) \ .
\end{aligned}
$$

- Well-typed expressions are defined in figure 16.5. All expressions are considered up to $\alpha$-renaming. Parallel composition has to be understood as an associative and commutative operator, with 0 as identity. Note that expressions of type behaviour are built up starting with the constant 0, for instance $(\lambda x : o.0)(c^{Ch(\sigma)}!d^\sigma) : b$.

---

$(\lambda x.e)(new)$. We keep both binders to simplify the comparison with the $\pi$-calculus.

$$(Asmp) \ \overline{z^\sigma : \sigma} \qquad\qquad (0) \ \overline{0 : b}$$

$$(\rightarrow_I) \ \frac{e : \alpha}{\lambda x^\sigma.e : \sigma \rightarrow \alpha} \qquad (\rightarrow_E) \ \frac{e : \sigma \rightarrow \alpha \quad e' : \sigma}{ee' : \alpha}$$

$$(!) \ \frac{e : Ch(\sigma) \quad e' : \sigma}{e!e' : o} \qquad (?) \ \frac{e : Ch(\sigma)}{e? : \sigma}$$

$$(\nu) \ \frac{e : \alpha}{\nu x^{Ch(\sigma)} e : \alpha} \qquad\qquad (|) \ \frac{e : b \quad e' : b}{e \mid e' : b}$$

Figure 16.5: Typing rules for the $\lambda_\|$-calculus

Expressions having a value type are called value expressions and they return a result upon termination. Expressions having type $b$ are called behaviour expressions and they *never* return a result. In particular their semantics is determined only by their interaction capabilities. Since we are in a call-by-value framework it does not make sense to allow behaviours as arguments of a function. The types' grammar is restricted accordingly in order to avoid such pathologies. It should be remarked that the interaction capabilities of an expression are not reflected by its type.

Next we describe a rewriting relation (up to structural equivalence) which is supposed to represent abstractly the possible internal computations of a well-typed $\lambda_\|$-expression. On top of this relation we build a notion of observation, and notions of barbed bisimulation and equivalence.

**Definition 16.2.1** *A program is a closed expression of type $b$. Values are specified as follows: $V ::= c \mid v \mid \lambda v.e$.*

In the definition above, variables are values because evaluation may take place under the $\nu$ operator. In the implementation these variables can be understood as fresh constants (cf. the abstract machine for the $\pi$-calculus in section 16.1).

*Local* evaluation contexts $E$ are standard evaluation contexts for call-by-value evaluation (cf. section 8.5). For historical reasons ! and ? are written here in infix and postfix notation, respectively. If one writes them in prefix notation then local evaluation contexts are literally call-by-value evaluation contexts.

$$E ::= [\,] \mid Ee \mid (\lambda v.e)E \mid E!e \mid z!E \mid E? .$$

Local evaluation contexts do not allow evaluation under restriction and parallel composition. In order to complete the description of the reduction relation we need to introduce a notion of *global* evaluation context $C$.

$$C ::= [\,] \mid (\nu v \, C) \mid (C \mid e) .$$

$$(\beta) \quad E[(\lambda x.e)V] \to E[e[V/x]] \qquad (\tau) \quad E[z!V] \mid E'[z?] \to E[*] \mid E'[V]$$

$$(cxt) \quad \frac{e \to e'}{C[e] \to C[e']} \qquad\qquad (\equiv) \quad \frac{e \equiv e_1 \quad e_1 \to e_1' \quad e_1' \equiv e'}{e \to e'}$$

Figure 16.6: Reduction rules for the $\lambda_\parallel$-calculus

Note that if $e : b$ then $C[e] : b$. As in the $\pi$-calculus, we consider expressions up to structural equivalence. We assume associativity and commutativity of the parallel composition, $e \mid 0 \equiv e$, and the following laws concerning the restriction operator $\nu$:

$$\begin{aligned}
\nu x\, e \mid e' &\equiv \nu x\,(e \mid e') \quad (x \notin FV(e')) \\
\nu x\, \nu y\, e &\equiv \nu y\, \nu x\, e \\
E[\nu x\, e] &\equiv \nu x\, E[e] \quad (x \notin FV(E),\ E[e] : b)\ .
\end{aligned}$$

We define the relation $\equiv$ as the least equivalence relation on $\lambda_\parallel$-expressions that contains the equations above and is closed under global contexts, that is $e \equiv e'$ implies $C[e] \equiv C[e']$. It would be also sensible to ask closure under arbitrary contexts (and so have a structural *congruence*), we do not do this to simplify the comparison with the $\pi$-calculus.

Using the notion of local evaluation context two basic reduction rules are defined in figure 16.6. The rule $(\beta)$ corresponds to local functional evaluation while the rule $(\tau)$ describes inter-process communication. The reduction relation describes the internal computation of a program, therefore it is assumed that $E, E'$ have type $b$. The definition of the rewriting relation is extended to all global contexts by the rule $(cxt)$.

The proof of a one-step reduction of an expression has the following structure, up to structural equivalence: (i) at most one application of the $(cxt)$ rule, and (ii) one application of one of the basic reduction rules $(\beta)$ and $(\tau)$. We write $e \to_r e'$ if the rule applied in (ii) is $r \in \{\beta, \tau\}$. We observe that by means of structural equivalences it is always possible to display a behaviour expression as follows:

$$\nu x_1 \dots \nu x_n\,(E_1[\Delta_1] \mid \cdots \mid E_m[\Delta_m]),$$

where the $\Delta_i$'s have the form $(\lambda v.e)V$, $z!V$, or $z?$, and $n, m \geq 0$. If $m = 0$ then the process can be identified with $0$. It is interesting to note that purely functional computations always terminate.

**Proposition 16.2.2** *Let $e$ be a program. Then all the reduction sequences not involving the communication rule $(\tau)$ are finite.*

PROOF. First, we eliminate restrictions, by observing that it is enough to prove termination for a calculus having just one channel for every value type. Second, we translate types as follows:

$$\langle o \rangle \;=\; o \qquad\qquad \langle b \rangle \;=\; o$$
$$\langle \sigma \to \alpha \rangle \;=\; \langle \sigma \rangle \to \langle \alpha \rangle \qquad \langle Ch(\sigma) \rangle \;=\; \langle \sigma \rangle \,.$$

Third, we associate with the $\lambda_{\parallel}$-operators $0, ?, !, |$ variables with suitable types. For instance to $|$ we associate a variable $x_|$ with type $o \to (o \to o)$, so $\langle e \mid e' \rangle = x_|\langle e\rangle\langle e'\rangle$. It is then possible to translate $\lambda_{\parallel}$ into a simply typed $\lambda$-calculus (which is known to be strongly normalizing, cf. theorem 2.2.9). In the translation every $\beta$-reduction in $\lambda_{\parallel}$ induces a $\beta$-reduction in the translated term. From this one can conclude the termination of every $\beta$-reduction sequence in $\lambda_{\parallel}$. $\qquad\square$

**Recursive behaviours.** If we allow $\tau$ reductions, then a program in the $\lambda_{\parallel}$-calculus may fail to terminate. Indeed behaviours can be recursively defined by means of a combinator $Y : ((o \to b) \to b) \to b$. This is obtained by a simple simulation of the combinator for call-by-value

$$Y_V \equiv \lambda f.\omega_V \omega_V \text{ where } \omega_V \equiv \lambda x.f(\lambda w.xx) \,. \tag{16.7}$$

Note that if $f$ is a value then:

$$Y_V f = f(\lambda w.\omega_V \omega_V) = f(\lambda w.f(\lambda w.\omega_V \omega_V)) = \cdots \,.$$

Being in a simply typed framework one expects problems in typing self application. The 'way out' is to simulate self application by a parallel composition of the function and the argument which communicate on a channel of type $o \to b$ (this exploits the fact that all behaviour expressions inhabit the same type). In the following $e!e'.0$ abbreviates $(\lambda w.0)(e!e')$.

$$Y_b \equiv \lambda f.\nu y\,(\omega_b \mid y!(\lambda w.\omega_b).0) \quad \text{ where } \quad \omega_b \equiv (\lambda x.f(\lambda w.(x* \mid (y!x).0)))y? \,.$$

Using $Y_b$ one may for instance define a behaviour *replicator* $Rep$ $e$, such that $Rep\ e \approx e \mid Rep\ e$, as follows: $Rep\ e \equiv Y_b f$ where $f \equiv (\lambda x'^{o \to b}.(x'* \mid e))$. We then have:

$$
\begin{aligned}
Y_b f \;\to\;& \nu y\,(\omega_b \mid y!(\lambda w.\omega_b).0) \\
\to\;& \nu y\,((\lambda x.f(\lambda w.(x* \mid y!x.0)))(\lambda w.\omega_b)) \\
\to\;& \nu y\,(f(\lambda w.((\lambda w.\omega_b)* \mid y!(\lambda w.\omega_b).0))) \\
\to\;& \nu y\,((\lambda w.((\lambda w.\omega_b)* \mid y!(\lambda w.\omega_b).0))* \mid e) \\
\to\;& \nu y\,((\lambda w.\omega_b)* \mid y!(\lambda w.\omega_b)).0 \mid e) \\
\to\;& \nu y\,(\omega_b \mid y!(\lambda w.\omega_b).0) \mid e \qquad\qquad \text{(as } y \notin FV(e)) \,.
\end{aligned}
$$

**Barbed equivalence.** It is easy to adapt the notions of barbed bisimulation and barbed equivalence to the $\lambda_{\parallel}$-calculus. Having already defined the reduction relation it just remains to fix the relation of immediate commitment. The relation $e \downarrow \beta$ where $e$ is a program (cf. definition 16.2.1), $\beta ::= \bar{c} \mid c$, and $c$ is a constant, is defined as follows:

$$e \downarrow \bar{c} \quad \text{if } e \equiv C[E[c!V]] \qquad\qquad e \downarrow c \quad \text{if } e \equiv C[E[c?]] \,.$$

As usual let $\to^*$ be the reflexive and transitive closure of $\to$ and define a weak commitment relation as $e \downarrow_* \beta$ if $\exists e'$ $(e \to^* e'$ and $e' \downarrow \beta)$. The notions of barbed bisimulation and barbed equivalence are then derived in a mechanic way. A binary relation $S$ between programs is a (weak) barbed simulation if $eSf$ implies:

(1) $\forall e'$ $(e \to^* e' \Rightarrow \exists f'$ $(f \to^* f'$ and $e'Sf'))$.

(2) $\forall \beta$ $(e \downarrow_* \beta \Rightarrow f \downarrow_* \beta)$.

$S$ is a barbed bisimulation if $S$ and $S^{-1}$ are barbed simulations. We write $e \overset{\bullet}{\approx} f$ if $e\,S\,f$ for some barbed bisimulation $S$.

The following exercises relate the $\lambda_{\|}$-calculus to environment machines and continuations, and consider a variant of the calculus based on asynchronous communication.

**Exercise\* 16.2.3** *Define an abstract machine that executes $\lambda_{\|}$-programs by combining the abstract machines defined for the call-by-value $\lambda$-calculus (section 8.3) and for the $\pi$-calculus (section 16.1).*

**Exercise\* 16.2.4** *Extend the calculus with a control operator $\mathcal{C}$ (cf. section 8.5) defined according to the following typing and reduction rules:*

$$\frac{e : (\sigma \to b) \to b}{\mathcal{C}e : \sigma} \qquad \frac{}{E[\mathcal{C}e] \to e(\lambda x^\sigma.E[x])} \; .$$

*The operator $\mathcal{C}$ catches the local evaluation context (the operator $\mathcal{A}$ of section 8.5 is useless here because, due to the particular handling of the behaviour type $b$, the only context in which it could be applied is the trivial one). Define a CPS translation from the $\lambda_{\|}$-calculus with control operator to the $\lambda_{\|}$-calculus.*

**Exercise\* 16.2.5** *Consider a variant of the $\lambda_{\|}$-calculus where we replace the 'synchronous' output operator '!' with an 'asynchronous' output operator '$!_a$' (when speaking on the telephone we communicate synchronously, when sending a letter we communicate asynchronously). Typing and reduction for the asynchronous output are defined as follows:*

$$\frac{e : Ch(\sigma) \quad e' : \sigma}{e!_a e' : b} \qquad \frac{}{E[z?] \mid z!_a V \to E[V]} \; .$$

*This calculus can be regarded as a restriction of the $\lambda_{\|}$-calculus by writing $e!_a e'$ as $(\lambda x : o.0)(e!e')$. Define a translation from the $\lambda_{\|}$-calculus into the corresponding calculus having asynchronous output. Hint: It is convenient to suppose first that the target calculus has the control operator defined in the previous exercise. Then the idea is to associate with an input an asynchronous output: rather than receiving a value one transmits the local evaluation context. Symmetrically one associates an output with an input: rather than transmitting a value one receives the local evaluation context where the value has to be evaluated, say $\langle c? \rangle = \mathcal{C}(\lambda f.c!_a f)$, $\langle c!V \rangle = \mathcal{C}(\lambda g.(f\langle V \rangle \mid g*))c?$.*

**Translation.** We will show that there is an adequate translation of the $\lambda_{\parallel}$-calculus into the $\pi$-calculus. This serves two goals:

- The encoding of the call-by-value $\lambda$-calculus and of the transmission of higher order processes gives a substantial example of the expressive power of the $\pi$-calculus.

- The translation elucidates the semantics of the $\lambda_{\parallel}$-calculus.

We will work with a polyadic $\pi$-calculus with a ground sort $o$ and a constant name $*$ of sort $o$.

The basic problem in the translation is that of finding a simulation of function transmission by means of channel transmission. The idea is that rather than transmitting a function one transmits a pointer to a function (a channel) and at the same time one 'stores' the function by means of the *replication* operator. Let us consider the following reduction sequence in $\lambda_{\parallel}$:

$$c!(\lambda x.e) \mid (\lambda f.(fn \mid fm))(c?) \to^+ [n/x]e \mid [m/x]e .$$

Supposing that there is some translation $\langle\!\langle\ \rangle\!\rangle$ such that:

$$\langle\!\langle c!(\lambda x.e)\rangle\!\rangle = \nu f\,(\overline{c}f \mid !(f(x).\langle\!\langle e\rangle\!\rangle)) \quad \langle\!\langle(\lambda f.(fn \mid fm))(c?)\rangle\!\rangle = c(f).(\overline{f}n \mid \overline{f}m) .$$

Then by parallel composition of the translations the following simulating reduction sequence in the $\pi$-calculus is obtained:

$$\nu f\,(\overline{c}f \mid !(f(x).\langle\!\langle e\rangle\!\rangle)) \mid c(f).(\overline{f}n \mid \overline{f}m) \quad \to \quad \nu f\,(!(f(x).\langle\!\langle e\rangle\!\rangle)) \mid \overline{f}n \mid \overline{f}m \to^+$$
$$\nu f\,(!(f(x).\langle\!\langle e\rangle\!\rangle)) \mid [n/x]\langle\!\langle e\rangle\!\rangle \mid [m/x]\langle\!\langle e\rangle\!\rangle) \quad \approx \quad \langle\!\langle[n/x]e \mid [m/x]e\rangle\!\rangle .$$

**Definition 16.2.6 (type translation)** *A function $\langle\!\langle\ \rangle\!\rangle$ from $\lambda_{\parallel}$ value types into $\pi$ sorts is defined as follows:*

$$\langle\!\langle o\rangle\!\rangle = o \qquad\qquad \langle\!\langle Ch(\sigma)\rangle\!\rangle = Ch(\langle\!\langle \sigma\rangle\!\rangle)$$
$$\langle\!\langle \sigma \to \sigma'\rangle\!\rangle = Ch(\langle\!\langle \sigma\rangle\!\rangle, Ch(\langle\!\langle \sigma'\rangle\!\rangle)) \qquad \langle\!\langle \sigma \to b\rangle\!\rangle = Ch(\langle\!\langle \sigma\rangle\!\rangle, Ch()) .$$

In figure 16.7 a function $\langle\!\langle\ \rangle\!\rangle$ from well-typed $\lambda_{\parallel}$-expressions into well-sorted $\pi$-processes is defined. It is possible to statically assign one out of three 'colours' to each $\pi$-variable involved in the translation. The colours are used to make the functionality of a channel explicit and classify the possible reductions of translated terms. To this end, we suppose that in the expression $e$ to be translated all variables of functional type $\sigma \to \alpha$ are represented with $f, g, \ldots$ Variables of channel or ground sort in the $\lambda_{\parallel}$-term are represented by $x, y, \ldots$ and channels used for 'internal book keeping' in the translation are represented by $u, t, v, \ldots$ Thus we suppose that $\pi$-variables include three infinite sets: $u, t, w, \ldots$; $f, g, \ldots$; and $x, y, \ldots$ Furthermore, we let $r, r', \ldots$ ambiguously denote constants $c, c', \ldots$, variables $x, y, \ldots$, and variables $f, g, \ldots$.

The translation is parameterized over a (fresh) channel $u$. If $e : \sigma$ is a value expression then $u$ has sort $Ch(\langle\!\langle \sigma\rangle\!\rangle)$ and it is used to transmit the value (or a pointer to the value) resulting from the evaluation of the expression $e$. If $e : b$ is a behaviour expression then $u$ is actually of *no use*, we conventionally assign the

$$\langle r \rangle u \;=\; \bar{u}r$$
$$\langle \lambda r.e \rangle u \;=\; \nu f\,(\bar{u}f \mid \langle f := \lambda r.e \rangle)$$
$$\text{where } \langle f := \lambda r.e \rangle \;=\; !(f(r,w).\langle e \rangle w)$$
$$\langle ee' \rangle u \;=\; \nu t\,\nu w\,(\langle e \rangle t \mid t(f).(\langle e' \rangle w \mid w(r).\bar{f}(r,u)))$$
$$\langle e!e' \rangle u \;=\; \nu t\,\nu w\,(\langle e \rangle t \mid t(x).(\langle e' \rangle w \mid w(r).\bar{x}r.\bar{u}*))$$
$$\langle e? \rangle u \;=\; \nu t\,(\langle e \rangle t \mid t(x).x(r).\bar{u}r)$$
$$\langle \nu x\,e \rangle u \;=\; \nu x\,\langle e \rangle u$$
$$\langle 0 \rangle u \;=\; 0$$
$$\langle e \mid e' \rangle u \;=\; \langle e \rangle u \mid \langle e' \rangle u$$

Figure 16.7: Expression translation

sort $Ch()$ to the channel $u$ (we choose to parameterize the behaviour expressions too in order to have a more uniform notation). Each rule using variables $r$ actually stands for *two* rules, one in which $r$ is replaced by a variable $x, y, \ldots$ or a constant and another where it is replaced by a variable $f, g, \ldots$ In the translation only the variables $x, y, \ldots$ can be instantiated by a constant. Note the use of polyadic channels in the translation of $\lambda$-abstraction.

As expected, reductions in the $\lambda_{\parallel}$-calculus are implemented by several reductions in the $\pi$-calculus. The need for a finer description of the computation in the $\pi$-calculus relates to two aspects:

(1) In the $\pi$-calculus there is no notion of application. The implicit order of evaluation given by the relative positions of the expressions in the $\lambda_{\parallel}$-calculus has to be explicitly represented in the $\pi$-calculus. In particular the 'computation' of the evaluation context is performed by means of certain administrative reductions.

(2) In the $\pi$-calculus it is not possible to transmit functions. Instead, a pointer to a function which is stored in the environment by means of the replication operator is transmitted. (There is an analogy with graph reduction of functional languages, see [Bou93] for a discussion.)

We will analyse this encoding in the next section 16.3. We conclude by sketching the encoding of call-by-name (as defined in figure 8.6). The translation is given parametrically with respect to a fresh name $a$ which should be interpreted as the channel on which the term will receive a pair consisting of (a pointer to) its next argument, and the channel name on which to receive the following pair.

$$[x]a \;=\; \bar{x}a$$
$$[\lambda x.M]a \;=\; a(x,b).[M]b$$
$$[MN]a \;=\; \nu b\,\nu c\,([M]b \mid \bar{b}(c,a) \mid !(c(d).[N]d))\;.$$

**Exercise* 16.2.7** *Prove that* $[(\lambda x.M)N]a \approx [M[N/x]]a$.

For more results on this translation we refer to [San92, BL94] where a characterization of the equivalence induced by the $\pi$-calculus encoding on $\lambda$-terms can be found. Related work on the representation of (higher order) processes in the π-calculus can be found in [Mil92, Ama93b, San92, Tho93]. The following is a challenging programming exercise.

**Exercise\* 16.2.8** *Define a translation of the $\lambda_\sqcup$-calculus (section 8.4) in the π-calculus which simulates reduction.*

# 16.3    Adequacy *

We provide a detailed analysis of the π-calculus encoding for call-by-value. To this end, it is useful to identify certain special reductions in the polyadic π-calculus which enjoy an interesting *confluence* property and which occur in the translation described in figure 16.7.

**Definition 16.3.1** *Administrative reductions: We write $Q \to_{ad} Q'$ if for some global context $D$ with one hole, $Q \equiv D[\nu u\,(\overline{u}\vec{z} \mid u(\vec{x}).P)]$ and $Q' \equiv D[P[\vec{z}/\vec{x}]]$, where $u \notin FV(P \cup \{\vec{z}\})$.*

*Beta reductions:    We write $Q \to_{beta} Q'$ if for some context $D$ with one hole, $Q \equiv D[\nu f\,(\overline{f}\vec{z} \mid !(f(\vec{x}).P) \mid P')]$ and $Q' \equiv D[\nu f\,(P[\vec{z}/\vec{x}] \mid !(f(\vec{x}).P) \mid P')]$, where $f \notin FV(P)$, and $f$ cannot occur free in $P'$ in input position, that is as $f(\vec{y}).P''$.*

In the translation, we need to do some pre-computations in order to bring out the redex $\Delta$, these pre-computations correspond to the *administrative* reductions. In first approximation, the reduction of a $\beta$-redex in the $\lambda_\parallel$-calculus corresponds (after some administrative reductions) to a *beta* reduction (hence the terminology). The correspondence is not exact because we do not actually perform the substitution of a term for a name but distribute the price of the substitution along the computation (a similar situation arises with the rule (*beta*) of figure 4.5).

We note that administrative reductions always terminate. Moreover we observe the following confluence property.

**Proposition 16.3.2** *Suppose $P \to P_1$ and $P \to_{ad,beta} P_2$. Then either $P_1 \equiv P_2$ or there is $P'$ such that $P_1 \to_{ad,beta} P'$ and $P_2 \to P'$.*

PROOF HINT. By a simple analysis of the relative positions of the redexes. In particular, we note that if two *beta* reductions superpose then they both refer to the same replicated receiving subprocess.    □

Next, we relate expressions of type behaviour to their π-calculus translation, via the notion of barbed bisimulation. We define $Pr_{\langle\!\langle\,\rangle\!\rangle}$ as the set of processes $P$ of the π-calculus which satisfy the following condition:

$$\exists\, u, e : b, V_1, \ldots, V_n, f_1, \ldots, f_n \;\; \nu f_1 \ldots \nu f_n\, (\langle\!\langle e \rangle\!\rangle u \mid \langle\!\langle f_1 := V_1 \rangle\!\rangle \mid \cdots \mid \langle\!\langle f_n := V_n \rangle\!\rangle \to^* P)\,.$$

Given a process $P \in Pr_{\langle\!\langle\,\rangle\!\rangle}$, let $\natural P$ be its normal form with respect to administrative reductions on channels coloured $u, t, w, \ldots$

**Definition 16.3.3** *A binary relation* $\mathcal{R}$ *between programs in the* $\lambda_{\parallel}$-*calculus and programs in the* $\pi$-*calculus is defined as follows, where* $u$ *is some fresh channel, and* $V_i$ *are* $\lambda$-*abstractions.*

$$e[V_1/f_1]\cdots[V_n/f_n]\ \mathcal{R}\ P \quad if$$
$$\natural P \equiv \natural\nu f_1\ldots\nu f_n\,(\langle\!|e|\!\rangle u \mid \langle\!|f_1 := V_1|\!\rangle \mid \cdots \mid \langle\!|f_n := V_n|\!\rangle)\ .$$

*Note that the substitution is iterated from left to right, as* $V_j$ *may depend on* $f_i$ *for* $i > j$.

Here are some explanations regarding the definition of $\mathcal{R}$. First we note that for some fresh channel $u$, $e\mathcal{R}\langle\!|e|\!\rangle u$, simply by taking the empty substitution. The translated term may need to perform a certain number of administrative reductions before a reduction corresponding to a reduction of the $\lambda_{\parallel}$-calculus emerges. We get rid of these administrative reductions by introducing the notion of normal form $\natural P$. A second issue concerns the substitution of a value for a variable which in the $\pi$-calculus is simulated by the substitution of a pointer to a value for a variable. Therefore, we have to relate, say, the term $e[V/f]$ with the term $\nu f.(\langle\!|e|\!\rangle \mid \langle\!|f := V|\!\rangle)$. It will be convenient to use the following abbreviations:

$$\nu\vec{f} \qquad \text{stands for} \quad \nu f_1\ldots\nu f_n$$
$$\langle\!|f := \vec{V}|\!\rangle \quad \text{stands for} \quad \langle\!|f_1 := V_1|\!\rangle \mid \cdots \mid \langle\!|f_n := V_n|\!\rangle$$
$$[\vec{V}/f] \qquad \text{stands for} \quad [V_1/f_1]\cdots[V_n/f_n] \quad (n \geq 0)\ .$$

In order to analyse the structure of $\natural\nu\vec{f}\,(\langle\!|e|\!\rangle u \mid \langle\!|f := \vec{V}|\!\rangle)$ we define an *optimized* translation. The optimization amounts to pre-computing the initial administrative steps of the translation (a similar idea was applied in section 8.5). To this end, we define an open redex and an open evaluation context, as a redex and an evaluation context, respectively, in which a functional variable may stand for a value (cf. definition 16.2.1). For instance, $fV$ is an open redex, and $fE$ is an open evaluation context. In this way we can speak about redexes which arise only after a substitution is carried out (the non-trivial open evaluation contexts and the open redexes are listed on the left hand sides of figures 16.8 and 16.9, respectively).

We note that if $e[\vec{V}/f] \equiv E[\Delta]$ then $e \equiv E'[\Delta']$, where $\Delta', E'$ are an open redex and an evaluation context, respectively, and $\Delta'[\vec{V}/f] \equiv \Delta$, $E'[\vec{V}/f] \equiv E$. This remark is extended componentwise to the case where:

$$e[\vec{V}/f] \equiv \nu\vec{x}\,(E_1[\Delta_1] \mid \cdots \mid E_n[\Delta_n])\ .$$

In the following definitions and proofs the reader may at first skip the part involving the input-output operators and concentrate on the $\lambda$-calculus fragment of the $\lambda_{\parallel}$-calculus.

We introduce in figure 16.8 a translation which pre-computes the administrative reductions induced by a local evaluation context. The translation is defined on open evaluation contexts $E$ such that $E \neq [\ ]$ and it is parametric in two names $u$ and $u'$. The process $\{E\}(u', u)$ receives on $u'$ and emits on $u$. We assume that $V$ is a $\lambda$-abstraction. The translation is used in the following lemma.

**Lemma 16.3.4 (administrative reductions)** *Suppose that* $E$ *is an open evaluation context such that* $E \neq [\ ]$, *and that* $V_j$ *are* $\lambda$-*abstractions which may depend on* $f_i$ *for* $i > j$. *Then:*

$$\nu\vec{f}\,(\langle\!|E[e]|\!\rangle u \mid \langle\!|f := \vec{V}|\!\rangle) \rightarrow^*_{ad} \nu\vec{f}\nu u'\,(\langle\!|e|\!\rangle u' \mid \{E\}(u', u) \mid \langle\!|f := \vec{V}|\!\rangle)\ .$$

$$\{[\ ]e\}(u',u) \quad = \quad \nu w\,(u'(f).\langle e\rangle w \mid w(r).\overline{f}(r,u))$$
$$\{V[\ ]\}(u',u) \quad = \quad \nu f\,(\langle f := V\rangle \mid u'(r).\overline{f}(r,u))$$
$$\{f[\ ]\}(u',u) \quad = \quad u'(r).\overline{f}(r,u)$$
$$\{[\ ]?\}(u',u) \quad = \quad u'(x).x(r).\overline{u}r$$
$$\{[\ ]!e\}(u',u) \quad = \quad \nu w\,(u'(x).(\langle e\rangle w \mid w(r).\overline{x}r.\overline{u}*))$$
$$\{z![\ ]\}(u',u) \quad = \quad u'(r).\overline{z}r.\overline{u}*$$
$$\{Ee\}(u',u) \quad = \quad \nu t\,\nu w\,(\{E\}(u',t) \mid t(f).\langle e\rangle w \mid w(r).\overline{f}(r,u))$$
$$\{VE\}(u',u) \quad = \quad \nu w\,\nu f\,(\langle f := V\rangle \mid \{E\}(u',w) \mid w(r).\overline{f}(r,u))$$
$$\{fE\}(u',u) \quad = \quad \nu w\,(\{E\}(u',w) \mid w(r).\overline{f}(r,u))$$
$$\{E?\}(u',u) \quad = \quad \nu w\,(\{E\}(u',w) \mid w(x).x(r).\overline{u}r)$$
$$\{E!e\}(u',u) \quad = \quad \nu t\,\nu w\,(\{E\}(u',t) \mid t(x).\langle e\rangle w \mid w(r).\overline{x}r.\overline{u}*)$$
$$\{z!E\}(u',u) \quad = \quad \nu t\,(\{E\}(u',t) \mid t(r).\overline{z}r.\overline{u}*)$$

Figure 16.8: Open context translation

---

PROOF. By induction on the structure of the evaluation context. There are 12 cases to consider, following the context translation in figure 16.8. We present two typical cases for illustration.

Case $Ee_1$.

$$\nu\vec{f}\,(\langle E[e]e_1\rangle u \mid \langle f := V\rangle) \equiv$$
$$\nu\vec{f}\,\nu t\,\nu w\,(\langle E[e]\rangle t \mid t(f).\langle e_1\rangle w \mid w(r).\overline{f}(r,u) \mid \langle f := V\rangle) \rightarrow^*_{ad} \quad \text{(by ind. hyp.)}$$
$$\nu\vec{f}\,\nu t\,\nu w\,\nu u'\,(\langle e\rangle u' \mid \{E\}(u',t) \mid t(f).\langle e_1\rangle w \mid w(r).\overline{f}(r,u) \mid \langle f := V\rangle) \equiv$$
$$\nu\vec{f}\,\nu u'\,(\langle e\rangle u' \mid \{Ee_1\}(u',u) \mid \langle f := V\rangle)\,.$$

Case $VE$.

$$\nu\vec{f}\,(\langle VE[e]\rangle u \mid \langle f := V\rangle) \equiv$$
$$\nu\vec{f}\,\nu t\,\nu w\,\nu f\,(\langle f := V\rangle \mid \overline{t}f \mid t(f).\langle E[e]\rangle w \mid w(r).\overline{f}(r,u) \mid \langle f := V\rangle) \rightarrow_{ad}$$
$$\nu\vec{f}\,\nu t\,\nu w\,\nu f\,(\langle f := V\rangle \mid \langle E[e]\rangle w \mid w(r).\overline{f}(r,u) \mid \langle f := V\rangle) \rightarrow^*_{ad} \quad \text{(by ind. hyp.)}$$
$$\nu\vec{f}\,\nu t\,\nu w\,\nu f\,\nu u'\,(\langle f := V\rangle \mid \langle e\rangle u' \mid \{E\}(u',w) \mid w(r).\overline{f}(r,u) \mid \langle f := V\rangle) \equiv$$
$$\nu\vec{f}\,\nu u'\,(\langle f := V\rangle \mid \langle e\rangle u' \mid \{VE\}(u',w) \mid \langle f := V\rangle)\,. \qquad \Box$$

**Remark 16.3.5** (1) *From the previous lemma 16.3.4 we can prove that if $e \equiv e'$ then* $\natural\langle e\rangle u \equiv \natural\langle e'\rangle u$.

(2) *Lemma 16.3.4 immediately extends to a general behaviour expression*

$$e \equiv \nu\vec{x}\,(E_1[\Delta_1] \mid \cdots \mid E_m[\Delta_m])$$

*as the expression translation distributes with respect to restriction and parallel composition.*

We present in figure 16.9 a translation that pre-computes the administrative reductions in an open redex (we assume that $V$ is a $\lambda$-abstraction). This translation is needed in the following proposition.

$$\{(\lambda r'.e)r\}u \;=\; \nu f\,(\langle\!| f := \lambda r'.e|\!\rangle \mid \overline{f}(r,u))$$
$$\{(\lambda f'.e)V\}u \;=\; \nu f\,\nu f'\,(\langle\!| f := \lambda f'.e|\!\rangle \mid \langle\!| f' := V|\!\rangle \mid \overline{f}(f',u))$$
$$\{fr\}u \;=\; \overline{f}(r,u)$$
$$\{fV\}u \;=\; \nu f'\,(\langle\!| f' := V|\!\rangle \mid \overline{f}(f',u))$$
$$\{z?\}u \;=\; z(r).\overline{u}r$$
$$\{z!r\}u \;=\; \overline{z}r.\overline{u}*$$
$$\{z!V\}u \;=\; \nu f'\,(\langle\!| f' := V|\!\rangle \mid \overline{z}f'.\overline{u}*)$$

Figure 16.9: Open redex translation

**Proposition 16.3.6** *The administrative normal form of the behaviour expression* $e \equiv \nu\vec{x}\,(E_1[\Delta_1] \mid \cdots \mid E_m[\Delta_m])$ *can be characterized as (supposing* $E_i \neq [\,]$, *for* $i = 1, \ldots, m$, *otherwise just drop the context translation):*

$$\natural\langle\!| e|\!\rangle u \equiv \nu\vec{x}\,\nu u_1 \ldots u_m\,(\{\Delta_1\}u_1 \mid \{E_1\}(u_1, u) \mid \cdots \mid \{\Delta_m\}u_m \mid \{E_m\}(u_m, u))\;.$$

PROOF HINT. By remark 16.3.5 and the observation that translations of open evaluation contexts and redexes do not admit administrative reductions.  □

With the help of the optimized translation described above, we derive the following lemma, which relates reductions and commitments modulo the relation $\mathcal{R}$.

**Lemma 16.3.7** *The following assertions relate reductions and commitments:*

(1) *If* $e\,\mathcal{R}\,P$ *and* $e \to e'$ *then for some* $P'$, $\natural P \to P'$ *and* $e'\,\mathcal{R}\,P'$.

(2) *Vice versa, if* $e\,\mathcal{R}\,P$ *and* $\natural P \to P'$ *then for some* $e'$, $e \to e'$ *and* $e'\,\mathcal{R}\,P'$.

(3) *Suppose* $e\,\mathcal{R}\,P$. *Then* $e \downarrow \beta$ *iff* $\natural P \downarrow \beta$.

PROOF. (1) By analysis of the redex, following the open redex translation in figure 16.9. We consider only two cases which should justify the definition of the relation $\mathcal{R}$. As a first case suppose $e\,\mathcal{R}\,P$ and:

$$e \equiv E[(\lambda f'.e)V][V\!/\!f] \to_\beta E[e[V/f']][V\!/\!f] \equiv e'$$

$$\natural P \equiv \natural\nu\vec{f}\,(\langle\!| E[(\lambda f'.e)V]|\!\rangle u \mid \langle\!| f := V|\!\rangle)\;.$$

Then $\natural P \to_{beta} P'$, where:

$$P' \equiv \nu\vec{f}\,\nu f'\,\nu u'\,(\langle\!| e|\!\rangle u' \mid \{E\}(u', u) \mid \langle\!| f' := V|\!\rangle \mid \langle\!| f := V|\!\rangle)$$

and $e'\,\mathcal{R}\,P'$, since $e' \equiv E[e][V/f'][V\!/\!f]$ , and by the administrative reduction lemma 16.3.4:

$$\natural P' \equiv \natural\nu\vec{f}\,\nu f'\,(\langle\!| E[e]|\!\rangle u \mid \langle\!| f' := V|\!\rangle \mid \langle\!| f := V|\!\rangle)\;.$$

As a second case suppose $e\,\mathcal{R}\,P$ and:

$$e \equiv (E[c!f_i] \mid E'[c?])[V\!/\!f] \to_\beta (E[*] \mid E'[f_i])[V\!/\!f] \equiv e'\;.$$

$$\natural P \equiv \natural \nu \vec{f}\, ((E[c!f_i])\flat u \mid (E'[c?])\flat u \mid (f := \vec{V})) \, .$$

Then $\natural P \to_\tau P'$, where:

$$P' \equiv \nu \vec{f}\, \nu u_1\, \nu u_2\, ((\flat * )\flat u_1 \mid \{E\}(u_1,u) \mid (f_i)\flat u_2 \mid \{E'\}(u_2,u) \mid (f := \vec{V})) \, ,$$

and observe $e'\, \mathcal{R}\, P'$, since by the administrative reduction lemma 16.3.4:

$$\natural P' \equiv \natural \nu \vec{f}\, ((E[*] \mid E'[f_i])\flat u \mid (f := \vec{V})) \, .$$

(2) Same analysis as in (1).

(3) This follows by the definition of the relation $\mathcal{R}$ and by proposition 16.3.6.          □

**Theorem 16.3.8** *Let $e, e'$ be programs in $\lambda_\parallel$. Then $(e)\flat u \overset{\bullet}{\approx} (e')\flat u$ iff $e \overset{\bullet}{\approx} e'$.*

PROOF. The previous lemma 16.3.7 allows us to go back and forth between (weak) reductions and (weak) commitments 'modulo $\mathcal{R}$'. Hence we can define the following relations and show that they are barbed bisimulations.

$$\begin{aligned} S &= \{(e, e') \mid \exists P, P'\ (e\,\mathcal{R}\,P \overset{\bullet}{\approx} P'\,\mathcal{R}^{-1}\,e')\} \\ S' &= \{(P, P') \mid \exists e, e'\ (P\,\mathcal{R}^{-1}\,e \overset{\bullet}{\approx} e'\,\mathcal{R}\,P')\} \, . \end{aligned}$$

The conclusion follows since by definition $e\,\mathcal{R}\,(e)\flat u$.          □

Unfortunately, theorem 16.3.8 does not extend to barbed equivalence, as there are equivalent $\lambda_\parallel$-terms whose $\pi$-calculus translations can be distinguished. The relationships between $\lambda$-calculus and $\pi$-calculus need to be further studied. For instance it is not known whether there is a 'natural' fully-abstract translation of the call-by-value $\lambda$-calculus into the $\pi$-calculus, or in another direction, whether there is a 'reasonable' extension of the $\lambda$-calculus that would make the translation considered here fully-abstract. Yet another research direction is to consider fragments of the $\pi$-calculus which are obtained by some restriction on the communication mechanism, and/or on the use of channel names (see, e.g., [HY95, Bou92, PS93, ACS96, Ama97]).

**Exercise 16.3.9** *Define an asynchronous variant of the $\pi$-calculus (cf. exercise 16.2.5) where the output prefix is always followed by 0. Find a simulation of the synchronous polyadic $\pi$-calculus in the asynchronous monadic $\pi$-calculus (cf. exercise 16.1.22).*

# Appendix 1
## Summary of recursion theory

Partial recursive, or computable functions, may be defined in a number of equivalent ways. This is what Church's thesis is about: all definitions of computability turn out to be equivalent. Church's thesis justifies some confidence in 'semi-formal' arguments, used to show that a given function is computable. These arguments can be accepted only if at any moment, upon request, the author of the argument is able to fully formalize it in one of the available axiomatizations.

In this summary, functions are always partial, unless otherwise specified.

## A1.1   Partial recursive functions

The most basic way of defining computable functions is by means of computing devices of which Turing machines are the most well known. A given Turing machine defines, for each $n$, a partial function $f : \omega^n \to \omega$. More mathematical presentations are by means of recursive program schemes, or by means of combinations of basic recursive functions.

**Theorem A1.1.1 (Gödel-Kleene)** *For any $n$, the set of Turing computable functions from $\omega^n$ to $\omega$ is the set of partial recursive functions from $\omega^n$ to $\omega$, where by definition the class of partial recursive (p.r.) functions is the smallest class containing:*

- $0 : \omega \to \omega$ *defined by* $0(x) = 0$.

- $succ : \omega \to \omega$ *(the successor function).*

- *Projections* $\pi_{n,i} : \omega^n \to \omega$ *defined by* $\pi_{n,i}(x_1, \ldots, x_n) = x_i$,

*and closed under the following constructions:*

- *Composition: If* $f_1 : \omega^m \to \omega, \ldots, f_n : \omega^m \to \omega$ *and* $g : \omega^n \to \omega$ *are partial recursive, then* $g \circ \langle f_1, \ldots, f_n \rangle : \omega^m \to \omega$ *is partial recursive.*

- *Primitive recursion: if* $f : \omega^n \to \omega$, $g : \omega^{n+2} \to \omega$ *are partial recursive, then so is $h$ defined by:*
$$
\begin{aligned}
h(\vec{x}, 0) &= f(\vec{x}) \\
h(\vec{x}, y + 1) &= g(\vec{x}, y, h(\vec{x}, y)) \ .
\end{aligned}
$$

- *Minimalization: if* $f : \omega^{n+1} \to \omega$ *is partial recursive, so is* $g : \omega^n \to \omega$ *defined by* $g(\vec{x}) = \mu y.(f(\vec{x}, y) = 0)$, *where $\mu y.P$ means: the smallest $y$ such that $P$.*

The source of partiality lies in minimalization. The total functions obtained by the combinations of Gödel-Kleene, except minimalization, are called primitive recursive.

The partial recursive functions which are total are called the recursive functions. The set of partial recursive functions from $\omega^n$ to $\omega$ is called $PR^n$ (we write $PR$ for $PR^1$).

Notice the use of the symbol $\rightharpoonup$ in $g : \omega^n \rightharpoonup \omega$. From now on, we shall use $\rightharpoonup$ for partial functions and $\rightarrow$ for total functions.

**Lemma A1.1.2 (encoding of pairs)** *The following functions are recursive and provide inverse bijections between $\omega \times \omega$ and $\omega$.*

- $\langle \_, \_ \rangle : \omega \times \omega \rightarrow \omega$ *defined by:* $\langle m, n \rangle = 2^m(2n + 1) - 1$,

- $\pi_1 : \omega \rightarrow \omega$ *where $\pi_1(n)$ is the exponent of 2 in the prime decomposition of $n + 1$,*

- $\pi_2 : \omega \rightarrow \omega$ *defined by:* $\pi_2(n) = ((n + 1)/2^{\pi_1(n)} - 1)/2$.

Hence a function $f : \omega \times \omega \rightharpoonup \omega$ is partial recursive iff $f \circ \langle \pi_1, \pi_2 \rangle : \omega \rightharpoonup \omega$ is partial recursive.

Turing machines can also be coded by natural numbers (a Turing machine is determined by a finite control which can be described by a finite string on a finite alphabet which in turn can be represented by a natural number). We call:

- $T_n$ the Turing machine which has code $n$.

- $\phi_n^m$ the partial function from $\omega^m$ to $\omega$ defined by $T_n$, for each $m$ (we write $\phi_n$ for $\phi_n^1$).

- $W_n^m = dom(\phi_n^m)$ (we write $W_n$ for $W_n^1$).

If $f = \phi_n^m$, $W = W_n^m$, we say that $n$ is an index of $f$, $W$, respectively. The principal properties of the sets $W_n^m$ are summarized in section A1.2.

**Lemma A1.1.3 (enumeration of $PR$)** *The mapping $\lambda n.\phi_n$ is a surjection of $\omega$ onto $PR$.*

As a first consequence, there are total functions that are not recursive.

**Exercise A1.1.4** *Show that $f$ defined by*

$$f(n) = \begin{cases} \phi_n(n) + 1 & \text{if } \phi_n(n) \downarrow \\ 0 & \text{otherwise} \end{cases}$$

*is not recursive. (But $g$ defined by $(g(n) \downarrow \phi_n(n) + 1$ iff $\phi_n(n) \downarrow$) is p.r, see theorem A1.1.6.) Show that there exist recursive, non primitive recursive functions. Hint: For the last part use an enumeration $\{\theta_n\}_{n \in \omega}$ of the primitive recursive functions, and take $\lambda x.\theta_x(x) + 1$.*

The next theorem says that some of the arguments of a partial recursive function can be frozen, uniformly.

**Theorem A1.1.5 (s-m-n)** *For each $m, n$ there is a total recursive $m + 1$-ary function $s_n^m$ (s for short) such that for all $\vec{x} = x_1, \ldots, x_m$, $\vec{y} = y_{m+1}, \ldots, y_{m+n}$ and $p : \phi_p^{m+n}(\vec{x}, \vec{y}) \cong \phi_{s(p,\vec{x})}^n(\vec{y})$.*

PROOF HINT. We can 'prefix' to $T_p$ instructions that input the frozen argument $\vec{x}$.  □

**Theorem A1.1.6 (universal Turing machine)** *There exists a Turing machine $T_U$ computing, for any $n$, the function $\psi_U^n : \omega^{n+1} \rightharpoonup \omega$ defined by: $\psi_U^n(p, \vec{y}) = \phi_p^n(\vec{y})$.*

PROOF HINT. Informally, $T_U$ decodes its first argument $p$ into the machine $T_p$, and then acts as $T_p$ on the remaining arguments.  □

# A1.2 Recursively enumerable sets

The theory of computable functions can be equivalently presented as a theory of computable predicates.

**Definition A1.2.1 (decidable, r.e.)** *A subset $W$ of $\omega^n$ is called* decidable, *or recursive, when its characteristic function $\chi$ defined by*

$$\chi(x) = \begin{cases} 0 & \text{if } x \in W \\ 1 & \text{otherwise} \end{cases}$$

*is recursive. A subset $W$ of $\omega^n$ is called* primitive recursive, *when its characteristic function is primitive recursive. A subset $W$ of $\omega^n$ is called* semi-decidable, *or recursively enumerable (r.e.), when its partial characteristic function $\chi_p$ ($\chi_p(x) \downarrow$ iff $x \in W$) is partial recursive.*

Clearly, every decidable set is recursively enumerable. A central example of a recursive set is the following.

**Proposition A1.2.2 (convergence in $t$ steps)** *Given a Turing machine $T$ computing the partial recursive function $f$, the set $\{(\vec{x}, y, t) \mid f(\vec{x}) \downarrow y$ in $t$ steps of $T\}$ is recursive.*

PROOF. Given a Turing machine $T$ computing $f$, the obvious informal algorithm is: perform at most $t$ steps of $T$ starting with input $\vec{x}$, and check whether result $y$ has been reached. □

**Remark A1.2.3** *A more careful analysis shows that the characteristic function of*

$$\{(\vec{x}, y, t) \mid f(\vec{x}) \downarrow y \text{ in } t \text{ steps}\}$$

*can be defined by means of primitive recursion only.*

There are a number of equivalent characterizations of recursive and recursively enumerable sets.

**Proposition A1.2.4** *The set $W \subseteq \omega^n$ is r.e. iff one of the following conditions holds:*

(1) $W = dom(f)$, *for some partial recursive function $f$.*

(2) *There exists a recursive set $W' \subseteq \omega^{n+1}$ such that $W = \{\vec{x} \mid \exists y \ (\vec{x}, y) \in W'\}$.*

(3) $W = \emptyset$ *or $W = im(h)$, for some recursive function $h : \omega^n \to \omega$.*

(4) $W = im(h)$, *for some partial recursive function $h : \omega^n \rightharpoonup \omega$.*

PROOF. (1) If $W = dom(f)$, then its partial characteristic function is $\mathbf{1} \circ f$, where $\mathbf{1}$ is constant 1.

(2) Let $W$ be $\{\vec{x} \mid \exists y \ (\vec{x}, y) \in W'\}$. Then $W = dom(\lambda \vec{x}.\mu y.((\vec{x}, y) \in W'))$. Conversely, if $W = dom(f)$, take $W' = \{(\vec{x}, y) \mid f(\vec{x}) \downarrow$ in $y$ steps$\}$.

(3) If $W = dom(f) \neq \emptyset$, pick an element $\vec{a} \in W$. Define:

$$g(\vec{x}, y) = \begin{cases} \vec{x} & \text{if } f(\vec{x}) \downarrow \text{ in } y \text{ steps} \\ \vec{a} & \text{otherwise .} \end{cases}$$

Then $W = im(g) = im(h)$ (where $h$ is the composition of $g$ with the encoding from $\omega^n$ to $\omega^{n+1}$).

(4) If $W = im(h)$, we have by proposition A1.2.2 that $\{(\vec{x}, y, t) \mid h(\vec{x}) \downarrow y \text{ in } t \text{ steps}\}$ is recursive. Thus $W = dom(\lambda \vec{x}.\mu z.(z = \langle y, t \rangle \text{ and } h(\vec{x}) \downarrow y \text{ in } t \text{ steps}))$.  □

In particular, the $W_n^m$'s (cf. section A1.1) provide an enumeration of all $m$-ary r.e. predicates.

**Remark A1.2.5** *The encodings used in the proof of proposition A1.2.4(3) 'hide' a useful technique, known as* dovetailing: *the informal way of obtaining $h$ is by trying the first step of $f(1)$, the first step of $f(2)$, the second step of $f(1)$, the first step of $f(3)$, the second step of $f(2)$, the third step of $f(1)$, the first step of $f(4) \dots$*

**Exercise A1.2.6** *Show that if $W \subseteq \omega^{n+1}$ is recursively enumerable, then $\{\vec{x} \mid \exists y \ (\vec{x}, y) \in W\}$ is recursively enumerable. Hint: Consider a recursive $W'$ such that $W = \{(\vec{x}, y) \mid \exists z \ (\vec{x}, y, z) \in W'\}$ is recursively enumerable.*

**Proposition A1.2.7** *A predicate $W \subseteq \omega^n$ is recursive iff $W$ and its complement $W^c$ are recursively enumerable.*

PROOF. If $W$ is decidable, it is r.e., and $W^c$ is decidable (with characteristic function $\neg \circ \chi$, where $\chi$ is the characteristic function of $W$). Conversely, if $W$ and $W^c$ are both r.e., the (total) characteristic function $\chi$ of $W$ can be computed by interleaving the computations of the partial characteristic functions $\chi'$ and $\chi''$ of $W$ and $W^c$. More precisely, if $T'$ and $T''$ are Turing machines computing $\chi'$ and the negation of $\chi''$, respectively, then a machine $T$ computing $\chi$ is obtained by performing alternatively one step on each of the machines $T$ and $T'$. The machine $T$ will always stop because $W \cup W^c = \omega^n$.  □

The following is a useful characterization of partial recursive functions.

**Proposition A1.2.8** *A function $f$ is partial recursive if and only if its graph $\{(\vec{x}, y) \mid f(\vec{x}) \downarrow y\}$ is recursively enumerable.*

PROOF. If $f$ is p.r., then by proposition A1.2.2 $\{(\vec{x}, y, t) \mid f(\vec{x}) \downarrow y \text{ in } t \text{ steps}\}$ is recursive. We conclude by proposition A1.2.4(2) that $\{(\vec{x}, y) \mid f(\vec{x}) \downarrow y\}$ is r.e., since $f(\vec{x}) \downarrow y$ iff $f(\vec{x}) \downarrow y$ in $t$ steps for some $t$.

Conversely, if $\{(\vec{x}, y) \mid f(\vec{x}) \downarrow y\}$ is r.e., let $W'$ be a recursive set such that $f(\vec{x}) \downarrow y$ iff $(\vec{x}, y, t) \in W'$ for some $t$. Then $f$ can be written as:

$$\pi_1 \circ (\lambda \vec{x}.\mu z.(z = \langle y, t \rangle \text{ and } (\vec{x}, y, t) \in W')),$$

and thus is partial recursive.  □

Here is an example of a semi-decidable, non decidable predicate.

**Proposition A1.2.9** (1) *The set $K = \{x \mid x \in W_x\}$ is recursively enumerable.*

(2) *The set $\{x \mid x \notin W_x\}$ is not recursively enumerable.*

PROOF. (1) We have $K = im(\lambda x.\phi_x(x)) = im(\psi_U \circ \langle id, id \rangle)$, thus $K$ is r.e. by proposition A1.2.4(4).

(2) Suppose $\{x \mid x \notin W_x\} = dom(f)$ for some p.r. function. Let $n$ be an index of $f$. We have: $\forall x \ (x \notin W_x \text{ iff } x \in W_n)$. We get a contradiction when taking $x = n$.  □

**Exercise A1.2.10** *Show that $\{x \mid \phi_x \text{ is recursive}\}$ is not recursively enumerable. Hint: Consider $g(x) = \phi_{f(x)}(x) + 1$, where $f$ is a claimed enumeration of the recursive functions.*

# A1.3   The Rice-Shapiro theorem

We end this summary with an important theorem, which is widely used in theoretical computer science. It gives evidence to the thesis: *computable implies continuous* (cf. theorem 1.3.1 and proposition 15.5.10). A partial function $\theta$ such that $dom(\theta)$ is finite is called finite. Clearly finite functions from $\omega$ to $\omega$ are computable. Partial functions may be ordered as follows:

$$f \leq g \text{ iff } \forall x \ (f(x) \downarrow y) \Rightarrow (g(x) \downarrow y) \ .$$

**Theorem A1.3.1 (Rice-Shapiro)** *Let $A \subseteq PR$ be such that $A' = \{x \mid \phi_x \in A\}$ is recursively enumerable. Then, for any partial recursive $f$, $f \in A$ iff there exists a finite function $\theta \leq f$ such that $\theta \in A$.*

PROOF. Let $T$ be a Turing machine computing the partial characteristic function of $K = \{x \mid x \in W_x\}$.

($\Leftarrow$) Suppose $f \in A$, and $\forall \theta \leq f$ ($\theta \notin A$). Let $g$ be the partial recursive function defined by $g(z,t) \downarrow y$ iff $T$ starting with $z$ does not terminate in less than $t$ steps, and $f(t) \downarrow y$. One has, by definition of $g$:

$$\lambda t.g(z,t) = \begin{cases} f & \text{if } z \notin K \\ \theta & \text{if } z \in K, \text{ where } \theta \leq_{fin} f \ . \end{cases}$$

Thus our assumption entails $z \notin K$ iff $\lambda t.g(z,t) \in A$. Let $s$ be a recursive function, given by theorem A1.1.5, such that $g(z,t) \cong \phi_{s(z)}(t)$. The above equivalence can be rephrased as: $z \notin K$ iff $s(z) \in A'$. But the predicate on the right is r.e. (cf. proposition A1.2.9(2)): contradiction.

($\Rightarrow$) Suppose $f \notin A$ and $\theta \in A$, for some finite $\theta \leq f$. We argue as in the previous case, defining now $g$ by:

$$g(z,t) \downarrow y \text{ iff } (\theta(t) \downarrow \text{ or } z \in K) \text{ and } f(t) \downarrow y \ .$$

$\square$

**Corollary A1.3.2 (Rice)** *If $B \subseteq PR$, $B \neq \emptyset$ and $B \neq PR$, then $\{x \mid \phi_x \in B\}$ is undecidable.*

PROOF. Let $A$ be as in the statement of the Rice-Shapiro theorem, and let $\perp$ be the totally undefined function. If $\perp \in A$, then, by the theorem, $A$ must be the whole of $PR$.

Now suppose that $\{x \mid \phi_x \in B\}$ is decidable. Then $B$ and $B^c$ both satisfy the conditions of the Rice-Shapiro theorem. Consider the totally undefined function $\perp$. We have: $\perp \in B$ or $\perp \in B^c$. We deduce that either $B = PR$ or $B^c = PR$: contradiction.$\square$

# Appendix 2
## Summary of category theory

Category theory has been tightly connected to abstract mathematics since the first paper on cohomology by Eilenberg and Mac Lane [EML45] which establishes its basic notions. This appendix is a reminder of a few elementary definitions and results in this branch of mathematics. We refer to [ML71, AL91] for adequate introductions and wider perspectives.

In mathematical practice, category theory is helpful in formalizing a problem, as it is a good habit to ask in which category we are working in, if a certain transformation is a functor, if a given subcategory is reflective, etc. Using category theoretical terminology, one can often express a result in a more modular and abstract way. A list of 'prescriptions' for the use of category theory in computer science can be found in [Gog91].

*Categorical logic* is a branch of category theory that arises from the observation due to Lawvere that logical connectives can be suitably expressed by means of universal properties. In this way one represents the models of, say, intuitionistic propositional logic, as categories with certain closure properties where sentences are interpreted as objects and proofs as morphisms (cf. section 4.3).

The tools developed in categorical logic begin to play a central role in the study of programming languages. A link between these two apparently distant topics is suggested by:

• The role of (typed) $\lambda$-calculi in the work of Landin, McCarthy, Strachey, and Scott on the foundations of programming languages.

• The Curry-Howard correspondence between systems of natural deduction and typed $\lambda$-calculi (cf. section 4.1).

• The categorical semantics of typed $\lambda$-calculi along the lines traced by Lambek and Scott (cf. section 4.4).

The basic idea in this study is to describe in the categorical language the 'models' of a given programming languages. For instance, in the case of the simply typed $\lambda$-calculus the models correspond to the cartesian closed categories. Along these lines, categorical logic has provided important insights in the study of *functional* languages. Moreover, promising attempts to describe categorically other features of programming languages such as modules, continuations, local variables, etc. are actively pursued.

# A2.1 Basic definitions

A category may be regarded as a directed labelled graph endowed with a partial operation of composition of edges which is associative and has an identity.

**Definition A2.1.1** *A category* **C** *is a sextuple* $(Ob, Mor, dom, cod, id, comp)$ *where* $Ob$ *is the class of objects,* $Mor$ *is the class of morphisms and:*

$$dom : Mor \to Ob \quad cod : Mor \to Ob$$
$$id : Ob \to Mor \quad comp : Comp \to Mor \ ,$$

*where* $Comp = \{(f, g) \in Mor \times Mor \mid dom(f) = cod(g)\}$. *Moreover:*

$$id \circ f = f \circ id = f \quad (identity)$$
$$f \circ (g \circ h) = (f \circ g) \circ h \quad (associativity),$$

*where* $f \circ g$ *is a shorthand for* $comp(f, g)$; *we write* $f \circ g$ *only if* $(f, g) \in Comp$, *and we omit to write the object to which id is applied in (identity).*

Let **C** be a category, $a, b \in Ob$, then

$$\mathbf{C}[a, b] = \{f \in Mor \mid dom(f) = a \text{ and } cod(f) = b\}$$

is the homset from $a$ to $b$. We also write $f : a \to b$ for $f \in \mathbf{C}[a, b]$, and $a \in \mathbf{C}$ for $a \in Ob$. When confusion may arise we decorate the components $Ob, Mor, \dots$ of a category with its name, hence writing $Ob_\mathbf{C}, Mor_\mathbf{C}, \dots$ A category **C** is *small* if $Mor_\mathbf{C}$ is a set, and it is *locally* small if for any $a, b \in \mathbf{C}$, $\mathbf{C}[a, b]$ is a set.

**Example A2.1.2 (basic categories)** *We just specify objects and morphisms. The operation of composition is naturally defined. The verification of the identity and associativity laws is immediate:*

- *Sets and functions,* **Set**.

- *Sets and partial functions,* **pSet**.

- *Sets and binary relations.*

- *Every preorder* $(P, \leq)$ *induces a category* **P** *with* $\sharp\mathbf{P}[a, b] = 1$ *if* $a \leq b$ *and* $\sharp\mathbf{P}[a, b] = 0$ *otherwise.*

- *Any set with just an identity morphism for each object (this is the* discrete *category).*

- *Every monoid induces a category with one object and its elements as morphisms.*

- *Posets (or preorders) and monotonic functions.*

- *Groups and homomorphisms.*

- *Topological spaces and continuous functions,* **Top**.

- *Directed unlabelled graphs and transformations that preserve domain and codomain of edges.*

**Definition A2.1.3 (dual category)** *Let* **C** *be a category. We define the dual category* $\mathbf{C}^{op}$ *as follows:*

$$Ob_{\mathbf{C}^{op}} = Ob_\mathbf{C} \quad \mathbf{C}^{op}[a, b] = \mathbf{C}[b, a]$$
$$id^{op} = id \quad f \circ^{op} g = g \circ f \ .$$

**Remark A2.1.4 (dual property)** *Given a property P for a category* **C** *and relative theorems it often makes sense to consider a* dual property $P^{op}$ *to which correspond* dual *theorems. This idea can be formalized using the notion of dual category as follows: given a property P, we say that* **C** *has property $P^{op}$ if $\mathbf{C}^{op}$ has property P.*

**Example A2.1.5 (categories built out of categories)** (1) *A* subcategory *is any sub-graph of a given category closed under composition and identity.*

(2) *If* **C** *and* **D** *are categories the* product category **C** × **D** *is defined by:*

$$Ob_{\mathbf{C}\times\mathbf{D}} = Ob_{\mathbf{C}} \times Ob_{\mathbf{D}}, \quad (\mathbf{C} \times \mathbf{D})[(a,b),(a',b')] = \mathbf{C}[a,a'] \times \mathbf{D}[b,b'] \ .$$

(3) *If* **C** *is a category and $a \in$* **C***, the* slice category **C** ↓ *a is defined as:* **C** ↓ $a = \bigcup_{b\in\mathbf{C}} \mathbf{C}[b,a]$, $(\mathbf{C} \downarrow a)[f,g] = \{h \mid g \circ h = f\}$.

**Definition A2.1.6 (terminal object)** *An object a in a category* **C** *is terminal if $\forall b \in$* **C** $\exists! f : b \to a$. *We denote a terminal object with* 1 *and with* $!_b$ *the unique morphism from b to* 1.

**Definition A2.1.7 (properties of morphisms)** *Let* **C** *be a category.*

• *A morphism $f : a \to b$ is a* mono *if $\forall h, k$ ($f \circ h = f \circ k \Rightarrow h = k$).*

• *A morphism f is* epi *if it is mono in $\mathbf{C}^{op}$, i.e., $\forall h, k$ ($h \circ f = k \circ f \Rightarrow h = k$).*

• *A morphism $f : a \to b$ is a* split mono *if there is a morphism $g : b \to a$ (called a split epi) such that $g \circ f = id$.*

• *A morphism $f : a \to b$ is an* iso *if there is an inverse morphism $g : b \to a$ such that $g \circ f = id$ and $f \circ g = id$. We write $a \cong b$ if there is an iso between a and b.*

**Exercise A2.1.8** *Prove the following properties: (1) Each object has a unique identity morphism. (2) The inverse of an iso is unique. (3) If $g \circ f = id$ then g is an epi and f is a mono. (4) f epi and split mono implies f iso. (5) f mono and epi does not imply f iso. (6) The terminal object is uniquely determined up to isomorphism.*

# A2.2  Limits

The notions of cone and limit of a diagram are presented. The main result explains how to build limits of arbitrary diagrams by combining limits of special diagrams, namely *products* and *equalizers*.

**Definition A2.2.1 (diagram)** *Let* **C** *be a category and $I = (Ob_I, Mor_I)$ be a graph. A diagram in* **C** *over I is a graph morphism $D : I \to$* **C***.*

We often represent a diagram $D$ as a pair $(\{d_i\}_{i\in Ob_I}, \{f_u\}_{u\in Mor_I})$.

**Definition A2.2.2 (category of cones)** *Let* **C** *be a category and $D : I \to$* **C** *be a diagram. We define the category of cones* $\mathbf{Cones}_\mathbf{C}D$ *as follows:*

$$\mathbf{Cones}_\mathbf{C}D = \{(c, \{h_i : c \to d_i\}_{i\in Ob_I}) \mid \forall u \in Mor_I \ (f_u : d_i \to d_j \Rightarrow h_j = f_u \circ h_i)\}$$
$$\mathbf{Cones}_\mathbf{C}D[(c, \{h_i\}_{i\in Ob_I}), (d, \{k_i\}_{i\in Ob_I})] = \{g : c \to d \mid \forall i \in Ob_I \ (h_i = k_i \circ g)\} \ .$$

**Definition A2.2.3 (limit)** *Let* **C** *be a category and* $D : I \to$ **C** *be a diagram. We say that* $D$ *has a limit if the category* $\mathbf{Cones}_{\mathbf{C}} D$ *has a terminal object.*

By the properties of terminal objects it follows that limits are determined up to isomorphism in $\mathbf{Cones}_{\mathbf{C}} D$. Hence we may improperly speak of a limit as an object of the category $\mathbf{Cones}_{\mathbf{C}} D$. We denote this object by $lim_{\mathbf{C}} D$. Also we say that the category **C** has *I-limits* if all diagrams indexed over $I$ have limits.

**Example A2.2.4 (special limits)** *We specialize the definition of limit to some recurring diagrams:*

(1) *If* $I = \emptyset$ *then the limit is a terminal object.*

(2) *If* $I$ *is a discrete graph (no morphisms) then a diagram over* $I$ *in* **C** *is just a family of objects* $\{a_i\}_{i \in Ob_I}$. *In this case a limit is also called a* product *and it is determined by a couple* $(c, \{\pi_i : c \to a_i\}_{i \in Ob_I})$ *such that for any cone* $(d, \{f_i : c \to a_i\}_{i \in Ob_I})$ *there exists a unique* $z : d \to c$ *such that* $\forall i \in Ob_I$ $(f_i = \pi_i \circ z)$. *We write* $c$ *as* $\Pi_{i \in Ob_I} a_i$, *and* $z$ *as* $\langle f_i \rangle$, *which is an abbreviation for* $\langle f_i \rangle_{i \in Ob_I}$. *The operation* $\langle \_ \rangle$ *is called* pairing.

(3) *Equalizers are limits of diagrams over a graph* $I$ *with two nodes, say* $x, y$, *and two edges from* $x$ *to* $y$. *If the image of the diagram is a pair of morphisms* $f, g : a \to b$ *then an equalizer (or limit) is a pair* $(c, e : c \to a)$ *with properties (i)* $f \circ e = g \circ e$, *and (ii) if* $(c', e' : c' \to a)$ *and* $f \circ e' = g \circ e'$ *then* $\exists ! z : c' \to c$ $(e \circ z = e')$.

(4) *Pullbacks are limits of diagrams over a graph* $I$ *with three nodes* $x, y, z$, *one edge from* $x$ *to* $z$, *and one edge from* $y$ *to* $z$. *If the image of the diagram is a pair of morphisms* $f : a \to d$, $g : b \to d$ *then a pullback (or limit) is a pair* $(c, \{h : c \to a, k : c \to b\})$ *with properties (i)* $f \circ h = g \circ k$, *and (ii) if* $(c', \{h' : c' \to a, k' : c' \to b\})$ *and* $f \circ h' = g \circ k'$ *then* $\exists ! z : c' \to c$ $(h \circ z = h'$ *and* $k \circ z = k')$.

The notions of *cocone*, *initial object*, and *colimit* are dual to the notions of cone, terminal object, and limit, respectively. We spell out the definition of coproduct which is often needed.

**Definition A2.2.5 (coproduct)** *The colimit of a family of objects* $\{a_i\}_{i \in Ob_I}$ *is called* coproduct. *It is determined by a couple* $(c, \{in_i : a_i \to c\}_{i \in Ob_I})$ *such that for any cocone* $(d, \{f_i : a_i \to d\}_{i \in Ob_I})$ *there exists a unique* $z : c \to d$ *such that* $\forall i \in Ob_I$ $(f_i = z \circ in_i)$. *We write* $c$ *as* $\Sigma_{i \in Ob_I} a_i$, *and* $z$ *as* $[f_i]_{i \in Ob_I}$, *or simply* $[f_i]$. *The operation* $[\_]$ *is called* copairing.

**Exercise A2.2.6** *Show that a category with terminal object and pullbacks has binary products and equalizers.*

**Theorem A2.2.7 (existence of I-limits)** *Let* **C** *be a category and* $I$ *be a graph, then* **C** *has I-limits if*

(1) **C** *has equalizers.*

(2) **C** *has all products indexed over* $Ob_I$ *and* $Mor_I$.

*In particular a category with equalizers and finite products has all finite limits.*

PROOF. Let $D : I \to \mathbf{C}$ be a diagram. We define:

$$P = \Pi_{i \in Ob_I} D(i) \qquad Q = \Pi_{u \in Mor_I} cod(D(u)) \, .$$

Next we define $f, g : P \to Q$, and $e : L \to P$ as follows, using $p$ and $q$ to denote the projections of $P$ and $Q$, respectively.

- $f$ is the unique morphism such that $D(u) \circ p_{dom(u)} = q_u \circ f$, for any $u \in Mor_I$.
- $g$ is the unique morphism such that $p_{cod(u)} = q_u \circ g$, for any $u \in Mor_I$.
- $e$ is the equalizer of $f$ and $g$.

We claim that $(L, \{p_i \circ e\}_{i \in Ob_I})$ is a limit of the diagram $D$. The proof of this fact takes several steps.

(1) $(L, \{p_i \circ e\}_{i \in Ob_I}) \in \mathbf{Cones_C} D$. We have to show $D(u) \circ p_{dom(u)} \circ e = p_{cod(u)} \circ e$, for any $u \in Mor_I$. We observe:

$$D(u) \circ p_{dom(u)} \circ e \;\; = \;\; q_u \circ f \circ e \;\; = \;\; q_u \circ g \circ e \;\; = \;\; p_{cod(u)} \circ e \, .$$

(2) Let $(F, \{l_i\}_{i \in Ob_I}) \in \mathbf{Cones_C} D$. Then there is a uniquely determined morphism $\langle l_i \rangle : F \to P$ such that $p_i \circ \langle l_i \rangle = l_i$, for any $i \in Ob_I$. We claim $f \circ \langle l_i \rangle = g \circ \langle l_i \rangle$. This follows from the observation that for any $u \in Mor_I$:

$$
\begin{aligned}
q_u \circ f \circ \langle l_i \rangle \;\; &= \;\; D(u) \circ p_{dom(u)} \circ \langle l_i \rangle \;\; = \;\; D(u) \circ l_{dom(u)} \;\; = \;\; l_{cod(u)} \\
&= \;\; p_{cod(u)} \circ \langle l_i \rangle \;\; = \;\; q_u \circ g \circ \langle l_i \rangle \, .
\end{aligned}
$$

(3) Hence there is a unique $z : F \to L$ such that $e \circ z = \langle l_i \rangle$. Moreover, $z : (F, \{l_i\}_{i \in Ob_I}) \to (L, \{p_i \circ e\}_{i \in Ob_I})$ is in $\mathbf{Cones_C} D$, since for any $i \in Ob_I$, $p_i \circ e \circ z = p_i \circ \langle l_i \rangle = l_i$.

(4) Finally suppose $z' : (F, \{l_i\}_{i \in Ob_I}) \to (L, \{p_i \circ e\}_{i \in Ob_I})$ in $\mathbf{Cones_C} D$. Then $z' : (F, \langle l_i \rangle) \to (L, e)$ as $p_i \circ e \circ z' = l_i$, for any $i \in Ob_I$ implies $e \circ z' = \langle l_i \rangle$ (cf. example A2.2.4(3)). Hence $z = z'$. $\square$

**Exercise A2.2.8** *Study the existence of (co-)limits in the categories introduced in example A2.1.2.*

# A2.3 Functors and natural transformations

A functor is a morphism between categories and a natural transformation is a morphism between functors. The main result presented here is that there is a full and faithful functor from any category $\mathbf{C}$ to the category of set-valued functors over $\mathbf{C}^{op}$.

**Definition A2.3.1 (functor)** *Let $\mathbf{C}$, $\mathbf{D}$ be categories, a functor $F : \mathbf{C} \to \mathbf{D}$ is a morphism between the underlying graphs that preserves identity and composition, that is:*

$$F_{Ob} : Ob_\mathbf{C} \to Ob_\mathbf{D} \qquad F_{Mor} : Mor_\mathbf{C} \to Mor_\mathbf{D}$$
$$F_{Mor}(id_a) = id_{F_{Ob}(a)} \qquad F_{Mor}(f \circ g) = F_{Mor}(f) \circ F_{Mor}(g) \, ,$$

*where if $f : a \to b$ then $F_{Mor}(f) : F_{Ob}(a) \to F_{Ob}(b)$.*

In the following we omit the indices $Ob$ and $Mor$ in a functor. We often write $Fa$ for $F(a)$. A *contravariant* functor $F$ from $\mathbf{C}$ to $\mathbf{D}$ is a functor $F : \mathbf{C}^{op} \to \mathbf{D}$. By opposition, a *covariant* functor from $\mathbf{C}$ to $\mathbf{D}$ is a functor $F : \mathbf{C} \to \mathbf{D}$.

**Exercise A2.3.2** *Show that small categories and functors form a category.*

**Definition A2.3.3 (hom-functor)** *Let* $\mathbf{C}$ *be a locally small category. We define the hom-functor* $\mathbf{C}[\_,\_] : \mathbf{C}^{op} \times \mathbf{C} \to \mathbf{Set}$ *as follows:*

$$\mathbf{C}[\_,\_](a, b) = \mathbf{C}[a, b] \quad \mathbf{C}[\_,\_](f, g) = \lambda h. g \circ h \circ f .$$

Given an object $c$ in the category $\mathbf{C}$ we denote with $\mathbf{C}[\_, c] : \mathbf{C}^{op} \to \mathbf{Set}$ and $\mathbf{C}[c, \_] : \mathbf{C} \to \mathbf{Set}$ the contravariant and covariant functors over $\mathbf{C}$ obtained by restricting the hom-functor to the first and second component, respectively.

**Exercise A2.3.4** *Suppose* $F : \mathbf{C} \to \mathbf{D}$ *is a functor,* $D : I \to \mathbf{C}$ *is a diagram and* $(a, \{l_i\}_{i \in Ob_I}) \in \mathbf{Cones_C}D$. *Show that* $(Fa, \{Fl_i\}_{i \in Ob_I}) \in \mathbf{Cones_D}(F \circ D)$.

**Definition A2.3.5 (limit preservation)** *Suppose* $F : \mathbf{C} \to \mathbf{D}$ *is a functor, and* $D : I \to \mathbf{C}$ *is a diagram. We say that* $F$ *preserves the limits of the diagram* $D$ *if*

$$(a, \{l_i\}_{i \in Ob_I}) \in lim_{\mathbf{C}}D \;\Rightarrow\; (Fa, \{Fl_i\}_{i \in Ob_I}) \in lim_{\mathbf{D}}(F \circ D) .$$

**Proposition A2.3.6** *Let* $\mathbf{C}$ *be a locally small category and* $c$ *be an object in* $\mathbf{C}$. *Then the covariant hom-functor* $\mathbf{C}[c, \_] : \mathbf{C} \to \mathbf{Set}$ *preserves limits.*

PROOF. Let $D = (\{d_i\}_{i \in Ob_I}, \{f_u\}_{u \in Mor_I})$ be a diagram and $(a, \{l_i\}_{i \in Ob_I}) \in lim_{\mathbf{C}}D$. Then $(\mathbf{C}[c, a], \{\lambda h. l_i \circ h\}_{i \in Ob_I}) \in \mathbf{Cones_{Set}}(\mathbf{C}[c, \_] \circ D)$. We suppose $(X, \{g_i\}_{i \in Ob_I}) \in \mathbf{Cones_{Set}}(\mathbf{C}[c, \_] \circ D)$, that is:

$$\forall u \in Mor_I \;\forall x \in X \;(f_u : d_i \to d_j \;\Rightarrow\; (f_u \circ g_i(x) = g_j(x))) .$$

Then $\forall x \in X \;(c, \{g_i(x)\}_{i \in Ob_I}) \in \mathbf{Cones_{Set}}D$. Hence there is a unique $h(x) : c \to a$ such that $g_i(x) = l_i \circ h(x)$, for any $i \in Ob_I$. We can then build a unique $z : X \to \mathbf{C}[c, a]$ such that $l_i \circ z = g_i$, for any $i \in Ob_I$. This $z$ is defined by $z(x) = h(x)$. $\square$

**Definition A2.3.7 (natural transformation)** *Let* $F, G : \mathbf{C} \to \mathbf{D}$ *be functors. A natural transformation* $\tau : F \to G$ *is a family* $\{\tau_a : Fa \to Ga\}_{a \in Ob_{\mathbf{C}}}$ *such that for any* $f : a \to b$, $\tau_b \circ Ff = Gf \circ \tau_a$. *A natural isomorphism* $\tau$ *is a natural transformation such that* $\tau_a$ *is an isomorphism, for any* $a$.

**Exercise A2.3.8** *Given categories* $\mathbf{C}, \mathbf{D}$ *show that the functors from* $\mathbf{C}$ *to* $\mathbf{D}$, *and their natural transformations form a category. We denote this new category with* $\mathbf{D}^{\mathbf{C}}$.

It can be shown that $\mathbf{D}^{\mathbf{C}}$ is actually an *exponent* in the sense of cartesian closed categories (see section A2.7). If $F, G : \mathbf{C} \to \mathbf{D}$ are functors, we also write $\mathbf{Nat}[F, G]$ for $\mathbf{D}^{\mathbf{C}}[F, G]$.

**Definition A2.3.9 (category of presheaves)** *Given a category* $\mathbf{C}$ *the category of presheaves over* $\mathbf{C}$ *is the category* $\mathbf{Set}^{\mathbf{C}^{op}}$ *of contravariant set-valued functors and natural transformations.*

Another important operation involving natural transformations is the composition with a functor.

**Proposition A2.3.10** *If* $G : \mathbf{B} \to \mathbf{C}$, $F, F' : \mathbf{C} \to \mathbf{C}'$ *and* $\delta : F \to F'$, *then* $\delta G :$
$F \circ G \to F' \circ G$ *is natural, where* $\delta G$ *is defined by set theoretical composition, i.e.,*
$(\delta G)_a = \delta_{Ga}$. *Likewise, if* $H : \mathbf{C}' \to \mathbf{B}'$, $F, F' : \mathbf{C} \to \mathbf{C}'$ *and* $\delta : F \to F'$, *then*
$H\delta : H \circ F \to H \circ F'$ *is natural, where* $(H\delta)_a = H(\delta_a)$.

The composition of natural transformations and functors extends to a notion of
*horizontal* composition of natural transformations (in contrast to the *vertical* one given
by the '∘').

**Proposition A2.3.11** *If* $F, F' : \mathbf{C} \to \mathbf{C}'$, $G, G' : \mathbf{C}' \to \mathbf{C}''$, $\delta : F \to F'$, $\epsilon : G \to G'$,
*then:*
$$(\epsilon F') \circ (G\delta) = (G'\delta) \circ (\epsilon F) : G \circ F \to G' \circ F' .$$
*We write* $\epsilon\delta$ *for the common value of both sides of this equation.*

**Exercise A2.3.12** *Show the following so-called* interchange law *(originally stated by
Godement), for all* $\delta, \delta', \epsilon, \epsilon'$ *of appropriate types* $(\epsilon' \circ \epsilon)(\delta' \circ \delta) = (\epsilon'\delta') \circ (\epsilon\delta)$.

**Definition A2.3.13** *A functor* $F : \mathbf{C} \to \mathbf{D}$ *is* full *if*

$$\forall a, b \; \forall h : Fa \to Fb \; \exists f : a \to b \; (Ff = h),$$

*and* faithful *if it is injective on each hom-set* $\mathbf{C}[a, b]$.

**Theorem A2.3.14 (Yoneda)** *For any category* $\mathbf{C}$ *there is a full and faithful functor*
$Y : \mathbf{C} \to \mathbf{Set}^{\mathbf{C}^{op}}$ *from* $\mathbf{C}$ *into the related category of presheaves, called the Yoneda
embedding, and defined as follows:*

$$Y(c) = \mathbf{C}[\_, c] \qquad Y(f) = \lambda h.h \circ f .$$

PROOF HINT. The key to the proof that $Y$ is full resides in the following lemma where
we take $F = \mathbf{C}[\_, d]$.                                                    □

**Lemma A2.3.15** *For any functor* $F : \mathbf{C}^{op} \to \mathbf{Set}$ *and any object* $c \in \mathbf{C}$, *the following
isomorphism holds in* $\mathbf{Set}$:
$$Fc \cong \mathrm{Nat}[\mathbf{C}[\_, c], F] .$$

PROOF. We define $i : Fc \to \mathrm{Nat}[\mathbf{C}[\_, c], F]$ with inverse $j : \mathrm{Nat}[\mathbf{C}[\_, c], F] \to Fc$ as
follows:
$$i(x) = \lambda d.\lambda l : d \to c.(Fl)(x) \qquad j(\tau) = \tau_c(id_c) .$$
First we verify that $i(x)$ is a natural transformation as:

$$(Ff)((i(x)_a)(l)) = (Ff)((Fl)(x)) = F(l \circ f)(x) = (i(x)_b)(l \circ f) .$$

Next we verify that $j$ is the inverse of $i$:

$$j(i(x)) = i(x)_c(id_c) = (Fid_c)(x) = (id)(x) = x$$
$$i(j(\tau)) = \lambda d.\lambda l : d \to c.(Fl)(\tau_c(id_c)) = \lambda d.\lambda l : d \to c.\tau_d(l) = \tau ,$$

as by applying the naturality of $\tau$ to $l : d \to c$ one gets $(Fl)(\tau_c(id_c)) = \tau_d(l)$.                □

# A2.4    Universal morphisms and adjunctions

A universal morphism is a rather simple abstraction of a frequent mathematical phenomenon.

**Example A2.4.1** (1)  *Given a signature $\Sigma$ consider the category of $\Sigma$-algebras and morphisms (cf. example 1.1.13). If $A$ is a $\Sigma$-algebra denote with $|A|$ its carrier (which is a set). There is a well known construction which associates to any set $X$ the free $\Sigma$-algebra $\Sigma(X)$ and which is characterized by the following property:*

$$\exists u : X \to |\Sigma(X)| \;\; \forall A \;\; \forall f : X \to |A| \;\; \exists! f' : \Sigma(X) \to A \;\; (f' \circ u = f) \; .$$

(2)  *Consider the category of metric spaces and continuous morphisms and the full subcategory of complete metric spaces. The Cauchy completion associates to any metric space $(X, d)$ a complete metric space $(X_c, d_c)$ which is characterized by:*

$$\exists u : (X, d) \to (X_c, d_c) \; \forall (Y, d') \text{ complete } \forall f : (X, d) \to (Y, d')$$
$$\exists! f' : (X_c, d_c) \to (Y, d') \;\; (f' \circ u = f) \; .$$

**Definition A2.4.2 (universal morphism)**  *Let $F : \mathbf{C} \to \mathbf{D}$ be a functor and $d$ an object in $\mathbf{D}$. Then the couple $(c_d, u : d \to F c_d)$ is* universal *from $d$ to $F$ (and we also write $(c_d, u) : d \to F$) if*

$$\forall c \; \forall f : d \to F c \; \exists! f' : c_d \to c \;\; (F f' \circ u = f) \; .$$

**Exercise A2.4.3**  *(1) Show that if $(c_d, u) : d \to F$ and $(c'_d, u') : d \to F$ then $c_d \cong c_{d'}$. (2) Make explicit the dual notion of co-universal. (3) Verify that the previous examples A2.4.1 fit the definition of universal morphism.*

The notion of *adjunction* is a fundamental one, and it has several equivalent characterizations. In particular, an adjunction arises whenever there is a 'natural' way of determining a universal morphism (cf. theorem A2.4.8).

**Definition A2.4.4 (adjunction)**  *An* adjunction *between two categories $\mathbf{C}, \mathbf{D}$ is a triple $(L, R, \tau)$, where $L : \mathbf{D} \to \mathbf{C}$ and $R : \mathbf{C} \to \mathbf{D}$ are functors and $\tau : \mathbf{C}[L\text{-}, \text{-}] \to \mathbf{D}[\text{-}, R\text{-}]$ is a natural isomorphism. We say that $L$ is the* left adjoint, *$R$ is the* right adjoint, *and we denote this situation by $L \dashv R$.*

**Exercise A2.4.5**  *With reference to example A2.4.1, define the 'free algebra' and 'Cauchy completion' functors. Verify that they are left adjoints to the forgetful and inclusion functors, respectively.*

In the following we develop some properties of adjunctions in the special case in which $\mathbf{C}$ and $\mathbf{D}$ are poset categories and therefore the functors $L$ and $R$ are monotonic functions. Let us first observe that the pair $(c_d, d \leq F c_d)$ is universal from $d$ to $F :$ $\mathbf{C} \to \mathbf{D}$ if

$$\forall c \; (d \leq F c \Rightarrow c_d \leq c) \; , \tag{2.1}$$

and the triple $(L, R, \tau)$ is an adjunction iff

$$\forall c, d \; (L d \leq c \text{ iff } d \leq R c) \; . \tag{2.2}$$

A pair of monotonic functions satisfying this property is also known as a Galois connection.

**Proposition A2.4.6** *Let* C, D *be poset categories. Then:*

(1) *Every component of an adjunction determines the other.*

(2) *The following conditions are equivalent for* $R : C \to D$, *and* $L : D \to C$: *(a)* $\forall c, d$ $(Ld \le c$ *iff* $d \le Rc)$, *and (b)* $L \circ R \le id_C$, $id_D \le R \circ L$.

(3) *If* $\forall d$ $(c_d, d \le Fc_d) : d \to F$ *then* $F$ *has a left adjoint* $L$ *where* $L(d) = c_d$.

(4) *Vice versa, if* $L \dashv R$, $R : C \to D$, *and* $L : D \to C$ *then* $\forall d$ $(Ld, d \le (R \circ L)d)$ *is universal from* $d$ *to* $R$, *and symmetrically* $\forall c$ $(Rc, (L \circ R)c \le c)$ *is co-universal from* $L$ *to* $c$.

PROOF. (1) We note that if $L \dashv R$ and $L \dashv R'$ then $d \le Rc$ iff $Ld \le c$ iff $d \le R'c$. For $d = Rc$ we get $Rc \le Rc$ iff $Rc \le R'c$. Hence $Rc \le R'c$, and symmetrically $R'c \le Rc$.

(2) We show $(a) \Rightarrow (b)$ by, e.g., $L(Rc) \le c$ iff $Rc \le Rc$, and $(b) \Rightarrow (a)$ by $Ld \le c$ implies $d \le R(Ld) \le Rc$, and $d \le Rc$ implies $Ld \le L(Rc) \le c$.

(3) If $d \le Fc$ then, by condition 2.1, $c_d \le c$, that is $Ld \le c$. By hypothesis $\forall d$ $(d \le F(Ld))$. Hence, $Ld \le c$ implies $d \le F(Ld) \le Fc$.

(4) Direct application of the characterizations (2) and (3). □

**Exercise A2.4.7** *Generalize point (1) of proposition A2.4.6 to arbitrary categories: if* $L \dashv R$ *and* $L \dashv R'$ *then* $R$ *and* $R'$ *are naturally isomorphic.*

The following theorem connects adjunctions with universal morphisms and generalizes points (2-4) of proposition A2.4.6.

**Theorem A2.4.8** *An adjunction* $(L, R, \tau)$ *determines:*

(1) *A natural transformation* $\eta : id_D \to R \circ L$ *(called the unit) such that (i) for each object* $d \in D$, $(Ld, \eta_d)$ *is universal from* $d$ *to* $R$, *and (ii) for each* $f : Ld \to c$, $\tau(f) = R(f) \circ \eta_d : d \to Rc$.

(2) *A natural transformation* $\epsilon : L \circ R \to id_C$ *(called the counit) such that (i) for each object* $c \in C$, $(Rc, \epsilon_c)$ *is co-universal from* $L$ *to* $c$, *and (ii) for each* $g : d \to Rc$, $\tau^{-1}(g) = \epsilon_c \circ L(g) : Ld \to c$.

(3) *Moreover the following equations hold:*

$$(R\epsilon) \circ (\eta R) = id_R \quad (\epsilon L) \circ (L\eta) = id_L .$$

**Exercise A2.4.9** *Show that an adjunction* $L \dashv R$ *is completely determined by (i) functors* $L : D \to C$ *and* $R : C \to D$, *(ii) natural transformations* $\epsilon : L \circ R \to id$, $\eta : id \to R \circ L$ *such that* $(R\epsilon) \circ (\eta R) = id_R$ *and* $(\epsilon L) \circ (L\eta) = id_L$.

**Exercise A2.4.10** *Let* C *be a category. Show the following properties:*

(1) C *has a terminal object iff the unique functor* $! : C \to 1$ *has a right adjoint.*

(2) C *has binary products iff the diagonal functor* $\Delta : C \to C \times C$ *has a right adjoint, where* $\Delta(a) = (a, a)$ *and* $\Delta(f) = (f, f)$.

(3) *Given a graph* $I$ *consider the category* $[I \to C]$ *of graphs and natural transformations (observe that the definition of natural transformation does not require* $I$ *to be a category). Define a generalized diagonal functor* $\Delta_I : C \to [I \to C]$ *and show that* C *has limits of* $I$-*indexed diagrams iff the functor* $\Delta_I$ *has a right adjoint.*

The definition of adjunction hides some redundancy, the following characterizations show different ways of optimizing it.

**Exercise A2.4.11** *Show that an adjunction $L \dashv R$ is determined by: (i) a functor $L : \mathbf{D} \to \mathbf{C}$, (ii) a function $R : Ob_{\mathbf{C}} \to Ob_{\mathbf{D}}$, and one of the following conditions:*

(1) *Bijections $\tau_{d,c} : \mathbf{C}[Ld, c] \to \mathbf{D}[d, Rc]$ for all $d, c$, such that for all $f, g$ of appropriate types: $\tau(f) \circ g = \tau(f \circ L(g))$. Hint: $R$ is uniquely extended to a functor by setting $Rh = \tau(h \circ \tau^{-1}(id))$.*

(2) *Functions $\tau_{d,c} : \mathbf{C}[Ld, c] \to \mathbf{D}[d, Rc]$ for all $c, d$, and morphisms $\epsilon_c : L(Rc) \to c$ ($\epsilon$ for short) for all $c$, such that for all $f, g$ of appropriate types $\epsilon \circ L(\tau(f)) = f$, $g = \tau(\epsilon \circ Lg)$. Hint: $\tau$ is proved bijective by setting $\tau^{-1}(g) = \epsilon \circ Lg$. The naturality of $\tau$ is also a consequence.*

(3) *Morphisms $\epsilon_c : L(Rc) \to c$, for all $c$, such that for all $c, d$, for all $f \in \mathbf{C}[Ld, c]$, there exists a unique morphism, written $\tau(f)$, satisfying $\epsilon \circ L(\tau(f)) = f$. Hint: The naturality of $\epsilon$ follows. Another way of saying this is that $(Rc, \epsilon_c)$ is co-universal from $L$ to $c$.*

# A2.5    Adjoints and limits

Given a functor $F$, the existence of a left (right) adjoint implies the preservation of limits (colimits). First consider the situation in **Poset**.

**Proposition A2.5.1** *Let $\mathbf{C}, \mathbf{D}$ be poset categories, and $L \dashv R$ be an adjunction with $R : \mathbf{C} \to \mathbf{D}$, and $L : \mathbf{D} \to \mathbf{C}$. Then $R$ preserves glb's (and $L$ lub's).*

PROOF. We suppose $X \subseteq \mathbf{C}$, and $\exists \bigwedge X$. Also we assume $\forall c \in X$ $(d \leq Rc)$. Then $\forall c \in X$ $(Ld \leq c)$. Hence $Ld \leq \bigwedge X$, which implies $d \leq R(\bigwedge X)$. Thus $R(\bigwedge X) = \bigwedge R(X)$. $\square$

The following theorem generalizes the previous proposition.

**Theorem A2.5.2** *If the functor $R : \mathbf{C} \to \mathbf{D}$ has a left adjoint, then $R$ preserves limits (and $L$ colimits).*

Vice versa one may wonder if the existence of limits helps in the construction of an adjunction. Consider again the situation in **Poset**.

**Proposition A2.5.3** *Let $\mathbf{C}, \mathbf{D}$ be poset categories. Suppose there is $R : \mathbf{C} \to \mathbf{D}$ and $\mathbf{C}$ has all glb's. Then $R$ has a left adjoint iff $R$ preserves glb's.*

PROOF. ($\Rightarrow$) This follows by A2.5.1.

($\Leftarrow$) Define $L(d) = \bigwedge_{\mathbf{C}}\{c' \mid d \leq Rc'\}$. Then $d \leq Rc$ implies $L(d) = \bigwedge_{\mathbf{C}}\{c' \mid d \leq Rc'\} \leq c$. On the other hand, if $L(d) \leq c$, then $d \leq \bigwedge_{\mathbf{C}}\{Rc' \mid d \leq Rc'\} = R(\bigwedge_{\mathbf{C}}\{c' \mid d \leq Rc'\}) = R(L(d)) \leq R(c)$. $\square$

There are several results which generalize the previous proposition. We mention just one of them without proof. Given a functor $R : \mathbf{C} \to \mathbf{D}$, where $\mathbf{C}$ is small and has all limits the following *Solution Set Condition* is enough to establish the existence of a left adjoint:

$$\forall d \in \mathbf{D} \; \exists \{(c_i, w_i : d \to Rc_i)\}_{i \in I} \; (I \text{ set})$$
$$\forall c' \in \mathbf{C} \; \forall f : d \to Rc' \; \exists i \in I \; \exists f' : c_i \to c' \; f = Rf' \circ w_i \,.$$

This can be understood as a weakening of the universal condition in the definition A2.4.2 of a universal morphism. Given an object $d \in \mathbf{D}$ we can find a set of objects and morphisms that commute (not in a unique way) with every morphism $f : d \to Rc'$.

**Exercise A2.5.4** *Show that if $R$ has a left adjoint then the solution set condition is always satisfied (cf. [BW85]).*

**Theorem A2.5.5 (Freyd)** *Let $\mathbf{C}$ be a category with all limits, and $R : \mathbf{C} \to \mathbf{D}$ be a functor. Then $R$ has a left adjoint iff $R$ preserves all limits and satisfies the Solution Set Condition.*

# A2.6  Equivalences and reflections

The notion of functor isomorphism is often too strong to express the idea that two categories enjoy the 'same properties' (e.g., the existence of limits). The following weaker notion of equivalence is more useful.

**Definition A2.6.1 (equivalence of categories)** *A functor $F : \mathbf{C} \to \mathbf{D}$ is an equivalence of categories if there is a functor $G : \mathbf{D} \to \mathbf{C}$ such that $F \circ G \cong id_{\mathbf{D}}$, and $G \circ F \cong id_{\mathbf{C}}$, via natural isomorphisms.*

**Theorem A2.6.2** *The following properties of a functor $F : \mathbf{C} \to \mathbf{D}$ are equivalent:*

(1) *$F$ is an equivalence of categories.*

(2) *$F$ is part of an adjoint $(F, G, \eta, \epsilon)$ such that $\eta$ and $\epsilon$ are natural isomorphisms.*

(3) *$F$ is full and faithful and $\forall d \in \mathbf{D} \; \exists c \in \mathbf{C} \; (d \cong Fc)$.*

**Exercise A2.6.3** *Give examples of equivalent but not isomorphic preorders.*

**Exercise A2.6.4** *Show that any adjunction cuts down to an equivalence between the full subcategory whose objects are those at which the counity and the unity, respectively, are iso.*

**Exercise A2.6.5** *(1) Let $L \dashv R$ be an adjunction where $L : \mathbf{D} \to \mathbf{C}$, $R : \mathbf{C} \to \mathbf{D}$. If $\mathbf{C}', \mathbf{D}'$ are full subcategories of $\mathbf{C}, \mathbf{D}$ such that $\forall a \in \mathbf{D}' \; La \in \mathbf{C}'$, and $\forall b \in \mathbf{C}' \; Rb \in \mathbf{D}'$, respectively, then the adjunction $L \dashv R$ restricts to an adjunction between $\mathbf{C}'$ and $\mathbf{D}'$. The same holds of equivalences. (2) If $L \dashv R$ is an equivalence between two categories $\mathbf{C}, \mathbf{D}$, if $\mathbf{D}'$ is a full subcategory of $\mathbf{D}$, closed under isomorphic objects, then the equivalence cuts down to an equivalence between $\mathbf{C}'$ and $\mathbf{D}'$ where $\mathbf{C}'$ is the full subcategory of $\mathbf{C}$ whose collection of objects is $\{a \mid Ra \in \mathbf{D}'\}$, which is equal to $\{a \mid \exists b \in \mathbf{D}' \; a \cong Lb\}$.*

**Exercise A2.6.6** *Suppose that $L \dashv R$ is an adjunction with counity $\epsilon$ such that $\epsilon_d$ is a mono for all $d$. Show the following equivalences: (1) $\epsilon$ is iso at $d$ iff $d$ is isomorphic to $Lc$ for some $c$. (2) $\eta$ is iso at $c$ iff $c$ is isomorphic to $Rd$ for some $d$ . Show the same properties under the assumption that $\eta_c$ is epi, for all $c$.*

*Reflection* is a condition weaker than equivalence. The following proposition illustrates the idea in the poset case.

**Proposition A2.6.7 (poset reflection)** *Let* $C, D$ *be poset categories. Suppose there is an adjunction* $L \dashv R$, $R : C \to D$, $L : D \to C$, *where* $R$ *is an inclusion. Then for any* $X \subseteq C$,

$$\exists \bigwedge_D X \quad \Rightarrow \quad \exists \bigwedge_C X \ \text{ and } \ \bigwedge_C X = \bigwedge_D X \ .$$

PROOF. We set $c = L(\bigwedge_D X)$, and show $c = \bigwedge_C X = \bigwedge_D X$. For any $x \in X$, $\bigwedge_D X \leq x$ implies, by the adjunction hypothesis, $c = L(\bigwedge_D X) \leq x$. Hence $c \leq \bigwedge_D X$. On the other hand, suppose $c' \in C$ is a lower bound for $X$, then $c' \leq \bigwedge_D X$, and therefore $Lc' \leq c$. We conclude by observing that $Lc' = c'$. By the adjunction condition, $c' \leq c'$ implies $Lc' \leq c'$, and $Lc' \leq Lc'$ implies $c' \leq Lc'$. □

**Definition A2.6.8** *If* $C$ *is a subcategory of* $D$ *we denote with* $Incl : C \to D$ *the inclusion functor. We say that* $C$ *is a reflective subcategory of* $D$ *if there is* $L$ *such that* $L \dashv Incl$. $L$ *is also called the* reflector *functor.*

The point (4) of the following theorem generalizes the previous example.

**Theorem A2.6.9** *For an adjunction* $(L, R, \eta, \epsilon)$ *the following holds:*

(1) $R$ *is faithful iff every component* $\epsilon_c : L(Rc) \to c$ *is an epi.*

(2) $R$ *is full iff every component* $\epsilon_c : L(Rc) \to c$ *is a split mono (i.e., it has a left inverse).*

(3) *Hence* $R$ *is full and faithful iff* $\epsilon_c : L(Rc) \to c$ *is an iso.*

(4) *If* $R : C \to D$ *is the inclusion functor then for any diagram* $D : I \to C$:

$$\exists lim_D D \quad \Rightarrow \quad \exists lim_C D \ \text{ and } \ lim_C D \cong lim_D D \ .$$

**Exercise A2.6.10** *Show that the full subcategory of Hausdorff topological spaces is reflective in the category of topological spaces and continuous functions, and that the full subcategory of posets is reflective in the category of preorders and monotonic morphisms. On the other hand show that the ideal completion of a poset to a directed complete poset does* not *provide a left adjoint to the inclusion of directed complete posets into the category of posets and monotonic morphisms.*

# A2.7 Cartesian closed categories

Cartesian closure formalizes the idea of closure of a category under function space. Chapter 4 provides some intuition for the genesis of the notion, several equivalent definitions, e.g., 4.2.5, and examples. We just recall here that a CCC is a category with finite products and such that the functor $\_ \times a : C \to C$ has a right adjoint, for any object $a$. In the following, we present small categories and presheaves as examples of CCC's.

**Example A2.7.1** *The category of small categories and functors is cartesian closed. The exponent object* $\mathbf{D}^\mathbf{C}$ *is given by the category of functors and natural transformations. Then we define:*

$$ev(F, a) = Fa \qquad ev(\delta, f) = Gf \circ \delta_a = \delta_b \circ Ff \quad (\delta : F \to G, f : a \to b)$$
$$\Lambda(F)ab = F(a, b) \qquad \Lambda(F)af = F(id_a, f) \qquad\qquad (\text{object part of } \Lambda(F))$$
$$\Lambda(F)fb = F(f, id_b) \qquad\qquad\qquad\qquad\qquad\qquad (\text{morphism part of } \Lambda(F)) \ .$$

**Example A2.7.2 (presheaves)** *Our next example of a CCC is* $\mathbf{Set}^{\mathbf{C}^{op}}$, *for any category* $\mathbf{C}$. *The cartesian structure is built* pointwise, *but this does not work for exponents (try to take* $(F \Rightarrow G)a = \mathbf{Set}[Fa, Ga]$, *how does one define* $(F \Rightarrow G)$ *on morphisms?). The solution is to use the Yoneda lemma A2.3.15. For* $F, G : \mathbf{C}^{op} \to \mathbf{Set}$ *we define:*

$$(F \Rightarrow G)(c) = \mathbf{Nat}[\mathbf{C}[\_, c] \times F, G] \ .$$

**Exercise A2.7.3** *If* $\mathbf{C}$ *is a preorder, we can recover a pointwise definition of* $F \Rightarrow G$. *Define* $\mathbf{C}_{\rceil a}$ *as the full subcategory of* $\mathbf{C}$ *with objects those* $b$ *such that* $b \le a$. *Given* $F : \mathbf{C}^{op} \to \mathbf{Set}$, *define* $F_{\rceil a} : (\mathbf{C}_{\rceil a})^{op} \to \mathbf{Set}$ *by restriction. Then show* $(F \Rightarrow G)a = \mathbf{Set}[F_{\rceil a}, G_{\rceil a}]$.

**Exercise A2.7.4** *Let* $\mathbf{C}$ *be a CCC which has an initial object* $0$. *Then show that for any* $a$: *(i)* $0 \times a \cong 0$, *(ii)* $\mathbf{C}[a, 0] \ne \emptyset$ *implies* $a \cong 0$ *(thus* $\mathbf{C}[a, 0]$ *has at most one element). If furthermore* $\mathbf{C}$ *has finite limits, show that, for any* $a$, *the unique morphism from* $0$ *to* $a$ *is mono. Hints:* $\mathbf{C}[0 \times a, b] \cong \mathbf{C}[0, b^a]$ *and consider in particular* $b = 0 \times a$. *Consider also* $!^{op} \circ \pi_1$. *Suppose* $f : a \to 0$. *Then consider* $\pi_2 \circ \langle f, id \rangle$.

**Exercise A2.7.5** *Let* $\mathbf{C}$ *be a CCC, and* $0$ *be an object such that the natural transformation* $\mu : \lambda x.x \to \lambda x.(x \Rightarrow 0) \Rightarrow 0$ *defined by* $\mu = \Lambda(ev \circ \langle \pi_2, \pi_1 \rangle)$ *is iso. Show that* $0$ *is initial and that* $\mathbf{C}$ *is a preorder (this is an important negative fact: there is no nontrivial categorical semantics of classical logic, thinking of* $0$ *as absurdity and of* $(x \Rightarrow 0) \Rightarrow 0$ *as double negation). Hints: (i)* $0 \Rightarrow 0 \cong 1$, *by observing* $1 \cong (1 \Rightarrow 0) \Rightarrow 0$, *and* $(1 \Rightarrow a) \cong a$, *for any* $a$. *(ii) For any* $a$:

$$\mathbf{C}[0, a] \cong \mathbf{C}[0, (a \Rightarrow 0) \Rightarrow 0] \cong \mathbf{C}[0 \times (a \Rightarrow 0), 0]$$
$$\cong \mathbf{C}[a \Rightarrow 0, 0 \Rightarrow 0] \cong \mathbf{C}[a \Rightarrow 0, 1] \ .$$

*(iii) For any* $a, b$: $\mathbf{C}[a, b] \cong \mathbf{C}[a, (b \Rightarrow 0) \Rightarrow 0] \cong \mathbf{C}[a \times (b \Rightarrow 0), 0]$.

# A2.8   Monads

The notion of monad (or triple) is an important category theoretical notion, we refer to [BW85, ML71] for more information and to chapter 8 for several applications of this notion in computer science.

**Definition A2.8.1 (monad)** *A monad over a category* $\mathbf{C}$ *is a triple* $(T, \eta, \mu)$ *where* $T : \mathbf{C} \to \mathbf{C}$ *is a functor,* $\eta : id_\mathbf{C} \to T$, $\mu : T^2 \to T$ *are natural transformations and the following equations hold:*

$$\mu_a \circ \eta_{Ta} = id_{Ta} \quad \mu_a \circ T\eta_a = id_{Ta} \quad \mu_a \circ \mu_{Ta} = \mu_a \circ T\mu_a \ .$$

**Exercise A2.8.2** *Show that if* **C** *is a poset then a monad can be characterized as a closure, i.e., a monotonic function* $T : \mathbf{C} \to \mathbf{C}$, *such that* $id \le T = T \circ T$.

From a monad $T$ we can build the category of $T$-algebras and the Kleisli category as follows.

**Definition A2.8.3 (category of $T$-algebras)** *Given a monad* $(T, \eta, \mu)$, *a $T$-algebra is a morphism* $\alpha : Td \to d$ *satisfying the following conditions:*

$$(T_\eta) \quad \alpha \circ \eta_d = id_d \qquad (T_\mu) \quad \alpha \circ T\alpha = \alpha \circ \mu_d \ .$$

*The category* $\mathbf{Alg}_T$ *has $T$-algebras as objects and morphisms as follows:*

$$\mathbf{Alg}_T[\alpha : Td \to d, \beta : Td' \to d'] = \{f : d \to d' \mid \beta \circ Tf = f \circ \alpha\} \ .$$

**Exercise A2.8.4** *With reference to example A2.4.1 and exercise A2.4.5, show that $\Sigma$-algebras are exactly the algebras for the monad associated with the adjunction $T_\Sigma \dashv Forget$, where $T_\Sigma$ is the 'free algebra' functor and Forget is the forgetful functor (cf. exercise A2.4.5).*

**Exercise A2.8.5** *Consider the powerset functor* $\mathcal{P} : \mathbf{Set} \to \mathbf{Set}$ *with* $\eta(x) = \{x\}$ *and* $\mu(X) = \bigcup X$. *(1) Show that these data define a monad. (2) Show that the category of complete lattices and functions preserving arbitrary glb's is isomorphic to the category of algebras for this monad. Hint: Show that a complete lattice can be presented as a set $X$ equipped with an operation* $\bigwedge : \mathcal{P}X \to X$ *such that* $\bigwedge\{x\} = x$ *and* $\bigwedge\{\bigwedge X_j \mid j \in J\} = \bigwedge(\bigcup_{j \in J} X_j)$ *for any indexed family of subsets $X_j$.*

**Definition A2.8.6 (Kleisli category)** *Given a monad* $(T, \eta, \mu)$ *over the category* **D**, *the Kleisli category* $\mathbf{K}_T$ *is defined as:*

$$\mathbf{K}_T = \mathbf{D} \qquad \mathbf{K}_T[d, d'] = \mathbf{D}[d, Td']$$
$$id_d = \eta_d : d \to Td \qquad f \circ g = \mu_{d''} \circ Tf \circ g \qquad (for\ g : d \to d', f : d' \to d''\ in\ \mathbf{K}_T) \ .$$

Every adjunction gives rise to a monad. Vice versa, given a monad $(T, \eta, \mu)$ we can use either the category of $T$-algebras or the Kleisli category to build an adjunction which corresponds to the monad.

**Theorem A2.8.7** *(1) Every adjunction* $(L, R, \eta, \epsilon)$ *gives rise to a monad:*

$$T(L \dashv R) = (R \circ L, \eta, R\epsilon L) \ .$$

*(2) Given a monad* $(T, \eta, \epsilon)$ *over the category* **D**, *consider the category of $T$-algebras* $\mathbf{Alg}_T$. *We can build an adjunction* $(L^A, R^A, \eta^A, \epsilon^A)$ *as follows:*

$$
\begin{array}{llll}
L^A(d) & = & \mu_d : T^2 d \to Td & L^A(f : d \to d') & = & T(f) \\
R^A(\alpha : Td \to d) & = & d & R^A(g : \alpha \to \beta) & = & g \\
\eta^A & = & \eta & \epsilon^A(\alpha : Td \to d) & = & \alpha \ .
\end{array}
$$

*Moreover the monad induced by this adjunction is again* $(T, \eta, \epsilon)$.

*(3) Given a monad* $(T, \eta, \epsilon)$ *over the category* **D**, *consider the Kleisli category* $\mathbf{K_T}$, *then we can build an adjunction* $(L^K, R^K, \eta^K, \epsilon^K)$ *as follows:*

$$
\begin{array}{llll}
L^K(d) & = & d & L^K(f : d \to d') & = & \eta_{d'} \circ f \\
R^K(d) & = & Td & R^K(f : d \to Td') & = & \mu_{d'} \circ Tf \\
\eta^K & = & \eta & \epsilon_d^K & = & id_{Td} \ .
\end{array}
$$

*Moreover the monad induced by this adjunction is again* $(T, \eta, \epsilon)$.

Given a monad $T$ the Kleisli adjunction and the $T$-algebra adjunction can be shown to be initial and final, respectively, in a suitable category of adjunctions generating the monad $T$.

# References and bibliography

[ABL86]    R. Amadio, K. Bruce, and G. Longo. The finitary projection model and the solution of higher order domain equations. In *Proc. IEEE Logic in Comp. Sci.*, pages 122–130, 1986.

[Abr90]    S. Abramsky. The lazy lambda calculus. In *Research topics in functional programming, Turner (ed.), Addison-Wesley*, 1990.

[Abr91a]   S. Abramsky. A domain equation for bisimulation. *Information and Computation*, 92:161–218, 1991.

[Abr91b]   S. Abramsky. Domain theory in logical form. *Annals of Pure and Applied Logic*, 51:1–77, 1991.

[AC03]     R. Amadio and L. Cardelli. Subtyping recursive types. *Transactions on Programming Languages and Systems*, 15(4):575–631, 1993.

[AC94]     R. Amadio and P.-L. Curien. Selected domains and lambda calculi. Technical report, *TR 161, INRIA-Lorraine*, 1994.

[ACC93]    M. Abadi, L. Cardelli, and P.-L. Curien. Formal parametric polymorphism. *Theoretical Computer Science*, 121(1-2):9–58, 1993. Böhm Festschrift Volume.

[ACCL92]   M. Abadi, L. Cardelli, P.-L. Curien, and J.-J. Lévy. Explicit substitutions. *Journal of Functional Programming*, 1-4:375–416, 1992.

[ACS96]    R. Amadio, I. Castellani, and D. Sangiorgi. On bisimulations for the asynchronous π-calculus. In *CONCUR 96, Springer Lect. Notes in Comp. Sci. 1119*, pages 147–162, 1996.

[Acz88]    P. Aczel. *Non-well founded sets*. CSLI Lecture Notes 14, 1988.

[AG]       A. Asperti and S. Guerrini. *The optimal implementation of functional programming languages*. Cambridge University Press. To appear.

[AHMP95]   A. Avron, F. Honsell, I. Mason, and R. Pollak. Using typed lambda calculus to implement formal systems on a machine. *J. of Automated Reasoning*, 1995.

[AJ92]     S. Abramsky and R. Jagadeesan. Games and full completeness for multiplicative linear logic. In *Proc. FST-TCS, Springer Lect. Notes in Comp. Sci. 652*, 1992.

[AJM95]    S. Abramsky, R. Jagadeesan, and P. Malacaria. Full abstraction for PCF. *Manuscript, Imperial College*, 1995.

[AL87]     R. Amadio and G. Longo. Type-free compiling of parametric types. In *IFIP Formal Description of Programming Concepts-III, Wirsing (ed.)*, pages 377–398. North Holland, 1987.

[AL91]     A. Asperti and G. Longo. *Categories, types, and structures*. MIT Press, 1991.

[AL93]     A. Asperti and C. Laneve. Paths, computations and labels in the λ-calculus. *Theoretical Computer Science*, 142(2):277–297, 1993.

[ALT95]    R. Amadio, L. Leth, and B. Thomsen. From a concurrent λ-calculus to the π-calculus. In Proc. Foundations of Computation Theory 95, Springer Lect. Notes in Comp. Sci. 965, pages 106–115, 1995.

[Ama91a]   R Amadio. Bifinite domains: Stable case. In Proc. Category Theory in Comp. Sci. 91, Springer Lect. Notes in Comp. Sci. 530, pages 16–33, 1991.

[Ama91b]   R. Amadio. Domains in a realizability framework. In Proc. CAAP 91, Springer Lect. Notes in Comp. Sci. 493, pages 241–263, 1991.

[Ama91c]   R. Amadio. Recursion over realizability structures. Information and Computation, 91(1):55–85, 1991.

[Ama93a]   R. Amadio. On the adequacy of per models. In Proc. Mathematical Foundations of Computer Science, Springer Lect. Notes in Comp. Sci. 711, pages 222–231, 1993.

[Ama93b]   R. Amadio. On the reduction of Chocs bisimulation to π-calculus bisimulation. In Proc. CONCUR 93, Springer Lect. Notes in Comp. Sci. 715, pages 112–126, 1993.

[Ama94]    R. Amadio. Translating core Facile. Technical report, TR 94-3, ECRC, Munich, 1994. Available at http://protis.univ-mrs.fr/~amadio/.

[Ama95]    R. Amadio. A quick construction of a retraction of all retractions for stable bifinites. Information and Computation, 116(2):272–274, 1995.

[Ama97]    R. Amadio. An asynchronous model of locality, failure, and process mobility. In Proc. Coordination 97, Springer Lect. Notes in Comp. Sci. 1282, 1997.

[AN80]     A. Arnold and M. Nivat. Metric interpretation of infinite trees and semantics of non-deterministic recursive programs. Theoretical Computer Science, 11:181–205, 1980.

[AP90]     M. Abadi and G. Plotkin. A per model of polymorphism and recursive types. In Proc. IEEE Logic in Comp. Sci., 1990.

[App92]    A. Appel. Compiling with continuations. Cambridge University Press, 1992.

[AZ84]     E. Astesiano and E. Zucca. Parametric channels via label expressions in CCS. Theoretical Computer Science, 33:45–64, 1984.

[Bar78]    M. Barr. *-autonomous categories. Springer Lect. Notes in Mathematics 752, 1978. Appendix by P.H. Chu.

[Bar84]    H. Barendregt. The lambda calculus; its syntax and semantics. North-Holland, 1984.

[Bar91a]   H. Barendregt. Introduction to generalized type systems. Journal of Functional Programming, 1:125–154, 1991.

[Bar91b]   M. Barr. *-autonomous categories and linear logic. Mathematical Structures in Computer Science, 1(2):159–178, 1991.

[BC82]     G. Berry and P.-L. Curien. Sequential algorithms on concrete data structures. Theoretical Computer Science, 20:265–321, 1982.

[BC85]     G. Berry and P.-L. Curien. Theory and practice of sequential algorithms: the kernel of the applicative language cds. In Algebraic methods in semantics, Nivat and Reynolds (eds.), pages 35–87. Cambridge University Press, 1985.

[BCD83]    H. Barendregt, M. Coppo, and M. Dezani. A filter lambda model and the completeness of type assignment. Journal of Symbolic Logic, 48:931–940, 1983.

[BCL85]    G. Berry, P.-L. Curien, and J.-J. Lévy. Full abstraction for sequential languages: state of the art. In Algebraic methods in semantics, Nivat and Reynolds (eds.), pages 89–132. Cambridge University Press, 1985.

[BE93]     A. Bucciarelli and T. Ehrhard. A theory of sequentiality. Theoretical Computer Science, 113:273–291, 1993.

[BE94]      A. Bucciarelli and T. Ehrhard. Sequentiality in an extensional framework. *Information and Computation*, 110:265–296, 1994.

[Ber78]     G. Berry. Stable models of typed lambda-calculi. In *Proc. ICALP, Springer Lect. Notes in Comp. Sci. 62*, 1978.

[Ber79]     G. Berry. Modèles complètement adéquats et stables des lambda-calculs typés. 1979. Thèse de Doctorat d'Etat, Université Paris VII.

[Ber91]     S. Berardi. Retractions on dI-domains as a model for type:type. *Information and Computation*, 94:204–231, 1991.

[Bet88]     I. Bethke. *Notes on partial combinatory algebras.* PhD thesis, Amsterdam, 1988.

[BGG91]     B. Berthomieu, D. Giralt, and J.-P. Gouyon. LCS User's Manual. Technical report, *TR 91226, LAAS/CNRS*, 1991.

[BH76]      B. Banaschewski and R. Herrlich. Subcategories defined by implications. *Houston J. Math.*, 2:149–171, 1976.

[Bie95]     G. Bierman. What is a categorical model of intuitionistic linear logic? In *Proc. Typed Lambda Calculi and Applications, Springer Lect. Notes in Comp. Sci. 902*, 1995.

[BL88]      K. Bruce and G. Longo. A modest model of records, inheritance, and bounded quantification. In *Proc. IEEE Logic in Comp. Sci.*, 1988.

[BL94]      G. Boudol and C. Laneve. The discriminating power of multiplicites in the λ-calculus. Technical report, *RR 2441, INRIA-Sophia-Antipolis*, 1994.

[Bla72]     A. Blass. Degrees of indeterminacy of games. *Fundamenta Mathematicae*, LXXVII:151–166, 1972.

[Bla92]     A. Blass. A game semantics for linear logic. *Annals of Pure and Applied Logic*, 56:183–220, 1992.

[Bon96]     M. Bonsangue. *Topological dualities in semantics.* PhD thesis, Vrije Universiteit Amsterdam, 1996.

[Bou92]     G. Boudol. Asynchrony and the π-calculus. Technical report, *RR 1702, INRIA, Sophia-Antipolis*, 1992.

[Bou93]     G. Boudol. Some chemical abstract machines. In *Proc. of REX School, Springer Lect. Notes in Comp. Sci. 803*, 1993.

[Bou94]     G. Boudol. Lambda calculi for (strict) parallel functions. *Information and Computation*, 108:51–127, 1994.

[BS83]      G. Buckley and A. Silberschatz. An effective implementation for the generalized input-output construct of CSP. *Transactions on Programming Languages and Systems*, 5(2):223–235, 1983.

[BTG91]     V. Breazu-Tannen and J. Gallier. Polymorphic rewriting conserves algebraic strong normalization. *Theoretical Computer Science*, 83:3–28, 1991.

[Buc93]     A. Bucciarelli. Another approach to sequentiality: Kleene's unimonotone functions. In *Proc. MFPS, Springer Lect. Notes in Comp. Sci. 802*, 1993.

[Buc97]     A. Bucciarelli. Logical reconstruction of bi-domains. In *Proc. Typed Lambda Calculi and Applications, Springer Lect. Notes in Comp. Sci. 1210*, 1997.

[BW85]      M. Barr and C. Wells. *Toposes, triples and theories.* Springer-Verlag, 1985.

[Car88]     L. Cardelli. A semantics of multiple inheritance. *Information and Computation*, 76:138–164, 1988.

[CCF94]     R. Cartwright, P.-L. Curien, and M. Felleisen. Fully abstract semantics for observably sequential languages. *Information and Computation*, 111(2):297–401, 1994.

[CCM87]  G. Cousineau, P.-L. Curien, and M. Mauny. The categorical abstract machine. *Sci. of Comp. Programming*, 8:173–202, 1987.

[CD78]  M. Coppo and M. Dezani. A new type assignment for lambda-terms. *Archiv. Math. Logik*, 19:139–156, 1978.

[CDC80]  M. Coppo and M. Dezani-Ciancaglini. An extension of the basic functionality theory for the λ-calculus. *Notre Dame Journal of Formal Logic*, 21(4):685–693, 1980.

[CDHL82]  M. Coppo, M. Dezani, F. Honsell, and G. Longo. Extended type structures and filter lambda models. In *Proc. Logic Coll., Lolli et al. (ed.), North-Holland*, 1982.

[CF58]  H. Curry and R. Feys. *Combinatory Logic, vol. 1*. North Holland, 1958.

[CF92]  R. Cartwright and M. Felleisen. Observable sequentiality and full abstraction. *Proc. ACM Principles of Prog. Lang.*, 1992.

[CGW88]  T. Coquand, C. Gunter, and G. Winskel. Domain theoretic models of polymorphism. *Information and Computation*, 81:123–167, 1988.

[CH88]  T. Coquand and G. Huet. A calculus of constructions. *Information and Computation*, 76:95–120, 1988.

[CH94]  P.-L. Curien and T. Hardin. Yet yet a counterexample for λ+SP. *Journal of Functional Programming*, 4(1):113–115, 1994.

[CHL96]  P.-L. Curien, T. Hardin, and J.-J. Lévy. Weak and strong confluent calculi of explicit substitutions. *Journal of the ACM*, 43(2), 1996.

[CHR96]  P.-L. Curien, T. Hardin, and A. Rios. Strong normalisation of substitutions. *Journal of Logic and Computation*, 6(6):799–817, 1996.

[Chu41]  A. Church. *The calculi of lambda-conversion*. Princeton University Press, 1941.

[CO88]  P.-L. Curien and A. Obtulowicz. Partiality, cartesian closedness and toposes. *Information and Computation*, 80:50–95, 1988.

[Col89]  L. Colson. About intensional behaviour of primitive recursive algorithms. In *Proc. ICALP, Springer Lect. Notes in Comp. Sci. 372*, 1989.

[Coq89]  T. Coquand. Categories of embeddings. *Theoretical Computer Science*, 68:221–237, 1989.

[Coq92]  T. Coquand. Une preuve directe du théorème d'ultime obstination. *Comptes Rendus de l'Académie des Sciences t. 314, Série I*, pages 489–492, 1992.

[Coq97]  T. Coquand. Computational content of classical logic. In *Semantics and Logics of Computation, Pitts and Dybjer (eds.), Cambridge University Press*, 1997.

[CPW96]  P.-L. Curien, G. Plotkin, and G. Winskel. Bistructures, bidomains and linear logic. *Milner's Festschrift*, 1996. MIT Press, to appear. Preliminary version by G. Plotkin and G. Winskel in Springer Lect. Notes in Comp. Sci. 820.

[Cur86]  P.-L. Curien. *Categorical combinators, sequential algorithms and functional programming*. Pitman, 1986. Revised edition, Birkhäuser, 1993.

[Cur91]  P.-L. Curien. An abstract framework for environment machines. *Theoretical Computer Science*, 82:389–402, 1991.

[Dam94]  M. Dam. On the decidability of process equivalence for the π-calculus. Technical report, *RR 94:20, SICS, Stockholm, Available at ftp.sics.se*, 1994.

[Dan90]  V. Danos. *La logique linéaire appliquée à l'étude de divers processus de normalisation (principalement le λ-calcul)*. PhD thesis, Université Paris VII, 1990.

[dB80]  N. G. de Bruijn. A survey of the project Automath. *In Curry Festschrift, Hindley and Seldin (eds.)*, pages 589–606, 1980. Academic Press.

[DF92]　O. Danvy and A. Filinski. Representing control: a study of the CPS transformation. *Mathematical Structures in Computer Science*, 2:361–391, 1992.

[DHR96]　V. Danos, H. Herbelin, and M. Regnier. Game semantics and abstract machines. In *Proc. IEEE Logic in Comp. Sci.*, 1996.

[DR93]　M. Droste and Göbel R. Universal domains and the amalgamation property. *Mathematical Structures in Computer Science*, 3:137–160, 1993.

[Dro89]　M. Droste. Event structures and domains. *Theoretical Computer Science*, 68:37–48, 1989.

[Eda95a]　A. Edalat. Domain theory and integration. *Theoretical Computer Science*, 151:163–193, 1995.

[Eda95b]　A. Edalat. Dynamical systems, measures and fractals via domain theory. *Information and Computation*, 120:32–48, 1995.

[EH96]　A. Edalat and R. Heckmann. A computational model for metric spaces. Manuscript, 1996.

[Ehr88]　T. Ehrhard. A categorical semantics of constructions. In *Proc. IEEE Logic in Comp. Sci.*, 1988.

[Ehr93]　T. Ehrhard. Hypercoherences: a strongly stable model of linear logic. *Mathematical Structures in Computer Science*, 3:365–385, 1993.

[Ehr96]　T. Ehrhard. A relative PCF-definability result for strongly stable functions. *Manuscript, LMD, Marseille*, 1996.

[EML45]　S. Eilenberg and S. Mac Lane. General theory of natural equivalences. *Trans. Am. Math. Soc.*, 58:231–241, 1945.

[EN86]　U. Engberg and M. Nielsen. A calculus of communicating systems with label passing. Technical report, *PB-208, Aarhus Computer Science Department*, 1986.

[Eng81]　E. Engeler. Algebras and combinators. *Algebra Universalis*, 13:389–392, 1981.

[Eng95]　E. Engeler. *The combinatory program*. Birkhäuser, 1995. With contributions by K. Aberer, B. Amrhein, O. Gloor, von M. von Mohrenshildt, D. Otth, G. Schwärzler, T. Weibel.

[Esc95]　M. Escardó. PCF extended with real numbers. *Theoretical Computer Science*, 162(1):79–115, 1995.

[FFKD87]　M. Felleisen, D. Friedman, E. Kohlbecker, and B. Duba. A syntactic theory of sequential control. *Theoretical Computer Science*, 52:205–237, 1987.

[Fio96]　M. Fiore. *Axiomatic domain theory in categories of partial maps*. Distinguished dissertations in computer science, Cambridge University Press, 1996.

[FMRS92]　P. Freyd, P. Mulry, G. Rosolini, and D. Scott. Extensional pers. *Information and Computation*, 98:211–227, 1992.

[FMS96]　M. Fiore, E. Moggi, and D. Sangiorgi. A fully-abstract model for the π-calculus. In *Proc. IEEE Logic in Comp. Sci.*, 1996.

[Fre91a]　P. Freyd. Algebraically complete categories. In *Proc. Category Theory, Springer Lecture Notes in Mathematics 1488*, 1991.

[Fre91b]　P. Freyd. Remarks on algebraically compact categories. In *Applications of Categories in Computer Science, Durham, Cambridge University Press*, 1991.

[Fri73]　H. Friedman. Equality between functionals. In *Proc. Logic Colloquium, Springer Lect. Notes in Mathematics 453*, 1973.

[Fri78]　H. Friedman. Classically and intuitionistically provably recursive functions. In *Higher set theory, Springer Lect. Notes in Mathematics 699*, 1978.

[GD62]    A. Gleason and R. Dilworth. A generalized Cantor theorem. In *Proc. Amer. Math. Soc. 13*, 1962.

[GHK⁺80]  G. Gierz, K. Hofmann, K. Keimel, J. Lawson, M. Mislove, and D. Scott. *A compendium of continuous lattices*. Springer-Verlag, 1980.

[Gir72]   J.-Y. Girard. Interprétation fonctionnelle et élimination des coupures dans l'arithmétique d'ordre supérieur. 1972. Thèse de Doctorat d'Etat, Université Paris VII.

[Gir86]   J.-Y. Girard. The system F of variable types, fifteen years later. *Theoretical Computer Science*, 45:159–192, 1986.

[Gir87]   J.-Y. Girard. Linear logic. *Theoretical Computer Science*, 50:1–102, 1987.

[GJ90]    C. Gunter and A. Jung. Coherence and consistency in domains. *J. of Pure and Applied Algebra*, 63:49–66, 1990.

[GLT89]   J.-Y. Girard, Y. Lafont, and P. Taylor. *Proofs and Types*. Cambridge University Press, 1989.

[GMP89]   A. Giacalone, P. Mishra, and S. Prasad. Facile: A symmetric integration of concurrent and functional programming. *International Journal of Parallel Programming*, 18(2):121–160, 1989.

[GN91]    H. Geuvers and M. Nederhof. Modular proof of strong normalization for the calculus of constructions. *Journal of Functional Programming*, 1(2):155–189, 1991.

[Gog91]   J. Goguen. A categorical manifesto. *Mathematical Structures in Computer Science*, 1:49–68, 1991.

[Gri90]   T. Griffin. A formulae-as-types notion of control. In *Proc. ACM Principles of Prog. Lang.*, 1990.

[Har89]   T. Hardin. Confluence results for the pure strong categorical combinatory logic CCL: lambda-calculi as subsytems of CCL. *Theoretical Computer Science*, 65:291–342, 1989.

[Hen50]   L. Henkin. Completeness in the theory of types. *Journal of Symbolic Logic*, 15:81–91, 1950.

[HF87]    C. Haynes and D. Friedman. Embedding continuations in procedural objects. *Transactions on Programming Languages and Systems*, 9(4):397–402, 1987.

[HHP93]   R. Harper, F. Honsell, and G. Plotkin. A framework for defining logics. *Journal of the ACM*, 40:143–184, 1993.

[Hin69]   R. Hindley. The principal type schema of an object in combinatory logic. *Trans. Amer. Math. Society*, 1969.

[Hin83]   R. Hindley. The completeness theorem for typing lambda-terms. *Theoretical Computer Science*, 22:1–17, 1983.

[HO80]    G. Huet and D. Oppen. Equations and rewrite rules: a survey. *Formal Language Theory: Perspectives and Open Problems, R. Book (ed.), Academic Press*, pages 349–405, 1980.

[HO94]    J. Hyland and L. Ong. On full abstraction for PCF. *Manuscript, Cambridge University*, 1994.

[How80]   W. Howard. The formulas-as-types notion of construction. *In Curry Festschrift, Hindley and Seldin (eds.)*, pages 479–490, 1980. Academic Press. Manuscript circulated since 1969.

[HP90]    H. Huwig and A. Poigné. A note on inconsistencies caused by fixpoints in a cartesian closed category. *Theoretical Computer Science*, 73:101–112, 1990.

[HS86]    R. Hindley and J. Seldin. *Introduction to combinators and lambda-calculus.* Cambridge University Press, 1986.

[HY95]    K. Honda and N. Yoshida. On reduction based process semantics. *Theoretical Computer Science*, 151:437–486, 1995.

[Hyl76]   M. Hyland. A syntactic characterization of the equality in some models of lambda calculus. *J. London Math. Soc.*, 2:361–370, 1976.

[Hyl82]   M. Hyland. The effective topos. *The Brouwer Symposium, Troelstra and Van Dalen (eds.)*, 1982.

[Hyl88]   M. Hyland. A small complete category. *Annals of Pure and Applied Logic*, 40:135–165, 1988.

[Hyl91]   M. Hyland. First steps in synthetic domain theory. In *Proc. Category Theory, Springer Lecture Notes in Mathematics 1488*. Springer-Verlag, 1991.

[Hyl97]   M. Hyland. Game semantics. In *Semantics and Logics of Computation, Pitts and Dybjer (eds.), Cambridge University Press*, 1997.

[Jec78]   T. Jech. *Set Theory.* Academic Press, 1978.

[JM94]    T. Jim and A. Meyer. Full abstraction and the context lemma. In *Proc. Theoretical Aspects of Computer Software, Springer Lect. Notes in Comp. Sci. 526*, 1994.

[JMS91]   B. Jacobs, E. Moggi, and T. Streicher. Relating models of impredicative type theories. In *Proc. CTCS 91, Springer Lect. Notes in Comp. Sci. 530*, 1991.

[Joh82]   P. Johnstone. *Stone Spaces.* Cambridge University Press, 1982.

[JT93]    A. Jung and J. Tiuryn. A new characterization of lambda-definability. In *Proc. Typed lambda-calculus and applications, Springer Lect. Notes in Comp. Sci. 664*, 1993.

[Jun88]   A. Jung. *Cartesian closed categories of domains.* CWI Tracts, Amsterdam, 1988.

[Jun90]   A. Jung. The classification of continuous domains. In *Proc. IEEE Logic in Comp. Sci.*, 1990.

[Jun96]   A. Jung. Domains and denotational semantics: history, accomplishments and open problems. *Bulletin European Association for Theoretical Computer Science*, 59:227–256, 1996. Collection of contributions edited by A. Jung.

[Kle45]   S. Kleene. On the interpretation of intuitionistic number theory. *Journal of Symbolic Logic*, 10:109–124, 1945.

[Kle78]   S. Kleene. Recursive functionals and quantifiers of finite types revisited I. In *Proc. General Recursion Theory II, Fenstad et al. (eds.), North-Holland*, 1978.

[Kle80]   S. Kleene. Recursive functionals and quantifiers of finite types revisited II. In *Proc. The Kleene Symposium, Barwise et al. (eds.), North-Holland*, 1980.

[Kle82]   S. Kleene. Recursive functionals and quantifiers of finite types revisited III. In *Proc. Patras Logic Symposium, North Holland*, 1982.

[Kle85]   S. Kleene. Unimonotone functions of finite types (recursive functionals and quantifiers of finite types revisited IV). In *Proc. Symposia in Pure Mathematics 42*, 1985.

[Klo85]   J.W. Klop. *Combinatory Reduction Systems.* PhD thesis, Utrecht University, 1985.

[Koc72]   A.. Kock. Strong functors and monoidal monads. *Archive Math.*, 23, 1972.

[KP93]    G. Kahn and G. Plotkin. Concrete domains. *Theoretical Computer Science*, 121:187–277, 1993. Appeared as TR IRIA-Laboria 336 in 1978.

[KPS93]   D. Kozen, J. Palsberg, and M. Schwartzbach. Efficient recursive subtyping. In *Proc. ACM Principles of Prog. Lang.* ACM, 1993.

[Kri91]   J.-L. Krivine. *Lambda-calcul, types et modèles.* Masson, 1991.

[Lam80]   J. Lamping. An algorithm for optimal lambda-calculus reductions. In *Proc. ACM Principles of Prog. Lang.*, 1980.

[Lam92a]  F. Lamarche. Games, additives and correctness criteria. *Manuscript*, 1992.

[Lam92b]  F. Lamarche. Sequentiality, games and linear logic. *Manuscript*, 1992.

[Lam94]   F. Lamarche. From Chu spaces to cpo's. *Manuscript*, 1994.

[Lan64]   P. Landin. The mechanical evaluation of expressions. *Computer Journal*, 6:308–320, 1964.

[Lan66]   P. Landin. The next 700 programming languages. *Communications of the ACM*, 3, 1966.

[Lev78]   J.-J. Levy. Réductions correctes et optimales dans le λ-calcul. 1978. Thèse de Doctorat d'Etat, Université Paris VII.

[Lis88]   B. Liskov. Data abstraction and hierarchy. In *Proc. OOPSLA, Sigplan Notices 23-5*, 1988.

[LM84]    G. Longo and E. Moggi. Cartesian closed categories of enumerations and effective type structures. In *Proc. Semantics of Data Types, Springer Lect. Notes in Comp. Sci. 173*, 1984.

[LM92]    G. Longo and E. Moggi. Constructive natural deduction and its modest interpretation. *Mathematical Structures in Computer Science*, 1:215–254, 1992.

[Loa94]   R. Loader. The undecidability of λ-definability. In *Proc. Church Festschrift CSLI/University of Chicago Press, Zeleny (ed.)*, 1994.

[Loa97]   R. Loader. Equational theories for inductive types. *Annals of Pure and Applied Logic*, 1997. To appear.

[LRS94]   Y. Lafont, B. Reus, and T. Streicher. Continuation semantics: Abstract machines and control operators. Manuscript, University of Munich, 1994.

[LS86]    J. Lambek and P. Scott. *Introduction to higher order categorical logic.* Cambridge University Press, 1986.

[LS95]    J. Longley and K. Simpson. A uniform approach to domain theory in realizability models. *University of Edinburgh, available at http://hypatia.dcs.qmw.ac.uk*, 1995.

[Mac60]   J. MacCarthy. Recursive functions of symbolic expressions and their computation by machine, part I. *Communications of the ACM*, 3:184–195, 1960.

[Mar76]   G. Markowsky. Chain-complete p.o. sets and directed sets with applications. *Algebra Universalis*, 6:53–68, 1976.

[McC84]   D. McCarty. *Realizability and recursive mathematics.* PhD thesis, Oxford University, 1984.

[Mil77]   R. Milner. Fully abstract models of typed lambda-calculi. *Theoretical Computer Science*, 4:1–23, 1977.

[Mil89]   R. Milner. *Communication and Concurrency.* Prentice Hall, 1989.

[Mil92]   R. Milner. Functions as processes. *Mathematical Structures in Computer Science*, 2(2):119–141, 1992.

[Mit88]   J. Mitchell. Polymorphic type inference and containment. *Information and Computation*, 76:211–249, 1988.

[ML71]    S. Mac Lane. *Categories for the working mathematician.* Springer-Verlag, New York, 1971.

[ML83]    P. Martin-Löf. Lecture notes on the domain interpretation of type theory. Technical report, *Workshop on Semantics of Programming Languages, Chalmers University of Technology,* 1983.

[ML84]    P. Martin-Löf. *Intuitionistic type theory.* Bibliopolis, 1984.

[Mog88]   E. Moggi. Partial morphisms in categories of effective objects. *Information and Computation,* 76:250–277, 1988.

[Mog89]   E. Moggi. Computational lambda-calculus and monads. *Information and Computation,* 93:55–92, 1989.

[MPW92]   R. Milner, J. Parrow, and D. Walker. A Calculus of Mobile Process, Parts 1-2. *Information and Computation,* 100(1):1–77, 1992.

[MS92]    R. Milner and D. Sangiorgi. Barbed bisimulation. In *Proc. ICALP 92, Springer Lect. Notes in Comp. Sci. 623,* 1992.

[Mul81]   P. Mulry. Generalized Banach-Mazur functionals in the topos of recursive sets. *J. of Pure and Applied Algebra,* 26:71–83, 1981.

[Mul89]   K. Mulmuley. *Full abstraction and semantic equivalence.* MIT Press, 1989.

[Mur91]   C. Murthy. An evaluation semantics for classical proofs. In *Proc. IEEE Logic in Comp. Sci.,* 1991.

[PA93]    G. Plotkin and M. Abadi. A logic for parametric polymorphism. In *Proc. Typed Lambda Calculi and Applications, Springer Lect. Notes in Comp. Sci. 664,* 1993.

[Par81]   D. Park. Concurrency and automata on infinite sequences. In *Proc. Theor. Comp. Sci., Springer Lect. Notes in Comp. Sci. 104,* 1981.

[Pau87]   L. Paulson. *Logic and Computation, Interactive proof with Cambridge LCF.* Cambridge University Press, 1987.

[Pho90]   W. Phoa. Effective domains and intrinsic structure. In *Proc. IEEE Logic in Comp. Sci.,* 1990.

[Pit96]   A. Pitts. Relational properties of domains. *Information and Computation,* 127:66–90, 1996.

[PJ87]    S.L. Peyton Jones. *The Implementation of Functional Programming Languages.* Prentice-Hall, 1987.

[Plo75]   G. Plotkin. Call-by-name, call-by-value and the lambda-calculus. *Theoretical Computer Science,* 1:125–159, 1975.

[Plo76]   G. Plotkin. A powerdomain construction. *SIAM J. of Computing,* 5:452–487, 1976.

[Plo77]   G. Plotkin. LCF as a programming language. *Theoretical Computer Science,* 5:223–257, 1977.

[Plo78]   G. Plotkin. $T^\omega$ as a universal domain. *Journal of Computer and System Sciences,* 17:209–236, 1978.

[Plo83]   G. Plotkin. Domains. *Lecture Notes, University of Edinburgh,* 1983.

[Plo85]   G. Plotkin. Denotational semantics with partial functions. *Lecture Notes, CSLI-Stanford,* 1985.

[Poi92]   A. Poigné. Basic category theory. *Handbook of Logic in Computer Science, Abramsky et al. (eds.), Clarendon Press, Oxford,* 1:413–640, 1992.

[Pra65]   D. Prawitz. *Natural deduction.* Almqvist and Wiksell, Stockholm, 1965.

[PS93]     B. Pierce and D. Sangiorgi. Typing and subtyping for mobile processes. In *Proc. IEEE Logic in Comp. Sci.*, 1993.

[RdR93]    S. Ronchi della Rocca. Fundamentals in lambda-calculus. *Summer School in Logic for Computer Science, Chambery*, 1993.

[Rep91]    J. Reppy. CML: A higher-order concurrent language. In *Proc. ACM-SIGPLAN 91, Conf. on Prog. Lang. Design and Impl.*, 1991.

[Rey70]    J. Reynolds. Gedanken: a simple typeless programming language based on the principle of completeness and the reference concept. *Communications of the ACM*, 5, 1970.

[Rey74]    J. Reynolds. Towards a theory of type structures. In *Colloque sur la Programmation, Springer Lect. Notes in Comp. Sci. 19*, 1974.

[Rey83]    J. Reynolds. Types, abstraction and parametric polymorphism. In *Information Processing, Mason (ed.)*. Elsevier Science, 1983.

[RK93]     R. Cartwright R. Kanneganti. What is a universal higher-order programming language? In *Proc ICALP, Springer Lect. Notes in Comp. Sci. 700*, 1993.

[Rog67]    H. Rogers. *Theory of recursive functions and effective computability*. McGraw Hill, 1967.

[Ros86]    G. Rosolini. *Continuity and effectivity in topoi*. PhD thesis, Oxford University, 1986.

[RR88]     E. Robinson and P. Rosolini. Categories of partial maps. *Information and Computation*, 79:95–130, 1988.

[Sal66]    A. Salomaa. Two complete systems for the algebra of complete events. *Journal of the ACM*, 13-1, 1966.

[San92]    D. Sangiorgi. *Expressing mobility in process algebras: first-order and higher order paradigms*. PhD thesis, University of Edinburgh, 1992.

[Sco72]    D. Scott. Continuous lattices. In *Proc. Toposes, Algebraic Geometry and Logic, Springer Lect. Notes in Mathematics 274*, pages 97–136, 1972.

[Sco76]    D. Scott. Data types as lattices. *SIAM J. of Computing*, 5:522–587, 1976.

[Sco80]    D. Scott. Relating theories of the lambda-calculus. *In Curry Festschrift, Hindley and Seldin (eds.)*, pages 589–606, 1980. Academic Press.

[Sco82]    D. Scott. Domains for denotational semantics. In *Proc ICALP, Springer Lect. Notes in Comp. Sci. 140*, 1982.

[Sco93]    D. Scott. A type-theoretical alternative to ISWIM, CUCH, OWHY. *Theoretical Computer Science*, 121:411–440, 1993. Manuscript circulated since 1969.

[See89]    R. Seely. Linear logic, *-autonomous categories and cofree coalgebras. *Applications of categories in logic and computer science, Contempory Mathematics*, 92, 1989.

[Sie92]    K. Sieber. Reasoning about sequential functions via logical relations. In *Applications of Categories in Computer Science, Cambridge University Press*, 1992.

[Smy78]    M. Smyth. Power domains. *Journal of Computer and System Sciences*, 16:23–36, 1978.

[Smy83a]   M. Smyth. The largest cartesian closed category of domains. *Theoretical Computer Science*, 27:109–119, 1983.

[Smy83b]   M. Smyth. Powerdomains and predicate transformers. In *Springer Lect. Notes in Comp. Sci. 154*, 1983.

[Smy92]    M. Smyth. Topology. *Handbook of Logic in Computer Science, Abramsky et al. (eds.), Clarendon Press, Oxford*, 1:641–761, 1992.

[Soa87]    R. Soare. *Recursively enumerable sets and degrees.* Springer-Verlag, 1987.

[SP82]     M. Smyth and G. Plotkin. The category-theoretic solution of recursive domain equations. *SIAM J. of Computing,* 11:761–783, 1982.

[Sta96]    I. Stark. A fully abstract domain model for the $\pi$-calculus. In *Proc. IEEE Logic in Comp. Sci.,* 1996.

[Sto94]    A. Stoughton. Mechanizing logical relations. In *Proc. Math. Found. Progr. Semantics, Springer Lect. Notes in Comp. Sci. 802,* 1994.

[SVV96]    G. Sambin, S. Valentini, and P. Virgili. Constructive domain theory as a branch of intuitionistic pointfree topology. *Theoretical Computer Science,* 169:319–342, 1996.

[Tay90a]   P. Taylor. An algebraic approach to stable domains. *J. of Pure and Applied Algebra,* 64:171–203, 1990.

[Tay90b]   P. Taylor. The trace factorisation of stable functors. *Manuscript, Imperial College,* 1990.

[Tho93]    B. Thomsen. Plain Chocs. *Acta Informatica,* 30:1–59, 1993.

[TLP$^+$93]  B. Thomsen, L. Leth, S. Prasad, T.M. Kuo, A. Kramer, F. Knabe, and A. Giacalone. Facile Antigua release programming guide. Technical report, *TR 93-20, ECRC, Munich,* 1993.

[TvD88]    A. Troelstra and D. van Dalen. *Constructivism in mathematics (2 volumes).* North-Holland, 1988.

[Vic89]    S. Vickers. *Topology via logic.* Cambridge University Press, 1989.

[vR96]     F. van Raamsdonk. *Confluence and normalisation for higher-order rewriting systems.* PhD thesis, Vrije Universitet Amsterdam, 1996.

[Vui74]    J. Vuillemin. Syntaxe, sémantique et axiomatique d'un langage de programmation simple. 1974. Thèse de Doctorat d'Etat, Université Paris VII.

[Wad76]    C. Wadsworth. The relation between computational and denotational properties for Scott's D-infinity models of the lambda-calculus. *SIAM J. of Computing,* 5:488–521, 1976.

[Wad89]    P. Wadler. Theorems for free. In *Proc. ACM Functional Programming Languages and Computer Architecture,* 1989.

[Wan79]    M. Wand. Fixed-point constructions in order-enriched categories. *Theoretical Computer Science,* 8:13–30, 1979.

[Wel94]    J. Wells. Typability and type-checking in the second order $\lambda$-calculus are equivalent and undecidable. In *Proc. IEEE Logic in Comp. Sci.,* 1994.

[Win80]    G. Winskel. *Events in computation.* PhD thesis, University of Edinburgh, 1980.

[Win86]    G. Winskel. Event structures. In *Springer Lect. Notes in Comp. Sci. 255,* 1986.

[Win93]    G. Winskel. *The formal semantics of programming languages.* MIT Press, 1993.

[Win94]    G. Winskel. Stable bistructure models of PCF. In *Proc. Mathematical Foundations of Programming Semantics, Springer Lect. Notes in Comp. Sci. 841,* 1994.

[Zha91]    G. Zhang. *Logic of domains.* Birkhäuser, 1991.

[Zha95]    G. Zhang. The largest cartesian closed category of stable domains. *TCS,* 166:203–219, 1995.

[Zha97]    G. Zhang. Back and forth through universal coherence spaces. *Manuscript,* 1997.

# Index

Printed in the United States
By Bookmasters